PROFESSIONAL C# 2012 AND .

M000286826

Continued

PROFESSIONAL

C# 2012 and .NET 4.5

PROFESSIONAL

C# 2012 and .NET 4.5

Christian Nagel
Bill Evjen
Jay Glynn
Karli Watson
Morgan Skinner

WILEY

John Wiley & Sons, Inc.

Professional C# 2012 and .NET 4.5

Published by
John Wiley & Sons, Inc.
10475 Crosspoint Boulevard
Indianapolis, IN 46256
www.wiley.com

Copyright © 2013 by John Wiley & Sons, Inc., Indianapolis, Indiana

Published simultaneously in Canada

ISBN: 978-1-118-31442-5
ISBN: 978-1-118-38800-6 (ebk)
ISBN: 978-1-118-33212-2 (ebk)
ISBN: 978-1-118-33538-3 (ebk)

Manufactured in the United States of America

10 9 8 7 6 5 4 3 2 1

No part of this publication may be reproduced, stored in a retrieval system or transmitted in any form or by any means, electronic, mechanical, photocopying, recording, scanning or otherwise, except as permitted under Sections 107 or 108 of the 1976 United States Copyright Act, without either the prior written permission of the Publisher, or authorization through payment of the appropriate per-copy fee to the Copyright Clearance Center, 222 Rosewood Drive, Danvers, MA 01923, (978) 750-8400, fax (978) 646-8600. Requests to the Publisher for permission should be addressed to the Permissions Department, John Wiley & Sons, Inc., 111 River Street, Hoboken, NJ 07030, (201) 748-6011, fax (201) 748-6008, or online at http://www.wiley.com/go/permissions.

Limit of Liability/Disclaimer of Warranty: The publisher and the author make no representations or warranties with respect to the accuracy or completeness of the contents of this work and specifically disclaim all warranties, including without limitation warranties of fitness for a particular purpose. No warranty may be created or extended by sales or promotional materials. The advice and strategies contained herein may not be suitable for every situation. This work is sold with the understanding that the publisher is not engaged in rendering legal, accounting, or other professional services. If professional assistance is required, the services of a competent professional person should be sought. Neither the publisher nor the author shall be liable for damages arising herefrom. The fact that an organization or Web site is referred to in this work as a citation and/or a potential source of further information does not mean that the author or the publisher endorses the information the organization or Web site may provide or recommendations it may make. Further, readers should be aware that Internet Web sites listed in this work may have changed or disappeared between when this work was written and when it is read.

For general information on our other products and services please contact our Customer Care Department within the United States at (877) 762-2974, outside the United States at (317) 572-3993 or fax (317) 572-4002.

Wiley publishes in a variety of print and electronic formats and by print-on-demand. Some material included with standard print versions of this book may not be included in e-books or in print-on-demand. If this book refers to media such as a CD or DVD that is not included in the version you purchased, you may download this material at http://booksupport.wiley.com. For more information about Wiley products, visit www.wiley.com.

Library of Congress Control Number: 2012944687

Trademarks: Wiley, the Wiley logo, Wrox, the Wrox logo, Programmer to Programmer, and related trade dress are trademarks or registered trademarks of John Wiley & Sons, Inc. and/or its affiliates, in the United States and other countries, and may not be used without written permission. All other trademarks are the property of their respective owners. John Wiley & Sons, Inc., is not associated with any product or vendor mentioned in this book.

To my family – Angela, Stephanie, and Matthias – I love you all!

—CHRISTIAN NAGEL

This work is dedicated to my wife and son. They are my world.

—JAY GLYNN

Love is as strong as death;
Many waters cannot quench love,
Neither can the floods drown it.

—MORGAN SKINNER

ABOUT THE AUTHORS

CHRISTIAN NAGEL is a Microsoft Regional Director and Microsoft MVP, an associate of thinktecture, and founder of CN innovation. A software architect and developer, he offers training and consulting on how to develop solutions using the Microsoft platform. He draws on more than 25 years of software development experience. Christian started his computing career with PDP 11 and VAX/VMS systems, covering a variety of languages and platforms. Since 2000, when .NET was just a technology preview, he has been working with various .NET technologies to build .NET solutions. Currently, he mainly coaches the development of Windows Store apps accessing Windows Azure services. With his profound knowledge of Microsoft technologies, he has written numerous books, and is certified as a Microsoft Certified Trainer and Professional Developer. Christian speaks at international conferences such as TechEd, Basta!, and TechDays, and he founded INETA Europe to support .NET user groups. You can contact Christian via his websites, www.cninnovation.com and www.thinktecture.com, and follow his tweets at @christiannagel.

JAY GLYNN started writing software more than 20 years ago, writing applications for the PICK operating system using PICK basic. Since then, he has created software using Paradox PAL and Object PAL, Delphi, VBA, Visual Basic, C, Java, and of course C#. He currently works for UL PureSafety as a senior software engineer writing web-based software.

MORGAN SKINNER began his computing career at a young age on the Sinclair ZX80 at school, where he was underwhelmed by some code a teacher had written and so began programming in assembly language. Since then he has used a wide variety of languages and platforms, including VAX Macro Assembler, Pascal, Modula2, Smalltalk, X86 assembly language, PowerBuilder, C/C++, VB, and currently C#. He's been programming in .NET since the PDC release in 2000, and liked it so much he joined Microsoft in 2001. He's now an independent consultant.

ABOUT THE TECHNICAL EDITORS

DAVID FRANSON has been a professional in the field of networking, programming, and 2D and 3D computer graphics since 1990. He is the author of *2D Artwork and 3D Modeling for Game Artists, The Dark Side of Game Texturing,* and *Game Character Design Complete.*

DON REAMEY is an architect/principal engineer for TIBCO Software working on TIBCO Spotfire business intelligence analytics software. Prior to TIBCO Don spent 12 years with Microsoft as a software development engineer working on SharePoint, SharePoint Online and InfoPath Forms Service. Don has also spent 10 years writing software in the financial service industry for capital markets.

MITCHEL SELLERS specializes in software development using Microsoft technologies. As the CEO of IowaComputerGurus Inc., he works with small and large companies worldwide. He is a Microsoft C# MVP, a Microsoft Certified Professional, and the author of *Professional DotNetNuke Module Programming* (Wrox Press, 2009). Mitchel frequently writes technical articles for online and print publications including SQL Server magazine, and he regularly speaks to user groups and conferences. He is also a DotNetNuke Core Team member as well as an active participant in the .NET and DotNetNuke development communities. Additional information on Mitchel's professional experience, certifications, and publications can be found at http://mitchelsellers.com/.

CREDITS

ACQUISITIONS EDITOR
Mary James

SENIOR PROJECT EDITOR
Adaobi Obi Tulton

TECHNICAL EDITORS
David Franson
Don Reamey
Mitchel Sellers

PRODUCTION EDITOR
Kathleen Wisor

COPY EDITOR
Luann Rouff

EDITORIAL MANAGER
Mary Beth Wakefield

FREELANCER EDITORIAL MANAGER
Rosemarie Graham

ASSOCIATE DIRECTOR OF MARKETING
David Mayhew

MARKETING MANAGER
Ashley Zurcher

BUSINESS MANAGER
Amy Knies

PRODUCTION MANAGER
Tim Tate

VICE PRESIDENT AND EXECUTIVE GROUP PUBLISHER
Richard Swadley

VICE PRESIDENT AND EXECUTIVE PUBLISHER
Neil Edde

ASSOCIATE PUBLISHER
Jim Minatel

PROJECT COORDINATOR, COVER
Katie Crocker

PROOFREADER
Word One, New York

INDEXER
Robert Swanson

COVER DESIGNER
Ryan Sneed

COVER IMAGE
© Punchstock

ACKNOWLEDGMENTS

I WOULD LIKE TO THANK Adaobi Obi Tulton, Maureen Spears, and Luann Rouff for making this text more readable; Mary James; and Jim Minatel; and everyone else at Wiley who helped to get another edition of this great book published. I would also like to thank my wife and children for supporting my writing. You're my inspiration.

—CHRISTIAN NAGEL

I WANT TO THANK my wife and son for putting up with the time and frustrations of working on a project like this. I also want to thank all the dedicated people at Wiley for getting this book out the door.

—JAY GLYNN

CONTENTS

PART V: PRESENTATION

INTRODUCTION

IF YOU WERE TO DESCRIBE THE C# LANGUAGE and its associated environment, the .NET Framework, as the most significant technology for developers available, you would not be exaggerating. .NET is designed to provide an environment within which you can develop almost any application to run on Windows, whereas C# is a programming language designed specifically to work with the .NET Framework. By using C#, you can, for example, write a dynamic web page, a Windows Presentation Foundation application, an XML web service, a component of a distributed application, a database access component, a classic Windows desktop application, or even a new smart client application that enables online and offline capabilities. This book covers the .NET Framework 4.5. If you code using any of the prior versions, there may be sections of the book that will not work for you. This book notifies you of items that are new and specific to the .NET Framework 4.5.

Don't be fooled by the .NET label in the Framework's name and think that this is a purely an Internet-focused framework. The NET bit in the name is there to emphasize Microsoft's belief that *distributed applications*, in which the processing is distributed between client and server, are the way forward. You must also understand that C# is not just a language for writing Internet or network-aware applications. It provides a means for you to code almost any type of software or component that you need to write for the Windows platform. Between them, C# and .NET have revolutionized the way that developers write their programs and have made programming on Windows much easier than it has ever been before.

So what's the big deal about .NET and C#?

THE SIGNIFICANCE OF .NET AND C#

To understand the significance of .NET, you must consider the nature of many of the Windows technologies that have appeared in the past 18 years. Although they may look quite different on the surface, all the Windows operating systems from Windows NT 3.1 (introduced in 1993) through Windows 8 and Windows Server 2012 have the same familiar Windows API for Windows desktop and server applications at their core. Progressing through new versions of Windows, huge numbers of new functions have been added to the API, but this has been a process to evolve and extend the API rather than replace it.

The same can be said for many of the technologies and frameworks used to develop software for Windows. For example, *Component Object Model* (COM) originated as *Object Linking and Embedding* (OLE). Originally, it was largely a means by which different types of Office documents could be linked so that you could place a small Excel spreadsheet in your Word document, for example. From that it evolved into COM, *Distributed* COM (DCOM), and eventually *COM+*—a sophisticated technology that formed the basis of the way almost all components communicated, as well as implementing transactions, messaging services, and object pooling.

Microsoft chose this evolutionary approach to software for the obvious reason that it is concerned about backward compatibility. Over the years, a huge base of third-party software has been written for Windows, and Windows would not have enjoyed the success it has had if every time Microsoft introduced a new technology it broke the existing code base!

Although backward compatibility has been a crucial feature of Windows technologies and one of the strengths of the Windows platform, it does have a big disadvantage. Every time some technology evolves and adds new features, it ends up a bit more complicated than it was before.

It was clear that something had to change. Microsoft could not go on forever extending the same development tools and languages, always making them more and more complex to satisfy the conflicting demands of keeping up with the newest hardware and maintaining backward compatibility with what was around when Windows first became popular in the early 1990s. There comes a point in which you must start with a clean slate if you want a simple yet sophisticated set of languages, environments, and developer tools, which makes it easy for developers to write state-of-the-art software.

This fresh start is what C# and .NET were all about in the first incarnation. Roughly speaking, .NET is a framework—an API—for programming on the Windows platform. Along with the .NET Framework, C# is a language that has been designed from scratch to work with .NET, as well as to take advantage of all the progress in developer environments and in your understanding of object-oriented programming principles that have taken place over the past 25 years.

Before continuing, you must understand that backward compatibility has not been lost in the process. Existing programs continue to work, and .NET was designed with the capability to work with existing software. Presently, communication between software components on Windows takes place almost entirely using COM. Taking this into account, the .NET Framework does have the capability to provide wrappers around existing COM components so that .NET components can talk to them.

It is true that you don't need to learn C# to write code for .NET. Microsoft has extended C++ and made substantial changes to Visual Basic to turn it into a more powerful language to enable code written in either of these languages to target the .NET environment. These other languages, however, are hampered by the legacy of having evolved over the years rather than having been written from the start with today's technology in mind.

This book can equip you to program in C#, while at the same time provides the necessary background in how the .NET architecture works. You not only cover the fundamentals of the C# language, but also see examples of applications that use a variety of related technologies, including database access, dynamic web pages, advanced graphics, and directory access.

While the Windows API just evolved and was extended since the early days of Windows NT in 1993, and the .NET Framework offered a major change on how programs are written since the year 2002, now in the year 2012 are the days of the next big change. Do such changes happen every 10 years? Windows 8 now offers a new API: the Windows Runtime (WinRT) for Windows Store apps. This runtime is a native API (like the Windows API) that is not build with the .NET runtime as its core, but offers great new features that are based on ideas of .NET. Windows 8 includes the first release of this API available for modern-style apps. While this is not based on .NET, you still can use a subset of .NET with Windows Store apps, and write the apps with C#. This new runtime will evolve in the next years to come with upcoming releases of Windows. This book will also give you a start in writing Windows Store apps with C# and WinRT.

ADVANTAGES OF .NET

So far, you've read in general terms about how great .NET is, but it can help to make your life as a developer easier. This section briefly identifies some of the features of .NET.

- ➤ **Object-oriented programming** — Both the .NET Framework and C# are entirely based on object-oriented principles from the start.
- ➤ **Good design** — A base class library, which is designed from the ground up in a highly intuitive way.
- ➤ **Language independence** — With .NET, all the languages—Visual Basic, C#, and managed C++— compile to a common *Intermediate Language*. This means that languages are interoperable in a way that has not been seen before.

➤ **Better support for dynamic web pages** — Though Classic ASP offered a lot of flexibility, it was also inefficient because of its use of interpreted scripting languages, and the lack of object-oriented design often resulted in messy ASP code. .NET offers an integrated support for web pages, using ASP.NET. With ASP.NET, code in your pages is compiled and may be written in a .NET-aware high-level language such as C# or Visual Basic 2010. .NET now takes it even further with outstanding support for the latest web technologies such as Ajax and jQuery.

➤ **Efficient data access** — A set of .NET components, collectively known as ADO.NET, provides efficient access to relational databases and a variety of data sources. Components are also available to enable access to the file system and to directories. In particular, XML support is built into .NET, enabling you to manipulate data, which may be imported from or exported to non-Windows platforms.

➤ **Code sharing** — .NET has completely revamped the way that code is shared between applications, introducing the concept of the *assembly*, which replaces the traditional DLL. Assemblies have formal facilities for versioning, and different versions of assemblies can exist side by side.

➤ **Improved security** — Each assembly can also contain built-in security information that can indicate precisely who or what category of user or process is allowed to call which methods on which classes. This gives you a fine degree of control over how the assemblies that you deploy can be used.

➤ **Zero-impact installation** — There are two types of assemblies: shared and private. Shared assemblies are common libraries available to all software, whereas private assemblies are intended only for use with particular software. A private assembly is entirely self-contained, so the process to install it is simple. There are no registry entries; the appropriate files are simply placed in the appropriate folder in the file system.

➤ **Support for web services** — .NET has fully integrated support for developing web services as easily as you would develop any other type of application.

➤ **Visual Studio 2012** — .NET comes with a developer environment, Visual Studio 2012, which can cope equally well with C++, C#, and Visual Basic 2012, as well as with ASP.NET or XML code. Visual Studio 2012 integrates all the best features of the respective language-specific environments of all the previous versions of this amazing IDE.

➤ **C#** — C# is a powerful and popular object-oriented language intended for use with .NET.

You look more closely at the benefits of the .NET architecture in Chapter 1, ".NET Architecture."

WHAT'S NEW IN THE .NET FRAMEWORK 4.5

The first version of the .NET Framework (1.0) was released in 2002 to much enthusiasm. The .NET Framework 2.0 was introduced in 2005 and was considered a major release of the Framework. The major new feature of 2.0 was generics support in C# and the runtime (IL code changed for generics), and new classes and interfaces. .NET 3.0 was based on the 2.0 runtime and introduced a new way to create UIs (WPF with XAML and vector-based graphics instead of pixel-based), and a new communication technology (WCF). .NET 3.5 together with C# 3 introduced LINQ, one query syntax that can be used for all data sources. .NET 4.0 was another major release of the product that also brought a new version of the runtime (4.0) and a new version of C# (4.0) to offer dynamic language integration and a huge new library for parallel programming. The .NET Framework 4.5 is based on an updated version of the 4.0 runtime with many outstanding new features.

With each release of the Framework, Microsoft has always tried to ensure that there were minimal breaking changes to code developed. Thus far, Microsoft has been successful at this goal.

The following section details some of the changes that are new to C# 2012 and the .NET Framework 4.5.

Asynchronous Programming

Blocking the UI is unfriendly to the user; the user becomes impatient if the UI does not react. Maybe you've this experience with Visual Studio as well. Good news: Visual Studio has become a lot better in reacting faster in many scenarios.

The .NET Framework always offered calling methods asynchronously. However, using synchronous methods was a lot easier than calling their asynchronous variant. This changed with C# 5. Programming asynchronously has become as easy as writing synchronous programs. New C# keywords are based on the .NET Parallel Library that is available since .NET 4. Now the language offers productivity features.

Windows Store Apps and the Windows Runtime

Windows Store apps can be programmed with C# using the Windows Runtime and a subset of the .NET Framework. The Windows Runtime is a new native API that offers classes, methods, properties, and events that look like .NET; although it is native. For using language projection features, the .NET runtime has been enhanced. With .NET 4.5, the .NET 4.0 runtime gets an in-place update.

Enhancements with Data Access

The ADO.NET Entity Framework offered important new features. Its version changed from 4.0 with .NET 4.0 to 5.0 with .NET 4.5. After the release of .NET 4.0, the Entity Framework already received updates with versions 4.1, 4.2, and 4.3. New features such as Code First, spatial types, using enums, and table-valued functions are now available.

Enhancements with WPF

Programming Windows desktop applications, WPF has been enhanced. Now you can fill collections from a non-UI thread; the ribbon control is now part of the framework; weak references with events have been made easier; validation can be done asynchronously with the INotifyDataErrorInfo interface; and live shaping allows easy dynamic sorting and grouping with data that changes.

ASP.NET MVC

Visual Studio 2010 included ASP.NET MVC 2.0. With the release of Visual Studio 2012, ASP.NET MVC 4.0 is available. ASP.NET MVC supplies you with the means to create ASP.NET using the model-view-controller model that many developers expect. ASP.NET MVC provides developers with testability, flexibility, and maintainability in the applications they build. ASP.NET MVC is not meant to be a replacement for ASP.NET Web Forms but is simply a different way to construct your applications.

WHERE C# FITS IN

In one sense, C# is the same thing to programming languages that .NET is to the Windows environment. Just as Microsoft has been adding more and more features to Windows and the Windows API over the past 15 years, Visual Basic 2012 and C++ have undergone expansion. Although Visual Basic and C++ have resulted in hugely powerful languages, both languages also suffer from problems because of the legacies left over from the way they evolved.

For Visual Basic 6 and earlier versions, the main strength of the language was that it was simple to understand and made many programming tasks easy, largely hiding the details of the Windows API and the COM component infrastructure from the developer. The downside to this was that Visual Basic was never truly object-oriented, so large applications quickly became disorganized and hard to maintain. As well, because Visual Basic's syntax was inherited from early versions of BASIC (which, in turn, was designed to be intuitively simple for beginning programmers to understand, rather than to write large commercial applications), it didn't lend itself to well-structured or object-oriented programs.

C++, on the other hand, has its roots in the ANSI C++ language definition. It is not completely ANSI-compliant for the simple reason that Microsoft first wrote its C++ compiler before the ANSI definition had become official, but it comes close. Unfortunately, this has led to two problems. First, ANSI C++ has its roots in a decade-old state of technology, and this shows up in a lack of support for modern concepts (such as Unicode strings and generating XML documentation) and for some archaic syntax structures designed for the compilers of yesteryear (such as the separation of declaration from definition of member functions). Second, Microsoft has been simultaneously trying to evolve C++ into a language designed for high-performance tasks on Windows, and to achieve that, it has been forced to add a huge number of Microsoft-specific keywords as well as various libraries to the language. The result is that on Windows, the language has become a complete mess. Just ask C++ developers how many definitions for a string they can think of: `char*`, `LPSTR`, `string`, `CString` (MFC version), `CString` (WTL version), `wchar_t*`, `OLECHAR*`, and so on.

Now enters .NET—a completely revolutionary environment that has brought forth new extensions to both languages. Microsoft has gotten around this by adding yet more Microsoft-specific keywords to C++ and by completely revamping Visual Basic to the current Visual Basic 2012, a language that retains some of the basic VB syntax but that is so different in design from the original VB that it can be considered, for all practical purposes, a new language.

It is in this context that Microsoft has provided developers an alternative—a language designed specifically for .NET and designed with a clean slate. C# is the result. Officially, Microsoft describes C# as a "simple, modern, object-oriented, and type-safe programming language derived from C and C++." Most independent observers would probably change that to "derived from C, C++, and Java." Such descriptions are technically accurate but do little to convey the beauty or elegance of the language. Syntactically, C# is similar to both C++ and Java, to such an extent that many keywords are the same, and C# also shares the same block structure with braces (`{}`) to mark blocks of code and semicolons to separate statements. The first impression of a piece of C# code is that it looks quite like C++ or Java code. Beyond that initial similarity, however, C# is a lot easier to learn than C++ and of comparable difficulty to Java. Its design is more in tune with modern developer tools than both of those other languages, and it has been designed to provide, simultaneously, the ease of use of Visual Basic and the high-performance, low-level memory access of C++, if required. Some of the features of C# follow:

➤ Full support for classes and object-oriented programming, including interface and implementation inheritance, virtual functions, and operator overloading.

➤ A consistent and well-defined set of basic types.

➤ Built-in support for an automatic generation of XML documentation.

➤ Automatic cleanup of dynamically allocated memory.

➤ The facility to mark classes or methods with user-defined attributes. This can be useful for documentation and can have some effects on compilation (for example, marking methods to be compiled only in debug builds).

➤ Full access to the .NET base class library and easy access to the Windows API (if you need it, which will not be often).

➤ Pointers and direct memory access are available if required, but the language has been designed in such a way that you can work without them in almost all cases.

➤ Support for properties and events in the style of Visual Basic.

➤ Just by changing the compiler options, you can compile either to an executable or to a library of .NET components that can be called up by other code in the same way as ActiveX controls (COM components).

➤ C# can be used to write ASP.NET dynamic web pages and XML web services.

Most of these statements, it should be pointed out, also apply to Visual Basic 2012 and Managed C++. Because C# is designed from the start to work with .NET, however, means that its support for the features of .NET is both more complete and offered within the context of a more suitable syntax than those of other languages. Although the C# language is similar to Java, there are some improvements; in particular, Java is not designed to work with the .NET environment.

Before leaving the subject, you must understand a couple of limitations of C#. The one area the language is not designed for is time-critical or extremely high-performance code—the kind where you are worried about whether a loop takes 1,000 or 1,050 machine cycles to run through, and you need to clean up your resources the millisecond they are no longer needed. C++ is likely to continue to reign supreme among low-level languages in this area. C# lacks certain key facilities needed for extremely high-performance apps, including the capability to specify inline functions and destructors guaranteed to run at particular points in the code. However, the proportions of applications that fall into this category are low.

WHAT YOU NEED TO WRITE AND RUN C# CODE

The .NET Framework 4.5 can run on the client operating systems Windows Vista, 7, 8, and the server operating systems Windows Server 2008, 2008 R2, and 2012. To write code using .NET, you need to install the .NET 4.5 SDK.

In addition, unless you intend to write your C# code using a text editor or some other third-party developer environment, you almost certainly also want Visual Studio 2012. The full SDK is not needed to run managed code, but the .NET runtime is needed. You may find you need to distribute the .NET runtime with your code for the benefit of those clients who do not have it already installed.

WHAT THIS BOOK COVERS

This book starts by reviewing the overall architecture of .NET in Chapter 1 to give you the background you need to write managed code. After that, the book is divided into a number of sections that cover both the C# language and its application in a variety of areas.

Part I: The C# Language

This section gives a good grounding in the C# language. This section doesn't presume knowledge of any particular language; although, it does assume you are an experienced programmer. You start by looking at C#'s basic syntax and data types and then explore the object-oriented features of C# before looking at more advanced C# programming topics.

Part II: Visual Studio

This section looks at the main IDE utilized by C# developers worldwide: Visual Studio 2012. The two chapters in this section look at the best way to use the tool to build applications based on the .NET Framework 4.5. In addition, this section also focuses on the deployment of your projects.

Part III: Foundation

In this section, you look at the principles of programming in the .NET environment. In particular, you look at security, threading, localization, transactions, how to build Windows services, and how to generate your own libraries as assemblies, among other topics. One part is interaction with native code and assemblies using platform invoke and COM interop. This section also gives information how the Windows Runtime differs from .NET and how to start writing Windows 8–style programs.

Part IV: Data

Here, you look at accessing data using ADO.NET and learn about the ADO.NET Entity Framework. You can use core ADO.NET to get the best performance; the ADO.NET Entity Framework offers ease of use with mapping objects to relations. Now, different programming models with Model First, Database First, and Code First are available that are all discussed. This part also extensively covers support in .NET for XML, using LINQ to query XML data sources.

Part V: Presentation

This section starts by showing you how to build applications based upon the Windows Presentation Foundation. Not only different control types, styles, resources, and data binding are covered, but you can also read about creating fixed and flow documents, and printing. Here, you can also read about creating Windows Store apps, use of pictures for a nicer UI, grids, and contracts to interact with other applications. Finally, this section includes coverage of the tremendous number of features that ASP.NET offers, building websites with ASP.NET Web Forms, ASP.NET MVC, and dynamic data.

Part VI: Communication

This section is all about communication. It covers services for platform-independent communication using Windows Communication Foundation (WCF) and WCF to access data with WCF Data Services. With Message Queuing, asynchronous disconnected communication is shown. This section looks at utilizing the Windows Workflow Foundation and peer-to-peer networking.

CONVENTIONS

To help you get the most from the text and keep track of what's happening, a number of conventions are used throughout the book.

> **WARNING** *Warnings hold important, not-to-be-forgotten information that is directly relevant to the surrounding text.*

> **NOTE** *Notes indicate notes, tips, hints, tricks, or and asides to the current discussion.*

As for styles in the text:

➤ We *highlight* new terms and important words when we introduce them.

➤ We show keyboard strokes like this: Ctrl+A.

➤ We show filenames, URLs, and code within the text like so: `persistence.properties`.

➤ We present code in two different ways:

```
We use a monofont type with no highlighting for most code examples.
```

We use bold to emphasize code that's particularly important in the present context or to show changes from a previous code snippet.

SOURCE CODE

As you work through the examples in this book, you may choose either to type in all the code manually or to use the source code files that accompany the book. All the source code used in this book is available for download at `http://www.wrox.com`. When at the site, simply locate the book's title (either by using the Search box or by using one of the title lists) and click the Download Code link on the book's detail page to obtain all the source code for the book.

> **NOTE** *Because many books have similar titles, you may find it easiest to search by ISBN; this book's ISBN is 978-1-118-31442-5.*

After you download the code, just decompress it with your favorite compression tool. Alternately, you can go to the main Wrox code download page at `http://www.wrox.com/dynamic/books/download.aspx` to see the code available for this book and all other Wrox books.

ERRATA

We make every effort to ensure that there are no errors in the text or in the code. However, no one is perfect, and mistakes do occur. If you find an error in one of our books, like a spelling mistake or faulty piece of code, we would be grateful for your feedback. By sending in errata you may save another reader hours of frustration, and at the same time you can help provide even higher quality information.

To find the errata page for this book, go to `http://www.wrox.com` and locate the title using the Search box or one of the title lists. Then, on the book details page, click the Book Errata link. On this page you can view all errata that has been submitted for this book and posted by Wrox editors. A complete book list including links to each book's errata is also available at www.wrox.com/misc-pages/booklist.shtml.

If you don't spot "your" error on the Book Errata page, go to www.wrox.com/contact/techsupport .shtml and complete the form there to send us the error you have found. We'll check the information and, if appropriate, post a message to the book's errata page and fix the problem in subsequent editions of the book.

P2P.WROX.COM

For author and peer discussion, join the P2P forums at p2p.wrox.com. The forums are a web-based system for you to post messages relating to Wrox books and related technologies and interact with other readers and technology users. The forums offer a subscription feature to e-mail you topics of interest of your choosing when new posts are made to the forums. Wrox authors, editors, other industry experts, and your fellow readers are present on these forums.

At http://p2p.wrox.com you can find a number of different forums to help you not only as you read this book, but also as you develop your own applications. To join the forums, just follow these steps:

1. Go to p2p.wrox.com and click the Register link.
2. Read the terms of use and click Agree.
3. Complete the required information to join and any optional information you want to provide, and click Submit.
4. You will receive an e-mail with information describing how to verify your account and complete the joining process.

> **NOTE** *You can read messages in the forums without joining P2P but to post your own messages, you must join.*

After you join, you can post new messages and respond to messages other users post. You can read messages at any time on the web. If you want to have new messages from a particular forum e-mailed to you, click the Subscribe to this Forum icon by the forum name in the forum listing.

For more information about how to use the Wrox P2P, read the P2P FAQs for answers to questions about how the forum software works as well as many common questions specific to P2P and Wrox books. To read the FAQs, click the FAQ link on any P2P page.

PART I
The C# Language

.NET Architecture

WHAT'S IN THIS CHAPTER?

- ➤ Compiling and running code that targets .NET
- ➤ Advantages of Microsoft Intermediate Language (MSIL)
- ➤ Value and reference types
- ➤ Data typing
- ➤ Understanding error handling and attributes
- ➤ Assemblies, .NET base classes, and namespaces

WROX.COM CODE DOWNLOADS FOR THIS CHAPTER

There are no code downloads for this chapter.

THE RELATIONSHIP OF C# TO .NET

This book emphasizes that the C# language must be considered in parallel with the .NET Framework, rather than viewed in isolation. The C# compiler specifically targets .NET, which means that all code written in C# always runs within the .NET Framework. This has two important consequences for the C# language:

1. The architecture and methodologies of C# reflect the underlying methodologies of .NET.
2. In many cases, specific language features of C# actually depend on features of .NET or of the .NET base classes.

Because of this dependence, you must gain some understanding of the architecture and methodology of .NET before you begin C# programming, which is the purpose of this chapter.

C# is a programming language newly designed for .NET. and is significant in two respects:

➤ It is specifically designed and targeted for use with Microsoft's .NET Framework (a feature-rich platform for the development, deployment, and execution of distributed applications).

➤ It is a language based on the modern object-oriented design methodology, and when designing it Microsoft learned from the experience of all the other similar languages that have been around since object-oriented principles came to prominence 20 years ago.

C# is a language in its own right. Although it is designed to generate code that targets the .NET environment, it is not part of .NET. Some features are supported by .NET but not by C#, and you might be surprised to learn that some features of the C# language are not supported by .NET (for example, some instances of operator overloading).

However, because the C# language is intended for use with .NET, you must understand this Framework if you want to develop applications in C# effectively. Therefore, this chapter takes some time to peek underneath the surface of .NET.

THE COMMON LANGUAGE RUNTIME

Central to the .NET Framework is its runtime execution environment, known as the *Common Language Runtime* (CLR) or the *.NET runtime*. Code running under the control of the CLR is often termed *managed code*.

However, before it can be executed by the CLR, any source code that you develop (in C# or some other language) needs to be compiled. Compilation occurs in two steps in .NET:

1. Compilation of source code to Microsoft Intermediate Language (IL).
2. Compilation of IL to platform-specific code by the CLR.

This two-stage compilation process is important because the existence of the Microsoft Intermediate Language is the key to providing many of the benefits of .NET.

IL shares with Java byte code the idea that it is a low-level language with a simple syntax (based on numeric codes rather than text), which can be quickly translated into native machine code. Having this well-defined universal syntax for code has significant advantages: platform independence, performance improvement, and language interoperability.

Platform Independence

First, platform independence means that the same file containing byte code instructions can be placed on any platform; at runtime, the final stage of compilation can then be easily accomplished so that the code can run on that particular platform. In other words, by compiling to IL you obtain platform independence for .NET in much the same way as compiling to Java byte code gives Java platform independence.

The platform independence of .NET is only theoretical at present because, at the time of writing, a complete implementation of .NET is available only for Windows. However, a partial, cross-platform implementation is available (see, for example, the Mono project, an effort to create an open source implementation of .NET, at www.go-mono.com).

Performance Improvement

Although previously compared to Java, IL is actually a bit more ambitious than Java byte code. IL is always *Just-in-Time* compiled (known as JIT compilation), whereas Java byte code was often interpreted. One of the disadvantages of Java was that, on execution, the process to translate from Java byte code to native executable resulted in a loss of performance (with the exception of more recent cases in which Java is JIT compiled on certain platforms).

Instead of compiling the entire application at one time (which could lead to a slow startup time), the JIT compiler simply compiles each portion of code as it is called (just in time). When code has been compiled once, the resultant native executable is stored until the application exits so that it does not need to be recompiled the next time that portion of code is run. Microsoft argues that this process is more efficient than compiling the entire application code at the start because of the likelihood that large portions of any application code will not actually be executed in any given run. Using the JIT compiler, such code can never be compiled.

This explains why you can expect that execution of managed IL code will be almost as fast as executing native machine code. What it does not explain is why Microsoft expects that you get a performance *improvement*. The reason given for this is that because the final stage of compilation takes place at runtime, the JIT compiler knows exactly what processor type the program runs on. This means that it can optimize the final executable code to take advantage of any features or particular machine code instructions offered by that particular processor.

Traditional compilers optimize the code, but they can perform optimizations that are only independent of the particular processor that the code runs on. This is because traditional compilers compile to native executable code before the software is shipped. This means that the compiler does not know what type of processor the code runs on beyond basic generalities, such as that it is an x86-compatible processor or an Alpha processor.

Language Interoperability

The use of IL not only enables platform independence, but it also facilitates *language interoperability*. Simply put, you can compile to IL from one language, and this compiled code should then be interoperable with code that has been compiled to IL from another language.

You are probably now wondering which languages aside from C# are interoperable with .NET. The following sections briefly discuss how some of the other common languages fit into .NET.

Visual Basic 2012

Visual Basic .NET 2002 underwent a complete revamp from Visual Basic 6 to bring it up to date with the first version of the .NET Framework. The Visual Basic language had dramatically evolved from VB6, which this meant that VB6 was not a suitable language to run .NET programs. For example, VB6 is heavily integrated into Component Object Model (COM) and works by exposing only event handlers as source code to the developer — most of the background code is not available as source code. Not only that, it does not support implementation inheritance, and the standard data types that Visual Basic 6 uses are incompatible with .NET.

Visual Basic 6 was upgraded to Visual Basic .NET in 2002, and the changes that were made to the language are so extensive you might as well regard Visual Basic as a new language. Existing Visual Basic 6 code does not compile to the present Visual Basic 2012 code (or to Visual Basic .NET 2002, 2003, 2005, 2008, and 2010 for that matter). Converting a Visual Basic 6 program to Visual Basic 2012 requires extensive changes to the code. However, Visual Studio 2012 (the upgrade of Visual Studio for use with .NET) can do most of the changes for you. If you attempt to read a Visual Basic 6 project into Visual Studio 2012, it can upgrade the project for you, which means that it can rewrite the Visual Basic 6 source code into Visual Basic 2012 source code. Although this means that the work involved for you is heavily reduced, you need to check through the new Visual Basic 2012 code to make sure that the project still works as intended because the conversion is not perfect.

One side effect of this language upgrade is that it is no longer possible to compile Visual Basic 2012 to native executable code. Visual Basic 2012 compiles only to IL, just as C# does. If you need to continue coding in Visual Basic 6, you can do so, but the executable code produced completely ignores the .NET Framework, and you need to keep Visual Studio 6 installed if you want to continue to work in this developer environment.

Visual C++ 2012

Visual C++ 6 already had a large number of Microsoft-specific extensions on Windows. With Visual C++ .NET, extensions have been added to support the .NET Framework. This means that existing C++ source code will continue to compile to native executable code without modification. It also means, however, that it will run independently of the .NET runtime. If you want your C++ code to run within the .NET Framework, you can simply add the following line to the beginning of your code:

```
#using <mscorlib.dll>
```

You can also pass the flag /clr to the compiler, which then assumes that you want to compile to managed code and will hence emit IL instead of native machine code. The interesting thing about C++ is that when you compile to managed code, the compiler can emit IL that contains an embedded native executable. This means that you can mix managed types and unmanaged types in your C++ code. Thus, the managed C++ code

```
class MyClass
{
```

defines a plain C++ class, whereas the code

```
ref class MyClass
{
```

gives you a managed class, just as if you had written the class in C# or Visual Basic 2012. The advantage to use managed C++ over C# code is that you can call unmanaged C++ classes from managed C++ code without resorting to COM interop.

The compiler raises an error if you attempt to use features not supported by .NET on managed types (for example, templates or multiple inheritances of classes). You can also find that you need to use nonstandard C++ features when using managed classes.

Writing C++ programs that uses .NET gives you different variants of interop scenarios. With the compiler setting /clr for Common Language Runtime Support, you can completely mix all native and managed C++ features. Other options such as /clr:safe and /clr:pure restrict the use of native C++ pointers and thus enable writing safe code like with C# and Visual Basic.

Visual C++ 2012 enables you to create programs for the Windows Runtime (WinRT) with Windows 8. This way C++ does not use managed code but instead accesses the WinRT natively.

COM and COM+

Technically speaking, COM and COM+ are not technologies targeted at .NET — components based on them cannot be compiled into IL. (Although you can do so to some degree using managed C++ if the original COM component were written in C++). However, COM+ remains an important tool because its features are not duplicated in .NET. Also, COM components can still work — and .NET incorporates COM interoperability features that make it possible for managed code to call up COM components and vice versa (discussed in Chapter 23, "Interop"). In general, you will probably find it more convenient for most purposes to code new components as .NET components so that you can take advantage of the .NET base classes and the other benefits of running as managed code.

Windows Runtime

Windows 8 offers a new runtime used by the new applications. You can use this runtime from Visual Basic, C#, C++, and JavaScript. When using the runtime with these different environments, it looks different. Using it from C# it looks like classes from the .NET Framework. Using it from JavaScript it looks like what

JavaScript developers are used to with JavaScript libraries. And using it from C++, methods looks like the Standard C++ Library. This is done by using language projection. The Windows Runtime and how it looks like from C# is discussed in Chapter 31, "Windows Runtime."

A CLOSER LOOK AT INTERMEDIATE LANGUAGE

From what you learned in the previous section, Microsoft Intermediate Language obviously plays a fundamental role in the .NET Framework. It makes sense now to take a closer look at the main features of IL because any language that targets .NET logically needs to support these characteristics.

Here are the important features of IL:

➤   Object orientation and the use of interfaces

➤   Strong distinction between value and reference types

➤   Strong data typing

➤   Error handling using exceptions

➤   Use of attributes

The following sections explore each of these features.

Support for Object Orientation and Interfaces

The language independence of .NET does have some practical limitations. IL is inevitably going to implement some particular programming methodology, which means that languages targeting it need to be compatible with that methodology. The particular route that Microsoft has chosen to follow for IL is that of classic object-oriented programming, with single implementation inheritance of classes.

In addition to classic object-oriented programming, IL also brings in the idea of interfaces, which saw their first implementation under Windows with COM. Interfaces built using .NET produce interfaces that are not the same as COM interfaces. They do not need to support any of the COM infrastructure. (For example, they are not derived from IUnknown and do not have associated globally unique identifiers, more commonly known as GUIDs.) However, they do share with COM interfaces the idea that they provide a contract, and classes that implement a given interface must provide implementations of the methods and properties specified by that interface.

You have now seen that working with .NET means compiling to IL, and that in turn means that you need to use traditional object-oriented methodologies. However, that alone is not sufficient to give you language interoperability. After all, C++ and Java both use the same object-oriented paradigms but are still not regarded as interoperable. You need to look a little more closely at the concept of language interoperability.

So what exactly is language interoperability?

After all, COM enabled components written in different languages to work together in the sense of calling each other's methods. What was inadequate about that? COM, by virtue of being a binary standard, did enable components to instantiate other components and call methods or properties against them, without worrying about the language in which the respective components were written. To achieve this, however, each object had to be instantiated through the COM runtime and accessed through an interface. Depending on the threading models of the relative components, there may have been large performance losses associated with marshaling data between apartments or running components or both on different threads. In the extreme case of components hosted as an executable rather than DLL files, separate processes would need to be created to run them. The emphasis was very much that components could talk to each other but only via the COM runtime. In no way with COM did components written in different languages directly communicate with each other, or instantiate instances of each other — it was always done with COM as an intermediary. Not only that, but the COM architecture did not permit implementation inheritance, which meant that it lost many of the advantages of object-oriented programming.

An associated problem was that, when debugging, you would still need to debug components written in different languages independently. It was not possible to step between languages in the debugger. Therefore, what you *actually* mean by language interoperability is that classes written in one language should talk directly to classes written in another language. In particular

➤ A class written in one language can inherit from a class written in another language.

➤ The class can contain an instance of another class, no matter what the languages of the two classes are.

➤ An object can directly call methods against another object written in another language.

➤ Objects (or references to objects) can be passed around between methods.

➤ When calling methods between languages, you can step between the method calls in the debugger, even when this means stepping between source code written in different languages.

This is all quite an ambitious aim, but amazingly .NET and IL have achieved it. In the case of stepping between methods in the debugger, this facility is actually offered by the Visual Studio integrated development environment (IDE) rather than by the CLR.

Distinct Value and Reference Types

As with any programming language, IL provides a number of predefined primitive data types. One characteristic of IL, however, is that it makes a strong distinction between value and reference types. *Value types* are those for which a variable directly stores its data, whereas *reference types* are those for which a variable simply stores the address at which the corresponding data can be found.

In C++ terms, using reference types is similar to accessing a variable through a pointer, whereas for Visual Basic the best analogy for reference types are objects, which in Visual Basic 6 are always accessed through references. IL also lays down specifications about data storage: Instances of reference types are always stored in an area of memory known as the *managed heap*, whereas value types are normally stored on the *stack*. (Although if value types are declared as fields within reference types, they will be stored inline on the heap.) Chapter 2, "Core C#," discusses the stack and the managed heap and how they work.

Strong Data Typing

One important aspect of IL is that it is based on exceptionally *strong data typing*. That means that all variables are clearly marked as being of a particular, specific data type. (There is no room in IL, for example, for the Variant data type recognized by Visual Basic and scripting languages.) In particular, IL does not normally permit any operations that result in ambiguous data types.

For instance, Visual Basic 6 developers are used to passing variables around without worrying too much about their types because Visual Basic 6 automatically performs type conversion. C++ developers are used to routinely casting pointers between different types. Performing this kind of operation can be great for performance, but it breaks type safety. Hence, it is permitted only under certain circumstances in some of the languages that compile to managed code. Indeed, pointers (as opposed to references) are permitted only in marked blocks of code in C#, and not at all in Visual Basic. (Although they are allowed in managed C++.) Using pointers in your code causes it to fail the memory type-safety checks performed by the CLR. Some languages compatible with .NET, such as Visual Basic 2010, still allow some laxity in typing but only because the compilers behind the scenes ensure that the type safety is enforced in the emitted IL.

Although enforcing type safety might initially appear to hurt performance, in many cases the benefits gained from the services provided by .NET that rely on type safety far outweigh this performance loss. Such services include the following:

➤ Language interoperability

➤ Garbage collection

➤ Security

➤ Application domains

The following sections take a closer look at why strong data typing is particularly important for these features of .NET.

Strong Data Typing as a Key to Language Interoperability

If a class is to derive from or contains instances of other classes, it needs to know about all the data types used by the other classes. This is why strong data typing is so important. Indeed, it is the absence of any agreed-on system for specifying this information in the past that has always been the real barrier to inheritance and interoperability across languages. This kind of information is simply not present in a standard executable file or DLL.

Suppose that one of the methods of a Visual Basic 2012 class is defined to return an `Integer` — one of the standard data types available in Visual Basic 2012. C# simply does not have any data type of that name. Clearly, you can derive from the class, use this method, and use the return type from C# code only if the compiler knows how to map Visual Basic 2012's `Integer` type to some known type defined in C#. So, how is this problem circumvented in .NET?

Common Type System

This data type problem is solved in .NET using the *Common Type System* (CTS). The CTS defines the predefined data types available in IL so that all languages that target the .NET Framework can produce compiled code ultimately based on these types.

For the previous example, Visual Basic 2012's `Integer` is actually a 32-bit signed integer, which maps exactly to the IL type known as `Int32`. Therefore, this is the data type specified in the IL code. Because the C# compiler is aware of this type, there is no problem. At source code-level, C# refers to `Int32` with the keyword `int`, so the compiler simply treats the Visual Basic 2012 method as if it returned an `int`.

The CTS does not specify merely primitive data types but a rich hierarchy of types, which includes well-defined points in the hierarchy at which code is permitted to define its own types. The hierarchical structure of the CTS reflects the single-inheritance object-oriented methodology of IL, and resembles Figure 1-1.

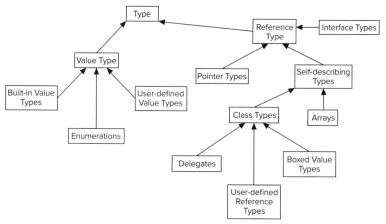

FIGURE 1-1

All of the built-in value types aren't here because they are covered in detail in Chapter 3, "Objects and Types." In C#, each predefined type is recognized by the compiler maps onto one of the IL built-in types. The same is true in Visual Basic 2012.

Common Language Specification

The *Common Language Specification* (CLS) works with the CTS to ensure language interoperability. The CLS is a set of minimum standards that all compilers targeting .NET must support. Because IL is a rich language, writers of most compilers prefer to restrict the capabilities of a given compiler to support only a subset of the facilities offered by IL and the CTS. That is fine as long as the compiler supports everything defined in the CLS.

For example, take case sensitivity. IL is case-sensitive. Developers who work with case-sensitive languages regularly take advantage of the flexibility that this case sensitivity gives them when selecting variable names. Visual Basic 2012, however, is not case-sensitive. The CLS works around this by indicating that CLS-compliant code should not expose any two names that differ only in their case. Therefore, Visual Basic 2012 code can work with CLS-compliant code.

This example shows that the CLS works in two ways:

1. Individual compilers do not need to be powerful enough to support the full features of .NET — this should encourage the development of compilers for other programming languages that target .NET.

2. If you restrict your classes to exposing only CLS-compliant features, then it guarantees that code written in any other compliant language can use your classes.

The beauty of this idea is that the restriction to using CLS-compliant features applies only to public and protected members of classes and public classes. Within the private implementations of your classes, you can write whatever non-CLS code you want because code in other assemblies (units of managed code; see later in the section Assemblies) cannot access this part of your code.

Without going into the details of the CLS specifications here, in general, the CLS does not affect your C# code much because of the few non-CLS-compliant features of C#.

> **NOTE** *It is perfectly acceptable to write non-CLS-compliant code. However, if you do, the compiled IL code is not guaranteed to be fully language interoperable.*

Garbage Collection

The *garbage collector* is .NET's answer to memory management and in particular to the question of what to do about reclaiming memory that running applications ask for. Up until now, two techniques have been used on the Windows platform for de-allocating memory that processes have dynamically requested from the system:

➤ Make the application code do it all manually.

➤ Make objects maintain reference counts.

Having the application code responsible for de-allocating memory is the technique used by lower-level, high-performance languages such as C++. It is efficient and has the advantage that (in general) resources are never occupied for longer than necessary. The big disadvantage, however, is the frequency of bugs. Code that requests memory also should explicitly inform the system when it no longer requires that memory. However, it is easy to overlook this, resulting in memory leaks.

Although modern developer environments do provide tools to assist in detecting memory leaks, they remain difficult bugs to track down. That's because they have no effect until so much memory has been leaked that Windows refuses to grant any more to the process. By this point, the entire computer may have appreciably slowed down due to the memory demands made on it.

Maintaining reference counts is favored in COM. The idea is that each COM component maintains a count of how many clients are currently maintaining references to it. When this count falls to zero, the component can destroy itself and free up associated memory and resources. The problem with this is that it still relies on the good behavior of clients to notify the component that they have finished with it. It takes only one client not to do so, and the object sits in memory. In some ways, this is a potentially more serious problem than a simple C++-style memory leak because the COM object may exist in its own process, which means that it can never be removed by the system. (At least with C++ memory leaks, the system can reclaim all memory when the process terminates.)

The .NET runtime relies on the garbage collector instead. The purpose of this program is to clean up memory. The idea is that all dynamically requested memory is allocated on the heap. (That is true for all languages; although in the case of .NET, the CLR maintains its own managed heap for .NET applications to use.) Sometimes, when .NET detects that the managed heap for a given process is becoming full and therefore needs tidying up, it calls the garbage collector. The garbage collector runs through variables currently in scope in your code, examining references to objects stored on the heap to identify which ones are accessible from your code — that is, which objects have references that refer to them. Any objects not referred to are deemed to be no longer accessible from your code and can therefore be removed. Java uses a system of garbage collection similar to this.

Garbage collection works in .NET because IL has been designed to facilitate the process. The principle requires that you cannot get references to existing objects other than by copying existing references and that IL is type safe. In this context, if any reference to an object exists, there is sufficient information in the reference to exactly determine the type of the object.

The garbage collection mechanism cannot be used with a language such as unmanaged C++, for example, because C++ enables pointers to be freely cast between types.

One important aspect of garbage collection is that it is not deterministic. In other words, you cannot guarantee when the garbage collector will be called. It will be called when the CLR decides that it is needed; though you can override this process and call up the garbage collector in your code. Calling the garbage collector in your code is good for testing purposes, but you shouldn't do this in a normal program.

Look at Chapter 14, "Memory Management and Pointers," for more information on the garbage collection process.

Security

.NET can excel in terms of complementing the security mechanisms provided by Windows because it can offer code-based security, whereas Windows offers only role-based security.

Role-based security is based on the identity of the account under which the process runs (that is, who owns and runs the process). *Code-based security*, by contrast, is based on what the code actually does and on how much the code is trusted. Because of the strong type safety of IL, the CLR can inspect code before running it to determine required security permissions. .NET also offers a mechanism by which code can indicate in advance what security permissions it requires to run.

The importance of code-based security is that it reduces the risks associated with running code of dubious origin (such as code that you have downloaded from the Internet). For example, even if code runs under the administrator account, you can use code-based security to indicate that the code should still not be permitted to perform certain types of operations that the administrator account would normally be allowed to do, such as read or write to environment variables, read or write to the registry, or access the .NET reflection features.

> **NOTE** *Security issues are covered in more depth in Chapter 22, "Security."*

Application Domains

Application domains are an important innovation in .NET and are designed to ease the overhead involved when running applications that need to be isolated from each other, but also need to communicate with each other. The classic example of this is a web server application, which may be simultaneously responding to a number of browser requests. It can, therefore, probably have a number of instances of the component responsible for servicing those requests running simultaneously.

In pre-.NET days, the choice would be between allowing those instances to share a process (with the resultant risk of a problem in one running instance bringing the whole website down) or isolating those instances in separate processes (with the associated performance overhead). Before .NET, isolation of code was only possible by using different processes. When you start a new application, it runs within the context of a process. Windows isolates processes from each other through address spaces. The idea is that each process has available 4GB of virtual memory in which to store its data and executable code (4GB is for 32-bit systems; 64-bit systems use more memory). Windows imposes an extra level of indirection by which this virtual

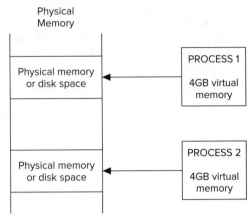

FIGURE 1-2

memory maps into a particular area of actual physical memory or disk space. Each process gets a different mapping, with no overlap between the actual physical memories that the blocks of virtual address space map to (see Figure 1-2).

In general, any process can access memory only by specifying an address in virtual memory — processes do not have direct access to physical memory. Hence, it is simply impossible for one process to access the memory allocated to another process. This provides an excellent guarantee that any badly behaved code cannot damage anything outside of its own address space.

Processes do not just serve as a way to isolate instances of running code from each other; they also form the unit to which security privileges and permissions are assigned. Each process has its own security token, which indicates to Windows precisely what operations that process is permitted to do.

Although processes are great for security reasons, their big disadvantage is in the area of performance. Often, a number of processes can actually work together, and therefore need to communicate with each other. The obvious example of this is where a process calls up a COM component, which is an executable and therefore is required to run in its own process. The same thing happens in COM when surrogates are used. Because processes cannot share any memory, a complex marshaling process must be used to copy data between the processes. This results in a significant performance hit. If you need components to work together and do not want that performance hit, you must use DLL-based components and have everything running in the same address space — with the associated risk that a badly behaved component can bring everything else down.

Application domains are designed as a way to separate components without resulting in the performance problems associated with passing data between processes. The idea is that any one process is divided into a number of application domains. Each application domain roughly corresponds to a single application, and each thread of execution can run in a particular application domain (see Figure 1-3).

If different executables run in the same process space, then they clearly can easily share data because theoretically they can directly see each other's data. However, although this is possible in principle, the CLR makes sure that this does not happen in practice by inspecting the code for each running application to ensure that the code cannot stray outside of its own data areas. This looks, at first, like an almost impossible task to pull off — after all, how can you tell what the program is going to do without actually running it?

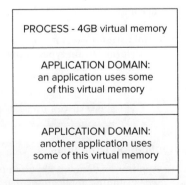

FIGURE 1-3

It is usually possible to do this because of the strong type safety of the IL. In most cases, unless code uses unsafe features such as pointers, the data types it uses ensures that memory is not accessed inappropriately. For example, .NET array types perform bounds checking to ensure that no out-of-bounds array operations are permitted. If a running application does need to communicate or share data with other applications running in different application domains, it must do so by calling on .NET's remoting services.

Code that has been verified to check that it cannot access data outside its application domain (other than through the explicit remoting mechanism) is *memory type safe*. Such code can safely be run alongside other type-safe code in different application domains within the same process.

Error Handling with Exceptions

The .NET Framework is designed to facilitate handling of error conditions using the same mechanism based on exceptions that is employed by Java and C++. C++ developers should note that because of IL's stronger typing system, there is no performance penalty associated with the use of exceptions with IL in the way that there is in C++. Also, the `finally` block, which has long been on many C++ developers' wish lists, is supported by .NET and by C#.

Exceptions are covered in detail in Chapter 16, "Errors and Exceptions." Briefly, the idea is that certain areas of code are designated as exception handler routines, with each one dealing with a particular error condition (for example, a file not being found, or being denied permission to perform some operation). These conditions can be defined as narrowly or as widely as you want. The exception architecture ensures that when an error condition occurs, execution can immediately jump to the exception handler routine that is most specifically geared to handle the exception condition in question.

The architecture of exception handling also provides a convenient means to pass an object containing precise details of the exception condition to an exception-handling routine. This object might include an appropriate message for the user and details of exactly where in the code the exception was detected.

Most exception-handling architecture, including the control of program flow when an exception occurs, is handled by the high-level languages (C#, Visual Basic 2012, C++), and is not supported by any special IL commands. C#, for example, handles exceptions using `try{}`, `catch{}`, and `finally{}` blocks of code. (For more details, see Chapter 16.)

What .NET does do, however, is provide the infrastructure to enable compilers that target .NET to support exception handling. In particular, it provides a set of .NET classes that can represent the exceptions and the language interoperability to enable the thrown exception objects to be interpreted by the exception-handling code, regardless of what language the exception-handling code is written in. This language independence is absent from both the C++ and Java implementations of exception handling; although it is present to a limited extent in the COM mechanism for handling errors, which involves returning error codes from methods and passing error objects around. Because exceptions are handled consistently in different languages is a crucial aspect of facilitating multi-language development.

Use of Attributes

Attributes are familiar to developers who use C++ to write COM components (through their use in Microsoft's COM Interface Definition Language [IDL]). The initial idea of an attribute was that it provided extra information concerning some item in the program that could be used by the compiler.

Attributes are supported in .NET — and now by C++, C#, and Visual Basic 2012. What is, however, particularly innovative about attributes in .NET is that you can define your own custom attributes in your source code. These user-defined attributes will be placed with the metadata for the corresponding data types or methods. This can be useful for documentation purposes, in which they can be used with reflection technology to perform programming tasks based on attributes. In addition, in common with the .NET philosophy of language independence, attributes can be defined in source code in one language and read by code written in another language.

> **NOTE** *Chapter 15, "Reflection," covers attributes.*

ASSEMBLIES

An *assembly* is the logical unit that contains compiled code targeted at the .NET Framework. This chapter doesn't cover assemblies in detail because they are covered thoroughly in Chapter 19, "Assemblies," but following are the main points.

An assembly is completely self-describing and is a logical rather than a physical unit, which means that it can be stored across more than one file. (Indeed, dynamic assemblies are stored in memory, not on file.) If an assembly is stored in more than one file, there will be one main file that contains the entry point and describes the other files in the assembly.

The same assembly structure is used for both executable code and library code. The only difference is that an executable assembly contains a main program entry point, whereas a library assembly does not.

An important characteristic of assemblies is that they contain metadata that describes the types and methods defined in the corresponding code. An assembly, however, also contains assembly metadata that describes the assembly. This assembly metadata, contained in an area known as the *manifest*, enables checks to be made on the version of the assembly and on its integrity.

> **NOTE** `ildasm`, *a Windows-based utility, can be used to inspect the contents of an assembly, including the manifest and metadata.* `ildasm` *is discussed in Chapter 19.*

Because an assembly contains program metadata means that applications or other assemblies that call up code in a given assembly do not need to refer to the registry, or to any other data source, to find out how to use that assembly. This is a significant break from the old COM way to do things, in which the GUIDs of the components and interfaces had to be obtained from the registry, and in some cases, the details of the methods and properties exposed would need to be read from a type library.

Having data spread out in up to three different locations meant there was the obvious risk of something getting out of synchronization, which would prevent other software from using the component successfully. With assemblies, there is no risk of this happening because all the metadata is stored with the program executable instructions. Even though assemblies are stored across several files, there are still no problems with data going out of synchronization. This is because the file that contains the assembly entry point also stores details of, and a hash of, the contents of the other files, which means that if one of the files is replaced, or in any way tampered with, this will almost certainly be detected and the assembly will refuse to load.

Assemblies come in two types: *private* and *shared* assemblies.

Private Assemblies

Private assemblies are the simplest type. They normally ship with software and are intended to be used only with that software. The usual scenario in which you ship private assemblies is when you supply an application in the form of an executable and a number of libraries, where the libraries contain code that should be used only with that application.

The system guarantees that private assemblies will not be used by other software because an application may load only private assemblies located in the same folder that the main executable is loaded in, or in a subfolder of it.

Because you would normally expect that commercial software would always be installed in its own directory, there is no risk of one software package overwriting, modifying, or accidentally loading private assemblies intended for another package. And, because private assemblies can be used only by the software package that they are intended for, you have much more control over what software uses them. There is, therefore, less need to take security precautions because there is no risk, for example, of some other commercial software overwriting one of your assemblies with some new version of it (apart from software designed specifically to perform malicious damage). There are also no problems with name collisions. If classes in your private assembly happen to have the same name as classes in someone else's private assembly, that does not matter because any given application can see only the one set of private assemblies.

Because a private assembly is entirely self-contained, the process to deploy it is simple. You simply place the appropriate file(s) in the appropriate folder in the file system. (No registry entries need to be made.) This process is known as *zero impact (xcopy) installation*.

Shared Assemblies

Shared assemblies are intended to be common libraries that any other application can use. Because any other software can access a shared assembly, more precautions need to be taken against the following risks:

> ➤ Name collisions, where another company's shared assembly implements types that have the same names as those in your shared assembly. Because client code can theoretically have access to both assemblies simultaneously, this could be a serious problem.

> ➤ The risk of an assembly being overwritten by a different version of the same assembly — the new version is incompatible with some existing client code.

The solution to these problems is placing shared assemblies in a special directory subtree in the file system, known as the *global assembly cache* (GAC). Unlike with private assemblies, this cannot be done by simply copying the assembly into the appropriate folder; it must be specifically installed into the cache. This process can be performed by a number of .NET utilities and requires certain checks on the assembly, as well as setting up of a small folder hierarchy within the assembly cache used to ensure assembly integrity.

To prevent name collisions, shared assemblies are given a name based on private key cryptography. (Private assemblies are simply given the same name as their main filename.) This name is known as a *strong name*; it is guaranteed to be unique and must be quoted by applications that reference a shared assembly.

Problems associated with the risk of overwriting an assembly are addressed by specifying version information in the assembly manifest and by allowing side-by-side installations.

Reflection

Because assemblies store metadata, including details of all the types and members of these types defined in the assembly, you can access this metadata programmatically. Full details of this are given in Chapter 15. This technique, known as reflection, raises interesting possibilities because it means that managed code can actually examine other managed code, and can even examine itself, to determine information about that code. This is most commonly used to obtain the details of attributes; although you can also use reflection, among other purposes, as an indirect way to instantiate classes or calling methods, given the names of those classes or methods as strings. In this way, you could select classes to instantiate methods to call at runtime, rather than at compile time, based on user input (dynamic binding).

Parallel Programming

The .NET Framework enables you to take advantage of all the multicore processors available today. The parallel computing capabilities provide the means to separate work actions and run these across multiple processors. The parallel programming APIs available now make writing safe multithreaded code simple; though you must realize that you still need to account for race conditions and things such as deadlocks.

The new parallel programming capabilities provide a new Task Parallel Library and a PLINQ Execution Engine. Chapter 21, "Tasks, Threads, and Synchronization," covers parallel programming.

Asynchronous Programming

Based on the `Task` from the Task Parallel Library are the new async features of C# 5. Since .NET 1.0, many classes from the .NET Framework offered asynchronous methods beside the synchronous variant. The user interface thread should not be blocked when doing a task that takes a while. You've probably seen several programs that have become unresponsive, which is annoying. A problem with the asynchronous methods was that they were difficult to use. The synchronous variant was a lot easier to program with, and thus this one was usually used.

Using the mouse the user is — with many years of experience — used to a delay. When moving objects or just using the scrollbar, a delay is normal. With new touch interfaces, if there's a delay the experience for the user can be extremely annoying. This can be solved by calling asynchronous methods. If a method with the WinRT might take more than 50 milliseconds, the WinRT offers only asynchronous method calls.

C# 5 now makes it easy to invoke new asynchronous methods. C# 5 defines two new keywords: `async` and `await`. These keywords and how they are used are discussed in Chapter 13, "Asynchronous Programming."

.NET FRAMEWORK CLASSES

Perhaps one of the biggest benefits to write managed code, at least from a developer's point of view, is that you can use the .NET *base class library*. The .NET base classes are a massive collection of managed code classes that enable you to do almost any of the tasks that were previously available through the Windows API. These classes follow the same object model that IL uses, based on single inheritance. This means that you can either instantiate objects of whichever .NET base class is appropriate or derive your own classes from them.

The great thing about the .NET base classes is that they have been designed to be intuitive and easy to use. For example, to start a thread, you call the `Start()` method of the `Thread` class. To disable a `TextBox`, you set the `Enabled` property of a `TextBox` object to `false`. This approach — though familiar to Visual Basic and Java developers whose respective libraries are just as easy to use — will be a welcome relief to C++ developers, who for years have had to cope with such API functions as `GetDIBits()`, `RegisterWndClassEx()`, and `IsEqualIID()`, and a plethora of functions that require Windows handles to be passed around.

However, C++ developers always had easy access to the entire Windows API, unlike Visual Basic 6 and Java developers who were more restricted in terms of the basic operating system functionality that they have access to from their respective languages. What is new about the .NET base classes is that they combine the ease of use that was typical of the Visual Basic and Java libraries with the relatively comprehensive coverage of the Windows API functions. Many features of Windows still are not available through the base classes, and for those you need to call into the API functions, but in general, these are now confined to the more exotic features. For everyday use, you can probably find the base classes adequate. Moreover, if you do need to call into an API function, .NET offers a *platform-invoke* that ensures data types are correctly converted, so the task is no harder than calling the function directly from C++ code would have been — regardless of whether you code in C#, C++, or Visual Basic 2012.

Although Chapter 3 is nominally dedicated to the subject of base classes, after you have completed the coverage of the syntax of the C# language, most of the rest of this book shows you how to use various classes within the .NET base class library for the .NET Framework 4.5. That is how comprehensive base classes are. As a rough guide, the areas covered by the .NET 4.5 base classes include the following:

➤ Core features provided by IL (including the primitive data types in the CTS discussed in Chapter 3)

➤ Windows UI support and controls (see Chapters 35–38)

➤ ASP.NET with Web Forms and MVC (see Chapters 39–42)

➤ Data access with ADO.NET and XML (see Chapters 32–34)

➤ File system and registry access (see Chapter 24, "Manipulating Files and Registry")

➤ Networking and web browsing (see Chapter 26, "Networking")

➤ .NET attributes and reflection (see Chapter 14)

➤ COM interoperability (see Chapter 23)

Incidentally, according to Microsoft sources, a large proportion of the .NET base classes have actually been written in C#.

NAMESPACES

Namespaces are the way that .NET avoids name clashes between classes. They are designed to prevent situations in which you define a class to represent a customer, name your class `Customer`, and then someone else does the same thing. (A likely scenario in which — the proportion of businesses that have customers seems to be quite high.)

A namespace is no more than a grouping of data types, but it has the effect that the names of all data types within a namespace are automatically prefixed with the name of the namespace. It is also possible to nest namespaces within each other. For example, most of the general-purpose .NET base classes are in a namespace called `System`. The base class `Array` is in this namespace, so its full name is `System.Array`.

.NET requires all types to be defined in a namespace; for example, you could place your `Customer` class in a namespace called `YourCompanyName.ProjectName`. This class would have the full name `YourCompanyName.ProjectName.Customer`.

> **NOTE** *If a namespace is not explicitly supplied, the type will be added to a nameless global namespace.*

Microsoft recommends that for most purposes you supply at least two nested namespace names: the first one represents the name of your company, and the second one represents the name of the technology or software package of which the class is a member, such as `YourCompanyName.SalesServices.Customer`. This protects, in most situations, the classes in your application from possible name clashes with classes written by other organizations.

Chapter 2 looks more closely at namespaces.

CREATING .NET APPLICATIONS USING C#

You can also use C# to create console applications: text-only applications that run in a DOS window. You can probably use console applications when unit testing class libraries and for creating UNIX or Linux daemon processes. More often, however, you can use C# to create applications that use many of the technologies associated with .NET. This section gives you an overview of the different types of applications that you can write in C#.

Creating ASP.NET Applications

The original introduction of ASP.NET 1.0 fundamentally changed the web programming model. ASP.NET 4.5 is a major release of the product and builds upon its earlier achievements. ASP.NET 4.5 follows on a series of major revolutionary steps designed to increase your productivity. The primary goal of ASP.NET is to enable you to build powerful, secure, dynamic applications using the least possible amount of code. As this is a C# book, there are many chapters showing you how to use this language to build the latest in web applications.

The following section explores the key features of ASP.NET. For more details, refer to Chapters 39 to 42.

Features of ASP.NET

With the invention of ASP.NET, there were only ASP.NET Web Forms, which had the goal of easily creating web applications in a way a Windows application developer was used to writing applications. It was the goal not to need to write HTML and JavaScript.

Nowadays this is difference again. HTML and JavaScript became important and modern again. And there's a new ASP.NET Framework that makes it easy to do this and gives a separation based on the well-known Model View Controller (MVC) pattern for easier unit testing: ASP.NET MVC.

ASP.NET was refactored to have a foundation available both for ASP.NET Web Forms and ASP.NET MVC, and then the UI frameworks are based on this foundation.

> **NOTE** *Chapter 39, "Core ASP.NET" covers the foundation of ASP.NET*

ASP.NET Web Forms

To make web page construction easy, Visual Studio 2012 supplies *Web Forms*. Web pages can be built graphically by dragging controls from a toolbox onto a form and then flipping over to the code aspect of that form and writing event handlers for the controls. When you use C# to create a Web Form, you create a C# class that inherits from the `Page` base class and an ASP.NET page that designates that class as its code-behind. Of course, you do not need to use C# to create a Web Form; you can use Visual Basic 2012 or another .NET-compliant language just as well.

ASP.NET Web Forms provide a rich functionality with controls that do not create only simple HTML code, but with controls that do input validation using both JavaScript and server-side validation logic, grids, data sources to access the database, offer Ajax features for dynamically rendering just parts of the page on the client and much more.

> **NOTE** *Chapter 40, "ASP.NET Web Forms" discusses ASP.NET Web Forms.*

Web Server Controls

The controls used to populate a Web Form are not controls in the same sense as ActiveX controls. Rather, they are XML tags in the ASP.NET namespace that the web browser dynamically transforms into HTML and client-side script when a page is requested. Amazingly, the web server can render the same server-side control in different ways, producing a transformation appropriate to the requestor's particular web browser. This means that it is now easy to write fairly sophisticated user interfaces for web pages, without worrying about how to ensure that your page can run on any of the available browsers — because Web Forms take care of that for you.

You can use C# or Visual Basic 2012 to expand the Web Form toolbox. Creating a new server-side control is simply a matter of implementing .NET's `System.Web.UI.WebControls.WebControl` class.

ASP.NET MVC

Visual Studio comes with *ASP.NET MVC* 4. This technology is already available in version 4. Contrary to Web Forms where HTML and JavaScript is abstracted away from the developer, with the advent of HTML 5 and jQuery, using these technologies has become more important again. With ASP.NET MVC the focus is on writing server-side code separated within model and controller and using views with just a little bit of server-side code to get information from the controller. This separation makes unit testing a lot easier and gives the full power to use HTML 5 and JavaScript libraries.

> **NOTE** *Chapter 41, "ASP.NET MVC" covers ASP.NET MVC.*

ASP.NET Dynamic Data

Creating data-driven web applications is fast using *ASP.NET Dynamic Data*. Using the Entity Framework and scaffolding options, forms to read and write data can be done in an efficient, rapid way. ASP.NET Dynamic Data is not a one-stop way to create forms; you can also customize the forms and form fields, classes that should be offered for data entry.

> **NOTE** *Chapter 42, "ASP.NET Dynamic Data" covers ASP.NET Dynamic Data.*

ASP.NET Web API

A new way for simple communication between the client and the server — a REST based style — is offered with the *ASP.NET Web API*. This new framework is based on ASP.NET MVC and makes use of controllers and routing. The client can receive JSON or Atom data based on the Open Data specification.

The features of this new API makes it easy to consume from web clients using JavaScript, but also from Windows 8 apps.

> **NOTE** *Because ASP.NET Web API is based on ASP.NET MVC, this technology is covered in Chapter 41.*

Windows Presentation Foundation (WPF)

For creating Windows desktop applications, two technologies are available: Windows Forms and Windows Presentation Foundation. Windows Forms consists of classes that just wrap native Windows controls and is thus based on pixel graphics. *Windows Presentation Foundation* (WPF) is the newer technology based on vector graphics.

WPF makes use of XAML in building applications. XAML stands for eXtensible Application Markup Language. This new way to create applications within a Microsoft environment is something introduced in 2006 and is part of the .NET Framework 3.0. This means that to run any WPF application, you need to make sure that at least the .NET Framework 3.0 is installed on the client machine. Of course, you get new WPF features with newer versions of the framework. With version 4.5, for example, the ribbon control and live shaping are new features among many new controls.

XAML is the XML declaration used to create a form that represents all the visual aspects and behaviors of the WPF application. Though you can work with a WPF application programmatically, WPF is a step in the direction of declarative programming, which the industry is moving to. *Declarative programming* means that instead of creating objects through programming in a compiled language such as C#, VB, or Java, you declare everything through XML-type programming. Chapter 29, "Core XAML," introduces XAML (which is also used with XML Paper Specification, Windows Workflow Foundation, and Windows Communication Foundation).

Chapter 35, "Core WPF," details how to build WPF applications using XAML and C#. Chapter 36 goes into more details on data-driven business applications with WPF and XAML. Printing and creating documents is another important aspect of WPF covered in Chapter 37, "Creating Documents with WPF."

Windows 8 Apps

Windows 8 starts a new paradigm with touch-first Windows 8 apps. With desktop applications the user usually gets a menu and a toolbar, receives a chrome with the application to see what he can do next. Windows 8 apps have the focus on the content. Chrome should be minimized to tasks the user can do with the content, and not on different options he has. The focus is on the current task, and not what the user might do next. This way the user remembers the application based on its content. Content and no chrome is a buzz phrase with this technology.

Windows 8 apps can be written with C# and XAML, using the Windows Runtime with a subset of the .NET Framework. Windows 8 apps offer huge new opportunities. The major disadvantage is that they are only available with Windows 8 and newer operating systems.

> **NOTE** *Chapter 38, "Windows 8 UI," covers creating Windows 8 apps.*

Windows Services

A Windows Service (originally called an NT Service) is a program designed to run in the background in Windows NT kernel based operating systems. Services are useful when you want a program to run continuously and ready to respond to events without having been explicitly started by the user. A good example is the World Wide Web Service on web servers, which listens for web requests from clients.

It is easy to write services in C#. .NET Framework base classes are available in the `System .ServiceProcess` namespace that handles many of the boilerplate tasks associated with services. In addition, Visual Studio .NET enables you to create a C# Windows Service project, which uses C# source code for a basic Windows Service. Chapter 27, "Windows Services," explores how to write C# Windows Services.

Windows Communication Foundation

One communication technology fused between client and server is the ASP.NET Web API. The ASP.NET Web API is easy to use but doesn't offer a lot of features such as offered from the SOAP protocol.

Windows Communication Foundation (WCF) is a feature-rich technology to offer a broad set of communication options. With WCF you can use a REST-based communication but also a SOAP-based communication with all the features used by standards-based Web services such as security, transactions, duplex and one-way communication, routing, discovery, and so on. WCF provides you with the ability to build your service one time and then expose this service in a multitude of ways (under different protocols even) by just making changes within a configuration file. You can find that WCF is a powerful new way to connect disparate systems. Chapter 43, "Windows Communication Foundation," covers this in detail. You can also find WCF-based technologies such as WCF Data Services and Message Queuing with WCF in Chapter 44, "WCF Data Services" and Chapter 47, "Message Queuing."

Windows Workflow Foundation

The *Windows Workflow Foundation* (WF) was introduced with the release of the .NET Framework 3.0 but had a good overhaul that many find more approachable now since .NET 4. There are some smaller improvements with .NET 4.5 as well. You can find that Visual Studio 2012 has greatly improved for working with WF and makes it easier to construct your workflows and write expressions using C# (instead of VB in the previous edition). You can also find a new state machine designer and new activities.

> **NOTE** *WF is covered in Chapter 45, "Windows Workflow Foundation."*

THE ROLE OF C# IN THE .NET ENTERPRISE ARCHITECTURE

New technologies are coming in a fast pace. What should you use for enterprise applications? There are many aspects that influence the decision. For example, what about the existing applications that have been developed with current technology knowledge of the developers. Can you integrate new features with legacy applications? Depending on the maintenance required, maybe it makes sense to rebuild some existing applications for easier use of new features. Usually, legacy and new can coexist for many years to come. What is the requirement for the client systems? Can the .NET Framework be upgraded to version 4.5, or is 2.0 a requirement? Or is .NET not available on the client?

There are many decisions to make, and .NET gives many options. You can use .NET on the client with Windows Forms, WPF, or Windows 8-style apps. You can use .NET on the web server hosted with IIS and the ASP.NET Runtime with ASP.NET Web Forms or ASP.NET MVC. Services can run within IIS, and you can host the services from within Windows Services. C# presents an outstanding opportunity for organizations interested in building robust, n-tiered client-server applications.

When combined with ADO.NET, C# has the capability to quickly and generically access data stores such as SQL Server or other databases with data providers. The ADO.NET Entity Framework can be an easy way to map database relations to object hierarchies. This is not only possible with SQL Server, but also many different databases where an Entity Framework provider is offered. The returned data can easily be manipulated using the ADO.NET object model or LINQ and automatically rendered as XML or JSON for transport across an office intranet.

After a database schema has been established for a new project, C# presents an excellent medium for implementing a layer of data access objects, each of which could provide insertion, updates, and deletion access to a different database table.

Because it's the first component-based C language, C# is a great language for implementing a business object tier, too. It encapsulates the messy plumbing for intercomponent communication, leaving developers free to focus on gluing their data access objects together in methods that accurately enforce their organizations' business rules.

To create an enterprise application with C#, you create a class library project for the data access objects and another for the business objects. While developing, you can use Console projects to test the methods on your classes. Fans of extreme programming can build Console projects that can be executed automatically from batch files to unit test that working code has not been broken.

On a related note, C# and .NET will probably influence the way you physically package your reusable classes. In the past, many developers crammed a multitude of classes into a single physical component because this arrangement made deployment a lot easier; if there were a versioning problem, you knew just where to look. Because deploying .NET components involves simply copying files into directories, developers can now package their classes into more logical, discrete components without encountering "DLL Hell."

Last, but not least, ASP.NET pages coded in C# constitute an excellent medium for user interfaces. Because ASP.NET pages compile, they execute quickly. Because they can be debugged in the Visual Studio 2012 IDE, they are robust. Because they support full-scale language features such as early binding, inheritance, and modularization, ASP.NET pages coded in C# are tidy and easily maintained.

After the hype of SOA and service-based programming, nowadays using services has becoming the norm. The new hype is cloud-based programming, with Windows Azure as Microsoft's offering. You can run .NET applications in a range from ASP.NET Web Forms, ASP.NET Web API, or WCF either on on-premise servers or in the cloud. Clients can make use of HTML 5 for a broad reach or make use of WPF or Windows 8 apps for rich functionality. Still with new technologies and options, .NET has a prosperous life.

SUMMARY

This chapter covered a lot of ground, briefly reviewing important aspects of the .NET Framework and C#'s relationship to it. It started by discussing how all languages that target .NET are compiled into Microsoft Intermediate Language (IL) before this is compiled and executed by the Common Language Runtime (CLR). This chapter also discussed the roles of the following features of .NET in the compilation and execution process:

➤ Assemblies and .NET base classes

➤ COM components

➤ JIT compilation

➤ Application domains

➤ Garbage collection

Figure 1-4 provides an overview of how these features come into play during compilation and execution.

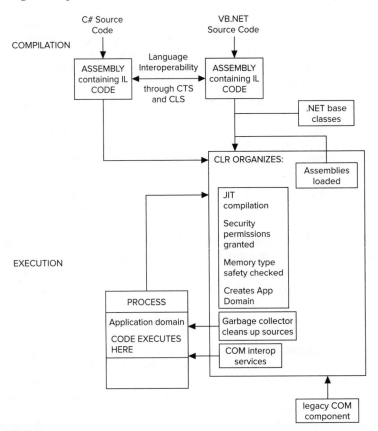

FIGURE 1-4

You learned about the characteristics of IL, particularly its strong data typing and object orientation, and how these characteristics influence the languages that target .NET, including C#. You also learned how the strongly typed nature of IL enables language interoperability, as well as CLR services such as garbage collection and security. There was also a focus on the Common Language Specification (CLS) and the Common Type System (CTS) to help deal with language interoperability.

Finally, you learned how C# can be used as the basis for applications built on several .NET technologies, including ASP.NET and WPF.

Chapter 2 discusses how to write code in C#.

Core C#

WHAT'S IN THIS CHAPTER?

- ➤ Declaring variables
- ➤ Initialization and scope of variables
- ➤ Predefined C# data types
- ➤ Dictating execution flow within a C# program using conditional statements, loops, and jump statements
- ➤ Enumerations
- ➤ Namespaces
- ➤ The `Main()` method
- ➤ Basic command-line C# compiler options
- ➤ Using `System.Console` to perform console I/O
- ➤ Using internal comments and documentation features
- ➤ Preprocessor directives
- ➤ Guidelines and conventions for good programming in C#

WROX.COM CODE DOWNLOADS FOR THIS CHAPTER

The wrox.com code downloads for this chapter are found at `http://www.wrox.com/remtitle.cgi?isbn=1118314425` on the Download Code tab. The code for this chapter is divided into the following major examples:

- ➤ ArgsExample.cs
- ➤ DoubleMain.cs
- ➤ ElseIf.cs
- ➤ First.cs
- ➤ MathClient.cs
- ➤ MathLibrary.cs
- ➤ NestedFor.cs
- ➤ Scope.cs

➤   ScopeBad.cs

➤   ScopeTest2.cs

➤   StringExample.cs

➤   Var.cs

FUNDAMENTAL C#

Now that you understand more about what C# can do, you will want to learn how to use it. This chapter gives you a good start in that direction by providing a basic understanding of the fundamentals of C# programming, which is built on in subsequent chapters. By the end of this chapter, you will know enough C# to write simple programs (though without using inheritance or other object-oriented features, which are covered in later chapters).

YOUR FIRST C# PROGRAM

Let's start by compiling and running the simplest possible C# program—a simple console app consisting of a class that writes a message to the screen.

> **NOTE** *Later chapters present a number of code samples. The most common technique for writing C# programs is to use Visual Studio 2011 to generate a basic project and add your own code to it. However, because the aim of Part I is to teach the C# language, we are going to keep things simple and avoid relying on Visual Studio 2011 until Chapter 17, "Visual Studio 2011." Instead, we present the code as simple files that you can type in using any text editor and compile from the command line.*

The Code

Type the following into a text editor (such as Notepad), and save it with a `.cs` extension (for example, `First.cs`). The `Main()` method is shown here (for more information, see "The Main Method" section later in this chapter):

```
using System;

namespace Wrox
{
   public class MyFirstClass
   {
      static void Main()
      {
         Console.WriteLine("Hello from Wrox.");
         Console.ReadLine();
         return;
      }
   }
}
```

Compiling and Running the Program

You can compile this program by simply running the C# command-line compiler (`csc.exe`) against the source file, like this:

```
csc First.cs
```

If you want to compile code from the command line using the csc command, you should be aware that the .NET command-line tools, including csc, are available only if certain environment variables have been set up. Depending on how you installed .NET (and Visual Studio 2011), this may or may not be the case on your machine.

> **NOTE** *If you do not have the environment variables set up, you have two options: The first is to run the batch file* %Microsoft Visual Studio 2011%\Common7\Tools\vsvars32.bat *from the command prompt before running* csc*, where* %Microsoft Visual Studio 2011% *is the folder to which Visual Studio 2011 has been installed. The second, and easier, way is to use the Visual Studio 2011 command prompt instead of the usual command prompt window. To find the Visual Studio 2011 command prompt from the Start menu, select Programs ⇨ Microsoft Visual Studio 2011 ⇨ Visual Studio Tools. It is simply a command prompt window that automatically runs* vsvars32.bat *when it opens.*

Compiling the code produces an executable file named First.exe, which you can run from the command line or from Windows Explorer like any other executable. Give it a try:

```
csc First.cs
Microsoft (R) Visual C# Compiler version 4.0.30319.17379
for Microsoft(R) .NET Framework 4.5
Copyright (C) Microsoft Corporation. All rights reserved.

First.exe
Hello from Wrox.
```

A Closer Look

First, a few general comments about C# syntax. In C#, as in other C-style languages, most statements end in a semicolon (;) and can continue over multiple lines without needing a continuation character. Statements can be joined into blocks using curly braces ({}). Single-line comments begin with two forward slash characters (//), and multiline comments begin with a slash and an asterisk (/*) and end with the same combination reversed (*/). In these aspects, C# is identical to C++ and Java but different from Visual Basic. It is the semicolons and curly braces that give C# code such a different visual appearance from Visual Basic code. If your background is predominantly Visual Basic, take extra care to remember the semicolon at the end of every statement. Omitting this is usually the biggest single cause of compilation errors among developers new to C-style languages. Another thing to remember is that C# is case sensitive. That means the variables named myVar and MyVar are two different variables.

The first few lines in the previous code example are related to *namespaces* (mentioned later in this chapter), which is a way to group together associated classes. The namespace keyword declares the namespace with which your class should be associated. All code within the braces that follow it is regarded as being within that namespace. The using statement specifies a namespace that the compiler should look at to find any classes that are referenced in your code but aren't defined in the current namespace. This serves the same purpose as the import statement in Java and the using namespace statement in C++.

```
using System;

namespace Wrox
{
```

The reason for the presence of the using statement in the First.cs file is that you are going to use a library class, System.Console. The using System statement enables you to refer to this class simply as Console (and similarly for any other classes in the System namespace). Without using, you would have to fully qualify the call to the Console.WriteLine method like this:

```
System.Console.WriteLine("Hello from Wrox.");
```

The standard `System` namespace is where the most commonly used .NET types reside. It is important to realize that everything you do in C# depends on the .NET base classes. In this case, you are using the `Console` class within the `System` namespace to write to the console window. C# has no built-in keywords of its own for input or output; it is completely reliant on the .NET classes.

> **NOTE** *Because almost every C# program uses classes in the* System *namespace, we will assume that a* using System; *statement is present in the file for all code snippets in this chapter.*

Next, you declare a class called `MyFirstClass`. However, because it has been placed in a namespace called `Wrox`, the fully qualified name of this class is `Wrox.MyFirstCSharpClass`:

```
class MyFirstCSharpClass
{
```

All C# code must be contained within a class. The class declaration consists of the `class` keyword, followed by the class name and a pair of curly braces. All code associated with the class should be placed between these braces.

Next, you declare a method called `Main()`. Every C# executable (such as console applications, Windows applications, and Windows services) must have an entry point—the `Main()` method (note the capital `M`):

```
public static void Main()
{
```

The method is called when the program is started. This method must return either nothing (`void`) or an integer (`int`). Note the format of method definitions in C#:

```
[modifiers] return_type MethodName([parameters])
{
    // Method body. NB. This code block is pseudo-code.
}
```

Here, the first square brackets represent certain optional keywords. Modifiers are used to specify certain features of the method you are defining, such as from where the method can be called. In this case, you have two modifiers: `public` and `static`. The `public` modifier means that the method can be accessed from anywhere, so it can be called from outside your class. The `static` modifier indicates that the method does not operate on a specific instance of your class and therefore is called without first instantiating the class. This is important because you are creating an executable rather than a class library. You set the return type to `void`, and in the example you don't include any parameters.

Finally, we come to the code statements themselves:

```
Console.WriteLine("Hello from Wrox.");
Console.ReadLine();
return;
```

In this case, you simply call the `WriteLine()` method of the `System.Console` class to write a line of text to the console window. `WriteLine()` is a `static` method, so you don't need to instantiate a `Console` object before calling it.

`Console.ReadLine()` reads user input. Adding this line forces the application to wait for the carriage-return key to be pressed before the application exits, and, in the case of Visual Studio 2011, the console window disappears.

You then call `return` to exit from the method (also, because this is the `Main()` method, you exit the program as well). You specified `void` in your method header, so you don't return any values.

Now that you have had a taste of basic C# syntax, you are ready for more detail. Because it is virtually impossible to write any nontrivial program without *variables*, we will start by looking at variables in C#.

VARIABLES

You declare variables in C# using the following syntax:

```
datatype identifier;
```

For example:

```
int i;
```

This statement declares an `int` named `i`. The compiler won't actually let you use this variable in an expression until you have initialized it with a value.

After it has been declared, you can assign a value to the variable using the assignment operator, `=`:

```
i = 10;
```

You can also declare the variable and initialize its value at the same time:

```
int i = 10;
```

If you declare and initialize more than one variable in a single statement, all the variables will be of the same data type:

```
int x = 10, y =20;    // x and y are both ints
```

To declare variables of different types, you need to use separate statements. You cannot assign different data types within a multiple-variable declaration:

```
int x = 10;
bool y = true;            // Creates a variable that stores true or false
int x = 10, bool y = true;    // This won't compile!
```

Notice the `//` and the text after it in the preceding examples. These are comments. The `//` character sequence tells the compiler to ignore the text that follows on this line because it is included for a human to better understand the program, not part of the program itself. We further explain comments in code later in this chapter.

Initialization of Variables

Variable initialization demonstrates an example of C#'s emphasis on safety. Briefly, the C# compiler requires that any variable be initialized with some starting value before you refer to that variable in an operation. Most modern compilers will flag violations of this as a warning, but the ever-vigilant C# compiler treats such violations as errors. This prevents you from unintentionally retrieving junk values from memory left over from other programs.

C# has two methods for ensuring that variables are initialized before use:

➤ Variables that are fields in a class or struct, if not initialized explicitly, are by default zeroed out when they are created (classes and structs are discussed later).

➤ Variables that are local to a method must be explicitly initialized in your code prior to any statements in which their values are used. In this case, the initialization doesn't have to happen when the variable is declared, but the compiler checks all possible paths through the method and flags an error if it detects any possibility of the value of a local variable being used before it is initialized.

For example, you can't do the following in C#:

```
public static int Main()
{
    int d;
    Console.WriteLine(d);   // Can't do this! Need to initialize d before use
    return 0;
}
```

Notice that this code snippet demonstrates defining `Main()` so that it returns an `int` instead of `void`.

If you attempt to compile the preceding lines, you will receive this error message:

```
Use of unassigned local variable 'd'
```

Consider the following statement:

```
Something objSomething;
```

In C#, this line of code would create only a *reference* for a `Something` object, but this reference would not yet actually refer to any object. Any attempt to call a method or property against this variable would result in an error.

Instantiating a reference object in C# requires use of the `new` keyword. You create a reference as shown in the previous example and then point the reference at an object allocated on the heap using the `new` keyword:

```
objSomething = new Something();   // This creates a Something on the heap
```

Type Inference

Type inference makes use of the `var` keyword. The syntax for declaring the variable changes somewhat. The compiler "infers" what the type of the variable is by what the variable is initialized to. For example:

```
int someNumber = 0;
```

becomes:

```
var someNumber = 0;
```

Even though `someNumber` is never declared as being an `int`, the compiler figures this out and `someNumber` is an `int` for as long as it is in scope. Once compiled, the two preceding statements are equal.

Here is a short program to demonstrate:

```
using System;

namespace Wrox
{
  class Program
  {
    static void Main(string[] args)
    {
      var name = "Bugs Bunny";
      var age = 25;
      var isRabbit = true;

      Type nameType = name.GetType();
      Type ageType = age.GetType();
      Type isRabbitType = isRabbit.GetType();

      Console.WriteLine("name is type " + nameType.ToString());
      Console.WriteLine("age is type " + ageType.ToString());
      Console.WriteLine("isRabbit is type " + isRabbitType.ToString());
    }
  }
}
```

The output from this program is as follows:

```
name is type System.String
age is type System.Int32
isRabbit is type System.Bool
```

There are a few rules that you need to follow:

➤ The variable must be initialized. Otherwise, the compiler doesn't have anything from which to infer the type.

➤ The initializer cannot be null.

➤ The initializer must be an expression.

➤ You can't set the initializer to an object unless you create a new object in the initializer.

We examine this more closely in the discussion of anonymous types in Chapter 3, "Objects and Types."

After the variable has been declared and the type inferred, the variable's type cannot be changed. When established, the variable's type follows all the strong typing rules that any other variable type must follow.

Variable Scope

The *scope* of a variable is the region of code from which the variable can be accessed. In general, the scope is determined by the following rules:

➤ A *field* (also known as a member variable) of a class is in scope for as long as its containing class is in scope.

➤ A *local variable* is in scope until a closing brace indicates the end of the block statement or method in which it was declared.

➤ A local variable that is declared in a `for`, `while`, or similar statement is in scope in the body of that loop.

Scope Clashes for Local Variables

It's common in a large program to use the same variable name for different variables in different parts of the program. This is fine as long as the variables are scoped to completely different parts of the program so that there is no possibility for ambiguity. However, bear in mind that local variables with the same name can't be declared twice in the same scope. For example, you can't do this:

```
int x = 20;
// some more code
int x = 30;
```

Consider the following code sample:

```
using System;
namespace Wrox.ProCSharp.Basics
{
    public class ScopeTest
    {
        public static int Main()
        {
            for (int i = 0; i < 10; i++)
            {
                Console.WriteLine(i);
            }   // i goes out of scope here
            // We can declare a variable named i again, because
            // there's no other variable with that name in scope
            for (int i = 9; i >= 0; i-)
            {
                Console.WriteLine(i);
            }   // i goes out of scope here.
            return 0;
        }
    }
}
```

This code simply prints out the numbers from 0 to 9, and then back again from 9 to 0, using two `for` loops. The important thing to note is that you declare the variable `i` twice in this code, within the same method. You can do this because `i` is declared in two separate loops, so each `i` variable is local to its own loop.

Here's another example:

```
public static int Main()
{
    int j = 20;
    for (int i = 0; i < 10; i++)
    {
        int j = 30;    // Can't do this—j is still in scope
        Console.WriteLine(j + i);
    }
    return 0;
}
```

If you try to compile this, you'll get an error like the following:

```
ScopeTest.cs(12,15): error CS0136: A local variable named 'j' cannot be declared in
this scope because it would give a different meaning to 'j', which is already used
in a 'parent or current' scope to denote something else.
```

This occurs because the variable `j`, which is defined before the start of the `for` loop, is still in scope within the `for` loop, and won't go out of scope until the `Main()` method has finished executing. Although the second `j` (the illegal one) is in the loop's scope, that scope is nested within the `Main()` method's scope. The compiler has no way to distinguish between these two variables, so it won't allow the second one to be declared.

Scope Clashes for Fields and Local Variables

In certain circumstances, however, you can distinguish between two identifiers with the same name (although not the same fully qualified name) and the same scope, and in this case the compiler allows you to declare the second variable. That's because C# makes a fundamental distinction between variables that are declared at the type level (fields) and variables that are declared within methods (local variables).

Consider the following code snippet:

```
using System;
namespace Wrox
{
    class ScopeTest2
    {
        static int j = 20;
        public static void Main()
        {
            int j = 30;
            Console.WriteLine(j);
            return;
        }
    }
}
```

This code will compile even though you have two variables named `j` in scope within the `Main()` method: the `j` that was defined at the class level, and doesn't go out of scope until the class is destroyed (when the `Main()` method terminates and the program ends); and the `j` defined in `Main()`. In this case, the new variable named `j` that you declare in the `Main()` method *hides* the class-level variable with the same name, so when you run this code, the number 30 is displayed.

What if you want to refer to the class-level variable? You can actually refer to fields of a class or struct from outside the object, using the syntax `object.fieldname`. In the previous example, you are accessing a static field (you'll learn what this means in the next section) from a static method, so you can't use an instance of the class; you just use the name of the class itself:

```
  ..
public static void Main()
{
   int j = 30;
   Console.WriteLine(j);
   Console.WriteLine(ScopeTest2.j);
}
  ..
```

If you were accessing an instance field (a field that belongs to a specific instance of the class), you would need to use the `this` keyword instead.

Constants

As the name implies, a constant is a variable whose value cannot be changed throughout its lifetime. Prefixing a variable with the `const` keyword when it is declared and initialized designates that variable as a constant:

```
const int a = 100;   // This value cannot be changed.
```

Constants have the following characteristics:

➤ They must be initialized when they are declared; and after a value has been assigned, it can never be overwritten.

➤ The value of a constant must be computable at compile time. Therefore, you can't initialize a constant with a value taken from a variable. If you need to do this, you must use a read-only field (this is explained in Chapter 3).

➤ Constants are always implicitly static. However, notice that you don't have to (and, in fact, are not permitted to) include the `static` modifier in the constant declaration.

At least three advantages exist for using constants in your programs:

➤ Constants make your programs easier to read by replacing magic numbers and strings with readable names whose values are easy to understand.

➤ Constants make your programs easier to modify. For example, assume that you have a `SalesTax` constant in one of your C# programs, and that constant is assigned a value of 6 percent. If the sales tax rate changes later, you can modify the behavior of all tax calculations simply by assigning a new value to the constant; you don't have to hunt through your code for the value `.06` and change each one, hoping you will find all of them.

➤ Constants help prevent mistakes in your programs. If you attempt to assign another value to a constant somewhere in your program other than at the point where the constant is declared, the compiler will flag the error.

PREDEFINED DATA TYPES

Now that you have seen how to declare variables and constants, let's take a closer look at the data types available in C#. As you will see, C# is much stricter about the types available and their definitions than some other languages.

Value Types and Reference Types

Before examining the data types in C#, it is important to understand that C# distinguishes between two categories of data type:

➤ Value types

➤ Reference types

The next few sections look in detail at the syntax for value and reference types. Conceptually, the difference is that a *value type* stores its value directly, whereas a *reference type* stores a reference to the value.

These types are stored in different places in memory; value types are stored in an area known as the *stack*, and reference types are stored in an area known as the *managed heap*. It is important to be aware of whether a type is a value type or a reference type because of the different effect each assignment has. For example, int is a value type, which means that the following statement results in two locations in memory storing the value 20:

```
// i and j are both of type int
i = 20;
j = i;
```

However, consider the following example. For this code, assume you have defined a class called Vector; and that Vector is a reference type and has an int member variable called Value:

```
Vector x, y;
x = new Vector();
x.Value = 30;    // Value is a field defined in Vector class
y = x;
Console.WriteLine(y.Value);
y.Value = 50;
Console.WriteLine(x.Value);
```

The crucial point to understand is that after executing this code, there is only one Vector object: x and y both point to the memory location that contains this object. Because x and y are variables of a reference type, declaring each variable simply reserves a reference—it doesn't instantiate an object of the given type. In neither case is an object actually created. To create an object, you have to use the new keyword, as shown. Because x and y refer to the same object, changes made to x will affect y and vice versa. Hence, the code will display 30 and then 50.

> **NOTE** *C++ developers should note that this syntax is like a reference, not a pointer. You use the . notation, not ->, to access object members. Syntactically, C# references look more like C++ reference variables. However, behind the superficial syntax, the real similarity is with C++ pointers.*

If a variable is a reference, it is possible to indicate that it does not refer to any object by setting its value to null:

```
y = null;
```

If a reference is set to null, then clearly it is not possible to call any nonstatic member functions or fields against it; doing so would cause an exception to be thrown at runtime.

In C#, basic data types such as bool and long are value types. This means that if you declare a bool variable and assign it the value of another bool variable, you will have two separate bool values in memory. Later, if you change the value of the original bool variable, the value of the second bool variable does not change. These types are copied by value.

In contrast, most of the more complex C# data types, including classes that you yourself declare, are reference types. They are allocated upon the heap, have lifetimes that can span multiple function calls, and can be accessed through one or several aliases. The Common Language Runtime (CLR) implements an elaborate algorithm to track which reference variables are still reachable and which have been orphaned. Periodically, the CLR will destroy orphaned objects and return the memory that they once occupied back to the operating system. This is done by the garbage collector.

C# has been designed this way because high performance is best served by keeping primitive types (such as int and bool) as value types, and larger types that contain many fields (as is usually the case with classes) as reference types. If you want to define your own type as a value type, you should declare it as a struct.

CTS Types

As mentioned in Chapter 1, ".NET Architecture," the basic predefined types recognized by C# are not intrinsic to the language but are part of the .NET Framework. For example, when you declare an `int` in C#, you are actually declaring an instance of a .NET struct, `System.Int32`. This may sound like a small point, but it has a profound significance: It means that you can treat all the primitive data types syntactically, as if they were classes that supported certain methods. For example, to convert an `int i` to a `string`, you can write the following:

```
string s = i.ToString();
```

It should be emphasized that behind this syntactical convenience, the types really are stored as primitive types, so absolutely no performance cost is associated with the idea that the primitive types are notionally represented by .NET structs.

The following sections review the types that are recognized as built-in types in C#. Each type is listed, along with its definition and the name of the corresponding .NET type (CTS type). C# has 15 predefined types, 13 value types, and 2 (`string` and `object`) reference types.

Predefined Value Types

The built-in CTS value types represent primitives, such as integer and floating-point numbers, character, and Boolean types.

Integer Types

C# supports eight predefined integer types, shown in the following table.

NAME	CTS TYPE	DESCRIPTION	RANGE (MIN:MAX)
sbyte	System.SByte	8-bit signed integer	-128:127 (-2^7:2^7-1)
short	System.Int16	16-bit signed integer	-32,768:32,767 (-2^{15}:$2^{15}-1$)
int	System.Int32	32-bit signed integer	-2,147,483,648:2,147,483,647 (-2^{31}:$2^{31}-1$)
long	System.Int64	64-bit signed integer	-9,223,372,036,854,775,808: 9,223,372,036,854,775,807 (-2^{63}:$2^{63}-1$)
byte	System.Byte	8-bit unsigned integer	0:255 (0:2^8-1)
ushort	System.UInt16	16-bit unsigned integer	0:65,535 (0:$2^{16}-1$)
uint	System.UInt32	32-bit unsigned integer	0:4,294,967,295 (0:$2^{32}-1$)
ulong	System.UInt64	64-bit unsigned integer	0:18,446,744,073,709,551,615 (0:$2^{64}-1$)

Some C# types have the same names as C++ and Java types but have different definitions. For example, in C# an `int` is always a 32-bit signed integer. In C++ an `int` is a signed integer, but the number of bits is platform-dependent (32 bits on Windows). In C#, all data types have been defined in a platform-independent manner to allow for the possible future porting of C# and .NET to other platforms.

A `byte` is the standard 8-bit type for values in the range 0 to 255 inclusive. Be aware that, in keeping with its emphasis on type safety, C# regards the `byte` type and the `char` type as completely distinct, and any programmatic conversions between the two must be explicitly requested. Also be aware that unlike the other types in the integer family, a `byte` type is by default unsigned. Its signed version bears the special name `sbyte`.

With .NET, a `short` is no longer quite so short; it is now 16 bits long. The `int` type is 32 bits long. The `long` type reserves 64 bits for values. All integer-type variables can be assigned values in decimal or hex notation. The latter requires the `0x` prefix:

```
long x = 0x12ab;
```

If there is any ambiguity about whether an integer is int, uint, long, or ulong, it will default to an int. To specify which of the other integer types the value should take, you can append one of the following characters to the number:

```
uint ui = 1234U;
long l = 1234L;
ulong ul = 1234UL;
```

You can also use lowercase u and l, although the latter could be confused with the integer 1 (one).

Floating-Point Types

Although C# provides a plethora of integer data types, it supports floating-point types as well.

NAME	CTS TYPE	DESCRIPTION	SIGNIFICANT FIGURES	RANGE (APPROXIMATE)
float	System.Single	32-bit, single-precision floating point	7	$\pm 1.5 \times 10^{245}$ to $\pm 3.4 \times 10^{38}$
double	System.Double	64-bit, double-precision floating point	15/16	$\pm 5.0 \times 10^{2324}$ to $\pm 1.7 \times 10^{308}$

The float data type is for smaller floating-point values, for which less precision is required. The double data type is bulkier than the float data type but offers twice the precision (15 digits).

If you hard-code a non-integer number (such as 12.3), the compiler will normally assume that you want the number interpreted as a double. To specify that the value is a float, append the character F (or f) to it:

```
float f = 12.3F;
```

The Decimal Type

The decimal type represents higher-precision floating-point numbers, as shown in the following table.

NAME	CTS TYPE	DESCRIPTION	SIGNIFICANT FIGURES	RANGE (APPROXIMATE)
decimal	System.Decimal	128-bit, high-precision decimal notation	28	$\pm 1.0 \times 10^{228}$ to $\pm 7.9 \times 10^{28}$

One of the great things about the CTS and C# is the provision of a dedicated decimal type for financial calculations. How you use the 28 digits that the decimal type provides is up to you. In other words, you can track smaller dollar amounts with greater accuracy for cents or larger dollar amounts with more rounding in the fractional portion. Bear in mind, however, that decimal is not implemented under the hood as a primitive type, so using decimal has a performance effect on your calculations.

To specify that your number is a decimal type rather than a double, float, or an integer, you can append the M (or m) character to the value, as shown here:

```
decimal d = 12.30M;
```

The Boolean Type

The C# bool type is used to contain Boolean values of either true or false.

NAME	CTS TYPE	DESCRIPTION	SIGNIFICANT FIGURES	RANGE (APPROXIMATE)
bool	System.Boolean	Represents true or false	NA	true or false

You cannot implicitly convert `bool` values to and from integer values. If a variable (or a function return type) is declared as a `bool`, you can only use values of `true` and `false`. You will get an error if you try to use zero for `false` and a nonzero value for `true`.

The Character Type

For storing the value of a single character, C# supports the `char` data type.

NAME	CTS TYPE	VALUES
char	System.Char	Represents a single 16-bit (Unicode) character

Literals of type `char` are signified by being enclosed in single quotation marks—for example, `'A'`. If you try to enclose a character in double quotation marks, the compiler will treat this as a string and throw an error.

As well as representing `char`s as character literals, you can represent them with four-digit hex Unicode values (for example, `'\u0041'`), as integer values with a cast (for example, `(char)65`), or as hexadecimal values (for example,`'\x0041'`). You can also represent them with an escape sequence, as shown in the following table.

ESCAPE SEQUENCE	CHARACTER
\'	Single quotation mark
\"	Double quotation mark
\\	Backslash
\0	Null
\a	Alert
\b	Backspace
\f	Form feed
\n	Newline
\r	Carriage return
\t	Tab character
\v	Vertical tab

Predefined Reference Types

C# supports two predefined reference types, `object` and `string`, described in the following table.

NAME	CTS TYPE	DESCRIPTION
object	System.Object	The root type. All other types (including value types) in the CTS are derived from `object`.
string	System.String	Unicode character string

The object Type

Many programming languages and class hierarchies provide a root type, from which all other objects in the hierarchy are derived. C# and .NET are no exception. In C#, the `object` type is the ultimate parent type from which all other intrinsic and user-defined types are derived. This means that you can use the `object` type for two purposes:

➤ You can use an `object` reference to bind to an object of any particular subtype. For example, in Chapter 7, "Operators and Casts," you will see how you can use the `object` type to box a value object on the stack to move it to the heap; `object` references are also useful in reflection, when code must manipulate objects whose specific types are unknown.

➤ The `object` type implements a number of basic, general-purpose methods, which include `Equals()`, `GetHashCode()`, `GetType()`, and `ToString()`. Responsible user-defined classes may need to provide replacement implementations of some of these methods using an object-oriented technique known as *overriding*, which is discussed in Chapter 4, "Inheritance." When you override `ToString()`, for example, you equip your class with a method for intelligently providing a string representation of itself. If you don't provide your own implementations for these methods in your classes, the compiler will pick up the implementations in `object`, which may or may not be correct or sensible in the context of your classes.

We examine the `object` type in more detail in subsequent chapters.

The string Type

C# recognizes the `string` keyword, which under the hood is translated to the .NET class, `System.String`. With it, operations like string concatenation and string copying are a snap:

```
string str1 = "Hello ";
string str2 = "World";
string str3 = str1 + str2; // string concatenation
```

Despite this style of assignment, `string` is a reference type. Behind the scenes, a `string` object is allocated on the heap, not the stack; and when you assign one string variable to another string, you get two references to the same string in memory. However, `string` differs from the usual behavior for reference types. For example, strings are immutable. Making changes to one of these strings creates an entirely new `string` object, leaving the other string unchanged. Consider the following code:

```
using System;
class StringExample
{
    public static int Main()
    {
        string s1 = "a string";
        string s2 = s1;
        Console.WriteLine("s1 is " + s1);
        Console.WriteLine("s2 is " + s2);
        s1 = "another string";
        Console.WriteLine("s1 is now " + s1);
        Console.WriteLine("s2 is now " + s2);
        return 0;
    }
}
```

The output from this is as follows:

```
s1 is a string
s2 is a string
s1 is now another string
s2 is now a string
```

Changing the value of `s1` has no effect on `s2`, contrary to what you'd expect with a reference type! What's happening here is that when `s1` is initialized with the value a string, a new string object is allocated on the heap. When `s2` is initialized, the reference points to this same object, so `s2` also has the value a string. However, when you now change the value of `s1`, instead of replacing the original value, a new object is allocated on the heap for the new value. The `s2` variable will still point to the original object, so its value is unchanged. Under the hood, this happens as a result of operator overloading, a topic that is explored in Chapter 7. In general, the `string` class has been implemented so that its semantics follow what you would normally intuitively expect for a string.

String literals are enclosed in double quotation marks (`". "`); if you attempt to enclose a string in single quotation marks, the compiler will take the value as a `char` and throw an error. C# strings can contain the same Unicode and hexadecimal escape sequences as `chars`. Because these escape sequences start with a backslash, you can't use this character unescaped in a string. Instead, you need to escape it with two backslashes (`\\`):

```
string filepath = "C:\\ProCSharp\\First.cs";
```

Even if you are confident that you can remember to do this all the time, typing all those double backslashes can prove annoying. Fortunately, C# gives you an alternative. You can prefix a string literal with the at character (@) and all the characters after it will be treated at face value; they won't be interpreted as escape sequences:

```
string filepath = @"C:\ProCSharp\First.cs";
```

This even enables you to include line breaks in your string literals:

```
string jabberwocky = @"'Twas brillig and the slithy toves
Did gyre and gimble in the wabe.";
```

In this case, the value of `jabberwocky` would be this:

```
'Twas brillig and the slithy toves
Did gyre and gimble in the wabe.
```

FLOW CONTROL

This section looks at the real nuts and bolts of the language: the statements that allow you to control the *flow* of your program rather than execute every line of code in the order it appears in the program.

Conditional Statements

Conditional statements allow you to branch your code depending on whether certain conditions are met or the value of an expression. C# has two constructs for branching code: the `if` statement, which allows you to test whether a specific condition is met; and the `switch` statement, which allows you to compare an expression with several different values.

The if Statement

For conditional branching, C# inherits the C and C++ `if..else` construct. The syntax should be fairly intuitive for anyone who has done any programming with a procedural language:

```
if (condition)
    statement(s)
else
    statement(s)
```

If more than one statement is to be executed as part of either condition, these statements need to be joined together into a block using curly braces (`{.}`). (This also applies to other C# constructs where statements can be joined into a block, such as the `for` and `while` loops):

```
bool isZero;
if (i == 0)
{
    isZero = true;
    Console.WriteLine("i is Zero");
}
else
{
    isZero = false;
    Console.WriteLine("i is Non-zero");
}
```

If you want to, you can use an `if` statement without a final `else` statement. You can also combine `else if` clauses to test for multiple conditions:

```
using System;
namespace Wrox
{
    class MainEntryPoint
    {
```

```
static void Main(string[] args)
{
    Console.WriteLine("Type in a string");
    string input;
    input = Console.ReadLine();
    if (input == "")
    {
        Console.WriteLine("You typed in an empty string.");
    }
    else if (input.Length < 5)
    {
        Console.WriteLine("The string had less than 5 characters.");
    }
    else if (input.Length < 10)
    {
        Console.WriteLine("The string had at least 5 but less than 10
            Characters.");
    }
    Console.WriteLine("The string was " + input);
}
}
```

There is no limit to how many `else if`s you can add to an `if` clause.

Note that the previous example declares a string variable called `input`, gets the user to enter text at the command line, feeds this into `input`, and then tests the length of this string variable. The code also shows how easy string manipulation can be in C#. To find the length of `input`, for example, use `input.Length`.

Another point to note about `if` is that you don't need to use the braces if there's only one statement in the conditional branch:

```
if (i == 0) Let's add some brackets here.
    Console.WriteLine("i is Zero");       // This will only execute if i == 0
Console.WriteLine("i can be anything");   // Will execute whatever the
                                          // value of i
```

However, for consistency, many programmers prefer to use curly braces whenever they use an `if` statement.

The `if` statements presented also illustrate some of the C# operators that compare values. Note in particular that C# uses == to compare variables for equality. Do not use = for this purpose. A single = is used to assign values.

In C#, the expression in the `if` clause must evaluate to a Boolean. It is not possible to test an integer directly (returned from a function, for example). You have to convert the integer that is returned to a Boolean `true` or `false`, for example, by comparing the value with zero or `null`:

```
if (DoSomething() != 0)
{
    // Non-zero value returned
}
else
{
    // Returned zero
}
```

The switch Statement

The `switch` / `case` statement is good for selecting one branch of execution from a set of mutually exclusive ones. It takes the form of a `switch` argument followed by a series of `case` clauses. When the expression in the `switch` argument evaluates to one of the values beside a `case` clause, the code immediately following the `case` clause executes. This is one example for which you don't need to use curly braces to join statements into blocks; instead, you mark the end of the code for each case using the `break` statement. You can also include a `default` case in the `switch` statement, which will execute if the expression evaluates to none of the other cases. The following `switch` statement tests the value of the `integerA` variable:

```
switch (integerA)
{
    case 1:
        Console.WriteLine("integerA =1");
        break;
    case 2:
        Console.WriteLine("integerA =2");
        break;
    case 3:
        Console.WriteLine("integerA =3");
        break;
    default:
        Console.WriteLine("integerA is not 1,2, or 3");
        break;
}
```

Note that the case values must be constant expressions; variables are not permitted.

Though the `switch.case` statement should be familiar to C and C++ programmers, C#'s `switch.case` is a bit safer than its C++ equivalent. Specifically, it prohibits fall-through conditions in almost all cases. This means that if a `case` clause is fired early on in the block, later clauses cannot be fired unless you use a `goto` statement to indicate that you want them fired, too. The compiler enforces this restriction by flagging every `case` clause that is not equipped with a `break` statement as an error:

```
Control cannot fall through from one case label ('case 2:') to another
```

Although it is true that fall-through behavior is desirable in a limited number of situations, in the vast majority of cases it is unintended and results in a logical error that's hard to spot. Isn't it better to code for the norm rather than for the exception?

By getting creative with `goto` statements, you can duplicate fall-through functionality in your `switch.cases`. However, if you find yourself really wanting to, you probably should reconsider your approach. The following code illustrates both how to use `goto` to simulate fall-through, and how messy the resultant code can be:

```
// assume country and language are of type string
switch(country)
{
    case "America":
        CallAmericanOnlyMethod();
        goto case "Britain";
    case "France":
        language = "French";
        break;
    case "Britain":
        language = "English";
        break;
}
```

There is one exception to the no-fall-through rule, however, in that you can fall through from one case to the next if that case is empty. This allows you to treat two or more cases in an identical way (without the need for `goto` statements):

```
switch(country)
{
    case "au":
    case "uk":
    case "us":
        language = "English";
        break;
```

```
      case "at":
      case "de":
         language = "German";
         break;
   }
```

One intriguing point about the `switch` statement in C# is that the order of the cases doesn't matter—you can even put the `default` case first! As a result, no two cases can be the same. This includes different constants that have the same value, so you can't, for example, do this:

```
// assume country is of type string
const string england = "uk";
const string britain = "uk";
switch(country)
{
   case england:
   case britain:     // This will cause a compilation error.
      language = "English";
      break;
}
```

The previous code also shows another way in which the `switch` statement is different in C# compared to C++: In C#, you are allowed to use a string as the variable being tested.

Loops

C# provides four different loops (`for`, `while`, `do. . .while`, and `foreach`) that enable you to execute a block of code repeatedly until a certain condition is met.

The for Loop

C# `for` loops provide a mechanism for iterating through a loop whereby you test whether a particular condition holds true before you perform another iteration. The syntax is

```
for (initializer; condition; iterator):
   statement(s)
```

where:

> ➤ The initializer is the expression evaluated before the first loop is executed (usually initializing a local variable as a loop counter).

> ➤ The condition is the expression checked before each new iteration of the loop (this must evaluate to `true` for another iteration to be performed).

> ➤ The iterator is an expression evaluated after each iteration (usually incrementing the loop counter).

The iterations end when the condition evaluates to `false`.

The `for` loop is a so-called pretest loop because the loop condition is evaluated before the loop statements are executed; therefore, the contents of the loop won't be executed at all if the loop condition is `false`.

The `for` loop is excellent for repeating a statement or a block of statements for a predetermined number of times. The following example demonstrates typical usage of a `for` loop. It will write out all the integers from 0 to 99:

```
for (int i = 0; i < 100; i=i+1)   // This is equivalent to
                                  // For i = 0 To 99 in VB.
{
   Console.WriteLine(i);
}
```

Here, you declare an `int` called `i` and initialize it to zero. This will be used as the loop counter. You then immediately test whether it is less than 100. Because this condition evaluates to `true`, you execute the code in the loop, displaying the value 0. You then increment the counter by one, and walk through the process again. Looping ends when i reaches 100.

Actually, the way the preceding loop is written isn't quite how you would normally write it. C# has a shorthand for adding 1 to a variable, so instead of i = i + 1, you can simply write i++:

```
for (int i = 0; i < 100; i++)
{
    // etc.
    }
```

You can also make use of type inference for the iteration variable i in the preceding example. Using type inference the loop construct would be as follows:

```
for (var i = 0; i < 100; i++)
..
```

It's not unusual to nest `for` loops so that an inner loop executes once completely for each iteration of an outer loop. This approach is typically employed to loop through every element in a rectangular multidimensional array. The outermost loop loops through every row, and the inner loop loops through every column in a particular row. The following code displays rows of numbers. It also uses another `Console` method, `Console.Write()`, which does the same thing as `Console.WriteLine()` but doesn't send a carriage return to the output:

```
using System;
namespace Wrox
{
    class MainEntryPoint
    {
        static void Main(string[] args)
        {
            // This loop iterates through rows
            for (int i = 0; i < 100; i+=10)
            {
                // This loop iterates through columns
                for (int j = i; j < i + 10; j++)
                {
                    Console.Write("  " + j);
                }
                Console.WriteLine();
            }
        }
    }
}
```

Although j is an integer, it is automatically converted to a string so that the concatenation can take place.

The preceding sample results in this output:

```
0   1   2   3   4   5   6   7   8   9
10  11  12  13  14  15  16  17  18  19
20  21  22  23  24  25  26  27  28  29
30  31  32  33  34  35  36  37  38  39
40  41  42  43  44  45  46  47  48  49
50  51  52  53  54  55  56  57  58  59
60  61  62  63  64  65  66  67  68  69
70  71  72  73  74  75  76  77  78  79
80  81  82  83  84  85  86  87  88  89
90  91  92  93  94  95  96  97  98  99
```

It is technically possible to evaluate something other than a counter variable in a `for` loop's test condition, but it is certainly not typical. It is also possible to omit one (or even all) of the expressions in the `for` loop. In such situations, however, you should consider using the `while` loop.

The while Loop

Like the for loop, while is a pretest loop. The syntax is similar, but while loops take only one expression:

```
while(condition)
    statement(s);
```

Unlike the for loop, the while loop is most often used to repeat a statement or a block of statements for a number of times that is not known before the loop begins. Usually, a statement inside the while loop's body will set a Boolean flag to false on a certain iteration, triggering the end of the loop, as in the following example:

```
bool condition = false;
while (!condition)
{
    // This loop spins until the condition is true.
    DoSomeWork();
    condition = CheckCondition();   // assume CheckCondition() returns a bool
}
```

The do...while Loop

The do...while loop is the post-test version of the while loop. This means that the loop's test condition is evaluated after the body of the loop has been executed. Consequently, do...while loops are useful for situations in which a block of statements must be executed at least one time, as in this example:

```
bool condition;
do
{
    // This loop will at least execute once, even if Condition is false.
    MustBeCalledAtLeastOnce();
    condition = CheckCondition();
} while (condition);
```

The foreach Loop

The foreach loop enables you to iterate through each item in a collection. For now, don't worry about exactly what a collection is (it is explained fully in Chapter 10, "Collections"); just understand that it is an object that represents a list of objects. Technically, to count as a collection, it must support an interface called IEnumerable. Examples of collections include C# arrays, the collection classes in the System. Collection namespaces, and user-defined collection classes. You can get an idea of the syntax of foreach from the following code, if you assume that arrayOfInts is (unsurprisingly) an array of ints:

```
foreach (int temp in arrayOfInts)
{
    Console.WriteLine(temp);
}
```

Here, foreach steps through the array one element at a time. With each element, it places the value of the element in the int variable called temp and then performs an iteration of the loop.

Here is another situation where type inference can be used. The foreach loop would become the following:

```
foreach (var temp in arrayOfInts)
    ..
```

temp would be inferred to int because that is what the collection item type is.

An important point to note with foreach is that you can't change the value of the item in the collection (temp in the preceding code), so code such as the following will not compile:

```
foreach (int temp in arrayOfInts)
{
    temp++;
    Console.WriteLine(temp);
}
```

If you need to iterate through the items in a collection and change their values, you must use a `for` loop instead.

Jump Statements

C# provides a number of statements that enable you to jump immediately to another line in the program. The first of these is, of course, the notorious `goto` statement.

The goto Statement

The `goto` statement enables you to jump directly to another specified line in the program, indicated by a *label* (this is just an identifier followed by a colon):

```
goto Label1;
    Console.WriteLine("This won't be executed");
Label1:
    Console.WriteLine("Continuing execution from here");
```

A couple of restrictions are involved with `goto`. You can't jump into a block of code such as a `for` loop, you can't jump out of a class, and you can't exit a `finally` block after `try.catch` blocks (Chapter 16, "Errors and Exceptions," looks at exception handling with `try.catch.finally`).

The reputation of the `goto` statement probably precedes it, and in most circumstances, its use is sternly frowned upon. In general, it certainly doesn't conform to good object-oriented programming practices.

The break Statement

You have already met the `break` statement briefly—when you used it to exit from a case in a `switch` statement. In fact, `break` can also be used to exit from `for`, `foreach`, `while`, or `do..while` loops. Control will switch to the statement immediately after the end of the loop.

If the statement occurs in a nested loop, control switches to the end of the innermost loop. If the break occurs outside of a `switch` statement or a loop, a compile-time error will occur.

The continue Statement

The `continue` statement is similar to `break`, and must also be used within a `for`, `foreach`, `while`, or `do..while` loop. However, it exits only from the current iteration of the loop, meaning that execution will restart at the beginning of the next iteration of the loop, rather than outside the loop altogether.

The return Statement

The `return` statement is used to exit a method of a class, returning control to the caller of the method. If the method has a return type, `return` must return a value of this type; otherwise, if the method returns `void`, you should use `return` without an expression.

ENUMERATIONS

An *enumeration* is a user-defined integer type. When you declare an enumeration, you specify a set of acceptable values that instances of that enumeration can contain. Not only that, but you can also give the values user-friendly names. If, somewhere in your code, you attempt to assign a value that is not in the acceptable set of values to an instance of that enumeration, the compiler will flag an error.

Creating an enumeration can save you a lot of time and headaches in the long run. At least three benefits exist to using enumerations instead of plain integers:

➤ As mentioned, enumerations make your code easier to maintain by helping to ensure that your variables are assigned only legitimate, anticipated values.

➤ Enumerations make your code clearer by allowing you to refer to integer values by descriptive names rather than by obscure "magic" numbers.

➤ Enumerations make your code easier to type, too. When you begin to assign a value to an instance of an enumerated type, the Visual Studio .NET IDE will, through IntelliSense, pop up a list box of acceptable values to save you some keystrokes and remind you of the possible options.

You can define an enumeration as follows:

```
public enum TimeOfDay
{
    Morning = 0,
    Afternoon = 1,
    Evening = 2
}
```

In this case, you use an integer value to represent each period of the day in the enumeration. You can now access these values as members of the enumeration. For example, TimeOfDay.Morning will return the value 0. You will typically use this enumeration to pass an appropriate value into a method and iterate through the possible values in a switch statement:

```
class EnumExample
{
    public static int Main()
    {
        WriteGreeting(TimeOfDay.Morning);
        return 0;
    }
    static void WriteGreeting(TimeOfDay timeOfDay)
    {
        switch(timeOfDay)
        {
            case TimeOfDay.Morning:
                Console.WriteLine("Good morning!");
                break;
            case TimeOfDay.Afternoon:
                Console.WriteLine("Good afternoon!");
                break;
            case TimeOfDay.Evening:
                Console.WriteLine("Good evening!");
                break;
            default:
                Console.WriteLine("Hello!");
                break;
        }
    }
}
```

The real power of enums in C# is that behind the scenes they are instantiated as structs derived from the base class, System.Enum. This means it is possible to call methods against them to perform some useful tasks. Note that because of the way the .NET Framework is implemented, no performance loss is associated with treating the enums syntactically as structs. In practice, after your code is compiled, enums will exist as primitive types, just like int and float.

You can retrieve the string representation of an enum, as in the following example, using the earlier TimeOfDay enum:

```
TimeOfDay time = TimeOfDay.Afternoon;
Console.WriteLine(time.ToString());
```

This returns the string Afternoon.

Alternatively, you can obtain an enum value from a string:

```
TimeOfDay time2 = (TimeOfDay) Enum.Parse(typeof(TimeOfDay), "afternoon", true);
Console.WriteLine((int)time2);
```

This code snippet illustrates both obtaining an enum value from a string and converting to an integer. To convert from a string, you need to use the static `Enum.Parse()` method, which, as shown, takes three parameters. The first is the type of enum you want to consider. The syntax is the keyword `typeof` followed by the name of the enum class in brackets. (Chapter 7 explores the `typeof` operator in more detail.) The second parameter is the string to be converted, and the third parameter is a `bool` indicating whether case should be ignored when doing the conversion. Finally, note that `Enum.Parse()` actually returns an object reference—you need to explicitly convert this to the required enum type (this is an example of an unboxing operation). For the preceding code, this returns the value 1 as an object, corresponding to the enum value of `TimeOfDay.Afternoon`. Converting explicitly to an `int`, this produces the value 1 again.

Other methods on `System.Enum` do things such as return the number of values in an enum definition or list the names of the values. Full details are in the MSDN documentation.

NAMESPACES

As you saw earlier in this chapter, namespaces provide a way to organize related classes and other types. Unlike a file or a component, a namespace is a logical, rather than a physical, grouping. When you define a class in a C# file, you can include it within a namespace definition. Later, when you define another class that performs related work in another file, you can include it within the same namespace, creating a logical grouping that indicates to other developers using the classes how they are related and used:

```
namespace CustomerPhoneBookApp
{
    using System;
    public struct Subscriber
    {
        // Code for struct here..
    }
}
```

Placing a type in a namespace effectively gives that type a long name, consisting of the type's namespace as a series of names separated with periods (.), terminating with the name of the class. In the preceding example, the full name of the `Subscriber` struct is `CustomerPhoneBookApp.Subscriber`. This enables distinct classes with the same short name to be used within the same program without ambiguity. This full name is often called the *fully qualified name*.

You can also nest namespaces within other namespaces, creating a hierarchical structure for your types:

```
namespace Wrox
{
    namespace ProCSharp
    {
        namespace Basics
        {
            class NamespaceExample
            {
                // Code for the class here..
            }
        }
    }
}
```

Each namespace name is composed of the names of the namespaces it resides within, separated with periods, starting with the outermost namespace and ending with its own short name. Therefore, the full name for the `ProCSharp` namespace is `Wrox.ProCSharp`, and the full name of the `NamespaceExample` class is `Wrox.ProCSharp.Basics.NamespaceExample`.

You can use this syntax to organize the namespaces in your namespace definitions too, so the previous code could also be written as follows:

```
namespace Wrox.ProCSharp.Basics
{
```

```
    class NamespaceExample
    {
        // Code for the class here..
    }
}
```

Note that you are not permitted to declare a multipart namespace nested within another namespace.

Namespaces are not related to assemblies. It is perfectly acceptable to have different namespaces in the same assembly or to define types in the same namespace in different assemblies.

Defining the namespace hierarchy should be planned out prior to the start of a project. Generally the accepted format is `CompanyName.ProjectName.SystemSection`. In the previous example, Wrox is the company name, ProCSharp is the project, and in the case of this chapter, Basics is the section.

The using Directive

Obviously, namespaces can grow rather long and tiresome to type, and the capability to indicate a particular class with such specificity may not always be necessary. Fortunately, as noted earlier in this chapter, C# allows you to abbreviate a class's full name. To do this, list the class's namespace at the top of the file, prefixed with the `using` keyword. Throughout the rest of the file, you can refer to the types in the namespace simply by their type names:

```
using System;
using Wrox.ProCSharp;
```

As remarked earlier, virtually all C# source code will have the statement `using System;` simply because so many useful classes supplied by Microsoft are contained in the `System` namespace.

If two namespaces referenced by `using` statements contain a type of the same name, you need to use the full (or at least a longer) form of the name to ensure that the compiler knows which type to access. For example, suppose classes called `NamespaceExample` exist in both the `Wrox.ProCSharp.Basics` and `Wrox.ProCSharp.OOP` namespaces. If you then create a class called `Test` in the `Wrox.ProCSharp` namespace, and instantiate one of the `NamespaceExample` classes in this class, you need to specify which of these two classes you're talking about:

```
using Wrox.ProCSharp.OOP;
using Wrox.ProCSharp.Basics;
namespace Wrox.ProCSharp
{
  class Test
  {
    public static int Main()
    {
      Basics.NamespaceExample nSEx = new Basics.NamespaceExample();
      // do something with the nSEx variable.
      return 0;
    }
  }
}
```

> **NOTE** *Because* using *statements occur at the top of C# files, in the same place that C and C++ list* #include *statements, it's easy for programmers moving from C++ to C# to confuse namespaces with C++-style header files. Don't make this mistake. The* using *statement does no physical linking between files, and C# has no equivalent to C++ header files.*

Your organization will probably want to spend some time developing a namespace convention so that its developers can quickly locate functionality that they need and so that the names of the organization's homegrown classes won't conflict with those in off-the-shelf class libraries. Guidelines on establishing your own namespace convention, along with other naming recommendations, are discussed later in this chapter.

Namespace Aliases

Another use of the using keyword is to assign aliases to classes and namespaces. If you need to refer to a very long namespace name several times in your code but don't want to include it in a simple using statement (for example, to avoid type name conflicts), you can assign an alias to the namespace. The syntax for this is as follows:

```
using alias = NamespaceName;
```

The following example (a modified version of the previous example) assigns the alias Introduction to the Wrox.ProCSharp.Basics namespace and uses this to instantiate a NamespaceExample object, which is defined in this namespace. Notice the use of the namespace alias qualifier (::). This forces the search to start with the Introduction namespace alias. If a class called Introduction had been introduced in the same scope, a conflict would occur. The :: operator enables the alias to be referenced even if the conflict exists. The NamespaceExample class has one method, GetNamespace(), which uses the GetType() method exposed by every class to access a Type object representing the class's type. You use this object to return a name of the class's namespace:

```
using System;
using Introduction =  Wrox.ProCSharp.Basics;
class Test
{
    public static int Main()
    {
        Introduction::NamespaceExample NSEx =
            new Introduction::NamespaceExample();
        Console.WriteLine(NSEx.GetNamespace());
        return 0;
    }
}
namespace Wrox.ProCSharp.Basics
{
    class NamespaceExample
    {
        public string GetNamespace()
        {
            return this.GetType().Namespace;
        }
    }
}
```

THE MAIN() METHOD

As described at the beginning of this chapter, C# programs start execution at a method named Main(). This must be a static method of a class (or struct), and must have a return type of either int or void.

Although it is common to specify the public modifier explicitly, because by definition the method must be called from outside the program, it doesn't actually matter what accessibility level you assign to the entry-point method—it will run even if you mark the method as private.

Multiple Main() Methods

When a C# console or Windows application is compiled, by default the compiler looks for exactly one Main() method in any class matching the signature that was just described and makes that class method the entry point for the program. If there is more than one `Main()` method, the compiler returns an error message. For example, consider the following code called `DoubleMain.cs`:

```
using System;
namespace Wrox
{
    class Client
    {
        public static int Main()
        {
            MathExample.Main();
            return 0;
        }
    }
    class MathExample
    {
        static int Add(int x, int y)
        {
            return x + y;
        }
        public static int Main()
        {
            int i = Add(5,10);
            Console.WriteLine(i);
            return 0;
        }
    }
}
```

This contains two classes, both of which have a `Main()` method. If you try to compile this code in the usual way, you will get the following errors:

```
csc DoubleMain.cs
Microsoft (R) Visual C# 2010 Compiler version 4.0.20506.1
Copyright (C) Microsoft Corporation. All rights reserved.
DoubleMain.cs(7,25): error CS0017: Program
        'DoubleMain.exe' has more than one entry point defined:
        'Wrox.Client.Main()'.  Compile with /main to specify the type that
        contains the entry point.
DoubleMain.cs(21,25): error CS0017: Program
        'DoubleMain.exe' has more than one entry point defined:
        'Wrox.MathExample.Main()'.  Compile with /main to specify the type that
        contains the entry point.
```

However, you can explicitly tell the compiler which of these methods to use as the entry point for the program by using the `/main` switch, together with the full name (including namespace) of the class to which the `Main()` method belongs:

```
csc DoubleMain.cs /main:Wrox.MathExample
```

Passing Arguments to Main()

The examples so far have shown only the `Main()` method without any parameters. However, when the program is invoked, you can get the CLR to pass any command-line arguments to the program by including a parameter. This parameter is a string array, traditionally called `args` (although C# will accept any name). The program can use this array to access any options passed through the command line when the program is started.

The following example, `ArgsExample.cs`, loops through the string array passed in to the `Main()` method and writes the value of each option to the console window:

```
using System;
namespace Wrox
{
```

```
class ArgsExample
{
    public static int Main(string[] args)
    {
        for (int i = 0; i < args.Length; i++)
        {
            Console.WriteLine(args[i]);
        }
        return 0;
    }
}
```

You can compile this as usual using the command line. When you run the compiled executable, you can pass in arguments after the name of the program, as shown here:

```
ArgsExample /a /b /c
/a
/b
/c
```

MORE ON COMPILING C# FILES

You have seen how to compile console applications using csc.exe, but what about other types of applications? What if you want to reference a class library? The full set of compilation options for the C# compiler is, of course, detailed in the MSDN documentation, but we list here the most important options.

To answer the first question, you can specify what type of file you want to create using the /target switch, often abbreviated as /t. This can be one of those shown in the following table.

OPTION	OUTPUT
/t:exe	A console application (the default)
/t:library	A class library with a manifest
/t:module	A component without a manifest
/t:winexe	A Windows application (without a console window)

If you want a nonexecutable file (such as a DLL) to be loadable by the .NET runtime, you must compile it as a library. If you compile a C# file as a module, no assembly will be created. Although modules cannot be loaded by the runtime, they can be compiled into another manifest using the /addmodule switch.

Another option to be aware of is /out. This enables you to specify the name of the output file produced by the compiler. If the /out option isn't specified, the compiler bases the name of the output file on the name of the input C# file, adding an extension according to the target type (for example, exe for a Windows or console application, or dll for a class library). Note that the /out and /t, or /target, options must precede the name of the file you want to compile.

If you want to reference types in assemblies that aren't referenced by default, you can use the /reference or /r switch, together with the path and filename of the assembly. The following example demonstrates how you can compile a class library and then reference that library in another assembly. It consists of two files:

➤ The class library
➤ A console application, which will call a class in the library

The first file is called MathLibrary.cs and contains the code for your DLL. To keep things simple, it contains just one (public) class, MathLib, with a single method that adds two ints:

```
namespace Wrox
{
    public class MathLib
    {
```

```
      public int Add(int x, int y)
      {
         return x + y;
      }
   }
}
```

You can compile this C# file into a .NET DLL using the following command:

```
csc /t:library MathLibrary.cs
```

The console application, `MathClient.cs`, will simply instantiate this object and call its `Add()` method, displaying the result in the console window:

```
using System;
namespace Wrox
{
   class Client
   {
      public static void Main()
      {
         MathLib mathObj = new MathLib();
         Console.WriteLine(mathObj.Add(7,8));
      }
   }
}
```

To compile this code, use the `/r` switch to point at or reference the newly compiled DLL:

```
csc MathClient.cs /r:MathLibrary.dll
```

You can then run it as normal just by entering `MathClient` at the command prompt. This displays the number 15 — the result of your addition.

CONSOLE I/O

By this point, you should have a basic familiarity with C#'s data types, as well as some knowledge of how the thread-of-control moves through a program that manipulates those data types. In this chapter, you have also used several of the `Console` class's static methods used for reading and writing data. Because these methods are so useful when writing basic C# programs, this section briefly reviews them in more detail.

To read a line of text from the console window, you use the `Console.ReadLine()` method. This reads an input stream (terminated when the user presses the `Return` key) from the console window and returns the input string. There are also two corresponding methods for writing to the console, which you have already used extensively:

➤   `Console.Write()` — Writes the specified value to the console window.

➤   `Console.WriteLine()` — Writes the specified value to the console window but adds a newline character at the end of the output.

Various forms (overloads) of these methods exist for all the predefined types (including `object`), so in most cases you don't have to convert values to strings before you display them.

For example, the following code lets the user input a line of text and then displays that text:

```
string s = Console.ReadLine();
Console.WriteLine(s);
```

`Console.WriteLine()` also allows you to display formatted output in a way comparable to C's `printf()` function. To use `WriteLine()` in this way, you pass in a number of parameters. The first is a string containing markers in curly braces where the subsequent parameters will be inserted into the text. Each marker contains a zero-based index for the number of the parameter in the following list. For example, {0} represents the first parameter in the list. Consider the following code:

```
int i = 10;
int j = 20;
Console.WriteLine("{0} plus {1} equals {2}", i, j, i + j);
```

The preceding code displays the following:

```
10 plus 20 equals 30
```

You can also specify a width for the value, and justify the text within that width, using positive values for right justification and negative values for left justification. To do this, use the format $\{n, w\}$, where n is the parameter index and w is the width value:

```
int i = 940;
int j = 73;
Console.WriteLine(" {0,4}\n+{1,4}\n--\n {2,4}", i, j, i + j);
```

The result of the preceding is as follows:

```
 940
+  73
 --
1013
```

Finally, you can also add a format string, together with an optional precision value. It is not possible to provide a complete list of potential format strings because, as you will see in Chapter 9, "Strings and Regular Expressions," you can define your own format strings. However, the main ones in use for the predefined types are described in the following table.

STRING	DESCRIPTION
C	Local currency format
D	Decimal format. Converts an integer to base 10, and pads with leading zeros if a precision specifier is given.
E	Scientific (exponential) format. The precision specifier sets the number of decimal places (6 by default). The case of the format string (e or E) determines the case of the exponential symbol.
F	Fixed-point format; the precision specifier controls the number of decimal places. Zero is acceptable.
G	General format. Uses E or F formatting, depending on which is more compact.
N	Number format. Formats the number with commas as the thousands separators—for example 32,767.44.
P	Percent format
X	Hexadecimal format. The precision specifier can be used to pad with leading zeros.

Note that the format strings are normally case insensitive, except for e/E.

If you want to use a format string, you should place it immediately after the marker that specifies the parameter number and field width, and separate it with a colon. For example, to format a decimal value as currency for the computer's locale, with precision to two decimal places, you would use C2:

```
decimal i = 940.23m;
decimal j = 73.7m;
Console.WriteLine(" {0,9:C2}\n+{1,9:C2}\n-----\n {2,9:C2}", i, j, i + j);
```

The output of this in U.S. currency is as follows:

```
  $940.23
+  $73.70
 -----
$1,013.93
```

As a final trick, you can also use placeholder characters instead of these format strings to map out formatting, as shown in this example:

```
double d = 0.234;
Console.WriteLine("{0:#.00}", d);
```

This displays as .23 because the # symbol is ignored if there is no character in that place, and zeros are either replaced by the character in that position if there is one or printed as a zero.

USING COMMENTS

The next topic—adding comments to your code—looks very simple on the surface, but can be complex. Comments can be beneficial to the other developers that may look at your code. Also, as you will see, they can be used to generate documentation of your code for developers to use.

Internal Comments within the Source Files

As noted earlier in this chapter, C# uses the traditional C-type single-line (//..) and multiline (/* .. */) comments:

```
// This is a single-line comment
/* This comment
   spans multiple lines. */
```

Everything in a single-line comment, from the // to the end of the line, is ignored by the compiler, and everything from an opening /* to the next */ in a multiline comment combination is ignored. Obviously, you can't include the combination */ in any multiline comments, because this will be treated as the end of the comment.

It is possible to put multiline comments within a line of code:

```
Console.WriteLine(/* Here's a comment! */ "This will compile.");
```

Use inline comments with care because they can make code hard to read. However, they can be useful when debugging if, for example, you temporarily want to try running the code with a different value somewhere:

```
DoSomething(Width, /*Height*/ 100);
```

Comment characters included in string literals are, of course, treated like normal characters:

```
string s = "/* This is just a normal string .*/";
```

XML Documentation

In addition to the C-type comments, illustrated in the preceding section, C# has a very neat feature that we want to highlight: the capability to produce documentation in XML format automatically from special comments. These comments are single-line comments but begin with three slashes (///) instead of the usual two. Within these comments, you can place XML tags containing documentation of the types and type members in your code.

The tags in the following table are recognized by the compiler.

TAG	DESCRIPTION
`<c>`	Marks up text within a line as code—for example, `<c>int i = 10;</c>`.
`<code>`	Marks multiple lines as code
`<example>`	Marks up a code example
`<exception>`	Documents an exception class. (Syntax is verified by the compiler.)
`<include>`	Includes comments from another documentation file. (Syntax is verified by the compiler.)
`<list>`	Inserts a list into the documentation

TAG	DESCRIPTION
`<para>`	Gives structure to text
`<param>`	Marks up a method parameter. (Syntax is verified by the compiler.)
`<paramref>`	Indicates that a word is a method parameter. (Syntax is verified by the compiler.)
`<permission>`	Documents access to a member. (Syntax is verified by the compiler.)
`<remarks>`	Adds a description for a member
`<returns>`	Documents the return value for a method
`<see>`	Provides a cross-reference to another parameter. (Syntax is verified by the compiler.)
`<seealso>`	Provides a "see also" section in a description. (Syntax is verified by the compiler.)
`<summary>`	Provides a short summary of a type or member
`<typeparam>`	Used in the comment of a generic type to describe a type parameter
`<typeparamref>`	The name of the type parameter
`<value>`	Describes a property

To see how this works, add some XML comments to the `MathLibrary.cs` file from the previous "More on Compiling C# Files" section. You will add a `<summary>` element for the class and for its `Add()` method, and a `<returns>` element and two `<param>` elements for the `Add()` method:

```
// MathLib.cs
namespace Wrox
{
    ///<summary>
    ///    Wrox.Math class.
    ///    Provides a method to add two integers.
    ///</summary>
    public class MathLib
    {
        ///<summary>
        ///    The Add method allows us to add two integers.
        ///</summary>
        ///<returns>Result of the addition (int)</returns>
        ///<param name="x">First number to add</param>
        ///<param name="y">Second number to add</param>
        public int Add(int x, int y)
        {
            return x + y;
        }
    }
}
```

The C# compiler can extract the XML elements from the special comments and use them to generate an XML file. To get the compiler to generate the XML documentation for an assembly, you specify the `/doc` option when you compile, together with the name of the file you want to be created:

```
csc /t:library /doc:MathLibrary.xml MathLibrary.cs
```

The compiler will throw an error if the XML comments do not result in a well-formed XML document.

The preceding will generate an XML file named `Math.xml`, which looks like this:

```
<?xml version="1.0"?>
<doc>
    <assembly>
        <name>MathLibrary</name>
    </assembly>
    <members>
        <member name="T:Wrox.MathLibrary">
            <summary>
```

```
            Wrox.MathLibrary class.
            Provides a method to add two integers.
        </summary>
    </member>
    <member name=
        "M:Wrox.MathLibrary.Add(System.Int32,System.Int32)">
        <summary>
            The Add method allows us to add two integers.
        </summary>
        <returns>Result of the addition (int)</returns>
        <param name="x">First number to add</param>
        <param name="y">Second number to add</param>
    </member>
  </members>
</doc>
```

Notice how the compiler has actually done some work for you; it has created an `<assembly>` element and added a `<member>` element for each type or member of a type in the file. Each `<member>` element has a name attribute with the full name of the member as its value, prefixed by a letter that indicates whether it is a type (`T:`), field (`F:`), or member (`M:`).

THE C# PREPROCESSOR DIRECTIVES

Besides the usual keywords, most of which you have now encountered, C# also includes a number of commands that are known as *preprocessor directives*. These commands are never actually translated to any commands in your executable code, but they affect aspects of the compilation process. For example, you can use preprocessor directives to prevent the compiler from compiling certain portions of your code. You might do this if you are planning to release two versions of it—a basic version and an enterprise version that will have more features. You could use preprocessor directives to prevent the compiler from compiling code related to the additional features when you are compiling the basic version of the software. In another scenario, you might have written bits of code that are intended to provide you with debugging information. You probably don't want those portions of code compiled when you actually ship the software.

The preprocessor directives are all distinguished by beginning with the # symbol.

> **NOTE** *C++ developers will recognize the preprocessor directives as something that plays an important part in C and C++. However, there aren't as many preprocessor directives in C#, and they are not used as often. C# provides other mechanisms, such as custom attributes, that achieve some of the same effects as C++ directives. Also, note that C# doesn't actually have a separate preprocessor in the way that C++ does. The so-called preprocessor directives are actually handled by the compiler. Nevertheless, C# retains the name preprocessor directive because these commands give the impression of a preprocessor.*

The following sections briefly cover the purposes of the preprocessor directives.

#define and #undef

`#define` is used like this:

```
#define DEBUG
```

This tells the compiler that a symbol with the given name (in this case DEBUG) exists. It is a little bit like declaring a variable, except that this variable doesn't really have a value—it just exists. Also, this symbol isn't part of your actual code; it exists only for the benefit of the compiler, while the compiler is compiling the code, and has no meaning within the C# code itself.

`#undef` does the opposite, and removes the definition of a symbol:

```
#undef DEBUG
```

If the symbol doesn't exist in the first place, then `#undef` has no effect. Similarly, `#define` has no effect if a symbol already exists.

You need to place any `#define` and `#undef` directives at the beginning of the C# source file, before any code that declares any objects to be compiled.

`#define` isn't much use on its own, but when combined with other preprocessor directives, especially `#if`, it becomes very powerful.

> **NOTE** *Incidentally, you might notice some changes from the usual C# syntax. Preprocessor directives are not terminated by semicolons and they normally constitute the only command on a line. That's because for the preprocessor directives, C# abandons its usual practice of requiring commands to be separated by semicolons. If the compiler sees a preprocessor directive, it assumes that the next command is on the next line.*

#if, #elif, #else, and #endif

These directives inform the compiler whether to compile a block of code. Consider this method:

```
int DoSomeWork(double x)
{
    // do something
    #if DEBUG
        Console.WriteLine("x is " + x);
    #endif
}
```

This code will compile as normal except for the `Console.WriteLine()` method call contained inside the `#if` clause. This line will be executed only if the symbol `DEBUG` has been defined by a previous `#define` directive. When the compiler finds the `#if` directive, it checks to see whether the symbol concerned exists, and compiles the code inside the `#if` clause only if the symbol does exist. Otherwise, the compiler simply ignores all the code until it reaches the matching `#endif` directive. Typical practice is to define the symbol `DEBUG` while you are debugging and have various bits of debugging-related code inside `#if` clauses. Then, when you are close to shipping, you simply comment out the `#define` directive, and all the debugging code miraculously disappears, the size of the executable file gets smaller, and your end users don't get confused by seeing debugging information. (Obviously, you would do more testing to ensure that your code still works without `DEBUG` defined.) This technique is very common in C and C++ programming and is known as *conditional compilation*.

The `#elif` (=else if) and `#else` directives can be used in `#if` blocks and have intuitively obvious meanings. It is also possible to nest `#if` blocks:

```
#define ENTERPRISE
#define W2K
// further on in the file
#if ENTERPRISE
    // do something
    #if W2K
        // some code that is only relevant to enterprise
        // edition running on W2K
    #endif
#elif PROFESSIONAL
    // do something else
#else
    // code for the leaner version
#endif
```

> **NOTE** *Unlike the situation in C++, using* #if *is not the only way to compile code conditionally. C# provides an alternative mechanism through the* Conditional *attribute, which is explored in Chapter 15, "Reflection."*

#if and #elif support a limited range of logical operators too, using the operators !, ==, !=, and ||. A symbol is considered to be true if it exists and false if it doesn't. For example:

```
#if W2K && (ENTERPRISE==false)    // if W2K is defined but ENTERPRISE isn't
```

#warning and #error

Two other very useful preprocessor directives are #warning and #error. These will respectively cause a warning or an error to be raised when the compiler encounters them. If the compiler sees a #warning directive, it displays whatever text appears after the #warning to the user, after which compilation continues. If it encounters a #error directive, it displays the subsequent text to the user as if it were a compilation error message and then immediately abandons the compilation, so no IL code will be generated.

You can use these directives as checks that you haven't done anything silly with your #define statements; you can also use the #warning statements to remind yourself to do something:

```
#if DEBUG && RELEASE
    #error "You've defined DEBUG and RELEASE simultaneously!"
#endif
#warning "Don't forget to remove this line before the boss tests the code!"
    Console.WriteLine("*I hate this job.*");
```

#region and #endregion

The #region and #endregion directives are used to indicate that a certain block of code is to be treated as a single block with a given name, like this:

```
#region Member Field Declarations
    int x;
    double d;
    Currency balance;
#endregion
```

This doesn't look that useful by itself; it doesn't affect the compilation process in any way. However, the real advantage is that these directives are recognized by some editors, including the Visual Studio .NET editor. These editors can use the directives to lay out your code better on the screen. You will see how this works in Chapter 17.

#line

The #line directive can be used to alter the filename and line number information that is output by the compiler in warnings and error messages. You probably won't want to use this directive very often. It's most useful when you are coding in conjunction with another package that alters the code you are typing in before sending it to the compiler. In this situation, line numbers, or perhaps the filenames reported by the compiler, won't match up to the line numbers in the files or the filenames you are editing. The #line directive can be used to restore the match. You can also use the syntax #line default to restore the line to the default line numbering:

```
#line 164 "Core.cs"   // We happen to know this is line 164 in the file
                       // Core.cs, before the intermediate
                       // package mangles it.
// later on
#line default          // restores default line numbering
```

#pragma

The #pragma directive can either suppress or restore specific compiler warnings. Unlike command-line options, the #pragma directive can be implemented on the class or method level, enabling fine-grained control over what warnings are suppressed and when. The following example disables the "field not used" warning and then restores it after the MyClass class compiles:

```
#pragma warning disable 169
public class MyClass
{
    int neverUsedField;
}
#pragma warning restore 169
```

C# PROGRAMMING GUIDELINES

This final section of the chapter supplies the guidelines you need to bear in mind when writing C# programs. These are guidelines that most C# developers will use. By using these guidelines other developers will feel comfortable working with your code.

Rules for Identifiers

This section examines the rules governing what names you can use for variables, classes, methods, and so on. Note that the rules presented in this section are not merely guidelines: they are enforced by the C# compiler.

Identifiers are the names you give to variables, to user-defined types such as classes and structs, and to members of these types. Identifiers are case sensitive, so, for example, variables named interestRate and InterestRate would be recognized as different variables. Following are a few rules determining what identifiers you can use in C#:

➤   They must begin with a letter or underscore, although they can contain numeric characters.

➤   You can't use C# keywords as identifiers.

The following table lists the C# reserved keywords.

abstract	event	new	struct
as	explicit	null	switch
base	extern	object	this
bool	false	operator	throw
break	finally	out	true
byte	fixed	override	try
case	float	params	typeof
catch	for	private	uint
char	foreach	protected	ulong
checked	goto	public	unchecked
class	if	readonly	unsafe
const	implicit	ref	ushort
continue	in	return	using
decimal	int	sbyte	virtual
default	interface	sealed	void

(continues)

(continued)

abstract	event	new	struct
delegate	internal	short	volatile
do	is	sizeof	while
double	lock	stackalloc	
else	long	static	
enum	namespace	string	

If you need to use one of these words as an identifier (for example, if you are accessing a class written in a different language), you can prefix the identifier with the @ symbol to indicate to the compiler that what follows should be treated as an identifier, not as a C# keyword (so abstract is not a valid identifier, but @ abstract is).

Finally, identifiers can also contain Unicode characters, specified using the syntax \u*XXXX*, where *XXXX* is the four-digit hex code for the Unicode character. The following are some examples of valid identifiers:

➤ Name

➤ Überfluß

➤ _Identifier

➤ \u005fIdentifier

The last two items in this list are identical and interchangeable (because 005f is the Unicode code for the underscore character), so obviously these identifiers couldn't both be declared in the same scope. Note that although syntactically you are allowed to use the underscore character in identifiers, this isn't recommended in most situations. That's because it doesn't follow the guidelines for naming variables that Microsoft has written to ensure that developers use the same conventions, making it easier to read one another's code.

Usage Conventions

In any development language, certain traditional programming styles usually arise. The styles are not part of the language itself but rather are conventions—for example, how variables are named or how certain classes, methods, or functions are used. If most developers using that language follow the same conventions, it makes it easier for different developers to understand each other's code—which in turn generally helps program maintainability. Conventions do, however, depend on the language and the environment. For example, C++ developers programming on the Windows platform have traditionally used the prefixes psz or lpsz to indicate strings—char *pszResult; char *lpszMessage; —but on Unix machines it's more common not to use any such prefixes: char *Result; char *Message;.

You'll notice from the sample code in this book that the convention in C# is to name variables without prefixes: string Result; string Message;.

> **NOTE** *The convention by which variable names are prefixed with letters that represent the data type is known as Hungarian notation. It means that other developers reading the code can immediately tell from the variable name what data type the variable represents. Hungarian notation is widely regarded as redundant in these days of smart editors and IntelliSense.*

Whereas with many languages usage conventions simply evolved as the language was used, with C# and the whole of the .NET Framework, Microsoft has written very comprehensive usage guidelines, which are detailed in the .NET/C# MSDN documentation. This means that, right from the start, .NET programs have a high degree of interoperability in terms of developers being able to understand code. The guidelines have also been developed with the benefit of some 20 years' hindsight in object-oriented programming. Judging by the relevant newsgroups, the guidelines have been carefully thought out and are well received in the developer community. Hence, the guidelines are well worth following.

Note, however, that the guidelines are not the same as language specifications. You should try to follow the guidelines when you can. Nevertheless, you won't run into problems if you have a good reason for not doing so—for example, you won't get a compilation error because you don't follow these guidelines. The general rule is that if you don't follow the usage guidelines, you must have a convincing reason. Departing from the guidelines should be a conscious decision rather than simply not bothering. Also, if you compare the guidelines with the samples in the remainder of this book, you'll notice that in numerous examples we have chosen not to follow the conventions. That's usually because the conventions are designed for much larger programs than our samples; and although they are great if you are writing a complete software package, they are not really suitable for small 20-line standalone programs. In many cases, following the conventions would have made our samples harder, rather than easier, to follow.

The full guidelines for good programming style are quite extensive. This section is confined to describing some of the more important guidelines, as well as those most likely to surprise you. To be absolutely certain that your code follows the usage guidelines completely, you need to refer to the MSDN documentation.

Naming Conventions

One important aspect of making your programs understandable is how you choose to name your items—and that includes naming variables, methods, classes, enumerations, and namespaces.

It is intuitively obvious that your names should reflect the purpose of the item and should not clash with other names. The general philosophy in the .NET Framework is also that the name of a variable should reflect the purpose of that variable instance and not the data type. For example, `height` is a good name for a variable, whereas `integerValue` isn't. However, you are likely to find that principle an ideal that is hard to achieve. Particularly when you are dealing with controls, in most cases you'll probably be happier sticking with variable names such as `confirmationDialog` and `chooseEmployeeListBox`, which do indicate the data type in the name.

The following sections look at some of the things you need to think about when choosing names.

Casing of Names

In many cases you should use *Pascal casing* for names. With Pascal casing, the first letter of each word in a name is capitalized: `EmployeeSalary`, `ConfirmationDialog`, `PlainTextEncoding`. You will notice that nearly all the names of namespaces, classes, and members in the base classes follow Pascal casing. In particular, the convention of joining words using the underscore character is discouraged. Therefore, try not to use names such as `employee_salary`. It has also been common in other languages to use all capitals for names of constants. This is not advised in C# because such names are harder to read—the convention is to use Pascal casing throughout:

```
const int MaximumLength;
```

The only other casing convention that you are advised to use is *camel casing*. Camel casing is similar to Pascal casing, except that the first letter of the first word in the name is not capitalized: `employeeSalary`, `confirmationDialog`, `plainTextEncoding`. Following are three situations in which you are advised to use camel casing:

➤ For names of all private member fields in types:

```
private int subscriberId;
```

Note, however, that often it is conventional to prefix names of member fields with an underscore:

```
private int _subscriberId;
```

➤ For names of all parameters passed to methods:

```
public void RecordSale(string salesmanName, int quantity);
```

➤ To distinguish items that would otherwise have the same name. A common example is when a property wraps around a field:

```
private string employeeName;
public string EmployeeName
{
    get
    {
        return employeeName;
    }
}
```

If you are doing this, you should always use camel casing for the private member and Pascal casing for the public or protected member, so that other classes that use your code see only names in Pascal case (except for parameter names).

You should also be wary about case sensitivity. C# is case sensitive, so it is syntactically correct for names in C# to differ only by the case, as in the previous examples. However, bear in mind that your assemblies might at some point be called from Visual Basic .NET applications—and *Visual Basic .NET is not case sensitive*. Hence, if you do use names that differ only by case, it is important to do so only in situations in which both names will never be seen outside your assembly. (The previous example qualifies as okay because camel case is used with the name that is attached to a `private` variable.) Otherwise, you may prevent other code written in Visual Basic .NET from being able to use your assembly correctly.

Name Styles

Be consistent about your style of names. For example, if one of the methods in a class is called `ShowConfirmationDialog()`, then you should not give another method a name such as `ShowDialogWarning()` or `WarningDialogShow()`. The other method should be called `ShowWarningDialog()`.

Namespace Names

It is particularly important to choose Namespace names carefully to avoid the risk of ending up with the same name for one of your namespaces as someone else uses. Remember, namespace names are the *only* way that .NET distinguishes names of objects in shared assemblies. Therefore, if you use the same namespace name for your software package as another package, and both packages are installed on the same computer, problems will occur. Because of this, it's almost always a good idea to create a top-level namespace with the name of your company and then nest successive namespaces that narrow down the technology, group, or department you are working in or the name of the package for which your classes are intended. Microsoft recommends namespace names that begin with `<CompanyName>.<TechnologyName>`, as in these two examples:

```
WeaponsOfDestructionCorp.RayGunControllers
WeaponsOfDestructionCorp.Viruses
```

Names and Keywords

It is important that the names do not clash with any keywords. In fact, if you attempt to name an item in your code with a word that happens to be a C# keyword, you'll almost certainly get a syntax error because the compiler will assume that the name refers to a statement. However, because of the possibility that your classes will be accessed by code written in other languages, it is also important that you don't use names that are keywords in other .NET languages. Generally speaking, C++ keywords are similar to C# keywords, so confusion with C++ is unlikely, and those commonly encountered keywords that are unique to Visual C++ tend to start with two underscore characters. As with C#, C++ keywords are spelled in lowercase, so if you hold to the convention of naming your public classes and members with Pascal-style names, they will always have at least one uppercase letter in their names, and there will be no risk of clashes with C++ keywords. However, you are more likely to have problems with Visual Basic .NET, which has many more keywords than C# does, and being non-case-sensitive means that you cannot rely on Pascal-style names for your classes and methods.

The following table lists the keywords and standard function calls in Visual Basic .NET, which you should avoid, if possible, in whatever case combination, for your public C# classes.

Abs	Do	Loc	RGB
Add	Double	Local	Right
AddHandler	Each	Lock	RmDir
AddressOf	Else	LOF	Rnd
Alias	ElseIf	Log	RTrim
And	Empty	Long	SaveSettings
Ansi	End	Loop	Second
AppActivate	Enum	LTrim	Seek
Append	EOF	Me	Select
As	Erase	Mid	SetAttr
Asc	Err	Minute	SetException
Assembly	Error	MIRR	Shared
Atan	Event	MkDir	Shell
Auto	Exit	Module	Short
Beep	Exp	Month	Sign
Binary	Explicit	MustInherit	Sin
BitAnd	ExternalSource	MustOverride	Single
BitNot	False	MyBase	SLN
BitOr	FileAttr	MyClass	Space
BitXor	FileCopy	Namespace	Spc
Boolean	FileDateTime	New	Split
ByRef	FileLen	Next	Sqrt
Byte	Filter	Not	Static
ByVal	Finally	Nothing	Step
Call	Fix	NotInheritable	Stop
Case	For	NotOverridable	Str
Catch	Format	Now	StrComp
CBool	FreeFile	NPer.	StrConv
CByte	Friend	NPV	Strict
CDate	Function	Null	String
CDbl	FV	Object	Structure
CDec	Get	Oct	Sub
ChDir	GetAllSettings	Off	Switch
ChDrive	GetAttr	On	SYD
Choose	GetException	Open	SyncLock
Chr	GetObject	Option	Tab
CInt	GetSetting	Optional	Tan
Class	GetType	Or	Text
Clear	GoTo	Overloads	Then
CLng	Handles	Overridable	Throw

(continues)

(continued)

Abs	Do	Loc	RGB
Close	Hex	Overrides	TimeOfDay
Collection	Hour	ParamArray	Timer
Command	If	Pmt	TimeSerial
Compare	Iif	PPmt	TimeValue
Const	Implements	Preserve	To
Cos	Imports	Print	Today
CreateObject	In	Private	Trim
CShort	Inherits	Property	Try
CSng	Input	Public	TypeName
CStr	InStr	Put	TypeOf
CurDir	Int	PV	UBound
Date	Integer	QBColor	UCase
DateAdd	Interface	Raise	Unicode
DateDiff	Ipmt	RaiseEvent	Unlock
DatePart	IRR	Randomize	Until
DateSerial	Is	Rate	Val
DateValue	IsArray	Read	Weekday
Day	IsDate	ReadOnly	While
DDB	IsDbNull	ReDim	Width
Decimal	IsNumeric	Remove	With
Declare	Item	RemoveHandler	WithEvents
Default	Kill	Rename	Write
Delegate	Lcase	Replace	WriteOnly
DeleteSetting	Left	Reset	Xor
Dim	Lib	Resume	Year

Use of Properties and Methods

One area that can cause confusion regarding a class is whether a particular quantity should be represented by a property or a method. The rules are not hard and fast, but in general you should use a property if something should look and behave like a variable. (If you're not sure what a property is, see Chapter 3.) This means, among other things, that:

➤ Client code should be able to read its value. Write-only properties are not recommended, so, for example, use a SetPassword() method, not a write-only Password property.

➤ Reading the value should not take too long. The fact that something is a property usually suggests that reading it will be relatively quick.

➤ Reading the value should not have any observable and unexpected side effect. Furthermore, setting the value of a property should not have any side effect that is not directly related to the property. Setting the width of a dialog has the obvious effect of changing the appearance of the dialog on the screen. That's fine, because that's obviously related to the property in question.

➤ It should be possible to set properties in any order. In particular, it is not good practice when setting a property to throw an exception because another related property has not yet been set. For example, to use a class that accesses a database, you need to set ConnectionString, UserName, and Password, and then the author of the class should ensure that the class is implemented such that users can set them in any order.

➤ Successive reads of a property should give the same result. If the value of a property is likely to change unpredictably, you should code it as a method instead. Speed, in a class that monitors the motion of an automobile, is not a good candidate for a property. Use a GetSpeed() method here; but, Weight and EngineSize are good candidates for properties because they will not change for a given object.

If the item you are coding satisfies all the preceding criteria, it is probably a good candidate for a property. Otherwise, you should use a method.

Use of Fields

The guidelines are pretty simple here. Fields should almost always be private, although in some cases it may be acceptable for constant or read-only fields to be public. Making a field public may hinder your ability to extend or modify the class in the future.

The previous guidelines should give you a foundation of good practices, and you should use them in conjunction with a good object-oriented programming style.

A final helpful note to keep in mind is that Microsoft has been relatively careful about being consistent and has followed its own guidelines when writing the .NET base classes, so a very good way to get an intuitive feel for the conventions to follow when writing .NET code is to simply look at the base classes—see how classes, members, and namespaces are named, and how the class hierarchy works. Consistency between the base classes and your classes will facilitate readability and maintainability.

SUMMARY

This chapter examined some of the basic syntax of C#, covering the areas needed to write simple C# programs. We covered a lot of ground, but much of it will be instantly recognizable to developers who are familiar with any C-style language (or even JavaScript).

You have seen that although C# syntax is similar to C++ and Java syntax, there are many minor differences. You have also seen that in many areas this syntax is combined with facilities to write code very quickly—for example, high-quality string handling facilities. C# also has a strongly defined type system, based on a distinction between value and reference types. Chapters 3 and 4, "Objects and Types" and "Inheritance" respectively, cover the C# object-oriented programming features.

Objects and Types

WHAT'S IN THIS CHAPTER?

➤ The differences between classes and structs

➤ Class members

➤ Passing values by value and by reference

➤ Method overloading

➤ Constructors and static constructors

➤ Read-only fields

➤ Partial classes

➤ Static classes

➤ Weak references

➤ The Object class, from which all other types are derived

WROX.COM CODE DOWNLOADS FOR THIS CHAPTER

The wrox.com code downloads for this chapter are found at `http://www.wrox.com/remtitle` `.cgi?isbn=1118314425` on the Download Code tab. The code for this chapter is divided into the following major examples:

➤ MathTest

➤ MathTestWeakReference

➤ ParameterTest

CREATING AND USING CLASSES

So far, you've been introduced to some of the building blocks of the C# language, including variables, data types, and program flow statements, and you have seen a few very short complete programs containing little more than the `Main()` method. What you haven't seen yet is how to put all these elements together to form a longer, complete program. The key to this lies in working with classes—the subject of this chapter. Note that we cover inheritance and features related to inheritance in Chapter 4, "Inheritance."

> **NOTE** *This chapter introduces the basic syntax associated with classes. However, we assume that you are already familiar with the underlying principles of using classes—for example, that you know what a constructor or a property is. This chapter is largely confined to applying those principles in C# code.*

CLASSES AND STRUCTS

Classes and structs are essentially templates from which you can create objects. Each object contains data and has methods to manipulate and access that data. The class defines what data and behavior each particular object (called an *instance*) of that class can contain. For example, if you have a class that represents a customer, it might define fields such as `CustomerID`, `FirstName`, `LastName`, and `Address`, which are used to hold information about a particular customer. It might also define functionality that acts upon the data stored in these fields. You can then instantiate an object of this class to represent one specific customer, set the field values for that instance, and use its functionality:

```
class PhoneCustomer
{
    public const string DayOfSendingBill = "Monday";
    public int CustomerID;
    public string FirstName;
    public string LastName;
}
```

Structs differ from classes in the way that they are stored in memory and accessed (classes are reference types stored in the heap; structs are value types stored on the stack), and in some of their features (for example, structs don't support inheritance). You typically use structs for smaller data types for performance reasons. In terms of syntax, however, structs look very similar to classes; the main difference is that you use the keyword `struct` instead of `class` to declare them. For example, if you wanted all `PhoneCustomer` instances to be allocated on the stack instead of the managed heap, you could write the following:

```
struct PhoneCustomerStruct
{
    public const string DayOfSendingBill = "Monday";
    public int CustomerID;
    public string FirstName;
    public string LastName;
}
```

For both classes and structs, you use the keyword `new` to declare an instance. This keyword creates the object and initializes it; in the following example, the default behavior is to zero out its fields:

```
PhoneCustomer myCustomer = new PhoneCustomer();        // works for a class
PhoneCustomerStruct myCustomer2 = new PhoneCustomerStruct();// works for a struct
```

In most cases, you'll use classes much more often than structs. Therefore, we discuss classes first and then the differences between classes and structs and the specific reasons why you might choose to use a struct instead of a class. Unless otherwise stated, however, you can assume that code presented for a class will work equally well for a struct.

CLASSES

The data and functions within a class are known as the class's *members*. Microsoft's official terminology distinguishes between data members and function members. In addition to these members, classes can contain nested types (such as other classes). Accessibility to the members can be `public`, `protected`, `internal protected`, `private`, or `internal`. These are described in detail in Chapter 5, "Generics."

Data Members

Data members are those members that contain the data for the class—fields, constants, and events. Data members can be `static`. A class member is always an instance member unless it is explicitly declared as `static`.

Fields are any variables associated with the class. You have already seen fields in use in the `PhoneCustomer` class in the previous example.

After you have instantiated a `PhoneCustomer` object, you can then access these fields using the `Object.FieldName` syntax, as shown in this example:

```
PhoneCustomer Customer1 = new PhoneCustomer();
Customer1.FirstName = "Simon";
```

Constants can be associated with classes in the same way as variables. You declare a constant using the `const` keyword. If it is declared as `public`, then it will be accessible from outside the class:

```
class PhoneCustomer
{
    public const string DayOfSendingBill = "Monday";
    public int CustomerID;
    public string FirstName;
    public string LastName;
}
```

Events are class members that allow an object to notify a subscriber whenever something noteworthy happens, such as a field or property of the class changing, or some form of user interaction occurring. The client can have code, known as an *event handler*, that reacts to the event. Chapter 8, "Delegates, Lambdas, and Events," looks at events in detail.

Function Members

Function members are those members that provide *some* functionality for manipulating the data in the class. They include methods, properties, constructors, finalizers, operators, and indexers.

➤ *Methods* are functions associated with a particular class. Like data members, function members are instance members by default. They can be made static by using the `static` modifier.

➤ *Properties* are sets of functions that can be accessed from the client in a similar way to the public fields of the class. C# provides a specific syntax for implementing read and write properties on your classes, so you don't have to use method names that have the words `Get` or `Set` embedded in them. Because there's a dedicated syntax for properties that is distinct from that for normal functions, the illusion of objects as actual things is strengthened for client code.

➤ *Constructors* are special functions that are called automatically when an object is instantiated. They must have the same name as the class to which they belong and cannot have a return type. Constructors are useful for initialization.

➤ *Finalizers* are similar to constructors but are called when the CLR detects that an object is no longer needed. They have the same name as the class, preceded by a tilde (~). It is impossible to predict precisely when a finalizer will be called. Finalizers are discussed in Chapter 14, "Memory Management and Pointers."

➤ *Operators*, at their simplest, are actions such as + or −. When you add two integers, you are, strictly speaking, using the + operator for integers. However, C# also allows you to specify how existing operators will work with your own classes (*operator overloading*). Chapter 7, "Operators and Casts," looks at operators in detail.

➤ *Indexers* allow your objects to be indexed in the same way as an array or collection.

Methods

Note that official C# terminology makes a distinction between functions and methods. In C# terminology, the term "function member" includes not only methods, but also other nondata members of a class or struct. This includes indexers, operators, constructors, destructors, and—perhaps somewhat surprisingly—properties. These are contrasted with data members: fields, constants, and events.

Declaring Methods

In C#, the definition of a method consists of any method modifiers (such as the method's accessibility), followed by the type of the return value, followed by the name of the method, followed by a list of input arguments enclosed in parentheses, followed by the body of the method enclosed in curly braces:

```
[modifiers] return_type MethodName([parameters])
{
    // Method body
}
```

Each parameter consists of the name of the type of the parameter, and the name by which it can be referenced in the body of the method. Also, if the method returns a value, a return statement must be used with the return value to indicate each exit point, as shown in this example:

```
public bool IsSquare(Rectangle rect)
{
    return (rect.Height == rect.Width);
}
```

This code uses one of the .NET base classes, System.Drawing.Rectangle, which represents a rectangle.

If the method doesn't return anything, specify a return type of void because you can't omit the return type altogether; and if it takes no arguments, you still need to include an empty set of parentheses after the method name. In this case, including a return statement is optional—the method returns automatically when the closing curly brace is reached. Note that a method can contain as many return statements as required:

```
public bool IsPositive(int value)
{
    if (value < 0)
        return false;
    return true;
}
```

Invoking Methods

The following example, MathTest, illustrates the syntax for definition and instantiation of classes, and definition and invocation of methods. Besides the class that contains the Main() method, it defines a class named MathTest, which contains a couple of methods and a field:

```
using System;

namespace Wrox
{
    class MainEntryPoint
    {
        static void Main()
        {
            // Try calling some static functions.
            Console.WriteLine("Pi is " + MathTest.GetPi());
            int x = MathTest.GetSquareOf(5);
            Console.WriteLine("Square of 5 is " + x);

            // Instantiate a MathTest object
            MathTest math = new MathTest();    // this is C#'s way of
```

```
                                            // instantiating a reference type

         // Call nonstatic methods
         math.value = 30;
         Console.WriteLine(
             "Value field of math variable contains " + math.value);
         Console.WriteLine("Square of 30 is " + math.GetSquare());
    }
}

// Define a class named MathTest on which we will call a method
class MathTest
{
    public int value;

    public int GetSquare()
    {
        return value*value;
    }

    public static int GetSquareOf(int x)
    {
        return x*x;
    }

    public static double GetPi()
    {
        return 3.14159;
    }
  }
}
```

Running the `MathTest` example produces the following results:

```
Pi is 3.14159
Square of 5 is 25
Value field of math variable contains 30
Square of 30 is 900
```

As you can see from the code, the `MathTest` class contains a field that contains a number, as well as a method to find the square of this number. It also contains two static methods: one to return the value of pi and one to find the square of the number passed in as a parameter.

Some features of this class are not really good examples of C# program design. For example, `GetPi()` would usually be implemented as a `const` field, but following good design here would mean using some concepts that have not yet been introduced.

Passing Parameters to Methods

In general, parameters can be passed into methods by reference or by value. When a variable is passed by reference, the called method gets the actual variable, or more to the point, a pointer to the variable in memory. Any changes made to the variable inside the method persist when the method exits. However, when a variable is passed by value, the called method gets an identical copy of the variable, meaning any changes made are lost when the method exits. For complex data types, passing by reference is more efficient because of the large amount of data that must be copied when passing by value.

In C#, reference types are passed by reference and value types are passed by value unless you specify otherwise. However, be sure you understand the implications of this for reference types. Because reference type variables hold only a reference to an object, it is this reference that is passed in as a parameter, not the object itself. Hence, changes made to the underlying object will persist. Value type variables, in contrast, hold the actual data, so a copy of the data itself is passed into the method. An `int`, for instance, is passed by value to a method, and any changes that the method makes to the value of that `int` do not change the value of the original int object. Conversely, if an array or any other reference type, such as a class, is passed into a method, and the method uses the reference to change a value in that array, the new value is reflected in the original array object.

Here is an example, `ParameterTest.cs`, which demonstrates the difference between value types and reference types used as parameters:

```
using System;

namespace Wrox
{
    class ParameterTest
    {
        static void SomeFunction(int[] ints, int i)
        {
            ints[0] = 100;
            i = 100;
        }

        public static int Main()
        {
            int i = 0;
            int[] ints = { 0, 1, 2, 4, 8 };
            // Display the original values.
            Console.WriteLine("i = " + i);
            Console.WriteLine("ints[0] = " + ints[0]);
            Console.WriteLine("Calling SomeFunction...");

            // After this method returns, ints will be changed,
            // but i will not.
            SomeFunction(ints, i);
            Console.WriteLine("i = " + i);
            Console.WriteLine("ints[0] = " + ints[0]);
            return 0;
        }
    }
}
```

The output of the preceding is as follows:

```
ParameterTest.exe
i = 0
ints[0] = 0
Calling SomeFunction...
i = 0
ints[0] = 100
```

Notice how the value of i remains unchanged, but the value changed in ints is also changed in the original array.

The behavior of strings is different again. This is because strings are immutable (if you alter a string's value, you create an entirely new string), so strings don't display the typical reference-type behavior. Any changes made to a string within a method call won't affect the original string. This point is discussed in more detail in Chapter 9, "Strings and Regular Expressions."

ref Parameters

As mentioned, passing variables by value is the default, but you can force value parameters to be passed by reference. To do so, use the `ref` keyword. If a parameter is passed to a method, and the input argument for that method is prefixed with the `ref` keyword, any changes that the method makes to the variable will affect the value of the original object:

```
static void SomeFunction(int[] ints, ref int i)
{
    ints[0] = 100;
    i = 100;      // The change to i will persist after SomeFunction() exits.
}
```

You also need to add the `ref` keyword when you invoke the method:

```
SomeFunction(ints, ref i);
```

Finally, it is important to understand that C# continues to apply initialization requirements to parameters passed to methods. Any variable must be initialized before it is passed into a method, whether it is passed in by value or by reference.

out Parameters

In C-style languages, it is common for functions to be able to output more than one value from a single routine. This is accomplished using output parameters, by assigning the output values to variables that have been passed to the method by reference. Often, the starting values of the variables that are passed by reference are unimportant. Those values will be overwritten by the function, which may never even look at any previous value.

It would be convenient if you could use the same convention in C#, but C# requires that variables be initialized with a starting value before they are referenced. Although you could initialize your input variables with meaningless values before passing them into a function that will fill them with real, meaningful ones, this practice is at best needless and at worst confusing. However, there is a way to circumvent the C# compiler's insistence on initial values for input arguments.

You do this with the `out` keyword. When a method's input argument is prefixed with `out`, that method can be passed a variable that has not been initialized. The variable is passed by reference, so any changes that the method makes to the variable will persist when control returns from the called method. Again, you must use the `out` keyword when you call the method, as well as when you define it:

```
static void SomeFunction(out int i)
{
    i = 100;
}

public static int Main()
{
    int i; // note how i is declared but not initialized.
    SomeFunction(out i);
    Console.WriteLine(i);
    return 0;
}
```

Named Arguments

Typically, parameters need to be passed into a method in the same order that they are defined. Named arguments allow you to pass in parameters in any order. So for the following method:

```
string FullName(string firstName, string lastName)
{
    return firstName + " " + lastName;
}
```

The following method calls will return the same full name:

```
FullName("John", "Doe");
FullName(lastName: "Doe", firstName: "John");
```

If the method has several parameters, you can mix positional and named arguments in the same call.

Optional Arguments

Parameters can also be optional. You must supply a default value for optional parameters, which must be the last ones defined. For example, the following method declaration would be incorrect:

```
void TestMethod(int optionalNumber = 10, int notOptionalNumber)
{
    System.Console.Write(optionalNumber + notOptionalNumber);
}
```

For this method to work, the `optionalNumber` parameter would have to be defined last.

Method Overloading

C# supports method overloading—several versions of the method that have different signatures (that is, the same name but a different number of parameters and/or different parameter data types). To overload methods, simply declare the methods with the same name but different numbers or types of parameters:

```
class ResultDisplayer
{
    void DisplayResult(string result)
    {
        // implementation
    }

    void DisplayResult(int result)
    {
        // implementation
    }
}
```

If optional parameters won't work for you, then you need to use method overloading to achieve the same effect:

```
class MyClass
{
    int DoSomething(int x)     // want 2nd parameter with default value 10
    {
        DoSomething(x, 10);
    }

    int DoSomething(int x, int y)
    {
        // implementation
    }
}
```

As in any language, method overloading carries with it the potential for subtle runtime bugs if the wrong overload is called. Chapter 4 discusses how to code defensively against these problems. For now, you should know that C# does place some minimum restrictions on the parameters of overloaded methods:

➤   It is not sufficient for two methods to differ only in their return type.

➤   It is not sufficient for two methods to differ only by virtue of a parameter having been declared as `ref` or `out`.

Properties

The idea of a property is that it is a method or a pair of methods dressed to look like a field. A good example of this is the `Height` property of a Windows form. Suppose that you have the following code:

```
// mainForm is of type System.Windows.Forms
mainForm.Height = 400;
```

On executing this code, the height of the window will be set to 400 px, and you will see the window resize on the screen. Syntactically, this code looks like you're setting a field, but in fact you are calling a property accessor that contains code to resize the form.

To define a property in C#, use the following syntax:

```csharp
public string SomeProperty
{
    get
    {
        return "This is the property value.";
    }
    set
    {
        // do whatever needs to be done to set the property.
    }
}
```

The `get` accessor takes no parameters and must return the same type as the declared property. You should not specify any explicit parameters for the `set` accessor either, but the compiler assumes it takes one parameter, which is of the same type again, and which is referred to as `value`. For example, the following code contains a property called `Age`, which sets a field called `age`. In this example, `age` is referred to as the backing variable for the property `Age`:

```csharp
private int age;

public int Age
{
    get
    {
        return age;
    }
    set
    {
        age = value;
    }
}
```

Note the naming convention used here. You take advantage of C#'s case sensitivity by using the same name, Pascal-case for the public property, and camel-case for the equivalent private field if there is one. Some developers prefer to use field names that are prefixed by an underscore: _age; this provides an extremely convenient way to identify fields.

Read-Only and Write-Only Properties

It is possible to create a read-only property by simply omitting the `set` accessor from the property definition. Thus, to make `Name` a read-only property, you would do the following:

```csharp
private string name;

public string Name
{
    get
    {
        return name;
    }
}
```

It is similarly possible to create a write-only property by omitting the `get` accessor. However, this is regarded as poor programming practice because it could be confusing to authors of client code. In general, it is recommended that if you are tempted to do this, you should use a method instead.

Access Modifiers for Properties

C# does allow the `set` and `get` accessors to have differing access modifiers. This would allow a property to have a public `get` and a private or protected `set`. This can help control how or when a property can be set. In the following code example, notice that the `set` has a private access modifier but the `get` does not. In this case, the `get` takes the access level of the property. One of the accessors must follow the access level of the property. A compile error will be generated if the `get` accessor has the `protected` access level associated with it because that would make both accessors have a different access level from the property.

```
public string Name
{
  get
  {
    return _name;
  }
  private set
  {
    _name = value;
  }
}
```

Auto-Implemented Properties

If there isn't going to be any logic in the properties `set` and `get`, then auto-implemented properties can be used. Auto-implemented properties implement the backing member variable automatically. The code for the earlier `Age` example would look like this:

```
public int Age {get; set;}
```

The declaration `private int Age;` is not needed. The compiler will create this automatically.

By using auto-implemented properties, validation of the property cannot be done at the property set. Therefore, in the last example you could not have checked to see if an invalid age is set. Also, both accessors must be present, so an attempt to make a property read-only would cause an error:

```
public int Age {get;}
```

However, the access level of each accessor can be different, so the following is acceptable:

```
public int Age {get; private set;}
```

> **A NOTE ABOUT INLINING**
>
> Some developers may be concerned that the previous sections have presented a number of situations in which standard C# coding practices have led to very small functions—for example, accessing a field via a property instead of directly. Will this hurt performance because of the overhead of the extra function call? The answer is no. There's no need to worry about performance loss from these kinds of programming methodologies in C#. Recall that C# code is compiled to IL, then JIT compiled at runtime to native executable code. The JIT compiler is designed to generate highly optimized code and will ruthlessly inline code as appropriate (in other words, it replaces function calls with inline code). A method or property whose implementation simply calls another method or returns a field will almost certainly be inlined. However, the decision regarding where to inline is made entirely by the CLR. You cannot control which methods are inlined by using, for example, a keyword similar to the inline keyword of C++.

Constructors

The syntax for declaring basic constructors is a method that has the same name as the containing class and that does not have any return type:

```
public class MyClass
{
    public MyClass()
    {
    }
    // rest of class definition
```

It's not necessary to provide a constructor for your class. We haven't supplied one for any of the examples so far in this book. In general, if you don't supply any constructor, the compiler will generate a default one behind the scenes. It will be a very basic constructor that just initializes all the member fields by zeroing them out (null reference for reference types, zero for numeric data types, and false for bools). Often, that will be adequate; if not, you'll need to write your own constructor.

Constructors follow the same rules for overloading as other methods—that is, you can provide as many overloads to the constructor as you want, provided they are clearly different in signature:

```
public MyClass()    // zeroparameter constructor
{
    // construction code
}
public MyClass(int number)    // another overload
{
    // construction code
}
```

However, if you supply any constructors that take parameters, the compiler will not automatically supply a default one. This is done only if you have not defined any constructors at all. In the following example, because a one-parameter constructor is defined, the compiler assumes that this is the only constructor you want to be available, so it will not implicitly supply any others:

```
public class MyNumber
{
    private int number;
    public MyNumber(int number)
    {
        this.number = number;
    }
}
```

This code also illustrates typical use of the this keyword to distinguish member fields from parameters of the same name. If you now try instantiating a MyNumber object using a no-parameter constructor, you will get a compilation error:

```
MyNumber numb = new MyNumber();    // causes compilation error
```

Note that it is possible to define constructors as private or protected, so that they are invisible to code in unrelated classes too:

```
public class MyNumber
{
    private int number;
    private MyNumber(int number)    // another overload
    {
        this.number = number;
    }
}
```

This example hasn't actually defined any public or even any protected constructors for MyNumber. This would actually make it impossible for MyNumber to be instantiated by outside code using the new operator (though you might write a public static property or method in `MyNumber` that can instantiate the class). This is useful in two situations:

➤ If your class serves only as a container for some static members or properties, and therefore should never be instantiated

➤ If you want the class to only ever be instantiated by calling a static member function (this is the so-called "class factory" approach to object instantiation)

Static Constructors

One novel feature of C# is that it is also possible to write a static no-parameter constructor for a class. Such a constructor is executed only once, unlike the constructors written so far, which are instance constructors that are executed whenever an object of that class is created:

```
class MyClass
{
    static MyClass()
    {
        // initialization code
    }
    // rest of class definition
}
```

One reason for writing a static constructor is if your class has some static fields or properties that need to be initialized from an external source before the class is first used.

The .NET runtime makes no guarantees about when a static constructor will be executed, so you should not place any code in it that relies on it being executed at a particular time (for example, when an assembly is loaded). Nor is it possible to predict in what order static constructors of different classes will execute. However, what is guaranteed is that the static constructor will run at most once, and that it will be invoked before your code makes any reference to the class. In C#, the static constructor is usually executed immediately before the first call, to any member of the class.

Note that the static constructor does not have any access modifiers. It's never called by any other C# code, but always by the .NET runtime when the class is loaded, so any access modifier such as `public` or `private` would be meaningless. For this same reason, the static constructor can never take any parameters, and there can be only one static constructor for a class. It should also be obvious that a static constructor can access only static members, not instance members, of the class.

It is possible to have a static constructor and a zero-parameter instance constructor defined in the same class. Although the parameter lists are identical, there is no conflict because the static constructor is executed when the class is loaded, but the instance constructor is executed whenever an instance is created. Therefore, there is no confusion about which constructor is executed or when.

If you have more than one class that has a static constructor, the static constructor that will be executed first is undefined. Therefore, you should not put any code in a static constructor that depends on other static constructors having been or not having been executed. However, if any static fields have been given default values, these will be allocated before the static constructor is called.

The next example illustrates the use of a static constructor. It is based on the idea of a program that has user preferences (which are presumably stored in some configuration file). To keep things simple, assume just one user preference, a quantity called `BackColor` that might represent the background color to be used in an application. Because we don't want to get into the details of writing code to read data from an external source here, assume also that the preference is to have a background color of red on weekdays and green on weekends. All the program does is display the preference in a console window, but that is enough to see a static constructor at work:

```
namespace Wrox.ProCSharp.StaticConstructorSample
{
    public class UserPreferences
    {
```

```
        public static readonly Color BackColor;

        static UserPreferences()
        {
            DateTime now = DateTime.Now;
            if (now.DayOfWeek == DayOfWeek.Saturday
                || now.DayOfWeek == DayOfWeek.Sunday)
                BackColor = Color.Green;
            else
                BackColor = Color.Red;
        }

        private UserPreferences()
        {
        }
    }
}
```

This code shows how the color preference is stored in a static variable, which is initialized in the static constructor. The field is declared as read-only, which means that its value can only be set in a constructor. You learn about read-only fields in more detail later in this chapter. The code uses a few helpful structs that Microsoft has supplied as part of the Framework class library. System.DateTime and System.Drawing.Color. DateTime implement a static property, Now, which returns the current time; and an instance property, DayOfWeek, which determines what day of the week a date-time represents. Color is used to store colors. It implements various static properties, such as Red and Green as used in this example, which return commonly used colors. To use Color, you need to reference the System.Drawing.dll assembly when compiling, and you must add a using statement for the System.Drawing namespace:

```
using System;
using System.Drawing;
```

You test the static constructor with this code:

```
class MainEntryPoint
{
    static void Main(string[] args)
    {
        Console.WriteLine("User-preferences: BackColor is: " +
                        UserPreferences.BackColor.ToString());
    }
}
```

Compiling and running the preceding code results in this output:

```
User-preferences: BackColor is: Color [Red]
```

Of course, if the code is executed during the weekend, your color preference would be Green.

Calling Constructors from Other Constructors

You might sometimes find yourself in the situation where you have several constructors in a class, perhaps to accommodate some optional parameters for which the constructors have some code in common. For example, consider the following:

```
class Car
{
    private string description;
    private uint nWheels;
    public Car(string description, uint nWheels)
    {
        this.description = description;
```

```
        this.nWheels = nWheels;
    }

    public Car(string description)
    {
        this.description = description;
        this.nWheels = 4;
    }
// etc.
```

Both constructors initialize the same fields. It would clearly be neater to place all the code in one location. C# has a special syntax known as a *constructor initializer* to enable this:

```
class Car
{
    private string description;
    private uint nWheels;

    public Car(string description, uint nWheels)
    {
        this.description = description;
        this.nWheels = nWheels;
    }

    public Car(string description): this(description, 4)
    {
    }
    // etc
```

In this context, the `this` keyword simply causes the constructor with the nearest matching parameters to be called. Note that any constructor initializer is executed before the body of the constructor. Suppose that the following code is run:

```
Car myCar = new Car("Proton Persona");
```

In this example, the two-parameter constructor executes before any code in the body of the one-parameter constructor (though in this particular case, because there is no code in the body of the one-parameter constructor, it makes no difference).

A C# constructor initializer may contain either one call to another constructor in the same class (using the syntax just presented) or one call to a constructor in the immediate base class (using the same syntax, but using the keyword `base` instead of `this`). It is not possible to put more than one call in the initializer.

readonly Fields

The concept of a constant as a variable that contains a value that cannot be changed is something that C# shares with most programming languages. However, constants don't necessarily meet all requirements. On occasion, you may have a variable whose value shouldn't be changed but the value is not known until runtime. C# provides another type of variable that is useful in this scenario: the `readonly` field.

The `readonly` keyword provides a bit more flexibility than `const`, allowing for situations in which you want a field to be constant but you also need to carry out some calculations to determine its initial value. The rule is that you can assign values to a `readonly` field inside a constructor, but not anywhere else. It's also possible for a `readonly` field to be an instance rather than a static field, having a different value for each instance of a class. This means that, unlike a `const` field, if you want a `readonly` field to be static, you have to declare it as such.

Suppose that you have an MDI program that edits documents, and for licensing reasons you want to restrict the number of documents that can be opened simultaneously. Assume also that you are selling different versions of the software, and it's possible for customers to upgrade their licenses to open more documents simultaneously. Clearly, this means you can't hard-code the maximum number in the source code. You would probably need a field to represent this maximum number. This field will have to be read in—perhaps from a registry key or some other file storage—each time the program is launched. Therefore, your code might look something like this:

```
public class DocumentEditor
{
    public static readonly uint MaxDocuments;

    static DocumentEditor()
    {
        MaxDocuments = DoSomethingToFindOutMaxNumber();
    }
}
```

In this case, the field is static because the maximum number of documents needs to be stored only once per running instance of the program. This is why it is initialized in the static constructor. If you had an instance `readonly` field, you would initialize it in the instance constructor(s). For example, presumably each document you edit has a creation date, which you wouldn't want to allow the user to change (because that would be rewriting the past!). Note that the field is also public—you don't normally need to make `readonly` fields private, because by definition they cannot be modified externally (the same principle also applies to constants).

As noted earlier, date is represented by the class `System.DateTime`. The following code uses a `System.DateTime` constructor that takes three parameters (year, month, and day of the month; for details about this and other `DateTime` constructors see the MSDN documentation):

```
public class Document
{
    public readonly DateTime CreationDate;

    public Document()
    {
        // Read in creation date from file. Assume result is 1 Jan 2002
        // but in general this can be different for different instances
        // of the class
        CreationDate = new DateTime(2002, 1, 1);
    }
}
```

`CreationDate` and `MaxDocuments` in the previous code snippet are treated like any other field, except that because they are read-only they cannot be assigned outside the constructors:

```
void SomeMethod()
{
    MaxDocuments = 10;    // compilation error here. MaxDocuments is readonly
}
```

It's also worth noting that you don't have to assign a value to a `readonly` field in a constructor. If you don't do so, it will be left with the default value for its particular data type or whatever value you initialized it to at its declaration. That applies to both static and instance `readonly` fields.

ANONYMOUS TYPES

Chapter 2, "Core C#" discussed the `var` keyword in reference to implicitly typed variables. When used with the `new` keyword, anonymous types can be created. An anonymous type is simply a nameless class that inherits from `object`. The definition of the class is inferred from the initializer, just as with implicitly typed variables.

For example, if you needed an object containing a person's first, middle, and last name, the declaration would look like this:

```
var captain = new {FirstName = "James", MiddleName = "T", LastName = "Kirk"};
```

This would produce an object with `FirstName`, `MiddleName`, and `LastName` properties. If you were to create another object that looked like:

```
var doctor = new {FirstName = "Leonard", MiddleName = "", LastName = "McCoy"};
```

then the types of `captain` and `doctor` are the same. You could set `captain = doctor`, for example.

If the values that are being set come from another object, then the initializer can be abbreviated. If you already have a class that contains the properties `FirstName`, `MiddleName`, and `LastName` and you have an instance of that class with the instance name `person`, then the `captain` object could be initialized like this:

```
var captain = new {person.FirstName, person.MiddleName, person.LastName};
```

The property names from the `person` object would be projected to the new object named `captain`, so the object named `captain` would have the `FirstName`, `MiddleName`, and `LastName` properties.

The actual type name of these new objects is unknown. The compiler "makes up" a name for the type, but only the compiler is ever able to make use of it. Therefore, you can't and shouldn't plan on using any type reflection on the new objects because you will not get consistent results.

STRUCTS

So far, you have seen how classes offer a great way to encapsulate objects in your program. You have also seen how they are stored on the heap in a way that gives you much more flexibility in data lifetime, but with a slight cost in performance. This performance cost is small thanks to the optimizations of managed heaps. However, in some situations all you really need is a small data structure. If so, a class provides more functionality than you need, and for best performance you probably want to use a struct. Consider the following example:

```
class Dimensions
{
    public double Length;
    public double Width;
}
```

This code defines a class called `Dimensions`, which simply stores the length and width of an item. Suppose you're writing a furniture-arranging program that enables users to experiment with rearranging their furniture on the computer, and you want to store the dimensions of each item of furniture. It might seem as though you're breaking the rules of good program design by making the fields public, but the point is that you don't really need all the facilities of a class for this. All you have is two numbers, which you'll find convenient to treat as a pair rather than individually. There is no need for a lot of methods, or for you to be able to inherit from the class, and you certainly don't want to have the .NET runtime go to the trouble of bringing in the heap, with all the performance implications, just to store two `double`s.

As mentioned earlier in this chapter, the only thing you need to change in the code to define a type as a struct instead of a class is to replace the keyword `class` with `struct`:

```
struct Dimensions
{
    public double Length;
    public double Width;
}
```

Defining functions for structs is also exactly the same as defining them for classes. The following code demonstrates a constructor and a property for a struct:

```
struct Dimensions
{
    public double Length;
    public double Width;

    public Dimensions(double length, double width)
```

```
    {
       Length = length;
       Width = width;
    }

    public double Diagonal
    {
       get
       {
          return Math.Sqrt(Length * Length + Width * Width);
       }
    }
  }
}
```

Structs are value types, not reference types. This means they are stored either in the stack or inline (if they are part of another object that is stored on the heap) and have the same lifetime restrictions as the simple data types:

➤ Structs do not support inheritance.

➤ There are some differences in the way constructors work for structs. In particular, the compiler always supplies a default no-parameter constructor, which you are not permitted to replace.

➤ With a struct, you can specify how the fields are to be laid out in memory (this is examined in Chapter 15, "Reflection," which covers attributes).

Because structs are really intended to group data items together, you'll sometimes find that most or all of their fields are declared as public. Strictly speaking, this is contrary to the guidelines for writing .NET code—according to Microsoft, fields (other than const fields) should always be private and wrapped by public properties. However, for simple structs, many developers consider public fields to be acceptable programming practice.

The following sections look at some of these differences between structs and classes in more detail.

Structs Are Value Types

Although structs are value types, you can often treat them syntactically in the same way as classes. For example, with the definition of the Dimensions class in the previous section, you could write this:

```
Dimensions point = new Dimensions();
point.Length = 3;
point.Width = 6;
```

Note that because structs are value types, the new operator does not work in the same way as it does for classes and other reference types. Instead of allocating memory on the heap, the new operator simply calls the appropriate constructor, according to the parameters passed to it, initializing all fields. Indeed, for structs it is perfectly legal to write this:

```
Dimensions point;
point.Length = 3;
point.Width = 6;
```

If Dimensions were a class, this would produce a compilation error, because point would contain an uninitialized reference—an address that points nowhere, so you could not start setting values to its fields. For a struct, however, the variable declaration actually allocates space on the stack for the entire struct, so it's ready to assign values to. The following code, however, would cause a compilation error, with the compiler complaining that you are using an uninitialized variable:

```
Dimensions point;
Double D = point.Length;
```

Structs follow the same rule as any other data type—everything must be initialized before use. A struct is considered fully initialized either when the new operator has been called against it or when values have been individually assigned to all its fields. Also, of course, a struct defined as a member field of a class is initialized by being zeroed out automatically when the containing object is initialized.

The fact that structs are value types affects performance, though depending on how you use your struct, this can be good or bad. On the positive side, allocating memory for structs is very fast because this takes place inline or on the stack. The same is true when they go out of scope. Structs are cleaned up quickly and don't need to wait on garbage collection. On the negative side, whenever you pass a struct as a parameter or assign a struct to another struct (as in A=B, where A and B are structs), the full contents of the struct are copied, whereas for a class only the reference is copied. This results in a performance loss that varies according to the size of the struct, emphasizing the fact that structs are really intended for small data structures. Note, however, that when passing a struct as a parameter to a method, you can avoid this performance loss by passing it as a `ref` parameter—in this case, only the address in memory of the struct will be passed in, which is just as fast as passing in a class. If you do this, though, be aware that it means the called method can, in principle, change the value of the struct.

Structs and Inheritance

Structs are not designed for inheritance. This means it is not possible to inherit from a struct. The only exception to this is that structs, in common with every other type in C#, derive ultimately from the class `System.Object`. Hence, structs also have access to the methods of `System.Object`, and it is even possible to override them in structs—an obvious example would be overriding the `ToString()` method. The actual inheritance chain for structs is that each struct derives from a class, `System.ValueType`, which in turn derives from `System.Object`. `ValueType` which does not add any new members to `Object` but provides implementations of some of them that are more suitable for structs. Note that you cannot supply a different base class for a struct: Every struct is derived from `ValueType`.

Constructors for Structs

You can define constructors for structs in exactly the same way that you can for classes, but you are not permitted to define a constructor that takes no parameters. This may seem nonsensical, but the reason is buried in the implementation of the .NET runtime. In some rare circumstances, the .NET runtime would not be able to call a custom zero-parameter constructor that you have supplied. Microsoft has therefore taken the easy way out and banned zero-parameter constructors for structs in C#.

That said, the default constructor, which initializes all fields to zero values, is always present implicitly, even if you supply other constructors that take parameters. It's also impossible to circumvent the default constructor by supplying initial values for fields. The following code will cause a compile-time error:

```
struct Dimensions
{
    public double Length = 1;     // error. Initial values not allowed
    public double Width = 2;      // error. Initial values not allowed
}
```

Of course, if `Dimensions` had been declared as a class, this code would have compiled without any problems.

Incidentally, you can supply a `Close()` or `Dispose()` method for a struct in the same way you do for a class. The `Dispose()` method is discussed in detail in Chapter 14, "Memory Management and Pointers."

WEAK REFERENCES

When the class or struct is instantiated in the application code, it will have a strong reference as long as there is any other code that references it. For example, if you have a class called `MyClass()` and you create a reference to objects based on that class and call the variable `myClassVariable` as follows, as long as `myClassVariable` is in scope there is a strong reference to the `MyClass` object:

```
MyClass myClassVariable = new MyClass();
```

This means that the garbage collector cannot clean up the memory used by the `MyClass` object. Generally this is a good thing because you may need to access the `MyClass` object; but what if `MyClass` were very large and perhaps wasn't accessed very often? Then a weak reference to the object can be created.

A weak reference allows the object to be created and used, but if the garbage collector happens to run (garbage collection is discussed in Chapter 14), it will collect the object and free up the memory. This is not something you would typically want to do because of potential bugs and performance issues, but there are certainly situations in which it makes sense.

Weak references are created using the `WeakReference` class. Because the object could be collected at any time, it's important that the existence of the object is valid before trying to reference it. Using the `MathTest` class from before, this time we'll create a weak reference to it using the `WeakReference` class:

```
static void Main()
{
    // Instantiate a weak reference to MathTest object
    WeakReference mathReference = new WeakReference(new MathTest());
    MathTest math;
    if(mathReference.IsAlive)
    {
        math = mathReference.Target as MathTest;
        math.Value = 30;
        Console.WriteLine("Value field of math variable contains " + math.Value);
        Console.WriteLine("Square of 30 is " + math.GetSquare());
    }
    else
    {
        Console.WriteLine("Reference is not available.");
    }

    GC.Collect();

    if(mathReference.IsAlive)
    {
        math = mathReference.Target as MathTest;
    }
    else
    {
        Console.WriteLine("Reference is not available.");
    }
}
```

When you create `mathReference` a new `MathTest` object is passed into the constructor. The `MathTest` object becomes the target of the `WeakReference` object. When you want to use the `MathTest` object, you have to check the `mathReference` object first to ensure it hasn't been collected. You use the `IsAlive` property for that. If the `IsAlive` property is true, then you can get the reference to the `MathTest` object from the target property. Notice that you have to cast to the `MathTest` type, as the `Target` property returns an `Object` type.

Next, you call the garbage collector (`GC.Collect()`) and try to get the `MathTest` object again. This time the `IsAlive` property returns false, and if you really wanted a `MathTest` object you would have to instantiate a new version.

PARTIAL CLASSES

The `partial` keyword allows the class, struct, method, or interface to span multiple files. Typically, a class resides entirely in a single file. However, in situations in which multiple developers need access to the same class, or, more likely, a code generator of some type is generating part of a class, having the class in multiple files can be beneficial.

To use the `partial` keyword, simply place `partial` before class, struct, or interface. In the following example, the class `TheBigClass` resides in two separate source files, `BigClassPart1.cs` and `BigClassPart2.cs`:

```
//BigClassPart1.cs
partial class TheBigClass
{
  public void MethodOne()
  {
  }
}
```

```
//BigClassPart2.cs
partial class TheBigClass
{
  public void MethodTwo()
  {
  }
}
```

When the project that these two source files are part of is compiled, a single type called `TheBigClass` will be created with two methods, `MethodOne()` and `MethodTwo()`.

If any of the following keywords are used in describing the class, the same must apply to all partials of the same type:

➤ `public`

➤ `private`

➤ `protected`

➤ `internal`

➤ `abstract`

➤ `sealed`

➤ `new`

➤ generic constraints

Nested partials are allowed as long as the `partial` keyword precedes the `class` keyword in the nested type. Attributes, XML comments, interfaces, generic-type parameter attributes, and members are combined when the partial types are compiled into the type. Given these two source files:

```
//BigClassPart1.cs
[CustomAttribute]
partial class TheBigClass: TheBigBaseClass, IBigClass
{
  public void MethodOne()
  {
  }
}
```

```
//BigClassPart2.cs
[AnotherAttribute]
partial class TheBigClass: IOtherBigClass
{
  public void MethodTwo()
  {
  }
}
```

the equivalent source file would be as follows after the compile:

```
[CustomAttribute]
[AnotherAttribute]
```

```
partial class TheBigClass: TheBigBaseClass, IBigClass, IOtherBigClass
{
  public void MethodOne()
  {
  }

  public void MethodTwo()
  {
  }
}
```

STATIC CLASSES

Earlier, this chapter discussed static constructors and how they allowed the initialization of static member variables. If a class contains nothing but static methods and properties, the class itself can become static. A static class is functionally the same as creating a class with a private static constructor. An instance of the class can never be created. By using the static keyword, the compiler can verify that instance members are never accidentally added to the class. If they are, a compile error occurs. This helps guarantee that an instance is never created. The syntax for a static class looks like this:

```
static class StaticUtilities
{
  public static void HelperMethod()
  {
  }
}
```

An object of type StaticUtilities is not needed to call the HelperMethod(). The type name is used to make the call:

```
StaticUtilities.HelperMethod();
```

THE OBJECT CLASS

As indicated earlier, all .NET classes are ultimately derived from System.Object. In fact, if you don't specify a base class when you define a class, the compiler automatically assumes that it derives from Object. Because inheritance has not been used in this chapter, every class you have seen here is actually derived from System.Object. (As noted earlier, for structs this derivation is indirect — a struct is always derived from System.ValueType, which in turn derives from System.Object.)

The practical significance of this is that, besides the methods, properties, and so on that you define, you also have access to a number of public and protected member methods that have been defined for the Object class. These methods are available in all other classes that you define.

System.Object Methods

For the time being, the following list summarizes the purpose of each method; the next section provides more details about the ToString() method in particular:

➤   ToString() — A fairly basic, quick-and-easy string representation. Use it when you just want a quick idea of the contents of an object, perhaps for debugging purposes. It provides very little choice regarding how to format the data. For example, dates can, in principle, be expressed in a huge variety of different formats, but DateTime.ToString() does not offer you any choice in this regard. If you need a more sophisticated string representation — for example, one that takes into account your formatting preferences or the culture (the locale) — then you should implement the IFormattable interface (see Chapter 9).

➤   GetHashCode() — If objects are placed in a data structure known as a map (also known as a hash table or dictionary), it is used by classes that manipulate these structures to determine where to place an object in the structure. If you intend your class to be used as a key for a dictionary, you need to override `GetHashCode()`. Some fairly strict requirements exist for how you implement your overload, which you learn about when you examine dictionaries in Chapter 10, "Collections."

➤ `Equals()` (both versions) and `ReferenceEquals()` — As you'll note by the existence of three different methods aimed at comparing the equality of objects, the .NET Framework has quite a sophisticated scheme for measuring equality. Subtle differences exist between how these three methods, along with the comparison operator, ==, are intended to be used. In addition, restrictions exist on how you should override the virtual, one-parameter version of `Equals()` if you choose to do so, because certain base classes in the `System.Collections` namespace call the method and expect it to behave in certain ways. You explore the use of these methods in Chapter 7 when you examine operators.

➤ `Finalize()` — Covered in Chapter 13, "Asynchronous Programming," this method is intended as the nearest that C# has to C++-style destructors. It is called when a reference object is garbage collected to clean up resources. The `Object` implementation of `Finalize()` doesn't actually do anything and is ignored by the garbage collector. You normally override `Finalize()` if an object owns references to unmanaged resources that need to be removed when the object is deleted. The garbage collector cannot do this directly because it only knows about managed resources, so it relies on any finalizers that you supply.

➤ `GetType()` — This object returns an instance of a class derived from `System.Type`, so it can provide an extensive range of information about the class of which your object is a member, including base type, methods, properties, and so on. `System.Type` also provides the entry point into .NET's reflection technology. Chapter 15 examines this topic.

➤ `MemberwiseClone()` — The only member of `System.Object` that isn't examined in detail anywhere in the book. That's because it is fairly simple in concept. It just makes a copy of the object and returns a reference (or in the case of a value type, a boxed reference) to the copy. Note that the copy made is a shallow copy, meaning it copies all the value types in the class. If the class contains any embedded references, then only the references are copied, not the objects referred to. This method is protected and cannot be called to copy external objects. Nor is it virtual, so you cannot override its implementation.

The ToString() Method

You've already encountered `ToString()` in Chapter 2. It provides the most convenient way to get a quick string representation of an object.

For example:

```
int i = 50;
string str = i.ToString();  // returns "50"
```

Here's another example:

```
enum Colors {Red, Orange, Yellow};
// later on in code...
Colors favoriteColor = Colors.Orange;
string str = favoriteColor.ToString();    // returns "Orange"
```

`Object.ToString()` is actually declared as virtual, and all these examples are taking advantage of the fact that its implementation in the C# predefined data types has been overridden for us to return correct string representations of those types. You might not think that the `Colors` enum counts as a predefined data type. It actually is implemented as a struct derived from `System.Enum`, and `System.Enum` has a rather clever override of `ToString()` that deals with all the enums you define.

If you don't override `ToString()` in classes that you define, your classes will simply inherit the `System .Object` implementation, which displays the name of the class. If you want `ToString()` to return a string that contains information about the value of objects of your class, you need to override it. To illustrate this, the following example, `Money`, defines a very simple class, also called `Money`, which represents U.S. currency amounts. `Money` simply acts as a wrapper for the decimal class but supplies a `ToString()` method. Note that this method must be declared as `override` because it is replacing (overriding) the `ToString()` method supplied by `Object`. Chapter 4 discusses overriding in more detail. The complete code for this example is as follows (note that it also illustrates use of properties to wrap fields):

```
using System;

namespace Wrox
{
    class MainEntryPoint
    {
        static void Main(string[] args)
        {
            Money cash1 = new Money();
            cash1.Amount = 40M;
            Console.WriteLine("cash1.ToString() returns: " + cash1.ToString());
            Console.ReadLine();
        }
    }
    public class Money
    {
        private decimal amount;

        public decimal Amount
        {
            get
            {
                return amount;
            }
            set
            {
                amount = value;
            }
        }
        public override string ToString()
        {
            return "$" + Amount.ToString();
        }
    }

}
```

This example is included just to illustrate syntactical features of C#. C# already has a predefined type to represent currency amounts, `decimal`, so in real life you wouldn't write a class to duplicate this functionality unless you wanted to add various other methods to it; and in many cases, due to formatting requirements, you'd probably use the `String.Format()` method (which is covered in Chapter 8) rather than `ToString()` to display a currency string.

In the `Main()` method, you first instantiate a `Money` object. The `ToString()` method is then called, which actually executes the overridden version of the method. Running this code gives the following results:

```
cash1.ToString() returns: $40
```

EXTENSION METHODS

There are many ways to extend a class. If you have the source for the class, then inheritance, which is covered in Chapter 4, is a great way to add functionality to your objects. If the source code isn't available, extension methods can help by enabling you to change a class without requiring the source code for the class.

Extension methods are static methods that can appear to be part of a class without actually being in the source code for the class. Let's say that the `Money` class from the previous example needs to have a method `AddToAmount(decimal amountToAdd)`. However, for whatever reason, the original source for the assembly cannot be changed directly. All you have to do is create a static class and add the AddToAmount method as a static method. Here is what the code would look like:

```
namespace Wrox
{
  public static class MoneyExtension
  {
    public static void AddToAmount(this Money money, decimal amountToAdd)
    {
      money.Amount += amountToAdd;
    }
  }
}
```

Notice the parameters for the AddToAmount method. For an extension method, the first parameter is the type that is being extended preceded by the this keyword. This is what tells the compiler that this method is part of the Money type. In this example, Money is the type that is being extended. In the extension method you have access to all the public methods and properties of the type being extended.

In the main program, the AddToAmount method appears just as another method. The first parameter doesn't appear, and you do not have to do anything with it. To use the new method, you make the call just like any other method:

```
cash1.AddToAmount(10M);
```

Even though the extension method is static, you use standard instance method syntax. Notice that you call AddToAmount using the cash1 instance variable and not using the type name.

If the extension method has the same name as a method in the class, the extension method will never be called. Any instance methods already in the class take precedence.

SUMMARY

This chapter examined C# syntax for declaring and manipulating objects. You have seen how to declare static and instance fields, properties, methods, and constructors. You have also seen that C# adds some new features not present in the OOP model of some other languages—for example, static constructors provide a means of initializing static fields, whereas structs enable you to define types that do not require the use of the managed heap, which could result in performance gains. You have also seen how all types in C# derive ultimately from the type System.Object, which means that all types start with a basic set of useful methods, including ToString(). We mentioned inheritance a few times throughout this chapter, and you'll examine implementation and interface inheritance in C# in Chapter 4.

Inheritance

WHAT'S IN THIS CHAPTER?

➤ Types of inheritance
➤ Implementing inheritance
➤ Access modifiers
➤ Interfaces

WROX.COM CODE DOWNLOADS FOR THIS CHAPTER

The wrox.com code downloads for this chapter are found at `http://www.wrox.com/remtitle`
`.cgi?isbn=1118314425` on the Download Code tab. The code for this chapter is divided into the
following major examples:

➤ BankAccounts.cs
➤ CurrentAccounts.cs
➤ MortimerPhones.cs

INHERITANCE

Chapter 3, "Objects and Types," examined how to use individual classes in C#. The focus in that
chapter was how to define methods, properties, constructors, and other members of a single class (or
a single struct). Although you learned that all classes are ultimately derived from the class `System`
`.Object`, you have not yet learned how to create a hierarchy of inherited classes. Inheritance is the
subject of this chapter, which explains how C# and the .NET Framework handle inheritance.

TYPES OF INHERITANCE

Let's start by reviewing exactly what C# does and does not support as far as inheritance is
concerned.

Implementation Versus Interface Inheritance

In object-oriented programming, there are two distinct types of inheritance—implementation inheritance and interface inheritance:

> ➤ **Implementation inheritance** means that a type derives from a base type, taking all the base type's member fields and functions. With implementation inheritance, a derived type adopts the base type's implementation of each function, unless the definition of the derived type indicates that a function implementation is to be overridden. This type of inheritance is most useful when you need to add functionality to an existing type, or when a number of related types share a significant amount of common functionality.

> ➤ **Interface inheritance** means that a type inherits only the signatures of the functions, not any implementations. This type of inheritance is most useful when you want to specify that a type makes certain features available.

C# supports both implementation inheritance and interface inheritance. Both are incorporated into the framework and the language from the ground up, thereby enabling you to decide which to use based on the application's architecture.

Multiple Inheritance

Some languages such as C++ support what is known as *multiple inheritance,* in which a class derives from more than one other class. The benefits of using multiple inheritance are debatable: On the one hand, you can certainly use multiple inheritance to write extremely sophisticated, yet compact code, as demonstrated by the C++ ATL library. On the other hand, code that uses multiple implementation inheritance is often difficult to understand and debug (a point that is equally well demonstrated by the C++ ATL library). As mentioned, making it easy to write robust code was one of the crucial design goals behind the development of C#. Accordingly, C# does not support multiple implementation inheritance. It does, however, allow types to be derived from multiple interfaces—multiple interface inheritance. This means that a C# class can be derived from one other class, and any number of interfaces. Indeed, we can be more precise: Thanks to the presence of System.Object as a common base type, every C# class (except for Object) has exactly one base class, and may additionally have any number of base interfaces.

Structs and Classes

Chapter 3 distinguishes between structs (value types) and classes (reference types). One restriction of using structs is that they do not support inheritance, beyond the fact that every struct is automatically derived from System.ValueType. Although it's true that you cannot code a type hierarchy of structs, it is possible for structs to implement interfaces. In other words, structs don't really support implementation inheritance, but they do support interface inheritance. The following summarizes the situation for any types that you define:

> ➤ **Structs** are always derived from System.ValueType. They can also be derived from any number of interfaces.

> ➤ **Classes** are always derived from either System.Object or one that you choose. They can also be derived from any number of interfaces.

IMPLEMENTATION INHERITANCE

If you want to declare that a class derives from another class, use the following syntax:

```
class MyDerivedClass: MyBaseClass
{
    // functions and data members here
}
```

> **NOTE** *This syntax is very similar to C++ and Java syntax. However, C++ programmers, who will be used to the concepts of public and private inheritance, should note that C# does not support private inheritance, hence the absence of a public or private qualifier on the base class name. Supporting private inheritance would have complicated the language for very little gain. In practice, private inheritance is very rarely in C++ anyway.*

If a class (or a struct) also derives from interfaces, the list of base class and interfaces is separated by commas:

```
public class MyDerivedClass: MyBaseClass, IInterface1, IInterface2
{
    // etc.
}
```

For a struct, the syntax is as follows:

```
public struct MyDerivedStruct: IInterface1, IInterface2
{
    // etc.
}
```

If you do not specify a base class in a class definition, the C# compiler will assume that `System.Object` is the base class. Hence, the following two pieces of code yield the same result:

```
class MyClass: Object  // derives from System.Object
{
    // etc.
}
```

and:

```
class MyClass    // derives from System.Object
{
    // etc.
}
```

For the sake of simplicity, the second form is more common.

Because C# supports the `object` keyword, which serves as a pseudonym for the `System.Object` class, you can also write this:

```
class MyClass: object   // derives from System.Object
{
    // etc.
}
```

If you want to reference the `Object` class, use the `object` keyword, which is recognized by intelligent editors such as Visual Studio .NET and thus facilitates editing your code.

Virtual Methods

By declaring a base class function as `virtual`, you allow the function to be overridden in any derived classes:

```
class MyBaseClass
{
    public virtual string VirtualMethod()
    {
        return "This method is virtual and defined in MyBaseClass";
    }
}
```

It is also permitted to declare a property as `virtual`. For a virtual or overridden property, the syntax is the same as for a nonvirtual property, with the exception of the keyword `virtual`, which is added to the definition. The syntax looks like this:

```
public virtual string ForeName
{
    get { return foreName;}
    set { foreName = value;}
}
private string foreName;
```

For simplicity, the following discussion focuses mainly on methods, but it applies equally well to properties.

The concepts behind virtual functions in C# are identical to standard OOP concepts. You can override a virtual function in a derived class; and when the method is called, the appropriate method for the type of object is invoked. In C#, functions are not virtual by default but (aside from constructors) can be explicitly declared as `virtual`. This follows the C++ methodology: For performance reasons, functions are not virtual unless indicated. In Java, by contrast, all functions are virtual. C# does differ from C++ syntax, though, because it requires you to declare when a derived class's function overrides another function, using the `override` keyword:

```
class MyDerivedClass: MyBaseClass
{
    public override string VirtualMethod()
    {
        return "This method is an override defined in MyDerivedClass.";
    }
}
```

This syntax for method overriding removes potential runtime bugs that can easily occur in C++, when a method signature in a derived class unintentionally differs slightly from the base version, resulting in the method failing to override the base version. In C#, this is picked up as a compile-time error because the compiler would see a function marked as `override` but no base method for it to override.

Neither member fields nor static functions can be declared as virtual. The concept simply wouldn't make sense for any class member other than an instance function member.

Hiding Methods

If a method with the same signature is declared in both base and derived classes but the methods are not declared as `virtual` and `override`, respectively, then the derived class version is said to *hide* the base class version.

In most cases, you would want to override methods rather than hide them. By hiding them you risk calling the wrong method for a given class instance. However, as shown in the following example, C# syntax is designed to ensure that the developer is warned at compile time about this potential problem, thus making it safer to hide methods if that is your intention. This also has versioning benefits for developers of class libraries.

Suppose that you have a class called `HisBaseClass`:

```
class HisBaseClass
{
    // various members
}
```

At some point in the future, you write a derived class that adds some functionality to `HisBaseClass`. In particular, you add a method called `MyGroovyMethod()`, which is not present in the base class:

```
class MyDerivedClass: HisBaseClass
{
    public int MyGroovyMethod()
    {
        // some groovy implementation
        return 0;
    }
}
```

One year later, you decide to extend the functionality of the base class. By coincidence, you add a method that is also called `MyGroovyMethod()` and that has the same name and signature as yours, but probably doesn't do the same thing. When you compile your code using the new version of the base class, you have a potential clash because your program won't know which method to call. It's all perfectly legal in C#, but because your `MyGroovyMethod()` is not intended to be related in any way to the base class `MyGroovyMethod()`, the result is that running this code does not yield the result you want. Fortunately, C# has been designed to cope very well with these types of conflicts.

In these situations, C# generates a compilation warning that reminds you to use the `new` keyword to declare that you intend to hide a method, like this:

```
class MyDerivedClass: HisBaseClass
{
    public new int MyGroovyMethod()
    {
        // some groovy implementation
        return 0;
    }
}
```

However, because your version of `MyGroovyMethod()` is not declared as `new`, the compiler picks up on the fact that it's hiding a base class method without being instructed to do so and generates a warning (this applies whether or not you declared `MyGroovyMethod()` as `virtual`). If you want, you can rename your version of the method. This is the recommended course of action because it eliminates future confusion. However, if you decide not to rename your method for whatever reason (for example, if you've published your software as a library for other companies, so you can't change the names of methods), all your existing client code will still run correctly, picking up your version of `MyGroovyMethod()`. This is because any existing code that accesses this method must be done through a reference to `MyDerivedClass` (or a further derived class).

Your existing code cannot access this method through a reference to `HisBaseClass`; it would generate a compilation error when compiled against the earlier version of `HisBaseClass`. The problem can only occur in client code you have yet to write. C# is designed to issue a warning that a potential problem might occur in future code—you need to pay attention to this warning and take care not to attempt to call your version of `MyGroovyMethod()` through any reference to `HisBaseClass` in any future code you add. However, all your existing code will still work fine. It may be a subtle point, but it's an impressive example of how C# is able to cope with different versions of classes.

Calling Base Versions of Functions

C# has a special syntax for calling base versions of a method from a derived class: `base.<MethodName>()`. For example, if you want a method in a derived class to return 90 percent of the value returned by the base class method, you can use the following syntax:

```
class CustomerAccount
{
    public virtual decimal CalculatePrice()
    {
        // implementation
        return 0.0M;
    }
}
class GoldAccount: CustomerAccount
{
    public override decimal CalculatePrice()
    {
        return base.CalculatePrice() * 0.9M;
    }
}
```

Note that you can use the `base.<MethodName>()` syntax to call any method in the base class—you don't have to call it from inside an override of the same method.

Abstract Classes and Functions

C# allows both classes and functions to be declared as abstract. An abstract class cannot be instantiated, whereas an abstract function does not have an implementation, and must be overridden in any non-abstract derived class. Obviously, an abstract function is *automatically* virtual (although you don't need to supply the `virtual` keyword; and doing so results in a syntax error). If any class contains any abstract functions, that class is also abstract and must be declared as such:

```
abstract class Building
{
    public abstract decimal CalculateHeatingCost();    // abstract method
}
```

> **NOTE** *C++ developers should note the slightly different terminology. In C++, abstract functions are often described as pure virtual; in the C# world, the only correct term to use is abstract.*

Sealed Classes and Methods

C# allows classes and methods to be declared as `sealed`. In the case of a class, this means you can't inherit from that class. In the case of a method, this means you can't override that method.

```
sealed class FinalClass
{
    // etc
}
class DerivedClass: FinalClass        // wrong. Will give compilation error
{
    // etc
}
```

The most likely situation in which you'll mark a class or method as `sealed` is if the class or method is internal to the operation of the library, class, or other classes that you are writing, to ensure that any attempt to override some of its functionality will lead to instability in the code. You might also mark a class or method as `sealed` for commercial reasons, in order to prevent a third party from extending your classes in a manner that is contrary to the licensing agreements. In general, however, be careful about marking a class or member as `sealed`, because by doing so you are severely restricting how it can be used. Even if you don't think it would be useful to inherit from a class or override a particular member of it, it's still possible that at some point in the future someone will encounter a situation you hadn't anticipated in which it is useful to do so. The .NET base class library frequently uses sealed classes to make these classes inaccessible to third-party developers who might want to derive their own classes from them. For example, `string` is a sealed class.

Declaring a method as `sealed` serves a purpose similar to that for a class:

```
class MyClass: MyClassBase
{
    public sealed override void FinalMethod()
    {
        // etc.
    }
}
class DerivedClass: MyClass
{
    public override void FinalMethod()        // wrong. Will give compilation error
    {
    }
}
```

In order to use the `sealed` keyword on a method or property, it must have first been overridden from a base class. If you do not want a method or property in a base class overridden, then don't mark it as virtual.

Constructors of Derived Classes

Chapter 3 discusses how constructors can be applied to individual classes. An interesting question arises as to what happens when you start defining your own constructors for classes that are part of a hierarchy, inherited from other classes that may also have custom constructors.

Assume that you have not defined any explicit constructors for any of your classes. This means that the compiler supplies default zeroing-out constructors for all your classes. There is actually quite a lot going on under the hood when that happens, but the compiler is able to arrange it so that things work out nicely throughout the class hierarchy and every field in every class is initialized to whatever its default value is. When you add a constructor of your own, however, you are effectively taking control of construction. This has implications right down through the hierarchy of derived classes, so you have to ensure that you don't inadvertently do anything to prevent construction through the hierarchy from taking place smoothly.

You might be wondering why there is any special problem with derived classes. The reason is that when you create an instance of a derived class, more than one constructor is at work. The constructor of the class you instantiate isn't by itself sufficient to initialize the class—the constructors of the base classes must also be called. That's why we've been talking about construction through the hierarchy.

To understand why base class constructors must be called, you're going to develop an example based on a cell phone company called MortimerPhones. The example contains an abstract base class, `GenericCustomer`, which represents any customer. There is also a (non-abstract) class, `Nevermore60Customer`, which represents any customer on a particular rate called the `Nevermore60` rate. All customers have a name, represented by a private field. Under the `Nevermore60` rate, the first few minutes of the customer's call time are charged at a higher rate, necessitating the need for the field `highCostMinutesUsed`, which details how many of these higher-cost minutes each customer has used. The class definitions look like this:

```
abstract class GenericCustomer
{
    private string name;
    // lots of other methods etc.
}
class Nevermore60Customer: GenericCustomer
{
    private uint highCostMinutesUsed;
    // other methods etc.
}
```

Don't worry about what other methods might be implemented in these classes because we are concentrating solely on the construction process here. If you download the sample code for this chapter, you'll find that the class definitions include only the constructors.

Take a look at what happens when you use the `new` operator to instantiate a `Nevermore60Customer`:

```
GenericCustomer customer = new Nevermore60Customer();
```

Clearly, both of the member fields `name` and `highCostMinutesUsed` must be initialized when `customer` is instantiated. If you don't supply constructors of your own, but rely simply on the default constructors, then you'd expect `name` to be initialized to the `null` reference, and `highCostMinutesUsed` initialized to zero. Let's look in a bit more detail at how this actually happens.

The `highCostMinutesUsed` field presents no problem: The default `Nevermore60Customer` constructor supplied by the compiler initializes this field to zero.

What about `name`? Looking at the class definitions, it's clear that the `Nevermore60Customer` constructor can't initialize this value. This field is declared as private, which means that derived classes don't have access to it. Therefore, the default `Nevermore60Customer` constructor won't know that this field exists. The only code items that have that knowledge are other members of `GenericCustomer`. Therefore, if `name` is going to be initialized, that must be done by a constructor in `GenericCustomer`. No matter how big your class hierarchy is, this same reasoning applies right down to the ultimate base class, `System.Object`.

Now that you have an understanding of the issues involved, you can look at what actually happens whenever a derived class is instantiated. Assuming that default constructors are used throughout, the compiler first grabs the constructor of the class it is trying to instantiate, in this case `Nevermore60Customer`. The first thing that the default `Nevermore60Customer` constructor does is attempt to run the default constructor for the immediate base class, `GenericCustomer`. The `GenericCustomer` constructor attempts to run the constructor for its immediate base class, `System.Object`; but `System.Object` doesn't have any base classes, so its constructor just executes and returns control to the `GenericCustomer` constructor. That constructor now executes, initializing `name` to `null`, before returning control to the `Nevermore60Customer` constructor. That constructor in turn executes, initializing `highCostMinutesUsed` to zero, and exits. At this point, the `Nevermore60Customer` instance has been successfully constructed and initialized.

The net result of all this is that the constructors are called in order of `System.Object` first, and then progress down the hierarchy until the compiler reaches the class being instantiated. Notice that in this process, each constructor handles initialization of the fields in its own class. That's how it should normally work, and when you start adding your own constructors you should try to stick to that principle.

Note the order in which this happens. It's always the base class constructors that are called first. This means there are no problems with a constructor for a derived class invoking any base class methods, properties, and any other members to which it has access, because it can be confident that the base class has already been constructed and its fields initialized. It also means that if the derived class doesn't like the way that the base class has been initialized, it can change the initial values of the data, provided that it has access to do so. However, good programming practice almost invariably means you'll try to prevent that situation from occurring if possible, and you will trust the base class constructor to deal with its own fields.

Now that you know how the process of construction works, you can start fiddling with it by adding your own constructors.

Adding a Constructor in a Hierarchy

This section takes the easiest case first and demonstrates what happens if you simply replace the default constructor somewhere in the hierarchy with another constructor that takes no parameters. Suppose that you decide that you want everyone's name to be initially set to the string `"<no name>"` instead of to the `null` reference. You'd modify the code in `GenericCustomer` like this:

```
public abstract class GenericCustomer
{
    private string name;
    public GenericCustomer()
     : base()   // We could omit this line without affecting the compiled code.
    {
        name = "<no name>";
    }
}
```

Adding this code will work fine. `Nevermore60Customer` still has its default constructor, so the sequence of events described earlier will proceed as before, except that the compiler uses the custom `GenericCustomer` constructor instead of generating a default one, so the `name` field is always initialized to `"<no name>"` as required.

Notice that in your constructor you've added a call to the base class constructor before the `GenericCustomer` constructor is executed, using a syntax similar to that used earlier when you saw how to get different overloads of constructors to call each other. The only difference is that this time you use the `base` keyword instead of `this` to indicate that it's a constructor to the base class, rather than a constructor to the current class, you want to call. There are no parameters in the brackets after the `base` keyword—that's important because it means you are not passing any parameters to the base constructor, so the compiler has to look for a parameterless constructor to call. The result of all this is that the compiler injects code to call the `System.Object` constructor, which is what happens by default anyway.

In fact, you can omit that line of code and write the following (as was done for most of the constructors so far in this chapter):

```
public GenericCustomer()
{
    name = "<no name>";
}
```

If the compiler doesn't see any reference to another constructor before the opening curly brace, it assumes that you wanted to call the base class constructor; this is consistent with how default constructors work.

The `base` and `this` keywords are the only keywords allowed in the line that calls another constructor. Anything else causes a compilation error. Also note that only one other constructor can be specified.

So far, this code works fine. One way to collapse the progression through the hierarchy of constructors, however, is to declare a constructor as `private`:

```
private GenericCustomer()
{
    name = "<no name>";
}
```

If you try this, you'll get an interesting compilation error, which could really throw you if you don't understand how construction down a hierarchy works:

```
'Wrox.ProCSharp.GenericCustomer.GenericCustomer()' is inaccessible due to its protection level
```

What's interesting here is that the error occurs not in the `GenericCustomer` class but in the derived class, `Nevermore60Customer`. That's because the compiler tried to generate a default constructor for `Nevermore60Customer` but was not able to, as the default constructor is supposed to invoke the no-parameter `GenericCustomer` constructor. By declaring that constructor as `private`, you've made it inaccessible to the derived class. A similar error occurs if you supply a constructor to `GenericCustomer`, which takes parameters, but at the same time you fail to supply a no-parameter constructor. In this case, the compiler won't generate a default constructor for `GenericCustomer`, so when it tries to generate the default constructors for any derived class, it again finds that it can't because a no-parameter base class constructor is not available. A workaround is to add your own constructors to the derived classes—even if you don't actually need to do anything in these constructors—so that the compiler doesn't try to generate any default constructors.

Now that you have all the theoretical background you need, you're ready to move on to an example demonstrating how you can neatly add constructors to a hierarchy of classes. In the next section, you start adding constructors that take parameters to the MortimerPhones example.

Adding Constructors with Parameters to a Hierarchy

You're going to start with a one-parameter constructor for `GenericCustomer`, which specifies that customers can be instantiated only when they supply their names:

```
abstract class GenericCustomer
{
    private string name;
    public GenericCustomer(string name)
    {
        this.name = name;
    }
}
```

So far, so good. However, as mentioned previously, this causes a compilation error when the compiler tries to create a default constructor for any derived classes because the default compiler-generated constructors for `Nevermore60Customer` will try to call a no-parameter `GenericCustomer` constructor, and `GenericCustomer` does not possess such a constructor. Therefore, you need to supply your own constructors to the derived classes to avoid a compilation error:

```
class Nevermore60Customer: GenericCustomer
{
    private uint highCostMinutesUsed;
    public Nevermore60Customer(string name)
    :   base(name)
    {
    }
```

Now instantiation of `Nevermore60Customer` objects can occur only when a string containing the customer's name is supplied, which is what you want anyway. The interesting thing here is what the `Nevermore60Customer` constructor does with this string. Remember that it can't initialize the `name` field itself because it has no access to private fields in its base class. Instead, it passes the name through to the base class for the `GenericCustomer` constructor to handle. It does this by specifying that the base class constructor to be executed first is the one that takes the name as a parameter. Other than that, it doesn't take any action of its own.

Now examine what happens if you have different overloads of the constructor as well as a class hierarchy to deal with. To this end, assume that `Nevermore60` customers might have been referred to MortimerPhones by a friend as part of one of those sign-up-a-friend-and-get-a-discount offers. This means that when you construct a `Nevermore60Customer`, you may need to pass in the referrer's name as well. In real life, the constructor would have to do something complicated with the name, such as process the discount, but here you'll just store the referrer's name in another field.

The `Nevermore60Customer` definition will now look like this:

```
class Nevermore60Customer: GenericCustomer
{
    public Nevermore60Customer(string name, string referrerName)
    : base(name)
    {
        this.referrerName = referrerName;
    }

    private string referrerName;
    private uint highCostMinutesUsed;
```

The constructor takes the name and passes it to the `GenericCustomer` constructor for processing; `referrerName` is the variable that is your responsibility here, so the constructor deals with that parameter in its main body.

However, not all `Nevermore60Customers` will have a referrer, so you still need a constructor that doesn't require this parameter (or a constructor that gives you a default value for it). In fact, you will specify that if there is no referrer, then the `referrerName` field should be set to `"<None>"`, using the following one-parameter constructor:

```
public Nevermore60Customer(string name)
  : this(name, "<None>")
{
}
```

You now have all your constructors set up correctly. It's instructive to examine the chain of events that occurs when you execute a line like this:

```
GenericCustomer customer=new Nevermore60Customer("Arabel Jones");
```

The compiler sees that it needs a one-parameter constructor that takes one string, so the constructor it identifies is the last one that you defined:

```
public Nevermore60Customer(string Name)
  : this(Name, "<None>")
```

When you instantiate `customer`, this constructor is called. It immediately transfers control to the corresponding `Nevermore60Customer` two-parameter constructor, passing it the values `"ArabelJones"`, and `"<None>"`. Looking at the code for this constructor, you see that it in turn immediately passes control to the one-parameter `GenericCustomer` constructor, giving it the string `"ArabelJones"`, and in turn that constructor passes control to the `System.Object` default constructor. Only now do the constructors execute. First, the `System.Object` constructor executes. Next is the `GenericCustomer` constructor, which initializes the name field. Then the `Nevermore60Customer` two-parameter constructor gets control back and sorts out initializing the `referrerName` to `"<None>"`. Finally, the `Nevermore60Customer` one-parameter constructor executes; this constructor doesn't do anything else.

As you can see, this is a very neat and well-designed process. Each constructor handles initialization of the variables that are obviously its responsibility; and, in the process, your class is correctly instantiated and prepared for use. If you follow the same principles when you write your own constructors for your classes, even the most complex classes should be initialized smoothly and without any problems.

MODIFIERS

You have already encountered quite a number of so-called modifiers—keywords that can be applied to a type or a member. Modifiers can indicate the visibility of a method, such as `public` or `private`, or the nature of an item, such as whether a method is `virtual` or `abstract`. C# has a number of modifiers, and at this point it's worth taking a minute to provide the complete list.

Visibility Modifiers

Visibility modifiers indicate which other code items can view an item.

MODIFIER	APPLIES TO	DESCRIPTION
public	Any types or members	The item is visible to any other code.
protected	Any member of a type, and any nested type	The item is visible only to any derived type.
internal	Any types or members	The item is visible only within its containing assembly.
private	Any member of a type, and any nested type	The item is visible only inside the type to which it belongs.
protected internal	Any member of a type, and any nested type	The item is visible to any code within its containing assembly and to any code inside a derived type.

Note that type definitions can be internal or public, depending on whether you want the type to be visible outside its containing assembly:

```
public class MyClass
{
   // etc.
```

You cannot define types as protected, private, or protected internal because these visibility levels would be meaningless for a type contained in a namespace. Hence, these visibilities can be applied only to members. However, you can define nested types (that is, types contained within other types) with these visibilities because in this case the type also has the status of a member. Hence, the following code is correct:

```
public class OuterClass
{
   protected class InnerClass
   {
      // etc.
   }
   // etc.
}
```

If you have a nested type, the inner type is always able to see all members of the outer type. Therefore, with the preceding code, any code inside `InnerClass` always has access to all members of `OuterClass`, even where those members are private.

Other Modifiers

The modifiers in the following table can be applied to members of types and have various uses. A few of these modifiers also make sense when applied to types.

MODIFIER	APPLIES TO	DESCRIPTION
new	Function members	The member hides an inherited member with the same signature.
static	All members	The member does not operate on a specific instance of the class.
virtual	Function members only	The member can be overridden by a derived class.
abstract	Function members only	A virtual member that defines the signature of the member but doesn't provide an implementation.
override	Function members only	The member overrides an inherited virtual or abstract member.
sealed	Classes, methods, and properties	For classes, the class cannot be inherited from. For properties and methods, the member overrides an inherited virtual member but cannot be overridden by any members in any derived classes. Must be used in conjunction with `override`.
extern	Static [DllImport] methods only	The member is implemented externally, in a different language.

INTERFACES

As mentioned earlier, by deriving from an interface, a class is declaring that it implements certain functions. Because not all object-oriented languages support interfaces, this section examines C#'s implementation of interfaces in detail. It illustrates interfaces by presenting the complete definition of one of the interfaces that has been predefined by Microsoft—`System.IDisposable`. `IDisposable` contains one method, `Dispose()`, which is intended to be implemented by classes to clean up code:

```
public interface IDisposable
{
    void Dispose();
}
```

This code shows that declaring an interface works syntactically in much the same way as declaring an abstract class. Be aware, however, that it is not permitted to supply implementations of any of the members of an interface. In general, an interface can contain only declarations of methods, properties, indexers, and events.

You can never instantiate an interface; it contains only the signatures of its members. An interface has neither constructors (how can you construct something that you can't instantiate?) nor fields (because that would imply some internal implementation). Nor is an interface definition allowed to contain operator overloads, although that's not because there is any problem with declaring them; there isn't, but because interfaces are usually intended to be public contracts, having operator overloads would cause some incompatibility problems with other .NET languages, such as Visual Basic .NET, which do not support operator overloading.

Nor is it permitted to declare modifiers on the members in an interface definition. Interface members are always implicitly `public`, and they cannot be declared as `virtual` or `static`. That's up to implementing classes to decide. Therefore, it is fine for implementing classes to declare access modifiers, as demonstrated in the example in this section.

For example, consider `IDisposable`. If a class wants to declare publicly that it implements the `Dispose()` method, it must implement `IDisposable`, which in C# terms means that the class derives from `IDisposable`:

```
class SomeClass: IDisposable
{
    // This class MUST contain an implementation of the
    // IDisposable.Dispose() method, otherwise
    // you get a compilation error.
    public void Dispose()
    {
        // implementation of Dispose() method
    }
    // rest of class
}
```

In this example, if `SomeClass` derives from `IDisposable` but doesn't contain a `Dispose()` implementation with the exact same signature as defined in `IDisposable`, you get a compilation error because the class is breaking its agreed-on contract to implement `IDisposable`. Of course, it's no problem for the compiler if a class has a `Dispose()` method but doesn't derive from `IDisposable`. The problem is that other code would have no way of recognizing that `SomeClass` has agreed to support the `IDisposable` features.

> **NOTE** `IDisposable` *is a relatively simple interface because it defines only one method. Most interfaces contain more members.*

Defining and Implementing Interfaces

This section illustrates how to define and use interfaces by developing a short program that follows the interface inheritance paradigm. The example is based on bank accounts. Assume that you are writing code that will ultimately allow computerized transfers between bank accounts. Assume also for this example that there are many companies that implement bank accounts but they have all mutually agreed that any classes representing bank accounts will implement an interface, `IBankAccount`, which exposes methods to deposit or withdraw money, and a property to return the balance. It is this interface that enables outside code to recognize the various bank account classes implemented by different bank accounts. Although the aim is to enable the bank accounts to communicate with each other to allow transfers of funds between accounts, that feature isn't introduced just yet.

To keep things simple, you will keep all the code for the example in the same source file. Of course, if something like the example were used in real life, you could surmise that the different bank account classes would not only be compiled to different assemblies, but also be hosted on different machines owned by the different banks. That's all much too complicated for our purposes here. However, to maintain some realism, you will define different namespaces for the different companies.

To begin, you need to define the `IBankAccount` interface:

```
namespace Wrox.ProCSharp
{
    public interface IBankAccount
    {
        void PayIn(decimal amount);
        bool Withdraw(decimal amount);
        decimal Balance { get; }
    }
}
```

Notice the name of the interface, `IBankAccount`. It's a best-practice convention to begin an interface name with the letter I, to indicate it's an interface.

> **NOTE** *Chapter 2, "Core C#," points out that in most cases, .NET usage guidelines discourage the so-called Hungarian notation in which names are preceded by a letter that indicates the type of object being defined. Interfaces are one of the few exceptions for which Hungarian notation is recommended.*

The idea is that you can now write classes that represent bank accounts. These classes don't have to be related to each other in any way; they can be completely different classes. They will all, however, declare that they represent bank accounts by the mere fact that they implement the IBankAccount interface.

Let's start off with the first class, a saver account run by the Royal Bank of Venus:

```csharp
namespace Wrox.ProCSharp.VenusBank
{
    public class SaverAccount: IBankAccount
    {
        private decimal balance;
        public void PayIn(decimal amount)
        {
            balance += amount;
        }
        public bool Withdraw(decimal amount)
        {
            if (balance >= amount)
            {
                balance -= amount;
                return true;
            }
            Console.WriteLine("Withdrawal attempt failed.");
            return false;
        }
        public decimal Balance
        {
            get
            {
                return balance;
            }
        }
        public override string ToString()
        {
            return String.Format("Venus Bank Saver: Balance = {0,6:C}", balance);
        }
    }
}
```

It should be obvious what the implementation of this class does. You maintain a private field, balance, and adjust this amount when money is deposited or withdrawn. You display an error message if an attempt to withdraw money fails because of insufficient funds. Notice also that because we are keeping the code as simple as possible, we are not implementing extra properties, such as the account holder's name! In real life that would be essential information, of course, but for this example it's unnecessarily complicated.

The only really interesting line in this code is the class declaration:

```csharp
public class SaverAccount: IBankAccount
```

You've declared that SaverAccount is derived from one interface, IBankAccount, and you have not explicitly indicated any other base classes (which of course means that SaverAccount is derived directly from System .Object). By the way, derivation from interfaces acts completely independently from derivation from classes.

Being derived from IBankAccount means that SaverAccount gets all the members of IBankAccount; but because an interface doesn't actually implement any of its methods, SaverAccount must provide its own implementations of all of them. If any implementations are missing, you can rest assured that the compiler will complain. Recall also that the interface just indicates the presence of its members. It's up to the class to determine whether it wants any of them to be `virtual` or `abstract` (though `abstract` functions are of course only allowed if the class itself is `abstract`). For this particular example, you don't have any reason to make any of the interface functions virtual.

To illustrate how different classes can implement the same interface, assume that the Planetary Bank of Jupiter also implements a class to represent one of its bank accounts—a Gold Account:

```
namespace Wrox.ProCSharp.JupiterBank
{
    public class GoldAccount: IBankAccount
    {
        // etc
    }
}
```

We won't present details of the `GoldAccount` class here; in the sample code, it's basically identical to the implementation of `SaverAccount`. We stress that `GoldAccount` has no connection with `SaverAccount`, other than they both happen to implement the same interface.

Now that you have your classes, you can test them. You first need a few `using` statements:

```
using System;
using Wrox.ProCSharp;
using Wrox.ProCSharp.VenusBank;
using Wrox.ProCSharp.JupiterBank;
```

Now you need a `Main()` method:

```
namespace Wrox.ProCSharp
{
    class MainEntryPoint
    {
        static void Main()
        {
            IBankAccount venusAccount = new SaverAccount();
            IBankAccount jupiterAccount = new GoldAccount();
            venusAccount.PayIn(200);
            venusAccount.Withdraw(100);
            Console.WriteLine(venusAccount.ToString());
            jupiterAccount.PayIn(500);
            jupiterAccount.Withdraw(600);
            jupiterAccount.Withdraw(100);
            Console.WriteLine(jupiterAccount.ToString());
        }
    }
}
```

This code (which if you download the sample, you can find in the file `BankAccounts.cs`) produces the following output:

```
C:> BankAccounts
Venus Bank Saver: Balance = £100.00
Withdrawal attempt failed.
Jupiter Bank Saver: Balance = £400.00
```

The main point to notice about this code is the way that you have declared both your reference variables as `IBankAccount` references. This means that they can point to any instance of any class that implements this interface. However, it also means that you can call only methods that are part of this interface through these references—if you want to call any methods implemented by a class that are not part of the interface, you need to cast the reference to the appropriate type. In the example code, you were able to call `ToString()` (not implemented by `IBankAccount`) without any explicit cast, purely because `ToString()` is a `System.Object` method, so the C# compiler knows that it will be supported by any class (put differently, the cast from any interface to `System.Object` is implicit). Chapter 7, "Operators and Casts," covers the syntax for performing casts.

Interface references can in all respects be treated as class references—but the power of an interface reference is that it can refer to any class that implements that interface. For example, this allows you to form arrays of interfaces, whereby each element of the array is a different class:

```
IBankAccount[] accounts = new IBankAccount[2];
accounts[0] = new SaverAccount();
accounts[1] = new GoldAccount();
```

Note, however, that you would get a compiler error if you tried something like this:

```
accounts[1] = new SomeOtherClass();    // SomeOtherClass does NOT implement
                                       // IBankAccount: WRONG!!
```

The preceding causes a compilation error similar to this:

```
Cannot implicitly convert type 'Wrox.ProCSharp. SomeOtherClass' to
  'Wrox.ProCSharp.IBankAccount'
```

Derived Interfaces

It's possible for interfaces to inherit from each other in the same way that classes do. This concept is illustrated by defining a new interface, `ITransferBankAccount`, which has the same features as `IBankAccount` but also defines a method to transfer money directly to a different account:

```
namespace Wrox.ProCSharp
{
    public interface ITransferBankAccount: IBankAccount
    {
        bool TransferTo(IBankAccount destination, decimal amount);
    }
}
```

Because `ITransferBankAccount` is derived from `IBankAccount`, it gets all the members of `IBankAccount` as well as its own. That means that any class that implements (derives from) `ITransferBankAccount` must implement all the methods of `IBankAccount`, as well as the new `TransferTo()` method defined in `ITransferBankAccount`. Failure to implement all these methods will result in a compilation error.

Note that the `TransferTo()` method uses an `IBankAccount` interface reference for the destination account. This illustrates the usefulness of interfaces: When implementing and then invoking this method, you don't need to know anything about what type of object you are transferring money to—all you need to know is that this object implements `IBankAccount`.

To illustrate `ITransferBankAccount`, assume that the Planetary Bank of Jupiter also offers a current account. Most of the implementation of the `CurrentAccount` class is identical to implementations of `SaverAccount` and `GoldAccount` (again, this is just to keep this example simple—that won't normally be the case), so in the following code only the differences are highlighted:

```
public class CurrentAccount: ITransferBankAccount
{
    private decimal balance;
    public void PayIn(decimal amount)
    {
        balance += amount;
    }
    public bool Withdraw(decimal amount)
    {
        if (balance >= amount)
        {
            balance -= amount;
```

```
            return true;
        }
        Console.WriteLine("Withdrawal attempt failed.");
        return false;
    }
    public decimal Balance
    {
        get
        {
            return balance;
        }
    }
    public bool TransferTo(IBankAccount destination, decimal amount)
    {
        bool result;
        result = Withdraw(amount);
        if (result)
        {
            destination.PayIn(amount);
        }
        return result;
    }
    public override string ToString()
    {
        return String.Format("Jupiter Bank Current Account: Balance = {0,6:C}",balance);
    }
}
```

The class can be demonstrated with this code:

```
static void Main()
{
    IBankAccount venusAccount = new SaverAccount();
    ITransferBankAccount jupiterAccount = new CurrentAccount();
    venusAccount.PayIn(200);
    jupiterAccount.PayIn(500);
    jupiterAccount.TransferTo(venusAccount, 100);
    Console.WriteLine(venusAccount.ToString());
    Console.WriteLine(jupiterAccount.ToString());
}
```

The preceding code (CurrentAccounts.cs) produces the following output, which, as you can verify, shows that the correct amounts have been transferred:

```
C:> CurrentAccount
Venus Bank Saver: Balance = £300.00
Jupiter Bank Current Account: Balance = £400.00
```

SUMMARY

This chapter described how to code inheritance in C#. You have seen that C# offers rich support for both multiple interface and single implementation inheritance. You have also learned that C# provides a number of useful syntactical constructs designed to assist in making code more robust. These include the override keyword, which indicates when a function should override a base function; the new keyword, which indicates when a function hides a base function; and rigid rules for constructor initializers that are designed to ensure that constructors are designed to interoperate in a robust manner.

Generics

WROX.COM CODE DOWNLOADS FOR THIS CHAPTER

The wrox.com code downloads for this chapter are found at http://www.wrox.com/remtitle.cgi?isbn=1118314425 on the Download Code tab. The code for this chapter is divided into the following major examples:

GENERICS OVERVIEW

Since the release of .NET 2.0, .NET has supported generics. Generics are not just a part of the C# programming language; they are deeply integrated with the IL (Intermediate Language) code in the assemblies. With generics, you can create classes and methods that are independent of contained types. Instead of writing a number of methods or classes with the same functionality for different types, you can create just one method or class.

Another option to reduce the amount of code is using the Object class. However, passing using types derived from the Object class is not type safe. Generic classes make use of generic types that are replaced with specific types as needed. This allows for type safety: the compiler complains if a specific type is not supported with the generic class.

Generics are not limited to classes; in this chapter, you also see generics with interfaces and methods. Generics with delegates can be found in Chapter 8, "Delegates, Lambdas, and Events."

Generics are not a completely new construct; similar concepts exist with other languages. For example, C++ templates have some similarity to generics. However, there's a big difference between C++ templates and .NET generics. With C++ templates, the source code of the template is required when a template is instantiated with a specific type. Unlike C++ templates, generics are not only a construct of the C# language, but are defined with the CLR. This makes it possible to instantiate generics with a specific type in Visual Basic even though the generic class was defined with C#.

The following sections explore the advantages and disadvantages of generics, particularly in regard to the following:

➤ Performance

➤ Type safety

➤ Binary code reuse

➤ Code bloat

➤ Naming guidelines

Performance

One of the big advantages of generics is performance. In Chapter 10, "Collections," you will see non-generic and generic collection classes from the namespaces `System.Collections` and `System.Collections.Generic`. Using value types with non-generic collection classes results in boxing and unboxing when the value type is converted to a reference type, and vice versa.

> **NOTE** *Boxing and unboxing are discussed in Chapter 7, "Operators and Casts." Here is just a short refresher about these terms.*

Value types are stored on the stack, whereas reference types are stored on the heap. C# classes are reference types; structs are value types. .NET makes it easy to convert value types to reference types, so you can use a value type everywhere an object (which is a reference type) is needed. For example, an `int` can be assigned to an object. The conversion from a value type to a reference type is known as *boxing*. Boxing occurs automatically if a method requires an object as a parameter, and a value type is passed. In the other direction, a boxed value type can be converted to a value type by using unboxing. With unboxing, the cast operator is required.

The following example shows the `ArrayList` class from the namespace `System.Collections`. `ArrayList` stores objects; the `Add()` method is defined to require an object as a parameter, so an integer type is boxed. When the values from an `ArrayList` are read, unboxing occurs when the object is converted to an integer type. This may be obvious with the cast operator that is used to assign the first element of the `ArrayList` collection to the variable i1, but it also happens inside the `foreach` statement where the variable i2 of type int is accessed:

```
var list = new ArrayList();
list.Add(44);    // boxing — convert a value type to a reference type

int i1 = (int)list[0];    // unboxing — convert a reference type to
                          // a value type
```

```
  foreach (int i2 in list)
  {
    Console.WriteLine(i2);    // unboxing
  }
```

Boxing and unboxing are easy to use but have a big performance impact, especially when iterating through many items.

Instead of using objects, the List<T> class from the namespace System.Collections.Generic enables you to define the type when it is used. In the example here, the generic type of the List<T> class is defined as int, so the int type is used inside the class that is generated dynamically from the JIT compiler. Boxing and unboxing no longer happen:

```
var list = new List<int>();
list.Add(44);  // no boxing — value types are stored in the List<int>

int i1 = list[0];  // no unboxing, no cast needed

foreach (int i2 in list)
{
  Console.WriteLine(i2);
}
```

Type Safety

Another feature of generics is type safety. As with the ArrayList class, if objects are used, any type can be added to this collection. The following example shows adding an integer, a string, and an object of type MyClass to the collection of type ArrayList:

```
var list = new ArrayList();
list.Add(44);
list.Add("mystring");
list.Add(new MyClass());
```

If this collection is iterated using the following foreach statement, which iterates using integer elements, the compiler accepts this code. However, because not all elements in the collection can be cast to an int, a runtime exception will occur:

```
foreach (int i in list)
{
  Console.WriteLine(i);
}
```

Errors should be detected as early as possible. With the generic class List<T>, the generic type T defines what types are allowed. With a definition of List<int>, only integer types can be added to the collection. The compiler doesn't compile this code because the Add() method has invalid arguments:

```
var list = new List<int>();
list.Add(44);
list.Add("mystring");   // compile time error
list.Add(new MyClass());   // compile time error
```

Binary Code Reuse

Generics enable better binary code reuse. A generic class can be defined once and can be instantiated with many different types. Unlike C++ templates, it is not necessary to access the source code.

For example, here the List<T> class from the namespace System.Collections.Generic is instantiated with an int, a string, and a MyClass type:

```
var list = new List<int>();
list.Add(44);

var stringList = new List<string>();
stringList.Add("mystring");

var myClassList = new List<MyClass>();
myClassList.Add(new MyClass());
```

Generic types can be defined in one language and used from any other .NET language.

Code Bloat

You might be wondering how much code is created with generics when instantiating them with different specific types. Because a generic class definition goes into the assembly, instantiating generic classes with specific types doesn't duplicate these classes in the IL code. However, when the generic classes are compiled by the JIT compiler to native code, a new class for every specific value type is created. Reference types share all the same implementation of the same native class. This is because with reference types, only a 4-byte memory address (with 32-bit systems) is needed within the generic instantiated class to reference a reference type. Value types are contained within the memory of the generic instantiated class; and because every value type can have different memory requirements, a new class for every value type is instantiated.

Naming Guidelines

If generics are used in the program, it helps when generic types can be distinguished from non-generic types. Here are naming guidelines for generic types:

➤ Generic type names should be prefixed with the letter T.

➤ If the generic type can be replaced by any class because there's no special requirement, and only one generic type is used, the character T is good as a generic type name:

```
public class List<T> { }

public class LinkedList<T> { }
```

➤ If there's a special requirement for a generic type (for example, it must implement an interface or derive from a base class), or if two or more generic types are used, descriptive names should be used for the type names:

```
public delegate void EventHandler<TEventArgs>(object sender,
  TEventArgs e);

public delegate TOutput Converter<TInput, TOutput>(TInput from);

public class SortedList<TKey, TValue> { }
```

CREATING GENERIC CLASSES

The example in this section starts with a normal, non-generic simplified linked list class that can contain objects of any kind, and then converts this class to a generic class.

With a linked list, one element references the next one. Therefore, you must create a class that wraps the object inside the linked list and references the next object. The class LinkedListNode contains a property named Value that is initialized with the constructor. In addition to that, the LinkedListNode class contains references to the next and previous elements in the list that can be accessed from properties (code file LinkedListObjects/LinkedListNode.cs):

```
public class LinkedListNode
{
  public LinkedListNode(object value)
  {
    this.Value = value;
  }

  public object Value { get; private set; }

  public LinkedListNode Next { get; internal set; }
  public LinkedListNode Prev { get; internal set; }
}
```

The LinkedList class includes First and Last properties of type LinkedListNode that mark the beginning and end of the list. The method AddLast() adds a new element to the end of the list. First, an object of type LinkedListNode is created. If the list is empty, then the First and Last properties are set to the new element; otherwise, the new element is added as the last element to the list. By implementing the GetEnumerator() method, it is possible to iterate through the list with the foreach statement. The GetEnumerator() method makes use of the yield statement for creating an enumerator type:

```
public class LinkedList: IEnumerable
{
  public LinkedListNode First { get; private set; }
  public LinkedListNode Last { get; private set; }

  public LinkedListNode AddLast(object node)
  {
    var newNode = new LinkedListNode(node);
    if (First == null)
    {
      First = newNode;
      Last = First;
    }
    else
    {
      LinkedListNode previous = Last;
      Last.Next = newNode;
      Last = newNode;
      Last.Prev = previous;
    }
    return newNode;
  }

  public IEnumerator GetEnumerator()
  {
    LinkedListNode current = First;
    while (current != null)
    {
      yield return current.Value;
      current = current.Next;
    }
  }
}
```

NOTE *The* yield *statement creates a state machine for an enumerator. This statement is explained in Chapter 6, "Arrays and Tuples."*

Now you can use the `LinkedList` class with any type. The following code segment instantiates a new `LinkedList` object and adds two integer types and one string type. As the integer types are converted to an object, boxing occurs as explained earlier. With the `foreach` statement, unboxing happens. In the `foreach` statement, the elements from the list are cast to an integer, so a runtime exception occurs with the third element in the list because casting to an `int` fails (code file `LinkedListObjects/Program.cs`):

```
var list1 = new LinkedList();
list1.AddLast(2);
list1.AddLast(4);
list1.AddLast("6");

foreach (int i in list1)
{
  Console.WriteLine(i);
}
```

Now let's make a generic version of the linked list. A generic class is defined similarly to a normal class with the generic type declaration. The generic type can then be used within the class as a field member, or with parameter types of methods. The class `LinkedListNode` is declared with a generic type `T`. The property `Value` is now type `T` instead of `object`; the constructor is changed as well to accept an object of type `T`. A generic type can also be returned and set, so the properties `Next` and `Prev` are now of type `LinkedListNode<T>` (code file `LinkedListSample/LinkedListNode.cs`):

```
public class LinkedListNode<T>
{
  public LinkedListNode(T value)
  {
    this.Value = value;
  }

  public T Value { get; private set; }
  public LinkedListNode<T> Next { get; internal set; }
  public LinkedListNode<T> Prev { get; internal set; }
}
```

In the following code the class `LinkedList` is changed to a generic class as well. `LinkedList<T>` contains `LinkedListNode<T>` elements. The type `T` from the `LinkedList` defines the type `T` of the properties `First` and `Last`. The method `AddLast()` now accepts a parameter of type `T` and instantiates an object of `LinkedListNode<T>`.

Besides the interface `IEnumerable`, a generic version is also available: `IEnumerable<T>`. `IEnumerable<T>` derives from `IEnumerable` and adds the `GetEnumerator()` method, which returns `IEnumerator<T>`. `LinkedList<T>` implements the generic interface `IEnumerable<T>` (code file `LinkedListSample/LinkedList.cs`):

> **NOTE** *Enumerations and the interfaces* `IEnumerable` *and* `IEnumerator` *are discussed in Chapter 6, "Arrays and Tuples."*

```
public class LinkedList<T>: IEnumerable<T>
{
  public LinkedListNode<T> First { get; private set; }
  public LinkedListNode<T> Last { get; private set; }

  public LinkedListNode<T> AddLast(T node)
  {
```

```csharp
  var newNode = new LinkedListNode<T>(node);
  if (First == null)
  {
    First = newNode;
    Last = First;
  }
  else
  {
    LinkedListNode<T> previous = Last;
    Last.Next = newNode;
    Last = newNode;
    Last.Prev = previous;
  }
  return newNode;
}

public IEnumerator<T> GetEnumerator()
{
  LinkedListNode<T> current = First;

  while (current != null)
  {
    yield return current.Value;
    current = current.Next;
  }
}

IEnumerator IEnumerable.GetEnumerator()
{
  return GetEnumerator();
}
}
```

Using the generic `LinkedList<T>`, you can instantiate it with an `int` type, and there's no boxing. Also, you get a compiler error if you don't pass an `int` with the method `AddLast()`. Using the generic `IEnumerable<T>`, the `foreach` statement is also type safe, and you get a compiler error if that variable in the `foreach` statement is not an `int` (code file `LinkedListSample/Program.cs`):

```csharp
var list2 = new LinkedList<int>();
list2.AddLast(1);
list2.AddLast(3);
list2.AddLast(5);

foreach (int i in list2)
{
  Console.WriteLine(i);
}
```

Similarly, you can use the generic `LinkedList<T>` with a `string` type and pass strings to the `AddLast()` method:

```csharp
var list3 = new LinkedList<string>();
list3.AddLast("2");
list3.AddLast("four");
list3.AddLast("foo");

foreach (string s in list3)
{
  Console.WriteLine(s);
}
```

> **NOTE** *Every class that deals with the object type is a possible candidate for a generic implementation. Also, if classes make use of hierarchies, generics can be very helpful in making casting unnecessary.*

GENERICS FEATURES

When creating generic classes, you might need some additional C# keywords. For example, it is not possible to assign null to a generic type. In this case, the keyword default can be used, as demonstrated in the next section. If the generic type does not require the features of the Object class but you need to invoke some specific methods in the generic class, you can define constraints.

This section discusses the following topics:

➤ Default values

➤ Constraints

➤ Inheritance

➤ Static members

This example begins with a generic document manager, which is used to read and write documents from and to a queue. Start by creating a new Console project named DocumentManager and add the class DocumentManager<T>. The method AddDocument() adds a document to the queue. The read-only property IsDocumentAvailable returns true if the queue is not empty (code file DocumentManager/DocumentManager.cs):

```
using System;
using System.Collections.Generic;

namespace Wrox.ProCSharp.Generics
{
  public class DocumentManager<T>
  {
    private readonly Queue<T> documentQueue = new Queue<T>();

    public void AddDocument(T doc)
    {
      lock (this)
      {
        documentQueue.Enqueue(doc);
      }
    }

    public bool IsDocumentAvailable
    {
      get { return documentQueue.Count > 0; }
    }
  }
}
```

Threading and the lock statement are discussed in Chapter 21, "Threads, Tasks, and Synchronization."

Default Values

Now you add a GetDocument() method to the DocumentManager<T> class. Inside this method the type T should be assigned to null. However, it is not possible to assign null to generic types. That's because a generic type can also be instantiated as a value type, and null is allowed only with reference types.

To circumvent this problem, you can use the `default` keyword. With the `default` keyword, `null` is assigned to reference types and `0` is assigned to value types:

```
public T GetDocument()
{
  T doc = default(T);
  lock (this)
  {
    doc = documentQueue.Dequeue();
  }
  return doc;
}
```

> **NOTE** *The* `default` *keyword has multiple meanings depending on the context, or where it is used. The* `switch` *statement uses a* `default` *for defining the default case, and with generics* `default` *is used to initialize generic types either to* `null` *or to* `0`, *depending on if it is a reference or value type.*

Constraints

If the generic class needs to invoke some methods from the generic type, you have to add constraints.

With `DocumentManager<T>`, all the document titles should be displayed in the `DisplayAllDocuments()` method. The `Document` class implements the interface `IDocument` with the properties `Title` and `Content` (code file `DocumentManager/Document.cs`):

```
public interface IDocument
{
  string Title { get; set; }
  string Content { get; set; }
}

public class Document: IDocument
{
  public Document()
  {
  }

  public Document(string title, string content)
  {
    this.Title = title;
    this.Content = content;
  }

  public string Title { get; set; }
  public string Content { get; set; }
}
```

To display the documents with the `DocumentManager<T>` class, you can cast the type `T` to the interface `IDocument` to display the title (code file `DocumentManager/DocumentManager.cs`):

```
public void DisplayAllDocuments()
{
  foreach (T doc in documentQueue)
  {
```

```
        Console.WriteLine(((IDocument)doc).Title);
    }
}
```

The problem here is that doing a cast results in a runtime exception if type `T` does not implement the interface `IDocument`. Instead, it would be better to define a constraint with the `DocumentManager` `<TDocument>` class specifying that the type `TDocument` must implement the interface `IDocument`. To clarify the requirement in the name of the generic type, `T` is changed to `TDocument`. The `where` clause defines the requirement to implement the interface `IDocument`:

```
public class DocumentManager<TDocument>
        where TDocument: IDocument
{
```

This way you can write the `foreach` statement in such a way that the type `TDocument` contains the property `Title`. You get support from Visual Studio IntelliSense and the compiler:

```
public void DisplayAllDocuments()
{
    foreach (TDocument doc in documentQueue)
    {
        Console.WriteLine(doc.Title);
    }
}
```

In the `Main()` method, the `DocumentManager<T>` class is instantiated with the type `Document` that implements the required interface `IDocument`. Then new documents are added and displayed, and one of the documents is retrieved (code file `DocumentManager/Program.cs`):

```
static void Main()
{
    var dm = new DocumentManager<Document>();
    dm.AddDocument(new Document("Title A", "Sample A"));
    dm.AddDocument(new Document("Title B", "Sample B"));

    dm.DisplayAllDocuments();

    if (dm.IsDocumentAvailable)
    {
        Document d = dm.GetDocument();
        Console.WriteLine(d.Content);
    }
}
```

The `DocumentManager` now works with any class that implements the interface `IDocument`.

In the sample application, you've seen an interface constraint. Generics support several constraint types, indicated in the following table.

CONSTRAINT	DESCRIPTION
`where T: struct`	With a struct constraint, type `T` must be a value type.
`where T: class`	The class constraint indicates that type `T` must be a reference type.
`where T: IFoo`	Specifies that type `T` is required to implement interface `IFoo`.
`where T: Foo`	Specifies that type `T` is required to derive from base class `Foo`.
`where T: new()`	A constructor constraint; specifies that type `T` must have a default constructor.
`where T1: T2`	With constraints it is also possible to specify that type `T1` derives from a generic type `T2`. This constraint is known as *naked type constraint*.

> **NOTE** *Constructor constraints can be defined only for the default constructor. It is not possible to define a constructor constraint for other constructors.*

With a generic type, you can also combine multiple constraints. The constraint `where T: IFoo, new()` with the `MyClass<T>` declaration specifies that type `T` implements the interface `IFoo` and has a default constructor:

```
public class MyClass<T>
   where T: IFoo, new()
{
   //...
```

> **NOTE** *One important restriction of the `where` clause with C# is that it's not possible to define operators that must be implemented by the generic type. Operators cannot be defined in interfaces. With the `where` clause, it is only possible to define base classes, interfaces, and the default constructor.*

Inheritance

The `LinkedList<T>` class created earlier implements the interface `IEnumerable<T>`:

```
public class LinkedList<T>: IEnumerable<T>
{
   //...
```

A generic type can implement a generic interface. The same is possible by deriving from a class. A generic class can be derived from a generic base class:

```
public class Base<T>
{
}

public class Derived<T>: Base<T>
{
}
```

The requirement is that the generic types of the interface must be repeated, or the type of the base class must be specified, as in this case:

```
public class Base<T>
{
}

public class Derived<T>: Base<string>
{
}
```

This way, the derived class can be a generic or non-generic class. For example, you can define an abstract generic base class that is implemented with a concrete type in the derived class. This enables you to write *generic specialization* for specific types:

```
public abstract class Calc<T>
{
   public abstract T Add(T x, T y);
```

```
    public abstract T Sub(T x, T y);
  }

  public class IntCalc: Calc<int>
  {
    public override int Add(int x, int y)
    {
      return x + y;
    }

    public override int Sub(int x, int y)
    {
      return x - y;
    }
  }
```

Static Members

Static members of generic classes are only shared with one instantiation of the class, and require special attention. Consider the following example, where the class `StaticDemo<T>` contains the static field x:

```
public class StaticDemo<T>
{
  public static int x;
}
```

Because the class `StaticDemo<T>` is used with both a `string` type and an `int` type, two sets of static fields exist:

```
StaticDemo<string>.x = 4;
StaticDemo<int>.x = 5;
Console.WriteLine(StaticDemo<string>.x);     // writes 4
```

GENERIC INTERFACES

Using generics, you can define interfaces that define methods with generic parameters. In the linked list sample, you've already implemented the interface `IEnumerable<out T>`, which defines a `GetEnumerator()` method to return `IEnumerator<out T>`. .NET offers a lot of generic interfaces for different scenarios; examples include `IComparable<T>`, `ICollection<T>`, and `IExtensibleObject<T>`. Often older, non-generic versions of the same interface exist; for example .NET 1.0 had an `IComparable` interface that was based on objects. `IComparable<in T>` is based on a generic type:

```
public interface IComparable<in T>
{
  int CompareTo(T other);
}
```

The older, non-generic `IComparable` interface requires an object with the `CompareTo()` method. This requires a cast to specific types, such as to the `Person` class for using the `LastName` property:

```
public class Person: IComparable
{
  public int CompareTo(object obj)
  {
    Person other = obj as Person;
    return this.lastname.CompareTo(other.LastName);
  }
  //
```

When implementing the generic version, it is no longer necessary to cast the `object` to a `Person`:

```
public class Person: IComparable<Person>
{
  public int CompareTo(Person other)
  {
    return this.LastName.CompareTo(other.LastName);
  }
  //...
```

Covariance and Contra-variance

Prior to .NET 4, generic interfaces were invariant. .NET 4 added important changes for generic interfaces and generic delegates: covariance and contra-variance. Covariance and contra-variance are used for the conversion of types with arguments and return types. For example, can you pass a `Rectangle` to a method that requests a `Shape`? Let's get into examples to see the advantages of these extensions.

With .NET, parameter types are covariant. Assume you have the classes `Shape` and `Rectangle`, and `Rectangle` derives from the `Shape` base class. The `Display()` method is declared to accept an object of the `Shape` type as its parameter:

```
public void Display(Shape o) { }
```

Now you can pass any object that derives from the `Shape` base class. Because `Rectangle` derives from `Shape`, a `Rectangle` fulfills all the requirements of a `Shape` and the compiler accepts this method call:

```
var r = new Rectangle { Width= 5, Height=2.5 };
Display(r);
```

Return types of methods are contra-variant. When a method returns a `Shape` it is not possible to assign it to a `Rectangle` because a `Shape` is not necessarily always a `Rectangle`; but the opposite is possible. If a method returns a `Rectangle` as the `GetRectangle()` method,

```
public Rectangle GetRectangle();
```

the result can be assigned to a `Shape`:

```
Shape s = GetRectangle();
```

Before version 4 of the .NET Framework, this behavior was not possible with generics. Since C# 4, the language is extended to support covariance and contra-variance with generic interfaces and generic delegates. Let's start by defining a `Shape` base class and a `Rectangle` class (code files `Variance/Shape.cs` and `Rectangle.cs`):

```
public class Shape
{
  public double Width { get; set; }
  public double Height { get; set; }

  public override string ToString()
  {
    return String.Format("Width: {0}, Height: {1}", Width, Height);
  }
}

public class Rectangle: Shape
{
}
```

Covariance with Generic Interfaces

A generic interface is covariant if the generic type is annotated with the out keyword. This also means that type T is allowed only with return types. The interface IIndex is covariant with type T and returns this type from a read-only indexer (code file Variance/IIndex.cs):

```
public interface IIndex<out T>
{
  T this[int index] { get; }
  int Count { get; }
}
```

The IIndex<T> interface is implemented with the RectangleCollection class. RectangleCollection defines Rectangle for generic type T:

> **NOTE** *If a read-write indexer is used with the IIndex interface, the generic type T is passed to the method and retrieved from the method. This is not possible with covariance; the generic type must be defined as invariant. Defining the type as invariant is done without out and in annotations (code file Variance/ RectangleCollection.cs):*

```
public class RectangleCollection: IIndex<Rectangle>
{
  private Rectangle[] data = new Rectangle[3]
  {
    new Rectangle { Height=2, Width=5 },
    new Rectangle { Height=3, Width=7 },
    new Rectangle { Height=4.5, Width=2.9 }
  };

  private static RectangleCollection coll;
  public static RectangleCollection GetRectangles()
  {
    return coll ?? (coll = new RectangleCollection());
  }

  public Rectangle this[int index]
  {
    get
    {
      if (index < 0 || index > data.Length)
        throw new ArgumentOutOfRangeException("index");
      return data[index];
    }
  }
  public int Count
  {
    get
    {
      return data.Length;
    }
  }
}
```

> **NOTE** *The* `RectangleCollection.GetRectangles()` *method makes use of the coalescing operator that is, explained later in this chapter. If the variable* `coll` *is null, the right side of operator is invoked to create a new instance of* `RectangleCollection` *and assign it to the variable* `coll`, *which is returned from this method afterwards.*

The `RectangleCollection.GetRectangles()` method returns a `RectangleCollection` that implements the `IIndex<Rectangle>` interface, so you can assign the return value to a variable `rectangle` of the `IIndex<Rectangle>` type. Because the interface is covariant, it is also possible to assign the returned value to a variable of `IIndex<Shape>`. `Shape` does not need anything more than a `Rectangle` has to offer. Using the `shapes` variable, the indexer from the interface and the `Count` property are used within the `for` loop (code file `Variance/Program.cs`):

```
static void Main()
{
  IIndex<Rectangle> rectangles = RectangleCollection.GetRectangles();
  IIndex<Shape> shapes = rectangles;

  for (int i = 0; i < shapes.Count; i++)
  {
    Console.WriteLine(shapes[i]);
  }
}
```

Contra-Variance with Generic Interfaces

A generic interface is contra-variant if the generic type is annotated with the in keyword. This way, the interface is only allowed to use generic type `T` as input to its methods (code file `Variance/IDisplay.cs`):

```
public interface IDisplay<in T>
{
  void Show(T item);
}
```

The `ShapeDisplay` class implements `IDisplay<Shape>` and uses a `Shape` object as an input parameter (code file Variance/ShapeDisplay.cs):

```
public class ShapeDisplay: IDisplay<Shape>
{
  public void Show(Shape s)
  {
    Console.WriteLine("{0} Width: {1}, Height: {2}", s.GetType().Name,
                      s.Width, s.Height);
  }
}
```

Creating a new instance of `ShapeDisplay` returns `IDisplay<Shape>`, which is assigned to the `shapeDisplay` variable. Because `IDisplay<T>` is contra-variant, it is possible to assign the result to `IDisplay<Rectangle>`, where `Rectangle` derives from `Shape`. This time the methods of the interface define only the generic type as input, and `Rectangle` fulfills all the requirements of a `Shape` (code file Variance/Program.cs):

```
static void Main()
{
  //...

  IDisplay<Shape> shapeDisplay = new ShapeDisplay();
```

```
    IDisplay<Rectangle> rectangleDisplay = shapeDisplay;
    rectangleDisplay.Show(rectangles[0]);
}
```

GENERIC STRUCTS

Similar to classes, structs can be generic as well. They are very similar to generic classes with the exception of inheritance features. In this section you look at the generic struct Nullable<T>, which is defined by the .NET Framework.

An example of a generic struct in the .NET Framework is Nullable<T>. A number in a database and a number in a programming language have an important difference: A number in the database can be null, whereas a number in C# cannot be null. Int32 is a struct, and because structs are implemented as value types, they cannot be null. This difference often causes headaches and a lot of additional work to map the data. The problem exists not only with databases but also with mapping XML data to .NET types.

One solution is to map numbers from databases and XML files to reference types, because reference types can have a null value. However, this also means additional overhead during runtime.

With the structure Nullable<T>, this can be easily resolved. The following code segment shows a simplified version of how Nullable<T> is defined. The structure Nullable<T> defines a constraint specifying that the generic type T needs to be a struct. With classes as generic types, the advantage of low overhead is eliminated; and because objects of classes can be null anyway, there's no point in using a class with the Nullable<T> type. The only overhead in addition to the T type defined by Nullable<T> is the hasValue Boolean field that defines whether the value is set or null. Other than that, the generic struct defines the read-only properties HasValue and Value and some operator overloads. The operator overload to cast the Nullable<T> type to T is defined as explicit because it can throw an exception in case hasValue is false. The operator overload to cast to Nullable<T> is defined as implicit because it always succeeds:

```
public struct Nullable<T>
    where T: struct
{
  public Nullable(T value)
  {
    this.hasValue = true;
    this.value = value;
  }
  private bool hasValue;
  public bool HasValue
  {
    get
    {
      return hasValue;
    }
  }

  private T value;
  public T Value
  {
    get
    {
      if (!hasValue)
      {
        throw new InvalidOperationException("no value");
      }
      return value;
    }
  }
}
```

```
public static explicit operator T(Nullable<T> value)
{
  return value.Value;
}
public static implicit operator Nullable<T>(T value)
{
  return new Nullable<T>(value);
}

public override string ToString()
{
  if (!HasValue)
    return String.Empty;
  return this.value.ToString();
}
}
}
```

In this example, `Nullable<T>` is instantiated with `Nullable<int>`. The variable x can now be used as an int, assigning values and using operators to do some calculation. This behavior is made possible by casting operators of the `Nullable<T>` type. However, x can also be null. The `Nullable<T>` properties `HasValue` and `Value` can check whether there is a value, and the value can be accessed:

```
Nullable<int> x;
x = 4;
x += 3;
if (x.HasValue)
{
  int y = x.Value;
}
x = null;
```

Because nullable types are used often, C# has a special syntax for defining variables of this type. Instead of using syntax with the generic structure, the `?` operator can be used. In the following example, the variables x1 and x2 are both instances of a nullable `int` type:

```
Nullable<int> x1;
int? x2;
```

A nullable type can be compared with `null` and numbers, as shown. Here, the value of x is compared with `null`, and if it is not `null` it is compared with a value less than 0:

```
int? x = GetNullableType();
if (x == null)
{
  Console.WriteLine("x is null");
}
else if (x < 0)
{
  Console.WriteLine("x is smaller than 0");
}
```

Now that you know how `Nullable<T>` is defined, let's get into using nullable types. Nullable types can also be used with arithmetic operators. The variable x3 is the sum of the variables x1 and x2. If any of the nullable types have a `null` value, the result is `null`:

```
int? x1 = GetNullableType();
int? x2 = GetNullableType();
int? x3 = x1 + x2;
```

> **NOTE** *The* `GetNullableType()` *method, which is called here, is just a placeholder for any method that returns a nullable* `int`. *For testing you can implement it to simply return* `null` *or to return any integer value.*

Non-nullable types can be converted to nullable types. With the conversion from a non-nullable type to a nullable type, an implicit conversion is possible where casting is not required. This type of conversion always succeeds:

```
int y1 = 4;
int? x1 = y1;
```

In the reverse situation, a conversion from a nullable type to a non-nullable type can fail. If the nullable type has a `null` value and the `null` value is assigned to a non-nullable type, then an exception of type `InvalidOperationException` is thrown. That's why the cast operator is required to do an explicit conversion:

```
int? x1 = GetNullableType();
int y1 = (int)x1;
```

Instead of doing an explicit cast, it is also possible to convert a nullable type to a non-nullable type with the coalescing operator. The coalescing operator uses the syntax `??` to define a default value for the conversion in case the nullable type has a value of `null`. Here, `y1` gets a `0` value if `x1` is `null`:

```
int? x1 = GetNullableType();
int y1 = x1 ?? 0;
```

GENERIC METHODS

In addition to defining generic classes, it is also possible to define generic methods. With a generic method, the generic type is defined with the method declaration. Generic methods can be defined within non-generic classes.

The method `Swap<T>()` defines `T` as a generic type that is used for two arguments and a variable `temp`:

```
void Swap<T>(ref T x, ref T y)
{
    T temp;
    temp = x;
    x = y;
    y = temp;
}
```

A generic method can be invoked by assigning the generic type with the method call:

```
int i = 4;
int j = 5;
Swap<int>(ref i, ref j);
```

However, because the C# compiler can get the type of the parameters by calling the `Swap()` method, it is not necessary to assign the generic type with the method call. The generic method can be invoked as simply as non-generic methods:

```
int i = 4;
int j = 5;
Swap(ref i, ref j);
```

Generic Methods Example

In this example, a generic method is used to accumulate all the elements of a collection. To show the features of generic methods, the following Account class, which contains Name and Balance properties, is used (code file GenericMethods/Account.cs):

```
public class Account
{
  public string Name { get; private set; }
  public decimal Balance { get; private set; }

  public Account(string name, Decimal balance)
  {
    this.Name = name;
    this.Balance = balance;
  }
}
```

All the accounts in which the balance should be accumulated are added to an accounts list of type List<Account> (code file GenericMethods/Program.cs):

```
var accounts = new List<Account>()
{
  new Account("Christian", 1500),
  new Account("Stephanie", 2200),
  new Account("Angela", 1800),
  new Account("Matthias", 2400)
};
```

A traditional way to accumulate all Account objects is by looping through them with a foreach statement, as shown here. Because the foreach statement uses the IEnumerable interface to iterate the elements of a collection, the argument of the AccumulateSimple() method is of type IEnumerable. The foreach statement works with every object implementing IEnumerable. This way, the AccumulateSimple() method can be used with all collection classes that implement the interface IEnumerable<Account>. In the implementation of this method, the property Balance of the Account object is directly accessed (code file GenericMethods/Algorithm.cs):

```
public static class Algorithm
{
  public static decimal AccumulateSimple(IEnumerable<Account> source)
  {
    decimal sum = 0;
    foreach (Account a in source)
    {
      sum += a.Balance;
    }
    return sum;
  }
}
```

The AccumulateSimple() method is invoked like this:

```
decimal amount = Algorithm.AccumulateSimple(accounts);
```

Generic Methods with Constraints

The problem with the first implementation is that it works only with Account objects. This can be avoided by using a generic method.

The second version of the Accumulate() method accepts any type that implements the interface IAccount. As you saw earlier with generic classes, generic types can be restricted with the where clause. The same clause that is used with generic classes can be used with generic methods. The parameter of the Accumulate() method is changed to IEnumerable<T>, a generic interface that is implemented by generic collection classes (code file GenericMethods/Algorithms.cs):

```
public static decimal Accumulate<TAccount>(IEnumerable<TAccount> source)
    where TAccount: IAccount
{
  decimal sum = 0;

  foreach (TAccount a in source)
  {
    sum += a.Balance;
  }
  return sum;
}
```

The Account class is now refactored to implement the interface IAccount (code file GenericMethods/Account.cs):

```
public class Account: IAccount
{
  //...
```

The IAccount interface defines the read-only properties Balance and Name (code file GenericMethods/IAccount.cs):

```
public interface IAccount
{
  decimal Balance { get; }
  string Name { get; }
}
```

The new Accumulate() method can be invoked by defining the Account type as a generic type parameter (code file GenericMethods/Program.cs):

```
decimal amount = Algorithm.Accumulate<Account>(accounts);
```

Because the generic type parameter can be automatically inferred by the compiler from the parameter type of the method, it is valid to invoke the Accumulate() method this way:

```
decimal amount = Algorithm.Accumulate(accounts);
```

Generic Methods with Delegates

The requirement for the generic types to implement the interface IAccount may be too restrictive. The following example hints at how the Accumulate() method can be changed by passing a generic delegate. Chapter 8, "Delegates, Lambdas, and Events" provides all the details about how to work with generic delegates, and how to use Lambda expressions.

This Accumulate() method uses two generic parameters, T1 and T2. T1 is used for the collection-implementing IEnumerable<T1> parameter, which is the first one of the methods. The second parameter uses the generic delegate Func<T1, T2, TResult>. Here, the second and third generic parameters are of the same T2 type. A method needs to be passed that has two input parameters (T1 and T2) and a return type of T2 (code file GenericMethods/Algorithm.cs).

```
public static T2 Accumulate<T1, T2>(IEnumerable<T1> source,
                                    Func<T1, T2, T2> action)
{
  T2 sum = default(T2);
  foreach (T1 item in source)
  {
    sum = action(item, sum);
  }
  return sum;
}
```

In calling this method, it is necessary to specify the generic parameter types because the compiler cannot infer this automatically. With the first parameter of the method, the accounts collection that is assigned is of type IEnumerable<Account>. With the second parameter, a Lambda expression is used that defines two parameters of type Account and decimal, and returns a decimal. This Lambda expression is invoked for every item by the Accumulate() method (code file GenericMethods/Program.cs):

```
decimal amount = Algorithm.Accumulate<Account, decimal>(
                     accounts, (item, sum) => sum += item.Balance);
```

Don't scratch your head over this syntax yet. The sample should give you a glimpse of the possible ways to extend the Accumulate() method. Chapter 8 covers Lambda expressions in detail.

Generic Methods Specialization

Generic methods can be overloaded to define specializations for specific types. This is true for methods with generic parameters as well. The Foo() method is defined in two versions. The first accepts a generic parameter; the second one is a specialized version for the int parameter. During compile time, the best match is taken. If an int is passed, then the method with the int parameter is selected. With any other parameter type, the compiler chooses the generic version of the method (code file Specialization/Program.cs):

```
public class MethodOverloads
{
  public void Foo<T>(T obj)
  {
    Console.WriteLine("Foo<T>(T obj), obj type: {0}", obj.GetType().Name);
  }

  public void Foo(int x)
  {
    Console.WriteLine("Foo(int x)");
  }

  public void Bar<T>(T obj)
  {
    Foo(obj);
  }
}
```

The Foo() method can now be invoked with any parameter type. The sample code passes an int and a string to the method:

```
static void Main()
{
  var test = new MethodOverloads();
  test.Foo(33);
  test.Foo("abc");
}
```

Running the program, you can see by the output that the method with the best match is taken:

```
Foo(int x)
Foo<T>(T obj), obj type: String
```

Be aware that the method invoked is defined during compile time and not runtime. This can be easily demonstrated by adding a generic `Bar()` method that invokes the `Foo()` method, passing the generic parameter value along:

```
public class MethodOverloads
{
  // ...

  public void Bar<T>(T obj)
  {
    Foo(obj);
  }
}
```

The `Main()` method is now changed to invoke the `Bar()` method passing an `int` value:

```
static void Main()
{
  var test = new MethodOverloads();
  test.Bar(44);
```

From the output on the console you can see that the generic `Foo()` method was selected by the `Bar()` method and not the overload with the `int` parameter. That's because the compiler selects the method that is invoked by the `Bar()` method during compile time. Because the `Bar()` method defines a generic parameter, and because there's a `Foo()` method that matches this type, the generic `Foo()` method is called. This is not changed during runtime when an `int` value is passed to the `Bar()` method:

```
Foo<T>(T obj), obj type: Int32
```

SUMMARY

This chapter introduced a very important feature of the CLR: generics. With generic classes you can create type-independent classes, and generic methods allow type-independent methods. Interfaces, structs, and delegates can be created in a generic way as well. Generics make new programming styles possible. You've seen how algorithms, particularly actions and predicates, can be implemented to be used with different classes — and all are type safe. Generic delegates make it possible to decouple algorithms from collections.

You will see more features and uses of generics throughout this book. Chapter 8, "Delegates, Lambdas, and Events," introduces delegates that are often implemented as generics; Chapter 10, "Collections," provides information about generic collection classes; and Chapter 11, "Language Integrated Query," discusses generic extension methods. The next chapter demonstrates the use of generic methods with arrays.

Arrays and Tuples

WROX.COM CODE DOWNLOADS FOR THIS CHAPTER

The wrox.com code downloads for this chapter are found at `http://www.wrox.com/remtitle` `.cgi?isbn=1118314425` on the Download Code tab. The code for this chapter is divided into the following major examples:

➤ SimpleArrays

➤ SortingSample

➤ ArraySegment

➤ YieldDemo

➤ StructuralComparison

MULTIPLE OBJECTS OF THE SAME AND DIFFERENT TYPES

If you need to work with multiple objects of the same type, you can use collections (see Chapter 10, "Collections") and arrays. C# has a special notation to declare, initialize, and use arrays. Behind the scenes, the `Array` class comes into play, which offers several methods to sort and filter the elements inside the array. Using an enumerator, you can iterate through all the elements of the array.

To use multiple objects of different types, the type `Tuple` can be used. See the "Tuples" section later in this chapter for details about this type.

SIMPLE ARRAYS

If you need to use multiple objects of the same type, you can use an array. An *array* is a data structure that contains a number of elements of the same type.

Array Declaration

An array is declared by defining the type of elements inside the array, followed by empty brackets and a variable name. For example, an array containing integer elements is declared like this:

```
int[] myArray;
```

Array Initialization

After declaring an array, memory must be allocated to hold all the elements of the array. An array is a reference type, so memory on the heap must be allocated. You do this by initializing the variable of the array using the new operator, with the type and the number of elements inside the array. Here, you specify the size of the array:

```
myArray = new int[4];
```

> **NOTE** *Value types and reference types are covered in Chapter 3, "Objects and Types."*

With this declaration and initialization, the variable myArray references four integer values that are allocated on the managed heap (see Figure 6-1).

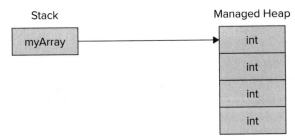

FIGURE 6-1

> **NOTE** *An array cannot be resized after its size is specified without copying all the elements. If you don't know how many elements should be in the array in advance, you can use a collection (see Chapter 10).*

Instead of using a separate line to declare and initialize an array, you can use a single line:

```
int[] myArray = new int[4];
```

You can also assign values to every array element using an array initializer. Array initializers can be used only while declaring an array variable, not after the array is declared:

```
int[] myArray = new int[4] {4, 7, 11, 2};
```

If you initialize the array using curly brackets, the size of the array can also be omitted, because the compiler can count the number of elements itself:

```
int[] myArray = new int[] {4, 7, 11, 2};
```

There's even a shorter form using the C# compiler. Using curly brackets you can write the array declaration and initialization. The code generated from the compiler is the same as the previous result:

```
int[] myArray = {4, 7, 11, 2};
```

Accessing Array Elements

After an array is declared and initialized, you can access the array elements using an indexer. Arrays support only indexers that have integer parameters.

With the indexer, you pass the element number to access the array. The indexer always starts with a value of 0 for the first element. Therefore, the highest number you can pass to the indexer is the number of elements minus one, because the index starts at zero. In the following example, the array *myArray* is declared and initialized with four integer values. The elements can be accessed with indexer values 0, 1, 2, and 3.

```
int[] myArray = new int[] {4, 7, 11, 2};
int v1 = myArray[0];   // read first element
int v2 = myArray[1];   // read second element
myArray[3] = 44;       // change fourth element
```

> **NOTE** *If you use a wrong indexer value where that is bigger than the length of the array, an exception of type* IndexOutOfRangeException *is thrown.*

If you don't know the number of elements in the array, you can use the Length property, as shown in this for statement:

```
for (int i = 0; i < myArray.Length; i++)
{
  Console.WriteLine(myArray[i]);
}
```

Instead of using a for statement to iterate through all the elements of the array, you can also use the foreach statement:

```
foreach (var val in myArray)
{
  Console.WriteLine(val);
}
```

> **NOTE** *The* foreach *statement makes use of the* IEnumerable *and* IEnumerator *interfaces, which are discussed later in this chapter.*

Using Reference Types

In addition to being able to declare arrays of predefined types, you can also declare arrays of custom types. Let's start with the following Person class, the properties FirstName and LastName using auto-implemented properties, and an override of the ToString() method from the Object class (code file SimpleArrays/Person.cs):

```
public class Person
{
  public string FirstName { get; set; }
```

```
    public string LastName { get; set; }

    public override string ToString()
    {
      return String.Format("{0} {1}", FirstName, LastName);
    }
  }
```

Declaring an array of two `Person` elements is similar to declaring an array of `int`:

```
Person[] myPersons = new Person[2];
```

However, be aware that if the elements in the array are reference types, memory must be allocated for every array element. If you use an item in the array for which no memory was allocated, a `NullReferenceException` is thrown.

> **NOTE** *For information about errors and exceptions, see Chapter 16, "Errors and Exceptions."*

You can allocate every element of the array by using an indexer starting from 0:

```
myPersons[0] = new Person { FirstName="Ayrton", LastName="Senna" };
myPersons[1] = new Person { FirstName="Michael", LastName="Schumacher" };
```

Figure 6-2 shows the objects in the managed heap with the `Person` array. `myPersons` is a variable that is stored on the stack. This variable references an array of `Person` elements that is stored on the managed heap. This array has enough space for two references. Every item in the array references a `Person` object that is also stored in the managed heap.

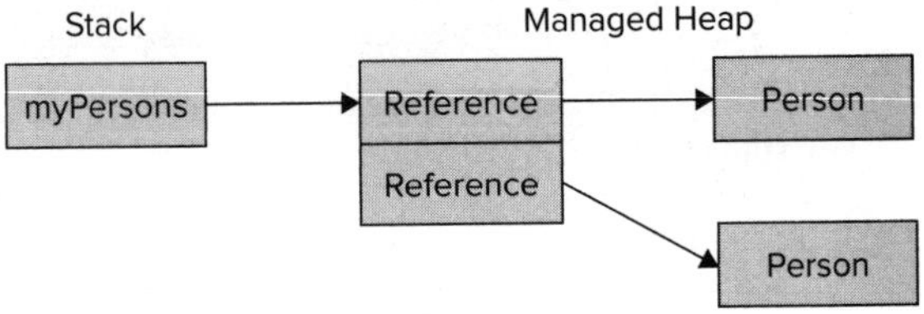

FIGURE 6-2

Similar to the `int` type, you can also use an array initializer with custom types:

```
Person[] myPersons2 =
{
  new Person { FirstName="Ayrton", LastName="Senna"},
  new Person { FirstName="Michael", LastName="Schumacher"}
};
```

MULTIDIMENSIONAL ARRAYS

Ordinary arrays (also known as one-dimensional arrays) are indexed by a single integer. A multidimensional array is indexed by two or more integers.

FIGURE 6-3

Figure 6-3 shows the mathematical notation for a two-dimensional array that has three rows and three columns. The first row has the values 1, 2, and 3, and the third row has the values 7, 8, and 9.

To declare this two-dimensional array with C#, you put a comma inside the brackets. The array is initialized by specifying the size of every dimension (also known as rank). Then the array elements can be accessed by using two integers with the indexer:

```
int[,] twodim = new int[3, 3];
twodim[0, 0] = 1;
```

```
twodim[0, 1] = 2;
twodim[0, 2] = 3;
twodim[1, 0] = 4;
twodim[1, 1] = 5;
twodim[1, 2] = 6;
twodim[2, 0] = 7;
twodim[2, 1] = 8;
twodim[2, 2] = 9;
```

> **NOTE** *After declaring an array, you cannot change the rank.*

You can also initialize the two-dimensional array by using an array indexer if you know the values for the elements in advance. To initialize the array, one outer curly bracket is used, and every row is initialized by using curly brackets inside the outer curly brackets:

```
int[,] twodim = {
                {1, 2, 3},
                {4, 5, 6},
                {7, 8, 9}
                };
```

> **NOTE** *When using an array initializer, you must initialize every element of the array. It is not possible to defer the initialization of some values until later.*

By using two commas inside the brackets, you can declare a three-dimensional array:

```
int[,,] threedim = {
                { { 1, 2 }, { 3, 4 } },
                { { 5, 6 }, { 7, 8 } },
                { { 9, 10 }, { 11, 12 } }
                };

Console.WriteLine(threedim[0, 1, 1]);
```

JAGGED ARRAYS

A two-dimensional array has a rectangular size (for example, 3 × 3 elements). A jagged array provides more flexibility in sizing the array. With a jagged array every row can have a different size.

Figure 6-4 contrasts a two-dimensional array that has 3 × 3 elements with a jagged array. The jagged array shown contains three rows, with the first row containing two elements, the second row containing six elements, and the third row containing three elements.

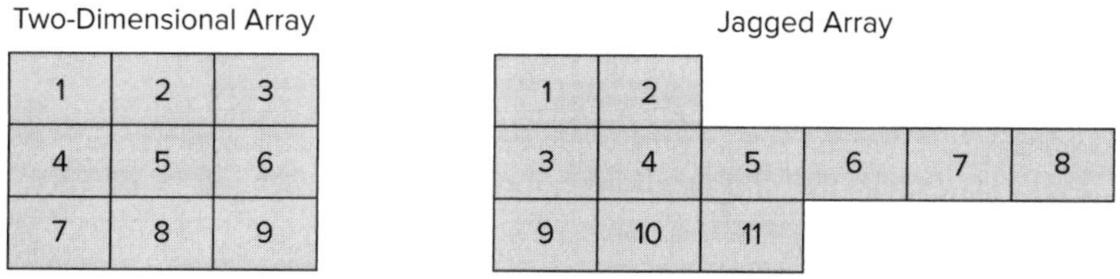

Two-Dimensional Array

1	2	3
4	5	6
7	8	9

Jagged Array

1	2				
3	4	5	6	7	8
9	10	11			

FIGURE 6-4

A jagged array is declared by placing one pair of opening and closing brackets after another. To initialize the jagged array, only the size that defines the number of rows in the first pair of brackets is set. The second brackets that define the number of elements inside the row are kept empty because every row has a different number of elements. Next, the element number of the rows can be set for every row:

```
int[][] jagged = new int[3][];
jagged[0] = new int[2] { 1, 2 };
jagged[1] = new int[6] { 3, 4, 5, 6, 7, 8 };
jagged[2] = new int[3] { 9, 10, 11 };
```

You can iterate through all the elements of a jagged array with nested `for` loops. In the outer `for` loop every row is iterated, and the inner `for` loop iterates through every element inside a row:

```
for (int row = 0; row < jagged.Length; row++)
{
  for (int element = 0; element < jagged[row].Length; element++)
  {
    Console.WriteLine("row: {0}, element: {1}, value: {2}", row, element,
                      jagged[row][element]);
  }
}
```

The output of the iteration displays the rows and every element within the rows:

```
row: 0, element: 0, value: 1
row: 0, element: 1, value: 2
row: 1, element: 0, value: 3
row: 1, element: 1, value: 4
row: 1, element: 2, value: 5
row: 1, element: 3, value: 6
row: 1, element: 4, value: 7
row: 1, element: 5, value: 8
row: 2, element: 0, value: 9
row: 2, element: 1, value: 10
row: 2, element: 2, value: 11
```

ARRAY CLASS

Declaring an array with brackets is a C# notation using the `Array` class. Using the C# syntax behind the scenes creates a new class that derives from the abstract base class `Array`. This makes it possible to use methods and properties that are defined with the `Array` class with every C# array. For example, you've already used the `Length` property or iterated through the array by using the `foreach` statement. By doing this, you are using the `GetEnumerator()` method of the `Array` class.

Other properties implemented by the `Array` class are `LongLength`, for arrays in which the number of items doesn't fit within an integer, and `Rank`, to get the number of dimensions.

Let's have a look at other members of the `Array` class by getting into various features.

Creating Arrays

The `Array` class is abstract, so you cannot create an array by using a constructor. However, instead of using the C# syntax to create array instances, it is also possible to create arrays by using the static `CreateInstance()` method. This is extremely useful if you don't know the type of elements in advance, because the type can be passed to the `CreateInstance()` method as a `Type` object.

The following example shows how to create an array of type `int` with a size of 5. The first argument of the `CreateInstance()` method requires the type of the elements, and the second argument defines the size. You can set values with the `SetValue()` method, and read values with the `GetValue()` method (code file `SimpleArrays/Program.cs`):

```
Array intArray1 = Array.CreateInstance(typeof(int), 5);
for (int i = 0; i < 5; i++)
{
  intArray1.SetValue(33, i);
}

for (int i = 0; i < 5; i++)
{
  Console.WriteLine(intArray1.GetValue(i));
}
```

You can also cast the created array to an array declared as `int[]`:

```
int[] intArray2 = (int[])intArray1;
```

The `CreateInstance()` method has many overloads to create multidimensional arrays and to create arrays that are not 0-based. The following example creates a two-dimensional array with 2 × 3 elements. The first dimension is 1-based; the second dimension is 10-based:

```
int[] lengths = { 2, 3 };
int[] lowerBounds = { 1, 10 };
Array racers = Array.CreateInstance(typeof(Person), lengths, lowerBounds);
```

Setting the elements of the array, the `SetValue()` method accepts indices for every dimension:

```
racers.SetValue(new Person
{
  FirstName = "Alain",
  LastName = "Prost"
}, index1: 1, index2: 10);
racers.SetValue(new Person
{
  FirstName = "Emerson",
  LastName = "Fittipaldi"
}, 1, 11);
racers.SetValue(new Person
{
  FirstName = "Ayrton",
  LastName = "Senna"
}, 1, 12);
racers.SetValue(new Person
{
  FirstName = "Michael",
  LastName = "Schumacher"
}, 2, 10);
racers.SetValue(new Person
{
  FirstName = "Fernando",
  LastName = "Alonso"
}, 2, 11);
racers.SetValue(new Person
{
  FirstName = "Jenson",
  LastName = "Button"
}, 2, 12);
```

Although the array is not 0-based, you can assign it to a variable with the normal C# notation. You just have to take care not to cross the boundaries:

```
Person[,] racers2 = (Person[,])racers;
Person first = racers2[1, 10];
Person last = racers2[2, 12];
```

Copying Arrays

Because arrays are reference types, assigning an array variable to another one just gives you two variables referencing the same array. For copying arrays, the array implements the interface `ICloneable`. The `Clone()` method that is defined with this interface creates a shallow copy of the array.

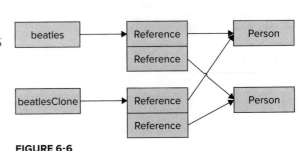

If the elements of the array are value types, as in the following code segment, all values are copied (see Figure 6-5):

```
int[] intArray1 = {1, 2};
int[] intArray2 = (int[])intArray1.Clone();
```

FIGURE 6-5

If the array contains reference types, only the references are copied, not the elements. Figure 6-6 shows the variables `beatles` and `beatlesClone`, where `beatlesClone` is created by calling the `Clone()` method from `beatles`. The `Person` objects that are referenced are the same for `beatles` and `beatlesClone`. If you change a property of an element of `beatlesClone`, you change the same object of `beatles` (code file `SimpleArray/Program.cs`):

FIGURE 6-6

```
Person[] beatles = {
                new Person { FirstName="John", LastName="Lennon" },
                new Person { FirstName="Paul", LastName="McCartney" }
            };
Person[] beatlesClone = (Person[])beatles.Clone();
```

Instead of using the `Clone()` method, you can use the `Array.Copy()` method, which also creates a shallow copy. However, there's one important difference with `Clone()` and `Copy()`: `Clone()` creates a new array; with `Copy()` you have to pass an existing array with the same rank and enough elements.

> **NOTE** *If you need a deep copy of an array containing reference types, you have to iterate the array and create new objects.*

Sorting

The `Array` class uses the Quicksort algorithm to sort the elements in the array. The `Sort()` method requires the interface `IComparable` to be implemented by the elements in the array. Simple types such as `System.String` and `System.Int32` implement `IComparable`, so you can sort elements containing these types.

With the sample program, the array name contains elements of type `string`, and this array can be sorted (code file `SortingSample/Program.cs`):

```
string[] names = {
        "Christina Aguilera",
        "Shakira",
        "Beyonce",
        "Lady Gaga"
    };

Array.Sort(names);
```

```
foreach (var name in names)
{
    Console.WriteLine(name);
}
```

The output of the application shows the sorted result of the array:

```
Beyonce
Christina Aguilera
Lady Gaga
Shakira
```

If you are using custom classes with the array, you must implement the interface IComparable. This interface defines just one method, CompareTo(), which must return 0 if the objects to compare are equal; a value smaller than 0 if the instance should go before the object from the parameter; and a value larger than 0 if the instance should go after the object from the parameter.

Change the Person class to implement the interface IComparable<Person>. The comparison is first done on the value of the LastName by using the Compare() method of the String class. If the LastName has the same value, the FirstName is compared (code file SortingSample/Person.cs):

```
public class Person: IComparable<Person>
{
    public int CompareTo(Person other)
    {
        if (other == null) return 1;

        int result = string.Compare(this.LastName, other.LastName);
        if (result == 0)
        {
            result = string.Compare(this.FirstName, other.FirstName);
        }
        return result;
    }
}
//...
```

Now it is possible to sort an array of Person objects by the last name (code file SortingSample/Program.cs):

```
Person[] persons = {
    new Person { FirstName="Damon", LastName="Hill" },
    new Person { FirstName="Niki", LastName="Lauda" },
    new Person { FirstName="Ayrton", LastName="Senna" },
    new Person { FirstName="Graham", LastName="Hill" }
};

Array.Sort(persons);
foreach (var p in persons)
{
    Console.WriteLine(p);
}
```

Using the sort of the Person class, the output returns the names sorted by last name:

```
Damon Hill
Graham Hill
Niki Lauda
Ayrton Senna
```

If the Person object should be sorted differently, or if you don't have the option to change the class that is used as an element in the array, you can implement the interface IComparer or IComparer<T>. These interfaces define the method `Compare()`. One of these interfaces must be implemented by the class that should be compared. The `IComparer` interface is independent of the class to compare. That's why the `Compare()` method defines two arguments that should be compared. The return value is similar to the `CompareTo()` method of the `IComparable` interface.

The class `PersonComparer` implements the `IComparer<Person>` interface to sort `Person` objects either by `firstName` or by `lastName`. The enumeration `PersonCompareType` defines the different sorting options that are available with `PersonComparer`: `FirstName` and `LastName`. How the compare should be done is defined with the constructor of the class `PersonComparer`, where a `PersonCompareType` value is set. The `Compare()` method is implemented with a `switch` statement to compare either by `LastName` or by `FirstName` (code file `SortingSample/PersonComparer.cs`):

```
public enum PersonCompareType
{
  FirstName,
  LastName
}

public class PersonComparer: IComparer<Person>
{
  private PersonCompareType compareType;

  public PersonComparer(PersonCompareType compareType)
  {
    this.compareType = compareType;
  }

  public int Compare(Person x, Person y)
  {
    if (x == null && y == null) return 0;
    if (x == null) return 1;
    if (y == null) return -1;

    switch (compareType)
    {
      case PersonCompareType.FirstName:
        return string.Compare(x.FirstName, y.FirstName);
      case PersonCompareType.LastName:
        return string.Compare(x.LastName, y.LastName);
      default:
        throw new ArgumentException("unexpected compare type");
    }
  }
}
```

Now you can pass a `PersonComparer` object to the second argument of the `Array.Sort()` method. Here, the persons are sorted by first name (code file `SortingSample/Program.cs`):

```
Array.Sort(persons, new PersonComparer(PersonCompareType.FirstName));
foreach (var p in persons)
{
  Console.WriteLine(p);
}
```

The persons array is now sorted by first name:

```
Ayrton Senna
Damon Hill
Graham Hill
Niki Lauda
```

NOTE *The* Array *class also offers* Sort *methods that require a delegate as an argument. With this argument you can pass a method to do the comparison of two objects, rather than rely on the* IComparable *or* IComparer *interfaces. Chapter 8, "Delegates, Lambdas, and Events," discusses how to use delegates.*

ARRAYS AS PARAMETERS

Arrays can be passed as parameters to methods, and returned from methods. Returning an array, you just have to declare the array as the return type, as shown with the following method GetPersons():

```
static Person[] GetPersons()
{
  return new Person[] {
      new Person { FirstName="Damon", LastName="Hill" },
      new Person { FirstName="Niki", LastName="Lauda" },
      new Person { FirstName="Ayrton", LastName="Senna" },
      new Person { FirstName="Graham", LastName="Hill" }
  };
}
```

Passing arrays to a method, the array is declared with the parameter, as shown with the method DisplayPersons():

```
static void DisplayPersons(Person[] persons)
{
    //...
```

Array Covariance

With arrays, covariance is supported. This means that an array can be declared as a base type and elements of derived types can be assigned to the elements.

For example, you can declare a parameter of type object[] as shown and pass a Person[] to it:

```
static void DisplayArray(object[] data)
{
  //...
}
```

NOTE *Array covariance is only possible with reference types, not with value types. In addition, array covariance has an issue that can only be resolved with runtime exceptions. If you assign a* Person *array to an object array, the object array can then be used with anything that derives from the object. The compiler accepts, for example, passing a string to array elements. However, because a* Person *array is referenced by the object array, a runtime exception,* ArrayTypeMismatchException, *occurs.*

ArraySegment<T>

The struct ArraySegment<T> represents a segment of an array. If you are working with a large array, and different methods work on parts of the array, you could copy the array part to the different methods. Instead of creating multiple arrays, it is more efficient to use one array and pass the complete array to the methods. The methods should only use a part of the array. For this, you can pass the offset into the array and the count of elements that the method should use in addition to the array. This way, at least three parameters are needed. When using an array segment, just a single parameter is needed. The `ArraySegment<T>` structure contains information about the segment (the offset and count).

The method `SumOfSegments` takes an array of `ArraySegment<int>` elements to calculate the sum of all the integers that are defined with the segments and returns the sum (code file `ArraySegmentSample/Program.cs`):

```
static int SumOfSegments(ArraySegment<int>[] segments)
{
  int sum = 0;
  foreach (var segment in segments)
  {
    for (int i = segment.Offset; i < segment.Offset +
        segment.Count; i++)
    {
      sum += segment.Array[i];
    }
  }
  return sum;
}
```

This method is used by passing an array of segments. The first array element references three elements of `ar1` starting with the first element; the second array element references three elements of `ar2` starting with the fourth element:

```
int[] ar1 = { 1, 4, 5, 11, 13, 18 };
int[] ar2 = { 3, 4, 5, 18, 21, 27, 33 };

var segments = new ArraySegment<int>[2]
{
  new ArraySegment<int>(ar1, 0, 3),
  new ArraySegment<int>(ar2, 3, 3)
};
var sum = SumOfSegments(segments);
```

> **NOTE** *Array segments don't copy the elements of the originating array. Instead, the originating array can be accessed through* `ArraySegment<T>`. *If elements of the array segment are changed, the changes can be seen in the original array.*

ENUMERATIONS

By using the `foreach` statement you can iterate elements of a collection (see Chapter 10, "Collections") without needing to know the number of elements inside the collection. The `foreach` statement uses an enumerator. Figure 6-7 shows the relationship between the client invoking the `foreach` method and the collection. The array or collection implements the `IEnumerable` interface with the `GetEnumerator()` method. The `GetEnumerator()` method returns an enumerator implementing the `IEnumerator` interface. The interface `IEnumerator` is then used by the `foreach` statement to iterate through the collection.

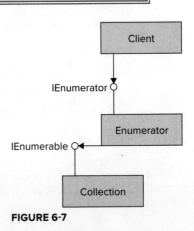

FIGURE 6-7

> **NOTE** *The* GetEnumerator() *method is defined with the interface* IEnumerable. *The* foreach *statement doesn't really need this interface implemented in the collection class. It's enough to have a method with the name* GetEnumerator() *that returns an object implementing the* IEnumerator *interface.*

IEnumerator Interface

The foreach statement uses the methods and properties of the IEnumerator interface to iterate all elements in a collection. For this, IEnumerator defines the property Current to return the element where the cursor is positioned, and the method MoveNext() to move to the next element of the collection. MoveNext() returns true if there's an element, and false if no more elements are available.

The generic version of this interface IEnumerator<T> derives from the interface IDisposable and thus defines a Dispose() method to clean up resources allocated by the enumerator.

> **NOTE** *The* IEnumerator *interface also defines the* Reset() *method for COM interoperability. Many .NET enumerators implement this by throwing an exception of type* NotSupportedException.

foreach Statement

The C# foreach statement is not resolved to a foreach statement in the IL code. Instead, the C# compiler converts the foreach statement to methods and properties of the IEnumerator interface. Here's a simple foreach statement to iterate all elements in the persons array and display them person by person:

```
foreach (var p in persons)
{
  Console.WriteLine(p);
}
```

The foreach statement is resolved to the following code segment. First, the GetEnumerator() method is invoked to get an enumerator for the array. Inside a while loop, as long as MoveNext() returns true, the elements of the array are accessed using the Current property:

```
IEnumerator<Person> enumerator = persons.GetEnumerator();
while (enumerator.MoveNext())
{
  Person p = enumerator.Current;
  Console.WriteLine(p);
}
```

yield Statement

Since the first release of C#, it has been easy to iterate through collections by using the foreach statement. With C# 1.0, it was still a lot of work to create an enumerator. C# 2.0 added the yield statement for creating enumerators easily. The yield return statement returns one element of a collection and moves the position to the next element, and yield break stops the iteration.

The next example shows the implementation of a simple collection using the yield return statement. The class HelloCollection contains the method GetEnumerator(). The implementation of the

GetEnumerator() method contains two yield return statements where the strings Hello and World are returned (code file YieldDemo/Program.cs):

```
using System;
using System.Collections;

namespace Wrox.ProCSharp.Arrays
{
  public class HelloCollection
  {
    public IEnumerator<string> GetEnumerator()
    {
      yield return "Hello";
      yield return "World";
    }
  }
}
```

> **NOTE** *A method or property that contains yield statements is also known as an* iterator *block. An iterator block must be declared to return an* IEnumerator *or* IEnumerable *interface, or the generic versions of these interfaces. This block may contain multiple* yield return *or* yield break *statements; a* return *statement is not allowed.*

Now it is possible to iterate through the collection using a foreach statement:

```
public void HelloWorld()
{
  var helloCollection = new HelloCollection();
  foreach (var s in helloCollection)
  {
    Console.WriteLine(s);
  }
}
```

With an iterator block, the compiler generates a yield type, including a state machine, as shown in the following code segment. The yield type implements the properties and methods of the interfaces IEnumerator and IDisposable. In the example, you can see the yield type as the inner class Enumerator. The GetEnumerator() method of the outer class instantiates and returns a new yield type. Within the yield type, the variable state defines the current position of the iteration and is changed every time the method MoveNext() is invoked. MoveNext() encapsulates the code of the iterator block and sets the value of the current variable so that the Current property returns an object depending on the position:

```
public class HelloCollection
{
  public IEnumerator GetEnumerator()
  {
    return new Enumerator(0);
  }

  public class Enumerator: IEnumerator<string>, IEnumerator, IDisposable
  {
    private int state;
    private string current;

    public Enumerator(int state)
    {
```

```
      this.state = state;
    }
    bool System.Collections.IEnumerator.MoveNext()
    {
      switch (state)
      {
        case 0:
          current = "Hello";
          state = 1;
          return true;
        case 1:
          current = "World";
          state = 2;
          return true;
        case 2:
          break;
      }

      return false;
    }

    void System.Collections.IEnumerator.Reset()
    {
      throw new NotSupportedException();
    }

    string System.Collections.Generic.IEnumerator<string>.Current
    {
      get
      {
        return current;
      }
    }
    object System.Collections.IEnumerator.Current
    {
      get
      {
        return current;
      }
    }

    void IDisposable.Dispose()
    {
    }
  }
}
```

> **NOTE** *Remember that the* yield *statement produces an enumerator, and not just a list filled with items. This enumerator is invoked by the* foreach *statement. As each item is accessed from the* foreach, *the enumerator is accessed. This makes it possible to iterate through huge amounts of data without reading all the data into memory in one turn.*

Different Ways to Iterate Through Collections

In a slightly larger and more realistic way than the Hello World example, you can use the yield return statement to iterate through a collection in different ways. The class MusicTitles enables iterating the titles in a default way with the `GetEnumerator()` method, in reverse order with the `Reverse()` method, and through a subset with the `Subset()` method (code file `YieldDemo/MusicTitles.cs`):

```
public class MusicTitles
{
  string[] names = { "Tubular Bells", "Hergest Ridge", "Ommadawn",
                     "Platinum" };

  public IEnumerator<string> GetEnumerator()
  {
    for (int i = 0; i < 4; i++)
    {
      yield return names[i];
    }
  }

  public IEnumerable<string> Reverse()
  {
    for (int i = 3; i >= 0; i--)
    {
      yield return names[i];
    }
  }

  public IEnumerable<string> Subset(int index, int length)
  {
    for (int i = index; i < index + length; i++)
    {
      yield return names[i];
    }
  }
}
```

> **NOTE** *The default iteration supported by a class is the* `GetEnumerator()` *method, which is defined to return* `IEnumerator`. *Named iterations return* `IEnumerable`.

The client code to iterate through the string array first uses the `GetEnumerator()` method, which you don't have to write in your code because it is used by default with the implementation of the `foreach` statement. Then the titles are iterated in reverse, and finally a subset is iterated by passing the index and number of items to iterate to the `Subset()` method (code file `YieldDemo/Program.cs`):

```
var titles = new MusicTitles();
foreach (var title in titles)
{
  Console.WriteLine(title);
}
Console.WriteLine();

Console.WriteLine("reverse");
foreach (var title in titles.Reverse())
{
  Console.WriteLine(title);
}
Console.WriteLine();

Console.WriteLine("subset");
```

```
      foreach (var title in titles.Subset(2, 2))
      {
        Console.WriteLine(title);
      }
```

Returning Enumerators with Yield Return

With the `yield` statement you can also do more complex things, such as return an enumerator from `yield return`. Using the following Tic-Tac-Toe game as an example, players alternate putting a cross or a circle in one of nine fields. These moves are simulated by the `GameMoves` class. The methods `Cross()` and `Circle()` are the iterator blocks for creating iterator types. The variables `cross` and `circle` are set to `Cross()` and `Circle()` inside the constructor of the `GameMoves` class. By setting these fields the methods are not invoked, but they are set to the iterator types that are defined with the iterator blocks. Within the `Cross()` iterator block, information about the move is written to the console and the move number is incremented. If the move number is higher than 8, the iteration ends with `yield break`; otherwise, the enumerator object of the circle yield type is returned with each iteration. The `Circle()` iterator block is very similar to the `Cross()` iterator block; it just returns the cross iterator type with each iteration (code file `YieldDemo/GameMoves.cs`):

```csharp
public class GameMoves
{
  private IEnumerator cross;
  private IEnumerator circle;

  public GameMoves()
  {
    cross = Cross();
    circle = Circle();
  }

  private int move = 0;
  const int MaxMoves = 9;

  public IEnumerator Cross()
  {
    while (true)
    {
      Console.WriteLine("Cross, move {0}", move);
      if (++move >= MaxMoves)
        yield break;
      yield return circle;
    }
  }

  public IEnumerator Circle()
  {
    while (true)
    {
      Console.WriteLine("Circle, move {0}", move);
      if (++move >= MaxMoves)
        yield break;
      yield return cross;
    }
  }
}
```

From the client program, you can use the class `GameMoves` as follows. The first move is set by setting enumerator to the enumerator type returned by `game.Cross()`. In a `while` loop, `enumerator.MoveNext()` is called. The first time this is invoked, the `Cross()` method is called, which returns the other enumerator with a `yield` statement. The returned value can be accessed with the `Current` property and is set to the enumerator variable for the next loop:

```
var game = new GameMoves();
IEnumerator enumerator = game.Cross();
while (enumerator.MoveNext())
{
    enumerator = enumerator.Current as IEnumerator;
}
```

The output of this program shows alternating moves until the last move:

```
Cross, move 0
Circle, move 1
Cross, move 2
Circle, move 3
Cross, move 4
Circle, move 5
Cross, move 6
Circle, move 7
Cross, move 8
```

TUPLES

Whereas arrays combine objects of the same type, tuples can combine objects of different types. Tuples have their origin in functional programming languages such as F# where they are used often. With the .NET Framework, tuples are available for all .NET languages.

The .NET Framework defines eight generic `Tuple` classes (since version 4.0) and one static `Tuple` class that act as a factory of tuples. The different generic `Tuple` classes support a different number of elements — e.g., `Tuple<T1>` contains one element, `Tuple<T1, T2>` contains two elements, and so on.

The method `Divide()` demonstrates returning a tuple with two members: `Tuple<int, int>`. The parameters of the generic class define the types of the members, which are both integers. The tuple is created with the static `Create()` method of the static `Tuple` class. Again, the generic parameters of the `Create()` method define the type of tuple that is instantiated. The newly created tuple is initialized with the `result` and `reminder` variables to return the result of the division (code file `TupleSamle/Program.cs`):

```
public static Tuple<int, int> Divide(int dividend, int divisor)
{
    int result = dividend / divisor;
    int reminder = dividend % divisor;

    return Tuple.Create<int, int>(result, reminder);
}
```

The following example demonstrates invoking the `Divide()` method. The items of the tuple can be accessed with the properties `Item1` and `Item2`:

```
var result = Divide(5, 2);
Console.WriteLine("result of division: {0}, reminder: {1}",
    result.Item1, result.Item2);
```

If you have more than eight items that should be included in a tuple, you can use the `Tuple` class definition with eight parameters. The last template parameter is named `TRest` to indicate that you must pass a tuple itself. That way you can create tuples with any number of parameters.

The following example demonstrates this functionality:

```
public class Tuple<T1, T2, T3, T4, T5, T6, T7, TRest>
```

Here, the last template parameter is a tuple type itself, so you can create a tuple with any number of items:

```
var tuple = Tuple.Create<string, string, string, int, int, int, double,
    Tuple<int, int>>("Stephanie", "Alina", "Nagel", 2009, 6, 2, 1.37,
        Tuple.Create<int, int>(52, 3490));
```

STRUCTURAL COMPARISON

Both arrays and tuples implement the interfaces IStructuralEquatable and IStructuralComparable. These interfaces are new since .NET 4 and compare not only references but also the content. This interface is implemented explicitly, so it is necessary to cast the arrays and tuples to this interface on use. IStructuralEquatable is used to compare whether two tuples or arrays have the same content; IStructuralComparable is used to sort tuples or arrays.

With the sample demonstrating IStructuralEquatable, the Person class implementing the interface IEquatable is used. IEquatable defines a strongly typed Equals() method where the values of the FirstName and LastName properties are compared (code file StructuralComparison/Person.cs):

```
public class Person: IEquatable<Person>
{
  public int Id { get; private set; }
  public string FirstName { get; set; }
  public string LastName { get; set; }

  public override string ToString()
  {
    return String.Format("{0}, {1} {2}", Id, FirstName, LastName);
  }

  public override bool Equals(object obj)
  {
    if (obj == null)
      return base.Equals(obj);
    return Equals(obj as Person);
  }

  public override int GetHashCode()
  {
    return Id.GetHashCode();
  }

  public bool Equals(Person other)
  {
    if (other == null)
      return base.Equals(other);

    return this.Id == other.Id && this.FirstName == other.FirstName &&
        this.LastName == other.LastName;
  }
}
```

Now two arrays containing Person items are created. Both arrays contain the same Person object with the variable name janet, and two different Person objects that have the same content. The comparison operator != returns true because there are indeed two different arrays referenced from two variable names, persons1 and persons2. Because the Equals() method with one parameter is not overridden by the Array class, the same happens as with the == operator to compare the references, and they are not the same (code file StructuralComparison/Program.cs):

```
var janet = new Person { FirstName = "Janet", LastName = "Jackson" };
Person[] persons1 = {
  new Person
  {
    FirstName = "Michael",
    LastName = "Jackson"
  },
  janet
};
Person[] persons2 = {
  new Person
  {
    FirstName = "Michael",
    LastName = "Jackson"
  },
  janet
};
if (persons1 != persons2)
  Console.WriteLine("not the same reference");
```

Invoking the Equals() method defined by the IStructuralEquatable interface—that is, the method with the first parameter of type object and the second parameter of type IEqualityComparer—you can define how the comparison should be done by passing an object that implements IEqualityComparer<T>. A default implementation of the IEqualityComparer is done by the EqualityComparer<T> class. This implementation checks whether the type implements the interface IEquatable, and invokes the IEquatable.Equals() method. If the type does not implement IEquatable, the Equals() method from the base class Object is invoked to do the comparison.

Person implements IEquatable<Person>, where the content of the objects is compared, and the arrays indeed contain the same content:

```
if ((persons1 as IStructuralEquatable).Equals(persons2,
    EqualityComparer<Person>.Default))
{
  Console.WriteLine("the same content");
}
```

Next, you'll see how the same thing can be done with tuples. Here, two tuple instances are created that have the same content. Of course, because the references t1 and t2 reference two different objects, the comparison operator != returns true:

```
var t1 = Tuple.Create<int, string>(1, "Stephanie");
var t2 = Tuple.Create<int, string>(1, "Stephanie");
if (t1 != t2)
  Console.WriteLine("not the same reference to the tuple");
```

The Tuple<> class offers two Equals() methods: one that is overridden from the Object base class with an object as parameter, and the second that is defined by the IStructuralEqualityComparer interface with object and IEqualityComparer as parameters. Another tuple can be passed to the first method as shown. This method uses EqualityComparer<object>.Default to get an ObjectEqualityComparer<object> for the comparison. This way, every item of the tuple is compared by invoking the Object.Equals() method. If every item returns true, the result of the Equals() method is true, which is the case here with the same int and string values:

```
    if (t1.Equals(t2))
      Console.WriteLine("the same content");
```

You can also create a custom IEqualityComparer, as shown in the following example, with the class TupleComparer. This class implements the two methods Equals() and GetHashCode() of the IEqualityComparer interface:

```
class TupleComparer: IEqualityComparer
{
  public new bool Equals(object x, object y)
  {
    return x.Equals(y);
  }

  public int GetHashCode(object obj)
  {
    return obj.GetHashCode();
  }
}
```

> **NOTE** *Implementation of the* Equals() *method of the* IEqualityComparer *interface requires the new modifier or an implicit interface implementation because the base class* Object *defines a static* Equals() *method with two parameters as well.*

The TupleComparer is used, passing a new instance to the Equals() method of the Tuple<T1, T2> class. The Equals() method of the Tuple class invokes the Equals() method of the TupleComparer for every item to be compared. Therefore, with the Tuple<T1, T2> class, the TupleComparer is invoked two times to check whether all items are equal:

```
    if (t1.Equals(t2, new TupleComparer()))
      Console.WriteLine("equals using TupleComparer");
```

SUMMARY

In this chapter, you've seen the C# notation to create and use simple, multidimensional, and jagged arrays. The Array class is used behind the scenes of C# arrays, enabling you to invoke properties and methods of this class with array variables.

You've seen how to sort elements in the array by using the IComparable and IComparer interfaces; and you've learned how to create and use enumerators, the interfaces IEnumerable and IEnumerator, and the yield statement.

Finally, you have seen how to unite objects of the same type to an array, and objects of different types to a tuple.

The next chapter focuses on operators and casts.

7

Operators and Casts

WHAT'S IN THIS CHAPTER?

➤ Operators in C#

➤ The idea of equality when dealing with reference and value types

➤ Data conversion between primitive data types

➤ Converting value types to reference types using boxing

➤ Converting between reference types by casting

➤ Overloading the standard operators for custom types

➤ Adding cast operators to custom types

WROX.COM CODE DOWNLOADS FOR THIS CHAPTER

The wrox.com code downloads for this chapter are found at `http://www.wrox.com/remtitle.cgi?isbn=1118314425` on the Download Code tab. The code for this chapter is divided into the following major examples:

➤ SimpleCurrency

➤ SimpleCurrency2

➤ VectorStruct

➤ VectorStructMoreOverloads

OPERATORS AND CASTS

The preceding chapters have covered most of what you need to start writing useful programs using C#. This chapter completes the discussion of the essential language elements and illustrates some powerful aspects of C# that enable you to extend its capabilities.

OPERATORS

Although most of C#'s operators should be familiar to C and C++ developers, this section discusses the most important operators for the benefit of new programmers and Visual Basic converts, and sheds light on some of the changes introduced with C#.

C# supports the operators listed in the following table:

CATEGORY	OPERATOR
Arithmetic	+ - * / %
Logical	& | ^ ~ && || !
String concatenation	+
Increment and decrement	++ --
Bit shifting	<< >>
Comparison	== != < > <= >=
Assignment	= += -= *= /= %= &= |= ^= <<= >>=
Member access (for objects and structs)	.
Indexing (for arrays and indexers)	[]
Cast	()
Conditional (the ternary operator)	?:
Delegate concatenation and removal (discussed in Chapter 8, "Delegates, Lambdas, and Events")	+ -
Object creation	new
Type information	sizeof is typeof as
Overflow exception control	checked unchecked
Indirection and address	[]
Namespace alias qualifier (discussed in Chapter 2, "Core C#")	::
Null coalescing operator	??

However, note that four specific operators (sizeof, *, ->, and &, listed in the following table) are available only in unsafe code (code that bypasses C#'s type-safety checking), which is discussed in Chapter 14, "Memory Management and Pointers." It is also important to note that the sizeof operator keywords, when used with the very early versions of the .NET Framework 1.0 and 1.1, required the unsafe mode. This is not a requirement since the .NET Framework 2.0.

CATEGORY	OPERATOR
Operator keywords	sizeof (for .NET Framework versions 1.0 and 1.1 only)
Operators	* -> &

One of the biggest pitfalls to watch out for when using C# operators is that, as with other C-style languages, C# uses different operators for assignment (=) and comparison (==). For instance, the following statement means "let x equal three":

```
x = 3;
```

If you now want to compare x to a value, you need to use the double equals sign ==:

```
if (x == 3)
{

}
```

Fortunately, C#'s strict type-safety rules prevent the very common C error whereby assignment is performed instead of comparison in logical statements. This means that in C# the following statement will generate a compiler error:

```
if (x = 3)
{

}
```

Visual Basic programmers who are accustomed to using the ampersand (&) character to concatenate strings will have to make an adjustment. In C#, the plus sign (+) is used instead for concatenation, whereas the & symbol denotes a bitwise AND between two different integer values. The pipe symbol, |, enables you to perform a bitwise OR between two integers. Visual Basic programmers also might not recognize the modulus (%) arithmetic operator. This returns the remainder after division, so, for example, x % 5 returns 2 if x is equal to 7.

You will use few pointers in C#, and therefore few indirection operators. More specifically, the only place you will use them is within blocks of unsafe code, because that is the only place in C# where pointers are allowed. Pointers and unsafe code are discussed in Chapter 14.

Operator Shortcuts

The following table shows the full list of shortcut assignment operators available in C#:

SHORTCUT OPERATOR	EQUIVALENT TO
x++, ++x	x = x + 1
x--, --x	x = x - 1
x += y	x = x + y
x -= y	x = x - y
x *= y	x = x * y
x /= y	x = x / y
x %= y	x = x % y
x >>= y	x = x >> y
x <<= y	x = x << y
x &= y	x = x & y
x |= y	x = x	y

You may be wondering why there are two examples each for the ++ increment and the -- decrement operators. Placing the operator *before* the expression is known as a prefix; placing the operator *after* the expression is known as a postfix. Note that there is a difference in the way they behave.

The increment and decrement operators can act both as entire expressions and within expressions. When used by themselves, the effect of both the prefix and postfix versions is identical and corresponds to the statement x = x + 1. When used within larger expressions, the prefix operator will increment the value of x *before* the expression is evaluated; in other words, x is incremented and the new value is used in the expression. Conversely, the postfix operator increments the value of x *after* the expression is evaluated—the expression is evaluated using the original value of x. The following example uses the increment operator (++) as an example to demonstrate the difference between the prefix and postfix behavior:

```
int x = 5;

if (++x == 6)  // true - x is incremented to 6 before the evaluation
{
    Console.WriteLine("This will execute");
}

if (x++ == 7) // false - x is incremented to 7 after the evaluation
{
    Console.WriteLine("This won't");
}
```

The first `if` condition evaluates to `true` because x is incremented from 5 to 6 *before* the expression is evaluated. The condition in the second `if` statement is `false`, however, because x is incremented to 7 only after the entire expression has been evaluated (while x == 6).

The prefix and postfix operators --x and x-- behave in the same way, but decrement rather than increment the operand.

The other shortcut operators, such as += and -=, require two operands, and are used to modify the value of the first operand by performing an arithmetic, logical, or bitwise operation on it. For example, the next two lines are equivalent:

```
x += 5;
x = x + 5;
```

The following sections look at some of the primary and cast operators that you will frequently use within your C# code.

The Conditional Operator (==)

The conditional operator (`?:`), also known as the ternary operator, is a shorthand form of the `if...else` construction. It gets its name from the fact that it involves three operands. It allows you to evaluate a condition, returning one value if that condition is true, or another value if it is false. The syntax is as follows:

```
condition ? true_value: false_value
```

Here, `condition` is the Boolean expression to be evaluated, `true_value` is the value that will be returned if `condition` is true, and `false_value` is the value that will be returned otherwise.

When used sparingly, the conditional operator can add a dash of terseness to your programs. It is especially handy for providing one of a couple of arguments to a function that is being invoked. You can use it to quickly convert a Boolean value to a string value of `true` or `false`. It is also handy for displaying the correct singular or plural form of a word:

```
int x = 1;
string s = x + " ";
s += (x == 1 ? "man": "men");
Console.WriteLine(s);
```

This code displays 1 man if x is equal to one but will display the correct plural form for any other number. Note, however, that if your output needs to be localized to different languages, you have to write more sophisticated routines to take into account the different grammatical rules of different languages.

The checked and unchecked Operators

Consider the following code:

```
byte b = 255;
b++;
Console.WriteLine(b.ToString());
```

The `byte` data type can hold values only in the range 0 to 255, so incrementing the value of b causes an overflow. How the CLR handles this depends on a number of issues, including compiler options; so whenever there's a risk of an unintentional overflow, you need some way to ensure that you get the result you want.

To do this, C# provides the `checked` and `unchecked` operators. If you mark a block of code as `checked`, the CLR will enforce overflow checking, throwing an `OverflowException` if an overflow occurs. The following changes the preceding code to include the `checked` operator:

```
byte b = 255;
checked
{
    b++;
}
Console.WriteLine(b.ToString());
```

When you try to run this code, you will get an error message like this:

```
Unhandled Exception: System.OverflowException: Arithmetic operation resulted in an
    overflow at Wrox.ProCSharp.Basics.OverflowTest.Main(String[] args)
```

> **NOTE** *You can enforce overflow checking for all unmarked code in your program by* *-specifying the* /checked *compiler option.*

If you want to suppress overflow checking, you can mark the code as unchecked:

```
byte b = 255;
unchecked
{
    b++;
}
Console.WriteLine(b.ToString());
```

In this case, no exception will be raised but you will lose data because the byte type cannot hold a value of 256, the overflowing bits will be discarded, and your b variable will hold a value of zero (0).

Note that unchecked is the default behavior. The only time you are likely to need to explicitly use the unchecked keyword is when you need a few unchecked lines of code inside a larger block that you have explicitly marked as checked.

The is Operator

The is operator allows you to check whether an object is compatible with a specific type. The phrase "is compatible" means that an object either is of that type or is derived from that type. For example, to check whether a variable is compatible with the object type, you could use the following bit of code:

```
int i = 10;
if (i is object)
{
    Console.WriteLine("i is an object");
}
```

int, like all C# data types, inherits from object; therefore, the expression i is object evaluates to true in this case, and the appropriate message will be displayed.

The as Operator

The as operator is used to perform explicit type conversions of reference types. If the type being converted is compatible with the specified type, conversion is performed successfully. However, if the types are incompatible, the as operator returns the value null. As shown in the following code, attempting to convert an object reference to a string will return null if the object reference does not actually refer to a string instance:

```
object o1 = "Some String";
object o2 = 5;

string s1 = o1 as string;    // s1 = "Some String"
string s2 = o2 as string;    // s2 = null
```

The as operator allows you to perform a safe type conversion in a single step without the need to first test the type using the is operator and then perform the conversion.

The sizeof Operator

You can determine the size (in bytes) required on the stack by a value type using the sizeof operator:

```
Console.WriteLine(sizeof(int));
```

This will display the number 4, because an `int` is 4 bytes long.

If you are using the `sizeof` operator with complex types (and not primitive types), you need to block the code within an `unsafe` block as illustrated here:

```
unsafe
{
    Console.WriteLine(sizeof(Customer));
}
```

Chapter 14 looks at unsafe code in more detail.

The typeof Operator

The `typeof` operator returns a `System.Type` object representing a specified type. For example, `typeof(string)` will return a `Type` object representing the `System.String` type. This is useful when you want to use reflection to find information about an object dynamically. For more information, see Chapter 15, "Reflection."

Nullable Types and Operators

Looking at the Boolean type, you have a true or false value that you can assign to this type. However, what if you wanted to define the value of the type as undefined? This is where using nullable types can add a distinct value to your applications. If you use nullable types in your programs, you must always consider the effect a `null` value can have when used in conjunction with the various operators. Usually, when using a unary or binary operator with nullable types, the result will be `null` if one or both of the operands is `null`. For example:

```
int? a = null;

int? b = a + 4;      // b = null
int? c = a * 5;      // c = null
```

However, when comparing nullable types, if only one of the operands is `null`, the comparison will always equate to `false`. This means that you cannot assume a condition is `true` just because its opposite is `false`, as often happens in programs using non-nullable types. For example:

```
int? a = null;
int? b = -5;

if (a > = b)
    Console.WriteLine("a > = b");
else
    Console.WriteLine("a < b");
```

> **NOTE** *The possibility of a* `null` *value means that you cannot freely combine nullable and non-nullable types in an expression. This is discussed in the section "Type Conversions" later in this chapter.*

The Null Coalescing Operator

The null coalescing operator (`??`) provides a shorthand mechanism to cater to the possibility of `null` values when working with nullable and reference types. The operator is placed between two operands—the first operand must be a nullable type or reference type, and the second operand must be of the same type as the first or of a type that is implicitly convertible to the type of the first operand. The null coalescing operator evaluates as follows:

➤   If the first operand is not `null`, then the overall expression has the value of the first operand.

➤   If the first operand is `null`, then the overall expression has the value of the second operand.

For example:

```
int? a = null;
int b;

b = a ?? 10;      // b has the value 10
a = 3;
b = a ?? 10;      // b has the value 3
```

If the second operand cannot be implicitly converted to the type of the first operand, a compile-time error is generated.

Operator Precedence

The following table shows the order of precedence of the C# operators. The operators at the top of the table are those with the highest precedence (that is, the ones evaluated first in an expression containing multiple operators).

GROUP	OPERATORS
Primary	`() . [] x++ x-- new typeof sizeof checked unchecked`
Unary	`+ — ! ~ ++x --x and casts`
Multiplication/division	`* / %`
Addition/subtraction	`+ -`
Bitwise shift operators	`<< >>`
Relational	`< ><= >= is as`
Comparison	`== !=`
Bitwise AND	`&`
Bitwise XOR	`^`
Bitwise OR	`|`
Boolean AND	`&&`
Boolean OR	`||`
Conditional operator	`?:`
Assignment	`= += -= *= /= %= &= |= ^= <<= >>= >>>=`

> **NOTE** *In complex expressions, avoid relying on operator precedence to produce the correct result. Using parentheses to specify the order in which you want operators applied clarifies your code and prevents potential confusion.*

TYPE SAFETY

Chapter 1, ".NET Architecture," noted that the Intermediate Language (IL) enforces strong type safety upon its code. Strong typing enables many of the services provided by .NET, including security and language interoperability. As you would expect from a language compiled into IL, C# is also strongly typed. Among other things, this means that data types are not always seamlessly interchangeable. This section looks at conversions between primitive types.

> **NOTE** *C# also supports conversions between different reference types and allows you to define how data types that you create behave when converted to and from other types. Both of these topics are discussed later in this chapter.*
>
> *Generics, however, enable you to avoid some of the most common situations in which you would need to perform type conversions. See Chapter 5, "Generics" and Chapter 10, "Collections," for details.*

Type Conversions

Often, you need to convert data from one type to another. Consider the following code:

```
byte value1 = 10;
byte value2 = 23;
byte total;
total = value1 + value2;
Console.WriteLine(total);
```

When you attempt to compile these lines, you get the following error message:

```
Cannot implicitly convert type 'int' to 'byte'
```

The problem here is that when you add 2 bytes together, the result will be returned as an int, not another byte. This is because a byte can contain only 8 bits of data, so adding 2 bytes together could very easily result in a value that cannot be stored in a single byte. If you want to store this result in a byte variable, you have to convert it back to a byte. The following sections discuss two conversion mechanisms supported by C#—*implicit* and *explicit*.

Implicit Conversions

Conversion between types can normally be achieved automatically (implicitly) only if you can guarantee that the value is not changed in any way. This is why the previous code failed; by attempting a conversion from an int to a byte, you were potentially losing 3 bytes of data. The compiler won't let you do that unless you explicitly specify that's what you want to do. If you store the result in a long instead of a byte, however, you will have no problems:

```
byte value1 = 10;
byte value2 = 23;
long total;                   // this will compile fine
total = value1 + value2;
Console.WriteLine(total);
```

Your program has compiled with no errors at this point because a long holds more bytes of data than a byte, so there is no risk of data being lost. In these circumstances, the compiler is happy to make the conversion for you, without your needing to ask for it explicitly.

The following table shows the implicit type conversions supported in C#:

FROM	TO
sbyte	short, int, long, float, double, decimal, BigInteger
byte	short, ushort, int, uint, long, ulong, float, double, decimal, BigInteger
short	int, long, float, double, decimal, BigInteger
ushort	int, uint, long, ulong, float, double, decimal, BigInteger
int	long, float, double, decimal, BigInteger
uint	long, ulong, float, double, decimal, BigInteger

FROM	TO
`long, ulong`	`float, double, decimal, BigInteger`
`float`	`double, BigInteger`
`char`	`ushort, int, uint, long, ulong, float, double, decimal, BigInteger`

As you would expect, you can perform implicit conversions only from a smaller integer type to a larger one, not from larger to smaller. You can also convert between integers and floating-point values; however, the rules are slightly different here. Though you can convert between types of the same size, such as `int`/`uint` to `float` and `long`/`ulong` to `double`, you can also convert from `long`/`ulong` back to `float`. You might lose 4 bytes of data doing this, but it only means that the value of the `float` you receive will be less precise than if you had used a `double`; the compiler regards this as an acceptable possible error because the magnitude of the value is not affected. You can also assign an unsigned variable to a signed variable as long as the value limits of the unsigned type fit between the limits of the signed variable.

Nullable types introduce additional considerations when implicitly converting value types:

➤ Nullable types implicitly convert to other nullable types following the conversion rules described for non-nullable types in the previous table; that is, `int?` implicitly converts to `long?`, `float?`, `double?`, and `decimal?`.

➤ Non-nullable types implicitly convert to nullable types according to the conversion rules described in the preceding table; that is, `int` implicitly converts to `long?`, `float?`, `double?`, and `decimal?`.

➤ Nullable types *do not* implicitly convert to non-nullable types; you must perform an explicit conversion as described in the next section. That's because there is a chance that a nullable type will have the value `null`, which cannot be represented by a non-nullable type.

Explicit Conversions

Many conversions cannot be implicitly made between types, and the compiler will return an error if any are attempted. These are some of the conversions that cannot be made implicitly:

➤ `int` to `short`—Data loss is possible.

➤ `int` to `uint`—Data loss is possible.

➤ `uint` to `int`—Data loss is possible.

➤ `float` to `int`—Everything is lost after the decimal point.

➤ Any numeric type to `char`—Data loss is possible.

➤ `decimal` to any numeric type—The decimal type is internally structured differently from both integers and floating-point numbers.

➤ `int?` to `int`—The nullable type may have the value `null`.

However, you can explicitly carry out such conversions using *casts*. When you cast one type to another, you deliberately force the compiler to make the conversion. A cast looks like this:

```
long val = 30000;
int i = (int)val;   // A valid cast. The maximum int is 2147483647
```

You indicate the type to which you are casting by placing its name in parentheses before the value to be converted. If you are familiar with C, this is the typical syntax for casts. If you are familiar with the C++ special cast keywords such as `static_cast`, note that these do not exist in C#; you have to use the older C-type syntax.

Casting can be a dangerous operation to undertake. Even a simple cast from a `long` to an `int` can cause problems if the value of the original `long` is greater than the maximum value of an `int`:

```
long val = 3000000000;
int i = (int)val;         // An invalid cast. The maximum int is 2147483647
```

In this case, you will not get an error, but nor will you get the result you expect. If you run this code and output the value stored in i, this is what you get:

```
-1294967296
```

It is good practice to assume that an explicit cast will not return the results you expect. As shown earlier, C# provides a checked operator that you can use to test whether an operation causes an arithmetic overflow. You can use the checked operator to confirm that a cast is safe and to force the runtime to throw an overflow exception if it is not:

```
long val = 3000000000;
int i = checked((int)val);
```

Bearing in mind that all explicit casts are potentially unsafe, take care to include code in your application to deal with possible failures of the casts. Chapter 16, "Errors and Exceptions," introduces structured exception handling using the try and catch statements.

Using casts, you can convert most primitive data types from one type to another; for example, in the following code, the value 0.5 is added to price, and the total is cast to an int:

```
double price = 25.30;
int approximatePrice = (int)(price + 0.5);
```

This gives the price rounded to the nearest dollar. However, in this conversion, data is lost—namely, everything after the decimal point. Therefore, such a conversion should never be used if you want to continue to do more calculations using this modified price value. However, it is useful if you want to output the approximate value of a completed or partially completed calculation—if you don't want to bother the user with a lot of figures after the decimal point.

This example shows what happens if you convert an unsigned integer into a char:

```
ushort c = 43;
char symbol = (char)c;
Console.WriteLine(symbol);
```

The output is the character that has an ASCII number of 43, the + sign. You can try any kind of conversion you want between the numeric types (including char) and it will work, such as converting a decimal into a char, or vice versa.

Converting between value types is not restricted to isolated variables, as you have seen. You can convert an array element of type double to a struct member variable of type int:

```
struct ItemDetails
{
    public string Description;
    public int ApproxPrice;
}

//..

double[] Prices = { 25.30, 26.20, 27.40, 30.00 };

ItemDetails id;
id.Description = "Hello there.";
id.ApproxPrice = (int)(Prices[0] + 0.5);
```

To convert a nullable type to a non-nullable type or another nullable type where data loss may occur, you must use an explicit cast. This is true even when converting between elements with the same basic underlying type—for example, int? to int or float? to float. This is because the nullable type may have the value null, which cannot be represented by the non-nullable type. As long as an explicit cast between two equivalent non-nullable types is possible, so is the explicit cast between nullable types. However, when casting from a nullable type to a non-nullable type and the variable has the value null, an InvalidOperationException is thrown. For example:

```
int? a = null;
int  b = (int)a;     // Will throw exception
```

Using explicit casts and a bit of care and attention, you can convert any instance of a simple value type to almost any other. However, there are limitations on what you can do with explicit type conversions—as far as value types are concerned, you can only convert to and from the numeric and char types and enum types. You cannot directly cast Booleans to any other type or vice versa.

If you need to convert between numeric and string, you can use methods provided in the .NET class library. The Object class implements a ToString() method, which has been overridden in all the .NET predefined types and which returns a string representation of the object:

```
int i = 10;
string s = i.ToString();
```

Similarly, if you need to parse a string to retrieve a numeric or Boolean value, you can use the Parse() method supported by all the predefined value types:

```
string s = "100";
int i = int.Parse(s);
Console.WriteLine(i + 50);   // Add 50 to prove it is really an int
```

Note that Parse() will register an error by throwing an exception if it is unable to convert the string (for example, if you try to convert the string Hello to an integer). Again, exceptions are covered in Chapter 15.

Boxing and Unboxing

In Chapter 2, "Core C#," you learned that all types—both the simple predefined types such as int and char, and the complex types such as classes and structs—derive from the object type. This means you can treat even literal values as though they are objects:

```
string s = 10.ToString();
```

However, you also saw that C# data types are divided into value types, which are allocated on the stack, and reference types, which are allocated on the managed heap. How does this square with the capability to call methods on an int, if the int is nothing more than a 4-byte value on the stack?

C# achieves this through a bit of magic called *boxing*. Boxing and its counterpart, *unboxing*, enable you to convert value types to reference types and then back to value types. We include this in the section on casting because this is essentially what you are doing—you are casting your value to the object type. Boxing is the term used to describe the transformation of a value type to a reference type. Basically, the runtime creates a temporary reference-type box for the object on the heap.

This conversion can occur implicitly, as in the preceding example, but you can also perform it explicitly:

```
int myIntNumber = 20;
object myObject = myIntNumber;
```

Unboxing is the term used to describe the reverse process, whereby the value of a previously boxed value type is cast back to a value type. We use the term cast here because this has to be done explicitly. The syntax is similar to explicit type conversions already described:

```
int myIntNumber = 20;
object myObject = myIntNumber;          // Box the int
int mySecondNumber = (int)myObject;     // Unbox it back into an int
```

A variable can be unboxed only if it has been boxed. If you execute the last line when myObject is not a boxed int, you will get a runtime exception thrown at runtime.

One word of warning: When unboxing, you have to be careful that the receiving value variable has enough room to store all the bytes in the value being unboxed. C#'s ints, for example, are only 32 bits long, so unboxing a `long` value (64 bits) into an `int`, as shown here, will result in an `InvalidCastException`:

```
long myLongNumber = 333333423;
object myObject = (object)myLongNumber;
int myIntNumber = (int)myObject;
```

COMPARING OBJECTS FOR EQUALITY

After discussing operators and briefly touching on the equality operator, it is worth considering for a moment what equality means when dealing with instances of classes and structs. Understanding the mechanics of object equality is essential for programming logical expressions and is important when implementing operator overloads and casts, the topic of the rest of this chapter.

The mechanisms of object equality vary depending on whether you are comparing reference types (instances of classes) or value types (the primitive data types, instances of structs, or enums). The following sections present the equality of reference types and value types independently.

Comparing Reference Types for Equality

You might be surprised to learn that `System.Object` defines three different methods for comparing objects for equality: `ReferenceEquals()` and two versions of `Equals()`. Add to this the comparison operator (`==`) and you actually have four ways to compare for equality. Some subtle differences exist between the different methods, which are examined next.

The ReferenceEquals() Method

`ReferenceEquals()` is a `static` method that tests whether two references refer to the same instance of a class, specifically whether the two references contain the same address in memory. As a `static` method, it cannot be overridden, so the `System.Object` implementation is what you always have. `ReferenceEquals()` always returns `true` if supplied with two references that refer to the same object instance, and `false` otherwise. It does, however, consider `null` to be equal to `null`:

```
SomeClass x, y;
x = new SomeClass();
y = new SomeClass();
bool B1 = ReferenceEquals(null, null);     // returns true
bool B2 = ReferenceEquals(null,x);         // returns false
bool B3 = ReferenceEquals(x, y);           // returns false because x and y
                                           // point to different objects
```

The Virtual Equals() Method

The `System.Object` implementation of the virtual version of `Equals()` also works by comparing references. However, because this method is virtual, you can override it in your own classes to compare objects by value. In particular, if you intend instances of your class to be used as keys in a dictionary, you need to override this method to compare values. Otherwise, depending on how you override `Object.GetHashCode()`, the dictionary class that contains your objects will either not work at all or work very inefficiently. Note that when overriding `Equals()`, your override should never throw exceptions. Again, that's because doing so can cause problems for dictionary classes and possibly some other .NET base classes that internally call this method.

The Static Equals() Method

The static version of `Equals()` actually does the same thing as the virtual instance version. The difference is that the static version takes two parameters and compares them for equality. This method is able to cope when either of the objects is `null`; therefore, it provides an extra safeguard against throwing exceptions if there is a risk that an object might be `null`. The static overload first checks whether the references it has been passed are `null`. If they are both `null`, it returns `true` (because `null` is considered to be equal to `null`). If just one of them is `null`, it returns `false`. If both references actually refer to something, it calls the virtual instance version of `Equals()`. This means that when you override the instance version of `Equals()`, the effect is the same as if you were overriding the static version as well.

Comparison Operator (==)

It is best to think of the comparison operator as an intermediate option between strict value comparison and strict reference comparison. In most cases, writing the following means that you are comparing references:

```
bool b = (x == y);    // x, y object references
```

However, it is accepted that there are some classes whose meanings are more intuitive if they are treated as values. In those cases, it is better to override the comparison operator to perform a value comparison. Overriding operators is discussed next, but the obvious example of this is the `System.String` class for which Microsoft has overridden this operator to compare the contents of the strings rather than their references.

Comparing Value Types for Equality

When comparing value types for equality, the same principles hold as for reference types: `ReferenceEquals()` is used to compare references, `Equals()` is intended for value comparisons, and the comparison operator is viewed as an intermediate case. However, the big difference is that value types need to be boxed to be converted to references so that methods can be executed on them. In addition, Microsoft has already overloaded the instance `Equals()` method in the `System.ValueType` class to test equality appropriate to value types. If you call `sA.Equals(sB)` where `sA` and `sB` are instances of some struct, the return value will be `true` or `false`, according to whether `sA` and `sB` contain the same values in all their fields. On the other hand, no overload of `==` is available by default for your own structs. Writing `(sA == sB)` in any expression will result in a compilation error unless you have provided an overload of `==` in your code for the struct in question.

Another point is that `ReferenceEquals()` always returns `false` when applied to value types because, to call this method, the value types need to be boxed into objects. Even if you write the following, you will still get the result of `false`:

```
bool b = ReferenceEquals(v,v);   // v is a variable of some value type
```

The reason is because `v` will be boxed separately when converting each parameter, which means you get different references. Therefore, there really is no reason to call `ReferenceEquals()` to compare value types because it doesn't make much sense.

Although the default override of `Equals()` supplied by `System.ValueType` will almost certainly be adequate for the vast majority of structs that you define, you might want to override it again for your own structs to improve performance. Also, if a value type contains reference types as fields, you might want to override `Equals()` to provide appropriate semantics for these fields because the default override of `Equals()` will simply compare their addresses.

OPERATOR OVERLOADING

This section looks at another type of member that you can define for a class or a struct: the operator overload. Operator overloading is something that will be familiar to C++ developers. However, because the concept is new to both Java and Visual Basic developers, we explain it here. C++ developers will probably prefer to skip ahead to the main operator overloading example.

The point of operator overloading is that you do not always just want to call methods or properties on objects. Often, you need to do things like add quantities together, multiply them, or perform logical operations such as comparing objects. Suppose you defined a class that represents a mathematical matrix. In the world of math, matrices can be added together and multiplied, just like numbers. Therefore, it is quite plausible that you would want to write code like this:

```
Matrix a, b, c;
// assume a, b and c have been initialized
Matrix d = c * (a + b);
```

By overloading the operators, you can tell the compiler what + and * do when used in conjunction with a `Matrix` object, enabling you to write code like the preceding. If you were coding in a language that did not support operator overloading, you would have to define methods to perform those operations. The result would certainly be less intuitive and would probably look something like this:

```
Matrix d = c.Multiply(a.Add(b));
```

With what you have learned so far, operators like + and * have been strictly for use with the predefined data types, and for good reason: The compiler knows what all the common operators mean for those data types. For example, it knows how to add two `longs` or how to divide one `double` by another `double`, and it can generate the appropriate intermediate language code. When you define your own classes or structs, however, you have to tell the compiler everything: what methods are available to call, what fields to store with each instance, and so on. Similarly, if you want to use operators with your own types, you have to tell the compiler what the relevant operators mean in the context of that class. You do that by defining overloads for the operators.

The other thing to stress is that overloading is not just concerned with arithmetic operators. You also need to consider the comparison operators, ==, <, >, !=, >=, and <=. Take the statement `if  (a==b)`. For classes, this statement will, by default, compare the references a and b. It tests whether the references point to the same location in memory, rather than checking whether the instances actually contain the same data. For the `string` class, this behavior is overridden so that comparing strings really does compare the contents of each string. You might want to do the same for your own classes. For structs, the == operator does not do anything at all by default. Trying to compare two structs to determine whether they are equal produces a compilation error unless you explicitly overload == to tell the compiler how to perform the comparison.

In many situations, being able to overload operators enables you to generate more readable and intuitive code, including the following:

➤ Almost any mathematical object such as coordinates, vectors, matrices, tensors, functions, and so on. If you are writing a program that does some mathematical or physical modeling, you will almost certainly use classes representing these objects.

➤ Graphics programs that use mathematical or coordinate-related objects when calculating positions on-screen.

➤ A class that represents an amount of money (for example, in a financial program).

➤ A word processing or text analysis program that uses classes representing sentences, clauses, and so on. You might want to use operators to combine sentences (a more sophisticated version of concatenation for strings).

However, there are also many types for which operator overloading is not relevant. Using operator overloading inappropriately will make any code that uses your types far more difficult to understand. For example, multiplying two `DateTime` objects does not make any sense conceptually.

How Operators Work

To understand how to overload operators, it's quite useful to think about what happens when the compiler encounters an operator. Using the addition operator (+) as an example, suppose that the compiler processes the following lines of code:

```
int myInteger = 3;
uint myUnsignedInt = 2;
double myDouble = 4.0;
long myLong = myInteger + myUnsignedInt;
double myOtherDouble = myDouble + myInteger;
```

Now consider what happens when the compiler encounters this line:

```
long myLong = myInteger + myUnsignedInt;
```

The compiler identifies that it needs to add two integers and assign the result to a `long`. However, the expression `myInteger + myUnsignedInt` is really just an intuitive and convenient syntax for calling a method that adds two numbers. The method takes two parameters, `myInteger` and `myUnsignedInt`, and returns their sum. Therefore, the compiler does the same thing it does for any method call: It looks for the best matching overload of the addition operator based on the parameter types—in this case, one that takes two integers. As with normal overloaded methods, the desired return type does not influence the compiler's choice as to which version of a method it calls. As it happens, the overload called in the example takes two `int` parameters and returns an `int`; this return value is subsequently converted to a `long`.

The next line causes the compiler to use a different overload of the addition operator:

```
double myOtherDouble = myDouble + myInteger;
```

In this instance, the parameters are a `double` and an `int`, but there is no overload of the addition operator that takes this combination of parameters. Instead, the compiler identifies the best matching overload of the addition operator as being the version that takes two `doubles` as its parameters, and it implicitly casts the `int` to a `double`. Adding two `doubles` requires a different process from adding two integers. Floating-point numbers are stored as a mantissa and an exponent. Adding them involves bit-shifting the mantissa of one of the `doubles` so that the two exponents have the same value, adding the mantissas, then shifting the mantissa of the result and adjusting its exponent to maintain the highest possible accuracy in the answer.

Now you are in a position to see what happens if the compiler finds something like this:

```
Vector vect1, vect2, vect3;
// initialize vect1 and vect2
vect3 = vect1 + vect2;
vect1 = vect1*2;
```

Here, `Vector` is the struct, which is defined in the following section. The compiler sees that it needs to add two `Vector` instances, `vect1` and `vect2`, together. It looks for an overload of the addition operator, which takes two `Vector` instances as its parameters.

If the compiler finds an appropriate overload, it calls up the implementation of that operator. If it cannot find one, it checks whether there is any other overload for + that it can use as a best match—perhaps something with two parameters of other data types that can be implicitly converted to `Vector` instances. If the compiler cannot find a suitable overload, it raises a compilation error, just as it would if it could not find an appropriate overload for any other method call.

Operator Overloading Example: The Vector Struct

This section demonstrates operator overloading through developing a struct named `Vector` that represents a three-dimensional mathematical vector. Don't worry if mathematics is not your strong point—the vector example is very simple. As far as you are concerned here, a 3D vector is just a set of three numbers (`doubles`) that tell you how far something is moving. The variables representing the numbers are called x, y, and z: the x tells you how far something moves east, y tells you how far it moves north, and z tells you how far it moves upward (in height). Combine the three numbers and you get the total movement. For example, if x=3.0, y=3.0, and z=1.0 (which you would normally write as (3.0, 3.0, 1.0), you're moving 3 units east, 3 units north, and rising upward by 1 unit.

You can add or multiply vectors by other vectors or by numbers. Incidentally, in this context, we use the term *scalar*, which is math-speak for a simple number—in C# terms that is just a `double`. The significance of addition should be clear. If you move first by the vector (3.0, 3.0, 1.0) then you move by the vector (2.0, -4.0, -4.0), the total amount you have moved can be determined by adding the two vectors. Adding vectors means adding each component individually, so you get (5.0, -1.0, -3.0). In this context, mathematicians write c=a+b, where a and b are the vectors and c is the resulting vector. You want to be able to use the `Vector` struct the same way.

> **NOTE** *The fact that this example is developed as a struct rather than a class is not significant. Operator overloading works in the same way for both structs and classes.*

Following is the definition for `Vector`—containing the member fields, constructors, a `ToString()` override so you can easily view the contents of a `Vector`, and, finally, that operator overload:

```
namespace Wrox.ProCSharp.OOCSharp
{
    struct Vector
    {
        public double x, y, z;

        public Vector(double x, double y, double z)
        {
            this.x = x;
            this.y = y;
            this.z = z;
        }

        public Vector(Vector rhs)
        {
            x = rhs.x;
            y = rhs.y;
            z = rhs.z;
        }

        public override string ToString()
        {
            return "( " + x + ", " + y + ", " + z + " )";
        }
```

This example has two constructors that require specifying the initial value of the vector, either by passing in the values of each component or by supplying another `Vector` whose value can be copied. Constructors like the second one, that takes a single `Vector` argument, are often termed *copy constructors* because they effectively enable you to initialize a class or struct instance by copying another instance. Note that to keep things simple, the fields are left as `public`. We could have made them `private` and written corresponding properties to access them, but it would not make any difference to the example, other than to make the code longer.

Here is the interesting part of the `Vector` struct—the operator overload that provides support for the addition operator:

```
        public static Vector operator + (Vector lhs, Vector rhs)
        {
            Vector result = new Vector(lhs);
            result.x += rhs.x;
            result.y += rhs.y;
            result.z += rhs.z;

            return result;
        }
    }
}
```

The operator overload is declared in much the same way as a method, except that the `operator` keyword tells the compiler it is actually an operator overload you are defining. The `operator` keyword is followed by the actual symbol for the relevant operator, in this case the addition operator (+). The return type is whatever type you get when you use this operator. Adding two vectors results in a vector; therefore, the return type is also a `Vector`. For this particular override of the addition operator, the return type is the same as the containing class, but that is not necessarily the case, as you will see later in this example. The two parameters are the things you are operating on. For binary operators (those that take two parameters), such as the addition and subtraction operators, the first parameter is the value on the left of the operator, and the second parameter is the value on the right.

> **NOTE** *It is conventional to name your left-hand parameters* lhs *(for left-hand side) and your right-hand parameters* rhs *(for right-hand side).*

C# requires that all operator overloads be declared as `public` and `static`, which means they are associated with their class or struct, not with a particular instance. Because of this, the body of the operator overload has no access to non-static class members or the `this` identifier. This is fine because the parameters provide all the input data the operator needs to know to perform its task.

Now that you understand the syntax for the addition operator declaration, examine what happens inside the operator:

```
{
    Vector result = new Vector(lhs);
    result.x += rhs.x;
    result.y += rhs.y;
    result.z += rhs.z;

    return result;
}
```

This part of the code is exactly the same as if you were declaring a method, and you should easily be able to convince yourself that this will return a vector containing the sum of lhs and rhs as defined. You simply add the members x, y, and z together individually.

Now all you need to do is write some simple code to test the `Vector` struct:

```
static void Main()
{
    Vector vect1, vect2, vect3;

    vect1 = new Vector(3.0, 3.0, 1.0);
    vect2 = new Vector(2.0, -4.0, -4.0);
    vect3 = vect1 + vect2;

    Console.WriteLine("vect1 = " + vect1.ToString());
    Console.WriteLine("vect2 = " + vect2.ToString());
    Console.WriteLine("vect3 = " + vect3.ToString());
}
```

Saving this code as `Vectors.cs` and compiling and running it returns this result:

```
vect1 = ( 3, 3, 1 )
vect2 = ( 2, -4, -4 )
vect3 = ( 5, -1, -3 )
```

Adding More Overloads

In addition to adding vectors, you can multiply and subtract them and compare their values. In this section, you develop the `Vector` example further by adding a few more operator overloads. You won't develop the complete set that you'd probably need for a fully functional `Vector` type, but just enough to demonstrate some other aspects of operator overloading. First, you'll overload the multiplication operator to support multiplying vectors by a scalar and multiplying vectors by another vector.

Multiplying a vector by a scalar simply means multiplying each component individually by the scalar: for example, `2 * (1.0, 2.5, 2.0)` returns `(2.0, 5.0, 4.0)`. The relevant operator overload looks similar to this:

```
public static Vector operator * (double lhs, Vector rhs)
{
```

```
        return new Vector(lhs * rhs.x, lhs * rhs.y, lhs * rhs.z);
}
```

This by itself, however, is not sufficient. If a and b are declared as type Vector, you can write code like this:

```
b = 2 * a;
```

The compiler will implicitly convert the integer 2 to a double to match the operator overload signature. However, code like the following will not compile:

```
b = a * 2;
```

The point is that the compiler treats operator overloads exactly like method overloads. It examines all the available overloads of a given operator to find the best match. The preceding statement requires the first parameter to be a Vector and the second parameter to be an integer, or something to which an integer can be implicitly converted. You have not provided such an overload. The compiler cannot start swapping the order of parameters, so the fact that you've provided an overload that takes a double followed by a Vector is not sufficient. You need to explicitly define an overload that takes a Vector followed by a double as well. There are two possible ways of implementing this. The first way involves breaking down the vector multiplication operation in the same way that you have done for all operators so far:

```
public static Vector operator * (Vector lhs, double rhs)
{
    return new Vector(rhs * lhs.x, rhs * lhs.y, rhs *lhs.z);
}
```

Given that you have already written code to implement essentially the same operation, however, you might prefer to reuse that code by writing the following:

```
public static Vector operator * (Vector lhs, double rhs)
{
    return rhs * lhs;
}
```

This code works by effectively telling the compiler that when it sees a multiplication of a Vector by a double, it can simply reverse the parameters and call the other operator overload. The sample code for this chapter uses the second version, because it looks neater and illustrates the idea in action. This version also makes the code more maintainable because it saves duplicating the code to perform the multiplication in two separate overloads.

Next, you need to overload the multiplication operator to support vector multiplication. Mathematics provides a couple of ways to multiply vectors, but the one we are interested in here is known as the *dot product* or *inner product*, which actually returns a scalar as a result. That's the reason for this example, to demonstrate that arithmetic operators don't have to return the same type as the class in which they are defined.

In mathematical terms, if you have two vectors (x, y, z) and (X, Y, Z), then the inner product is defined to be the value of x*X + y*Y + z*Z. That might look like a strange way to multiply two things together, but it is actually very useful because it can be used to calculate various other quantities. If you ever write code that displays complex 3D graphics, such as using Direct3D or DirectDraw, you will almost certainly find that your code needs to work out inner products of vectors quite often as an intermediate step in calculating where to place objects on the screen. What concerns us here is that we want users of your Vector to be able to write double X = a*b to calculate the inner product of two Vector objects (a and b). The relevant overload looks like this:

```
public static double operator * (Vector lhs, Vector rhs)
{
    return lhs.x * rhs.x + lhs.y * rhs.y + lhs.z * rhs.z;
}
```

Now that you understand the arithmetic operators, you can confirm that they work using a simple test method:

```
static void Main()
{
    // stuff to demonstrate arithmetic operations
    Vector vect1, vect2, vect3;
    vect1 = new Vector(1.0, 1.5, 2.0);
```

```
        vect2 = new Vector(0.0, 0.0, -10.0);

        vect3 = vect1 + vect2;

        Console.WriteLine("vect1 = " + vect1);
        Console.WriteLine("vect2 = " + vect2);
        Console.WriteLine("vect3 = vect1 + vect2 = " + vect3);
        Console.WriteLine("2*vect3 = " + 2*vect3);
        vect3 += vect2;

        Console.WriteLine("vect3+=vect2 gives " + vect3);

        vect3 = vect1*2;

        Console.WriteLine("Setting vect3=vect1*2 gives " + vect3);

        double dot = vect1*vect3;

        Console.WriteLine("vect1*vect3 = " + dot);
    }
```

Running this code (`Vectors2.cs`) produces the following result:

VECTORS2

```
vect1 = ( 1, 1.5, 2 )
vect2 = ( 0, 0, -10 )
vect3 = vect1 + vect2 = ( 1, 1.5, -8 )
2*vect3 = ( 2, 3, -16 )
vect3+=vect2 gives ( 1, 1.5, -18 )
Setting vect3=vect1*2 gives ( 2, 3, 4 )
vect1*vect3 = 14.5
```

This shows that the operator overloads have given the correct results; but if you look at the test code closely, you might be surprised to notice that it actually used an operator that wasn't overloaded—the addition assignment operator, +=:

```
        vect3 += vect2;

        Console.WriteLine("vect3 += vect2 gives " + vect3);
```

Although += normally counts as a single operator, it can be broken down into two steps: the addition and the assignment. Unlike the C++ language, C# does not allow you to overload the = operator; but if you overload +, the compiler will automatically use your overload of + to work out how to perform a += operation. The same principle works for all the assignment operators, such as -=, *=, /=, &=, and so on.

Overloading the Comparison Operators

As shown earlier in the section "Operators," C# has six comparison operators, and they are paired as follows:

➤ == and !=

➤ > and <

➤ >= and <=

The C# language requires that you overload these operators in pairs. That is, if you overload ==, you must overload != too; otherwise, you get a compiler error. In addition, the comparison operators must return a bool. This is the fundamental difference between these operators and the arithmetic operators. The result of adding or subtracting two quantities, for example, can theoretically be any type depending on the quantities. You have already seen that multiplying two Vector objects can be implemented to give a scalar. Another example involves the .NET base class System.DateTime. It's possible to subtract two DateTime instances, but the result is not a DateTime; instead it is a System.TimeSpan instance. By contrast, it doesn't really make much sense for a comparison to return anything other than a bool.

> **NOTE** *If you overload* `==` *and* `!=`, *you must also override the* `Equals()` *and* `GetHashCode()` *methods inherited from* `System.Object`; *otherwise, you'll get a compiler warning. The reasoning is that the* `Equals()` *method should implement the same kind of equality logic as the* `==` *operator.*

Apart from these differences, overloading the comparison operators follows the same principles as overloading the arithmetic operators. However, comparing quantities isn't always as simple as you might think. For example, if you simply compare two object references, you will compare the memory address where the objects are stored. This is rarely the desired behavior of a comparison operator, so you must code the operator to compare the value of the objects and return the appropriate Boolean response. The following example overrides the `==` and `!=` operators for the `Vector` struct. Here is the implementation of `==`:

```
public static bool operator == (Vector lhs, Vector rhs)
{
    if (lhs.x == rhs.x && lhs.y == rhs.y && lhs.z == rhs.z)
        return true;
    else
        return false;
}
```

This approach simply compares two `Vector` objects for equality based on the values of their components. For most structs, that is probably what you will want to do, though in some cases you may need to think carefully about what you mean by equality. For example, if there are embedded classes, should you simply compare whether the references point to the same object (shallow comparison) or whether the values of the objects are the same (deep comparison)?

With a shallow comparison, the objects point to the same point in memory, whereas deep comparisons work with values and properties of the object to deem equality. You want to perform equality checks depending on the depth to help you decide what you want to verify.

> **NOTE** *Don't be tempted to overload the comparison operator by calling the instance version of the* `Equals()` *method inherited from* `System.Object`. *If you do and then an attempt is made to evaluate* `(objA == objB)`, *when* `objA` *happens to be null, you will get an exception, as the .NET runtime tries to evaluate* `null.Equals(objB)`. *Working the other way around (overriding* `Equals()` *to call the comparison operator) should be safe.*

You also need to override the `!=` operator. Here is the simple way to do this:

```
public static bool operator != (Vector lhs, Vector rhs)
{
    return ! (lhs == rhs);
}
```

As usual, you should quickly confirm that your override works with some test code. This time you'll define three `Vector` objects and compare them:

```
static void Main()
{
    Vector vect1, vect2, vect3;

    vect1 = new Vector(3.0, 3.0, -10.0);
    vect2 = new Vector(3.0, 3.0, -10.0);
    vect3 = new Vector(2.0, 3.0, 6.0);

    Console.WriteLine("vect1==vect2 returns  " + (vect1==vect2));
    Console.WriteLine("vect1==vect3 returns  " + (vect1==vect3));
```

```
    Console.WriteLine("vect2==vect3 returns  " + (vect2==vect3));

    Console.WriteLine();

    Console.WriteLine("vect1!=vect2 returns  " + (vect1!=vect2));
    Console.WriteLine("vect1!=vect3 returns  " + (vect1!=vect3));
    Console.WriteLine("vect2!=vect3 returns  " + (vect2!=vect3));
}
```

Compiling this code (the `Vectors3.cs` sample in the code download) generates the following compiler warning because you haven't overridden `Equals()` for your `Vector`. For our purposes here, that doesn't, so we will ignore it:

```
Microsoft (R) Visual C# 2010 Compiler version 4.0.21006.1
for Microsoft (R) .NET Framework version 4.0
Copyright (C) Microsoft Corporation. All rights reserved.


Vectors3.cs(5,11): warning CS0660: 'Wrox.ProCSharp.OOCSharp.Vector' defines
        operator == or operator != but does not override Object.Equals(object o)
Vectors3.cs(5,11): warning CS0661: 'Wrox.ProCSharp.OOCSharp.Vector' defines
        operator == or operator != but does not override Object.GetHashCode()
```

Running the example produces these results at the command line:

VECTORS3

```
vect1==vect2 returns  True
vect1==vect3 returns  False
vect2==vect3 returns  False

vect1!=vect2 returns  False
vect1!=vect3 returns  True
vect2!=vect3 returns  True
```

Which Operators Can You Overload?

It is not possible to overload all the available operators. The operators that you can overload are listed in the following table:

CATEGORY	OPERATORS	RESTRICTIONS
Arithmetic binary	+, *, /, −, %	None
Arithmetic unary	+, −, ++, --	None
Bitwise binary	&, |, ^, <<, >>	None
Bitwise unary	!, ~true, false	The true and false operators must be overloaded as a pair.
Comparison	==, !=, >=, <=>, <,	Comparison operators must be overloaded in pairs.
Assignment	+=, −=, *=, /=, >>=, <<=, %=, &=, |=, ^=	You cannot explicitly overload these operators; they are overridden implicitly when you override the individual operators such as +, -, %, and so on.
Index	[]	You cannot overload the index operator directly. The indexer member type, discussed in Chapter 2, allows you to support the index operator on your classes and structs.
Cast	()	You cannot overload the cast operator directly. User-defined casts (discussed next) allow you to define custom cast behavior.

USER-DEFINED CASTS

Earlier in this chapter (see the "Explicit Conversions" section), you learned that you can convert values between predefined data types through a process of casting. You also saw that C# allows two different types of casts: implicit and explicit. This section looks at these types of casts.

For an explicit cast, you explicitly mark the cast in your code by including the destination data type inside parentheses:

```
int I = 3;
long l = I;              // implicit
short s = (short)I;      // explicit
```

For the predefined data types, explicit casts are required where there is a risk that the cast might fail or some data might be lost. The following are some examples:

➤ When converting from an `int` to a `short`, the `short` might not be large enough to hold the value of the `int`.

➤ When converting from signed to unsigned data types, incorrect results are returned if the signed variable holds a negative value.

➤ When converting from floating-point to integer data types, the fractional part of the number will be lost.

➤ When converting from a nullable type to a non-nullable type, a value of `null` causes an exception.

By making the cast explicit in your code, C# forces you to affirm that you understand there is a risk of data loss, and therefore presumably you have written your code to take this into account.

Because C# allows you to define your own data types (structs and classes), it follows that you need the facility to support casts to and from those data types. The mechanism is to define a cast as a member operator of one of the relevant classes. Your cast operator must be marked as either `implicit` or `explicit` to indicate how you are intending it to be used. The expectation is that you follow the same guidelines as for the predefined casts: if you know that the cast is always safe regardless of the value held by the source variable, then you define it as `implicit`. Conversely, if you know there is a risk of something going wrong for certain values—perhaps some loss of data or an exception being thrown—then you should define the cast as `explicit`.

> **NOTE** *You should define any custom casts you write as explicit if there are any source data values for which the cast will fail or if there is any risk of an exception being thrown.*

The syntax for defining a cast is similar to that for overloading operators discussed earlier in this chapter. This is not a coincidence—a cast is regarded as an operator whose effect is to convert from the source type to the destination type. To illustrate the syntax, the following is taken from an example `struct` named `Currency`, which is introduced later in this section:

```
public static implicit operator float (Currency value)
{
    // processing
}
```

The return type of the operator defines the target type of the cast operation, and the single parameter is the source object for the conversion. The cast defined here allows you to implicitly convert the value of a `Currency` into a `float`. Note that if a conversion has been declared as `implicit`, the compiler permits its use either implicitly or explicitly. If it has been declared as `explicit`, the compiler only permits it to be used explicitly. In common with other operator overloads, casts must be declared as both `public` and `static`.

> **NOTE** *C++ developers will notice that this is different from C++, in which casts are instance members of classes.*

Implementing User-Defined Casts

This section illustrates the use of implicit and explicit user-defined casts in an example called SimpleCurrency (which, as usual, is available in the code download). In this example, you define a struct, Currency, which holds a positive USD ($) monetary value. C# provides the decimal type for this purpose, but it is possible you will still want to write your own struct or class to represent monetary values if you need to perform sophisticated financial processing and therefore want to implement specific methods on such a class.

> **NOTE** *The syntax for casting is the same for structs and classes. This example happens to be for a struct, but it would work just as well if you declared Currency as a class.*

Initially, the definition of the Currency struct is as follows:

```
struct Currency
{
    public uint Dollars;
    public ushort Cents;

    public Currency(uint dollars, ushort cents)
    {
        this.Dollars = dollars;
        this.Cents = cents;
    }

    public override string ToString()
    {
        return string.Format("${0}.{1,-2:00}", Dollars,Cents);
    }
}
```

The use of unsigned data types for the Dollar and Cents fields ensures that a Currency instance can hold only positive values. It is restricted this way to illustrate some points about explicit casts later. You might want to use a class like this to hold, for example, salary information for company employees (people's salaries tend not to be negative!). To keep the class simple, the fields are public, but usually you would make them private and define corresponding properties for the dollars and cents.

Start by assuming that you want to be able to convert Currency instances to float values, where the integer part of the float represents the dollars. In other words, you want to be able to write code like this:

```
Currency balance = new Currency(10,50);
float f = balance; // We want f to be set to 10.5
```

To be able to do this, you need to define a cast. Hence, you add the following to your Currency definition:

```
public static implicit operator float (Currency value)
{
    return value.Dollars + (value.Cents/100.0f);
}
```

The preceding cast is implicit. It is a sensible choice in this case because, as it should be clear from the definition of Currency, any value that can be stored in the currency can also be stored in a float. There is no way that anything should ever go wrong in this cast.

> **NOTE** *There is a slight cheat here: in fact, when converting a* uint *to a* float, *there can be a loss in precision, but Microsoft has deemed this error sufficiently marginal to count the* uint-to-float *cast as implicit.*

However, if you have a float that you would like to be converted to a Currency, the conversion is not guaranteed to work. A float can store negative values, which Currency instances can't, and a float can store numbers of a far higher magnitude than can be stored in the (uint) Dollar field of Currency. Therefore, if a float contains an inappropriate value, converting it to a Currency could give unpredictable results. Because of this risk, the conversion from float to Currency should be defined as explicit. Here is the first attempt, which will not return quite the correct results, but it is instructive to examine why:

```
public static explicit operator Currency (float value)
{
    uint dollars = (uint)value;
    ushort cents = (ushort)((value-dollars)*100);
    return new Currency(dollars, cents);
}
```

The following code will now successfully compile:

```
float amount = 45.63f;
Currency amount2 = (Currency)amount;
```

However, the following code, if you tried it, would generate a compilation error, because it attempts to use an explicit cast implicitly:

```
float amount = 45.63f;
Currency amount2 = amount;    // wrong
```

By making the cast explicit, you warn the developer to be careful because data loss might occur. However, as you will soon see, this is not how you want your Currency struct to behave. Try writing a test harness and running the sample. Here is the Main() method, which instantiates a Currency struct and attempts a few conversions. At the start of this code, you write out the value of balance in two different ways (this will be needed to illustrate something later in the example):

```
static void Main()
{
    try
    {
        Currency balance = new Currency(50,35);

        Console.WriteLine(balance);
        Console.WriteLine("balance is " + balance);
        Console.WriteLine("balance is (using ToString()) " + balance.ToString());

        float balance2= balance;

        Console.WriteLine("After converting to float, = " + balance2);

        balance = (Currency) balance2;

        Console.WriteLine("After converting back to Currency, = " + balance);
        Console.WriteLine("Now attempt to convert out of range value of " +
                          "-$50.50 to a Currency:");

        checked
        {
            balance = (Currency) (-50.50);
            Console.WriteLine("Result is " + balance.ToString());
        }
    }
```

```
    }
    catch(Exception e)
    {
        Console.WriteLine("Exception occurred: " + e.Message);
    }
}
```

Notice that the entire code is placed in a `try` block to catch any exceptions that occur during your casts. In addition, the lines that test converting an out-of-range value to `Currency` are placed in a `checked` block in an attempt to trap negative values. Running this code produces the following output:

SIMPLECURRENCY

```
50.35
Balance is $50.35
Balance is (using ToString()) $50.35
After converting to float, = 50.35
After converting back to Currency, = $50.34
Now attempt to convert out of range value of -$100.00 to a Currency:
Result is $4294967246.00
```

This output shows that the code did not quite work as expected. First, converting back from `float` to `Currency` gave a wrong result of $50.34 instead of $50.35. Second, no exception was generated when you tried to convert an obviously out-of-range value.

The first problem is caused by rounding errors. If a cast is used to convert from a `float` to a `uint`, the computer will truncate the number rather than round it. The computer stores numbers in binary rather than decimal, and the fraction 0.35 cannot be exactly represented as a binary fraction (just as ⅓ cannot be represented exactly as a decimal fraction; it comes out as 0.3333 recurring). The computer ends up storing a value very slightly lower than 0.35 that can be represented exactly in binary format. Multiply by 100 and you get a number fractionally less than 35, which is truncated to 34 cents. Clearly, in this situation, such errors caused by truncation are serious, and the way to avoid them is to ensure that some intelligent rounding is performed in numerical conversions instead.

Luckily, Microsoft has written a class that does this: `System.Convert`. The `System.Convert` object contains a large number of static methods to perform various numerical conversions, and the one that we want is `Convert.ToUInt16()`. Note that the extra care taken by the `System.Convert` methods does come at a performance cost. You should use them only when necessary.

Let's examine the second problem—why the expected overflow exception wasn't thrown. The issue here is this: The place where the overflow really occurs isn't actually in the `Main()` routine at all—it is inside the code for the cast operator, which is called from the `Main()` method. The code in this method was not marked as `checked`.

The solution is to ensure that the cast itself is computed in a `checked` context too. With both this change and the fix for the first problem, the revised code for the conversion looks like the following:

```
public static explicit operator Currency (float value)
{
    checked
    {
        uint dollars = (uint)value;
        ushort cents = Convert.ToUInt16((value-dollars)*100);
        return new Currency(dollars, cents);
    }
}
```

Note that you use `Convert.ToUInt16()` to calculate the cents, as described earlier, but you do not use it for calculating the dollar part of the amount. `System.Convert` is not needed when calculating the dollar amount because truncating the `float` value is what you want there.

> **NOTE** *The* `System.Convert` *methods also carry out their own overflow checking. Hence, for the particular case we are considering, there is no need to place the call to* `Convert.ToUInt16()` *inside the checked context. The checked context is still required, however, for the explicit casting of* `value` *to dollars.*

You won't see a new set of results with this new `checked` cast just yet because you have some more modifications to make to the `SimpleCurrency` example later in this section.

> **NOTE** *If you are defining a cast that will be used very often, and for which performance is at an absolute premium, you may prefer not to do any error checking. That is also a legitimate solution, provided that the behavior of your cast and the lack of error checking are very clearly documented.*

Casts Between Classes

The `Currency` example involves only classes that convert to or from `float` — one of the predefined data types. However, it is not necessary to involve any of the simple data types. It is perfectly legitimate to define casts to convert between instances of different structs or classes that you have defined. You need to be aware of a couple of restrictions, however:

➤ You cannot define a cast if one of the classes is derived from the other (these types of casts already exist, as you will see).

➤ The cast must be defined inside the definition of either the source or the destination data type.

To illustrate these requirements, suppose that you have the class hierarchy shown in Figure 7-1.

In other words, classes C and D are indirectly derived from A. In this case, the only legitimate user-defined cast between A, B, C, or D would be to convert between classes C and D, because these classes are not derived from each other. The code to do so might look like the following (assuming you want the casts to be explicit, which is usually the case when defining casts between user-defined classes):

```
public static explicit operator D(C value)
{
    // and so on
}
public static explicit operator C(D value)
{
    // and so on
}
```

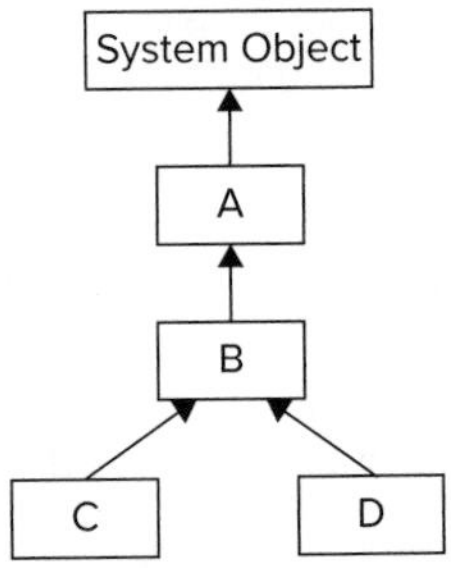

For each of these casts, you can choose where you place the definitions — inside the class definition of C or inside the class definition of D, but not anywhere else. C# requires you to put the definition of a cast inside either the source class (or struct) or the destination class (or struct). A side effect of this is that you cannot define a cast between two classes unless you have access to edit the source code for at least one of them. This is sensible because it prevents third parties from introducing casts into your classes.

FIGURE 7-1

After you have defined a cast inside one of the classes, you cannot also define the same cast inside the other class. Obviously, there should be only one cast for each conversion; otherwise, the compiler would not know which one to use.

Casts Between Base and Derived Classes

To see how these casts work, start by considering the case in which both the source and the destination are reference types, and consider two classes, `MyBase` and `MyDerived`, where `MyDerived` is derived directly or indirectly from `MyBase`.

First, from `MyDerived` to `MyBase`, it is always possible (assuming the constructors are available) to write this:

```
MyDerived derivedObject = new MyDerived();
MyBase baseCopy = derivedObject;
```

Here, you are casting implicitly from `MyDerived` to `MyBase`. This works because of the rule that any reference to a type `MyBase` is allowed to refer to objects of class `MyBase` or anything derived from `MyBase`. In OO programming, instances of a derived class are, in a real sense, instances of the base class, plus something extra. All the functions and fields defined on the base class are defined in the derived class too.

Alternatively, you can write this:

```
MyBase derivedObject = new MyDerived();
MyBase baseObject = new MyBase();
MyDerived derivedCopy1 = (MyDerived) derivedObject;   // OK
MyDerived derivedCopy2 = (MyDerived) baseObject;       // Throws exception
```

This code is perfectly legal C# (in a syntactic sense, that is) and illustrates casting from a base class to a derived class. However, the final statement will throw an exception when executed. When you perform the cast, the object being referred to is examined. Because a base class reference can, in principle, refer to a derived class instance, it is possible that this object is actually an instance of the derived class that you are attempting to cast to. If that is the case, the cast succeeds, and the derived reference is set to refer to the object. If, however, the object in question is not an instance of the derived class (or of any class derived from it), the cast fails and an exception is thrown.

Notice that the casts that the compiler has supplied, which convert between base and derived class, do not actually do any data conversion on the object in question. All they do is set the new reference to refer to the object if it is legal for that conversion to occur. To that extent, these casts are very different in nature from the ones that you normally define yourself. For example, in the `SimpleCurrency` example earlier, you defined casts that convert between a `Currency` struct and a `float`. In the `float`-to-`Currency` cast, you actually instantiated a new `Currency` struct and initialized it with the required values. The predefined casts between base and derived classes do not do this. If you want to convert a `MyBase` instance into a real `MyDerived` object with values based on the contents of the `MyBase` instance, you cannot use the cast syntax to do this. The most sensible option is usually to define a derived class constructor that takes a base class instance as a parameter, and have this constructor perform the relevant initializations:

```
class DerivedClass: BaseClass
{
   public DerivedClass(BaseClass rhs)
   {
      // initialize object from the Base instance
   }
   // etc.
```

Boxing and Unboxing Casts

The previous discussion focused on casting between base and derived classes where both participants were reference types. Similar principles apply when casting value types, although in this case it is not possible to simply copy references—some copying of data must occur.

It is not, of course, possible to derive from structs or primitive value types. Casting between base and derived structs invariably means casting between a primitive type or a struct and `System.Object`. (Theoretically, it is possible to cast between a struct and `System.ValueType`, though it is hard to see why you would want to do this.)

The cast from any struct (or primitive type) to `object` is always available as an implicit cast—because it is a cast from a derived type to a base type—and is just the familiar process of boxing. For example, using the `Currency` struct:

```
Currency balance = new Currency(40,0);
object baseCopy = balance;
```

When this implicit cast is executed, the contents of `balance` are copied onto the heap into a boxed object, and the `baseCopy` object reference is set to this object. What actually happens behind the scenes is this: When you originally defined the `Currency` struct, the .NET Framework implicitly supplied another (hidden) class, a boxed `Currency` class, which contains all the same fields as the `Currency` struct but is a reference type, stored on the heap. This happens whenever you define a value type, whether it is a `struct` or an `enum`, and similar boxed reference types exist corresponding to all the primitive value types of `int`, `double`, `uint`, and so on. It is not possible, or necessary, to gain direct programmatic access to any of these boxed classes in source code, but they are the objects that are working behind the scenes whenever a value type is cast to `object`. When you implicitly cast `Currency` to `object`, a boxed `Currency` instance is instantiated and initialized with all the data from the `Currency` struct. In the preceding code, it is this boxed `Currency` instance to which `baseCopy` refers. By these means, it is possible for casting from derived to base type to work syntactically in the same way for value types as for reference types.

Casting the other way is known as unboxing. Like casting between a base reference type and a derived reference type, it is an explicit cast because an exception will be thrown if the object being cast is not of the correct type:

```
object derivedObject = new Currency(40,0);
object baseObject = new object();
Currency derivedCopy1 = (Currency)derivedObject;    // OK
Currency derivedCopy2 = (Currency)baseObject;        // Exception thrown
```

This code works in a way similar to the code presented earlier for reference types. Casting `derivedObject` to `Currency` works fine because `derivedObject` actually refers to a boxed `Currency` instance—the cast is performed by copying the fields out of the boxed `Currency` object into a new `Currency` struct. The second cast fails because `baseObject` does not refer to a boxed `Currency` object.

When using boxing and unboxing, it is important to understand that both processes actually copy the data into the new boxed or unboxed object. Hence, manipulations on the boxed object, for example, will not affect the contents of the original value type.

Multiple Casting

One thing you will have to watch for when you are defining casts is that if the C# compiler is presented with a situation in which no direct cast is available to perform a requested conversion, it will attempt to find a way of combining casts to do the conversion. For example, with the `Currency` struct, suppose the compiler encounters a few lines of code like this:

```
Currency balance = new Currency(10,50);
long amount = (long)balance;
double amountD = balance;
```

You first initialize a `Currency` instance, and then you attempt to convert it to a `long`. The trouble is that you haven't defined the cast to do that. However, this code still compiles successfully. What will happen is that the compiler will realize that you have defined an implicit cast to get from `Currency` to `float`, and the compiler already knows how to explicitly cast a `float` to a `long`. Hence, it will compile that line of code into IL code that converts `balance` first to a `float`, and then converts that result to a `long`. The same thing happens in the final line of the code, when you convert `balance` to a `double`. However, because the cast from `Currency` to `float` and the predefined cast from `float` to `double` are both implicit, you can write this conversion in your code as an implicit cast. If you prefer, you could also specify the casting route explicitly:

```
Currency balance = new Currency(10,50);
long amount = (long)(float)balance;
double amountD = (double)(float)balance;
```

However, in most cases, this would be seen as needlessly complicating your code. The following code, by contrast, produces a compilation error:

```
Currency balance = new Currency(10,50);
long amount = balance;
```

The reason is that the best match for the conversion that the compiler can find is still to convert first to `float` and then to `long`. The conversion from `float` to `long` needs to be specified explicitly, though.

Not all of this by itself should give you too much trouble. The rules are, after all, fairly intuitive and designed to prevent any data loss from occurring without the developer knowing about it. However, the problem is that if you are not careful when you define your casts, it is possible for the compiler to select a path that leads to unexpected results. For example, suppose that it occurs to someone else in the group writing the `Currency` struct that it would be useful to be able to convert a `uint` containing the total number of cents in an amount into a `Currency` (cents, not dollars, because the idea is not to lose the fractions of a dollar). Therefore, this cast might be written to try to achieve this:

```
public static implicit operator Currency (uint value)
{
    return new Currency(value/100u, (ushort)(value%100));
} // Do not do this!
```

Note the u after the first 100 in this code to ensure that `value/100u` is interpreted as a `uint`. If you had written `value/100`, the compiler would have interpreted this as an `int`, not a `uint`.

The comment `Do not do this!` is clearly noted in this code, and here is why: The following code snippet merely converts a `uint` containing 350 into a `Currency` and back again; but what do you think `bal2` will contain after executing this?

```
uint bal = 350;
Currency balance = bal;
uint bal2 = (uint)balance;
```

The answer is not 350 but 3! Moreover, it all follows logically. You convert 350 implicitly to a `Currency`, giving the result `balance.Dollars = 3`, `balance.Cents = 50`. Then the compiler does its usual figuring out of the best path for the conversion back. `Balance` ends up being implicitly converted to a `float` (value 3.5), and this is converted explicitly to a `uint` with value 3.

Of course, other instances exist in which converting to another data type and back again causes data loss. For example, converting a `float` containing 5.8 to an `int` and back to a `float` again will lose the fractional part, giving you a result of 5, but there is a slight difference in principle between losing the fractional part of a number and dividing an integer by more than 100. `Currency` has suddenly become a rather dangerous class that does strange things to integers!

The problem is that there is a conflict between how your casts interpret integers. The casts between `Currency` and `float` interpret an integer value of 1 as corresponding to one dollar, but the latest `uint`-to-`Currency` cast interprets this value as one cent. This is an example of very poor design. If you want your classes to be easy to use, you should ensure that all your casts behave in a way that is mutually compatible, in the sense that they intuitively give the same results. In this case, the solution is obviously to rewrite the `uint`-to-`Currency` cast so that it interprets an integer value of 1 as one dollar:

```
public static implicit operator Currency (uint value)
{
    return new Currency(value, 0);
}
```

Incidentally, you might wonder whether this new cast is necessary at all. The answer is that it could be useful. Without this cast, the only way for the compiler to carry out a `uint`-to-`Currency` conversion would be via a `float`. Converting directly is a lot more efficient in this case, so having this extra cast provides performance benefits, though you need to ensure that it provides the same result as via a `float`, which you have now done. In other situations, you may also find that separately defining casts for different predefined data types enables more conversions to be implicit rather than explicit, though that is not the case here.

A good test of whether your casts are compatible is to ask whether a conversion will give the same results (other than perhaps a loss of accuracy as in `float`-to-`int` conversions) regardless of which path it takes. The `Currency` class provides a good example of this. Consider this code:

```
Currency balance = new Currency(50, 35);
ulong bal = (ulong) balance;
```

At present, there is only one way that the compiler can achieve this conversion: by converting the `Currency` to a `float` implicitly, then to a `ulong` explicitly. The `float-to-ulong` conversion requires an explicit conversion, but that is fine because you have specified one here.

Suppose, however, that you then added another cast, to convert implicitly from a `Currency` to a `uint`. You will actually do this by modifying the `Currency` struct by adding the casts both to and from `uint`. This code is available as the `SimpleCurrency2` example:

```
public static implicit operator Currency (uint value)
{
    return new Currency(value, 0);
}

public static implicit operator uint (Currency value)
{
    return value.Dollars;
}
```

Now the compiler has another possible route to convert from `Currency` to `ulong`: to convert from `Currency` to `uint` implicitly, then to `ulong` implicitly. Which of these two routes will it take? C# has some precise rules about the best route for the compiler when there are several possibilities. (The rules are not covered in this book, but if you are interested in the details, see the MSDN documentation.) The best answer is that you should design your casts so that all routes give the same answer (other than possible loss of precision), in which case it doesn't really matter which one the compiler picks. (As it happens in this case, the compiler picks the `Currency-to-uint-to-ulong` route in preference to `Currency-to-float-to-ulong`.)

To test the `SimpleCurrency2` sample, add this code to the test code for `SimpleCurrency`:

```
try
{
    Currency balance = new Currency(50,35);

    Console.WriteLine(balance);
    Console.WriteLine("balance is " + balance);
    Console.WriteLine("balance is (using ToString()) " + balance.ToString());

    uint balance3 = (uint) balance;

    Console.WriteLine("Converting to uint gives " + balance3);
```

Running the sample now gives you these results:

SIMPLECURRENCY2

```
50
balance is $50.35
balance is (using ToString()) $50.35
Converting to uint gives 50
After converting to float, = 50.35
After converting back to Currency, = $50.34
Now attempt to convert out of range value of -$50.50 to a Currency:
Result is $4294967246.00
```

The output shows that the conversion to `uint` has been successful, though as expected, you have lost the cents part of the `Currency` in making this conversion. Casting a negative `float` to `Currency` has also produced the expected overflow exception now that the `float-to-Currency` cast itself defines a `checked` context.

However, the output also demonstrates one last potential problem that you need to be aware of when working with casts. The very first line of output does not display the balance correctly, displaying `50` instead of `$50.35`. Consider these lines:

```
Console.WriteLine(balance);
Console.WriteLine("balance is " + balance);
Console.WriteLine("balance is (using ToString()) " + balance.ToString());
```

Only the last two lines correctly display the Currency as a string. So what is going on? The problem here is that when you combine casts with method overloads, you get another source of unpredictability. We will look at these lines in reverse order.

The third Console.WriteLine() statement explicitly calls the Currency.ToString() method, ensuring that the Currency is displayed as a string. The second does not. However, the string literal "balance is" passed to Console.WriteLine() makes it clear to the compiler that the parameter is to be interpreted as a string. Hence, the Currency.ToString() method is called implicitly.

The very first Console.WriteLine() method, however, simply passes a raw Currency struct to Console .WriteLine(). Now, Console.WriteLine() has many overloads, but none of them takes a Currency struct. Therefore, the compiler will start fishing around to see what it can cast the Currency to in order to make it match up with one of the overloads of Console.WriteLine(). As it happens, one of the Console .WriteLine() overloads is designed to display uints quickly and efficiently, and it takes a uint as a parameter—you have now supplied a cast that converts Currency implicitly to uint.

In fact, Console.WriteLine() has another overload that takes a double as a parameter and displays the value of that double. If you look closely at the output from the first SimpleCurrency example, you will see that the first line of output displayed Currency as a double, using this overload. In that example, there wasn't a direct cast from Currency to uint, so the compiler picked Currency-to-float-to-double as its preferred way of matching up the available casts to the available Console.WriteLine() overloads. However, now that there is a direct cast to uint available in SimpleCurrency2, the compiler has opted for that route.

The upshot of this is that if you have a method call that takes several overloads and you attempt to pass it a parameter whose data type doesn't match any of the overloads exactly, then you are forcing the compiler to decide not only what casts to use to perform the data conversion, but also which overload, and hence which data conversion, to pick. The compiler always works logically and according to strict rules, but the results may not be what you expected. If there is any doubt, you are better off specifying which cast to use explicitly.

SUMMARY

This chapter looked at the standard operators provided by C#, described the mechanics of object equality, and examined how the compiler converts the standard data types from one to another. It also demonstrated how you can implement custom operator support on your data types using operator overloads. Finally, you looked at a special type of operator overload, the cast operator, which enables you to specify how instances of your types are converted to other data types.

Delegates, Lambdas, and Events

WHAT'S IN THIS CHAPTER?

- ➤ Delegates
- ➤ Lambda expressions
- ➤ Closures
- ➤ Events
- ➤ Weak Events

WROX.COM CODE DOWNLOADS FOR THIS CHAPTER

The wrox.com code downloads for this chapter are found at `http://www.wrox.com/remtitle` `.cgi?isbn=1118314425` on the Download Code tab. The code for this chapter is divided into the following major examples:

- ➤ Simple Delegates
- ➤ Bubble Sorter
- ➤ Lambda Expressions
- ➤ Events Sample
- ➤ Weak Events

REFERENCING METHODS

Delegates are the .NET variant of addresses to methods. Compare this to C++, where a function pointer is nothing more than a pointer to a memory location that is not type-safe. You have no idea what a pointer is really pointing to, and items such as parameters and return types are not known.

This is completely different with .NET; delegates are type-safe classes that define the return types and types of parameters. The delegate class not only contains a reference to a method, but can hold references to multiple methods.

Lambda expressions are directly related to delegates. When the parameter is a delegate type, you can use a lambda expression to implement a method that's referenced from the delegate.

This chapter explains the basics of delegates and lambda expressions, and shows you how to implement methods called by delegates with lambda expressions. It also demonstrates how .NET uses delegates as the means of implementing events.

DELEGATES

Delegates exist for situations in which you want to pass methods around to other methods. To see what that means, consider this line of code:

```
int i = int.Parse("99");
```

You are so used to passing data to methods as parameters, as in this example, that you don't consciously think about it, so the idea of passing methods around instead of data might sound a little strange. However, sometimes you have a method that does something, and rather than operate on data, the method might need to do something that involves invoking another method. To complicate things further, you do not know at compile time what this second method is. That information is available only at runtime and hence will need to be passed in as a parameter to the first method. That might sound confusing, but it should become clearer with a couple of examples:

➤ **Starting threads and tasks** — It is possible in C# to tell the computer to start a new sequence of execution in parallel with what it is currently doing. Such a sequence is known as a thread, and starting one is done using the `Start` method on an instance of one of the base classes, `System` `.Threading.Thread`. If you tell the computer to start a new sequence of execution, you have to tell it where to start that sequence; that is, you have to supply the details of a method in which execution can start. In other words, the constructor of the `Thread` class takes a parameter that defines the method to be invoked by the thread.

➤ **Generic library classes** — Many libraries contain code to perform various standard tasks. It is usually possible for these libraries to be self-contained, in the sense that you know when you write to the library exactly how the task must be performed. However, sometimes the task contains a subtask, which only the individual client code that uses the library knows how to perform. For example, say that you want to write a class that takes an array of objects and sorts them in ascending order. Part of the sorting process involves repeatedly taking two of the objects in the array and comparing them to see which one should come first. If you want to make the class capable of sorting arrays of any object, there is no way that it can tell in advance how to do this comparison. The client code that hands your class the array of objects must also tell your class how to do this comparison for the particular objects it wants sorted. The client code has to pass your class details of an appropriate method that can be called to do the comparison.

➤ **Events** — The general idea here is that often you have code that needs to be informed when some event takes place. GUI programming is full of situations similar to this. When the event is raised, the runtime needs to know what method should be executed. This is done by passing the method that handles the event as a parameter to a delegate. This is discussed later in this chapter.

In C and C++, you can just take the address of a function and pass it as a parameter. There's no type safety with C. You can pass any function to a method where a function pointer is required. Unfortunately, this direct approach not only causes some problems with type safety, but also neglects the fact that when you are doing object-oriented programming, methods rarely exist in isolation, but usually need to be associated with a class instance before they can be called. Because of these problems, the .NET Framework does not syntactically permit this direct approach. Instead, if you want to pass methods around, you have to wrap the details of the method in a new kind of object, a delegate. Delegates, quite simply, are a special type of object — special in the sense that, whereas all the objects defined up to now contain data, a delegate contains the address of a method, or the address of multiple methods.

Declaring Delegates

When you want to use a class in C#, you do so in two stages. First, you need to define the class — that is, you need to tell the compiler what fields and methods make up the class. Then (unless you are using only static methods), you instantiate an object of that class. With delegates it is the same process. You start by declaring the delegates you want to use. Declaring delegates means telling the compiler what kind of method a delegate of that type will represent. Then, you have to create one or more instances of that delegate. Behind the scenes, the compiler creates a class that represents the delegate.

The syntax for declaring delegates looks like this:

```
delegate void IntMethodInvoker(int x);
```

This declares a delegate called `IntMethodInvoker`, and indicates that each instance of this delegate can hold a reference to a method that takes one `int` parameter and returns `void`. The crucial point to understand about delegates is that they are type-safe. When you define the delegate, you have to provide full details about the signature and the return type of the method that it represents.

> **NOTE** *One good way to understand delegates is to think of a delegate as something that gives a name to a method signature and the return type.*

Suppose that you want to define a delegate called `TwoLongsOp` that will represent a method that takes two `longs` as its parameters and returns a `double`. You could do so like this:

```
delegate double TwoLongsOp(long first, long second);
```

Or, to define a delegate that will represent a method that takes no parameters and returns a `string`, you might write this:

```
delegate string GetAString();
```

The syntax is similar to that for a method definition, except there is no method body and the definition is prefixed with the keyword `delegate`. Because what you are doing here is basically defining a new class, you can define a delegate in any of the same places that you would define a class — that is to say, either inside another class, outside of any class, or in a namespace as a top-level object. Depending on how visible you want your definition to be, and the scope of the delegate, you can apply any of the normal access modifiers to delegate definitions — `public`, `private`, `protected`, and so on:

> **NOTE** *We really mean what we say when we describe defining a delegate as defining a new class. Delegates are implemented as classes derived from the class* `System` `.MulticastDelegate`, *which is derived from the base class* `System.Delegate`. *The C# compiler is aware of this class and uses its delegate syntax to hide the details of the operation of this class. This is another good example of how C# works in conjunction with the base classes to make programming as easy as possible.*

```
public delegate string GetAString();
```

After you have defined a delegate, you can create an instance of it so that you can use it to store details about a particular method.

> **NOTE** *There is an unfortunate problem with terminology here. When you are talking about classes, there are two distinct terms — class, which indicates the broader definition, and object, which means an instance of the class. Unfortunately, with delegates there is only the one term; delegate can refer to both the class and the object. When you create an instance of a delegate, what you have created is also referred to as a delegate. You need to be aware of the context to know which meaning is being used when we talk about delegates.*

Using Delegates

The following code snippet demonstrates the use of a delegate. It is a rather long-winded way of calling the `ToString` method on an `int` (code file `GetAStringDemo/Program.cs`):

```
private delegate string GetAString();

static void Main()
    {
      int x = 40;
      GetAString firstStringMethod = new GetAString(x.ToString);
      Console.WriteLine("String is {0}", firstStringMethod());
      // With firstStringMethod initialized to x.ToString(),
      // the above statement is equivalent to saying
      // Console.WriteLine("String is {0}", x.ToString());
    }
```

This code instantiates a delegate of type `GetAString` and initializes it so it refers to the `ToString` method of the integer variable x. Delegates in C# always syntactically take a one-parameter constructor, the parameter being the method to which the delegate refers. This method must match the signature with which you originally defined the delegate. In this case, you would get a compilation error if you tried to initialize the variable `firstStringMethod` with any method that did not take any parameters and return a string. Notice that because `int.ToString` is an instance method (as opposed to a static one), you need to specify the instance (x) as well as the name of the method to initialize the delegate properly.

The next line actually uses the delegate to display the string. In any code, supplying the name of a delegate instance, followed by parentheses containing any parameters, has exactly the same effect as calling the method wrapped by the delegate. Hence, in the preceding code snippet, the `Console.WriteLine` statement is completely equivalent to the commented-out line.

In fact, supplying parentheses to the delegate instance is the same as invoking the `Invoke` method of the delegate class. Because `firstStringMethod` is a variable of a delegate type, the C# compiler replaces `firstStringMethod` with `firstStringMethod.Invoke`:

```
firstStringMethod();
firstStringMethod.Invoke();
```

For less typing, at every place where a delegate instance is needed, you can just pass the name of the address. This is known by the term *delegate inference*. This C# feature works as long as the compiler can resolve the delegate instance to a specific type. The example initialized the variable firstStringMethod of type GetAString with a new instance of the delegate GetAString:

```
GetAString firstStringMethod = new GetAString(x.ToString);
```

You can write the same just by passing the method name with the variable x to the variable firstStringMethod:

```
GetAString firstStringMethod = x.ToString;
```

The code that is created by the C# compiler is the same. The compiler detects that a delegate type is required with firstStringMethod, so it creates an instance of the delegate type GetAString and passes the address of the method with the object x to the constructor.

> **NOTE** *Be aware that you can't type the brackets to the method name as* x.ToString *and pass it to the delegate variable. This would be an invocation of the method. The invocation of* x.ToString *returns a string object that can't be assigned to the delegate variable. You can only assign the address of a method to the delegate variable.*

Delegate inference can be used anywhere a delegate instance is required. Delegate inference can also be used with events because events are based on delegates (as you will see later in this chapter).

One feature of delegates is that they are type-safe to the extent that they ensure that the signature of the method being called is correct. However, interestingly, they don't care what type of object the method is being called against or even whether the method is a static method or an instance method.

> **NOTE** *An instance of a given delegate can refer to any instance or static method on any object of any type, provided that the signature of the method matches the signature of the delegate.*

To demonstrate this, the following example expands the previous code snippet so that it uses the firstStringMethod delegate to call a couple of other methods on another object — an instance method and a static method. For this, you use the Currency struct. The Currency struct has its own overload of ToString and a static method with the same signature to GetCurrencyUnit. This way, the same delegate variable can be used to invoke these methods (code file GetAStringDemo/Currency.cs):

```
struct Currency
{
  public uint Dollars;
  public ushort Cents;

  public Currency(uint dollars, ushort cents)
  {
    this.Dollars = dollars;
    this.Cents = cents;
  }

  public override string ToString()
  {
    return string.Format("${0}.{1,2:00}", Dollars,Cents);
  }
```

```
public static string GetCurrencyUnit()
{
  return "Dollar";
}

public static explicit operator Currency (float value)
{
  checked
  {
    uint dollars = (uint)value;
    ushort cents = (ushort)((value - dollars) * 100);
    return new Currency(dollars, cents);
  }
}

public static implicit operator float (Currency value)
{
  return value.Dollars + (value.Cents / 100.0f);
}

public static implicit operator Currency (uint value)
{
  return new Currency(value, 0);
}

public static implicit operator uint (Currency value)
{
  return value.Dollars;
}
}
```

Now you can use the GetAString instance as follows:

```
private delegate string GetAString();

static void Main()
{
  int x = 40;
  GetAString firstStringMethod = x.ToString;
  Console.WriteLine("String is {0}", firstStringMethod());

  Currency balance = new Currency(34, 50);

  // firstStringMethod references an instance method
  firstStringMethod = balance.ToString;
  Console.WriteLine("String is {0}", firstStringMethod());

  // firstStringMethod references a static method
  firstStringMethod = new GetAString(Currency.GetCurrencyUnit);
  Console.WriteLine("String is {0}", firstStringMethod());
}
```

This code shows how you can call a method via a delegate and subsequently reassign the delegate to refer to different methods on different instances of classes, even static methods or methods against instances of different types of class, provided that the signature of each method matches the delegate definition.

When you run the application, you get the output from the different methods that are referenced by the delegate:

```
String is 40
String is $34.50
String is Dollar
```

However, you still haven't seen the process of actually passing a delegate to another method. Nor has this actually achieved anything particularly useful yet. It is possible to call the `ToString` method of `int` and `Currency` objects in a much more straightforward way than using delegates. Unfortunately, the nature of delegates requires a fairly complex example before you can really appreciate their usefulness. The next section presents two delegate examples. The first one simply uses delegates to call a couple of different operations. It illustrates how to pass delegates to methods and how you can use arrays of delegates — although arguably it still doesn't do much that you couldn't do a lot more simply without delegates. The second, much more complex, example presents a `BubbleSorter` class, which implements a method to sort arrays of objects into ascending order. This class would be difficult to write without using delegates.

Simple Delegate Example

This example defines a `MathOperations` class that uses a couple of static methods to perform two operations on doubles. Then you use delegates to invoke these methods. The math class looks like this:

```
class MathOperations
{
  public static double MultiplyByTwo(double value)
  {
    return value * 2;
  }

  public static double Square(double value)
  {
    return value * value;
  }
}
```

You invokethese methods as follows (code file `SimpleDelegate/Program.cs`):

```
using System;

namespace Wrox.ProCSharp.Delegates
{
  delegate double DoubleOp(double x);

  class Program
  {
    static void Main()
    {
      DoubleOp[] operations =
      {
        MathOperations.MultiplyByTwo,
        MathOperations.Square
      };

      for (int i=0; i < operations.Length; i++)
      {
        Console.WriteLine("Using operations[{0}]:", i);
        ProcessAndDisplayNumber(operations[i], 2.0);
        ProcessAndDisplayNumber(operations[i], 7.94);
        ProcessAndDisplayNumber(operations[i], 1.414);
        Console.WriteLine();
```

```
        }
      }

      static void ProcessAndDisplayNumber(DoubleOp action, double value)
      {
        double result = action(value);
        Console.WriteLine("Value is {0}, result of operation is {1}",
                          value, result);
      }
    }
  }
```

In this code, you instantiate an array of `DoubleOp` delegates (remember that after you have defined a delegate class, you can basically instantiate instances just as you can with normal classes, so putting some into an array is no problem). Each element of the array is initialized to refer to a different operation implemented by the `MathOperations` class. Then, you loop through the array, applying each operation to three different values. This illustrates one way of using delegates — to group methods together into an array so that you can call several methods in a loop.

The key lines in this code are the ones in which you actually pass each delegate to the `ProcessAndDisplayNumber` method, such as here:

```
ProcessAndDisplayNumber(operations[i], 2.0);
```

The preceding passes in the name of a delegate but without any parameters. Given that `operations[i]` is a delegate, syntactically:

➤   `operations[i]` means the *delegate* (that is, the method represented by the delegate)

➤   `operations[i](2.0)` means *actually call this method, passing in the value in parentheses*

The `ProcessAndDisplayNumber` method is defined to take a delegate as its first parameter:

```
static void ProcessAndDisplayNumber(DoubleOp action, double value)
```

Then, when in this method, you call:

```
double result = action(value);
```

This actually causes the method that is wrapped up by the `action` delegate instance to be called and its return result stored in `Result`. Running this example gives you the following:

```
SimpleDelegate
Using operations[0]:
Value is 2, result of operation is 4
Value is 7.94, result of operation is 15.88
Value is 1.414, result of operation is 2.828

Using operations[1]:
Value is 2, result of operation is 4
Value is 7.94, result of operation is 63.0436
Value is 1.414, result of operation is 1.999396
```

Action<T> and Func<T> Delegates

Instead of defining a new delegate type with every parameter and return type, you can use the `Action<T>` and `Func<T>` delegates. The generic `Action<T>` delegate is meant to reference a method with `void` return. This delegate class exists in different variants so that you can pass up to 16 different parameter types. The `Action` class without the generic parameter is for calling methods without parameters. `Action<in T>` is for calling a method with one parameter; Action<in T1, in T2> for a method with two parameters; and Action<in T1, in T2, in T3, in T4, in T5, in T6, in T7, in T8> for a method with eight parameters.

The Func<T> delegates can be used in a similar manner. Func<T> allows you to invoke methods with a return type. Similar to Action<T>, Func<T> is defined in different variants to pass up to 16 parameter types and a return type. Func<out TResult> is the delegate type to invoke a method with a return type and without parameters. Func<in T, out TResult> is for a method with one parameter, and Func<in T1, in T2, in T3, in T4, out TResult> is for a method with four parameters.

The example in the preceding section declared a delegate with a double parameter and a double return type:

```
delegate double DoubleOp(double x);
```

Instead of declaring the custom delegate DoubleOp you can use the Func<in T, out TResult> delegate. You can declare a variable of the delegate type, or as shown here, an array of the delegate type:

```
Func<double, double>[] operations =
{
  MathOperations.MultiplyByTwo,
  MathOperations.Square
};
```

and use it with the ProcessAndDisplayNumber() method as a parameter:

```
static void ProcessAndDisplayNumber(Func<double, double> action,
                                    double value)
{
  double result = action(value);
  Console.WriteLine("Value is {0}, result of operation is {1}",
                    value, result);
}
```

BubbleSorter Example

You are now ready for an example that shows the real usefulness of delegates. You are going to write a class called BubbleSorter. This class implements a static method, Sort, which takes as its first parameter an array of objects, and rearranges this array into ascending order. For example, if you were to pass it this array of ints, {0, 5, 6, 2, 1}, it would rearrange this array into {0, 1, 2, 5, 6}.

The bubble-sorting algorithm is a well-known and very simple way to sort numbers. It is best suited to small sets of numbers, because for larger sets of numbers (more than about 10), far more efficient algorithms are available. It works by repeatedly looping through the array, comparing each pair of numbers and, if necessary, swapping them, so that the largest numbers progressively move to the end of the array. For sorting ints, a method to do a bubble sort might look similar to this:

```
bool swapped = true;
do
{
  swapped = false;
  for (int i = 0; i < sortArray.Length - 1; i++)
  {
    if (sortArray[i] > sortArray[i+1])) // problem with this test
    {
      int temp = sortArray[i];
      sortArray[i] = sortArray[i + 1];
      sortArray[i + 1] = temp;
      swapped = true;
    }
  }
} while (swapped);
```

This is all very well for ints, but you want your Sort method to be able to sort any object. In other words, if some client code hands you an array of Currency structs or any other class or struct that it may have defined, you need to be able to sort the array. This presents a problem with the line if(sortArray[i] < sortArray[i+1]) in the preceding code, because that requires you to compare two objects on the array to determine which one is greater. You can do that for ints, but how do you do it for a new class that doesn't implement the < operator? The answer is that the client code that knows about the class will have to pass in a delegate wrapping a method that does the comparison. Also, instead of using an int type for the *temp* variable, a generic Sort method can be implemented using a generic type.

With a generic Sort<T> method accepting type T, a comparison method is needed that has two parameters of type T and a return type of bool for the if comparison. This method can be referenced from a Func<T1, T2, TResult> delegate, where T1 and T2 are the same type: Func<T, T, bool>.

This way, you give your Sort<T> method the following signature:

```
static public void Sort<T>(IList<T> sortArray, Func<T, T, bool> comparison)
```

The documentation for this method states that comparison must refer to a method that takes two arguments, and returns true if the value of the first argument is *smaller than* the second one.

Now you are all set. Here's the definition for the BubbleSorter class (code file BubbleSorter/BubbleSorter.cs):

```
class BubbleSorter
{
  static public void Sort<T>(IList<T> sortArray, Func<T, T, bool> comparison)
  {
    bool swapped = true;
    do
    {
      swapped = false;
      for (int i = 0; i < sortArray.Count − 1; i++)
      {
        if (comparison(sortArray[i+1], sortArray[i]))
        {
          T temp = sortArray[i];
          sortArray[i] = sortArray[i + 1];
          sortArray[i + 1] = temp;
          swapped = true;
        }
      }
    } while (swapped);
  }
}
```

To use this class, you need to define another class, which you can use to set up an array that needs sorting. For this example, assume that the Mortimer Phones mobile phone company has a list of employees and wants them sorted according to salary. Each employee is represented by an instance of a class, Employee, which looks similar to this (code file BubbleSorter/Employee.cs):

```
class Employee
{
  public Employee(string name, decimal salary)
  {
    this.Name = name;
    this.Salary = salary;
  }

  public string Name { get; private set; }
  public decimal Salary { get; private set; }
```

```
    public override string ToString()
    {
      return string.Format("{0}, {1:C}", Name, Salary);
    }

    public static bool CompareSalary(Employee e1, Employee e2)
    {
      return e1.Salary < e2.Salary;
    }
  }
```

Note that to match the signature of the `Func<T, T, bool>` delegate, you have to define `CompareSalary` in this class as taking two `Employee` references and returning a Boolean. In the implementation, the comparison based on salary is performed.

Now you are ready to write some client code to request a sort (code file `BubbleSorter/Program.cs`):

```
using System;

namespace Wrox.ProCSharp.Delegates
{
  class Program
  {
    static void Main()
    {
      Employee[] employees =
      {
        new Employee("Bugs Bunny", 20000),
        new Employee("Elmer Fudd", 10000),
        new Employee("Daffy Duck", 25000),
        new Employee("Wile Coyote", 1000000.38m),
        new Employee("Foghorn Leghorn", 23000),
        new Employee("RoadRunner", 50000)
      };

      BubbleSorter.Sort(employees, Employee.CompareSalary);

      foreach (var employee in employees)
      {
        Console.WriteLine(employee);
      }
    }
  }
}
```

Running this code shows that the `Employees` are correctly sorted according to salary:

```
BubbleSorter
Elmer Fudd, $10,000.00
Bugs Bunny, $20,000.00
Foghorn Leghorn, $23,000.00
Daffy Duck, $25,000.00
RoadRunner, $50,000.00
Wile Coyote, $1,000,000.38
```

Multicast Delegates

So far, each of the delegates you have used wraps just one method call. Calling the delegate amounts to calling that method. If you want to call more than one method, you need to make an explicit call through a delegate more than once. However, it is possible for a delegate to wrap more than one method. Such a delegate is known as a *multicast delegate.* When a multicast delegate is called, it successively calls each method in order. For this to work, the delegate signature should return a void; otherwise, you would only get the result of the last method invoked by the delegate.

With a void return type, the Action<double> delegate can be used (code file MulticastDelegates/Program.cs):

```
class Program
{
  static void Main()
  {
    Action<double> operations = MathOperations.MultiplyByTwo;
    operations += MathOperations.Square;
```

In the earlier example, you wanted to store references to two methods, so you instantiated an array of delegates. Here, you simply add both operations into the same multicast delegate. Multicast delegates recognize the operators + and +=. Alternatively, you can expand the last two lines of the preceding code, as in this snippet:

```
Action<double> operation1 = MathOperations.MultiplyByTwo;
Action<double> operation2 = MathOperations.Square;
Action<double> operations = operation1 + operation2;
```

Multicast delegates also recognize the operators – and -= to remove method calls from the delegate.

> **NOTE** *In terms of what's going on under the hood, a multicast delegate is a class derived from* System.MulticastDelegate, *which in turn is derived from* System .Delegate. System.MulticastDelegate, *and has additional members to allow the chaining of method calls into a list.*

To illustrate the use of multicast delegates, the following code recasts the SimpleDelegate example into a new example, MulticastDelegate. Because you now need the delegate to refer to methods that return void, you have to rewrite the methods in the MathOperations class so they display their results instead of returning them:

```
class MathOperations
{
  public static void MultiplyByTwo(double value)
  {
    double result = value * 2;
    Console.WriteLine("Multiplying by 2: {0} gives {1}", value, result);
  }

  public static void Square(double value)
  {
    double result = value * value;
    Console.WriteLine("Squaring: {0} gives {1}", value, result);
  }
}
```

To accommodate this change, you also have to rewrite ProcessAndDisplayNumber:

```
static void ProcessAndDisplayNumber(Action<double> action, double value)
{
  Console.WriteLine();
```

```
        Console.WriteLine("ProcessAndDisplayNumber called with value = {0}",
                          value);
        action(value);
    }
```

Now you can try out your multicast delegate:

```
    static void Main()
    {
        Action<double> operations = MathOperations.MultiplyByTwo;
        operations += MathOperations.Square;

        ProcessAndDisplayNumber(operations, 2.0);
        ProcessAndDisplayNumber(operations, 7.94);
        ProcessAndDisplayNumber(operations, 1.414);
        Console.WriteLine();
    }
```

Each time `ProcessAndDisplayNumber` is called now, it will display a message saying that it has been called. Then the following statement will cause each of the method calls in the `action` delegate instance to be called in succession:

```
        action(value);
```

Running the preceding code produces this result:

```
    MulticastDelegate

    ProcessAndDisplayNumber called with value = 2
    Multiplying by 2: 2 gives 4
    Squaring: 2 gives 4

    ProcessAndDisplayNumber called with value = 7.94
    Multiplying by 2: 7.94 gives 15.88
    Squaring: 7.94 gives 63.0436

    ProcessAndDisplayNumber called with value = 1.414
    Multiplying by 2: 1.414 gives 2.828
    Squaring: 1.414 gives 1.999396
```

If you are using multicast delegates, be aware that the order in which methods chained to the same delegate will be called is formally undefined. Therefore, avoid writing code that relies on such methods being called in any particular order.

Invoking multiple methods by one delegate might cause an even bigger problem. The multicast delegate contains a collection of delegates to invoke one after the other. If one of the methods invoked by a delegate throws an exception, the complete iteration stops. Consider the following `MulticastIteration` example. Here, the simple delegate `Action` that returns `void` without arguments is used. This delegate is meant to invoke the methods `One` and `Two`, which fulfill the parameter and return type requirements of the delegate. Be aware that method `One` throws an exception (code file `MulticastDelegateWithIteration/Program.cs`):

```
    using System;

    namespace Wrox.ProCSharp.Delegates
    {
      class Program
      {
        static void One()
        {
```

```
      Console.WriteLine("One");
      throw new Exception("Error in one");
   }

   static void Two()
   {
      Console.WriteLine("Two");
   }
```

In the `Main` method, delegate `d1` is created to reference method `One`; next, the address of method `Two` is added to the same delegate. `d1` is invoked to call both methods. The exception is caught in a `try`/`catch` block:

```
   static void Main()
   {
      Action d1 = One;
      d1 += Two;

      try
      {
         d1();
      }
      catch (Exception)
      {
         Console.WriteLine("Exception caught");
      }
   }
}
```

Only the first method is invoked by the delegate. Because the first method throws an exception, iterating the delegates stops here and method `Two()` is never invoked. The result might differ because the order of calling the methods is not defined:

```
One
Exception Caught
```

> **NOTE** *Errors and exceptions are explained in detail in Chapter 16, "Errors and Exceptions."*

In such a scenario, you can avoid the problem by iterating the list on your own. The `Delegate` class defines the method `GetInvocationList` that returns an array of `Delegate` objects. You can now use this delegate to invoke the methods associated with them directly, catch exceptions, and continue with the next iteration:

```
   static void Main()
   {
      Action d1 = One;
      d1 += Two;

      Delegate[] delegates = d1.GetInvocationList();
      foreach (Action d in delegates)
      {
         try
         {
            d();
```

```
        }
        catch (Exception)
        {
          Console.WriteLine("Exception caught");
        }
      }
    }
```

When you run the application with the code changes, you can see that the iteration continues with the next method after the exception is caught:

```
One
Exception caught
Two
```

Anonymous Methods

Up to this point, a method must already exist for the delegate to work (that is, the delegate is defined with the same signature as the method(s) it will be used with). However, there is another way to use delegates — with *anonymous methods*. An anonymous method is a block of code that is used as the parameter for the delegate.

The syntax for defining a delegate with an anonymous method doesn't change. It's when the delegate is instantiated that things change. The following very simple console application shows how using an anonymous method can work (code file AnonymousMethods/Program.cs):

```
using System;

namespace Wrox.ProCSharp.Delegates
{
  class Program
  {
    static void Main()
    {
      string mid = ", middle part,";

      Func<string, string> anonDel = delegate(string param)
      {
        param += mid;
        param += " and this was added to the string.";
        return param;
      };
      Console.WriteLine(anonDel("Start of string"));

    }
  }
}
```

The delegate Func<string, string> takes a single string parameter and returns a string. anonDel is a variable of this delegate type. Instead of assigning the name of a method to this variable, a simple block of code is used, prefixed by the delegate keyword, followed by a string parameter.

As you can see, the block of code uses a method-level string variable, mid, which is defined outside of the anonymous method and adds it to the parameter that was passed in. The code then returns the string value. When the delegate is called, a string is passed in as the parameter and the returned string is output to the console.

The benefit of using anonymous methods is that it reduces the amount of code you have to write. You don't need to define a method just to use it with a delegate. This becomes evident when defining the delegate for an event (events are discussed later in this chapter), and it helps reduce the complexity of code, especially where several events are defined. With anonymous methods, the code does not perform faster. The compiler still defines a method; the method just has an automatically assigned name that you don't need to know.

A couple of rules must be followed when using anonymous methods. You can't have a jump statement (break, goto, or continue) in an anonymous method that has a target outside of the anonymous method. The reverse is also true — a jump statement outside the anonymous method cannot have a target inside the anonymous method.

Unsafe code cannot be accessed inside an anonymous method, and the ref and out parameters that are used outside of the anonymous method cannot be accessed. Other variables defined outside of the anonymous method can be used.

If you have to write the same functionality more than once, don't use anonymous methods. In this case, instead of duplicating the code, write a named method. You only have to write it once and reference it by its name.

Beginning with C# 3.0, you can use lambda expressions instead of writing anonymous methods.

LAMBDA EXPRESSIONS

Since C# 3.0, you can use a different syntax for assigning code implementation to delegates: *lambda expressions*. Lambda expressions can be used whenever you have a delegate parameter type. The previous example using anonymous methods is modified here to use a lambda expression.

> **NOTE** *The syntax of lambda expressions is simpler than the syntax of anonymous methods. In a case where a method to be invoked has parameters and you don't need the parameters, the syntax of anonymous methods is simpler, as you don't need to supply parameters in that case.*

```csharp
using System;

namespace Wrox.ProCSharp.Delegates
{
  class Program
  {
    static void Main()
    {
      string mid = ", middle part,";

      Func<string, string> lambda = param =>
        {
          param += mid;
          param += " and this was added to the string.";
          return param;
        };

      Console.WriteLine(lambda("Start of string"));
    }
  }
}
```

The left side of the lambda operator, =>, lists the parameters needed. The right side following the lambda operator defines the implementation of the method assigned to the variable lambda.

Parameters

With lambda expressions there are several ways to define parameters. If there's only one parameter, just the name of the parameter is enough. The following lambda expression uses the parameter named *s*. Because the delegate type defines a string parameter, *s* is of type string. The implementation invokes the String .Format method to return a string that is finally written to the console when the delegate is invoked: change uppercase TEST:

```
Func<string, string> oneParam = s =>
    String.Format("change uppercase {0}", s.ToUpper());
Console.WriteLine(oneParam("test"));
```

If a delegate uses more than one parameter, you can combine the parameter names inside brackets. Here, the parameters *x* and *y* are of type double as defined by the Func<double, double, double> delegate:

```
Func<double, double, double> twoParams = (x, y) => x * y;
Console.WriteLine(twoParams(3, 2));
```

For convenience, you can add the parameter types to the variable names inside the brackets. If the compiler can't match an overloaded version, using parameter types can help resolve the matching delegate:

```
Func<double, double, double> twoParamsWithTypes = (double x, double y) => x * y;
Console.WriteLine(twoParamsWithTypes(4, 2));
```

Multiple Code Lines

If the lambda expression consists of a single statement, a method block with curly brackets and a return statement are not needed. There's an implicit return added by the compiler:

```
Func<double, double> square = x => x * x;
```

It's completely legal to add curly brackets, a return statement, and semicolons. Usually it's just easier to read without them:

```
Func<double, double> square = x =>
{
  return x * x;
}
```

However, if you need multiple statements in the implementation of the lambda expression, curly brackets and the return statement are required:

```
Func<string, string> lambda = param =>
{
  param += mid;
  param += " and this was added to the string.";
  return param;
};
```

Closures

With lambda expressions you can access variables outside the block of the lambda expression. This is known by the term *closure*. Closures are a great feature but they can also be very dangerous if not used correctly.

In the following example here, a lambda expression of type `Func<int, int>` requires one `int` parameter and returns an `int`. The parameter for the lambda expression is defined with the variable x. The implementation also accesses the variable `someVal`, which is outside the lambda expression. As long as you do not assume that the lambda expression creates a new method that is used later when `f` is invoked, this might not look confusing at all. Looking at this code block, the returned value calling `f` should be the value from x plus 5, but this might not be the case:

```
int someVal = 5;
Func<int, int> f = x => x + someVal;
```

Assuming the variable `someVal` is later changed, and then the lambda expression invoked, the new value of `someVal` is used. The result here invoking `f(3)` is `10`:

```
someVal = 7;
Console.WriteLine(f(3));
```

In particular, when the lambda expression is invoked by a separate thread, you might not know when the invocation happened and thus what value the outside variable currently has.

Now you might wonder how it is possible at all to access variables outside of the lambda expression from within the lambda expression. To understand this, consider what the compiler does when you define a lambda expression. With the lambda expression x => x + someVal, the compiler creates an anonymous class that has a constructor to pass the outer variable. The constructor depends on how many variables you access from the outside. With this simple example, the constructor accepts an `int`. The anonymous class contains an anonymous method that has the implementation as defined by the lambda expression, with the parameters and return type:

```
public class AnonymousClass
{
  private int someVal;
  public AnonymousClass(int someVal)
  {
    this.someVal = someVal;
  }
  public int AnonymousMethod(int x)
  {
    return x + someVal;
  }
}
```

Using the lambda expression and invoking the method creates an instance of the anonymous class and passes the value of the variable from the time when the call is made.

Closures with Foreach Statements

`foreach` statements have an important change with C# 5 in regard to closures. In the following example, first a list named `values` is filled with the values 10, 20, and 30. The `funcs` variable references a generic list in which each object references a delegate of type `Func<int>`. The elements of the `funcs` list are added within the first `foreach` statement. The function added to the items is defined with a lambda expression. This lambda expression makes use of the variable `val` that is declared outside of the lambda as a loop variable with the `foreach` statement. The second `foreach` statement iterates through the list of `funcs` to invoke every method that is referenced:

```
var values = new List<int>() { 10, 20, 30 };
var funcs = new List<Func<int>>();

foreach (var val in values)
```

```
    {
      funcs.Add(() => val);
    }
    foreach (var f in funcs)
    {
      Console.WriteLine((f()));
    }
```

The outcome of this code snippet changed with C# 5. Using C# 4 or earlier versions of the compiler, 30 is written to the console three times. Using a closure with the first `foreach` loop, the functions that are created don't take the value of the `val` variable during the time of the iteration, but instead when the functions are invoked. As you've already seen in Chapter 6, "Arrays and Tuples," the compiler creates a `while` loop out from the `foreach` statement. With C# 4 the compiler defines the loop variable outside of the while loop and reuses it with every iteration. Thus, at the end of the loop the variable has the value from the last iteration. To get 10, 20, 30 with the result of the code using C# 4, it's necessary to change the code to use a local variable that is passed to the lambda expression. Here, a different value is retained with every iteration.

```
    var values = new List<int>() { 10, 20, 30 };
    var funcs = new List<Func<int>>();

    foreach (var val in values)
    {
      var v = val;
      funcs.Add(() => v);
    }
    foreach (var f in funcs)
    {
      Console.WriteLine((f()));
    }
```

Using C# 5 the code change to have a local variable is no longer necessary. C# now creates the loop variable differently locally within the block of the while loop and thus the value is retained automatically. You just need to be aware of these different behaviors of C# 4 and 5.

> **NOTE** *Lambda expressions can be used anywhere the type is a delegate. Another use of lambda expressions is when the type is* Expression *or* Expression<T>. *, in which case the compiler creates an expression tree. This feature is discussed in Chapter 11, "Language Integrated Query."*

EVENTS

Events are based on delegates and offer a publish/subscribe mechanism to delegates. You can find events everywhere across the framework. In Windows applications, the `Button` class offers the `Click` event. This type of event is a delegate. A handler method that is invoked when the `Click` event is fired needs to be defined, with the parameters as defined by the delegate type.

In the code example shown in this section, events are used to connect `CarDealer` and `Consumer` classes. The `CarDealer` offers an event when a new car arrives. The `Consumer` class subscribes to the event to be informed when a new car arrives.

Event Publisher

We start with a `CarDealer` class that offers a subscription based on events. `CarDealer` defines the event named `NewCarInfo` of type `EventHandler<CarInfoEventArgs>` with the `event` keyword. Inside the method `NewCar`, the event `NewCarInfo` is fired by invoking the method `RaiseNewCarInfo`.

The implementation of this method verifies if the delegate is not null, and raises the event (code file EventSample/CarDealer.cs):

```csharp
using System;

namespace Wrox.ProCSharp.Delegates
{
  public class CarInfoEventArgs: EventArgs
  {
    public CarInfoEventArgs(string car)
    {
      this.Car = car;
    }

    public string Car { get; private set; }
  }

  public class CarDealer
  {
    public event EventHandler<CarInfoEventArgs> NewCarInfo;

    public void NewCar(string car)
    {
      Console.WriteLine("CarDealer, new car {0}", car);

      RaiseNewCarInfo(car);
    }

    protected virtual void RaiseNewCarInfo(string car)
    {
      EventHandler<CarInfoEventArgs> newCarInfo = NewCarInfo;
      if (newCarInfo != null)
      {
        newCarInfo(this, new CarInfoEventArgs(car));
      }
    }
  }
}
```

The class `CarDealer` offers the event `NewCarInfo` of type `EventHandler<CarInfoEventArgs>`. As a convention, events typically use methods with two parameters; the first parameter is an object and contains the sender of the event, and the second parameter provides information about the event. The second parameter is different for various event types. .NET 1.0 defined several hundred delegates for events for all different data types. That's no longer necessary with the generic delegate `EventHandler<T>`. `EventHandler<TEventArgs>` defines a handler that returns `void` and accepts two parameters. With `EventHandler<TEventArgs>`, the first parameter needs to be of type `object`, and the second parameter is of type `T`. `EventHandler<TEventArgs>` also defines a constraint on `T`; it must derive from the base class `EventArgs`, which is the case with `CarInfoEventArgs`:

```csharp
public event EventHandler<CarInfoEventArgs> NewCarInfo;
```

The delegate `EventHandler<TEventArgs>` is defined as follows:

```csharp
public delegate void EventHandler<TEventArgs>(object sender, TEventArgs e)
    where TEventArgs: EventArgs
```

Defining the event in one line is a C# shorthand notation. The compiler creates a variable of the delegate type `EventHandler<CarInfoEventArgs>` and adds methods to subscribe and unsubscribe from the delegate. The long form of the shorthand notation is shown next. This is very similar to auto-properties and full properties. With events, the add and remove keywords are used to add and remove a handler to the delegate:

```
private delegate EventHandler<CarInfoEventArgs> newCarInfo;
public event EventHandler<CarInfoEventArgs> NewCarInfo
{
  add
  {
    newCarInfo += value;
  }
  remove
  {
    newCarInfo = value;
  }
}
```

> **NOTE** *The long notation to define events is useful if more needs to be done than just adding and removing the event handler, such as adding synchronization for multiple thread access. The WPF controls make use of the long notation to add bubbling and tunneling functionality with the events. You can read more about event bubbling and tunneling events in Chapter 29, "Core XAML."*

The class CarDealer fires the event in the method RaiseNewCarInfo. Using the delegate NewCarInfo with brackets invokes all the handlers that are subscribed to the event. Remember, as shown with multicast delegates, the order of the methods invoked is not guaranteed. To have more control over calling the handler methods you can use the Delegate class method GetInvocationList to access every item in the delegate list and invoke each on its own, as shown earlier.

Before firing the event, it is necessary to check whether the delegate NewCarInfo is not null. If no one subscribed, the delegate is null:

```
protected virtual void RaiseNewCarInfo(string car)
{
  var newCarInfo = NewCarInfo;
  if (newCarInfo != null)
  {
    newCarInfo(this, new CarInfoEventArgs(car));
  }
}
```

Event Listener

The class Consumer is used as the event listener. This class subscribes to the event of the CarDealer and defines the method NewCarIsHere that in turn fulfills the requirements of the EventHandler<CarInfoEventArgs> delegate with parameters of type object and CarInfoEventArgs (code file EventsSample/Consumer.cs):

```
using System;

namespace Wrox.ProCSharp.Delegates
{
  public class Consumer
  {
```

```
    private string name;

    public Consumer(string name)
    {
      this.name = name;
    }

    public void NewCarIsHere(object sender, CarInfoEventArgs e)
    {
      Console.WriteLine("{0}: car {1} is new", name, e.Car);
    }
  }
}
```

Now the event publisher and subscriber need to connect. This is done by using the `NewCarInfo` event of the `CarDealer` to create a subscription with `+=`. The consumer *Michael* subscribes to the event, then the consumer *Sebastian*, and next *Michael* unsubscribes with `-=` (code file `EventsSample/Program.cs`):

```
namespace Wrox.ProCSharp.Delegates
{
  class Program
  {
    static void Main()
    {
      var dealer = new CarDealer();

      var michael = new Consumer("Michael");
      dealer.NewCarInfo += michael.NewCarIsHere;

      dealer.NewCar("Ferrari");

      var sebastian = new Consumer("Sebastian");
      dealer.NewCarInfo += sebastian.NewCarIsHere;

      dealer.NewCar("Mercedes");

      dealer.NewCarInfo -= michael.NewCarIsHere;

      dealer.NewCar("Red Bull Racing");
    }
  }
}
```

Running the application, a Ferrari arrived and Michael was informed. Because after that Sebastian registers for the subscription as well, both Michael and Sebastian are informed about the new Mercedes. Then Michael unsubscribes and only Sebastian is informed about the Red Bull:

```
CarDealer, new car Ferrari
Michael: car Ferrari is new
CarDealer, new car Mercedes
Michael: car Mercedes is new
Sebastian: car Mercedes is new
CarDealer, new car Red Bull
Sebastian: car Red Bull is new
```

Weak Events

With events, the publisher and listener are directly connected. This can be a problem with garbage collection. For example, if a listener is not directly referenced any more, there's still a reference from the publisher. The garbage collector cannot clean up memory from the listener, as the publisher still holds a reference and fires events to the listener.

This strong connection can be resolved by using the weak event pattern and using the WeakEventManager as an intermediary between the publisher and listeners.

The preceding example with the CarDealer as publisher and the Consumer as listener is modified in this section to use the weak event pattern.

> **NOTE** *With subscribers that are created dynamically, in order to not be in danger of having resource leaks, you need to pay special attention to events. That is, you need to either ensure that you unsubscribe events before the subscribers go out of scope (are not needed any longer), or use weak events.*

Weak Event Manager

To use weak events you need to create a class that derives from WeakEventManager, which is defined in the namespace System.Windows in the assembly WindowsBase.

The class WeakCarInfoEventManager is the weak event manager class that manages the connection between the publisher and the listener for the NewCarInfo event. This class implements a singleton pattern so that only one instance is created. The static property CurrentManager creates an object of type WeakCarInfoEventManager if it doesn't exist, and returns a reference to it. WeakCarInfoEventManager .CurrentManager is used to access the singleton object from the WeakCarInfoEventManager.

With the weak event pattern, the weak event manager class needs the static methods AddListener and RemoveListener. The listener is connected and disconnected to the events of the publisher with these methods, instead of using the events from the publisher directly. The listener also needs to implement the interface IWeakEventListener, which is shown shortly. With the AddListener and RemoveListener methods, methods from the base class WeakEventManager are invoked to add and remove the listeners.

With the WeakCarInfoEventManager class you also need to override the StartListening and StopListening methods from the base class. StartListening is called when the first listener is added, StopListening when the last listener is removed. StartListening and StopListening subscribes and unsubscribes, respectively, a method from the weak event manager to listen for the event from the publisher. In case the weak event manager class needs to connect to different publisher types, you can check the type information from the source object before doing the cast. The event is then forwarded to the listeners by calling the DeliverEvent method from the base class, which in turn invokes the method ReceiveWeakEvent from the IWeakEventListener interface in the listeners (code file WeakEventsSample/ WeakCarInfoEventManger.cs):

```
using System.Windows;

namespace Wrox.ProCSharp.Delegates
{
  public class WeakCarInfoEventManager: WeakEventManager
  {
    public static void AddListener(object source, IWeakEventListener listener)
    {
      CurrentManager.ProtectedAddListener(source, listener);
    }

    public static void RemoveListener(object source, IWeakEventListener listener)
    {
      CurrentManager.ProtectedRemoveListener(source, listener);
    }
```

```
    public static WeakCarInfoEventManager CurrentManager
    {
      get
      {
        var manager = GetCurrentManager(typeof(WeakCarInfoEventManager))
            as WeakCarInfoEventManager;
        if (manager == null)
        {
          manager = new WeakCarInfoEventManager();
          SetCurrentManager(typeof(WeakCarInfoEventManager), manager);
        }
        return manager;
      }
    }

    protected override void StartListening(object source)
    {
      (source as CarDealer).NewCarInfo += CarDealer_NewCarInfo;
    }

    void CarDealer_NewCarInfo(object sender, CarInfoEventArgs e)
    {
      DeliverEvent(sender, e);
    }

    protected override void StopListening(object source)
    {
      (source as CarDealer).NewCarInfo = CarDealer_NewCarInfo;
    }
  }
}
```

> **NOTE** *WPF makes use of the weak event pattern with the event manager classes:* `CollectionChangedEventManager`, `CurrentChangedEventManager`, `CurrentChangingEventManager`, `PropertyChangedEventManager`, `DataChangedEventManager`, *and* `LostFocusEventManager`.

With the publisher class `CarDealer` there's no need to change anything. It has the same implementation as before.

Event Listener

The listener needs to be changed to implement the interface `IWeakEventListener`. This interface defines the method `ReceiveWeakEvent` that is called from the weak event manager when the event arrives. The method implementation acts as a proxy and in turn invokes the method `NewCarIsHere` (code file `WeakEventsSample/Consumer.cs`):

```
using System;
using System.Windows;

namespace Wrox.ProCSharp.Delegates
{
  public class Consumer: IWeakEventListener
  {
    private string name;

    public Consumer(string name)
```

```
      {
        this.name = name;
      }

      public void NewCarIsHere(object sender, CarInfoEventArgs e)
      {
        Console.WriteLine("{0}: car {1} is new", name, e.Car);
      }

      bool IWeakEventListener.ReceiveWeakEvent(Type managerType, object sender,
            EventArgs e)
      {
        NewCarIsHere(sender, e as CarInfoEventArgs);
        return true;
      }
    }
  }
```

Inside the `Main` method, where the publisher and listeners are connected, the connection is now made by using the static `AddListener` and `RemoveListener` methods from the `WeakCarInfoEventManager` class (code file `WeakEventsSample/Program.cs`):

```
static void Main()
{
  var dealer = new CarDealer();

  var michael = new Consumer("Michael");
  WeakCarInfoEventManager.AddListener(dealer, michael);

  dealer.NewCar("Mercedes");

  var sebastian = new Consumer("Sebastian");
  WeakCarInfoEventManager.AddListener(dealer, sebastian);

  dealer.NewCar("Ferrari");

  WeakCarInfoEventManager.RemoveListener(dealer, michael);

  dealer.NewCar("Red Bull Racing");
}
```

With this additional work of implementing the weak event pattern, the publisher and listeners are no longer strongly connected. When a listener is not referenced anymore, it can be garbage collected.

Generic Weak Event Manager

.NET 4.5 has a new implementation of a weak event manager. The generic class `WeakEventManager<TEventSource, TEventArgs>` derives from the base class `WeakEventManager` and makes dealing with weak events a lot easier. Using this class it's no longer necessary to implement a custom weak event manager class for every event, nor is it necessary that the consumer implements the interface `IWeakEventsListener`. All that is required is using the generic weak event manager on subscribing to the events.

The main program to subscribe to the events is now changed to use the generic `WeakEventManager` with the event source being the `CarDealer` type, and the event args that are passed with the event the `CarInfoEventArgs` type. The class defines the `AddHandler` method to subscribe to an event, and the `RemoveHandler` method to unsubscribe. Then the program works as before but with a lot less code:

```
var dealer = new CarDealer();

var michael = new Consumer("Michael");
```

```
WeakEventManager<CarDealer, CarInfoEventArgs>.AddHandler(dealer,
    "NewCarInfo", michael.NewCarIsHere);

dealer.NewCar("Mercedes");

var sebastian = new Consumer("Sebastian");
WeakEventManager<CarDealer, CarInfoEventArgs>.AddHandler(dealer,
    "NewCarInfo", sebastian.NewCarIsHere);

dealer.NewCar("Ferrari");

WeakEventManager<CarDealer, CarInfoEventArgs>.RemoveHandler(dealer,
    "NewCarInfo", michael.NewCarIsHere);

dealer.NewCar("Red Bull Racing");
```

SUMMARY

This chapter provided the basics of delegates, lambda expressions, and events. You learned how to declare a delegate and add methods to the delegate list; you learned how to implement methods called by delegates with lambda expressions; and you learned the process of declaring event handlers to respond to an event, as well as how to create a custom event and use the patterns for raising the event.

As a .NET developer, you will use delegates and events extensively, especially when developing Windows applications. Events are the means by which the .NET developer can monitor the various Windows messages that occur while the application is executing. Otherwise, you would have to monitor the WndProc function and catch the WM_MOUSEDOWN message instead of getting the mouse Click event for a button.

Using delegates and events in the design of a large application can reduce dependencies and the coupling of layers. This enables you to develop components that have a higher reusability factor.

Lambda expressions are C# language features on delegates. With these, you can reduce the amount of code you need to write. Lambda expressions are not only used with delegates, as you will see in Chapter 11, "Language Integrated Query."

The next chapter covers the use of strings and regular expressions.

Strings and Regular Expressions

➤ Building strings

➤ Formatting expressions

➤ Using regular expressions

WROX.COM CODE DOWNLOADS FOR THIS CHAPTER

The wrox.com code downloads for this chapter are found at `http://www.wrox.com/remtitle` `.cgi?isbn=1118314425` on the Download Code tab. The code for this chapter is divided into the following major examples:

➤ Encoder.cs

➤ Encoder2.cs

➤ FormattableVector.cs

➤ RegularExpressionPlayground.cs

➤ StringEncoder.cs

Strings have been used consistently since the beginning of this book, but you might not have realized that the stated mapping that the `string` keyword in C# actually refers to is the `System.String` .NET base class. `System.String` is a very powerful and versatile class, but it is by no means the only string-related class in the .NET armory. This chapter begins by reviewing the features of `System.String` and then looks at some nifty things you can do with strings using some of the other .NET classes — in particular those in the `System.Text` and `System.Text.RegularExpressions` namespaces. This chapter covers the following areas:

➤ **Building strings** — If you're performing repeated modifications on a string — for example, to build a lengthy string prior to displaying it or passing it to some other method or application — the `String` class can be very inefficient. When you find yourself in this kind of situation, another class, `System.Text.StringBuilder`, is more suitable because it has been designed exactly for this scenario.

➤ **Formatting expressions** — This chapter takes a closer look at the formatting expressions that have been used in the `Console.WriteLine()` method throughout the past few chapters. These formatting expressions are processed using two useful interfaces, `IFormatProvider` and `IFormattable`. By implementing these interfaces on your own classes, you can define your own formatting sequences so that `Console.WriteLine()` and similar classes display the values of your classes in whatever way you specify.

➤ **Regular expressions** — .NET also offers some very sophisticated classes that deal with cases in which you need to identify or extract substrings that satisfy certain fairly sophisticated criteria; for example, finding all occurrences within a string where a character or set of characters is repeated: finding all words that begin with "s" and contain at least one "n:" or strings that adhere to an employee ID or a social security number construction. Although you can write methods to perform this kind of processing using the `String` class, writing such methods is cumbersome. Instead, some classes, specifically those from `System.Text.RegularExpressions`, are designed to perform this kind of processing.

EXAMINING SYSTEM.STRING

Before digging into the other string classes, this section briefly reviews some of the available methods in the `String` class itself.

`System.String` is a class specifically designed to store a string and allow a large number of operations on the string. In addition, due to the importance of this data type, C# has its own keyword and associated syntax to make it particularly easy to manipulate strings using this class.

You can concatenate strings using operator overloads:

```
string message1 = "Hello";  // returns "Hello"
message1 += ", There"; // returns "Hello, There"
string message2 = message1 + "!"; // returns "Hello, There!"
```

C# also allows extraction of a particular character using an indexer-like syntax:

```
string message = "Hello";
char char4 = message[4];    // returns 'o'. Note the string is zero-indexed
```

This enables you to perform such common tasks as replacing characters, removing whitespace, and changing case. The following table introduces the key methods.

METHOD	DESCRIPTION
Compare	Compares the contents of strings, taking into account the culture (locale) in assessing equivalence between certain characters.
CompareOrdinal	Same as Compare but doesn't take culture into account.
Concat	Combines separate string instances into a single instance.
CopyTo	Copies a specific number of characters from the selected index to an entirely new instance of an array.
Format	Formats a string containing various values and specifiers for how each value should be formatted.
IndexOf	Locates the first occurrence of a given substring or character in the string.
IndexOfAny	Locates the first occurrence of any one of a set of characters in a string.
Insert	Inserts a string instance into another string instance at a specified index.
Join	Builds a new string by combining an array of strings.
LastIndexOf	Same as IndexOf but finds the last occurrence.
LastIndexOfAny	Same as IndexOf Any but finds the last occurrence.

PadLeft	Pads out the string by adding a specified repeated character to the left side of the string.
PadRight	Pads out the string by adding a specified repeated character to the right side of the string.
Replace	Replaces occurrences of a given character or substring in the string with another character or substring.
Split	Splits the string into an array of substrings; the breaks occur wherever a given character occurs.
Substring	Retrieves the substring starting at a specified position in a string.
ToLower	Converts the string to lowercase.
ToUpper	Converts the string to uppercase.
Trim	Removes leading and trailing whitespace.

> **NOTE** *Please note that this table is not comprehensive; it is intended to give you an idea of the features offered by strings.*

Building Strings

As you have seen, String is an extremely powerful class that implements a large number of very useful methods. However, the String class has a shortcoming that makes it very inefficient for making repeated modifications to a given string — it is actually an *immutable* data type, which means that after you initialize a string object, that string object can never change. The methods and operators that appear to modify the contents of a string actually create new strings, copying across the contents of the old string if necessary. For example, consider the following code:

```
string greetingText = "Hello from all the guys at Wrox Press. ";
greetingText += "We do hope you enjoy this book as much as we enjoyed writing it.";
```

When this code executes, first an object of type System.String is created and initialized to hold the text Hello from all the guys at Wrox Press. (Note the space *after* the period.) When this happens, the .NET runtime allocates just enough memory in the string to hold this text (39 chars), and the variable greetingText is set to refer to this string instance.

In the next line, syntactically it looks like more text is being added onto the string, but it is not. Instead, a new string instance is created with just enough memory allocated to store the combined text — that's 103 characters in total. The original text, Hello from all the people at Wrox Press., is copied into this new string instance along with the extra text: We do hope you enjoy this book as much as we enjoyed writing it. Then, the address stored in the variable greetingText is updated, so the variable correctly points to the new String object. The old String object is now unreferenced — there are no variables that refer to it — so it will be removed the next time the garbage collector comes along to clean out any unused objects in your application.

By itself, that doesn't look too bad, but suppose you wanted to create a very simple encryption scheme by adding 1 to the ASCII value of each character in the string. This would change the string to Ifmmp gspn bmm uif hvst bu Xspy Qsftt. Xf ep ipqf zpv fokpz uijt cppl bt nvdi bt xf fokpzfe xsjujoh ju. Several ways of doing this exist, but the simplest and (if you are restricting yourself to using the String class) almost certainly the most efficient way is to use the String.Replace() method, which replaces all occurrences of a given substring in a string with another substring. Using `Replace()`, the code to encode the text looks like this:

```
string greetingText = "Hello from all the guys at Wrox Press. ";
greetingText += "We do hope you enjoy this book as much as we enjoyed writing it.";

for(int i = 'z'; i>= 'a'; i--)
{
   char old1 = (char)i;
   char new1 = (char)(i+1);
   greetingText = greetingText.Replace(old1, new1);
}

for(int i = 'Z'; i>='A'; i--)
{
   char old1 = (char)i;
   char new1 = (char)(i+1);
   greetingText = greetingText.Replace(old1, new1);
}

Console.WriteLine("Encoded:\n" + greetingText);
```

> **NOTE** *Simply this code does not wrap Z to A or z to a. These letters are encoded to [and {, respectively.*

In this example, the `Replace()` method works in a fairly intelligent way, to the extent that it won't actually create a new string unless it actually makes changes to the old string. The original string contained 23 different lowercase characters and three different uppercase ones. The `Replace()` method will therefore have allocated a new string 26 times in total, with each new string storing 103 characters. That means because of the encryption process, there will be string objects capable of storing a combined total of 2,678 characters now sitting on the heap waiting to be garbagecollected! Clearly, if you use strings to do text processing extensively, your applications will run into severe performance problems.

To address this kind of issue, Microsoft supplies the `System.Text.StringBuilder` class. `StringBuilder` is not as powerful as `String` in terms of the number of methods it supports. The processing you can do on a `StringBuilder` is limited to substitutions and appending or removing text from strings. However, it works in a much more efficient way.

When you construct a string using the `String` class, just enough memory is allocated to hold the string object. The `StringBuilder`, however, normally allocates more memory than is actually needed. You, as a developer, have the option to indicate how much memory the `StringBuilder` should allocate; but if you do not, the amount defaults to a value that varies according to the size of the string with which the `StringBuilder` instance is initialized. The `StringBuilder` class has two main properties:

➤ `Length` — Indicates the length of the string that it actually contains
➤ `Capacity` — Indicates the maximum length of the string in the memory allocation

Any modifications to the string take place within the block of memory assigned to the `StringBuilder` instance, which makes appending substrings and replacing individual characters within strings very efficient. Removing or inserting substrings is inevitably still inefficient because it means that the following part of the string has to be moved. Only if you perform an operation that exceeds the capacity of the string is it necessary to allocate new memory and possibly move the entire contained string. In adding extra capacity, based on our experiments the StringBuilder appears to double its capacity if it detects that the capacity has been exceeded and no new value for capacity has been set.

For example, if you use a StringBuilder object to construct the original greeting string, you might write this code:

```
StringBuilder greetingBuilder =
    new StringBuilder("Hello from all the guys at Wrox Press. ", 150);
greetingBuilder.AppendFormat("We do hope you enjoy this book as much as we enjoyed
    writing it");
```

> **NOTE** *To use the* StringBuilder *class, you need a* System.Text *reference in your code.*

This code sets an initial capacity of 150 for the StringBuilder. It is always a good idea to set a capacity that covers the likely maximum length of a string, to ensure that the StringBuilder does not need to relocate because its capacity was exceeded. By default, the capacity is set to 16. Theoretically, you can set a number as large as the number you pass in an int, although the system will probably complain that it does not have enough memory if you actually try to allocate the maximum of two billion characters (the theoretical maximum that a StringBuilder instance is allowed to contain).

When the preceding code is executed, it first creates a StringBuilder object that looks like Figure 9-1.

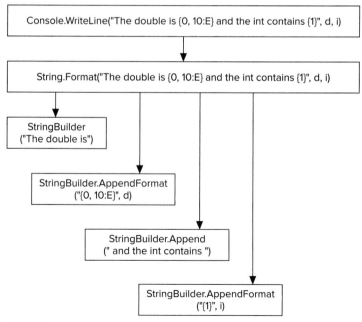

FIGURE 9-1

Then, on calling the `AppendFormat()` method, the remaining text is placed in the empty space, without the need to allocate more memory. However, the real efficiency gain from using a `StringBuilder` is realized when you make repeated text substitutions. For example, if you try to encrypt the text in the same way as before, you can perform the entire encryption without allocating any more memory whatsoever:

```
StringBuilder greetingBuilder =
    new StringBuilder("Hello from all the guys at Wrox Press. ", 150);
greetingBuilder.AppendFormat("We do hope you enjoy this book as much as we " +
    "enjoyed writing it");

Console.WriteLine("Not Encoded:\n" + greetingBuilder);

for(int i = 'z'; i>='a'; i--)
{
    char old1 = (char)i;
    char new1 = (char)(i+1);
    greetingBuilder = greetingBuilder.Replace(old1, new1);
}

for(int i = 'Z'; i>='A'; i--)
{
    char old1 = (char)i;
    char new1 = (char)(i+1);
    greetingBuilder = greetingBuilder.Replace(old1, new1);
}

Console.WriteLine("Encoded:\n" + greetingBuilder);
```

This code uses the `StringBuilder.Replace()` method, which does the same thing as `String.Replace()` but without copying the string in the process. The total memory allocated to hold strings in the preceding code is 150 characters for the `StringBuilder` instance, as well as the memory allocated during the string operations performed internally in the final `Console.WriteLine()` statement.

Normally, you want to use `StringBuilder` to perform any manipulation of strings, and `String` to store or display the final result.

StringBuilder Members

You have seen a demonstration of one constructor of `StringBuilder`, which takes an initial string and capacity as its parameters. There are others. For example, you can supply only a string:

```
StringBuilder sb = new StringBuilder("Hello");
```

Or you can create an empty `StringBuilder` with a given capacity:

```
StringBuilder sb = new StringBuilder(20);
```

Apart from the `Length` and `Capacity` properties, there is a read-only `MaxCapacity` property that indicates the limit to which a given `StringBuilder` instance is allowed to grow. By default, this is specified by `int.MaxValue` (roughly two billion, as noted earlier), but you can set this value to something lower when you construct the `StringBuilder` object:

```
// This will both set initial capacity to 100, but the max will be 500.
// Hence, this StringBuilder can never grow to more than 500 characters,
// otherwise it will raise exception if you try to do that.
StringBuilder sb = new StringBuilder(100, 500);
```

You can also explicitly set the capacity at any time, though an exception will be raised if you set it to a value less than the current length of the string or a value that exceeds the maximum capacity:

```
StringBuilder sb = new StringBuilder("Hello");
sb.Capacity = 100;
```

The following table lists the main `StringBuilder` methods.

METHOD	DESCRIPTION
`Append()`	Appends a string to the current string.
`AppendFormat()`	Appends a string that has been formatted from a format specifier.
`Insert()`	Inserts a substring into the current string.
`Remove()`	Removes characters from the current string.
`Replace()`	Replaces all occurrences of a character with another character or a substring with another substring in the current string.
`ToString()`	Returns the current string cast to a `System.String` object (overridden from `System.Object`).

Several overloads of many of these methods exist.

> **NOTE** `AppendFormat()` *is actually the method that is ultimately called when you call* `Console.WriteLine()`, *which is responsible for determining what all the format expressions like {0:D} should be replaced with. This method is examined in the next section.*

There is no cast (either implicit or explicit) from `StringBuilder` to `String`. If you want to output the contents of a `StringBuilder` as a `String`, you must use the `ToString()` method.

Now that you have been introduced to the `StringBuilder` class and have learned some of the ways in which you can use it to increase performance, be aware that this class does not always deliver the increased performance you are seeking. Basically, the `StringBuilder` class should be used when you are manipulating multiple strings. However, if you are just doing something as simple as concatenating two strings, you will find that `System.String` performs better.

Format Strings

So far, a large number of classes and structs have been written for the code samples presented in this book, and they have normally implemented a `ToString()` method in order to display the contents of a given variable. However, users often want the contents of a variable to be displayed in different, often culture- and locale-dependent ways. The .NET base class, `System.DateTime`, provides the most obvious example of this. For example, you might want to display the same date as 10 June 2012, 10 Jun 2012, 6/10/12 (USA), 10/6/12 (UK), or 10.06.2012 (Germany).

Similarly, the `Vector` struct in Chapter 7, "Operators and Casts," implements the `Vector.ToString()` method to display the vector in the format (4, 56, 8). There is, however, another very common way to write vectors, whereby this vector would appear as 4i + 56j + 8k. If you want the classes that you write to be user-friendly, they need to support the capability to display string representations in any of the formats that users are likely to want to use. The .NET runtime defines a standard way in which this should be done: the `IFormattable` interface. Learning how to add this important feature to your classes and structs is the subject of this section.

As you probably know, you need to specify the format in which you want a variable displayed when you call `Console.WriteLine()`. Therefore, this section uses this method as an example, although most of the discussion applies to any situation in which you want to format a string. For example, if you want to display the value of a variable in a list box or text box, you normally use the `String.Format()` method to obtain the appropriate string representation of the variable. However, the actual format specifiers you use to request a particular format are identical to those passed to `Console.WriteLine()`. Hence, this section focuses on `Console.WriteLine()` as an example. It begins by examining what actually happens when you supply a format string to a primitive type, and from this you will see how you can plug format specifiers for your own classes and structs into the process.

Chapter 2, "Core C#," uses format strings in `Console.Write()` and `Console.WriteLine()` like this:

```
double d = 13.45;
int i = 45;
Console.WriteLine("The double is {0,10:E} and the int contains {1}", d, i);
```

The format string itself consists mostly of the text to be displayed; but wherever a variable needs to be formatted, its index in the parameter list appears in braces. You might also include other information inside the braces concerning the format of that item, such as the following:

➤ The number of characters to be occupied by the representation of the item, prefixed by a comma. A negative number indicates that the item should be left-justified, whereas a positive number indicates that it should be right-justified. If the item occupies more characters than have been requested, it will still appear in full.

➤ A format specifier, preceded by a colon. This indicates how you want the item to be formatted. For example, you can indicate whether you want a number to be formatted as a currency or displayed in scientific notation.

The following table lists the common format specifiers for the numeric types, which were briefly discussed in Chapter 2.

SPECIFIER	APPLIES TO	MEANING	EXAMPLE
C	Numeric types	Locale-specific monetary value	$4834.50 (USA) £4834.50 (UK)
D	Integer types only	General integer	4834
E	Numeric types	Scientific notation	4.834E+003
F	Numeric types	Fixed-point decimal	4384.50
G	Numeric types	General number	4384.5
N	Numeric types	Common locale-specific format for numbers	4,384.50 (UK/USA)4 384,50 (continental Europe)
P	Numeric types	Percentage notation	432,000.00%
X	Integer types only	Hexadecimal format	1120 (If you want to display 0x1120, you will have to write out the 0x separately)

If you want an integer to be padded with zeros, you can use the format specifier 0 (zero) repeated as many times as the number length requires. For example, the format specifier 0000 will cause 3 to be displayed as 0003, and 99 to be displayed as 0099, and so on.

It is not possible to provide a complete list, because other data types can add their own specifiers. The aim here is to demonstrate how to define your own specifiers for your own classes.

How the String Is Formatted

As an example of how strings are formatted, consider executing the following statement:

```
Console.WriteLine("The double is {0,10:E} and the int contains {1}", d, i);
```

In the preceding example, `Console.WriteLine()` just passes the entire set of parameters to the static method, `String.Format()`. This is the same method that you would call if you wanted to format these values for use in a string to be displayed in a text box, for example. The implementation of the three-parameter overload of `WriteLine()` basically does this:

```
// Likely implementation of Console.WriteLine()

public void WriteLine(string format, object arg0, object arg1)
{
    this.WriteLine(string.Format(this.FormatProvider, format,
        new object[]{arg0, arg1}));
}
```

The one-parameter overload of this method, which is in turn called in the preceding code sample, simply writes out the contents of the string it has been passed, without doing any further formatting on it.

`String.Format()` now needs to construct the final string by replacing each format specifier with a suitable string representation of the corresponding object. However, as shown earlier, for this process of building up a string you need a `StringBuilder` instance, rather than a `string` instance. In this example, a `StringBuilder` instance is created and initialized with the first known portion of the string, the text "The double is". Next, the `StringBuilder.AppendFormat()` method is called, passing in the first format specifier, `{0,10:E}`, as well as the associated object, `double`, to add the string representation of this object to the string object being constructed. This process continues with `StringBuilder.Append()` and `StringBuilder.AppendFormat()` being called repeatedly until the entire formatted string has been obtained.

Now the interesting part: `StringBuilder.AppendFormat()` has to figure out how to format the object. First, it probes the object to determine whether it implements an interface in the `System` namespace called `IFormattable`. This can be done quite simply by trying to cast an object to this interface and seeing whether the cast succeeds, or by using the C# `is` keyword. If this test fails, `AppendFormat()` calls the object's `ToString()` method, which all objects either inherit from `System.Object` or override. This is exactly what happens here because none of the classes written so far has implemented this interface. That is why the overrides of `Object.ToString()` have been sufficient to allow the structs and classes from earlier chapters, such as `Vector`, to be displayed in `Console.WriteLine()` statements.

However, all the predefined primitive numeric types do implement this interface, which means that for those types, and in particular for `double` and `int` in the example, the basic `ToString()` method inherited from `System.Object` will not be called. To understand what happens instead, you need to examine the `IFormattable` interface.

`IFormattable` defines just one method, which is also called `ToString()`. However, this method takes two parameters as opposed to the `System.Object` version, which doesn't take any parameters. The following code shows the definition of `IFormattable`:

```
interface IFormattable
{
    string ToString(string format, IFormatProvider formatProvider);
}
```

The first parameter that this overload of `ToString()` expects is a string that specifies the requested format. In other words, it is the specifier portion of the string that appears inside the braces (`{}`) in the string originally passed to `Console.WriteLine()` or `String.Format()`. For example, in the example the original statement was as follows:

```
Console.WriteLine("The double is {0,10:E} and the int contains {1}", d, i);
```

Hence, when evaluating the first specifier, {0,10:E}, this overload is called against the double variable, d, and the first parameter passed to it will be E. The StringBuilder.AppendFormat() method will pass in here the text that appears after the colon in the appropriate format specifier from the original string.

We won't worry about the second ToString() parameter in this book. It is a reference to an object that implements the IFormatProvider interface. This interface provides further information that ToString() might need to consider when formatting the object, such as culture-specific details (a .NET culture is similar to a Windows locale; if you are formatting currencies or dates, you need this information). If you are calling this ToString() overload directly from your source code, you might want to supply such an object. However, StringBuilder.AppendFormat() passes in null for this parameter. If formatProvider is null, then ToString() is expected to use the culture specified in the system settings.

Getting back to the example, the first item you want to format is a double, for which you are requesting exponential notation, with the format specifier E. The StringBuilder.AppendFormat() method establishes that the double does implement IFormattable, and will therefore call the two-parameter ToString() overload, passing it the string E for the first parameter and null for the second parameter. It is now up to the double's implementation of this method to return the string representation of the double in the appropriate format, taking into account the requested format and the current culture. StringBuilder.AppendFormat() will then sort out padding the returned string with spaces, if necessary, to fill the 10 characters specified by the format string.

The next object to be formatted is an int, for which you are not requesting any particular format (the format specifier was simply {1}). With no format requested, StringBuilder.AppendFormat() passes in a null reference for the format string. The two-parameter overload of int.ToString() is expected to respond appropriately. No format has been specifically requested; therefore, it calls the no-parameter ToString() method.

This entire string formatting process is summarized in Figure 9-2.

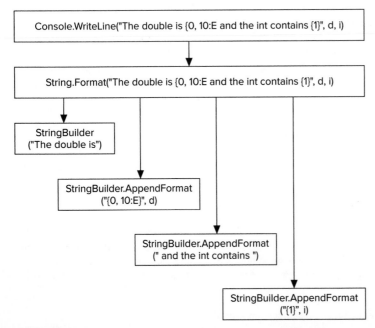

FIGURE 9-2

The FormattableVector Example

Now that you know how format strings are constructed, this section extends the Vector example from Chapter 7, "Operators and Casts," so that you can format vectors in a variety of ways. You can download the code for this example from www.wrox.com; the filename is FormattableVector.cs. With your new knowledge of the principles involved now in hand, you will discover that the actual coding is quite simple. All you need to do is implement IFormattable and supply an implementation of the ToString() overload defined by that interface.

The format specifiers you are going to support are as follows:

➤ N — Should be interpreted as a request to supply a quantity known as the Norm of the Vector. This is just the sum of the squares of its components, which for mathematics buffs happens to be equal to the square of the length of the Vector, and is usually displayed between double vertical bars, like this: ||34.5||.

➤ VE — Should be interpreted as a request to display each component in scientific format, just as the specifier E applied to a double indicates (2.3E+01, 4.5E+02, 1.0E+00)

➤ IJK — Should be interpreted as a request to display the vector in the form 23i + 450j + 1k

➤ Anything else should simply return the default representation of the Vector (23, 450, 1.0).

To keep things simple, you are not going to implement any option to display the vector in combined IJK and scientific format. However, you will test the specifier in a case-insensitive way, so that you allow ijk instead of IJK. Note that it is entirely up to you which strings you use to indicate the format specifiers.

To achieve this, you first modify the declaration of Vector so it implements IFormattable:

```
struct Vector: IFormattable
{
    public double x, y, z;

    // Beginning part of Vector
```

Now you add your implementation of the two-parameter ToString() overload:

```
public string ToString(string format, IFormatProvider formatProvider)
{
    if (format == null)
    {
        return ToString();
    }

    string formatUpper = format.ToUpper();

    switch (formatUpper)
    {
      case "N":
          return "|| " + Norm().ToString() + " ||";
      case "VE":
          return String.Format("( {0:E}, {1:E}, {2:E} )", x, y, z);
      case "IJK":
          StringBuilder sb = new StringBuilder(x.ToString(), 30);
          sb.AppendFormat(" i + ");
          sb.AppendFormat(y.ToString());
          sb.AppendFormat(" j + ");
          sb.AppendFormat(z.ToString());
          sb.AppendFormat(" k");
          return sb.ToString();
      default:
          return ToString();
    }
}
```

That is all you have to do! Notice how you take the precaution of checking whether format is null before you call any methods against this parameter — you want this method to be as robust as reasonably possible. The format specifiers for all the primitive types are case insensitive, so that is the behavior that other developers will expect from your class, too. For the format specifier VE, you need each component to be formatted in scientific notation, so you just use String.Format() again to achieve this. The fields x, y, and z are all doubles. For the case of the IJK format specifier, quite a few substrings need to be added to the string, so you use a StringBuilder object to improve performance.

For completeness, you also reproduce the no-parameter ToString() overload developed earlier:

```
public override string ToString()
{
    return "( " + x + ", " + y + ", " + z + " )";
}
```

Finally, you need to add a Norm() method that computes the square (norm) of the vector because you didn't actually supply this method when you developed the Vector struct:

```
public double Norm()
{
    return x*x + y*y + z*z;
}
```

Now you can try your formattable vector with some suitable test code:

```
static void Main()
{
    Vector v1 = new Vector(1,32,5);
    Vector v2 = new Vector(845.4, 54.3, -7.8);
    Console.WriteLine("\nIn IJK format,\nv1 is {0,30:IJK}\nv2 is {1,30:IJK}",
                      v1, v2);
    Console.WriteLine("\nIn default format,\nv1 is {0,30}\nv2 is {1,30}", v1, v2);
    Console.WriteLine("\nIn VE format\nv1 is {0,30:VE}\nv2 is {1,30:VE}", v1, v2);
    Console.WriteLine("\nNorms are:\nv1 is {0,20:N}\nv2 is {1,20:N}", v1, v2);
}
```

The result of running this sample is as follows:

```
FormattableVector
In IJK format,
v1 is                 1 i + 32 j + 5 k
v2 is      845.4 i + 54.3 j + -7.8 k

In default format,
v1 is                   ( 1, 32, 5 )
v2 is          ( 845.4, 54.3, -7.8 )

In VE format
v1 is ( 1.000000E+000, 3.200000E+001, 5.000000E+000 )
v2 is ( 8.454000E+002, 5.430000E+001, -7.800000E+000 )

Norms are:
v1 is              || 1050 ||
v2 is        || 717710.49 ||
```

This indicates that your custom specifiers are being picked up correctly.

REGULAR EXPRESSIONS

Regular expressions are one of those small technology aids that are incredibly useful in a wide range of programs. You can think of regular expressions as a mini-programming language with one specific purpose: to locate substrings within a large string expression. It is not a new technology; it originated in the UNIX environment and is commonly used with the Perl programming language. Microsoft ported it onto Windows, where up until recently it has been used mostly with scripting languages. Today, regular expressions are supported by a number of .NET classes in the namespace `System.Text .RegularExpressions`. You can also find the use of regular expressions in various parts of the .NET Framework. For instance, they are used within the ASP.NET validation server controls.

If you are not familiar with the regular expressions language, this section introduces both regular expressions and their related .NET classes. If you are familiar with regular expressions, you will probably want to just skim through this section to pick out the references to the .NET base classes. You might like to know that the .NET regular expression engine is designed to be mostly compatible with Perl 5 regular expressions, although it has a few extra features.

Introduction to Regular Expressions

The regular expressions language is designed specifically for string processing. It contains two features:

A set of escape codes for identifying specific types of characters. You will be familiar with the use of the * character to represent any substring in DOS expressions. (For example, the DOS command `Dir Re*` lists the files with names beginning with `Re`.) Regular expressions use many sequences like this to represent items such as *any one character, a word break, one optional character,* and so on.

➤ A system for grouping parts of substrings and intermediate results during a search operation

With regular expressions, you can perform very sophisticated and high-level operations on strings. For example, you can do all of the following:

➤ Identify (and perhaps either flag or remove) all repeated words in a string (e.g., "The computer books books" to "The computer books")

➤ Convert all words to title case (e.g., "this is a Title" to "This Is A Title")

➤ Convert all words longer than three characters to title case (e.g., "this is a Title" to "This is a Title")

➤ Ensure that sentences are properly capitalized

➤ Separate the various elements of a URI (e.g., given `http://www.wrox.com,` extract the protocol, computer name, filename, and so on)

Of course, all these tasks can be performed in C# using the various methods on `System.String` and `System.Text.StringBuilder`. However, in some cases, this would require writing a fair amount of C# code. Using regular expressions, this code can normally be compressed to just a couple of lines. Essentially, you instantiate a `System.Text.RegularExpressions.RegEx` object (or, even simpler, invoke a static `RegEx()` method), pass it the string to be processed, and pass in a regular expression (a string containing the instructions in the regular expressions language), and you're done.

A regular expression string looks at first sight rather like a regular string, but interspersed with escape sequences and other characters that have a special meaning. For example, the sequence \b indicates the beginning or end of a word (a word boundary), so if you wanted to indicate you were looking for the characters th at the beginning of a word, you would search for the regular expression, \bth (that is, the sequence word boundary-t-h). If you wanted to search for all occurrences of th at the end of a word, you would write th\b (the sequence t-h-word boundary). However, regular expressions are much more sophisticated than that and include, for example, facilities to store portions of text that are found in a search operation. This section only scratches the surface of the power of regular expressions.

> **NOTE** *For more on regular expressions, please see Andrew Watt's* Beginning Regular
> Expressions *(John Wiley & Sons, 2005).*

Suppose your application needed to convert U.S. phone numbers to an international format. In the United States, the phone numbers have the format 314-123-1234, which is often written as (314) 123-1234. When converting this national format to an international format, you have to include +1 (the country code of the United States) and add brackets around the area code: +1 (314) 123-1234. As find-and-replace operations go, that is not too complicated. It would still require some coding effort if you were going to use the String class for this purpose (meaning you would have to write your code using the methods available from System.String). The regular expressions language enables you to construct a short string that achieves the same result.

This section is intended only as a very simple example, so it concentrates on searching strings to identify certain substrings, not on modifying them.

The RegularExpressionsPlayaround Example

The rest of this section develops a short example called RegularExpressionsPlayaround that illustrates some of the features of regular expressions, and how to use the .NET regular expressions engine in C# by performing and displaying the results of some searches. The text you are going to use as your sample document is the introduction to a book on ASP.NET, *Professional ASP.NET 4: in C# and VB* (Wiley, 2010):

```
const string myText =
@"This comprehensive compendium provides a broad and thorough investigation of all
aspects of programming with ASP.NET. Entirely revised and updated for the fourth
release of .NET, this book will give you the information you need to
master ASP.NET and build a dynamic, successful, enterprise Web application.";
```

> **NOTE** *This code is valid C# code, despite all the line breaks. It nicely illustrates the
> utility of verbatim strings that are prefixed by the @ symbol.*

This text is referred to as the *input string.* To get your bearings and get used to the regular expressions of .NET classes, you start with a basic plain-text search that does not feature any escape sequences or regular expression commands. Suppose that you want to find all occurrences of the string "ion". This search string is referred to as the *pattern.* Using regular expressions and the Text variable declared previously, you could write the following:

```
const string pattern = "ion";
MatchCollection myMatches = Regex.Matches(myText, pattern,
                                 RegexOptions.IgnoreCase |
                                 RegexOptions.ExplicitCapture);

foreach (Match nextMatch in myMatches)
{
    Console.WriteLine(nextMatch.Index);
}
```

This code uses the static method Matches() of the Regex class in the System.Text.RegularExpressions namespace. This method takes as parameters some input text, a pattern, and a set of optional flags taken from the RegexOptions enumeration. In this case, you have specified that all searching should be caseinsensitive. The other flag, ExplicitCapture, modifies how the match is collected in a way that, for your purposes, makes the search a bit more efficient — you'll see why this is later (although it does have other uses that we won't explore here). Matches() returns a reference to a MatchCollection object. A *match* is the technical term for the results of finding an instance of the pattern in the expression. It is represented by the class System.Text.RegularExpressions.Match. Therefore, you return a MatchCollection that contains all the matches, each represented by a Match object. In the preceding code, you simply iterate over the collection and use the Index property of the Match class, which returns the index in the input text where the match was found. Running this code results in three matches. The following table details some of the RegexOptions enumerations.

MEMBER NAME	DESCRIPTION
CultureInvariant	Specifies that the culture of the string is ignored.
ExplicitCapture	Modifies the way the match is collected by making sure that valid captures are the ones that are explicitly named.
IgnoreCase	Ignores the case of the string that is input.
IgnorePatternWhitespace	Removes unescaped whitespace from the string and enables comments that are specified with the pound or hash sign.
Multiline	Changes the characters ^ and $ so that they are applied to the beginning and end of each line and not just to the beginning and end of the entire string.
RightToLeft	Causes the inputted string to be read from right to left instead of the default left to right (ideal for some Asian and other languages that are read in this direction).
Singleline	Specifies a single-line mode where the meaning of the dot (.) is changed to match every character.

So far, nothing is new from the preceding example apart from some .NET base classes. However, the power of regular expressions comes from that pattern string. The reason is because the pattern string is not limited to only plain text. As hinted earlier, it can also contain what are known as *meta-characters*, which are special characters that provide commands, as well as escape sequences, which work in much the same way as C# escape sequences. They are characters preceded by a backslash (\) and have special meanings.

For example, suppose you wanted to find words beginning with n. You could use the escape sequence \b, which indicates a word boundary (a word boundary is just a point where an alphanumeric character precedes or follows a whitespace character or punctuation symbol):

```
const string pattern = @"\bn";
MatchCollection myMatches = Regex.Matches(myText, pattern,
                            RegexOptions.IgnoreCase |
                            RegexOptions.ExplicitCapture);
```

Notice the @ character in front of the string. You want the \b to be passed to the .NET regular expressions engine at runtime — you don't want the backslash intercepted by a well-meaning C# compiler that thinks it's an escape sequence in your source code. If you want to find words ending with the sequence ion, you write this:

```
const string pattern = @"ion\b";
```

If you want to find all words beginning with the letter a and ending with the sequence ion (which has as its only match the word *application* in the example), you have to put a bit more thought into your code. You clearly need a pattern that begins with \ba and ends with ion\b, but what goes in the middle? You need to somehow tell the application that between the a and the ion there can be any number of characters as long as none of them are whitespace. In fact, the correct pattern looks like this:

```
const string pattern = @"\ba\S*ion\b";
```

Eventually you will get used to seeing weird sequences of characters like this when working with regular expressions. It actually works quite logically. The escape sequence \S indicates any character that is not a whitespace character. The * is called a *quantifier*. It means that the preceding character can be repeated any number of times, including zero times. The sequence \S* means *any number of characters as long as they are not whitespace characters*. The preceding pattern will, therefore, match any single word that begins with a and ends with ion.

The following table lists some of the main special characters or escape sequences that you can use. It is not comprehensive, but a fuller list is available in the MSDN documentation.

SYMBOL	DESCRIPTION	EXAMPLE	MATCHES
^	Beginning of input text	^B	B, but only if first character in text
$	End of input text	X$	X, but only if last character in text
.	Any single character except the newline character (\ )	i.ation	isation, ization
*	Preceding character may be repeated zero or more times	ra*t	rt, rat, raat, raaat, and so on
+	Preceding character may be repeated one or more times	ra+t	rat, raat, raaat and so on, but not rt
?	Preceding character may be repeated zero or one time	ra?t	rt and rat only
\s	Any whitespace character	\sa	[space]a, \ta, \na (\t and \n have the same meanings as in C#)
\S	Any character that isn't whitespace	\SF	aF, rF, cF, but not \tf
\b	Word boundary	ion\b	Any word ending in ion
\B	Any position that isn't a word boundary	\BX\B	Any X in the middle of a word

If you want to search for one of the meta-characters, you can do so by escaping the corresponding character with a backslash. For example, . (a single period) means any single character other than the newline character, whereas \. means a dot.

You can request a match that contains alternative characters by enclosing them in square brackets. For example, [1|c] means one character that can be either 1 or c. If you wanted to search for any occurrence of the words map or man, you would use the sequence ma[n|p]. Within the square brackets, you can also indicate a range, for example [a-z], to indicate any single lowercase letter, [A-E] to indicate any uppercase letter between A and E (including the letters A and E themselves), or [0-9] to represent a single digit. If you wanted to search for an integer (that is, a sequence that contains only the characters 0 through 9), you could write [0-9]+.

> **NOTE** *The use of the + character specifies there must be at least one such digit, but there may be more than one — so this would match 9, 83, 854, and so on.*

Displaying Results

In this section, you code the `RegularExpressionsPlayaround` example to get a feel for how regular expressions work.

The core of the example is a method called `WriteMatches()`, which writes out all the matches from a `MatchCollection` in a more detailed format. For each match, it displays the index of where the match was found in the input string, the string of the match, and a slightly longer string, which consists of the match plus up to 10 surrounding characters from the input text — up to five characters before the match and up to five afterward. (It is fewer than five characters if the match occurred within five characters of the beginning or end of the input text.) In other words, a match on the word `messaging` that occurs near the end of the input text quoted earlier would display `and messaging of d` (five characters before and after the match), but a match on the final word `data` would display `g of data.` (only one character after the match), because after that you get to the end of the string. This longer string enables you to see more clearly where the regular expression locates the match:

```
static void WriteMatches(string text, MatchCollection matches)
{
    Console.WriteLine("Original text was: \n\n" + text + "\n");
    Console.WriteLine("No. of matches: " + matches.Count);

    foreach (Match nextMatch in matches)
    {
        int index = nextMatch.Index;
        string result = nextMatch.ToString();
        int charsBefore = (index < 5) ? index: 5;
        int fromEnd = text.Length-index-result.Length;
        int charsAfter = (fromEnd < 5) ? fromEnd: 5;
        int charsToDisplay = charsBefore + charsAfter + result.Length;

        Console.WriteLine("Index: {0}, \tString: {1}, \t{2}",
            index, result, text.Substring(index-charsBefore, charsToDisplay));
    }
}
```

The bulk of the processing in this method is devoted to the logic of figuring out how many characters in the longer substring it can display without overrunning the beginning or end of the input text. Note that you use another property on the `Match` object, `Value`, which contains the string identified for the match. Other than that, `RegularExpressionsPlayaround` simply contains a number of methods with names such as `Find1`, `Find2`, and so on, which perform some of the searches based on the examples in this section. For example, `Find2` looks for any string that contains a at the beginning of a word:

```
static void Find2()
{
    string text = @"This comprehensive compendium provides a broad and thorough
        investigation of all aspects of programming with ASP.NET. Entirely revised and
        updated for the 3.5 Release of .NET, this book will give you the information
        you need to master ASP.NET and build a dynamic, successful, enterprise Web
        application.";
    string pattern = @"\ba";
    MatchCollection matches = Regex.Matches(text, pattern,
        RegexOptions.IgnoreCase);
    WriteMatches(text, matches);
}
```

Along with this is a simple `Main()` method that you can edit to select one of the `Find<n>()` methods:

```
static void Main()
{
    Find1();
    Console.ReadLine();
}
```

The code also needs to make use of the `RegularExpressions` namespace:

```
using System;
using System.Text.RegularExpressions;
```

Running the example with the `Find2()` method shown previously gives these results:

```
RegularExpressionsPlayaround
Original text was:

This comprehensive compendium provides a broad and thorough investigation of all
aspects of programming with ASP.NET. Entirely revised and updated for the 3.5
Release of .NET, this book will give you the information you need to master ASP.NET
and build a dynamic, successful, enterprise Web application.

No. of matches: 1
Index: 291,     String: application,     Web application.
```

Matches, Groups, and Captures

One nice feature of regular expressions is that you can group characters. It works the same way as compound statements in C#. In C#, you can group any number of statements by putting them in braces, and the result is treated as one compound statement. In regular expression patterns, you can group any characters (including meta-characters and escape sequences), and the result is treated as a single character. The only difference is that you use parentheses instead of braces. The resultant sequence is known as a group.

For example, the pattern `(an)+` locates any recurrences of the sequence an. The + quantifier applies only to the previous character, but because you have grouped the characters together, it now applies to repeats of an treated as a unit. This means that if you apply `(an)+` to the input text, `bananas came to Europe late in the annals of history`, the anan from `bananas` is identified; however, if you write an+, the program selects the ann from `annals`, as well as two separate sequences of an from `bananas`. The expression `(an)+` identifies occurrences of an, anan, ananan, and so on, whereas the expression an+ identifies occurrences of an, ann, annn, and so on.

> **NOTE** *You might be wondering why with the preceding example* (an)+ *selects anan from the word "banana" but doesn't identify either of the two occurrences of an from the same word. The rule is that matches must not overlap. If a couple of possibilities would overlap, then by default the longest possible sequence is matched.*

However, groups are actually more powerful than that. By default, when you form part of the pattern into a group, you are also asking the regular expression engine to remember any matches against just that group, as well as any matches against the entire pattern. In other words, you are treating that group as a pattern to be matched and returned in its own right. This can be extremely useful if you want to break up strings into component parts.

For example, URIs have the format `<protocol>://<address>:<port>`, where the port is optional. An example of this is `http://www.wrox.com:4355`. Suppose you want to extract the protocol, the address, and the port from a URI in which there may or may not be whitespace (but no punctuation) immediately following the URI. You could do so using this expression:

```
\b(\S+)://([^:]+)(?::(\S+))?\b
```

Here is how this expression works: First, the leading and trailing `\b` sequences ensure that you consider only portions of text that are entire words. Within that, the first group, `(\S+)://`, identifies one or more characters that don't count as whitespace, and that are followed by `://` — the `http://` at the start of an HTTP URI. The brackets cause the `http` to be stored as a group. Next, `([^:]+)` identifies the string `www.wrox.com` in the URI. This group will end either when it encounters the end of the word (the closing `\b`) or a colon (`:`) as marked by the next group.

The next group identifies the port (`:4355`). The following `?` indicates that this group is optional in the match — if there is no: xxxx, this won't prevent a match from being marked. This is very important because the port number is not always specified in a URI — in fact, it is usually absent. However, things are a bit more complicated than that. You want to indicate that the colon might or might not appear too, but you don't want to store this colon in the group. You achieved this by using two nested groups. The inner `(\S+)` identifies anything that follows the colon (for example, `4355`). The outer group contains the inner group preceded by the colon, and this group in turn is preceded by the sequence `?:`. This sequence indicates that the group in question should not be saved (you only want to save `4355`; you don't need `:4355` as well!). Don't be confused by the two colons following each other — the first colon is part of the `?:` sequence that says "don't save this group," and the second is text to be searched for.

If you run this pattern on the following string, you'll get one match: `http://www.wrox.com`:

```
Hey I've just found this amazing URI at
http:// what was it --oh yes http://www.wrox.com
```

Within this match you will find the three groups just mentioned, as well as a fourth group that represents the match itself. Theoretically, it is possible for each group itself to return no, one, or more than one match. Each of these individual matches is known as a *capture*. Therefore, the first group, `(\S+)`, has one capture, `http`. The second group also has one capture (`www.wrox.com`). The third group, however, has no captures, because there is no port number on this URI.

Notice that the string contains a second `http://`. Although this does match up to the first group, it will not be captured by the search because the entire search expression does not match this part of the text.

There isn't space here to show examples of C# code that uses groups and captures, but you should know that the .NET `RegularExpressions` classes support groups and captures through classes known as `Group` and `Capture`. Also, the `GroupCollection` and `CaptureCollection` classes represent collections of groups and captures, respectively. The `Match` class exposes the `Groups` property, which returns the corresponding `GroupCollection` object. The `Group` class correspondingly implements the `Captures` property, which returns a `CaptureCollection`. The relationship between the objects is shown in Figure 9-3.

You might not want to return a `Group` object every time you just want to group some characters. A fair amount of overhead is involved in instantiating the object, which is not necessary if all you want to do is group some characters as part of your search pattern. You can disable this by starting the group with the character sequence `?:` for an individual group, as was done for the URI example, or for all groups by specifying the `RegExOptions.ExplicitCaptures` flag on the `RegEx.Matches()` method, as was done in the earlier examples.

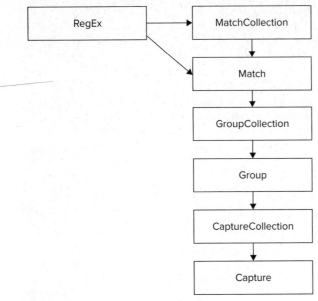

FIGURE 9-3

SUMMARY

You have quite a number of available data types at your disposal when working with the .NET Framework. One of the most frequently used types in your applications (especially applications that focus on submitting and retrieving data) is the `string` data type. The importance of `string` is the reason why this book has an entire chapter that focuses on how to use the `string` data type and manipulate it in your applications.

When working with strings in the past, it was quite common to just slice and dice the strings as needed using concatenation. With the .NET Framework, you can use the `StringBuilder` class to accomplish a lot of this task with better performance than before.

Last, but hardly least, advanced string manipulation using regular expressions is an excellent tool to search through and validate your strings.

10

Collections

WROX.COM CODE DOWNLOADS FOR THIS CHAPTER

The wrox.com code downloads for this chapter are found at `http://www.wrox.com/remtitle .cgi?isbn=1118314425` on the Download Code tab. The code for this chapter is divided into the following major examples:

➤ List Samples

➤ Queue Sample

➤ Linked List Sample

➤ Sorted List Sample

➤ Dictionary Sample

➤ Set Sample

➤ Observable Collection Sample

➤ BitArray Sample

➤ Pipeline Sample

OVERVIEW

In Chapter 6, "Arrays and Tuples," you learned about arrays and the interfaces implemented by the `Array` class. The size of arrays is fixed. If the number of elements is dynamic, you should use a collection class instead of an array.

List<T> is a collection class that can be compared to arrays; but there are also other kinds of collections: queues, stacks, linked lists, dictionaries, and sets. The other collection classes have partly different APIs to access the elements in the collection and often a different internal structure for how the items are stored in memory. This chapter covers all of these collection classes and their differences, including performance differences.

You can also read about bit arrays and concurrent collections that can be used from multiple threads.

> **NOTE** *Version 1 of the .NET Framework included only non-generic collection classes such as* ArrayList *and* HashTable. *CLR 2.0 added support for generics and added generic collection classes. The focus of this chapter is just on the newer group of collection classes and ignores the old ones, as they are not needed with new applications.*

COLLECTION INTERFACES AND TYPES

Most collection classes can be found in the System.Collections and System.Collections.Generic namespaces. Generic collection classes are located in the System.Collections.Generic namespace. Collection classes that are specialized for a specific type are located in the System.Collections .Specialized namespace. Thread-safe collection classes are in the System.Collections.Concurrent namespace.

Of course, there are also other ways to group collection classes. Collections can be grouped into lists, collections, and dictionaries based on the interfaces that are implemented by the collection class.

> **NOTE** *You can read detailed information about the interfaces IEnumerable and IEnumerator in Chapter 6.*

The following table describes interfaces implemented by collections and lists.

INTERFACE	DESCRIPTION
IEnumerable<T>	The interface IEnumerable is required by the foreach statement. This interface defines the method GetEnumerator which returns an enumerator that implements the IEnumerator interface.
ICollection<T>	ICollection<T> is implemented by generic collection classes. With this you can get the number of items in the collection (Count property), and copy the collection to an array (CopyTo method). You can also add and remove items from the collection (Add, Remove, Clear).
IList<T>	The IList<T> interface is for lists where elements can be accessed from their position. This interface defines an indexer, as well as ways to insert or remove items from specific positions (Insert, RemoveAt methods). IList<T> derives from ICollection<T>.

INTERFACE	DESCRIPTION
ISet<T>	This interface is implemented by sets. Sets allow combining different sets into a union, getting the intersection of two sets, and checking whether two sets overlap. ISet<T> derives from ICollection<T>.
IDictionary<TKey, TValue>	The interface IDictionary<TKey, TValue> is implemented by generic collection classes that have a key and a value. With this interface all the keys and values can be accessed, items can be accessed with an indexer of type key, and items can be added or removed.
ILookup<TKey, TValue>	Similar to the IDictionary<TKey, TValue> interface, lookups have keys and values. However, with lookups the collection can contain multiple values with one key.
IComparer<T>	The interface IComparer<T> is implemented by a comparer and used to sort elements inside a collection with the Compare method.
IEqualityComparer<T>	IEqualityComparer<T> is implemented by a comparer that can be used for keys in a dictionary. With this interface the objects can be compared for equality. Since .NET 4, this interface is also implemented by arrays and tuples.
IProducerConsumerCollection<T>	The interface IProducerConsumerCollection<T> is new since .NET 4 to support new thread-safe collection classes.

LISTS

For dynamic lists, the .NET Framework offers the generic class List<T>. This class implements the IList, ICollection, IEnumerable, IList<T>, ICollection<T>, and IEnumerable<T> interfaces.

The following examples use the members of the class Racer as elements to be added to the collection to represent a Formula-1 racer. This class has five properties: Id, FirstName, LastName, Country, and the number of Wins. With the constructors of the class, the name of the racer and the number of wins can be passed to set the members. The method ToString is overridden to return the name of the racer. The class Racer also implements the generic interface IComparable<T> for sorting racer elements and IFormattable (code file ListSamples/Racer.cs):

```
[Serializable]
public class Racer: IComparable<Racer>, IFormattable
{
  public int Id { get; private set; }
  public string FirstName { get; set; }
  public string LastName { get; set; }
  public string Country { get; set; }
  public int Wins { get; set; }

  public Racer(int id, string firstName, string lastName,
               string country)
    :this(id, firstName, lastName, country, wins: 0)
  { }

  public Racer(int id, string firstName, string lastName,
               string country, int wins)
  {
    this.Id = id;
```

```
      this.FirstName = firstName;
      this.LastName = lastName;
      this.Country = country;
      this.Wins = wins;
   }

   public override string ToString()
   {
      return String.Format("{0} {1}", FirstName, LastName);
   }

   public string ToString(string format, IFormatProvider formatProvider)
   {
      if (format == null) format = "N";
      switch (format.ToUpper())
      {
        case "N": // name
          return ToString();
        case "F": // first name
          return FirstName;
        case "L": // last name
          return LastName;
        case "W": // Wins
          return String.Format("{0}, Wins: {1}", ToString(), Wins);
        case "C": // Country
          return String.Format("{0}, Country: {1}", ToString(), Country);
        case "A": // All
          return String.Format("{0}, {1} Wins: {2}", ToString(), Country,
                               Wins);
        default:
          throw new FormatException(String.Format(formatProvider,
                    "Format {0} is not supported", format));
      }
   }

   public string ToString(string format)
   {
      return ToString(format, null);
   }

   public int CompareTo(Racer other)
   {
      if (other == null) return -1;
      int compare = string.Compare(this.LastName, other.LastName);
      if (compare == 0)
        return string.Compare(this.FirstName, other.FirstName);
      return compare;
   }
}
```

Creating Lists

You can create list objects by invoking the default constructor. With the generic class List<T>, you must specify the type for the values of the list with the declaration. The following code shows how to declare a List<T> with int and a list with Racer elements. ArrayList is a non-generic list that accepts any Object type for its elements.

Using the default constructor creates an empty list. As soon as elements are added to the list, the capacity of the list is extended to allow four elements. If the fifth element is added, the list is resized to allow eight elements. If eight elements are not enough, the list is resized again to contain 16 elements. With every resize the capacity of the list is doubled.

```
var intList = new List<int>();
var racers = new List<Racer>();
```

If the capacity of the list changes, the complete collection is reallocated to a new memory block. With the implementation of `List<T>`, an array of type `T` is used. With reallocation, a new array is created, and `Array.Copy` copies the elements from the old array to the new array. To save time, if you know the number of elements in advance, that should be in the list; you can define the capacity with the constructor. The following example creates a collection with a capacity of 10 elements. If the capacity is not large enough for the elements added, the capacity is resized to 20 and then to 40 elements — doubled again:

```
List<int> intList = new List<int>(10);
```

You can get and set the capacity of a collection by using the `Capacity` property:

```
intList.Capacity = 20;
```

The capacity is not the same as the number of elements in the collection. The number of elements in the collection can be read with the `Count` property. Of course, the capacity is always larger or equal to the number of items. As long as no element was added to the list, the count is 0:

```
Console.WriteLine(intList.Count);
```

If you are finished adding elements to the list and don't want to add any more, you can get rid of the unneeded capacity by invoking the `TrimExcess` method; however, because the relocation takes time, `TrimExcess` has no effect if the item count is more than 90 percent of capacity:

```
intList.TrimExcess();
```

Collection Initializers

You can also assign values to collections using collection initializers. The syntax of collection initializers is similar to array initializers, explained in Chapter 6. With a collection initializer, values are assigned to the collection within curly brackets at the time the collection is initialized:

```
var intList = new List<int>() {1, 2};
var stringList = new List<string>() {"one", "two"};
```

> **NOTE** *Collection initializers are not reflected within the IL code of the compiled assembly. The compiler converts the collection initializer to invoke the* Add *method for every item from the initializer list.*

Adding Elements

You can add elements to the list with the `Add` method, shown in the following example. The generic instantiated type defines the parameter type of the `Add` method:

```
var intList = new List<int>();
intList.Add(1);
intList.Add(2);
```

```
var stringList = new List<string>();
stringList.Add("one");
stringList.Add("two");
```

The variable `racers` is defined as type `List<Racer>`. With the `new` operator, a new object of the same type is created. Because the class `List<T>` was instantiated with the concrete class `Racer`, now only `Racer` objects can be added with the `Add` method. In the following sample code, five Formula-1 racers are created and added to the collection. The first three are added using the collection initializer, and the last two are added by invoking the `Add` method explicitly (code file `ListSamples/Program.cs`):

```
var graham = new Racer(7, "Graham", "Hill", "UK", 14);
var emerson = new Racer(13, "Emerson", "Fittipaldi", "Brazil", 14);
var mario = new Racer(16, "Mario", "Andretti", "USA", 12);

var racers = new List<Racer>(20) {graham, emerson, mario};

racers.Add(new Racer(24, "Michael", "Schumacher", "Germany", 91));
racers.Add(new Racer(27, "Mika", "Hakkinen", "Finland", 20));
```

With the `AddRange` method of the `List<T>` class, you can add multiple elements to the collection at once. The method `AddRange` accepts an object of type `IEnumerable<T>`, so you can also pass an array as shown here:

```
racers.AddRange(new Racer[] {
    new Racer(14, "Niki", "Lauda", "Austria", 25),
    new Racer(21, "Alain", "Prost", "France", 51)});
```

> **NOTE** *The collection initializer can be used only during declaration of the collection. The `AddRange` method can be invoked after the collection is initialized.*

If you know some elements of the collection when instantiating the list, you can also pass any object that implements `IEnumerable<T>` to the constructor of the class. This is very similar to the `AddRange` method:

```
var racers = new List<Racer>(
    new Racer[] {
        new Racer(12, "Jochen", "Rindt", "Austria", 6),
        new Racer(22, "Ayrton", "Senna", "Brazil", 41) });
```

Inserting Elements

You can insert elements at a specified position with the `Insert` method:

```
racers.Insert(3, new Racer(6, "Phil", "Hill", "USA", 3));
```

The method `InsertRange` offers the capability to insert a number of elements, similar to the `AddRange` method shown earlier.

If the index set is larger than the number of elements in the collection, an exception of type `ArgumentOutOfRangeException` is thrown.

Accessing Elements

All classes that implement the `IList` and `IList<T>` interface offer an indexer, so you can access the elements by using an indexer and passing the item number. The first item can be accessed with an index value 0. By specifying `racers[3]`, for example, you access the fourth element of the list:

```
Racer r1 = racers[3];
```

Getting the number of elements with the `Count` property, you can do a `for` loop to iterate through every item in the collection, and use the indexer to access every item:

```
for (int i = 0; i < racers.Count; i++)
{
  Console.WriteLine(racers[i]);
}
```

> **NOTE** *Indexed access to collection classes is available with* `ArrayList`, `StringCollection`, *and* `List<T>`.

Because `List<T>` implements the interface `IEnumerable`, you can iterate through the items in the collection using the `foreach` statement as well:

```
foreach (Racer r in racers)
{
  Console.WriteLine(r);
}
```

> **NOTE** *How the foreach statement is resolved by the compiler to make use of the* `IEnumerable` *and* `IEnumerator` *interfaces is explained in Chapter 6.*

Instead of using the `foreach` statement, the `List<T>` class also offers a `ForEach` method that is declared with an `Action<T>` parameter:

```
public void ForEach(Action<T> action);
```

The implementation of `ForEach` is shown next. `ForEach` iterates through every item of the collection and invokes the method that is passed as parameter for every item:

```
public class List<T>: IList<T>
{
  private T[] items;

  //...

  public void ForEach(Action<T> action)
  {
    if (action == null) throw new ArgumentNullException("action");

    foreach (T item in items)
    {
      action(item);
    }
  }
  //...
}
```

To pass a method with `ForEach`, `Action<T>` is declared as a delegate that defines a method with a `void` return type and parameter `T`:

```
public delegate void Action<T>(T obj);
```

With a list of `Racer` items, the handler for the `ForEach` method must be declared with a `Racer` object as parameter and a `void` return type:

```
public void ActionHandler(Racer obj);
```

Because one overload of the `Console.WriteLine` method accepts `Object` as a parameter, you can pass the address of this method to the `ForEach` method, and every racer of the collection is written to the console:

```
racers.ForEach(Console.WriteLine);
```

You can also write a lambda expression that accepts a `Racer` object as parameter and contains an implementation to write a string to the console using `Console.WriteLine`. Here, the format `A` is used with the `ToString` method of the `IFormattable` interface to display all information about the racer:

```
racers.ForEach(r => Console.WriteLine("{0:A}", r));
```

> **NOTE** *Lambda expressions are explained in Chapter 8, "Delegates, Lambdas, and Events."*

Removing Elements

You can remove elements by index or pass the item that should be removed. Here, the fourth element is removed from the collection:

```
racers.RemoveAt(3);
```

You can also directly pass a `Racer` object to the `Remove` method to remove this element. Removing by index is faster, because here the collection must be searched for the item to remove. The `Remove` method first searches in the collection to get the index of the item with the `IndexOf` method, and then uses the index to remove the item. `IndexOf` first checks if the item type implements the interface `IEquatable<T>`. If it does, the `Equals` method of this interface is invoked to find the item in the collection that is the same as the one passed to the method. If this interface is not implemented, the `Equals` method of the `Object` class is used to compare the items. The default implementation of the `Equals` method in the `Object` class does a bitwise compare with value types, but compares only references with reference types.

> **NOTE** *Chapter 7, "Operators and Casts," explains how you can override the `Equals` method.*

In the following example, the racer referenced by the variable `graham` is removed from the collection. The variable `graham` was created earlier when the collection was filled. Because the interface `IEquatable<T>` and the `Object.Equals` method are not overridden with the `Racer` class, you cannot create a new object with the same content as the item that should be removed and pass it to the `Remove` method:

```
if (!racers.Remove(graham))
{
  Console.WriteLine("object not found in collection");
}
```

The method `RemoveRange` removes a number of items from the collection. The first parameter specifies the index where the removal of items should begin; the second parameter specifies the number of items to be removed:

```
int index = 3;
int count = 5;
racers.RemoveRange(index, count);
```

To remove all items with some specific characteristics from the collection, you can use the `RemoveAll` method. This method uses the `Predicate<T>` parameter when searching for elements, which is discussed next. To remove all elements from the collection, use the `Clear` method defined with the `ICollection<T>` interface.

Searching

There are different ways to search for elements in the collection. You can get the index to the found item, or the item itself. You can use methods such as `IndexOf`, `LastIndexOf`, `FindIndex`, `FindLastIndex`, `Find`, and `FindLast`. To just check whether an item exists, the `List<T>` class offers the `Exists` method.

The method `IndexOf` requires an object as parameter and returns the index of the item if it is found inside the collection. If the item is not found, –1 is returned. Remember that `IndexOf` is using the `IEquatable<T>` interface to compare the elements:

```
int index1 = racers.IndexOf(mario);
```

With the `IndexOf` method, you can also specify that the complete collection should not be searched, instead specifying an index where the search should start and the number of elements that should be iterated for the comparison.

Instead of searching a specific item with the `IndexOf` method, you can search for an item that has some specific characteristics that you can define with the `FindIndex` method. `FindIndex` requires a parameter of type `Predicate`:

```
public int FindIndex(Predicate<T> match);
```

The `Predicate<T>` type is a delegate that returns a Boolean value and requires type `T` as parameter. This delegate can be used similarly to the `Action` delegate shown earlier with the `ForEach` method. If the predicate returns `true`, there's a match and the element is found. If it returns `false`, the element is not found and the search continues.

```
public delegate bool Predicate<T>(T obj);
```

With the `List<T>` class that is using `Racer` objects for type `T`, you can pass the address of a method that returns a `bool` and defines a parameter of type `Racer` to the `FindIndex` method. Finding the first racer of a specific country, you can create the `FindCountry` class as shown next. The `FindCountryPredicate` method has the signature and return type defined by the `Predicate<T>` delegate. The `Find` method uses the variable `country` to search for a country that you can pass with the constructor of the class.

```
public class FindCountry
{
  public FindCountry(string country)
  {
```

```
      this.country = country;
   }
   private string country;

   public bool FindCountryPredicate(Racer racer)
   {
      Contract.Requires<ArgumentNullException>(racer != null);

      return racer.Country == country;
   }
}
```

With the `FindIndex` method, you can create a new instance of the `FindCountry` class, pass a country string to the constructor, and pass the address of the `Find` method. In the following example, after `FindIndex` completes successfully, `index2` contains the index of the first item where the `Country` property of the racer is set to `Finland`:

```
int index2 = racers.FindIndex(new FindCountry("Finland").
                     FindCountryPredicate);
```

Instead of creating a class with a handler method, you can use a lambda expression here as well. The result is exactly the same as before. Now the lambda expression defines the implementation to search for an item where the `Country` property is set to `Finland`:

```
int index3 = racers.FindIndex(r => r.Country == "Finland");
```

Similar to the `IndexOf` method, with the `FindIndex` method you can also specify the index where the search should start and the count of items that should be iterated through. To do a search for an index beginning from the last element in the collection, you can use the `FindLastIndex` method.

The method `FindIndex` returns the index of the found item. Instead of getting the index, you can also go directly to the item in the collection. The `Find` method requires a parameter of type `Predicate<T>`, much as the `FindIndex` method. The `Find` method in the following example searches for the first racer in the list that has the `FirstName` property set to `Niki`. Of course, you can also do a `FindLast` search to find the last item that fulfills the predicate.

```
Racer racer = racers.Find(r => r.FirstName == "Niki");
```

To get not only one, but all the items that fulfill the requirements of a predicate, you can use the `FindAll` method. The `FindAll` method uses the same `Predicate<T>` delegate as the `Find` and `FindIndex` methods. The `FindAll` method does not stop when the first item is found but instead iterates through every item in the collection and returns all items for which the predicate returns `true`.

With the `FindAll` method invoked in the next example, all racer items are returned where the property `Wins` is set to more than 20. All racers who won more than 20 races are referenced from the `bigWinners` list:

```
List<Racer> bigWinners = racers.FindAll(r => r.Wins > 20);
```

Iterating through the variable `bigWinners` with a `foreach` statement gives the following result:

```
foreach (Racer r in bigWinners)
{
   Console.WriteLine("{0:A}", r);
}
```

```
Michael Schumacher, Germany Wins: 91
```

```
Niki Lauda, Austria Wins: 25
Alain Prost, France Wins: 51
```

The result is not sorted, but you'll see that done next.

Sorting

The `List<T>` class enables sorting its elements by using the `Sort` method. `Sort` uses the quick sort algorithm whereby all elements are compared until the complete list is sorted.

You can use several overloads of the `Sort` method. The arguments that can be passed are a generic delegate `Comparison<T>`, the generic interface `IComparer<T>`, and a range together with the generic interface `IComparer<T>`:

```
public void List<T>.Sort();
public void List<T>.Sort(Comparison<T>);
public void List<T>.Sort(IComparer<T>);
public void List<T>.Sort(Int32, Int32, IComparer<T>);
```

Using the `Sort` method without arguments is possible only if the elements in the collection implement the interface `IComparable`.

Here, the class `Racer` implements the interface `IComparable<T>` to sort racers by the last name:

```
racers.Sort();
racers.ForEach(Console.WriteLine);
```

If you need to do a sort other than the default supported by the item types, you need to use other techniques, such as passing an object that implements the `IComparer<T>` interface.

The class `RacerComparer` implements the interface `IComparer<T>` for `Racer` types. This class enables you to sort by either the first name, last name, country, or number of wins. The kind of sort that should be done is defined with the inner enumeration type `CompareType`. The `CompareType` is set with the constructor of the class `RacerComparer`. The interface `IComparer<Racer>` defines the method `Compare`, which is required for sorting. In the implementation of this method, the `Compare` and `CompareTo` methods of the `string` and `int` types are used (code file `ListSamples/RacerComparer.cs`):

```
public class RacerComparer: IComparer<Racer>
{
  public enum CompareType
  {
    FirstName,
    LastName,
    Country,
    Wins
  }

  private CompareType compareType;
  public RacerComparer(CompareType compareType)
  {
    this.compareType = compareType;
  }

  public int Compare(Racer x, Racer y)
  {
    if (x == null && y == null) return 0;
    if (x == null) return -1;
    if (y == null) return 1;

    int result;
```

```
switch (compareType)
{
  case CompareType.FirstName:
    return string.Compare(x.FirstName, y.FirstName);
  case CompareType.LastName:
    return string.Compare(x.LastName, y.LastName);
  case CompareType.Country:
    result = string.Compare(x.Country, y.Country);
    if (result == 0)
      return string.Compare(x.LastName, y.LastName);
    else
      return result;
  case CompareType.Wins:
    return x.Wins.CompareTo(y.Wins);
  default:
    throw new ArgumentException("Invalid Compare Type");
}
}
}
```

> **NOTE** *The* Compare *method returns 0 if the two elements passed to it are equal with the order. If a value less than 0 is returned, the first argument is less than the second. With a value larger than 0, the first argument is greater than the second. Passing null with an argument, the method shouldn't throw a* NullReferenceException. *Instead, null should take its place before any other element, thus –1 is returned if the first argument is null, and +1 if the second argument is null.*

An instance of the RacerComparer class can now be used with the Sort method. Passing the enumeration RacerComparer.CompareType.Country sorts the collection by the property Country:

```
racers.Sort(new RacerComparer(RacerComparer.CompareType.Country));
racers.ForEach(Console.WriteLine);
```

Another way to do the sort is by using the overloaded Sort method, which requires a Comparison<T> delegate:

```
public void List<T>.Sort(Comparison<T>);
```

Comparison<T> is a delegate to a method that has two parameters of type T and a return type int. If the parameter values are equal, the method must return 0. If the first parameter is less than the second, a value less than zero must be returned; otherwise, a value greater than zero is returned:

```
public delegate int Comparison<T>(T x, T y);
```

Now you can pass a lambda expression to the Sort method to do a sort by the number of wins. The two parameters are of type Racer, and in the implementation the Wins properties are compared by using the int method CompareTo. Also in the implementation, r2 and r1 are used in reverse order, so the number of wins is sorted in descending order. After the method has been invoked, the complete racer list is sorted based on the racer's number of wins:

```
racers.Sort((r1, r2) => r2.Wins.CompareTo(r1.Wins));
```

You can also reverse the order of a complete collection by invoking the Reverse method.

Type Conversion

With the List<T> method ConvertAll<TOutput>, all types of a collection can be converted to a different type. The ConvertAll<TOutput> method uses a Converter delegate that is defined like this:

```
public sealed delegate TOutput Converter<TInput, TOutput>(TInput from);
```

The generic types TInput and TOutput are used with the conversion. TInput is the argument of the delegate method, and TOutput is the return type.

In this example, all Racer types should be converted to Person types. Whereas the Racer type contains a firstName, lastName, country, and the number of wins, the Person type contains just a name. For the conversion, the country of the racer and the number of race wins can be ignored, but the name must be converted:

```
[Serializable]
public class Person
{
  private string name;

  public Person(string name)
  {
    this.name = name;
  }

  public override string ToString()
  {
    return name;
  }
}
```

The conversion happens by invoking the racers.ConvertAll<Person> method. The argument of this method is defined as a lambda expression with an argument of type Racer and a Person type that is returned. In the implementation of the lambda expression, a new Person object is created and returned. For the Person object, the FirstName and LastName are passed to the constructor:

```
List<Person> persons =
    racers.ConvertAll<Person>(
        r => new Person(r.FirstName + " " + r.LastName));
```

The result of the conversion is a list containing the converted Person objects: persons of type List<Person>.

Read-Only Collections

After collections are created they are read/write of course; otherwise, you couldn't fill them with any values. However, after the collection is filled, you can create a read-only collection. The List<T> collection has the method AsReadOnly that returns an object of type ReadOnlyCollection<T>. The class ReadOnlyCollection<T> implements the same interfaces as List<T>, but all methods and properties that change the collection throw a NotSupportedException.

QUEUES

A queue is a collection whose elements are processed *first in, first out* (FIFO), meaning the item that is put first in the queue is read first. Examples of queues are standing in line at the airport, a human resources queue to process employee applicants, print jobs waiting to be processed in a print queue, and a thread waiting for the CPU in a round-robin fashion. Sometimes the elements of a queue differ in their priority. For example, in the queue at the airport, business passengers are processed before economy passengers. In this case, multiple queues can be used, one queue for each priority. At the airport this is easily handled with separate check-in queues for business and economy passengers. The same is true for print queues and threads. You can have an array or a list of queues whereby one item in the array stands for a priority. Within every array item there's a queue, where processing happens using the FIFO principle.

> **NOTE** *Later in this chapter, a different implementation with a linked list is used to define a list of priorities.*

A queue is implemented with the `Queue<T>` class in the namespace `System.Collections.Generic`. Internally, the `Queue<T>` class is using an array of type `T`, similar to the `List<T>` type. It implements the interfaces `IEnumerable<T>` and `ICollection`; but not `ICollection<T>`, which is not implemented because this interface defines `Add` and `Remove` methods that shouldn't be available for queues.

The `Queue<T>` class does not implement the interface `IList<T>`, so you cannot access the queue using an indexer. The queue just allows you to add an item to it, which is put at the end of the queue (with the `Enqueue` method), and to get items from the head of the queue (with the `Dequeue` method).

Figure 10-1 shows the items of a queue. The `Enqueue` method adds items to one end of the queue; the items are read and removed at the other end of the queue with the `Dequeue` method. Invoking the `Dequeue` method once more removes the next item from the queue.

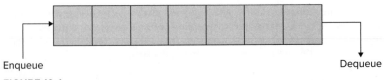

Enqueue   Dequeue

FIGURE 10-1

Methods of the `Queue<T>` class are described in the following table.

SELECTED QUEUE <T> MEMBERS	DESCRIPTION
Count	Returns the number of items in the queue.
Enqueue	Adds an item to the end of the queue.
Dequeue	Reads and removes an item from the head of the queue. If there are no more items in the queue when the `Dequeue` method is invoked, an exception of type `InvalidOperationException` is thrown.
Peek	Reads an item from the head of the queue but does not remove the item.
TrimExcess	Resizes the capacity of the queue. The `Dequeue` method removes items from the queue, but it doesn't resize the capacity of the queue. To get rid of the empty items at the beginning of the queue, use the `TrimExcess` method.

When creating queues, you can use constructors similar to those used with the List<T> type. The default constructor creates an empty queue, but you can also use a constructor to specify the capacity. As items are added to the queue, the capacity is increased to hold 4, 8, 16, and 32 items if the capacity is not defined. Similar to the List<T> class, the capacity is always doubled as required. The default constructor of the non-generic Queue class is different, because it creates an initial array of 32 empty items. With an overload of the constructor, you can also pass any other collection that implements the IEnumerable<T> interface that is copied to the queue.

The following example demonstrating the use of the Queue<T> class is a document management application. One thread is used to add documents to the queue, and another thread reads documents from the queue and processes them.

The items stored in the queue are of type Document. The Document class defines a title and content (code file QueueSample/Document.cs):

```
public class Document
{
  public string Title { get; private set; }
  public string Content { get; private set; }

  public Document(string title, string content)
  {
    this.Title = title;
    this.Content = content;
  }
}
```

The DocumentManager class is a thin layer around the Queue<T> class. It defines how to handle documents: adding documents to the queue with the AddDocument method, and getting documents from the queue with the GetDocument method.

Inside the AddDocument method, the document is added to the end of the queue using the Enqueue method. The first document from the queue is read with the Dequeue method inside GetDocument. Because multiple threads can access the DocumentManager concurrently, access to the queue is locked with the lock statement.

> **NOTE** *Threading and the* lock *statement are discussed in Chapter 21, "Threads, Tasks, and Synchronization."*

IsDocumentAvailable is a read-only Boolean property that returns true if there are documents in the queue, and false if not (code file QueueSample/DocumentManager.cs):

```
public class DocumentManager
{
  private readonly Queue<Document> documentQueue = new Queue<Document>();

  public void AddDocument(Document doc)
  {
    lock (this)
    {
      documentQueue.Enqueue(doc);
    }
  }

  public Document GetDocument()
```

```
  {
    Document doc = null;
    lock (this)
    {
      doc = documentQueue.Dequeue();
    }
    return doc;
  }

  public bool IsDocumentAvailable
  {
    get
    {
      return documentQueue.Count > 0;
    }
  }
}
```

The class `ProcessDocuments` processes documents from the queue in a separate task. The only method that can be accessed from the outside is `Start`. In the `Start` method, a new task is instantiated. A `ProcessDocuments` object is created to starting the task, and the `Run` method is defined as the start method of the task. The `StartNew` method of the `TaskFactory` (which is accessed from the static `Factory` property of the `Task` class) requires a delegate `Action` parameter where the address of the `Run` method can be passed to. The `StartNew` method of the `TaskFactory` immediately starts the task.

With the `Run` method of the `ProcessDocuments` class, an endless loop is defined. Within this loop, the property `IsDocumentAvailable` is used to determine whether there is a document in the queue. If so, the document is taken from the `DocumentManager` and processed. Processing in this example is writing information only to the console. In a real application, the document could be written to a file, written to the database, or sent across the network (code file `QueueSample/ProcessDocuments.cs`):

```
public class ProcessDocuments
{
  public static void Start(DocumentManager dm)
  {
    Task.Factory.StartNew(new ProcessDocuments(dm).Run);
  }

  protected ProcessDocuments(DocumentManager dm)
  {
    if (dm == null)
      throw new ArgumentNullException("dm");
    documentManager = dm;
  }

  private DocumentManager documentManager;

  protected void Run()
  {
    while (true)
    {
      if (documentManager.IsDocumentAvailable)
      {
        Document doc = documentManager.GetDocument();
        Console.WriteLine("Processing document {0}", doc.Title);
      }
      Thread.Sleep(new Random().Next(20));
    }
  }
}
```

In the `Main` method of the application, a `DocumentManager` object is instantiated, and the document processing task is started. Then 1,000 documents are created and added to the `DocumentManager` (code file `QueueSample/Program.cs`):

```
class Program
{
  static void Main()
  {
    var dm = new DocumentManager();

    ProcessDocuments.Start(dm);

    // Create documents and add them to the DocumentManager
    for (int i = 0; i < 1000; i++)
    {
      var doc = new Document("Doc " + i.ToString(), "content");
      dm.AddDocument(doc);
      Console.WriteLine("Added document {0}", doc.Title);
      Thread.Sleep(new Random().Next(20));
    }
  }
}
```

When you start the application, the documents are added to and removed from the queue, and you get output similar to the following:

```
Added document Doc 279
Processing document Doc 236
Added document Doc 280
Processing document Doc 237
Added document Doc 281
Processing document Doc 238
Processing document Doc 239
Processing document Doc 240
Processing document Doc 241
Added document Doc 282
Processing document Doc 242
Added document Doc 283
Processing document Doc 243
```

A real-life scenario using the task described with the sample application might be an application that processes documents received with a Web service.

STACKS

A stack is another container that is very similar to the queue. You just use different methods to access the stack. The item that is added last to the stack is read first, so the stack is a *last in, first out* (LIFO) container.

Figure 10-2 shows the representation of a stack where the `Push` method adds an item to the stack, and the `Pop` method gets the item that was added last.

Similar to the `Queue<T>` class, the `Stack<T>` class implements the interfaces `IEnumerable<T>` and `ICollection`.

Members of the `Stack<T>` class are listed in the following table.

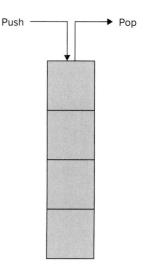

FIGURE 10-2

SELECTED STACK<T> MEMBERS	DESCRIPTION
Count	Returns the number of items in the stack.
Push	Adds an item on top of the stack.
Pop	Removes and returns an item from the top of the stack. If the stack is empty, an exception of type InvalidOperationException is thrown.
Peek	Returns an item from the top of the stack but does not remove the item.
Contains	Checks whether an item is in the stack and returns true if it is.

In this example, three items are added to the stack with the Push method. With the foreach method, all items are iterated using the IEnumerable interface. The enumerator of the stack does not remove the items; it just returns them item by item (code file StackSample/Program.cs):

```
var alphabet = new Stack<char>();
alphabet.Push('A');
alphabet.Push('B');
alphabet.Push('C');

foreach (char item in alphabet)
{
  Console.Write(item);
}
Console.WriteLine();
```

Because the items are read in order from the last item added to the first, the following result is produced:

```
CBA
```

Reading the items with the enumerator does not change the state of the items. With the Pop method, every item that is read is also removed from the stack. This way, you can iterate the collection using a while loop and verify the Count property if items still exist:

```
var alphabet = new Stack<char>();
alphabet.Push('A');
alphabet.Push('B');
alphabet.Push('C');

Console.Write("First iteration: ");
foreach (char item in alphabet)
{
  Console.Write(item);
}
Console.WriteLine();

Console.Write("Second iteration: ");
while (alphabet.Count > 0)
{
  Console.Write(alphabet.Pop());
}
Console.WriteLine();
```

The result gives CBA twice, once for each iteration. After the second iteration, the stack is empty because the second iteration used the Pop method:

```
First iteration: CBA
Second iteration: CBA
```

LINKED LISTS

LinkedList<T> is a doubly linked list, whereby one element references the next and the previous one, as shown in Figure 10-3. This way you can easily walk through the complete list forward by moving to the next element, or backward by moving to the previous element.

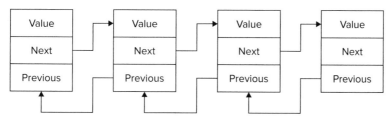

FIGURE 10-3

The advantage of a linked list is that if items are inserted in the middle of a list, the linked list is very fast. When an item is inserted, only the Next reference of the previous item and the Previous reference of the next item must be changed to reference the inserted item. With the List<T> class, when an element is inserted all subsequent elements must be moved.

Of course, there's also a disadvantage with linked lists. Items of linked lists can be accessed only one after the other. It takes a long time to find an item that's somewhere in the middle or at the end of the list.

A linked list cannot just store the items inside the list; together with every item, the linked list must have information about the next and previous items. That's why the LinkedList<T> contains items of type LinkedListNode<T>. With the class LinkedListNode<T>, you can get to the next and previous items in the list. The LinkedListNode<T> class defines the properties List, Next, Previous, and Value. The List property returns the LinkedList<T> object that is associated with the node. Next and Previous are for iterating through the list and accessing the next or previous item. Value returns the item that is associated with the node. Value is of type T.

The LinkedList<T> class itself defines members to access the first (First) and last (Last) item of the list, to insert items at specific positions (AddAfter, AddBefore, AddFirst, AddLast), to remove items from specific positions (Remove, RemoveFirst, RemoveLast), and to find elements where the search starts from either the beginning (Find) or the end (FindLast) of the list.

The sample application to demonstrate linked lists uses a linked list together with a list. The linked list contains documents as in the queue example, but the documents have an additional priority associated with them. The documents will be sorted inside the linked list depending on the priority. If multiple documents have the same priority, the elements are sorted according to the time when the document was inserted.

Figure 10-4 describes the collections of the sample application. LinkedList<Document> is the linked list containing all the Document objects. The figure shows the title and priority of the documents. The title indicates when the document was added to the list: The first document added has the title "One", the second document has the title "Two", and so on. You can see that the documents One and Four have the same priority, 8, but because One was added before Four, it is earlier in the list.

When new documents are added to the linked list, they should be added after the last document that has the same priority. The LinkedList<Document> collection contains elements of type

`LinkedListNode<Document>`. The class `LinkedListNode<T>` adds `Next` and `Previous` properties to walk from one node to the next. For referencing such elements, the `List<T>` is defined as `List<LinkedListNode<Document>>`. For fast access to the last document of every priority, the collection `List<LinkedListNode>` contains up to 10 elements, each referencing the last document of every priority. In the upcoming discussion, the reference to the last document of every priority is called the *priority node*.

Using the previous example, the `Document` class is extended to contain the priority, which is set with the constructor of the class (code file `LinkedListSample/Document.cs`):

```
public class Document
{
    public string Title { get; private set; }
    public string Content { get; private set; }
    public byte Priority { get; private set; }

    public Document(string title, string content, byte priority)
    {
        this.Title = title;
        this.Content = content;
        this.Priority = priority;
    }
}
```

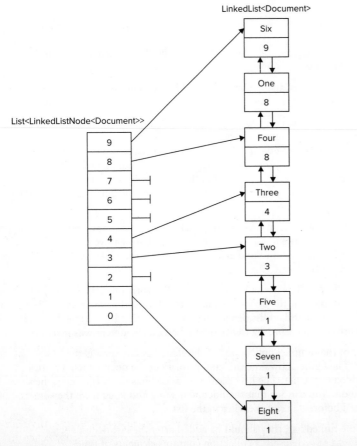

FIGURE 10-4

The heart of the solution is the `PriorityDocumentManager` class. This class is very easy to use. With the public interface of this class, new `Document` elements can be added to the linked list, the first document can be retrieved, and for testing purposes it also has a method to display all elements of the collection as they are linked in the list.

The class `PriorityDocumentManager` contains two collections. The collection of type `LinkedList<Document>` contains all documents. The collection of type `List<LinkedListNode<Document>>` contains references of up to 10 elements that are entry points for adding new documents with a specific priority. Both collection variables are initialized with the constructor of the class `PriorityDocumentManager`. The list collection is also initialized with `null` (code file `LinkedListSample/PriorityDocumentManager.cs`):

```
public class PriorityDocumentManager
{
    private readonly LinkedList<Document> documentList;

    // priorities 0.9
    private readonly List<LinkedListNode<Document>> priorityNodes;

    public PriorityDocumentManager()
    {
        documentList = new LinkedList<Document>();

        priorityNodes = new List<LinkedListNode<Document>>(10);
        for (int i = 0; i < 10; i++)
        {
            priorityNodes.Add(new LinkedListNode<Document>(null));
        }
    }
}
```

Part of the public interface of the class is the method `AddDocument`. `AddDocument` does nothing more than call the private method `AddDocumentToPriorityNode`. The reason for having the implementation inside a different method is that `AddDocumentToPriorityNode` may be called recursively, as you will see soon:

```
public void AddDocument(Document d)
{
    if (d == null) throw new ArgumentNullException("d");

    AddDocumentToPriorityNode(d, d.Priority);
}
```

The first action that is done in the implementation of `AddDocumentToPriorityNode` is a check to see if the priority fits in the allowed priority range. Here, the allowed range is between 0 and 9. If a wrong value is passed, an exception of type `ArgumentException` is thrown.

Next, you check whether there's already a priority node with the same priority as the priority that was passed. If there's no such priority node in the list collection, `AddDocumentToPriorityNode` is invoked recursively with the priority value decremented to check for a priority node with the next lower priority.

If there's no priority node with the same priority or any priority with a lower value, the document can be safely added to the end of the linked list by calling the method `AddLast`. In addition, the linked list node is referenced by the priority node that's responsible for the priority of the document.

If there's an existing priority node, you can get the position inside the linked list where the document should be inserted. In the following example, you must determine whether a priority node already exists with the correct priority, or if there's just a priority node that references a document with a lower priority. In the first case, you can insert the new document after the position referenced by the priority node. Because the priority node always must reference the last document with a specific priority, the reference of the priority node must be set. It gets more complex if only a priority node referencing a document with a lower priority exists. Here, the document must be inserted before all documents with the same priority as the priority node. To get the first document of the same priority, a `while` loop iterates through all linked list nodes, using the `Previous` property, until a linked list node is reached that has a different priority. This way, you know the position where the document must be inserted, and the priority node can be set:

```csharp
private void AddDocumentToPriorityNode(Document doc, int priority)
{
  if (priority > 9 || priority < 0)
    throw new ArgumentException("Priority must be between 0 and 9");

  if (priorityNodes[priority].Value == null)
  {
    --priority;
    if (priority >= 0)
    {
      // check for the next lower priority
      AddDocumentToPriorityNode(doc, priority);
    }
    else // now no priority node exists with the same priority or lower
         // add the new document to the end
    {
      documentList.AddLast(doc);
      priorityNodes[doc.Priority] = documentList.Last;
    }
    return;
  }
  else // a priority node exists
  {
    LinkedListNode<Document> prioNode = priorityNodes[priority];
    if (priority == doc.Priority)
        // priority node with the same priority exists
    {
      documentList.AddAfter(prioNode, doc);

      // set the priority node to the last document with the same priority
      priorityNodes[doc.Priority] = prioNode.Next;
    }
    else // only priority node with a lower priority exists
    {
      // get the first node of the lower priority
      LinkedListNode<Document> firstPrioNode = prioNode;

      while (firstPrioNode.Previous != null &&
          firstPrioNode.Previous.Value.Priority == prioNode.Value.Priority)
      {
        firstPrioNode = prioNode.Previous;
        prioNode = firstPrioNode;
      }

      documentList.AddBefore(firstPrioNode, doc);

      // set the priority node to the new value
      priorityNodes[doc.Priority] = firstPrioNode.Previous;
    }
  }
}
```

Now only simple methods are left for discussion. `DisplayAllNodes` does a `foreach` loop to display the priority and the title of every document to the console.

The method `GetDocument` returns the first document (the document with the highest priority) from the linked list and removes it from the list:

```
public void DisplayAllNodes()
{
  foreach (Document doc in documentList)
  {
    Console.WriteLine("priority: {0}, title {1}", doc.Priority, doc.Title);
  }
}

// returns the document with the highest priority
// (that's first in the linked list)
public Document GetDocument()
{
  Document doc = documentList.First.Value;
  documentList.RemoveFirst();
  return doc;
}
}
```

In the `Main` method, the `PriorityDocumentManager` is used to demonstrate its functionality. Eight new documents with different priorities are added to the linked list, and then the complete list is displayed (code file `LinkedListSample/Program.cs`):

```
static void Main()
{
  var pdm =  new PriorityDocumentManager();
  pdm.AddDocument(new Document("one", "Sample", 8));
  pdm.AddDocument(new Document("two", "Sample", 3));
  pdm.AddDocument(new Document("three", "Sample", 4));
  pdm.AddDocument(new Document("four", "Sample", 8));
  pdm.AddDocument(new Document("five", "Sample", 1));
  pdm.AddDocument(new Document("six", "Sample", 9));
  pdm.AddDocument(new Document("seven", "Sample", 1));
  pdm.AddDocument(new Document("eight", "Sample", 1));

  pdm.DisplayAllNodes();
}
```

With the processed result, you can see that the documents are sorted first by priority and second by when the document was added:

```
priority: 9, title six
priority: 8, title one
priority: 8, title four
priority: 4, title three
priority: 3, title two
priority: 1, title five
priority: 1, title seven
priority: 1, title eight
```

SORTED LIST

If the collection you need should be sorted based on a key, you can use the `SortedList<TKey, TValue>`. This class sorts the elements based on a key. You can use any type for the value, and also for the key.

The following example creates a sorted list for which both the key and the value are of type string. The default constructor creates an empty list, and then two books are added with the Add method. With overloaded constructors, you can define the capacity of the list and pass an object that implements the interface IComparer<TKey>, which is used to sort the elements in the list.

The first parameter of the Add method is the key (the book title); the second parameter is the value (the ISBN number). Instead of using the Add method, you can use the indexer to add elements to the list. The indexer requires the key as index parameter. If a key already exists, the Add method throws an exception of type ArgumentException. If the same key is used with the indexer, the new value replaces the old value (code file SortedListSample/Program.cs):

```
var books = new SortedList<string, string>();
books.Add("Professional WPF Programming", "978-0-470-04180-2");
books.Add("Professional ASP.NET MVC 3", "978-1-1180-7658-3");

books["Beginning Visual C# 2010"] = "978-0-470-50226-6";
books["Professional C# 4 and .NET 4"] = "978-0-470-50225-9";
```

> **NOTE** SortedList<TKey, TValue> *allows only one value per key. If you need multiple values per key you can use* Lookup<TKey, TElement>.

You can iterate through the list using a foreach statement. Elements returned by the enumerator are of type KeyValuePair<TKey, TValue>, which contains both the key and the value. The key can be accessed with the Key property, and the value can be accessed with the Value property:

```
foreach (KeyValuePair<string, string> book in books)
{
   Console.WriteLine("{0}, {1}", book.Key, book.Value);
}
```

The iteration displays book titles and ISBN numbers ordered by the key:

```
Beginning Visual C# 2010, 978-0-470-50226-6
Professional ASP.NET MVC 3, 978-1-1180-7658-3
Professional C# 4 and .NET 4, 978-0-470-50225-9
Professional WPF Programming, 978-0-470-04180-2
```

You can also access the values and keys by using the Values and Keys properties. The Values property returns IList<TValue> and the Keys property returns IList<TKey>, so you can use these properties with a foreach:

```
foreach (string isbn in books.Values)
{
   Console.WriteLine(isbn);
}

foreach (string title in books.Keys)
{
   Console.WriteLine(title);
}
```

The first loop displays the values, and next the keys:

```
978-0-470-50226-6
978-1-1180-7658-3
```

```
978-0-470-50225-9
978-0-470-04180-2
Beginning Visual C# 2010
Professional ASP.NET MVC 3
Professional C# 4 and .NET 4
Professional WPF Programming
```

If you try to access an element with an indexer and passing a key that does not exist, an exception of type `KeyNotFoundException` is thrown. To avoid that exception you can use the method `ContainsKey`, which returns `true` if the key passed exists in the collection, or you can invoke the method `TryGetValue`, which tries to get the value but doesn't throw an exception if it isn't found:

```
string isbn;
string title = "Professional C# 7.0";
if (!books.TryGetValue(title, out isbn))
{
  Console.WriteLine("{0} not found", title);
}
```

DICTIONARIES

A dictionary represents a sophisticated data structure that enables you to access an element based on a key. Dictionaries are also known as hash tables or maps. The main feature of dictionaries is fast lookup based on keys. You can also add and remove items freely, a bit like a `List<T>`, but without the performance overhead of having to shift subsequent items in memory.

Figure 10-5 shows a simplified representation of a dictionary. Here `employee-ids` such as B4711 are the keys added to the dictionary. The key is transformed into a hash. With the hash a number is created to associate an index with the values. The index then contains a link to the value. The figure is simplified because it is possible for a single index entry to be associated with multiple values, and the index can be stored as a tree.

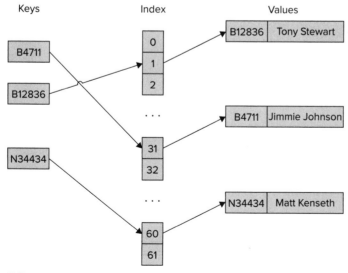

FIGURE 10-5

The .NET Framework offers several dictionary classes. The main class you to use is `Dictionary<TKey, TValue>`.

Key Type

A type that is used as a key in the dictionary must override the method `GetHashCode` of the `Object` class. Whenever a dictionary class needs to determine where an item should be located, it calls the `GetHashCode` method. The `int` that is returned by `GetHashCode` is used by the dictionary to calculate an index of where to place the element. We won't go into this part of the algorithm; what you should know is that it involves prime numbers, so the capacity of a dictionary is a prime number.

The implementation of `GetHashCode` must satisfy the following requirements:

➤ The same object should always return the same value.

➤ Different objects can return the same value.

➤ It should execute as quickly as possible; it must be inexpensive to compute.

➤ It must not throw exceptions.

➤ It should use at least one instance field.

➤ The hash code value should be evenly distributed across the entire range of numbers that an `int` can store.

➤ The hash code should not change during the lifetime of the object.

> **NOTE** *Good performance of the dictionary is based on a good implementation of the method* `GetHashCode`.

What's the reason for having hash code values evenly distributed across the range of integers? If two keys return hashes that have the same index, the dictionary class needs to start looking for the nearest available free location to store the second item — and it will have to do some searching to retrieve this item later. This is obviously going to hurt performance. In addition, if a lot of your keys are tending to provide the same storage indexes for where they should be stored, this kind of clash becomes more likely. However, because of the way that Microsoft's part of the algorithm works, this risk is minimized when the calculated hash values are evenly distributed between `int.MinValue` and `int.MaxValue`.

Besides having an implementation of `GetHashCode`, the key type also must implement the `IEquatable<T>`. `Equals` method or override the `Equals` method from the `Object` class. Because different key objects may return the same hash code, the method `Equals` is used by the dictionary comparing keys. The dictionary examines whether two keys, such as A and B, are equal, it invoking `A.Equals(B)`. This means that you must ensure that the following is always true:

If `A.Equals(B)` is true, then `A.GetHashCode` and `B.GetHashCode` must always return the same hash code.

This may seem a fairly subtle point, but it is crucial. If you contrived some way of overriding these methods so that the preceding statement were not always true, a dictionary that uses instances of this class as its keys would not work properly. Instead, you'd find funny things happening. For example, you might place an object in the dictionary and then discover that you could never retrieve it, or you might try to retrieve an entry and have the wrong entry returned.

> **NOTE** *For this reason, the C# compiler displays a compilation warning if you supply an override for* `Equals` *but don't supply an override for* `GetHashCode`.

For `System.Object` this condition is true because `Equals` simply compares references, and `GetHashCode` actually returns a hash that is based solely on the address of the object. This means that hash tables based on a key that doesn't override these methods will work correctly. However, the problem with this approach is that keys are regarded as equal only if they are the same object. That means when you place an object in the dictionary, you have to hang onto the reference to the key; you can't simply instantiate another key object later with the same value. If you don't override `Equals` and `GetHashCode`, the type is not very convenient to use in a dictionary.

Incidentally, `System.String` implements the interface `IEquatable` and overloads `GetHashCode` appropriately. `Equals` provides value comparison, and `GetHashCode` returns a hash based on the value of the string. Strings can be used conveniently as keys in dictionaries.

Number types such as `Int32` also implement the interface `IEquatable` and overload `GetHashCode`. However, the hash code returned by these types simply maps to the value. If the number you would like to use as a key is not itself distributed around the possible values of an integer, using integers as keys doesn't fulfill the rule of evenly distributing key values to get the best performance. `Int32` is not meant to be used in a dictionary.

If you need to use a key type that does not implement `IEquatable` and override `GetHashCode` according to the key values you store in the dictionary, you can create a comparer implementing the interface `IEqualityComparer<T>`. `IEqualityComparer<T>` defines the methods `GetHashCode` and `Equals` with an argument of the object passed, so you can offer an implementation different from the object type itself. An overload of the `Dictionary<TKey, TValue>` constructor allows passing an object implementing `IEqualityComparer<T>`. If such an object is assigned to the dictionary, this class is used to generate the hash codes and compare the keys.

Dictionary Example

The dictionary example in this section is a program that sets up a dictionary of employees. The dictionary is indexed by `EmployeeId` objects, and each item stored in the dictionary is an `Employee` object that stores details of an employee.

The struct `EmployeeId` is implemented to define a key to be used in a dictionary. The members of the class are a prefix character and a number for the employee. Both of these variables are read-only and can be initialized only in the constructor to ensure that keys within the dictionary shouldn't change, and this way that is guaranteed. The fields are filled within the constructor. The `ToString` method is overloaded to get a string representation of the employee ID. As required for a key type, `EmployeeId` implements the interface `IEquatable` and overloads the method `GetHashCode` (code file `DictionarySample/EmployeeId.cs`):

```
[Serializable]
public class EmployeeIdException : Exception
{
  public EmployeeIdException(string message) : base(message)  { }
}

[Serializable]
public struct EmployeeId : IEquatable<EmployeeId>
{
  private readonly char prefix;
  private readonly int number;

  public EmployeeId(string id)
  {
    Contract.Requires<ArgumentNullException>(id != null);

    prefix = (id.ToUpper())[0];
    int numLength = id.Length  1;
    try
```

```
    {
      number = int.Parse(id.Substring(1, numLength > 6 ? 6 : numLength));
    }
    catch (FormatException)
    {
      throw new EmployeeIdException("Invalid EmployeeId format");
    }
  }

  public override string ToString()
  {
      return prefix.ToString() + string.Format("{0,6:000000}", number);
  }

  public override int GetHashCode()
  {
    return (number ^ number << 16) * 0x15051505;
  }

  public bool Equals(EmployeeId other)
  {
    if (other == null) return false;

    return (prefix == other.prefix && number == other.number);
  }

  public override bool Equals(object obj)
  {
    return Equals((EmployeeId)obj);
  }

  public static bool operator ==(EmployeeId left, EmployeeId right)
  {
    return left.Equals(right);
  }

  public static bool operator !=(EmployeeId left, EmployeeId right)
  {
    return !(left == right);
  }
}
```

The `Equals` method that is defined by the `IEquatable<T>` interface compares the values of two `EmployeeId` objects and returns `true` if both values are the same. Instead of implementing the `Equals` method from the `IEquatable<T>` interface, you can also override the `Equals` method from the `Object` class:

```
public bool Equals(EmployeeId other)
{
  if (other == null) return false;
  return (prefix == other.prefix && number == other.number);
}
```

With the number variable, a value from 1 to around 190,000 is expected for the employees. This doesn't fill the range of an integer. The algorithm used by `GetHashCode` shifts the number 16 bits to the left, then does an XOR with the original number, and finally multiplies the result by the hex value 15051505. The hash code is fairly evenly distributed across the range of an integer:

```
public override int GetHashCode()
{
  return (number ^ number << 16) * 0x15051505;
}
```

> **NOTE** *On the Internet, you can find a lot more complex algorithms that have a better distribution across the integer range. You can also use the* GetHashCode *method of a string to return a hash.*

The Employee class is a simple entity class containing the name, salary, and ID of the employee. The constructor initializes all values, and the method ToString returns a string representation of an instance. The implementation of ToString uses a format string to create the string representation for performance reasons (code file DictionarySample/Employee.cs):

```
[Serializable]
public class Employee
{
  private string name;
  private decimal salary;
  private readonly EmployeeId id;

  public Employee(EmployeeId id, string name, decimal salary)
  {
    this.id = id;
    this.name = name;
    this.salary = salary;
  }

  public override string ToString()
  {
    return String.Format("{0}: {1, -20} {2:C}",
      id.ToString(), name, salary);
  }
}
```

In the Main method of the sample application, a new Dictionary<TKey, TValue> instance is created, where the key is of type EmployeeId and the value is of type Employee. The constructor allocates a capacity of 31 elements. Remember that capacity is based on prime numbers. However, when you assign a value that is not a prime number, you don't need to worry. The Dictionary<TKey, TValue> class itself takes the next prime number that follows the integer passed to the constructor to allocate the capacity. The employee objects and IDs are created and added to the dictionary with the Add method. Instead of using the Add method, you can also use the indexer to add keys and values to the dictionary, as shown here with the employees Matt and Brad (code file DictionarySample/Program.cs):

```
static void Main()
{
  var employees = new Dictionary<EmployeeId, Employee>(31);

  var idTony = new EmployeeId("C3755");
  var tony = new Employee(idTony, "Tony Stewart", 379025.00m);
  employees.Add(idTony, tony);
  Console.WriteLine(tony);

  var idCarl = new EmployeeId("F3547");
  var carl = new Employee(idCarl, "Carl Edwards", 403466.00m);
```

```
employees.Add(idCarl, carl);
Console.WriteLine(carl);

var idKevin = new EmployeeId("C3386");
var kevin = new Employee(idKevin, "Kevin Harwick", 415261.00m);
employees.Add(idKevin, kevin);
Console.WriteLine(kevin);

var idMatt = new EmployeeId("F3323");
var matt = new Employee(idMatt, "Matt Kenseth", 1589390.00m);
employees[idMatt] = matt;
Console.WriteLine(matt);

var idBrad = new EmployeeId("D3234");
var brad = new Employee(idBrad, "Brad Keselowski", 322295.00m);
employees[idBrad] = brad;
Console.WriteLine(brad);
```

After the entries are added to the dictionary, inside a `while` loop employees are read from the dictionary. The user is asked to enter an employee number to store in the variable `userInput`, and the user can exit the application by entering **X**. If the key is in the dictionary, it is examined with the `TryGetValue` method of the `Dictionary<TKey, TValue>` class. `TryGetValue` returns `true` if the key is found and `false` otherwise. If the value is found, the value associated with the key is stored in the employee variable. This value is written to the console.

> **NOTE** *You can also use an indexer of the* `Dictionary<TKey, TValue>` *class instead of* `TryGetValue` *to access a value stored in the dictionary. However, if the key is not found, the indexer throws an exception of type* `KeyNotFoundException`.

```
while (true)
{
  Console.Write("Enter employee id (X to exit)> ");
  var userInput = Console.ReadLine();
  userInput = userInput.ToUpper();
  if (userInput == "X") break;

  EmployeeId id;
  try
  {
    id = new EmployeeId(userInput);


    Employee employee;
    if (!employees.TryGetValue(id, out employee))
    {
      Console.WriteLine("Employee with id {0} does not exist",
          id);
    }
    else
    {
      Console.WriteLine(employee);
    }
  }
  catch (EmployeeIdException ex)
```

```
        {
          Console.WriteLine(ex.Message);
        }
      }
    }
  }
```

Running the application produces the following output:

```
Enter employee id (X to exit)> C3386
C003386: Kevin Harwick        $415,261.00
Enter employee id (X to exit)> F3547
F003547: Carl Edwards         $403,466.00
Enter employee id (X to exit)> X
Press any key to continue ...
```

Lookups

Dictionary<TKey, TValue> supports only one value per key. The class Lookup<TKey, TElement> resembles a Dictionary<TKey, TValue> but maps keys to a collection of values. This class is implemented in the assembly System.Core and defined with the namespace System.Linq.

Lookup<TKey, TElement> cannot be created as a normal dictionary. Instead, you have to invoke the method ToLookup, which returns a Lookup<TKey, TElement> object. The method ToLookup is an extension method that is available with every class implementing IEnumerable<T>. In the following example, a list of Racer objects is filled. Because List<T> implements IEnumerable<T>, the ToLookup method can be invoked on the racers list. This method requires a delegate of type Func<TSource, TKey> that defines the selector of the key. Here, the racers are selected based on their country by using the lambda expression r => r.Country. The foreach loop accesses only the racers from Australia by using the indexer (code file LookupSample/Program.cs):

```
var racers = new List<Racer>();
racers.Add(new Racer("Jacques", "Villeneuve", "Canada", 11));
racers.Add(new Racer("Alan", "Jones", "Australia", 12));
racers.Add(new Racer("Jackie", "Stewart", "United Kingdom", 27));
racers.Add(new Racer("James", "Hunt", "United Kingdom", 10));
racers.Add(new Racer("Jack", "Brabham", "Australia", 14));

var lookupRacers = racers.ToLookup(r => r.Country);

foreach (Racer r in lookupRacers["Australia"])
{
    Console.WriteLine(r);
}
```

> **NOTE** *You can read more about extension methods in Chapter 11, "Language Integrated Query." Lambda expressions are explained in Chapter 8, "Delegates, Lambdas, and Events."*

The output shows the racers from Australia:

```
Alan Jones
Jack Brabham
```

Sorted Dictionaries

`SortedDictionary<TKey, TValue>` is a binary search tree in which the items are sorted based on the key. The key type must implement the interface `IComparable<TKey>`. If the key type is not sortable, you can also create a comparer implementing `IComparer<TKey>` and assign the comparer as a constructor argument of the sorted dictionary.

Earlier in this chapter you read about `SortedList<TKey, TValue>`. `SortedDictionary<TKey, TValue>` and `SortedList<TKey, TValue>` have similar functionality, but because `SortedList<TKey, TValue>` is implemented as a list that is based on an array, and `SortedDictionary<TKey, TValue>` is implemented as a dictionary, the classes have different characteristics:

➤ `SortedList<TKey, TValue>` uses less memory than `SortedDictionary<TKey, TValue>`.

➤ `SortedDictionary<TKey, TValue>` has faster insertion and removal of elements.

➤ When populating the collection with already sorted data, `SortedList<TKey, TValue>` is faster if capacity changes are not needed.

> **NOTE** `SortedList` *consumes less memory than* `SortedDictionary`. `SortedDictionary` *is faster with inserts and the removal of unsorted data.*

SETS

A collection that contains only distinct items is known by the term *set*. The .NET Framework includes two sets, `HashSet<T>` and `SortedSet<T>`, that both implement the interface `ISet<T>`. `HashSet<T>` contains an unordered list of distinct items; with `SortedSet<T>` the list is ordered.

The `ISet<T>` interface offers methods to create a union of multiple sets, an intersection of sets, or to provide information if one set is a superset or subset of another.

In the following sample code, three new sets of type string are created and filled with Formula-1 cars. The `HashSet<T>` class implements the `ICollection<T>` interface. However, the `Add` method is implemented explicitly and a different `Add` method is offered by the class, as you can see here. The `Add` method differs by the return type; a Boolean value is returned to provide the information if the element was added. If the element was already in the set, it is not added, and `false` is returned (code file `SetSample/Program.cs`):

```
var companyTeams = new HashSet<string>()
{ "Ferrari", "McLaren", "Mercedes" };
var traditionalTeams = new HashSet<string>() { "Ferrari", "McLaren" };
var privateTeams = new HashSet<string>()
{ "Red Bull", "Toro Rosso", "Force India", "Sauber" };

if (privateTeams.Add("Williams"))
    Console.WriteLine("Williams added");
if (!companyTeams.Add("McLaren"))
    Console.WriteLine("McLaren was already in this set");
```

The result of these two `Add` methods is written to the console:

```
Williams added
McLaren was already in this set
```

The methods `IsSubsetOf` and `IsSupersetOf` compare a set with a collection that implements the `IEnumerable<T>` interface and returns a Boolean result. Here, `IsSubsetOf` verifies whether every element in `traditionalTeams` is contained in `companyTeams`, which is the case; `IsSupersetOf` verifies whether `traditionalTeams` has any additional elements compared to `companyTeams`:

```
if (traditionalTeams.IsSubsetOf(companyTeams))
{
  Console.WriteLine("traditionalTeams is subset of companyTeams");
}

if (companyTeams.IsSupersetOf(traditionalTeams))
{
  Console.WriteLine("companyTeams is a superset of traditionalTeams");
}
```

The output of this verification is shown here:

```
traditionalTeams is a subset of companyTeams
companyTeams is a superset of traditionalTeams
```

Williams is a traditional team as well, which is why this team is added to the `traditionalTeams` collection:

```
traditionalTeams.Add("Williams");
if (privateTeams.Overlaps(traditionalTeams))
{
  Console.WriteLine("At least one team is the same with the " +
      "traditional and private teams");
}
```

Because there's an overlap, this is the result:

```
At least one team is the same with the traditional and private teams.
```

The variable `allTeams` that references a new `SortedSet<string>` is filled with a union of `companyTeams`, `privateTeams`, and `traditionalTeams` by calling the `UnionWith` method:

```
var allTeams = new SortedSet<string>(companyTeams);
allTeams.UnionWith(privateTeams);
allTeams.UnionWith(traditionalTeams);

Console.WriteLine();
Console.WriteLine("all teams");
foreach (var team in allTeams)
{
  Console.WriteLine(team);
}
```

Here, all teams are returned but every team is listed just once because the set contains only unique values; and because the container is a `SortedSet<string>`, the result is ordered:

```
Ferrari
Force India
Lotus
McLaren
Mercedes
Red Bull
Sauber
Toro Rosso
Williams
```

The method `ExceptWith` removes all private teams from the `allTeams` set:

```
allTeams.ExceptWith(privateTeams);
Console.WriteLine();
Console.WriteLine("no private team left");
foreach (var team in allTeams)
{
    Console.WriteLine(team);
}
```

The remaining elements in the collection do not contain any private team:

```
Ferrari
McLaren
Mercedes
```

OBSERVABLE COLLECTIONS

In case you need information when items in the collection are removed or added, you can use the `ObservableCollection<T>` class. This class was defined for WPF so that the UI is informed about collection changes; therefore, this class is defined in the assembly WindowsBase and you need to reference it. The namespace of this class is `System.Collections.ObjectModel`.

`ObservableCollection<T>` derives from the base class `Collection<T>` that can be used to create custom collections and it uses `List<T>` internal. From the base class, the virtual methods `SetItem` and `RemoveItem` are overridden to fire the `CollectionChanged` event. Clients of this class can register to this event by using the interface `INotifyCollectionChanged`.

The next example demonstrates using an `ObservableCollection<string>` where the method `Data_CollectionChanged` is registered to the `CollectionChanged` event. Two items are added to the end — one item is inserted, and one item is removed (code file `ObservableCollectionSample/Program.cs`):

```
var data = new ObservableCollection<string>();
data.CollectionChanged += Data_CollectionChanged;
data.Add("One");
data.Add("Two");
data.Insert(1, "Three");
data.Remove("One");
```

The method `Data_CollectionChanged` receives `NotifyCollectionChangedEventArgs` containing information about changes to the collection. The `Action` property provides information if an item was added or removed. With removed items, the `OldItems` property is set and lists the removed items. With added items, the `NewItems` property is set and lists the new items:

```
static void Data_CollectionChanged(object sender,
                                   NotifyCollectionChangedEventArgs e)
{
  Console.WriteLine("action: {0}", e.Action.ToString());

  if (e.OldItems != null)
  {
    Console.WriteLine("starting index for old item(s): {0}",
                      e.OldStartingIndex);
    Console.WriteLine("old item(s):");
    foreach (var item in e.OldItems)
```

```
      {
        Console.WriteLine(item);
      }
    }
    if (e.NewItems != null)
    {
      Console.WriteLine("starting index for new item(s): {0}",
                        e.NewStartingIndex);
      Console.WriteLine("new item(s): ");
      foreach (var item in e.NewItems)
      {
        Console.WriteLine(item);
      }
    }
    Console.WriteLine();
}
```

Running the application results in the following output. First the items One and Two are added to the collection, and thus the Add action is shown with the index 0 and 1. The third item, Three, is inserted on position 1 so it shows the action Add with index 1. Finally, the item One is removed as shown with the action Remove and index 0:

```
action: Add
starting index for new item(s): 0
new item(s):
One

action: Add
starting index for new item(s): 1
new item(s):
Two

action: Add
starting index for new item(s): 1
new item(s):
Three

action: Remove
starting index for old item(s): 0
old item(s):
One
```

BIT ARRAYS

If you need to deal with a number of bits, you can use the class BitArray and the struct BitVector32. BitArray is located in the namespace System.Collections; BitVector32 is in the namespace System .Collections.Specialized. The most important difference between these two types is that BitArray is resizable, which is useful if you don't know the number of bits needed in advance, and it can contain a large number of bits. BitVector32 is stack-based and therefore faster. BitVector32 contains only 32 bits, which are stored in an integer.

BitArray

The class BitArray is a reference type that contains an array of ints, where for every 32 bits a new integer is used. Members of this class are described in the following table.

BITARRAY MEMBERS	DESCRIPTION
Count Length	The get accessor of both Count and Length return the number of bits in the array. With the Length property, you can also define a new size and resize the collection.
Item Get Set	You can use an indexer to read and write bits in the array. The indexer is of type bool. Instead of using the indexer, you can also use the Get and Set methods to access the bits in the array.
SetAll	The method SetAll sets the values of all bits according to the parameter passed to the method.
Not	The method Not generates the inverse of all bits of the array.
And Or Xor	With the methods And, Or, and Xor, you can combine two BitArray objects. The And method does a binary AND, where the result bits are set only if the bits from both input arrays are set. The Or method does a binary OR, where the result bits are set if one or both of the input arrays are set. The Xor method is an exclusive OR, where the result is set if only one of the input bits is set.

The helper method DisplayBits iterates through a BitArray and displays 1 or 0 to the console, depending on whether or not the bit is set (code file BitArraySample/Program.cs):

```
static void DisplayBits(BitArray bits)
{
    foreach (bool bit in bits)
    {
        Console.Write(bit ? 1: 0);
    }
}
```

The example to demonstrate the BitArray class creates a bit array with 8 bits, indexed from 0 to 7. The SetAll method sets all 8 bits to true. Then the Set method changes bit 1 to false. Instead of the Set method, you can also use an indexer, as shown with index 5 and 7:

```
var bits1 = new BitArray(8);
bits1.SetAll(true);
bits1.Set(1, false);
bits1[5] = false;
bits1[7] = false;
Console.Write("initialized: ");
DisplayBits(bits1);
Console.WriteLine();
```

This is the displayed result of the initialized bits:

```
initialized: 10111010
```

The Not method generates the inverse of the bits of the BitArray:

```
Console.Write(" not ");
DisplayBits(bits1);
bits1.Not();
Console.Write(" = ");
DisplayBits(bits1);
Console.WriteLine();
```

The result of Not is all bits inversed. If the bit were true, it is false; and if it were false, it is true:

```
not 10111010 = 01000101
```

In the following example, a new BitArray is created. With the constructor, the variable bits1 is used to initialize the array, so the new array has the same values. Then the values for bits 0, 1, and 4 are set to different values. Before the Or method is used, the bit arrays bits1 and bits2 are displayed. The Or method changes the values of bits1:

```
var bits2 = new BitArray(bits1);
bits2[0] = true;
bits2[1] = false;
bits2[4] = true;
DisplayBits(bits1);
Console.Write(" or ");
DisplayBits(bits2);
Console.Write(" = ");
bits1.Or(bits2);
DisplayBits(bits1);
Console.WriteLine();
```

With the Or method, the set bits are taken from both input arrays. In the result, the bit is set if it was set with either the first or the second array:

```
01000101 or 10001101 = 11001101
```

Next, the And method is used to operate on bits2 and bits1:

```
DisplayBits(bits2);
Console.Write(" and ");
DisplayBits(bits1);
Console.Write(" = ");
bits2.And(bits1);
DisplayBits(bits2);
Console.WriteLine();
```

The result of the And method only sets the bits where the bit was set in both input arrays:

```
10001101 and 11001101 = 10001101
```

Finally, the Xor method is used for an exclusive OR:

```
DisplayBits(bits1);
Console.Write(" xor ");
DisplayBits(bits2);
bits1.Xor(bits2);
Console.Write(" = ");
DisplayBits(bits1);
Console.WriteLine();
```

With the Xor method, the resultant bits are set only if the bit was set either in the first or the second input, but not both:

```
11001101 xor 10001101 = 01000000
```

BitVector32

If you know the number of bits you need in advance, you can use the `BitVector32` structure instead of `BitArray`. `BitVector32` is more efficient because it is a value type and stores the bits on the stack inside an integer. With a single integer you have a place for 32 bits. If you need more bits, you can use multiple `BitVector32` values or the `BitArray`. The `BitArray` can grow as needed; this is not an option with `BitVector32`.

The following table shows the members of `BitVector` that are very different from `BitArray`:

BITVECTOR MEMBERS	DESCRIPTION
Data	The property `Data` returns the data behind the `BitVector32` as an integer.
Item	The values for the `BitVector32` can be set using an indexer. The indexer is overloaded — you can get and set the values using a mask or a section of type `BitVector32.Section`.
CreateMask	`CreateMask` is a static method that you can use to create a mask for accessing specific bits in the `BitVector32`.
CreateSection	`CreateSection` is a static method that you can use to create several sections within the 32 bits.

The following example creates a `BitVector32` with the default constructor, whereby all 32 bits are initialized to `false`. Then masks are created to access the bits inside the bit vector. The first call to `CreateMask` creates a mask to access the first bit. After `CreateMask` is invoked, `bit1` has a value of 1. Invoking `CreateMask` once more and passing the first mask as a parameter to `CreateMask` returns a mask to access the second bit, which is 2. `bit3` then has a value of 4 to access bit number 3, and `bit4` has a value of 8 to access bit number 4.

Then the masks are used with the indexer to access the bits inside the bit vector and to set the fields accordingly (code file `BitArraySample/Program.cs`):

```
var bits1 = new BitVector32();
int bit1 = BitVector32.CreateMask();
int bit2 = BitVector32.CreateMask(bit1);
int bit3 = BitVector32.CreateMask(bit2);
int bit4 = BitVector32.CreateMask(bit3);
int bit5 = BitVector32.CreateMask(bit4);

bits1[bit1] = true;
bits1[bit2] = false;
bits1[bit3] = true;
bits1[bit4] = true;
bits1[bit5] = true;
Console.WriteLine(bits1);
```

The `BitVector32` has an overridden `ToString` method that not only displays the name of the class but also 1 or 0 if the bits are set or not, respectively:

```
BitVector32{00000000000000000000000000011101}
```

Instead of creating a mask with the `CreateMask` method, you can define the mask yourself; you can also set multiple bits at once. The hexadecimal value `abcdef` is the same as the binary value `1010 1011 1100 1101 1110 1111`. All the bits defined with this value are set:

```
        bits1[0xabcdef] = true;
        Console.WriteLine(bits1);
```

With the output shown you can verify the bits that are set:

```
BitVector32{00000000101010111100110111101111}
```

Separating the 32 bits to different sections can be extremely useful. For example, an IPv4 address is defined as a four-byte number that is stored inside an integer. You can split the integer by defining four sections. With a multicast IP message, several 32-bit values are used. One of these 32-bit values is separated in these sections: 16 bits for the number of sources, 8 bits for a querier's query interval code, 3 bits for a querier's robustness variable, a 1-bit suppress flag, and 4 bits that are reserved. You can also define your own bit meanings to save memory.

The following example simulates receiving the value `0x79abcdef` and passes this value to the constructor of `BitVector32`, so that the bits are set accordingly:

```
        int received = 0x79abcdef;

        BitVector32 bits2 = new BitVector32(received);
        Console.WriteLine(bits2);
```

The bits are shown on the console as initialized:

```
BitVector32{01111001101010111100110111101111}
```

Then six sections are created. The first section requires 12 bits, as defined by the hexadecimal value `0xfff` (12 bits are set); section B requires 8 bits; section C, 4 bits; section D and E, 3 bits; and section F, 2 bits. The first call to `CreateSection` just receives `0xfff` to allocate the first 12 bits. With the second call to `CreateSection`, the first section is passed as an argument, so the next section continues where the first section ended. `CreateSection` returns a value of type `BitVector32.Section` that contains the offset and the mask for the section:

```
// sections: FF EEE DDD CCCC BBBBBBBB
// AAAAAAAAAAAA
BitVector32.Section sectionA = BitVector32.CreateSection(0xfff);
BitVector32.Section sectionB = BitVector32.CreateSection(0xff, sectionA);
BitVector32.Section sectionC = BitVector32.CreateSection(0xf, sectionB);
BitVector32.Section sectionD = BitVector32.CreateSection(0x7, sectionC);
BitVector32.Section sectionE = BitVector32.CreateSection(0x7, sectionD);
BitVector32.Section sectionF = BitVector32.CreateSection(0x3, sectionE);
```

Passing a `BitVector32.Section` to the indexer of the `BitVector32` returns an int just mapped to the section of the bit vector. As shown next, a helper method, `IntToBinaryString`, retrieves a string representation of the int number:

```
        Console.WriteLine("Section A: {0}",
                        IntToBinaryString(bits2[sectionA], true));
        Console.WriteLine("Section B: {0}",
                        IntToBinaryString(bits2[sectionB], true));
        Console.WriteLine("Section C: {0}",
                        IntToBinaryString(bits2[sectionC], true));
        Console.WriteLine("Section D: {0}",
                        IntToBinaryString(bits2[sectionD], true));
        Console.WriteLine("Section E: {0}",
```

```
                                    IntToBinaryString(bits2[sectionE], true));
            Console.WriteLine("Section F: {0}",
                                    IntToBinaryString(bits2[sectionF], true));
```

The method `IntToBinaryString` receives the bits in an integer and returns a string representation containing 0 and 1. With the implementation, 32 bits of the integer are iterated through. In the iteration, if the bit is set, 1 is appended to the `StringBuilder`; otherwise, 0 is appended. Within the loop, a bit shift occurs to check if the next bit is set:

```
static string IntToBinaryString(int bits, bool removeTrailingZero)
{
  var sb = new StringBuilder(32);

  for (int i = 0; i < 32; i++)
  {
    if ((bits & 0x80000000) != 0)
    {
      sb.Append("1");
    }
    else
    {
      sb.Append("0");
    }
    bits = bits << 1;
  }
  string s = sb.ToString();
  if (removeTrailingZero)
  {
    return s.TrimStart('0');
  }
  else
  {
    return s;
  }
}
```

The result displays the bit representation of sections A to F, which you can now verify with the value that was passed into the bit vector:

```
Section A: 110111101111
Section B: 10111100
Section C: 1010
Section D: 1
Section E: 111
Section F: 1
```

CONCURRENT COLLECTIONS

Since version 4 of the .NET Framework, .NET offers thread-safe collection classes within the namespace `System.Collections.Concurrent`. Thread-safe collections are guarded against multiple threads accessing them in conflicting ways.

For thread-safe access of collections, the interface `IProducerConsumerCollection<T>` is defined. The most important methods of this interface are `TryAdd` and `TryTake`. `TryAdd` tries to add an item to the collection, but this might fail if the collection is locked from adding items. To provide this information, the method returns a Boolean value indicating success or failure. `TryTake` works the same way to inform the caller about success or failure, and returns on success an item from the collection. The following list describes the collection classes from the `System.Collections.Concurrent` namespace and its functionality:

➤ `ConcurrentQueue<T>` — This class is implemented with a lock-free algorithm and uses 32 item arrays that are combined in a linked list internally. Methods to access the elements of the queue are `Enqueue`, `TryDequeue`, and `TryPeek`. The naming of these methods is very similar to the methods of `Queue<T>` that you know already, with the difference of the "Try" prefix to indicate the method call might fail.

Because this class implements the interface `IProducerConsumerCollection<T>`, the methods `TryAdd` and `TryTake` just invoke `Enqueue` and `TryDequeue`.

➤ `ConcurrentStack<T>` — Very similar to `ConcurrentQueue<T>` but with other item access methods, this class defines the methods `Push`, `PushRange`, `TryPeek`, `TryPop`, and `TryPopRange`. Internally this class uses a linked list of its items.

➤ `ConcurrentBag<T>` — This class doesn't define any order in which to add or take items. It uses a concept that maps threads to arrays used internally and thus tries to reduce locks. The methods to access elements are `Add`, `TryPeek`, and `TryTake`.

➤ `ConcurrentDictionary<TKey, TValue>` — This is a thread-safe collection of keys and values. `TryAdd`, `TryGetValue`, `TryRemove`, and `TryUpdate` are methods to access the members in a non-blocking fashion. Because the items are based on keys and values, `ConcurrentDictionary<TKey, TValue>` does not implement `IProducerConsumerCollection<T>`.

➤ `BlockingCollection<T>` — A collection that blocks and waits until it is possible to do the task by adding or taking the item, `BlockingCollection<T>` offers an interface to add and remove items with the `Add` and `Take` methods. These methods block the thread and wait until the task becomes possible. The `Add` method has an overload whereby you also can pass a `CancellationToken`. This token enables cancelling a blocking call. If you don't want the thread to wait for an endlessly time, and you don't want to cancel the call from the outside, the methods `TryAdd` and `TryTake` are offered as well, whereby you can also specify a timeout value for the maximum amount of time you would like to block the thread and wait before the call should fail.

The `ConcurrentXXX` collection classes are thread-safe, returning false if an action is not possible with the current state of threads. You always have to check whether adding or taking the item was successful before moving on. You can't trust the collection to always fulfill the task.

`BlockingCollection<T>` is a decorator to any class implementing the `IProducerConsumerCollection<T>` interface and by default uses `ConcurrentQueue<T>`. With the constructor you can also pass any other class that implements `IProducerConsumerCollection<T>`, e.g., `ConcurrentBag<T>` and `ConcurrentStack<T>`.

Creating Pipelines

A great use for these concurrent collection classes is with pipelines. One task writes some content to a collection class while another task can read from the collection at the same time.

The following sample application demonstrates the use of the `BlockingCollection<T>` class with multiple tasks that form a pipeline. The first pipeline is shown in Figure 10-6. The task for the first stage reads filenames and adds them to a queue. While this task is running, the task for stage two can already start to read the filenames from the queue and load their content. The result is written to another queue. Stage 3 can be started at the same time to read the content from the second queue and process it. Here, the result is written to a dictionary.

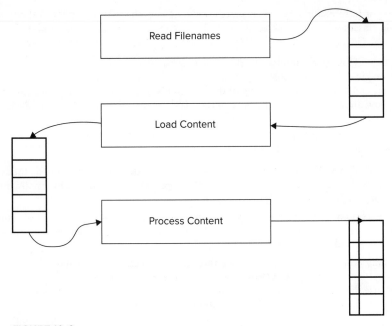

FIGURE 10-6

In this scenario, the next stage can only start when stage 3 is completed and the content is finally processed with a full result in the dictionary. The next steps are shown in Figure 10-7. Stage 4 reads from the dictionary, converts the data, and writes it to a queue. Stage 5 adds color information to the items and puts them in another queue. The last stage displays the information. Stages 4 to 6 can run concurrently as well.

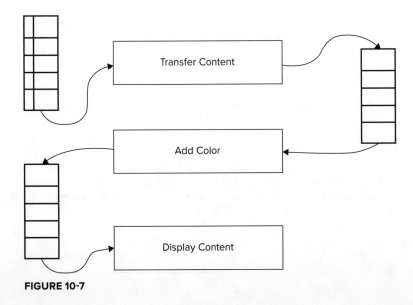

FIGURE 10-7

Looking at the code of this sample application, the complete pipeline is managed within the method StartPipeline. Here, the collections are instantiated and passed to the various stages of the pipeline. The first stage is processed with ReadFilenamesAsync, and the second and third stages, LoadContentAsync and ProcessContentAsync, are running simultaneously. The fourth stage, however, can only start when the first three stages are completed (code file PipelineSample/Program.cs):

```csharp
private static async void StartPipeline()
{
  var fileNames = new BlockingCollection<string>();
  var lines = new BlockingCollection<string>();
  var words = new ConcurrentDictionary<string, int>();
  var items = new BlockingCollection<Info>();
  var coloredItems = new BlockingCollection<Info>();

  Task t1 = PipelineStages.ReadFilenamesAsync(@"../../..", fileNames);
  ConsoleHelper.WriteLine("started stage 1");
  Task t2 = PipelineStages.LoadContentAsync(fileNames, lines);
  ConsoleHelper.WriteLine("started stage 2");
  Task t3 = PipelineStages.ProcessContentAsync(lines, words);
  await Task.WhenAll(t1, t2, t3);
  ConsoleHelper.WriteLine("stages 1, 2, 3 completed");

  Task t4 = PipelineStages.TransferContentAsync(words, items);
  Task t5 = PipelineStages.AddColorAsync(items, coloredItems);
  Task t6 = PipelineStages.ShowContentAsync(coloredItems);
  ConsoleHelper.WriteLine("stages 4, 5, 6 started");

  await Task.WhenAll(t4, t5, t6);

  ConsoleHelper.WriteLine("all stages finished");
}
```

> **NOTE** *This example application makes use of tasks and the* async *and* await *keywords, which that are explained in detail in Chapter 13, "Asynchronous Programming." You can read more about threads, tasks, and synchronization in Chapter 21. File I/O is discussed in Chapter 24, "Manipulating Files and the Registry."*

The example writes information to the console using the ConsoleHelper class. This class provides an easy way to change the color for console output and uses synchronization to avoid returning output with the wrong colors (code file PipelineSample/ConsoleHelper.cs):

```csharp
using System;

namespace Wrox.ProCSharp.Collections
{
  public class ConsoleHelper
  {
    private static object syncOutput = new object();

    public static void WriteLine(string message)
    {
      lock (syncOutput)
      {
        Console.WriteLine(message);
      }
    }
  }
```

```
    public static void WriteLine(string message, string color)
  {
    lock (syncOutput)
    {
      Console.ForegroundColor = (ConsoleColor)Enum.Parse(
          typeof(ConsoleColor), color);
      Console.WriteLine(message);
      Console.ResetColor();
    }
  }
 }
}
```

Using BlockingCollection

Let's get into the first stage of the pipeline. `ReadFilenamesAsync` receives a `BlockingCollection<T>` where it can write its output. The implementation of this method uses an enumerator to iterate C# files within the specified directory and its subdirectories. The filenames are added to the `BlockingCollection<T>` with the `Add` method. After adding filenames is completed, the `CompleteAdding` method is invoked to inform all readers that they should not wait for any additional items in the collection (code file `PipelineSample/PipelineStages.cs`):

```
using System.Collections.Concurrent;
using System.IO;
using System.Linq;
using System.Threading.Tasks;

namespace Wrox.ProCSharp.Collections
{
  public static class PipelineStages
  {
    public static Task ReadFilenamesAsync(string path,
        BlockingCollection<string> output)
    {
      return Task.Run(() =>
        {
          foreach (string filename in Directory.EnumerateFiles(path, "*.cs",
              SearchOption.AllDirectories))
          {
            output.Add(filename);
            ConsoleHelper.WriteLine(string.Format("stage 1: added {0}",
                filename));
          }
          output.CompleteAdding();
        });
    }
```

> **NOTE** If you have a reader that reads from a `BlockingCollection<T>` at the same time a writer adds items, it is important to invoke the `CompleteAdding` method. Otherwise, the reader would wait for more items to arrive within the `foreach` loop.

The next stage is to read the file and add its content to another collection , which is done from the `LoadContentAsync` method. This method uses the filenames passed with the input collection, opens the file, and adds all lines of the file to the output collection. With the `foreach` loop, the method

`GetConsumingEnumerable` is invoked with the input blocking collection to iterate the items. It's possible to use the `input` variable directly without invoking `GetConsumingEnumerable`, but this would only iterate the current state of the collection, and not the items that are added afterwards.

```
public static async Task LoadContentAsync(BlockingCollection<string> input,
    BlockingCollection<string> output)
{
  foreach (var filename in input.GetConsumingEnumerable())
  {
    using (FileStream stream = File.OpenRead(filename))
    {
      var reader = new StreamReader(stream);
      string line = null;
      while ((line = await reader.ReadLineAsync()) != null)
      {
        output.Add(line);
        ConsoleHelper.WriteLine(string.Format("stage 2: added {0}", line));
      }
    }
  }
  output.CompleteAdding();
}
```

> **NOTE** *If a reader is reading a collection at the same time while it is filled, you need to get the enumerator of the blocking collection with the method* `GetConsumingEnumerable` *instead of iterating the collection directly.*

Using ConcurrentDictionary

Stage 3 is implemented in the `ProcessContentAsync` method. This method gets the lines from the input collection, and then splits and filters words to and output dictionary. The method `AddOrIncrementValue` is a helper method implemented as an extension method for dictionaries is shown next.:

```
public static Task ProcessContentAsync(BlockingCollection<string> input,
    ConcurrentDictionary<string, int> output)
{
  return Task.Run(() =>
    {
      foreach (var line in input.GetConsumingEnumerable())
      {
        string[] words = line.Split(' ', ';', '\t', '{', '}', '(', ')',
            ':', ',', '"');
        foreach (var word in words.Where(w => !string.IsNullOrEmpty(w)))
        {
          output.AddOrIncrementValue(word);
          ConsoleHelper.WriteLine(string.Format("stage 3: added {0}",
              word));
        }
      }
    });
}
```

Remember that stage 3 in the pipeline adds a word to the dictionary if it doesn't exist yet, and increments a value in the dictionary if the word is already in there. This functionality is implemented in the extension method `AddOrIncrementValue`. Because the dictionary cannot be used with the `BlockingCollection<T>`, there are no blocking methods that wait until adding values succeeds. Instead, TryXXX methods can be used where it's necessary to verify if adding or updating the value succeeded. If another thread were updating a value at the same time, updates can fail. The implementation makes use of TryGetValue to check if an item is already in the dictionary, TryUpdate to update a value, and TryAdd to add a value (code file PipelineSample/ConcurrentDictionaryExtensions.cs):

```
using System.Collections.Concurrent;

namespace Wrox.ProCSharp.Collections
{
  public static class ConcurrentDictionaryExtension
  {
    public static void AddOrIncrementValue(
        this ConcurrentDictionary<string, int> dict, string key)
    {
      bool success = false;
      while (!success)
      {
        int value;
        if (dict.TryGetValue(key, out value))
        {
          if (dict.TryUpdate(key, value + 1, value))
          {
            success = true;
          }
        }
        else
        {
          if (dict.TryAdd(key, 1))
          {
            success = true;
          }
        }
      }
    }
  }
}
```

> **NOTE** *Extension methods are explained in Chapter 3, "Objects and Types."*

Running the application with the first three stages, you'll see output like the following, with one where the stages operate interleaved:

```
stage 3: added get
stage 3: added set
stage 3: added public
stage 3: added int
stage 3: added Wins
stage 2: added    public static class Pipeline
stage 2: added    {
stage 2: added        public static Task ReadFil
stage 2: added        {
stage 2: added            return Task.Run(() =>
```

Completing the Pipeline

After the first three stages are completed, the next three stages can run in parallel again. `TransferContentAsync` gets the data from the dictionary, converts it to the type `Info`, and puts it into the output `BlockingCollectiony<T>` (code file `PipelineSample/PipelineStages.cs`):

```
public static Task TransferContentAsync(
    ConcurrentDictionary<string, int> input,
    BlockingCollection<Info> output)
{
  return Task.Run(() =>
    {
      foreach (var word in input.Keys)
      {
        int value;
        if (input.TryGetValue(word, out value))
        {
          var info = new Info { Word = word, Count = value };
          output.Add(info);
          ConsoleHelper.WriteLine(string.Format("stage 4: added {0}",
              info));
        }
      }
      output.CompleteAdding();
    });
}
```

The pipeline stage `AddColorAsync` sets the `Color` property of the `Info` type depending on the value of the `Count` property.:

```
public static Task AddColorAsync(BlockingCollection<Info> input,
    BlockingCollection<Info> output)
{
  return Task.Run(() =>
    {
      foreach (var item in input.GetConsumingEnumerable())
      {
        if (item.Count > 40)
        {
          item.Color = "Red";
        }
        else if (item.Count > 20)
        {
          item.Color = "Yellow";
        }
        else
        {
          item.Color = "Green";
        }
        output.Add(item);
        ConsoleHelper.WriteLine(string.Format(
            "stage 5: added color {1} to {0}", item, item.Color));
      }
      output.CompleteAdding();
    });
}
```

The last stage writes the resulting items to the console in the specified color:

```
public static Task ShowContentAsync(BlockingCollection<Info> input)
{
  return Task.Run(() =>
```

```
        {
          foreach (var item in input.GetConsumingEnumerable())
          {
            ConsoleHelper.WriteLine(string.Format("stage 6: {0}", item),
                item.Color);
          }
        });
      }
```

Running the application results in the output shown in Figure 10-8.

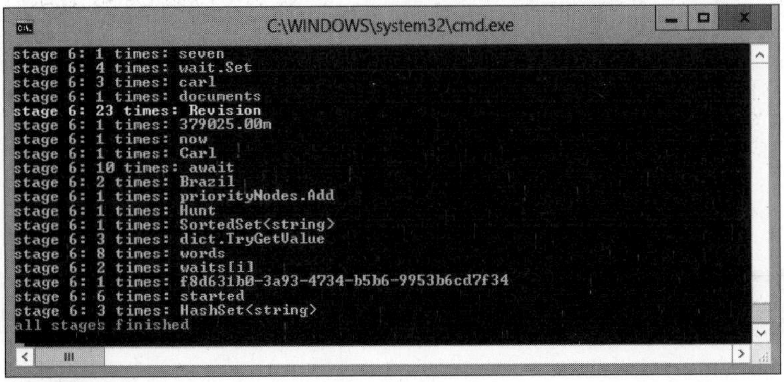

FIGURE 10-8

PERFORMANCE

Many collection classes offer the same functionality as others; for example, SortedList offers nearly the same features as SortedDictionary. However, often there's a big difference in performance. Whereas one collection consumes less memory, the other collection class is faster with retrieval of elements. The MSDN documentation often provides performance hints about methods of the collection, giving you information about the time the operation requires in *big-O* notation:

```
O(1)
O(log n)
O(n)
```

O(1) means that the time this operation needs is constant no matter how many items are in the collection. For example, the ArrayList has an Add method with O(1) behavior. No matter how many elements are in the list, it always takes the same amount of time when adding a new element to the end of the list. The Count property provides the number of items, so it is easy to find the end of the list.

O(n) means it takes the worst case time of N to perform an operation on the collection. The Add method of ArrayList can be an O(n) operation if a reallocation of the collection is required. Changing the capacity causes the list to be copied, and the time for the copy increases linearly with every element.

O(log n) means that the time needed for the operation increases with every element in the collection,. but the increase of time for each element is not linear but logarithmic. SortedDictionary<TKey, TValue> has O(log n) behavior for inserting operations inside the collection; SortedList<TKey, TValue> has O(n) behavior for the same functionality. Here, SortedDictionary<TKey, TValue> is a lot faster because it is more efficient to insert elements into a tree structure than into a list.

The following table lists collection classes and their performance for different actions such as adding, inserting, and removing items. Using this table you can select the best collection class for the purpose of your use. The left column lists the collection class. The Add column gives timing information about adding items to the collection. The List<T> and the HashSet<T> classes define Add methods to add items to the collection. With other collection classes use a different method to add elements to the collection; for example, the

Stack<T> class defines a Push method, and the Queue<T> class defines an Enqueue method. You can find this information in the table as well.

If there are multiple big-O values in a cell, the reason is because if a collection needs to be resized, resizing takes a while. For example, with the List<T> class, adding items needs O(1). If the capacity of the collection is not large enough and the collection needs to be resized, the resize requires O(n) time. The larger the collection, the longer the resize operation takes. It's best to avoid resizes by setting the capacity of the collection to a value that can hold all the elements.

If the table cell contents is *n/a,* the operation is *not applicable* with this collection type.

COLLECTION	ADD	INSERT	REMOVE	ITEM	SORT	FIND
List<T>	O(1) or O(n) if the collection must be resized	O(n)	O(n)	O(1)	O (n log n), worst case O(n ^ 2)	O(n)
Stack<T>	Push, O(1) or O(n) if the stack must be resized	n/a	Pop, O(1)	n/a	n/a	n/a
Queue<T>	Enqueue, O(1) or O(n) if the queue must be resized	n/a	Dequeue, O(1)	n/a	n/a	n/a
HashSet<T>	O(1) or O(n) if the set must be resized	Add O(1) or O(n)	O(1)	n/a	n/a	n/a
SortedSet<T>	O(1) or O(n) if the set must be resized	Add O(1) or O(n)	O(1)	n/a	n/a	n/a
LinkedList<T>	AddLast O(1)	Add After O(1)	O(1)	n/a	n/a	O(n)
Dictionary <TKey, TValue>	O(1) or O(n)	n/a	O(1)	O(1)	n/a	n/a
SortedDictionary <TKey, TValue>	O(log n)	n/a	O(log n)	O(log n)	n/a	n/a
SortedList <TKey, TValue>	O(n) for unsorted data, O(log n) for end of list, O(n) if resize is needed	n/a	O(n)	O(log n) to read/write, O(log n) if the key is in the list, O(n) if the key is not in the list	n/a	n/a

SUMMARY

This chapter took a look at working with different kinds of collections. Arrays are fixed in size, but you can use lists for dynamically growing collections. For accessing elements on a first-in, first-out basis, there's a queue; and you can use a stack for last-in, first-out operations. Linked lists allow for fast insertion and removal of elements but are slow for searching. With keys and values, you can use dictionaries, which are fast for searching and inserting elements. Sets are useful for unique items and can be ordered (SortedSet<T>) or not ordered (HashSet<T>). ObservableCollection<T> raises events when items change in the list.

You've also looked at several interfaces and classes in this chapter, including how to use them for accessing and sorting collections. Finally, you looked at some specialized collections, such as BitArray and BitVector32, which are optimized for working with a collection of bits.

Chapter 11 gives you details about Language Integrated Query (LINQ).

11

Language Integrated Query

WHAT'S IN THIS CHAPTER?

➤ Traditional queries across objects using List

➤ Extension methods

➤ LINQ query operators

➤ Parallel LINQ

➤ Expression trees

WROX.COM CODE DOWNLOADS FOR THIS CHAPTER

The wrox.com code downloads for this chapter are found at `http://www.wrox.com/remtitle
.cgi?isbn=1118314425` on the Download Code tab. The code for this chapter is divided into the
following major examples:

➤ LINQ Intro

➤ Enumerable Sample

➤ Parallel LINQ

➤ Expression Trees

LINQ OVERVIEW

LINQ (Language Integrated Query) integrates query syntax inside the C# programming language,
making it possible to access different data sources with the same syntax. LINQ accomplishes this by
offering an abstraction layer.

This chapter describes the core principles of LINQ and the language extensions for C# that make the
C# LINQ Query possible.

> **NOTE** *For details about using LINQ across the database, you should read Chapter
> 33, "ADO.NET Entity Framework." For information about querying XML data, read
> Chapter 34, "Manipulating XML," after reading this chapter.*

This chapter starts with a simple LINQ query before diving into the full potential of LINQ. The C# language offers integrated query language that is converted to method calls. This section shows you what the conversion looks like so you can use all the possibilities of LINQ.

Lists and Entities

The LINQ queries in this chapter are performed on a collection containing Formula-1 champions from 1950 to 2011. This data needs to be prepared with entity classes and lists.

For the entities, the type `Racer` is defined. `Racer` defines several properties and an overloaded `ToString` method to display a racer in a string format. This class implements the interface `IFormattable` to support different variants of format strings, and the interface `IComparable<Racer>`, which can be used to sort a list of racers based on the `LastName`. For more advanced queries, the class `Racer` contains not only single-value properties such as `FirstName`, `LastName`, `Wins`, `Country`, and `Starts`, but also multivalue properties such as `Cars` and `Years`. The `Years` property lists all the years of the championship title. Some racers have won more than one title. The `Cars` property is used to list all the cars used by the driver during the title years (code file `DataLib/Racer.cs`):

```
using System;
using System.Collections.Generic;

namespace Wrox.ProCSharp.LINQ
{
  [Serializable]
  public class Racer: IComparable<Racer>, IFormattable
  {
    public Racer(string firstName, string lastName, string country,
        int starts, int wins)
      : this(firstName, lastName, country, starts, wins, null, null)
    {
    }
    public Racer(string firstName, string lastName, string country,
        int starts, int wins, IEnumerable<int> years, IEnumerable<string> cars)
    {
      this.FirstName = firstName;
      this.LastName = lastName;
      this.Country = country;
      this.Starts = starts;
      this.Wins = wins;
      this.Years = new List<int>(years);
      this.Cars = new List<string>(cars);
    }

    public string FirstName {get; set;}
    public string LastName {get; set;}
    public int Wins {get; set;}
    public string Country {get; set;}
    public int Starts {get; set;}
    public IEnumerable<string> Cars { get; private set; }
    public IEnumerable<int> Years { get; private set; }

    public override string ToString()
    {
      return String.Format("{0} {1}", FirstName, LastName);
    }

    public int CompareTo(Racer other)
    {
      if (other == null) return -1;
```

```
        return string.Compare(this.LastName, other.LastName);
      }

      public string ToString(string format)
      {
        return ToString(format, null);
      }

      public string ToString(string format, IFormatProvider formatProvider)
      {
        switch (format)
        {
          case null:
          case "N":
            return ToString();
          case "F":
            return FirstName;
          case "L":
            return LastName;
          case "C":
            return Country;
          case "S":
            return Starts.ToString();
          case "W":
            return Wins.ToString();
          case "A":
            return String.Format("{0} {1}, {2}; starts: {3}, wins: {4}",
                        FirstName, LastName, Country, Starts, Wins);
          default:
            throw new FormatException(String.Format(
                        "Format {0} not supported", format));
        }
      }
    }
  }
```

A second entity class is `Team`. This class just contains the name and an array of years for constructor championships. Similar to a driver championship, there's a constructor championship for the best team of a year (code file `DataLib/Team.cs`):

```
[Serializable]
public class Team
{
  public Team(string name, params int[] years)
  {
    this.Name = name;
    this.Years = new List<int>(years);
  }
  public string Name { get; private set; }
  public IEnumerable<int> Years { get; private set; }
}
```

The class `Formula1` returns a list of racers in the method `GetChampions`. The list is filled with all Formula-1 champions from the years 1950 to 2011 (code file `DataLib/Formula1.cs`):

```
using System.Collections.Generic;

namespace Wrox.ProCSharp.LINQ
{
  public static class Formula1
```

```
{
  private static List<Racer> racers;

  public static IList<Racer> GetChampions()
  {
    if (racers == null)
    {
      racers = new List<Racer>(40);
      racers.Add(new Racer("Nino", "Farina", "Italy", 33, 5,
          new int[] { 1950 }, new string[] { "Alfa Romeo" }));
      racers.Add(new Racer("Alberto", "Ascari", "Italy", 32, 10,
          new int[] { 1952, 1953 }, new string[] { "Ferrari" }));
      racers.Add(new Racer("Juan Manuel", "Fangio", "Argentina", 51, 24,
          new int[] { 1951, 1954, 1955, 1956, 1957 },
          new string[] { "Alfa Romeo", "Maserati", "Mercedes", "Ferrari" }));
      racers.Add(new Racer("Mike", "Hawthorn", "UK", 45, 3,
          new int[] { 1958 }, new string[] { "Ferrari" }));
      racers.Add(new Racer("Phil", "Hill", "USA", 48, 3, new int[] { 1961 },
          new string[] { "Ferrari" }));
      racers.Add(new Racer("John", "Surtees", "UK", 111, 6,
          new int[] { 1964 }, new string[] { "Ferrari" }));
      racers.Add(new Racer("Jim", "Clark", "UK", 72, 25,
          new int[] { 1963, 1965 }, new string[] { "Lotus" }));
      racers.Add(new Racer("Jack", "Brabham", "Australia", 125, 14,
          new int[] { 1959, 1960, 1966 },
          new string[] { "Cooper", "Brabham" }));
      racers.Add(new Racer("Denny", "Hulme", "New Zealand", 112, 8,
          new int[] { 1967 }, new string[] { "Brabham" }));
      racers.Add(new Racer("Graham", "Hill", "UK", 176, 14,
          new int[] { 1962, 1968 }, new string[] { "BRM", "Lotus" }));
      racers.Add(new Racer("Jochen", "Rindt", "Austria", 60, 6,
          new int[] { 1970 }, new string[] { "Lotus" }));
      racers.Add(new Racer("Jackie", "Stewart", "UK", 99, 27,
          new int[] { 1969, 1971, 1973 },
          new string[] { "Matra", "Tyrrell" }));
      //...

      return racers;
    }
  }
}
```

Where queries are done across multiple lists, the GetConstructorChampions method that follows returns the list of all constructor championships (these championships have been around since 1958):

```
private static List<Team> teams;
public static IList<Team> GetContructorChampions()
{
  if (teams == null)
  {
    teams = new List<Team>()
    {
      new Team("Vanwall", 1958),
      new Team("Cooper", 1959, 1960),
      new Team("Ferrari", 1961, 1964, 1975, 1976, 1977, 1979, 1982,
              1983, 1999, 2000, 2001, 2002, 2003, 2004, 2007, 2008),
      new Team("BRM", 1962),
      new Team("Lotus", 1963, 1965, 1968, 1970, 1972, 1973, 1978),
      new Team("Brabham", 1966, 1967),
      new Team("Matra", 1969),
      new Team("Tyrrell", 1971),
```

```
              new Team("McLaren", 1974, 1984, 1985, 1988, 1989, 1990, 1991, 1998),
              new Team("Williams", 1980, 1981, 1986, 1987, 1992, 1993, 1994, 1996,
                      1997),
              new Team("Benetton", 1995),
              new Team("Renault", 2005, 2006),
              new Team("Brawn GP", 2009),
              new Team("Red Bull Racing", 2010, 2011)
          };
      }
      return teams;
  }
```

LINQ Query

Using these prepared lists and entities, you can do a LINQ query — for example, a query to get all world champions from Brazil sorted by the highest number of wins. To accomplish this you could use methods of the List<T> class; e.g., the FindAll and Sort methods. However, using LINQ there's a simpler syntax as soon as you get used to it (code file LINQIntro/Program.cs):

```
      private static void LinqQuery()
      {
        var query = from r in Formula1.GetChampions()
                    where r.Country == "Brazil"
                    orderby r.Wins descending
                    select r;

        foreach (Racer r in query)
        {
          Console.WriteLine("{0:A}", r);
        }
      }
```

The result of this query shows world champions from Brazil ordered by number of wins:

```
    Ayrton Senna, Brazil; starts: 161, wins: 41
    Nelson Piquet, Brazil; starts: 204, wins: 23
    Emerson Fittipaldi, Brazil; starts: 143, wins: 14
```

The statement

```
    from r in Formula1.GetChampions()
    where r.Country == "Brazil"
    orderby r.Wins descending
    select r;
```

is a LINQ query. The clauses from, where, orderby, descending, and select are predefined keywords in this query.

The query expression must begin with a from clause and end with a select or group clause. In between you can optionally use where, orderby, join, let, and additional from clauses.

> **NOTE** *The variable* query *just has the LINQ query assigned to it. The query is not performed by this assignment, but rather as soon as the query is accessed using the* foreach *loop. This is discussed in more detail later in the section "Deferred Query Execution."*

Extension Methods

The compiler converts the LINQ query to invoke method calls instead of the LINQ query. LINQ offers various extension methods for the `IEnumerable<T>` interface, so you can use the LINQ query across any collection that implements this interface. An *extension method* is defined as a static method whose first parameter defines the type it extends, and it is declared in a static class.

Extension methods make it possible to write a method to a class that doesn't already offer the method at first. You can also add a method to any class that implements a specific interface, so multiple classes can make use of the same implementation.

For example, wouldn't you like to have a Foo method with the `String` class? The `String` class is sealed, so it is not possible to inherit from this class; but you can create an extension method, as shown in the following code:

```
public static class StringExtension
{
  public static void Foo(this string s)
  {
    Console.WriteLine("Foo invoked for {0}", s);
  }
}
```

An *extension method* is defined as a static method where the first parameter defines the type it extends and it is declared in a static class. The Foo method extends the `string` class, as is defined with the first parameter. For differentiating extension methods from normal static methods, the extension method also requires the `this` keyword with the first parameter.

Indeed, it is now possible to use the Foo method with the `string` type:

```
string s = "Hello";
s.Foo();
```

The result shows `Foo invoked for Hello` in the console, because `Hello` is the string passed to the Foo method.

This might appear to be breaking object-oriented rules because a new method is defined for a type without changing the type or deriving from it. However, this is not the case. The extension method cannot access private members of the type it extends. Calling an extension method is just a new syntax for invoking a static method. With the string you can get the same result by calling the method Foo this way:

```
string s = "Hello";
StringExtension.Foo(s);
```

To invoke the static method, write the class name followed by the method name. Extension methods are a different way to invoke static methods. You don't have to supply the name of the class where the static method is defined. Instead, because of the parameter type the static method is selected by the compiler. You just have to import the namespace that contains the class to get the Foo extension method in the scope of the `String` class.

One of the classes that define LINQ extension methods is `Enumerable` in the namespace `System.Linq`. You just have to import the namespace to open the scope of the extension methods of this class. A sample implementation of the `Where` extension method is shown in the following code. The first parameter of the `Where` method that includes the `this` keyword is of type `IEnumerable<T>`. This enables the `Where` method to be used with every type that implements `IEnumerable<T>`. A few examples of types that implement this interface are arrays and `List<T>`. The second parameter is a `Func<T, bool>` delegate that references a method that returns a Boolean value and requires a parameter of type T. This predicate is invoked within the implementation to examine whether the item from the `IEnumerable<T>` source should be added into the destination collection. If the method is referenced by the delegate, the `yield return` statement returns the item from the source to the destination:

```
public static IEnumerable<TSource> Where<TSource>(
        this IEnumerable<TSource> source,
        Func<TSource, bool> predicate)
{
  foreach (TSource item in source)
    if (predicate(item))
      yield return item;
}
```

Because `Where` is implemented as a generic method, it works with any type that is contained in a collection. Any collection implementing `IEnumerable<T>` is supported.

> **NOTE** *The extension methods here are defined in the namespace* `System.Linq` *in the assembly* `System.Core`.

Now it's possible to use the extension methods `Where`, `OrderByDescending`, and `Select` from the class `Enumerable`. Because each of these methods returns `IEnumerable<TSource>`, it is possible to invoke one method after the other by using the previous result. With the arguments of the extension methods, anonymous methods that define the implementation for the delegate parameters are used (code file `LINQIntro/Program.cs`):

```
static void ExtensionMethods()
{
  var champions = new List<Racer>(Formula1.GetChampions());
  IEnumerable<Racer> brazilChampions =
      champions.Where(r => r.Country == "Brazil").
              OrderByDescending(r => r.Wins).
              Select(r => r);

  foreach (Racer r in brazilChampions)
  {
    Console.WriteLine("{0:A}", r);
  }
}
```

Deferred Query Execution

When the query expression is defined during runtime, the query does not run. The query runs when the items are iterated.

Let's have a look once more at the extension method `Where`. This extension method makes use of the `yield return` statement to return the elements where the predicate is true. Because the `yield return` statement is used, the compiler creates an enumerator and returns the items as soon as they are accessed from the enumeration:

```
public static IEnumerable<T> Where<T>(this IEnumerable<T> source,
                                      Func<T, bool> predicate)
{
  foreach (T item in source)
  {
    if (predicate(item))
    {
      yield return item;
    }
  }
}
```

This has a very interesting and important effect. In the following example a collection of `string` elements is created and filled with first names. Next, a query is defined to get all names from the collection whose first letter is `J`. The collection should also be sorted. The iteration does not happen when the query is defined. Instead, the iteration happens with the `foreach` statement, where all items are iterated. Only one element of the collection fulfills the requirements of the `where` expression by starting with the letter J: `Juan`. After the iteration is done and `Juan` is written to the console, four new names are added to the collection. Then the iteration is done again:

```
var names = new List<string> { "Nino", "Alberto", "Juan", "Mike", "Phil" };

var namesWithJ = from n in names
                 where n.StartsWith("J")
                 orderby n
                 select n;

Console.WriteLine("First iteration");
foreach (string name in namesWithJ)
{
  Console.WriteLine(name);
}
Console.WriteLine();

names.Add("John");
names.Add("Jim");
names.Add("Jack");
names.Add("Denny");

Console.WriteLine("Second iteration");
foreach (string name in namesWithJ)
{
  Console.WriteLine(name);
}
```

Because the iteration does not happen when the query is defined, but does happen with every `foreach`, changes can be seen, as the output from the application demonstrates:

```
First iteration
Juan

Second iteration
Jack
Jim
John
Juan
```

Of course, you also must be aware that the extension methods are invoked every time the query is used within an iteration. Most of the time this is very practical, because you can detect changes in the source data. However, sometimes this is impractical. You can change this behavior by invoking the extension methods `ToArray`, `ToList`, and the like. In the following example, you can see that `ToList` iterates through the collection immediately and returns a collection implementing `IList<string>`. The returned list is then iterated through twice; in between iterations, the data source gets new names:

```
var names = new List<string>
                 { "Nino", "Alberto", "Juan", "Mike", "Phil" };
var namesWithJ = (from n in names
                  where n.StartsWith("J")
                  orderby n
                  select n).ToList();

Console.WriteLine("First iteration");
```

```
        foreach (string name in namesWithJ)
        {
          Console.WriteLine(name);
        }
        Console.WriteLine();

        names.Add("John");
        names.Add("Jim");
        names.Add("Jack");
        names.Add("Denny");

        Console.WriteLine("Second iteration");
        foreach (string name in namesWithJ)
        {
          Console.WriteLine(name);
        }
```

The result indicates that in between the iterations the output stays the same although the collection values have changed:

```
    First iteration
    Juan

    Second iteration
    Juan
```

STANDARD QUERY OPERATORS

Where, OrderByDescending, and Select are only a few of the query operators defined by LINQ. The LINQ query defines a declarative syntax for the most common operators. There are many more query operators available with the Enumerable class.

The following table lists the standard query operators defined by the Enumerable class.

STANDARD QUERY OPERATORS	DESCRIPTION
Where OfType<TResult>	*Filtering operators* define a restriction to the elements returned. With the Where query operator you can use a predicate; for example, a Lambda expression that returns a bool. OfType<TResult> filters the elements based on the type and returns only the elements of the type TResult.
Select SelectMany	*Projection operators* are used to transform an object into a new object of a different type. Select and SelectMany define a projection to select values of the result based on a selector function.
OrderBy ThenBy OrderByDescending ThenByDescending Reverse	*Sorting operators* change the order of elements returned. OrderBy sorts values in ascending order; OrderByDescending sorts values in descending order. ThenBy and ThenByDescending operators are used for a secondary sort if the first sort gives similar results. Reverse reverses the elements in the collection.
Join GroupJoin	*Join operators* are used to combine collections that might not be directly related to each other. With the Join operator a join of two collections based on key selector functions can be done. This is similar to the JOIN you know from SQL. The GroupJoin operator joins two collections and groups the results.
GroupBy ToLookup	*Grouping operators* put the data into groups. The GroupBy operator groups elements with a common key. ToLookup groups the elements by creating a one-to-many dictionary.

(continues)

(continued)

STANDARD QUERY OPERATORS	DESCRIPTION
Any All Contains	*Quantifier operators* return a Boolean value if elements of the sequence satisfy a specific condition. Any, All, and Contains are quantifier operators. Any determines if any element in the collection satisfies a predicate function; All determines if all elements in the collection satisfy a predicate. Contains checks whether a specific element is in the collection.
Take Skip TakeWhile SkipWhile	*Partitioning operators* return a subset of the collection. Take, Skip, TakeWhile, and SkipWhile are partitioning operators. With these, you get a partial result. With Take, you have to specify the number of elements to take from the collection; Skip ignores the specified number of elements and takes the rest. TakeWhile takes the elements as long as a condition is true.
Distinct Union Intersect Except Zip	*Set operators* return a collection set. Distinct removes duplicates from a collection. With the exception of Distinct, the other set operators require two collections. Union returns unique elements that appear in either of the two collections. Intersect returns elements that appear in both collections. Except returns elements that appear in just one collection. Zip combines two collections into one.
First FirstOrDefault Last LastOrDefault ElementAt ElementAtOrDefault Single SingleOrDefault	*Element operators* return just one element. First returns the first element that satisfies a condition. FirstOrDefault is similar to First, but it returns a default value of the type if the element is not found. Last returns the last element that satisfies a condition. With ElementAt, you specify the position of the element to return. Single returns only the one element that satisfies a condition. If more than one element satisfies the condition, an exception is thrown.
Count Sum Min Max Average Aggregate	*Aggregate operators* compute a single value from a collection. With aggregate operators, you can get the sum of all values, the number of all elements, the element with the lowest or highest value, an average number, and so on.
ToArray AsEnumerable ToList ToDictionary Cast<TResult>	*Conversion operators* convert the collection to an array: IEnumerable, IList, IDictionary, and so on.
Empty Range Repeat	*Generation* operators return a new sequence. The collection is empty using the Empty operator; Range returns a sequence of numbers, and Repeat returns a collection with one repeated value.

The following sections provide examples demonstrating how to use these operators.

Filtering

This section looks at some examples for a query.

With the `where` clause, you can combine multiple expressions — for example, get only the racers from Brazil and Austria who won more than 15 races. The result type of the expression passed to the `where` clause just needs to be of type `bool`:

```
var racers = from r in Formula1.GetChampions()
             where r.Wins > 15 &&
                   (r.Country == "Brazil" || r.Country == "Austria")
             select r;

foreach (var r in racers)
{
  Console.WriteLine("{0:A}", r);
}
```

Starting the program with this LINQ query returns Niki Lauda, Nelson Piquet, and Ayrton Senna, as shown here:

```
Niki Lauda, Austria, Starts: 173, Wins: 25
Nelson Piquet, Brazil, Starts: 204, Wins: 23
Ayrton Senna, Brazil, Starts: 161, Wins: 41
```

Not all queries can be done with the LINQ query syntax, and not all extension methods are mapped to LINQ query clauses. Advanced queries require using extension methods. To better understand complex queries with extension methods, it's good to see how simple queries are mapped. Using the extension methods `Where` and `Select` produces a query very similar to the LINQ query done before:

```
var racers = Formula1.GetChampions().
    Where(r => r.Wins > 15 &&
          (r.Country == "Brazil" || r.Country == "Austria")).
    Select(r => r);
```

Filtering with Index

One scenario in which you can't use the LINQ query is an overload of the `Where` method. With an overload of the `Where` method, you can pass a second parameter that is the index. The index is a counter for every result returned from the filter. You can use the index within the expression to do some calculation based on the index. In the following example, the index is used within the code that is called by the `Where` extension method to return only racers whose last name starts with A if the index is even (code file `EnumerableSample/Program.cs`):

```
var racers = Formula1.GetChampions().
    Where((r, index) => r.LastName.StartsWith("A") && index % 2 != 0);
foreach (var r in racers)
{
  Console.WriteLine("{0:A}", r);
}
```

The racers with last names beginning with the letter A are Alberto Ascari, Mario Andretti, and Fernando Alonso. Because Mario Andretti is positioned within an index that is odd, he is not in the result:

```
Alberto Ascari, Italy; starts: 32, wins: 10
Fernando Alonso, Spain; starts: 177, wins: 27
```

Type Filtering

For filtering based on a type you can use the `OfType` extension method. Here the array data contains both `string` and `int` objects. Using the extension method `OfType`, passing the string class to the generic parameter returns only the strings from the collection (code file `EnumerableSample/Program.cs`):

```
object[] data = { "one", 2, 3, "four", "five", 6 };
var query = data.OfType<string>();
foreach (var s in query)
{
  Console.WriteLine(s);
}
```

Running this code, the strings one, four, and five are displayed:

```
one
four
five
```

Compound from

If you need to do a filter based on a member of the object that itself is a sequence, you can use a compound `from`. The `Racer` class defines a property `Cars`, where `Cars` is a string array. For a filter of all racers who were champions with a Ferrari, you can use the LINQ query shown next. The first `from` clause accesses the `Racer` objects returned from `Formula1.GetChampions`. The second `from` clause accesses the `Cars` property of the `Racer` class to return all cars of type `string`. Next the cars are used with the `where` clause to filter only the racers who were champions with a Ferrari (code file `EnumerableSample/Program.cs`):

```
var ferrariDrivers = from r in Formula1.GetChampions()
                     from c in r.Cars
                     where c == "Ferrari"
                     orderby r.LastName
                     select r.FirstName + " " + r.LastName;
```

If you are curious about the result of this query, following are all Formula-1 champions driving a Ferrari:

```
Alberto Ascari
Juan Manuel Fangio
Mike Hawthorn
Phil Hill
Niki Lauda
Kimi Räikkönen
Jody Scheckter
Michael Schumacher
John Surtees
```

The C# compiler converts a compound `from` clause with a LINQ query to the `SelectMany` extension method. `SelectMany` can be used to iterate a sequence of a sequence. The overload of the `SelectMany` method that is used with the example is shown here:

```
public static IEnumerable<TResult> SelectMany<TSource, TCollection, TResult> (
    this IEnumerable<TSource> source,
    Func<TSource,
    IEnumerable<TCollection>> collectionSelector,
    Func<TSource, TCollection, TResult> resultSelector);
```

The first parameter is the implicit parameter that receives the sequence of `Racer` objects from the `GetChampions` method. The second parameter is the `collectionSelector` delegate where the inner sequence is defined. With the lambda expression `r => r.Cars`, the collection of cars should be returned. The third parameter is a delegate that is now invoked for every car and receives the `Racer` and `Car` objects. The lambda expression creates an anonymous type with a `Racer` and a `Car` property. As a result of this `SelectMany` method, the hierarchy of racers and cars is flattened and a collection of new objects of an anonymous type for every car is returned.

This new collection is passed to the `Where` method so that only the racers driving a Ferrari are filtered. Finally, the `OrderBy` and `Select` methods are invoked:

```
var ferrariDrivers = Formula1.GetChampions().
    SelectMany(r => r.Cars,
        (r, c) => new { Racer = r, Car = c }).
        Where(r => r.Car == "Ferrari").
        OrderBy(r => r.Racer.LastName).
        Select(r => r.Racer.FirstName + " " + r.Racer.LastName);
```

Resolving the generic `SelectMany` method to the types that are used here, the types are resolved as follows. In this case the source is of type `Racer`, the filtered collection is a `string` array, and of course the name of the anonymous type that is returned is not known and is shown here as `TResult`:

```
public static IEnumerable<TResult> SelectMany<Racer, string, TResult> (
    this IEnumerable<Racer> source,
    Func<Racer, IEnumerable<string>> collectionSelector,
    Func<Racer, string, TResult> resultSelector);
```

Because the query was just converted from a LINQ query to extension methods, the result is the same as before.

Sorting

To sort a sequence, the `orderby` clause was used already. This section reviews the earlier example, now with the `orderby descending` clause. Here the racers are sorted based on the number of wins as specified by the key selector in descending order (code file `EnumerableSample/Program.cs`):

```
var racers = from r in Formula1.GetChampions()
             where r.Country == "Brazil"
             orderby r.Wins descending
             select r;
```

The `orderby` clause is resolved to the `OrderBy` method, and the `orderby descending` clause is resolved to the `OrderByDescending` method:

```
var racers = Formula1.GetChampions().
    Where(r => r.Country == "Brazil").
    OrderByDescending(r => r.Wins).
    Select(r => r);
```

The `OrderBy` and `OrderByDescending` methods return `IOrderedEnumerable<TSource>`. This interface derives from the interface `IEnumerable<TSource>` but contains an additional method, `CreateOrdered Enumerable<TSource>`. This method is used for further ordering of the sequence. If two items are the same based on the key selector, ordering can continue with the `ThenBy` and `ThenByDescending` methods. These methods require an `IOrderedEnumerable<TSource>` to work on but return this interface as well. Therefore, you can add any number of `ThenBy` and `ThenByDescending` methods to sort the collection.

Using the LINQ query, you just add all the different keys (with commas) for sorting to the `orderby` clause. In the next example, the sort of all racers is done first based on country, next on last name, and finally on first name. The `Take` extension method that is added to the result of the LINQ query is used to return the first 10 results:

```
var racers = (from r in Formula1.GetChampions()
                orderby r.Country, r.LastName, r.FirstName
                select r).Take(10);
```

The sorted result is shown here:

```
Argentina: Fangio, Juan Manuel
Australia: Brabham, Jack
Australia: Jones, Alan
Austria: Lauda, Niki
Austria: Rindt, Jochen
Brazil: Fittipaldi, Emerson
Brazil: Piquet, Nelson
Brazil: Senna, Ayrton
Canada: Villeneuve, Jacques
Finland: Hakkinen, Mika
```

Doing the same with extension methods makes use of the `OrderBy` and `ThenBy` methods:

```
var racers = Formula1.GetChampions().
    OrderBy(r => r.Country).
    ThenBy(r => r.LastName).
    ThenBy(r => r.FirstName).
    Take(10);
```

Grouping

To group query results based on a key value, the `group` clause can be used. Now the Formula-1 champions should be grouped by country, and the number of champions within a country should be listed. The clause `group r by r.Country into g` groups all the racers based on the `Country` property and defines a new identifier g that can be used later to access the group result information. The result from the `group` clause is ordered based on the extension method `Count` that is applied on the group result; and if the count is the same, the ordering is done based on the key. This is the country because this was the key used for grouping. The `where` clause filters the results based on groups that have at least two items, and the `select` clause creates an anonymous type with the `Country` and `Count` properties (code file `EnumerableSample/Program.cs`):

```
var countries = from r in Formula1.GetChampions()
                group r by r.Country into g
                orderby g.Count() descending, g.Key
                where g.Count() >= 2
                select new {
                        Country = g.Key,
                        Count = g.Count()
                };

foreach (var item in countries)
{
    Console.WriteLine("{0, -10} {1}", item.Country, item.Count);
}
```

The result displays the collection of objects with the `Country` and `Count` properties:

```
UK          10
Brazil      3
```

```
Finland    3
Australia  2
Austria    2
Germany    2
Italy      2
USA        2
```

Doing the same with extension methods, the groupby clause is resolved to the GroupBy method. What's interesting with the declaration of the GroupBy method is that it returns an enumeration of objects implementing the IGrouping interface. The IGrouping interface defines the Key property, so you can access the key of the group after defining the call to this method:

```
public static IEnumerable<IGrouping<TKey, TSource>> GroupBy<TSource, TKey>(
        this IEnumerable<TSource> source, Func<TSource, TKey> keySelector);
```

The group r by r.Country into g clause is resolved to GroupBy(r => r.Country) and returns the group sequence. The group sequence is first ordered by the OrderByDecending method, then by the ThenBy method. Next, the Where and Select methods that you already know are invoked:

```
var countries = Formula1.GetChampions().
    GroupBy(r => r.Country).
    OrderByDescending(g => g.Count()).
    ThenBy(g => g.Key).
    Where(g => g.Count() >= 2).
    Select(g => new { Country = g.Key,
                      Count = g.Count() });
```

Grouping with Nested Objects

If the grouped objects should contain nested sequences, you can do that by changing the anonymous type created by the select clause. With this example, the returned countries should contain not only the properties for the name of the country and the number of racers, but also a sequence of the names of the racers. This sequence is assigned by using an inner from/in clause assigned to the Racers property. The inner from clause is using the g group to get all racers from the group, order them by last name, and create a new string based on the first and last name (code file EnumerableSample/Program.cs):

```
var countries = from r in Formula1.GetChampions()
                group r by r.Country into g
                orderby g.Count() descending, g.Key
                where g.Count() >= 2
                select new
                {
                  Country = g.Key,
                  Count = g.Count(),
                  Racers = from r1 in g
                           orderby r1.LastName
                           select r1.FirstName + " " + r1.LastName
                };
foreach (var item in countries)
{
  Console.WriteLine("{0, -10} {1}", item.Country, item.Count);
  foreach (var name in item.Racers)
  {
    Console.Write("{0}; ", name);
  }
  Console.WriteLine();
}
```

The output now lists all champions from the specified countries:

```
UK          10
Jenson Button; Jim Clark; Lewis Hamilton; Mike Hawthorn; Graham Hill;
Damon Hill; James Hunt; Nigel Mansell; Jackie Stewart; John Surtees;
Brazil      3
Emerson Fittipaldi; Nelson Piquet; Ayrton Senna;
Finland     3
Mika Hakkinen; Kimi Raikkonen; Keke Rosberg;
Australia  2
Jack Brabham; Alan Jones;
Austria     2
Niki Lauda; Jochen Rindt;
Germany     2
Michael Schumacher; Sebastian Vettel;
Italy       2
Alberto Ascari; Nino Farina;
USA         2
Mario Andretti; Phil Hill;
```

Inner Join

You can use the `join` clause to combine two sources based on specific criteria. First, however, let's get two lists that should be joined. With Formula-1, there are drivers and a constructors championships. The drivers are returned from the method `GetChampions`, and the constructors are returned from the method `GetConstructorChampions`. It would be interesting to get a list by year in which every year lists the driver and the constructor champions.

To do this, the first two queries for the racers and the teams are defined (code file `EnumerableSample/Program.cs`):

```
var racers = from r in Formula1.GetChampions()
             from y in r.Years
             select new
             {
               Year = y,
               Name = r.FirstName + " " + r.LastName
             };

var teams = from t in Formula1.GetContructorChampions()
            from y in t.Years
            select new
            {
              Year = y,
              Name = t.Name
            };
```

Using these two queries, a join is done based on the year of the driver champion and the year of the team champion with the `join` clause. The `select` clause defines a new anonymous type containing `Year`, `Racer`, and `Team` properties:

```
var racersAndTeams = (from r in racers
                      join t in teams on r.Year equals t.Year
                      select new
                      {
                        r.Year,
                        Champion = r.Name,
                        Constructor = t.Name
                      }).Take(10);
```

```
Console.WriteLine("Year  World Champion\t   Constructor Title");
foreach (var item in racersAndTeams)
{
  Console.WriteLine("{0}: {1,-20} {2}", item.Year, item.Champion,
      item.Constructor);
}
```

Of course you can also combine this to just one LINQ query, but that's a matter of taste:

```
var racersAndTeams =
    (from r in
        from r1 in Formula1.GetChampions()
        from yr in r1.Years
        select new
        {
          Year = yr,
          Name = r1.FirstName + " " + r1.LastName
        }
    join t in
        from t1 in Formula1.GetContructorChampions()
        from yt in t1.Years
        select new
        {
          Year = yt,
          Name = t1.Name
        }
    on r.Year equals t.Year
    orderby t.Year
    select new
    {
      Year = r.Year,
      Racer = r.Name,
      Team = t.Name
    }).Take(10);
```

The output displays data from the anonymous type for the first 10 years in which both a drivers and constructor championship took place:

```
Year  World Champion       Constructor Title
1958: Mike Hawthorn        Vanwall
1959: Jack Brabham         Cooper
1960: Jack Brabham         Cooper
1961: Phil Hill            Ferrari
1962: Graham Hill          BRM
1963: Jim Clark            Lotus
1964: John Surtees         Ferrari
1965: Jim Clark            Lotus
1966: Jack Brabham         Brabham
1967: Denny Hulme          Brabham
```

Left Outer Join

The output from the previous join sample started with the year 1958 — the first year when both the drivers' and constructor championship started. The drivers' championship started earlier, in the year 1950. With an inner join, results are returned only when matching records are found. To get a result with all the years included, a left outer join can be used. A left outer join returns all the elements in the left sequence even when no match is found in the right sequence.

The earlier LINQ query is changed to a left outer join. A left outer join is defined with the `join` clause together with the `DefaultIfEmpty` method. If the left side of the query (the racers) does not have a matching constructor champion, the default value for the right side is defined by the `DefaultIfEmpty` method (code file `EnumerableSample/Program.cs`):

```
var racersAndTeams =
  (from r in racers
   join t in teams on r.Year equals t.Year into rt
   from t in rt.DefaultIfEmpty()
   orderby r.Year
   select new
   {
     Year = r.Year,
     Champion = r.Name,
     Constructor = t == null ? "no constructor championship" : t.Name
   }).Take(10);
```

Running the application with this query, the output starts with the year 1950 as shown here:

```
Year  Champion              Constructor Title
1950: Nino Farina           no constructor championship
1951: Juan Manuel Fangio    no constructor championship
1952: Alberto Ascari        no constructor championship
1953: Alberto Ascari        no constructor championship
1954: Juan Manuel Fangio    no constructor championship
1955: Juan Manuel Fangio    no constructor championship
1956: Juan Manuel Fangio    no constructor championship
1957: Juan Manuel Fangio    no constructor championship
1958: Mike Hawthorn         Vanwall
1959: Jack Brabham          Cooper
```

Group Join

A left outer join makes use of a group join together with the `into` clause. It uses partly the same syntax as the group join. The group join just doesn't need the `DefaultIfEmpty` method.

With a group join, two independent sequences can be joined, whereby one sequence contains a list of items for one element of the other sequence.

The following example uses two independent sequences. One is the list of champions that you already know from previous examples. The second sequence is a collection of `Championship` types. The `Championship` type is shown in the next code snippet. This class contains the year of the championship and the racers with the first, second, and third position of the year with the properties `Year`, `First`, `Second`, and `Third` (code file `DataLib/Championship.cs`):

```
public class Championship
{
  public int Year { get; set; }
  public string First { get; set; }
  public string Second { get; set; }
  public string Third { get; set; }
}
```

The collection of championships is returned from the method `GetChampionships` as shown in the following code snippet (code file `DataLib/Formula1.cs`):

```
private static List<Championship> championships;
public static IEnumerable<Championship> GetChampionships()
{
  if (championships == null)
  {
    championships = new List<Championship>();
    championships.Add(new Championship
```

```
    {
      Year = 1950,
      First = "Nino Farina",
      Second = "Juan Manuel Fangio",
      Third = "Luigi Fagioli"
    });
    championships.Add(new Championship
    {
      Year = 1951,
      First = "Juan Manuel Fangio",
      Second = "Alberto Ascari",
      Third = "Froilan Gonzalez"
    });
    //...
```

The list of champions should be combined with the list of racers that are found within the first three positions in every year of championships, and the results for every year should be displayed.

The information that should be shown is defined with the `RacerInfo` class, as shown here (code file `EnumerableSample/RacerInfo.cs`):

```
public class RacerInfo
{
  public int Year { get; set; }
  public int Position { get; set; }
  public string FirstName { get; set; }
  public string LastName { get; set; }
}
```

With a join statement the racers from both lists can be combined.

Because in the list of championships every item contains three racers, this list needs to be flattened first. One way to do this is by using the `SelectMany` method. `SelectMany` makes use of a lambda expression that returns a list of three items for every item in the list. Within the implementation of the lambda expression, because the `RacerInfo` contains the `FirstName` and the `LastName` properties, and the collection received just contains only a name with `First`, `Second`, and `Third` properties, the string needs to be divided. This is done with the help of the extension methods `FirstName` and `SecondName` (code file `EnumerableSample/Program.cs`):

```
var racers = Formula1.GetChampionships()
  .SelectMany(cs => new List<RacerInfo>()
  {
    new RacerInfo {
      Year = cs.Year,
      Position = 1,
      FirstName = cs.First.FirstName(),
      LastName = cs.First.LastName()
    },
    new RacerInfo {
      Year = cs.Year,
      Position = 2,
      FirstName = cs.Second.FirstName(),
      LastName = cs.Second.LastName()
    },
    new RacerInfo {
      Year = cs.Year,
      Position = 3,
      FirstName = cs.Third.FirstName(),
      LastName = cs.Third.LastName()
    }
  });
```

The extension methods `FirstName` and `SecondName` just use the last blank character to split up the string:

```
public static class StringExtension
{
  public static string FirstName(this string name)
  {
    int ix = name.LastIndexOf(' ');
    return name.Substring(0, ix);
  }
  public static string LastName(this string name)
  {
    int ix = name.LastIndexOf(' ');
    return name.Substring(ix + 1);
  }
}
```

Now the two sequences can be joined. `Formula1.GetChampions` returns a list of `Racers`, and the `racers` variable returns the list of `RacerInfo` that contains the year, the result, and the names of racers. It's not enough to compare the items from these two collections by using the last name. Sometimes a racer and his father can be found in the list (e.g., Damon Hill and Graham Hill), so it's necessary to compare the items by both `FirstName` and `LastName`. This is done by creating a new anonymous type for both lists. Using the `into` clause, the result from the second collection is put into the variable `yearResults`. `yearResults` is created for every racer in the first collection and contains the results of the matching first name and last name from the second collection. Finally, with the LINQ query a new anonymous type is created that contains the needed information:

```
var q = (from r in Formula1.GetChampions()
         join r2 in racers on
         new
         {
            FirstName = r.FirstName,
            LastName = r.LastName
         }
         equals
         new
         {
            FirstName = r2.FirstName,
            LastName = r2.LastName
         }
         into yearResults
         select new
         {
            FirstName = r.FirstName,
            LastName = r.LastName,
            Wins = r.Wins,
            Starts = r.Starts,
            Results = yearResults
         });

foreach (var r in q)
{
  Console.WriteLine("{0} {1}", r.FirstName, r.LastName);
  foreach (var results in r.Results)
  {
    Console.WriteLine("{0} {1}.", results.Year, results.Position);
  }
}
```

The last results from the `foreach` loop are shown next. Lewis Hamilton has been twice among the top three, 2007 as second and 2008 as first. Jenson Button is found three times, 2004, 2009, and 2011; and Sebastian Vettel was world champion two times and had the second position in 2009:

```
Lewis Hamilton
2007 2.
2008 1.
Jenson Button
2004 3.
2009 1.
2011 2.
Sebastian Vettel
2009 2.
2010 1.
2011 1.
```

Set Operations

The extension methods `Distinct`, `Union`, `Intersect`, and `Except` are set operations. The following example creates a sequence of Formula-1 champions driving a Ferrari and another sequence of Formula-1 champions driving a McLaren, and then determines whether any driver has been a champion driving both of these cars. Of course, that's where the `Intersect` extension method can help.

First, you need to get all champions driving a Ferrari. This uses a simple LINQ query with a compound `from` to access the property `Cars` that's returning a sequence of string objects (code file `EnumerableSample/Program.cs`):

```
var ferrariDrivers = from r in
                     Formula1.GetChampions()
                     from c in r.Cars
                     where c == "Ferrari"
                     orderby r.LastName
                     select r;
```

Now the same query with a different parameter of the `where` clause is needed to get all McLaren racers. It's not a good idea to write the same query again. One option is to create a method in which you can pass the parameter `car`:

```
private static IEnumerable<Racer> GetRacersByCar(string car)
{
  return from r in Formula1.GetChampions()
         from c in r.Cars
         where c == car
         orderby r.LastName
         select r;
}
```

However, because the method wouldn't be needed in other places, defining a variable of a delegate type to hold the LINQ query is a good approach. The variable `racersByCar` needs to be of a delegate type that requires a string parameter and returns `IEnumerable<Racer>`, similar to the method implemented earlier. To do this, several generic `Func<>` delegates are defined, so you do not need to declare your own delegate. A lambda expression is assigned to the variable `racersByCar`. The left side of the lambda expression defines a car variable of the type that is the first generic parameter of the `Func` delegate (a string). The right side defines the LINQ query that uses the parameter with the `where` clause:

```
Func<string, IEnumerable<Racer>> racersByCar =
     car => from r in Formula1.GetChampions()
            from c in r.Cars
            where c == car
            orderby r.LastName
            select r;
```

Now you can use the `Intersect` extension method to get all racers who won the championship with a Ferrari and a McLaren:

```
Console.WriteLine("World champion with Ferrari and McLaren");
foreach (var racer in racersByCar("Ferrari").Intersect(
            racersByCar("McLaren")))
{
    Console.WriteLine(racer);
}
```

The result is just one racer, Niki Lauda:

```
World champion with Ferrari and McLaren
Niki Lauda
```

> **NOTE** *The set operations compares the objects by invoking the* `GetHashCode` *and* `Equals` *methods of the entity class. For custom comparisons, you can also pass an object that implements the interface* `IEqualityComparer<T>`. *In the preceding example here, the* `GetChampions` *method always returns the same objects, so the default comparison works. If that's not the case, the set methods offer overloads in which a comparison can be defined.*

Zip

The `Zip` method is new since .NET 4 and enables you to merge two related sequences into one with a predicate function.

First, two related sequences are created, both with the same filtering (country Italy) and ordering. For merging this is important, as item 1 from the first collection is merged with item 1 from the second collection, item 2 with item 2, and so on. In case the count of the two sequences is different, `Zip` stops when the end of the smaller collection is reached.

The items in the first collection have a `Name` property and the items in the second collection have `LastName` and `Starts` properties.

Using the `Zip` method on the collection `racerNames` requires the second collection `racerNamesAndStarts` as the first parameter. The second parameter is of type `Func<TFirst, TSecond, TResult>`. This parameter is implemented as a lambda expression and receives the elements of the first collection with the parameter `first`, and the elements of the second collection with the parameter `second`. The implementation creates and returns a string containing the `Name` property of the first element and the `Starts` property of the second element (code file `EnumerableSample/Program.cs`):

```
var racerNames = from r in Formula1.GetChampions()
                 where r.Country == "Italy"
                 orderby r.Wins descending
                 select new
                 {
                     Name = r.FirstName + " " + r.LastName
                 };

var racerNamesAndStarts = from r in Formula1.GetChampions()
                          where r.Country == "Italy"
                          orderby r.Wins descending
                          select new
                          {
                              LastName = r.LastName,
```

```
                               Starts = r.Starts
                            };

         var racers = racerNames.Zip(racerNamesAndStarts,
            (first, second) => first.Name + ", starts: " + second.Starts);
         foreach (var r in racers)
         {
           Console.WriteLine(r);
         }
```

The result of this merge is shown here:

```
    Alberto Ascari, starts: 32
    Nino Farina, starts: 33
```

Partitioning

Partitioning operations such as the extension methods `Take` and `Skip` can be used for easy paging — for example, to display just 5 racers on the first page, and continue with the next 5 on the following pages.

With the LINQ query shown here, the extension methods `Skip` and `Take` are added to the end of the query. The `Skip` method first ignores a number of items calculated based on the page size and the actual page number; the `Take` method then takes a number of items based on the page size (code file `EnumerableSample/Program.cs`):

```
        int pageSize = 5;

        int numberPages = (int)Math.Ceiling(Formula1.GetChampions().Count() /
           (double)pageSize);

        for (int page = 0; page < numberPages; page++)
        {
          Console.WriteLine("Page {0}", page);

          var racers =
              (from r in Formula1.GetChampions()
               orderby r.LastName, r.FirstName
               select r.FirstName + " " + r.LastName).
               Skip(page * pageSize).Take(pageSize);

          foreach (var name in racers)
          {
            Console.WriteLine(name);
          }
          Console.WriteLine();
        }
```

Here is the output of the first three pages:

```
    Page 0
    Fernando Alonso
    Mario Andretti
    Alberto Ascari
    Jack Brabham
    Jenson Button

    Page 1
    Jim Clark
    Juan Manuel Fangio
    Nino Farina
```

```
Emerson Fittipaldi
Mika Hakkinen

Page 2
Lewis Hamilton
Mike Hawthorn
Damon Hill
Graham Hill
Phil Hill
```

Paging can be extremely useful with Windows or web applications, showing the user only a part of the data.

> **NOTE** *Note an important behavior of this paging mechanism: because the query is done with every page, changing the underlying data affects the results. New objects are shown as paging continues. Depending on your scenario, this can be advantageous to your application. If this behavior is not what you need, you can do the paging not over the original data source but by using a cache that maps to the original data.*

With the `TakeWhile` and `SkipWhile` extension methods you can also pass a predicate to retrieve or skip items based on the result of the predicate.

Aggregate Operators

The aggregate operators such as `Count`, `Sum`, `Min`, `Max`, `Average`, and `Aggregate` do not return a sequence but a single value instead.

The `Count` extension method returns the number of items in the collection. In the following example, the `Count` method is applied to the `Years` property of a `Racer` to filter the racers and return only those who won more than three championships. Because the same count is needed more than once in the same query, a variable `numberYears` is defined by using the `let` clause (code file `EnumerableSample/Program.cs`):

```
var query = from r in Formula1.GetChampions()
            let numberYears = r.Years.Count()
            where numberYears >= 3
            orderby numberYears descending, r.LastName
            select new
            {
              Name = r.FirstName + " " + r.LastName,
              TimesChampion = numberYears
            };

foreach (var r in query)
{
  Console.WriteLine("{0} {1}", r.Name, r.TimesChampion);
}
```

The result is shown here:

```
Michael Schumacher 7
Juan Manuel Fangio 5
Alain Prost 4
Jack Brabham 3
Niki Lauda 3
Nelson Piquet 3
Ayrton Senna 3
Jackie Stewart 3
```

The Sum method summarizes all numbers of a sequence and returns the result. In the next example, Sum is used to calculate the sum of all race wins for a country. First the racers are grouped based on country; then, with the new anonymous type created, the Wins property is assigned to the sum of all wins from a single country:

```
var countries =
  (from c in
     from r in Formula1.GetChampions()
     group r by r.Country into c
     select new
     {
       Country = c.Key,
       Wins = (from r1 in c
               select r1.Wins).Sum()
     }
     orderby c.Wins descending, c.Country
     select c).Take(5);

foreach (var country in countries)
{
  Console.WriteLine("{0} {1}", country.Country, country.Wins);
}
```

The most successful countries based on the Formula-1 race champions are as follows:

```
UK 167
Germany 112
Brazil 78
France 51
Finland 42
```

The methods Min, Max, Average, and Aggregate are used in the same way as Count and Sum. Min returns the minimum number of the values in the collection, and Max returns the maximum number. Average calculates the average number. With the Aggregate method you can pass a lambda expression that performs an aggregation of all the values.

Conversion Operators

In this chapter you've already seen that query execution is deferred until the items are accessed. Using the query within an iteration, the query is executed. With a conversion operator, the query is executed immediately and the result is returned in an array, a list, or a dictionary.

In the next example, the ToList extension method is invoked to immediately execute the query and put the result into a List<T> (code file EnumerableSample/Program.cs):

```
List<Racer> racers = (from r in Formula1.GetChampions()
                      where r.Starts > 150
                      orderby r.Starts descending
                      select r).ToList();
foreach (var racer in racers)
{
  Console.WriteLine("{0} {0:S}", racer);
}
```

It's not that simple to get the returned objects into the list. For example, for fast access from a car to a racer within a collection class, you can use the new class Lookup<TKey, TElement>.

> **NOTE** *The* `Dictionary<TKey, TValue>` *class supports only a single value for a key. With the class* `Lookup<TKey TElement>` *from the namespace* `System.Linq`, *you can have multiple values for a single key. These classes are covered in detail in Chapter 10, "Collections."*

Using the compound `from` query, the sequence of racers and cars is flattened, and an anonymous type with the properties `Car` and `Racer` is created. With the lookup that is returned, the key should be of type `string` referencing the car, and the value should be of type `Racer`. To make this selection, you can pass a key and an element selector to one overload of the `ToLookup` method. The key selector references the `Car` property, and the element selector references the `Racer` property:

```
var racers = (from r in Formula1.GetChampions()
              from c in r.Cars
              select new
              {
                Car = c,
                Racer = r
              }).ToLookup(cr => cr.Car, cr => cr.Racer);
if (racers.Contains("Williams"))
{
  foreach (var williamsRacer in racers["Williams"])
  {
    Console.WriteLine(williamsRacer);
  }
}
```

The result of all "Williams" champions accessed using the indexer of the `Lookup` class is shown here:

```
Alan Jones
Keke Rosberg
Nigel Mansell
Alain Prost
Damon Hill
Jacques Villeneuve
```

In case you need to use a LINQ query over an untyped collection, such as the `ArrayList`, you can use the `Cast` method. In the following example, an `ArrayList` collection that is based on the `Object` type is filled with `Racer` objects. To make it possible to define a strongly typed query, you can use the `Cast` method:

```
var list = new System.Collections.ArrayList(Formula1.GetChampions()
    as System.Collections.ICollection);

var query = from r in list.Cast<Racer>()
            where r.Country == "USA"
            orderby r.Wins descending
            select r;
foreach (var racer in query)
{
  Console.WriteLine("{0:A}", racer);
}
```

Generation Operators

The generation operators `Range`, `Empty`, and `Repeat` are not extension methods, but normal static methods that return sequences. With LINQ to Objects, these methods are available with the `Enumerable` class.

Have you ever needed a range of numbers filled? Nothing is easier than using the `Range` method. This method receives the start value with the first parameter and the number of items with the second parameter:

```
var values = Enumerable.Range(1, 20);
foreach (var item in values)
{
  Console.Write("{0} ", item);
}
Console.WriteLine();
```

> **NOTE** *The* `Range` *method does not return a collection filled with the values as defined. This method does a deferred query execution similar to the other methods. It returns a* `RangeEnumerator` *that simply does a* `yield` *return with the values incremented.*

Of course, the result now looks like this:

```
1 2 3 4 5 6 7 8 9 10 11 12 13 14 15 16 17 18 19 20
```

You can combine the result with other extension methods to get a different result — for example, using the `Select` extension method:

```
var values = Enumerable.Range(1, 20).Select(n => n * 3);
```

The `Empty` method returns an iterator that does not return values. This can be used for parameters that require a collection for which you can pass an empty collection.

The `Repeat` method returns an iterator that returns the same value a specific number of times.

PARALLEL LINQ

The class `ParallelEnumerable` in the `System.Linq` namespace to splits the work of queries across multiple threads. Although the `Enumerable` class defines extension methods to the `IEnumerable<T>` interface, most extension methods of the `ParallelEnumerable` class are extensions for the class `ParallelQuery<TSource>`. One important exception is the `AsParallel` method, which extends `IEnumerable<TSource>` and returns `ParallelQuery<TSource>`, so a normal collection class can be queried in a parallel manner.

Parallel Queries

To demonstrate Parallel LINQ (PLINQ), a large collection is needed. With small collections you won't see any effect when the collection fits inside the CPU's cache. In the following code, a large `int` collection is filled with random values (code file `ParallelLinqSample/Program.cs`):

```
static IEnumerable<int> SampleData()
{
  const int arraySize = 100000000;
  var r = new Random();
  return Enumerable.Range(0, arraySize).Select(x => r.Next(140)).ToList();
}
```

Now you can use a LINQ query to filter the data, do some calculations, and get an average of the filtered data. The query defines a filter with the `where` clause to summarize only the items with values < 20, and then the aggregation function sum is invoked. The only difference to the LINQ queries you've seen so far is the call to the AsParallel method:

```
var res = (from x in data.AsParallel()
              where Math.Log(x) < 4
              select x).Average();
```

Like the LINQ queries shown already, the compiler changes the syntax to invoke the methods AsParallel, Where, Select, and Average. AsParallel is defined with the ParallelEnumerable class to extend the IEnumerable<T> interface, so it can be called with a simple array. AsParallel returns ParallelQuery<TSource>. Because of the returned type, the Where method chosen by the compiler is ParallelEnumerable.Where instead of Enumerable.Where. In the following code, the Select and Average methods are from ParallelEnumerable as well. In contrast to the implementation of the Enumerable class, with the ParallelEnumerable class the query is *partitioned* so that multiple threads can work on the query. The collection can be split into multiple parts whereby different threads work on each part to filter the remaining items. After the partitioned work is completed, *merging* must occur to get the summary result of all parts:

```
var res = data.AsParallel().Where(x => Math.Log(x) < 4).
              Select(x => x).Average();
```

Running this code starts the task manager so you can confirm that all CPUs of your system are busy. If you remove the AsParallel method, multiple CPUs might not be used. Of course, if you don't have multiple CPUs on your system, then don't expect to see an improvement with the parallel version.

Partitioners

The AsParallel method is an extension not only to the IEnumerable<T> interface, but also to the Partitioner class. With this you can influence the partitions to be created.

The Partitioner class is defined within the namespace System.Collections.Concurrent and has different variants. The Create method accepts arrays or objects implementing IList<T>. Depending on that, as well as on the parameter loadBalance , which is of type Boolean and available with some overloads of the method, a different partitioner type is returned. For arrays, .NET 4 includes DynamicPartitionerFor Array<TSource> and StaticPartitionerForArray<TSource>, both of which derive from the abstract base class OrderablePartitioner<TSource>.

In the following example, the code from the "Parallel Queries" section is changed to manually create a partitioner instead of relying on the default one:

```
var result = (from x in Partitioner.Create(data, true).AsParallel()
                 where Math.Log(x) < 4
                 select x).Average();
```

You can also influence the parallelism by invoking the methods WithExecutionMode and WithDegreeOfParallelism. With WithExecutionMode you can pass a value of ParallelExecutionMode, which can be Default or ForceParallelism. By default, Parallel LINQ avoids parallelism with high overhead. With the method WithDegreeOfParallelism you can pass an integer value to specify the maximum number of tasks that should run in parallel. This is useful if not all CPU cores should be used by the query.

Cancellation

.NET offers a standard way to cancel long-running tasks, and this is also true for Parallel LINQ.

To cancel a long-running query, you can add the method WithCancellation to the query and pass a CancellationToken to the parameter. The CancellationToken is created from the

CancellationTokenSource. The query is run in a separate thread where the exception of type OperationCanceledException is caught. This exception is fired if the query is cancelled. From the main thread the task can be cancelled by invoking the Cancel method of the CancellationTokenSource:

```
var cts = new CancellationTokenSource();

Task.Factory.StartNew(() =>
  {
    try
    {
      var res = (from x in data.AsParallel().WithCancellation(cts.Token)
                 where Math.Log(x) < 4
                 select x).Average();
      Console.WriteLine("query finished, sum: {0}", res);
    }
    catch (OperationCanceledException ex)
    {
      Console.WriteLine(ex.Message);
    }
  });

Console.WriteLine("query started");
Console.Write("cancel? ");
string input = Console.ReadLine();
if (input.ToLower().Equals("y"))
{
  // cancel!
  cts.Cancel();
}
```

> **NOTE** *You can read more about cancellation and the* CancellationToken *in Chapter 21, "Threads, Tasks, and Synchronization."*

EXPRESSION TREES

With LINQ to Objects, the extension methods require a delegate type as parameter; this way, a lambda expression can be assigned to the parameter. Lambda expressions can also be assigned to parameters of type Expression<T>. The C# compiler defines different behavior for lambda expressions depending on the type. If the type is Expression<T>, the compiler creates an expression tree from the lambda expression and stores it in the assembly. The expression tree can be analyzed during runtime and optimized for querying against the data source.

Let's turn to a query expression that was used previously (code file ExpressionTreeSample/Program.cs):

```
var brazilRacers = from r in racers
                   where r.Country == "Brazil"
                   orderby r.Wins
                   select r;
```

The preceding query expression uses the extension methods Where, OrderBy, and Select. The Enumerable class defines the Where extension method with the delegate type Func<T, bool> as parameter predicate:

```
public static IEnumerable<TSource> Where<TSource>(
    this IEnumerable<TSource> source, Func<TSource, bool> predicate);
```

This way, the lambda expression is assigned to the predicate. Here, the lambda expression is similar to an anonymous method, as explained earlier:

```
Func<Racer, bool> predicate = r => r.Country == "Brazil";
```

The `Enumerable` class is not the only class for defining the `Where` extension method. The `Where` extension method is also defined by the class `Queryable<T>`. This class has a different definition of the `Where` extension method:

```
public static IQueryable<TSource> Where<TSource>(
    this IQueryable<TSource> source,
    Expression<Func<TSource, bool>> predicate);
```

Here, the lambda expression is assigned to the type `Expression<T>`, which behaves differently:

```
Expression<Func<Racer, bool>> predicate = r => r.Country == "Brazil";
```

Instead of using delegates, the compiler emits an expression tree to the assembly. The expression tree can be read during runtime. Expression trees are built from classes derived from the abstract base class `Expression`. The `Expression` class is not the same as `Expression<T>`. Some of the expression classes that inherit from `Expression` include `BinaryExpression`, `ConstantExpression`, `InvocationExpression`, `LambdaExpression`, `NewExpression`, `NewArrayExpression`, `TernaryExpression`, `UnaryExpression`, and more. The compiler creates an expression tree resulting from the lambda expression.

For example, the lambda expression `r.Country == "Brazil"` makes use of `ParameterExpression`, `MemberExpression`, `ConstantExpression`, and `MethodCallExpression` to create a tree and store the tree in the assembly. This tree is then used during runtime to create an optimized query to the underlying data source.

The method `DisplayTree` is implemented to display an expression tree graphically on the console. In the following example, an `Expression` object can be passed, and depending on the expression type some information about the expression is written to the console. Depending on the type of the expression, `DisplayTree` is called recursively:

> **NOTE** *This method does not deal with all expression types, only the types that are used with the following example expression.*

```
private static void DisplayTree(int indent, string message,
                                Expression expression)
{
  string output = String.Format("{0} {1} ! NodeType: {2}; Expr: {3} ",
      "".PadLeft(indent, '>'), message, expression.NodeType, expression);

  indent++;
  switch (expression.NodeType)
  {
    case ExpressionType.Lambda:
      Console.WriteLine(output);
      LambdaExpression lambdaExpr = (LambdaExpression)expression;
      foreach (var parameter in lambdaExpr.Parameters)
      {
        DisplayTree(indent, "Parameter", parameter);
      }
      DisplayTree(indent, "Body", lambdaExpr.Body);
      break;
```

```
      case ExpressionType.Constant:
        ConstantExpression constExpr = (ConstantExpression)expression;
        Console.WriteLine("{0} Const Value: {1}", output, constExpr.Value);
        break;
      case ExpressionType.Parameter:
        ParameterExpression paramExpr = (ParameterExpression)expression;
        Console.WriteLine("{0} Param Type: {1}", output,
                          paramExpr.Type.Name);
        break;
      case ExpressionType.Equal:
      case ExpressionType.AndAlso:
      case ExpressionType.GreaterThan:
        BinaryExpression binExpr = (BinaryExpression)expression;
        if (binExpr.Method != null)
        {
          Console.WriteLine("{0} Method: {1}", output,
                            binExpr.Method.Name);
        }
        else
        {
          Console.WriteLine(output);
        }
        DisplayTree(indent, "Left", binExpr.Left);
        DisplayTree(indent, "Right", binExpr.Right);
        break;
      case ExpressionType.MemberAccess:
        MemberExpression memberExpr = (MemberExpression)expression;
        Console.WriteLine("{0} Member Name: {1}, Type: {2}", output,
            memberExpr.Member.Name, memberExpr.Type.Name);
        DisplayTree(indent, "Member Expr", memberExpr.Expression);
        break;
      default:
        Console.WriteLine();
        Console.WriteLine("{0} {1}", expression.NodeType,
                          expression.Type.Name);
        break;
    }
  }
}
```

The expression that is used for showing the tree is already well known. It's a lambda expression with a Racer parameter, and the body of the expression takes racers from Brazil only if they have won more than six races:

```
Expression<Func<Racer, bool>> expression =
    r => r.Country == "Brazil" && r.Wins > 6;

DisplayTree(0, "Lambda", expression);
```

Looking at the tree result, you can see from the output that the lambda expression consists of a Parameter and an AndAlso node type. The AndAlso node type has an Equal node type to the left and a GreaterThan node type to the right. The Equal node type to the left of the AndAlso node type has a MemberAccess node type to the left and a Constant node type to the right, and so on:

```
Lambda! NodeType: Lambda; Expr: r => ((r.Country == "Brazil")
    AndAlso (r.Wins > 6))
> Parameter! NodeType: Parameter; Expr: r  Param Type: Racer
> Body! NodeType: AndAlso; Expr: ((r.Country == "Brazil")
    AndAlso (r.Wins > 6))
>> Left! NodeType: Equal; Expr: (r.Country == "Brazil")  Method: op_Equality
```

```
>>> Left! NodeType: MemberAccess; Expr: r.Country
    Member Name: Country, Type: String
>>>> Member Expr! NodeType: Parameter; Expr: r  Param Type: Racer
>>> Right! NodeType: Constant; Expr: "Brazil" Const Value: Brazil
>> Right! NodeType: GreaterThan; Expr: (r.Wins > 6)
>>> Left! NodeType: MemberAccess; Expr: r.Wins  Member Name: Wins, Type: Int32
>>>> Member Expr! NodeType: Parameter; Expr: r  Param Type: Racer
>>> Right! NodeType: Constant; Expr: 6  Const Value: 6
```

Examples where the `Expression<T>` type is used are with the ADO.NET Entity Framework and the client provider for WCF Data Services. These technologies define methods with `Expression<T>` parameters. This way the LINQ provider accessing the database can create a runtime-optimized query by reading the expressions to get the data from the database.

LINQ PROVIDERS

.NET includes several LINQ providers. A LINQ provider implements the standard query operators for a specific data source. LINQ providers might implement more extension methods than are defined by LINQ, but the standard operators must at least be implemented. LINQ to XML implements additional methods that are particularly useful with XML, such as the methods `Elements`, `Descendants`, and `Ancestors` defined by the class `Extensions` in the `System.Xml.Linq` namespace.

Implementation of the LINQ provider is selected based on the namespace and the type of the first parameter. The namespace of the class that implements the extension methods must be opened; otherwise, the extension class is not in scope. The parameter of the `Where` method defined by LINQ to Objects and the `Where` method defined by LINQ to Entities is different.

The `Where` method of LINQ to Objects is defined with the `Enumerable` class:

```
public static IEnumerable<TSource> Where<TSource>(
    this IEnumerable<TSource> source, Func<TSource, bool> predicate);
```

Inside the `System.Linq` namespace is another class that implements the operator `Where`. This implementation is used by LINQ to Entities. You can find the implementation in the class `Queryable`:

```
public static IQueryable<TSource> Where<TSource>(
    this IQueryable<TSource> source,
    Expression<Func<TSource, bool>> predicate);
```

Both of these classes are implemented in the `System.Core` assembly in the `System.Linq` namespace. How does the compiler select what method to use, and what's the magic with the Expression type? The lambda expression is the same regardless of whether it is passed with a `Func<TSource, bool>` parameter or an `Expression<Func<TSource, bool>>` parameter—only the compiler behaves differently. The selection is done based on the `source` parameter. The method that matches best based on its parameters is chosen by the compiler. The `CreateQuery<T>` method of the `ObjectContext` class that is defined by ADO.NET Entity Framework returns an `ObjectQuery<T>` object that implements `IQueryable<TSource>`, and thus the Entity Framework uses the `Where` method of the `Queryable` class.

SUMMARY

This chapter described and demonstrated the LINQ query and the language constructs on which the query is based, such as extension methods and lambda expressions. You've looked at the various LINQ query operators — not only for filtering and ordering of data sources, but also for partitioning, grouping, doing conversions, joins, and so on.

With Parallel LINQ, you've seen how longer queries can easily be parallelized.

Another important concept of this chapter is the expression tree. Expression trees enable building the query to the data source at runtime because the tree is stored in the assembly. You can read about its great advantages in Chapter 33, "ADO.NET Entity Framework." LINQ is a very in-depth topic, and you can see Chapters 33 and 34, "Manipulating XML," for more information. Other third-party providers are also available for download, such as LINQ to MySQL, LINQ to Amazon, LINQ to Flickr, LINQ to LDAP, and LINQ to SharePoint. No matter what data source you have, with LINQ you can use the same query syntax.

12

Dynamic Language Extensions

WHAT'S IN THIS CHAPTER?

➤ Understanding the Dynamic Language Runtime

➤ The dynamic type

➤ The DLR ScriptRuntime

➤ Creating dynamic objects with DynamicObject and ExpandoObject

WROX.COM CODE DOWNLOADS FOR THIS CHAPTER

The wrox.com code downloads for this chapter are found at `http://www.wrox.com/remtitle
.cgi?isbn=1118314425` on the Download Code tab. The code for this chapter is divided into the
following major examples:

➤ DLRHost

➤ Dynamic

➤ DynamicFileReader

➤ ErrorExample

The growth of languages such as Ruby and Python, and the increased use of JavaScript, have
intensified interest in dynamic programming. In previous versions of the .NET Framework, the `var`
keyword and anonymous methods started C# down the "dynamic" road. In version 4, the `dynamic`
type was added. Although C# is still a statically typed language, these additions give it the dynamic
capabilities that some developers are looking for.

In this chapter, you'll look at the `dynamic` type and the rules for using it. You'll also see what an
implementation of `DynamicObject` looks like and how it can be used. `ExpandoObject`, which is the
frameworks implementation of `DynamicObject`, will also be covered.

DYNAMIC LANGUAGE RUNTIME

The dynamic capabilities of C# 4 are part of the dynamic language runtime (DLR). The DLR is a set
of services that is added to the common language runtime (CLR) to enable the addition of dynamic
languages such as Ruby and Python. It also enables C# to take on some of the same
dynamic capabilities that these dynamic languages have.

There is a version of the DLR that is open source and resides on the CodePlex website. This same version is included with the .NET 4.5 Framework, with some additional support for language implementers.

In the .NET Framework, the DLR is found in the `System.Dynamic` namespace as well as a few additional classes in the `System.Runtime.CompilerServices` namespace.

IronRuby and IronPython, which are open-source versions of the Ruby and Python languages, use the DLR. Silverlight also uses the DLR. It's possible to add scripting capabilities to your applications by hosting the DLR. The scripting runtime enables you to pass variables to and from the script.

THE DYNAMIC TYPE

The `dynamic` type enables you to write code that bypasses compile-time type checking. The compiler will assume that whatever operation is defined for an object of type `dynamic` is valid. If that operation isn't valid, the error won't be detected until runtime. This is shown in the following example:

```
class Program
{
    static void Main(string[] args)
    {
        var staticPerson = new Person();
        dynamic dynamicPerson = new Person();
        staticPerson.GetFullName("John", "Smith");
        dynamicPerson.GetFullName("John", "Smith");
    }
}

class Person
{
    public string FirstName { get; set; }
    public string LastName { get; set; }
    public string GetFullName()
    {
        return string.Concat(FirstName, " ", LastName);
    }
}
```

This example will not compile because of the call to `staticPerson.GetFullName`. There isn't a method on the `Person` object that takes two parameters, so the compiler raises the error. If that line of code were to be commented out, the example would compile. If executed, a runtime error would occur. The exception that is raised is `RuntimeBinderException`. The `RuntimeBinder` is the object in the runtime that evaluates the call to determine whether `Person` really does support the method that was called. Binding is discussed later in the chapter.

Unlike the var keyword, an object that is defined as *dynamic* can change type during runtime. Remember that when the var keyword is used, the determination of the object's type is delayed. Once the type is defined, it can't be changed. Not only can you change the type of a dynamic object, you can change it many times. This differs from casting an object from one type to another. When you cast an object, you are creating a new object with a different but compatible type. For example, you cannot cast an int to a `Person` object. In the following example, you can see that if the object is a dynamic object, you can change it from int to `Person`:

```
dynamic dyn;

dyn = 100;
Console.WriteLine(dyn.GetType());
Console.WriteLine(dyn);
```

```
dyn = "This is a string";
Console.WriteLine(dyn.GetType());
Console.WriteLine(dyn);

dyn = new Person() { FirstName = "Bugs", LastName = "Bunny" };
Console.WriteLine(dyn.GetType());
Console.WriteLine("{0} {1}", dyn.FirstName, dyn.LastName);
```

Executing this code would show that the `dyn` object actually changes type from `System.Int32` to `System.String` to `Person`. If `dyn` had been declared as an `int` or `string`, the code would not have compiled.

Note a couple of limitations to the `dynamic` type. A dynamic object does not support extension methods. Nor can anonymous functions (lambda expressions) be used as parameters to a dynamic method call, so LINQ does not work well with dynamic objects. Most LINQ calls are extension methods, and lambda expressions are used as arguments to those extension methods.

Dynamic Behind the Scenes

So what's going on behind the scenes to make this happen? C# is still a statically typed language. That hasn't changed. Take a look at the IL (Intermediate Language) that's generated when the `dynamic` type is used.

First, this is the example C# code that you're looking at:

```
using System;

namespace DeCompile
{
    class Program
    {
        static void Main(string[] args)
        {
            StaticClass staticObject = new StaticClass();
            DynamicClass dynamicObject = new DynamicClass();
            Console.WriteLine(staticObject.IntValue);
            Console.WriteLine(dynamicObject.DynValue);
            Console.ReadLine();
        }
    }

    class StaticClass
    {
        public int IntValue = 100;
    }

    class DynamicClass
    {
        public dynamic DynValue = 100;
    }
}
```

You have two classes, `StaticClass` and `DynamicClass`. `StaticClass` has a single field that returns an `int`. `DynamicClass` has a single field that returns a `dynamic` object. The `Main` method just creates these objects and prints out the value that the methods return. Simple enough.

Now comment out the references to the `DynamicClass` in `Main` like this:

```
static void Main(string[] args)
{
    StaticClass staticObject = new StaticClass();
    //DynamicClass dynamicObject = new DynamicClass();
```

```
        Console.WriteLine(staticObject.IntValue);
        //Console.WriteLine(dynamicObject.DynValue);
        Console.ReadLine();
    }
```

Using the `ildasm` tool (discussed in Chapter 19, "Assemblies"), you can look at the IL that is generated for the `Main` method:

```
.method private hidebysig static void  Main(string[] args) cil managed
{
  .entrypoint
  // Code size       26 (0x1a)
  .maxstack  1
  .locals init ([0] class DeCompile.StaticClass staticObject)
  IL_0000:  nop
  IL_0001:  newobj     instance void DeCompile.StaticClass::.ctor()
  IL_0006:  stloc.0
  IL_0007:  ldloc.0
  IL_0008:  ldfld      int32 DeCompile.StaticClass::IntValue
  IL_000d:  call       void [mscorlib]System.Console::WriteLine(int32)
  IL_0012:  nop
  IL_0013:  call       string [mscorlib]System.Console::ReadLine()
  IL_0018:  pop
  IL_0019:  ret
} // end of method Program::Main
```

Without going into the details of IL but just looking at this section of code, you can still pretty much tell what's going on. Line 0001, the `StaticClass` constructor, is called. Line 0008 calls the `IntValue` field of `StaticClass`. The next line writes out the value.

Now comment out the `StaticClass` references and uncomment the `DynamicClass` references:

```
static void Main(string[] args)
{
    //StaticClass staticObject = new StaticClass();
    DynamicClass dynamicObject = new DynamicClass();
    Console.WriteLine(staticObject.IntValue);
    //Console.WriteLine(dynamicObject.DynValue);
    Console.ReadLine();
}
```

Compile the application again and this is what is generated:

```
.method private hidebysig static void  Main(string[] args) cil managed
{
  .entrypoint
  // Code size       121 (0x79)
  .maxstack  9
  .locals init ([0] class DeCompile.DynamicClass dynamicObject,
           [1] class
[Microsoft.CSharp]Microsoft.CSharp.RuntimeBinder.CSharpArgumentInfo[]
                CS$0$0000)
  IL_0000:  nop
  IL_0001:  newobj     instance void DeCompile.DynamicClass::.ctor()
  IL_0006:  stloc.0
  IL_0007:  ldsfld     class [System.Core]System.Runtime.CompilerServices.CallSite`1
                       <class [mscorlib]
System.Action`3<class
[System.Core]System.Runtime.CompilerServices.CallSite,class [mscorlib]
System.Type,object>> DeCompile.Program/'<Main>o__SiteContainer0'::'<>p__Site1'
```

```
  IL_000c:  brtrue.s    IL_004d
  IL_000e:  ldc.i4.0
  IL_000f:  ldstr "WriteLine"
  IL_0014:  ldtoken     DeCompile.Program
  IL_0019:  call        class [mscorlib]System.Type
[mscorlib]System.Type::GetTypeFromHandle
(valuetype [mscorlib]System.RuntimeTypeHandle)
  IL_001e:  ldnull
  IL_001f:  ldc.i4.2
  IL_0020:  newarr
[Microsoft.CSharp]Microsoft.CSharp.RuntimeBinder.CSharpArgumentInfo
  IL_0025:  stloc.1
  IL_0026:  ldloc.1
  IL_0027:  ldc.i4.0
  IL_0028:  ldc.i4.s    33
  IL_002a:  ldnull
  IL_002b:  newobj      instance void [Microsoft.CSharp]Microsoft.CSharp.RuntimeBinder
.CSharpArgumentInfo::.ctor(valuetype [Microsoft.CSharp]Microsoft.CSharp.RuntimeBinder
.CSharpArgumentInfoFlags, string)
  IL_0030:  stelem.ref
  IL_0031:  ldloc.1
  IL_0032:  ldc.i4.1
  IL_0033:  ldc.i4.0
  IL_0034:  ldnull
  IL_0035:  newobj      instance void [Microsoft.CSharp]Microsoft.CSharp.RuntimeBinder
.CSharpArgumentInfo::.ctor(valuetype [Microsoft.CSharp]Microsoft.CSharp.RuntimeBinder
.CSharpArgumentInfoFlags, string)
  IL_003a:  stelem.ref
  IL_003b:  ldloc.1
  IL_003c:  newobj      instance void [Microsoft.CSharp]Microsoft.CSharp.RuntimeBinder
.CSharpInvokeMemberBinder::.ctor(valuetype Microsoft.CSharp]Microsoft.CSharp
.RuntimeBinder.CSharpCallFlags, string)
class [mscorlib]System.Type,
class [mscorlib]System.Collections.Generic.IEnumerable'1
<class [mscorlib]System.Type>,
class [mscorlib]System.Collections.Generic.IEnumerable'1
<class [Microsoft.CSharp]Microsoft.CSharp.RuntimeBinder.CSharpArgumentInfo>)
  IL_0041:  call        class [System.Core]System.Runtime.CompilerServices.CallSite'1
<!0> class [System.Core]System.Runtime.CompilerServices.CallSite'1
<class [mscorlib]System.Action'3
<class [System.Core]System.Runtime.CompilerServices.CallSite,
class [mscorlib]System.Type,object>>::Create(class
[System.Core]System.Runtime.CompilerServices.CallSiteBinder)
  IL_0046:  stsfld      class [System.Core]System.Runtime.CompilerServices.CallSite'1
<class [mscorlib]System.Action'3
<class [System.Core]System.Runtime.CompilerServices.CallSite,
class [mscorlib]System.Type,object>>
DeCompile.Program/'<Main>o__SiteContainer0'::'<>p__Site1'
  IL_004b:  br.s        IL_004d
  IL_004d:  ldsfld      class [System.Core]System.Runtime.CompilerServices.CallSite'1
<class [mscorlib]System.Action'3
<class [System.Core]System.Runtime.CompilerServices.CallSite,
class [mscorlib]System.Type,object>>
DeCompile.Program/'<Main>o__SiteContainer0'::'<>p__Site1'
  IL_0052:  ldfld       !0 class [System.Core]System.Runtime.CompilerServices.CallSite'1
<class [mscorlib]System.Action'3
<class [System.Core]System.Runtime.CompilerServices.CallSite,
class [mscorlib]System.Type,object>>::Target
  IL_0057:  ldsfld      class [System.Core]System.Runtime.CompilerServices.CallSite'1
<class [mscorlib]System.Action'3
<class [System.Core]System.Runtime.CompilerServices.CallSite,
class [mscorlib]System.Type,object>>
```

```
DeCompile.Program/'<Main>o__SiteContainer0'::'<>p__Site1'
  IL_005c:  ldtoken      [mscorlib]System.Console
  IL_0061:  call         class [mscorlib]System.Type
[mscorlib]System.Type::GetTypeFromHandle
(valuetype [mscorlib]System.RuntimeTypeHandle)
  IL_0066:  ldloc.0
  IL_0067:  ldfld        object DeCompile.DynamicClass::DynValue
  IL_006c:  callvirt     instance void class [mscorlib]System.Action'3
               <class [System.Core]System.Runtime.CompilerServices.CallSite, class
               [mscorlib]System.Type,object>::Invoke(!0,!1,!2)
  IL_0071:  nop
  IL_0072:  call         string [mscorlib]System.Console::ReadLine()
  IL_0077:  pop
  IL_0078:  ret
} // end of method Program::Main
```

It's safe to say that the C# compiler is doing a little extra work to support the dynamic type. Looking at the generated code, you can see references to System.Runtime.CompilerServices.CallSite and System .Runtime.CompilerServices.CallSiteBinder.

The CallSite is a type that handles the lookup at runtime. When a call is made on a dynamic object at runtime, something has to check that object to determine whether the member really exists. The call site caches this information so the lookup doesn't have to be performed repeatedly. Without this process, performance in looping structures would be questionable.

After the CallSite does the member lookup, the CallSiteBinder is invoked. It takes the information from the call site and generates an expression tree representing the operation to which the binder is bound.

There is obviously a lot going on here. Great care has been taken to optimize what would appear to be a very complex operation. Clearly, although using the dynamic type can be useful, it does come with a price.

HOSTING THE DLR SCRIPTRUNTIME

Imagine being able to add scripting capabilities to an application, or passing values in and out of the script so the application can take advantage of the work that the script does. These are the kind of capabilities that hosting the DLR's ScriptRuntime in your app gives you. Currently, IronPython, IronRuby, and JavaScript are supported as hosted scripting languages.

The ScriptRuntime enables you to execute snippets of code or a complete script stored in a file. You can select the proper language engine or allow the DLR to figure out which engine to use. The script can be created in its own app domain or in the current one. Not only can you pass values in and out of the script, you can call methods on dynamic objects created in the script.

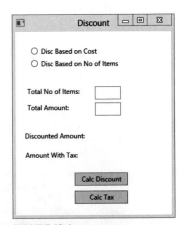

This degree of flexibility provides countless uses for hosting the ScriptRuntime. The following example demonstrates one way that you can use the ScriptRuntime. Imagine a shopping cart application. One of the requirements is to calculate a discount based on certain criteria. These discounts change often as new sales campaigns are started and completed. There are many ways to handle such a requirement; this example shows how it could be done using the ScriptRuntime and a little Python scripting.

For simplicity, the example is a Windows client app. It could be part of a larger web application or any other application. Figure 12-1 shows a sample screen for the application.

FIGURE 12-1

Using the values provided for the number of items and the total cost of the items, the application applies a discount based on which radio button is selected. In a real application, the system would use a slightly more sophisticated technique to determine the discount to apply, but for this example the radio buttons will suffice.

Here is the code that performs the discount:

```
private void button1_Click(object sender, RoutedEventArgs e)
{
    string scriptToUse;
    if (CostRadioButton.IsChecked.Value)
    {
        scriptToUse = "AmountDisc.py";
    }
    else
    {
        scriptToUse = "CountDisc.py";
    }
    ScriptRuntime scriptRuntime = ScriptRuntime.CreateFromConfiguration();
    ScriptEngine pythEng = scriptRuntime.GetEngine("Python");
    ScriptSource source = pythEng.CreateScriptSourceFromFile(scriptToUse);
    ScriptScope scope = pythEng.CreateScope();
    scope.SetVariable("prodCount", Convert.ToInt32(totalItems.Text));
    scope.SetVariable("amt", Convert.ToDecimal(totalAmt.Text));
    source.Execute(scope);
    label5.Content = scope.GetVariable("retAmt").ToString();
}
```

The first part just determines which script to apply, `AmountDisc.py` or `CountDisc.py`. `AmountDisc.py` does the discount based on the amount of the purchase:

```
discAmt = .25
retAmt = amt
if amt > 25.00:
   retAmt = amt-(amt*discAmt)
```

The minimum amount needed for a discount to be applied is $25. If the amount is less than that, then no discount is applied; otherwise, a discount of 25 percent is applied.

`ContDisc.py` applies the discount based on the number of items purchased:

```
discCount = 5
discAmt = .1
retAmt = amt
if prodCount > discCount:
   retAmt = amt-(amt*discAmt)
```

In this Python script, the number of items purchased must be more than 5 for a 10 percent discount to be applied to the total cost.

The next step is getting the `ScriptRuntime` environment set up. For this, four specific tasks are performed: creating the `ScriptRuntime` object, setting the proper `ScriptEngine`, creating the `ScriptSource`, and creating the `ScriptScope`.

The `ScriptRuntime` object is the starting point, or base, for hosting. It contains the global state of the hosting environment. The `ScriptRuntime` is created using the `CreateFromConfiguration` static method. This is what the `app.config` file looks like:

```
<configuration>
  <configSections>
    <section
```

```
        name="microsoft.scripting"
        type="Microsoft.Scripting.Hosting.Configuration.Section,
            Microsoft.Scripting,
            Version=0.9.6.10,
            Culture=neutral,
            PublicKeyToken=null"
            requirePermission="false" />
    </configSections>

    <microsoft.scripting>
      <languages>
        <language
          names="IronPython;Python;py"
          extensions=".py"
          displayName="IronPython 2.6 Alpha"
          type="IronPython.Runtime.PythonContext,
                IronPython,
                Version=2.6.0.1,
                Culture=neutral,
                PublicKeyToken=null" />
      </languages>
    </microsoft.scripting>
</configuration>
```

The code defines a section for "microsoft.scripting" and sets a couple of properties for the IronPython language engine.

Next, you get a reference to the ScriptEngine from the ScriptRuntime. In the example, you specify that you want the Python engine, but the ScriptRuntime would have been able to determine this on its own because of the py extension on the script.

The ScriptEngine does the work of executing the script code. There are several methods for executing scripts from files or from snippets of code. The ScriptEngine also gives you the ScriptSource and ScriptScope.

The ScriptSource object is what gives you access to the script. It represents the source code of the script. With it you can manipulate the source of the script, load it from a disk, parse it line by line, and even compile the script into a CompiledCode object. This is handy if the same script is executed multiple times.

The ScriptScope object is essentially a namespace. To pass a value into or out of a script, you bind a variable to the ScriptScope. In the following example, you call the SetVariable method to pass into the Python script the prodCount variable and the amt variable. These are the values from the totalItems text box and the totalAmt text box. The calculated discount is retrieved from the script by using the GetVariable method. In this example, the retAmt variable has the value you're looking for.

The CalcTax button illustrates how to call a method on a Python object. The script CalcTax.py is a very simple method that takes an input value, adds 7.5 percent tax, and returns the new value. Here's what the code looks like:

```
def CalcTax(amount):
    return amount*1.075
```

Here is the C# code to call the CalcTax method:

```
private void button2_Click(object sender, RoutedEventArgs e)
{
    ScriptRuntime scriptRuntime = ScriptRuntime.CreateFromConfiguration();
    dynamic calcRate = scriptRuntime.UseFile("CalcTax.py");
    label16.Content = calcRate.CalcTax(Convert.ToDecimal(label5.Content)).ToString();
}
```

A very simple process — you create the `ScriptRuntime` object using the same configuration settings as before. `calcRate` is a `ScriptScope` object. You defined it as dynamic so you can easily call the `CalcTax` method. This is an example of the how the dynamic type can make life a little easier.

DYNAMICOBJECT AND EXPANDOOBJECT

What if you want to create your own dynamic object? You have a couple of options for doing that: by deriving from `DynamicObject` or by using `ExpandoObject`. Using `DynamicObject` is a little more work because you have to override a couple of methods. `ExpandoObject` is a sealed class that is ready to use.

DynamicObject

Consider an object that represents a person. Normally, you would define properties for the first name, middle name, and last name. Now imagine the capability to build that object during runtime, with the system having no prior knowledge of what properties the object may have or what methods the object may support. That's what having a `DynamicObject`-based object can provide. There may be very few times when you need this sort of functionality, but until now the C# language had no way of accommodating such a requirement.

First take a look at what the `DynamicObject` looks like:

```
class WroxDynamicObject : DynamicObject
{
    Dictionary<string, object> _dynamicData = new Dictionary<string, object>();

    public override bool TryGetMember(GetMemberBinder binder, out object result)
    {
        bool success = false;
        result = null;
        if (_dynamicData.ContainsKey(binder.Name))
        {
            result = _dynamicData[binder.Name];
            success = true;
        }
        else
        {
            result = "Property Not Found!";
            success = false;
        }
        return success;
    }

    public override bool TrySetMember(SetMemberBinder binder, object value)
    {
        _dynamicData[binder.Name] = value;
        return true;
    }

    public override bool TryInvokeMember(InvokeMemberBinder binder,
                                         object[] args,
                                         out object result)
    {
        dynamic method = _dynamicData[binder.Name];
        result = method((DateTime)args[0]);
        return result != null;
    }

}
```

In this example, you're overriding three methods: TrySetMember, TryGetMember, and TryInvokeMember.

TrySetMember adds the new method, property, or field to the object. In this case, you store the member information in a Dictionary object. The SetMemberBinder object that is passed into the TrySetMember method contains the Name property, which is used to identify the element in the Dictionary.

The TryGetMember retrieves the object stored in the Dictionary based on the GetMemberBinder Name property.

Here is the code that makes use of the new dynamic object just created:

```
dynamic wroxDyn = new WroxDynamicObject();
wroxDyn.FirstName = "Bugs";
wroxDyn.LastName = "Bunny";
Console.WriteLine(wroxDyn.GetType());
Console.WriteLine("{0} {1}", wroxDyn.FirstName, wroxDyn.LastName);
```

It looks simple enough, but where is the call to the methods you overrode? That's where the .NET Framework helps. DynamicObject handles the binding for you; all you have to do is reference the properties FirstName and LastName as if they were there all the time.

Adding a method is also easily done. You can use the same WroxDynamicObject and add a GetTomorrowDate method to it. It takes a DateTime object and returns a date string representing the next day. Here's the code:

```
dynamic wroxDyn = new WroxDynamicObject();
Func<DateTime, string> GetTomorrow = today => today.AddDays(1).ToShortDateString();
wroxDyn.GetTomorrowDate = GetTomorrow;
Console.WriteLine("Tomorrow is {0}", wroxDyn.GetTomorrowDate(DateTime.Now));
```

You create the delegate GetTomorrow using Func<T, TResult>. The method the delegate represents is the call to AddDays. One day is added to the Date that is passed in, and a string of that date is returned. The delegate is then set to GetTomorrowDate on the wroxDyn object. The last line calls the new method, passing in the current day's date. Hence the dynamic magic and you have an object with a valid method.

ExpandoObject

ExpandoObject works similarly to the WroxDynamicObject created in the previous section. The difference is that you don't have to override any methods, as shown in the following code example:

```
static void DoExpando()
{
    dynamic expObj = new ExpandoObject();
    expObj.FirstName = "Daffy";
    expObj.LastName = "Duck";
    Console.WriteLine(expObj.FirstName + " " + expObj.LastName);
    Func<DateTime, string> GetTomorrow = today => today.AddDays(1).ToShortDateString();
    expObj.GetTomorrowDate = GetTomorrow;
    Console.WriteLine("Tomorrow is {0}", expObj.GetTomorrowDate(DateTime.Now));

    expObj.Friends = new List<Person>();
    expObj.Friends.Add(new Person() { FirstName = "Bob", LastName = "Jones" });
    expObj.Friends.Add(new Person() { FirstName = "Robert", LastName = "Jones" });
    expObj.Friends.Add(new Person() { FirstName = "Bobby", LastName = "Jones" });

    foreach (Person friend in expObj.Friends)
    {
        Console.WriteLine(friend.FirstName + " " + friend.LastName);
    }
}
```

Notice that this code is almost identical to what you did earlier. You add a `FirstName` and `LastName` property, add a `GetTomorrow` function, and then do one additional thing — add a collection of `Person` objects as a property of the object.

At first glance it may seem that this is no different from using the `dynamic` type, but there are a couple of subtle differences that are important. First, you can't just create an empty `dynamic` typed object. The `dynamic` type has to have something assigned to it. For example, the following code won't work:

```
dynamic dynObj;
dynObj.FirstName = "Joe";
```

As shown in the previous example, this is possible with `ExpandoObject`.

Second, because the `dynamic` type has to have something assigned to it, it will report back the type assigned to it if you do a `GetType` call. For example, if you assign an `int`, it will report back that it is an `int`. This won't happen with `ExpandoObject` or an object derived from `DynamicObject`.

If you have to control the addition and access of properties in your dynamic object, then deriving from `DynamicObject` is your best option. With `DynamicObject`, you can use several methods to override and control exactly how the object interacts with the runtime. For other cases, using the `dynamic` type or the `ExpandoObject` may be appropriate.

Following is another example of using dynamic and `ExpandoObject`. Assume that the requirement is to develop a general-purpose comma-separated values (CSV) file parsing tool. You won't know from one execution to another what data will be in the file, only that the values will be comma-separated and that the first line will contain the field names.

First, open the file and read in the stream. A simple helper method can be used to do this:

```
private StreamReader OpenFile(string fileName)
{
  if(File.Exists(fileName))
  {
    return new StreamReader(fileName);
  }
  return null;
}
```

This just opens the file and creates a new `StreamReader` to read the file contents.

Now you want to get the field names. This is easily done by reading in the first line from the file and using the `Split` function to create a string array of field names:

```
string[] headerLine = fileStream.ReadLine().Split(',');
```

Next is the interesting part. You read in the next line from the file, create a string array just like you did with the field names, and start creating your dynamic objects. Here's what the code looks like:

```
var retList = new List<dynamic>();
while (fileStream.Peek() > 0)
{
  string[] dataLine = fileStream.ReadLine().Split(',');
  dynamic dynamicEntity = new ExpandoObject();
  for(int i=0;i<headerLine.Length;i++)
  {
    ((IDictionary<string,object>)dynamicEntity).Add(headerLine[i],dataLine[i]);
  }
  retList.Add(dynamicEntity);
}
```

Once you have the string array of field names and data elements, you create a new `ExpandoObject` and add the data to it. Notice that you cast the `ExpandoObject` to a `Dictionary` object. You use the field name as the key and the data as the value. Then you can add the new object to the `retList` object you created and return it to the code that called the method.

What makes this nice is you have a section of code that can handle any data you give it. The only requirements in this case are ensuring that the field names are the first line and that everything is comma-separated. This concept could be expanded to other file types or even to a `DataReader`.

SUMMARY

In this chapter we looked at how the dynamic type can change the way you look at C# programming. Using `ExpandoObject` in place of multiple objects can reduce the number of lines of code significantly. Also using the DLR and adding scripting languages like Python or Ruby can help building a more polymorphic application that can be changed easily without re-compiling.

Dynamic development is becoming increasingly popular because it enables you to do things that are very difficult in a statically typed language. The `dynamic` type and the DLR enable C# programmers to make use of some dynamic capabilities.

13

Asynchronous Programming

WHAT'S IN THIS CHAPTER?

➤ Why asynchronous programming is important

➤ Asynchronous patterns

➤ Foundations of the async and await keywords

➤ Creating and using asynchronous methods

➤ Error handling with asynchronous methods

WROX.COM CODE DOWNLOADS FOR THIS CHAPTER

The wrox.com code downloads for this chapter are found at `http://www.wrox.com/remtitle` `.cgi?isbn=1118314425` on the Download Code tab. The code for this chapter is divided into the following major examples:

➤ Async Patterns

➤ Foundations

➤ Error Handling

WHY ASYNCHRONOUS PROGRAMMING IS IMPORTANT

The most important change of C# 5 is the advances provided with asynchronous programming. C# 5 adds only two new keywords: async and await. These two keywords are the main focus of this chapter.

With *asynchronous programming* a method is called that runs in the background (typically with the help of a thread or task), and the calling thread is not blocked.

In this chapter, you can read about different patterns on asynchronous programming such as the *asynchronous pattern*, the *event-based asynchronous pattern*, and the new *task-based asynchronous pattern* (TAP). TAP makes use of the async and await keywords. Comparing these patterns you can see the real advantage of the new style of asynchronous programming.

After discussing the different patterns, you will see the foundation of asynchronous programming by creating tasks and invoking asynchronous methods. You'll learn about what's behind the scenes with continuation tasks and the synchronization context.

Error handling needs some special emphasis; as with asynchronous tasks, some scenarios require some different handling with errors.

The last part of this chapter discusses how cancellation can be done. Background tasks can take a while and there might be a need to cancel the task while it is still running. How this can be done, you'll also read in this chapter.

Chapter 21, "Threads, Tasks, and Synchronization," covers other information about parallel programming.

Users find it annoying when an application does not immediately react to requests. With the mouse, we have become accustomed to experiencing a delay, as we've learned that behavior over several decades. With a touch UI, an application needs to immediately react to requests. Otherwise, the user tries to redo the action.

Because asynchronous programming was hard to achieve with older versions of the .NET Framework, it was not always done when it should have been. One of the applications that blocked the UI thread fairly often is Visual Studio 2010. With that version, opening a solution containing hundreds of projects meant you could take a long coffee break. With Visual Studio 2012, that's no longer the case, as projects are loaded asynchronously in the background, with the selected project loaded first. This loading behavior is just one example of important changes built into Visual Studio 2012 related to asynchronous programming. Similarly, users of Visual Studio 2010 are likely familiar with the experience of a dialog not reacting. This is less likely to occur with Visual Studio 2012.

Many APIs with the .NET Framework offer both a synchronous and an asynchronous version. Because the synchronous version of the API was a lot easier to use, it was often used where it wasn't appropriate. With the new Windows Runtime (WinRT), if an API call is expected to take longer than 40 milliseconds, only an asynchronous version is available. Now, with .NET 4.5 programming, asynchronously is as easy as programming in a synchronous manner, so there shouldn't be any barrier to using the asynchronous APIs.

ASYNCHRONOUS PATTERNS

Before stepping into the new `async` and `await` keywords it is best to understand asynchronous patterns from the .NET Framework. Asynchronous features have been available since .NET 1.0, and many classes in the .NET Framework implement one or more such patterns. The asynchronous pattern is also available with the delegate type.

Because doing updates on the UI, both with Windows Forms, and WPF with the asynchronous pattern is quite complex, .NET 2.0 introduced the *event-based asynchronous pattern*. With this pattern, an event handler is invoked from the thread that owns the synchronization context, so updating UI code is easily handled with this pattern. Previously, this pattern was also known with the name *asynchronous component pattern*.

Now, with .NET 4.5, another new way to achieve asynchronous programming is introduced: the *task-based asynchronous pattern* (TAP). This pattern is based on the `Task` type that was new with .NET 4 and makes use of a compiler feature with the keywords `async` and `await`.

To understand the advantage of the `async` and `await` keywords, the first sample application makes use of Windows Presentation Foundation (WPF) and network programming to provide an overview of asynchronous programming. If you have no experience with WPF and network programming, don't despair. You can still follow the essentials here and gain an understanding of how asynchronous programming can be done. The following examples demonstrate the differences between the asynchronous patterns. After looking at these, you'll learn the basics of asynchronous programming with some simple console applications.

> **NOTE** *WPF is covered in detail in Chapters 35, "Core WPF," and 36, "Business Applications with WPF," and network programming is discussed in Chapter 26, "Networking."*

The sample application to show the differences between the asynchronous patterns is a WPF application that makes use of types in a class library. The application is used to find images on the web using services from Bing and Flickr. The user can enter a search term to find images, and the search term is sent to Bing and Flickr services with a simple HTTP request.

The UI design from the Visual Studio designer is shown in Figure 13-1. On top of the screen is a text input field followed by several buttons that start the search or clear the result list. The left side below the control area contains a ListBox for displaying all the images found. On the right side is an Image control to display the image that is selected within the ListBox control in a version with a higher resolution.

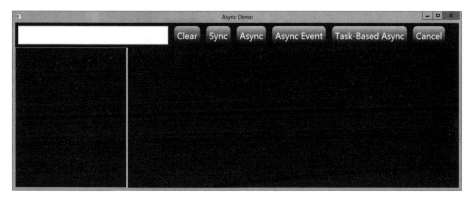

FIGURE 13-1

To understand the sample application we will start with the class library AsyncLib, which contains several helper classes. These classes are used by the WPF application.

The class SearchItemResult represents a single item from a result collection that is used to display the image together with a title and the source of the image. This class just defines simple properties: Title, Url, ThumbnailUrl, and Source. The property ThumbnailIUrl is used to reference a thumbnail image, the Url property contains a link to a larger-size image. Title contains some text to describe the image. The base class of SearchItemResult is BindableBase. This base class just implements a notification mechanism by implementing the interface INotifyPropertyChanged that is used by WPF to make updates with data binding (code file AsyncLib/SearchItemResult.cs):

```
namespace Wrox.ProCSharp.Async
{
  public class SearchItemResult : BindableBase
  {
    private string title;
    public string Title
    {
      get { return title; }
      set { SetProperty(ref title, value); }
    }

    private string url;
    public string Url
    {
      get { return url; }
      set { SetProperty(ref url, value); }
    }
```

```
    private string thumbnailUrl;
    public string ThumbnailUrl
    {
      get { return thumbnailUrl; }
      set { SetProperty(ref thumbnailUrl, value); }
    }

    private string source;
    public string Source
    {
      get { return source; }
      set { SetProperty(ref source, value); }
    }
  }
}
```

The class `SearchInfo` is another class used with data binding. The property `SearchTerm` contains the user input to search for images with that type. The `List` property returns a list of all found images represented with the `SearchItemResult` type (code file `AsyncLib/SearchInfo.cs`):

```
using System.Collections.ObjectModel;

namespace Wrox.ProCSharp.Async
{
  public class SearchInfo : BindableBase
  {
    public SearchInfo()
    {
      list = new ObservableCollection<SearchItemResult>();
      list.CollectionChanged += delegate { OnPropertyChanged("List"); };
    }

    private string searchTerm;
    public string SearchTerm
    {
      get { return searchTerm; }
      set { SetProperty(ref searchTerm, value); }
    }

    private ObservableCollection<SearchItemResult> list;
    public ObservableCollection<SearchItemResult> List
    {
      get
      {
        return list;
      }
    }
  }
}
```

In the XAML code, a `TextBox` is used to enter the search term. This control is bound to the `SearchTerm` property of the `SearchInfo` type. Several `Button` controls are used to activate an event handler, e.g., the Sync button invokes the `OnSearchSync` method (XAML file `AsyncPatterns/MainWindow.xaml`):

```
    <StackPanel Orientation="Horizontal" Grid.Row="0">
      <StackPanel.LayoutTransform>
        <ScaleTransform ScaleX="2" ScaleY="2" />
      </StackPanel.LayoutTransform>
      <TextBox Text="{Binding SearchTerm}" Width="200" Margin="4" />
      <Button Click="OnClear">Clear</Button>
      <Button Click="OnSearchSync">Sync</Button>
      <Button Click="OnSeachAsyncPattern">Async</Button>
```

```
<Button Click="OnAsyncEventPattern">Async Event</Button>
<Button Click="OnTaskBasedAsyncPattern">Task Based Async</Button>
</StackPanel>
```

The second part of the XAML code contains a `ListBox`. To have a special representation for the items in the `ListBox`, an `ItemTemplate` is used. Every item is represented with two `TextBlock` controls and one `Image` control. The `ListBox` is bound to the `List` property of the `SearchInfo` class, and properties of the item controls are bound to properties of the `SearchItemResult` type:

```
<Grid Grid.Row="1">
  <Grid.ColumnDefinitions>
    <ColumnDefinition Width="*" />
    <ColumnDefinition Width="3*" />
  </Grid.ColumnDefinitions>
  <ListBox Grid.IsSharedSizeScope="True" ItemsSource="{Binding List}"
      Grid.Column="0" IsSynchronizedWithCurrentItem="True"
      Background="Black">
    <ListBox.ItemTemplate>
      <DataTemplate>
        <Grid>
          <Grid.ColumnDefinitions>
            <ColumnDefinition SharedSizeGroup="ItemTemplateGroup" />
          </Grid.ColumnDefinitions>
          <StackPanel HorizontalAlignment="Stretch" Orientation="Vertical"
              Background="{StaticResource linearBackgroundBrush}">
            <TextBlock Text="{Binding Source}" Foreground="White" />
            <TextBlock Text="{Binding Title}" Foreground="White" />
            <Image HorizontalAlignment="Center"
                Source="{Binding ThumbnailUrl}" Width="100" />
          </StackPanel>
        </Grid>
      </DataTemplate>
    </ListBox.ItemTemplate>
  </ListBox>
  <GridSplitter Grid.Column="1" Width="3" HorizontalAlignment="Left" />
  <Image Grid.Column="1" Source="{Binding List/Url}" />
</Grid>
```

Now let's get into the `BingRequest` class. This class contains some information about how to make a request to the Bing service. The `Url` property of this class returns a URL string that can be used to make a request for images. The request is comprised of the search term, a number of images that should be requested (`Count`), and a number of images to skip (`Offset`). With Bing, authentication is needed. The user ID is defined with the `AppId`, and used with the `Credentials` property that returns a `NetworkCredential` object. To run the application, you need to register with Windows Azure Marketplace and sign up for the Bing Search API. At the time of this writing, up to 5000 transactions per month are free—this should be enough for running the sample application. Every search is one transaction. The link for the registration to the Bing Search API is `https://datamarket.azure.com/dataset/bing/search`. After registration you need to copy the application ID. After obtaining the application ID, add it to the `BingRequest` class.

After sending a request to Bing by using the created URL, Bing returns XML. The `Parse` method of the `BingRequest` class parses the XML and returns a collection of `SearchItemResult` objects (code file `AsyncLib/BingRequest.cs`):

> **NOTE** *The* `Parse` *methods in the classes* `BingRequest` *and* `FlickrRequest` *make use of LINQ to XML. How to use LINQ to XML is covered in Chapter 34, "Manipulating XML."*

```csharp
using System.Collections.Generic;
using System.Linq;
using System.Net;
using System.Xml.Linq;

namespace Wrox.ProCSharp.Async
{
  public class BingRequest : IImageRequest
  {
    private const string AppId = "enter your Bing AppId here";

    public BingRequest()
    {
      Count = 50;
      Offset = 0;
    }
    private string searchTerm;
    public string SearchTerm
    {
      get { return searchTerm; }
      set { searchTerm = value; }
    }

    public ICredentials Credentials
    {
      get
      {
        return new NetworkCredentials(AppId, AppId);
      }
    }

    public string Url
    {
      get
      {
        return string.Format("https://api.datamarket.azure.com/" +
          "Data.ashx/Bing/Search/v1/Image?Query=%27{0}%27&" +
          "$top={1}&$skip={2}&$format=Atom",
          SearchTerm, Count, Offset);
      }
    }

    public int Count { get; set; }
    public int Offset { get; set; }

    public IEnumerable<SearchItemResult> Parse(string xml)
    {
      XElement respXml = XElement.Parse(xml);
      // XNamespace atom = XNamespace.Get("http://www.w3.org/2005/Atom");
      XNamespace d = XNamespace.Get(
        "http://schemas.microsoft.com/ado/2007/08/dataservices");
      XNamespace m = XNamespace.Get(
        "http://schemas.microsoft.com/ado/2007/08/dataservices/metadata");

      return (from item in respXml.Descendants(m + "properties")
              select new SearchItemResult
              {
                Title = new string(item.Element(d +
                  "Title").Value.Take(50).ToArray()),
                Url = item.Element(d + "MediaUrl").Value,
                ThumbnailUrl = item.Element(d + "Thumbnail").
                  Element(d + "MediaUrl").Value,
```

```
                    Source = "Bing"
                }).ToList();
        }
    }
}
```

Both the `BingRequest` class and the `FlickrRequest` class implement the interface `IImageRequest`. This interface defines the properties `SearchTerm` and `Url`, and the method `Parse`, which enables easy iteration through both image service providers (code file `AsyncLib/IImageRequest.cs`):

```csharp
using System;
using System.Collections.Generic;
using System.Net;

namespace Wrox.ProCSharp.Async
{
  public interface IImageRequest
  {
    string SearchTerm { get; set; }
    string Url { get; }

    IEnumerable<SearchItemResult> Parse(string xml);

    ICredentials Credentials { get; }
  }
}
```

The `FlickrRequest` class is very similar to `BingRequest`. It just creates a different URL to request an image with a search term, and has a different implementation of the `Parse` method, just as the returned XML from Flickr differs from the returned XML from Bing. As with Bing, to create an application ID for Flickr, you need to register with Flickr and request it: http://www.flickr.com/services/apps/create/apply/.

```csharp
using System.Collections.Generic;
using System.Linq;
using System.Xml.Linq;

namespace Wrox.ProCSharp.Async
{
  public class FlickrRequest : IImageRequest
  {
    private const string AppId = "Enter your Flickr AppId here";

    public FlickrRequest()
    {
      Count = 50;
      Page = 1;
    }

    private string searchTerm;
    public string SearchTerm
    {
      get { return searchTerm; }
      set { searchTerm = value; }
    }

    public string Url
    {
      get
```

```
      {
        return string.Format("http://api.flickr.com/services/rest?" +
            "api_key={0}&method=flickr.photos.search&content_type=1&" +
            "text={1}&per_page={2}&page={3}", AppId, SearchTerm, Count, Page);
      }
    }

    public ICredentials Credentials
    {
      get { return null; }
    }

    public int Count { get; set; }
    public int Page { get; set; }

    public IEnumerable<SearchItemResult> Parse(string xml)
    {
      XElement respXml = XElement.Parse(xml);
      return (from item in respXml.Descendants("photo")
              select new SearchItemResult
              {
                Title = new string(item.Attribute("title").Value.
                    Take(50).ToArray()),
                Url = string.Format("http://farm{0}.staticflickr.com/" +
                    "{1}/{2}_{3}_z.jpg",
                  item.Attribute("farm").Value, item.Attribute("server").Value,
                  item.Attribute("id").Value, item.Attribute("secret").Value),
                ThumbnailUrl = string.Format("http://farm{0}." +
                    "staticflickr.com/{1}/{2}_{3}_t.jpg",
                    item.Attribute("farm").Value,
                    item.Attribute("server").Value,
                    item.Attribute("id").Value,
                    item.Attribute("secret").Value),
                Source = "Flickr"
              }).ToList();
    }
  }
}
```

Now you just need to connect the types from the library and the WPF application. In the constructor of the MainWindow class, an instance of SearchInfo is created, and the DataContext of the window is set to this instance. Now data binding can take place, shown earlier with the XAML code (code file AsyncPatterns/MainWindow.xaml.cs):

```
public partial class MainWindow : Window
{
  private SearchInfo searchInfo;

  public MainWindow()
  {
    InitializeComponent();
    searchInfo = new SearchInfo();
    this.DataContext = searchInfo;
  }
```

The MainWindow class also contains the helper method GetSearchRequests, which returns a collection of IImageRequest objects in the form of BingRequest and FlickrRequest types. In case you only registered with one of these services, you can change this code to return only the one with which you registered. Of course, you can also create IImageRequest types of other services, e.g., using Google or Yahoo. Then add these request types to the collection returned:

```
private IEnumerable<IImageRequest> GetSearchRequests()
{
  return new List<IImageRequest>
  {
    new BingRequest { SearchTerm = searchInfo.SearchTerm },
    new FlickrRequest { SearchTerm = searchInfo.SearchTerm}
  };
}
```

Synchronous Call

Now that everything is set up, let's start with a synchronous call to these services. The click handler of the Sync button, OnSearchSync, iterates through all search requests returned from GetSearchRequests and uses the Url property to make an HTTP request with the WebClient class. The method DownloadString blocks until the result is received. The resulting XML is assigned to the resp variable. The XML content is parsed with the help of the Parse method, which returns a collection of SearchItemResult objects. The items of these collections are then added to the list contained within searchInfo (code file AsyncPatterns/MainWindow.xaml.cs):

```
private void OnSearchSync(object sender, RoutedEventArgs e)
{
  foreach (var req in GetSearchRequests())
  {
    var client = new WebClient();
    client.Credentials = req.Credentials;
    string resp = client.DownloadString(req.Url);
    IEnumerable<SearchItemResult> images = req.Parse(resp);
    foreach (var image in images)
    {
      searchInfo.List.Add(image);
    }
  }
}
```

Running the application (see Figure 13-2), the user interface is blocked until the method OnSearchSync is finished making network calls to Bing and Flickr, as well as parsing the results. The amount of time needed to complete these calls varies according to the speed of your network and the current workload of Bing and Flickr. Whatever it is, however, the wait is unpleasant to the user.

FIGURE 13-2

Therefore, make the call asynchronously instead.

Asynchronous Pattern

One way to make the call asynchronously is by using the asynchronous pattern. The asynchronous pattern defines a Begin*XXX* method and an End*XXX* method. For example, if a synchronous method DownloadString is offered, the asynchronous variants would be BeginDownloadString and EndDownloadString. The Begin*XXX* method takes all input arguments of the synchronous method, and End*XXX* takes the output arguments and return type to return the result. With the asynchronous pattern, the Begin*XXX* method also defines a parameter of AsyncCallback, which accepts a delegate that is invoked as soon as the asynchronous method is completed. The Begin*XXX* method returns IAsyncResult, which can be used for polling to verify whether the call is completed, and to wait for the end of the method.

The WebClient class doesn't offer an implementation of the asynchronous pattern. Instead, the HttpWebRequest class could be used, which offers this pattern with the methods BeginGetResponse and EndGetResponse. This is not done in the following sample. Instead, a delegate is used. The delegate type defines an Invoke method to make a synchronous method call, and BeginInvoke and EndInvoke methods to use it with the asynchronous pattern. Here, the delegate downloadString of type Func<string, string> is declared to reference a method that has a string parameter and returns a string. The method that is referenced by the downloadString variable is implemented as a Lambda expression and invokes the synchronous method DownloadString of the WebClient type. The delegate is invoked asynchronously by calling the BeginInvoke method. This method uses a thread from the thread pool to make an asynchronous call.

The first parameter of the BeginInvoke method is the first generic string parameter of the Func delegate where the URL can be passed. The second parameter is of type AsyncCallback. AsyncCallback is a delegate that requires IAsyncResult as a parameter. The method referenced by this delegate is invoked as soon as the asynchronous method is completed. When that happens, downloadString.EndInvoke is invoked to retrieve the result, which is dealt with in the same manner as before to parse the XML content and get the collection of items. However, here it is not possible to directly go back to the UI, as the UI is bound to a single thread, and the callback method is running within a background thread. Therefore, it's necessary to switch back to the UI thread by using the Dispatcher property from the window. The Invoke method of the Dispatcher requires a delegate as a parameter; that's why the Action<SearchItemResult> delegate is specified, which adds an item to the collection bound to the UI (code file AsyncPatterns/MainWindow .xaml.cs):

```
private void OnSeachAsyncPattern(object sender, RoutedEventArgs e)
{
  Func<string, ICredentials, string> downloadString = (address, cred) =>
    {
      var client = new WebClient();
      client.Credentials = cred;
      return client.DownloadString(address);
    };

  Action<SearchItemResult> addItem = item => searchInfo.List.Add(item);

  foreach (var req in GetSearchRequests())
  {
    downloadString.BeginInvoke(req.Url, req.Credentials, ar =>
      {
        string resp = downloadString.EndInvoke(ar);
        IEnumerable<SearchItemResult> images = req.Parse(resp);
        foreach (var image in images)
        {
          this.Dispatcher.Invoke(addItem, image);
        }
      }, null);
  }
}
```

An advantage of the asynchronous pattern is that it can be implemented easily just by using the functionality of delegates. The program now behaves as it should; the UI is no longer blocked. However, using the asynchronous pattern is difficult. Fortunately, .NET 2.0 introduced the event-based asynchronous pattern, which makes it easier to deal with UI updates. This pattern is discussed next.

> **NOTE** *Delegate types and Lambda expressions are explained in Chapter 8, "Delegates, Lambdas, and Events." Threads and thread pools are covered in Chapter 21, "Threads, Tasks, and Synchronization."*

Event-Based Asynchronous Pattern

The method `OnAsyncEventPattern` makes use of the event-based asynchronous pattern. This pattern is implemented by the `WebClient` class and thus it can be directly used.

This pattern defines a method with the suffix `"Async"`. Therefore, for example, for the synchronous method `DownloadString`, the `WebClient` class offers the asynchronous variant `DownloadStringAsync`. Instead of defining a delegate that is invoked when the asynchronous method is completed, an event is defined. The `DownloadStringCompleted` event is invoked as soon as the asynchronous method `DownloadStringAsync` is completed. The method assigned to the event handler is implemented within a Lambda expression. The implementation is very similar to before, but now it is possible to directly access UI elements because the event handler is invoked from the thread that has the synchronization context, and this is the UI thread in the case of Windows Forms and WPF applications (code file `AsyncPatterns/MainWindow.xaml.cs`):

```
private void OnAsyncEventPattern(object sender, RoutedEventArgs e)
{
  foreach (var req in GetSearchRequests())
  {
    var client = new WebClient();
    client.Credentials = req.Credentials;
    client.DownloadStringCompleted += (sender1, e1) =>
      {
        string resp = e1.Result;
        IEnumerable<SearchItemResult> images = req.Parse(resp);
        foreach (var image in images)
        {
          searchInfo.List.Add(image);
        }
      };
    client.DownloadStringAsync(new Uri(req.Url));
  }
}
```

An advantage of the event-based asynchronous pattern is that it is easy to use. Note, however, that it is not that easy to implement this pattern in a custom class. One way to use an existing implementation of this pattern to make synchronous methods asynchronous is with the `BackgroundWorker` class. `BackgroundWorker` implements the event-based asynchronous pattern.

This makes the code a lot simpler. However, the order is reversed compared to synchronous method calls. Before invoking the asynchronous method, you need to define what happens when the method call is completed. The following section plunges into the new world of asynchronous programming with the `async` and `await` keywords.

Task-Based Asynchronous Pattern

The WebClient class is updated with .NET 4.5 to offer the task-based asynchronous pattern (TAP) as well. This pattern defines a suffix Async method that returns a Task type. Because the WebClient class already offers a method with the Async suffix to implement the task-based asynchronous pattern, the new method has the name DownloadStringTaskAsync.

The method DownloadStringTaskAsync is declared to return Task<string>. You do not need to declare a variable of Task<string> to assign the result from DownloadStringTaskAsync; instead, a variable of type string can be declared, and the await keyword used. The await keyword unblocks the thread (in this case the UI thread) to do other tasks. As soon as the method DownloadStringTaskAsync completes its background processing, the UI thread can continue and get the result from the background task to the string variable resp. Also, the code following this line continues (code file AsyncPatterns/MainWindow.xaml.cs):

```
private async void OnTaskBasedAsyncPattern(object sender,
    RoutedEventArgs e)
{
  foreach (var req in GetSearchRequests())
  {
    var client = new WebClient();
    client.Credentials = req.Credentials;
    string resp = await client.DownloadStringTaskAsync(req.Url);

    IEnumerable<SearchItemResult> images = req.Parse(resp);
    foreach (var image in images)
    {
      searchInfo.List.Add(image);
    }
  }
}
```

> **NOTE** *The* async *keyword creates a state machine similar to the* yield *return statement, which is discussed in Chapter 6, "Arrays and Tuples."*

The code is much simpler now. There is no blocking, and no manually switching back to the UI thread, as this is done automatically; and the code has the same order as you're used to with synchronous programming.

Next, the code is changed to use a different class from WebClient, one in which the task-based event pattern is more directly implemented and synchronous methods are not offered. This class, new with .NET 4.5, is HttpClient. Doing an asynchronous GET request is done with the GetAsync method. Then, to read the content another asynchronous method is needed. ReadAsStringAsync returns the content formatted in a string:

```
private async void OnTaskBasedAsyncPattern(object sender,
    RoutedEventArgs e)
{
  foreach (var req in GetSearchRequests())
  {
    var clientHandler = new HttpClientHandler
    {
      Credentials = req.Credentials
    };
    var client = new HttpClient(clientHandler);
```

```
var response = await client.GetAsync(req.Url);
string resp = await response.Content.ReadAsStringAsync();

IEnumerable<SearchItemResult> images = req.Parse(resp);
foreach (var image in images)
{
  searchInfo.List.Add(image);
}
    }
  }
}
```

Parsing of the XML string to could take a while. Because the parsing code is running in the UI thread, the UI thread cannot react to user requests at that time. To create a background task from synchronous functionality, Task.Run can be used. In the following example, Task.Run wraps the parsing of the XML string to return the SearchItemResult collection:

```
private async void OnTaskBasedAsyncPattern(object sender,
    RoutedEventArgs e)
{
  foreach (var req in GetSearchRequests())
  {
    var clientHandler = new HttpClientHandler
    {
      Credentials = req.Credentials
    };
    var client = new HttpClient(clientHandler);
    var response = await client.GetAsync(req.Url, cts.Token);
    string resp = await response.Content.ReadAsStringAsync();

    await Task.Run(() =>
    {
      IEnumerable<SearchItemResult> images = req.Parse(resp);
      foreach (var image in images)
      {
        searchInfo.List.Add(image);
      }
    }
  }
}
```

Because the method passed to the Task.Run method is running in a background thread, here we have the same problem as before referencing some UI code. One solution would be to just do req.Parse within the Task.Run method, and do the foreach loop outside of the task to add the result to the list in the UI thread. WPF with .NET 4.5 offers a better solution, however, that enables filling collections that are bound to the UI from a background thread. This extension only requires enabling the collection for synchronization using BindingOperations.EnableCollectionSynchronization, as shown in the following code snippet:

```
public partial class MainWindow : Window
{
  private SearchInfo searchInfo;
  private object lockList = new object();

  public MainWindow()
  {
    InitializeComponent();
    searchInfo = new SearchInfo();
    this.DataContext = searchInfo;

    BindingOperations.EnableCollectionSynchronization(
        searchInfo.List, lockList);
  }
```

Having looked at the advantages of the async and await keywords, the next section examines the programming foundation behind these keywords.

FOUNDATION OF ASYNCHRONOUS PROGRAMMING

The async and await keywords are just a compiler feature. The compiler creates code by using the Task class. Instead of using the new keywords, you could get the same functionality with C# 4 and methods of the Task class; it's just not as convenient.

This section gives information about what the compiler does with the async and await keywords, an easy way to create an asynchronous method, how you can invoke multiple asynchronous methods in parallel, and how you can change a class that just offers the asynchronous pattern to use the new keywords.

Creating Tasks

Let's start with the synchronous method Greeting, which takes a while before returning a string (code file Foundations/Program.cs):

```
static string Greeting(string name)
{
  Thread.Sleep(3000);
  return string.Format("Hello, {0}", name);
}
```

To make such a method asynchronously, the method GreetingAsync is defined. The task-based asynchronous pattern specifies that an asynchronous method is named with the Async suffix and returns a task. GreetingAsync is defined to have the same input parameters as the Greeting method but returns Task<string>. Task<string>, which defines a task that returns a string in the future. A simple way to return a task is by using the Task.Run method. The generic version Task.Run<string>() creates a task that returns a string:

```
static Task<string> GreetingAsync(string name)
{
  return Task.Run<string>(() =>
    {
      return Greeting(name);
    });
}
```

Calling an Asynchronous Method

You can call this asynchronous method GreetingAsync by using the await keyword on the task that is returned. The await keyword requires the method to be declared with the async modifier. The code within this method does not continue before the GreetingAsync method is completed. However, the thread that started the CallerWithAsync method can be reused. This thread is not blocked:

```
private async static void CallerWithAsync()
{
  string result = await GreetingAsync("Stephanie");
  Console.WriteLine(result);
}
```

Instead of passing the result from the asynchronous method to a variable, you can also use the await keyword directly within parameters. Here, the result from the GreetingAsync method is awaited like in the previously code snippet, but this time the result is directly passed to the Console.WriteLine method:

```
private async static void CallerWithAsync2()
{
  Console.WriteLine(await GreetingAsync("Stephanie"));
}
```

> **NOTE** *The* async *modifier can only be used with methods returning a* Task *or* void. *It cannot be used with the entry point of a program, the* Main *method.* await *can only be used with methods returning a* Task.

In the next section you'll see what's driving this await keyword. Behind the scenes, continuation tasks are used.

Continuation with Tasks

GreetingAsync returns a Task<string> object. The Task object contains information about the task created, and allows waiting for its completion. The ContinueWith method of the Task class defines the code that should be invoked as soon as the task is finished. The delegate assigned to the ContinueWith method receives the completed task with its argument, which allows accessing the result from the task using the Result property:

```
private static void CallerWithContinuationTask()
{
  Task<string> t1 = GreetingAsync("Stephanie");
  t1.ContinueWith(t =>
    {
      string result = t.Result;
      Console.WriteLine(result);
    });
}
```

The compiler converts the await keyword by putting all the code that follows within the block of a ContinueWith method.

Synchronization Context

If you verify the thread that is used within the methods you will find that in both methods, CallerWithAsync and CallerWithContinuationTask, different threads are used during the lifetime of the methods. One thread is used to invoke the method GreetingAsync, and another thread takes action after the await keyword or within the code block in the ContinueWith method.

With a console application usually this is not an issue. However, you have to ensure that at least one foreground thread is still running before all background tasks that should be completed are finished. The sample application invokes Console.ReadLine to keep the main thread running until the return key is pressed.

With applications that are bound to a specific thread for some actions (e.g., with WPF applications, UI elements can only be accessed from the UI thread), this is an issue.

Using the async and await keywords you don't have to do any special actions to access the UI thread after an await completion. By default the generated code switches the thread to the thread that has the synchronization context. A WPF application sets a DispatcherSynchronizationContext, and a Windows Forms application sets a WindowsFormsSynchronizationContext. If the calling thread of the asynchronous method is assigned to the synchronization context, then with the continuous execution after the await, by default the same synchronization context is used. If the same synchronization context shouldn't be used, you must invoke the `Task` method `ConfigureAwait(continueOnCapturedContext: false)`. An example that illustrates this usefulness is a WPF application in which the code that follows the `await` is not using any UI elements. In this case, it is faster to avoid the switch to the synchronization context.

Using Multiple Asynchronous Methods

Within an asynchronous method you can call not only one but multiple asynchronous methods. How you code this depends on whether the results from one asynchronous method are needed by another.

Calling Asynchronous Methods Sequentially

The `await` keyword can be used to call every asynchronous method. In cases where one method is dependent on the result of another method, this is very useful. Here, the second call to `GreetingAsync` is completely independent of the result of the first call to `GreetingAsync`. Thus, the complete method `MultipleAsyncMethods` could return the result faster if `await` is not used with every single method, as shown in the following example:

```
private async static void MultipleAsyncMethods()
{
  string s1 = await GreetingAsync("Stephanie");
  string s2 = await GreetingAsync("Matthias");
  Console.WriteLine("Finished both methods.\n " +
      "Result 1: {0}\n Result 2: {1}", s1, s2);
}
```

Using Combinators

If the asynchronous methods are not dependent on each other, it is a lot faster not to `await` on each separately, and instead assign the return of the asynchronous method to a `Task` variable. The `GreetingAsync` method returns `Task<string>`. Both these methods can now run in parallel. *Combinators* can help with this. A combinator accepts multiple parameters of the same type and returns a value of the same type. The passed parameters are "combined" to one. `Task` combinators accept multiple `Task` objects as parameter and return a `Task`.

The sample code invokes the `Task.WhenAll` combinator method that you can `await` to have both tasks finished:

```
private async static void MultipleAsyncMethodsWithCombinators1()
{
  Task<string> t1 = GreetingAsync("Stephanie");
  Task<string> t2 = GreetingAsync("Matthias");
  await Task.WhenAll(t1, t2);
  Console.WriteLine("Finished both methods.\n " +
      "Result 1: {0}\n Result 2: {1}", t1.Result, t2.Result);
}
```

The `Task` class defines the `WhenAll` and `WhenAny` combinators. The `Task` returned from the `WhenAll` method is completed as soon as all tasks passed to the method are completed; the `Task` returned from the `WhenAny` method is completed as soon as one of the tasks passed to the method is completed.

The `WhenAll` method of the `Task` type defines several overloads. If all the tasks return the same type, an array of this type can be used for the result of the `await`. The `GreetingAsync` method returns a `Task<string>`, and awaiting for this method results in a `string`. Therefore, `Task.WhenAll` can be used to return a `string` array:

```
private async static void MultipleAsyncMethodsWithCombinators2()
{
  Task<string> t1 = GreetingAsync("Stephanie");
```

```
        Task<string> t2 = GreetingAsync("Matthias");
        string[] result =  await Task.WhenAll(t1, t2);
        Console.WriteLine("Finished both methods.\n " +
            "Result 1: {0}\n Result 2: {1}", result[0], result[1]);
    }
```

Converting the Asynchronous Pattern

Not all classes from the .NET Framework introduced the new asynchronous method style with .NET 4.5. There are still many classes just offering the asynchronous pattern with Begin*XXX* and End*XXX* methods and not task-based asynchronous methods as you will see when working with different classes from the framework.

First, let's create an asynchronous method from the previously-defined synchronous method Greeting with the help of a delegate. The Greeting method receives a string as parameter and returns a string, thus a variable of Func<string, string> delegate is used to reference this method. According to the asynchronous pattern, the BeginGreeting method receives a string parameter in addition to AsyncCallback and object parameters and returns IAsyncResult. The EndGreeting method returns the result from the Greeting method—a string—and receives an IAsyncResult parameter. With the implementation just the delegate is used to make the implementation asynchronously.

```
        private static Func<string, string> greetingInvoker = Greeting;

        static IAsyncResult BeginGreeting(string name, AsyncCallback callback,
          object state)
        {
          return greetingInvoker.BeginInvoke(name, callback, state);
        }

        static string EndGreeting(IAsyncResult ar)
        {
          return greetingInvoker.EndInvoke(ar);
        }
```

Now the BeginGreeting and EndGreeting methods are available, and these should be converted to use the async and await keywords to get the results. The TaskFactory class defines the FromAsync method that allows converting methods using the asynchronous pattern to the TAP.

With the sample code, the first generic parameter of the Task type, Task<string>, defines the return value from the method that is invoked. The generic parameter of the FromAsync method defines the input type of the method. In this case the input type is again of type string. With the parameters of the FromAsync method, the first two parameters are delegate types to pass the addresses of the BeginGreeting and EndGreeting methods. After these two parameters, the input parameters and the object state parameter follow. The object state is not used, so null is assigned to it. Because the FromAsync method returns a Task type, in the sample code Task<string>, an await can be used as shown:

```
        private static async void ConvertingAsyncPattern()
        {
          string s = await Task<string>.Factory.FromAsync<string>(
            BeginGreeting, EndGreeting, "Angela", null);
          Console.WriteLine(s);
        }
```

ERROR HANDLING

Chapter 16, "Errors and Exceptions," provides detailed coverage of errors and exception handling. However, in the context of asynchronous methods, you should be aware of some special handling of errors.

Let's start with a simple method that throws an exception after a delay (code file ErrorHandling/Program.cs):

```
static async Task ThrowAfter(int ms, string message)
{
  await Task.Delay(ms);
  throw new Exception(message);
}
```

If you call the asynchronous method without awaiting it, you can put the asynchronous method within a try/catch block—and the exception will not be caught. That's because the method DontHandle has already completed before the exception from ThrowAfter is thrown. You need to await the ThrowAfter method, as shown in the following example:

```
private static void DontHandle()
{
  try
  {
    ThrowAfter(200, "first");
    // exception is not caught because this method is finished
    // before the exception is thrown
  }
  catch (Exception ex)
  {
    Console.WriteLine(ex.Message);
  }
}
```

> **WARNING** *Asynchronous methods that return* void *cannot be awaited. The issue with this is that exceptions that are thrown from* async void *methods cannot be caught. That's why it is best to return a* Task *type from an asynchronous method. Handler methods or overridden base methods are exempted from this rule.*

Handling Exceptions with Asynchronous Methods

A good way to deal with exceptions from asynchronous methods is to use await and put a try/catch statement around it, as shown in the following code snippet. The HandleOneError method releases the thread after calling the ThrowAfter method asynchronously, but it keeps the Task referenced to continue as soon as the task is completed. When that happens (which in this case is when the exception is thrown after two seconds), the catch matches and the code within the catch block is invoked:

```
private static async void HandleOneError()
{
  try
  {
    await ThrowAfter(2000, "first");
  }
  catch (Exception ex)
  {
    Console.WriteLine("handled {0}", ex.Message);
  }
}
```

Exceptions with Multiple Asynchronous Methods

What if two asynchronous methods are invoked that each throw exceptions? In the following example, first the ThrowAfter method is invoked, which throws an exception with the message first after two seconds. After this method is completed, the ThrowAfter method is invoked, throwing an exception after one second. Because the first call to ThrowAfter already throws an exception, the code within the try block does not continue to invoke the second method, instead landing within the catch block to deal with the first exception:

```
private static async void StartTwoTasks()
{
  try
  {
    await ThrowAfter(2000, "first");
    await ThrowAfter(1000, "second"); // the second call is not invoked
                                      // because the first method throws
                                      // an exception
  }
  catch (Exception ex)
  {
    Console.WriteLine("handled {0}", ex.Message);
  }
}
```

Now let's start the two calls to ThrowAfter in parallel. The first method throws an exception after two seconds, the second one after one second. With Task.WhenAll you wait until both tasks are completed, whether an exception is thrown or not. Therefore, after a wait of about two seconds, Task.WhenAll is completed, and the exception is caught with the catch statement. However, you will only see the exception information from the first task that is passed to the WhenAll method. It's not the task that threw the exception first (which is the second task), but the first task in the list:

```
private async static void StartTwoTasksParallel()
{
  try
  {
    Task t1 = ThrowAfter(2000, "first");
    Task t2 = ThrowAfter(1000, "second");
    await Task.WhenAll(t1, t2);
  }
  catch (Exception ex)
  {
    // just display the exception information of the first task
    // that is awaited within WhenAll
    Console.WriteLine("handled {0}", ex.Message);
  }
}
```

One way to get the exception information from all tasks is to declare the task variables t1 and t2 outside of the try block, so they can be accessed from within the catch block. Here you can check the status of the task to determine whether they are in a faulted state with the IsFaulted property. In case of an exception, the IsFaulted property returns true. The exception information itself can be accessed by using Exception.InnerException of the Task class. Another, and usually better, way to retrieve exception information from all tasks is demonstrated next.

Using AggregateException Information

To get the exception information from all failing tasks, the result from Task.WhenAll can be written to a Task variable. This task is then awaited until all tasks are completed. Otherwise the exception would still be missed. As described in the last section, with the `catch` statement just the exception of the first task can be retrieved. However, now you have access to the `Exception` property of the outer task. The `Exception` property is of type `AggregateException`. This exception type defines the property `InnerExceptions` (not only `InnerException`), which contains a list of all the exceptions from the awaited for. Now you can easily iterate through all the exceptions:

```
private static async void ShowAggregatedException()
{
  Task taskResult = null;
  try
  {
    Task t1 = ThrowAfter(2000, "first");
    Task t2 = ThrowAfter(1000, "second");
    await (taskResult = Task.WhenAll(t1, t2));
  }
  catch (Exception ex)
  {
    Console.WriteLine("handled {0}", ex.Message);
    foreach (var ex1 in taskResult.Exception.InnerExceptions)
    {
      Console.WriteLine("inner exception {0}", ex1.Message);
    }
  }
}
```

CANCELLATION

With background tasks that can run longer in some scenarios, it is useful to cancel the tasks. For cancellation, .NET offers a standard mechanism that has been available since .NET 4. This mechanism can be used with the task-based asynchronous pattern.

The cancellation framework is based on cooperative behavior; it is not forceful. A long-running task needs to check itself if it is canceled, in which case it is the responsibility of the task to cleanup any open resources and finish its work.

Cancellation is based on the `CancellationTokenSource` class, which can be used to send cancel requests. Requests are sent to tasks that reference the `CancellationToken` that is associated with the `CancellationTokenSource`. The following section looks at an example by modifying the `AsyncPatterns` sample created earlier in this chapter to add support for cancellation.

Starting a Cancellation

First, a variable `cts` of type `CancellationTokenSource` is defined with the private field members of the class `MainWindow`. This member will be used to cancel tasks and pass tokens to the methods that should be cancelled (code file `AsyncPatterns/MainWindow.xaml.cs`):

```
public partial class MainWindow : Window
{
  private SearchInfo searchInfo;
  private object lockList = new object();
  private CancellationTokenSource cts;
```

For a new button that can be activated by the user to cancel the running task, the event handler method `OnCancel` is added. Within this method, the variable `cts` is used to cancel the tasks with the `Cancel` method:

```
private void OnCancel(object sender, RoutedEventArgs e)
{
  if (cts != null)
    cts.Cancel();
}
```

The `CancellationTokenSource` also supports cancellation after a specified amount of time. The method `CancelAfter` enables passing a value, in milliseconds, after which a task should be cancelled.

Cancellation with Framework Features

Now let's pass the `CancellationToken` to an asynchronous method. Several of the asynchronous methods in the framework support cancellation by offering an overload whereby a `CancellationToken` can be passed. One example is the `GetAsync` method of the `HttpClient` class. The overloaded `GetAsync` method accepts a `CancellationToken` in addition to the URI string. The token from the `CancellationTokenSource` can be retrieved by using the `Token` property.

The implementation of the `GetAsync` method periodically checks whether the operation should be cancelled. If so, it does a cleanup of resources before throwing the exception `OperationCanceledException`. This exception is caught with the `catch` handler in the following code snippet:

```
private async void OnTaskBasedAsyncPattern(object sender,
    RoutedEventArgs e)
{
  cts = new CancellationTokenSource();
  try
  {
    foreach (var req in GetSearchRequests())
    {
      var client = new HttpClient();
      var response = await client.GetAsync(req.Url, cts.Token);
      string resp = await response.Content.ReadAsStringAsync();

      //...
    }
  }
  catch (OperationCanceledException ex)
  {
    MessageBox.Show(ex.Message);
  }
}
```

Cancellation with Custom Tasks

What about custom tasks that should be cancelled? The `Run` method of the `Task` class offers an overload to pass a `CancellationToken` as well. However, with custom tasks it is necessary to check whether cancellation is requested. In the following example, this is implemented within the `foreach` loop. The token can be checked by using the `IsCancellationRequsted` property. If you need to do some cleanup before throwing the exception, it is best to verify that cancellation is requested. If cleanup is not needed, an exception can be fired immediately after the check, which is done with the `ThrowIfCancellationRequested` method:

```
await Task.Run(() =>
{
  var images = req.Parse(resp);
  foreach (var image in images)
```

```
    {
        cts.Token.ThrowIfCancellationRequested();
        searchInfo.List.Add(image);
    }
}, cts.Token);
```

Now the user can cancel long-running tasks.

SUMMARY

This chapter introduced the `async` and `await` keywords that are new with C# 5. Having looked at several examples, you've seen the advantages of the task-based asynchronous pattern compared to the asynchronous pattern and the event-based asynchronous pattern available with earlier editions of .NET.

You've also seen how easy it is to create asynchronous methods with the help of the `Task` class, and learned how to use the `async` and `await` keywords to wait for these methods without blocking threads. Finally, you looked at the error-handling aspect of asynchronous methods.

For more information on parallel programming, and details about threads and tasks, see Chapter 21.

The next chapter continues with core features of C# and .NET and gives detailed information on memory and resource management.

14

Memory Management and Pointers

WHAT'S IN THIS CHAPTER?

➤ Allocating space on the stack and heap at runtime

➤ Garbage collection

➤ Releasing unmanaged resources using destructors and the `System .IDisposable` interface

➤ The syntax for using pointers in C#

➤ Using pointers to implement high-performance stack-based arrays

WROX.COM CODE DOWNLOADS FOR THIS CHAPTER

The wrox.com code downloads for this chapter are found at `http://www.wrox.com/remtitle .cgi?isbn=1118314425` on the Download Code tab. The code for this chapter is divided into the following major examples:

➤ PointerPlayground

➤ PointerPlayground2

➤ QuickArray

MEMORY MANAGEMENT

This chapter presents various aspects of memory management and memory access. Although the runtime removes much of the responsibility for memory management from the programmer, it is useful to understand how memory management works, and important to know how to work with unmanaged resources efficiently.

A good understanding of memory management and knowledge of the pointer capabilities provided by C# will better enable you to integrate C# code with legacy code and perform efficient memory manipulation in performance-critical systems.

MEMORY MANAGEMENT UNDER THE HOOD

One of the advantages of C# programming is that the programmer does not need to worry about detailed memory management; the garbage collector deals with the problem of memory clean up on your behalf. As a result, you get something that approximates the efficiency of languages such as C++ without the complexity of having to handle memory management yourself as you do in C++. However, although you do not have to manage memory manually, it still pays to understand what is going on behind the scenes. Understanding how your program manages memory under the covers will help you increase the speed and performance of your applications. This section looks at what happens in the computer's memory when you allocate variables.

> **NOTE** *The precise details of many of the topics of this section are not presented here. This section serves as an abbreviated guide to the general processes rather than as a statement of exact implementation.*

Value Data Types

Windows uses a system known as *virtual addressing*, in which the mapping from the memory address seen by your program to the actual location in hardware memory is entirely managed by Windows. As a result, each process on a 32-bit processor sees 4GB of available memory, regardless of how much hardware memory you actually have in your computer (on 64-bit processors this number is greater). This memory contains everything that is part of the program, including the executable code, any DLLs loaded by the code, and the contents of all variables used when the program runs. This 4GB of memory is known as the *virtual address space* or *virtual memory*. For convenience, this chapter uses the shorthand *memory*.

Each memory location in the available 4GB is numbered starting from zero. To access a value stored at a particular location in memory, you need to supply the number that represents that memory location. In any compiled high-level language, including C#, Visual Basic, C++, and Java, the compiler converts human-readable variable names into memory addresses that the processor understands.

Somewhere inside a processor's virtual memory is an area known as the *stack*. The stack stores value data types that are not members of objects. In addition, when you call a method, the stack is used to hold a copy of any parameters passed to the method. To understand how the stack works, you need to understand the importance of variable *scope* in C#. If variable a goes into scope before variable b, then b will always go out of scope first. Consider the following code:

```
{
    int a;
    // do something
    {
        int b;
        // do something else
    }
}
```

First, a is declared. Then, inside the inner code block, b is declared. Then the inner code block terminates and b goes out of scope, then a goes out of scope. Therefore, the lifetime of b is entirely contained within the lifetime of a. The idea that you always deallocate variables in the reverse order of how you allocate them is crucial to the way the stack works.

Note that b is in a different block from code (defined by a different nesting of curly braces). For this reason, it is contained within a different scope. This is termed as *block scope* or *structure scope*.

You do not know exactly where in the address space the stack is—you don't need to know for C# development. A *stack pointer* (a variable maintained by the operating system) identifies the next free location on the stack. When your program first starts running, the stack pointer will point to just past the end of the block of memory that is reserved for the stack. The stack fills downward, from high memory addresses to low addresses. As data is put on the stack, the stack pointer is adjusted accordingly, so it always points to just past the next free location. This is illustrated in Figure 14-1, which shows a stack pointer with a value of 800000 (0xC3500 in hex); the next free location is the address 799999.

The following code tells the compiler that you need space in memory to store an integer and a double, and these memory locations are referred to as nRacingCars and engineSize. The line that declares each variable indicates the point at which you start requiring access to this variable. The closing curly brace of the block in which the variables are declared identifies the point at which both variables go out of scope:

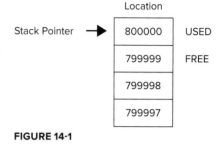

FIGURE 14-1

```
{
    int nRacingCars = 10;
    double engineSize = 3000.0;
    // do calculations;
}
```

Assuming that you use the stack shown in Figure 14-1, when the variable nRacingCars comes into scope and is assigned the value 10, the value 10 is placed in locations 799996 through 799999, the 4 bytes just below the location pointed to by the stack pointer (4 bytes because that's how much memory is needed to store an int.) To accommodate this, 4 is subtracted from the value of the stack pointer, so it now points to the location 799996, just after the new first free location (799995).

The next line of code declares the variable engineSize (a double) and initializes it to the value 3000.0. A double occupies eight bytes, so the value 3000.0 is placed in locations 799988 through 799995 on the stack, and the stack pointer is decremented by eight, so that it again points to the location just after the next free location on the stack.

When engineSize goes out of scope, the runtime knows that it is no longer needed. Because of the way variable lifetimes are always nested, you can guarantee that whatever happened while engineSize was in scope, the stack pointer is now pointing to the location where engineSize is stored. To remove engineSize from the stack, the stack pointer is incremented by eight and it now points to the location immediately after the end of engineSize. At this point in the code, you are at the closing curly brace, so nRacingCars also goes out of scope. The stack pointer is incremented by 4. When another variable comes into scope after engineSize and nRacingCars have been removed from the stack, it overwrites the memory descending from location 799999, where nRacingCars was stored.

If the compiler hits a line such as int i, j, then the order of variables coming into scope looks indeterminate. Both variables are declared at the same time and go out of scope at the same time. In this situation, it does not matter in what order the two variables are removed from memory. The compiler internally always ensures that the one that was put in memory first is removed last, thus preserving the rule that prohibits crossover of variable lifetimes.

Reference Data Types

Although the stack provides very high performance, it is not flexible enough to be used for all variables. The requirement that the lifetime of a variable must be nested is too restrictive for many purposes. Often, you need to use a method to allocate memory for storing data and keeping that data available long after that method has exited. This possibility exists whenever storage space is requested with the new operator—as is the case for all reference types. That is where the *managed heap* comes in.

If you have done any C++ coding that required low-level memory management, you are familiar with the heap. The managed heap is not quite the same as the heap C++ uses, however; the managed heap works under the control of the garbage collector and provides significant benefits compared to traditional heaps.

The managed heap (or heap for short) is just another area of memory from the processor's available 4GB. The following code demonstrates how the heap works and how memory is allocated for reference data types:

```
void DoWork()
{
   Customer arabel;
   arabel = new Customer();
   Customer otherCustomer2 = new EnhancedCustomer();
}
```

This code assumes the existence of two classes, `Customer` and `EnhancedCustomer`. The `EnhancedCustomer` class extends the `Customer` class.

First, you declare a `Customer` reference called `arabel`. The space for this is allocated on the stack, but remember that this is only a reference, not an actual `Customer` object. The `arabel` reference occupies 4 bytes, enough space to hold the address at which a `Customer` object will be stored. (You need 4 bytes to represent a memory address as an integer value between 0 and 4GB.)

The next line,

```
arabel = new Customer();
```

does several things. First, it allocates memory on the heap to store a `Customer` object (a real object, not just an address). Then it sets the value of the variable `arabel` to the address of the memory it has allocated to the new `Customer` object. (It also calls the appropriate `Customer` constructor to initialize the fields in the class instance, but we won't worry about that here.)

The `Customer` instance is not placed on the stack—it is placed on the heap. In this example, you don't know precisely how many bytes a `Customer` object occupies, but assume for the sake of argument that it is 32. These 32 bytes contain the instance fields of `Customer` as well as some information that .NET uses to identify and manage its class instances.

To find a storage location on the heap for the new `Customer` object, the .NET runtime looks through the heap and grabs the first adjacent, unused block of 32 bytes. Again for the sake of argument, assume that this happens to be at address `200000`, and that the `arabel` reference occupied locations `799996` through `799999` on the stack. This means that before instantiating the `arabel` object, the memory content will look similar to Figure 14-2.

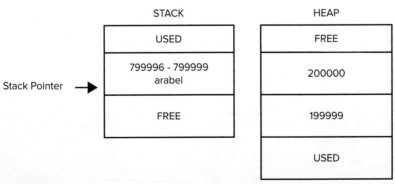

FIGURE 14-2

After allocating the new `Customer` object, the content of memory will look like Figure 14-3. Note that unlike the stack, memory in the heap is allocated upward, so the free space can be found above the used space.

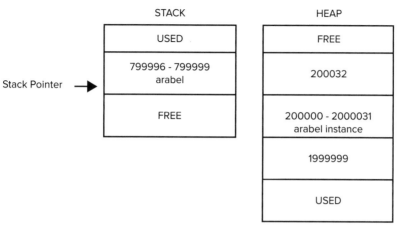

FIGURE 14-3

The next line of code both declares a `Customer` reference and instantiates a `Customer` object. In this instance, space on the stack for the `otherCustomer2` reference is allocated and space for the `mrJones` object is allocated on the heap in a single line of code:

```
Customer otherCustomer2 = new EnhancedCustomer();
```

This line allocates 4 bytes on the stack to hold the `otherCustomer2` reference, stored at locations `799992` through `799995`. The `otherCustomer2` object is allocated space on the heap starting at location `200032`.

It is clear from the example that the process of setting up a reference variable is more complex than that for setting up a value variable, and there is a performance overhead. In fact, the process is somewhat oversimplified here, because the .NET runtime needs to maintain information about the state of the heap, and this information needs to be updated whenever new data is added to the heap. Despite this overhead, you now have a mechanism for allocating variables that is not constrained by the limitations of the stack. By assigning the value of one reference variable to another of the same type, you have two variables that reference the same object in memory. When a reference variable goes out of scope, it is removed from the stack as described in the previous section, but the data for a referenced object is still sitting on the heap. The data remains on the heap until either the program terminates or the garbage collector removes it, which happens only when it is no longer referenced by any variables.

That is the power of reference data types, and you will see this feature used extensively in C# code. It means that you have a high degree of control over the lifetime of your data, because it is guaranteed to exist in the heap as long as you are maintaining some reference to it.

Garbage Collection

The previous discussion and diagrams show the managed heap working very much like the stack, to the extent that successive objects are placed next to each other in memory. This means that you can determine where to place the next object by using a heap pointer that indicates the next free memory location, which is adjusted as you add more objects to the heap. However, things are complicated by the fact that the lives of the heap-based objects are not coupled to the scope of the individual stack-based variables that reference them.

When the garbage collector runs, it removes all those objects from the heap that are no longer referenced. Immediately after doing this, the heap will have objects scattered on it, mixed up with memory that has just been freed (see Figure 14-4).

If the managed heap stayed like this, allocating space for new objects would be an awkward process, with the runtime having to search through the heap for a block of memory big enough to store each new object. However, the garbage collector does not leave the heap in this state. As soon as the garbage collector has freed up all the objects it can, it compacts the heap by moving all the remaining objects to form one continuous block of memory. This means that the heap can continue working just like the stack, as far as locating where to store new objects. Of course, when the objects are moved about, all the references to those objects need to be updated with the correct new addresses, but the garbage collector handles that too.

In use
Free
In use
In use
Free

FIGURE 14-4

This action of compacting by the garbage collector is where the managed heap works very differently from old, unmanaged heaps. With the managed heap, it is just a question of reading the value of the heap pointer, rather than iterating through a linked list of addresses to find somewhere to put the new data. For this reason, instantiating an object under .NET is much faster. Interestingly, accessing objects tends to be faster too, because the objects are compacted toward the same area of memory on the heap, resulting in less page swapping. Microsoft believes that these performance gains more than compensate for the performance penalty you get whenever the garbage collector needs to do some work to compact the heap and change all those references to objects it has moved.

> **NOTE** *Generally, the garbage collector runs when the .NET runtime determines that garbage collection is required. You can force the garbage collector to run at a certain point in your code by calling* System.GC.Collect. *The* System.GC *class is a .NET class that represents the garbage collector, and the* Collect *method initiates a garbage collection. The* GC *class is intended for rare situations in which you know that it's a good time to call the garbage collector; for example, if you have just de-referenced a large number of objects in your code. However, the logic of the garbage collector does not guarantee that all unreferenced objects will be removed from the heap in a single garbage collection pass.*

When the garbage collector runs, it actually hurts the performance of your application as it is impossible for your application to continue running while the garbage collector finishes its tasks. Because of this, it's best to let the runtime decide when to do garbage collection and not try to optimize it yourself.

When objects are created, they are placed within the managed heap. The first section of the heap is called the generation 0 section, or gen 0. As your new objects are created, they are moved into this section of the heap. Therefore, this is where the youngest objects reside.

Your objects remain there until the first collection of objects occurs through the garbage collection process. The objects that remain alive after this cleansing are compacted and then moved to the next section or generational part of the heap—the generation 1, or gen 1, section.

At this point, the generation 0 section is empty, and all new objects are again placed in this section. Older objects that survived the GC (garbage collection) process are found further down in the generation 1 section. This movement of aged items actually occurs one more time. The next collection process that occurs is then repeated. This means that the items that survived the GC process from the generation 1 section are moved to the generation 2 section, and the gen 0 items go to gen 1, again leaving gen 0 open for new objects.

> **NOTE** *Interestingly, a garbage collection will occur when you allocate an item that exceeds the capacity of the generation 0 section or when a* GC.Collect *is called.*

This process greatly improves the performance of your application. Typically, your youngest objects are the ones that can be collected, and a large number of younger-related objects might be reclaimed as well. If these objects reside next to each other in the heap, then the garbage collection process will be faster. In addition, because related objects are residing next to each other, program execution will be faster all around.

Another performance-related aspect of garbage collection in .NET is how the framework deals with larger objects that are added to the heap. Under the covers of .NET, larger objects have their own managed heap, referred to as the Large Object Heap. When objects greater than 85,000 bytes are utilized, they go to this special heap rather than the main heap. Your .NET application doesn't know the difference, as this is all managed for you. Because compressing large items in the heap is expensive, it isn't done for the objects residing in the Large Object Heap.

FREEING UNMANAGED RESOURCES

The presence of the garbage collector means that you usually do not need to worry about objects you no longer need; you simply allow all references to those objects to go out of scope and let the garbage collector free memory as required. However, the garbage collector does not know how to free unmanaged resources (such as file handles, network connections, and database connections). When managed classes encapsulate direct or indirect references to unmanaged resources, you need to make special provisions to ensure that the unmanaged resources are released when an instance of the class is garbage collected.

When defining a class, you can use two mechanisms to automate the freeing of unmanaged resources. These mechanisms are often implemented together because each provides a slightly different approach:

➤   Declare a *destructor* (or finalizer) as a member of your class.
➤   Implement the System.IDisposable interface in your class.

The following sections discuss each of these mechanisms in turn, and then look at how to implement them together for best results.

Destructors

You have seen that constructors enable you to specify actions that must take place whenever an instance of a class is created. Conversely, destructors are called before an object is destroyed by the garbage collector. Given this behavior, a destructor would initially seem like a great place to put code to free unmanaged resources and perform a general clean up. Unfortunately, things are not so straightforward.

> **NOTE** *Although we talk about destructors in C#, in the underlying .NET architecture these are known as* finalizers. *When you define a destructor in C#, what is emitted into the assembly by the compiler is actually a* Finalize *method. It doesn't affect any of your source code, but you need to be aware of it when examining the content of an assembly.*

The syntax for a destructor will be familiar to C++ developers. It looks like a method, with the same name as the containing class, but prefixed with a tilde (~). It has no return type, and takes no parameters or access modifiers. Here is an example:

```
class MyClass
{
    ~MyClass()
    {
        // destructor implementation
    }
}
```

When the C# compiler compiles a destructor, it implicitly translates the destructor code to the equivalent of a `Finalize` method, which ensures that the `Finalize` method of the parent class is executed. The following example shows the C# code equivalent to the Intermediate Language (IL) that the compiler would generate for the ~`MyClass` destructor:

```
protected override void Finalize()
{
    try
    {
        // destructor implementation
    }
    finally
    {
        base.Finalize();
    }
}
```

As shown, the code implemented in the ~`MyClass` destructor is wrapped in a `try` block contained in the `Finalize` method. A call to the parent's `Finalize` method is ensured by placing the call in a `finally` block. You can read about `try` and `finally` blocks in Chapter 16, "Errors and Exceptions."

Experienced C++ developers make extensive use of destructors, sometimes not only to clean up resources but also to provide debugging information or perform other tasks. C# destructors are used far less than their C++ equivalents. The problem with C# destructors as compared to their C++ counterparts is that they are nondeterministic. When a C++ object is destroyed, its destructor runs immediately. However, because of the way the garbage collector works when using C#, there is no way to know when an object's destructor will actually execute. Hence, you cannot place any code in the destructor that relies on being run at a certain time, and you should not rely on the destructor being called for different class instances in any particular order. When your object is holding scarce and critical resources that need to be freed as soon as possible, you do not want to wait for garbage collection.

Another problem with C# destructors is that the implementation of a destructor delays the final removal of an object from memory. Objects that do not have a destructor are removed from memory in one pass of the garbage collector, but objects that have destructors require two passes to be destroyed: The first pass calls the destructor without removing the object, and the second pass actually deletes the object. In addition, the runtime uses a single thread to execute the `Finalize` methods of all objects. If you use destructors frequently, and use them to execute lengthy clean-up tasks, the impact on performance can be noticeable.

The IDisposable Interface

In C#, the recommended alternative to using a destructor is using the `System.IDisposable` interface. The `IDisposable` interface defines a pattern (with language-level support) that provides a deterministic mechanism for freeing unmanaged resources and avoids the garbage collector–related problems inherent with destructors. The `IDisposable` interface declares a single method named `Dispose`, which takes no parameters and returns `void`. Here is an implementation for `MyClass`:

```
class MyClass: IDisposable
{
    public void Dispose()
    {
        // implementation
    }
}
```

The implementation of `Dispose` should explicitly free all unmanaged resources used directly by an object and call `Dispose` on any encapsulated objects that also implement the `IDisposable` interface. In this way, the `Dispose` method provides precise control over when unmanaged resources are freed.

Suppose that you have a class named `ResourceGobbler`, which relies on the use of some external resource and implements `IDisposable`. If you want to instantiate an instance of this class, use it, and then dispose of it, you could do so like this:

```
ResourceGobbler theInstance = new ResourceGobbler();

// do your processing

theInstance.Dispose();
```

Unfortunately, this code fails to free the resources consumed by `theInstance` if an exception occurs during processing, so you should write the code as follows using a `try` block (as covered in detail in Chapter 16):

```
ResourceGobbler theInstance = null;

try
{
    theInstance = new ResourceGobbler();

    // do your processing
}
finally
{
    if (theInstance != null)
    {
        theInstance.Dispose();
    }
}
```

This version ensures that `Dispose` is always called on `theInstance` and that any resources consumed by it are always freed, even if an exception occurs during processing. However, if you always had to repeat such a construct, it would result in confusing code. C# offers a syntax that you can use to guarantee that `Dispose` is automatically called against an object that implements `IDisposable` when its reference goes out of scope. The syntax to do this involves the `using` keyword—though now in a very different context, which has nothing to do with namespaces. The following code generates IL code equivalent to the `try` block just shown:

```
using (ResourceGobbler theInstance = new ResourceGobbler())
{
    // do your processing
}
```

The `using` statement, followed in brackets by a reference variable declaration and instantiation, causes that variable to be scoped to the accompanying statement block. In addition, when that variable goes out of scope, its `Dispose` method will be called automatically, even if an exception occurs. However, if you are already using `try` blocks to catch other exceptions, it is cleaner and avoids additional code indentation if you avoid the `using` statement and simply call `Dispose` in the `finally` clause of the existing `try` block.

> **NOTE** *For some classes, the notion of a* Close *method is more logical than* Dispose, *such as when dealing with files or database connections. In these cases, it is common to implement the* IDisposable *interface and then implement a separate* Close *method that simply calls* Dispose. *This approach provides clarity in the use of your classes and supports the* using *statement provided by C#.*

Implementing IDisposable and a Destructor

The previous sections discussed two alternatives for freeing unmanaged resources used by the classes you create:

➤ The execution of a destructor is enforced by the runtime but is nondeterministic and places an unacceptable overhead on the runtime because of the way garbage collection works.

➤ The IDisposable interface provides a mechanism that enables users of a class to control when resources are freed but requires discipline to ensure that Dispose is called.

In general, the best approach is to implement both mechanisms to gain the benefits of both while overcoming their limitations. You implement IDisposable on the assumption that most programmers will call Dispose correctly, but implement a destructor as a safety mechanism in case Dispose is not called. Here is an example of a dual implementation:

```
using System;

public class ResourceHolder: IDisposable
{

    private bool isDisposed = false;

    public void Dispose()
    {
       Dispose(true);
       GC.SuppressFinalize(this);
    }

    protected virtual void Dispose(bool disposing)
    {
       if (!isDisposed)
       {
          if (disposing)
          {
             // Cleanup managed objects by calling their
             // Dispose() methods.
          }
          // Cleanup unmanaged objects
       }
       isDisposed = true;
    }

    ~ResourceHolder()
    {
       Dispose (false);
    }

    public void SomeMethod()
    {
```

```
        // Ensure object not already disposed before execution of any method
        if(isDisposed)
        {
            throw new ObjectDisposedException("ResourceHolder");
        }

        // method implementation...
    }
}
```

You can see from this code that there is a second `protected` overload of `Dispose` that takes one `bool` parameter—and this is the method that does all the cleaning up. `Dispose(bool)` is called by both the destructor and by `IDisposable.Dispose`. The point of this approach is to ensure that all clean-up code is in one place.

The parameter passed to `Dispose(bool)` indicates whether `Dispose(bool)` has been invoked by the destructor or by `IDisposable.Dispose`—`Dispose(bool)` should not be invoked from anywhere else in your code. The idea is this:

➤ If a consumer calls `IDisposable.Dispose`, that consumer is indicating that all managed and unmanaged resources associated with that object should be cleaned up.

➤ If a destructor has been invoked, all resources still need to be cleaned up. However, in this case, you know that the destructor must have been called by the garbage collector and you should not attempt to access other managed objects because you can no longer be certain of their state. In this situation, the best you can do is clean up the known unmanaged resources and hope that any referenced managed objects also have destructors that will perform their own cleaning up.

The `isDisposed` member variable indicates whether the object has already been disposed of and ensures that you do not try to dispose of member variables more than once. It also allows you to test whether an object has been disposed of before executing any instance methods, as shown in `SomeMethod`. This simplistic approach is not thread-safe and depends on the caller ensuring that only one thread is calling the method concurrently. Requiring a consumer to enforce synchronization is a reasonable assumption and one that is used repeatedly throughout the .NET class libraries (in the `Collection` classes, for example). Threading and synchronization are discussed in Chapter 21, "Threads, Tasks, and Synchronization."

Finally, `IDisposable.Dispose` contains a call to the method `System.GC.SuppressFinalize`. `GC` is the class that represents the garbage collector, and the `SuppressFinalize` method tells the garbage collector that a class no longer needs to have its destructor called. Because your implementation of `Dispose` has already done all the clean up required, there's nothing left for the destructor to do. Calling `SuppressFinalize` means that the garbage collector will treat that object as if it doesn't have a destructor at all.

UNSAFE CODE

As you have just seen, C# is very good at hiding much of the basic memory management from the developer, thanks to the garbage collector and the use of references. However, sometimes you will want direct access to memory. For example, you might want to access a function in an external (non-.NET) DLL that requires a pointer to be passed as a parameter (as many Windows API functions do), or possibly for performance reasons. This section examines the C# facilities that provide direct access to the content of memory.

Accessing Memory Directly with Pointers

Although we are introducing *pointers* as if they were a new topic, in reality pointers are not new at all. You have been using references freely in your code, and a reference is simply a type-safe pointer. You have already seen how variables that represent objects and arrays actually store the memory address of where the corresponding data (the *referent*) is stored. A pointer is simply a variable that stores the address of something else in the same way as a reference. The difference is that C# does not allow you direct access to the address contained in a reference variable. With a reference, the variable is treated syntactically as if it stores the actual content of the referent.

C# references are designed to make the language simpler to use and to prevent you from inadvertently doing something that corrupts the contents of memory. With a pointer, however, the actual memory address is available to you. This gives you a lot of power to perform new kinds of operations. For example, you can add 4 bytes to the address in order to examine or even modify whatever data happens to be stored 4 bytes further in memory.

There are two main reasons for using pointers:

➤ **Backward compatibility**—Despite all the facilities provided by the .NET runtime, it is still possible to call native Windows API functions, and for some operations this may be the only way to accomplish your task. These API functions are generally written in C and often require pointers as parameters. However, in many cases it is possible to write the `DllImport` declaration in a way that avoids use of pointers—for example, by using the `System.IntPtr` class.

➤ **Performance**—On those occasions when speed is of the utmost importance, pointers can provide a route to optimized performance. If you know what you are doing, you can ensure that data is accessed or manipulated in the most efficient way. However, be aware that more often than not, there are other areas of your code where you can likely make the necessary performance improvements without resorting to using pointers. Try using a code profiler to look for the bottlenecks in your code—one is included with Visual Studio.

Low-level memory access has a price. The syntax for using pointers is more complex than that for reference types, and pointers are unquestionably more difficult to use correctly. You need good programming skills and an excellent ability to think carefully and logically about what your code is doing to use pointers successfully. Otherwise, it is very easy to introduce subtle, difficult-to-find bugs into your program when using pointers. For example, it is easy to overwrite other variables, cause stack overflows, access areas of memory that don't store any variables, or even overwrite information about your code that is needed by the .NET runtime, thereby crashing your program.

In addition, if you use pointers your code must be granted a high level of trust by the runtime's code access security mechanism or it will not be allowed to execute. Under the default code access security policy, this is only possible if your code is running on the local machine. If your code must be run from a remote location, such as the Internet, users must grant your code additional permissions for it to work. Unless the users trust you and your code, they are unlikely to grant these permissions. Code access security is discussed in more detail in Chapter 22, "Security."

Despite these issues, pointers remain a very powerful and flexible tool in the writing of efficient code.

> **WARNING** *We strongly advise against using pointers unnecessarily because your code will not only be harder to write and debug, but it will also fail the memory type safety checks imposed by the CLR, which is discussed in Chapter 1, ".NET Architecture."*

Writing Unsafe Code with the unsafe Keyword

As a result of the risks associated with pointers, C# allows the use of pointers only in blocks of code that you have specifically marked for this purpose. The keyword to do this is `unsafe`. You can mark an individual method as being `unsafe` like this:

```
unsafe int GetSomeNumber()
{
    // code that can use pointers
}
```

Any method can be marked as unsafe, regardless of what other modifiers have been applied to it (for example, static methods or virtual methods). In the case of methods, the unsafe modifier applies to the method's parameters, allowing you to use pointers as parameters. You can also mark an entire class or struct as unsafe, which means that all its members are assumed unsafe:

```
unsafe class MyClass
{
    // any method in this class can now use pointers
}
```

Similarly, you can mark a member as unsafe:

```
class MyClass
{
    unsafe int* pX;    // declaration of a pointer field in a class
}
```

Or you can mark a block of code within a method as unsafe:

```
void MyMethod()
{
    // code that doesn't use pointers
    unsafe
    {
        // unsafe code that uses pointers here
    }
    // more 'safe' code that doesn't use pointers
}
```

Note, however, that you cannot mark a local variable by itself as unsafe:

```
int MyMethod()
{
    unsafe int *pX;    // WRONG
}
```

If you want to use an unsafe local variable, you need to declare and use it inside a method or block that is unsafe. There is one more step before you can use pointers. The C# compiler rejects unsafe code unless you tell it that your code includes unsafe blocks. The flag to do this is unsafe. Hence, to compile a file named MySource.cs that contains unsafe blocks (assuming no other compiler options), the command is

```
csc /unsafe MySource.cs
```
or
```
csc -unsafe MySource.cs
```

> **NOTE** *If you are using Visual Studio 2005, 2008, 2010, or 2012 you will also find the option to compile unsafe code in the Build tab of the project properties window.*

Pointer Syntax

After you have marked a block of code as `unsafe`, you can declare a pointer using the following syntax:

```
int* pWidth, pHeight;
double* pResult;
byte*[] pFlags;
```

This code declares four variables: `pWidth` and `pHeight` are pointers to integers, `pResult` is a pointer to a `double`, and `pFlags` is an array of pointers to bytes. It is common practice to use the prefix `p` in front of names of pointer variables to indicate that they are pointers. When used in a variable declaration, the symbol `*` indicates that you are declaring a pointer (that is, something that stores the address of a variable of the specified type).

> **NOTE** *C++ developers should be aware of the syntax difference between C++ and C#. The C# statement* `int* pX, pY;` *corresponds to the C++ statement* `int *pX, *pY;`*. In C#, the * symbol is associated with the type, rather than the variable name.*

When you have declared variables of pointer types, you can use them in the same way as normal variables, but first you need to learn two more operators:

➤ `&` means *take the address of*, and converts a value data type to a pointer—for example `int` to `*int`. This operator is known as the *address operator*.

➤ `*` means *get the content of this address*, and converts a pointer to a value data type—for example, `*float` to `float`. This operator is known as the *indirection operator* (or the *dereference operator*).

You can see from these definitions that `&` and `*` have opposite effects.

> **NOTE** *You might be wondering how it is possible to use the symbols & and * in this manner because these symbols also refer to the operators of bitwise AND (&) and multiplication (*). Actually, it is always possible for both you and the compiler to know what is meant in each case because with the pointer meanings, these symbols always appear as unary operators—they act on only one variable and appear in front of that variable in your code. By contrast, bitwise AND and multiplication are binary operators—they require two operands.*

The following code shows examples of how to use these operators:

```
int x = 10;
int* pX, pY;
pX = &x;
pY = pX;
*pY = 20;
```

You start by declaring an integer, `x`, with the value `10` followed by two pointers to integers, `pX` and `pY`. You then set `pX` to point to `x` (that is, you set the content of `pX` to the address of `x`). Then you assign the value of `pX` to `pY`, so that `pY` also points to `x`. Finally, in the statement `*pY = 20`, you assign the value 20 as the contents of the location pointed to by `pY`—in effect changing `x` to 20 because `pY` happens to point to `x`. Note that there is no particular connection between the variables `pY` and `x`. It is just that at the present time, `pY` happens to point to the memory location at which `x` is held.

To get a better understanding of what is going on, consider that the integer x is stored at memory locations 0x12F8C4 through 0x12F8C7 (1243332 to 1243335 in decimal) on the stack (there are four locations because an int occupies 4 bytes). Because the stack allocates memory downward, this means that the variables pX will be stored at locations 0x12F8C0 to 0x12F8C3, and pY will end up at locations 0x12F8BC to 0x12F8BF. Note that pX and pY also occupy 4 bytes each. That is not because an int occupies 4 bytes, but because on a 32-bit processor you need 4 bytes to store an address. With these addresses, after executing the previous code, the stack will look like Figure 14-5.

> **NOTE** *Although this process is illustrated with integers, which are stored consecutively on the stack on a 32-bit processor, this does not happen for all data types. The reason is because 32-bit processors work best when retrieving data from memory in 4-byte chunks. Memory on such machines tends to be divided into 4-byte blocks, and each block is sometimes known under Windows as a DWORD because this was the name of a 32-bit unsigned int in pre-.NET days. It is most efficient to grab DWORDs from memory—storing data across DWORD boundaries normally results in a hardware performance hit. For this reason, the .NET runtime normally pads out data types so that the memory they occupy is a multiple of 4. For example, a short occupies 2 bytes, but if a short is placed on the stack, the stack pointer will still be decremented by 4, not 2, so the next variable to go on the stack will still start at a DWORD boundary.*

You can declare a pointer to any value type (that is, any of the predefined types uint, int, byte, and so on, or to a struct). However, it is not possible to declare a pointer to a class or an array; this is because doing so could cause problems for the garbage collector. To work properly, the garbage collector needs to know exactly what class instances have been created on the heap, and where they are; but if your code started manipulating classes using pointers, you could very easily corrupt the information on the heap concerning classes that the .NET runtime maintains for the garbage collector. In this context, any data type that the garbage collector can access is known as a *managed type*. Pointers can only be declared as *unmanaged* types because the garbage collector cannot deal with them.

Casting Pointers to Integer Types

Because a pointer really stores an integer that represents an address, you won't be surprised to know that the address in any pointer can be converted to or from any integer type. Pointer-to-integer-type conversions must be explicit. Implicit conversions are not available for such conversions. For example, it is perfectly legitimate to write the following:

0x12F8C4-0x12F8C7	x=20 (=0x14)
0x12F8C0-0x12F8C3	pX=0x12F8C4
0x12F8BC-0x12F8BF	pY=012F8C4

FIGURE 14-5

```
int x = 10;
int* pX, pY;
pX = &x;
pY = pX;
*pY = 20;
uint y = (uint)pX;
int* pD = (int*)y;
```

The address held in the pointer pX is cast to a uint and stored in the variable y. You have then cast y back to an int* and stored it in the new variable pD. Hence, now pD also points to the value of x.

The primary reason for casting a pointer value to an integer type is to display it. The `Console.Write` and `Console.WriteLine` methods do not have any overloads that can take pointers, but they will accept and display pointer values that have been cast to integer types:

```
Console.WriteLine("Address is " + pX);       // wrong -- will give a
                                             // compilation error
Console.WriteLine("Address is " + (uint)pX);    // OK
```

You can cast a pointer to any of the integer types. However, because an address occupies 4 bytes on 32-bit systems, casting a pointer to anything other than a `uint`, `long`, or `ulong` is almost certain to lead to overflow errors. (An `int` causes problems because its range is from roughly –2 billion to 2 billion, whereas an address runs from zero to about 4 billion.) When C# is released for 64-bit processors, an address will occupy 8 bytes. Hence, on such systems, casting a pointer to anything other than `ulong` is likely to lead to overflow errors.

It is also important to be aware that the `checked` keyword does not apply to conversions involving pointers. For such conversions, exceptions will not be raised when overflows occur, even in a `checked` context. The .NET runtime assumes that if you are using pointers, you know what you are doing and are not worried about possible overflows.

Casting Between Pointer Types

You can also explicitly convert between pointers pointing to different types. For example, the following is perfectly legal code:

```
byte aByte = 8;
byte* pByte= &aByte;
double* pDouble = (double*)pByte;
```

However, if you try something like this, be careful. In this example, if you look at the `double` value pointed to by pDouble, you will actually be looking up some memory that contains a `byte` (aByte), combined with some other memory, and treating it as if this area of memory contained a `double`, which will not give you a meaningful value. However, you might want to convert between types to implement the equivalent of a C union, or you might want to cast pointers from other types into pointers to `sbyte` to examine individual bytes of memory.

void Pointers

If you want to maintain a pointer but not specify to what type of data it points, you can declare it as a pointer to a `void`:

```
int* pointerToInt;
void* pointerToVoid;
pointerToVoid = (void*)pointerToInt;
```

The main use of this is if you need to call an API function that requires `void*` parameters. Within the C# language, there isn't a great deal that you can do using `void` pointers. In particular, the compiler will flag an error if you attempt to dereference a `void` pointer using the * operator.

Pointer Arithmetic

It is possible to add or subtract integers to and from pointers. However, the compiler is quite clever about how it arranges this. For example, suppose that you have a pointer to an `int` and you try to add 1 to its value. The compiler will assume that you actually mean you want to look at the memory location following the `int`, and hence it will increase the value by 4 bytes—the size of an `int`. If it is a pointer to a `double`, adding 1 will actually increase the value of the pointer by 8 bytes, the size of a `double`. Only if the pointer points to a byte or sbyte (1 byte each), will adding 1 to the value of the pointer actually change its value by 1.

You can use the operators +, -, +=, -=, ++, and -- with pointers, with the variable on the right side of these operators being a long or ulong.

> **NOTE** *It is not permitted to carry out arithmetic operations on void pointers.*

For example, assume the following definitions:

```
uint u = 3;
byte b = 8;
double d = 10.0;
uint* pUint= &u;          // size of a uint is 4
byte* pByte = &b;         // size of a byte is 1
double* pDouble = &d;     // size of a double is 8
```

Next, assume the addresses to which these pointers point are as follows:

➤   pUint: 1243332

➤   pByte: 1243328

➤   pDouble: 1243320

Then execute this code:

```
++pUint;                 // adds (1*4) = 4 bytes to pUint
pByte -= 3;              // subtracts (3*1) = 3 bytes from pByte
double* pDouble2 = pDouble + 4; // pDouble2 = pDouble + 32 bytes (4*8 bytes)
```

The pointers now contain this:

➤   pUint: 1243336

➤   pByte: 1243325

➤   pDouble2: 1243352

> **NOTE** *The general rule is that adding a number X to a pointer to type T with value P gives the result P + X*(sizeof(T)). If successive values of a given type are stored in successive memory locations, pointer addition works very well, allowing you to move pointers between memory locations. If you are dealing with types such as byte or char, though, with sizes not in multiples of 4, successive values will not, by default, be stored in successive memory locations.*

You can also subtract one pointer from another pointer, if both pointers point to the same data type. In this case, the result is a long whose value is given by the difference between the pointer values divided by the size of the type that they represent:

```
double* pD1 = (double*)1243324;   // note that it is perfectly valid to
                                  // initialize a pointer like this.
double* pD2 = (double*)1243300;
long L = pD1-pD2;                 // gives the result 3 (=24/sizeof(double))
```

The sizeof Operator

This section has been referring to the size of various data types. If you need to use the size of a type in your code, you can use the `sizeof` operator, which takes the name of a data type as a parameter and returns the number of bytes occupied by that type, as shown in this example:

```
int x = sizeof(double);
```

This will set x to the value 8.

The advantage of using `sizeof` is that you don't have to hard-code data type sizes in your code, making your code more portable. For the predefined data types, `sizeof` returns the following values:

```
sizeof(sbyte) = 1;  sizeof(byte) = 1;
sizeof(short) = 2;  sizeof(ushort) = 2;
sizeof(int) = 4;    sizeof(uint) = 4;
sizeof(long) = 8;   sizeof(ulong) = 8;
sizeof(char) = 2;   sizeof(float) = 4;
sizeof(double) = 8; sizeof(bool) = 1;
```

You can also use `sizeof` for structs that you define yourself, although in that case, the result depends on what fields are in the struct. You cannot use `sizeof` for classes.

Pointers to Structs: The Pointer Member Access Operator

Pointers to structs work in exactly the same way as pointers to the predefined value types. There is, however, one condition—the struct must not contain any reference types. This is due to the restriction mentioned earlier that pointers cannot point to any reference types. To avoid this, the compiler will flag an error if you create a pointer to any struct that contains any reference types.

Suppose that you had a struct defined like this:

```
struct MyStruct
{
   public long X;
   public float F;
}
```

You could define a pointer to it as follows:

```
MyStruct* pStruct;
```

Then you could initialize it like this:

```
MyStruct Struct = new MyStruct();
pStruct = &Struct;
```

It is also possible to access member values of a struct through the pointer:

```
(*pStruct).X = 4;
(*pStruct).F = 3.4f;
```

However, this syntax is a bit complex. For this reason, C# defines another operator that enables you to access members of structs through pointers using a simpler syntax. It is known as the *pointer member access operator*, and the symbol is a dash followed by a greater-than sign, so it looks like an arrow: ->.

> **NOTE** C++ *developers will recognize the pointer member access operator because C++* *uses the same symbol for the same purpose.*

Using the pointer member access operator, the previous code can be rewritten like this:

```
pStruct->X = 4;
pStruct->F = 3.4f;
```

You can also directly set up pointers of the appropriate type to point to fields within a struct:

```
long* pL = &(Struct.X);
float* pF = &(Struct.F);
```

or

```
long* pL = &(pStruct->X);
float* pF = &(pStruct->F);
```

Pointers to Class Members

As indicated earlier, it is not possible to create pointers to classes. That is because the garbage collector does not maintain any information about pointers, only about references, so creating pointers to classes could cause garbage collection to not work properly.

However, most classes do contain value type members, and you might want to create pointers to them. This is possible but requires a special syntax. For example, suppose that you rewrite the struct from the previous example as a class:

```
class MyClass
{
    public long X;
    public float F;
}
```

Then you might want to create pointers to its fields, X and F, in the same way as you did earlier. Unfortunately, doing so will produce a compilation error:

```
MyClass myObject = new MyClass();
long* pL = &(myObject.X);    // wrong -- compilation error
float* pF = &(myObject.F);   // wrong -- compilation error
```

Although X and F are unmanaged types, they are embedded in an object, which sits on the heap. During garbage collection, the garbage collector might move MyObject to a new location, which would leave pL and pF pointing to the wrong memory addresses. Because of this, the compiler will not let you assign addresses of members of managed types to pointers in this manner.

The solution is to use the fixed keyword, which tells the garbage collector that there may be pointers referencing members of certain objects, so those objects must not be moved. The syntax for using fixed looks like this if you just want to declare one pointer:

```
MyClass myObject = new MyClass();
fixed (long* pObject = &(myObject.X))
{
    // do something
}
```

You define and initialize the pointer variable in the brackets following the keyword `fixed`. This pointer variable (`pObject` in the example) is scoped to the `fixed` block identified by the curly braces. As a result, the garbage collector knows not to move the `myObject` object while the code inside the `fixed` block is executing.

If you want to declare more than one pointer, you can place multiple `fixed` statements before the same code block:

```
MyClass myObject = new MyClass();
fixed (long* pX = &(myObject.X))
fixed (float* pF = &(myObject.F))
{
    // do something
}
```

You can nest entire `fixed` blocks if you want to fix several pointers for different periods:

```
MyClass myObject = new MyClass();
fixed (long* pX = &(myObject.X))
{
    // do something with pX
    fixed (float* pF = &(myObject.F))
    {
        // do something else with pF
    }
}
```

You can also initialize several variables within the same `fixed` block, if they are of the same type:

```
MyClass myObject = new MyClass();
MyClass myObject2 = new MyClass();
fixed (long* pX = &(myObject.X), pX2 = &(myObject2.X))
{
    // etc.
}
```

In all these cases, it is immaterial whether the various pointers you are declaring point to fields in the same or different objects or to static fields not associated with any class instance.

Pointer Example: PointerPlayground

This section presents an example that uses pointers. The following code is an example named `PointerPlayground`. It does some simple pointer manipulation and displays the results, enabling you to see what is happening in memory and where variables are stored:

```
using System;

namespace PointerPlayground
{
    class MainEntryPoint
    {
        static unsafe void Main()
        {
            int x=10;
            short y = -1;
            byte y2 = 4;
            double z = 1.5;
            int* pX = &x;
            short* pY = &y;
            double* pZ = &z;
```

```
            Console.WriteLine(
               "Address of x is 0x{0:X}, size is {1}, value is {2}",
               (uint)&x, sizeof(int), x);
            Console.WriteLine(
               "Address of y is 0x{0:X}, size is {1}, value is {2}",
               (uint)&y, sizeof(short), y);
            Console.WriteLine(
               "Address of y2 is 0x{0:X}, size is {1}, value is {2}",
               (uint)&y2, sizeof(byte), y2);
            Console.WriteLine(
               "Address of z is 0x{0:X}, size is {1}, value is {2}",
               (uint)&z, sizeof(double), z);
            Console.WriteLine(
               "Address of pX=&x is 0x{0:X}, size is {1}, value is 0x{2:X}",
               (uint)&pX, sizeof(int*), (uint)pX);
            Console.WriteLine(
               "Address of pY=&y is 0x{0:X}, size is {1}, value is 0x{2:X}",
               (uint)&pY, sizeof(short*), (uint)pY);
            Console.WriteLine(
               "Address of pZ=&z is 0x{0:X}, size is {1}, value is 0x{2:X}",
               (uint)&pZ, sizeof(double*), (uint)pZ);

            *pX = 20;
            Console.WriteLine("After setting *pX, x = {0}", x);
            Console.WriteLine("*pX = {0}", *pX);

            pZ = (double*)pX;
            Console.WriteLine("x treated as a double = {0}", *pZ);

            Console.ReadLine();
         }
      }
   }
```

This code declares four value variables:

➤   An int x
➤   A short y
➤   A byte y2
➤   A double z

It also declares pointers to three of these values: pX, pY, and pZ.

Next, you display the value of these variables as well as their size and address. Note that in taking the address of pX, pY, and pZ, you are effectively looking at a pointer *to* a pointer—an address of an address of a value. Also, in accordance with the usual practice when displaying addresses, you have used the {0:X} format specifier in the Console.WriteLine commands to ensure that memory addresses are displayed in hexadecimal format.

Finally, you use the pointer pX to change the value of x to 20 and do some pointer casting to see what happens if you try to treat the content of x as if it were a double.

Compiling and running this code results in the following output. This screen output demonstrates the effects of attempting to compile both with and without the /unsafe flag:

```
csc PointerPlayground.cs
Microsoft (R) Visual C# Compiler version 4.0.30319.17379
for Microsoft(R) .NET Framework 4.5
Copyright (C) Microsoft Corporation. All rights reserved.
```

```
PointerPlayground.cs(7,26): error CS0227: Unsafe code may only appear if
        compiling with /unsafe

csc /unsafe PointerPlayground.cs
Microsoft (R) Visual C# Compiler version 4.0.30319.17379
for Microsoft(R) .NET Framework 4.5
Copyright (C) Microsoft Corporation. All rights reserved.

PointerPlayground
Address of x is 0x12F4B0, size is 4, value is 10
Address of y is 0x12F4AC, size is 2, value is -1
Address of y2 is 0x12F4A8, size is 1, value is 4
Address of z is 0x12F4A0, size is 8, value is 1.5
Address of pX=&x is 0x12F49C, size is 4, value is 0x12F4B0
Address of pY=&y is 0x12F498, size is 4, value is 0x12F4AC
Address of pZ=&z is 0x12F494, size is 4, value is 0x12F4A0
After setting *pX, x = 20
*pX = 20
x treated as a double = 2.86965129997082E-308
```

Checking through these results confirms the description of how the stack operates presented in the "Memory Management Under the Hood" section earlier in this chapter. It allocates successive variables moving downward in memory. Notice how it also confirms that blocks of memory on the stack are always allocated in multiples of 4 bytes. For example, y is a short (of size 2), and has the (decimal) address 1242284, indicating that the memory locations reserved for it are locations 1242284 through 1242287. If the .NET runtime had been strictly packing up variables next to each other, Y would have occupied just two locations, 1242284 and 1242285.

The next example illustrates pointer arithmetic, as well as pointers to structs and class members. This example is named PointerPlayground2. To start, you define a struct named CurrencyStruct, which represents a currency value as dollars and cents. You also define an equivalent class named CurrencyClass:

```
internal struct CurrencyStruct
{
    public long Dollars;
    public byte Cents;

    public override string ToString()
    {
        return "$" + Dollars + "." + Cents;
    }
}

internal class CurrencyClass
{
    public long Dollars;
    public byte Cents;

    public override string ToString()
    {
        return "$" + Dollars + "." + Cents;
    }
}
```

Now that you have your struct and class defined, you can apply some pointers to them. Following is the code for the new example. Because the code is fairly long, we will go through it in detail. You start by displaying the size of CurrencyStruct, creating a couple of CurrencyStruct instances and creating some CurrencyStruct pointers. You use the pAmount pointer to initialize the members of the amount1 CurrencyStruct and then display the addresses of your variables:

```
public static unsafe void Main()
{
    Console.WriteLine(
        "Size of CurrencyStruct struct is " + sizeof(CurrencyStruct));
    CurrencyStruct amount1, amount2;
    CurrencyStruct* pAmount = &amount1;
    long* pDollars = &(pAmount->Dollars);
    byte* pCents = &(pAmount->Cents);

    Console.WriteLine("Address of amount1 is 0x{0:X}", (uint)&amount1);
    Console.WriteLine("Address of amount2 is 0x{0:X}", (uint)&amount2);
    Console.WriteLine("Address of pAmount is 0x{0:X}", (uint)&pAmount);
    Console.WriteLine("Address of pDollars is 0x{0:X}", (uint)&pDollars);
    Console.WriteLine("Address of pCents is 0x{0:X}", (uint)&pCents);
    pAmount->Dollars = 20;
    *pCents = 50;
    Console.WriteLine("amount1 contains " + amount1);
```

Now you do some pointer manipulation that relies on your knowledge of how the stack works. Due to the order in which the variables were declared, you know that amount2 will be stored at an address immediately below amount1. The sizeof(CurrencyStruct) operator returns 16 (as demonstrated in the screen output coming up), so CurrencyStruct occupies a multiple of 4 bytes. Therefore, after you decrement your currency pointer, it points to amount2:

```
--pAmount;    // this should get it to point to amount2
Console.WriteLine("amount2 has address 0x{0:X} and contains {1}",
    (uint)pAmount, *pAmount);
```

Notice that when you call Console.WriteLine, you display the contents of amount2, but you haven't yet initialized it. What is displayed will be random garbage—whatever happened to be stored at that location in memory before execution of the example. There is an important point here: Normally, the C# compiler would prevent you from using an uninitialized variable, but when you start using pointers, it is very easy to circumvent many of the usual compilation checks. In this case, you have done so because the compiler has no way of knowing that you are actually displaying the contents of amount2. Only you know that, because your knowledge of the stack means that you can tell what the effect of decrementing pAmount will be. Once you start doing pointer arithmetic, you will find that you can access all sorts of variables and memory locations that the compiler would usually stop you from accessing, hence the description of pointer arithmetic as unsafe.

Next, you do some pointer arithmetic on your pCents pointer. pCents currently points to amount1.Cents, but the aim here is to get it to point to amount2.Cents, again using pointer operations instead of directly telling the compiler that's what you want to do. To do this, you need to decrement the address pCents contains by sizeof(Currency):

```
// do some clever casting to get pCents to point to cents
// inside amount2
CurrencyStruct* pTempCurrency = (CurrencyStruct*)pCents;
pCents = (byte*) ( --pTempCurrency );
Console.WriteLine("Address of pCents is now 0x{0:X}", (uint)&pCents);
```

Finally, you use the fixed keyword to create some pointers that point to the fields in a class instance and use these pointers to set the value of this instance. Notice that this is also the first time that you have been able to look at the address of an item stored on the heap, rather than the stack:

```
Console.WriteLine("\nNow with classes");
// now try it out with classes
CurrencyClass amount3 = new CurrencyClass();
```

```
      fixed(long* pDollars2 = &(amount3.Dollars))
      fixed(byte* pCents2 = &(amount3.Cents))
      {
         Console.WriteLine(
            "amount3.Dollars has address 0x{0:X}", (uint)pDollars2);
         Console.WriteLine(
            "amount3.Cents has address 0x{0:X}", (uint) pCents2);
         *pDollars2 = -100;
         Console.WriteLine("amount3 contains " + amount3);
      }
```

Compiling and running this code gives output similar to this:

```
csc /unsafe PointerPlayground2.cs
Microsoft (R) Visual C# 2010 Compiler version 4.0.21006.1
Copyright (C) Microsoft Corporation. All rights reserved.

PointerPlayground2
Size of CurrencyStruct struct is 16
Address of amount1 is 0x12F4A4
Address of amount2 is 0x12F494
Address of pAmount is 0x12F490
Address of pDollars is 0x12F48C
Address of pCents is 0x12F488
amount1 contains $20.50
amount2 has address 0x12F494 and contains $0.0
Address of pCents is now 0x12F488

Now with classes
amount3.Dollars has address 0xA64414
amount3.Cents has address 0xA6441C
amount3 contains $-100.0
```

Notice in this output the uninitialized value of amount2 that is displayed, and notice that the size of the
CurrencyStruct struct is 16 — somewhat larger than you would expect given the size of its fields (a long
and a byte should total 9 bytes).

Using Pointers to Optimize Performance

Until now, all the examples have been designed to demonstrate the various things that you can do with
pointers. We have played around with memory in a way that is probably interesting only to people who like
to know what's happening under the hood, but that doesn't really help you write better code. Now you're
going to apply your understanding of pointers and see an example of how judicious use of pointers has a
significant performance benefit.

Creating Stack-Based Arrays

This section explores one of the main areas in which pointers can be useful: creating high-performance,
low-overhead arrays on the stack. As discussed in Chapter 2, C# includes rich support for handling arrays.
Although C# makes it very easy to use both 1-dimensional and rectangular or jagged multidimensional
arrays, it suffers from the disadvantage that these arrays are actually objects; they are instances of System.
Array. This means that the arrays are stored on the heap, with all the overhead that this involves. There
may be occasions when you need to create a short-lived, high-performance array and don't want the
overhead of reference objects. You can do this by using pointers, although as you see in this section, this is
easy only for 1-dimensional arrays.

To create a high-performance array, you need to use a new keyword: `stackalloc`. The `stackalloc` command instructs the .NET runtime to allocate an amount of memory on the stack. When you call `stackalloc`, you need to supply it with two pieces of information:

➤ The type of data you want to store

➤ The number of these data items you need to store

For example, to allocate enough memory to store 10 `decimal` data items, you can write the following:

```
decimal* pDecimals = stackalloc decimal[10];
```

This command simply allocates the stack memory; it does not attempt to initialize the memory to any default value. This is fine for the purpose of this example because you are creating a high-performance array, and initializing values unnecessarily would hurt performance.

Similarly, to store 20 `double` data items, you write this:

```
double* pDoubles = stackalloc double[20];
```

Although this line of code specifies the number of variables to store as a constant, this can equally be a quantity evaluated at runtime. Therefore, you can write the previous example like this:

```
int size;
size = 20;   // or some other value calculated at runtime
double* pDoubles = stackalloc double[size];
```

You can see from these code snippets that the syntax of `stackalloc` is slightly unusual. It is followed immediately by the name of the data type you want to store (which must be a value type) and then by the number of items you need space for, in square brackets. The number of bytes allocated will be this number multiplied by `sizeof(data type)`. The use of square brackets in the preceding code sample suggests an array, which is not too surprising. If you have allocated space for 20 `doubles`, then what you have is an array of 20 `doubles`. The simplest type of array that you can have is a block of memory that stores one element after another (see Figure 14-6).

This diagram also shows the pointer returned by `stackalloc`, which is always a pointer to the allocated data type that points to the top of the newly allocated memory block. To use the memory block, you simply dereference the returned pointer. For example, to allocate space for 20 `doubles` and then set the first element (element 0 of the array) to the value `3.0`, write this:

```
double* pDoubles = stackalloc double[20];
*pDoubles = 3.0;
```

To access the next element of the array, you use pointer arithmetic. As described earlier, if you add 1 to a pointer, its value will be increased by the size of whatever data type it points to. In this case, that's just enough to take you to the next free memory location in the block that you have allocated. Therefore, you can set the second element of the array (element number 1) to the value `8.4`:

```
double* pDoubles = stackalloc double [20];
*pDoubles = 3.0;
*(pDoubles+1) = 8.4;
```

By the same reasoning, you can access the element with index X of the array with the expression `*(pDoubles+X)`.

Effectively, you have a means by which you can access elements of your array, but for general-purpose use, this syntax is too complex. Fortunately, C# defines an alternative syntax using square brackets. C# gives a very precise meaning to square brackets when they are applied to pointers; if the variable p is any pointer type and X is an integer, then the expression p[X] is always interpreted by the compiler as meaning *(p+X). This is true for all pointers, not only those initialized using stackalloc. With this shorthand notation, you now have a very convenient syntax for accessing your array. In fact, it means that you have exactly the same syntax for accessing 1-dimensional, stack-based arrays as you do for accessing heap-based arrays that are represented by the System.Array class:

```
double* pDoubles = stackalloc double [20];
pDoubles[0] = 3.0;   // pDoubles[0] is the same as *pDoubles
pDoubles[1] = 8.4;   // pDoubles[1] is the same as *(pDoubles+1)
```

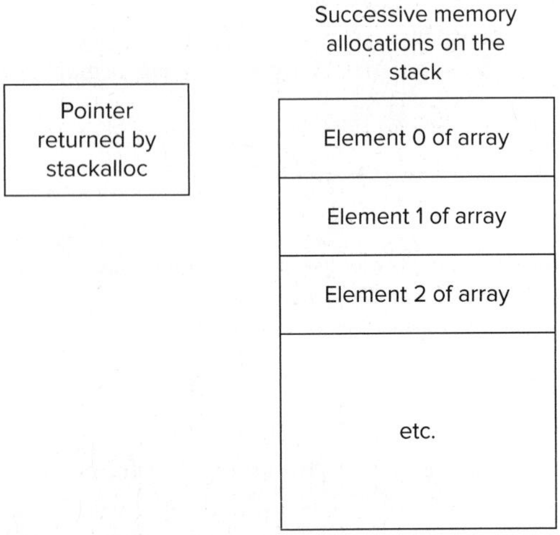

FIGURE 14-6

> **NOTE** *This idea of applying array syntax to pointers is not new. It has been a fundamental part of both the C and the C++ languages ever since those languages were invented. Indeed, C++ developers will recognize the stack-based arrays they can obtain using* stackalloc *as being essentially identical to classic stack-based C and C++ arrays. This syntax and the way it links pointers and arrays is one reason why the C language became popular in the 1970s, and the main reason why the use of pointers became such a popular programming technique in C and C++.*

Although your high-performance array can be accessed in the same way as a normal C# array, a word of caution is in order. The following code in C# raises an exception:

```
double[] myDoubleArray = new double [20];
myDoubleArray[50] = 3.0;
```

The exception occurs because you are trying to access an array using an index that is out of bounds; the index is 50, whereas the maximum allowed value is 19. However, if you declare the equivalent array using stackalloc, there is no object wrapped around the array that can perform bounds checking. Hence, the following code will *not* raise an exception:

```
double* pDoubles = stackalloc double [20];
pDoubles[50] = 3.0;
```

In this code, you allocate enough memory to hold 20 `doubles`. Then you set `sizeof(double)` memory locations, starting at the location given by the start of this memory + `50*sizeof(double)` to hold the double value `3.0`. Unfortunately, that memory location is way outside the area of memory that you have allocated for the doubles. There is no knowing what data might be stored at that address. At best, you may have used some currently unused memory, but it is equally possible that you may have just overwritten some locations in the stack that were being used to store other variables or even the return address from the method currently being executed. Again, you see that the high performance to be gained from pointers comes at a cost; you need to be certain you know what you are doing, or you will get some very strange runtime bugs.

QuickArray Example

Our discussion of pointers ends with a `stackalloc` example called `QuickArray`. In this example, the program simply asks users how many elements they want to be allocated for an array. The code then uses `stackalloc` to allocate an array of `longs` that size. The elements of this array are populated with the squares of the integers starting with `0` and the results are displayed on the console:

```
using System;

namespace QuickArray
{
    internal class Program
    {
        private static unsafe void Main()
        {
            Console.Write("How big an array do you want? \n> ");
            string userInput = Console.ReadLine();
            uint size = uint.Parse(userInput);

            long* pArray = stackalloc long[(int) size];
            for (int i = 0; i < size; i++)
            {
                pArray[i] = i*i;
            }

            for (int i = 0; i < size; i++)
            {
                Console.WriteLine("Element {0} = {1}", i, *(pArray + i));
            }

            Console.ReadLine();
        }
    }
}
```

Here is the output from the `QuickArray` example:

```
How big an array do you want?
> 15
Element 0 = 0
Element 1 = 1
Element 2 = 4
Element 3 = 9
Element 4 = 16
Element 5 = 25
Element 6 = 36
Element 7 = 49
Element 8 = 64
Element 9 = 81
Element 10 = 100
```

```
Element 11 = 121
Element 12 = 144
Element 13 = 169
Element 14 = 196
_
```

SUMMARY

Remember that in order to become a truly proficient C# programmer, you must have a solid understanding of how memory allocation and garbage collection work. This chapter described how the CLR manages and allocates memory on the heap and the stack. It also illustrated how to write classes that free unmanaged resources correctly, and how to use pointers in C#. These are both advanced topics that are poorly understood and often implemented incorrectly by novice programmers.

This chapter should be treated as a companion to what you learn from Chapter 16 on error handling and from Chapter 21 about dealing with threading. The next chapter of this book looks at reflection in C#.

15

Reflection

WHAT'S IN THIS CHAPTER?

➤ Using custom attributes

➤ Inspecting the metadata at runtime using reflection

➤ Building access points from classes that enable reflection

WROX.COM CODE DOWNLOADS FOR THIS CHAPTER

The wrox.com code downloads for this chapter are found at `http://www.wrox.com/remtitle .cgi?isbn=1118314425` on the Download Code tab. The code for this chapter is divided into the following major examples:

➤ LookupWhatsNew

➤ TypeView

➤ VectorClass

➤ WhatsNewAttributes

MANIPULATING AND INSPECTING CODE AT RUNTIME

This chapter focuses on custom attributes and reflection. Custom attributes are mechanisms that enable you to associate custom metadata with program elements. This metadata is created at compile time and embedded in an assembly. *Reflection* is a generic term that describes the capability to inspect and manipulate program elements at runtime. For example, reflection allows you to do the following:

➤ Enumerate the members of a type

➤ Instantiate a new object

➤ Execute the members of an object

➤ Find out information about a type

➤ Find out information about an assembly

➤ Inspect the custom attributes applied to a type

➤ Create and compile a new assembly

This list represents a great deal of functionality and encompasses some of the most powerful and complex capabilities provided by the .NET Framework class library. Because one chapter does not have the space to cover all the capabilities of reflection, it focuses on those elements that you are likely to use most frequently.

To demonstrate custom attributes and reflection, in this chapter you first develop an example based on a company that regularly ships upgrades of its software and wants to have details about these upgrades documented automatically. In the example, you define custom attributes that indicate the date when program elements were last modified, and what changes were made. You then use reflection to develop an application that looks for these attributes in an assembly and can automatically display all the details about what upgrades have been made to the software since a given date.

Another example in this chapter considers an application that reads from or writes to a database and uses custom attributes as a way to mark which classes and properties correspond to which database tables and columns. By reading these attributes from the assembly at runtime, the program can automatically retrieve or write data to the appropriate location in the database, without requiring specific logic for each table or column.

CUSTOM ATTRIBUTES

You have already seen in this book how you can define attributes on various items within your program. These attributes have been defined by Microsoft as part of the .NET Framework class library, and many of them receive special support from the C# compiler. This means that for those particular attributes, the compiler can customize the compilation process in specific ways—for example, laying out a struct in memory according to the details in the `StructLayout` attributes.

The .NET Framework also enables you to define your own attributes. Obviously, these attributes won't have any effect on the compilation process because the compiler has no intrinsic awareness of them. However, these attributes will be emitted as metadata in the compiled assembly when they are applied to program elements.

By itself, this metadata might be useful for documentation purposes, but what makes attributes really powerful is that by using reflection, your code can read this metadata and use it to make decisions at runtime. This means that the custom attributes that you define can directly affect how your code runs. For example, custom attributes can be used to enable declarative code access security checks for custom permission classes, to associate information with program elements that can then be used by testing tools, or when developing extensible frameworks that allow the loading of plug-ins or modules.

Writing Custom Attributes

To understand how to write your own custom attributes, it is useful to know what the compiler does when it encounters an element in your code that has a custom attribute applied to it. To take the database example, suppose that you have a C# property declaration that looks like this:

```
[FieldName("SocialSecurityNumber")]
public string SocialSecurityNumber
{
    get {
        // etc.
```

When the C# compiler recognizes that this property has an attribute applied to it (`FieldName`), it first appends the string `Attribute` to this name, forming the combined name `FieldNameAttribute`. The compiler then searches all the namespaces in its search path (those namespaces that have been mentioned in a `using` statement) for a class with the specified name. Note that if you mark an item with an attribute whose name already ends in the string `Attribute`, the compiler will not add the string to the name a second time; it will leave the attribute name unchanged. Therefore, the preceding code is equivalent to this:

```
[FieldNameAttribute("SocialSecurityNumber")]
public string SocialSecurityNumber
{
    get {
    // etc.
```

The compiler expects to find a class with this name, and it expects this class to be derived directly or indirectly from `System.Attribute`. The compiler also expects that this class contains information governing the use of the attribute. In particular, the attribute class needs to specify the following:

➤ The types of program elements to which the attribute can be applied (classes, structs, properties, methods, and so on)

➤ Whether it is legal for the attribute to be applied more than once to the same program element

➤ Whether the attribute, when applied to a class or interface, is inherited by derived classes and interfaces

➤ The mandatory and optional parameters the attribute takes

If the compiler cannot find a corresponding attribute class, or if it finds one but the way that you have used that attribute does not match the information in the attribute class, the compiler will raise a compilation error. For example, if the attribute class indicates that the attribute can be applied only to classes but you have applied it to a struct definition, a compilation error will occur.

Continuing with the example, assume that you have defined the `FieldName` attribute like this:

```
[AttributeUsage(AttributeTargets.Property,
    AllowMultiple=false,
    Inherited=false)]
public class FieldNameAttribute: Attribute
{
    private string name;
    public FieldNameAttribute(string name)
    {
        this.name = name;
    }
}
```

The following sections discuss each element of this definition.

AttributeUsage Attribute

The first thing to note is that the attribute class itself is marked with an attribute—the `System .AttributeUsage` attribute. This is an attribute defined by Microsoft for which the C# compiler provides special support. (You could argue that `AttributeUsage` isn't an attribute at all; it is more like a meta-attribute, because it applies only to other attributes, not simply to any class.) The primary purpose of `AttributeUsage` is to identify the types of program elements to which your custom attribute can be applied. This information is provided by the first parameter of the `AttributeUsage` attribute. This parameter is mandatory, and it is of an enumerated type, `AttributeTargets`. In the previous example, you have indicated that the `FieldName` attribute can be applied only to properties, which is fine, because that is exactly what you have applied it to in the earlier code fragment. The members of the `AttributeTargets` enumeration are as follows:

➤ `All`

➤ `Assembly`

➤ `Class`

➤ `Constructor`

➤ `Delegate`

➤ `Enum`

- ➤ Event
- ➤ Field
- ➤ GenericParameter (.NET 2.0 and higher only)
- ➤ Interface
- ➤ Method
- ➤ Module
- ➤ Parameter
- ➤ Property
- ➤ ReturnValue
- ➤ Struct

This list identifies all the program elements to which you can apply attributes. Note that when applying the attribute to a program element, you place the attribute in square brackets immediately before the element. However, two values in the preceding list do not correspond to any program element: `Assembly` and `Module`. An attribute can be applied to an assembly or a module as a whole, rather than to an element in your code; in this case the attribute can be placed anywhere in your source code, but it must be prefixed with the `Assembly` or `Module` keyword:

```
[assembly:SomeAssemblyAttribute(Parameters)]
[module:SomeAssemblyAttribute(Parameters)]
```

When indicating the valid target elements of a custom attribute, you can combine these values using the bitwise `OR` operator. For example, if you want to indicate that your `FieldName` attribute can be applied to both properties and fields, you would use the following:

```
[AttributeUsage(AttributeTargets.Property | AttributeTargets.Field,
    AllowMultiple=false,
    Inherited=false)]
public class FieldNameAttribute: Attribute
```

You can also use `AttributeTargets.All` to indicate that your attribute can be applied to all types of program elements. The `AttributeUsage` attribute also contains two other parameters, `AllowMultiple` and `Inherited`. These are specified using the syntax of `<ParameterName>=<ParameterValue>`, instead of simply specifying the values for these parameters. These parameters are optional—you can omit them.

The `AllowMultiple` parameter indicates whether an attribute can be applied more than once to the same item. The fact that it is set to `false` here indicates that the compiler should raise an error if it sees something like this:

```
[FieldName("SocialSecurityNumber")]
[FieldName("NationalInsuranceNumber")]
public string SocialSecurityNumber
{
    // etc.
```

If the `Inherited` parameter is set to `true`, an attribute applied to a class or interface will also automatically be applied to all derived classes or interfaces. If the attribute is applied to a method or property, it will automatically apply to any overrides of that method or property, and so on.

Specifying Attribute Parameters

This section demonstrates how you can specify the parameters that your custom attribute takes. When the compiler encounters a statement such as the following, it examines the parameters passed into the attribute—which is a string—and looks for a constructor for the attribute that takes exactly those parameters:

```
[FieldName("SocialSecurityNumber")]
public string SocialSecurityNumber
{

    // etc.
```

If the compiler finds an appropriate constructor, it emits the specified metadata to the assembly. If the compiler does not find an appropriate constructor, a compilation error occurs. As discussed later in this chapter, reflection involves reading metadata (attributes) from assemblies and instantiating the attribute classes they represent. Because of this, the compiler must ensure that an appropriate constructor exists that will allow the runtime instantiation of the specified attribute.

In the example, you have supplied just one constructor for FieldNameAttribute, and this constructor takes one string parameter. Therefore, when applying the FieldName attribute to a property, you must supply one string as a parameter, as shown in the preceding code.

To allow a choice of what types of parameters should be supplied with an attribute, you can provide different constructor overloads, although normal practice is to supply just one constructor and use properties to define any other optional parameters, as explained next.

Specifying Optional Attribute Parameters

As demonstrated with the AttributeUsage attribute, an alternative syntax enables optional parameters to be added to an attribute. This syntax involves specifying the names and values of the optional parameters. It works through public properties or fields in the attribute class. For example, suppose that you modify the definition of the SocialSecurityNumber property as follows:

```
[FieldName("SocialSecurityNumber", Comment="This is the primary key field")]
public string SocialSecurityNumber
{

    // etc.
```

In this case, the compiler recognizes the <ParameterName>=<ParameterValue> syntax of the second parameter and does not attempt to match this parameter to a FieldNameAttribute constructor. Instead, it looks for a public property or field (although public fields are not considered good programming practice, so normally you will work with properties) of that name that it can use to set the value of this parameter. If you want the previous code to work, you have to add some code to FieldNameAttribute:

```
[AttributeUsage(AttributeTargets.Property,
    AllowMultiple=false,
    Inherited=false)]
public class FieldNameAttribute: Attribute
{
    private string comment;
    public string Comment
    {
      get
      {
        return comment;
      }
      set
      {
        comment = value;
      }
    }

        // etc
}
```

Custom Attribute Example: WhatsNewAttributes

In this section you start developing the example mentioned at the beginning of the chapter. WhatsNewAttributes provides for an attribute that indicates when a program element was last modified. This is a more ambitious code example than many of the others in that it consists of three separate assemblies:

> ➤ WhatsNewAttributes—Contains the definitions of the attributes
>
> ➤ VectorClass—Contains the code to which the attributes have been applied
>
> ➤ LookUpWhatsNew—Contains the project that displays details about items that have changed

Of these, only the LookUpWhatsNew assembly is a console application of the type that you have used up until now. The remaining two assemblies are libraries—they each contain class definitions but no program entry point. For the VectorClass assembly, this means that the entry point and test harness class have been removed from the VectorAsCollection sample, leaving only the Vector class. These classes are represented later in this chapter.

Managing three related assemblies by compiling at the command line is tricky. Although the commands for compiling all these source files are provided separately, you might prefer to edit the code sample (which you can download from the Wrox web site at www.wrox.com) as a combined Visual Studio solution, as discussed in Chapter 17, "Visual Studio 2012." The download includes the required Visual Studio 2012 solution files.

The WhatsNewAttributes Library Assembly

This section starts with the core WhatsNewAttributes assembly. The source code is contained in the file WhatsNewAttributes.cs, which is located in the WhatsNewAttributes project of the WhatsNewAttributes solution in the example code for this chapter. The syntax for this is quite simple. At the command line, you supply the flag target:library to the compiler. To compile WhatsNewAttributes, type the following:

```
csc /target:library WhatsNewAttributes.cs
```

The WhatsNewAttributes.cs file defines two attribute classes, LastModifiedAttribute and Supports WhatsNewAttribute. You use the attribute LastModifiedAttribute to mark when an item was last modified. It takes two mandatory parameters (parameters that are passed to the constructor): the date of the modification and a string containing a description of the changes. One optional parameter named issues (for which a public property exists) can be used to describe any outstanding issues for the item.

In practice, you would probably want this attribute to apply to anything. To keep the code simple, its usage is limited here to classes and methods. You will allow it to be applied more than once to the same item (AllowMultiple=true) because an item might be modified more than once, and each modification has to be marked with a separate attribute instance.

SupportsWhatsNew is a smaller class representing an attribute that doesn't take any parameters. The purpose of this assembly attribute is to mark an assembly for which you are maintaining documentation via the LastModifiedAttribute. This way, the program that examines this assembly later knows that the assembly it is reading is one on which you are actually using your automated documentation process. Here is the complete source code for this part of the example (code file WhatsNewAttributes.cs):

```
using System;

namespace WhatsNewAttributes
{
    [AttributeUsage(
        AttributeTargets.Class | AttributeTargets.Method,
        AllowMultiple=true, Inherited=false)]
    public class LastModifiedAttribute: Attribute
```

```
    {
        private readonly DateTime _dateModified;
        private readonly string _changes;

        public LastModifiedAttribute(string dateModified, string changes)
        {
            dateModified = DateTime.Parse(dateModified);
            _changes = changes;
        }

        public DateTime DateModified
        {
            get { return _dateModified; }
        }

        public string Changes
        {
            get { return _changes; }
        }

        public string Issues { get; set; }
    }

    [AttributeUsage(AttributeTargets.Assembly)]
    public class SupportsWhatsNewAttribute: Attribute
    {
    }
}
```

Based on what has been discussed, this code should be fairly clear. Notice, however, that we have not bothered to supply set accessors to the Changes and DateModified properties. There is no need for these accessors because you are requiring these parameters to be set in the constructor as mandatory parameters. You need the get accessors so that you can read the values of these attributes.

The VectorClass Assembly

To use these attributes, you will be using a modified version of the earlier VectorAsCollection example. Note that you need to reference the WhatsNewAttributes library that you just created. You also need to indicate the corresponding namespace with a using statement so the compiler can recognize the attributes:

```
using System;
using System.Collections;
using System.Text;
using WhatsNewAttributes;

[assembly: SupportsWhatsNew]
```

This code also adds the line that marks the assembly itself with the SupportsWhatsNew attribute.

Now for the code for the Vector class. You are not making any major changes to this class; you only add a couple of LastModified attributes to mark the work that you have done on this class in this chapter. Then Vector is defined as a class instead of a struct to simplify the code (of the next iteration of the example) that displays the attributes. (In the VectorAsCollection example, Vector is a struct, but its enumerator is a class. This means that the next iteration of the example would have had to pick out both classes and structs when looking at the assembly, which would have made the example less straightforward.)

```
namespace VectorClass
{
    [LastModified("14 Feb 2010", "IEnumerable interface implemented " +
        "So Vector can now be treated as a collection")]
```

```
[LastModified("10 Feb 2010", "IFormattable interface implemented " +
    "So Vector now responds to format specifiers N and VE")]
class Vector: IFormattable, IEnumerable
{
    public double x, y, z;

    public Vector(double x, double y, double z)
    {
       this.x = x;
       this.y = y;
       this.z = z;
    }

    [LastModified("10 Feb 2010",
                "Method added in order to provide formatting support")]
    public string ToString(string format, IFormatProvider formatProvider)
    {
       if (format == null)
       {
          return ToString();
       }
```

You also mark the contained `VectorEnumerator` class as new:

```
[LastModified("14 Feb 2010",
             "Class created as part of collection support for Vector")]
private class VectorEnumerator: IEnumerator
{
```

To compile this code from the command line, type the following:

```
csc /target:library /reference:WhatsNewAttributes.dll VectorClass.cs
```

That's as far as you can get with this example for now. You are unable to run anything yet because all you have are two libraries. After taking a look at reflection in the next section, you will develop the final part of the example, in which you look up and display these attributes.

USING REFLECTION

In this section, you take a closer look at the `System.Type` class, which enables you to access information concerning the definition of any data type. You'll also look at the `System.Reflection.Assembly` class, which you can use to access information about an assembly or to load that assembly into your program. Finally, you will combine the code in this section with the code in the previous section to complete the `WhatsNewAttributes` example.

The System.Type Class

So far you have used the `Type` class only to hold the reference to a type as follows:

```
Type t = typeof(double);
```

Although previously referred to as a class, `Type` is an abstract base class. Whenever you instantiate a `Type` object, you are actually instantiating a class derived from `Type`. `Type` has one derived class corresponding to each actual data type, though in general the derived classes simply provide different overloads of the various `Type` methods and properties that return the correct data for the corresponding data type. They do not typically add new methods or properties. In general, there are three common ways to obtain a `Type` reference that refers to any given type.

➤ You can use the C# `typeof` operator as shown in the preceding code. This operator takes the name of the type (not in quotation marks, however) as a parameter.

➤ You can use the `GetType` method, which all classes inherit from `System.Object`:

```
double d = 10;
Type t = d.GetType();
```

`GetType` is called against a variable, rather than taking the name of a type. Note, however, that the `Type` object returned is still associated with only that data type. It does not contain any information that relates to that instance of the type. The `GetType` method can be useful if you have a reference to an object but you are not sure what class that object is actually an instance of.

➤ You can call the static method of the `Type` class, `GetType`:

```
Type t = Type.GetType("System.Double");
```

`Type` is really the gateway to much of the reflection functionality. It implements a huge number of methods and properties—far too many to provide a comprehensive list here. However, the following subsections should give you a good idea of the kinds of things you can do with the `Type` class. Note that the available properties are all read-only; you use `Type` to find out about the data type—you cannot use it to make any modifications to the type!

Type Properties

You can divide the properties implemented by `Type` into three categories. First, a number of properties retrieve the strings containing various names associated with the class, as shown in the following table:

PROPERTY	RETURNS
Name	The name of the data type
FullName	The fully qualified name of the data type (including the namespace name)
Namespace	The name of the namespace in which the data type is defined

Second, it is possible to retrieve references to further type objects that represent related classes, as shown in the following table.

PROPERTY	RETURNS TYPE REFERENCE CORRESPONDING TO
BaseType	The immediate base type of this type
UnderlyingSystemType	The type to which this type maps in the .NET runtime (recall that certain .NET base types actually map to specific predefined types recognized by IL)

A number of Boolean properties indicate whether this type is, for example, a class, an enum, and so on. These properties include `IsAbstract`, `IsArray`, `IsClass`, `IsEnum`, `IsInterface`, `IsPointer`, `IsPrimitive` (one of the predefined primitive data types), `IsPublic`, `IsSealed`, and `IsValueType`. The following example uses a primitive data type:

```
Type intType = typeof(int);
Console.WriteLine(intType.IsAbstract);     // writes false
Console.WriteLine(intType.IsClass);        // writes false
Console.WriteLine(intType.IsEnum);         // writes false
Console.WriteLine(intType.IsPrimitive);    // writes true
Console.WriteLine(intType.IsValueType);    // writes true
```

This example uses the `Vector` class:

```
Type vecType = typeof(Vector);
Console.WriteLine(vecType.IsAbstract);      // writes false
Console.WriteLine(vecType.IsClass);         // writes true
Console.WriteLine(vecType.IsEnum);          // writes false
Console.WriteLine(vecType.IsPrimitive);     // writes false
Console.WriteLine(vecType.IsValueType);     // writes false
```

Finally, you can also retrieve a reference to the assembly in which the type is defined. This is returned as a reference to an instance of the `System.Reflection.Assembly` class, which is examined shortly:

```
Type t = typeof (Vector);
Assembly contai6ningAssembly = new Assembly(t);
```

Methods

Most of the methods of `System.Type` are used to obtain details about the members of the corresponding data type—the constructors, properties, methods, events, and so on. Quite a large number of methods exist, but they all follow the same pattern. For example, two methods retrieve details about the methods of the data type: `GetMethod` and `GetMethods`. `GetMethod()` returns a reference to a `System.Reflection.MethodInfo` object, which contains details about a method. `GetMethods` returns an array of such references. As the names suggest, the difference is that `GetMethods` returns details about all the methods, whereas `GetMethod` returns details about just one method with a specified parameter list. Both methods have overloads that take an extra parameter, a `BindingFlags` enumerated value that indicates which members should be returned—for example, whether to return public members, instance members, static members, and so on.

For example, the simplest overload of `GetMethods` takes no parameters and returns details about all the public methods of the data type:

```
Type t = typeof(double);
MethodInfo[] methods = t.GetMethods();
foreach (MethodInfo nextMethod in methods)
{
    // etc.
        }
```

The member methods of `Type` that follow the same pattern are shown in the following table. Note that plural names return an array.

TYPE OF OBJECT RETURNED	METHOD(S)
ConstructorInfo	GetConstructor(), GetConstructors()
EventInfo	GetEvent(), GetEvents()
FieldInfo	GetField(), GetFields()
MemberInfo	GetMember(), GetMembers(), GetDefaultMembers()
MethodInfo	GetMethod(), GetMethods()
PropertyInfo	GetProperty(), GetProperties()

The `GetMember` and `GetMembers` methods return details about any or all members of the data type, regardless of whether these members are constructors, properties, methods, and so on.

The TypeView Example

This section demonstrates some of the features of the `Type` class with a short example, `TypeView`, which you can use to list the members of a data type. The example demonstrates how to use `TypeView` for a `double`; however, you can swap this type with any other data type just by changing one line of the code in the example. `TypeView` displays far more information than can be displayed in a console window, so we're going to take a break from our normal practice and display the output in a message box. Running `TypeView` for a `double` produces the results shown in Figure 15-1.

The message box displays the name, full name, and namespace of the data type as well as the name of the underlying type and the base type. Next, it simply iterates through all the public instance members of the data type, displaying for each member the declaring type, the type of member (method, field, and so on), and the name of the member. The *declaring type* is the name of the class that actually declares the type member (for example, `System.Double` if it is defined or overridden in `System.Double`, or the name of the relevant base type if the member is simply inherited from a base class).

`TypeView` does not display signatures of methods because you are retrieving details about all public instance members through `MemberInfo` objects, and information about parameters is not available through a `MemberInfo` object. To retrieve that information, you would need references to `MethodInfo` and other more specific objects, which means that you would need to obtain details about each type of member separately.

`TypeView` does display details about all public instance members; but for doubles, the only ones defined are fields and methods. For this example, you will compile `TypeView` as a console application—there is no problem with displaying a message box from a console application. However, because you are using a message box, you need to reference the base class assembly `System.Windows.Forms.dll`, which contains the classes in the `System.Windows.Forms` namespace in which the `MessageBox` class that you will need is defined. The code for `TypeView` is as follows. To begin, you need to add a few `using` statements:

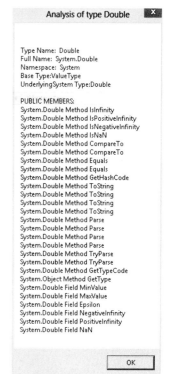

FIGURE 15-1

```
using System;
using System.Reflection;
using System.Text;
using System.Windows.Forms;
```

You need `System.Text` because you will be using a `StringBuilder` object to build up the text to be displayed in the message box, and `System.Windows.Forms` for the message box itself. The entire code is in one class, `MainClass`, which has a couple of `static` methods and one `static` field, a `StringBuilder` instance called `OutputText`, which will be used to build the text to be displayed in the message box. The main method and class declaration look like this:

```
class MainClass
{
    static StringBuilder OutputText = new StringBuilder();

    static void Main()
    {
        // modify this line to retrieve details of any
        // other data type
        Type t = typeof(double);

        AnalyzeType(t);
```

```
            MessageBox.Show(OutputText.ToString(), "Analysis of type "
                                                  + t.Name);
            Console.ReadLine();
    }
```

The `Main` method implementation starts by declaring a `Type` object to represent your chosen data type. You then call a method, `AnalyzeType`, which extracts the information from the `Type` object and uses it to build the output text. Finally, you show the output in a message box. Using the `MessageBox` class is fairly intuitive. You just call its `static` `Show` method, passing it two strings, which will, respectively, be the text in the box and the caption. `AnalyzeType` is where the bulk of the work is done:

```
static void AnalyzeType(Type t)
{
    AddToOutput("Type Name: " + t.Name);
    AddToOutput("Full Name: " + t.FullName);
    AddToOutput("Namespace: " + t.Namespace);

    Type tBase = t.BaseType;

    if (tBase != null)
    {
        AddToOutput("Base Type:" + tBase.Name);
    }

    Type tUnderlyingSystem = t.UnderlyingSystemType;

    if (tUnderlyingSystem != null)
    {
        AddToOutput("UnderlyingSystem Type:" + tUnderlyingSystem.Name);
    }

    AddToOutput("\nPUBLIC MEMBERS:");
    MemberInfo [] Members = t.GetMembers();

    foreach (MemberInfo NextMember in Members)
    {
        AddToOutput(NextMember.DeclaringType + " " +
        NextMember.MemberType + " " + NextMember.Name);
    }
}
```

You implement the `AnalyzeType` method by calling various properties of the `Type` object to get the information you need concerning the type names, then call the `GetMembers` method to get an array of `MemberInfo` objects that you can use to display the details for each member. Note that you use a helper method, `AddToOutput`, to build the text to be displayed in the message box:

```
static void AddToOutput(string Text)
{
    OutputText.Append("\n" + Text);
}
```

Compile the `TypeView` assembly using this command:

```
csc /reference:System.Windows.Forms.dll Program.cs
```

The Assembly Class

The `Assembly` class is defined in the `System.Reflection` namespace and provides access to the metadata for a given assembly. It also contains methods that enable you to load and even execute an assembly—assuming that the assembly is an executable. As with the `Type` class, `Assembly` contains too many methods and properties to cover here, so this section is confined to covering those methods and properties that you need to get started and that you will use to complete the WhatsNewAttributes example.

Before you can do anything with an Assembly instance, you need to load the corresponding assembly into the running process. You can do this with either the static members Assembly.Load or Assembly .LoadFrom. The difference between these methods is that Load takes the name of the assembly, and the runtime searches in a variety of locations in an attempt to locate the assembly. These locations include the local directory and the global assembly cache. LoadFrom takes the full path name of an assembly and does not attempt to find the assembly in any other location:

```
Assembly assembly1 = Assembly.Load("SomeAssembly");
Assembly assembly2 = Assembly.LoadFrom
    (@"C:\My Projects\Software\SomeOtherAssembly");
```

A number of other overloads of both methods exist, which supply additional security information. After you have loaded an assembly, you can use various properties on it to find out, for example, its full name:

```
string name = assembly1.FullName;
```

Getting Details About Types Defined in an Assembly

One nice feature of the Assembly class is that it enables you to obtain details about all the types that are defined in the corresponding assembly. You simply call the Assembly.GetTypes method, which returns an array of System.Type references containing details about all the types. You can then manipulate these Type references as explained in the previous section:

```
Type[] types = theAssembly.GetTypes();

foreach(Type definedType in types)
{
    DoSomethingWith(definedType);
}
```

Getting Details About Custom Attributes

The methods you use to find out which custom attributes are defined on an assembly or type depend on the type of object to which the attribute is attached. If you want to find out what custom attributes are attached to an assembly as a whole, you need to call a static method of the Attribute class, GetCustomAttributes, passing in a reference to the assembly:

> **NOTE** *This is actually quite significant. You may have wondered why, when you defined custom attributes, you had to go to all the trouble of actually writing classes for them, and why Microsoft didn't come up with some simpler syntax. Well, the answer is here. The custom attributes genuinely exist as objects, and when an assembly is loaded you can read in these attribute objects, examine their properties, and call their methods.*

```
Attribute[] definedAttributes =
        Attribute.GetCustomAttributes(assembly1);
        // assembly1 is an Assembly object
```

GetCustomAttributes, which is used to get assembly attributes, has a few overloads. If you call it without specifying any parameters other than an assembly reference, it simply returns all the custom attributes defined for that assembly. You can also call GetCustomAttributes by specifying a second parameter, which is a `Type` object that indicates the attribute class in which you are interested. In this case, `GetCustomAttributes` returns an array consisting of all the attributes present that are of the specified type.

Note that all attributes are retrieved as plain `Attribute` references. If you want to call any of the methods or properties you defined for your custom attributes, you need to cast these references explicitly to the relevant custom attribute classes. You can obtain details about custom attributes that are attached to a given data type by calling another overload of `Assembly.GetCustomAttributes`, this time passing a `Type` reference that describes the type for which you want to retrieve any attached attributes. To obtain attributes that are attached to methods, constructors, fields, and so on, however, you need to call a `GetCustomAttributes` method that is a member of one of the classes `MethodInfo`, `ConstructorInfo`, `FieldInfo`, and so on.

If you expect only a single attribute of a given type, you can call the `GetCustomAttribute` method instead, which returns a single `Attribute` object. You will use `GetCustomAttribute` in the `WhatsNewAttributes` example to find out whether the `SupportsWhatsNew` attribute is present in the assembly. To do this, you call `GetCustomAttribute`, passing in a reference to the `WhatsNewAttributes` assembly, and the type of the `SupportsWhatsNewAttribute` attribute. If this attribute is present, you get an `Attribute` instance. If no instances of it are defined in the assembly, you get `null`. If two or more instances are found, `GetCustomAttribute` throws a `System.Reflection.AmbiguousMatchException`. This is what that call would look like:

```
Attribute supportsAttribute =
        Attribute.GetCustomAttributes(assembly1,
        typeof(SupportsWhatsNewAttribute));
```

Completing the WhatsNewAttributes Example

You now have enough information to complete the `WhatsNewAttributes` example by writing the source code for the final assembly in the sample, the `LookUpWhatsNew` assembly. This part of the application is a console application. However, it needs to reference the other assemblies of `WhatsNewAttributes` and `VectorClass`. Although this is going to be a command-line application, you will follow the previous `TypeView` example in that you actually display the results in a message box because there is a lot of text output—too much to show in a console window screenshot.

The file is called `LookUpWhatsNew.cs`, and the command to compile it is as follows:

```
csc /reference:WhatsNewAttributes.dll /reference:VectorClass.dll LookUpWhatsNew.cs
```

In the source code of this file, you first indicate the namespaces you want to infer. `System.Text` is there because you need to use a `StringBuilder` object again:

```
using System;
using System.Reflection;
using System.Windows.Forms;
using System.Text;
using WhatsNewAttributes;

namespace LookUpWhatsNew
{
```

The class that contains the main program entry point as well as the other methods is `WhatsNewChecker`. All the methods you define are in this class, which also has two static fields—`outputText`, which contains the text as you build it in preparation for writing it to the message box, and `backDateTo`, which stores the date you have selected. All modifications made since this date will be displayed. Normally, you would display a dialog inviting the user to pick this date, but we don't want to get sidetracked into that kind of code. For this reason, `backDateTo` is hard-coded to a value of 1 Feb 2010. You can easily change this date when you download the code:

```
internal class WhatsNewChecker
{
    private static readonly StringBuilder outputText = new StringBuilder(1000);
    private static DateTime backDateTo = new DateTime(2010, 2, 1);

    static void Main()
    {
        Assembly theAssembly = Assembly.Load("VectorClass");
        Attribute supportsAttribute =
            Attribute.GetCustomAttribute(
                theAssembly, typeof(SupportsWhatsNewAttribute));
        string name = theAssembly.FullName;

        AddToMessage("Assembly: " + name);

        if (supportsAttribute == null)
        {
            AddToMessage(
                "This assembly does not support WhatsNew attributes");
            return;
        }
        else
        {
            AddToMessage("Defined Types:");
        }

        Type[] types = theAssembly.GetTypes();

        foreach(Type definedType in types)
            DisplayTypeInfo(definedType);

        MessageBox.Show(outputText.ToString(),
            "What\'s New since " + backDateTo.ToLongDateString());
        Console.ReadLine();
    }
```

The Main method first loads the VectorClass assembly, and then verifies that it is marked with the SupportsWhatsNew attribute. You know VectorClass has the SupportsWhatsNew attribute applied to it because you have only recently compiled it, but this is a check that would be worth making if users were given a choice of which assembly they wanted to check.

Assuming that all is well, you use the Assembly.GetTypes method to get an array of all the types defined in this assembly, and then loop through them. For each one, you call a method, DisplayTypeInfo, which adds the relevant text, including details regarding any instances of LastModifiedAttribute, to the outputText field. Finally, you show the message box with the complete text. The DisplayTypeInfo method looks like this:

```
private static void DisplayTypeInfo(Type type)
{
    // make sure we only pick out classes
    if (!(type.IsClass))
    {
        return;
    }

    AddToMessage("\nclass " + type.Name);

    Attribute [] attribs = Attribute.GetCustomAttributes(type);

    if (attribs.Length == 0)
    {
```

```
            AddToMessage("No changes to this class\n");
      }
      else
      {
         foreach (Attribute attrib in attribs)
         {
            WriteAttributeInfo(attrib);
         }
      }

      MethodInfo [] methods = type.GetMethods();
      AddToMessage("CHANGES TO METHODS OF THIS CLASS:");

      foreach (MethodInfo nextMethod in methods)
      {
         object [] attribs2 =
            nextMethod.GetCustomAttributes(
               typeof(LastModifiedAttribute), false);

         if (attribs2 != null)
         {
            AddToMessage(
               nextMethod.ReturnType + " " + nextMethod.Name + "()");
            foreach (Attribute nextAttrib in attribs2)
            {
               WriteAttributeInfo(nextAttrib);
            }
         }
      }
   }
}
```

Notice that the first thing you do in this method is check whether the Type reference you have been passed actually represents a class. Because, to keep things simple, you have specified that the LastModified attribute can be applied only to classes or member methods, you would be wasting time by doing any processing if the item is not a class (it could be a class, delegate, or enum).

Next, you use the Attribute.GetCustomAttributes method to determine whether this class has any LastModifiedAttribute instances attached to it. If so, you add their details to the output text, using a helper method, WriteAttributeInfo.

Finally, you use the Type.GetMethods method to iterate through all the member methods of this data type, and then do the same with each method as you did for the class—check whether it has any LastModifiedAttribute instances attached to it; if so, you display them using WriteAttributeInfo.

The next bit of code shows the WriteAttributeInfo method, which is responsible for determining what text to display for a given LastModifiedAttribute instance. Note that this method is passed an Attribute reference, so it needs to cast this to a LastModifiedAttribute reference first. After it has done that, it uses the properties that you originally defined for this attribute to retrieve its parameters. It confirms that the date of the attribute is sufficiently recent before actually adding it to the text for display:

```
      private static void WriteAttributeInfo(Attribute attrib)
      {

         LastModifiedAttribute lastModifiedAttrib =
            attrib as LastModifiedAttribute;

         if (lastModifiedAttrib == null)
         {
            return;
         }
```

```
// check that date is in range
DateTime modifiedDate = lastModifiedAttrib.DateModified;

if (modifiedDate < backDateTo)
{
   return;
}

AddToMessage(" MODIFIED: " +
   modifiedDate.ToLongDateString() + ":");
AddToMessage(" " + lastModifiedAttrib.Changes);

if (lastModifiedAttrib.Issues != null)
{
   AddToMessage(" Outstanding issues:" +
      lastModifiedAttrib.Issues);
}
}
}
```

Finally, here is the helper `AddToMessage` method:

```
static void AddToMessage(string message)
{
   outputText.Append("\n" + message);
}
}
}
```

Running this code produces the results shown in Figure 15-2.

Note that when you list the types defined in the `VectorClass` assembly, you actually pick up two classes: `Vector` and the embedded `VectorEnumerator` class. In addition, note that because the `backDateTo` date of 1 Feb is hard-coded in this example, you actually pick up the attributes that are dated 14 Feb (when you added the collection support) but not those dated 10 Feb (when you added the `IFormattable` interface).

SUMMARY

No chapter can cover the entire topic of reflection, an extensive subject worthy of a book of its own. Instead, this chapter illustrated the `Type` and `Assembly` classes, which are the primary entry points through which you can access the extensive capabilities provided by reflection.

In addition, this chapter demonstrated a specific aspect of reflection that you are likely to use more often than any other—the inspection of custom attributes. You learned how to define and apply your own custom attributes, and how to retrieve information about custom attributes at runtime.

FIGURE 15-2

16

Errors and Exceptions

WROX.COM CODE DOWNLOADS FOR THIS CHAPTER

The wrox.com code downloads for this chapter are found at `http://www.wrox.com/remtitle .cgi?isbn=1118314425` on the Download Code tab. The code for this chapter is divided into the following major examples:

➤ Simple Exceptions

➤ Solicit Cold Call

➤ Caller Information

INTRODUCTION

Errors happen, and they are not always caused by the person who coded the application. Sometimes your application will generate an error because of an action that was initiated by the end user of the application, or it might be simply due to the environmental context in which your code is running. In any case, you should anticipate errors occurring in your applications and code accordingly.

The .NET Framework has enhanced the ways in which you deal with errors. C#'s mechanism for handling error conditions enables you to provide custom handling for each type of error condition, as well as to separate the code that identifies errors from the code that handles them.

No matter how good your coding is, your programs should be capable of handling any possible errors that may occur. For example, in the middle of some complex processing of your code, you may discover that it doesn't have permission to read a file; or, while it is sending network requests, the network may go down. In such exceptional situations, it is not enough for a method to simply return an appropriate error code — there might be 15 or 20 nested method calls, so what you really want the program to do is jump back up through all those calls to exit the task completely and take the appropriate counteractions. The C# language has very good facilities to handle this kind of situation, through the mechanism known as *exception handling*.

This chapter covers catching and throwing exceptions in many different scenarios. You will see exception types from different namespaces and their hierarchy, and learn about how to create custom exception types. You will learn different ways to catch exceptions, e.g. how to catch exceptions with the exact exception type or a base class. You will learn how to deal with nested `try` blocks, and how you could catch exceptions that way. For code that should be invoked no matter if an exception occurs or the code continues with any error, you will learn creating `try`/`finally` code blocks.

A new C# 5 feature that helps with handling errors enables the retrieval of caller information such as the file path, the line number, and the member name. This new feature is covered in the chapter as well.

By the end of this chapter, you will have a good grasp of advanced exception handling in your C# applications.

EXCEPTION CLASSES

In C#, an exception is an object created (or *thrown*) when a particular exceptional error condition occurs. This object contains information that should help identify the problem. Although you can create your own exception classes (and you will be doing so later), .NET includes many predefined exception classes — too many to provide a comprehensive list here. The class hierarchy diagram in Figure 16-1 shows a few of these classes to give you a sense of the general pattern. This section provides a quick survey of some of the exceptions available in the .NET base class library.

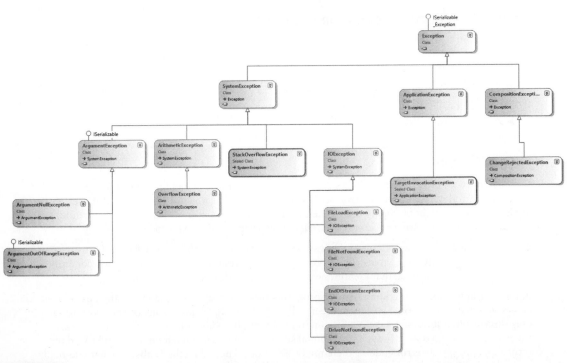

FIGURE 16-1

All the classes in Figure 16-1 are part of the System namespace, except for IOException and CompositionException and the classes derived from these two classes. IOException and its derived classes are part of the namespace System.IO. The System.IO namespace deals with reading from and writing to files. CompositionException and its derived classes are part of the namespace System.ComponentModel .Composition. This namespace deals with dynamically loading parts and components. In general, there is no specific namespace for exceptions. Exception classes should be placed in whatever namespace is appropriate to the classes that can generate them — hence, I/O-related exceptions are in the System.IO namespace. You will find exception classes in quite a few of the base class namespaces.

The generic exception class, System.Exception, is derived from System.Object, as you would expect for a .NET class. In general, you should not throw generic System.Exception objects in your code, because they provide no specifics about the error condition.

Two important classes in the hierarchy are derived from System.Exception:

➤ SystemException — This class is for exceptions that are usually thrown by the .NET runtime or that are considered to be of a generic nature and might be thrown by almost any application. For example, StackOverflowException is thrown by the .NET runtime if it detects that the stack is full. However, you might choose to throw ArgumentException or its subclasses in your own code if you detect that a method has been called with inappropriate arguments. Subclasses of SystemException include classes that represent both fatal and nonfatal errors.

➤ ApplicationException — With the initial design of the .NET Framework, this class was meant to be the base class for custom application exception classes. However, some exception classes that are thrown by the CLR derive from this base class (e.g., TargetInvocationException), and exceptions thrown from applications derive from SystemException (e.g., ArgumentException). Therefore, it's no longer a good practice to derive custom exception types from ApplicationException, as this doesn't offer any benefits. Instead, custom exception classes can derive directly from the Exception base class. Many exception classes in the .NET Framework directly derive from Exception.

Other exception classes that might come in handy include the following:

➤ StackOverflowException — This exception is thrown when the area of memory allocated to the stack is full. A stack overflow can occur if a method continuously calls itself recursively. This is generally a fatal error, because it prevents your application from doing anything apart from terminating (in which case it is unlikely that even the finally block will execute). Trying to handle errors like this yourself is usually pointless; instead, you should have the application gracefully exit.

➤ EndOfStreamException — The usual cause of an EndOfStreamException is an attempt to read past the end of a file. A *stream* represents a flow of data between data sources. Streams are covered in detail in Chapter 26, "Networking."

➤ OverflowException — An example when this occurs is if you attempt to cast an int containing a value of -40 to a uint in a checked context.

The other exception classes shown in Figure 16-1 are not discussed here.

The class hierarchy for exceptions is somewhat unusual in that most of these classes do not add any functionality to their respective base classes. However, in the case of exception handling, the common reason for adding inherited classes is to indicate more specific error conditions. Often, it isn't necessary to override methods or add any new ones (although it is not uncommon to add extra properties that carry extra information about the error condition). For example, you might have a base ArgumentException class intended for method calls whereby inappropriate values are passed in, and an ArgumentNullException class derived from it, which is intended to handle a null argument if passed.

CATCHING EXCEPTIONS

Given that the .NET Framework includes a selection of predefined base class exception objects, this section describes how you use them in your code to trap error conditions. In dealing with possible error conditions in C# code, you will typically divide the relevant part of your program into blocks of three different types:

➤ try blocks encapsulate the code that forms part of the normal operation of your program and that might encounter some serious error conditions.

➤ catch blocks encapsulate the code dealing with the various error conditions that your code might have encountered by working through any of the code in the accompanying try block. This block could also be used for logging errors.

➤ finally blocks encapsulate the code that cleans up any resources or takes any other action that you normally want handled at the end of a try or catch block. It is important to understand that the finally block is executed whether or not an exception is thrown. Because the purpose of the finally block is to contain cleanup code that should always be executed, the compiler will flag an error if you place a return statement inside a finally block. An example of using the finally block is closing any connections that were opened in the try block. Understand that the finally block is completely optional. If your application does not require any cleanup code (such as disposing of or closing any open objects), then there is no need for this block.

The following steps outline how these blocks work together to trap error conditions:

1. The execution flow first enters the try block.

2. If no errors occur in the try block, execution proceeds normally through the block, and when the end of the try block is reached, the flow of execution jumps to the finally block if one is present (Step 5). However, if an error does occur within the try block, execution jumps to a catch block (Step 3).

3. The error condition is handled in the catch block.

4. At the end of the catch block, execution automatically transfers to the finally block if one is present.

5. The finally block is executed (if present).

The C# syntax used to bring all this about looks roughly like this:

```
try
{
   // code for normal execution
}
catch
{
   // error handling
}
finally
{
   // clean up
}
```

Actually, a few variations on this theme exist:

➤ You can omit the finally block because it is optional.

➤ You can also supply as many catch blocks as you want to handle specific types of errors. However, you don't want to get too carried away and have a huge number of catch blocks.

➤ You can omit the catch blocks altogether, in which case the syntax serves not to identify exceptions, but as a way to guarantee that code in the finally block will be executed when execution leaves the try block. This is useful if the try block contains several exit points.

So far so good, but the question that has yet to be answered is this: If the code is running in the try block, how does it know when to switch to the catch block if an error occurs? If an error is detected, the code does something known as *throwing an exception*. In other words, it instantiates an exception object class and throws it:

```
throw new OverflowException();
```

Here, you have instantiated an exception object of the OverflowException class. As soon as the application encounters a throw statement inside a try block, it immediately looks for the catch block associated with that `try` block. If more than one `catch` block is associated with the `try` block, it identifies the correct `catch` block by checking which exception class the `catch` block is associated with. For example, when the `OverflowException` object is thrown, execution jumps to the following `catch` block:

```
catch (OverflowException ex)
{
   // exception handling here
}
```

In other words, the application looks for the `catch` block that indicates a matching exception class instance of the same class (or of a base class).

With this extra information, you can expand the `try` block just demonstrated. Assume, for the sake of argument, that two possible serious errors can occur in the `try` block: an overflow and an array out of bounds. Assume also that your code contains two Boolean variables, `Overflow` and `OutOfBounds`, which indicate whether these conditions exist. You have already seen that a predefined exception class exists to indicate overflow (`OverflowException`); similarly, an `IndexOutOfRangeException` class exists to handle an array that is out of bounds.

Now your `try` block looks like this:

```
try
{
   // code for normal execution

   if (Overflow == true)
   {
      throw new OverflowException();
   }

   // more processing

   if (OutOfBounds == true)
   {
      throw new IndexOutOfRangeException();
   }

   // otherwise continue normal execution
}
catch (OverflowException ex)
{
   // error handling for the overflow error condition
}
catch (IndexOutOfRangeException ex)
{
   // error handling for the index out of range error condition
}
finally
{
   // clean up
}
```

So far, this might not look that much different from what you could have done a long time ago if you ever used the Visual Basic 6 `On Error GoTo` statement (with the possible exception that the different parts of the code are separated). C#, however, provides a far more powerful and flexible mechanism for error handling.

This is because you can have `throw` statements that are nested in several method calls inside the `try` block, but the same `try` block continues to apply even as execution flow enters these other methods. If the application encounters a `throw` statement, it immediately goes back up through all the method calls on the stack, looking for the end of the containing `try` block and the start of the appropriate `catch` block. During this process, all the local variables in the intermediate method calls will correctly go out of scope. This makes the `try...catch` architecture well suited to the situation described at the beginning of this section, whereby the error occurs inside a method call that is nested inside 15 or 20 method calls, and processing has to stop immediately.

As you can probably gather from this discussion, `try` blocks can play a very significant role in controlling the flow of your code's execution. However, it is important to understand that exceptions are intended for exceptional conditions, hence their name. You wouldn't want to use them as a way of controlling when to exit a `do...while` loop.

Implementing Multiple Catch Blocks

The easiest way to see how `try...catch...finally` blocks work in practice is with a couple of examples. The first example is called `SimpleExceptions`. It repeatedly asks the user to type in a number and then displays it. However, for the sake of this example, imagine that the number has to be between 0 and 5; otherwise, the program won't be able to process the number properly. Therefore, you will throw an exception if the user types in anything outside of this range. The program then continues to ask for more numbers for processing until the user simply presses the Enter key without entering anything.

> **NOTE** *You should note that this code does not provide a good example of when to use exception handling, but it shows good practice on how to use exception handling. As their name suggests, exceptions are provided for other than normal circumstances. Users often type in silly things, so this situation doesn't really count. Normally, your program will handle incorrect user input by performing an instant check and asking the user to retype the input if it isn't valid. However, generating exceptional situations is difficult in a small example that you can read through in a few minutes, so we will tolerate this less than ideal one to demonstrate how exceptions work. The examples that follow present more realistic situations.*

The code for `SimpleExceptions` looks like this (code file `SimpleExceptions/Program.cs`):

```csharp
using System;

namespace Wrox.ProCSharp.ErrorsAndExceptions
{
  public class Program
  {
    public static void Main()
    {
      while (true)
      {
        try
        {
          string userInput;

          Console.Write("Input a number between 0 and 5 " +
              "(or just hit return to exit)> ");
          userInput = Console.ReadLine();

          if (userInput == "")
          {
            break;
          }

          int index = Convert.ToInt32(userInput);

          if (index < 0 || index > 5)
          {
            throw new IndexOutOfRangeException("You typed in " + userInput);
          }

          Console.WriteLine("Your number was " + index);
```

```
      }
      catch (IndexOutOfRangeException ex)
      {
        Console.WriteLine("Exception: " +
            "Number should be between 0 and 5. {0}", ex.Message);
      }
      catch (Exception ex)
      {
        Console.WriteLine(
            "An exception was thrown. Message was: {0}", ex.Message);
      }
      finally
      {
        Console.WriteLine("Thank you");
      }
    }
  }
}
```

The core of this code is a `while` loop, which continually uses `Console.ReadLine` to ask for user input. `ReadLine` returns a string, so your first task is to convert it to an `int` using the `System.Convert.ToInt32` method. The `System.Convert` class contains various useful methods to perform data conversions, and it provides an alternative to the `int.Parse` method. In general, `System.Convert` contains methods to perform various type conversions. Recall that the C# compiler resolves `int` to instances of the `System.Int32` base class.

> **NOTE** *It is also worth pointing out that the parameter passed to the* `catch` *block is scoped to that* `catch` *block — which is why you are able to use the same parameter name, ex, in successive* `catch` *blocks in the preceding code.*

In the preceding example, you also check for an empty string, because this is your condition for exiting the `while` loop. Notice how the `break` statement actually breaks right out of the enclosing `try` block as well as the `while` loop because this is valid behavior. Of course, when execution breaks out of the `try` block, the `Console.WriteLine` statement in the `finally` block is executed. Although you just display a greeting here, more commonly you will be doing tasks like closing file handles and calling the `Dispose` method of various objects to perform any cleanup. After the application leaves the `finally` block, it simply carries on executing into the next statement that it would have executed had the `finally` block not been present. In the case of this example, though, you iterate back to the start of the `while` loop and enter the `try` block again (unless the `finally` block was entered as a result of executing the `break` statement in the `while` loop, in which case you simply exit the `while` loop).

Next, you check for your exception condition:

```
if (index < 0 || index > 5)
{
  throw new IndexOutOfRangeException("You typed in " + userInput);
}
```

When throwing an exception, you need to specify what type of exception to throw. Although the class `System.Exception` is available, it is intended only as a base class. It is considered bad programming practice to throw an instance of this class as an exception, because it conveys no information about the nature of the error condition. Instead, the .NET Framework contains many other exception classes that are derived from `System.Exception`. Each of these matches a particular type of exception condition, and you are free to define your own as well. The goal is to provide as much information as possible about the particular exception condition by throwing an instance of a class that matches the particular error condition.

In the preceding example, `System.IndexOutOfRangeException` is the best choice for the circumstances. `IndexOutOfRangeException` has several constructor overloads. The one chosen in the example takes a string describing the error. Alternatively, you might choose to derive your own custom `Exception` object that describes the error condition in the context of your application.

Suppose that the user next types a number that is not between 0 and 5. This will be picked up by the `if` statement and an `IndexOutOfRangeException` object will be instantiated and thrown. At this point, the application will immediately exit the `try` block and hunt for a `catch` block that handles `IndexOutOfRangeException`. The first `catch` block it encounters is this:

```
catch (IndexOutOfRangeException ex)
{
  Console.WriteLine(
      "Exception: Number should be between 0 and 5. {0}", ex.Message);
}
```

Because this `catch` block takes a parameter of the appropriate class, the `catch` block will receive the exception instance and be executed. In this case, you display an error message and the `Exception.Message` property (which corresponds to the string passed to the `IndexOutOfRangeException`'s constructor). After executing this `catch` block, control then switches to the `finally` block, just as if no exception had occurred.

Notice that in the example you have also provided another `catch` block:

```
catch (Exception ex)
{
  Console.WriteLine("An exception was thrown. Message was: {0}",
      ex.Message);
}
```

This `catch` block would also be capable of handling an `IndexOutOfRangeException` if it weren't for the fact that such exceptions will already have been caught by the previous `catch` block. A reference to a base class can also refer to any instances of classes derived from it, and all exceptions are derived from `System .Exception`. This `catch` block isn't executed because the application executes only the first suitable `catch` block it finds from the list of available `catch` blocks. This second `catch` block is here, however, because not only your own code is covered by the `try` block. Inside the block, you actually make three separate calls to methods in the `System` namespace (`Console.ReadLine`, `Console.Write`, and `Convert.ToInt32`), and any of these methods might throw an exception.

If the user types in something that is not a number — say a or `hello` — the `Convert.ToInt32` method will throw an exception of the class `System.FormatException` to indicate that the string passed into `ToInt32` is not in a format that can be converted to an `int`. When this happens, the application will trace back through the method calls, looking for a handler that can handle this exception. Your first `catch` block (the one that takes an `IndexOutOfRangeException`) will not do. The application then looks at the second `catch` block. This one will do because `FormatException` is derived from `Exception`, so a `FormatException` instance can be passed in as a parameter here.

The structure of the example is actually fairly typical of a situation with multiple `catch` blocks. You start with `catch` blocks that are designed to trap very specific error conditions. Then, you finish with more general blocks that cover any errors for which you have not written specific error handlers. Indeed, the order of the `catch` blocks is important. Had you written the previous two blocks in the opposite order, the code would not have compiled, because the second `catch` block is unreachable (the `Exception` `catch` block would catch all exceptions). Therefore, the uppermost `catch` blocks should be the most granular options available, ending with the most general options.

Now that you have analyzed the code for the example, you can run it. The following output illustrates what happens with different inputs and demonstrates both the `IndexOutOfRangeException` and the `FormatException` being thrown:

```
SimpleExceptions
Input a number between 0 and 5 (or just hit return to exit)> 4
Your number was 4
Thank you
Input a number between 0 and 5 (or just hit return to exit)> 0
Your number was 0
Thank you
Input a number between 0 and 5 (or just hit return to exit)> 10
Exception: Number should be between 0 and 5. You typed in 10
Thank you
Input a number between 0 and 5 (or just hit return to exit)> hello
An exception was thrown. Message was: Input string was not in a correct format.
Thank you
Input a number between 0 and 5 (or just hit return to exit)>
Thank you
```

Catching Exceptions from Other Code

The previous example demonstrates the handling of two exceptions. One of them, IndexOutOfRangeException, was thrown by your own code. The other, FormatException, was thrown from inside one of the base classes. It is very common for code in a library to throw an exception if it detects that a problem has occurred, or if one of the methods has been called inappropriately by being passed the wrong parameters. However, library code rarely attempts to catch exceptions; this is regarded as the responsibility of the client code.

Often, exceptions are thrown from the base class libraries while you are debugging. The process of debugging to some extent involves determining why exceptions have been thrown and removing the causes. Your aim should be to ensure that by the time the code is actually shipped, exceptions occur only in very exceptional circumstances; and if possible, are handled appropriately in your code.

System.Exception Properties

The example illustrated the use of only the Message property of the exception object. However, a number of other properties are available in System.Exception, as shown in the following table.

PROPERTY	DESCRIPTION
Data	Enables you to add key/value statements to the exception that can be used to supply extra information about it
HelpLink	A link to a help file that provides more information about the exception
InnerException	If this exception was thrown inside a catch block, then InnerException contains the exception object that sent the code into that catch block.
Message	Text that describes the error condition
Source	The name of the application or object that caused the exception
StackTrace	Provides details about the method calls on the stack (to help track down the method that threw the exception)
TargetSite	A .NET reflection object that describes the method that threw the exception

Of these properties, StackTrace and TargetSite are supplied automatically by the .NET runtime if a stack trace is available. Source will always be filled in by the .NET runtime as the name of the assembly in which the exception was raised (though you might want to modify the property in your code to give more specific information), whereas Data, Message, HelpLink, and InnerException must be filled in by the code that threw the exception, by setting these properties immediately before throwing the exception. For example, the code to throw an exception might look something like this:

```
if (ErrorCondition == true)
{
    var myException = new ClassMyException("Help!!!!");
    myException.Source = "My Application Name";
    myException.HelpLink = "MyHelpFile.txt";
    myException.Data["ErrorDate"] = DateTime.Now;
    myException.Data.Add("AdditionalInfo",
        "Contact Bill from the Blue Team");
    throw myException;
}
```

Here, `ClassMyException` is the name of the particular exception class you are throwing. Note that it is common practice for the names of all exception classes to end with `Exception`. In addition, note that the `Data` property is assigned in two possible ways.

What Happens If an Exception Isn't Handled?

Sometimes an exception might be thrown but there is no `catch` block in your code that is able to handle that kind of exception. The `SimpleExceptions` example can serve to illustrate this. Suppose, for example, that you omitted the `FormatException` and catch-all `catch` blocks, and supplied only the block that traps an `IndexOutOfRangeException`. In that circumstance, what would happen if a `FormatException` were thrown?

The answer is that the .NET runtime would catch it. Later in this section, you learn how you can nest `try` blocks; and in fact, there is already a nested `try` block behind the scenes in the example. The .NET runtime has effectively placed the entire program inside another huge `try` block — it does this for every .NET program. This `try` block has a `catch` handler that can catch any type of exception. If an exception occurs that your code does not handle, the execution flow will simply pass right out of your program and be trapped by this `catch` block in the .NET runtime. However, the results of this probably will not be what you want, as the execution of your code will be terminated promptly. The user will see a dialog that complains that your code has not handled the exception, and that provides any details about the exception the .NET runtime was able to retrieve. At least the exception will have been caught! This is what happened earlier in Chapter 2, "Core C#," in the `Vector` example when the program threw an exception.

In general, if you are writing an executable, try to catch as many exceptions as you reasonably can and handle them in a sensible way. If you are writing a library, it is normally best not to handle exceptions (unless a particular exception represents something wrong in your code that you can handle); instead, assume that the calling code will handle any errors it encounters. However, you may nevertheless want to catch any Microsoft-defined exceptions, so that you can throw your own exception objects that give more specific information to the client code.

Nested try Blocks

One nice feature of exceptions is that you can nest `try` blocks inside each other, like this:

```
try
{
    // Point A
    try
    {
        // Point B
    }
    catch
    {
        // Point C
```

```
      }
      finally
      {
        // clean up
      }
      // Point D
   }
   catch
   {
      // error handling
   }
   finally
   {
      // clean up
   }
```

Although each `try` block is accompanied by only one `catch` block in this example, you could string several `catch` blocks together, too. This section takes a closer look at how nested `try` blocks work.

If an exception is thrown inside the outer `try` block but outside the inner `try` block (points A and D), the situation is no different from any of the scenarios you have seen before: Either the exception is caught by the outer `catch` block and the outer `finally` block is executed, or the `finally` block is executed and the .NET runtime handles the exception.

If an exception is thrown in the inner `try` block (point B), and a suitable inner `catch` block can handle the exception, then, again, you are in familiar territory: The exception is handled there, and the inner `finally` block is executed before execution resumes inside the outer `try` block (at point D).

Now suppose that an exception occurs in the inner `try` block but there *isn't* a suitable inner `catch` block to handle it. This time, the inner `finally` block is executed as usual, but then the .NET runtime has no choice but to leave the entire inner `try` block to search for a suitable exception handler. The next obvious place to look is in the outer `catch` block. If the system finds one here, then that handler will be executed and then the outer `finally` block is executed. If there is no suitable handler here, the search for one continues. In this case, it means the outer `finally` block will be executed, and then, because there are no more `catch` blocks, control will be transferred to the .NET runtime. Note that the code beyond point D in the outer `try` block is not executed at any point.

An even more interesting thing happens when an exception is thrown at point C. If the program is at point C, it must be already processing an exception that was thrown at point B. It is quite legitimate to throw another exception from inside a `catch` block. In this case, the exception is treated as if it had been thrown by the outer `try` block, so flow of execution immediately leaves the inner `catch` block, and executes the inner `finally` block, before the system searches the outer `catch` block for a handler. Similarly, if an exception is thrown in the inner `finally` block, control is immediately transferred to the best appropriate handler, with the search starting at the outer `catch` block.

> **NOTE** *It is perfectly legitimate to throw exceptions from* catch *and* finally *blocks. You can either just throw the same exception again using the* throw *keyword without passing any exception information, or throw a new exception object. Throwing a new exception you can assign the original exception with the constructor of the new object as inner exception. This is covered in "Modifying the Type of Exception" next.*

Although the situation has been shown with just two `try` blocks, the same principles hold no matter how many `try` blocks you nest inside each other. At each stage, the .NET runtime will smoothly transfer control up through the `try` blocks, looking for an appropriate handler. At each stage, as control leaves a `catch` block, any cleanup code in the corresponding `finally` block (if present) will be executed, but no code outside any `finally` block will be run until the correct `catch` handler has been found and run.

The nesting of `try` blocks can also occur between methods themselves. For example, if method A calls method B from within a `try` block, then method B itself has a `try` block within it as well.

Now that you have seen how having nested `try` blocks can work, let's get into scenarios where this is very useful:

➤ To modify the type of exception thrown
➤ To enable different types of exception to be handled in different places in your code

Modifying the Type of Exception

Modifying the type of the exception can be useful when the original exception thrown does not adequately describe the problem. What typically happens is that something — possibly the .NET runtime — throws a fairly low-level exception indicating that something such as an overflow occurred (`OverflowException`), or an argument passed to a method was incorrect (a class derived from `ArgumentException`). However, because of the context in which the exception occurred, you will know that this reveals some other underlying problem (for example, an overflow can only happen at that point in your code because a file you just read contained incorrect data). In that case, the most appropriate thing that your handler for the first exception can do is throw another exception that more accurately describes the problem, thereby enabling another `catch` block further along to deal with it more appropriately. In this case, it can also forward the original exception through a property implemented by `Exception` called `InnerException`, which simply contains a reference to any other related exception that was thrown — in case the ultimate handler routine needs this extra information.

Of course, an exception might occur inside a `catch` block. For example, you might normally read in a configuration file that contains detailed instructions for handling the error but it turns out that this file is not there.

Handling Different Exceptions in Different Places

The second reason to have nested `try` blocks is so that different types of exceptions can be handled at different locations in your code. A good example of this is if you have a loop in which various exception conditions can occur. Some of these might be serious enough that you need to abandon the entire loop, whereas others might be less serious and simply require that you abandon that iteration and move on to the next iteration around the loop. You could achieve this by having a `try` block inside the loop, which handles the less serious error conditions, and an outer `try` block outside the loop, which handles the more serious error conditions. You will see how this works in the next exceptions example.

USER-DEFINED EXCEPTION CLASSES

You are now ready to look at a second example that illustrates exceptions. This example, called `SolicitColdCall`, contains two nested `try` blocks and illustrates the practice of defining your own custom exception classes and throwing another exception from inside a `try` block.

This example assumes that a sales company wants to increase its customer base. The company's sales team is going to phone a list of people to invite them to become customers, a practice known in sales jargon as *cold-calling*. To this end, you have a text file available that contains the names of the people to be cold-called. The file should be in a well-defined format in which the first line contains the number of people in the file and each subsequent line contains the name of the next person. In other words, a correctly formatted file of names might look like this:

```
4
George Washington
Benedict Arnold
John Adams
Thomas Jefferson
```

This version of cold-calling is designed to display the name of the person on the screen (perhaps for the salesperson to read). That is why only the names and not the phone numbers of the individuals are contained in the file.

For this example, your program will ask the user for the name of the file and then simply read it in and display the names of people. That sounds like a simple task, but even so a couple of things can go wrong and require you to abandon the entire procedure:

➤ The user might type the name of a file that does not exist. This will be caught as a `FileNotFound` exception.

➤ The file might not be in the correct format. There are two possible problems here. One, the first line of the file might not be an integer. Two, there might not be as many names in the file as the first line of the file indicates. In both cases, you want to trap this oddity as a custom exception that has been written especially for this purpose, `ColdCallFileFormatException`.

There is something else that can go wrong that, while not causing you to abandon the entire process, will mean you need to abandon a person's name and move on to the next name in the file (and therefore trap it by an inner `try` block). Some people are spies working for rival sales companies, so you obviously do not want to let these people know what you are up to by accidentally phoning one of them. For simplicity, assume that you can identify who the spies are because their names begin with B. Such people should have been screened out when the data file was first prepared, but just in case any have slipped through, you need to check each name in the file and throw a `SalesSpyFoundException` if you detect a sales spy. This, of course, is another custom exception object.

Finally, you will implement this example by coding a class, `ColdCallFileReader`, which maintains the connection to the cold-call file and retrieves data from it. You will code this class in a very safe way, which means that its methods will all throw exceptions if they are called inappropriately — for example, if a method that reads a file is called before the file has even been opened. For this purpose, you will write another exception class, `UnexpectedException`.

Catching the User-Defined Exceptions

Let's start with the `Main` method of the `SolicitColdCall` sample, which catches your user-defined exceptions. Note that you need to call up file-handling classes in the `System.IO` namespace as well as the `System` namespace (code file `SolicitColdCall/Program.cs`):

```
using System;
using System.IO;

namespace Wrox.ProCSharp.ErrorsAndExceptions
{
  class Program
  {
    static void Main()
    {
      Console.Write("Please type in the name of the file " +
          "containing the names of the people to be cold called > ");
      string fileName = Console.ReadLine();
      var peopleToRing = new ColdCallFileReader();

      try
      {
        peopleToRing.Open(fileName);
        for (int i = 0; i < peopleToRing.NPeopleToRing; i++)
        {
          peopleToRing.ProcessNextPerson();
        }
```

```
      Console.WriteLine("All callers processed correctly");
  }
  catch(FileNotFoundException)
  {
      Console.WriteLine("The file {0} does not exist", fileName);
  }
  catch(ColdCallFileFormatException ex)
  {
      Console.WriteLine("The file {0} appears to have been corrupted",
          fileName);
      Console.WriteLine("Details of problem are: {0}", ex.Message);
      if (ex.InnerException != null)
      {
        Console.WriteLine(
            "Inner exception was: {0}", ex.InnerException.Message);
      }
  }
  catch(Exception ex)
  {
      Console.WriteLine("Exception occurred:\n" + ex.Message);
  }
  finally
  {
      peopleToRing.Dispose();
  }
  Console.ReadLine();
    }
  }
```

This code is a little more than just a loop to process people from the file. You start by asking the user for the name of the file. Then you instantiate an object of a class called `ColdCallFileReader`, which is defined shortly. The `ColdCallFileReader` class is the class that handles the file reading. Notice that you do this outside the initial `try` block — that's because the variables that you instantiate here need to be available in the subsequent `catch` and `finally` blocks, and if you declared them inside the `try` block they would go out of scope at the closing curly brace of the `try` block, where the compiler would complain about.

In the `try` block, you open the file (using the `ColdCallFileReader.Open` method) and loop over all the people in it. The `ColdCallFileReader.ProcessNextPerson` method reads in and displays the name of the next person in the file, and the `ColdCallFileReader.NPeopleToRing` property indicates how many people should be in the file (obtained by reading the file's first line). There are three `catch` blocks: one for `FileNotFoundException`, one for `ColdCallFileFormatException`, and one to trap any other .NET exceptions.

In the case of a `FileNotFoundException`, you display a message to that effect. Notice that in this `catch` block, the exception instance is not actually used at all. This `catch` block is used to illustrate the user-friendliness of the application. Exception objects generally contain technical information that is useful for developers, but not the sort of stuff you want to show to end users. Therefore, in this case you create a simpler message of your own.

For the `ColdCallFileFormatException` handler, you have done the opposite, specifying how to obtain fuller technical information, including details about the inner exception, if one is present.

Finally, if you catch any other generic exceptions, you display a user-friendly message, instead of letting any such exceptions fall through to the .NET runtime. Note that here you are not handling any other exceptions not derived from `System.Exception`, because you are not calling directly into non-.NET code.

The `finally` block is there to clean up resources. In this case, that means closing any open file — performed by the `ColdCallFileReader.Dispose` method.

> **NOTE** *C# offers a the* using *statement where the compiler itself creates a* try/finally *block calling the* Dispose *method in the finally block. The using statement is available on objects implementing a Dispose method. You can read the details of the using statement in Chapter 14.*

Throwing the User-Defined Exceptions

Now take a look at the definition of the class that handles the file reading and (potentially) throws your user-defined exceptions: ColdCallFileReader. Because this class maintains an external file connection, you need to ensure that it is disposed of correctly in accordance with the principles outlined for the disposing of objects in Chapter 4, "Inheritance." Therefore, you derive this class from IDisposable.

First, you declare some private fields (code file SolicitColdCall/ColdCallFileReader.cs):

```
public class ColdCallFileReader: IDisposable
{
  private FileStream fs;
  private StreamReader sr;
  private uint nPeopleToRing;
  private bool isDisposed = false;
  private bool isOpen = false;
```

FileStream and StreamReader, both in the System.IO namespace, are the base classes that you will use to read the file. FileStream enables you to connect to the file in the first place, whereas StreamReader is designed to read text files and implements a method, ReadLine, which reads a line of text from a file. You look at StreamReader more closely in Chapter 24, "Manipulating Files and the Registry," which discusses file handling in depth.

The isDisposed field indicates whether the Dispose method has been called. ColdCallFileReader is implemented so that after Dispose has been called, it is not permitted to reopen connections and reuse the object. isOpen is also used for error checking — in this case, checking whether the StreamReader actually connects to an open file.

The process of opening the file and reading in that first line — the one that tells you how many people are in the file — is handled by the Open method:

```
public void Open(string fileName)
{
  if (isDisposed)
    throw new ObjectDisposedException("peopleToRing");

  fs = new FileStream(fileName, FileMode.Open);
  sr = new StreamReader(fs);

  try
  {
    string firstLine = sr.ReadLine();
    nPeopleToRing = uint.Parse(firstLine);
    isOpen = true;
  }
  catch (FormatException ex)
  {
    throw new ColdCallFileFormatException(
        "First line isn\'t an integer", ex);
  }
}
```

The first thing you do in this method (as with all other `ColdCallFileReader` methods) is check whether the client code has inappropriately called it after the object has been disposed of, and if so, throw a pre-defined `ObjectDisposedException` object. The `Open` method checks the `isDisposed` field to determine whether `Dispose` has already been called. Because calling `Dispose` implies that the caller has now finished with this object, you regard it as an error to attempt to open a new file connection if `Dispose` has been called.

Next, the method contains the first of two inner `try` blocks. The purpose of this one is to catch any errors resulting from the first line of the file not containing an integer. If that problem arises, the .NET runtime throws a `FormatException`, which you trap and convert to a more meaningful exception that indicates a problem with the format of the cold-call file. Note that `System.FormatException` is there to indicate format problems with basic data types, not with files, so it's not a particularly useful exception to pass back to the calling routine in this case. The new exception thrown will be trapped by the outermost `try` block. Because no cleanup is needed here, there is no need for a `finally` block.

If everything is fine, you set the `isOpen` field to `true` to indicate that there is now a valid file connection from which data can be read.

The `ProcessNextPerson` method also contains an inner `try` block:

```
public void ProcessNextPerson()
{
    if (isDisposed)
    {
        throw new ObjectDisposedException("peopleToRing");
    }

    if (!isOpen)
    {
        throw new UnexpectedException(
            "Attempted to access coldcall file that is not open");
    }

    try
    {
        string name;
        name = sr.ReadLine();
        if (name == null)
        {
            throw new ColdCallFileFormatException("Not enough names");
        }
        if (name[0] == 'B')
        {
            throw new SalesSpyFoundException(name);
        }
        Console.WriteLine(name);
    }
    catch(SalesSpyFoundException ex)
    {
        Console.WriteLine(ex.Message);
    }
    finally
    {
    }
}
```

Two possible problems exist with the file here (assuming there actually is an open file connection; the `ProcessNextPerson` method checks this first). One, you might read in the next name and discover that it is a sales spy. If that condition occurs, then the exception is trapped by the first `catch` block in this method. Because that exception has been caught here, inside the loop, it means that execution can subsequently continue in the Main method of the program, and the subsequent names in the file will continue to be processed.

A problem might also occur if you try to read the next name and discover that you have already reached the end of the file. The way that the StreamReader object's ReadLine method works is if it has gone past the end of the file, it doesn't throw an exception but simply returns null. Therefore, if you find a null string, you know that the format of the file was incorrect because the number in the first line of the file indicated a larger number of names than were actually present in the file. If that happens, you throw a ColdCallFileFormatException, which will be caught by the outer exception handler (which causes the execution to terminate).

Again, you don't need a finally block here because there is no cleanup to do; however, this time an empty finally block is included just to show that you can do so, if you want.

The example is nearly finished. You have just two more members of ColdCallFileReader to look at: the NPeopleToRing property, which returns the number of people that are supposed to be in the file, and the Dispose method, which closes an open file. Notice that the Dispose method returns only if it has already been called — this is the recommended way of implementing it. It also confirms that there actually is a file stream to close before closing it. This example is shown here to illustrate defensive coding techniques:

```csharp
public uint NPeopleToRing
{
  get
  {
    if (isDisposed)
    {
      throw new ObjectDisposedException("peopleToRing");
    }

    if (!isOpen)
    {
      throw new UnexpectedException(
          "Attempted to access cold-call file that is not open");
    }

    return nPeopleToRing;
  }
}

public void Dispose()
{
  if (isDisposed)
  {
    return;
  }

  isDisposed = true;
  isOpen = false;

  if (fs != null)
  {
    fs.Close();
    fs = null;
  }
}
```

Defining the User-Defined Exception Classes

Finally, you need to define your own three exception classes. Defining your own exception is quite easy because there are rarely any extra methods to add. It is just a case of implementing a constructor to ensure that the base class constructor is called correctly. Here is the full implementation of SalesSpyFoundException (code file SolicitColdCall/SalesSpyFoundException.cs):

```
public class SalesSpyFoundException: Exception
{
  public SalesSpyFoundException(string spyName)
    : base("Sales spy found, with name " + spyName)
  {
  }

  public SalesSpyFoundException(string spyName, Exception innerException)
    : base("Sales spy found with name " + spyName, innerException)
  {
  }
}
```

Notice that it is derived from Exception, as you would expect for a custom exception. In fact, in practice, you would probably have added an intermediate class, something like ColdCallFileException, derived from Exception, and then derived both of your exception classes from this class. This ensures that the handling code has that extra-fine degree of control over which exception handler handles each exception. However, to keep the example simple, you will not do that.

You have done one bit of processing in SalesSpyFoundException. You have assumed that the message passed into its constructor is just the name of the spy found, so you turn this string into a more meaningful error message. You have also provided two constructors: one that simply takes a message, and one that also takes an inner exception as a parameter. When defining your own exception classes, it is best to include, at a minimum, at least these two constructors (although you will not actually be using the second SalesSpyFoundException constructor in this example).

Now for the ColdCallFileFormatException. This follows the same principles as the previous exception, but you don't do any processing on the message (code file SolicitColdCall/ColdCallFileFormatException.cs):

```
public class ColdCallFileFormatException: Exception
{
  public ColdCallFileFormatException(string message)
    : base(message)
  {
  }

  public ColdCallFileFormatException(string message, Exception innerException)
    : base(message, innerException)
  {
  }
}
```

Finally, UnexpectedException, which looks much the same as ColdCallFileFormatException (code file SolicitColdCall/UnexpectedException.cs):

```
public class UnexpectedException: Exception
{
  public UnexpectedException(string message)
    : base(message)
  {
  }
```

```
        public UnexpectedException(string message, Exception innerException)
          : base(message, innerException)
        {
        }
    }
```

Now you are ready to test the program. First, try the `people.txt` file. The contents are defined here:

```
4
George Washington
Benedict Arnold
John Adams
Thomas Jefferson
```

This has four names (which match the number given in the first line of the file), including one spy. Then try the following `people2.txt` file, which has an obvious formatting error:

```
49
George Washington
Benedict Arnold
John Adams
Thomas Jefferson
```

Finally, try the example but specify the name of a file that does not exist, such as `people3.txt`. Running the program three times for the three filenames returns these results:

```
SolicitColdCall
Please type in the name of the file containing the names of the people to be cold
  called > people.txt
George Washington
Sales spy found, with name Benedict Arnold
John Adams
Thomas Jefferson
All callers processed correctly
```

```
SolicitColdCall
Please type in the name of the file containing the names of the people to be cold
  called > people2.txt
George Washington
Sales spy found, with name Benedict Arnold
John Adams
Thomas Jefferson
The file people2.txt appears to have been corrupted.
Details of the problem are: Not enough names
```

```
SolicitColdCall
Please type in the name of the file containing the names of the people to be cold
  called > people3.txt
The file people3.txt does not exist.
```

This application has demonstrated a number of different ways in which you can handle the errors and exceptions that you might find in your own applications.

CALLER INFORMATION

When dealing with errors, it is often helpful to get information about the error where it occurred. C# 5 has a new feature to get this information with the help of attributes and optional parameters. The attributes `CallerLineNumber`, `CallerFilePath`, and `CallerMemberName`, defined within the namespace

`System.Runtime.CompilerServices`, can be applied to parameters. Normally with optional parameters, the compiler assigns the default values on method invocation in case these parameters are not supplied with the call information. With caller information attributes, the compiler doesn't fill in the default values, but instead fills in the line number, file path, and member name.

The `Log` method from the following code snippet demonstrates how to use these attributes. With the implementation, the information is written to the console (code file `CallerInformation/Program.cs`):

```
public void Log([CallerLineNumber] int line = -1,
  [CallerFilePath] string path = null,
  [CallerMemberName] string name = null)
{
  Console.WriteLine((line < 0) ? "No line" : "Line " + line);
  Console.WriteLine((path == null) ? "No file path" : path);
  Console.WriteLine((name == null) ? "No member name" : name);
  Console.WriteLine();
}
```

Let's invoke this method with some different scenarios. In the following `Main` method, the `Log` method is called by using an instance of the `Program` class, within the set accessor of the property, and within a lambda expression. Argument values are not assigned to the method, enabling the compiler to fill it in:

```
static void Main()
{
  var p = new Program();
  p.Log();
  p.SomeProperty = 33;

  Action a1 = () => p.Log();
  a1();
}

private int someProperty;
public int SomeProperty
{
  get { return someProperty; }
  set
  {
    this.Log();
    someProperty = value;
  }
}
```

The result of the running program is shown next. Where the `Log` method was invoked, you can see the line numbers, the filename, and the caller member name. With the `Log` inside the `Main` method, the member name is `Main`. The invocation of the `Log` method inside the set accessor of the property `SomeProperty` shows `SomeProperty`. The Log method inside the lambda expression doesn't show the name of the generated method, but instead the name of the method where the lambda expression was invoked (`Main`), which is of course more useful.

```
Line 11
c:\ProCSharp\ErrorsAndExceptions\CallerInformation\Program.cs
Main

Line 24
c:\ProCSharp\ErrorsAndExceptions\CallerInformation\Program.cs
SomeProperty

Line 14
c:\ProCSharp\ErrorsAndExceptions\CallerInformation\Program.cs
Main
```

Using the `Log` method within a constructor, the caller member name shows `ctor`. With a destructor, the caller member name is `Finalize`, as this is the method name generated.

> **NOTE** *A great use of the* `CallerMemberName` *attribute is with the implementation of the interface* `INotifyPropertyChanged`. *This interface requires the name of the property to be passed with the method implementation. You can see the implementation of this interface in several chapters in this book — for example, Chapter 36, "Business Applications with WPF."*

SUMMARY

This chapter examined the rich mechanism C# provides for dealing with error conditions through exceptions. You are not limited to the generic error codes that could be output from your code; instead, you have the capability to go in and uniquely handle the most granular of error conditions. Sometimes these error conditions are provided to you through the .NET Framework itself; but at other times, you might want to code your own error conditions as illustrated in this chapter. In either case, you have many ways to protect the workflow of your applications from unnecessary and dangerous faults.

The next chapter enables you to implement a lot of what you learned so far in this book within the .NET developer's IDE — Visual Studio 2012.

PART II
Visual Studio

17

Visual Studio 2012

WHAT'S IN THIS CHAPTER?

➤ Using Visual Studio 2012

➤ Architecture tools

➤ Analyzing applications

➤ Testing

➤ Refactoring with Visual Studio

➤ Visual Studio 2012's multi-targeting capabilities

➤ Working with various technologies — WPF, WCF, WF, and more

WROX.COM CODE DOWNLOADS FOR THIS CHAPTER

There are no code downloads for this chapter.

WORKING WITH VISUAL STUDIO 2012

At this point, you should be familiar with the C# language and almost ready to move on to the applied sections of the book, which cover how to use C# to program a variety of applications. Before doing that, however, it's important to understand how you can use Visual Studio and some of the features provided by the .NET environment to get the best from your programs.

This chapter explains what programming in the .NET environment means in practice. It covers Visual Studio, the main development environment in which you will write, compile, debug, and optimize your C# programs, and provides guidelines for writing good applications. Visual Studio is the main IDE used for numerous purposes, including writing ASP.NET applications, Windows Forms, Windows Presentation Foundation (WPF) applications, Windows Store apps accessing WCF services or the Web API, and more.

This chapter also explores what it takes to build applications that are targeted at the .NET Framework 4.5. Working with Visual Studio 2012 enables you to work with the latest application types, such as WPF, the Windows Communication Foundation (WCF), and the Windows Workflow Foundation (WF), directly.

Visual Studio 2012 is a fully integrated development environment. It is designed to make the process of writing your code, debugging it, and compiling it to an assembly to be shipped as easy as possible. This means that Visual Studio gives you a very sophisticated multiple-document–interface application in which you can do just about everything related to developing your code. It offers the following features:

➤ **Text editor**—Using this editor, you can write your C# (as well as Visual Basic 2012, C++, F#, JavaScript, XAML, and SQL) code. This text editor is quite sophisticated. For example, as you type, it automatically lays out your code by indenting lines, matching start and end brackets of code blocks, and color-coding keywords. It also performs some syntax checks as you type, and underlines code that causes compilation errors, also known as design-time debugging. In addition, it features IntelliSense, which automatically displays the names of classes, fields, or methods as you begin to type them. As you start typing parameters to methods, it also shows you the parameter lists for the available over-loads. Figure 17-1 shows the IntelliSense feature in action with one of the .NET base classes, ListBox.

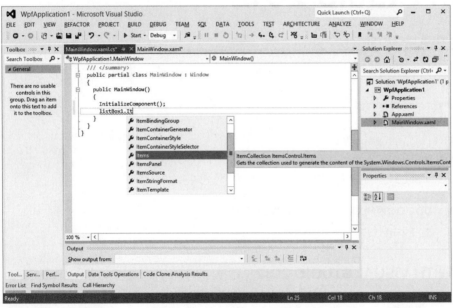

FIGURE 17-1

> **NOTE** *By pressing Ctrl+Space, you can bring back the IntelliSense list box if you need it or if for any reason it is not visible.*

➤ **Design view editor**—This editor enables you to place user-interface and data-access controls in your project; Visual Studio automatically adds the necessary C# code to your source files to instantiate these controls in your project. (This is possible because all .NET controls are instances of particular base classes.)

➤ **Supporting windows**—These windows enable you to view and modify aspects of your project, such as the classes in your source code, as well as the available properties (and their startup values) for Windows Forms and Web Forms classes. You can also use these windows to specify compilation options, such as which assemblies your code needs to reference.

➤ **The capability to compile from within the environment**—Instead of needing to run the C# compiler from the command line, you can simply select a menu option to compile the project, and Visual Studio will call the compiler for you and pass it all the relevant command-line parameters, detailing such things as which assemblies to reference and what type of assembly you want to be emitted (executable or library .dll, for example). If you want, it can also run the compiled executable for you so that you can see whether it runs satisfactorily. You can even choose between different build configurations (for example, a release or debug build).

➤ **Integrated debugger**—It is in the nature of programming that your code will not run correctly the first time you try it. Or the second time. Or the third time. Visual Studio seamlessly links up to a debugger for you, enabling you to set breakpoints and watches on variables from within the environment.

➤ **Integrated MSDN help**—Visual Studio enables you to access the MSDN documentation from within the IDE. For example, if you are not sure of the meaning of a keyword while using the text editor, simply select the keyword and press the F1 key, and Visual Studio will access MSDN to show you related topics. Similarly, if you are not sure what a certain compilation error means, you can bring up the documentation for that error by selecting the error message and pressing F1.

➤ **Access to other programs**—Visual Studio can also access a number of other utilities that enable you to examine and modify aspects of your computer or network, without your having to leave the developer environment. With the tools available, you can check running services and database connections, look directly into your SQL Server tables, and even browse the Web using an Internet Explorer window.

Visual Studio 2010 redesigned the shell to be based on WPF instead of native Windows controls. Visual Studio 2012 has some user interface (UI) changes based on this. In particular, the UI has been enhanced in the way of the Modern UI style. The heart of the Modern UI style is content, rather than chrome. Of course, with a tool like Visual Studio, it's not possible to remove all the chrome; but given the importance of working with the code editor, Visual Studio 2012 provides more space for it. Menus and toolbars are reduced in size; and by default, only one toolbar is opened. Eliminating the borders from menus and toolbars has also provided more space for the editor. In addition, whereas with Visual Studio 2010 a lot of other tool windows were usually open, now many features are integrated within the new Solution Explorer.

Along with the Windows 8 modern-style look, the use of color has been modified. If you worked with previous versions of Visual Studio, you may have occasionally found yourself unable to edit the code, only to realize a few moments later that you were running in the debugger. Now, the status of your project can be clearly identified by its color in the status bar.

Better responsiveness was a major goal for Visual Studio 2012. In previous versions, if you opened a solution consisting of many projects, you could probably take your first coffee break before working with the solution. Now, all the projects are loaded asynchronously; the files that are opened for editing are loaded first, with the others opened later in the background. This way, you can already do some work before loading is done. New asynchronous features can be found in many places. For example, while the IntelliSense thread is starting and loading information, you can already start typing the methods you know in the editor. The assemblies from the Add Reference dialog are searched asynchronously as well. Because more operations are taking place in the background, Visual Studio 2012 is a lot more responsive than previous editions.

For XAML code editing, Visual Studio 2010 and Expression Blend 4 had different editor engines. Now, the teams within Microsoft have been merged, and Visual Studio 2012 includes the same editor as Expression Blend. This is great news if you want to work with both tools, as they now work very similarly. Template editing is also strongly integrated into Visual Studio 2012.

Another improvement to Visual Studio 2012 is search. There are many places where search can be used, and in previous versions of Visual Studio it was not unusual to need a feature but not be able to find the menu entry. Now you can use the Quick Launch located at the top-right corner of the window to search for menus, toolbars, and options (see Figure 17-2). Search functionality is also available from the toolbox, Solution Explorer, the code editor (which you can invoke by selecting Ctrl+F), the assemblies on the Reference Manager, and more.

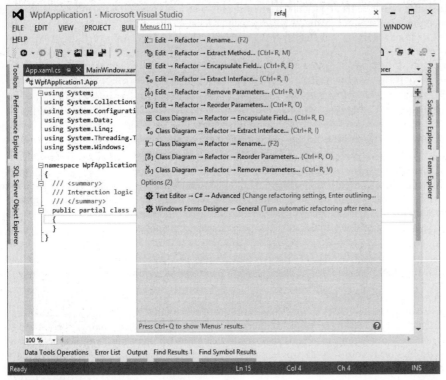

FIGURE 17-2

Project File Changes

When you opened a project with Visual Studio 2010 that was created with Visual Studio 2008, the project file was converted and you could no longer open the project with Visual Studio 2008. This behavior is different in Visual Studio 2012. If you open a Visual Studio 2010 project with Visual Studio 2012, you can still open the file with Visual Studio 2010. This enables a team of members working with different versions of Visual Studio to work with the same project. However, as soon as you change a project to use .NET Framework 4.5, the project can no longer be opened with Visual Studio 2010. Visual Studio 2010 supports only .NET programs from version 2.0 to version 4.0.

If you install Visual Studio 2012 on a Windows 8 system, you can create a completely new category of applications: Windows Store apps. You can create these applications with C# and XAML and use the new Windows Runtime in addition to a subset of the .NET Framework. These applications can run on Windows 8 and Windows RT.

Visual Studio Editions

Visual Studio 2012 is available in several editions. The least expensive is Visual Studio 2012 Express Edition, as this edition is free! Available for purchase are the Professional, Premium, and Ultimate editions. Only the Ultimate edition includes all the features. What you will miss with Visual Studio Professional 2012 is code metrics, a lot of testing tools, checking for code clones, as well as architecting and modeling tools. Exclusive to the Ultimate edition is IntelliTrace, load testing, the Microsoft Fakes framework (unit test isolation), and some architecture tools. This chapter's tour of Visual Studio 2012 includes a few features that are available only with specific editions. For detailed information about the features of each edition of Visual Studio 2012, see http://www.microsoft.com/visualstudio/11/en-us/products/compare.

Visual Studio Settings

When you start Visual Studio the first time, you are asked to select a settings collection that matches your environment, e.g., General Development, Visual Basic, Visual C#, Visual C++, or Web Development. These different settings reflect the different tools historically used for these languages. When writing applications on the Microsoft platform, different tools are used to create Visual Basic, C++, and Web applications. Similarly, Visual Basic, Visual C++, and Visual InterDev have completely different programming environments, with completely different settings and tool options.

After choosing the main category of settings to define keyboard shortcuts, menus, and the position of tool windows, you can change every setting with Tools ⇨ Customize... (toolbars and commands), and Tools ⇨ Options... (here you find the settings for all the tools). You can also reset the settings collection with Tools ⇨ Import and Export Settings..., which invokes a wizard that enables you to select a new default collection of settings (see Figure 17-3).

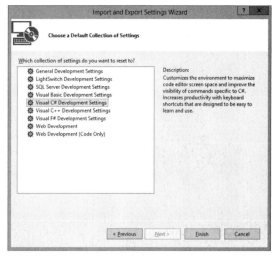

FIGURE 17-3

The following sections walk through the process of creating, coding, and debugging a project, demonstrating what Visual Studio can do to help you at each stage.

CREATING A PROJECT

After installing Visual Studio 2012, you will want to start your first project. With Visual Studio, you rarely start with a blank file and then add C# code, in the way that you have been doing in the previous chapters in this book. (Of course, the option of asking for an empty application project is there if you really do want to start writing your code from scratch or if you are going to create a solution that will contain a number of projects.)

Instead, the idea is that you tell Visual Studio roughly what type of project you want to create, and it will generate the files and C# code that provide a framework for that type of project. You then proceed to add your code to this outline. For example, if you want to build a Windows client application (a WPF application), Visual Studio will start you off with a XAML file and a file containing C# source code that creates a basic form. This form is capable of communicating with Windows and receiving events. It can be maximized, minimized, or resized; all you need to do is add the controls and functionality you want. If your application is intended to be a command-line utility (a console application), Visual Studio gives you a basic namespace, a class, and a `Main` method to get you started.

Last, but hardly least, when you create your project, Visual Studio also sets up the compilation options that you are likely to supply to the C# compiler—whether it is to compile to a command-line application, a library, or a WPF application. It also tells the compiler which base class libraries you will need to reference (a WPF GUI application will need to reference many of the WPF-related libraries; a console application probably will not). Of course, you can modify all these settings as you are editing if necessary.

The first time you start Visual Studio, you are presented with an IDE containing menus, a toolbar, and a page with getting started information, how-to videos, and latest news (see Figure 17-4). The Start Page contains various links to useful web sites and enables you to open existing projects or start a new project altogether.

FIGURE 17-4

In this case, the Start Page reflects what is shown after you have already used Visual Studio 2012, as it includes a list of the most recently edited projects. You can just click one of these projects to open it again.

Multi-Targeting the .NET Framework

Visual Studio 2012 enables you to target the version of the .NET Framework that you want to work with. When you open the New Project dialog, shown in Figure 17-5, a drop-down list in the top area of the dialog displays the available options.

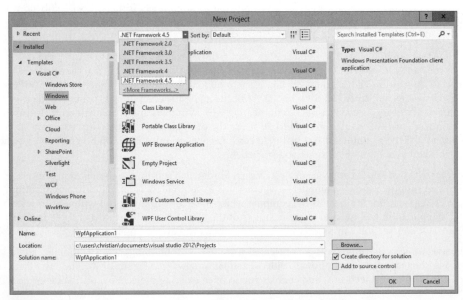

FIGURE 17-5

In this case, you can see that the drop-down list enables you to target the .NET Frameworks 2.0, 3.0, 3.5, 4, and 4.5. You can also install other versions of the .NET Framework by clicking the More Frameworks link. This link opens a web site from which you can download other versions of the .NET Framework, e.g., 4.01, 4.02, and 4.03.

When you use the Upgrade dialog to upgrade a Visual Studio 2010 solution to Visual Studio 2012, it is important to understand that you are only upgrading the solution to *use* Visual Studio 2012; you are not upgrading your project to the .NET Framework 4.5. Your project will stay on the framework version you were using, but now you will be able to use the new Visual Studio 2012 to work on your project.

If you want to change the version of the framework the solution is using, right-click the project and select the properties of the solution. If you are working with an ASP.NET project, you will see the dialog shown in Figure 17-6.

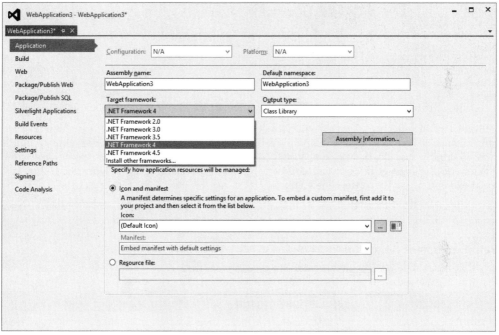

FIGURE 17-6

From this dialog, the Application tab enables you to change the version of the framework that the application is using.

Selecting a Project Type

To create a new project, select File ➪ New Project from the Visual Studio menu. The New Project dialog will appear (see Figure 17-7)—giving you your first inkling of the variety of different projects you can create.

FIGURE 17-7

Using this dialog, you effectively select the initial framework files and code you want Visual Studio to generate for you, the type of compilation options you want, and the compiler you want to compile your code with—either Visual C#, LightSwitch, Visual Basic, Visual C++, Visual F#, or JavaScript. You can immediately see the language integration that Microsoft has promised for .NET at work here! This particular example uses a C# console application.

The following tables describe all the options that are available to you under the Visual C# projects. Note that some other, more specialized C# template projects are available under the Other Projects option.

Using Windows Project Templates

The first table lists the projects available with the Windows category:

IF YOU CHOOSE…	YOU GET THE C# CODE AND COMPILATION OPTIONS TO GENERATE…
Windows Forms Application	A basic empty form that responds to events. Windows Forms wraps native Windows controls and uses pixel-based graphics with GDI+.
WPF Application	A basic empty form that responds to events. Although the project type is similar to the Windows Forms Application project type (Windows Forms), this Windows Application project type enables you to build an XAML-based smart client solution with vector-based graphics and styles.
Console Application	An application that runs at the command-line prompt or in a console window.
Class Library	A .NET class library that can be called up by other code.
Portable Class Library	A class library that can be used by WPF, Silverlight, Windows Phone, and Windows Store apps.
WPF Browser Application	Quite similar to the Windows Application for WPF, this variant enables you to build a XAML-based application that is targeted at the browser. Nowadays, you should think about using a different technology for this, such as a WPF application with ClickOnce, a Silverlight project, or HTML 5.
Empty Project	An empty project that just contains an application configuration file and settings for a console application.

IF YOU CHOOSE...	YOU GET THE C# CODE AND COMPILATION OPTIONS TO GENERATE...
Windows Service	A Windows Service that can automatically start up with Windows and act on behalf of a privileged local system account.
WPF Custom Control Library	A custom control that can be used in a Windows Presentation Foundation application.
WPF User Control Library	A user control library built using Windows Presentation Foundation.
Windows Forms Control Library	A project for creating controls for use in Windows Forms applications.

Using Windows Store Project Templates

The next table covers Windows Store apps. These templates are available only if Visual Studio is installed on Windows 8. The templates are used to create applications that run within the new modern UI on Windows 8 and Windows RT.

IF YOU CHOOSE...	YOU GET THE C# CODE AND COMPILATION OPTIONS TO GENERATE...
Blank App (XAML)	A basic empty Windows Store app with XAML, without styles and other base classes. The styles and base classes can be added easily later.
Grid App (XAML)	A Windows Store app with three pages for displaying groups and item details.
Split App (XAML)	A Windows Store app with two pages for displaying groups and the items of a group.
Class Library (Windows Store apps)	A .NET class library that can be called up by other Windows Store apps programmed with .NET.
Windows Runtime Component	A Windows Runtime class library that can be called up by other Windows Store apps developed with different programming languages (C#, C++, JavaScript).
Unit Test Library (Windows Store apps)	A library that contains unit tests for Windows Store apps.

Using Web Project Templates

With the Web project templates described in the following table, you can create ASP.NET Web applications using either ASP.NET Web Forms or the newer technology, ASP.NET MVC.

IF YOU CHOOSE...	YOU GET THE C# CODE AND COMPILATION OPTIONS TO GENERATE...
ASP.NET Web Forms Application	An ASP.NET Web Forms web application: ASP.NET pages and C# classes that generate the HTML response sent to browsers from those pages. This option includes a base demo application.
ASP.NET MVC 4 (3) Web Application	A project type that enables you to create an ASP.NET MVC application. This template has options for an empty, Internet or Intranet, or Web API project.
ASP.NET Empty Web Application	An ASP.NET-based web application with only a configuration file. This template allows adding Web Forms and Web API items later.
ASP.NET Dynamic Data Entities Web Application	A project type that enables you to build an ASP.NET application that takes advantage of ASP.NET Dynamic Data using LINQ to Entities.
ASP.NET AJAX Server Control	A custom server control for use within ASP.NET applications.
ASP.NET AJAX Control Extender	A project type that enables you to create extenders for ASP.NET server controls.
ASP.NET Server Control	A control that can be called by ASP.NET Web Forms pages to generate the HTML code that provides the appearance when displayed in the browser.

Using WCF Project Templates

To create a Windows Communication Foundation (WCF) application that enables communication between the client and server, you can select from the following WCF project templates.

IF YOU CHOOSE...	YOU GET THE C# CODE AND COMPILATION OPTIONS TO GENERATE...
WCF Service Library	A library that contains a sample service contract and implementation, as well as the configuration. The project is configured to start a WCF service host that hosts the service and a test client application.
WCF Service Application	A Web project that contains a WCF contract and service implementation.
WCF Workflow Service Application	A Web project that hosts a WCF service with the Workflow runtime.
Syndication Service Library	A WCF service library with a WCF contract and implementation that hosts RSS or ATOM feeds.

Workflow Project Templates

This table describes the project templates available for creating Windows Workflow Foundation (WF) projects.

IF YOU CHOOSE...	YOU GET THE C# CODE AND COMPILATION OPTIONS TO GENERATE...
Workflow Console Application	A Windows Workflow Foundation executable that hosts a workflow.
WCF Workflow Service Application	A Web project that hosts a WCF service with the Workflow runtime.
Activity Library	A workflow activity library that can be used with workflows.
Activity Designer Library	A library that is used to create XAML user interfaces for activities to show and configure activities in the workflow designer.

This is not a full list of the Visual Studio 2012 project templates, but it reflects some of the most commonly used templates. The main additions to this version of Visual Studio are the Windows Store project templates. These new capabilities are covered in other chapters later in this book. Be sure to look at Chapter 31, "Windows Runtime", and Chapter 38, "Windows Store Apps" in particular. You can also find new project templates online using the search capability available through the New Project dialog.

EXPLORING AND CODING A PROJECT

This section looks at the features that Visual Studio provides to help you add and explore code with your project. You will learn about using the Solution Explorer to explore files and code, use features from the editor such as IntelliSense and code snippets, and explore other windows such as the Properties window and the Document Outline.

Solution Explorer

After creating a project, the most important tool you will use besides the code editor is the *Solution Explorer*. With this tool you can navigate through all files and items of your project, and see all the classes and members of classes. The Solution Explorer has been greatly enhanced in Visual Studio 2012.

> **NOTE** *When running a console application from within Visual Studio, there's a common misconception that it's necessary to have a* `Console.ReadLine` *method at the last line of the* `Main` *method to keep the console window open. That's not the case. You can start the application with Debug ➪ Start without Debugging (or press Ctrl+F5) instead of Debug ➪ Start Debugging (or F5). This keeps the window open until a key is pressed. Using F5 to start the application makes sense if breakpoints are set, and then Visual Studio halts at the breakpoints anyway.*

Working with Projects and Solutions

The Solution Explorer displays your projects and solutions. It's important to understand the distinction between these:

➤ A *project* is a set of all the source-code files and resources that will compile into a single assembly (or in some cases, a single module). For example, a project might be a class library or a Windows GUI application.

➤ A *solution* is the set of all the projects that make up a particular software package (application).

To understand this distinction, consider what happens when you ship a project, which consists of more than one assembly. For example, you might have a user interface, custom controls, and other components that ship as libraries of parts of the application. You might even have a different user interface for administrators, and a service that is called across the network. Each of these parts of the application might be contained in a separate assembly, and hence they are regarded by Visual Studio as separate projects. However, it is quite likely that you will be coding these projects in parallel and in conjunction with one another. Thus, it is quite useful to be able to edit them all as one single unit in Visual Studio. Visual Studio enables this by regarding all the projects as forming one solution, and treating the solution as the unit that it reads in and allows you to work on.

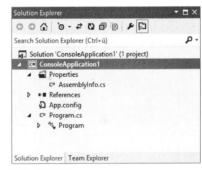

FIGURE 17-8

Up until now, this chapter has been loosely talking about creating a console project. In fact, in the example you are working on, Visual Studio has actually created a solution for you—although this particular solution contains just one project. You can see this scenario reflected in the Solution Explorer (see Figure 17-8), which contains a tree structure that defines your solution.

In this case, the project contains your source file, `Program.cs`, as well as another C# source file, `AssemblyInfo.cs` (found in the `Properties` folder), which enables you to provide information that describes the assembly and specify versioning information. (You look at this file in detail in Chapter 19, "Assemblies.") The Solution Explorer also indicates the assemblies that your project references. You can see this by expanding the `References` folder in the Solution Explorer.

If you have not changed any of the default settings in Visual Studio, you will probably find the Solution Explorer in the top-right corner of your screen. If you cannot see it, just go to the View menu and select Solution Explorer.

The solution is described by a file with the extension `.sln`—in this example, it is `ConsoleApplication1.sln`. The solution file is a text file that contains information about all the projects contained within the solution, as well as global items that can be used with all contained projects.

The C# project is described by a file with the extension `.csproj`—in this example, it is `ConsoleApplication1.csproj`. This is an XML file that you can open directly from within Solution Explorer. However, to do this, you need to unload the project first, which you can do by clicking on the project name and selecting Unload Project in the context menu. After the project is unloaded, the context menu contains the entry Edit `ConsoleApplication1.csproj`, from which you can directly access the XML code.

> ### REVEALING HIDDEN FILES
>
> By default, Solution Explorer hides some files. By clicking the button Show All Files on the Solution Explorer toolbar, you can display all hidden files. For example, the bin and obj directories store compiled and intermediate files. Subfolders of obj hold various temporary or intermediate files; subfolders of bin hold the compiled assemblies.

Adding Projects to a Solution

As you work through the following sections, you will see how Visual Studio works with Windows desktop applications and console applications. To that end, you create a Windows project called BasicForm that you will add to your current solution, ConsoleApplication1.

> **NOTE** *Doing this means that you will end up with a solution containing a WPF application and a console application. That is not a very common scenario—you are more likely to have one application and a number of libraries—but it enables you to see more code! You might, however, create a solution like this if, for example, you are writing a utility that you want to run either as a WPF application or as a command-line utility.*

You can create the new project in several ways. One way is to select New ⇨ Project from the File menu (as you have done already) or you can select Add ⇨ New Project from the File menu. Selecting Add ⇨ New Project from the File menu brings up the familiar Add New Project dialog; as shown in Figure 17-9, however, Visual Studio wants to create the new project in the preexisting ConsoleApplication1 project location.

FIGURE 17-9

If you select this option, a new project is added, so the ConsoleApplication1 solution now contains a console application and a WPF application.

> **NOTE** *In accordance with Visual Studio's language independence, the new project does not need to be a C# project. It is perfectly acceptable to put a C# project, a Visual Basic project, and a C++ project in the same solution. We will stick with C# here because this is a C# book!*

Of course, this means that `ConsoleApplication1` is not really an appropriate name for the solution anymore. To change the name, you can right-click the name of the solution and select Rename from the context menu. Call the new solution `DemoSolution`. The Solution Explorer window should now look like Figure 17-10.

As you can see, Visual Studio has made your newly added WPF project automatically reference some of the extra base classes that are important for WPF functionality.

Note that if you look in Windows Explorer, the name of the solution file has changed to **DemoSolution.sln**. In general, if you want to rename any files, the Solution Explorer window is the best place to do so, because Visual Studio will then automatically update any references to that file in the other project files. If you rename files using only Windows Explorer, you might break the solution because Visual Studio will not be able to locate all the files it needs to read into the IDE. As a result, you will need to manually edit the project and solution files to update the file references.

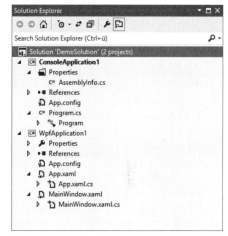

FIGURE 17-10

Setting the Startup Project

Bear in mind that if you have multiple projects in a solution, you need to configure which one should run as the startup project. You can also configure multiple projects to start simultaneously. There are a lot of ways to do this. After selecting a project in the Solution Explorer, the context menu offers a Set as Startup Project option, which enables one startup project at a time. You can also use the context menu Debug ➪ Start new instance to start one project after the other. To simultaneously start more than one project, click the solution in the Solution Explorer and select the context menu Set Startup Projects. This opens the dialog shown in Figure 17-11. After you check Multiple startup projects, you can define what projects should be started.

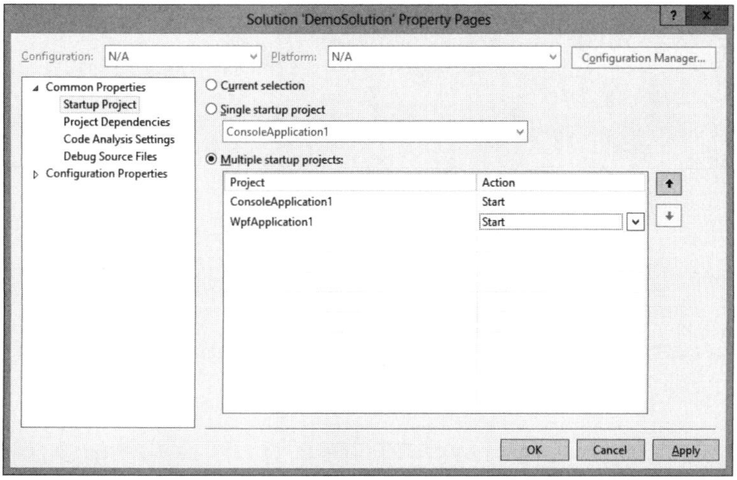

FIGURE 17-11

Discovering Types and Members

A WPF application contains a lot more initial code than a console application when Visual Studio first creates it. That is because creating a window is an intrinsically more complex process. Chapter 35, "Core WPF," discusses the code for a WPF application in detail. For now, have a look at the XAML code in `MainWindow.xaml`, and in the C# source code `MainWindow.xaml.cs`. There's also some hidden generated C# code. Iterating through the tree in the Solution Explorer, below `MainWindow.xaml.cs` you can find the class `MainWindow`. With all the code files, the Solution Explorer shows the types within that file.

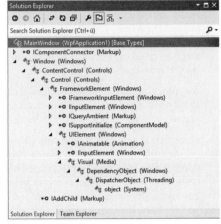

Within the type `MainWindow` you can see the members of the class. `_contentLoaded` is a field of type `bool`. Clicking on this field opens the file `MainWindow.g.i.cs`. This file—a part of the `MainWindow` class—is generated by the designer and contains initialization code.

Being able to view the classes, methods, properties, events, and fields within the Solution Explorer is new with Visual Studio 2012 and reduces the need to use the Class View tool.

FIGURE 17-12

Using Scopes

Setting scopes allows you to focus on a specific part of the solution. The list of items shown by the Solution Explorer can grow really huge. For example, opening the context menu of a type enables you to select the base type from the menu Base Types. Here you can see the complete inheritance hierarchy of the type, as shown in Figure 17-12.

Because Solution Explorer contains more information than you can easily view with one screen, you can open multiple Solution Explorer windows at once with the menu option New Solution Explorer View, and you can set the scope to a specific element, e.g., to a project or a class, by selecting Scope to This from the context menu. To return to the previous scope, click the Back button.

Adding Items to a Project

Directly from within Solution Explorer you can add different items to the project. Selecting the project and opening the context menu Add ⇨ New Item opens the dialog shown in Figure 17-13. Another way to get to the same dialog is by using the main menu Project ⇨ Add New Item. Here you find many different categories, such as code items to add classes or interfaces, data items for using the Entity Framework or other data access technologies, and a lot more.

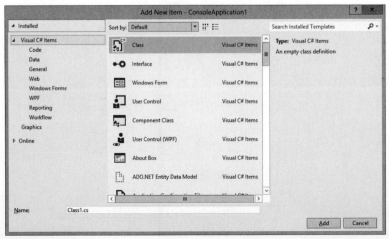

FIGURE 17-13

Managing References

The Reference Manager, shown in Figure 17-14, has been greatly enhanced with Visual Studio 2012. Selecting References in Solution Explorer and clicking the context menu Add Reference opens this dialog. Here you can add references to other assemblies in the same solution, assemblies from the .NET Framework, COM type libraries, and browse for assemblies on the disk.

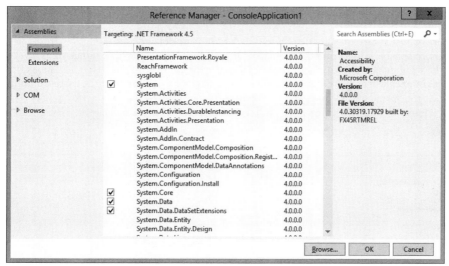

FIGURE 17-14

Using NuGet Packages to Install and Update Microsoft and Third-party Tools

The NuGet Package Manager, shown in Figure 17-15, is an important tool for installing and updating Microsoft and third-party libraries and tools. Some parts of the .NET Framework need a separate installation, e.g., version 5.0 of the Entity Framework, or TPL DataFlow; and some JavaScript libraries such as jQuery and Modernizr. If your project contains packages installed by the NuGet Package Manager, you will be automatically informed when a new version of a package is available.

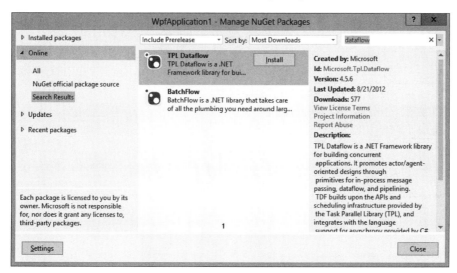

FIGURE 17-15

Working with the Code Editor

The Visual Studio code editor is where most of your development work takes place. This editor increased in size in Visual Studio 2012 after the removal of some toolbars from the default configuration, and the removal of borders from the menus, toolbars, and tab headers. The following sections take a look at some of the most useful features of this editor.

The Folding Editor

One notable feature of Visual Studio is its use of a folding editor as its default code editor. Figure 17-16 shows the code for the console application that you generated earlier. Notice the little minus signs on the left-hand side of the window. These signs mark the points where the editor assumes that a new block of code (or documentation comment) begins. You can click these icons to close up the view of the corresponding block of code just as you would close a node in a tree control (see Figure 17-17).

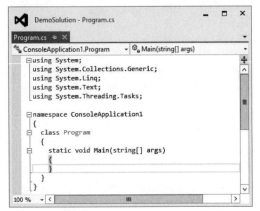

FIGURE 17-16

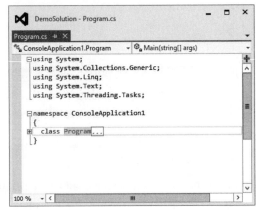

FIGURE 17-17

This means that while you are editing you can focus on just the areas of code you want to look at, hiding the bits of code you are not interested in working with at that moment. If you do not like the way the editor has chosen to block off your code, you can indicate your own blocks of collapsible code with the C# preprocessor directives, `#region` and `#endregion`. For example, to collapse the code inside the `Main` method, you would add the code shown in Figure 17-18.

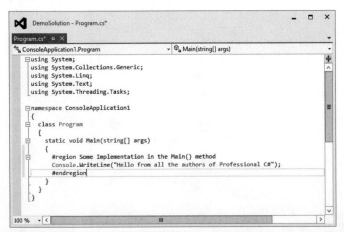

FIGURE 17-18

The code editor automatically detects the `#region` block and places a new minus sign by the `#region` directive, enabling you to close the region. Enclosing this code in a region enables the editor to close it (see Figure 17-19), marking the area with the comment you specified in the `#region` directive. The compiler, however, ignores the directives and compiles the `Main` method as normal.

```
DemoSolution - Program.cs*                                    _  □  ×
Program.cs* ⊕ ×
ConsoleApplication1.Program          ▼  Main(string[] args)        ▼

 using System;
 using System.Collections.Generic;
 using System.Linq;
 using System.Text;
 using System.Threading.Tasks;

 namespace ConsoleApplication1
 {
    class Program
    {
       static void Main(string[] args)
       {
          Some Implementation in the Main() method
       }
    }
 }

100 %  ▼ ‹                                                          ›
```

FIGURE 17-19

IntelliSense

In addition to the folding editor feature, Visual Studio's code editor also incorporates Microsoft's popular *IntelliSense* capability, which not only saves you typing but also ensures that you use the correct parameters. IntelliSense remembers your preferred choices and starts with these initially instead of at the beginning of the sometimes rather lengthy lists that IntelliSense can now provide.

The code editor also performs some syntax checking on your code, underlining these errors with a short wavy line, even before you compile the code. Hovering the mouse pointer over the underlined text brings up a small box that contains a description of the error.

Using Code Snippets

Great productivity features from the code editor are *code snippets*. Just by writing `cw<tab><tab>` in the editor, the editor creates a `Console.WriteLine();`. Visual Studio comes with many code snippets, e.g., with the shortcuts `do`, `for`, `forr`, `foreach`, `while` for creating loops, `equals` for an implementation of the `Equals` method, `attribute` and `exception` for creating `Attribute`- and `Exception`- derived types, and many more. You can see all the code snippets available with the Code Snippets Manager (see Figure 17-20) by selecting Tools ⇨ Code Snippets Manager. You can also create custom snippets.

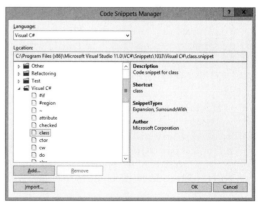

FIGURE 17-20

Learning and Understanding Other Windows

In addition to the code editor and Solution Explorer, Visual Studio provides a number of other windows that enable you to view and or manage your projects from different points of view.

> **NOTE** *The rest of this section describes several other windows. If any of these windows are not visible on your monitor, you can select it from the View menu. To show the design view and code editor, right-click the filename in Solution Explorer and select View Designer or View Code from the context menu, or select the item from the toolbar at the top of Solution Explorer. The design view and code editor share the same tabbed window.*

Using the Design View Window

If you are designing a user interface application, such as a WPF application, Windows control library, or ASP.NET Web Forms application, you can use the Design View window. This window presents a visual overview of what your form will look like. You normally use the Design View window in conjunction with a window known as the *toolbox*. The toolbox contains a large number of .NET components that you can drag onto your program. Toolbox components vary according to project type. Figure 17-21 shows the items displayed within a WPF application.

To add your own custom categories to the toolbox, execute the following steps:

1. Right-click any category.
2. Select Add Tab from the context menu.

You can also place other tools in the toolbox by selecting Choose Items from the same context menu—this is particularly useful for adding your own custom components or components from the .NET Framework that are not present in the toolbox by default.

Using the Properties Window

You know from the first part of the book that .NET classes can implement properties. The Properties window is available with projects, files, and when selecting items using the Design view. Figure 17-22 shows the Properties view with a Windows Service.

With this window you can see all the properties of an item and configure it accordingly. Some properties can be changed by entering text in a text box, others have predefined selections, and others have a custom editor (such as the More Colors dialog for ASP.NET Web Forms, shown in Figure 17-23). You can also add event handlers to events with the Properties window.

FIGURE 17-21

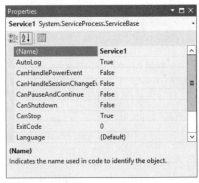

FIGURE 17-22

With WPF applications, the Properties window looks very different, as you can see in Figure 17-24. This window provides much more graphical feedback and allows graphical configuration of the properties. If it looks familiar, that might be because it originated in Expression Blend. As mentioned earlier, beginning with Visual Studio 2012, many aspects of Expression Blend and Visual Studio have been integrated.

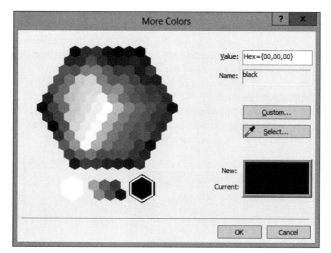

FIGURE 17-23

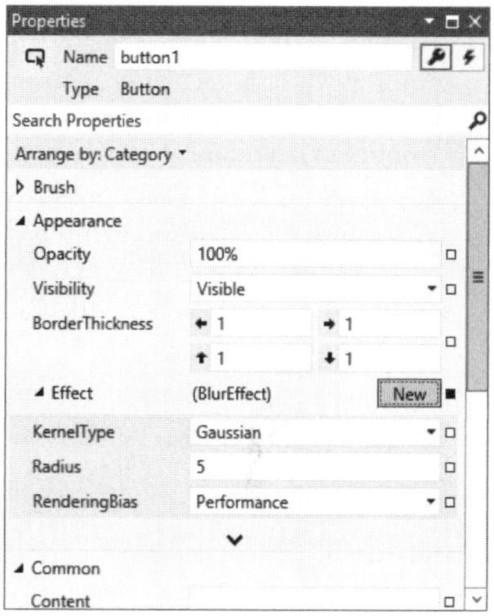

FIGURE 17-24

> **NOTE** *Interestingly, the standard Properties window is implemented as a* `System.Windows.Forms.PropertyGrid` *instance, which internally uses the reflection technology described in Chapter 15, "Reflection," to identify the properties and property values to display.*

Using the Class View Window

While the Solution Explorer can show classes and members of classes, that's the normal job of the Class View (see Figure 17-25). To invoke the class view, select View ⇨ Class View. The Class View shows the hierarchy of the namespaces and classes in your code. It provides a tree view that you can expand to see which namespaces contain what classes, and what classes contain what members.

A nice feature of the Class View is that if you right-click the name of any item for which you have access to the source code, then the context menu displays the Go To Definition

FIGURE 17-25

option, which takes you to the definition of the item in the code editor. Alternatively, you can do this by double-clicking the item in Class View (or, indeed, by right-clicking the item you want in the source code editor and choosing the same option from the resulting context menu). The context menu also enables you to add a field, method, property, or indexer to a class. In other words, you specify the details for the relevant member in a dialog, and the code is added for you. This feature can be particularly useful for adding properties and indexers, as it can save you quite a bit of typing.

Using the Object Browser Window

An important aspect of programming in the .NET environment is being able to find out what methods and other code items are available in the base classes and any other libraries that you are referencing from your assembly. This feature is available through a window called the Object Browser. You can access this window by selecting Object Browser from the View menu in Visual Studio 2012. With this tool you can browse for and select existing component sets such as .NET 4.5, .NET 4, .NET 3.5, .NET for Windows Store apps, and view the classes and members of the classes that are available with this subset. You can also select the Windows Runtime by selecting Windows in the Browse drop-down (as shown in Figure 17-26) to find all namespaces, types, and methods of this native new API for Windows 8.

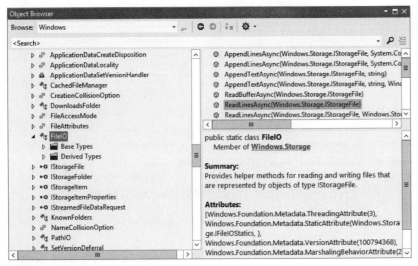

FIGURE 17-26

Using the Server Explorer Window

You can use the Server Explorer window, shown in Figure 17-27, to find out about aspects of the computers in your network while coding. With the Servers section, you can find information about services running (which is extremely useful developing Windows Services), create new performance counts, and access the event logs. The Data Connections section enables not only connecting to existing databases and querying data, but also creating a new database. Visual Studio 2012 also has a lot of Windows Azure information built in to Server Explorer, including options for Windows Azure Compute, Storage, Service Bus, and Virtual Machines.

Using the Document Outline

A window available with WPF applications is the Document Outline. Figure 17-28 shows this window opened with an application from Chapter 36, "Business Applications with WPF." Here, you can view the logical structure and hierarchy of the XAML elements, lock elements to prevent changing them unintentionally, easily move elements within the hierarchy, group elements within a new container element, and change layout types.

Arranging Windows

While exploring Visual Studio, you might have noticed that many of the windows have some interesting functionality more reminiscent of toolbars. In particular, they can all either float (also on a second display), or they can be docked. When they are docked, they display an extra icon that looks like a pin next to the minimize button in the top-right corner of each window. This icon really does act like a pin—it can be used to pin the window open. A pinned window (the pin is displayed vertically), behaves just like the regular windows you are used to. When they are unpinned, however (the pin is displayed horizontally), they remain open only as long as they have the focus. As soon as they lose the focus (because you clicked or moved your mouse somewhere else), they smoothly retreat into the main border around the entire Visual Studio application. Pinning and unpinning windows provides another way to make the best use of the limited space on your screen.

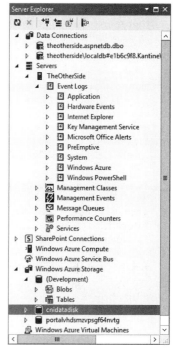

FIGURE 17-27

BUILDING A PROJECT

Visual Studio is not only about coding your projects. It is actually an IDE that manages the full life cycle of your project, including the building or compiling of your solutions. This section examines the options that Visual Studio provides for building your project.

Building, Compiling, and Making

Before examining the various build options, it is important to clarify some terminology. You will often see three different terms used in connection with the process of getting from your source code to some sort of executable code: *compiling*, *building*, and *making*. The origin of these three terms reflects the fact that until recently, the process of getting from source code to executable code involved more than one step (this is still the case in C++). This was due in large part to the number of source files in a program.

FIGURE 17-28

In C++, for example, each source file needs to be compiled individually. This results in what are known as *object files*, each containing something like executable code, but where each object file relates to only one source file. To generate an executable, these object files need to be linked together, a process that is officially known as *linking*. The combined process was usually referred to—at least on the Windows platform—as building your code. However, in C# terms the compiler is more sophisticated, able to read in and treat all your source files as one block. Hence, there is not really a separate linking stage, so in the context of C#, the terms *compile* and *build* are used interchangeably.

The term *make* basically means the same thing as *build,* although it is not really used in the context of C#. The term make originated on old mainframe systems on which, when a project was composed of many source files, a separate file would be written containing instructions to the compiler on how to build a project—which files to include and what libraries to link to, and so on. This file was generally known as a *makefile* and it is still quite standard on UNIX systems. The project file is in reality something like the old makefile, it's just a new advanced XML variant. You can use the MSBuild command with the project file as input, and all the sources will be compiled. Using build files is very helpful on a separate build server on which all developers check their code in, and overnight the build process is done.

Debugging and Release Builds

The idea of having separate builds is very familiar to C++ developers, and to a lesser degree to those with a Visual Basic background. The point here is that when you are debugging, you typically want your executable to behave differently from when you are ready to ship the software. When you are ready to ship your software, you want the executable to be as small and fast as possible. Unfortunately, these two requirements are not compatible with your needs when you are debugging code, as explained in the following sections.

Optimization

High performance is achieved partly by the compiler's many optimizations of the code. This means that the compiler actively looks at your source code as it is compiling to identify places where it can modify the precise details of what you are doing in a way that does not change the overall effect but makes things more efficient. For example, suppose the compiler encountered the following source code:

```
double InchesToCm(double ins)
{
  return ins*2.54;
}

// later on in the code
Y = InchesToCm(X);
```

It might replace it with this:

```
Y = X * 2.54;
```

Similarly, it might replace

```
{
  string message = "Hi";
  Console.WriteLine(message);
}
```

with this:

```
Console.WriteLine("Hi");
```

By doing so, the compiler bypasses having to declare any unnecessary object reference in the process.

It is not possible to exactly pin down what optimizations the C# compiler does—nor whether the two previous examples would actually occur with any particular situation—because those kinds of details are not documented. (Chances are good that for managed languages such as C#, the previous optimizations would occur at JIT compilation time, not when the C# compiler compiles source code to assembly.) Obviously, for proprietary reasons, companies that write compilers are usually quite reluctant to provide many details about the tricks that their compilers use. Note that optimizations do not affect your source code—they affect only the contents of the executable code. However, the previous examples should give you a good idea of what to expect from optimizations.

The problem is that although optimizations like the examples just shown help a great deal in making your code run faster, they are detrimental for debugging. In the first example, suppose that you want to set a breakpoint inside the InchesToCm method to see what is going on in there. How can you possibly do that if the executable code does not actually have an InchesToCm method because the compiler has removed it? Moreover, how can you set a watch on the Message variable when that does not exist in the compiled code either?

Debugger Symbols

During debugging, you often have to look at the values of variables, and you specify them by their source code names. The trouble is that executable code generally does not contain those names—the compiler replaces the names with memory addresses. .NET has modified this situation somewhat to the extent that certain items in assemblies are stored with their names, but this is true of only a small minority of items—such as public classes and methods—and those names will still be removed when the assembly is JIT-compiled. Asking the debugger to tell you the value in the variable called HeightInInches is not going to get you very far if, when the debugger examines the executable code, it sees only addresses and no reference to the name HeightInInches anywhere.

Therefore, to debug properly, you need to make extra debugging information available in the executable. This information includes, among other things, names of variables and line information that enables the debugger to match up which executable machine assembly language instructions correspond to your original source code instructions. You will not, however, want that information in a release build, both for proprietary reasons (debugging information makes it a lot easier for other people to disassemble your code) and because it increases the size of the executable.

Extra Source Code Debugging Commands

A related issue is that quite often while you are debugging there will be extra lines in your code to display crucial debugging-related information. Obviously, you want the relevant commands removed entirely from the executable before you ship the software. You could do this manually, but wouldn't it be so much easier if you could simply mark those statements in some way so that the compiler ignores them when it is compiling your code to be shipped? You've already seen in the first part of the book how this can be done in C# by defining a suitable processor symbol, and possibly using this in conjunction with the Conditional attribute, giving you what is known as *conditional compilation*.

What all these factors add up to is that you need to compile almost all commercial software in a slightly different way when debugging than in the final product that is shipped. Visual Studio can handle this because, as you have already seen, it stores details about all the options it is supposed to pass to the compiler when it has your code compiled. All that Visual Studio has to do to support different types of builds is store more than one set of such details. These different sets of build information are referred to as *configurations*. When you create a project, Visual Studio automatically gives you two configurations, Debug and Release:

➤ **Debug**—This configuration commonly specifies that no optimizations are to take place, extra debugging information is to be present in the executable, and the compiler is to assume that the debug preprocessor symbol Debug is present unless it is explicitly #undefined in the source code.

➤ **Release**—This configuration specifies that the compiler should optimize the compilation, that there should be no extra debugging information in the executable, and that the compiler should not assume that any particular preprocessor symbol is present.

You can define your own configurations as well. You might want to do this, for example, to set up professional-level builds and enterprise-level builds so that you can ship two versions of the software. In the past, because of issues related to Unicode character encodings being supported on Windows NT but not on Windows 95, it was common for C++ projects to feature a Unicode configuration and an MBCS (multi-byte character set) configuration.

Selecting a Configuration

At this point you might be wondering how Visual Studio, given that it stores details about more than one configuration, determines which one to use when arranging for a project to be built. The answer is that there is always an active configuration, which is the configuration that is used when you ask Visual Studio to build a project. (Note that configurations are set for each project, rather than each solution.)

By default, when you create a project, the Debug configuration is the active configuration. You can change which configuration is the active one by clicking the Build menu option and selecting the Configuration Manager item. It is also available through a drop-down menu in the main Visual Studio toolbar.

Editing Configurations

In addition to choosing the active configuration, you can also examine and edit the configurations. To do this, select the relevant project in Solution Explorer and then select Properties from the Project menu. This brings up a sophisticated dialog. (Alternatively, you can access the same dialog by right-clicking the name of the project in Solution Explorer and then selecting Properties from the context menu.)

This dialog contains a tabbed view that enables you to select many different general areas to examine or edit. Space does not permit showing all of these areas, but this section outlines a couple of the most important ones.

Figure 17-29 shows a tabbed view of the available properties for a particular application. This screenshot shows the general application settings for the `ConsoleApplication1` project that you created earlier in the chapter.

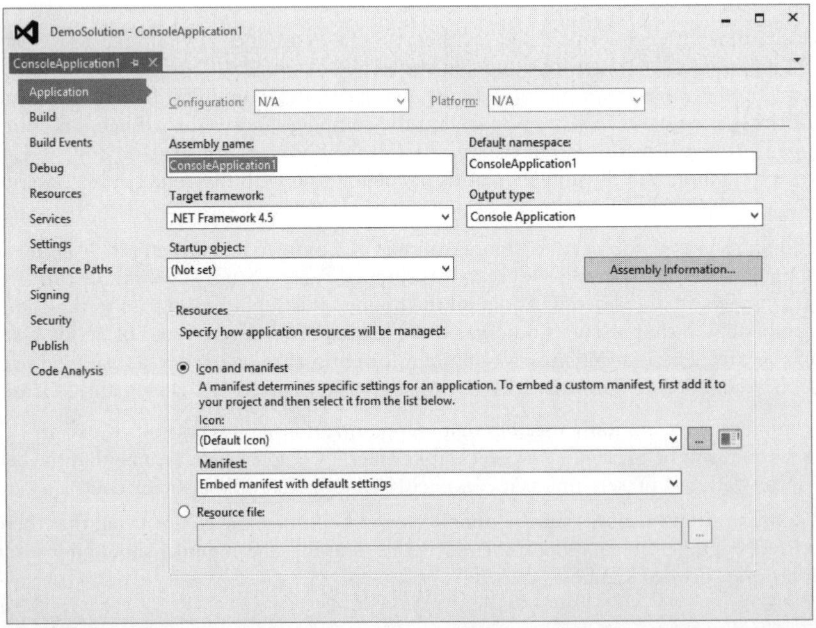

FIGURE 17-29

Among the points to note are that you can select the name of the assembly as well as the type of assembly to be generated. The options here are Console Application, Windows Application, and Class Library. Of course, you can change the assembly type if you want (though arguably, you might wonder why you did not pick the correct project type when you asked Visual Studio to generate the project for you in the first place)!

Figure 17-30 shows the build configuration properties. Note that a list box near the top of the dialog enables you to specify which configuration you want to look at. You can see—in the case of the Debug configuration—that the compiler assumes that the DEBUG and TRACE preprocessor symbols have been defined. In addition, the code is not optimized and extra debugging information is generated.

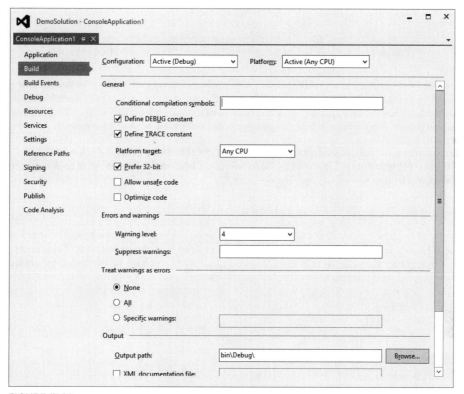

FIGURE 17-30

In general, you won't need to adjust the configuration settings; but if you ever do need to modify them, you are now familiar with the different available configuration properties.

DEBUGGING YOUR CODE

At this point, you are ready to run and debug the application. In C#, as in pre-.NET languages, the main technique involved in debugging is simply setting breakpoints and using them to examine what is going on in your code at a certain point in its execution.

Setting Breakpoints

You can set breakpoints from Visual Studio on any line of your code that is actually executed. The simplest way is to click the line in the code editor, within the shaded area near the far left of the document window (or press the F9 key when the appropriate line is selected). This sets up a breakpoint on that particular line, which pauses execution and transfers control to the debugger as soon as that line is reached in the execution process. As in previous versions of Visual Studio, a breakpoint is indicated by a red circle to the left of the line in the code editor. Visual Studio also highlights the line by displaying the text and background in a different color. Clicking the circle again removes the breakpoint.

If breaking every time at a particular line is not adequate for your particular problem, you can also set conditional breakpoints. To do this, select Debug ⇨ Windows ⇨ Breakpoints. This brings up a dialog that requests details about the breakpoint you want to set. Among the options available, you can do the following:

➤ Specify that execution should break only after the breakpoint has been passed a certain number of times.

➤ Specify that the breakpoint should be activated only after the line has been reached a defined number of times—for example, every twentieth time a line is executed. (This is useful when debugging large loops.)

➤ Set the breakpoints relative to a variable, rather than an instruction. In this case, the value of the variable will be monitored and the breakpoints triggered whenever the value of this variable changes. You might find, however, that using this option slows down your code considerably. Checking whether the value of a variable has changed after every instruction adds a lot of processor time.

With this dialog you also have the option to export and import breakpoint settings, which is useful for working with different breakpoint arrangements depending on what scenario you want to debug into, and to store the debug settings.

Using Data Tips and Debugger Visualizers

After a breakpoint has been hit, you will usually want to investigate the values of variables. The simplest way to do this is to hover the mouse cursor over the name of the variable in the code editor. This causes a little *data tip* box that shows the value of that variable to pop up, which can also be expanded for greater detail. This data tip box is shown in Figure 17-31.

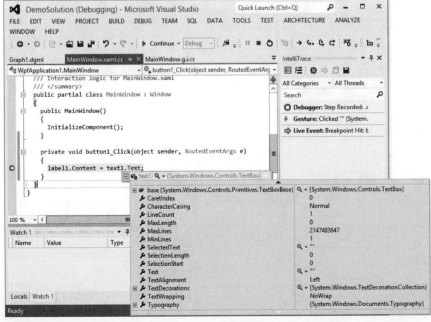

FIGURE 17-31

Some of the values shown in the data tip offer a magnifying glass. Clicking this magnifying class provides one or more options to use a *debugger visualizer*—depending on the type. With WPF controls, the WPF Visualizer enables you to take a closer look at the control (see Figure 17-32). With this visualizer you can view the visual tree that is used during runtime, including all the actual property settings. This visual tree also gives you a preview of the element that you select within the tree.

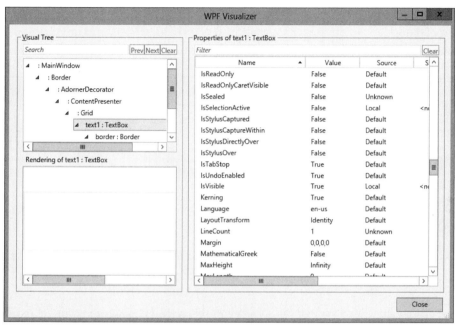

FIGURE 17-32

Figure 17-33 shows the XML Visualizer, which displays XML content. Many other visualizers are available as well, such as HTML and Text visualizers, and visualizers that display the content of a DataTable or DataSet.

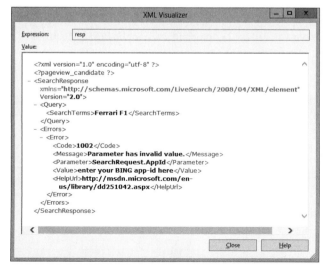

FIGURE 17-33

Monitoring and Changing Variables

Sometimes you might prefer to have a more continuous look at values. For that you can use the *Autos*, *Locals*, and *Watch* windows to examine the contents of variables. Each of these windows is designed to monitor different variables:

➤ **Autos**—Monitors the last few variables that have been accessed as the program was executing.

➤ **Locals**—Monitors variables that are accessible in the method currently being executed.

➤ **Watch**—Monitors any variables that you have explicitly specified by typing their names into the Watch window. You can drag and drop variables to the Watch window.

These windows are only visible when the program is running under the debugger. If you do not see them, select Debug ➪ Windows, and then select the desired menu. The Watch window offers four different windows in case there's so much to watch and you want to group that. With all these windows you can both watch and change the values, enabling you to try different paths in the program without leaving the debugger. The Locals window is shown in Figure 17-34.

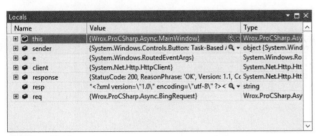

FIGURE 17-34

Another window that not directly relates to the other windows discussed, but is still an important one on monitoring and changing variables is the *Immediate window*. This window also enables looking at variable values. You can use this window to enter code and run it. This is very helpful when doing some tests during a debug session, enabling you to hone in on details, try a method out, and change a debug run dynamically.

Exceptions

Exceptions are great when you are ready to ship your application, ensuring that error conditions are handled appropriately. Used well, they can ensure that users are never presented with technical or annoying dialogs. Unfortunately, exceptions are not so great when you are trying to debug your application. The problem is twofold:

➤ If an exception occurs when you are debugging, you often do not want it to be handled automatically—especially if automatically handling it means retiring gracefully and terminating execution! Rather, you want the debugger to help you determine why the exception has occurred. Of course, if you have written good, robust, defensive code, your program will automatically handle almost anything—including the bugs that you want to detect!

➤ If an exception for which you have not written a handler occurs, the .NET runtime will still search for one. Unfortunately, by the time it discovers there isn't one, it will have terminated your program. There will not be a call stack left, and you will not be able to look at the values of any of your variables because they will all have gone out of scope.

Of course, you can set breakpoints in your catch blocks, but that often does not help very much because when the catch block is reached, flow of execution will, by definition, have exited the corresponding try block. That means the variables you probably wanted to examine the values of, to figure out what has gone wrong, will have gone out of scope. You will not even be able to look at the stack trace to find what method was being executed when the throw statement occurred, because control will have left that method. Setting the breakpoints at the throw statement will obviously solve this; but if you are coding defensively, there will be many throw statements in your code. How can you tell which one threw the exception?

Visual Studio provides a very neat answer to all of this. In the main Debug menu is an item called Exceptions. Clicking this item opens the Exceptions dialog (see Figure 17-35), where you can specify what happens when an exception is thrown. You can choose to continue execution or to stop and start debugging—in which case execution stops and the debugger steps in at the throw statement.

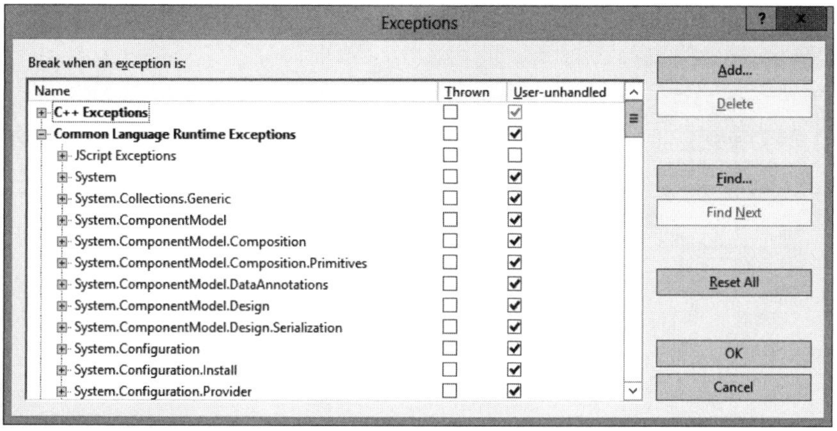

FIGURE 17-35

What makes this a really powerful tool is that you can customize the behavior according to which class of exception is thrown. You can configure to break into the debugger whenever it encounters any exception thrown by a .NET base class, but not to break into the debugger for specific exception types.

Visual Studio is aware of all the exception classes available in the .NET base classes, and of quite a few exceptions that can be thrown outside the .NET environment. Visual Studio is not automatically aware of any custom exception classes that you write, but you can manually add your exception classes to the list, and specify which of your exceptions should cause execution to stop immediately. To do this, just click the Add button (which is enabled when you have selected a top-level node from the tree) and type in the name of your exception class.

Multithreading

Visual Studio also offers great support for debugging multithreaded programs. When debugging multi-threaded programs, you must understand that the program behaves differently depending on whether it is running in the debugger or not. If you reach a breakpoint, Visual Studio stops all threads of the program, so you have the chance to access the current state of all the threads. To switch between different threads you can enable the Debug Location toolbar. This toolbar contains a combo box for all processes and another combo box for all threads of the running application. Selecting a different thread you'll find the code line where the thread currently halts, and the variables currently accessible from different threads. The Parallel Tasks window (shown in Figure 17-36) shows all running tasks, including their status, location, task name, the current thread that's used by the task, the application domain, and the process identifier. This window also indicates when different threads block each other, causing a deadlock.

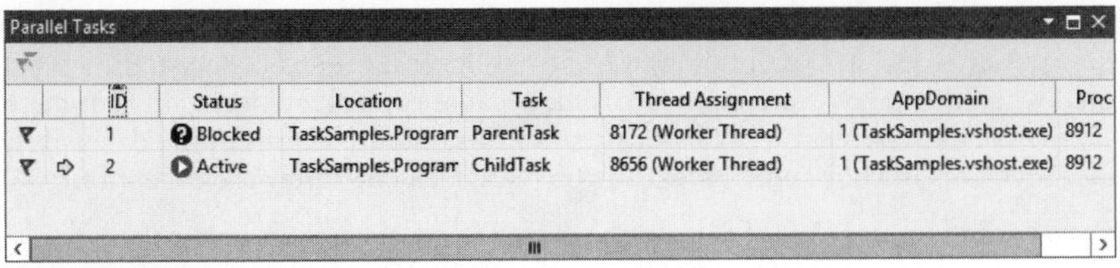

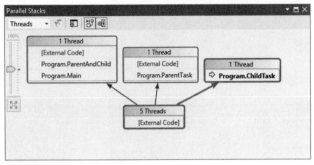

FIGURE 17-36

Figure 17-37 shows the Parallel Stacks window, where you can see different threads or tasks (depending on the selection) in a hierarchical view. You can jump to the source code directly by clicking the task or thread.

FIGURE 17-37

IntelliTrace

Another great debugging feature is *IntelliTrace*, which is available only with Visual Studio 2012 Ultimate Edition. IntelliTrace, also known as *historical debugging,* provides historical information. Hitting a breakpoint, you can have a look at previous information in time (see Figure 17-38), such as previous breakpoints, exceptions that were thrown, database access, ASP.NET events, tracing, or gestures from a user such as clicking a button. By clicking on previous events you can have a look at local variables, the call stack, and method calls that were done. This makes it easy to find problems without restarting a debug session and setting breakpoints to methods that have been invoked before seeing the issue.

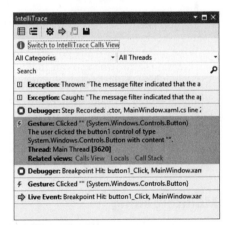

FIGURE 17-38

REFACTORING TOOLS

Many developers develop their applications first for functionality; then, once the functionality is in place, they *rework* their applications to make them more manageable and more readable. This process is called *refactoring.* Refactoring involves reworking code for readability and performance, providing type safety, and ensuring that applications adhere to standard OO (object-oriented) programming practices. Reworking also happens when updates are made to applications.

The C# environment of Visual Studio 2012 includes a set of refactoring tools, which you can find under the Refactoring option in the Visual Studio menu. To see this in action, create a new class called `Car` in Visual Studio:

```
namespace ConsoleApplication1
{
  public class Car
  {
    public string color;
    public string doors;

    public int Go()
    {
      int speedMph = 100;
      return speedMph;
    }
  }
}
```

Now suppose that for the purpose of refactoring, you want to change the code a bit so that the `color` and `door` variables are encapsulated in public .NET properties. The refactoring capabilities of Visual Studio 2012 enable you to simply right-click either of these properties in the document window and select Refactor ⇨ Encapsulate Field. This will pull up the Encapsulate Field dialog, shown in Figure 17-39.

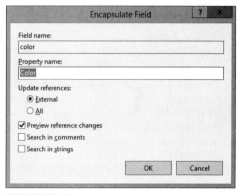

FIGURE 17-39

From this dialog you can provide the name of the property and click the OK button, which changes the selected public field into a private field, while also encapsulating the field in a public .NET property. After you click OK, the code is reworked into the following (after redoing both fields):

```
namespace ConsoleApplication1
{
  public class Car
  {
    private string color;
    public string Color
    {
      get { return color; }
      set { color = value; }
    }

    private string doors;
    public string Doors
    {
      get { return doors; }
      set { doors = value; }
    }

    public int Go()
    {
      int speedMph = 100;
      return speedMph;
    }
  }
}
```

As you can see, these wizards make it quite simple to refactor your code—not only on one page but throughout an entire application. Also included are capabilities to do the following:

➤ Rename method names, local variables, fields, and more

➤ Extract methods from a selection of code

➤ Extract interfaces based on a set of existing type members

➤ Promote local variables to parameters

➤ Rename or reorder parameters

You will find that the refactoring capabilities provided by Visual Studio 2012 offer a great way to get cleaner, more readable, and better-structured code.

ARCHITECTURE TOOLS

Before starting with coding programs, you should have an architectural viewpoint to your solution, analyze requirements and define a solution architecture. Architecture tools are available with the Visual Studio Ultimate 2012. Reading the diagrams is also possible with Visual Studio Premium 2012.

Figure 17-40 shows the Add New Item dialog that appears after creating a modeling project. It provides options to create a UML use case diagram, a class diagram, a sequence diagram, and an activity diagram. The standard UML diagrams are not discussed in this chapter, as you can find several books covering this group. Instead, this section looks at two Microsoft-specific diagrams: *Directed Graph Document* (or *Dependency Graph*) and *Layer Diagram*.

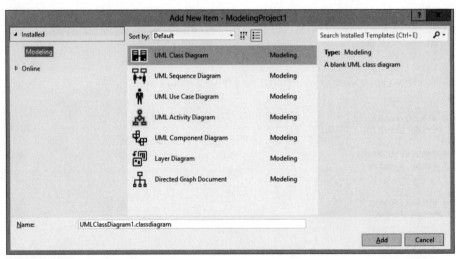

FIGURE 17-40

Dependency Graph

With the dependency graph you can see dependencies between assemblies, classes, and even members of classes. Figure 17-41 shows the dependency graph of a Calculator example from Chapter 30, "Managed Extensibility Framework" that includes a calculator hosting application and several libraries, such as a contract assembly and the add-in assemblies SimpleCalculator, FuelEconomy, and TemparatureConversion. The dependency graph is created by selecting Architecture ➪ Generate Dependency Graph ➪ For Solution. This activity analyzes all projects of the solution, displaying all the assemblies in a single diagram and drawing lines between the assemblies to show dependencies. In Figure 17-41 the external dependencies have been removed to show only the dependencies between the assemblies of the solution. The varying thickness of the lines between the assemblies reflects the degree of dependency. An assembly contains several types and members of types, and a number of types and its members are used from other assemblies.

You can dig deeper into the dependencies too. Figure 17-42 shows a more detailed diagram, including the classes of the `Calculator` assembly and their dependencies. The dependency on the `CalculatorContract` assembly is shown here as well. For simplicity, other assemblies have been removed from the diagram. In a large graph you can also zoom in and out of several parts of the graph.

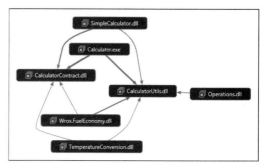

FIGURE 17-41

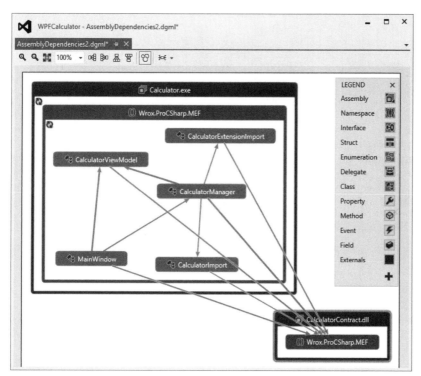

FIGURE 17-42

You can even go deeper, displaying fields, properties, methods, and events, and how they depend on each other.

Layer Diagram

The *layer diagram* is very much related with the dependency graph. You can create the layer diagram out of the dependency graph (or from Solution Explorer by selecting assemblies or classes), or create the layer diagram from scratch before doing any development.

Different layers can define client and server parts in a distributed solution, e.g., a layer for a Windows application, one for the service, and one for the data access library, or layers based on assemblies. A layer can also contain other layers.

Figure 17-43 shows a layer diagram with the main layers Calculator UI, CalculatorUtils, Contracts, and AddIns. The AddIns layer contains inner layers FuelEconomy, TemperatureConversion, and Calculator. The number that's displayed with the layer reflects the number of items that are linked to that layer.

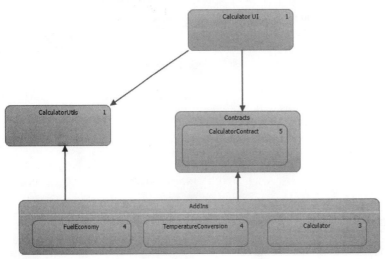

FIGURE 17-43

To create a layer diagram, select Architecture ⇨ New Diagram ⇨ Layer Diagram. This creates an empty diagram to which you can add layers from the toolbox or the Architecture Explorer. The Architecture Explorer contains a Solution View and a Class View from which you can select all items of the solution to add them to the layer diagram. Selecting items and dragging them to the layer is all you need to do build the layer diagram. Selecting a layer and clicking the context menu View Links opens the Layer Explorer, shown in Figure 17-44, which displays all the items contained in the selected layer(s).

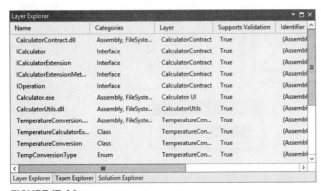

FIGURE 17-44

During application development, the layer diagram can be validated to analyze whether all the dependencies are on track. If a layer has a dependency in a wrong direction, or has a dependency on a layer that it shouldn't, this architecture validation returns with errors.

ANALYZING APPLICATIONS

The architectural diagrams discussed in the preceding section—the dependency graph and the layer diagram—are not only of interest before the coding starts, they also help in analyzing the application and keeping it on the right track to ensure that it doesn't generate inaccurate dependencies. There are many more useful tools available with Visual Studio 2012 that can help you analyze and proactively troubleshoot your application. This section looks at some of these Visual Studio analysis tools.

Sequence Diagram

To better understand a single method, you can create a sequence diagram from the method. Sequence diagrams can be created directly from within the editor by clicking a method name and selecting the context menu Generate Sequence Diagram. Within the dialog to create the sequence diagram, you can specify the call depth for the analysis; whether you want to include calls from the current project, the solution, or the solution and external references; and whether calls to properties and System objects should be excluded.

The sample diagram shown in Figure 17-45 is created from the WPFCalculator project created in the Managed Extensibility Framework sample in Chapter 30. It illustrates the sequence diagram of the method OnCalculate. Here, you can see that OnCalculate is an instance method in the MainWindow. At first, a condition is checked that verifies the length of currentOperands, and only continues if the value is 2. If this is successful, InvokeCalculatorAsync is invoked on the CalculatorManager class. The CalculatorManger class invokes the Run method of the Task type, and a deferred call started from the Run method invokes the Operate method on some object that implements the ICalculator interface.

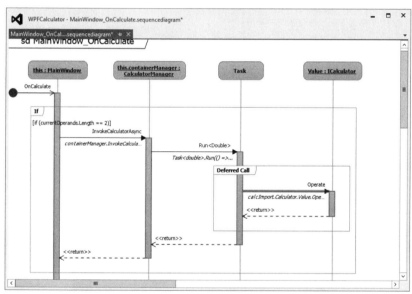

FIGURE 17-45

Profiler

To analyze a complete run of the application, you can use the profiler. This performance tool enables you to find what methods are called how often, how much time is spent in what methods, how much memory is used, and much more. An easy way to start using profiling is to open the Performance Wizard by selecting Analyze ⇨ Launch Performance Wizard. Figure 17-46 shows the different profiling methods available. The first option, which has the least overhead, is CPU sampling. Using this option, performance information is sampled after specific time intervals. You don't see all method calls invoked, in particular if they are running just for a short time. Again, the advantage of this option is low overhead. When running a profiling session, you must always be aware that you're monitoring not only the performance of the application, but the performance of getting the data. You shouldn't profile all data at once, as sampling all of the data influences the outcome. Collecting information about .NET memory allocation helps you identify memory leaks and provides information about what type of objects need how much memory. Resource contention data helps with the analysis of threads, enabling you to easily identify whether different threads block each other.

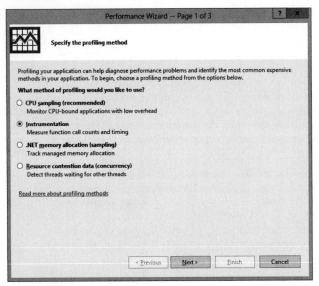

FIGURE 17-46

After configuring the options in the Performance Explorer, you can immediately start the application and run profiling after exiting the wizard. You can also change some options afterward by modifying the properties of a profiling setting. Using these settings, you can decide to add memory profiling with an instrumentation session, and add CPU counters and Windows counters to the profiling session to see this information in conjunction with the other profiled data.

Figure 17-47 shows the summary screen of a profiling session. Here you can see CPU usage by the application, a *hot path* indicating which functions are taking the most time, and a sorted list of the functions that have used most CPU time.

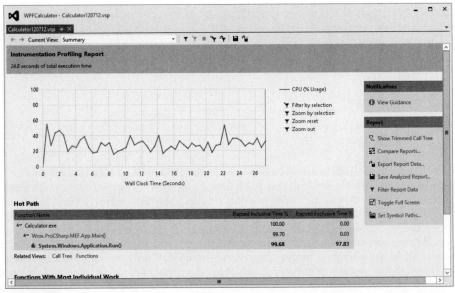

FIGURE 17-47

The profiler has many more screens, too many to show here. One view is a function view that you can sort based on the number of calls made to the function, or the elapsed inclusive and exclusive times used by the function. This information can help you identify methods deserving of another look in terms of performance, while others might not be worthwhile because they are not called very often or they do not take an inordinate amount of time.

Clicking within a function, you can invoke details about it, as shown in Figure 17-48. This enables you to see which functions are called and immediately step into the source code. The Caller/Callee view also provides information about what functions have been called by what function.

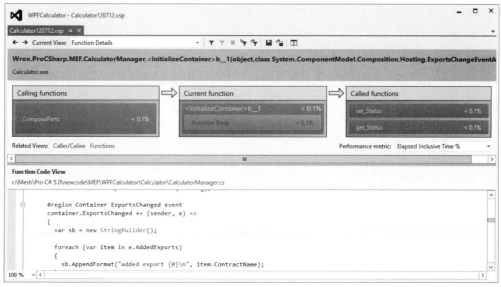

FIGURE 17-48

Profiling is available with Visual Studio Professional Edition. Using the Premium Edition, you can configure tier interaction profiling that enables you to view the SQL statements generated and the time spent on ADO.NET queries, as well as information on ASP.NET pages.

Concurrency Visualizer

The Concurrency Visualizer helps you to analyze threading issues with applications. Running this analyzer tool provides a summary screen like the one shown in Figure 17-49. Here, you can compare the amount of CPU needed by the application with overall system performance. You can also switch to a Threads view that displays information about all the running application threads and what state they were in over time. Switching to the Cores view displays information about how many cores have been used. If your application just makes use of one CPU core and it is busy all the time, adding some parallelism features might improve performance by making use of more cores. You might see that different threads are active over time but only one thread is active at any given point in time. In that case, you should probably change your locking behavior. You can also see if threads are working on I/O. If the I/O rate is high with multiple threads, the disk might be the bottleneck and threads just wait on each other to complete I/O. This behavior might warrant reducing the number of threads doing I/O, or using an SSD drive. Clearly, these analysis tools provide a great deal of useful information.

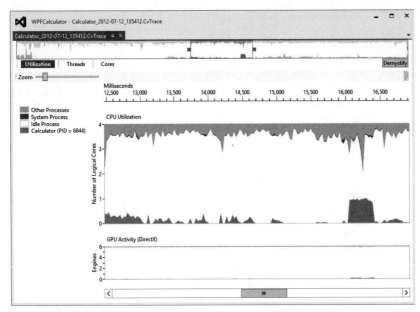

FIGURE 17-49

Code Analysis

You can verify the code with code analysis rules. Static code analysis is available with the Professional Edition of Visual Studio 2012. Clicking the properties of a project, you can see the Code Analysis tab, where you can select and edit a set of code analysis rules that should be run upon building the project, or with s separate start of Run Code Analysis. A single rule set can be configured as shown in Figure 17-50. With the rule set you can also specify whether the rule should result in a warning or an error.

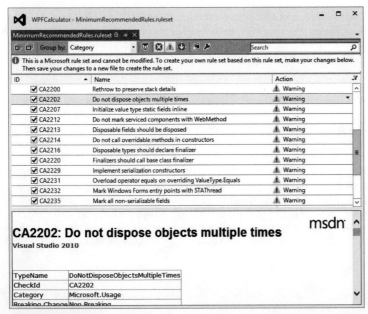

FIGURE 17-50

Before running the code analysis, you should define the rules that apply. Microsoft defines various rule sets for predefined rules, such as Microsoft Managed Recommended Rules or Microsoft Extended Design Guideline Rules. You can create your own rule set, or define the rule set to use. Even when applying a rule set, you might not agree with some of the rules, which is fine. You can configure the rule set to exclude that rule and/or add custom rules that fit your needs. You can also suppress rules, either on a per-project basis or just with classes or methods where the rule applies. For example, suppose one rule specifies that the spelling of `Wrox` should match what is used in the namespace. The spell-checking that is used by Visual Studio does not include "Wrox." However, this term should be allowed as a namespace name. To not receive an error message for this term, you can ignore the rule. When the error comes up with the Analysis window, the erroneous rule can be selected to be suppressed. On suppression, either an attribute is added to the identifier where the error occurred or the rule is suppressed globally with the application in `GlobalSuppressions.cs`:

```
[assembly: System.Diagnostics.CodeAnalysis.SuppressMessage("Microsoft.Naming",
  "CA1704:IdentifiersShouldBeSpelledCorrectly", MessageId = "Wrox",
  Scope = "namespace", Target = "Wrox.ProCSharp.MEF")]
```

Code Metrics

Checking code metrics provides information about how maintainable the code is. The code metrics shown in Figure 17-51 display a maintainability index for the complete namespace `Wrox.ProCSharp.MEF` of 82, and includes details about every class and method. These ratings are color-coded: A red rating, in the range of 0 to 9, means low maintainability; a yellow rating, in the range of 10 to 19, means moderate maintainability; and a green rating, in the range of 20 to 100, means high maintainability. The *cyclomatic complexity* provides feedback about the different code paths. More code paths means more unit tests are required to go through every option. The *depth of inheritance* reflects the hierarchy of the types. The greater the number of base classes, the harder it is to find the one to which a field belongs. The value for *class coupling* indicates how tightly types are coupled, e.g., used with parameters or locals. More coupling means more complexity in terms of maintaining the code.

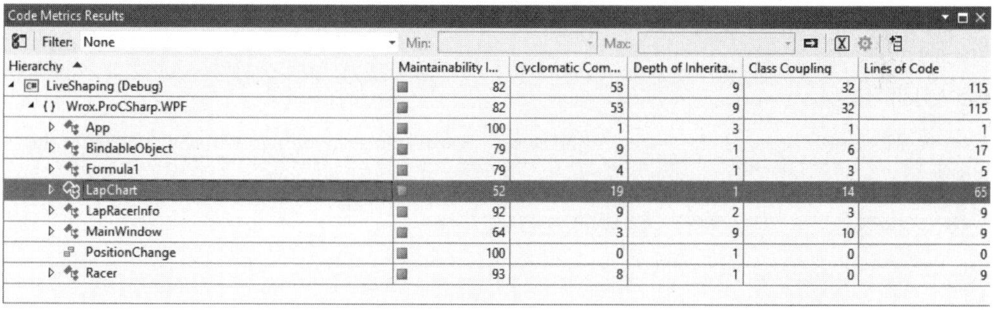

Hierarchy ▲	Maintainability I...	Cyclomatic Com...	Depth of Inherita...	Class Coupling	Lines of Code
▲ ▣ LiveShaping (Debug)	82	53	9	32	115
▲ {} Wrox.ProCSharp.WPF	82	53	9	32	115
▷ App	100	1	3	1	1
▷ BindableObject	79	9	1	6	17
▷ Formula1	79	4	1	3	5
▷ LapChart	52	19	1	14	65
▷ LapRacerInfo	92	9	2	3	9
▷ MainWindow	64	3	9	10	9
PositionChange	100	0	1	0	0
▷ Racer	93	8	1	0	9

FIGURE 17-51

UNIT TESTS

Writing unit tests helps with code maintenance. For example, when performing a code update, you want to be confident that the update won't break something else. Having automatic unit tests in place helps to ensure that all functionality is retained after code changes are made. Visual Studio 2012 offers a robust unit testing framework.

Creating Unit Tests

The following example tests a very simple method. The class `DeepThought` contains the `TheAnswerToTheUltimateQuestionOfLifeTheUniverseAndEverything` method, which returns `42` as a result. To ensure that nobody changes the method to return a wrong result (maybe someone who didn't read *The Hitchhiker's Guide to the Galaxy*), a unit test is created:

```
public class DeepThought
{
  public int TheAnswerToTheUltimateQuestionOfLifeTheUniverseAndEverything()
  {
    return 42;
  }
}
```

To create a unit test, the Unit Test Project template is available within the group of Visual C# projects. A unit test class is marked with the `TestClass` attribute, and a test method with the `TestMethod` attribute. The implementation creates an instance of `DeepThought` and invokes the method that is to be tested, `TheAnswerToTheUltimateQuestionOfLifeTheUniverseAndEverything`. The return value is compared with the value `42` using `Assert.AreEqual`. In case `Assert.AreEqual` fails, the test fails:

```
[TestClass]
public class TestProgram
{
  [TestMethod]
  public void
    TestTheAnswerToTheUltimateQuestionOfLifeTheUniverseAndEverything()
  {
    int expected = 42;
    DeepThought f1 = new DeepThought();
    int actual =
      f1.TheAnswerToTheUltimateQuestionOfLifeTheUniverseAndEverything();
    Assert.AreEqual(expected, actual);
  }
}
```

Running Unit Tests

Using the Test Explorer (opened via Test ➪ Windows ➪ Test Explorer), you can run the tests from the solution (see Figure 17-52).

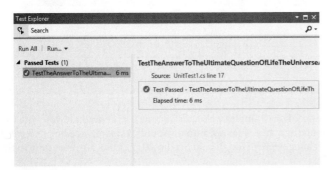

FIGURE 17-52

Figure 17-53 shows a failed test, which includes all details about the failure.

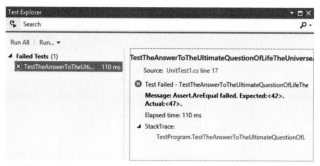

FIGURE 17-53

Of course, this was a very simple scenario, so the tests are not usually that simple. For example, methods can throw exceptions; they can have different routes to return other values; and they can make use of other code (e.g., database access code, or services that are invoked) that shouldn't be tested with the single unit. Now you'll look at a more involved scenario for unit testing.

The following class `StringSample` defines a constructor with a string parameter and contains the method `GetStringDemo`, which uses different paths depending on the `first` and `second` parameter and returns a string that results from these parameters, and a field member of the class:

```csharp
public class StringSample
{
  public StringSample(string init)
  {
    if (init == null)
      throw new ArgumentNullException("init");
    this.init = init;
  }
  private string init;

  public string GetStringDemo(string first, string second)
  {
    if (first == null)
      throw new ArgumentNullException("first");
    if (string.IsNullOrEmpty(first))
      throw new ArgumentException("empty string is not allowed", first);
    if (second == null)
      throw new ArgumentNullException("second");
    if (second.Length > first.Length)
      throw new ArgumentOutOfRangeException("second",
        "must be shorter than first");

    int startIndex = first.IndexOf(second);
    if (startIndex < 0)
    {
      return string.Format("{0} not found in {1}", second, first);
    }
    else if (startIndex < 5)
    {
      return string.Format("removed {0} from {1}: {2}", second, first,
        first.Remove(startIndex, second.Length));
    }
    else
    {
      return init.ToUpperInvariant();
    }
  }
}
```

A unit test should test every possible execution route, and check for exceptions, discussed next.

Expecting Exceptions

Invoking the constructor of the `StringSample` class and calling the method `GetStringDemo` with null, an `ArgumentNullException` is expected. This can be done with testing code easily, applying the `ExpectedException` attribute to the test method as shown in the following example. This way, the test method succeeds with the exception:

```
[TestMethod]
[ExpectedException(typeof(ArgumentNullException))]
public void TestStringSampleNull()
{
    StringSample sample = new StringSample(null);
}
```

The exception thrown by the `GetStringDemo` method can be dealt with similarly.

Testing All Code Paths

To test all code paths, multiple tests can be created, with each one taking a different route. The following test sample passes the strings a and b to the `GetStringDemo` method. Because the second string is not contained within the first string, the first path of the `if` statement applies. The result is checked accordingly:

```
[TestMethod]
public void GetStringDemoAB()
{
    string expected = "b not found in a";
    StringSample sample = new StringSample(String.Empty);
    string actual = sample.GetStringDemo("a", "b");
    Assert.AreEqual(expected, actual);
}
```

The next test method verifies another path of the `GetStringDemo` method. Here, the second string is found in the first one, and the index is lower than 5; therefore, it results in the second code block of the `if` statement:

```
[TestMethod]
public void GetStringDemoABCDBC()
{
    string expected = "removed bc from abcd: ad";
    StringSample sample = new StringSample(String.Empty);
    string actual = sample.GetStringDemo("abcd", "bc");
    Assert.AreEqual(expected, actual);
}
```

All other code paths can be tested similarly. To see what code is covered by unit tests, and what code is still missing, you can open the Code Coverage Results window, shown in Figure 17-54.

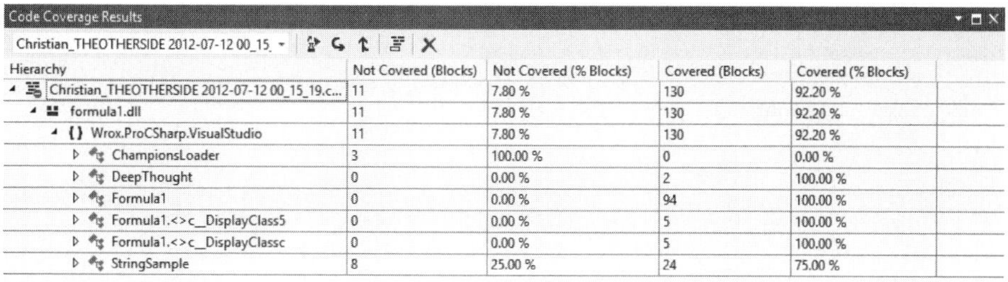

Hierarchy	Not Covered (Blocks)	Not Covered (% Blocks)	Covered (Blocks)	Covered (% Blocks)	
Christian_THEOTHERSIDE 2012-07-12 00_15_19.c...	11	7.80 %	130	92.20 %	
formula1.dll	11	7.80 %	130	92.20 %	
{} Wrox.ProCSharp.VisualStudio	11	7.80 %	130	92.20 %	
ChampionsLoader	3	100.00 %	0	0.00 %	
DeepThought	0	0.00 %	2	100.00 %	
Formula1	0	0.00 %	94	100.00 %	
Formula1.<>c__DisplayClass5	0	0.00 %	5	100.00 %	
Formula1.<>c__DisplayClassc	0	0.00 %	5	100.00 %	
StringSample	8	25.00 %	24	75.00 %	

FIGURE 17-54

External Dependencies

Many methods are dependent on some functionality outside of the application's control, e.g., calling a web service or accessing a database. Maybe the service or database is not available during some test runs, which tests the availability of these external resources. Or worse, maybe the database or service returns different data over time, and it's hard to compare this with expected data. This must be excluded from the unit test.

The following example is dependent on some functionality outside. The method `ChampionsByCountry` accesses an XML file from a web server that contains a list of Formula-1 world champions with `Firstname`, `Lastname`, `Wins`, and `Country` elements. This list is filtered by country, and numerically ordered using the value from the `Wins` element. The returned data is a `XElement` that contains converted XML code:

```
public XElement ChampionsByCountry(string country)
{
  XElement champions = XElement.Load(
    "http://www.cninnovation.com/downloads/Racers.xml");
  var q = from r in champions.Elements("Racer")
          where r.Element("Country").Value == country
          orderby int.Parse(r.Element("Wins").Value) descending
          select new XElement("Racer",
            new XAttribute("Name", r.Element("Firstname").Value + " " +
              r.Element("Lastname").Value),
            new XAttribute("Country", r.Element("Country").Value),
            new XAttribute("Wins", r.Element("Wins").Value));
  return new XElement("Racers", q.ToArray());
}
```

> **NOTE** *For more information on LINQ to XML, read Chapter 34, "Manipulating XML."*

For this method a unit test should be done. The test should not be dependent on the source from the server. Server unavailability is one issue, but it can also be expected that the data on the server changes over time to return new champions, and other values. The current test should ensure that filtering is done as expected, returning a correctly filtered list, and in the correct order.

One way to create a unit test that is independent of the data source is to refactor the implementation of the `ChampionsByCountry` method by using a factory that returns a `XElement` to replace the `XElement` `.Load` method with something that can be independent of the data source. The interface `IChampionsLoader` defines an interface with the method `LoadChampions` that can replace the aforementioned method:

```
public interface IChampionsLoader
{
  XElement LoadChampions();
}
```

The class ChampionsLoader, which implements the interface IChampionsLoader, implements the interface by using the XElement.Load method:

```
public class ChampionsLoader : IChampionsLoader
{
   public XElement LoadChampions()
   {
      return XElement.Load("http://www.cninnovation.com/downloads/Racers.xml");
   }
}
```

Now it's possible to change the implementation of the ChampionsByCountry method (the new method is named ChampionsByCountry2 to make both variants available for unit testing) by using an interface to load the champions instead of using XElement.Load directly. The IChampionsLoader is passed with the constructor of the class Formula1, and this loader is then used by ChampionsByCountry2:

```
public class Formula1
{
   private IChampionsLoader loader;
   public Formula1(IChampionsLoader loader)
   {
      this.loader = loader;
   }

   public XElement ChampionsByCountry2(string country)
   {
      var q = from r in loader.LoadChampions().Elements("Racer")
              where r.Element("Country").Value == country
              orderby int.Parse(r.Element("Wins").Value) descending
              select new XElement("Racer",
                new XAttribute("Name", r.Element("Firstname").Value + " " +
                  r.Element("Lastname").Value),
                new XAttribute("Country", r.Element("Country").Value),
                new XAttribute("Wins", r.Element("Wins").Value));
      return new XElement("Racers", q.ToArray());
   }
}
```

With a typical implementation, a ChampionsLoader instance would be passed to the Formula1 constructor to retrieve the racers from the server.

Creating the unit test, a custom method can be implemented that returns sample Formula-1 champions, as shown in the method Formula1SampleData:

```
internal static string Formula1SampleData()
{
   return @"
<Racers>
  <Racer>
    <Firstname>Nelson</Firstname>
    <Lastname>Piquet</Lastname>
    <Country>Brazil</Country>
    <Starts>204</Starts>
    <Wins>23</Wins>
  </Racer>
  <Racer>
    <Firstname>Ayrton</Firstname>
    <Lastname>Senna</Lastname>
    <Country>Brazil</Country>
    <Starts>161</Starts>
```

```
    <Wins>41</Wins>
  </Racer>
  <Racer>
    <Firstname>Nigel</Firstname>
    <Lastname>Mansell</Lastname>
    <Country>England</Country>
    <Starts>187</Starts>
    <Wins>31</Wins>
  </Racer>
  //... more sample data
```

For verifying the results that should be returned, verification data is created that matches the request with the sample data with the `Formula1VerificationData` method:

```
    internal static XElement Formula1VerificationData()
    {
      return XElement.Parse(@"
<Racers>
  <Racer Name=""Mika Hakkinen"" Country=""Finland"" Wins=""20"" />
  <Racer Name=""Kimi Raikkonen"" Country=""Finland"" Wins=""18"" />
</Racers>");
    }
```

The loader of the test data implements the same interface—`IChampionsLoader`—as the `ChampionsLoader` class. This loader just makes use of the sample data; it doesn't access the web server:

```
    public class F1TestLoader : IChampionsLoader
    {
      public XElement LoadChampions()
      {
        return XElement.Parse(Formula1SampleData());
      }
    }
```

Now it's easy to create a unit test that makes use of the sample data:

```
    [TestMethod]
    public void TestChampionsByCountry2()
    {

      Formula1 f1 = new Formula1(new F1TestLoader());
      XElement actual = f1.ChampionsByCountry2("Finland");

      Assert.AreEqual(Formula1VerificationData().ToString(),
        actual.ToString());
    }
```

Of course, a real test should not only cover a case that passes Finland as a string and two champions are returned with the test data. Other tests should be written to pass a string with no matching result, a case in which more than two champions are returned, and probably a case in which the number sort order would be different from the alphanumeric sort order.

Fakes Framework

It's not always possible to refactor the method that should be tested to be independent of a data source. This is when the *Fakes Framework* becomes very useful. This framework is part of Visual Studio Ultimate Edition.

The ChampionsByCountry method is tested as it was before. The implementation makes use of XElement .Load, which directly accesses a file on the web server. The Fakes Framework enables you to change the implementation of the ChampionsByCountry method just for the testing case by replacing the XElement .Load method with something else:

```
public XElement ChampionsByCountry(string country)
{
  XElement champions = XElement.Load(
    "http://www.cninnovation.com/downloads/Racers.xml");
  var q = from r in champions.Elements("Racer")
          where r.Element("Country").Value == country
          orderby int.Parse(r.Element("Wins").Value) descending
          select new XElement("Racer",
            new XAttribute("Name", r.Element("Firstname").Value + " " +
              r.Element("Lastname").Value),
            new XAttribute("Country", r.Element("Country").Value),
            new XAttribute("Wins", r.Element("Wins").Value));
  return new XElement("Racers", q.ToArray());
}
```

To use the Fakes Framework with the references of the unit testing project, select the assembly that contains the XElement class. XElement is within the System.Xml.Linq assembly. Opening the context menu while the System.Xml.Linq assembly is selected provides the menu option Add Fakes Assembly. Selecting this creates the System.Xml.Linq.4.0.0.0.Fakes assembly, which contains shim classes in the namespace System.Xml.Linq.Fakes. You will find all the types of the System.Xml.Linq assembly with a shimmed version, e.g., ShimXAttribute for XAttribute, and ShimXDocument for XDocument. For the example, only ShimXElement is needed. ShimXElement contains a member for every public over-loaded member of the XElement class. The Load method of XElement is overloaded to receive a string, a Stream, a TextReader, and an XmlReader, and overloads exist with a second LoadOptions parameter. ShimXElement defines members named LoadString, LoadStream, LoadTextReader, LoadXmlReader, and others with LoadOptions as well, such as LoadStringLoadOptions and LoadStreamLoadOptions. All these members are of a delegate type that allows specifying a custom method that should be invoked in place of the method call in the method that should be tested. The unit test method TestChampionsByCountry replaces the XElement.Load method with one parameter in the Formula1.ChampionsByCountry method with the call to XElement.Parse, accessing the sample data. ShimXElement.LoadString specifies the new implementation. Using shims, it's necessary to create a context, which you can do using ShimsContext .Create. The context is active until the Dispose method is invoked by the end of the using block:

```
[TestMethod]
public void TestChampionsByCountry()
{
  using (ShimsContext.Create())
  {
    ShimXElement.LoadString = s => XElement.Parse(Formula1SampleData());

    Formula1 f1 = new Formula1();
    XElement actual = f1.ChampionsByCountry("Finland");

    Assert.AreEqual(Formula1VerificationData().ToString(),
      actual.ToString());
  }
}
```

Although it is best to have a flexible implementation of the code that should be tested, the Fakes Framework offers a useful way to change an implementation such that it is not dependent on outside resources for testing purposes.

WINDOWS 8, WCF, WF, AND MORE

This last section of the chapter looks at some specific application types. We've already covered console and WPF applications; now let's get into WCF, WF, and Windows 8 applications. Windows 8 applications are new with Visual Studio 2012, but only if you're running on a Windows 8 system, of course.

Building WCF Applications with Visual Studio 2012

A WCF service library is a project template for creating a service that can be called from a client application using requests that use either the SOAP protocol across HTTP, TCP, or other networking protocols, or a REST-style form of communication.

The template for the WCF service application automatically creates a service contract, an operation contract, a data contract, and a service implementation file—all you need to provide is a small sample implementation.

Running the application starts both a server and a client application to test the service. The dialog of the server application is shown in Figure 17-55. If the host fails to start for some reason, you can access this dialog from the Windows notification area to determine the cause. If the host shouldn't be started, you can disable it with the WCF options in the project properties.

FIGURE 17-55

The WCF Test client (see Figure 17-56) is started because of the debug command-line argument settings `/client:"WcfTestClient.exe"`. Using this dialog you can invoke many different kinds of service calls (not all calls are supported). It enables easy testing that also provides information about the SOAP message that is sent.

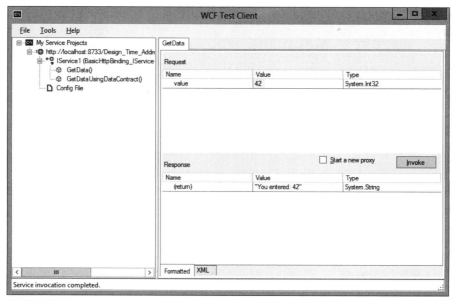

FIGURE 17-56

WCF applications are discussed in detail in Chapter 43, "Windows Communication Foundation."

Building WF Applications with Visual Studio 2012

Another dramatically different application style (when it comes to building the application from within Visual Studio) is the Windows Workflow application type. For an example of this, select the Workflow Console Application project type from the Workflow section of the New Project dialog. This will create a console application with a `Workflow1.xaml` file.

When building applications that make use of Windows Workflow Foundation, you'll notice that there is a heavy dependency on the design view. With the designer, you can create variables and drop many different activities from the toolbox onto the design view. Looking closely at the workflow (see Figure 17-57), you can see that it consists of a `while` loop, a sequence, and actions based on conditions (such as an `if-else` statement).

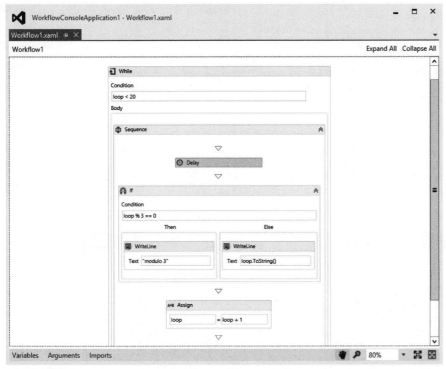

FIGURE 17-57

Windows Workflow Foundation is covered in detail in Chapter 45, "Windows Workflow Foundation"

Building Windows Store apps with Visual Studio 2012

A complete new category of Visual Studio project templates is available for Windows Store apps: Windows Store. The Grid App (XAML) template already contains three pages with sample data. Using this template, you'll find several files in Solution Explorer. The `Assets` folder contains some predefined icons. The `Common` folder contains some helper classes such as a base class for bindable objects, converters, a suspension manager, and a base page class that is aware of layout changes. The `DataModel` folder contains classes that produce sample data, and there are some XAML pages with code-behind. A package Manifest Editor opens when you click the `Package.appxmanifest` file (see Figure 17-58). This editor, which is specific to Windows Store apps, enables configuration of the UI to define names and tiles, capabilities and declarations, and how the application should be packaged.

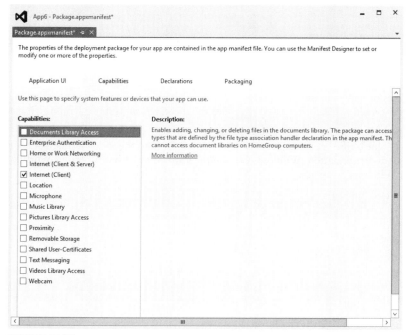

FIGURE 17-58

Running the application (see Figure 17-59), you can see that the template already defined formatting and styles as required by the Windows Store app guidelines. Clearly, it's a lot easier to start with this, rather than create all the styles from scratch. You likely already know some Windows Store apps that were started with this project template.

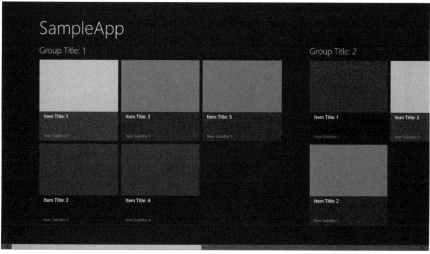

FIGURE 17-59

Windows Store apps are covered in more detail in Chapters 31, "Windows Runtime," and 38, "Windows Store apps."

SUMMARY

This chapter explored one of the most important programming tools in the .NET environment: Visual Studio 2012. The bulk of the chapter examined how this tool facilitates writing code in C#.

Visual Studio 2012 is one of the easiest development environments to work with in the programming world. Not only does Visual Studio make rapid application development (RAD) easy to achieve, it enables you to dig deeply into the mechanics of how your applications are created. This chapter focused on using Visual Studio for refactoring, multi-targeting, analyzing existing code, and creating unit tests and making use of the Fakes Framework.

This chapter also looked at some of the latest projects available to you through the .NET Framework 4.5, including Windows Presentation Foundation, Windows Communication Foundation, Windows Workflow Foundation, and of course Windows Store apps.

Chapter 18 is on deployment of applications.

18

Deployment

WROX.COM CODE DOWNLOADS FOR THIS CHAPTER

The wrox.com code downloads for this chapter are found at http://www.wrox.com/remtitle .cgi?isbn=1118314425 on the Download Code tab. The code for this chapter is found in the following examples:

➤ WPFSampleApp

➤ WebSampleApp

➤ Win8SplitApp

➤ Win8PackageSample

DEPLOYMENT AS PART OF THE APPLICATION LIFE CYCLE

The development process does not end when the source code is compiled and the testing is complete. At that stage, the job of getting the application into the user's hands begins. Whether it's an ASP.NET application, a WPF client application, or an application built for Windows 8, the software must be deployed to a target environment.

Deployment should be considered very early in the design of the application, as this can influence the technology to be used for the application itself.

The .NET Framework has made deployment much easier than it was in the past. The pains of registering COM components and writing new hives to the registry have been eliminated.

This chapter looks at the options that are available for application deployment, both from an ASP.NET perspective and from the rich client perspective including Windows 8 Apps.

PLANNING FOR DEPLOYMENT

Often, deployment is an afterthought in the development process that can lead to nasty, if not costly, surprises. To avoid grief in deployment scenarios, you should plan the deployment process during the initial design stage. Any special deployment considerations — such as server capacity, desktop security, or where assemblies will be loaded from — should be built into the design from the start, resulting in a much smoother deployment process.

Another issue that you should address early in the development process is the environment in which to test the deployment. Whereas unit testing of application code and deployment options can be done on the developer's system, the deployment must be tested in an environment that resembles the target system. This is important to eliminate the dependencies that don't exist on a targeted computer. An example of this might be a third-party library that has been installed on the developer's computer early in the project. The target computer might not have this library on it. It can be easy to forget to include it in the deployment package. Testing on the developer's system would not uncover the error because the library already exists. Documenting dependencies can help to eliminate this potential problem.

Deployment processes can be complex for a large application. Planning for the deployment can save time and effort when the deployment process is actually implemented.

Choosing the proper deployment option must be done with the same care and planning as any other aspect of the system being developed. Choosing the wrong option makes the process of getting the software into the users' hands difficult and frustrating.

Overview of Deployment Options

This section provides an overview of the deployment options that are available to .NET developers. Most of these options are discussed in greater detail later in this chapter:

➤ **xcopy** — The xcopy utility lets you copy an assembly or group of assemblies to an application folder, reducing your development time. Because assemblies are self-discovering (that is, the metadata that describes the assembly is included in the assembly), you do not need to register anything in the registry.

Each assembly keeps track of what other assemblies it requires to execute. By default, the assembly looks in the current application folder for the dependencies. The process of moving (or probing) assemblies to other folders is discussed later in this chapter.

➤ **ClickOnce** — The ClickOnce technology offers a way to build self-updating Windows-based applications. ClickOnce enables an application to be published to a website, a file share, or even a CD. As updates and new builds are made to the application, they can be published to the same location or site by the development team. As the application is used by the end user, it can automatically check the location to see if an update is available. If so, an update is attempted.

➤ **Windows Installer** — There are some restrictions when ClickOnce doesn't work. If the installation requires administrative privileges (e.g., for deploying Windows Services), Windows Installer can be the best option.

➤ **Deploying web applications** — When a website is deployed, a virtual site is created with IIS, and the files needed to run the application are copied to the server. With Visual Studio you have different options to copy the files: using the FTP protocol, accessing a network share, or using a commonly used option in previous years, FrontPage Server Extensions (FPSE). A newer technology is creating *Web Deploy* packages, which are discussed later in this chapter.

➤ **Windows 8 apps** — These apps can be deployed from the Windows Store, or by using PowerShell scripts from an enterprise environment. Creating packages from Windows 8 apps is covered later in this chapter.

Deployment Requirements

It is instructive to look at the runtime requirements of a .NET-based application. The CLR has certain requirements on the target platform before any managed application can execute.

The first requirement that must be met is the operating system. Currently, the following operating systems can run .NET 4.5–based applications:

- ➤ Windows Vista SP2
- ➤ Windows 7
- ➤ Windows 8 (.NET 4.5 is already included)

The following server platforms are supported:

- ➤ Windows Server 2008 SP2
- ➤ Windows Server 2008 R2
- ➤ Windows Server 2012 (.NET 4.5 is already included)

For Windows 8 apps, Windows 8 is the required operating system.

You also must consider hardware requirements when deploying .NET applications. The minimum hardware requirements for both the client and the server are a CPU with 1GHz and 512MB of RAM.

For best performance, increase the amount of RAM — the more RAM the better your .NET application runs. This is especially true for server applications. You can use the Performance Monitor to analyze the RAM usage of your applications.

Deploying the .NET Runtime

When an application is developed using .NET, there is a dependency on the .NET runtime. This may seem rather obvious, but sometimes the obvious can be overlooked. The following table shows the version number and the filename that would have to be distributed. With Windows 8 and Windows Server 2012, .NET 4.5 is already included.

.NET VERSION	FILENAME
2.0.50727.42	`dotnetfx.exe`
3.0.4506.30	`dotnetfx3.exe` (includes x86 and x64)
3.5.21022.8	`dotnetfx35.exe` (includes x86, x64, and ia64)
4.0.0.0	`dotnetfx40.exe` (includes x86, x64, and ia64)
4.5.50501	`dotnetFx45.exe` (includes x86 and x64)

TRADITIONAL DEPLOYMENT

If deployment is part of an application's original design considerations, deployment can be as simple as copying a set of files to the target computer. This section discusses simple deployment scenarios and different options for deployment.

To see the first deployment option in action, you must have an application to deploy. At first, the `ClientWPF` solution is used, which requires the library `AppSupport`.

`ClientWPF` is a rich client application using WPF. `AppSupport` is a class library containing one simple class that returns a string with the current date and time.

The sample applications use AppSupport to fill a label with a string containing the current date. To use the examples, first load and build AppSupport. Then, in the ClientWPF project, set a reference to the newly built AppSupport.dll.

Here is the code for the AppSupport assembly:

```
using System;

namespace AppSupport
{
  public class DateService
  {
    public string GetLongDateInfoString()
    {
      return string.Format("Today's date is {0:D}", DateTime.Today);
    }

    public string GetShortDateInfoString()
    {
      return string.Format("Today's date is {0:d}", DateTime.Today);
    }
  }
}
```

This simple assembly suffices to demonstrate the deployment options available to you.

xcopy Deployment

xcopy deployment is a term used for the process of copying a set of files to a folder on the target machine and then executing the application on the client. The term comes from the DOS command xcopy.exe. Regardless of the number of assemblies, if the files are copied into the same folder, the application will execute — rendering the task of editing the configuration settings or registry obsolete.

To see how an xcopy deployment works, execute the following steps:

1. Open the ClientWPF solution (ClientWPF.sln) that is part of the sample download file.
2. Change the target to Release and do a full compile.
3. Use the File Explorer to navigate to the project folder \ClientWPF\bin\Release and double-click ClientWPF.exe to run the application.
4. Click the button to see the current date displayed in the two text boxes. This verifies that the application functions properly. Of course, this folder is where Visual Studio placed the output, so you would expect the application to work.
5. Create a new folder and call it ClientWPFTest. Copy just the two assemblies (AppSupport.dll and ClientWPFTest.exe) from the release folder to this new folder and then delete the release folder. Again, double-click the ClientWPF.exe file to verify that it's working.

That's all there is to it; xcopy deployment provides the capability to deploy a fully functional application simply by copying the assemblies to the target machine. Although the example used here is simple, you can use this process for more complex applications. There really is no limit to the size or number of assemblies that can be deployed using this method.

Scenarios in which you might not want to use xcopy deployment are when you need to place assemblies in the global assembly cache (GAC) or add icons to the Start menu. Also, if your application still relies on a COM library of some type, you will not be able to register the COM components easily.

xcopy and Web Applications

xcopy deployment can also work with web applications, with the exception of the folder structure. You must establish the virtual directory of your web application and configure the proper user rights. This process is generally accomplished with the IIS administration tool.

After the virtual directory is set up, the web application files can be copied to the virtual directory. Copying a web application's files can be a bit tricky. A couple of configuration files, as well as any images that the pages might be using, need to be accounted for.

Windows Installer

ClickOnce is Microsoft's preferred technology for installing Windows applications; it is discussed later in more depth. However, ClickOnce has some restrictions. ClickOnce installation doesn't require administrator rights and installs applications in a directory where the user has rights. If multiple users are working on one system, the application needs to be installed for all users. Also, it is not possible to install shared COM components and configure them in the registry, install assemblies to the GAC, and register Windows services. All these tasks require administrative privileges.

> **NOTE** *For information about installing assemblies to the GAC, read Chapter 19, "Assemblies."*

To do these administrative tasks, you need to create a Windows installer package. Installer packages are MSI files (which can be started from `setup.exe`) that make use of the Windows Installer technology.

Creating Windows installer packages is no longer part of Visual Studio 2012 (it was part of Visual Studio 2010). You can use InstallShield Limited Edition, which is free, with Visual Studio 2012. A project template includes information for the download and registration with Flexera Software.

InstallShield Limited Edition offers a simple wizard to create an installation package based on application information (name, website, version number); installation requirements (supported operating systems and prerequisite software before the installation can start); application files and their shortcuts on the Start menu and the desktop; and, settings for the registry. You can optionally prompt the user for a license agreement.

If this is all that you need, and you don't need to add custom dialogs to the installation experience, InstallShield Limited Edition can provide an adequate deployment solution. Otherwise, you need to install another product such as the full version of InstallShield (`www.flexerasoftware.com/products/installshield.htm`), or the free WiX toolset (`http://wix.codeplex.com`).

ClickOnce, Web Deploy packages, and deployment of Windows 8 apps are discussed in detail later in this chapter.

CLICKONCE

ClickOnce is a deployment technology that enables applications to be self-updating. Applications are published to a file share, website, or media such as a CD. When published, ClickOnce apps can be automatically updated with minimal user input.

ClickOnce also solves the security permission problem. Normally, to install an application the user needs Administrative rights. With ClickOnce, a user without admin rights can install and run the application. However, the application is installed in a user-specific directory. In case multiple users log in to the same system, every user needs to install the application.

ClickOnce Operation

ClickOnce applications have two XML-based manifest files associated with them. One is the application manifest, and the other is the deployment manifest. These two files describe everything that is required to deploy an application.

The *application manifest* contains information about the application such as permissions required, assemblies to include, and other dependencies. The *deployment manifest* contains details about the application's deployment, such as settings and location of the application manifest. The complete schemas for the manifests are in the .NET SDK documentation.

As mentioned earlier, ClickOnce has some limitations, such as assemblies cannot be added to the GAC, and Windows Services cannot be configured in the registry. In such scenarios, Windows Installer is clearly a better choice. ClickOnce can still be used for a large number of applications, however.

Publishing a ClickOnce Application

Because everything that ClickOnce needs to know is contained in the two manifest files, the process of publishing an application for ClickOnce deployment is simply generating the manifests and placing the files in the proper location. The manifest files can be generated in Visual Studio 2012. There is also a command-line tool (mage.exe) and a version with a GUI (mageUI.exe).

You can create the manifest files in Visual Studio 2012 in two ways. At the bottom of the Publish tab on the Project Properties dialog are two buttons: Publish Wizard and Publish Now. The Publish Wizard asks several questions about the deployment of the application and then generates the manifest files and copies all the needed files to the deployment location. The Publish Now button uses the values that have been set in the Publish tab to create the manifest files and copies the files to the deployment location.

To use the command-line tool, mage.exe, the values for the various ClickOnce properties must be passed in. Manifest files can be both created and updated using mage.exe. Typing **mage.exe -help** at the command prompt gives the syntax for passing in the values required.

The GUI version of mage.exe (mageUI.exe) is similar in appearance to the Publish tab in Visual Studio 2012. An application and deployment manifest file can be created and updated using the GUI tool.

ClickOnce applications appear in the Install/Uninstall Programs control panel applet just like any other installed application. One big difference is that the user is presented with the choice of either uninstalling the application or rolling back to the previous version. ClickOnce keeps the previous version in the ClickOnce application cache.

Let's start with the process of creating a ClickOnce installation. As a prerequisite for this process, you need to have IIS installed on the system, and Visual Studio must be started with elevated privileges. The ClickOnce installation program will be directly published to the local IIS, which requires administrative privileges.

Open the ClientWPF project with Visual Studio, select the Publish tab in the Project properties, and click the Publish Wizard button. The first screen, shown in Figure 18-1, asks for the publish location. Use the local IIS http://localhost/ProCSharpSample.

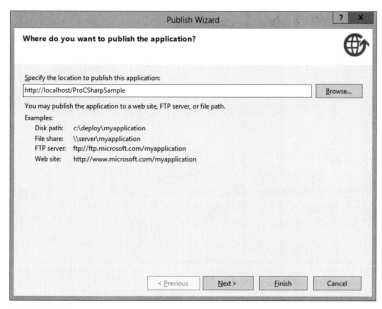

FIGURE 18-1

The next screen provides the option to place a shortcut on the Start menu to make the application available online or offline. Leave the default option. Then you are ready to publish, and a browser window is opened to install the application (see Figure 18-2).

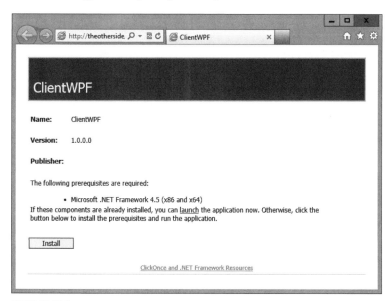

FIGURE 18-2

Before clicking the Install button, we'll have a look at the ClickOnce settings that have been made by the wizard.

ClickOnce Settings

Several properties are available for both manifest files. You can configure many of these properties with the Publish tab (see Figure 18-3) within the Visual Studio project settings. The most important property is the location from which the application should be deployed. We've used IIS with the sample, but a network share or CD could be used as well.

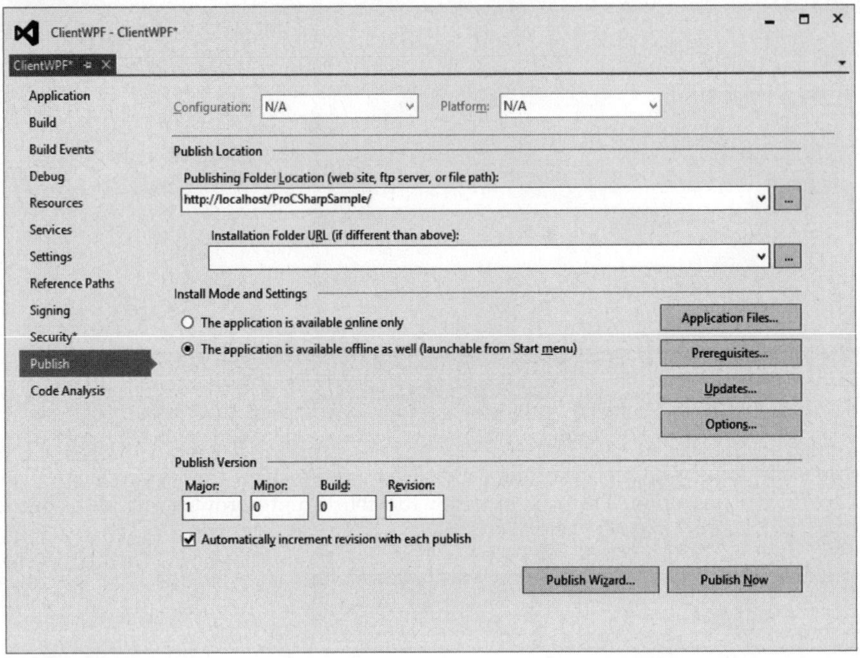

FIGURE 18-3

The Publish tab has an Application Files button that invokes a dialog that lists all assemblies and configuration files required by the application. The Prerequisite button displays a list of common prerequisites that can be installed along with the application. These prerequisites are defined by Microsoft Installer packages and need to be installed before the ClickOnce application can be installed. Referring back to Figure 18-2, you can see the .NET Framework 4.5 listed as a prerequisite before the application can be installed using the web page. You have the choice of installing the prerequisites from the same location from which the application is being published or from the vendor's website.

The Updates button displays a dialog (see Figure 18-4) containing information about how the application should be updated. As new versions of an application are made available, ClickOnce can be used to update the application.

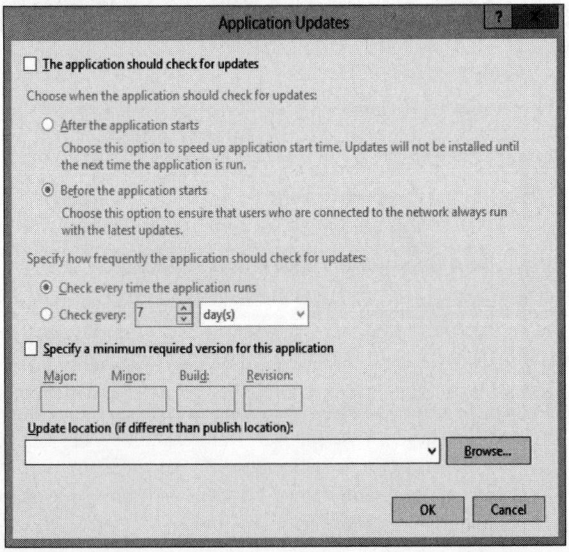

FIGURE 18-4

Options include checking for updates every time the application starts or checking in the background. If the background option is selected, a specified period of time between checks can be entered. Options for allowing the user to be able to decline or accept the update are available. This can be used to force an update in the background so that users are never aware that the update is occurring. The next time the application is run, the new version is used instead of the older version. A separate location for the update files can be used as well. This way, the original installation package can be located in one location and installed for new users, and all the updates can be staged in another location.

You can set the application up so that it will run in either online or offline mode. In offline mode the application can be run from the Start menu and acts as if it were installed using the Windows Installer. Online mode means that the application will run only if the installation folder is available.

Using the Publish Wizard made more changes with the project settings than you can see in the Publish tab. With the Signing tab, you can see that the ClickOnce manifest is signed. For the current deployment, a test certificate was created. The test certificate is only good for testing. Before changing to production you need to get an application signing certificate from a certification authority, and sign the manifest with this. Looking at the Security tab, you can see that ClickOnce security has been enabled, and by default the application is configured as a full-trust application. This configuration gives the application the same rights the user has, and it can do all the things the user is allowed to do. Users are prompted with the installation regarding whether they trust the application. The configuration can be changed to a partial-trust application, which applies lower ClickOnce security permissions. For example, with the Internet zone the application can only read and write from isolated storage instead of accessing the complete file system. You can read more about the .NET code access security in Chapter 22.

Application Cache for ClickOnce Files

Applications distributed with ClickOnce are not installed in the `Program Files` folder. Instead, they are placed in an application cache that resides in the `Local Settings` folder under the current user's `Documents And Settings` folder. Controlling this aspect of the deployment means that multiple versions of an application can reside on the client PC at the same time. If the application is set to run online, every version that the user has accessed is retained. For applications that are set to run locally, the current and previous versions are retained.

This makes it a very simple process to roll back a ClickOnce application to its previous version. If the user selects the Install/Uninstall Programs control panel applet, the dialog presented contains the options to remove the ClickOnce application or roll back to the previous version (see Figure 18-5). An administrator can change the manifest file to point to the previous version. If the administrator does this, the next time the user runs that application, a check is made for an update. Instead of finding new assemblies to deploy, the application will restore the previous version without any interaction from the user.

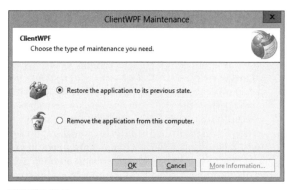

FIGURE 18-5

Application Installation

Now let's start the application installation from the browser screen shown earlier (refer to Figure 18-2). Running on Windows 8, you will get a message from Windows SmartScreen as shown in Figure 18-6. Because the certificate that is used does not come from a trusted certification authority, and thus the publisher is unknown, a warning is shown for the user: Windows protected your PC. To continue the installation you need to click on the Run Anyway button.

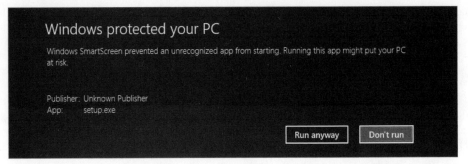

FIGURE 18-6

Next, you will see the dialog as shown in Figure 18-7, which that is also appears on Windows 7 and older systems. It's the same issue with the certificate, the publisher is unknown. Clicking on the More Information link, the user can get more information about the certificate, and see that the application wants full-trust access. If the user trusts the application, he or she can click the Install button to install the application.

After the installation, you can find the application with the Start menu, and it's also listed with Programs And Features in the control panel.

FIGURE 18-7

ClickOnce Deployment API

With the ClickOnce settings you can configure the application to automatically check for updates as discussed earlier, but often. Often this is not a practical approach. Maybe some super-users should get a new version of the application earlier. If they are happy with the new version, other users should be privileged to receive the update as well. With such a scenario, you can use your own user-management information database, and update the application programmatically.

For programmatic updates, the assembly `System.Deployment` and classes from the `System.Deployment` namespace can be used to check application version information and do an update. The following code snippet (code file `MainWindow.xaml.cs`) contains a click handler for an Update button in the application. It first checks whether the application is a ClickOnce-deployed application by checking the `IsNetworkDeployed` property from the `ApplicationDeployment` class. Using the `CheckForUpdateAsync` method, it determines whether a newer version is available on the server (in the update directory specified by the ClickOnce settings). On receiving the information about the update, the `CheckForUpdateCompleted` event is fired. With this event handler, the second argument (type `CheckForUpdateCompletedEventArgs`) contains information on the update, the version number, and whether it is a mandatory update. If an update is available, it is installed automatically by calling the `UpdateAsync` method:

```
private void OnUpdate(object sender, RoutedEventArgs e)
{
  if (ApplicationDeployment.IsNetworkDeployed)
  {
    ApplicationDeployment.CurrentDeployment.CheckForUpdateCompleted +=
      (sender1, e1) =>
      {
        if (e1.UpdateAvailable)
        {
          ApplicationDeployment.CurrentDeployment.UpdateCompleted +=
            (sender2, e2) =>
```

```
        {
            MessageBox.Show("Update completed");
        };
        ApplicationDeployment.CurrentDeployment.UpdateAsync();
    }
    else
    {
        MessageBox.Show("No update available");
    }

    };
    ApplicationDeployment.CurrentDeployment.CheckForUpdateAsync();
    }
}
```

Using the Deployment API code, you can manually test for updates directly from the application.

WEB DEPLOYMENT

With web applications, binaries for controllers (MVC) or code-behind (Web Forms), as well as HTML, JavaScript files, style sheets, and configuration files need to be deployed.

The easiest way to deploy a web application is to use Web Deploy. This feature is available both with on-premises IIS as well as Windows Azure websites. With Web Deploy, a package is created that can be directly uploaded with IIS. This package is a zip file that contains all the content needed for a web application, including database files.

Web Application

To demonstrate Web Deploy, a new ASP.NET MVC 4 project using the template Internet Application is created. This automatically creates an application with Home and About pages, including login and registration, as shown in Figure 18-8.

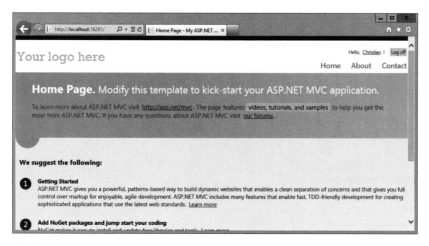

FIGURE 18-8

Configuration Files

One important part of the web application is the configuration file. In terms of deployment, you have to consider different versions of this file. For example, if you are using a different database for the web application that is running on the local system, there's a special testing database for the staging server, and of course a live database for the production server. The connection string is different for these servers, just as the debug configuration differs. If you create separate `Web.config` files for these scenarios and then add a new configuration value to the local `Web.config` file, it would be easy to overlook changing the other configuration files.

Visual Studio offers a special feature to deal with that. You can create one configuration file, and define how the file should be transformed to the staging and deployment servers. By default, with an ASP.NET web project, in the Solution Explorer you can see a `Web.config` file alongside `Web.debug.config` and `Web.release.config`. These two later files contain only transformations. You can also add other configuration files, e.g., for a staging server, as well. This can be done by selecting the solution in Solution Explorer, opening the Configuration Manager, and adding a new configuration (e.g., a Staging configuration). As soon as a new configuration is available, you can select the `Web.config` file, and choose the Add Config Transform option from the context menu. This then adds a config transformation file with the name of the configuration, e.g., `Web.Staging.config`.

The content of the transformation configuration files just defines transformations from the original configuration file, e.g., the compilation element below `system.web` is changed to remove the `debug` attribute as follows:

```
<system.web>
  <compilation xdt:Transform="RemoveAttributes(debug)" />
```

Creating a Web Deploy Package

To define the deployment for a web application, the project properties provide the Package/Publish Web settings (see Figure 18-9). With the configuration, you can select to publish only the files needed to run the application. This excludes all the C# source code files. Other options are to publish all files in the project, or all files in the project folder.

With the items to deploy, you can specify including databases with the package that are defined with the separate Package/Publish SQL tab. There you can import databases from the configuration file, and create SQL scripts to create the schema and also load data. These scripts can be included with the package to create a database on the target system.

The other configuration options with Package/Publish Web are the name of the zip file and the name of the IIS application. When deploying the package to IIS, the name defined with the package is the default unless the proposed. The administrator deploying the web application overrides it with a different name.

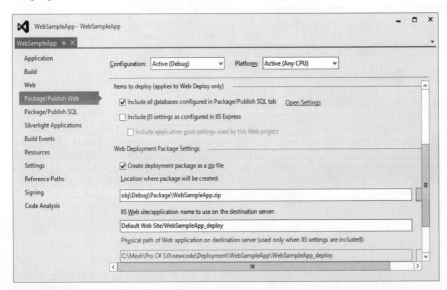

FIGURE 18-9

After the package is configured, the Publish menu in the context menu of the Solution Explorer can be selected to create a package. The first dialog enables creating or selecting a profile. Profiles can be used to deploy packages to different servers, e.g., you can define one profile to deploy to the staging server, and one profile for the production server. If you are running your site on Windows Azure websites, you can download a profile from Windows Azure that can be imported with the Publish Web tool. This profile contains a URL for the server as well as a username and password. The the second dialog of this wizard enables to specify the publish method. Valid options are to create a Web Deploy Package (which you do now), directly perform a Web Deploy to a server, or use FTP, the file system, or the FrontPage Server Extensions. Figure 18-10 shows the Web Deploy Package selected, and thus allows defining the package location and the name of the website. The third dialog enables you to specify the configuration that should be deployed to the package. If you created the Staging configuration earlier, now Debug, Release, and Staging configurations are available.

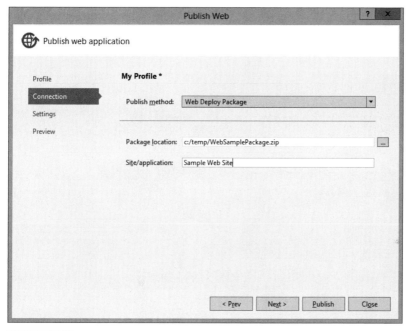

FIGURE 18-10

After completing the wizard and clicking the Publish button, the Web Deploy package is created. You can open it to see the files in the package. If you have IIS running, you can open the IIS Manager to deploy the zip file and create a new web application.

WINDOWS 8 APPS

Installing Windows 8 apps is a completely different story. With normal .NET applications, copying the executable with the DLLs as shown earlier with xcopy deployment is one way to go. This is not an option with Windows 8 apps. Unpackaged apps can only be used on systems with a developer license.

Windows 8 apps need to be packaged. This enables the app in the Windows Store to make the application broadly available in the Windows Store. There's also a different option to deploy Windows 8 apps in an environment without adding it to the Windows Store. This is known as *sideloading*. With all these options it is necessary to create an app package, so let's start with that.

Creating an App Package

A Windows 8 app package is a file with the .appx file extension, which that is really just a zip file. This file contains all the XAML files, binaries, pictures, and configurations. You can create a package with either Visual Studio or the command-line utility MakeAppx.exe.

A simple Windows 8 app that already contains some core functionality can be created with the Visual Studio application template Split App (XAML) that is in the Windows Store category. This template includes two pages that can be navigated. The sample app has the name Win8SplitApp.

What's important for the packaging are images in the Assets folder. The files Logo, SmallLogo, and StoreLogo represent logos of the application that should be replaced by custom application logos. The file Package.appxmanifest is a XML file that contains all the definitions needed for the app package. Opening this file invokes the Package Editor, which contains four tabs: Application UI, Capabilities, Declarations, and Packaging. The Packaging dialog is shown in Figure 18-11. Here you can configure the package name, the logo for the store, the version number and the certificate. By default, only just a certificate for testing purposes is created. Before deploying the application, the certificate must be replaced with a certificate from a certification authority that is trusted by Windows.

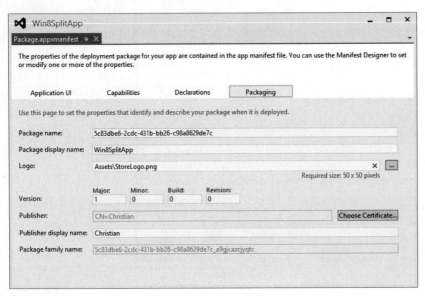

FIGURE 18-11

The Application UI tab enables configuration of the application name, a description of the application, and small and wide logos. Configurable capabilities vary according to the system features and the devices the application is using, e.g., the Music Library, or the webcam, etc. The user is informed about which capabilities the application is using. If the application does not specify the capabilities it needs, during runtime the application is not allowed to use it. With the Declarations tab, the application can register more features, e.g., to use it as a share target, or to specify whether some functionality should run in the background.

Using Visual Studio, you can create a package by clicking the project in Solution Explorer, and selecting the Store ⇨ Create App Package context menu. The first selection with this Create App Package wizard is to specify whether the application should be uploaded to the Windows Store. If that's not the case, sideloading can be used to deploy the package, as discussed later. In case you didn't register your account with the Windows Store yet, select the sideloading option. In the second dialog of the wizard, select Release instead of Debug Code for the package; you can also select the platforms for which the package should be generated: x86, x64, and ARM CPUs. This is all that's needed to build the package. To view what's in the package you can rename the .appx file to a .zip file extension, and find all the images, metadata, and binaries.

Windows App Certification Kit

Upon creation of the app package, the last dialog of the wizard enables the Windows App Certification Kit. The command line for this tool is `appcertui.exe`. You can use this command line and pass the package for testing.

When you deploy your application to the Windows Store, it is necessary for the application to fulfill some requirements. You can check most of the requirements beforehand.

Running this tool you should give the application some time. It requires several minutes to test the application and get the results. During this time you shouldn't interact with the tool or your running application. The following table shows what is tested with the application:

TEST	DESCRIPTION
Crashes and hangs test	The application may not crash or stop responding. Long-running tasks should be done asynchronously to prevent blocking the application.
App manifest compliance test	Verifies that the app manifest content is correct. Also, the application might only have one tile after the installation. The user can add additional tiles while configuring the application, but for the start only one tile is allowed.
Windows security features test	Verifies that the application does not delete the user's data without consent, and it won't be an entry point for viruses or malware.
Supported API test	The app may only use Windows 8 APIs (Windows Runtime and a subset of .NET), and cannot depend on libraries that don't have this limitation. The app may only depend on software from the Windows Store.
Performance test	The app must launch in 5 seconds or less, and suspend in 2 seconds or less.
App manifest resources test	The app must contain localized resources for all the languages it supports.

Figure 18-12 shows a partial result of a successful run of the tests.

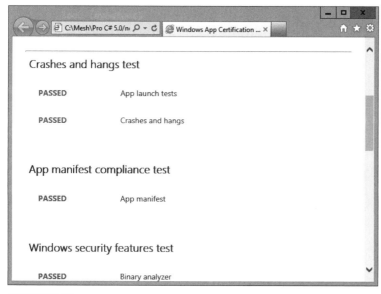

FIGURE 18-12

Sideloading

For the broadest set of customers, you should publish the app to the Windows Store. With the store you have flexibility in terms of licensing; that is, you can have a version for sale to individuals, or volume licensing whereby you can identify who is running the app based on a unique ID and device.

For enterprise scenarios, when the application shouldn't be in the Windows Store, sideloading can be used.

Sideloading has some requirements for the participating systems: the PC needs to be joined with an Active Directory, and a group policy that allows all trusted apps to be installed needs to be in place. This group policy adds the registry key `HKEY_LOCAL_MACHINE\Software\Policies\Microsoft\Windows\Appx\AllowAllTrustedApps` with a value of 1. The last requirement is that the application must be signed with a certificate that is trusted. This can also be a custom certificate whereby the certification server is listed as a trusted root certification authority.

> **NOTE** *Windows 8 Enterprise edition has sideloading enabled by default.*

Custom applications can be preinstalled for all users on an initial Windows 8 image that is distributed to all client systems, or installed with the following PowerShell cmdlet:

```
add-appxpackage Package.appx
```

Windows Deployment API

The new Windows Runtime defines the namespace `Windows.Management.Deployment`, which contains the `PackageManager` class, which can be used to deploy Windows 8 packages programmatically. The `AddPackageAsync` method adds a package to the system, `RemovePackageAsync` removes it.

The following code snippet (code file `Win8PackageSample/Program.cs`) demonstrates the use of the `PackageManager` class. The `PackageManager` can only be used from desktop applications, which is why a .NET console application was created:

```
using System;
using System.Collections.Generic;
using System.IO;
using Windows.ApplicationModel;
using Windows.Management.Deployment;

namespace Win8PackageSample
{
  class Program
  {
    static void Main()
    {
      var pm = new PackageManager();
      IEnumerable<Package> packages = pm.FindPackages();
      foreach (var package in packages)
      {
        try
        {
          Console.WriteLine("Architecture: {0}",
            package.Id.Architecture.ToString());
          Console.WriteLine("Family: {0}", package.Id.FamilyName);
          Console.WriteLine("Full name: {0}", package.Id.FullName);
          Console.WriteLine("Name: {0}", package.Id.Name);
          Console.WriteLine("Publisher: {0}", package.Id.Publisher);
```

```
            Console.WriteLine("Publisher Id: {0}", package.Id.PublisherId);
            if (package.InstalledLocation != null)
              Console.WriteLine(package.InstalledLocation.Path);
            Console.WriteLine();
          }
          catch (FileNotFoundException ex)
          {
            Console.WriteLine("{0}, file: {1}", ex.Message, ex.FileName);
          }
        }
        Console.ReadLine();
      }
    }
  }
```

> **NOTE** *To reference the Windows Runtime from .NET applications, the Windows tab in the Reference Manager can be used to add the reference to Windows. This tab can be enabled by adding* `<TargetPlatformVersion>8.0</TargetPlatformVersion>` *to the project file. The reference to the* `System.Runtime` *assembly must be added to the project file manually as well:* `<Reference Include="System.Runtime" />`

Because the `PackageManager` class requires administrator rights, an application manifest with the `requestedExecutionLevel` `requireAdministrator` is added to the project. This automatically starts the application in elevated mode:

```xml
<?xml version="1.0" encoding="utf-8"?>
<asmv1:assembly manifestVersion="1.0" xmlns="urn:schemas-microsoft-com:asm.v1"
xmlns:asmv1="urn:schemas-microsoft-com:asm.v1" xmlns:asmv2="urn:schemas-microsoft-com:asm.v2"
xmlns:xsi="http://www.w3.org/2001/XMLSchema-instance">
  <assemblyIdentity version="1.0.0.0" name="MyApplication.app" />
  <trustInfo xmlns="urn:schemas-microsoft-com:asm.v2">
    <security>
      <requestedPrivileges xmlns="urn:schemas-microsoft-com:asm.v3">
        <requestedExecutionLevel level="requireAdministrator"
          uiAccess="false" />
      </requestedPrivileges>
    </security>
  </trustInfo>
</asmv1:assembly>
```

Running the application provides information about all the packages installed on the system. This is an extract of the output:

```
Architecture: Neutral
Family: windows.immersivecontrolpanel_cw5n1h2txyewy
Full name: windows.immersivecontrolpanel_6.2.0.0_neutral_neutral_cw5n1h2txyewy
Name: windows.immersivecontrolpanel
Publisher: CN=Microsoft Windows, O=Microsoft Corporation, L=Redmond, S=Washington, C=US
Publisher Id: cw5n1h2txyewy
C:\Windows\ImmersiveControlPanel

Architecture: Neutral
Family: WinStore_cw5n1h2txyewy
Full name: WinStore_1.0.0.0_neutral_neutral_cw5n1h2txyewy
Name: WinStore
Publisher: CN=Microsoft Windows, O=Microsoft Corporation, L=Redmond, S=Washington, C=US
Publisher Id: cw5n1h2txyewy
```

```
C:\Windows\WinStore

Architecture: X64
Family: Microsoft.BingFinance_8wekyb3d8bbwe
Full name: Microsoft.BingFinance_1.1.1.43_x64__8wekyb3d8bbwe
Name: Microsoft.BingFinance
Publisher: CN=Microsoft Corporation, O=Microsoft Corporation, L=Redmond, S=Washington, C=US
Publisher Id: 8wekyb3d8bbwe
C:\Program Files\WindowsApps\Microsoft.BingFinance_1.1.1.43_x64__8wekyb3d8bbwe

Architecture: Neutral
Family: Microsoft.WinJS.1.0.RC_8wekyb3d8bbwe
Full name: Microsoft.WinJS.1.0.RC_1.0.8377.0_neutral__8wekyb3d8bbwe
Name: Microsoft.WinJS.1.0.RC
Publisher: CN=Microsoft Corporation, O=Microsoft Corporation, L=Redmond, S=Washington, C=US
Publisher Id: 8wekyb3d8bbwe
C:\Program Files\WindowsApps\Microsoft.WinJS.1.0.RC_1.0.8377.
0_neutral__8wekyb3d8bbwe

Architecture: X64
Family: Microsoft.BingMaps_8wekyb3d8bbwe
Full name: Microsoft.BingMaps_1.1.1.41_x64__8wekyb3d8bbwe
Name: Microsoft.BingMaps
Publisher: CN=Microsoft Corporation, O=Microsoft Corporation, L=Redmond, S=Washi
ngton, C=US
Publisher Id: 8wekyb3d8bbwe
C:\Program Files\WindowsApps\Microsoft.BingMaps_1.1.1.41_x64__8wekyb3d8bbwe

Architecture: X64
Family: Microsoft.BingNews_8wekyb3d8bbwe
Full name: Microsoft.BingNews_1.1.1.41_x64__8wekyb3d8bbwe
Name: Microsoft.BingNews
Publisher: CN=Microsoft Corporation, O=Microsoft Corporation, L=Redmond, S=Washington, C=US
Publisher Id: 8wekyb3d8bbwe
C:\Program Files\WindowsApps\Microsoft.BingNews_1.1.1.41_x64__8wekyb3d8bbwe
```

SUMMARY

Deployment is an important part of the application life cycle that should be thought about from the beginning of the project, as it also influences the technology used. Deploying different application types have been shown in this chapter.

You've seen the deployment of Windows applications using ClickOnce. ClickOnce offers an easy automatic update capability that can also be triggered directly from within the application, as you've seen with the `System.Deployment` API. In the section on deploying web applications, you looked at the Web Deploy package, which can be deployed easily with a custom managed IIS as well as Windows Azure websites.

You also learned how to deploy Windows 8 applications, which you can publish in the Windows Store, but also deploy using PowerShell in an enterprise environment without using the store.

The next chapter is the first of a group covering the foundations of the .NET Framework, assemblies.

PART III
Foundation

19

Assemblies

WROX.COM CODE DOWNLOADS FOR THIS CHAPTER

The wrox.com code downloads for this chapter are found at http://www.wrox.com/remtitle .cgi?isbn=1118314425 on the Download Code tab. The code for this chapter is divided into the following major examples:

➤ Application Domains

➤ Dynamic Assembly

➤ Shared Demo

WHAT ARE ASSEMBLIES?

An *assembly* is the .NET term for a deployment and configuration unit. This chapter discusses exactly what assemblies are, how they can be applied, and why they are such a useful feature.

You will learn how to create assemblies dynamically, how to load assemblies into application domains, and how to share assemblies between different applications. The chapter also covers versioning, which is an important aspect of sharing assemblies.

Assemblies are the deployment units of .NET applications, which consist of one or more assemblies. .NET executables, with the usual extension .EXE or .DLL, are known by the term assembly. What's the difference between an assembly and a native DLL or EXE? Although they both have the same file extension, .NET assemblies include metadata that describes all the types that are defined in the assembly, with information about its members — methods, properties, events, and fields.

The metadata of .NET assemblies also provides information about the files that belong to the assembly, version information, and the exact information about assemblies that are used. .NET assemblies are the answer to the DLL hell we've seen previously with native DLLs.

Assemblies are self-describing installation units, consisting of one or more files. One assembly could be a single DLL or EXE that includes metadata, or it can consist of different files — for example, resource files, modules, and an EXE.

Assemblies can be private or shared. With simple .NET applications, using only private assemblies is the best way to work. No special management, registration, versioning, and so on is needed with private assemblies. The only application that could have version problems with private assemblies is your own application. Other applications are not influenced because they have their own copies of the assemblies. The private components you use within your application are installed at the same time as the application itself. Private assemblies are located in the same directory as the application or subdirectories thereof. This way, you shouldn't have any versioning problems with the application. No other application will ever overwrite your private assemblies. Of course, it is still a good idea to use version numbers for private assemblies, too. This helps a lot with code changes (as you can detect on your own: these assemblies have a different version, there must be some changes), but it's not a requirement of .NET.

With shared assemblies, several applications can use the same assembly and have a dependency on it. Shared assemblies reduce the need for disk and memory space. With shared assemblies, many rules must be fulfilled — a shared assembly must have a version number and a unique name, and usually it's installed in the *global assembly cache (GAC)*. The GAC enables you to share different versions of the same assembly on a system.

Assembly Features

The features of an assembly can be summarized as follows:

➤ Assemblies are *self-describing*. It's no longer necessary to pay attention to registry keys for apartments, to get the type library from some other place, and so on. Assemblies include metadata that describes the assembly. The metadata includes the types exported from the assembly and a manifest; the next section describes the function of a manifest.

➤ *Version dependencies* are recorded inside an assembly manifest. Storing the version of any referenced assemblies in the manifest makes it possible to easily find deployment faults because of wrong versions available. The version of the referenced assembly that will be used can be configured by the developer and the system administrator. Later in this chapter, you'll learn which version policies are available and how they work.

➤ Assemblies can be loaded *side by side*. Beginning with Windows 2000, a side-by-side feature enables different versions of the same DLL to be used on a system. Did you ever check the directory `<windows>\winsxs`? .NET allows different versions of the same assembly to be used inside a single process! How is this useful? If assembly A references version 1 of the shared assembly `Shared`, and assembly B uses version 2 of the shared assembly `Shared`, and you are using both assembly A and B, you need both versions of the shared assembly `Shared` in your application — and with .NET both versions are loaded and used. The .NET 4 runtime even allows multiple CLR versions (2 and 4) inside one process. This enables, for example, loading plugins with different CLR requirements. While there's no direct .NET way to communicate between objects in different CLR versions inside one process, you can use other techniques, such as COM.

➤ Application isolation is ensured by using *application domains*. With application domains, a number of applications can run independently inside a single process. Faults in one application running in one application domain cannot directly affect other applications inside the same process running in another application domain.

➤ Installation can be as easy as copying the files that belong to an assembly. An xcopy can be enough. This feature is named *ClickOnce deployment*. However, in some cases ClickOnce deployment cannot be applied, and a normal Windows installation is required. Deployment of applications is discussed in Chapter 18, "Deployment."

Assembly Structure

An assembly consists of assembly metadata describing the complete assembly, type metadata describing the exported types and methods, MSIL code, and resources. All these parts can be inside of one file or spread across several files.

In the first example (see Figure 19-1), the assembly metadata, type metadata, MSIL code, and resources are all in one file — `Component.dll`. The assembly consists of a single file.

The second example shows a single assembly spread across three files (see Figure 19-2). `Component.dll` has assembly metadata, type metadata, and MSIL code, but no resources. The assembly uses a picture from `picture.jpeg` that is not embedded inside `Component.dll` but referenced from within the assembly metadata. The assembly metadata also references a module called `util.netmodule`, which itself includes only type metadata and MSIL code for a class. A module has no assembly metadata; thus, the module itself has no version information, nor can it be installed separately. All three files in this example make up a single assembly; the assembly is the installation unit. It would also be possible to put the manifest in a different file.

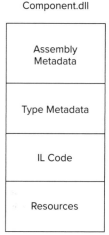

Component.dll

FIGURE 19-1

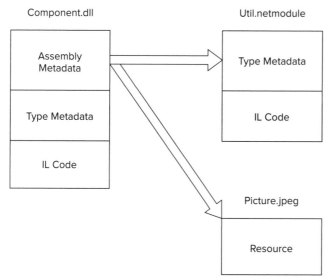

FIGURE 19-2

Assembly Manifests

An important part of an assembly is a *manifest,* which is part of the metadata. It describes the assembly with all the information that's needed to reference it and lists all its dependencies. The parts of the manifest are as follows:

➤ **Identity** — Name, version, culture, and public key.

➤ **A list of files** — Files belonging to this assembly. A single assembly must have at least one file but may contain a number of files.

➤ **A list of referenced assemblies** — All assemblies used from the assembly are documented inside the manifest. This reference information includes the version number and the public key, which is used to uniquely identify assemblies. The public key is discussed later in this chapter.

➤ **A set of permission requests** — These are the permissions needed to run this assembly. You can find more information about permissions in Chapter 22, "Security."

➤ **Exported types** — These are included if they are defined within a module and the module is referenced from the assembly; otherwise, they are not part of the manifest. A module is a unit of reuse. The type description is stored as metadata inside the assembly. You can get the structures and classes with the properties and methods from the metadata. This replaces the type library that was used with COM to describe the types. For the use of COM clients, it's easy to generate a type library from the manifest. The reflection mechanism uses the information about the exported types for late binding to classes. See Chapter 15, "Reflection," for more information about reflection.

Namespaces, Assemblies, and Components

You might be a little bit confused by the meanings of namespaces, types, assemblies, and components. How does a namespace fit into the assembly concept? The namespace is completely independent of an assembly. You can have different namespaces in a single assembly, but the same namespace can be spread across assemblies. The namespace is just an extension of the type name — it belongs to the name of the type.

For example, the assemblies `mscorlib` and `system` contain the namespace `System.Threading` among many other namespaces. Although the assemblies contain the same namespaces, you will not find the same class names.

Private and Shared Assemblies

Assemblies can be private or shared. A *private assembly* is found either in the same directory as the application or within one of its subdirectories. With a private assembly, it's not necessary to think about naming conflicts with other classes or versioning problems. The assemblies that are referenced during the build process are copied to the application directory. Private assemblies are the usual way to build assemblies, especially when applications and components are built within the same company.

> **NOTE** *Although it is still possible to have naming conflicts with private assemblies (multiple private assemblies may be part of the application and they could have conflicts, or a name in a private assembly might conflict with a name in a shared assembly used by the application), naming conflicts are greatly reduced. If you you will be using multiple private assemblies or working with shared assemblies in other applications, it's a good idea to use well-named namespaces and types to minimize naming conflicts.*

When using *shared assemblies*, you have to be aware of some rules. The assembly must be unique; therefore, it must also have a unique name, called a *strong name*. Part of the strong name is a mandatory version number. Shared assemblies are mostly used when a vendor other than the application vendor builds the component, or when a large application is split into subprojects. Also, some technologies, such as .NET Enterprise Services, require shared assemblies in specific scenarios.

Satellite Assemblies

A *satellite assembly* is an assembly that contains only resources. This is extremely useful for localization. Because an assembly has a culture associated with it, the resource manager looks for satellite assemblies containing the resources of a specific culture.

> **NOTE** *You can read more about satellite assemblies in Chapter 28, "Localization."*

Viewing Assemblies

You can view assemblies by using the command-line utility `ildasm`, the MSIL disassembler. You can open an assembly by starting `ildasm` from the command line with the assembly as an argument or by selecting File ⇨ Open from the menu.

Figure 19-3 shows `ildasm` opening the example that you will build a little later in the chapter, `SharedDemo.dll`. Note the manifest and the `SharedDemo` type in the `Wrox.ProCSharp.Assemblies` namespace. When you open the manifest, you can see the version number and the assembly attributes, as well as the referenced assemblies and their versions. You can see the MSIL code by opening the methods of the class.

FIGURE 19-3

Creating Assemblies

Now that you know what assemblies are, it is time to build some. Of course, you have already built assemblies in previous chapters, because a .NET executable counts as an assembly. This section looks at special options for building assemblies.

Creating Modules and Assemblies

All C# project types in Visual Studio create an assembly. Whether you choose a DLL or EXE project type, an assembly is always created. With the command-line C# compiler, `csc`, it's also possible to create modules. A module is a DLL without assembly attributes (so it's not an assembly, but it can be added to assemblies later). The command:

```
csc /target:module hello.cs
```

creates a module `hello.netmodule`. You can view this module using `ildasm`.

A module also has a manifest, but there is no `.assembly` entry inside the manifest (except for the external assemblies that are referenced) because a module has no assembly attributes. It's not possible to configure versions or permissions with modules; that can be done only at the assembly scope. You can find references to assemblies in the manifest of the module. With the `/addmodule` option of `csc`, it's possible to add modules to existing assemblies.

To compare modules to assemblies, create a simple class `A` and compile it by using the following command:

```
csc /target:module A.cs
```

The compiler generates the file `A.netmodule`, which doesn't include assembly information (as you can see using `ildasm` to look at the manifest information). The manifest of the module shows the referenced assembly `mscorlib` and the `.module` entry (see Figure 19-4).

Next, create an assembly B, which includes the module A.netmodule. It's not necessary to have a source file to generate this assembly. The command to build the assembly is as follows:

```
csc /target:library /addmodule:A.
netmodule /out:B.dll
```

Looking at the assembly using ildasm, you can find only a manifest. In the manifest, the assembly mscorlib is referenced. Next, you see the assembly section with a hash algorithm and the version. The number of the algorithm defines the type of the algorithm used to create the hash code of the assembly. When creating an assembly programmatically, it is possible to select the algorithm. Part of the manifest is a list of all modules belonging to the assembly. Figure 19-5 shows

FIGURE 19-4

.file A.netmodule, which belongs to the assembly. Classes exported from modules are part of the assembly manifest; classes exported from the assembly itself are not.

Modules enable the faster startup of assemblies because not all types are inside a single file. The modules are loaded only when needed. Another reason to use modules is if you want to create an assembly with more than one programming language. One module could be written using Visual Basic, another module could be written using C#, and these two modules could be included in a single assembly.

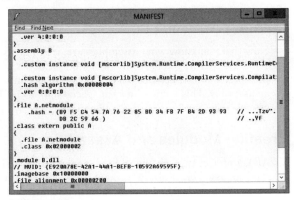

FIGURE 19-5

Assembly Attributes

When creating a Visual Studio project, the source file AssemblyInfo.cs is generated automatically. It is located below Properties in Solution Explorer. You can use the normal source code editor to configure the assembly attributes in this file. This is the file generated from the project template:

```
using System.Reflection;
using System.Runtime.CompilerServices;
using System.Runtime.InteropServices;
//
// General Information about an assembly is controlled through the following
// set of attributes. Change these attribute values to modify the information
// associated with an assembly.
[assembly: AssemblyTitle("ClassLibrary1")]
[assembly: AssemblyDescription("")]
[assembly: AssemblyConfiguration("")]
[assembly: AssemblyCompany("CN innovation")]
[assembly: AssemblyProduct("ClassLibrary1")]
[assembly: AssemblyCopyright("Copyright @ CN innovation 2012")]
[assembly: AssemblyTrademark("")]
[assembly: AssemblyCulture("")]

// Setting ComVisible to false makes the types in this assembly not visible
// to COM components.  If you need to access a type in this assembly from
// COM, set the ComVisible attribute to true on that type.
[assembly: ComVisible(false)]
```

```
// The following GUID is for the ID of the typelib if this project is exposed
// to COM
[assembly: Guid("21649c19-6609-4607-8fc0-d75f1f27a8ff")]

//
// Version information for an assembly consists of the following four
// values:
//
//        Major Version
//        Minor Version
//        Build Number
//        Revision
//
// You can specify all the values or you can default the Build and Revision
// Numbers by using the '*' as shown below:
// [assembly: AssemblyVersion("1.0.*")]
[assembly: AssemblyVersion("1.0.0.0")]
[assembly: AssemblyFileVersion("1.0.0.0")]
```

This file is used for configuration of the assembly manifest. The compiler reads the assembly attributes to inject the specific information into the manifest.

The `assembly:` prefix with the attribute marks an assembly-level attribute. Assembly-level attributes are, in contrast to the other attributes, not attached to a specific language element. The arguments that can be used for the assembly attribute are classes of the namespaces `System.Reflection`, `System.Runtime` `.CompilerServices`, and `System.Runtime.InteropServices`.

> **NOTE** *You can read more about attributes and how to create and use custom attributes in Chapter 15.*

The following table describes the assembly attributes defined within the `System.Reflection` namespace.

ASSEMBLY ATTRIBUTE	DESCRIPTION
AssemblyCompany	Specifies the company name.
AssemblyConfiguration	Specifies build information such as retail or debugging information.
AssemblyCopyright and AssemblyTrademark	Holds the copyright and trademark information.
AssemblyDefaultAlias	Can be used if the assembly name is not easily readable (such as a GUID when the assembly name is created dynamically). With this attribute an alias name can be specified.
AssemblyDescription	Describes the assembly or the product. Looking at the properties of the executable file, this value shows up as Comments.
AssemblyProduct	Specifies the name of the product where the assembly belongs.
AssemblyTitle	Used to give the assembly a friendly name. The friendly name can include spaces. With the file properties you can see this value as Description.
AssemblyCulture	Defines the culture of the assembly. This attribute is important for satellite assemblies.

(continues)

(continued)

ASSEMBLY ATTRIBUTE	DESCRIPTION
AssemblyInformationalVersion	This attribute isn't used for version checking when assemblies are referenced; it is for information only. It is very useful to specify the version of an application that uses multiple assemblies. Opening the properties of the executable you can see this value as the Product Version.
AssemblyVersion	Provides the version number of the assembly. Versioning is discussed later in this chapter.
AssemblyFileVersion	Defines the version of the file. The value shows up with the Windows file properties dialog, but it doesn't have any influence on .NET behavior.

Here's an example of how these attributes might be configured:

```
[assembly: AssemblyTitle("Professional C#")]
[assembly: AssemblyDescription("Sample Application")]
[assembly: AssemblyConfiguration("Retail version")]
[assembly: AssemblyCompany("Wrox Press")]
[assembly: AssemblyProduct("Wrox Professional Series")]
[assembly: AssemblyCopyright("Copyright (C) Wrox Press
2012")]
[assembly: AssemblyTrademark("Wrox is a registered
trademark of " +
     "John Wiley & Sons, Inc.")]
[assembly: AssemblyCulture("")]

[assembly: AssemblyVersion("1.0.0.0")]
[assembly: AssemblyFileVersion("1.0.0.0")]
```

FIGURE 19-6

With Visual Studio 2012, you can configure these attributes with the project properties, select the tab Application, and click the button Assembly Information, as shown in Figure 19-6.

Creating and Loading Assemblies Dynamically

During development, you add a reference to an assembly so that it is included with the assembly references, and the types of the assembly are available to the compiler. During runtime, the referenced assembly is loaded as soon as a type of the assembly is instantiated or a method of the type is used. Instead of using this automatic behavior, you can also load assemblies programmatically. To load assemblies programmatically, you can use the class `Assembly` with the static method `Load()`. This method is overloaded, meaning you can pass the name of the assembly using `AssemblyName`, the name of the assembly, or a byte array.

It is also possible to create an assembly on the fly, as shown in the next example. Here, C# code is entered in a text box, a new assembly is dynamically created by starting the C# compiler, and the compiled code is invoked.

To compile C# code dynamically, you can use the class `CSharpCodeProvider` from the namespace `Microsoft.CSharp`. Using this class, you can compile code and generate assemblies from a DOM tree, from a file, and from source code.

The UI of the application is created by using WPF. You can see the design view of the UI in Figure 19-7. The window is made up of a `TextBox` to enter C# code, a `Button`, and a `TextBlock` WPF control that spans all columns of the last row to display the result.

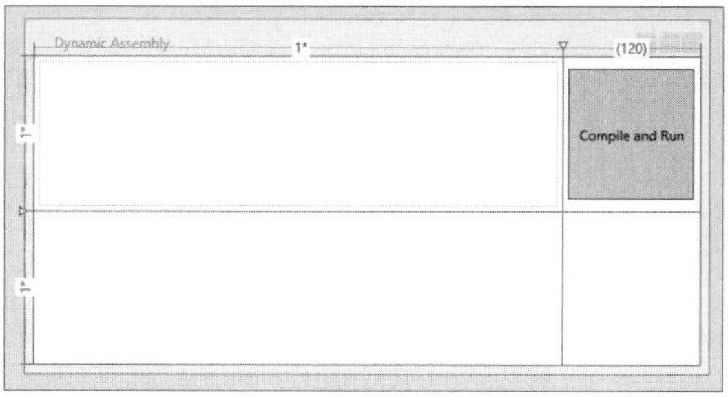

To dynamically compile and run C# code, the class `CodeDriver` defines the method `CompileAndRun()`. This method compiles the code from the text box and starts the generated method (code file `DynamicAssembly/CodeDriver.cs`):

FIGURE 19-7

```csharp
using System;
using System.CodeDom.Compiler;
using System.IO;
using System.Reflection;
using System.Text;
using Microsoft.CSharp;

namespace Wrox.ProCSharp.Assemblies
{
  public class CodeDriver
  {
    private string prefix =
        "using System;" +
        "public static class Driver" +
        "{" +
        "   public static void Run()" +
        "   {";

    private string postfix =
        "   }" +
        "}";


    public string CompileAndRun(string input, out bool hasError)
    {
      hasError = false;
      string returnData = null;

      CompilerResults results = null;
      using (var provider = new CSharpCodeProvider())
      {
        var options = new CompilerParameters();
        options.GenerateInMemory = true;

        var sb = new StringBuilder();
        sb.Append(prefix);
        sb.Append(input);
        sb.Append(postfix);

        results = provider.CompileAssemblyFromSource(options, sb.ToString());
      }

      if (results.Errors.HasErrors)
      {
        hasError = true;
        var errorMessage = new StringBuilder();
        foreach (CompilerError error in results.Errors)
```

```
        {
          errorMessage.AppendFormat("{0} {1}", error.Line,
              error.ErrorText);
        }
        returnData = errorMessage.ToString();
      }
      else
      {
        TextWriter temp = Console.Out;
        var writer = new StringWriter();
        Console.SetOut(writer);
        Type driverType = results.CompiledAssembly.GetType("Driver");

        driverType.InvokeMember("Run", BindingFlags.InvokeMethod |
            BindingFlags.Static | BindingFlags.Public, null, null, null);
        Console.SetOut(temp);

        returnData = writer.ToString();
      }

      return returnData;
    }
  }
}
```

The method `CompileAndRun()` requires a string input parameter in which one or multiple lines of C# code can be passed. Because every method that is called must be included in a method and a class, the variables `prefix` and `postfix` define the structure of the dynamically created class `Driver` and the method `Run()` that surround the code from the parameter. Using a `StringBuilder`, the `prefix`, `postfix`, and the code from the `input` variable are merged to create a complete class that can be compiled. Using this resultant string, the code is compiled with the `CSharpCodeProvider` class. The method `CompileAssemblyFromSource()` dynamically creates an assembly. Because this assembly is needed only in memory, the compiler parameter option `GenerateInMemory` is set.

If the source code that was passed contains some errors, these will appear in the `Errors` collection of `CompilerResults`. The errors are returned with the return data, and the variable `hasError` is set to `true`.

If the source code compiles successfully, the `Run()` method of the new `Driver` class is invoked. Invocation of this method is done using reflection. From the newly compiled assembly that can be accessed using `CompilerResults.CompiledType`, the new class `Driver` is referenced by the `driverType` variable. Then the `InvokeMember()` method of the `Type` class is used to invoke the method `Run()`. Because this method is defined as a public static method, the `BindingFlags` must be set accordingly. To see a result of the program that is written to the console, the console is redirected to a `StringWriter` to finally return the complete output of the program with the `returnData` variable.

> **NOTE** *Running the code with the* `InvokeMember()` *method makes use of .NET reflection. Reflection is discussed in Chapter 15.*

The `Click` event of the WPF button is connected to the `Compile_Click()` method where the `CodeDriver` class is instantiated, and the `CompileAndRun()` method is invoked. The input is taken from the `TextBox` named `textCode`, and the result is written to the `TextBlock` `textOutput` (code file `DynamicAssembly/DynamicAssemblyWindow.xaml.cs`):

```
private void Compile_Click(object sender, RoutedEventArgs e)
{
  textOutput.Background = Brushes.White;
```

```
var driver = new CodeDriver();
bool isError;
textOutput.Text = driver.CompileAndRun(textCode.Text, out isError);
if (isError)
{
    textOutput.Background = Brushes.Red;
}
}
```

Now you can start the application; enter C# code in the TextBox as shown in Figure 19-8, and compile and run the code.

The program as written so far has the disadvantage that every time you click the Compile and Run button, a new assembly is created and loaded, so the program always needs more and more memory. You cannot unload an

FIGURE 19-8

assembly from the application. To unload assemblies, application domains are needed.

APPLICATION DOMAINS

Before .NET, processes were used as isolation boundaries, with each process having its private virtual memory, an application running in one process could not write to the memory of another application and thereby crash the other application. The process was used as an isolation and security boundary between applications. With the .NET architecture, you have a new boundary for applications: *application domains*. With managed IL code, the runtime can ensure that access to the memory of another application inside a single process can't happen. Multiple applications can run in a single process within multiple application domains (see Figure 19-9).

An assembly is loaded into an application domain. In Figure 19-9, you can see process 4711 with two application domains. In application domain A, objects one and two are instantiated, object one in assembly one, and object two in assembly two. The second application domain in process 4711 has

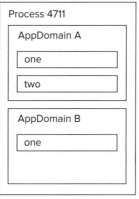
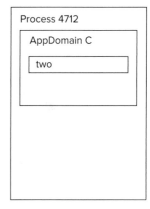

FIGURE 19-9

an instance of object one. To minimize memory consumption, the code of assemblies is loaded only once into an application domain. Instance and static members are not shared among application domains. It's not possible to directly access objects within another application domain; a proxy is needed instead. Therefore, in Figure 19-9, the object one in application domain B cannot directly access the objects one or two in application domain A without a proxy.

The AppDomain class is used to create and terminate application domains, load and unload assemblies and types, and enumerate assemblies and threads in a domain. In this section, you program a small example to see application domains in action.

First, create a C# console application called AssemblyA. In the Main() method, add a Console. WriteLine() so that you can see when this method is called. In addition, add the class Demo with a constructor with two int values as arguments, which will be used to create instances with the AppDomain class. The `AssemblyA.exe` assembly will be loaded from the second application that will be created (code file `AssemblyA/Program.cs`):

```
using System;

namespace Wrox.ProCSharp.Assemblies
{
  public class Demo
  {
    public Demo(int val1, int val2)
    {
      Console.WriteLine("Constructor with the values {0}, {1} in domain " +
          "{2} called", val1, val2, AppDomain.CurrentDomain.FriendlyName);
    }
  }

  class Program
  {
    static void Main()
    {
      Console.WriteLine("Main in domain {0} called",
          AppDomain.CurrentDomain.FriendlyName);
    }
  }
}
```

Running the application produces this output:

```
Main in domain AssemblyA.exe called.
```

The second project you create is again a C# console application: `DomainTest`. First, display the name of the current domain using the property `FriendlyName` of the `AppDomain` class. With the `CreateDomain()` method, a new application domain with the friendly name `New AppDomain` is created. Next, load the assembly `AssemblyA` into the new domain and call the `Main()` method by calling `ExecuteAssembly()` (code file `DomainTest/Program.cs`):

```
using System;
using System.Reflection;

namespace Wrox.ProCSharp.Assemblies
{
  class Program
  {
    static void Main()
    {
      AppDomain currentDomain = AppDomain.CurrentDomain;
      Console.WriteLine(currentDomain.FriendlyName);
      AppDomain secondDomain = AppDomain.CreateDomain("New AppDomain");
      secondDomain.ExecuteAssembly("AssemblyA.exe");
    }
  }
}
```

Before starting the program `DomainTest.exe`, reference the assembly `AssemblyA.exe` with the `DomainTest` project. Referencing the assembly with Visual Studio 2012 copies the assembly to the project directory so that the assembly can be found. If the assembly cannot be found, a `System.IO.FileNotFoundException` exception is thrown.

When `DomainTest.exe` is run, you get the following console output. `DomainTest.exe` is the friendly name of the first application domain. The second line is the output of the newly loaded assembly in the `New`

AppDomain. With a process viewer, you will not see the process AssemblyA.exe executing because no new process is created. AssemblyA is loaded into the process DomainTest.exe.

```
DomainTest.exe
Main in domain New AppDomain called
```

Instead of calling the Main() method in the newly loaded assembly, you can also create a new instance. In the following example, replace the ExecuteAssembly() method with a CreateInstance(). The first argument is the name of the assembly, AssemblyA. The second argument defines the type that should be instantiated: Wrox.ProCSharp.Assemblies.AppDomains.Demo. The third argument, true, means that case is ignored. System.Reflection.BindingFlags.CreateInstance is a binding flag enumeration value to specify that the constructor should be called:

```
AppDomain secondDomain = AppDomain.CreateDomain("New AppDomain");
// secondDomain.ExecuteAssembly("AssemblyA.exe");
secondDomain.CreateInstance("AssemblyA",
    "Wrox.ProCSharp.Assemblies.Demo", true,
    BindingFlags.CreateInstance, null, new object[] {7, 3},
    null, null);
```

The results of a successful run of the application are as follows:

```
DomainTest.exe
Constructor with the values 7, 3 in domain New AppDomain called
```

Now you have seen how to create and call application domains. In runtime hosts, application domains are created automatically. Most application types just have the default application domain. ASP.NET creates an application domain for each web application that runs on a web server. Internet Explorer creates application domains in which managed controls will run. For applications, it can be useful to create application domains if you want to unload an assembly. You can unload assemblies only by terminating an application domain.

> **NOTE** *Application domains are an extremely useful construct if assemblies are loaded dynamically and there is a requirement to unload assemblies after use. Within the primary application domain, it is not possible to get rid of loaded assemblies. However, it is possible to end application domains such that all assemblies loaded only within the application domain are cleaned from the memory.*

With this knowledge about application domains, it is now possible to change the WPF program created earlier. The new class CodeDriverInAppDomain creates a new application domain using AppDomain .CreateDomain. Inside this new application domain, the class CodeDriver is instantiated using CreateInstanceAndUnwrap(). Using the CodeDriver instance, the CompileAndRun() method is invoked before the new application domain is unloaded again:

```
using System;
using System.Runtime.Remoting;

namespace Wrox.ProCSharp.Assemblies
{
  public class CodeDriverInAppDomain
  {
    public string CompileAndRun(string code, out bool hasError)
    {
      AppDomain codeDomain = AppDomain.CreateDomain("CodeDriver");

      CodeDriver codeDriver = (CodeDriver)
```

```
        codeDomain.CreateInstanceAndUnwrap("DynamicAssembly",
            "Wrox.ProCSharp.Assemblies.CodeDriver");

    string result = codeDriver.CompileAndRun(code, out hasError);

    AppDomain.Unload(codeDomain);

    return result;
    }
  }
}
```

> **NOTE** *The class* CodeDriver *itself now is used both in the main application domain and in the new application domain; that's why it is not possible to get rid of the code that this class is using. If you want to do that, you can define an interface that is implemented by the* CodeDriver *and just use the interface in the main application domain. However, here this is not an issue because it's only necessary to get rid of the dynamically created assembly with the* Driver *class.*

To access the class CodeDriver from a different application domain, the class CodeDriver must derive from the base class MarshalByRefObject. Only classes that derive from this base type can be accessed across another application domain. In the main application domain, a proxy is instantiated to invoke the methods of this class across an inter-application domain channel (code file DynamicAssembly/CodeDriver.cs):

```
using System;
using System.CodeDom.Compiler;
using System.IO;
using System.Reflection;
using System.Text;
using Microsoft.CSharp;

namespace Wrox.ProCSharp.Assemblies
{
  public class CodeDriver: MarshalByRefObject
  {
```

The Compile_Click() event handler can now be changed to use the CodeDriverInAppDomain class instead of the CodeDriver class (code file DynamicAssembly/DynamicAssemblyWindow.xaml.cs):

```
    private void Compile_Click(object sender, RoutedEventArgs e)
    {
      var driver = new CodeDriverInAppDomain();
      bool isError;
      textOutput.Text = driver.CompileAndRun(textCode.Text, out isError);
      if (isError)
      {
        textOutput.Background = Brushes.Red;
      }
    }
```

Now you can click the Compile and Run button of the application any number of times and the generated assembly is always unloaded.

> **NOTE** *You can see the loaded assemblies in an application domain with the* GetAssemblies() *method of the* AppDomain *class.*

SHARED ASSEMBLIES

Assemblies can be isolated for use by a single application — not sharing an assembly is the default. When using shared assemblies, specific requirements must be followed. This section explores everything that's needed for sharing assemblies. Strong names are required to uniquely identify a shared assembly. You can create a strong name by signing the assembly. This section also explains the process of delayed signing. Shared assemblies are typically installed into the global assembly cache (GAC). You will read about how to use the GAC in this section.

Strong Names

A shared assembly name must be globally unique, and it must be possible to protect the name. At no time can any other person create an assembly using the same name.

COM solved the first requirement by using a globally unique identifier (GUID). The second issue, however, still existed because anyone could steal the GUID and create a different object with the same identifier. Both issues are solved with *strong names* of .NET assemblies.

A strong name consists of the following:

> ➤ The *name* of the assembly itself.
> ➤ A *version number* enables the use of different versions of the same assembly at the same time. Different versions can also work side by side and can be loaded concurrently inside the same process.
> ➤ A *public key* guarantees that the strong name is unique. It also guarantees that a referenced assembly cannot be replaced from a different source.
> ➤ A *culture* (cultures are discussed in Chapter 28).

> **NOTE** *A shared assembly must have a strong name to uniquely identify it.*

A strong name is a simple text name accompanied by a version number, a public key, and a culture. You wouldn't create a new public key with every assembly; you'd have one in your company, so the key uniquely identifies your company's assemblies.

However, this key cannot be used as a trust key. Assemblies can carry Authenticode signatures to build a trust. The key for the Authenticode signature can be a different one from the key used for the strong name.

> **NOTE** *For development purposes, a different public key can be used and later exchanged easily with the real key. This feature is discussed later in the section "Delayed Signing of Assemblies."*

To uniquely identify the assemblies in your companies, a useful namespace hierarchy should be used to name your classes. Here is a simple example showing how to organize namespaces: Wrox Press could use the major namespace `Wrox` for its classes and namespaces. In the hierarchy below the namespace, the namespaces must be organized so that all classes are unique. Every chapter of this book uses a different namespace of the form `Wrox.ProCSharp.<Chapter>`; this chapter uses `Wrox.ProCSharp` `.Assemblies`. Therefore, if there is a class `Hello` in two different chapters, there's no conflict because of different namespaces. Utility classes that are used across different books can go into the namespace `Wrox.Utilities`.

A company name commonly used as the first part of the namespace is not necessarily unique, so something else must be used to build a strong name. For this the public key is used. Because of the public/private key principle in strong names, no one without access to your private key can destructively create an assembly that could be unintentionally called by the client.

Integrity Using Strong Names

A public/private key pair must be used to create a shared component. The compiler writes the public key to the manifest, creates a hash of all files that belong to the assembly, and signs the hash with the private key, which is not stored within the assembly. It is then guaranteed that no one can change your assembly. The signature can be verified with the public key.

During development, the client assembly must reference the shared assembly. The compiler writes the public key of the referenced assembly to the manifest of the client assembly. To reduce storage, it is not the public key that is written to the manifest of the client assembly, but a public key token. The public key token consists of the last eight bytes of a hash of the public key and is unique.

At runtime, during loading of the shared assembly (or at install time if the client is installed using the native image generator), the hash of the shared component assembly can be verified by using the public key stored inside the client assembly. Only the owner of the private key can change the shared component assembly. There is no way a component `Math` that was created by vendor A and referenced from a client can be replaced by a component from a hacker. Only the owner of the private key can replace the shared component with a new version. Integrity is guaranteed insofar as the shared assembly comes from the expected publisher.

Figure 19-10 shows a shared component with a public key referenced by a client assembly that has a public key token of the shared assembly inside the manifest.

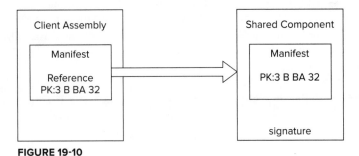

FIGURE 19-10

Global Assembly Cache

The *global assembly cache (GAC)* is, as the name implies, a cache for globally available assemblies. Most shared assemblies are installed inside this cache; otherwise, a shared directory (also on a server) can be used.

The GAC is located in the directory `<windows>\Microsoft.NET\assembly`. Inside this directory, you can find multiple `GACxxx` directories. The `GACxxx` directories contain shared assemblies. `GAC_MSIL` contains the assemblies with pure .NET code; `GAC_32` contains the assemblies that are specific to a 32-bit platform. On a 64-bit system, you can also find the directory `GAC_64` with assemblies specific for 64 bit platforms.

In the directory `<windows>\assembly\NativeImages_<runtime version>`, you can find the assemblies compiled to native code. If you go deeper in the directory structure, you will find directory names that are similar to the assembly names, and below that a version directory and the assemblies themselves. This enables installation of different versions of the same assembly.

`gacutil.exe` is a utility to install, uninstall, and list assemblies using the command line. The following list explains some of the `gacutil` options:

➤ `gacutil /l`—Lists all assemblies from the assembly cache.

➤ `gacutil /i mydll`—Installs the shared assembly `mydll` into the assembly cache. With the option `/f` you can force the installation to the GAC even if the assembly is already installed. This is useful if you changed the assembly but didn't change the version number.

➤ `gacutil /u mydll`—Uninstalls the assembly `mydll`.

> **NOTE** *For production you should use an installer program to install shared assemblies to the GAC. Deployment is covered in Chapter 18, "Deployment."*

> **NOTE** *The directory for shared assemblies prior to .NET 4 is at* <windows>\ assembly. *This directory includes a Windows shell extension to give it a nicer look for displaying assemblies and version numbers. This shell extension is not available for .NET 4 assemblies.*

Creating a Shared Assembly

In the next example, you create a shared assembly and a client that uses it. Creating shared assemblies is not much different from creating private assemblies. Create a simple Visual C# class library project with the name SharedDemo. Change the namespace to Wrox.ProCSharp.Assemblies and the class name to SharedDemo. Enter the following code. In the constructor of the class, all lines of a file are read into an array. The name of the file is passed as an argument to the constructor. The method GetQuoteOfTheDay() just returns a random string of the array (code file SharedDemo/SharedDemo.cs).

```
using System;
using System.IO;

namespace Wrox.ProCSharp.Assemblies
{
  public class SharedDemo
  {
    private string[] quotes;
    private Random random;

    public SharedDemo(string filename)
    {
      quotes = File.ReadAllLines(filename);
      random = new Random();
    }

    public string GetQuoteOfTheDay()
    {
      int index = random.Next(1, quotes.Length);
      return quotes[index];
    }
  }
}
```

Creating a Strong Name

A strong name is needed to share this assembly. You can create such a name with the *strong name tool* (sn):

```
sn -k mykey.snk
```

The strong name utility generates and writes a public/private key pair, and writes this pair to a file; here the file is mykey.snk.

With Visual Studio 2012, you can sign the assembly with the project properties by selecting the Signing tab, as shown in Figure 19-11. You can also create keys with this tool. However, you should not create a key file for every project. Just a few keys for the complete company can be used instead. It is useful to create different keys depending on security requirements (see Chapter 22).

Setting the signing option with Visual Studio adds the `/keyfile` option to the compiler setting. Visual Studio also allows you to create a keyfile that is secured with a password. As shown in the figure, such a file has the file extension `.pfx`.

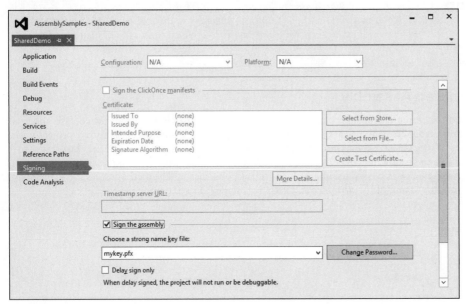

FIGURE 19-11

After rebuilding, the public key can be found inside the manifest. You can verify this using `ildasm`, as shown in Figure 19-12.

Installing the Shared Assembly

With a public key in the assembly, you can now install it in the global assembly cache using the global assembly cache tool, `gacutil`, with the `/i` option. The `/f` option forces you to write the assembly to the GAC, even if it is already there:

```
gacutil /i SharedDemo.dll /f
```

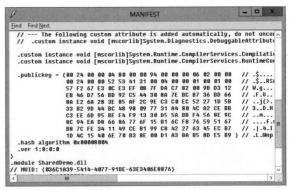

FIGURE 19-12

Then you can use the Global Assembly Cache Viewer or `gacutil /l SharedDemo` to check the version of the shared assembly to see if it is successfully installed.

Using the Shared Assembly

To use the shared assembly, create a C# console application called `Client`. Change the name of the namespace to `Wrox.ProCSharp.Assemblies`. The shared assembly can be referenced in the same way as a private assembly: by selecting Project ➪ Add Reference from the menu.

> **NOTE** *With shared assemblies the reference property* `Copy Local` *can be set to* `false`. *This way, the assembly is not copied to the directory of the output files but will be loaded from the GAC instead.*

Add the file `quotes.txt` to the project items, and set the property `Copy to Output Directory` to `Copy if newer`.

Here's the code for the client application (code file `Client/Program.cs`):

```csharp
using System;
namespace Wrox.ProCSharp.Assemblies
{
  class Program
  {
    static void Main()
    {
      var quotes = new SharedDemo("Quotes.txt");
      for (int i=0; i < 3; i++)
      {
        Console.WriteLine(quotes.GetQuoteOfTheDay());
        Console.WriteLine();
      }
    }
  }
}
```

Looking at the manifest in the client assembly using `ildasm` (see Figure 19-13), you can see the reference to the shared assembly `SharedDemo`: `.assembly extern SharedDemo`. Part of this referenced information is the version number, discussed next, and the token of the public key.

FIGURE 19-13

The token of the public key can also be seen within the shared assembly using the strong name utility: `sn -T` shows the token of the public key in the assembly, and `sn -Tp` shows the token and the public key. Note the use of the uppercase T!

The result of your program with a sample quotes file is shown here:

```
"We don't like their sound. And guitar music is on the way out."
- Decca Recording, Co., in rejecting the Beatles, 1962

"The ordinary 'horseless carriage' is at present a luxury for the wealthy; and
although its price will probably fall in the future, it will never come into as
common use as the bicycle." - The Literary Digest, 1889

"Landing and moving around the moon offers so many serious problems for human
beings that it may take science another 200 years to lick them", Lord Kelvin
(1824-1907)
```

Delayed Signing of Assemblies

The private key of a company should be safely stored. Most companies don't give all developers access to the private key; only a few security people have it. That's why the signature of an assembly can be added at a later date, such as before distribution. When the assembly attribute `AssemblyDelaySign` is set to `true`, no signature is stored in the assembly, but enough free space is reserved so that it can be added later. Without using a key, you cannot test the assembly and install it in the GAC; however, you can use a temporary key for testing purposes, later replacing this key with the real company key.

The following steps are required to delay signing of assemblies:

1. Create a public/private key pair with the strong name utility `sn`. The generated file `mykey.snk` includes both the public and private keys.

   ```
   sn -k mykey.snk
   ```

2. Extract the public key to make it available to developers. The option `-p` extracts the public key of the keyfile. The file `mykeypub.snk` holds only the public key.

   ```
   sn -p mykey.snk mykeypub.snk
   ```

   All developers in the company can use this keyfile `mykeypub.snk` and compile the assembly with the `/delaysign+` option. This way, the signature is not added to the assembly, but it can be added afterward. In Visual Studio 2012, the delay sign option can be set with a check box in the Signing settings.

3. Turn off verification of the signature, because the assembly doesn't have a signature:

   ```
   sn -Vr SharedDemo.dll
   ```

4. Before distribution the assembly can be re-signed with the `sn` utility. Use the `-R` option to re-sign previously signed or delayed signed assemblies. Re-signing of the assembly can be done by the person who creates the deployment package for the application and has access to the private key that is used for distribution.

   ```
   sn -R MyAssembly.dll mykey.snk
   ```

> **NOTE** *The signature verification should be turned off only during the development process. Never distribute an assembly without verification, as it would be possible for the assembly to be replaced with a malicious one.*

> **NOTE** *Re-signing of assemblies can be automated by defining the tasks in an MSBuild file. This is discussed in Chapter 17, "Visual Studio."*

References

Assemblies in the GAC can have references associated with them. These references are responsible for the fact that a cached assembly cannot be deleted if it is still needed by an application. For example, if a shared assembly is installed by a Microsoft installer package (`.msi` file), it can only be deleted by uninstalling the application, not by deleting it directly from the GAC. Trying to delete the assembly from the GAC results in the following error message:

```
"Assembly <name> could not be uninstalled because it is required by other
applications."
```

You can set a reference to the assembly by using the `gacutil` utility with the option `/r`. The option `/r` requires a reference type, a reference ID, and a description. The type of the reference can be one of three options: UNINSTALL_KEY, FILEPATH, or OPAQUE. UNINSTALL_KEY is used by MSI when a registry key is defined that is also needed for the uninstallation. A directory can be specified with FILEPATH. A useful directory would be the root directory of the application. The OPAQUE reference type enables you to set any type of reference.

The command line:

```
gacutil /i shareddemo.dll /r FILEPATH c:\ProCSharp\Assemblies\Client "Shared Demo"
```

installs the assembly shareddemo in the GAC with a reference to the directory of the client application. Another installation of the same assembly is possible with a different path, or an OPAQUE ID, such as in this command line:

```
gacutil /i shareddemo.dll /r OPAQUE 4711 "Opaque installation"
```

Now, the assembly is in the GAC only once, but it has two references. To delete the assembly from the GAC, both references must be removed:

```
gacutil /u shareddemo /r OPAQUE 4711 "Opaque installation"
gacutil /u shareddemo /r FILEPATH c:\ProCSharp\Assemblies\Client "Shared Demo"
```

> **NOTE** *To remove a shared assembly, the option* /u *requires the assembly name without the file extension* .DLL. *Conversely, the option* /i *to install a shared assembly requires the complete filename, including the file extension.*

> **NOTE** *Chapter 18 covers the deployment of assemblies in which the reference count is being dealt with in an MSI package.*

Native Image Generator

With the native image generator, Ngen.exe, you can compile the IL code to native code at installation time. This way, the program can start faster because the compilation during runtime is no longer necessary. Comparing precompiled assemblies to assemblies for which the JIT compiler needs to run is not different from a performance perspective after the IL code is compiled. The biggest improvement you get with the native image generator is that the application starts faster because there's no need to run JIT. Also, during runtime JIT is not needed as the IL code is already compiled. If your application is not using a lot of CPU time, you might not see a big improvement here. Reducing the startup time of the application might be enough reason to use the native image generator. If you do create a native image from the executable, you should also create native images from all the DLLs that are loaded by the executable. Otherwise, the JIT compiler still needs to run.

The ngen utility installs the native image in the native image cache. The physical directory of the native image cache is <windows>\assembly\NativeImages<RuntimeVersion>.

With ngen install myassembly, you can compile the MSIL code to native code and install it into the native image cache. This should be done from an installation program if you would like to put the assembly in the native image cache.

With ngen, you can also display all assemblies from the native image cache with the option display. If you add an assembly name to the display option, you get information about all assemblies that are dependent on the assembly; and after the long list, you can see all versions of this assembly installed:

```
C:\>ngen display System.Core
Microsoft (R) CLR Native Image Generator - Version 4.0.30319.17626
```

```
Copyright (c) Microsoft Corporation.  All rights reserved.

NGEN Roots that depend on "System.Core":

C:\Program Files (x86)\Common Files\Microsoft Shared\VSTA\Pipeline.v10.0\
AddInViews\Microsoft.VisualStudio.Tools.Applications.Runtime.v10.0.dll
C:\Program Files (x86)\Common Files\Microsoft Shared\VSTA\Pipeline.v10.0\
HostSideAdapters\Microsoft.VisualStudio.Tools.Office.Excel.HostAdapter.v10.0.
dll
C:\Program Files (x86)\Common Files\Microsoft Shared\VSTA\Pipeline.v10.0\
HostSideAdapters\Microsoft.VisualStudio.Tools.Office.HostAdapter.v10.0.dll
c:\Program Files (x86)\Microsoft Expression\Blend 4\
Microsoft.Windows.Design.Extensibility\
Microsoft.Windows.Design.Extensibility.dll
...

Native Images:

System.AddIn, Version=3.5.0.0, Culture=neutral, PublicKeyToken=b77a5c561934e089
System.AddIn, Version=4.0.0.0, Culture=neutral, PublicKeyToken=b77a5c561934e089
```

In case the security of the system changes, it is not sure if the precompiled native image has the security requirements it needs for running the application. This is why the native images become invalid with a system configuration change. With the command ngen update, all native images are rebuilt to include the new configurations.

Installing .NET 4.5 also installs the Native Runtime Optimization Service, which can be used to defer compilation of native images and regenerate native images that have been invalidated.

The command ngen install myassembly /queue can be used by an installation program to defer compilation of myassembly to a native image using the Native Image Service. ngen update /queue regenerates all native images that have been invalidated. With the ngen queue options pause, continue, and status, you can control the service and get status information.

> **NOTE** *You might be wondering why the native images cannot be created on the developer system, enabling you to just distribute them to the production system. The reason is because the native image generator takes care of the CPU that is installed with the target system, and compiles the code optimized for the CPU type. During installation of the application, the CPU is known.*

CONFIGURING .NET APPLICATIONS

Previous to COM, application configuration typically was using INI files. In the following application generation, the registry was the major place for configuration. All COM components are configured in the registry. The first version of Internet Information Server (IIS) had its complete configuration in the registry as well. The registry has its advantage on a centralized place for all configuration. One disadvantage was the open API where applications put configuration values to places in the registry that wasn't meant to. Also, xcopy deployment is not possible with registry configuration. IIS later changed to a custom binary configuration format that is only accessible via IIS Admin APIs. Nowadays, IIS uses XML files for its configuration. XML configuration files are also the preferred place to store configuration values for .NET applications. Configuration files can simply be copied. The configuration files use XML syntax to specify startup and runtime settings for applications.

This section explores the following:

➤   What you can configure using the XML base configuration files

➤   How you can redirect a strongly named referenced assembly to a different version

➤   How you can specify the directory of assemblies to find private assemblies in subdirectories and shared assemblies in common directories or on a server

Configuration Categories

The configuration can be grouped into the following categories:

➤   **Startup settings** — Enable you to specify the version of the required runtime. It's possible that different versions of the runtime could be installed on the same system. The version of the runtime can be specified with the `<startup>` element.

➤   Runtime settings — Enable you to specify how garbage collection is performed by the runtime and how the binding to assemblies works. You can also specify the version policy and the code base with these settings. You take a more detailed look into the runtime settings later in this chapter.

➤   **WCF settings** — Used to configure applications using WCF. You deal with these configurations in Chapter 43, "Windows Communication Foundation."

➤   **Security settings** — Covered in Chapter 22, configuration for cryptography and permissions is handled here.

These settings can be provided in three types of configuration files:

➤   **Application configuration files** — Include specific settings for an application, such as binding information to assemblies, configuration for remote objects, and so on. Such a configuration file is placed into the same directory as the executable; it has the same name as the executable with a `.config` extension. ASP.NET configuration files are named `web.config`.

➤   **Machine configuration files** — Used for system-wide configurations. You can also specify assembly binding and remoting configurations here. During a binding process, the machine configuration file is consulted before the application configuration file. The application configuration can override settings from the machine configuration. The application configuration file should be the preferred place for application-specific settings so that the machine configuration file remains smaller and more manageable. Machine configuration files are located at `%runtime_install_path%\config\Machine.config`.

➤   **Publisher policy files** — Can be used by a component creator to specify that a shared assembly is compatible with older versions. If a new assembly version just fixes a bug of a shared component, it is not necessary to put application configuration files in every application directory that uses this component; the publisher can mark it as compatible by adding a publisher policy file instead. If the component doesn't work with all applications, it is possible to override the publisher policy setting in an application configuration file. In contrast to the other configuration files, publisher policy files are stored in the GAC.

To understand how these configuration files are used, recall that how a client finds an assembly (also called *binding*) depends on whether the assembly is private or shared. Private assemblies must be in the directory of the application or a subdirectory thereof. A process called *probing* is used to find such an assembly. If the assembly doesn't have a strong name, the version number is not used with probing.

Shared assemblies can be installed in the GAC or placed in a directory, on a network share, or on a website. You specify such a directory with the configuration of the `codeBase` shortly. The public key, version, and culture are all important aspects when binding to a shared assembly. The reference of the required assembly is recorded in the manifest of the client assembly, including the name, the version, and the public key token. All configuration files are checked to apply the correct version policy. The GAC and code bases specified in the configuration files are checked, followed by the application directories, and probing rules are then applied.

Binding to Assemblies

You've already seen how to install a shared assembly to the GAC. Instead of doing that, you can configure a specific shared directory by using configuration files. This feature can be used if you want to make the shared components available on a server. Another possible scenario is when you want to share an assembly between your applications but you don't want to make it publicly available in the GAC, so you put it into a shared directory instead.

There are two ways to find the correct directory for an assembly: the codeBase element in an XML configuration file, or through probing. The codeBase configuration is available only for shared assemblies, and probing is done for private assemblies.

<codeBase>

The <codeBase> element can be configured with an application configuration file. The following application configuration file redirects the search for the assembly SharedDemo to load it from the network:

```xml
<?xml version="1.0" encoding="utf-8" ?>
<configuration>
  <runtime>
    <assemblyBinding xmlns="urn:schemas-microsoft-com:asm.v1">
      <dependentAssembly>
        <assemblyIdentity name="SharedDemo" culture="neutral"
             publicKeyToken="f946433fdae2512d" />
        <codeBase version="1.0.0.0"
             href="http://www.christiannagel.com/WroxUtils/SharedDemo.dll" />
      </dependentAssembly>
    </assemblyBinding>
  </runtime>
</configuration>
```

The <codeBase> element has the attributes version and href. With version, the original referenced version of the assembly must be specified. With href, you can define the directory from which the assembly should be loaded. In the preceding example, a path using the HTTP protocol is used. A directory on a local system or a share is specified by using href="file://C:/WroxUtils/SharedDemo.dll".

<probing>

When the <codeBase> is not configured and the assembly is not stored in the GAC, the runtime tries to find an assembly through probing. The .NET runtime tries to find assemblies with either a .dll or an .exe file extension in the application directory or in one of its subdirectories that has the same name as the assembly searched for. If the assembly is not found here, the search continues. You can configure search directories with the <probing> element in the <runtime> section of application configuration files. This XML configuration can also be done easily by selecting the properties of the application with the .NET Framework Configuration tool. You can configure the directories where the probing should occur by using the search path in the .NET Framework configuration.

The XML file produced has the following entries:

```xml
<?xml version="1.0" encoding="utf-8" ?>
<configuration>
  <runtime>
    <assemblyBinding xmlns="urn:schemas-microsoft-com:asm.v1">
      <probing privatePath="bin;utils;" />
    </assemblyBinding>
  </runtime>
</configuration>
```

The <probing> element has just a single required attribute: privatePath. This application configuration file tells the runtime that assemblies should be searched for in the base directory of the application, followed by the `bin` and `util` directories. Both directories are subdirectories of the application base directory. It's not possible to reference a private assembly outside the application base directory or a subdirectory thereof. An assembly outside of the application base directory must have a shared name and can be referenced using the `<codeBase>` element, as shown earlier.

VERSIONING

For private assemblies, versioning is not important because the referenced assemblies are copied with the client. The client uses the assembly it has in its private directories. This is different for shared assemblies, however. This section looks at the traditional problems that can occur with sharing.

With shared components, more than one client application can use the same component. The new version can break existing clients when updating a shared component with a newer version. You can't stop shipping new versions because new features will be requested and introduced with new versions of existing components. You can try to program carefully for backward compatibility, but that's not always possible.

A solution to this dilemma could be an architecture that allows installation of different versions of shared components, with clients using the version that they referenced during the build process. This solves a lot of problems but not all of them. What happens if you detect a bug in a component that's referenced from the client? You would like to update this component and ensure that the client uses the new version instead of the version that was referenced during the build process.

Therefore, depending on the type in the fix of the new version, you sometimes want to use a newer version, and you also want to use the older referenced version. The .NET architecture enables both scenarios. In .NET, the original referenced assembly is used by default. You can redirect the reference to a different version by using configuration files. Versioning plays a key role in the binding architecture — how the client gets the right assembly where the components reside.

Version Numbers

Assemblies have a four-part version number — for example, `1.1.400.3300`. The parts are `<Major>`, `<Minor>`, `<Build>`, `<Revision>`. How these numbers are used depends on your application configuration.

> **NOTE** *It's a good policy to change the major or minor number on changes incompatible with the previous version, but just the build or revision number with compatible changes. This way, it can be assumed that redirecting an assembly to a new version where just the build and revision have changed is safe.*

With Visual Studio 2012, you can define the version number of the assembly with the assembly information in the project settings. The project settings write the assembly attribute `[AssemblyVersion]` to the file `AssemblyInfo.cs`:

```
[assembly: AssemblyVersion("1.0.0.0")]
```

Instead of defining all four version numbers, you can also place an asterisk in the third or fourth place:

```
[assembly: AssemblyVersion("1.0.*")]
```

With this setting, the first two numbers specify the major and minor version, and the asterisk (*) means that the build and revision numbers are auto-generated. The build number is the number of days since January 1, 2000, and the revision is the number of seconds since midnight divided by two. Though the automatic versioning might help during development time, before shipping it is a good practice to define a specific version number.

This version is stored in the .assembly section of the manifest.

Referencing the assembly in the client application stores the version of the referenced assembly in the manifest of the client application.

Getting the Version Programmatically

To enable checking the version of the assembly that is used from the client application, add the read-only property FullName to the SharedDemo class created earlier to return the strong name of the assembly. For easy use of the Assembly class, you have to import the System.Reflection namespace (code file SharedDemo/SharedDemo.cs):

```
public string FullName
{
   get
   {
      return Assembly.GetExecutingAssembly().FullName;
   }
}
```

The FullName property of the Assembly class holds the name of the class, the version, the locality, and the public key token, as shown in the following output, when calling FullName in your client application.

In the client application, just add a call to FullName in the Main() method after creating the shared component (code file Client/Program.cs):

```
static void Main()
{
   var quotes = new SharedDemo("Quotes.txt");
   Console.WriteLine(quotes.FullName);
```

Be sure to register the new version of the shared assembly SharedDemo again in the GAC, using gacutil. If the referenced version cannot be found, you will get a System.IO.FileLoadException, because the binding to the correct assembly failed.

With a successful run, you can see the full name of the referenced assembly:

```
SharedDemo, Version=1.0.0.0, Culture=neutral, PublicKeyToken= f946433fdae2512d
```

This client program can now be used to test different configurations of this shared component.

Binding to Assembly Versions

With a configuration file, you can specify that the binding should happen to a different version of a shared assembly. Assume that you create a new version of the shared assembly SharedDemo with major and minor versions 1.1. Maybe you don't want to rebuild the client but just want the new version of the assembly to be used with the existing client instead. This is useful in cases where either a bug is fixed with the shared assembly or you just want to get rid of the old version because the new version is compatible.

By running gacutil.exe, you can see that the versions 1.0.0.0 and 1.0.3300.0 are installed for the SharedDemo assembly:

```
> gacutil -l SharedDemo

Microsoft (R) .NET Global Assembly Cache Utility.  Version 4.0.30319.17626
Copyright (c) Microsoft Corporation.  All rights reserved.

The Global Assembly Cache contains the following assemblies:
   SharedDemo, Version=1.0.0.0, Culture=neutral,
   PublicKeyToken=f946433fdae2512d, processorArchitecture=x86
```

```
SharedDemo, Version=1.0.3300.0, Culture=neutral,
PublicKeyToken=f946433fdae2512d, processorArchitecture=x86

Number of items = 2
```

Figure 19-14 shows the manifest of the client application for which the client references version 1.0.0.0 of the assembly SharedDemo.

Now, again, an application configuration file is needed. As before, the assembly that is redirected needs to be specified with the <assemblyIdentity> element. This element identifies the assembly using the name, culture, and public key token. For a redirect to a different

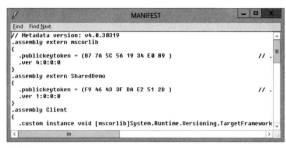

FIGURE 19-14

version, the <bindingRedirect> element is used. The oldVersion attribute specifies what version of the assembly should be redirected to a new version. With oldVersion you can specify a range like the one shown, with all assemblies from version 1.0.0.0 to 1.0.3300.0 to be redirected. The new version is specified with the newVersion attribute (configuration file Client/App.config):

```xml
<?xml version="1.0" encoding="utf-8" ?>
<configuration>
  <runtime>
    <assemblyBinding xmlns="urn:schemas-microsoft-com:asm.v1">
      <dependentAssembly>
        <assemblyIdentity name="SharedDemo" culture="neutral"
                          publicKeyToken="f946433fdae2512d" />
        <bindingRedirect oldVersion="1.0.0.0-1.0.3300.0"
                          newVersion="1.0.3300.0" />
      </dependentAssembly>
    </assemblyBinding>
  </runtime>
</configuration>
```

Publisher Policy Files

Using assemblies shared from the GAC enables you to use publisher policies to override versioning issues. Assume that you have an assembly used by some applications. What can be done if a critical bug is found in the shared assembly? You have seen that it is not necessary to rebuild all the applications that use this shared assembly, because you can use configuration files to redirect to the new version of this shared assembly. Maybe you don't know all the applications that use this shared assembly, but you want to get the bug fix to all of them. In that case, you can create publisher policy files to redirect all applications to the new version of the shared assembly.

> **NOTE** *Publisher policy files apply only to shared assemblies installed in the GAC.*

To set up publisher policies, you have to do the following:

➤ Create a publisher policy file.
➤ Create a publisher policy assembly.
➤ Add the publisher policy assembly to the GAC.

Creating a Publisher Policy File

A publisher policy file is an XML file that redirects an existing version or version range to a new version. The syntax used here is the same as that used for application configuration files, so you can use the file you created earlier to redirect the old versions 1.0.0.0 through 1.0.3300.0 to the new version 1.0.3300.0. Rename the previously created file to `mypolicy.config` to use it as a publisher policy file.

Creating a Publisher Policy Assembly

To associate the publisher policy file with the shared assembly, it is necessary to create a publisher policy assembly and place it in the GAC. The tool you can use to create such a file is the assembly linker, `al`. The option `/linkresource` adds the publisher policy file to the generated assembly. The name of the generated assembly must start with policy, followed by the major and minor version number of the assembly that should be redirected, and the filename of the shared assembly. In this case the publisher policy assembly must be named `policy.1.0.SharedDemo.dll` to redirect the assemblies `SharedDemo` with the major version 1 and minor version 0. The key that must be added to this publisher key with the option `/keyfile` is the same key that was used to sign the shared assembly `SharedDemo` to guarantee that the version redirection is from the same publisher:

```
al /linkresource:mypolicy.config /out:policy.1.0.SharedDemo.dll
/keyfile:.\.\mykey.snk
```

Adding the Publisher Policy Assembly to the GAC

The publisher policy assembly can now be added to the GAC with the utility `gacutil`:

```
gacutil -i policy.1.0.SharedDemo.dll
```

Do not forget the `-f` option if the same policy file was already published. Then remove the application configuration file that was placed in the directory of the client application and start the client application. Although the client assembly references 1.0.0.0, you use the new version 1.0.3300.0 of the shared assembly because of the publisher policy.

Overriding Publisher Policies

With a publisher policy, the publisher of the shared assembly guarantees that a new version of the assembly is compatible with the old version. As you know from changes to traditional DLLs, such guarantees don't always hold. Maybe all applications except one are working with the new shared assembly. To fix the one application that has a problem with the new release, the publisher policy can be overridden by using an application configuration file.

You can disable the publisher policy by adding the XML element `<publisherPolicy>` with the attribute `apply="no"` (configuration file `Client/App.config`):

```xml
<?xml version="1.0" encoding="utf-8" ?>
<configuration>
  <runtime>
    <assemblyBinding xmlns="urn:schemas-microsoft-com:asm.v1">
      <dependentAssembly>
        <assemblyIdentity name="SharedDemo" culture="neutral"
                          publicKeyToken="f946433fdae2512d" />
        <publisherPolicy apply="no" />
      </dependentAssembly>
    </assemblyBinding>
  </runtime>
</configuration>
```

By disabling the publisher policy, you can configure different version redirection in the application configuration file.

Runtime Version

Installing and using multiple versions is not only possible with assemblies but also with the .NET runtime (CLR). The versions 1.0, 1.1, 2.0, and 4.0 (and later versions) of the CLR can be installed on the same operating system side by side. Visual Studio 2012 targets applications running on CLR 2.0 with .NET 2.0, 3.0, and 3.5, and CLR 4.0 with .NET 4 and 4.5.

If the application is built with CLR 2.0, it might run without changes on a system where only CLR version 4.0 is installed. The reverse is not true: If the application is built with CLR 4.0, it cannot run on a system on which only CLR 2.0 is installed.

In an application configuration file, not only can you redirect versions of referenced assemblies, you can also define the required version of the runtime. You can specify the version that's required for the application in an application configuration file. The element `<supportedRuntime>` marks the runtime versions that are supported by the application. The order of `<supportedRuntime>` elements defines the preference if multiple runtime versions are available on the system. The following configuration prefers the .NET 4 runtime and supports 2.0. Remember that in order for this to be possible, the application must be built with the target framework .NET 2.0, 3.0 or 3.5.

```xml
<?xml version="1.0"?>
<configuration>
  <startup>
    <supportedRuntime version="v4.0" />
    <supportedRuntime version="v2.0.50727" />
  </startup>
</configuration>
```

Optionally, the SKUs can be defined with the `sku` attribute. The SKU defines the .NET Framework version, e.g., 4.0 with SP1, or the client profile. The following snippet requires the full version of .NET 4.5:

```xml
<supportedRuntime version="v4.0" sku=".NET Framework,Version=4.5" />
```

To specify the client profile of .NET 4.0 with SP2, this string is specified:

```
.NET Framework,Version=4.02,Profile=Client
```

All the possible SKUs can be found in the registry key `HKLM\SOFTWARE\Microsoft\.NETFramework\v4.0.30319\SKUs`.

SHARING ASSEMBLIES BETWEEN DIFFERENT TECHNOLOGIES

Sharing assemblies is not limited to different .NET applications; you can also share code or assemblies between different technologies — for example, between .NET and Windows 8 Metro applications. This section describes the different options available, including their advantages and disadvantages. Your requirements will determine which option is most appropriate for your environment.

Sharing Source Code

The first option is not really a variant of sharing assemblies; instead, source code is shared. To share source code between different technologies, you can use C# preprocessor directives and define conditional compilation symbols, as shown in the following code snippet. Here, the method `PlatformString` returns a string, which varies according to whether the symbol `SILVERLIGHT` or `NETFX_CORE` or neither of these symbols is defined:

```csharp
    public string PlatformString()
    {
#if SILVERLIGHT
        return "Silverlight";
#elif NETFX_CORE
        return "Windows 8 Metro";
#else
        return "Default";
#endif
    }
```

You can define the code with these platform dependencies within a normal .NET library. With other libraries, such as a Windows Metro-style class library or a Silverlight 5 class library, symbols are defined as shown in Figure 19-15, which in this case uses a Windows Metro-style class library.

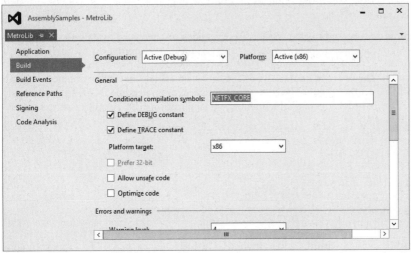

FIGURE 19-15

With other projects, existing items can be added with the option Add as Link from Solution Explorer. This way, the source code only exists once, and can be edited from all projects where the link was added. Depending on the project in which the file is opened for editing, the Visual Studio editor highlights the code from the part of the current active #if block. In Figure 19-16, three different projects have the same file, Demo.cs, linked. The links have a different symbol within Solution Explorer.

When sharing source code, every project type can take full advantage of all its features. However, it's necessary to define different code segments to handle the differences. For that, preprocessor directives can be used to deal with different method implementations, or different methods, or even different implementations of complete types.

FIGURE 19-16

Portable Class Library

Sharing the binary assembly instead of the source code can be done with the portable class library. Visual Studio 2012 provides a new template for creating portable class libraries. With this library you can configure multiple target frameworks, as shown in Figure 19-17. Here, the target frameworks .NET 4.5 and .NET for Metro-style apps are selected. This enables all references, classes, and methods to be used with all the selected frameworks.

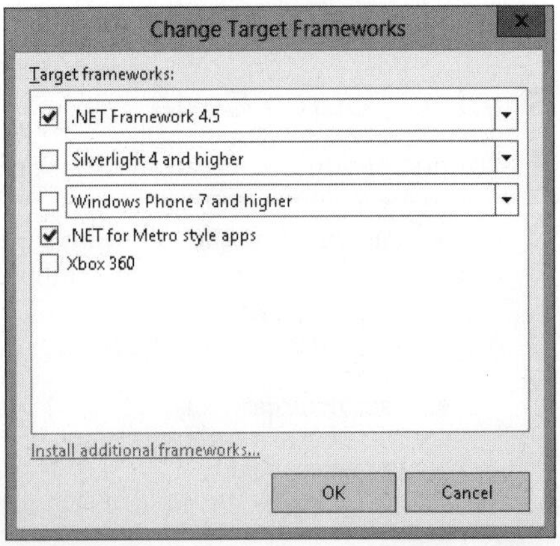

If all the frameworks are selected, of course, the classes that can be used are very limited. The available classes and class members are displayed within the Object Browser, as shown in Figure 19-18.

FIGURE 19-17

For example, using .NET Framework 4.5 and .NET for Metro-style apps, a subset of MEF and WCF, is available. Classes from WPF, Windows Forms, ASP.NET, and ADO.NET are not available. It's possible to create a view model within the portable library to be used with the MVVM pattern. With the portable library, the view model classes cannot use libraries that reference ADO.NET. Of course, it's a common scenario to use a database from a Windows application. To do this you can use some server-side code that accesses the database and use a communication protocol to access the service.

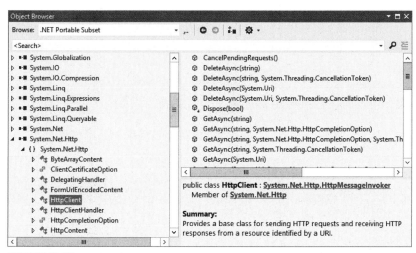

FIGURE 19-18

> **NOTE** *The MVVM Pattern (Model-View-ViewModel) separates the user interface (view) from the data (model) using a layer between (view-model). This pattern is often used with WPF applications.*

SUMMARY

Assemblies are the installation unit for the .NET platform. Microsoft learned from problems with previous architectures (like COM) and did a complete redesign to avoid them. This chapter discussed the main features of assemblies: that they are self-describing, and require no type library or registry information.

Because version dependencies are exactly recorded with assemblies, the old DLL hell no longer exists, and development, deployment, and administration have become a lot easier.

You learned the differences between private and shared assemblies and saw how shared assemblies can be created. With private assemblies, you don't have to pay attention to uniqueness and versioning issues because these assemblies are copied and only used by a single application. Sharing assemblies requires the use of a key for uniqueness and to define the version. You also looked at the GAC, which can be used as an intelligent store for shared assemblies.

You can have faster application startup by using the native image generator. With this, the JIT compiler does not need to run because the native code is created during installation.

You looked at all the aspects of assembly versioning, including overriding the policy to use a version of an assembly different from the one that was used during development; this is achieved using publisher policies and application configuration files. You learned how probing works with private assemblies.

The chapter also discussed loading assemblies dynamically and creating assemblies during runtime. If you want more information on this, read about the plugin model of .NET 4 in Chapter 30, "Managed Extensibility Framework."

The next chapter is on diagnostics, to find failures with applications not only during development but also on a production system.

20

Diagnostics

WROX.COM CODE DOWNLOADS FOR THIS CHAPTER

The wrox.com code downloads for this chapter are found at `http://www.wrox.com/remtitle .cgi?isbn=1118314425` on the Download Code tab. The code for this chapter is divided into the following major examples:

➤ Code Contracts

➤ Tracing Demo

➤ Tracing Demo with `EventLog`

➤ Event Log

➤ Event Log Reader

➤ Performance Counter

DIAGNOSTICS OVERVIEW

This chapter explains how to get real-time information about your running application in order to identify any issues that it might have during production or to monitor resource usage to ensure that higher user loads can be accommodated. This is where the namespace `System.Diagnostics` comes into play. This namespace offers classes for tracing, event logging, performance counts, and code contracts.

One way to deal with errors in your application, of course, is by throwing exceptions. However, an application might not fail with an exception, but still not behave as expected. The application might be running well on most systems but have a problem on a few. On the live system, you can change the log behavior by changing a configuration value and get detailed live information about what's going on in the application. This can be done with tracing.

If there are problems with applications, the system administrator needs to be informed. The *Event Viewer* is a commonly used tool that not only the system administrator should be aware of. With the Event Viewer, you can both interactively monitor problems with applications and be informed about specific events that happen by adding subscriptions. The *event-logging* mechanism enables you to write information about the application.

To analyze resources needed by applications, you can monitor applications with specified time intervals, e.g. get counts every 5 minutes. This way you can have data for 24 hours or a week without filling terabytes, and can plan for a different application distribution or the extension of system resources. The *Performance Monitor (PerfMon)* can be used to get these data. You can write live data from your application by using performance counts.

Design by contract is another feature offered by the .NET Framework. A method signature defines the type of parameters. It doesn't give you any information about the values that you can pass to the method. This is a feature of design by contract. Using classes from the namespace `System.Diagnostics.Contracts` you can define preconditions, postconditions, and invariants. These contracts can be checked during runtime but also with a static contract analyzer. This chapter explains these facilities and demonstrates how you can use them from your applications.

CODE CONTRACTS

Design by contract is an idea from the Eiffel programming language that defines preconditions, postconditions, and invariants. .NET includes classes for static and runtime checks of code within the namespace `System.Diagnostics.Contracts` that can be used by all .NET languages. With this functionality you can define preconditions, postconditions, and invariants within a method. The preconditions specify what requirements the parameters must fulfill, the postconditions define the requirements on returned data, and the invariants define the requirements of variables within the method itself.

Contract information can be compiled both into the debug code and the release code. It is also possible to define a separate contract assembly, and many checks can be made statically without running the application. You can also define contracts on interfaces that cause the implementations of the interface to fulfill the contracts. Contract tools can rewrite the assembly to inject contract checks within the code for runtime checks, check the contracts during compile time, and add contract information to the generated XML documentation.

Figure 20-1 shows the project properties for the code contracts in Visual Studio 2012. Here, you can define what level of runtime checking should be done, indicate whether assert dialogs should be opened on contract failures, and configure static checking. Setting the Perform Runtime Contract Checking to Full defines the symbol `CONTRACTS_FULL`. Because many of the contract methods are annotated with the attribute `[Conditional("CONTRACTS_FULL")]`, all runtime checks are performed with this setting only.

> **NOTE** *To work with code contracts you can use classes available with .NET 4 in the namespace* `System.Diagnostics.Contracts`*. However, no tool is included with Visual Studio 2012. You need to download an extension to Visual Studio from Microsoft DevLabs:* `http://msdn.microsoft.com/en-us/devlabs/dd491992.aspx`*.*

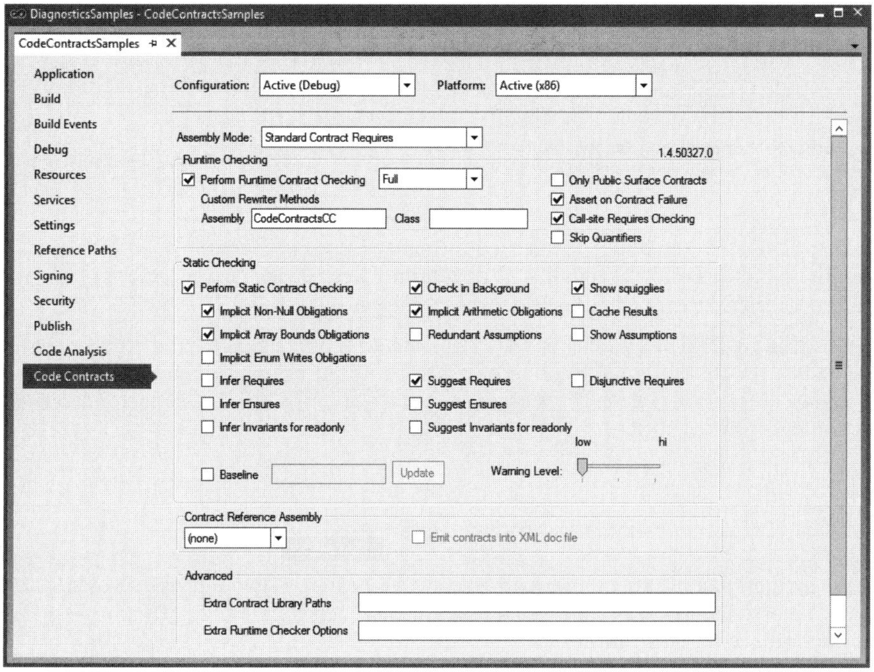

FIGURE 20-1

Code contracts are defined with the `Contract` class. All contract requirements that you define in a method, whether they are preconditions or postconditions, must be placed at the beginning of the method. You can also assign a global event handler to the event `ContractFailed` that is invoked for every failed contract during runtime. Invoking `SetHandled` with the e parameter of type `ContractFailedEventArgs` stops the standard behavior of failures that would throw an exception (code file CodeContractSamples/Program.cs).

```
Contract.ContractFailed += (sender, e) =>
{
  Console.WriteLine(e.Message);
  e.SetHandled();
};
```

Preconditions

Preconditions check the parameters that are passed to a method. With the `Contract` class, preconditions are defined with the `Requires` method. With the `Requires` method, a Boolean value must be passed, and an optional message string with the second parameter that is shown when the condition does not succeed. The following example requires that the argument `min` be less than or equal to the argument `max`:

```
static void MinMax(int min, int max)
{
  Contract.Requires(min <= max);
  //...
}
```

Using the generic variant of the `Requires` method enables specifying an exception type that should be invoked in case the condition is not fulfilled. The following contract throws an `ArgumentNullException` if the argument `o` is null. The exception is not thrown if an event handler sets the `ContractFailed` event to handled. Also, if the Assert on Contract Failure setting is configured, `Trace.Assert` is used to stop the program instead of throwing the exception defined.

```
static void Preconditions(object o)
{
  Contract.Requires<ArgumentNullException>(o != null,
      "Preconditions, o may not be null");
  //...
```

`Requires<TException>` is not annotated with the attribute `[Conditional("CONTRACTS_FULL")];` nor does it have a condition on the DEBUG symbol, so this runtime check is done in any case. `Requires<TException>` throws the defined exception if the condition is not fulfilled.

For checking collections that are used as arguments, the `Contract` class offers `Exists` and `ForAll` methods. `ForAll` checks every item in the collection if the condition succeeds. In the example, it checks whether every item in the collection has a value smaller than 12. With the `Exists` method, it checks whether any one element in the collection meets the condition:

```
static void ArrayTest(int[] data)
{
  Contract.Requires(Contract.ForAll(data, i => i < 12));
```

Both the methods `Exists` and `ForAll` have an overload whereby you can pass two integers, `fromInclusive` and `toExclusive`, instead of `IEnumerable<T>`. A range from the numbers (excluding `toExclusive`) is passed to the predicate defined with the third parameter. `Exists` and `ForAll` can be used with preconditions, postconditions, and invariants.

Postconditions

Postconditions define guarantees about shared data and return values after the method has completed. Although they define some guarantees on return values, they must be written at the beginning of a method; all contract requirements must be at the beginning of the method.

`Ensures` and `EnsuresOnThrow<TException>` are postconditions. The following contract ensures that the variable `sharedState` is less than 6 at the end of the method (the value can change in between):

```
private static int sharedState = 5;
static void Postcondition()
{
  Contract.Ensures(sharedState < 6);

  sharedState = 9;
  Console.WriteLine("change sharedState invariant {0}", sharedState);
  sharedState = 3;
  Console.WriteLine("before returning change it to a valid value {0}",
      sharedState);
}
```

With `EnsuresOnThrow<TException>`, it is guaranteed that a shared state meets a condition if a specified exception is thrown.

To guarantee a return value, the special value `Result<T>` can be used with an `Ensures` contract. In the next example, the result is of type `int` as is also defined with the generic type `T` for the `Result` method. The `Ensures` contract guarantees that the `return` value is less than 6:

```
static int ReturnValue()
{
  Contract.Ensures(Contract.Result<int>() < 6);
  return 3;
}
```

You can also compare a current value to an old value. This is done with the OldValue<T> method, which returns the original value on method entry for the variable passed. The following contract ensures that the result returned from the method is larger than the old value received from the argument x:

```
static int ReturnLargerThanInput(int x)
{
  Contract.Ensures(Contract.Result<int>() > Contract.OldValue<int>(x));
  return x + 3;
}
```

If a method returns values with the out modifier instead of just with the return statement, conditions can be defined with ValueAtReturn. The following contract defines that the x variable must be larger than 5 and smaller than 20 on return, and with the y variable modulo 5 must equal 0 on return:

```
static void OutParameters(out int x, out int y)
{
  Contract.Ensures(Contract.ValueAtReturn<int>(out x) > 5 &&
    Contract.ValueAtReturn<int>(out x) < 20);
  Contract.Ensures(Contract.ValueAtReturn<int>(out y) % 5 == 0);
  x = 8;
  y = 10;
}
```

Invariants

Invariants define contracts for variables during the object's lifetime. Contract.Requires defines input requirements of a method, and Contract.Ensures defines requirements on method end. Contract.Invariant defines conditions that must succeed during the whole lifetime of an object.

The following code snippet shows an invariant check of the member variable x, which must be larger than 5. With the initialization of x, x is initialized to 10, which fulfills the contract. The call to Contract.Invariant can only be placed within a method that has the ContractInvariantMethod attribute applied. This method can be public or private, can have any name (the name ObjectInvariant is suggested), and can only contain contract invariant checks.

```
private int x = 10;

[ContractInvariantMethod]
private void ObjectInvariant()
{
  Contract.Invariant(x > 5);
}
```

Invariant verification is always done at the end of public methods. In the next example, the method Invariant assigns 3 to the variable x, which results in a contract failure at the end of this method:

```
public void Invariant()
{
  x = 3;
  Console.WriteLine("invariant value: {0}", x);

  // contract failure at the end of the method
}
```

Purity

You can use custom methods within contract methods, but these methods must be pure. Pure means that the method doesn't change any visible state of the object.

You can mark methods and types as pure by applying the Pure attribute. Get accessors of properties are assumed to be pure by default. With the current version of the code contract tools, purity is not enforced.

Contracts for Interfaces

With interfaces you can define methods, properties, and events that a class derived from the interface must implement. With the interface declaration you cannot define how the interface must be implemented, but now this is possible using code contracts.

In the following example, the interface IPerson defines FirstName, LastName, and Age properties, and the method ChangeName. What's special about this interface is the attribute ContractClass. This attribute is applied to the interface IPerson and defines that the PersonContract class is used as the code contract for the interface (code file CodeContractsSamples/IPerson.cs).

```
[ContractClass(typeof(PersonContract))]
public interface IPerson
{
  string FirstName { get; set; }
  string LastName { get; set; }
  int Age { get; set; }
  void ChangeName(string firstName, string lastName);
}
```

The class PersonContract implements the interface IPerson and defines code contracts for all the members. This is defined with the get accessors of the properties but can also be defined with all methods that are not allowed to change state. The FirstName and LastName get accessors also define that the result must be a string with Contract.Result. The get accessor of the Age property defines a postcondition, ensuring that the returned value is between 0 and 120. The set accessor of the FirstName and LastName properties requires that the value passed is not null. The set accessor of the Age property defines a precondition that the passed value is between 0 and 120 (code file CodeContractSamples/Person Contract.cs).

```
[ContractClassFor(typeof(IPerson))]
public abstract class PersonContract : IPerson
{
  string IPerson.FirstName
  {
    get { return Contract.Result<String>(); }
    set { Contract.Requires(value != null); }
  }
  string IPerson.LastName
  {
    get { return Contract.Result<String>(); }
    set { Contract.Requires(value != null); }
  }
  int IPerson.Age
  {
    get
    {
      Contract.Ensures(Contract.Result<int>() >= 0 &&
                       Contract.Result<int>() < 121);
      return Contract.Result<int>();
    }
    set
```

```
      {
        Contract.Requires(value >= 0 && value < 121);
      }
    }
    void IPerson.ChangeName(string firstName, string lastName)
    {
      Contract.Requires(firstName != null);
      Contract.Requires(lastName != null);
    }
  }
```

Now a class implementing the `IPerson` interface must fulfill all the contract requirements. The class `Person` is a simple implementation of the interface that fulfills the contract (code file `CodeContractsSamples/Person.cs`):

```
public class Person : IPerson
{
  public Person(string firstName, string lastName)
  {
    this.FirstName = firstName;
    this.LastName = lastName;
  }

  public string FirstName { get; private set; }
  public string LastName { get; private set; }
  public int Age { get; set; }


  public void ChangeName(string firstName, string lastName)
  {
    this.FirstName = firstName;
    this.LastName = lastName;
  }
}
```

When using the class `Person`, the contract must also be fulfilled. For example, assigning null to a property is not allowed:

```
var p = new Person { FirstName = "Tom", LastName = null };
// contract error
```

Nor is it allowed to assign an invalid value to the `Age` property:

```
var p = new Person { FirstName = "Tom", LastName = "Turbo" };
p.Age = 133; // contract error
```

Abbreviations

A new feature of .NET 4.5 and code contracts are abbreviations. If some contracts are required repeatedly, a reuse mechanism is available. A method that contains multiple contracts can be attributed with the `ContractAbbreviator` attribute, and thus it can be used within other methods requiring this contract:

```
[ContractAbbreviator]
private static void CheckCollectionContract(int[] data)
{
  Contract.Requires<ArgumentNullException>(data != null);
  Contract.Requires(Contract.ForAll(data, x => x < 12));
}
```

Now the method `CheckCollectionContract` can be used within a method, checking for both null for the parameter and the values of the collection:

```
private static void Abbrevations(int[] data)
{
  CheckCollectionContract(data);
}
```

Contracts and Legacy Code

With a lot of legacy code, arguments are often checked with `if` statements and throw an exception if a condition is not fulfilled. With code contracts, it is not necessary to rewrite the verification; just add one line of code:

```
static void PrecondtionsWithLegacyCode(object o)
{
  if (o == null) throw new ArgumentNullException("o");
    Contract.EndContractBlock();
```

The `EndContractBlock` defines that the preceding code should be handled as a contract. If other contract statements are used as well, the `EndContractBlock` is not necessary.

> **NOTE** *When using assemblies with legacy code, with the code contracts configuration the assembly mode must be set to Custom Parameter Validation.*

TRACING

Tracing enables you to see informational messages about the running application. To get information about a running application, you can start the application in the debugger. During debugging, you can walk through the application step by step and set breakpoints at specific lines and when you reach specific conditions. The problem with debugging is that a program with release code can behave differently from a program with debug code. For example, while the program is stopping at a breakpoint, other threads of the application are suspended as well. Also, with a release build, the compiler-generated output is optimized and, thus, different effects can occur. With optimized release code, garbage collection is much more aggressive than with debug code. The order of calls within a method can be changed, and some methods can be removed completely and be called in-place. There is a need to have runtime information from the release build of a program as well. Trace messages are written with both debug and release code.

A scenario showing how tracing helps is described here. After an application is deployed, it runs on one system without problems, while on another system intermittent problems occur. When you enable verbose tracing, the system with the problems gives you detailed information about what's happening inside the application. The system that is running without problems has tracing configured just for error messages redirected to the Windows event log system. Critical errors are seen by the system administrator. The overhead of tracing is very small because you configure a trace level only when needed.

The tracing architecture has four major parts:

- ➤ **Source** — The originator of the trace information. You use the source to send trace messages.
- ➤ **Switch** — Defines the level of information to log. For example, you can request just error information or detailed verbose information.
- ➤ **Listeners** — Trace listeners define the location to which the trace messages should be written.
- ➤ **Filters** — Listeners can have filters attached. The filter defines what trace messages should be written by the listener. This way, you can have different listeners for the same source that write different levels of information.

Figure 20-2 shows a Visual Studio class diagram illustrating the major classes for tracing and how they are connected. The `TraceSource` uses a switch to define what information to log. It has a `TraceListenerCollection` associated with it, to which trace messages are forwarded. The collection consists of `TraceListener` objects, and every listener has a `TraceFilter` connected.

> **NOTE** *Several .NET technologies make use of trace sources, which you just need to enable to see what's going on. For example, WPF defines, among others, sources such as* `System.Windows.Data`*,* `System.Windows.RoutedEvent`*,* `System.Windows.Markup`*, and* `System.Windows.Media.Animation`*. However, with WPF, you need to enable tracing not only by configuring listeners but also by setting within the registry key* `HKEY_CURRENT_USER\Software\MicrosoftTracing\WPF` *a new* `DWORD` *named* `ManagedTracing` *and the value 1 — or turn it on programmatically.*
>
> *Classes from the* `System.Net` *namespace use the trace source* `System.Net`*; WCF uses the trace sources* `System.ServiceModel` *and* `System.ServiceModel.MessageLogging`*. WCF tracing is discussed in Chapter 43, "Windows Communication Foundation."*

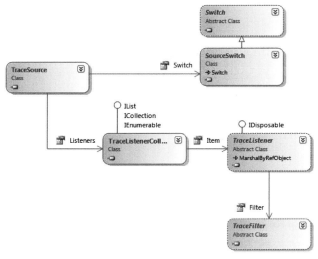

FIGURE 20-2

Trace Sources

You can write trace messages with the `TraceSource` class. Tracing requires the `Trace` flag of the compiler settings. With a Visual Studio project, the `Trace` flag is set by default with debug and release builds, but you can change it through the Build properties of the project.

> **NOTE** *The* `TraceSource` *class is more difficult to use compared to the* `Trace` *class when writing trace messages, but it provides more options.*

To write trace messages, you need to create a new `TraceSource` instance. In the constructor, the name of the trace source is defined. The method `TraceInformation` writes an informational message to the trace output. Instead of just writing informational messages, the `TraceEvent` method requires an enumeration value of type `TraceEventType` to define the type of the trace message. `TraceEventType.Error` specifies the message as an error message. You can define it with a trace switch to see only error messages.

The second argument of the `TraceEvent` method requires an identifier. The ID can be used within the application itself. For example, you can use id 1 for entering a method and id 2 for exiting a method. The method `TraceEvent` is overloaded, so the `TraceEventType` and the ID are the only required parameters. Using the third parameter of an overloaded method, you can pass the message written to the trace. `TraceEvent` also supports passing a format string with any number of parameters, in the same way as `Console.WriteLine`. `TraceInformation` does nothing more than invoke `TraceEvent` with an identifier of 0. `TraceInformation` is just a simplified version of `TraceEvent`. With the `TraceData` method, you can pass any object — for example, an exception instance — instead of a message.

To ensure that data is written by the listeners and does not stay in memory, you need to do a `Flush`. If the source is no longer needed, you can invoke the `Close` method, which closes all listeners associated with the trace source. `Close` does a `Flush` as well (code file `TracingDemo/Program.cs`).

```
public class Program
{
  internal static TraceSource trace =
      new TraceSource("Wrox.ProCSharp.Instrumentation");

  static void TraceSourceDemo1()
  {
    trace.TraceInformation("Info message");

    trace.TraceEvent(TraceEventType.Error, 3, "Error message");
    trace.TraceData(TraceEventType.Information, 2, "data1", 4, 5);
    trace.Close();
  }
```

> **NOTE** *You can use different trace sources within your application. It makes sense to define different sources for different libraries, so that you can enable different trace levels for different parts of your application. To use a trace source, you need to know its name. A common naming convention is to use the same name as the assembly name.*

The `TraceEventType` enumeration that is passed as an argument to the `TraceEvent` method defines the following levels to indicate the severity of the problem: `Verbose`, `Information`, `Warning`, `Error`, and `Critical`. `Critical` defines a fatal error or application crash; `Error` defines a recoverable error. Trace messages at the `Verbose` level provide detailed debugging information. `TraceEventType` also defines action levels `Start`, `Stop`, `Suspend`, and `Resume`, which define timely events inside a logical operation. As the code is written now, it does not display any trace message because the switch associated with the trace source is turned off.

Trace Switches

To enable or disable trace messages, you can configure a trace switch. Trace switches are classes derived from the abstract base class `Switch`. Derived classes are `BooleanSwitch`, `TraceSwitch`, and `SourceSwitch`. The class `BooleanSwitch` can be turned on and off, and the other two classes provide a range level. One range is defined by the `SourceLevels` enumeration. To configure trace switches, you must know the values associated with the `SourceLevels` enumeration. `SourceLevels` defines the values `Off`, `Error`, `Warning`, `Info`, and `Verbose`.

You can associate a trace switch programmatically by setting the `Switch` property of the `TraceSource`. In the following example, the associated switch is of type `SourceSwitch`, has the name `Wrox.ProCSharp` `.Diagnostics`, and has the level `Verbose`:

```
internal static SourceSwitch traceSwitch =
    new SourceSwitch("Wrox.ProCSharp.Diagnostics")
    { Level = SourceLevels.Verbose };
internal static TraceSource trace =
    new TraceSource("Wrox.ProCSharp.Diagnostics")
    { Switch = traceSwitch };
```

Setting the level to `Verbose` means that all trace messages should be written. If you set the value to `Error`, only error messages are displayed. Setting the value to `Information` means that error, warning, and info messages are shown. By writing the trace messages once more, you can see the messages while running the debugger in the Output window.

Usually, you would want to change the switch level not by recompiling the application, but instead by changing the configuration. The trace source can be configured in the application configuration file. Tracing is configured within the `<system.diagnostics>` element. The trace source is defined with the `<source>` element as a child element of `<sources>`. The name of the source in the configuration file must exactly match the name of the source in the program code. In the next example, the trace source has a switch of type `System.Diagnostics.SourceSwitch` associated with the name `MySourceSwitch`. The switch itself is defined within the `<switches>` section, and the level of the switch is set to `verbose` (config file `TracingDemo/App.config`):

```xml
<?xml version="1.0" encoding="utf-8" ?>
<configuration>
  <system.diagnostics>
    <sources>
      <source name="Wrox.ProCSharp.Diagnostics" switchName="MySourceSwitch"
        switchType="System.Diagnostics.SourceSwitch" />
    </sources>
    <switches>
      <add name="MySourceSwitch" value="Verbose"/>
    </switches>
  </system.diagnostics>
</configuration>
```

Now you can change the trace level just by changing the configuration file; there's no need to recompile the code. After the configuration file is changed, you must restart the application.

Trace Listeners

By default, trace information is written to the Output window of the Visual Studio debugger; but by changing the application's configuration, you can redirect the trace output to different locations.

Where the tracing results should be written to is defined by trace listeners. A trace listener is derived from the abstract base class `TraceListener`. NET includes several trace listeners to write the trace events to different targets. For file-based trace listeners, the base class `TextWriterTraceListener` is used, along with the derived classes `XmlWriterTraceListener` to write to XML files and `DelimitedListTraceListener` to write to delimited files. Writing to the event log is done with either the `EventLogTraceListener` or the `EventProviderTraceListener`. The latter uses the event file format available since Windows Vista. You can also combine web tracing with `System.Diagnostics` tracing and use the `WebPageTraceListener` to write `System.Diagnostics` tracing to the web trace file, `trace.axd`.

.NET Framework delivers many listeners to which trace information can be written; but if the provided listeners don't fulfill your requirements, you can create a custom listener by deriving a class from the base class `TraceListener`. With a custom listener, you can, for example, write trace information to a web service, write messages to your mobile phone, and so on. It's not usually desirable to receive hundreds of messages on your phone, however, and with verbose tracing this can become really expensive.

You can configure a trace listener programmatically by creating a listener object and assigning it to the `Listeners` property of the `TraceSource` class. However, usually it is more interesting to just change a configuration to define a different listener.

You can configure listeners as child elements of the `<source>` element. With the listener, you define the type of the listener class and use `initializeData` to specify where the output of the listener should go. The following configuration defines the `XmlWriterTraceListener` to write to the file `demotrace.xml`, and the `DelimitedListTraceListener` to write to the file `demotrace.txt` (config file `TracingDemo/App.config`):

```xml
<?xml version="1.0" encoding="utf-8" ?>
<configuration>
  <system.diagnostics>
    <sources>
      <source name="Wrox.ProCSharp.Diagnostics" switchName="MySourceSwitch"
          switchType="System.Diagnostics.SourceSwitch">
        <listeners>
          <add name="xmlListener"
              type="System.Diagnostics.XmlWriterTraceListener"
              traceOutputOptions="None"
              initializeData="c:/logs/mytrace.xml" />
          <add name="delimitedListener" delimiter=":"
              type="System.Diagnostics.DelimitedListTraceListener"
              traceOutputOptions="DateTime, ProcessId"
              initializeData="c:/logs/mytrace.txt" />
        </listeners>
      </source>
    </sources>
    <switches>
      <add name="MySourceSwitch" value="Verbose"/>
    </switches>
  </system.diagnostics>
</configuration>
```

With the listener, you can also specify what additional information should be written to the trace log. This information is specified with the `traceOutputOptions` XML attribute and is defined by the `TraceOptions` enumeration. The enumeration defines `Callstack`, `DateTime`, `LogicalOperationStack`, `ProcessId`, `ThreadId`, and `None`. You can add this comma-separated information to the `traceOutputOptions` XML attribute, as shown with the delimited trace listener.

The delimited file output from the `DelimitedListTraceListener`, including the process ID and date/time, is shown here:

```
"Wrox.ProCSharp.Diagnostics":Start:0:"Main started"::7724:""::
"2012-05-11T14:31:50.8677211Z"::
"Wrox.ProCSharp.Diagnostics":Information:0:"Info message"::7724:"Main"::
"2012-05-11T14:31:50.8797132Z"::
"Wrox.ProCSharp.Diagnostics":Error:3:"Error message"::7724:"Main"::
"2012-05-11T14:31:50.8817119Z"::
"Wrox.ProCSharp.Diagnostics":Information:2::"data1","4","5":7724:"Main"::
"2012-05-11T14:31:50.8817119Z"::
```

The XML output from the `XmlWriterTraceListener` always contains the name of the computer, the process ID, the thread ID, the message, the time created, the source, and the activity ID. Other fields, such as the call stack, logical operation stack, and timestamp, vary according to the trace output options.

> **NOTE** *You can use the* `XmlDocument`, `XPathNavigator` *, and* `XElement` *classes to analyze the content from the XML file. These classes are covered in Chapter 34 , "Manipulating XML."*

If a listener should be used by multiple trace sources, you can add the listener configuration to the element `<sharedListeners>`, which is independent of the trace source. The name of the listener that is configured with a shared listener must be referenced from the listeners of the trace source:

```xml
<?xml version="1.0" encoding="utf-8" ?>
<configuration>
  <system.diagnostics>
    <sources>
      <source name="Wrox.ProCSharp.Diagnostics" switchName="MySourceSwitch"
          switchType="System.Diagnostics.SourceSwitch">
        <listeners>
          <add name="xmlListener"
              type="System.Diagnostics.XmlWriterTraceListener"
              traceOutputOptions="None"
              initializeData="c:/logs/mytrace.xml" />
          <add name="delimitedListener" />
        </listeners>
      </source>
    </sources>
    <sharedListeners>
      <add  name="delimitedListener" delimiter=":"
          type="System.Diagnostics.DelimitedListTraceListener"
          traceOutputOptions="DateTime, ProcessId"
          initializeData="c:/logs/mytrace.txt" />
    </sharedListeners>
    <switches>
      <add name="MySourceSwitch" value="Verbose"/>
    </switches>
  </system.diagnostics>
</configuration>
```

Filters

Every listener has a `Filter` property that defines whether the listener should write the trace message. For example, multiple listeners can be used with the same trace source. One of the listeners writes verbose messages to a log file, and another listener writes error messages to the event log. Before a listener writes a trace message, it invokes the `ShouldTrace` method of the associated filter object to determine whether the trace message should be written.

A filter is a class that is derived from the abstract base class `TraceFilter`. .NET offers two filter implementations: `SourceFilter` and `EventTypeFilter`. With the source filter, you can specify that trace messages are to be written only from specific sources. The event type filter is an extension of the switch functionality. With a switch, it is possible to define, according to the trace severity level, whether the event source should forward the trace message to the listeners. If the trace message is forwarded, then the listener can then use the filter to determine whether the message should be written.

The changed configuration now defines that the delimited listener should write trace messages only if the severity level is of type warning or higher, because of the defined `EventTypeFilter`. The XML listener specifies a `SourceFilter` and accepts trace messages only from the source `Wrox.ProCSharp.Tracing`. If you have a large number of sources defined to write trace messages to the same listener, you can change the configuration for the listener to concentrate on trace messages from a specific source.

```xml
<?xml version="1.0" encoding="utf-8" ?>
<configuration>
  <system.diagnostics>
    <sources>
      <source name="Wrox.ProCSharp.Tracing" switchName="MySourceSwitch"
          switchType="System.Diagnostics.SourceSwitch">
        <listeners>
          <add name="xmlListener" />
          <add name="delimitedListener" />
        </listeners>
      </source>
    </sources>
    <sharedListeners>
        <add name="delimitedListener" delimiter=":"
            type="System.Diagnostics.DelimitedListTraceListener"
            traceOutputOptions="DateTime, ProcessId"
            initializeData="c:/logs/mytrace.txt">
          <filter type="System.Diagnostics.EventTypeFilter"
              initializeData="Warning" />
        </add>
        <add name="xmlListener"
            type="System.Diagnostics.XmlWriterTraceListener"
            traceOutputOptions="None"
            initializeData="c:/logs/mytrace.xml">
          <filter type="System.Diagnostics.SourceFilter"
              initializeData="Wrox.ProCSharp.Diagnostics" />
        </add>
    </sharedListeners>
    <switches>
      <add name="MySourceSwitch" value="Verbose"/>
    </switches>
  </system.diagnostics>
</configuration>
```

The tracing architecture can be extended. Just as you can write a custom listener derived from the base class `TraceListener`, you can create a custom filter derived from `TraceFilter`. With that capability, you can create a filter that specifies writing trace messages depending, for example, on the time, on an exception that occurred lately, or on the weather.

Correlation

With trace logs, you can see the relationship of different methods in several ways. To see the call stack of the trace events, a configuration only needs to track the call stack with the XML listener. You can also define a logical call stack that can be shown in the log messages; and you can define activities to map trace messages.

To show the call stack and the logical call stack with the trace messages, the `XmlWriterTraceListener` can be configured to the corresponding `traceOuputOptions`. The MSDN documentation (`http://msdn .microsoft.com/en-us/library/System.Diagnostics.XmlWriterTraceListener(v=vs.110).aspx`) provides details about all the other options you can configure for tracing with this listener.

```xml
<sharedListeners>
  <add name="xmlListener" type="System.Diagnostics.XmlWriterTraceListener"
      traceOutputOptions="LogicalOperationStack, Callstack"
      initializeData="c:/logs/mytrace.xml">
  </add>
</sharedListeners>
```

So you can see the correlation with trace logs, in the `Main` method a new activity ID is assigned to the `CorrelationManager` by setting the `ActivityID` property. Events of type `TraceEventType`.

`Start` and `TraceEventType.Stop` are done at the beginning and end of the `Main` method. In addition, a logical operation named `"Main"` is started and stopped with the `StartLogicalOperation` and `StopLogicalOperation` methods:

```
static void Main()
{
  // start a new activity
  if (Trace.CorrelationManager.ActivityId == Guid.Empty)
  {
    Guid newGuid = Guid.NewGuid();
    Trace.CorrelationManager.ActivityId = newGuid;
  }
  trace.TraceEvent(TraceEventType.Start, 0, "Main started");

  // start a logical operation
  Trace.CorrelationManager.StartLogicalOperation("Main");

  TraceSourceDemo1();
  StartActivityA();
  Trace.CorrelationManager.StopLogicalOperation();
  Thread.Sleep(3000);
  trace.TraceEvent(TraceEventType.Stop, 0, "Main stopped");
}
```

The method `StartActivityA` that is called from within the `Main` method creates a new activity by setting the `ActivityId` of the `CorrelationManager` to a new GUID. Before the activity stops, the `ActivityId` of the `CorrelationManager` is reset to the previous value. This method invokes the `Foo` method and creates a new task with the `Task.Factory.StartNew` method. This task is created so that you can see how different threads are displayed in a trace viewer.

> **NOTE** *Tasks are explained in Chapter 21, "Threads, Tasks, and Synchronization."*

```
private static void StartActivityA()
{
  Guid oldGuid = Trace.CorrelationManager.ActivityId;
  Guid newActivityId = Guid.NewGuid();
  Trace.CorrelationManager.ActivityId = newActivityId;

  Trace.CorrelationManager.StartLogicalOperation("StartActivityA");

  trace.TraceEvent(TraceEventType.Verbose, 0,
      "starting Foo in StartNewActivity");
  Foo();

  trace.TraceEvent(TraceEventType.Verbose, 0,
      "starting a new task");
  Task.Run(() => WorkForATask());

  Trace.CorrelationManager.StopLogicalOperation();
  Trace.CorrelationManager.ActivityId = oldGuid;
}
```

The `Foo` method that is started from within the `StartActivityA` method starts a new logical operation. The logical operation `Foo` is started within the `StartActivityA` logical operation:

```
private static void Foo()
{
  Trace.CorrelationManager.StartLogicalOperation("Foo operation");

  trace.TraceEvent(TraceEventType.Verbose, 0, "running Foo");

  Trace.CorrelationManager.StopLogicalOperation();
}
```

The task that is created from within the StartActivityA method runs the method WorkForATask. Here, only simple trace events with start and stop information, and verbose information, are written to the trace:

```
private static void WorkForATask()
{
  trace.TraceEvent(TraceEventType.Start, 0, "WorkForATask started");

  trace.TraceEvent(TraceEventType.Verbose, 0, "running WorkForATask");

  trace.TraceEvent(TraceEventType.Stop, 0, "WorkForATask completed");
}
```

To analyze the trace information, the tool Service Trace Viewer, svctraceviewer.exe, can be started. This tool is mainly used to analyze WCF traces, but you can also use it to analyze any trace that is written with the XmlWriterTraceListener. Figure 20-3 shows the Activity tab of Service Trace Viewer, with each activity displayed on the left, and the events displayed on the right. When you select an event you can choose to display either the complete message in XML or a formatted view. The latter displays basic information, application data, the logical operation stack, and the call stack in a nicely formatted manner.

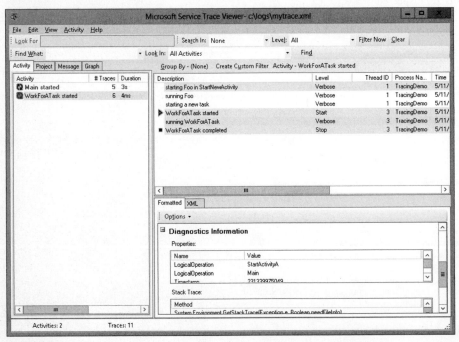

FIGURE 20-3

Figure 20-4 shows the Graph tab of the dialog. Using this view, different processes or threads can be selected for display in separate swimlanes. As a new thread is created with the `Task` class, a second swimlane appears by selecting the thread view.

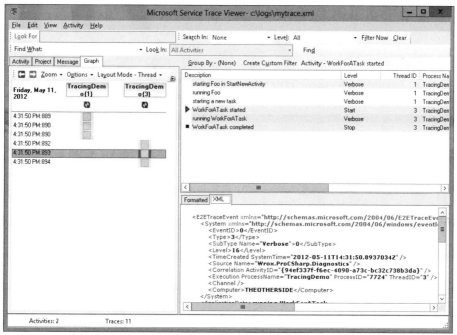

FIGURE 20-4

Tracing with ETW

A fast way to do tracing is by using Event Tracing for Windows (ETW). ETW is used by Windows for tracing, event logging, and performance counts. To write traces with ETW, the `EventProviderTraceListener` can be configured as a listener, as shown in the following snippet. The `type` attribute is used to find the class dynamically. The class name is specified with the strong name of the assembly together with the class name. With the `initializeData` attribute, a GUID needs to be specified to uniquely identify your listener. You can create a GUID by using the command-line tool uuidgen or the graphical tool guidgen.

```
<sharedListeners>
  <add name="etwListener"
       type="System.Diagnostics.Eventing.EventProviderTraceListener,
       System.Core, Version=4.0.0.0, Culture=neutral,
       PublicKeyToken=b77a5c561934e089"
       initializeData="{8ADA630A-F1CD-48BD-89F7-02CE2E7B9625}"/>
```

After changing the configuration, before you run the program once more to write traces using ETW, you need to start a trace session by using the `logman` command. The `start` option starts a new session to log. The `-p` option defines the name of the provider; here the GUID is used to identify the provider.

The `-o` option defines the output file, and the `-ets` option sends the command directly to the event trace system without scheduling:

```
logman start mysession -p {8ADA630A-F1CD-48BD-89F7-02CE2E7B9625}
  -o mytrace.etl -ets
```

After running the application, the trace session can be stopped with the `stop` command:

```
logman stop mysession -ets
```

The log file is in a binary format. To get a readable representation, the utility `tracerpt` can be used. With this tool it's possible to extract CSV, XML, and EVTX formats, as specified with the `-of` option:

```
tracerpt mytrace.etl -o mytrace.xml -of XML
```

> **NOTE** *The command-line tools* logman *and* tracerpt *are included with the Windows operating system.*

EVENT LOGGING

System administrators use the Event Viewer to get critical messages about the health of the system and applications, and informational messages. You should write error messages from your application to the event log so that the information can be read with the Event Viewer.

Trace messages can be written to the event log if you configure the `EventLogTraceListener` class. The `EventLogTraceListener` has an `EventLog` object associated with it to write the event log entries. You can also use the `EventLog` class directly to write and read event logs.

In this section, you explore the following:

➤ Event-logging architecture

➤ Classes for event logging from the `System.Diagnostics` namespace

➤ Adding event logging to services and other application types

➤ Creating an event log listener with the `EnableRaisingEvents` property of the `EventLog` class

➤ Using a resource file to define messages

Figure 20-5 shows an example of a log entry resulting from a failed access with Distributed COM.

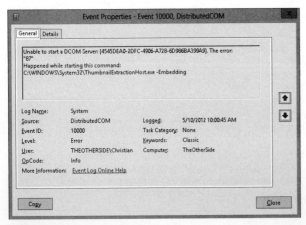

FIGURE 20-5

For custom event logging, you can use classes from the `System.Diagnostics` namespace.

Event-Logging Architecture

Event log information is stored in several log files. The most important ones are application, security, and system. Looking at the registry configuration of the event log service, you will notice several entries under `HKEY_LOCAL_MACHINE\System\CurrentControlSet\Services\Eventlog` with configurations pointing to the specific files. The system log file is used from the system and device drivers. Applications and services write to the application log. The security log is a read-only log for applications. The auditing feature of the operating system uses the security log. Every application can also create a custom category and write event log entries there, such as Media Center.

You can read these events by using the Event Viewer administrative tool. To open it directly from the Server Explorer of Visual Studio, right-click the Event Logs item and select the Launch Event Viewer entry from the context menu. The Event Viewer dialog is shown in Figure 20-6.

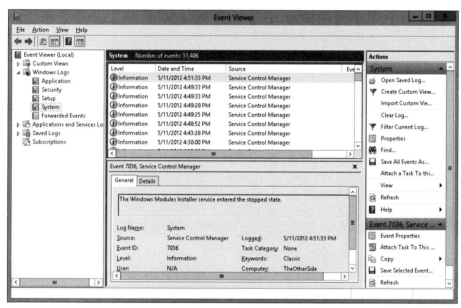

FIGURE 20-6

The event log contains the following information:

➤ **Type** — The main types are Information, Warning, or Error. Information is an infrequently used type that denotes a successful operation; Warning denotes a problem that is not immediately significant; and Error denotes a major problem. Additional types are `FailureAudit` and `SuccessAudit`, but these types are used only for the security log.

➤ **Date** — Date and Time show the day and time that the event occurred.

➤ **Source** — The Source is the name of the software that logs the event. The source for the application log is configured in the following registry key:

```
HKEY_LOCAL_MACHINE\System\CurrentControlSet\Services\Eventlog\
    Application\[ApplicationName]
```

Within this key, the value `EventMessageFile` is configured to point to a resource DLL that holds error messages:

➤ **Event ID** — The event identifier specifies a particular event message.

➤ **Category** — A category can be defined so that event logs can be filtered when using the Event Viewer. Categories can be defined according to an event source.

Event-Logging Classes

For writing event logs, two different Windows APIs exist. One API, available since Windows Vista, is wrapped by the classes in the namespace `System.Diagnostics.Eventing`. The other wrapper classes are in the `System.Diagnostics` namespace.

> **NOTE** *This book covers event logs using the* `System.Diagnostics` *namespace. The other event logs from the* `System.Diagnostics.Eventing` *namespace don't have strong support for .NET, require several command-line tools, and unsafe C# code. If you want to use* `System.Diagnostics.Eventing`*, you can find a procedure at* `http://weblogs.thinktecture.com/cnagel` *to do so.*

The `System.Diagnostics` namespace has the following classes for event logging.

CLASS	DESCRIPTION
EventLog	With the `EventLog` class, you can read and write entries in the event log, and establish applications as event sources.
EventLogEntry	The `EventLogEntry` class represents a single entry in the event log. With the `EventLogEntryCollection`, you can iterate through `EventLogEntry` items.
EventLogInstaller	The `EventLogInstaller` class is the installer for an `EventLog` component. `EventLogInstaller` calls `EventLog.CreateEventSource` to create an event source.
EventLogTraceListener	With the help of the `EventLogTraceListener`, traces can be written to the event log. This class implements the abstract class `TraceListener`.

The `EventLog` class is the heart of event logging. The members of this class are explained in the following table.

> **NOTE** *Chapter 18, "Deployment," explains how to create installation programs.*

EVENTLOG MEMBER	DESCRIPTION
Entries	With the `Entries` property, you can read event logs. `Entries` returns an `EventLogEntryCollection` that contains `EventLogEntry` objects holding information about the events. There is no need to invoke a `Read` method. The collection is filled as soon as you access this property.
Log	Specifies the log for reading or writing event logs.
LogDisplayName	A read-only property that returns the display name of the log.

EVENTLOG MEMBER	DESCRIPTION
MachineName	Specifies the system on which to read or write log entries.
Source	Specifies the source of the event entries to write.
CreateEventSource()	Creates a new event source and a new log file.
DeleteEventSource()	Invoke this to get rid of an event source.
SourceExists()	Using this element, you can verify whether the source already exists before creating an event source.
WriteEntry() WriteEvent()	Write event log entries with either the WriteEntry or WriteEvent method. WriteEntry is simpler, because you just need to pass a string. WriteEvent is more flexible, because you can use message files that are independent of the application and that support localization.
Clear()	Removes all entries from an event log.
Delete()	Deletes a complete event log.

Creating an Event Source

Before writing events, you must create an event source. You can use either the CreateEventSource method of the EventLog class or the class EventLogInstaller. Because you need administrative privileges when creating an event source, an installation program is best for defining the new source.

The following example verifies that an event log source named EventLogDemoApp already exists. If it doesn't exist, then an object of type EventSourceCreationData is instantiated that defines the source name EventLogDemoApp and the log name ProCSharpLog. Here, all events of this source are written to the ProCSharpLog event log. The default is the application log.

```
string logName = "ProCSharpLog";
string sourceName = "EventLogDemoApp";

if (!EventLog.SourceExists(sourceName))
{
  var eventSourceData = new EventSourceCreationData(sourceName, logName);

  EventLog.CreateEventSource(eventSourceData);
}
```

The name of the event source is an identifier of the application that writes the events. For the system administrator reading the log, the information helps to identify the event log entries in order to map them to application categories. Examples of names for event log sources are LoadPerf for the Performance Monitor, MSSQLSERVER for Microsoft SQL Server, MsiInstaller for the Windows Installer, Winlogon, Tcpip, Time-Service, and so on.

Setting the name "Application" for the event log writes event log entries to the application log. You can also create your own log by specifying a different application log name. Log files are located in the directory <windows>\System32\WinEvt\Logs.

With the EventSourceCreationData class, you can also specify several more characteristics for the event log, as described in the following table.

EVENTSOURCECREATIONDATA	DESCRIPTION
Source	Gets or sets the name of the event source.
LogName	Defines the log where event log entries are written. The default is the application log.

continues

(continued)

EVENTSOURCECREATIONDATA	DESCRIPTION
MachineName	Defines the system to read or write log entries.
CategoryResourceFile	Defines a resource file for categories. Categories enable easier filtering of event log entries within a single source.
CategoryCount	Defines the number of categories in the category resource file.
MessageResourceFile	Instead of specifying that the message should be written to the event log in the program that writes the events, messages can be defined in a resource file that is assigned to the MessageResourceFile property. Messages from the resource file are localizable.
ParameterResourceFile	Messages in a resource file can have parameters. The parameters can be replaced by strings defined in a resource file that is assigned to the ParameterResourceFile property.

Writing Event Logs

For writing event log entries, you can use the WriteEntry or WriteEvent methods of the EventLog class. The EventLog class has both a static and an instance method WriteEntry. The static method WriteEntry requires a parameter of the source. The source can also be set with the constructor of the EventLog class. In the following example, the log name, the local machine, and the event source name are defined in the constructor. Next, three event log entries are written with the message as the first parameter of the WriteEntry method. WriteEntry is overloaded. The second parameter you can assign is an enumeration of type EventLogEntryType. With EventLogEntryType, you can define the severity of the event log entry. Possible values are Information, Warning, and Error; and for auditing, SuccessAudit and FailureAudit. Depending on the type, different icons are shown in the Event Viewer. With the third parameter, you can specify an application-specific event ID that can be used by the application itself. In addition, you can pass application-specific binary data and a category.

```
using (var log = new EventLog(logName, ".", sourceName))
{
    log.WriteEntry("Message 1");
    log.WriteEntry("Message 2", EventLogEntryType.Warning);
    log.WriteEntry("Message 3", EventLogEntryType.Information, 33);
}
```

Resource Files

Instead of defining the messages for the event log in the C# code and passing it to the WriteEntry method, you can create a *message resource file*, define messages in the resource file, and pass message identifiers to the WriteEvent method. Resource files also support localization.

> **NOTE** *Message resource files are native resource files that have nothing in common with .NET resource files. .NET resource files are covered in Chapter 28, "Localization."*
>
> *A message file is a text file with the mc file extension. The syntax that this file uses to define messages is very strict. The sample file EventLogMessages.mc contains four categories followed by event messages. Every message has an ID that can be used by the application writing event entries. Parameters that can be passed from the application are defined with % syntax in the message text (resource file EventLogDemo/EventLogDemoMessages.mc):*
>
> ```
> ; // EventLogDemoMessages.mc
> ; // **********************************************************
> ```

```
; // - Event categories -
; // Categories must be numbered consecutively starting at 1.
; // *********************************************************

MessageId=0x1
Severity=Success
SymbolicName=INSTALL_CATEGORY
Language=English
Installation
.

MessageId=0x2
Severity=Success
SymbolicName=DATA_CATEGORY
Language=English
Database Query
.

MessageId=0x3
Severity=Success
SymbolicName=UPDATE_CATEGORY
Language=English
Data Update
.

MessageId=0x4
Severity=Success
SymbolicName=NETWORK_CATEGORY
Language=English
Network Communication
.

; // - Event messages -
; // *******************************

MessageId = 1000
Severity = Success
Facility = Application
SymbolicName = MSG_CONNECT_1000
Language=English
Connection successful.
.

MessageId = 1001
Severity = Error
Facility = Application
SymbolicName = MSG_CONNECT_FAILED_1001
Language=English
Could not connect to server %1.
.

MessageId = 1002
Severity = Error
Facility = Application
SymbolicName = MSG_DB_UPDATE_1002
Language=English
Database update failed.
.
```

continues

continued

```
        MessageId = 1003
        Severity = Success
        Facility = Application
        SymbolicName = APP_UPDATE
        Language=English
        Application %%5002 updated.
        .


        ; // - Event log display name -
        ; // *********************************************************

        MessageId = 5001
        Severity = Success
        Facility = Application
        SymbolicName = EVENT_LOG_DISPLAY_NAME_MSGID
        Language=English
        Professional C# Sample Event Log
        .


        ; // - Event message parameters -
        ; //     Language independent insertion strings
        ; // *********************************************************


        MessageId = 5002
        Severity = Success
        Facility = Application
        SymbolicName = EVENT_LOG_SERVICE_NAME_MSGID
        Language=English
        EventLogDemo.EXE
        .
```

For the exact syntax of message files, check the MSDN documentation for Message Text Files (http://msdn.microsoft.com/en-us/library/windows/desktop/dd996906(v=vs.85).aspx).

Use the Messages Compiler, `mc.exe`, to create a binary message file. The following command compiles the source file containing the messages to a messages file with the `.bin` extension and the file `Messages.rc`, which contains a reference to the binary message file:

```
mc -s EventLogDemoMessages.mc
```

Next, you must use the Resource Compiler, `rc.exe`. The following command creates the resource file `EventLogDemoMessages.RES`:

```
rc EventLogDemoMessages.rc
```

With the linker, you can bind the binary message file `EventLogDemoMessages.RES` to a native DLL:

```
link /DLL /SUBSYSTEM:WINDOWS /NOENTRY /MACHINE:x86 EventLogDemoMessages.RES
```

Now, you can register an event source that defines the resource files as shown in the following code. First, a check is done to determine whether the event source named `EventLogDemoApp` exists. If the event log must be created because it does not exist, the next check verifies that the resource file is available. Some samples in the MSDN documentation demonstrate writing the message file to the `<windows>\system32` directory, but you shouldn't do that. Copy the message DLL to a program-specific directory that you can get with the

SpecialFolder enumeration value ProgramFiles. If you need to share the messages file among multiple applications, you can put it into Environment.SpecialFolder.CommonProgramFiles.

If the file exists, a new object of type EventSourceCreationData is instantiated. In the constructor, the name of the source and the name of the log are defined. You use the properties CategoryResourceFile, MessageResourceFile, and ParameterResourceFile to define a reference to the resource file. After the event source is created, you can find the information on the resource files in the registry with the event source. The method CreateEventSource registers the new event source and log file. Finally, the method RegisterDisplayName from the EventLog class specifies the name of the log as it is displayed in the Event Viewer. The ID 5001 is taken from the message file (code file EventLogDemo/Program.cs):

```csharp
string logName = "ProCSharpLog";
string sourceName = "EventLogDemoApp";
string resourceFile = Environment.GetFolderPath(
    Environment.SpecialFolder.ProgramFiles) +
    @"\procsharp\EventLogDemoMessages.dll";

if (!EventLog.SourceExists(sourceName))
{
    if (!File.Exists(resourceFile))
    {
        Console.WriteLine("Message resource file does not exist");
        return;
    }

    var eventSource = new EventSourceCreationData(sourceName, logName);

    eventSource.CategoryResourceFile = resourceFile;
    eventSource.CategoryCount = 4;
    eventSource.MessageResourceFile = resourceFile;
    eventSource.ParameterResourceFile = resourceFile;

    EventLog.CreateEventSource(eventSource);
}
else
{
    logName = EventLog.LogNameFromSourceName(sourceName, ".");
}

var evLog = new EventLog(logName, ".", sourceName);
evLog.RegisterDisplayName(resourceFile, 5001);
```

> **NOTE** *To delete a previously created event source, you can use* EventLog.Delete EventSource(sourceName). *To delete a log, you can invoke* EventLog.Delete (logName).

Now you can use the WriteEvent method instead of WriteEntry to write the event log entry. WriteEvent requires an object of type EventInstance as a parameter. With the EventInstance, you can assign the message ID, the category, and the severity of type EventLogEntryType. In addition to the EventInstance parameter, WriteEvent accepts parameters for messages that have parameters and binary data in the form of a byte array:

```csharp
using (var log = new EventLog(logName, ".", sourceName))
{
    var info1 = new EventInstance(1000, 4,
        EventLogEntryType.Information);
```

```
        log.WriteEvent(info1);
        var info2 = new EventInstance(1001, 4,
            EventLogEntryType.Error);
        log.WriteEvent(info2, "avalon");

        var info3 = new EventInstance(1002, 3,
            EventLogEntryType.Error);
        byte[] additionalInfo = { 1, 2, 3 };
        log.WriteEvent(info3, additionalInfo);
    }
```

> **NOTE** *For the message identifiers, define a class with* const *values, which provide a more meaningful name for the identifiers in the application.*

You can read the event log entries with the Event Viewer.

PERFORMANCE MONITORING

Performance monitoring can be used to get information about the normal behavior of applications, to compare ongoing system behavior with previously established norms, and to observe changes and trends, particularly in applications running on the server. When you have a scenario of more and more users accessing the application, before the first user complains about a performance issue, the system administrator can already act and increase resources where needed. The Performance Monitor (PerfMon) is a great tool to see all the performance counts for acting early. As a developer, this tool also helps a lot to understand the running application and its foundation technologies.

Microsoft Windows has many performance objects, such as System, Memory, Objects, Process, Processor, Thread, Cache, and so on. Each of these objects has many counts to monitor. For example, with the Process object, the user time, handle count, page faults, thread count, and so on can be monitored for all processes or for specific process instances. The .NET Framework and several applications, such as SQL Server, also add application-specific objects.

Performance-Monitoring Classes

The System.Diagnostics namespace provides the following classes for performance monitoring:

➤ PerformanceCounter — Can be used both to monitor counts and to write counts. New performance categories can also be created with this class.

➤ PerformanceCounterCategory — Enables you to step through all existing categories, as well as create new ones. You can programmatically obtain all the counters in a category.

➤ PerformanceCounterInstaller — Used for the installation of performance counters. Its use is similar to that of the EventLogInstaller discussed previously.

Performance Counter Builder

The sample application PerformanceCounterDemo is a simple Windows application with just two buttons to demonstrate writing performance counts. The handler of one button registers a performance counter category; the handler of the other button writes a performance counter value. In a similar way to the sample application, you can add performance counters to a Windows Service (see Chapter 27, "Windows Services"), to a network application (see Chapter 26, "Networking"), or to any other application from which you would like to receive live counts.

Using Visual Studio, you can create a new performance counter category by selecting Performance Counters in Server Explorer and then selecting Create New Category from the context menu. This launches the Performance Counter Builder (see Figure 20-7). Set the name of the performance counter category to **Wrox Performance Counters**. The following table shows all performance counters of the sample application.

> **NOTE** *In order to create a performance counter category with Visual Studio, Visual Studio must be started in elevated mode.*

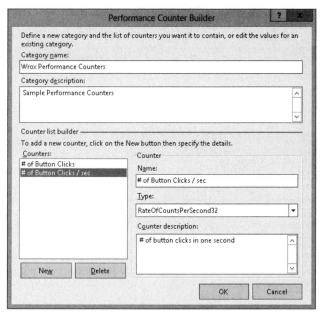

FIGURE 20-7

PERFORMANCE COUNTER	DESCRIPTION	TYPE
# of button clicks	Total # of button clicks	`NumberOfItems32`
# of button clicks/sec	# of button clicks per second	`RateOfCountsPerSecond32`
# of mouse move events	Total # of mouse move events	`NumberOfItems32`
# of mouse move events/sec	# of mouse move events per second	`RateOfCountsPerSecond32`

Performance Counter Builder writes the configuration to the performance database. This can also be done dynamically by using the `Create` method of the `PerformanceCounterCategory` class in the `System.Diagnostics` namespace. An installer for other systems can easily be added later using Visual Studio.

The following code snippet shows how a performance category can be added programmatically. With the tool from Visual Studio, you can only create a global performance category that doesn't have different values for different processes of running applications. Creating a performance category programmatically enables you to monitor performance counts from different applications, which is done here.

First, a `const` for the category name is defined, as well as `SortedList<TKey, TValue>`, which contains the names of the performance counts (code file `PerformanceCounterDemo/MainWindow.xaml.cs`):

```
private const string perfomanceCounterCategoryName =
    "Wrox Performance Counters";
private SortedList<string, Tuple<string, string>> perfCountNames;
```

The list of the `perfCountNames` variable is filled in within the method `InitializePerformanceCountNames`. The value of the sorted list is defined as `Tuple<string, string>` to define both the name and the description of the performance counter:

```
private void InitializePerfomanceCountNames()
{
  perfCountNames = new SortedList<string, Tuple<string, string>>();
  perfCountNames.Add("clickCount", Tuple.Create("# of button Clicks",
      "Total # of button clicks"));
  perfCountNames.Add("clickSec", Tuple.Create("# of button clicks/sec",
      "# of mouse button clicks in one second"));
  perfCountNames.Add("mouseCount", Tuple.Create("# of mouse move events",
      "Total # of mouse move events"));
  perfCountNames.Add("mouseSec", Tuple.Create("# of mouse move events/sec",
      "# of mouse move events in one second"));
}
```

The performance counter category is created next, in the method `OnRegisterCounts`. After a check to verify that the category does not already exist, the array `CounterCreationData` is created, which is filled with the types and names of the performance counts. Next, `PerformanceCounterCategory.Create` creates the new category. `PerformanceCounterCategoryType.MultiInstance` defines that the counts are not global, but rather that different values for different instances can exist:

```
private void OnRegisterCounts(object sender, RoutedEventArgs e)
{
  if (!PerformanceCounterCategory.Exists(
      perfomanceCounterCategoryName))
  {
    var counterCreationData = new CounterCreationData[4];
    counterCreationData[0] = new CounterCreationData
    {
      CounterName = perfCountNames["clickCount"].Item1,
      CounterType = PerformanceCounterType.NumberOfItems32,
      CounterHelp = perfCountNames["clickCount"].Item2
    };
    counterCreationData[1] = new CounterCreationData
    {
      CounterName = perfCountNames["clickSec"].Item1,
      CounterType = PerformanceCounterType.RateOfCountsPerSecond32,
      CounterHelp = perfCountNames["clickSec"].Item2,
    };
    counterCreationData[2] = new CounterCreationData
    {
      CounterName = perfCountNames["mouseCount"].Item1,
      CounterType = PerformanceCounterType.NumberOfItems32,
      CounterHelp = perfCountNames["mouseCount"].Item2,
    };
    counterCreationData[3] = new CounterCreationData
    {
      CounterName = perfCountNames["mouseSec"].Item1,
      CounterType = PerformanceCounterType.RateOfCountsPerSecond32,
      CounterHelp = perfCountNames["mouseSec"].Item2,
```

```
    };
    var counters = new CounterCreationDataCollection(counterCreationData);

    var category = PerformanceCounterCategory.Create(
        perfomanceCounterCategoryName,
        "Sample Counters for Professional C#",
        PerformanceCounterCategoryType.MultiInstance,
        counters);

    MessageBox.Show(String.Format("category {0} successfully created",
        category.CategoryName));
}
```

Adding PerformanceCounter Components

With Windows Forms or Windows Service applications, you can add PerformanceCounter components from the toolbox or from Server Explorer by dragging and dropping to the designer surface.

With WPF applications that's not possible. However, it's not a lot of work to define the performance counters manually, as this is done with the method InitializePerformanceCounters. In the following example, the CategoryName for all performance counts is set from the const string performanceCounterCategoryName; the CounterName is set from the sorted list. Because the application writes performance counts, the ReadOnly property must be set to false. When writing an application that only reads performance counts for display purposes, you can use the default value of the ReadOnly property, which is true. The InstanceName of the PerformanceCounter object is set to an application name. If the counters are configured to be global counts, then InstanceName may not be set:

```
private PerformanceCounter performanceCounterButtonClicks;
private PerformanceCounter performanceCounterButtonClicksPerSec;
private PerformanceCounter performanceCounterMouseMoveEvents;
private PerformanceCounter performanceCounterMouseMoveEventsPerSec;

private void InitializePerformanceCounters()
{
  performanceCounterButtonClicks = new PerformanceCounter
  {
    CategoryName = perfomanceCounterCategoryName,
    CounterName = perfCountNames["clickCount"].Item1,
    ReadOnly = false,
    MachineName = ".",
    InstanceLifetime = PerformanceCounterInstanceLifetime.Process,
    InstanceName = this.instanceName
  };
  performanceCounterButtonClicksPerSec = new PerformanceCounter
  {
    CategoryName = perfomanceCounterCategoryName,
    CounterName = perfCountNames["clickSec"].Item1,
    ReadOnly = false,
    MachineName = ".",
    InstanceLifetime = PerformanceCounterInstanceLifetime.Process,
    InstanceName = this.instanceName
  };
  performanceCounterMouseMoveEvents = new PerformanceCounter
  {
    CategoryName = perfomanceCounterCategoryName,
    CounterName = perfCountNames["mouseCount"].Item1,
    ReadOnly = false,
    MachineName = ".",
    InstanceLifetime = PerformanceCounterInstanceLifetime.Process,
    InstanceName = this.instanceName
```

```
    };
    performanceCounterMouseMoveEventsPerSec = new PerformanceCounter
    {
      CategoryName = perfomanceCounterCategoryName,
      CounterName = perfCountNames["mouseSec"].Item1,
      ReadOnly = false,
      MachineName = ".",
      InstanceLifetime = PerformanceCounterInstanceLifetime.Process,
      InstanceName = this.instanceName
    };
}
```

To calculate the performance values, you need to add the fields `clickCountPerSec` and `mouseMoveCountPerSec`:

```
public partial class MainWindow : Window
{
  // Performance monitoring counter values
  private int clickCountPerSec = 0;
  private int mouseMoveCountPerSec = 0;
```

Add an event handler to the `Click` event of the button, add an event handler to the `MouseMove` event of the button, and add the following code to the handlers:

```
private void OnButtonClick(object sender, RoutedEventArgs e)
{
  this.performanceCounterButtonClicks.Increment();
  this.clickCountPerSec++;
}

private void OnMouseMove(object sender, MouseEventArgs e)
{
  this.performanceCounterMouseMoveEvents.Increment();
  this.mouseMoveCountPerSec++;
}
```

The `Increment` method of the `PerformanceCounter` object increments the counter by one. If you need to increment the counter by more than one — for example, to add information about a byte count sent or received — you can use the `IncrementBy` method. For the performance counts that show the value in seconds, just the two variables, `clickCountPerSec` and `mouseMovePerSec`, are incremented.

To show updated values every second, add a `DispatcherTimer` to the members of the `MainWindow`:

```
private DispatcherTimer timer;
```

This timer is configured and started in the constructor. The `DispatcherTimer` class is a timer from the namespace `System.Windows.Threading`. For other than WPF applications, you can use other timers as discussed in Chapter 21, "Threads, Tasks, and Synchronization." The code that is invoked by the timer is defined with an anonymous method:

```
public MainWindow()
{
  InitializeComponent();
  InitializePerfomanceCountNames();
  InitializePerformanceCounts();
  if (PerformanceCounterCategory.Exists(perfomanceCounterCategoryName))
  {
```

```
            buttonCount.IsEnabled = true;
            timer = new DispatcherTimer(TimeSpan.FromSeconds(1),
                DispatcherPriority.Background,
                delegate
                {
                  this.performanceCounterButtonClicksPerSec.RawValue =
                      this.clickCountPerSec;
                  this.clickCountPerSec = 0;
                  this.performanceCounterMouseMoveEventsPerSec.RawValue =
                      this.mouseMoveCountPerSec;
                  this.mouseMoveCountPerSec = 0;
                },
                Dispatcher.CurrentDispatcher);
            timer.Start();
        }
    }
```

perfmon.exe

Now you can monitor the application. You can start Performance Monitor from the Administrative Tools applet in the control panel. Within Performance Monitor, click the + button in the toolbar; there, you can add performance counts. Wrox Performance Counters shows up as a performance object. All the counters that have been configured appear in the Available counters list, as shown in Figure 20-8.

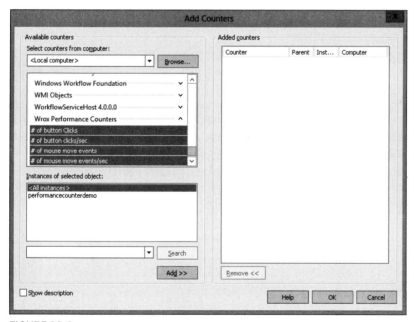

FIGURE 20-8

After you have added the counters to the performance monitor, you can view the actual values of the service over time (see Figure 20-9). Using this performance tool, you can also create log files to analyze the performance data later.

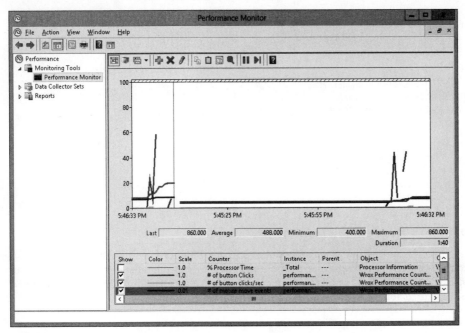

FIGURE 20-9

SUMMARY

In this chapter, you have looked at tracing and logging facilities that can help you find intermittent problems in your applications. You should plan early, building these features into your applications, as this will help you avoid many troubleshooting problems later.

With tracing, you can write debugging messages to an application that can also be used for the final product delivered. If there are problems, you can turn tracing on by changing configuration values, and find the issues.

Event logging provides the system administrator with information that can help identify some of the critical issues with the application. Performance monitoring helps in analyzing the load from applications and enables proactive planning for resources that might be required.

21

Tasks, Threads, and Synchronization

WHAT'S IN THIS CHAPTER?

➤ An overview of multi-threading

➤ Working with the `Parallel` class

➤ Tasks

➤ Cancellation framework

➤ `Thread` class and thread pools

➤ Threading issues

➤ Synchronization techniques

➤ Timers

WROX.COM CODE DOWNLOADS FOR THIS CHAPTER

The wrox.com code downloads for this chapter are found at `http://www.wrox.com/remtitle` `.cgi?isbn=1118314425` on the Download Code tab. The code for this chapter is divided into the following major examples:

➤ Parallel

➤ Task

➤ Cancellation

➤ ThreadClass

➤ Synchronization

➤ DataFlow

OVERVIEW

There are several reasons for using threading. Suppose that you are making a network call from an application that might take some time. You don't want to stall the user interface and force the user to wait idly until the response is returned from the server. The user could perform some other actions in the meantime or even cancel the request that was sent to the server. Using threads can help.

For all activities that require a wait—for example, because of file, database, or network access—a new thread can be started to fulfill other tasks at the same time. Even if you have only processing-intensive tasks to do, threading can help. Multiple threads of a single process can run on different CPUs, or, nowadays, on different cores of a multiple-core CPU, at the same time.

You must be aware of some issues when running multiple threads, however. Because they can run during the same time, you can easily get into problems if the threads access the same data. To avoid that, you must implement synchronization mechanisms.

> **NOTE** *The use of asynchronous methods with the new* async *and* await *keywords is covered in Chapter 13, "Asynchronous Programming."*

This chapter provides the foundation you need to program applications with multiple threads. The major namespaces in this chapter are System.Threading and System.Threading.Tasks.

A thread is an independent stream of instructions in a program. All the C# example programs up to this point have one entry point—the Main method. Execution starts with the first statement in the Main method and continues until that method returns.

This program structure is all very well for programs in which there is one identifiable sequence of tasks, but often a program needs to do more than one thing at the same time. Threads are important both for client-side and server-side applications. While you type C# code in the Visual Studio editor, the code is analyzed to underline missing semicolons or other syntax errors. This is done by a background thread. The same thing is done by the spell checker in Microsoft Word. One thread is waiting for input from the user, while the other does some background research. A third thread can store the written data in an interim file, while another one downloads some additional data from the Internet.

In an application that is running on the server, one thread, the listener thread, waits for a request from a client. As soon as the request comes in, the request is forwarded to a separate worker thread, which continues the communication with the client. The listener thread immediately comes back to get the next request from the next client.

A process contains resources, such as Window handles, handles to the file system, or other kernel objects. Every process has virtual memory allocated. A process contains at least one thread, and the operating system schedules threads. A thread has a priority, a program counter for the program location where it is actually processing, and a stack in which to store its local variables. Every thread has its own stack, but the memory for the program code and the heap are shared among all threads of a single process. This makes communication among threads of one process fast—the same virtual memory is addressed by all threads of a process. However, this also makes things difficult because multiple threads can change the same memory location.

A process manages resources, which include virtual memory and Window handles, and contains at least one thread. A thread is required to run the program. Prior to .NET 4 you had to program threads directly with the Thread and ThreadPool classes. Nowadays you can use an abstraction of these classes, working with Parallel and Task classes. In some special scenarios, the Thread and ThreadPool classes are still needed. It's good practice to use the classes that are the easiest ones to work with and just use the more complex classes when advanced functionality is really needed. Most programs are written without handcrafted IL code. However, there are some cases when even this is needed.

In order to write code that takes advantage of parallel features, you have to differentiate between two main scenarios: *task parallelism* and *data parallelism*. With task parallelism, code that's using the CPU is parallelized. Multiple cores of the CPU can be used to fulfill an activity that consists of multiple tasks a lot faster, instead of just doing one task after the other in a single core. With data parallelism, data collections are used. The work on the collection can be split up into multiple tasks. Of course, there are variants that mix task and data parallelism.

> **NOTE** *One variant of task parallelism is offered by Parallel LINQ, covered in Chapter 11, "Language Integrated Query."*

PARALLEL CLASS

One great abstraction of threads is the `Parallel` class. With this class, both data and task parallelism is offered. This class is in the namespace `System.Threading.Tasks`.

The `Parallel` class defines static methods for a parallel `for` and `foreach`. With the C# statements `for` and `foreach`, the loop is run from one thread. The `Parallel` class uses multiple tasks and, thus, multiple threads for this job.

While the `Parallel.For` and `Parallel.ForEach` methods invoke the same code during each iteration, `Parallel.Invoke` allows you to invoke different methods concurrently. `Parallel.Invoke` is for task parallelism, `Parallel.ForEach` for data parallelism.

Looping with the Parallel.For Method

The `Parallel.For` method is similar to the C# `for` loop statement to perform a task a number of times. With `Parallel.For`, the iterations run in parallel. The order of iteration is not defined.

With the `For` method, the first two parameters define the start and end of the loop. The following example has the iterations from 0 to 9. The third parameter is an `Action<int>` delegate. The integer parameter is the iteration of the loop that is passed to the method referenced by the delegate. The return type of `Parallel.For` is the struct `ParallelLoopResult`, which provides information if the loop is completed (code file `ParallelSamples/Program.cs`):

```
ParallelLoopResult result =
  Parallel.For(0, 10, i =>
  {
    Console.WriteLine("{0}, task: {1}, thread: {2}", i,
      Task.CurrentId, Thread.CurrentThread.ManagedThreadId);
    Thread.Sleep(10);
  });
Console.WriteLine("Is completed: {0}", result.IsCompleted);
```

In the body of `Parallel.For`, the index, task identifier, and thread identifier are written to the console. As shown in the following output, the order is not guaranteed. You will see different results if you run this program once more. This run of the program had the order 0-2-4-6-8... with five tasks and five threads. A task does not necessarily map to one thread. A thread could also be reused by different tasks.

```
0, task: 1, thread: 1
2, task: 2, thread: 3
4, task: 3, thread: 4
6, task: 4, thread: 5
8, task: 5, thread: 6
5, task: 3, thread: 4
7, task: 4, thread: 5
9, task: 5, thread: 6
```

```
3, task: 2, thread: 3
1, task: 1, thread: 1
Is completed: True
```

In the previous example, the method `Thread.Sleep` is used instead of `Task.Delay`, which is new with .NET 4.5. `Task.Delay` is an asynchronous method that releases the thread for other jobs to do. Using the `await` keyword, the code following is invoked as soon as the delay is completed. The code after the delay can run in another thread than the code before.

Let's change the previous example to now use the `Task.Delay` method, writing task thread and loop iteration information to the console as soon as the delay is finished:

```
ParallelLoopResult result =
    Parallel.For(0, 10, async i =>
        {
            Console.WriteLine("{0}, task: {1}, thread: {2}", i,
                Task.CurrentId, Thread.CurrentThread.ManagedThreadId);

            await Task.Delay(10);
            Console.WriteLine("{0}, task: {1}, thread: {2}", i,
                Task.CurrentId, Thread.CurrentThread.ManagedThreadId);
        });
Console.WriteLine("is completed: {0}", result.IsCompleted);
```

The result of this follows. With the output after the `Thread.Delay` method you can see the thread change. For example, loop iteration 2, which had thread ID 3 before the delay, has thread ID 4 after the delay. You can also see that tasks no longer exist, only threads, and here previous threads are reused. Another important aspect is that the `For` method of the `Parallel` class is completed without waiting for the delay. The `Parallel` class just waits for the tasks it created, but not other background activity. It is also possible that you won't see the output from the methods after the delay at all—if the main thread (which is a foreground thread) is finished, all the background threads are stopped. Foreground and background threads are discussed later in this chapter.

```
2, task: 2, thread: 3
0, task: 1, thread: 1
4, task: 3, thread: 5
6, task: 4, thread: 6
8, task: 5, thread: 4
3, task: 2, thread: 3
7, task: 2, thread: 3
9, task: 5, thread: 4
5, task: 3, thread: 5
1, task: 1, thread: 1
is completed: True
5, task: , thread: 6
6, task: , thread: 6
7, task: , thread: 6
3, task: , thread: 6
8, task: , thread: 6
4, task: , thread: 6
0, task: , thread: 6
9, task: , thread: 5
2, task: , thread: 4
1, task: , thread: 3
```

> **WARNING** *As demonstrated here, although using async features with .NET 4.5 and C# 5 is very easy, it's still important to know what's happening behind the scenes, and you have to pay attention to some issues.*

Stopping Parallel.For Early

You can also break the `Parallel.For` early without looping through all the iterations. A method overload of the `For` method accepts a third parameter of type `Action<int, ParallelLoopState>`. By defining a method with these parameters, you can influence the outcome of the loop by invoking the `Break` or `Stop` methods of the `ParallelLoopState`.

Remember, the order of iterations is not defined (code file `ParallelSamples/Program.cs`):

```
ParallelLoopResult result =
  Parallel.For(10, 40, async (int i, ParallelLoopState pls) =>
  {
    Console.WriteLine("i: {0} task {1}", i, Task.CurrentId);
    await Task.Delay(10);
    if (i > 15)
      pls.Break();
  });
Console.WriteLine("Is completed: {0}", tresult.IsCompleted);
Console.WriteLine("lowest break iteration: {0}",
  result.LowestBreakIteration);
```

This run of the application demonstrates that the iteration breaks up with a value higher than 15, but other tasks can simultaneously run and tasks with other values can run. With the help of the `LowestBreak Iteration` property, you can specify ignoring results from other tasks:

```
10 task 1
24 task 3
31 task 4
38 task 5
17 task 2
11 task 1
12 task 1
13 task 1
14 task 1
15 task 1
16 task 1
Is completed: False
lowest break iteration: 16
```

`Parallel.For` might use several threads to do the loops. If you need an initialization that should be done with every thread, you can use the `Parallel.For<TLocal>` method. The generic version of the `For` method accepts—besides the `from` and `to` values—three delegate parameters. The first parameter is of type `Func<TLocal>`. Because the example here uses a `string` for `TLocal`, the method needs to be defined as `Func<string>`, a method returning a `string`. This method is invoked only once for each thread that is used to do the iterations.

The second delegate parameter defines the delegate for the body. In the example, the parameter is of type `Func<int, ParallelLoopState, string, string>`. The first parameter is the loop iteration; the second parameter, `ParallelLoopState`, enables stopping the loop, as shown earlier. With the third parameter, the body method receives the value that is returned from the `init` method. The body method also needs to return a value of the type that was defined with the generic `For` parameter.

The last parameter of the `For` method specifies a delegate, `Action<TLocal>`; in the example, a string is received. This method, a thread exit method, is called only once for each thread:

```
Parallel.For<string>(0, 20, () =>
  {
    // invoked once for each thread
    Console.WriteLine("init thread {0}, task {1}",
```

```
              Thread.CurrentThread.ManagedThreadId, Task.CurrentId);
            return String.Format("t{0}",
              Thread.CurrentThread.ManagedThreadId);
          },
          (i, pls, str1) =>
          {
            // invoked for each member
            Console.WriteLine("body i {0} str1 {1} thread {2} task {3}", i, str1,
              Thread.CurrentThread.ManagedThreadId, Task.CurrentId);
            Thread.Sleep(10);
            return String.Format("i {0}", i);
          },
          (str1) =>
          {
            // final action on each thread
            Console.WriteLine("finally {0}", str1);
          });
```

The result of running this program once is shown here:

```
init thread 1, task 1
init thread 5, task 4
init thread 3, task 2
init thread 4, task 3
init thread 6, task 5
body i 10 str1 t4 thread 4 task 3
body i 1 str1 i 0 thread 1 task 1
body i 1 str1 t6 thread 6 task 5
body i 15 str1 t5 thread 5 task 4
body i 5 str1 t3 thread 3 task 2
body i 11 str1 i 10 thread 4 task 3
body i 16 str1 i 15 thread 5 task 4
body i 2 str1 i 1 thread 6 task 5
body i 4 str1 i 0 thread 1 task 1
body i 17 str1 i 16 thread 5 task 4
body i 3 str1 i 2 thread 6 task 5
body i 6 str1 i 4 thread 1 task 1
body i 13 str1 i 5 thread 3 task 2
body i 12 str1 i 11 thread 4 task 3
body i 7 str1 i 6 thread 1 task 1
finally i 3
body i 14 str1 i 13 thread 3 task 2
finally i 17
body i 18 str1 i 12 thread 4 task 3
finally i 14
body i 8 str1 i 7 thread 1 task 1
body i 19 str1 i 18 thread 4 task 3
body i 9 str1 i 8 thread 1 task 1
finally i 19
finally i 9
```

Looping with the Parallel.ForEach Method

Parallel.ForEach iterates through a collection implementing IEnumerable in a way similar to the foreach statement, but in an asynchronous manner. Again, the order is not guaranteed:

```
string[] data = {"zero", "one", "two", "three", "four", "five",
  "six", "seven", "eight", "nine", "ten", "eleven", "twelve"};
ParallelLoopResult result =
  Parallel.ForEach<string>(data, s =>
```

```
  {
    Console.WriteLine(s);
  });
```

If you need to break up the loop, you can use an overload of the ForEach method with a ParallelLoop
State parameter. You can do this in the same way it was done earlier with the For method. An overload of
the ForEach method can also be used to access an indexer to get the iteration number, as shown here:

```
Parallel.ForEach<string>(data, (s, pls, l) =>
  {
    Console.WriteLine("{0} {1}", s, l);
  });
```

Invoking Multiple Methods with the Parallel.Invoke Method

If multiple tasks should run in parallel, you can use the Parallel.Invoke method, which offers the task
parallelism pattern. Parallel.Invoke allows the passing of an array of Action delegates, whereby you can
assign methods that should run. The example code passes the Foo and Bar methods to be invoked in parallel
(code file ParallelSamples/Program.cs):

```
static void ParallelInvoke()
{
  Parallel.Invoke(Foo, Bar);
}

static void Foo()
{
  Console.WriteLine("foo");
}

static void Bar()
{
  Console.WriteLine("bar");
}
```

The Parallel class is very easy to use—both for task and data parallelism. If more control is needed, and
you don't want to wait until the action started with the Parallel class is completed, the Task class comes
in handy. Of course, it's also possible to combine the Task and Parallel classes.

TASKS

For more control over the parallel actions, the Task class from the namespace System.Threading.Tasks
can be used. A *task* represents some unit of work that should be done. This unit of work can run in a separate
thread; and it is also possible to start a task in a synchronized manner, which results in a wait for the
calling thread. With tasks, you have an abstraction layer but also a lot of control over the underlying threads.

Tasks provide much more flexibility in organizing the work you need to do. For example, you can define
continuation work—what should be done after a task is complete. This can be differentiated based on
whether the task was successful or not. You can also organize tasks in a hierarchy. For example, a parent
task can create new children tasks. Optionally, this can create a dependency, so canceling a parent task also
cancels its child tasks.

Starting Tasks

To start a task, you can use either the TaskFactory or the constructor of the Task and the Start method.
The Task constructor just gives you more flexibility in creating the task.

When starting a task, an instance of the Task class can be created, and the code that should run can be assigned with an Action or Action<object> delegate, with either no parameters or one object parameter. In the following example, a method is defined with one parameter. In the implementation, the ID of the task and the ID of the thread are written to the console, as well as information if the thread is coming from a thread pool, and if the thread is a background thread. Writing multiple messages to the console is synchronized by using the lock keyword with the taskMethodLock synchronization object. This way, parallel calls to TaskMethod can be done, and multiple writes to the console are not interleaving each other. Otherwise the title could be written by one task, and the thread information follows by another task (code file TaskSamples/Program.cs):

```
static object taskMethodLock = new object();
static void TaskMethod(object title)
{
  lock (taskMethodLock)
  {
    Console.WriteLine(title);
    Console.WriteLine("Task id: {0}, thread: {1}",
      Task.CurrentId == null ? "no task" : Task.CurrentId.ToString(),
      Thread.CurrentThread.ManagedThreadId);
    Console.WriteLine("is pooled thread: {0}",
      Thread.CurrentThread.IsThreadPoolThread);
    Console.WriteLine("is background thread: {0}",
      Thread.CurrentThread.IsBackground);
    Console.WriteLine();
  }
}
```

The following sections describe different ways to start a new task.

Tasks Using the Thread Pool

In this section, different ways are shown to start a task that uses a thread from the thread pool. The thread pool offers a pool of background threads and is discussed in more detail in the section "Thread Pools." For now, it's helpful to know that the thread pool manages threads on its own, increasing or decreasing the number of threads within the pool as needed. Threads from the pool are used to fulfill some actions, and returned to the pool afterward.

The first way to create a task is with an instantiated TaskFactory, where the method TaskMethod is passed to the StartNew method, and the task is immediately started. The second approach uses the static Factory property of the Task class to get access to the TaskFactory, and to invoke the StartNew method. This is very similar to the first version in that it uses a factory, but there's less control over factory creation. The third approach uses the constructor of the Task class. When the Task object is instantiated, the task does not run immediately. Instead, it is given the status Created. The task is then started by calling the Start method of the Task class. The fourth approach, new with .NET 4.5, calls the Run method of the Task that immediately starts the task. The Run method doesn't have an overloaded variant to pass an Action<object> delegate, but it's easy to simulate this by assigning a Lambda expression of type Action, and using the parameter within its implementation.

```
static void TasksUsingThreadPool()
{
  var tf = new TaskFactory();
  Task t1 = tf.StartNew(TaskMethod, "using a task factory");

  Task t2 = Task.Factory.StartNew(TaskMethod, "factory via a task");

  var t3 = new Task(TaskMethod, "using a task constructor and Start");
```

```
        t3.Start();

        Task t4 = Task.Run(() => TaskMethod("using the Run method"));

    }
```

The output returned with these variants is as follows. All these versions create a new task, and a thread from the thread pool is used:

```
using a task factory
Task id: 1, thread: 6
is pooled thread: True
is background thread: True

factory via a task
Task id: 2, thread: 4
is pooled thread: True
is background thread: True

using the Run method
Task id: 3, thread: 5
is pooled thread: True
is background thread: True

using a task constructor and Start
Task id: 4, thread: 3
is pooled thread: True
is background thread: True
```

With both the Task constructor and the StartNew method of the TaskFactory, you can pass values from the enumeration TaskCreationOptions. Using this creation option you can change how the task should behave differently, as is shown in the next sections.

Synchronous Tasks

A task does not necessarily mean to use a thread from a thread pool—it can use other threads as well. Tasks can also run synchronously, with the same thread as the calling thread. The following code snippet uses the method RunSynchronously of the Task class:

```
        private static void RunSynchronousTask()
        {
          TaskMethod("just the main thread");
          var t1 = new Task(TaskMethod, "run sync");
          t1.RunSynchronously();
        }
```

Here, the TaskMethod is first called directly from the main thread before it is invoked from the newly created Task. As you can see from the following console output, the main thread doesn't have a task ID, it is a foreground thread, and it is not a pooled thread. Calling the method RunSynchronously uses exactly the same thread as the calling thread, but creates a task if one wasn't created previously:

```
just the main thread
Task id: no task, thread: 1
is pooled thread: False
is background thread: False

run sync
Task id: 1, thread: 1
is pooled thread: False
is background thread: False
```

Tasks Using a Separate Thread

If the code of a task should run for a longer time, `TaskCreationOptions.LongRunning` should be used to instruct the task scheduler to create a new thread, rather than use a thread from the thread pool. This way, the thread doesn't need to be managed by the thread pool. When a thread is taken from the thread pool, the task scheduler can decide to wait for an already running task to be completed and use this thread instead of creating a new thread with the pool. With a long-running thread, the task scheduler knows immediately that it doesn't make sense to wait for this one. The following code snippet creates a long running task:

```
private static void LongRunningTask()
{
  var t1 = new Task(TaskMethod, "long running",
    TaskCreationOptions.LongRunning);
  t1.Start();
}
```

Indeed, using the option `TaskCreationOptions.LongRunning`, a thread from the thread pool is not used. Instead, a new thread is created:

```
long running
Task id: 1, thread: 3
is pooled thread: False
is background thread: True
```

Futures—Results from Tasks

When a task is finished, it can write some stateful information to a shared object. Such a shared object must be thread-safe. Another option is to use a task that returns a result. Such a task is also known as future as it returns a result in the future. With early versions of the Task Parallel Library (TPL), the class had the name `Future` as well. Now it is a generic version of the `Task` class. With this class it is possible to define the type of the result that is returned with a task.

A method that is invoked by a task to return a result can be declared with any return type. The following example method `TaskWithResult` returns two `int` values with the help of a `Tuple`. The input of the method can be void or of type `object`, as shown here (code file `TaskSamples/Program.cs`):

```
static Tuple<int, int> TaskWithResult(object division)
{
  Tuple<int, int> div = (Tuple<int, int>)division;
  int result = div.Item1 / div.Item2;
  int reminder = div.Item1 % div.Item2;
  Console.WriteLine("task creates a result...");

  return Tuple.Create<int, int>(result, reminder);
}
```

> **NOTE** *Tuples are explained in Chapter 6, "Arrays and Tuples."*

When defining a task to invoke the method `TaskWithResult`, the generic class `Task<TResult>` is used. The generic parameter defines the return type. With the constructor, the method is passed to the `Func` delegate, and the second parameter defines the input value. Because this task needs two input values in the `object` parameter, a tuple is created as well. Next, the task is started. The `Result` property of the `Task` instance t1 blocks and waits until the task is completed. Upon task completion, the `Result` property contains the result from the task:

```
var t1 = new Task<Tuple<int,int>>(TaskWithResult,
  Tuple.Create<int, int>(8, 3));
t1.Start();
Console.WriteLine(t1.Result);
t1.Wait();
Console.WriteLine("result from task: {0} {1}", t1.Result.Item1,
  t1.Result.Item2);
```

Continuation Tasks

With tasks, you can specify that after a task is finished another specific task should start to run—for example, a new task that uses a result from the previous one or should do some cleanup if the previous task failed.

Whereas the task handler has either no parameter or one object parameter, the continuation handler has a parameter of type Task. Here, you can access information about the originating task (code file TaskSamples/Program.cs):

```
static void DoOnFirst()
{
  Console.WriteLine("doing some task {0}", Task.CurrentId);
  Thread.Sleep(3000);
}

static void DoOnSecond(Task t)
{
  Console.WriteLine("task {0} finished", t.Id);
  Console.WriteLine("this task id {0}", Task.CurrentId);
  Console.WriteLine("do some cleanup");
  Thread.Sleep(3000);
}
```

A continuation task is defined by invoking the ContinueWith method on a task. You could also use the TaskFactory for this. t1.OnContinueWith(DoOnSecond) means that a new task invoking the method DoOnSecond should be started as soon as the task t1 is finished. You can start multiple tasks when one task is finished, and a continuation task can have another continuation task, as this next example demonstrates:

```
Task t1 = new Task(DoOnFirst);
Task t2 = t1.ContinueWith(DoOnSecond);
Task t3 = t1.ContinueWith(DoOnSecond);
Task t4 = t2.ContinueWith(DoOnSecond);
```

So far, the continuation tasks have been started when the previous task was finished, regardless of the result. With values from TaskContinuationOptions, you can define that a continuation task should only start if the originating task was successful (or faulted). Some of the possible values are OnlyOnFaulted, NotOnFaulted, OnlyOnCanceled, NotOnCanceled, and OnlyOnRanToCompletion:

```
Task t5 = t1.ContinueWith(DoOnError,
  TaskContinuationOptions.OnlyOnFaulted);
```

> **NOTE** *The compiler-generated code from the* await *keyword discussed in Chapter 13 makes use of continuation tasks.*

Task Hierarchies

With task continuations, one task is started after another. Tasks can also form a hierarchy. When a task itself starts a new task, a parent/child hierarchy is started.

In the code snippet that follows, within the task of the parent, a new task object is created, and the task is started. The code to create a child task is the same as that to create a parent task. The only difference is that the task is created from within another task:

```
static void ParentAndChild()
{
  var parent = new Task(ParentTask);
  parent.Start();
  Thread.Sleep(2000);
  Console.WriteLine(parent.Status);
  Thread.Sleep(4000);
  Console.WriteLine(parent.Status);
}

static void ParentTask()
{
  Console.WriteLine("task id {0}", Task.CurrentId);
  var child = new Task(ChildTask);
  child.Start();
  Thread.Sleep(1000);
  Console.WriteLine("parent started child");
}

static void ChildTask()
{
  Console.WriteLine("child");
  Thread.Sleep(5000);
  Console.WriteLine("child finished");
}
```

If the parent task is finished before the child task, the status of the parent task is shown as `WaitingFor ChildrenToComplete`. The parent task is completed with the status `RanToCompletion` as soon as all children tasks are completed as well. Of course, this is not the case if the parent creates a task with the `TaskCreationOption DetachedFromParent`.

Canceling a parent task also cancels the children. The cancellation framework is discussed next.

CANCELLATION FRAMEWORK

.NET 4.5 includes a cancellation framework to enable the canceling of long-running tasks in a standard manner. Every blocking call should support this mechanism. Of course, not every blocking call currently implements this new technology, but more and more are doing so. Among the technologies that offer this mechanism already are tasks, concurrent collection classes, and Parallel LINQ, as well as several synchronization mechanisms.

The cancellation framework is based on cooperative behavior; it is not forceful. A long-running task checks whether it is canceled and returns control accordingly.

A method that supports cancellation accepts a `CancellationToken` parameter. This class defines the property `IsCancellationRequested`, whereby a long operation can check if it should abort. Other ways for a long operation to check for cancellation include using a `WaitHandle` property that is signaled when the token is canceled, or using the `Register` method. The `Register` method accepts parameters of type `Action` and `ICancelableOperation`. The method that is referenced by the `Action` delegate is invoked when the token is canceled. This is similar to the `ICancelableOperation`, whereby the `Cancel` method of an object implementing this interface is invoked when the cancellation is done.

Cancellation of Parallel.For

This section starts with a simple example using the `Parallel.For` method. The `Parallel` class provides overloads for the `For` method, whereby you can pass a parameter of type `ParallelOptions`. With

ParallelOptions, you can pass a CancellationToken. The CancellationToken is generated by creating a CancellationTokenSource. CancellationTokenSource implements the interface ICancelableOperation and can therefore be registered with the CancellationToken and allows cancellation with the Cancel method. The example doesn't call the Cancel method directly, but makes use of a new .NET 4.5 method to cancel the token after 500 milliseconds with the CancelAfter method.

Within the implementation of the For loop, the Parallel class verifies the outcome of the Cancellation Token and cancels the operation. Upon cancellation, the For method throws an exception of type OperationCanceledException, which is caught in the example. With the CancellationToken, it is possible to register for information when the cancellation is done. This is accomplished by calling the Register method and passing a delegate that is invoked on cancellation (code file CancellationSamples/Program.cs):

```csharp
var cts = new CancellationTokenSource();
cts.Token.Register(() => Console.WriteLine("*** token canceled"));

// send a cancel after 500 ms
cts.CancelAfter(500);

try
{
  ParallelLoopResult result =
    Parallel.For(0, 100, new ParallelOptions()
      {
        CancellationToken = cts.Token,
      },
      x =>
      {
        Console.WriteLine("loop {0} started", x);
        int sum = 0;
        for (int i = 0; i < 100; i++)
        {
          Thread.Sleep(2);
          sum += i;
        }
        Console.WriteLine("loop {0} finished", x);
      });
}
catch (OperationCanceledException ex)
{
  Console.WriteLine(ex.Message);
}
```

Running the application, you will get output similar to the following. Iteration 0, 1, 25, 75, and 50 were all started. This is on a system with a quad-core CPU. With the cancellation, all other iterations were canceled before starting. The iterations that were started are allowed to finish because cancellation is always done in a cooperative way to avoid the risk of resource leaks when iterations are canceled somewhere in between:

```
loop 0 started
loop 1 started
loop 25 started
loop 75 started
loop 50 started
** token cancelled
loop 75 finished
loop 0 finished
loop 50 finished
loop 25 finished
loop 1 finished
The operation was canceled.
```

Cancellation of Tasks

The same cancellation pattern is used with tasks. First, a new `CancellationTokenSource` is created. If you need just one cancellation token, you can use a default token by accessing `Task.Factory .CancellationToken`. Then, similar to the previous code, the task is canceled after 500 milliseconds. The task doing the major work within a loop receives the cancellation token via the `TaskFactory` object. The cancellation token is assigned to the `TaskFactory` by setting it in the constructor. This cancellation token is used by the task to check if cancellation is requested by checking the `IsCancellationRequested` property of the `CancellationToken`:

```
static void CancelTask()
{
  var cts = new CancellationTokenSource();
  cts.Token.Register(() => Console.WriteLine("*** task cancelled"));

  // send a cancel after 500 ms
  cts.CancelAfter(500);

  Task t1 = Task.Run(() =>
    {
      Console.WriteLine("in task");
      for (int i = 0; i < 20; i++)
      {
        Thread.Sleep(100);
        CancellationToken token = cts.Token;
        if (token.IsCancellationRequested)
        {
          Console.WriteLine("cancelling was requested, " +
            "cancelling from within the task");
          token.ThrowIfCancellationRequested();
          break;
        }
        Console.WriteLine("in loop");
      }
      Console.WriteLine("task finished without cancellation");
    }, cts.Token);

  try
  {
    t1.Wait();
  }
  catch (AggregateException ex)
  {
    Console.WriteLine("exception: {0}, {1}", ex.GetType().Name, ex.Message);
    foreach (var innerException in ex.InnerExceptions)
    {
      Console.WriteLine("inner excepion: {0}, {1}",
        ex.InnerException.GetType().Name, ex.InnerException.Message);
    }
  }
}
```

When running the application, you can see that the task starts, runs for a few loops, and gets the cancellation request. The task is canceled and throws a `TaskCanceledException`, which is initiated from the method call `ThrowIfCancellationRequested`. With the caller waiting for the task, you can see that the exception `AggregateException` is caught and contains the inner exception `TaskCanceledException`. This is used for a hierarchy of cancellations—for example, if you run a `Parallel.For` within a task that is canceled as well. The final status of the task is `Canceled`:

```
in task
in loop
in loop
in loop
in loop
*** task cancelled
cancelling was requested, cancelling from within the task
exception: AggregateException, One or more errors occurred.
inner excepion: TaskCanceledException, A task was canceled.
```

THREAD POOLS

This section takes a look at what's behind the scenes of tasks: thread pools. Creating threads takes time. When you have different short tasks to do, you can create a number of threads in advance and send requests as they should be done. It would be nice if this number of threads increased as more were needed, and decreased as needed to release resources.

There is no need to create such a list on your own. The list is managed by the `ThreadPool` class. This class increases and decreases the number of threads in the pool as they are needed, up to the maximum number of threads, which is configurable. With a quad-core CPU, the default is currently set to 1,023 worker threads and 1,000 I/O threads. You can specify the minimum number of threads that should be started immediately when the pool is created and the maximum number of threads that are available in the pool. If the number of jobs to process exceeds the maximum number of threads in the pool, the newest jobs are queued and must wait for a thread to complete its work.

The following sample application first reads the maximum number of worker and I/O threads and writes this information to the console. Then, in a `for` loop, the method `JobForAThread` is assigned to a thread from the thread pool by invoking the method `ThreadPool.QueueUserWorkItem` and passing a delegate of type `WaitCallback`. The thread pool receives this request and selects one of the threads from the pool to invoke the method. If the pool is not already running, the pool is created and the first thread is started. If the pool is already running and one thread is free to do the task, the job is forwarded to that thread (code file `ThreadPoolSamples/Program.cs`):

```csharp
using System;
using System.Threading;

namespace Wrox.ProCSharp.Threading
{
  class Program
  {
    static void Main()
    {
      int nWorkerThreads;
      int nCompletionPortThreads;
      ThreadPool.GetMaxThreads(out nWorkerThreads, out nCompletionPortThreads);
      Console.WriteLine("Max worker threads: {0}, " +
        "I/O completion threads: {1}", nWorkerThreads, nCompletionPortThreads);

      for (int i = 0; i < 5; i++)
      {
        ThreadPool.QueueUserWorkItem(JobForAThread);
      }
      Thread.Sleep(3000);
    }

    static void JobForAThread(object state)
    {
      for (int i = 0; i < 3; i++)
      {
```

```
            Console.WriteLine("loop {0}, running inside pooled thread {1}",
              i, Thread.CurrentThread.ManagedThreadId);
            Thread.Sleep(50);
        }
      }
    }
  }
```

When you run the application, you can see that 1,023 worker threads are possible with the current settings. The five jobs are processed by four pooled threads (because this is a quad-core system). Your results may vary, and you can change the job's sleep time and the number of jobs to process to get very different results:

```
Max worker threads: 1023, I/O completion threads: 1000
loop 0, running inside pooled thread 4
loop 0, running inside pooled thread 6
loop 0, running inside pooled thread 5
loop 0, running inside pooled thread 3
loop 1, running inside pooled thread 3
loop 1, running inside pooled thread 6
loop 1, running inside pooled thread 5
loop 1, running inside pooled thread 4
loop 2, running inside pooled thread 6
loop 2, running inside pooled thread 4
loop 2, running inside pooled thread 5
loop 2, running inside pooled thread 3
loop 0, running inside pooled thread 4
loop 1, running inside pooled thread 4
loop 2, running inside pooled thread 4
```

Thread pools are very easy to use, but there are some restrictions:

➤ All thread pool threads are background threads. If all foreground threads of a process are finished, all background threads are stopped. You cannot change a pooled thread to a foreground thread.

➤ You cannot set the priority or name of a pooled thread.

➤ For COM objects, all pooled threads are multithreaded apartment (MTA) threads. Many COM objects require a single-threaded apartment (STA) thread.

➤ Use pooled threads only for a short task. If a thread should run all the time (for example, the spell-checker thread of Word), create a thread with the Thread class (or use the LongRunning option on creating a Task).

THE THREAD CLASS

If more control is needed, the Thread class can be used. This class enables you to create foreground threads and set different priorities with threads.

With the Thread class, you can create and control threads. The code here is a very simple example of creating and starting a new thread. The constructor of the Thread class is overloaded to accept a delegate parameter of type ThreadStart or ParameterizedThreadStart. The ThreadStart delegate defines a method with a void return type and without arguments. After the Thread object is created, you can start the thread with the Start method (code file ThreadSamples/Program.cs):

```
using System;
using System.Threading;

namespace Wrox.ProCSharp.Threading
{
  class Program
  {
    static void Main()
```

```
    {
      var t1 = new Thread(ThreadMain);
      t1.Start();
      Console.WriteLine("This is the main thread.");
    }

    static void ThreadMain()
    {
      Console.WriteLine("Running in a thread.");
    }
  }
}
```

When you run the application, you get the output of the two threads:

```
This is the main thread.
Running in a thread.
```

There is no guarantee regarding what output comes first. Threads are scheduled by the operating system; which thread comes first can be different each time.

You have seen how a Lambda expression can be used with an asynchronous delegate. You can use it with the Thread class as well by passing the implementation of the thread method to the argument of the Thread constructor:

```
using System;
using System.Threading;

namespace Wrox.ProCSharp.Threading
{
  class Program
  {
    static void Main()
    {
      var t1 = new Thread(() => Console.WriteLine("running in a thread, id: {0}",
        Thread.CurrentThread.ManagedThreadId));
      t1.Start();
      Console.WriteLine("This is the main thread, id: {0}",
        Thread.CurrentThread.ManagedThreadId);
    }
  }
}
```

The output of the application shows both the thread name and the ID:

```
This is the main thread, id: 1
Running in a thread, id: 3.
```

Passing Data to Threads

There are two ways to pass some data to a thread. You can either use the Thread constructor with the ParameterizedThreadStart delegate or create a custom class and define the method of the thread as an instance method so that you can initialize data of the instance before starting the thread.

For passing data to a thread, a class or struct that holds the data is needed. Here, the struct Data containing a string is defined, but you can pass any object you want:

```
public struct Data
{
  public string Message;
}
```

If the `ParameterizedThreadStart` delegate is used, the entry point of the thread must have a parameter of type `object` and a `void` return type. The object can be cast to what it is, and here the message is written to the console:

```
static void ThreadMainWithParameters(object o)
{
  Data d = (Data)o;
  Console.WriteLine("Running in a thread, received {0}", d.Message);
}
```

With the constructor of the `Thread` class, you can assign the new entry point `ThreadMainWithParameters` and invoke the `Start` method, passing the variable `d`:

```
static void Main()
{
  var d = new Data { Message = "Info" };
  var t2 = new Thread(ThreadMainWithParameters);
  t2.Start(d);
}
```

Another way to pass data to the new thread is to define a class (see the class `MyThread`), whereby you define the fields that are needed as well as the main method of the thread as an instance method of the class:

```
public class MyThread
{
  private string data;

  public MyThread(string data)
  {
    this.data = data;
  }

  public void ThreadMain()
  {
    Console.WriteLine("Running in a thread, data: {0}", data);
  }
}
```

This way, you can create an object of `MyThread` and pass the object and the method `ThreadMain` to the constructor of the `Thread` class. The thread can access the data:

```
var obj = new MyThread("info");
var t3 = new Thread(obj.ThreadMain);
t3.Start();
```

Background Threads

The process of the application keeps running as long as at least one foreground thread is running. If more than one foreground thread is running and the `Main` method ends, the process of the application remains active until all foreground threads finish their work.

A thread you create with the `Thread` class, by default, is a foreground thread. Thread pool threads are always background threads.

When you create a thread with the `Thread` class, you can define whether it should be a foreground or background thread by setting the property `IsBackground`. The `Main` method sets the `IsBackground` property of the thread t1 to `false` (which is the default). After starting the new thread, the main thread just writes an end message to the console. The new thread writes a start and an end message, and in between it sleeps for three seconds, which gives the main thread a good chance to finish before the new thread completes its work:

```
class Program
{
  static void Main()
  {
    var t1 = new Thread(ThreadMain)
      { Name = "MyNewThread", IsBackground = false };
    t1.Start();
    Console.WriteLine("Main thread ending now.");
  }

  static void ThreadMain()
  {
    Console.WriteLine("Thread {0} started", Thread.CurrentThread.Name);
    Thread.Sleep(3000);
    Console.WriteLine("Thread {0} completed", Thread.CurrentThread.Name);
  }
}
```

When you start the application, you will still see the completion message written to the console, although the main thread completed its work earlier. The reason is that the new thread is a foreground thread as well:

```
Main thread ending now.
Thread MyNewThread1 started
Thread MyNewThread1 completed
```

If you change the IsBackground property used to start the new thread to true, the result shown on the console is different. You might have the same result shown here—the start message of the new thread is shown but never the end message. Alternatively, you might not see the start message either, if the thread was prematurely ended before it had a chance to kick off:

```
Main thread ending now.
Thread MyNewThread1 started
```

Background threads are very useful for background tasks. For example, when you close the Word application, it doesn't make sense for the spell-checker to keep its process running. The spell-checker thread can be killed when the application is closed. However, the thread organizing the Outlook message store should remain active until it is finished, even if Outlook is closed.

Thread Priority

You have learned that the operating system schedules threads, and you have had a chance to influence the scheduling by assigning a priority to the thread. Before changing the priority, you must understand the thread scheduler. The operating system schedules threads based on a priority, and the thread with the highest priority is scheduled to run in the CPU. A thread stops running and gives up the CPU if it waits for a resource.

There are several reasons why a thread must wait, such as in response to a sleep instruction, while waiting for disk I/O to complete, while waiting for a network packet to arrive, and so on. If the thread does not give up the CPU on its own, it is preempted by the thread scheduler. A thread has a *time quantum*, which means it can use the CPU continuously until this time is reached (in case there isn't a thread with a higher priority). If multiple threads are running with the same priority, waiting to get the CPU, the thread scheduler uses a *round-robin* scheduling principle to give the CPU to one thread after another. If a thread is preempted, it is added last to the queue.

The time quantum and round-robin principles are used only if multiple threads are running with the same priority. The priority is dynamic. If a thread is CPU-intensive (requires the CPU continuously without waiting for resources), the priority is lowered to the level of the base priority that is defined with the thread. If a thread is waiting for a resource, the thread gets a priority boost and the priority is increased. Because of the boost, there is a good chance that the thread gets the CPU the next time that the wait ends.

With the `Thread` class, you can influence the base priority of the thread by setting the `Priority` property. The `Priority` property requires a value that is defined by the `ThreadPriority` enumeration. The levels defined are `Highest`, `AboveNormal`, `Normal`, `BelowNormal`, and `Lowest`.

> **NOTE** *Be careful when giving a thread a higher priority, because this may decrease the chance for other threads to run. You can change the priority for a short time if necessary.*

Controlling Threads

The thread is created by invoking the `Start` method of a `Thread` object. However, after invoking the `Start` method, the new thread is still not in the `Running` state, but in the `Unstarted` state. The thread changes to the `Running` state as soon as the operating system thread scheduler selects the thread to run. You can read the current state of a thread by reading the property `Thread.ThreadState`.

With the `Thread.Sleep` method, a thread goes into the `WaitSleepJoin` state and waits until it is woken up again after the time span defined by the `Sleep` method has elapsed.

To stop another thread, you can invoke the method `Thread.Abort`. When this method is called, an exception of type `ThreadAbortException` is thrown in the thread that receives the abort. With a handler to catch this exception, the thread can do some cleanup before it ends. The thread also has a chance to continue running after receiving the `ThreadAbortException` as a result of invoking `Thread.ResetAbort`. The state of the thread receiving the abort request changes from `AbortRequested` to the `Aborted` state if the thread does not reset the abort.

If you need to wait for a thread to end, you can invoke the `Thread.Join` method. `Thread.Join` blocks the current thread and sets it to the `WaitSleepJoin` state until the thread that is joined is completed.

THREADING ISSUES

Programming with multiple threads is challenging. When starting multiple threads that access the same data, you can get intermittent problems that are hard to find. The problems are the same whether you use tasks, Parallel LINQ, or the `Parallel` class. To avoid getting into trouble, you must pay attention to synchronization issues and the problems that can occur with multiple threads. This section covers two in particular: race conditions and deadlocks.

Race Conditions

A race condition can occur if two or more threads access the same objects and access to the shared state is not synchronized. To demonstrate a race condition, the following example defines the class `StateObject`, with an `int` field and the method `ChangeState`. In the implementation of `ChangeState`, the state variable is verified to determine whether it contains 5; if it does, the value is incremented. `Trace.Assert` is the next statement, which immediately verifies that state now contains the value 6.

After incrementing by 1 a variable that contains the value 5, you might assume that the variable now has the value 6; but this is not necessarily the case. For example, if one thread has just completed the `if (state == 5)` statement, it might be preempted, with the scheduler running another thread. The second thread now goes into the `if` body and, because the state still has the value 5, the state is incremented by 1 to 6. The first thread is then scheduled again, and in the next statement the state is incremented to 7. This is when the race condition occurs and the assert message is shown (code file `ThreadingIssues/SampleTask.cs`):

```
public class StateObject
{
  private int state = 5;

  public void ChangeState(int loop)
  {
    if (state == 5)
    {
      state++;
      Trace.Assert(state == 6, "Race condition occurred after " +
        loop + " loops");
    }
    state = 5;
  }
}
```

You can verify this by defining a method for a task. The method `RaceCondition` of the class `SampleTask` gets a `StateObject` as a parameter. Inside an endless `while` loop, the `ChangeState` method is invoked. The variable `i` is used just to show the loop number in the assert message:

```
public class SampleTask
{
  public void RaceCondition(object o)
  {
    Trace.Assert(o is StateObject, "o must be of type StateObject");
    StateObject state = o as StateObject;

    int i = 0;
    while (true)
    {
      state.ChangeState(i++);
    }
  }
}
```

In the `Main` method of the program, a new `StateObject` is created that is shared among all the tasks. `Task` objects are created by invoking the `RaceCondition` method with the Lambda expression that is passed to the `Run` method of the `Task`. The main thread then waits for user input. However, there's a good chance that the program halts before reading user input, as a race condition will happen:

```
static void RaceConditions()
{
  var state = new StateObject();
  for (int i = 0; i < 2; i++)
  {
    Task.Run(() => new SampleTask().RaceCondition(state));
  }
}
```

When you start the program, you will get race conditions. How long it takes until the first race condition happens depends on your system and whether you build the program as a release build or a debug build. With a release build, the problem will happen more often because the code is optimized. If you have multiple CPUs in your system or dual/quad-core CPUs, where multiple threads can run concurrently, the problem will also occur more often than with a single-core CPU. The problem will occur with a single-core CPU because thread scheduling is preemptive, but not that often.

Figure 21-1 shows an assertion of the program in which the race condition occurred after 4,076 loops. If you start the application multiple times, you will always get different results.

FIGURE 21-1

You can avoid the problem by locking the shared object. You do this inside the thread by locking the variable state, which is shared among the threads, with the `lock` statement, as shown in the following example. Only one thread can exist inside the lock block for the state object. Because this object is shared among all threads, a thread must wait at the lock if another thread has the lock for state. As soon as the lock is accepted, the thread owns the lock, and gives it up at the end of the lock block. If every thread changing the object referenced with the state variable is using a lock, the race condition no longer occurs:

```
public class SampleTask
{
  public void RaceCondition(object o)
  {
    Trace.Assert(o is StateObject, "o must be of type StateObject");
    StateObject state = o as StateObject;

    int i = 0;
    while (true)
    {
      lock (state)  // no race condition with this lock
      {
        state.ChangeState(i++);
      }
    }
  }
}
```

Instead of performing the lock when using the shared object, you can make the shared object thread-safe. In the following code, the ChangeState method contains a lock statement. Because you cannot lock the state variable itself (only reference types can be used for a lock), the variable sync of type object is defined and used with the lock statement. If a lock is done using the same synchronization object every time the value state is changed, race conditions no longer happen:

```csharp
public class StateObject
{
  private int state = 5;
  private object sync = new object();

  public void ChangeState(int loop)
  {
    lock (sync)
    {
      if (state == 5)
      {
        state++;
        Trace.Assert(state == 6, "Race condition occurred after " +
          loop + " loops");
      }
      state = 5;
    }
  }
}
```

Deadlocks

Too much locking can get you in trouble as well. In a deadlock, at least two threads halt and wait for each other to release a lock. As both threads wait for each other, a deadlock occurs and the threads wait endlessly.

To demonstrate deadlocks, the following code instantiates two objects of type StateObject and passes them with the constructor of the SampleTask class. Two tasks are created: one task running the method Deadlock1 and the other task running the method Deadlock2 (code file ThreadingIssues/Program.cs):

```csharp
var state1 = new StateObject();
var state2 = new StateObject();
new Task(new SampleTask(state1, state2).Deadlock1).Start();
new Task(new SampleTask(state1, state2).Deadlock2).Start();
```

The methods Deadlock1 and Deadlock2 now change the state of two objects: s1 and s2. That's why two locks are generated. Deadlock1 first does a lock for s1 and next for s2. Deadlock2 first does a lock for s2 and then for s1. Now, it may happen occasionally that the lock for s1 in Deadlock1 is resolved. Next, a thread switch occurs, and Deadlock2 starts to run and gets the lock for s2. The second thread now waits for the lock of s1. Because it needs to wait, the thread scheduler schedules the first thread again, which now waits for s2. Both threads now wait and don't release the lock as long as the lock block is not ended. This is a typical deadlock (code file ThreadingIssues/SampleTask.cs):

```csharp
public class SampleTask
{
  public SampleTask(StateObject s1, StateObject s2)
  {
    this.s1 = s1;
    this.s2 = s2;
  }

  private StateObject s1;
```

```csharp
private StateObject s2;

public void Deadlock1()
{
  int i = 0;
  while (true)
  {
    lock (s1)
    {
      lock (s2)
      {
        s1.ChangeState(i);
        s2.ChangeState(i++);
        Console.WriteLine("still running, {0}", i);
      }
    }
  }
}

public void Deadlock2()
{
  int i = 0;
  while (true)
  {
    lock (s2)
    {
      lock (s1)
      {
        s1.ChangeState(i);
        s2.ChangeState(i++);
        Console.WriteLine("still running, {0}", i);
      }
    }
  }
}
```

As a result, the program will run a number of loops and soon become unresponsive. The message "still running" is just written a few times to the console. Again, how soon the problem occurs depends on your system configuration, and the result will vary.

With Visual Studio 2012, you can run the program in debug mode, click the Break All button, and open the Parallel Tasks window (see Figure 21-2). Here, you can see that the threads have the status Deadlock.

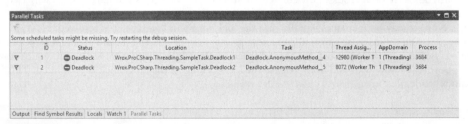

FIGURE 21-2

A deadlock problem is not always as obvious as it is here. One thread locks s1 and then s2; the other thread locks s2 and then s1. In this case, you just need to change the order so that both threads perform the locks in the same order. However, the locks might be hidden deeply inside a method. You can prevent this problem by designing a good lock order in the initial architecture of the application, and by defining timeouts for the locks, as demonstrated in the next section.

SYNCHRONIZATION

It is best to avoid synchronization issues by not sharing data between threads. Of course, this is not always possible. If data sharing is necessary, you must use synchronization techniques so that only one thread at a time accesses and changes shared state. Remember the synchronization issues with race conditions and deadlocks. If you don't pay attention to these issues, finding the source of problems in an application is difficult because threading issues occur only from time to time.

This section discusses synchronization technologies that you can use with multiple threads:

➤ `lock` statement

➤ `Interlocked` class

➤ `Monitor` class

➤ `SpinLock` struct

➤ `WaitHandle` class

➤ `Mutex` class

➤ `Semaphore` class

➤ `Events` classes

➤ `Barrier` class

➤ `ReaderWriterLockSlim` class

You can use the `lock`, `Interlocked`, and `Monitor` classes for synchronization within a process. The classes `Mutex`, `Event`, `SemaphoreSlim`, and `ReaderWriterLockSlim` also offer synchronization among threads of multiple processes.

The lock Statement and Thread Safety

C# has its own keyword for the synchronization of multiple threads: the `lock` statement. The `lock` statement provides an easy way to hold and release a lock. Before adding `lock` statements, however, let's look at another race condition. The class `SharedState` demonstrates using shared state between threads and shares an integer value (code file `SynchronizationSamples/SharedState.cs`):

```
public class SharedState
{
  public int State { get; set; }
}
```

The class `Job` contains the method `DoTheJob`, which is the entry point for a new task. With the implementation, the `State` of `SharedState` is incremented 50,000 times. The variable `sharedState` is initialized in the constructor of this class (code file `SynchronizationSamples/Job.cs`):

```
public class Job
{
  SharedState sharedState;
  public Job(SharedState sharedState)
  {
    this.sharedState = sharedState;
  }
  public void DoTheJob()
  {
    for (int i = 0; i < 50000; i++)
    {
      sharedState.State += 1;
    }
  }
}
```

In the `Main` method, a `SharedState` object is created and passed to the constructor of 20 `Task` objects. All tasks are started. After starting the tasks, the `Main` method does another loop to wait until every one of the 20 tasks is completed. After the tasks are completed, the summarized value of the shared state is written to the console. With 50,000 loops and 20 tasks, a value of 1,000,000 could be expected. Often, however, this is not the case (code file SynchronizationSamples/Program.cs):

```
class Program
{
  static void Main()
  {
    int numTasks = 20;
    var state = new SharedState();
    var tasks = new Task[numTasks];

    for (int i = 0; i < numTasks; i++)
    {
      tasks[i] = Task.Run(() => new Job(state).DoTheJob());
    }

    for (int i = 0; i < numTasks; i++)
    {
      tasks[i].Wait();
    }
    Console.WriteLine("summarized {0}", state.State);
  }
}
```

The results of multiple runs of the application are as follows:

```
summarized 314430
summarized 310683
summarized 315653
summarized 299973
summarized 326617
```

The behavior is different every time, but none of the results are correct. As noted earlier, you will see big differences between debug and release builds, and according to the type of CPU that you are using. If you change the loop count to smaller values, you will often get correct values—but not every time. In this case the application is small enough to see the problem easily; in a large application, the reason for such a problem can be hard to find.

You must add synchronization to this program. To do so, use the `lock` keyword. Defining the object with the `lock` statement means that you wait to get the lock for the specified object. You can pass only a reference type. Locking a value type would just lock a copy, which wouldn't make any sense. In any case, the C# compiler issues an error if value types are used with the `lock` statement. As soon as the lock is granted—only one thread gets the lock—the block of the `lock` statement can run. At the end of the `lock` statement block, the lock for the object is released, and another thread waiting for the lock can be granted access to it:

```
lock (obj)
{
    // synchronized region
}
```

To lock static members, you can place the lock on the type object:

```
lock (typeof(StaticClass))
{
}
```

You can make the instance members of a class thread-safe by using the `lock` keyword. This way, only one thread at a time can access the methods DoThis and DoThat for the same instance:

```
public class Demo
{
  public void DoThis()
  {
    lock (this)
    {
      // only one thread at a time can access the DoThis and DoThat methods
    }
  }
  public void DoThat()
  {
    lock (this)
    {
    }
  }
}
```

However, because the object of the instance can also be used for synchronized access from the outside, and you can't control this from the class itself, you can apply the SyncRoot pattern. With the SyncRoot pattern, a private object named `syncRoot` is created, and this object is used with the `lock` statements:

```
public class Demo
{
  private object syncRoot = new object();

  public void DoThis()
  {
    lock (syncRoot)
    {
      // only one thread at a time can access the DoThis and DoThat methods
    }
  }
  public void DoThat()
  {
    lock (syncRoot)
    {
    }
  }
}
```

Using locks costs time and is not always needed. You can create two versions of a class: synchronized and nonsynchronized. This is demonstrated in the next example code by changing the class `Demo`. The class `Demo` itself is not synchronized, as shown in the implementation of the `DoThis` and `DoThat` methods. The class also defines the `IsSynchronized` property, whereby the client can get information about the synchronization option of the class. To make a synchronized variant of the class, the static method `Synchronized` can be used to pass a nonsynchronized object, and this method returns an object of type `SynchronizedDemo`. `SynchronizedDemo` is implemented as an inner class that is derived from the base class `Demo` and overrides the virtual members of the base class. The overridden members make use of the SyncRoot pattern:

```
public class Demo
{
  private class SynchronizedDemo: Demo
  {
    private object syncRoot = new object();
    private Demo d;

    public SynchronizedDemo(Demo d)
    {
      this.d = d;
    }
```

```
    public override bool IsSynchronized
    {
      get { return true; }
    }

    public override void DoThis()
    {
      lock (syncRoot)
      {
        d.DoThis();
      }
    }

    public override void DoThat()
    {
      lock (syncRoot)
      {
        d.DoThat();
      }
    }
  }

  public virtual bool IsSynchronized
  {
    get { return false; }
  }

  public static Demo Synchronized(Demo d)
  {
    if (!d.IsSynchronized)
    {
      return new SynchronizedDemo(d);
    }
    return d;
  }

  public virtual void DoThis()
  {
  }

  public virtual void DoThat()
  {
  }
}
```

Bear in mind that when using the SynchronizedDemo class, only methods are synchronized. There is no synchronization for invoking two members of this class.

Now, we'll change the SharedState class that was not synchronized at first to use the SyncRoot pattern. If you try to make the SharedState class thread-safe by locking access to the properties with the SyncRoot pattern, you still get the race condition shown earlier in the "Race Conditions" section (code file SynchronizationSamples/SharedState.cs):

```
public class SharedState
{
  private int state = 0;
  private object syncRoot = new object();

  public int State // there's still a race condition,
                   // don't do this!
  {
```

```
      get { lock (syncRoot) {return state; }}
      set { lock (syncRoot) {state = value; }}
    }
  }
```

The thread invoking the DoTheJob method is accessing the get accessor of the SharedState class to get the current value of the state, and then the get accessor sets the new value for the state. In between calling the get and set accessors, the object is not locked, and another thread can read the interim value (code file SynchronizationSamples/Job.cs):

```
public void DoTheJob()
{
  for (int i = 0; i < 50000; i++)
  {
    sharedState.State += 1;
  }
}
```

Therefore, it is better to leave the SharedState class as it was earlier, without thread safety (code file SynchronizationSamples/SharedState.cs):

```
public class SharedState
{
  public int State { get; set; }
}
```

In addition, add the lock statement where it belongs, inside the method DoTheJob (code file SynchronizationSamples/Job.cs):

```
public void DoTheJob()
{
  for (int i = 0; i < 50000; i++)
  {
    lock (sharedState)
    {
      sharedState.State += 1;
    }
  }
}
```

This way, the results of the application are always as expected:

```
summarized 1000000
```

> **NOTE** *Using the* lock *statement in one place does not mean that all other threads accessing the object are waiting. You have to explicitly use synchronization with every thread accessing the shared state.*

Of course, you can also change the design of the SharedState class and offer incrementing as an atomic operation. This is a design question—what should be an atomic functionality of the class? The next code snippet just keeps the increment locked (code file SynchronizationSamples/SharedState.cs):

```
public class SharedState
{
  private int state = 0;
```

```
private object syncRoot = new object();

public int State
{
  get { return state; }
}

public int IncrementState()
{
  lock (syncRoot)
  {
    return ++state;
  }
}
}
```

There is, however, a faster way to lock the increment of the state, as shown next.

Interlocked

The `Interlocked` class is used to make simple statements for variables atomic. `i++` is not thread-safe. It consists of getting a value from the memory, incrementing the value by 1, and storing the value back in memory. These operations can be interrupted by the thread scheduler. The `Interlocked` class provides methods for incrementing, decrementing, exchanging, and reading values in a thread-safe manner.

Using the `Interlocked` class is much faster than other synchronization techniques. However, you can use it only for simple synchronization issues.

For example, instead of using the `lock` statement to lock access to the variable `someState` when setting it to a new value, in case it is null, you can use the `Interlocked` class, which is faster (code file `SynchronizationSamples/SharedState.cs`):

```
lock (this)
{
  if (someState == null)
  {
    someState = newState;
  }
}
```

The faster version with the same functionality uses the `Interlocked.CompareExchange` method:

```
Interlocked.CompareExchange<SomeState>(ref someState,
  newState, null);
```

Instead of performing incrementing inside a `lock` statement as shown here:

```
public int State
{
  get
  {
    lock (this)
    {
      return ++state;
    }
  }
}
```

You can use `Interlocked.Increment`, which is faster:

```
public int State
{
  get
  {
    return Interlocked.Increment(ref state);
  }
}
```

Monitor

The C# compiler resolves the `lock` statement to use the `Monitor` class. The following `lock` statement

```
lock (obj)
{
  // synchronized region for obj
}
```

is resolved to invoke the `Enter` method, which waits until the thread gets the lock of the object. Only one thread at a time may be the owner of the object lock. As soon as the lock is resolved, the thread can enter the synchronized section. The `Exit` method of the `Monitor` class releases the lock. The compiler puts the `Exit` method into a `finally` handler of a `try` block so that the lock is also released if an exception is thrown (code file `SynchronizationSamples/Program.cs`):

```
Monitor.Enter(obj);
try
{
  // synchronized region for obj
}
finally
{
  Monitor.Exit(obj);
}
```

> **NOTE** *Chapter 16, "Errors and Exceptions," covers the* `try/finally` *block.*

The `Monitor` class has a big advantage over the `lock` statement of C#: you can add a timeout value for waiting to get the lock. Therefore, instead of endlessly waiting to get the lock, you can use the `TryEnter` method shown in the following example, passing a timeout value that defines the maximum amount of time to wait for the lock. If the lock for `obj` is acquired, `TryEnter` sets the Boolean `ref` parameter to `true` and performs synchronized access to the state guarded by the object `obj`. If `obj` is locked for more than 500 milliseconds by another thread, `TryEnter` sets the variable `lockTaken` to `false`, and the thread does not wait any longer but is used to do something else. Maybe later, the thread can try to acquire the lock again.

```
bool lockTaken = false;
Monitor.TryEnter(obj, 500, ref lockTaken);
if (lockTaken)
{
  try
  {
    // acquired the lock
    // synchronized region for obj
  }
  finally
  {
    Monitor.Exit(obj);
  }
```

```
    }
    else
    {
      // didn't get the lock, do something else
    }
```

SpinLock

If the overhead on object-based lock objects (`Monitor`) would be too high because of garbage collection, the `SpinLock` struct can be used. Available since .NET 4, `SpinLock` is useful if you have a large number of locks (for example, for every node in a list) and hold times are always extremely short. You should avoid holding more than one `SpinLock`, and don't call anything that might block.

Other than the architectural differences, `SpinLock` is very similar in usage to the `Monitor` class. You acquire the lock with `Enter` or `TryEnter`, and release the lock with `Exit`. `SpinLock` also offers two properties to provide information about whether it is currently locked: `IsHeld` and `IsHeldByCurrentThread`.

> **NOTE** *Be careful when passing* `SpinLock` *instances around. Because* `SpinLock` *is defined as a* `struct`, *assigning one variable to another creates a copy. Always pass* `SpinLock` *instances by reference.*

WaitHandle

`WaitHandle` is an abstract base class that you can use to wait for a signal to be set. You can wait for different things, because `WaitHandle` is a base class and some classes are derived from it.

When describing asynchronous delegates earlier in this chapter, the `WaitHandle` was already in use. The method `BeginInvoke` of the asynchronous delegate returns an object that implements the interface `IAsyncResult`. Using `IAsyncResult`, you can access a `WaitHandle` with the property `AsyncWaitHandle`. When you invoke the method `WaitOne`, the thread waits until a signal is received that is associated with the wait handle (code file `AsyncDelegate/Program.cs`):

```
static void Main()
{
  TakesAWhileDelegate d1 = TakesAWhile;

  IAsyncResult ar = d1.BeginInvoke(1, 3000, null, null);
  while (true)
  {
    Console.Write(".");
    if (ar.AsyncWaitHandle.WaitOne(50, false))
    {
      Console.WriteLine("Can get the result now");
      break;
    }
  }
  int result = d1.EndInvoke(ar);
  Console.WriteLine("result: {0}", result);
}
```

With `WaitHandle`, you can wait for one signal to occur (`WaitOne`), multiple objects that all must be signaled (`WaitAll`), or one of multiple objects (`WaitAny`). `WaitAll` and `WaitAny` are static members of the `WaitHandle` class and accept an array of `WaitHandle` parameters.

`WaitHandle` has a `SafeWaitHandle` property whereby you can assign a native handle to an operating system resource and wait for that handle. For example, you can assign a `SafeFileHandle` to wait for a file I/O operation to complete, or a custom `SafeTransactionHandle` as shown in Chapter 25, "Transactions."

The classes `Mutex`, `EventWaitHandle`, and `Semaphore` are derived from the base class `WaitHandle`, so you can use any of these with waits.

Mutex

`Mutex` (mutual exclusion) is one of the classes of the .NET Framework that offers synchronization across multiple processes. It is very similar to the `Monitor` class in that there is just one owner. That is, only one thread can get a lock on the mutex and access the synchronized code regions that are secured by the mutex.

With the constructor of the `Mutex` class, you can define whether the mutex should initially be owned by the calling thread, define a name for the mutex, and determine whether the mutex already exists. In the following example, the third parameter is defined as an `out` parameter to receive a Boolean value if the mutex was newly created. If the value returned is `false`, the mutex was already defined. The mutex might be defined in a different process, because a mutex with a name is known to the operating system and is shared among different processes. If no name is assigned to the mutex, the mutex is unnamed and not shared among different processes.

```
bool createdNew;
Mutex mutex = new Mutex(false, "ProCSharpMutex", out createdNew);
```

To open an existing mutex, you can also use the method `Mutex.OpenExisting`, which doesn't require the same .NET privileges as creating the mutex with the constructor.

Because the `Mutex` class derives from the base class `WaitHandle`, you can do a `WaitOne` to acquire the mutex lock and be the owner of the mutex during that time. The mutex is released by invoking the `ReleaseMutex` method:

```
if (mutex.WaitOne())
{
  try
  {
    // synchronized region
  }
  finally
  {
    mutex.ReleaseMutex();
  }
}
else
{
  // some problem happened while waiting
}
```

Because a named mutex is known system-wide, you can use it to keep an application from being started twice. In the following Windows Forms application, the constructor of the `Mutex` object is invoked. Then it is verified whether the mutex with the name `SingletonWinAppMutex` exists already. If it does, the application exits:

```
static class Program
{
  [STAThread]
  static void Main()
  {
    bool createdNew;
    var mutex = new Mutex(false, "SingletonWinAppMutex",
      out createdNew);
    if (!createdNew)
    {
```

```
        MessageBox.Show("You can only start one instance " +
          "of the application");
        Application.Exit();
        return;
      }

    Application.EnableVisualStyles();
    Application.SetCompatibleTextRenderingDefault(false);
    Application.Run(new Form1());
    }
  }
```

Semaphore

A semaphore is very similar to a mutex; but unlike the mutex, the semaphore can be used by multiple threads at once. A semaphore is a counting mutex, meaning that with a semaphore you can define the number of threads that are allowed to access the resource guarded by the semaphore simultaneously. This is useful if you need to limit the number of threads that can access the resources available. For example, if a system has three physical I/O ports available, three threads can access them simultaneously, but a fourth thread needs to wait until the resource is released by one of the other threads.

.NET 4.5 provides two classes with semaphore functionality: Semaphore and SemaphoreSlim. Semaphore can be named, can use system-wide resources, and allows synchronization between different processes. SemaphoreSlim is a lightweight version that is optimized for shorter wait times.

In the following example application, in the Main method six tasks are created and one semaphore with a count of 3. In the constructor of the Semaphore class, you can define the count for the number of locks that can be acquired with the semaphore (the second parameter) and the number of locks that are free initially (the first parameter). If the first parameter has a lower value than the second parameter, the difference between the values defines the already allocated semaphore count. As with the mutex, you can also assign a name to the semaphore to share it among different processes. Here, no name is defined with the semaphore, so it is used only within this process. After the SemaphoreSlim object is created, six tasks are started, and they all get the same semaphore:

```
using System;
using System.Threading;
using System.Threading.Tasks;

namespace Wrox.ProCSharp.Threading
{
  class Program
  {
    static void Main()
    {
      int taskCount = 6;
      int semaphoreCount = 3;
      var semaphore = new SemaphoreSlim(semaphoreCount, semaphoreCount);
      var tasks = new Task[taskCount];

      for (int i = 0; i < taskCount; i++)
      {
        tasks[i] = Task.Run(() => TaskMain(semaphore));
      }

      Task.WaitAll(tasks);

      Console.WriteLine("All tasks finished");
    }
```

In the task's main method, TaskMain, the task does a Wait to lock the semaphore. Remember that the semaphore has a count of 3, so three tasks can acquire the lock. Task 4 must wait; and here the timeout of 600 milliseconds is defined as the maximum wait time. If the lock cannot be acquired after the wait time has elapsed, the task writes a message to the console and repeats the wait in a loop. As soon as the lock is acquired, the thread writes a message to the console, sleeps for some time, and releases the lock. Again, with the release of the lock it is important that the resource be released in all cases. That's why the Release method of the Semaphore class is invoked in a finally handler:

```
static void TaskMain(SemaphoreSlim semaphore)
{
  bool isCompleted = false;
  while (!isCompleted)
  {
    if (semaphore.Wait(600))
    {
      try
      {
        Console.WriteLine("Task {0} locks the semaphore", Task.CurrentId);
        Thread.Sleep(2000);
      }
      finally
      {
        Console.WriteLine("Task {0} releases the semaphore", Task.CurrentId);
        semaphore.Release();
        isCompleted = true;
      }
    }
    else
    {
      Console.WriteLine("Timeout for task {0}; wait again",
        Task.CurrentId);
    }
  }
}
```

When you run the application, you can indeed see that with four threads, the lock is made immediately. The tasks with IDs 4 and 5 must wait. The wait continues in the loop until one of the other threads releases the semaphore:

```
Task 1 locks the semaphore
Task 2 locks the semaphore
Task 3 locks the semaphore
Timeout for task 4; wait again
Timeout for task 4; wait again
Timeout for task 5; wait again
Timeout for task 4; wait again
Task 2 releases the semaphore
Task 5 locks the semaphore
Task 1 releases the semaphore
Task 6 locks the semaphore
Task 3 releases the semaphore
Task 4 locks the semaphore
Task 6 releases the semaphore
Task 5 releases the semaphore
Task 4 releases the semaphore
All tasks finished
```

Events

Like mutex and semaphore objects, events are also system-wide synchronization resources. For using system events from managed code, the .NET Framework offers the classes `ManualResetEvent`, `AutoResetEvent`, `ManualResetEventSlim`, and `CountdownEvent` in the namespace `System.Threading`. `ManualResetEventSlim` and `CountdownEvent` were new with .NET 4.

> **NOTE** *The* event *keyword from C# that is covered in Chapter 8, "Delegates, Lambdas, and Events" has nothing to do with the event classes from the namespace* System. Threading; *the* event *keyword is based on delegates. However, both event classes are .NET wrappers to the system-wide native event resource for synchronization.*

You can use events to inform other tasks that some data is present, that something is completed, and so on. An event can be signaled or not signaled. A task can wait for the event to be in a signaled state with the help of the `WaitHandle` class, discussed earlier.

A `ManualResetEventSlim` is signaled by invoking the `Set` method, and returned to a nonsignaled state with the `Reset` method. If multiple threads are waiting for an event to be signaled and the `Set` method is invoked, then all threads waiting are released. In addition, if a thread just invokes the `WaitOne` method but the event is already signaled, the waiting thread can continue immediately.

An `AutoResetEvent` is also signaled by invoking the `Set` method; and you can set it back to a nonsignaled state with the `Reset` method. However, if a thread is waiting for an auto-reset event to be signaled, the event is automatically changed into a nonsignaled state when the wait state of the first thread is finished. This way, if multiple threads are waiting for the event to be set, only one thread is released from its wait state. It is not the thread that has been waiting the longest for the event to be signaled, but the thread waiting with the highest priority.

To demonstrate events with the `ManualResetEventSlim` class, the following class `Calculator` defines the method `Calculation`, which is the entry point for a task. With this method, the task receives input data for calculation and writes the result to the variable result that can be accessed from the `Result` property. As soon as the result is completed (after a random amount of time), the event is signaled by invoking the `Set` method of the `ManualResetEventSlim` (code file `EventSample/Calculator.cs`):

```
public class Calculator
{
  private ManualResetEventSlim mEvent;

  public int Result { get; private set; }

  public Calculator(ManualResetEventSlim ev)
  {
    this.mEvent = ev;
  }

  public void Calculation(int x, int y)
  {
    Console.WriteLine("Task {0} starts calculation", Task.Current.Id);
    Thread.Sleep(new Random().Next(3000));
    Result = x + y;

    // signal the event-completed!
    Console.WriteLine("Task {0} is ready", Task.Current.Id);
    mEvent.Set();
  }
}
```

The `Main` method of the program defines arrays of four `ManualResetEventSlim` objects and four `Calculator` objects. Every `Calculator` is initialized in the constructor with a `ManualResetEventSlim` object, so every task gets its own event object to signal when it is completed. Now, the `Task` class is used to enable different tasks to run the calculation (code file `EventSample/Program.cs`):

```
class Program
{
  static void Main()
  {
    const int taskCount = 4;

    var mEvents = new ManualResetEventSlim[taskCount];
    var waitHandles = new WaitHandle[taskCount];
    var calcs = new Calculator[taskCount];

    for (int i = 0; i < taskCount; i++)
    {
      int i1 = i;
      mEvents[i] = new ManualResetEventSlim(false);
      waitHandles[i] = mEvents[i].WaitHandle;
      calcs[i] = new Calculator(mEvents[i]);

      Task.Run(() => calcs[i1].Calculation(i1 + 1, i1 + 3));
    }
    //...
```

The `WaitHandle` class is now used to wait for any one of the events in the array. `WaitAny` waits until any one of the events is signaled. In contrast to `ManualResetEvent`, `ManualResetEventSlim` does not derive from `WaitHandle`. That's why a separate collection of `WaitHandle` objects is kept, which is filled from the `WaitHandle` property of the `ManualResetEventSlim` class. `WaitAny` returns an index value that provides information about the event that was signaled. The returned value matches the index of the event array that is passed to `WaitAny`. Using this index, information from the signaled event can be read:

```
    for (int i = 0; i < taskCount; i++)
    {
      int index = WaitHandle.WaitAny(mEvents);
      if (index == WaitHandle.WaitTimeout)
      {
        Console.WriteLine("Timeout!!");
      }
      else
      {
        mEvents[index].Reset();
        Console.WriteLine("finished task for {0}, result: {1}",
          index, calcs[index].Result);
      }
    }
  }
}
```

When starting the application, you can see the tasks doing the calculation and setting the event to inform the main thread that it can read the result. At random times, depending on whether the build is a debug or release build and on your hardware, you might see different orders and a different number of tasks performing calls:

```
Task 2 starts calculation
Task 3 starts calculation
Task 4 starts calculation
Task 1 starts calculation
Task 1 is ready
```

```
Task 4 is ready
finished task for 0, result: 4
Task 3 is ready
finished task for 3, result: 10
finished task for 1, result: 6
Task 2 is ready
finished task for 2, result: 8
```

In a scenario like this, to fork some work into multiple tasks and later join the result, the new CountdownEvent class can be very useful. Instead of creating a separate event object for every task, you need to create only one. CountdownEvent defines an initial number for all the tasks that set the event, and after the count is reached, the CountdownEvent is signaled.

The Calculator class is modified to use the CountdownEvent instead of the ManualResetEvent. Rather than set the signal with the Set method, CountdownEvent defines the Signal method (code file EventSample/Calculator.cs):

```
public class Calculator
{
  private CountdownEvent cEvent;

  public int Result { get; private set; }

  public Calculator(CountdownEvent ev)
  {
    this.cEvent = ev;
  }

  public void Calculation(int x, int y)
  {
    Console.WriteLine("Task {0} starts calculation", Task.Current.Id);
    Thread.Sleep(new Random().Next(3000));
    Result = x + y;

    // signal the event-completed!
    Console.WriteLine("Task {0} is ready", Task.Current.Id);
    cEvent.Signal();
  }
}
```

The Main method can now be simplified so that it's only necessary to wait for the single event. If you don't deal with the results separately as it was done before, this new edition might be all that's needed:

```
const int taskCount = 4;
var cEvent = new CountdownEvent(taskCount);
var calcs = new Calculator[taskCount];

for (int i = 0; i < taskCount; i++)
{
  calcs[i] = new Calculator(cEvent);

  taskFactory.StartNew(calcs[i].Calculation,
                            Tuple.Create(i + 1, i + 3));
}

cEvent.Wait();
Console.WriteLine("all finished");
for (int i = 0; i < taskCount; i++)
{
  Console.WriteLine("task for {0}, result: {1}", i, calcs[i].Result);
}
```

Barrier

For synchronization, the `Barrier` class is great for scenarios in which work is forked into multiple tasks and the work must be joined afterward. `Barrier` is used for participants that need to be synchronized. While the job is active, additional participants can be added dynamically—for example, child tasks that are created from a parent task. Participants can wait until the work is done by all the other participants before continuing.

The following application uses a collection containing 2,000,000 strings. Multiple tasks are used to iterate through the collection and count the number of strings, starting with a, b, c, and so on.

The method `FillData` creates a collection and fills it with random strings (code file `BarrierSample/Program.cs`):

```
public static IEnumerable<string> FillData(int size)
{
  var data = new List<string>(size);
  var r = new Random();
  for (int i = 0; i < size; i++)
  {
    data.Add(GetString(r));
  }
  return data;
}
private static string GetString(Random r)
{
  var sb = new StringBuilder(6);
  for (int i = 0; i < 6; i++)
  {
    sb.Append((char)(r.Next(26) + 97));
  }
  return sb.ToString();
}
```

The `CalculationInTask` method defines the job performed by a task. With the parameter, a tuple containing four items is received. The third parameter is a reference to the `Barrier` instance. When the job is done by the task, the task removes itself from the barrier with the `RemoveParticipant` method:

```
static int[] CalculationInTask(int jobNumber, int partitionSize,
  Barrier barrier, IList<string> coll)
{
  List<string> data = new List<string>(coll);

  int start = jobNumber * partitionSize;
  int end = start + partitionSize;
  Console.WriteLine("Task {0}: partition from {1} to {2}",
    Task.Current.Id, start, end);
  int[] charCount = new int[26];
  for (int j = start; j < end; j++)
  {
    char c = data[j][0];
    charCount[c - 97]++;
  }
  Console.WriteLine("Calculation completed from task {0}. {1} " +
    "times a, {2} times z", Task.Current.Id, charCount[0],
    charCount[25]);

  barrier.RemoveParticipant();
  Console.WriteLine("Task {0} removed from barrier, " +
    "remaining participants {1}", Task.Current.Id,
    barrier.ParticipantsRemaining);
  return charCount;
}
```

With the `Main` method, a `Barrier` instance is created. In the constructor, you can specify the number of participants. In the example, this number is 3 (`numberTasks + 1`) because there are two created tasks, and the `Main` method itself is a participant as well. Using `Task.Run`, two tasks are created to fork the iteration through the collection into two parts. After starting the tasks, using `SignalAndWait`, the main method signals its completion and waits until all remaining participants either signal their completion or remove themselves as participants from the barrier. As soon as all participants are ready, the results from the tasks are zipped together with the `Zip` extension method:

```
static void Main()
{
  const int numberTasks = 2;
  const int partitionSize = 1000000;
  var data = new List<string>(FillData(partitionSize * numberTasks));

  var barrier = new Barrier(numberTasks + 1);

  var tasks = new Task<int[]>[numberTasks];
  for (int i = 0; i < participants; i++)
  {
    int jobNumber = i;
    tasks[i] = Task.Run(() => CalculationInTask(jobNumber, partitionSize,
      barrier, data);

    barrier.SignalAndWait();
    var resultCollection = tasks[0].Result.Zip(tasks[1].Result, (c1, c2) =
    {
      return c1 + c2;
    });

    char ch = 'a';
    int sum = 0;
    foreach (var x in resultCollection)
    {
      Console.WriteLine("{0}, count: {1}", ch++, x);
      sum += x;
    }

    Console.WriteLine("main finished {0}", sum);
    Console.WriteLine("remaining {0}", barrier.ParticipantsRemaining);
  }
```

ReaderWriterLockSlim

In order for a locking mechanism to allow multiple readers, but only one writer, for a resource, the class `ReaderWriterLockSlim` can be used. This class offers a locking functionality whereby multiple readers can access the resource if no writer locked it, and only a single writer can lock the resource.

The `ReaderWriterLockSlim` class has properties to acquire a read lock that are blocking and nonblocking, such as `EnterReadLock` and `TryEnterReadLock`, and to acquire a write lock with `EnterWriteLock` and `TryEnterWriteLock`. If a task reads first and writes afterward, it can acquire an upgradable read lock with `EnterUpgradableReadLock` or `TryEnterUpgradableReadLock`. With this lock, the write lock can be acquired without releasing the read lock.

Several properties of this class offer information about the held locks, such as `CurrentReadCount`, `WaitingReadCount`, `WaitingUpgradableReadCount`, and `WaitingWriteCount`.

The following example creates a collection containing six items and a `ReaderWriterLockSlim` object. The method `ReaderMethod` acquires a read lock to read all items of the list and write them to the console. The method `WriterMethod` tries to acquire a write lock to change all values of the collection. In the `Main` method, six threads are started that invoke either the method ReaderMethod or the method WriterMethod (code file ReaderWriterSample/Program.cs):

```csharp
using System;
using System.Collections.Generic;
using System.Threading;
using System.Threading.Tasks;

namespace Wrox.ProCSharp.Threading
{
  class Program
  {
    private static List<int> items = new List<int>() { 0, 1, 2, 3, 4, 5};
    private static ReaderWriterLockSlim rwl =
      new ReaderWriterLockSlim(LockRecursionPolicy.SupportsRecursion);

    static void ReaderMethod(object reader)
    {
      try
      {
        rwl.EnterReadLock();

        for (int i = 0; i < items.Count; i++)
        {
          Console.WriteLine("reader {0}, loop: {1}, item: {2}",
            reader, i, items[i]);
          Thread.Sleep(40);
        }
      }
      finally
      {
        rwl.ExitReadLock();
      }
    }

    static void WriterMethod(object writer)
    {
      try
      {
        while (!rwl.TryEnterWriteLock(50))
        {
          Console.WriteLine("Writer {0} waiting for the write lock",
            writer);
          Console.WriteLine("current reader count: {0}",
            rwl.CurrentReadCount);
        }
        Console.WriteLine("Writer {0} acquired the lock", writer);
        for (int i = 0; i < items.Count; i++)
        {
          items[i]++;
          Thread.Sleep(50);
        }
        Console.WriteLine("Writer {0} finished", writer);
      }
      finally
      {
        rwl.ExitWriteLock();
      }
    }

    static void Main()
```

```
    {
      var taskFactory = new TaskFactory(TaskCreationOptions.LongRunning,
        TaskContinuationOptions.None);
      var tasks = new Task[6];
      tasks[0] = taskFactory.StartNew(WriterMethod, 1);
      tasks[1] = taskFactory.StartNew(ReaderMethod, 1);
      tasks[2] = taskFactory.StartNew(ReaderMethod, 2);
      tasks[3] = taskFactory.StartNew(WriterMethod, 2);
      tasks[4] = taskFactory.StartNew(ReaderMethod, 3);
      tasks[5] = taskFactory.StartNew(ReaderMethod, 4);

      for (int i = 0; i < 6; i++)
      {
        tasks[i].Wait();
      }
    }
  }
}
```

Running the application, the following shows that the first writer gets the lock first. The second writer and all readers need to wait. Next, the readers can work concurrently, while the second writer still waits for the resource:

```
Writer 1 acquired the lock
Writer 2 waiting for the write lock
current reader count: 0
Writer 2 waiting for the write lock
current reader count: 0
Writer 2 waiting for the write lock
current reader count: 0
Writer 2 waiting for the write lock
current reader count: 0
Writer 1 finished
reader 4, loop: 0, item: 1
reader 1, loop: 0, item: 1
Writer 2 waiting for the write lock
current reader count: 4
reader 2, loop: 0, item: 1
reader 3, loop: 0, item: 1
reader 4, loop: 1, item: 2
reader 1, loop: 1, item: 2
reader 3, loop: 1, item: 2
reader 2, loop: 1, item: 2
Writer 2 waiting for the write lock
current reader count: 4
reader 4, loop: 2, item: 3
reader 1, loop: 2, item: 3
reader 2, loop: 2, item: 3
reader 3, loop: 2, item: 3
Writer 2 waiting for the write lock
current reader count: 4
reader 4, loop: 3, item: 4
reader 1, loop: 3, item: 4
reader 2, loop: 3, item: 4
reader 3, loop: 3, item: 4
reader 4, loop: 4, item: 5
reader 1, loop: 4, item: 5
Writer 2 waiting for the write lock
current reader count: 4
reader 2, loop: 4, item: 5
reader 3, loop: 4, item: 5
```

```
reader 4, loop: 5, item: 6
reader 1, loop: 5, item: 6
reader 2, loop: 5, item: 6
reader 3, loop: 5, item: 6
Writer 2 waiting for the write lock
current reader count: 4
Writer 2 acquired the lock
Writer 2 finished
```

TIMERS

The .NET Framework offers several `Timer` classes that can be used to invoke a method after a given time interval. The following table lists the `Timer` classes and their namespaces, as well as their functionality:

NAMESPACE	DESCRIPTION
System.Threading	The `Timer` class from the `System.Threading` namespace offers core functionality. In the constructor, you can pass a delegate that should be invoked at the time interval specified.
System.Timers	The `Timer` class from the `System.Timers` namespace is a component, because it derives from the `Component` base class. Therefore, you can drag-and-drop it from the toolbox to the design surface of a server application such as a Windows service. This `Timer` class uses `System.Threading.Timer` but provides an event-based mechanism instead of a delegate.
System.Windows.Forms	With the `Timer` classes from the namespaces `System.Threading` and `System.Timers`, the callback or event methods are invoked from a different thread than the calling thread. Windows Forms controls are bound to the creator thread. Calling back into this thread is done by the `Timer` class from the `System.Windows.Forms` namespace.
System.Web.UI	The `Timer` from this namespace is an AJAX Extension that can be used with web pages.
System.Windows.Threading	The `DispatcherTimer` class from the `System.Windows.Threading` namespace is used by WPF applications. `DispatcherTimer` runs on the UI thread.

Using the `System.Threading.Timer` class, you can pass the method to be invoked as the first parameter in the constructor. This method must fulfill the requirements of the `TimerCallback` delegate, which defines a `void` return type and an `object` parameter. With the second parameter, you can pass any object, which is then received with the object argument in the callback method. For example, you can pass an `Event` object to signal the caller. The third parameter specifies the time span during which the callback should be invoked the first time. With the last parameter, you specify the repeating interval for the callback. If the timer should fire only once, set the fourth parameter to the value –1.

If the time interval should be changed after creating the `Timer` object, you can pass new values with the `Change` method (code file `TimerSample/Program.cs`):

```
private static void ThreadingTimer()
{
  var t1 = new System.Threading.Timer(TimeAction, null,
    TimeSpan.FromSeconds(2), TimeSpan.FromSeconds(3));

  Thread.Sleep(15000);

  t1.Dispose();
```

```
    }

    static void TimeAction(object o)
    {
        Console.WriteLine("System.Threading.Timer {0:T}", DateTime.Now);
    }
```

The constructor of the `Timer` class from the `System.Timers` namespace requires only a time interval. The method that should be invoked after the interval is specified by the `Elapsed` event. This event requires a delegate of type `ElapsedEventHandler`, which requires `object` and `ElapsedEventArgs` parameters, as shown in the following example with the `TimeAction` method. The `AutoReset` property specifies whether the timer should be fired repeatedly. If you set this property to `false`, the event is fired only once. Calling the `Start` method enables the timer to fire the events. Instead of calling the `Start` method, you can set the `Enabled` property to `true`. Behind the scenes, `Start` does nothing else. The `Stop` method sets the `Enabled` property to `false` to stop the timer:

```
    private static void TimersTimer()
    {
        var t1 = new System.Timers.Timer(1000);
        t1.AutoReset = true;
        t1.Elapsed += TimeAction;
        t1.Start();
        Thread.Sleep(10000);
        t1.Stop();

        t1.Dispose();
    }

    static void TimeAction(object sender, System.Timers.ElapsedEventArgs e)
    {
        Console.WriteLine("System.Timers.Timer {0:T}", e.SignalTime );
    }
```

DATA FLOW

The `Parallel` and `Task` classes, and Parallel LINQ, help a lot with data parallelism. However, these classes do not directly support dealing with data flow, transform data in parallel. For this *Task Parallel Library Data Flow*, or *TPL Data Flow*, can be used. This library must be installed as a NuGet package. This package includes the assembly `System.Threading.Tasks.DataFlow` with the namespace `System.Threading.Tasks.DataFlow`.

> **NOTE** *Installation of NuGet Packages is discussed in Chapter 17, "Visual Studio."*

Using an Action Block

The heart of TPL Data Flow are data blocks. These blocks can act as a source to offer some data or a target to receive data, or both. Let's start with a simple example, a data block that receives some data and writes it to the console. The following code snippet defines an `ActionBlock` that receives a string and writes information to the console. The `Main` method reads user input within a `while` loop, and posts every string read to the `ActionBlock` by calling the `Post` method. The `Post` method posts an item to the `ActionBlock`, which deals with the message asynchronously, writing the information to the console:

```
static void Main()
{
  var processInput = new ActionBlock<string>(s =>
    {
      Console.WriteLine("user input: {0}", s);
    });

  bool exit = false;
  while (!exit)
  {
    string input = Console.ReadLine();
    if (string.Compare(input, "exit", ignoreCase: true) == 0)
    {
      exit = true;
    }
    else
    {
      processInput.Post(input);
    }
  }
}
```

Source and Target Blocks

When the method assigned to the `ActionBlock` from the previous example executes, the `ActionBlock` uses a task to do the execution in parallel. You could verify this by checking the task and thread identifiers, and writing these to the console. Every block implements the interface `IDataflowBlock`, which contains the property `Completion`, which returns a `Task`, and the methods `Complete` and `Fault`. Invoking the `Complete` method, the block no longer accepts any input or produces any more output. Invoking the `Fault` method puts the block into a faulting state.

As mentioned earlier, a block can be either a source or a target, or both. In this case, the `ActionBlock` is a target block and thus implements the interface `ITargetBlock`. `ITargetBlock` derives from `IDataflowBlock` and defines the `OfferMessage` method, in addition to the members of the `IDataBlock` interface. `OfferMessage` sends a message that can be consumed by the block. An easier to use API than `OfferMessage` is the `Post` method, which is implemented as an extension method for the `ITargetBlock` interface. The `Post` method was also used by the sample application.

The `ISourceBlock` interface is implemented by blocks that can act as a data source. `ISourceBlock` offers methods in addition to the members of the `IDataBlock` interface to link to a target block and to consume messages.

The `BufferBlock` acts both as a source and a target, implementing both `ISourceBlock` and `ITargetBlock`. In the next example, this `BufferBlock` is used to both post messages and receive messages:

```
static BufferBlock<string> buffer = new BufferBlock<string>();
```

The `Producer` method reads strings from the console and writes them to the `BufferBlock` by invoking the `Post` method:

```
static void Producer()
{
  bool exit = false;
  while (!exit)
  {
    string input = Console.ReadLine();
    if (string.Compare(input, "exit", ignoreCase: true) == 0)
    {
      exit = true;
```

```
      }
      else
      {
        buffer.Post(input);
      }
    }
  }
```

The `Consumer` method contains a loop to receive data from the `BufferBlock` by invoking the `ReceiveAsync` method. `ReceiveAsync` is an extension method for the `ISourceBlock` interface:

```
static async void Consumer()
{
  while (true)
  {
    string data = await buffer.ReceiveAsync();
    Console.WriteLine("user input: {0}", data);
  }
}
```

Now, you just need to start the producer and consumer. This is done with two independent tasks in the `Main` method:

```
static void Main()
{
  Task t1 = Task.Run(() => Producer());
  Task t2 = Task.Run(() => Consumer());
  Task.WaitAll(t1, t2);
}
```

Running the application, the producer task reads data from the console, and the consumer receives the data to write it to the console.

Connecting Blocks

This section creates a pipeline by connecting multiple blocks. First, three methods are created that will be used by the blocks. The `GetFileNames` method receives a directory path and yields the filenames that end with the `.cs` extension:

```
static IEnumerable<string> GetFileNames(string path)
{
  foreach (var fileName in Directory.EnumerateFiles(path, "*.cs"))
  {
    yield return fileName;
  }
}
```

The `LoadLines` method receives a list of filenames and yields every line of the files:

```
static IEnumerable<string> LoadLines(IEnumerable<string> fileNames)
{
  foreach (var fileName in fileNames)
  {
    using (FileStream stream = File.OpenRead(fileName))
    {
      var reader = new StreamReader(stream);
      string line = null;
      while ((line = reader.ReadLine()) != null)
      {
        // Console.WriteLine("LoadLines {0}", line);
```

```
        yield return line;
      }
    }
  }
}
```

The third method, GetWords, receives the lines collection and splits it up line by line to yield return a list of words:

```
static IEnumerable<string> GetWords(IEnumerable<string> lines)
{
  foreach (var line in lines)
  {
    string[] words = line.Split(' ', ';', '(', ')', '{', '}', '.', ',');
    foreach (var word in words)
    {
      if (!string.IsNullOrEmpty(word))
        yield return word;
    }
  }
}
```

To create the pipeline, the SetupPipeline method creates three TransformBlock objects. The Transform Block is a source and target block that transforms the source by using a delegate. The first TransformBlock is declared to transform a string to IEnumerable<string>. The transformation is done by the GetFileNames method that is invoked within the Lambda expression passed to the constructor of the first block. Similarly, the next two TransformBlock objects are used to invoke the LoadLines and GetWords methods:

```
static ITargetBlock<string> SetupPipeline()
{
  var fileNamesForPath = new TransformBlock<string, IEnumerable<string>>(
    path =>
    {
      return GetFileNames(path);
    });

  var lines = new TransformBlock<IEnumerable<string>, IEnumerable<string>>(
    fileNames =>
    {
      return LoadLines(fileNames);
    });

  var words = new TransformBlock<IEnumerable<string>, IEnumerable<string>>(
    lines2 =>
      {
        return GetWords(lines2);
      });
```

The last block defined is an ActionBlock. This block has been used before and is just a target block to receive data:

```
  var display = new ActionBlock<IEnumerable<string>>(
    coll =>
    {
      foreach (var s in coll)
      {
        Console.WriteLine(s);
      }
    });
```

Finally, the blocks are connected to each other. `fileNamesForPath` is linked to the `lines` block. The result from `fileNamesForPath` is passed to the `lines` block. The `lines` block links to the `words` block, and the `words` block links to the `display` block. Last, the block to start the pipeline is returned:

```
        fileNamesForPath.LinkTo(lines);
        lines.LinkTo(words);
        words.LinkTo(display);

        return fileNamesForPath;
    }
```

The `Main` method now just needs to kick off the pipeline. Invoking the `Post` method to pass a directory, the pipeline starts and finally writes words from the C# source code to the console. Here, it would be possible to start multiple requests for the pipeline, passing more than one directory, and doing these tasks in parallel:

```
    static void Main()
    {
      var target = SetupPipeline();
      target.Post("../..");
      Console.ReadLine();
    }
```

With this brief introduction to the TPL Data Flow library, you've seen the principal way to work with this technology. This library offers a lot more functionality, such as different blocks that deal with data differently. The `BroadcastBlock` allows passing the input source to multiple targets (e.g., writing data to a file and displaying it), the `JoinBlock` joins multiple sources to one target, and the `BatchBlock` batches input into arrays. Using `DataflowBlockOptions` options allows configuration of a block, such as the maximum number of items that are processed within a single task, and passing a cancellation token that allows canceling a pipeline. With links, messages can be filtered to pass only specified messages, and you can configure not passing messages to the end of a target source but instead to the beginning for faster processing of the last messages.

SUMMARY

This chapter explored how to code applications that use multiple threads by using the `System.Threading` namespace, and multiple tasks by using the `System.Threading.Tasks` namespace. Using multithreading in your applications takes careful planning. Too many threads can cause resource issues, and not enough threads can cause your application to be sluggish and perform poorly. With tasks, you get an abstraction to threads. This abstraction helps you avoid creating too many threads because threads are reused from a pool.

You've seen various ways to create multiple tasks, such as the `Parallel` class, which offers both task and data parallelism with `Parallel.Invoke`, `Parallel.ForEach`, and `Parallel.For`. With the `Task` class, you've seen how to gain more control over parallel programming. Tasks can run synchronously in the calling thread, using a thread from a thread pool, and a separate new thread can be created. Tasks also offer a hierarchical model that enables the creation of child tasks, also providing a way to cancel a complete hierarchy.

The cancellation framework offers a standard mechanism that can be used in the same manner with different classes to cancel a task early.

You've seen what's used behind the scenes with tasks, particularly the `ThreadPool` class and the `Thread` class, which you can also use on your own. The `Thread` class gives you control over threads to define foreground and background behavior, and to assign priorities to threads.

The System.Threading namespace in the .NET Framework provides multiple ways to manipulate threads, although this does not mean that the .NET Framework handles all the difficult tasks of multithreading for you. You need to consider the thread priority and synchronization issues described in this chapter, and code for them appropriately in your C# applications as demonstrated. You also looked at the problems associated with deadlocks and race conditions. Just keep in mind that if you are going to use multithreading in your C# applications, careful planning must be a major part of your efforts.

Here are some final guidelines regarding threading:

➤ Try to keep synchronization requirements to a minimum. Synchronization is complex and blocks threads. You can avoid it if you try to avoid sharing state. Of course, this is not always possible.

➤ Static members of a class should be thread-safe. Usually, this is the case with classes in the .NET Framework.

➤ Instance state does not need to be thread-safe. For best performance, synchronization is best used outside of the class where it is needed, and not with every member of the class. Instance members of .NET Framework classes usually are not thread-safe. In the MSDN library, you can find this information documented for every class of the .NET Framework in the "Thread Safety" section.

The next chapter gives information on another core .NET topic: security.

22

Security

WHAT'S IN THIS CHAPTER?

➤ Authentication and authorization

➤ Cryptography

➤ Access control to resources

➤ Code access security

WROX.COM CODE DOWNLOADS FOR THIS CHAPTER

The wrox.com code downloads for this chapter are found at `http://www.wrox.com/remtitle.cgi?isbn=1118314425` on the Download Code tab. The code for this chapter is divided into the following major examples:

➤ Authentication Samples

    ➤ Windows Principal

    ➤ Role Based Security

    ➤ Application Services

➤ Encryption Samples

    ➤ Signature

    ➤ Secure Transfer

➤ File Access Control

➤ Code Access Security

    ➤ Permissions

INTRODUCTION

Security has several key elements that you need to consider in order to make your applications secure. The primary one, of course, is the user of the application. Is the user actually the person authorized to access the application, or someone posing as the user? How can this user be trusted? As you will see in this chapter, ensuring the security of an application in regard of the user is a two-part process: First, users need to be authenticated, and then they need to be authorized to verify that they are allowed to use the requested resources.

What about data that is stored or sent across the network? Is it possible for someone to access this data, for example, by using a network sniffer? Encryption of data is important in this regard. Some technologies, such as Windows Communication Foundation (WCF) provide encryption capabilities by simple configuration, so you can see what's done behind the scenes.

Yet another aspect is the application itself. If the application is hosted by a web provider, how is the application restricted from doing harm to the server?

This chapter explores the features available in .NET to help you manage security, demonstrating how .NET protects you from malicious code, how to administer security policies, and how to access the security subsystem programmatically.

AUTHENTICATION AND AUTHORIZATION

Two fundamental pillars of security are authentication and authorization. *Authentication* is the process of identifying the user, and *authorization* occurs afterward to verify that the identified user is allowed to access a specific resource.

Identity and Principal

You can identify the user running the application by using an *identity*. The WindowsIdentity class represents a Windows user. If you don't identify the user with a Windows account, you can use other classes that implement the interface IIdentity. With this interface you have access to the name of the user, information about whether the user is authenticated, and the authentication type.

A *principal* is an object that contains the identity of the user and the roles to which the user belongs. The interface IPrincipal defines the property Identity, which returns an IIdentity object, and the method IsInRole with which you can verify that the user is a member of a specific role. A *role* is a collection of users who have the same security permissions, and it is the unit of administration for users. Roles can be Windows groups or just a collection of strings that you define.

The principal classes available with .NET are WindowsPrincipal, GenericPrincipal, and RolePrinciplal. Beginning with .NET 4.5, these principal types derive from the base class ClaimsPrinicipal. You can also create a custom principal class that implements the interface IPrincipal or derives from ClaimsPrincipal.

The following example creates a console application that provides access to the principal in an application that, in turn, enables you to access the underlying Windows account. You need to import the System .Security.Principal and System.Security.Claims namespaces. First, you must specify that .NET should automatically hook up the principal with the underlying Windows account. This must be done because .NET, by default, only populates the principal with a generic principal. You can do it like this (code file WindowsPrincipal/Program.cs):

```
using System;
using System.Security.Claims;
using System.Security.Principal;

namespace Wrox.ProCSharp.Security
{
  class Program
  {
    static void Main()
    {
      AppDomain.CurrentDomain.SetPrincipalPolicy(
          PrincipalPolicy.WindowsPrincipal);
```

The `SetPrincipalPolicy` method specifies that the principal in the current thread should hold a `WindowsIdentity` object. Other options that can be specified with `SetPrinicpalPolicy` are `NoPrincipal` and `UnauthenticatedPrincipal`. All identity classes, such as `WindowsIdentity`, implement the `IIdentity` interface, which contains three properties—`AuthenticationType`, `IsAuthenticated`, and `Name`—for all derived identity classes to implement.

Add the following code to access the principal's properties:

```
var principal = WindowsPrincipal.Current as WindowsPrincipal;
var identity = principal.Identity as WindowsIdentity;
Console.WriteLine("IdentityType: {0}", identity.ToString());
Console.WriteLine("Name: {0}", identity.Name);
Console.WriteLine("'Users'?: {0} ",
    principal.IsInRole(WindowsBuiltInRole.User));
Console.WriteLine("'Administrators'? {0}",
    principal.IsInRole(WindowsBuiltInRole.Administrator));
Console.WriteLine("Authenticated: {0}", identity.IsAuthenticated);
Console.WriteLine("AuthType: {0}", identity.AuthenticationType);
Console.WriteLine("Anonymous? {0}", identity.IsAnonymous);
Console.WriteLine("Token: {0}", identity.Token);
```

The output from this console application looks similar to the following; it varies according to your machine's configuration and the roles associated with the account under which you are signed in. Here, the account is a Windows Live account mapped to the Windows 8 account, and thus the `AuthType` is `LiveSSP`:

```
IdentityType: System.Security.Principal.WindowsIdentity
Name: THEOTHERSIDE\Christian
'Users'?: True
'Administrators'? False
Authenticated: True
AuthType: LiveSSP
Anonymous? False
Token: 488
```

It is enormously beneficial to be able to easily access details about the current users and their roles. With this information, you can make decisions about what actions should be permitted or denied. The ability to make use of roles and Windows user groups provides the added benefit that administration can be handled using standard user administration tools, and you can usually avoid altering the code when user roles change. The following section looks at roles in more detail.

Roles

Role-based security is especially useful when access to resources is an issue. A primary example is the finance industry, in which employees' roles define what information they can access and what actions they can perform.

Role-based security is also ideal for use in conjunction with Windows accounts, or a custom user directory to manage access to web-based resources. For example, a web site could restrict access to its content until a user registers with the site, and then additionally provide access to special content only if the user is a paying subscriber. In many ways, ASP.NET makes role-based security easier because much of the code is based on the server.

For example, to implement a Web service that requires authentication, you could use the account subsystem of Windows and write the web method in such a way that it ensures that the user is a member of a specific Windows user group before allowing access to the method's functionality.

Imagine a scenario with an intranet application that relies on Windows accounts. The system has a group called `Manager` and a group called `Assistant`; users are assigned to these groups according to their role within the organization. Suppose the application contains a feature that displays information about employees that should be accessed only by users in the Manager group. You can easily use code that checks whether the current user is a member of the Manager group and therefore permitted or denied access.

However, if you decide later to rearrange the account groups and introduce a group called Personnel that also has access to employee details, you will have a problem. You will need to go through all the code and update it to include rules for this new group.

A better solution would be to create a permission called something like ReadEmployeeDetails and assign it to groups where necessary. If the code applies a check for the ReadEmployeeDetails permission, updating the application to allow those in the Personnel group access to employee details is simply a matter of creating the group, placing the users in it, and assigning the ReadEmployeeDetails permission.

Declarative Role-Based Security

Just as with code access security, you can implement role-based security requests ("the user must be in the Administrators group") using imperative requests by calling the IsInRole() method from the IPrincipal interface, or using attributes. You can state permission requirements declaratively at the class or method level using the PrincipalPermission attribute (code file RoleBasedSecurity/Program.cs):

```csharp
using System;
using System.Security;
using System.Security.Principal;
using System.Security.Permissions;

namespace Wrox.ProCSharp.Security
{
  class Program
  {
    static void Main()
    {
      AppDomain.CurrentDomain.SetPrincipalPolicy(
          PrincipalPolicy.WindowsPrincipal);
      try
      {
        ShowMessage();
      }
      catch (SecurityException exception)
      {
        Console.WriteLine("Security exception caught ({0})",
                          exception.Message);
        Console.WriteLine("The current principal must be in the local" +
                          "Users group");
      }
    }

    [PrincipalPermission(SecurityAction.Demand, Role = "BUILTIN\\Users")]
    static void ShowMessage()
    {
      Console.WriteLine("The current principal is logged in locally ");
      Console.WriteLine("(member of the local Users group)");
    }
  }
}
```

The ShowMessage method will throw an exception unless you execute the application in the context of a user in the Windows local Users group. For a web application, the account under which the ASP.NET code is running must be in the group, although in a real-world scenario you would certainly avoid adding this account to the administrators group!

If you run the preceding code using an account in the local Users group, the output will look like this:

```
The current principal is logged in locally
(member of the local Users group)
```

Claims

Instead of using roles, claims can be used to access information about a user. Claims are associated with an entity and describe the capabilities of the entity. An entity is usually a user, but can be an application as well. Capabilities describe what the entity is allowed to do. This way, claims are much more flexible than the role model is.

With .NET 4.5, all the principal classes derive from the base class `ClaimsPrincipal`. This way, it's possible to access claims from users with the `Claims` property of a principal object. Using the following code snippet, information about all claims is written to the console:

```
Console.WriteLine();
Console.WriteLine("Claims");
foreach (var claim in principal.Claims)
{
  Console.WriteLine("Subject: {0}", claim.Subject);
  Console.WriteLine("Issuer: {0}", claim.Issuer);
  Console.WriteLine("Type: {0}", claim.Type);
  Console.WriteLine("Value type: {0}", claim.ValueType);
  Console.WriteLine("Value: {0}", claim.Value);
  foreach (var prop in claim.Properties)
  {
    Console.WriteLine("\tProperty: {0} {1}", prop.Key, prop.Value);
  }
  Console.WriteLine();
}
```

Here is an extract of the claims from the Windows Live account, which provides information about the name, the primary ID, and the group identifiers:

```
Claims
Subject: System.Security.Principal.WindowsIdentity
Issuer: AD AUTHORITY
Type: http://schemas.xmlsoap.org/ws/2005/05/identity/claims/name
Value type: http://www.w3.org/2001/XMLSchema#string
Value: THEOTHERSIDE\Christian

Subject: System.Security.Principal.WindowsIdentity
Issuer: AD AUTHORITY
Type: http://schemas.microsoft.com/ws/2008/06/identity/claims/primarysid
Value type: http://www.w3.org/2001/XMLSchema#string
Value: S-1-5-21-1413171500-312083878-1364686672-1001
        Property: http://schemas.microsoft.com/ws/2008/06/identity/claims/
        windowssubauthority NTAuthority

Subject: System.Security.Principal.WindowsIdentity
Issuer: AD AUTHORITY
Type: http://schemas.microsoft.com/ws/2008/06/identity/claims/groupsid
Value type: http://www.w3.org/2001/XMLSchema#string
Value: S-1-1-0
        Property: http://schemas.microsoft.com/ws/2008/06/identity/claims/
        windowssubauthority WorldAuthority

Subject: System.Security.Principal.WindowsIdentity
Issuer: AD AUTHORITY
Type: http://schemas.microsoft.com/ws/2008/06/identity/claims/groupsid
```

```
Value type: http://www.w3.org/2001/XMLSchema#string
Value: S-1-5-21-1413171500-312083878-1364686672-1008
        Property: http://schemas.microsoft.com/ws/2008/06/identity/claims/
        windowssubauthority NTAuthority
```

...

Client Application Services

Visual Studio makes it easy to use authentication services that were previously built for ASP.NET web applications. With this service, it is possible to use the same authentication mechanism with both Windows and web applications. This is a provider model that is primarily based on the classes `Membership` and `Roles` in the namespace `System.Web.Security`. With the `Membership` class you can validate, create, delete, and find users; change the password; and do other things related to users. With the `Roles` class you can add and delete roles, get the roles for a user, and change roles for a user.

Where the roles and users are stored depends on the provider. The `ActiveDirectoryMembershipProvider` accesses users and roles in the Active Directory; the `SqlMembershipProvider` uses a SQL Server database. With .NET 4.5 these providers exist for client application services `ClientFormsAuthenticationMembershipProvider` and `ClientWindowsAuthenticationMembershipProvider`.

In the next section, you use client application services with Forms authentication. To do this, first you need to start an application server, and then you can use this service from Windows Forms or Windows Presentation Foundation (WPF).

Application Services

To use client application services, you can create a WCF service project that offers application services. The project needs a membership provider. You can use an existing one, but you can also easily create a custom provider. The following code defines the class `SampleMembershipProvider`, which is derived from the base class `MembershipProvider`, which is defined in the namespace `System.Web.Security` in the assembly `System.Web.ApplicationServices`. You must override all abstract methods from the base class. For login, the only implementation needed is the method `ValidateUser`. All other methods can throw a `NotSupportedException`, as shown with the property `ApplicationName`. The sample code here uses a `Dictionary<string, string>` that contains usernames and passwords. Of course, you can change it to your own implementation—for example, to read a username and password from the database (code file `AppServices/SampleMembershipProvider.cs`).

```csharp
using System;
using System.Collections.Generic;
using System.Collections.Specialized;
using System.Web.Security;

namespace Wrox.ProCSharp.Security
{
  public class SampleMembershipProvider: MembershipProvider
  {
    private Dictionary<string, string> users =
        new Dictionary<string, string>();
    internal static string ManagerUserName = "Manager".ToLowerInvariant();
    internal static string EmployeeUserName = "Employee".ToLowerInvariant();

    public override void Initialize(string name, NameValueCollection config)
    {
      users.Add(ManagerUserName, "secret@Pa$$w0rd");
      users.Add(EmployeeUserName, "s0me@Secret");

      base.Initialize(name, config);
```

```
    }

    public override string ApplicationName
    {
      get
      {
        throw new NotImplementedException();
      }
      set
      {
        throw new NotImplementedException();
      }
    }

    // override abstract Membership members
    // ...

    public override bool ValidateUser(string username, string password)
    {
      if (users.ContainsKey(username.ToLowerInvariant()))
      {
        return password.Equals(users[username.ToLowerInvariant()]);
      }
      return false;
    }
  }
}
```

When using roles, you also need to implement a role provider. The class SampleRoleProvider derives from the base class RoleProvider and implements the methods GetRolesForUser and IsUserInRole (code AppServices/SampleRoleProvider.cs):

```
using System;
using System.Collections.Specialized;
using System.Web.Security;

namespace Wrox.ProCSharp.Security
{
  public class SampleRoleProvider: RoleProvider
  {
    internal static string ManagerRoleName = "Manager".ToLowerInvariant();
    internal static string EmployeeRoleName = "Employee".ToLowerInvariant();

    public override void Initialize(string name, NameValueCollection config)
    {
      base.Initialize(name, config);
    }

    public override void AddUsersToRoles(string[] usernames,
        string[] roleNames)
    {
      throw new NotImplementedException();
    }

    // override abstract RoleProvider members
    // ...

    public override string[] GetRolesForUser(string username)
    {
      if (string.Compare(username, SampleMembershipProvider.ManagerUserName,
          true) == 0)
      {
        return new string[] { ManagerRoleName };
```

```
      }
      else if (string.Compare(username,
          SampleMembershipProvider.EmployeeUserName, true) == 0)
      {
        return new string[] { EmployeeRoleName };
      }
      else
      {
        return new string[0];
      }
    }

    public override bool IsUserInRole(string username, string roleName)
    {
      string[] roles = GetRolesForUser(username);
      foreach (var role in roles)
      {
        if (string.Equals(role, roleName))
        {
          return true;
        }
      }
      return false;
    }
  }
}
```

Authentication services must be configured in the `Web.config` file. On the production system, it would be useful from a security standpoint to configure SSL with the server hosting application services (config file `AppServices/web.config`):

```
<system.web.extensions>
  <scripting>
    <webServices>
      <authenticationService enabled="true" requireSSL="false"/>
      <roleService enabled="true"/>
    </webServices>
  </scripting>
</system.web.extensions>
```

Within the `<system.web>` section, the `membership` and `roleManager` elements must be configured to reference the classes that implement the membership and role provider:

```
<system.web>
  <membership defaultProvider="SampleMembershipProvider">
    <providers>
      <add name="SampleMembershipProvider"
           type="Wrox.ProCSharp.Security.SampleMembershipProvider"/>
    </providers>
  </membership>
  <roleManager enabled="true" defaultProvider="SampleRoleProvider">
    <providers>
      <add name="SampleRoleProvider"
           type="Wrox.ProCSharp.Security.SampleRoleProvider"/>
    </providers>
  </roleManager>
```

For debugging, you can assign a port number and virtual path by selecting the Web tab of project properties. The sample application uses the port `55555` and the virtual path `/AppServices`. If you use different values, you need to change the configuration of the client application accordingly.

Now the application service can be used from a client application.

Client Application

With the client application, WPF is used. Visual Studio has a project setting named Services that enables the use of client application services. Here, you can set Forms authentication and the location of the authentication and roles service to the address defined previously: http://localhost:55555/AppServices. This project configuration merely references the assemblies System.Web and System.Web.Extensions, and changes the application's configuration file to configure membership and role providers that use the classes ClientAuthenticationMembershipProvider and ClientRoleProvider and the address of the Web service used by these providers (config file AuthenticationServices/App.config):

```xml
<?xml version="1.0" encoding="utf-8"?>
<configuration>
  <system.web>
    <membership defaultProvider="ClientAuthenticationMembershipProvider">
      <providers>
        <add name="ClientAuthenticationMembershipProvider"
            type="System.Web.ClientServices.Providers.
            ClientFormsAuthenticationMembershipProvider,
            System.Web.Extensions, Version=4.0.0.0, Culture=neutral,
            PublicKeyToken=31bf3856ad364e35" serviceUri=
"http://localhost:55555/AppServices/Authentication_JSON_AppService.axd" />
      </providers>
    </membership>
    <roleManager defaultProvider="ClientRoleProvider" enabled="true">
      <providers>
        <add name="ClientRoleProvider"
            type="System.Web.ClientServices.Providers.ClientRoleProvider,
            System.Web.Extensions, Version=4.0.0.0, Culture=neutral,
            PublicKeyToken=31bf3856ad364e35" serviceUri=
            "http://localhost:55555/AppServices/Role_JSON_AppService.axd"
            cacheTimeout="86400" />
      </providers>
    </roleManager>
  </system.web>
</configuration>
```

The Windows application just uses Label, TextBox, PasswordBox, and Button controls, as shown in Figure 22-1. The label with the content "User Validated" is displayed only when the logon is successful.

The handler of the Button.Click event invokes the ValidateUser method of the Membership class. For the membership API, the ClientAuthenticationMembershipProvider is configured. This provider invokes the Web service and calls the method ValidateUser of the SampleMembershipProvider class to verify a successful logon. With success, the label labelValidatedInfo is made visible; otherwise, a message box is displayed (code file AuthenticationServices/MainWindow.xaml.cs):

FIGURE 22-1

```csharp
private void OnLogin(object sender, RoutedEventArgs e)
{
  try
  {
```

```
      if (Membership.ValidateUser(textUsername.Text,
        textPassword.Password))
    {
      // user validated!
      labelValidatedInfo.Visibility = Visibility.Visible;
    }
    else
    {
      MessageBox.Show("Username or password not valid",
          "Client Authentication Services", MessageBoxButton.OK,
          MessageBoxImage.Warning);
    }
  }
  catch (WebException ex)
  {
    MessageBox.Show(ex.Message, "Client Application Services",
        MessageBoxButton.OK, MessageBoxImage.Error);
  }
}
```

ENCRYPTION

Confidential data should be secured so that it cannot be read by unprivileged users. This is valid both for data that is sent across the network, or stored data. You can encrypt such data with symmetric or asymmetric encryption keys.

With a symmetric key, the same key can be used for encryption and decryption. With asymmetric encryption, different keys are used for encryption and decryption: a public key and a private key. Something encrypted using a public key can be decrypted with the corresponding private key. This also works the other way around: Something encrypted using a private key can be decrypted by using the corresponding public key, but not the private key.

Public and private keys are always created as a pair. The public key can be made available to everybody, and even put on a web site, but the private key must be safely locked away. Following are some examples that demonstrate how public and private keys are used for encryption.

If Alice sends a message to Bob (see Figure 22-2), and she wants to ensure that no one other than Bob can read the message, she uses Bob's public key. The message is encrypted using Bob's public key. Bob opens the

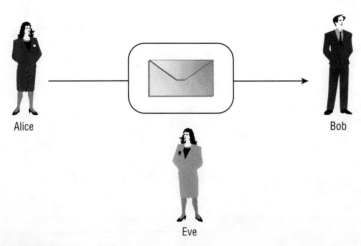

Alice

Bob

Eve

FIGURE 22-2

message and can decrypt it using his secretly stored private key. This key exchange guarantees that no one but Bob can read Alice's message.

There is one problem, however: Bob can't be sure that the mail comes from Alice. Eve can use Bob's public key to encrypt messages sent to Bob and pretend to be Alice. We can extend this principle using public/ private keys. Let's start again with Alice sending a message to Bob. Before Alice encrypts the message using Bob's public key, she adds her signature and encrypts the signature using her own private key. Then she encrypts the mail using Bob's public key. Therefore, it is guaranteed that no one other than Bob can read the message. When Bob decrypts it, he detects an encrypted signature. The signature can be decrypted using Alice's public key. For Bob, it is not a problem to access Alice's public key because the key is public. After decrypting the signature, Bob can be sure that it was Alice who sent the message.

The encryption and decryption algorithms using symmetric keys are a lot faster than those using asymmetric keys. The problem with symmetric keys is that the keys must be exchanged in a safe manner. With network communication, one way to do this is by using asymmetric keys first for the key exchange and then symmetric keys for encryption of the data that is sent across the wire.

The .NET Framework contains classes for encryption in the namespace `System.Security.Cryptography`. Several symmetric and asymmetric algorithms are implemented. You can find algorithm classes for many different purposes. Some of the classes have a `Cng` prefix or suffix. CNG is short for *Cryptography Next Generation*, which is a newer version of the native Crypto API. This API makes it possible to write a program independently of the algorithm by using a provider-based model.

The following table lists encryption classes from the namespace `System.Security.Cryptography` and their purpose. The classes without a `Cng`, `Managed`, or `CryptoServiceProvider` suffix are abstract base classes, such as `MD5`. The `Managed` suffix means that this algorithm is implemented with managed code; other classes might wrap native Windows API calls. The suffix `CryptoServiceProvider` is used with classes that implement the abstract base class. The `Cng` suffix is used with classes that make use of the new Cryptography CNG API.

CATEGORY	CLASSES	DESCRIPTION
Hash	MD5, MD5Cng SHA1, SHA1Managed, SHA1Cng, SHA256, SHA256Managed, SHA256Cng, SHA384, SHA384Managed, SHA384Cng, SHA512, SHA512Managed, SHA512Cng, RIPEMD160, RIPEMD160Managed	The purpose of hash algorithms is to create a fixed-length hash value from binary strings of arbitrary length. These algorithms are used with digital signatures and for data integrity. If the same binary string is hashed again, the same hash result is returned. MD5 (Message Digest Algorithm 5), developed at RSA Laboratories, is faster than SHA1. SHA1 is stronger against brute force attacks. The SHA algorithms were designed by the National Security Agency (NSA). MD5 uses a 128-bit hash size; SHA1 uses 160 bits. The other SHA algorithms contain the hash size in the name. SHA512 is the strongest of these algorithms, with a hash size of 512 bits; it is also the slowest. RIPEDM160 uses a hash size of 160 bits; it is meant to be a replacement for 128-bit MD4 and MD5. RIPEDM was developed from an EU project named RIPE (Race Integrity Primitives Evaluation).

(continues)

(continued)

CATEGORY	CLASSES	DESCRIPTION
Symmetric	DES, DESCryptoServiceProvider, TripleDES TripleDESCryptoServiceProvider, Aes, AesCryptoServiceProvider, AesManaged, RC2, RC2CryptoServiceProvider, Rijandel, RijandelManaged	Symmetric key algorithms use the same key for encryption and decryption of data. Data Encryption Standard (DES) is now considered insecure because it uses only 56 bits for the key size and can be broken in less than 24 hours. Triple-DES is the successor to DES and has a key length of 168 bits, but the effective security it provides is only 112-bit. Advanced Encryption Standard (AES) has a key size of 128, 192, or 256 bits. Rijandel is very similar to AES but offers more key size options. AES is an encryption standard adopted by the U.S. government.
Asymmetric	DSA, DSACryptoServiceProvider, ECDsa, ECDsaCng ECDiffieHellman, ECDiffieHellmanCng RSA, RSACryptoServiceProvider	Asymmetric algorithms use different keys for encryption and decryption. The Rivest, Shamir, Adleman (RSA) algorithm was the first one used for signing as well as encryption. This algorithm is widely used in e-commerce protocols. Digital Signature Algorithm (DSA) is a United States Federal Government standard for digital signatures. Elliptic Curve DSA (ECDSA) and EC Diffie-Hellman use algorithms based on elliptic curve groups. These algorithms are more secure, with shorter key sizes. For example, having a key size of 1024 bits for DSA is similar in security to 160 bits for ECDSA. As a result, ECDSA is much faster. EC Diffie-Hellman is an algorithm used to exchange private keys in a secure way over a public channel.

The following section includes some examples demonstrating how these algorithms can be used programmatically.

Signature

The first example demonstrates a signature using the ECDSA algorithm, described in the preceding table, for signing. Alice creates a signature that is encrypted with her private key and can be accessed using her public key. This way, it is guaranteed that the signature is from Alice.

First, take a look at the major steps in the `Main` method: Alice's keys are created, and the string `"Alice"` is signed and then verified to be the signature actually from Alice by using the public key. The message that is signed is converted to a byte array by using the `Encoding` class. To write the encrypted signature to the console, the byte array that contains the signature is converted to a string with the method `Convert` `.ToBase64String` (code file `SigningDemo/Program.cs`):

```
using System;
using System.Security.Cryptography;
using System.Text;
```

```
namespace Wrox.ProCSharp.Security
{
  class Program
  {
    internal static CngKey aliceKeySignature;
    internal static byte[] alicePubKeyBlob;

    static void Main()
    {
      CreateKeys();

      byte[] aliceData = Encoding.UTF8.GetBytes("Alice");
      byte[] aliceSignature = CreateSignature(aliceData, aliceKeySignature);
      Console.WriteLine("Alice created signature: {0}",
          Convert.ToBase64String(aliceSignature));

      if (VerifySignature(aliceData, aliceSignature, alicePubKeyBlob))
      {
        Console.WriteLine("Alice signature verified successfully");
      }
    }
```

> **WARNING** *Never convert encrypted data to a string using the* Encoding *class. The* Encoding *class verifies and converts invalid values that are not allowed with Unicode; therefore, converting the string back to a byte array yields a different result.*

CreateKeys is the method that creates a new key pair for Alice. This key pair is stored in a static field, so it can be accessed from the other methods. The Create method of CngKey gets the algorithm as an argument to define a key pair for the algorithm. With the Export method, the public key of the key pair is exported. This public key can be given to Bob for verification of the signature. Alice keeps the private key. Instead of creating a key pair with the CngKey class, you can open existing keys that are stored in the key store. Usually Alice would have a certificate containing a key pair in her private store, and the store could be accessed with CngKey.Open:

```
static void CreateKeys()
{
  aliceKeySignature = CngKey.Create(CngAlgorithm.ECDsaP256);
  alicePubKeyBlob = aliceKeySignature.Export(
      CngKeyBlobFormat.GenericPublicBlob);
}
```

With the key pair, Alice can create the signature using the ECDsaCng class. The constructor of this class receives the CngKey from Alice that contains both the public and private keys. The private key is used signing the data with the SignData method:

```
static byte[] CreateSignature(byte[] data, CngKey key)
{
  byte[] signature;
  using (var signingAlg = new ECDsaCng(key))
  {
    signature = signingAlg.SignData(data);
    signingAlg.Clear();
  }
  return signature;
}
```

To verify that the signature was really from Alice, Bob checks the signature by using the public key from Alice. The byte array containing the public key blob can be imported to a CngKey object with the static Import method. The ECDsaCng class is then used to verify the signature by invoking VerifyData:

```
static bool VerifySignature(byte[] data, byte[] signature, byte[] pubKey)
{
  bool retValue = false;
  using (CngKey key = CngKey.Import(pubKey,
      CngKeyBlobFormat.GenericPublicBlob))
  using (var signingAlg = new ECDsaCng(key))
  {
    retValue = signingAlg.VerifyData(data, signature);
    signingAlg.Clear();
  }
  return retValue;
}
  }
}
```

Key Exchange and Secure Transfer

This section uses a more-complex example to demonstrate exchanging a symmetric key for a secure transfer by using the EC Diffie-Hellman algorithm. The Main method contains the primary functionality. Alice creates an encrypted message and sends it to Bob. Before the message is created and sent, key pairs are created for Alice and Bob. Bob has access only to Alice's public key, and Alice has access only to Bob's public key (code file SecureTransfer/Program.cs):

```
using System;
using System.IO;
using System.Security.Cryptography;
using System.Text;
using System.Threading.Tasks;

namespace Wrox.ProCSharp.Security
{
  class Program
  {
    static CngKey aliceKey;
    static CngKey bobKey;
    static byte[] alicePubKeyBlob;
    static byte[] bobPubKeyBlob;

    static void Main()
    {
      Run();
      Console.ReadLine();
    }

    private async static void Run()
    {
      try
      {
        CreateKeys();
        byte[] encrytpedData = await AliceSendsData("secret message");
        await BobReceivesData(encrytpedData);
      }
      catch (Exception ex)
      {
        Console.WriteLine(ex.Message);
      }
    }
```

In the implementation of the `CreateKeys` method, keys are created to be used with the EC Diffie-Hellman 256 algorithm:

```
private static void CreateKeys()
{
  aliceKey = CngKey.Create(CngAlgorithm.ECDiffieHellmanP256);
  bobKey = CngKey.Create(CngAlgorithm.ECDiffieHellmanP256);
  alicePubKeyBlob = aliceKey.Export(CngKeyBlobFormat.EccPublicBlob);
  bobPubKeyBlob = bobKey.Export(CngKeyBlobFormat.EccPublicBlob);
}
```

In the method `AliceSendsData`, the string that contains text characters is converted to a byte array by using the `Encoding` class. An `ECDiffieHellmanCng` object is created and initialized with the key pair from Alice. Alice creates a symmetric key by using her key pair and the public key from Bob, calling the method `DeriveKeyMaterial`. The returned symmetric key is used with the symmetric algorithm AES to encrypt the data. `AesCryptoServiceProvider` requires the key and an initialization vector (IV). The IV is generated dynamically from the method `GenerateIV`. The symmetric key is exchanged with the help of the EC Diffie-Hellman algorithm, but the IV must also be exchanged. From a security standpoint, it is OK to transfer the IV unencrypted across the network—only the key exchange must be secured. The IV is stored first as content in the memory stream, followed by the encrypted data where the `CryptoStream` class uses the `encryptor` created by the `AesCryptoServiceProvider` class. Before the encrypted data is accessed from the memory stream, the crypto stream must be closed. Otherwise, end bits would be missing from the encrypted data:

```
private async static Task<byte[]> AliceSendsData(string message)
{
  Console.WriteLine("Alice sends message: {0}", message);
  byte[] rawData = Encoding.UTF8.GetBytes(message);
  byte[] encryptedData = null;

  using (var aliceAlgorithm = new ECDiffieHellmanCng(aliceKey))
  using (CngKey bobPubKey = CngKey.Import(bobPubKeyBlob,
        CngKeyBlobFormat.EccPublicBlob))
  {
    byte[] symmKey = aliceAlgorithm.DeriveKeyMaterial(bobPubKey);
    Console.WriteLine("Alice creates this symmetric key with " +
        "Bobs public key information: {0}",
        Convert.ToBase64String(symmKey));

    using (var aes = new AesCryptoServiceProvider())
    {
      aes.Key = symmKey;
      aes.GenerateIV();
      using (ICryptoTransform encryptor = aes.CreateEncryptor())
      using (MemoryStream ms = new MemoryStream())
      {
        // create CryptoStream and encrypt data to send
        var cs = new CryptoStream(ms, encryptor, CryptoStreamMode.Write);

        // write initialization vector not encrypted
        await ms.WriteAsync(aes.IV, 0, aes.IV.Length);
        cs.Write(rawData, 0, rawData.Length);
        cs.Close();
        encryptedData = ms.ToArray();
      }
      aes.Clear();
    }
  }
  Console.WriteLine("Alice: message is encrypted: {0}",
      Convert.ToBase64String(encryptedData));;
  Console.WriteLine();
  return encryptedData;
}
```

Bob receives the encrypted data in the argument of the method `BobReceivesData()`. First, the unencrypted initialization vector must be read. The `BlockSize` property of the class `AesCryptoServiceProvider` returns the number of bits for a block. The number of bytes can be calculated by dividing by 8, and the fastest way to do this is by doing a bit shift of 3 bits (shifting by 1 bit is a division by 2, 2 bits by 4, and 3 bits by 8). With the `for` loop, the first bytes of the raw bytes that contain the IV unencrypted are written to the array `iv`. Next, an `ECDiffieHellmanCng` object is instantiated with the key pair from Bob. Using the public key from Alice, the symmetric key is returned from the method `DeriveKeyMaterial`.

Comparing the symmetric keys created from Alice and Bob shows that the same key value is created. Using this symmetric key and the initialization vector, the message from Alice can be decrypted with the `AesCryptoServiceProvider` class:

```
private static void BobReceivesData(byte[] encryptedData)
{
  Console.WriteLine("Bob receives encrypted data");
  byte[] rawData = null;

  var aes = new AesCryptoServiceProvider();

  int nBytes = aes.BlockSize  3;
  byte[] iv = new byte[nBytes];
  for (int i = 0; i < iv.Length; i++)
    iv[i] = encryptedData[i];

  using (var bobAlgorithm = new ECDiffieHellmanCng(bobKey))
  using (CngKey alicePubKey = CngKey.Import(alicePubKeyBlob,
        CngKeyBlobFormat.EccPublicBlob))
  {
    byte[] symmKey = bobAlgorithm.DeriveKeyMaterial(alicePubKey);
    Console.WriteLine("Bob creates this symmetric key with " +
      "Alices public key information: {0}",
      Convert.ToBase64String(symmKey));

    aes.Key = symmKey;
    aes.IV = iv;

    using (ICryptoTransform decryptor = aes.CreateDecryptor())
    using (MemoryStream ms = new MemoryStream())
    {
      var cs = new CryptoStream(ms, decryptor, CryptoStreamMode.Write);
      cs.Write(encryptedData, nBytes, encryptedData.Length - nBytes);
      cs.Close();

      rawData = ms.ToArray();

      Console.WriteLine("Bob decrypts message to: {0}",
          Encoding.UTF8.GetString(rawData));
    }
    aes.Clear();
  }
}
```

Running the application returns output similar to the following. The message from Alice is encrypted, and then decrypted by Bob with the securely exchanged symmetric key.

```
Alice sends message: secret message
Alice creates this symmetric key with Bobs public key information:
5NWat8AemzFCYo1IIae9S3Vn4AXyai4aL8ATFo41vbw=
Alice: message is encrypted: 3C5U9CpYxnoFTk3Ew2V0T5Po0Jgryc5R7Te8ztau5N0=
```

```
Bob receives encrypted message
Bob creates this symmetric key with Alices public key information:
5NWat8AemzFCYo1IIae9S3Vn4AXyai4aL8ATFo41vbw=
Bob decrypts message to: secret message
```

ACCESS CONTROL TO RESOURCES

Operating system resources such as files and registry keys, as well as handles of a named pipe, are secured by using an access control list (ACL). Figure 22-3 shows the structure mapping this. Associated with the resource is a security descriptor that contains information about the owner of the resource. It references two access control lists: a discretionary access control list (DACL) and a system access control list (SACL). The DACL defines who has access; the SACL defines audit rules for security event logging. An ACL contains a list of access control entries (ACEs), which contain a type, a security identifier, and rights. With the DACL, the ACE can be of type access allowed or access denied. Some of the rights that you can set and get with a file are create, read, write, delete, modify, change permissions, and take ownership.

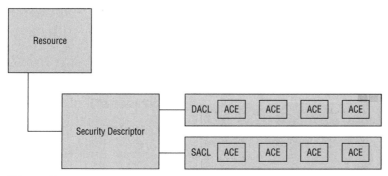

FIGURE 22-3

The classes to read and modify access control are located in the namespace `System.Security.AccessControl`. The following program demonstrates reading the access control list from a file.

The `FileStream` class defines the `GetAccessControl` method, which returns a `FileSecurity` object. `FileSecurity` is the .NET class that represents a security descriptor for files. `FileSecurity` derives from the base classes `ObjectSecurity`, `CommonObjectSecurity`, `NativeObjectSecurity`, and `FileSystemSecurity`. Other classes that represent a security descriptor are `CryptoKeySecurity`, `EventWaitHandleSecurity`, `MutexSecurity`, `RegistrySecurity`, `SemaphoreSecurity`, `PipeSecurity`, and `ActiveDirectorySecurity`. All of these objects can be secured using an access control list. In general, the corresponding .NET class defines the method `GetAccessControl` to return the corresponding security class; for example, the `Mutex.GetAccessControl` method returns a `MutexSecurity`, and the `PipeStream.GetAccessControl` method returns a `PipeSecurity`.

The `FileSecurity` class defines methods to read and change the DACL and SACL. The method `GetAccessRules` returns the DACL in the form of the class `AuthorizationRuleCollection`. To access the SACL, you can use the method `GetAuditRules`.

With the method `GetAccessRules`, you can specify whether inherited access rules, and not only access rules directly defined with the object, should be used. The last parameter defines the type of the security identifier that should be returned. This type must derive from the base class `IdentityReference`. Possible types are `NTAccount` and `SecurityIdentifier`. Both of these classes represent users or groups; the `NTAccount` class finds the security object by its name and the `SecurityIdentifier` class finds the security object by a unique security identifier.

The returned `AuthorizationRuleCollection` contains `AuthorizationRule` objects. The `AuthorizationRule` is the .NET representation of an ACE. In the following example, a file is accessed, so the `AuthorizationRule` can be cast to a `FileSystemAccessRule`. With ACEs of other resources, different .NET representations exist, such as `MutexAccessRule` and `PipeAccessRule`. With the `FileSystemAccessRule` class, the properties `AccessControlType`, `FileSystemRights`, and `IdentityReference` return information about the ACE (code file `FileAccessControl/Program.cs`).

```csharp
using System;
using System.IO;
using System.Security.AccessControl;
using System.Security.Principal;

namespace Wrox.ProCSharp.Security
{
  class Program
  {
    static void Main(string[] args)
    {
      string filename = null;
      if (args.Length == 0)
        return;

      filename = args[0];

      using (FileStream stream = File.Open(filename, FileMode.Open))
      {
        FileSecurity securityDescriptor = stream.GetAccessControl();
        AuthorizationRuleCollection rules =
            securityDescriptor.GetAccessRules(true, true,
            typeof(NTAccount));

        foreach (AuthorizationRule rule in rules)
        {
          var fileRule = rule as FileSystemAccessRule;
          Console.WriteLine("Access type: {0}", fileRule.AccessControlType);
          Console.WriteLine("Rights: {0}", fileRule.FileSystemRights);
          Console.WriteLine("Identity: {0}", fileRule.IdentityReference.Value);
          Console.WriteLine();
        }
      }
    }
  }
}
```

By running the application and passing a filename, you can see the access control list for the file. The following output lists full control to Administrators and System, modification rights to authenticated users, and read and execute rights to all users belonging to the group Users:

```
Access type: Allow
Rights: FullControl
Identity: BUILTIN\Administrators

Access type: Allow
Rights: FullControl
Identity: NT AUTHORITY\SYSTEM

Access type: Allow
Rights: FullControl
Identity: BUILTIN\Administrators
```

```
Access type: Allow
Rights: FullControl
Identity: TheOtherSide\Christian
```

Setting access rights is very similar to reading access rights. To set access rights, several resource classes that can be secured offer the `SetAccessControl` and `ModifyAccessControl` methods. The following code modifies the access control list of a file by invoking the `SetAccessControl` method from the `File` class. To this method a `FileSecurity` object is passed. The `FileSecurity` object is filled with `FileSystemAccessRule` objects. The access rules listed here deny write access to the Sales group, give read access to the Everyone group, and give full control to the Developers group:

> **NOTE** *This program runs on your system only if the Windows groups Sales and Developers are defined. You can change the program to use groups that are available in your environment.*

```csharp
private static void WriteAcl(string filename)
{
  var salesIdentity = new NTAccount("Sales");
  var developersIdentity = new NTAccount("Developers");
  var everyOneIdentity = new NTAccount("Everyone");

  var salesAce = new FileSystemAccessRule(salesIdentity,
      FileSystemRights.Write, AccessControlType.Deny);
  var everyoneAce = new FileSystemAccessRule(everyOneIdentity,
      FileSystemRights.Read, AccessControlType.Allow);
  var developersAce = new FileSystemAccessRule(developersIdentity,
      FileSystemRights.FullControl, AccessControlType.Allow);

  var securityDescriptor = new FileSecurity();
  securityDescriptor.SetAccessRule(everyoneAce);
  securityDescriptor.SetAccessRule(developersAce);
  securityDescriptor.SetAccessRule(salesAce);

  File.SetAccessControl(filename, securityDescriptor);
}
```

> **NOTE** *You can verify the access rules by opening the Properties window and selecting a file in Windows Explorer. Select the Security tab to see the access control list.*

CODE ACCESS SECURITY

Similar to role-based security, which enables you to define what the user is allowed to do, code access security defines what the code is allowed to do. .NET 4 simplified this model by removing the complex policy configuration that existed prior to .NET 4 and adding the security transparency level 2. Security transparency level 2 distinguishes between code that is allowed to make privileged calls (such as calling native code) and code that is not allowed to do so. The code is grouped into three categories:

➤ **Security-critical**—Any code can run. This code cannot be called by transparent code.

➤ **Safe-critical**—Code can be called by transparent code. Security verifications are done with this code.

➤ **Transparent**—Code is very limited in what it can do. This code is allowed to run in a specified permission set and it runs in a sandbox. It cannot contain unsafe or unverifiable code, and it cannot call security-critical code.

If you write Windows applications, the restricted code permissions do not apply. Applications running on the desktop have full trust privileges and can contain any code—if it's not otherwise defined by the system administrators. Sandboxing is used with Silverlight applications as well as ASP.NET applications that are hosted from a web provider, or with custom functionality, such as running add-ins with the Managed Add-In Framework.

This section discusses how you can apply security transparency level 2, and how you can make use of .NET permissions as is required with transparent code.

Security Transparency Level 2

You can annotate an assembly with the attribute `SecurityRules` and set the `SecurityRuleSet.Level2` for applying the newer level with .NET 4. (This is the default since .NET 4.) For backward compatibility, set it to `Level1`.

```
[assembly: SecurityRules(SecurityRuleSet.Level2)]
```

If you set the attribute `SecurityTransparent`, the entire assembly will not do anything privileged or unsafe. This assembly can only call other transparent code or safe-critical code. This attribute can be applied only to the complete assembly:

```
[assembly: SecurityTransparent()]
```

The attribute `AllowPartiallyTrustedCallers` is somewhere between transparent and the other categories. With this attribute, the code defaults to transparent, but individual types or members can have other attributes:

```
[assembly: AllowPartiallyTrustedCallers()]
```

If none of these attributes are applied, the code is security critical. However, you can apply the attribute `SecuritySafeCritical` to individual types and members to make them callable from transparent code:

```
[assembly: SecurityCritical()]
```

Permissions

If code runs inside a sandbox, the sandbox can define what the code is allowed to do by defining .NET permissions. While the full trust applies to applications running on the desktop, applications running in a sandbox are only allowed to perform the actions defined by the permissions that the host gives to the sandbox. You can also define permissions for an application domain that is started from a desktop application. This is done with the Sandbox API.

> **NOTE** *Application domains are discussed in Chapter 19, "Assemblies."*

Permissions refer to the actions that each code group is allowed to perform (or is prevented from performing). For example, permissions include "read files from the file system," "write to the Active Directory," and "use sockets to open network connections." Several predefined permissions exist, but you can also create your own permissions.

.NET permissions are independent of operating system permissions. .NET permissions are just verified by the CLR. An assembly demands a permission for a specific operation (for example, the `File` class demands the `FileIOPermission`), and the CLR verifies that the assembly has the permission granted so that it can continue.

You can apply a very fine-grained list of permissions to an assembly or a request from code. The following list describes a few of the code access permissions provided by the CLR; as you can see, you have a lot of control over what code is or is not permitted to do:

PERMISSION	DESCRIPTION
DirectoryServicesPermission	Controls access to Active Directory through the System.DirectoryServices classes
DnsPermission	Controls use of the TCP/IP Domain Name System (DNS)
EnvironmentPermission	Controls the use of read and write environment variables
EventLogPermission	Controls the ability to read and write to the event log
FileDialogPermission	Controls access to files that have been selected by the user in the Open dialog. This permission is commonly used when FileIOPermission is not granted in order to maintain limited access to files.
FileIOPermission	Controls the ability to work with files (reading, writing, and appending to files, as well as creating, altering, and accessing folders)
IsolatedStorageFilePermission	Controls access to private virtual file systems
IsolatedStoragePermission	Controls access to isolated storage—storage associated with an individual user and with some aspect of the code's identity. Isolated storage is discussed in Chapter 24.
MessageQueuePermission	Controls the use of message queues through the Microsoft Message Queue
PerformanceCounterPermission	Controls the use of performance counters
PrintingPermission	Controls the ability to print
ReflectionPermission	Controls the ability to discover information about a type at runtime by using System.Reflection
RegistryPermission	Controls the ability to read, write, create, or delete registry keys and values
SecurityPermission	Controls the ability to execute, assert permissions, call into unmanaged code, skip verification, and other rights
ServiceControllerPermission	Controls the ability to control Windows Services
SQLClientPermission	Controls access to SQL Server databases with the .NET data provider for SQL Server
UIPermission	Controls access to the user interface
WebPermission	Controls the ability to make or accept connections to or from the Web

With each of these permission classes, it is often possible to specify an even deeper level of granularity; for example, the DirectoryServicesPermission enables you to differentiate between read and write access, and to define which entries in the directory services are allowed or denied access.

Permission Sets

A *permission set* is a collection of permissions. Using a permission set, it is not necessary to apply every single permission to code; permissions are grouped into a permission set. For example, an assembly that has the FullTrust permission set has full access to all resources. With the LocalIntranet permission set, the assembly is restricted; that is, it is not allowed to write to the file system other than using the isolated storage. You can create a custom permission set that includes required permissions.

By assigning the permission to code groups, there is no need to deal with every single permission. Instead, the permissions are applied in blocks, which is why .NET has the concept of permission sets, lists of code access permissions grouped into a named set. The following list explains the seven named permission sets included out of the box:

- ➤ **FullTrust**—No permission restrictions.
- ➤ **SkipVerification**—Verification is not performed.
- ➤ **Execution**—Grants the ability to run, but not access, any protected resources.
- ➤ **Nothing**—Grants no permissions and prevents the code from executing.
- ➤ **LocalIntranet**—Specifies a subset of the full set of permissions. For example, file I/O is restricted to read access on the share where the assembly originates. With .NET 3.5 and earlier editions (before .NET 3.5 SP1), this permission set was used when an application was running from a network share.
- ➤ **Internet**—Specifies the default policy for code of unknown origin. This is the most restrictive policy. For example, code executing in this permission set has no file I/O capability, cannot read or write event logs, and cannot read or write environment variables.
- ➤ **Everything**—Grants all the permissions listed under this set, except the permission to skip code verification. The administrator can alter any of the permissions in this permission set. This is useful when the default policy needs to be tighter.

> **NOTE** *You can change the definitions of only the Everything permission set; the other sets are fixed and cannot be changed. Of course, you can also create your own permission set.*

Demanding Permissions Programmatically

An assembly can demand permissions declaratively or programmatically. The following code snippet demonstrates how permissions can be demanded with the method `DemandFileIOPermissions`. If you import the namespace `System.Security.Permissions`, you can check for permissions by creating a `FileIOPermission` object, and calling its `Demand` method. This verifies whether the caller of the method, here the caller of the method `DemandFileIOPermissions`, has the required permissions. In case the `Demand` method fails, an exception of type `SecurityException` is thrown. It's OK not to catch the exception and let it be handled by the caller (code file `DemandPermissionDemo/DemandPermissions.cs`).

```
using System;
using System.Security;
using System.Security.Permissions;

[assembly: AllowPartiallyTrustedCallers()]

namespace Wrox.ProCSharp.Security
{
  [SecuritySafeCritical]
  public class DemandPermissions
  {
    public void DemandFileIOPermissions(string path)
    {
      var fileIOPermission = new
          FileIOPermission(PermissionState.Unrestricted);
```

```
                fileIOPermission.Demand();

                //...
            }
        }
    }
```

`FileIOPermission` is contained within the `System.Security.Permissions` namespace, which is home to the full set of permissions and also provides classes for declarative permission attributes and enumerations for the parameters that are used to create permissions objects (for example, creating a `FileIOPermission` specifying whether read-only or full access is needed).

To catch exceptions thrown by the CLR when code attempts to act contrary to its granted permissions, you can catch the exception of the type `SecurityException`, which provides access to a number of useful pieces of information, including a human-readable stack trace (`SecurityException.StackTrace`) and a reference to the method that threw the exception (`SecurityException.TargetSite`). `SecurityException` even provides you with the `SecurityException.PermissionType` property, which returns the type of `Permission` object that caused the security exception to occur.

If you just use the .NET classes for file I/O, you don't have to demand the `FileIOPermission` yourself, as it is required by the .NET classes doing file I/O. However, you need to make the demand yourself if you wrap native API calls such as `CreateFileTransacted`. In addition, you can use this mechanism to demand custom permissions from the caller.

Using the Sandbox API to Host Unprivileged Code

By default, with a desktop application, the application has full trust. Using the Sandbox API, you can create an app-domain that doesn't have full trust.

To see the Sandbox API in action, first create a C# library project named **RequireFileIOPermissionsDemo**. This library contains the class `RequirePermissionsDemo` with the method `RequireFilePermissions`. This method returns `true` or `false`, depending on whether the code has file permissions. With the implementation of this code, the `File` class creates a file whereby the path is passed with the argument variable `path`. In case writing the file fails, an exception of type `SecurityException` is thrown. The `File` class checks for the `FileIOSecurity` as described earlier with the DemandPermissonDemo sample. If the security check fails, a `SecurityException` is thrown by the `Demand` method of the `FileIOSecurity` class. Here, the `SecurityException` is caught to return `false` from the `RequireFilePermissions` method (code file RequireFileIOPermissionDemo/RequirePermissionsDemo.cs):

```csharp
using System;
using System.IO;
using System.Security;

[assembly: AllowPartiallyTrustedCallers()]

namespace Wrox.ProCSharp.Security
{
  [SecuritySafeCritical]
  public class RequirePermissionsDemo : MarshalByRefObject
  {
    public bool RequireFilePermissions(string path)
    {
      bool accessAllowed = true;

      try
      {
        StreamWriter writer = File.CreateText(path);
        writer.WriteLine("written successfully");
```

```
      writer.Close();
    }
    catch (SecurityException)
    {
      accessAllowed = false;
    }

    return accessAllowed;
  }
 }
}
```

The hosting application where the Sandbox API is used in the project AppDomainHost, a simple C# console application. The Sandbox API is an overload of the `AppDomain.CreateDomain` method that creates a new app-domain in a sandbox. This method requires four parameters, including the name of the app-domain, the evidence that is taken from the current app-domain, the `AppDomainSetup` information, and a permission set. The permission set that is created only contains `SecurityPermission` with the flag `SecurityPermissionFlag.Execution` so that the code is allowed to execute—nothing more. In the new sandboxed app-domain, the object of type `DemandPermissions` in the assembly `DemandPermission` is instantiated.

Calling across app-domains requires .NET Remoting. That's why the class `RequirePermissionsDemo` needs to derive from the base class `MarshalByRefObject`. Unwrapping the returned `ObjectHandle` returns a transparent proxy to the object in the other app-domain to invoke the method `RequireFilePermissions` (code file `AppDomainHost/Program.cs`):

```csharp
using System;
using System.Runtime.Remoting;
using System.Security;
using System.Security.Permissions;

namespace Wrox.ProCSharp.Security
{
  class Program
  {
    static void Main()
    {
      var permSet = new PermissionSet(PermissionState.None);
      permSet.AddPermission(new SecurityPermission(
          SecurityPermissionFlag.Execution));

      AppDomainSetup setup = AppDomain.CurrentDomain.SetupInformation;
      AppDomain newDomain = AppDomain.CreateDomain("Sandboxed domain",
          AppDomain.CurrentDomain.Evidence, setup, permSet);
      ObjectHandle oh = newDomain.CreateInstance(
          "RequireFileIOPermissionsDemo",
          "Wrox.ProCSharp.Security.RequirePermissionsDemo");
      object o = oh.Unwrap();
      var io = o as RequirePermissionsDemo;
      string path = @"c:\temp\file.txt";
      Console.WriteLine("has {0}permissions to write to {1}",
          io.RequireFilePermissions(path) ? null : "no ", path);
    }
  }
}
```

After running the application, you can see from the result that the called assembly doesn't have the necessary permissions to create the file. If you add the `FileIOPermissionSet` to the permission set of the created app-domain as shown in the following code change, writing the file succeeds:

```
var permSet = new PermissionSet(PermissionState.None);
permSet.AddPermission(new SecurityPermission(
    SecurityPermissionFlag.Execution));
permSet.AddPermission(new FileIOPermission(
    FileIOPermissionAccess.AllAccess, "c:/temp"));
```

Implicit Permissions

When permissions are granted, there is often an implicit understanding that other permissions are also granted. For example, if you assign the `FileIOPermission` for `C:\`, there is an implicit assumption access to its subdirectories is also allowed.

To check whether a granted permission implicitly allows another permission as a subset, you can do this (code file `ImplicitPermissions/Program.cs`):

```
class Program
{
  static void Main()
  {
    CodeAccessPermission permissionA =
        new FileIOPermission(FileIOPermissionAccess.AllAccess, @"C:\");
    CodeAccessPermission permissionB =
        new FileIOPermission(FileIOPermissionAccess.Read, @"C:\temp");
    if (permissionB.IsSubsetOf(permissionA))
    {
      Console.WriteLine("PermissionB is a subset of PermissionA");
    }
  }
}
```

The output looks like this:

```
PermissionB is a subset of PermissionA
```

DISTRIBUTING CODE USING CERTIFICATES

You can make use of digital certificates and sign assemblies so that consumers of the software can verify the identity of the software publisher. Depending on where the application is used, certificates may be required. For example, with ClickOnce, the user installing the application can verify the certificate to trust the publisher. Using Windows Error Reporting, Microsoft uses the certificate to determine which vendor to map to the error report.

> **NOTE** *ClickOnce is explained in Chapter 18, "Deployment."*

In a commercial environment, you obtain a certificate from a company such as Verisign or Thawte. The advantage of buying a certificate from a supplier instead of creating your own is that it provides a high level of trust in the authenticity of the certificate; the supplier acts as a trusted third party. For test purposes, however, .NET includes a command-line utility you can use to create a test certificate. The process of creating certificates and using them for publishing software is complex, but this section walks through a simple example.

The example code is for a fictitious company called ABC Corporation. The company's software product (`simple.exe`) should be trusted. First, create a test certificate by typing the following command:

```
>makecert -sv abckey.pvk -r -n "CN=ABC Corporation" abccorptest.cer
```

The command creates a test certificate under the name ABC Corporation and saves it to a file called abccorptest.cer. The -sv abckey.pvk argument creates a key file to store the private key. When creating the key file, you are asked for a password that you should remember.

After creating the certificate, you can create a software publisher test certificate with the Software Publisher Certificate Test tool (Cert2spc.exe):

```
>cert2spc abccorptest.cer abccorptest.spc
```

With a certificate that is stored in an spc file and the key file that is stored in a pvk file, you can create a pfx file that contains both with the pvk2pfx utility:

```
>pvk2pfx -pvk abckey.pvk -spc abccorptest.spc -pfx abccorptest.pfx
```

Now the assembly can be signed with the signtool.exe utility. The sign option is used for signing, -f specifies the certificate in the pfx file, and -v is for verbose output:

```
>signtool sign -f abccorptest.pfx -v simple.exe
```

To establish trust for the certificate, install it with the Trusted Root Certification Authorities and the Trusted Publishers using the Certificate Manager, certmgr, or the MMC snap-in Certificates. Then you can verify the successful signing with the signtool:

```
>signtool verify -v -a simple.exe
```

SUMMARY

This chapter covered several aspects of security with .NET applications. Authentication and authorization with role-based security enable you to programmatically determine which users are allowed to access application features. Users are represented by identities and principals, classes that implement the interface IIdentity and IPrincipal. Role verification can be done within the code but also in a simple way using attributes.

A brief overview of cryptography demonstrated how the signing and encrypting of data enable the exchange of keys in a secure way. .NET offers both symmetric and asymmetric cryptography algorithms.

With access control lists you can read and modify access to operating system resources such as files. Programming ACLs is done similarly to the programming of secure pipes, registry keys, Active Directory entries, and many other operating system resources.

If your applications are used in different regions and with different languages, in the next chapter you can read about interop with native code.

23

Interop

WHAT'S IN THIS CHAPTER?

➤ COM and .NET technologies

➤ Using COM objects from within .NET applications

➤ Using .NET components from within COM clients

➤ Platform invoke for invoking native methods

WROX.COM CODE DOWNLOADS FOR THIS CHAPTER

The wrox.com code downloads for this chapter are found at `http://www.wrox.com/remtitle .cgi?isbn=1118314425` on the Download Code tab. The code for this chapter is divided into the following major examples:

➤ COMServer

➤ DotnetServer

➤ PInvokeSample

.NET AND COM

If you have Windows programs written prior to .NET, you probably don't have the time and resources to rewrite everything for .NET. Sometimes rewriting code is useful for refactoring or rethinking the application architecture. A rewrite can also help with productivity in the long term, when adding new features is easier to do with the new technology. However, there is no reason to rewrite old code just because a new technology is available. You might have thousands of lines of existing, running code, which would require too much effort to rewrite just to move it into the managed environment.

The same applies to Microsoft. With the namespace `System.DirectoryServices`, Microsoft hasn't rewritten the COM objects accessing the hierarchical data store; the classes inside this namespace are wrappers accessing the ADSI COM objects instead. The same thing happens with `System.Data .OleDb`, where the OLE DB providers that are used by classes from this namespace do have quite complex COM interfaces.

The same issue may apply to your own solutions. If you have existing COM objects that should be used from .NET applications, or the other way around, if you want to write .NET components that should be used in old COM clients, this chapter is a starter for using COM interoperability (or *interop*).

If you don't have existing COM components you want to integrate with your application, or old COM clients that should use some .NET components, you can skip this chapter.

The major namespace for this chapter is System.Runtime.InteropServices.

COM is the predecessor technology to .NET. COM defines a component model in which components can be written in different programming languages. A component written with C++ can be used from a Visual Basic client. Components can also be used locally inside a process, across processes, or across the network. Does this sound familiar? Of course, .NET has similar goals. However, the way in which these goals are achieved is different. The COM concepts became increasingly complex to use and turned out not to be extensible enough. .NET fulfills goals similar to those of COM but introduces new concepts to make your job easier.

Even today, when using COM interop the prerequisite is to know COM. It doesn't matter whether .NET components are used by COM clients or whether COM components are used by .NET applications — you must know COM. Therefore, this section compares COM and .NET functionality.

If you already have a good grasp of COM technologies, this section may refresh your COM knowledge. Otherwise, it introduces you to the concepts of COM — which now, using .NET, you happily don't have to deal with anymore in your daily work. However, all the problems that existed with COM still apply when COM technology is integrated into .NET applications.

COM and .NET do have many similar concepts, with very different approaches to using them, including the following:

- ➤ Metadata
- ➤ Freeing memory
- ➤ Interfaces
- ➤ Method binding
- ➤ Data types
- ➤ Registration
- ➤ Threading
- ➤ Error handling
- ➤ Event handling

These concepts, plus the marshaling mechanism, are covered in the following sections.

Metadata

With COM, all information about the component is stored inside the type library. The type library includes information such as names and IDs of interfaces, methods, and arguments. With .NET, all this information can be found inside the assembly itself, as shown in Chapter 15, "Reflection," and Chapter 19, "Assemblies." The problem with COM is that the type library is not extensible. With C++, IDL (Interface Definition Language) files have been used to describe the interfaces and methods. Some of the IDL modifiers cannot be found inside the type library, because Visual Basic (and the Visual Basic team was responsible for the type library) couldn't use these IDL modifiers. With .NET, this problem doesn't exist because the .NET metadata is extensible using custom attributes.

As a result of this behavior, some COM components have a type library and others don't. When no type library is available, a C++ header file can be used that describes the interfaces and methods. With .NET, it is easier to use COM components that do have a type library, but it is also possible to use COM components without a type library. In that case, it is necessary to redefine the COM interface by using C# code.

Freeing Memory

With .NET, memory is released by the garbage collector. This is completely different with COM. COM relies on reference counts. The interface `IUnknown`, which is the interface required to be implemented by every COM object, offers three methods. Two of these methods are related to reference counts. The method `AddRef` must be called by the client if another interface pointer is needed; this method increments the reference count. The method `Release` decrements the reference count, and if the resulting reference count is 0, the object destroys itself to free the memory.

Interfaces

Interfaces are the heart of COM. They distinguish between a contract used between the client and the object, and the implementation. The interface (the contract) defines the methods that are offered by the component and that can be used by the client. With .NET, interfaces play an important part, too. COM distinguishes among three interface types: *custom*, *dispatch*, and *dual*.

Custom Interfaces

Custom interfaces derive from the interface `IUnknown`. A custom interface defines the order of the methods in a *virtual table* (*vtable*), so that the client can access the methods of the interface directly. This also means that the client needs to know the vtable during development time, because binding to the methods happens by using memory addresses. As a result, custom interfaces cannot be used by scripting clients. Figure 23-1 shows the vtable of the custom interface `IMath`, which provides the methods `Add` and `Sub` in addition to the methods of the `IUnknown` interface.

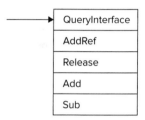

FIGURE 23-1

Dispatch Interfaces

Because a scripting client (and earlier Visual Basic clients) doesn't support custom interfaces, a different interface type is needed. With dispatch interfaces, the interface available for the client is always `IDispatch`. `IDispatch` derives from `IUnknown` and offers four methods in addition to the `IUnknown` methods. The two most important methods are `GetIDsOfNames` and `Invoke`. As shown in Figure 23-2, with a dispatch interface two tables are needed. The first one maps the method or property name to a dispatch ID; the second one maps the dispatch ID to the implementation of the method or property.

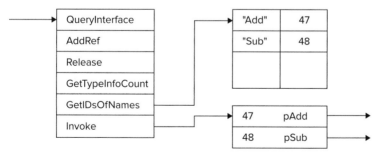

FIGURE 23-2

When the client invokes a method in the component, it first calls the method `GetIDsOfNames`, passing the name of the method it wants to call. `GetIDsOfNames` makes a lookup into the name-to-ID table to return the dispatch ID. This ID is used by the client to call the `Invoke` method.

> **NOTE** *Usually, the two tables for the* IDispatch *interface are stored inside the type library, but this is not a requirement, and some components have the tables in other places.*

Dual Interfaces

As you can imagine, on the one hand, dispatch interfaces are a lot slower than custom interfaces. On the other hand, custom interfaces cannot be used by scripting clients. A dual interface can solve this dilemma. As shown in Figure 23-3, a dual interface is derived from IDispatch but provides the additional methods of the interface directly in the vtable. Scripting clients can use the IDispatch interface to invoke the Add and Sub methods, whereas clients aware of the vtable can call the Add and Sub methods directly.

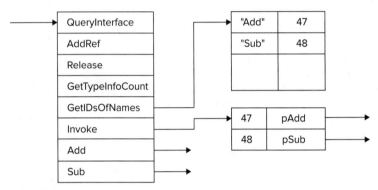

FIGURE 23-3

Casting and QueryInterface

If a .NET class implements multiple interfaces, casts can be done to get one interface or another. With COM, the interface IUnknown offers a similar mechanism with the method QueryInterface. As discussed in the previous section, the interface IUnknown is the base interface of every interface, so QueryInterface is available anyway.

Method Binding

How a client maps to a method is defined with the terms *early binding* and *late binding.* Late binding means that the method to invoke is looked for during runtime. .NET uses the System.Reflection namespace to make this possible (see Chapter 15). COM uses the IDispatch interface discussed earlier for late binding. Late binding is possible with dispatch and dual interfaces.

With COM, early binding has two different options. One way of early binding, also known as vtable binding, is to use the vtable directly — this is possible with custom and dual interfaces. The second option for early binding is also known as ID binding. Here, the dispatch ID is stored inside the client code, so during runtime only a call to Invoke is necessary. GetIdsOfNames is called during design time. With such clients, it is important to remember that the dispatch ID must not be changed.

Data Types

For dual and dispatch interfaces, the data types that can be used with COM are restricted to a list of automation-compatible data types. The Invoke method of the IDispatch interface accepts an array of VARIANT data types. The VARIANT is a union of many different data types, such as BYTE, SHORT, LONG, FLOAT, DOUBLE, BSTR, IUnknown*, IDispatch*, and so on. VARIANTs have been easy to use from Visual Basic, but it was complex to use them from C++. .NET has the Object class instead of VARIANTs.

With custom interfaces, all data types available with C++ can be used with COM. However, this also restricts the clients that can use this component to certain programming languages.

Registration

.NET distinguishes between private and shared assemblies, as discussed in Chapter 19. With COM, all components are globally available through a registry configuration.

All COM objects have a unique identifier that consists of a 128-bit number, also known as a class ID (CLSID). The COM API call to create COM objects, CoCreateInstance, just looks into the registry to find the CLSID and the path to the DLL or EXE to load the DLL or launch the EXE and instantiate the component.

Because such a 128-bit number cannot be easily remembered, many COM objects also have a ProgID. The ProgID is an easy-to-remember name, such as Excel.Application, that just maps to the CLSID.

In addition to the CLSID, COM objects also have a unique identifier for each interface (IID) and for the type library (typelib ID). Information in the registry is discussed in more detail later in the chapter.

Threading

COM uses apartment models to relieve the programmer of having to deal with threading issues. However, this also adds some more complexity. Different apartment types have been added with different releases of the operating system. This section discusses the single-threaded apartment and the multithreaded apartment.

> **NOTE** *Threading with .NET is discussed in Chapter 21, "Threads, Tasks, and Synchronization."*

Single-Threaded Apartment

The *single-threaded apartment (STA)* was introduced with Windows NT 3.51. With an STA, only one thread (the thread that created the instance) is allowed to access the component. However, it is legal to have multiple STAs inside one process, as shown in Figure 23-4.

In this figure, the inner rectangles with the lollipop represent COM components. Components and threads (curved arrows) are surrounded by apartments. The outer rectangle represents a process.

With STAs, there's no need to protect instance variables from multiple-thread access, because this protection is provided by a COM facility, and only one thread accesses the component.

A COM object that is not programmed with thread safety marks the requirements for an STA in the registry with the registry key ThreadingModel set to Apartment.

Multithreaded Apartment

Windows NT 4.0 introduced the concept of a *multithreaded apartment (MTA)*. With an MTA, multiple threads can access the component simultaneously. Figure 23-5 shows a process with one MTA and two STAs.

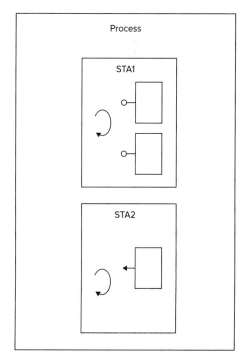

FIGURE 23-4

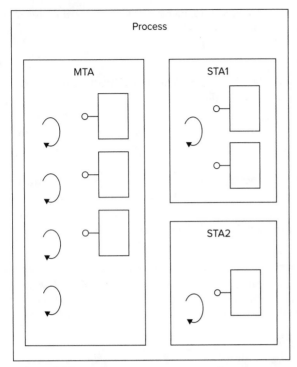

FIGURE 23-5

A COM object programmed with thread safety in mind marks the requirement for an MTA in the registry with the key `ThreadingModel` set to `Free`. The value `Both` is used for thread-safe COM objects that don't mind the apartment type.

> **NOTE** *Visual Basic 6.0 didn't offer support for multithreaded apartments. If you're using COM objects that have been developed with VB6, it's important to know that.*

> **NOTE** *Windows 2000 introduced another apartment model, the Thread Neutral Apartment (TNA). This apartment model is only used for COM components configured as COM+ applications. The value* `Both` *for the* `ThreadingModel` *accepts any of the three apartments: STA, MTA, and TNA.*

Error Handling

With .NET, errors are generated by throwing exceptions. With the older COM technology, errors are defined by returning HRESULT values with the methods. An HRESULT value of S_OK means that the method was successful.

If a more detailed error message is offered by the COM component, the COM component implements the interface ISupportErrorInfo, whereby not only an error message but also a link to a help file and the source of the error are returned with an error information object on the return of the method. Objects that implement ISupportErrorInfo are automatically mapped to more detailed error information with an exception in .NET.

> **NOTE** *How to trace and log errors is discussed in Chapter 20, "Diagnostics."*

Events

.NET offers a callback mechanism with the C# keywords event and delegate (see Chapter 8, "Delegates, Lambdas, and Events"). Figure 23-6 shows the COM event-handling architecture. With COM events, the component has to implement the interface IConnectionPointContainer and one or more connection point objects (CPOs) that implement the interface IConnectionPoint. The component also defines an outgoing interface — ICompletedEvents in Figure 23-6 — that is invoked by the CPO. The client must implement this outgoing interface in the sink object, which itself is a COM object. During runtime, the client queries the server for the interface IConnectionPointContainer. With the help of this interface, the client asks for a CPO by invoking the method FindConnectionPoint. The method FindConnectionPoint returns a pointer to IConnectionPoint. This interface pointer is used by the client to call the Advise method, where a pointer to the sink object is passed to the server. In turn, the component.

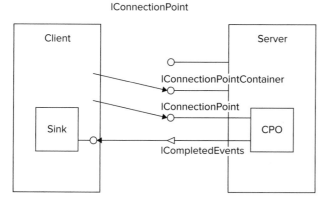

FIGURE 23-6

Later in this chapter, you learn how the .NET events and the COM events can be mapped so that COM events can be handled by a .NET client and vice versa.

Marshaling

Data passed from .NET to the COM component and the other way around must be converted to the corresponding representation. This mechanism is known as *marshaling*. What happens here depends on the data type of the data that is passed: you have to differentiate between blittable and nonblittable data types.

Blittable data types have a common representation with both .NET and COM, and no conversion is needed. Simple data types such as byte, short, int, long, and classes and arrays that contain only these simple data types belong to the blittable data types. Arrays must be one-dimensional to be blittable.

A conversion is needed with *nonblittable* data types. The following table lists some of the nonblittable COM data types with their .NET-related data types. Nonblittable types have a higher overhead because of the conversion.

COM DATA TYPE	.NET DATA TYPE
SAFEARRAY	Array
VARIANT	Object
BSTR	String
IUnknown* IDispatch*	Object

USING A COM COMPONENT FROM A .NET CLIENT

To see how a .NET application can use a COM component, you first have to create a COM component. Creating COM components is not possible with C# or Visual Basic 2012; you need either Visual Basic 6.0 or C++ (or any other language that supports COM). This chapter uses the Active Template Library (ATL) and C++ with Visual Studio 2012.

Here we will begin by creating a simple COM component and use this from a runtime callable wrapper (RCW). We will also use the component with the new C# 4 dynamic language extensions. Threading issues are discussed, and finally COM connection points are mapped to .NET events.

> **NOTE** *A short note about building COM components with Visual Basic 11 and C#: With Visual Basic 11 and C# 5 it is possible to build .NET components that can be used as COM objects by using a wrapper that is the real COM component. It would make no sense for a .NET component that is wrapped from a COM component to be used by a .NET client with COM interop.*

> **NOTE** *Because this is not a COM book, it does not discuss all aspects of the code but only what you need to build the sample.*

Creating a COM Component

To create a COM component with ATL and C++, create a new ATL Project. You can find the ATL Project Wizard within the Visual C++ Projects group when you select File ⇨ New Project. Set the name to **COMServer**. Within the Application Settings, select Dynamic Link Library and click Finish.

> **NOTE** *Because a build step registers the COM component in the registry, which requires admin privileges, Visual Studio should be started in elevated mode to write ATL COM objects.*

The ATL Project Wizard just creates the foundation for the server. A COM object is still needed. Add a class in Solution Explorer and select ATL Simple Object. In the dialog that appears, enter **COMDemo** in the Short name field. The other fields will be filled in automatically, but change the interface name to IWelcome and the ProgID to COMServer.COMDemo (see Figure 23-7). Click Finish to create the stub code for the class and the interface.

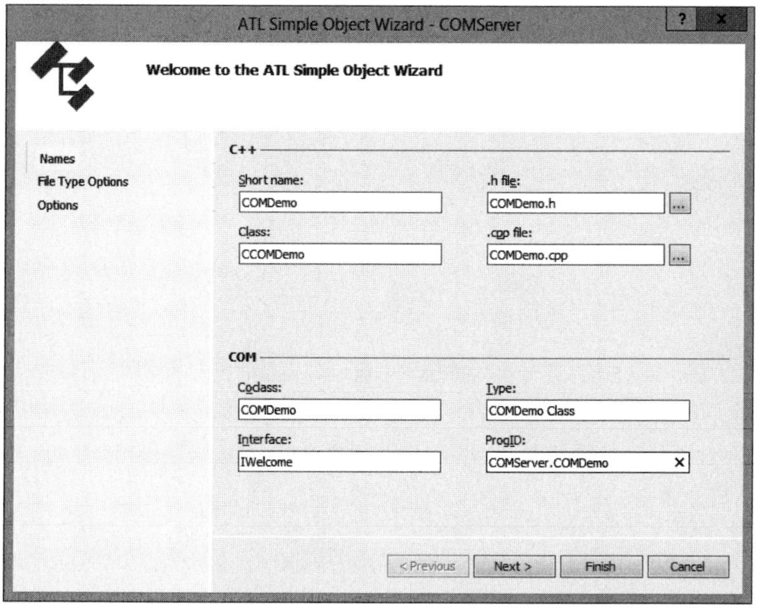

FIGURE 23-7

The COM component offers two interfaces so that you can see how QueryInterface is mapped from .NET, and just three simple methods so that you can see how the interaction takes place. In class view, select the interface IWelcome and add the method Greeting (see Figure 23-8) with the following parameters:

```
HRESULT Greeting([in] BSTR name, [out, retval] BSTR* message);
```

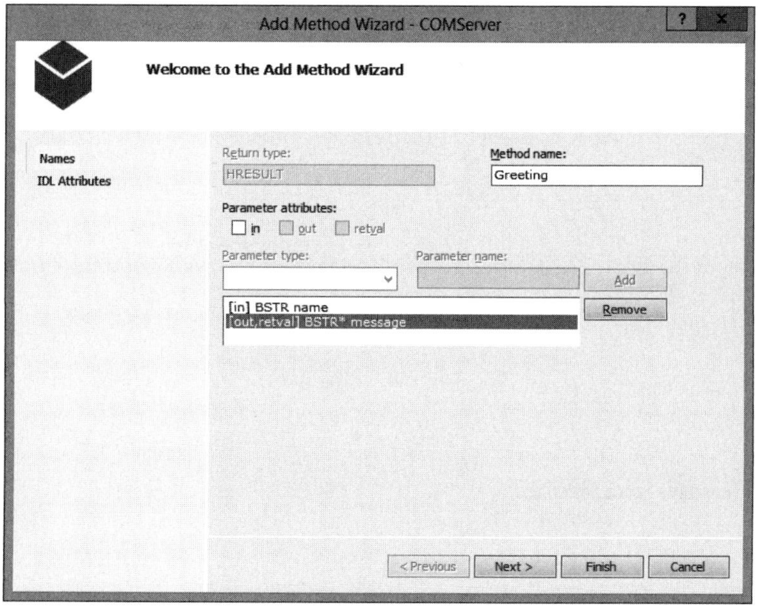

FIGURE 23-8

The IDL file COMServer.idl defines the interface for COM. Your wizard-generated code from the file COMServer.idl should look similar to the following code. The unique identifiers (uuids) will differ. The interface IWelcome defines the Greeting method. The brackets before the keyword interface define some attributes for the interface. uuid defines the interface ID and dual marks the type of the interface (code file COMServer/COMServer.idl):

```
[
  object,
  uuid(AF05C6E6-BF95-411F-B2FA-531D911C5C5C),
  dual,
  nonextensible,
  pointer_default(unique)
]
interface IWelcome : IDispatch{
  [id(1)] HRESULT Greeting([in] BSTR name, [out,retval] BSTR* message);
};
```

The IDL file also defines the content of the type library, which is the COM object (coclass) that implements the interface IWelcome:

```
[
  uuid(8FCA0342-FAF3-4481-9D11-3BC613A7F5C6),
  version(1.0),
]
library COMServerLib
{
  importlib("stdole2.tlb");
  [
    uuid(9015EDE5-D106-4005-9998-DE44849EFA3D)
  ]
  coclass COMDemo
  {
    [default] interface IWelcome;
  };
};
```

> **NOTE** With custom attributes, you can change the name of the class and interfaces that are generated by a .NET wrapper class. You just have to add the attribute custom with the identifier 0F21F359-AB84-41e8-9A78-36D110E6D2F9, and the name under which it should appear within .NET.

Add the custom attribute with the same identifier and the name Wrox.ProCSharp.Interop.Server .IWelcome to the header section of the IWelcome interface. Add the same attribute with a corresponding name to the coclass COMDemo:

```
[
  object,
  uuid(EB1E5898-4DAB-4184-92E2-BBD8F9341AFD),
  dual,
  nonextensible,
  pointer_default(unique),
  custom(0F21F359-AB84-41e8-9A78-36D110E6D2F9,
  "Wrox.ProCSharp.Interop.Server.IWelcome")
]
interface IWelcome : IDispatch{
  [id(1)] HRESULT Greeting([in] BSTR name, [out,retval] BSTR* message);
};
```

```
[
  uuid(8C123EAE-F567-421F-ACBE-E11F89909160),
  version(1.0),
]
library COMServerLib
{
  importlib("stdole2.tlb");
  [
    uuid(ACB04E72-EB08-4D4A-91D3-34A5DB55D4B4),
    custom(0F21F359-AB84-41e8-9A78-36D110E6D2F9,
    "Wrox.ProCSharp.Interop.Server.COMDemo")
  ]
  coclass COMDemo
  {
    [default] interface IWelcome;
  };
};
```

Now add a second interface to the file COMServer.idl. You can copy the header section of the IWelcome interface to the header section of the new IMath interface, but be sure to change the unique identifier that is defined with the uuid keyword. You can generate such an ID with the guidgen utility. The interface IMath offers the methods Add and Sub:

```
// IMath
[
    object,
    uuid(2158751B-896E-461d-9012-EF1680BE0628),
    dual,
    nonextensible,
    pointer_default(unique),
    custom(0F21F359-AB84-41e8-9A78-36D110E6D2F9,
    "Wrox.ProCSharp.Interop.Server.IMath")
]
interface IMath: IDispatch
{
    [id(1)] HRESULT Add([in] LONG val1, [in] LONG val2,
                        [out, retval] LONG* result);
    [id(2)] HRESULT Sub([in] LONG val1, [in] LONG val2,
                        [out, retval] LONG* result);
};
```

The coclass COMDemo must also be changed so that it implements both the interfaces IWelcome and Math. The IWelcome interface is the default interface:

```
    importlib("stdole2.tlb");
    [
        uuid(ACB04E72-EB08-4D4A-91D3-34A5DB55D4B4),
        helpstring("COMDemo Class"),
        custom(0F21F359-AB84-41e8-9A78-36D110E6D2F9,
        "Wrox.ProCSharp.Interop.Server.COMDemo")
    ]
    coclass COMDemo
    {
        [default] interface IWelcome;
        interface IMath;
    };
```

Now, you can set the focus away from the IDL file toward the C++ code. In the file COMDemo.h is the class definition of the COM object. The class CCOMDemo uses multiple inheritances to derive from the template classes CComObjectRootEx, CComCoClass, and IDisplatchImpl. The CComObjectRootEx class offers an implementation of the IUnknown interface functionality such as implementation of the AddRef and Release methods. The CComCoClass class creates a factory that instantiates objects of the template argument, which here is CComDemo. IDispatchImpl offers an implementation of the methods from the IDispatch interface.

With the macros that are surrounded by BEGIN_COM_MAP and END_COM_MAP, a map is created to define all the COM interfaces that are implemented by the COM class. This map is used by the implementation of the QueryInterface method (code file COMServer/COMDemo.h):

```
class ATL_NO_VTABLE CCOMDemo:
    public CComObjectRootEx<CComSingleThreadModel>,
    public CComCoClass<CCOMDemo, &CLSID_COMDemo>,
    public IDispatchImpl<IWelcome, &IID_IWelcome, &LIBID_COMServerLib,
        /*wMajor =*/ 1, /*wMinor =*/ 0>
{
public:
  CCOMDemo()
  {
  }

DECLARE_REGISTRY_RESOURCEID(IDR_COMDEMO)

BEGIN_COM_MAP(CCOMDemo)
   COM_INTERFACE_ENTRY(IWelcome)
   COM_INTERFACE_ENTRY(IDispatch)
END_COM_MAP()

  DECLARE_PROTECT_FINAL_CONSTRUCT()

  HRESULT FinalConstruct()
  {
    return S_OK;
  }

  void FinalRelease()
  {
  }

public:
  STDMETHOD(Greeting)(BSTR name, BSTR* message);
};

OBJECT_ENTRY_AUTO(__uuidof(COMDemo), CCOMDemo)
```

With this class definition, you have to add the second interface, IMath, as well as the methods that are defined with the IMath interface:

```
class ATL_NO_VTABLE CCOMDemo:
    public CComObjectRootEx<CComSingleThreadModel>,
    public CComCoClass<CCOMDemo, &CLSID_COMDemo>,
    public IDispatchImpl<IWelcome, &IID_IWelcome, &LIBID_COMServerLib,
        /*wMajor =*/ 1, /*wMinor =*/ 0>
    public IDispatchImpl<IMath, &IID_IMath, &LIBID_COMServerLib, 1, 0>
{
public:
  CCOMDemo()
  {
  }

DECLARE_REGISTRY_RESOURCEID(IDR_COMDEMO)
```

```
BEGIN_COM_MAP(CCOMDemo)
  COM_INTERFACE_ENTRY(IWelcome)
  COM_INTERFACE_ENTRY(IMath)
  COM_INTERFACE_ENTRY2(IDispatch, IWelcome)
END_COM_MAP()

  DECLARE_PROTECT_FINAL_CONSTRUCT()

  HRESULT FinalConstruct()
  {
    return S_OK;
  }

  void FinalRelease()
  {
  }

public:
  STDMETHOD(Greeting)(BSTR name, BSTR* message);
  STDMETHOD(Add)(long val1, long val2, long* result);
  STDMETHOD(Sub)(long val1, long val2, long* result);
};

OBJECT_ENTRY_AUTO(__uuidof(COMDemo), CCOMDemo)
```

Now you can implement the three methods in the file COMDemo.cpp with the following code. The CComBSTR is an ATL class that makes it easier to deal with BSTRs. In the Greeting method, only a welcome message is returned, which adds the name passed in the first argument to the message that is returned. The Add method just does a simple addition of two values, and the Sub method does a subtraction and returns the result (code file COMServer/COMDemo.cpp):

```
STDMETHODIMP CCOMDemo::Greeting(BSTR name, BSTR* message)
{
  CComBSTR tmp("Welcome, ");
  tmp.Append(name);
  *message = tmp;
  return S_OK;
}

STDMETHODIMP CCOMDemo::Add(LONG val1, LONG val2, LONG* result)
{
  *result = val1 + val2;
  return S_OK;
}

STDMETHODIMP CCOMDemo::Sub(LONG val1, LONG val2, LONG* result)
{
  *result = val1 - val2;
  return S_OK;
}
```

Now you can build the component. The build process also configures the component in the registry.

Creating a Runtime Callable Wrapper

To use the COM component from within .NET, you must create a runtime callable wrapper (RCW). Using the RCW, the .NET client sees a .NET object instead of the COM component; there is no need to deal with the COM characteristics because this is done by the wrapper. An RCW hides the IUnknown and IDispatch interfaces (see Figure 23-9) and deals itself with the reference counts of the COM object.

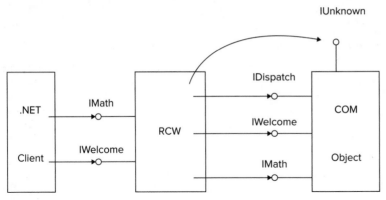

FIGURE 23-9

The RCW can be created by using the command-line utility `tlbimp` or by using Visual Studio. Starting the command:

```
tlbimp COMServer.dll /out:Interop.COMServer.dll
```

creates the file `Interop.COMServer.dll`, which contains a .NET assembly with the wrapper class. In this generated assembly, you can find the namespace `COMWrapper` with the class `CCOMDemoClass` and the interfaces `CCOMDemo`, `IMath`, and `IWelcome`. The name of the namespace can be changed by using options of the `tlbimp` utility. The option `/namespace` enables you to specify a different namespace, and with `/asmversion` you can define the version number of the assembly.

> **NOTE** *Another important option of this command-line utility is* `/keyfile`, *which is used to assign a strong name to the generated assembly. Strong names are discussed in Chapter 19, "Assemblies."*

An RCW can also be created by using Visual Studio. To create a simple sample application, create a C# console project. In Solution Explorer, add a reference to the COM server by selecting the COM tab in the Add Reference dialog, and scroll down to the entry `COMServerLib`. Here are listed all COM objects that are configured in the registry. Selecting a COM component from the list creates an RCW class. With Visual Studio 2012, this wrapper class can be created in the main assembly of the project by setting the property `Embed Interop Types` to `true`, which is the default. Setting it to `false` creates a separate interop assembly that needs to be deployed with the application.

Using the RCW

After creating the wrapper class, you can write the code for the application to instantiate and access the component. Because of the custom attributes in the C++ file, the generated namespace of the RCW class is `Wrox.ProCSharp.COMInterop.Server`. Add this namespace, as well as the namespace `System.Runtime .InteropServices`, to the declarations. From the namespace `System.Runtime.InteropServices`, the `Marshal` class will be used to release the COM object (code file `DotnetClient/Program.cs`):

```
using System;
using System.Runtime.InteropServices;
using Wrox.ProCSharp.Interop.Server
```

```
namespace Wrox.ProCSharp.Interop.Client
{
  class Program
  {
    [STAThread]
    static void Main()
    {
```

Now the COM component can be used similarly to a .NET class. `obj` is a variable of type `COMDemo`. `COMDemo` is a .NET interface that offers the methods of both the `IWelcome` and `IMath` interfaces. However, it is also possible to cast to a specific interface such as `IWelcome`. With a variable that is declared as type `IWelcome`, the method `Greeting` can be called:

```
var obj = new COMDemo();
IWelcome welcome = obj;
Console.WriteLine(welcome.Greeting("Stephanie"));
```

> **NOTE** *Although* COMDemo *is an interface, you can instantiate new objects of type* COMDemo. *Unlike normal interfaces, you can do this with wrapped COM interfaces.*

If the object offers multiple interfaces, as it does in this case, a variable of the other interface can be declared; and by using a simple assignment with the cast operator, the wrapper class does a `QueryInterface` with the COM object to return the second interface pointer. With the `I Math` variable, the methods of the `IMath` interface can be called:

```
IMath math;
math = (IMath)welcome;
int x = math.Add(4, 5);
Console.WriteLine(x);
```

If the COM object should be released before the garbage collector cleans up the object, the static method `Marshal.ReleaseComObject` invokes the `Release` method of the component so that the component can destroy itself and free up memory:

```
Marshal.ReleaseComObject(math);
    }
  }
}
```

> **NOTE** *Earlier you learned that the COM object is released as soon as the reference count is 0.* Marshal.ReleaseComObject *decrements the reference count by 1 by invoking the* Release *method. Because the RCW makes just one call to* AddRef *to increment the reference count, a single call to* Marshal.ReleaseComObject *is enough to release the object, regardless of how many references to the RCW you keep.*

After releasing the COM object using `Marshal.ReleaseComObject`, you may not use any variable that references the object. In the example, the COM object is released by using the variable `math`. The variable `welcome`, which references the same object, cannot be used after releasing the object. Otherwise, you will get an exception of type `InvalidComObjectException`.

> **NOTE** *Releasing COM objects when they are no longer needed is extremely important. COM objects make use of the native memory heap, whereas .NET objects make use of the managed memory heap. The garbage collector only deals with managed memory.*

As you can see, with a runtime callable wrapper, a COM component can be used similarly to a .NET object.

Using the COM Server with Dynamic Language Extensions

Since version 4, C# includes an extension for using dynamic languages from C#. This is also an advantage for using COM servers that offer the `IDispatch` interface. As you read earlier in the "Dispatch Interfaces" section, this interface is resolved at runtime with the methods `GetIdsOfNames` and `Invoke`. With the `dynamic` keyword and the help of a COM binder that is used behind the scenes, the COM component can be called without creating an RCW object.

Declaring a variable of type `dynamic` and assigning a COM object to it uses the COM binder, and you can invoke the methods of the default interface as shown. You can create an instance of the COM object without using an RCW by getting the `Type` object using `Type.GetTypeFromProgID`, and instantiating the COM object with the `Activator.CreateInstance` method. You don't get IntelliSense with the `dynamic` keyword, but you can use the optional parameters that are very common with COM (code file `DynamicDotnetClient/Program.cs`):

```
using System;

namespace Wrox.ProCSharp.Interop
{
  class Program
  {
    static void Main()
    {
      Type t = Type.GetTypeFromProgID("COMServer.COMDemo");
      dynamic o = Activator.CreateInstance(t);
      Console.WriteLine(o.Greeting("Angela"));
    }
  }
}
```

> **NOTE** *The dynamic language extensions of C# are explained in Chapter 12.*

Threading Issues

As discussed earlier in this chapter, a COM component marks the apartment (STA or MTA) in which it should reside, based on whether or not it is implemented as thread-safe. However, the thread has to join an apartment. What apartment the thread should join can be defined with the `[STAThread]` and `[MTAThread]` attributes, which can be applied to the `Main` method of an application. The attribute `[STAThread]` means that the thread joins an STA, whereas the attribute `[MTAThread]` means that the thread joins an MTA. Joining an MTA is the default if no attribute is applied.

It is also possible to set the apartment state programmatically with the `ApartmentState` property of the `Thread` class. The `ApartmentState` property enable you to set a value from the `ApartmentState` enumeration. `ApartmentState` has the possible values `STA` and `MTA` (and `Unknown` if it wasn't set). Be aware that the apartment state of a thread can be set only once. If it is set a second time, the second setting is ignored.

> **NOTE** *What happens if the thread chooses a different apartment from the apartments supported by the component? The correct apartment for the COM component is created automatically by the COM runtime, but performance decreases if apartment boundaries are crossed while calling the methods of a component.*

Adding Connection Points

To see how COM events can be handled in a .NET application, the COM component must be extended. First, you have to add another interface to the interface definition file COMDemo.idl. The interface _ICompletedEvents is implemented by the client, which is the .NET application, and called by the component. In this example, the method Completed is called by the component when the calculation is ready. Such an interface is also known as an *outgoing interface*. An outgoing interface must be either a dispatch or a custom interface. Dispatch interfaces are supported by all clients. The custom attribute with the ID 0F21F359-AB84-41e8-9A78-36D110E6D2F9 defines the name of the interface that will be created in the RCW. The outgoing interface must also be written to the interfaces supported by the component inside the coclass section, and marked as a source interface (code file COMServer/COMServer.idl):

```
library COMServerLib
{
  importlib("stdole2.tlb");
  [
    uuid(5CFF102B-0961-4EC6-8BB4-759A3AB6EF48),
    helpstring("_ICompletedEvents Interface"),
    custom(0F21F359-AB84-41e8-9A78-36D110E6D2F9,
    "Wrox.ProCSharp.Interop.Server.ICompletedEvents"),
  ]
  dispinterface _ICompletedEvents
  {
    properties:
    methods:
      [id(1)] void Completed(void);
  };
  [
    uuid(ACB04E72-EB08-4D4A-91D3-34A5DB55D4B4),
    helpstring("COMDemo Class")
    custom(0F21F359-AB84-41e8-9A78-36D110E6D2F9,
      "Wrox.ProCSharp.COMInterop.Server.COMDemo")
  ]
  coclass COMDemo
  {
    [default] interface IWelcome;
    interface IMath;
    [default, source] dispinterface _ICompletedEvents;
  };
```

You can use a wizard to create an implementation that fires the event back to the client. Open the class view, select the class CComDemo, open the context menu, and select Add ➪ Add Connection Point ... to start the Implement Connection Point Wizard (see Figure 23-10). Select the source interface ICompletedEvents for implementation with the connection point.

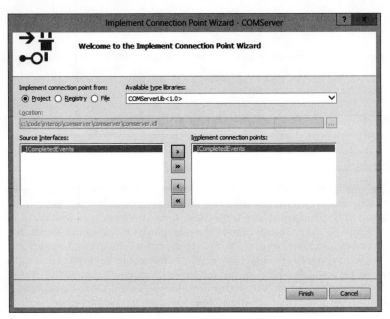

FIGURE 23-10

The wizard creates the proxy class `CProxy_ICompletedEvents` to fire the events to the client, and the class `CCOMDemo` is changed. The class now inherits from `IConnectionPointContainerImpl` and the proxy class. The interface `IConnectionPointContainer` is added to the interface map, and a connection point map is added to the source interface `_ICompletedEvents` (code file `COMServer/COMDemo.h`):

```
class ATL_NO_VTABLE CCOMDemo :
  public CComObjectRootEx<CComSingleThreadModel>,
  public CComCoClass<CCOMDemo, &CLSID_COMDemo>,
  public IDispatchImpl<IWelcome, &IID_IWelcome, &LIBID_COMServerLib,
    /*wMajor =*/ 1, /*wMinor =*/ 0>,
  public IDispatchImpl<IMath, &IID_IMath, &LIBID_COMServerLib, 1, 0>,
  public IConnectionPointContainerImpl<CCOMDemo>,
  public CProxy_ICompletedEvents<CCOMDemo>
{
public:
//...
BEGIN_COM_MAP(CCOMDemo)
  COM_INTERFACE_ENTRY(IWelcome)
  COM_INTERFACE_ENTRY(IMath)
  COM_INTERFACE_ENTRY2(IDispatch, IWelcome)
  COM_INTERFACE_ENTRY(IConnectionPointContainer)
END_COM_MAP()
//...
public:
  BEGIN_CONNECTION_POINT_MAP(CCOMDemo)
    CONNECTION_POINT_ENTRY(__uuidof(_ICompletedEvents))
  END_CONNECTION_POINT_MAP()
};
```

Finally, the method `Fire_Completed` from the proxy class can be called inside the methods `Add` and `Sub` in the file `COMDemo.cpp`:

```
STDMETHODIMP CCOMDemo::Add(LONG val1, LONG val2, LONG* result)
{
  *result = val1 + val2;
  Fire_Completed();
  return S_OK;
}

STDMETHODIMP CCOMDemo::Sub(LONG val1, LONG val2, LONG* result)
{
  *result = val1 - val2;
  Fire_Completed();
  return S_OK;
}
```

After rebuilding the COM DLL, you can change the .NET client to use these COM events just like a normal .NET event (code file `DotnetClient/Program.cs`):

```
static void Main()
{
  var obj = new COMDemo();

  IWelcome welcome = obj;
  Console.WriteLine(welcome.Greeting("Stephanie"));

  obj.Completed += () => Console.WriteLine("Calculation completed");

  IMath math = (IMath)welcome;
  int result = math.Add(3, 5);
  Console.WriteLine(result);

  Marshal.ReleaseComObject(math);
}
```

As you can see, the RCW offers automatic mapping from COM events to .NET events. COM events can be used similarly to .NET events in a .NET client.

USING A .NET COMPONENT FROM A COM CLIENT

So far, you have seen how to access a COM component from a .NET client. Equally interesting is finding a solution for accessing .NET components on an old COM client that is using Visual Basic 6.0, or C++ with Microsoft Foundation Classes (MFC) or the Active Template Library (ATL).

In this section, a COM object is defined with .NET code that is used by a COM client with the help of a COM callable wrapper (CCW). By using the object from a COM client, you will see how to create a type library from the .NET assembly, use different .NET attributes to specify COM interop behaviors, and register the .NET assembly as a COM component. Then, a COM client with C++ is created to use the CCW. Finally, the .NET component is expanded to offer COM connection points.

COM Callable Wrapper

If you want to access a COM component with a .NET client, you have to work with an RCW. To access a .NET component from a COM client application, you must use a CCW. Figure 23-11 shows the CCW that wraps a .NET class and offers COM interfaces that a COM client expects to use. The CCW offers interfaces such as `IUnknown`, `IDispatch`, and others. It also offers interfaces such as `IConnectionPointContainer` and `IConnectionPoint` for events. Of course, the CCW also provides the custom interfaces that are defined by the .NET class such as `IWelcome` and `IMath`. A COM client gets what it expects from a COM object — although a .NET component operates behind the scenes. The wrapper deals with methods such as `AddRef`, `Release`, and `QueryInterface` from the `IUnknown` interface, whereas in the .NET object you can count on the garbage collector without the need to deal with reference counts.

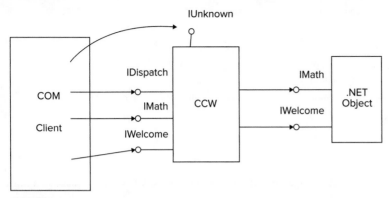

FIGURE 23-11

Creating a .NET Component

In the following example, you build the same functionality into a .NET class that you have previously built into a COM component. Start by creating a C# class library, and name it **DotNetServer**. Then add the interfaces IWelcome and IMath, and the class DotNetComponent that implements these interfaces. The attribute ComVisible(true) makes the class and interfaces available for COM (code file DotnetServer/DotnetServer.cs):

```
using System;
using System.Runtime.InteropServices;

namespace Wrox.ProCSharp.Interop.Server
{
  [ComVisible(true)]
  public interface IWelcome
  {
    string Greeting(string name);
  }

  [ComVisible(true)]
  public interface IMath
  {
    int Add(int val1, int val2);
    int Sub(int val1, int val2);
  }

  [ComVisible(true)]
  public class DotnetComponent: IWelcome, IMath
  {
    public DotnetComponent()
    {
    }

    public string Greeting(string name)
    {
      return "Hello " + name;
    }

    public int Add(int val1, int val2)
    {
      return val1 + val2;
    }

    public int Sub(int val1, int val2)
    {
```

```
            return val1 - val2;
        }
    }
}
```

After building the project, you can create a type library.

Creating a Type Library

A type library can be created by using the command-line utility `tlbexp`. The command:

```
tlbexp DotnetServer.dll
```

creates the type library `DotnetServer.tlb`. You can view the type library with the utility *OLE/COM Object Viewer,* `oleview.exe`. This tool is part of the Microsoft SDK, and you can start it from the Visual Studio 2012 command prompt. Select File ➪ View TypeLib to open the type library. Now you can see the interface definition, which is very similar to the interfaces created with the COM server earlier.

The name of the type library is created from the name of the assembly. The header of the type library also defines the full name of the assembly in a custom attribute, and all the interfaces are forward declared before they are defined:

```
// Generated .IDL file (by the OLE/COM Object Viewer)
//
// typelib filename: <could not determine filename>

[
  uuid(EEA130ED-40E1-4BF8-B06E-6CCA0FD21788),
  version(1.0),
  custom(90883F05-3D28-11D2-8F17-00A0C9A6186D, "DotnetServer, Version=1.0.0.0,
          Culture=neutral, PublicKeyToken=null")
]
library DotnetServer
{
    // TLib :      // TLib : mscorlib.dll :
      // {BED7F4EA-1A96-11D2-8F08-00A0C9A6186D}
    importlib("mscorlib.tlb");
    // TLib : OLE Automation : {00020430-0000-0000-c260-000000000046}
    importlib("stdole2.tlb");

    // Forward declare all types defined in this typelib
    interface IWelcome;
    interface IMath;
    interface _DotnetComponent;
```

In the following generated code, you can see that the interfaces `IWelcome` and `IMath` are defined as COM dual interfaces. All the methods that have been declared in the C# code are listed here in the type library definition. The parameters changed; the .NET types are mapped to COM types (for example, from the `String` class to the `BSTR` type), and the signature is changed, so that an `HRESULT` is returned. Because the interfaces are dual, dispatch IDs are also generated:

```
    [
      odl,
      uuid(6AE7CB9C-7471-3B6A-9E13-51C2294266F0),
      version(1.0),
      dual,
      oleautomation,
      custom(0F21F359-AB84-41E8-9A78-36D110E6D2F9,
        "Wrox.ProCSharp.Interop.Server.IWelcome")
    ]
```

```
interface IWelcome : IDispatch {
  [id(0x60020000)]
  HRESULT Greeting(
    [in] BSTR name,
    [out, retval] BSTR* pRetVal);
};


[
  odl,
  uuid(AED00E6F-3A60-3EB8-B974-1556096350CB),
  version(1.0),
  dual,
  oleautomation,
  custom(0F21F359-AB84-41E8-9A78-36D110E6D2F9,
    "Wrox.ProCSharp.Interop.Server.IMath")
]
interface IMath : IDispatch {
  [id(0x60020000)]
  HRESULT Add(
    [in] long val1,
    [in] long val2,
    [out, retval] long* pRetVal);
  [id(0x60020001)]
  HRESULT Sub(
    [in] long val1,
    [in] long val2,
    [out, retval] long* pRetVal);
};
```

The `coclass` section marks the COM object itself. The `uuid` in the header is the CLSID used to instantiate the object. The class `DotnetComponent` supports the interfaces `_DotnetComponent`, `_Object`, `IWelcome`, and `IMath`. `_Object` is defined in the file `mscorlib.tlb` included in an earlier code section and offers the methods of the base class `Object`. The default interface of the component is `_DotnetComponent`, which is defined after the `coclass` section as a dispatch interface. In the interface declaration, it is marked as dual, but because no methods are included, it is a dispatch interface. With this interface, it is possible to access all methods of the component using late binding:

```
[
  uuid(2F1E78D4-1147-33AC-9233-C0F51121DAAA),
  version(1.0),
  custom(0F21F359-AB84-41E8-9A78-36D110E6D2F9,
    "Wrox.ProCSharp.Interop.Server.DotnetComponent")
]
coclass DotnetComponent {
  [default] interface _DotnetComponent;
  interface _Object;
  interface IWelcome;
  interface IMath;
};


[
  odl,
  uuid(2B36C1BF-61F7-3E84-87B2-EAB52144046D),
  hidden,
  dual,
  oleautomation,
  custom(0F21F359-AB84-41E8-9A78-36D110E6D2F9,
    "Wrox.ProCSharp.Interop.Server.DotnetComponent")
]
interface _DotnetComponent : IDispatch {
};
};
```

There are quite a few defaults for generating the type library. However, often it is advantageous to change some of the default .NET to COM mappings. This can be done with several attributes in the System .Runtime.InteropServices namespaces.

COM Interop Attributes

Applying attributes from the namespace System.Runtime.InteropServices to classes, interfaces, or methods enables you to change the implementation of the CCW. The following table describes these attributes.

ATTRIBUTE	DESCRIPTION
Guid	This attribute can be assigned to the assembly, interfaces, and classes. Using the Guid as an assembly attribute defines the type-library ID, applying it to interfaces defines the interface ID (IID), and setting the attribute to a class defines the class ID (CLSID). You can create the unique IDs that must be defined with this attribute with the utility guidgen. The CLSID and type-library IDs are changed automatically with every build. If you don't want that behavior, you can change it by using this attribute. The IID is changed only if the signature of the interface changes—for example, if a method is added or removed, or some parameters are changed. Because with COM the IID should change with every new version of this interface, this is a very good default behavior, and usually there's no need to apply the IID with the Guid attribute. The only time you want to apply a fixed IID for an interface is when the .NET interface is an exact representation of an existing COM interface and the COM client already expects this identifier.
ProgId	This attribute can be applied to a class to specify what name should be used when the object is configured in the registry.
ComVisible	In the Assembly Information settings of the Project properties you can configure whether all the types of the assembly should be visible by COM. The default setting is false, which is a useful default that makes it necessary to explicitly mark the classes, interfaces, and delegates with the ComVisible attribute to create a COM representation. If the default setting is changed to make all types visible by COM, you can set the ComVisible attribute to false for the types for which a COM representation should not be created.
InterfaceType	This attribute, if set to a ComInterfaceType enumeration value, enables you to modify the default dual interface type that is created for .NET interfaces. ComInterfaceType has the values InterfaceIsDual, InterfaceIsIDispatch, and InterfaceIsIUnknown. To apply a custom interface type to a .NET interface, set the attribute like this: InterfaceType(ComInterfaceType.InterfaceIsIUnknown).
ClassInterface	This attribute enables you to modify the default dispatch interface that is created for a class. ClassInterface accepts an argument of a ClassInterfaceType enumeration. The possible values are AutoDispatch, AutoDual, and None. In the previous example, the default is AutoDispatch because a dispatch interface is created. If the class should be accessible only by the defined interfaces, apply the attribute ClassInterface(ClassInterfaceType.None) to the class.
DispId	This attribute can be used with dual and dispatch interfaces to define the DispId of methods and properties.
In Out	With COM the direction of parameter types can be specified. Use the attribute In if the parameter should be sent to the component. For returning a value from the parameter, specify Out. For using both directions, use both attributes In, Out.
Optional	Parameters of COM methods may be optional. You can mark optional parameters with the Optional attribute.

Now you can change the C# code to specify a dual interface type for the `IWelcome` interface and a custom interface type for the `IMath` interface. With the class `DotnetComponent`, the attribute `ClassInterface` with the argument `ClassInterfaceType.None` specifies that no separate COM interface will be generated. The attributes `ProgId` and `Guid` specify a ProgID and a GUID, respectively (code file `DotnetServer/DotnetServer.cs`):

```
[InterfaceType(ComInterfaceType.InterfaceIsDual)]
[ComVisible(true)]
public interface IWelcome
{
    [DispId(60040)]
    string Greeting(string name);
}

[InterfaceType(ComInterfaceType.InterfaceIsIUnknown)]
[ComVisible(true)]
public interface IMath
{
    int Add(int val1, int val2);
    int Sub(int val1, int val2);
}

[ClassInterface(ClassInterfaceType.None)]
[ProgId("Wrox.DotnetComponent")]
[Guid("77839717-40DD-4876-8297-35B98A8402C7")]
[ComVisible(true)]
public class DotnetComponent: IWelcome, IMath
{
    public DotnetComponent()
    {
    }
```

Rebuilding the class library and the type library changes the interface definition. You can verify this with `OleView.exe`. `IWelcome` is now a dual interface, `IMath` a custom interface that derives from `IUnknown` instead of `IDispatch`, and the `coclass` section no longer has a `_DotnetComponent` interface.

COM Registration

Before the .NET component can be used as a COM object, it is necessary to configure it in the registry. Also, if you don't want to copy the assembly into the same directory as the client application, it is necessary to install the assembly in the global assembly cache. The global assembly cache itself is discussed in Chapter 19.

To install the assembly in the global assembly cache, you must sign it with a strong name (using Visual Studio 2012, you can define a strong name in properties of the solution). Then you can register the assembly in the global assembly cache:

```
gacutil -i DotnetServer.dll
```

Now you can use the `regasm` utility to configure the component inside the registry. The option `/tlb` extracts the type library and configures the type library in the registry:

```
regasm DotnetServer.dll /tlb
```

The information for the .NET component that is written to the registry is as follows. The `All` COM configuration is in the hive `HKEY_CLASSES_ROOT` (`HKCR`). The key of the ProgID (in this example, it is `Wrox.DotnetComponent`) is written directly to this hive, along with the CLSID.

The key HKCR\CLSID\{CLSID}\InProcServer32 has the following entries:

➤ mscoree.dll — Represents the CCW. This is a real COM object that is responsible for hosting the .NET component. This COM object accesses the .NET component to offer COM behavior for the client. The file mscoree.dll is loaded and instantiated from the client via the normal COM instantiation mechanism.

➤ ThreadingModel=Both — This is an attribute of the mscoree.dll COM object. This component is programmed in a way that offers support both for STA and MTA.

➤ Assembly=DotnetServer, Version=1.0.0.0, Culture=neutral, PublicKeyToken=5cd57c93b4d9c41a — The value of the Assembly stores the assembly full name, including the version number and the public key token, so that the assembly can be uniquely identified. The assembly registered here will be loaded by mscoree.dll.

➤ Class=Wrox.ProCSharp.Interop.Server.DotnetComponent — The name of the class is also used by mscoree.dll. This is the class that will be instantiated.

➤ RuntimeVersion=v4.0.20826 — The registry entry RuntimeVersion specifies the version of the .NET runtime that will be used to host the .NET assembly.

In addition to the configurations shown here, all the interfaces and the type library are configured with their identifiers, too.

> **NOTE** *If the .NET component was developed with the platform target Any CPU (which is the Visual Studio 2012 default setting for libraries), it can be configured as a 32-bit or 64-bit COM component. Starting regasm from the VS2012 x86 Native Tools Command Prompt uses* regasm *from the directory* <windows>\Microsoft .NET\Framework\v4.0.30319. *Starting* regasm *from the VS2012 x64 Native Tools Command Prompt (in case you have a 64-bit Windows) uses* regasm *from the directory* <windows>\Microsoft.NET\Framework64\v4.0.30319. *Depending on which tool is used, the component is registered with either* HKCR\WOW6432Node\CLSID *or* HKCR\ CLSID.

Creating a COM Client Application

Now it's time to create a COM client. Start by creating a simple C++ Win32 Console application project, and name it COMClient. You can leave the default options selected and click Finish in the Project Wizard.

At the beginning of the file COMClient.cpp, add a preprocessor command to include the <iostream> header file and to import the type library that you created for the .NET component. The import statement creates a "smart pointer" class that makes it easier to deal with COM objects. During a build process, the import statement creates .tlh and .tli files that you can find in the debug directory of your project, which includes the smart pointer class. Then add using namespace directives to open the namespace std, which will be used to write output messages to the console, and the namespace DotnetServer that is created inside the smart pointer class (code file COMClient\COMClient.cpp):

```
// COMClient.cpp: Defines the entry point for the console application.
//

#include "stdafx.h"
#include <iostream>
#import "./DotNetServer/bin/debug/DotnetServer.tlb" named_guids

using namespace std;
using namespace DotnetServer;
```

In the _tmain method, the first thing to do before any other COM call is the initialization of COM with the API call `CoInitialize`, which creates and enters an STA for the thread. The variable `spWelcome` is of type `IWelcomePtr`, which is a smart pointer. The smart pointer method `CreateInstance` accepts the ProgID as an argument to create the COM object by using the COM API `CoCreateInstance`. The operator `->` is overridden with the smart pointer so that you can invoke the methods of the COM object, such as `Greeting`:

```
int _tmain(int argc, _TCHAR* argv[])
{
  HRESULT hr;
  hr = CoInitialize(NULL);

  try
  {
    IWelcomePtr spWelcome;

    // CoCreateInstance()
    hr = spWelcome.CreateInstance("Wrox.DotnetComponent");

    cout << spWelcome->Greeting("Bill") << endl;
```

The second interface supported by your .NET component is `IMath`, and there is a smart pointer that wraps the COM interface: `IMathPtr`. You can directly assign one smart pointer to another, as in `spMath = spWelcome;`. In the implementation of the smart pointer (the = operator is overridden), the `QueryInterface` method is called. With a reference to the `IMath` interface, you can call the `Add` method:

```
    IMathPtr spMath;
    spMath = spWelcome;    // QueryInterface()

    long result = spMath->Add(4, 5);
    cout << "result:" << result << endl;
  }
```

If an `HRESULT` error value is returned by the COM object (this is done by the CCW that returns `HRESULT` errors if the .NET component generates exceptions), the smart pointer wraps the `HRESULT` errors and generates _com_error exceptions instead. Errors are handled in the `catch` block. At the end of the program, the COM DLLs are closed and unloaded using `CoUninitialize`:

```
  catch (_com_error& e)
  {
    cout << e.ErrorMessage() << endl;
  }

  CoUninitialize();
  return 0;
}
```

If you run the application, you will get outputs from the `Greeting` and the `Add` methods to the console. You can also try to debug into the smart pointer class, where you can see the COM API calls directly.

> **NOTE** *If you get an exception stating that the component cannot be found, check whether the same version of the assembly that is configured in the registry is installed in the global assembly cache.*

Adding Connection Points

Adding support for COM events to the .NET components requires some changes to the implementation of your .NET class. Offering COM events is not a simple matter of using the `event` and `delegate` keywords; it is necessary to add some other COM interop attributes.

First, you have to add an interface to the .NET project: `IMathEvents`. This interface is the source or outgoing interface for the component, and it will be implemented by the `sink` object in the client. A source interface must be either a dispatch interface or a custom interface. A scripting client supports only dispatch interfaces. Dispatch interfaces are usually preferred as source interfaces (code file `DotnetServer/DotnetServer.cs`):

```
[InterfaceType(ComInterfaceType.InterfaceIsIDispatch)]
[ComVisible(true)]
public interface IMathEvents
{
  [DispId(46200)]
  void CalculationCompleted();
}
```

With the class `DotnetComponent`, a source interface must be specified. This can be done with the attribute `[ComSourceInterfaces]`. Add this attribute, and specify the outgoing interface declared earlier. You can add more than one source interface with different constructors of the attribute class; however, the only client language that supports more than one source interface is C++. Visual Basic 6.0 clients support only one source interface:

```
[ClassInterface(ClassInterfaceType.None)]
[ProgId("Wrox.DotnetComponent")]
[Guid("77839717-40DD-4876-8297-35B98A8402C7")]
[ComSourceInterfaces(typeof(IMathEvents))]
[ComVisible(true)]
public class DotnetComponent : IWelcome, IMath
{
  public DotnetComponent()
  {
  }
```

Inside the class `DotnetComponent`, you have to declare an event for every method of the source interface. The type of the method must be the name of the delegate, and the name of the event must be exactly the same as the name of the method inside the source interface. You can add the event calls to the `Add` and `Sub` methods. This step is the normal .NET way to invoke events, as discussed in Chapter 8:

```
public event Action CalculationCompleted;

public int Add(int val1, int val2)
{
  int result = val1 + val2;
  if (CalculationCompleted != null)
    CalculationCompleted();
  return result;
}

public int Sub(int val1, int val2)
{
  int result = val1 - val2;
  if (CalculationCompleted != null)
    CalculationCompleted();
  return result;
}
}
```

> **NOTE** *The name of the event must be the same as the name of the method inside the source interface. Otherwise, the events cannot be mapped for COM clients.*

Creating a Client with a Sink Object

After you've built and registered the .NET assembly and installed it into the global assembly cache, you can build a client application by using the event sources. Implementing a callback or sink object that implements the IDispatch interface was — using Visual Basic 6.0 — just a matter of adding the With Events keyword, very similar to how Visual Basic deals with .NET events today. It's more work with C++, but here the Active Template Library (ATL) helps.

Open the C++ Console application created in the section "Creating a COM Client Application" and add the following includes to the file stdafx.h:

```
#include <atlbase.h>
extern CComModule _Module;
#include <atlcom.h>
```

The file stdafx.cpp requires an include of the ATL implementation file atlimpl.cpp:

```
#include <atlimpl.cpp>
```

Add the new class CEventHandler to the file COMClient.cpp. This class contains the implementation of the IDispatch interface to be called by the component. The implementation of the IDispatch interface is done by the base class IDispEventImpl. This class reads the type library to match the dispatch IDs of the methods and the parameters to the methods of the class. The template parameters of the class IDispatchEventImpl require an ID of the sink object (here the ID 4 is used), the class that implements the callback methods (CEventHandler), the interface ID of the callback interface (DIID_IMathEvents), the ID of the type library (LIBID_DotnetComponent), and the version number of the type library. You can find the named IDs DIID_IMathEvents and LIBID_DotnetComponent in the file dotnetcomponent.tlh that was created from the #import statement.

The sink map that is surrounded by BEGIN_SINK_MAP and END_SINK_MAP defines the methods that are implemented by the sink object. SINK_ENTRY_EX maps the method OnCalcCompleted to the dispatch ID 46200. This dispatch ID was defined with the method CalculationCompleted of the IMathEvents interface in the .NET component (code file COMClient/COMClient.cpp):

```
class CEventHandler: public IDispEventImpl<4, CEventHandler,
    &DIID_IMathEvents, &LIBID_DotnetServer, 1, 0>
{
public:
  BEGIN_SINK_MAP(CEventHandler)
    SINK_ENTRY_EX(4, DIID_IMathEvents, 46200, OnCalcCompleted)
  END_SINK_MAP()

  HRESULT __stdcall OnCalcCompleted()
  {
    cout << "calculation completed" << endl;
    return S_OK;
  }
};
```

The main method now needs a change to advise the component of the existence of the event sink object, so that the component can call back into the sink. This can be done with the method `DispEventAdvise` of the `CEventHandler` class by passing an `IUnknown` interface pointer. The method `DispEventUnadvise` unregisters the sink object again:

```cpp
int _tmain(int argc, _TCHAR* argv[])
{
  HRESULT hr;
  hr = CoInitialize(NULL);

  try
  {
    IWelcomePtr spWelcome;
    hr = spWelcome.CreateInstance("Wrox.DotnetComponent");

    IUnknownPtr spUnknown = spWelcome;

    cout << spWelcome->Greeting("Bill") << endl;

    CEventHandler* eventHandler = new CEventHandler();
    hr = eventHandler->DispEventAdvise(spUnknown);

    IMathPtr spMath;
    spMath = spWelcome;    // QueryInterface()

    long result = spMath->Add(4, 5);
    cout << "result:" << result << endl;

    eventHandler->DispEventUnadvise(spWelcome.GetInterfacePtr());
    delete eventHandler;
  }
  catch (_com_error& e)
  {
    cout << e.ErrorMessage() << endl;
  }

  CoUninitialize();
  return 0;
}
```

PLATFORM INVOKE

Not all the features of Windows API calls are available from the .NET Framework. This is true not only for old Windows API calls but also for very new features from Windows 8 or Windows Server 2012. Maybe you've written some DLLs that export unmanaged methods and you would like to use them from C# as well.

To reuse an unmanaged library that doesn't contain COM objects, but only exported functions, platform invoke (p/invoke) can be used. With p/invoke, the CLR loads the DLL that includes the function that should be called and marshals the parameters.

To use the unmanaged function, first you have to determine the name of the function as it is exported. You can do this by using the `dumpbin` tool with the `/exports` option.

For example, the command:

```
dumpbin /exports c:\windows\system32\kernel32.dll | more
```

lists all exported functions from the DLL `kernel32.dll`. In the example, you use the `CreateHardLink` Windows API function to create a hard link to an existing file. With this API call, you can have several filenames that reference the same file as long as the filenames are on one hard disk only. This API call is not available from .NET Framework 4.5, so platform invoke must be used.

To call a native function, you have to define a C# external method with the same number of arguments, and the argument types that are defined with the unmanaged method must have mapped types with managed code.

The Windows API call `CreateHardLink` has this definition in C++:

```
BOOL CreateHardLink(
    LPCTSTR lpFileName,
    LPCTSTR lpExistingFileName,
    LPSECURITY_ATTRIBUTES lpSecurityAttributes);
```

This definition must be mapped to .NET data types. The return type is a `BOOL` with unmanaged code; this simply maps to the `bool` data type. `LPCTSTR` defines a `long` pointer to a `const` string. The Windows API uses the Hungarian naming convention for the data type. `LP` is a `long` pointer, `C` is a const, and `STR` is a null-terminated string. The `T` marks the type as a generic type, and the type is resolved to either `LPCSTR` (an ANSI string) or `LPWSTR` (a wide Unicode string), depending on the compiler's settings. C strings map to the .NET type `String`. `LPSECURITY_ATTRIBUTES`, which is a long pointer to a struct of type `SECURITY_ATTRIBUTES`. Because you can pass `NULL` to this argument, mapping this type to `IntPtr` is okay. The C# declaration of this method must be marked with the `extern` modifier, because there's no implementation of this method within the C# code. Instead, the method implementation is found in the DLL `kernel32.dll`, which is referenced with the attribute `[DllImport]`. The return type of the .NET declaration `CreateHardLink` is of type `bool`, and the native method `CreateHardLink` returns a `BOOL`, so some additional clarification is useful. Because there are different Boolean data types with C++ (for example, the native `bool` and the Windows-defined `BOOL`, which have different values), the attribute `[MarshalAs]` specifies to what native type the .NET type `bool` should map:

```
[DllImport("kernel32.dll", SetLastError="true",
        EntryPoint="CreateHardLink", CharSet=CharSet.Unicode)]
[return: MarshalAs(UnmanagedType.Bool)]
public static extern bool CreateHardLink(string newFileName,
                                string existingFilename,
                                IntPtr securityAttributes);
```

> **NOTE** *The website* `http://www.pinvoke.net` *and the tool P/Invoke Interop Assistant, which can be downloaded from* `http://www.codeplex.com`, *are very helpful with the conversion from native to managed code.*

The settings that you can specify with the attribute `[DllImport]` are listed in the following table.

DLLIMPORT PROPERTY OR FIELD	DESCRIPTION
EntryPoint	You can give the C# declaration of the function a different name than the one it has with the unmanaged library. The name of the method in the unmanaged library is defined in the field EntryPoint.
CallingConvention	Depending on the compiler or compiler settings that were used to compile the unmanaged function, different calling conventions can be used. The calling convention defines how the parameters are handled and where to put them on the stack. You can define the calling convention by setting an enumerable value. The Windows API usually uses the StdCall calling convention on the Windows operating system, and it uses the Cdecl calling convention on Windows CE. Setting the value to CallingConvention.Winapi works for the Windows API in both the Windows and the Windows CE environments.
CharSet	String parameters can be either ANSI or Unicode. With the CharSet setting, you can define how strings are managed. Possible values that are defined with the CharSet enumeration are Ansi, Unicode, and Auto. CharSet.Auto uses Unicode on the Windows NT platform, and ANSI on Windows 98 and Windows ME.
SetLastError	If the unmanaged function sets an error by using the Windows API SetLastError, you can set the SetLastError field to true. This way, you can read the error number afterward by using Marshal .GetLastWin32Error.

To make the CreateHardLink method easier to use from a .NET environment, you should follow these guidelines:

➤ Create an internal class named NativeMethods that wraps the platform invoke method calls.

➤ Create a public class to offer the native method functionality to .NET applications.

➤ Use security attributes to mark the required security.

In the following example (code file PInvokeSample/NativeMethods.cs), the public method CreateHardLink in the class FileUtility is the method that can be used by .NET applications. This method has the filename arguments reversed compared to the native Windows API method CreateHardLink. The first argument is the name of the existing file, and the second argument is the new file. This is similar to other classes in the framework, such as File.Copy. Because the third argument used to pass the security attributes for the new filename is not used with this implementation, the public method has just two parameters. The return type is changed as well. Instead of returning an error by returning the value false, an exception is thrown. In case of an error, the unmanaged method CreateHardLink sets the error number with the unmanaged API SetLastError. To read this value from .NET, the [DllImport] field SetLastError is set to true. Within the managed method CreateHardLink, the error number is read by calling Marshal.GetLastWin32Error. To create an error message from this number, the Win32Exception class from the namespace System.ComponentModel is used. This class accepts an error number with the constructor, and returns a localized error message. In case of an error, an exception of type IOException is thrown, which has an inner exception of type Win32Exception. The public method CreateHardLink has the FileIOPermission attribute applied to check whether the caller has the necessary permission. You can read more about .NET security in Chapter 22.

```
using System;
using System.ComponentModel;
using System.IO;
using System.Runtime.InteropServices;
using System.Security;
using System.Security.Permissions;
```

```csharp
namespace Wrox.ProCSharp.Interop
{
  [SecurityCritical]
  internal static class NativeMethods
  {
    [DllImport("kernel32.dll", SetLastError = true,
      EntryPoint = "CreateHardLinkW", CharSet = CharSet.Unicode)]
    [return: MarshalAs(UnmanagedType.Bool)]
    private static extern bool CreateHardLink(
      [In, MarshalAs(UnmanagedType.LPWStr)] string newFileName,
      [In, MarshalAs(UnmanagedType.LPWStr)] string existingFileName,
      IntPtr securityAttributes);


    internal static void CreateHardLink(string oldFileName,
                                        string newFileName)
    {
      if (!CreateHardLink(newFileName, oldFileName, IntPtr.Zero))
      {
        var ex = new Win32Exception(Marshal.GetLastWin32Error());
        throw new IOException(ex.Message, ex);
      }
    }
  }

  public static class FileUtility
  {
    [FileIOPermission(SecurityAction.LinkDemand, Unrestricted = true)]
    public static void CreateHardLink(string oldFileName,
                                      string newFileName)
    {
      NativeMethods.CreateHardLink(oldFileName, newFileName);
    }
  }
}
```

This class can now be used to create hard links very easily (code file `PInvokeSample/Program.cs`). If the file passed with the first argument of the program does not exist, you will get an exception with the message "The system cannot find the file specified." If the file exists, you get a new filename referencing the original file. You can easily verify this by changing text in one file; it will show up in the other file as well:

```csharp
using System;
using System.IO;

namespace Wrox.ProCSharp.Interop
{
  class Program
  {
    static void Main(string[] args)
    {
      if (args.Length != 2)
      {
        Console.WriteLine("usage: PInvokeSample " +
          "existingfilename newfilename");
        return;
      }
      try
      {
        FileUtility.CreateHardLink(args[0], args[1]);
      }
      catch (IOException ex)
      {
        Console.WriteLine(ex.Message);
```

```
          }

      }
    }
  }
```

With native method calls, often you have to use Windows handles. A Window handle is a 32-bit value for which, depending on the handle types, some values are not allowed. With .NET 1.0 for handles, usually the `IntPtr` structure was used because you can set every possible 32-bit value with this structure. However, with some handle types, this led to security problems and possible threading race conditions and leaked handles with the finalization phase. That's why .NET 2.0 introduced the `SafeHandle` class. The class `SafeHandle` is an abstract base class for every Windows handle. Derived classes inside the `Microsoft.Win32.SafeHandles` namespace are `SafeHandleZeroOrMinusOneIsInvalid` and `SafeHandleMinusOneIsInvalid`. As the name indicates, these classes do not accept invalid 0 or −1 values. Further derived handle types are `SafeFileHandle`, `SafeWaitHandle`, `SafeNCryptHandle`, and `SafePipeHandle`, which can be used by the specific Windows API calls.

For example, to map the Windows API `CreateFile`, you can use the following declaration to return a `SafeFileHandle`. Of course, usually you could use the .NET classes `File` and `FileInfo` instead.

```
[DllImport("Kernel32.dll", SetLastError = true,
         CharSet = CharSet.Unicode)]
internal static extern SafeFileHandle CreateFile(
   string fileName,
   [MarshalAs(UnmanagedType.U4)] FileAccess fileAccess,
   [MarshalAs(UnmanagedType.U4)] FileShare fileShare,
   IntPtr securityAttributes,
   [MarshalAs(UnmanagedType.U4)] FileMode creationDisposition,
   int flags,
   SafeFileHandle template);
```

> **NOTE** *In Chapter 25, "Transactions," you can learn how to create a custom* `SafeHandle` *class to work with the transacted file API from Windows, which has been available since Windows Vista.*

SUMMARY

In this chapter, you have seen how the different generations of COM and .NET applications can interact. Instead of rewriting applications and components, a COM component can be used from a .NET application just like a .NET class. The tool that makes this possible is `tlbimp`, which creates a runtime callable wrapper (RCW) that hides the COM object behind a .NET façade.

Likewise, `tlbexp` creates a type library from a .NET component that is used by the COM callable wrapper (CCW). The CCW hides the .NET component behind a COM façade. Using .NET classes as COM components makes it necessary to use some attributes from the namespace `System.Runtime.InteropServices` to define specific COM characteristics that are needed by the COM client.

With platform invoke, you've seen how native methods can be invoked using C#. Platform invoke requires redefining the native method with C# and .NET data types. After defining the mapping, you can invoke the native method as if it were a C# method.

The next chapter is on accessing the file system with files and streams.

24

Manipulating Files and the Registry

WHAT'S IN THIS CHAPTER?

- ➤ Exploring the directory structure
- ➤ Moving, copying, and deleting files and folders
- ➤ Reading and writing text in files
- ➤ Reading and writing keys in the registry
- ➤ Reading and writing to isolated storage

WROX.COM CODE DOWNLOADS FOR THIS CHAPTER

The wrox.com code downloads for this chapter are found at `http://www.wrox.com/remtitle .cgi?isbn=1118314425` on the Download Code tab. The code for this chapter is divided into the following major examples:

- ➤ BinaryFileReader
- ➤ DriveViewer
- ➤ FileProperties
- ➤ FilePropertiesAndMovement
- ➤ MappedMemoryFiles
- ➤ ReadingACLs
- ➤ ReadingACLsFromDirectory
- ➤ ReadingFiles
- ➤ ReadWriteText

FILE AND THE REGISTRY

This chapter examines how to perform tasks involving reading from and writing to files and the C# system registry. Microsoft has provided very intuitive object models covering these areas, and in this chapter you learn how to use .NET base classes to perform the listed tasks. In the case of file system operations, the relevant classes are almost all found in the `System.IO` namespace, whereas registry operations are dealt with by classes in the `Microsoft.Win32` namespace.

> **NOTE** *The .NET base classes also include a number of classes and interfaces in the* `System.Runtime.Serialization` *namespace. concerned with serialization—that is, the process of converting data (for example, the contents of a document) into a stream of bytes for storage. This chapter does not focus on these classes; it focuses on the classes that give you direct access to files.*

Note that security is particularly important when modifying either files or registry entries. Security is covered entirely in Chapter 22, "Security." In this chapter, however, we assume that you have sufficient access rights to run all the examples that modify files or registry entries, which should be the case if you are running from an account with administrator privileges.

MANAGING THE FILE SYSTEM

The classes used to browse around the file system and perform operations such as moving, copying, and deleting files are shown in Figure 24-1.

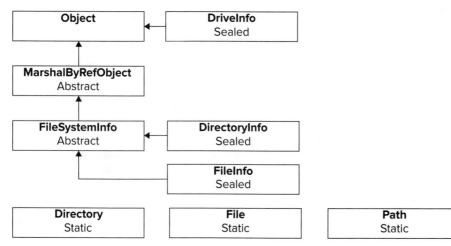

FIGURE 24-1

The following list explains the function of these classes:

➤ `System.MarshalByRefObject`—The base object class for .NET classes that are remotable; permits marshaling of data between application domains. The rest of the items in this list are part of the `System.IO` namespace.

➤ `FileSystemInfo`—The base class that represents any file system object

➤ `FileInfo` and `File`—These classes represent a file on the file system.

➤ `DirectoryInfo` and `Directory`—These classes represent a folder on the file system.

➤ `Path`—This class contains static members that you can use to manipulate pathnames.

➤ `DriveInfo`—This class provides properties and methods that provide information about a selected drive.

> **NOTE** *In Windows, the objects that contain files and that are used to organize the file system are termed* folders. *For example, in the path* C:\My Documents\ReadMe.txt, ReadMe.txt *is a file and* My Documents *is a folder. Folder is a very Windows-specific term. On virtually every other operating system, the term "directory" is used in place of folder; and in accordance with Microsoft's goal to design .NET as a platform-independent technology, the corresponding .NET base classes are called* Directory *and* DirectoryInfo. *However, due to the potential for confusion with LDAP directories and because this is a Windows book, we'll stick to the term folder in this discussion.*

.NET Classes That Represent Files and Folders

You will notice in the previous list that two classes are used to represent a folder and two classes are used to represent a file. Which one of these classes you use depends largely on how many times you need to access that folder or file:

> ➤ Directory and File contain only static methods and are never instantiated. You use these classes by supplying the path to the appropriate file system object whenever you call a member method. If you want to do only one operation on a folder or file, using these classes is more efficient because it saves the overhead of instantiating a .NET class.

> ➤ DirectoryInfo and FileInfo implement roughly the same public methods as Directory and File, as well as some public properties and constructors, but they are stateful and the members of these classes are not static. You need to instantiate these classes before each instance is associated with a particular folder or file. This means that these classes are more efficient if you are performing multiple operations using the same object. That's because they read in the authentication and other information for the appropriate file system object on construction, and then do not need to read that information again, no matter how many methods and so on you call against each object (class instance). In comparison, the corresponding stateless classes need to check the details of the file or folder again with every method you call.

This section mostly uses the FileInfo and DirectoryInfo classes, but it so happens that many (though not all) of the methods called are also implemented by File and Directory (although in those cases these methods require an extra parameter—the pathname of the file system object; also, a couple of the methods have slightly different names). For example,

```
FileInfo myFile = new FileInfo(@"C:\Program Files\My Program\ReadMe.txt");
myFile.CopyTo(@"D:\Copies\ReadMe.txt");
```

has the same effect as

```
File.Copy(@"C:\Program Files\My Program\ReadMe.txt", @"D:\Copies\ReadMe.txt");
```

The first code snippet takes slightly longer to execute because of the need to instantiate a FileInfo object, myFile, but it leaves myFile ready for you to perform further actions on the same file. By using the second example, there is no need to instantiate an object to copy the file.

You can instantiate a FileInfo or DirectoryInfo class by passing to the constructor a string containing the path to the corresponding file system object. You have just seen the process for a file. For a folder, the code looks similar:

```
DirectoryInfo myFolder = new DirectoryInfo(@"C:\Program Files");
```

If the path represents an object that does not exist, an exception is not thrown at construction, but is instead thrown the first time you call a method that actually requires the corresponding file system object to be there. You can find out whether the object exists and is of the appropriate type by checking the `Exists` property, which is implemented by both of these classes:

```
FileInfo test = new FileInfo(@"C:\Windows");
Console.WriteLine(test.Exists.ToString());
```

Note that for this property to return `true`, the corresponding file system object must be of the appropriate type. In other words, if you instantiate a `FileInfo` object, supplying the path of a folder, or you instantiate a `DirectoryInfo` object, giving it the path of a file, `Exists` will have the value `false`. Most of the properties and methods of these objects return a value if possible—they won't necessarily throw an exception just because the wrong type of object has been called, unless they are asked to do something that is impossible. For example, the preceding code snippet might first display `false` (because `C:\Windows` is a folder), but it still displays the time the folder was created because a folder has that information. However, if you tried to open the folder as if it were a file, using the `FileInfo.Open` method, you'd get an exception.

After you have established whether the corresponding file system object exists, you can (if you are using the `FileInfo` or `DirectoryInfo` class) find out information about it using the properties in the following table:

PROPERTY	DESCRIPTION
`CreationTime`	Indicates when the file or folder was created
`DirectoryName` (`FileInfo` only)	Full pathname of the containing folder
`Parent` (`DirectoryInfo` only)	The parent directory of a specified subdirectory
`Exists`	Specifies whether a file or folder exists
`Extension`	Extension of the file; it returns blank for folders
`FullName`	Full pathname of the file or folder
`LastAccessTime`	Indicates when the file or folder was last accessed
`LastWriteTime`	Indicates when the file or folder was last modified
`Name`	Name of the file or folder
`Root` (`DirectoryInfo` only)	The root portion of the path
`Length` (`FileInfo` only)	Size of the file, in bytes

You can also perform actions on the file system object using the methods in the following table:

METHOD	DESCRIPTION
`Create()`	Creates a folder or empty file of the given name. For a `FileInfo` this also returns a stream object to let you write to the file. (Streams are covered later in this chapter.)
`Delete()`	Deletes the file or folder. For folders, there is an option for the `Delete` to be recursive.
`MoveTo()`	Moves and/or renames the file or folder.
`CopyTo()`	(`FileInfo` only) Copies the file. Note that there is no copy method for folders. If you are copying complete directory trees you need to individually copy each file and create new folders corresponding to the old folders.
`GetDirectories()`	(`DirectoryInfo` only) Returns an array of `DirectoryInfo` objects representing all folders contained in this folder.
`GetFiles()`	(`DirectoryInfo` only) Returns an array of `FileInfo` objects representing all files contained in this folder.
`EnumerateFiles()`	Returns an `IEnumerable<string>` of filenames. You can act on the items in the list before the entire list is returned.
`GetFileSystemInfos()`	(`DirectoryInfo` only) Returns `FileInfo` and `DirectoryInfo` objects representing all objects contained in the folder as an array of `FileSystemInfo` references.

Note that these tables list the main properties and methods; they are not intended to be exhaustive.

> **NOTE** *The preceding tables do not list most of the properties or methods that allow you to write to or read the data in files. This is actually done using stream objects, which are covered later in this chapter.* FileInfo *also implements a number of methods,* Open, OpenRead, OpenText, OpenWrite, Create, *and* CreateText, *that return stream objects for this purpose.*

Interestingly, the creation time, last access time, and last write time are all writable:

```
// displays the creation time of a file,
// then changes it and displays it again
FileInfo test = new FileInfo(@"C:\MyFile.txt");
Console.WriteLine(test.Exists.ToString());
Console.WriteLine(test.CreationTime.ToString());
test.CreationTime = new DateTime(2010, 1, 1, 7, 30, 0);
Console.WriteLine(test.CreationTime.ToString());
```

Running this application produces results similar to the following:

```
True
2/5/2009 2:59:32 PM
1/1/2010 7:30:00 AM
```

Being able to manually modify these properties might seem strange at first, but it can be quite useful. For example, if you have a program that effectively modifies a file by simply reading it in, deleting it, and creating a new file with the new contents, you would probably want to modify the creation date to match the original creation date of the old file.

The Path Class

The Path class is not a class that you would instantiate. Rather, it exposes some static methods that make operations on pathnames easier. For example, suppose that you want to display the full pathname for a file, ReadMe.txt, in the folder C:\My Documents. You could find the path to the file using the following code:

```
Console.WriteLine(Path.Combine(@"C:\My Documents", "ReadMe.txt"));
```

Using the Path class is a lot easier than using separation symbols manually, especially because the Path class is aware of different formats for pathnames on different operating systems. At the time of this writing, Windows is the only operating system supported by .NET. However, if .NET is ported to UNIX, Path would be able to cope with UNIX paths, in which case /, rather than \, would be used as a separator in pathnames. Path.Combine is the method of this class that you are likely to use most often, but Path also implements other methods that supply information about the path or the required format for it.

Some of the static fields available to the Path class include those in the following table:

PROPERTY	DESCRIPTION
AltDirectorySeparatorChar	Provides a platform-agnostic way to specify an alternative character to separate directory levels. In Windows, a / symbol is used, whereas in UNIX, a \ symbol is used.
DirectorySeparatorChar	Provides a platform-agnostic way to specify a character to separate directory levels. In Windows, a / symbol is used, whereas in UNIX, a \ symbol is used.

continues

(continued)

PROPERTY	DESCRIPTION
PathSeparator	Provides a platform-agnostic way to specify path strings that divide environmental variables. The default value of this setting is a semicolon.
VolumeSeparatorChar	Provides a platform-agnostic way to specify a volume separator. The default value of this setting is a colon.

The following example illustrates how to browse directories and view the properties of files.

A FileProperties Sample

This section presents a sample C# application called `FileProperties`. This application presents a simple user interface that enables you to browse the file system and view the creation time, last access time, last write time, and size of files. (You can download the sample code for this application from the Wrox website at `www.wrox.com`.)

The `FileProperties` application works as follows. You type in the name of a folder or file in the main text box at the top of the window and click the Display button. If you type in the path to a folder, its contents are listed in the list boxes. If you type in the path to a file, its details are displayed in the text boxes at the bottom of the form and the contents of its parent folder are displayed in the list boxes. Figure 24-2 shows the `FileProperties` sample application in action.

The user can very easily navigate around the file system by clicking any folder in the right-hand list box to move down to that folder or by clicking the Up button to move up to the parent folder. Figure 24-2 shows the contents of the Users folder. The user can also select a file by clicking its name in the list box. This displays the file's properties in the text boxes at the bottom of the application (see Figure 24-3).

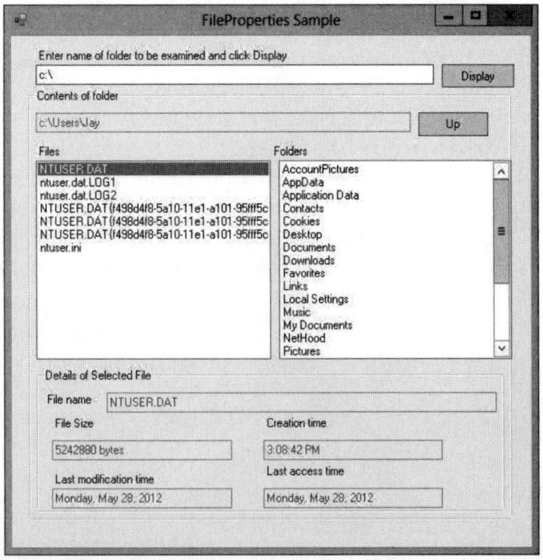

Note that you can also display the creation time, last access time, and last modification time for folders using the `DirectoryInfo` property. In this case, these properties are displayed only for a selected file to keep things simple.

You create the project as a standard C# Windows application in Visual Studio 2012. Add the various text boxes and the list box from the Windows Forms area of the toolbox. You also rename the controls with the more intuitive names of `textBoxInput`, `textBoxFolder`, `buttonDisplay`, `buttonUp`, `listBoxFiles`, `listBoxFolders`, `textBoxFileName`, `textBoxCreationTime`, `textBoxLastAccessTime`, `textBoxLastWriteTime`, and `textBoxFileSize`.

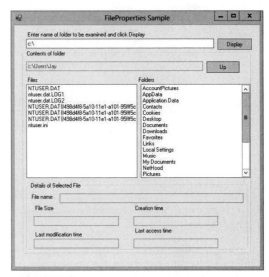

FIGURE 24-2

FIGURE 24-3

Next, you need to indicate that you will be using the `System.IO` namespace:

```
using System;
using System.IO;
using System.Windows.Forms;
```

You need to do this for all the file-system–related examples in this chapter, but this part of the code is not explicitly shown in the remaining examples. You then add a member field to the main form:

```
public partial class Form1: Form
{
    private string currentFolderPath;
```

`currentFolderPath` stores the path of the folder whose contents are displayed in the list boxes.

Now you need to add event handlers for the user-generated events. The possible user inputs are as follows:

➤ **User clicks the Display button**—You need to determine whether what the user has typed in the main text box is the path to a file or folder. If it is a folder, you list the files and subfolders of this folder in the list boxes. If it is a file, you still do this for the folder containing that file, but you also display the file properties in the lower text boxes.

➤ **User clicks a filename in the Files list box**—You display the properties of this file in the lower text boxes.

➤ **User clicks a folder name in the Folders list box**—You clear all the controls and then display the contents of this subfolder in the list boxes.

➤ **User clicks the Up button**—You clear all the controls and then display the contents of the parent of the currently selected folder.

Before looking at the code for the event handlers, here is the code for the methods that do all the work. First, you need to clear the contents of all the controls. This method is fairly self-explanatory:

```
protected void ClearAllFields()
{
    listBoxFolders.Items.Clear();
    listBoxFiles.Items.Clear();
    textBoxFolder.Text = "";
    textBoxFileName.Text = "";
    textBoxCreationTime.Text = "";
    textBoxLastAccessTime.Text = "";
    textBoxLastWriteTime.Text = "";
    textBoxFileSize.Text = "";
}
```

Next, you define a method, `DisplayFileInfo`, that handles the process of displaying the information for a given file in the text boxes. This method takes one parameter, the full pathname of the file as a `String`, and then creates a `FileInfo` object based on this path:

```
protected void DisplayFileInfo(string fileFullName)
{
    FileInfo theFile = new FileInfo(fileFullName);

    if (!theFile.Exists)
    {
        throw new FileNotFoundException("File not found: " + fileFullName);
    }

    textBoxFileName.Text = theFile.Name;
    textBoxCreationTime.Text = theFile.CreationTime.ToLongTimeString();
```

```
            textBoxLastAccessTime.Text = theFile.LastAccessTime.ToLongDateString();
            textBoxLastWriteTime.Text = theFile.LastWriteTime.ToLongDateString();
            textBoxFileSize.Text = theFile.Length.ToString() + " bytes";
        }
```

Note that you take the precaution of throwing an exception if there are any problems locating a file at the specified location. The exception itself will be handled in the calling routine (one of the event handlers). Finally, you define a method, DisplayFolderList, which displays the contents of a given folder in the two list boxes. The full pathname of the folder is passed in as a parameter to this method:

```
        protected void DisplayFolderList(string folderFullName)
        {
            DirectoryInfo theFolder = new DirectoryInfo(folderFullName);

            if (!theFolder.Exists)
            {
                throw new DirectoryNotFoundException("Folder not found: " + folderFullName);
            }

            ClearAllFields();
            textBoxFolder.Text = theFolder.FullName;
            currentFolderPath = theFolder.FullName;

            // list all subfolders in folder
            foreach(DirectoryInfo nextFolder in theFolder.GetDirectories())
                listBoxFolders.Items.Add(nextFolder.Name);

            // list all files in folder
            foreach(FileInfo nextFile in theFolder.GetFiles())
                listBoxFiles.Items.Add(nextFile.Name);
        }
```

The event handler that manages the event triggered when the user clicks the Display button is the most complex because it needs to handle three different possibilities for the text the user enters in the text box. For instance, it could be the pathname of a folder, the pathname of a file, or neither of these:

```
        protected void OnDisplayButtonClick(object sender, EventArgs e)
        {
            try
            {
                string folderPath = textBoxInput.Text;
                DirectoryInfo theFolder = new DirectoryInfo(folderPath);

                if (theFolder.Exists)
                {
                    DisplayFolderList(theFolder.FullName);
                    return;
                }

                FileInfo theFile = new FileInfo(folderPath);

                if (theFile.Exists)
                {
                    DisplayFolderList(theFile.Directory.FullName);
                    int index = listBoxFiles.Items.IndexOf(theFile.Name);
                    listBoxFiles.SetSelected(index, true);
                    return;
                }
```

```
            throw new FileNotFoundException("There is no file or folder with "
                                        + "this name: " + textBoxInput.Text);
      }
      catch(Exception ex)
      {
         MessageBox.Show(ex.Message);
      }
   }
```

This code establishes whether the supplied text represents a folder or a file by instantiating `DirectoryInfo` and `FileInfo` instances and examining the `Exists` property of each object. If neither exists, you throw an exception. If it's a folder, you call `DisplayFolderList` to populate the list boxes. If it's a file, you need to populate the list boxes and sort out the text boxes that display the file properties. You handle this case by first populating the list boxes. You then programmatically select the appropriate filename in the Files list box. This has exactly the same effect as if the user had selected that item—it raises the item-selected event. You can then simply exit the current event handler, knowing that the selected item event handler will immediately be called to display the file properties.

The following code is the event handler that is called when an item in the Files list box is selected, either by the user or, as indicated previously, programmatically. It simply constructs the full pathname of the selected file, and passes it to the `DisplayFileInfo` method presented earlier:

```
protected void OnListBoxFilesSelected(object sender, EventArgs e)
{
   try
   {
      string selectedString = listBoxFiles.SelectedItem.ToString();
      string fullFileName = Path.Combine(currentFolderPath, selectedString);
      DisplayFileInfo(fullFileName);
   }
   catch(Exception ex)
   {
      MessageBox.Show(ex.Message);
   }
}
```

The event handler for the selection of a folder in the Folders list box is implemented in a very similar way, except that in this case you call `DisplayFolderList` to update the contents of the list boxes:

```
protected void OnListBoxFoldersSelected(object sender, EventArgs e)
{
   try
   {
      string selectedString = listBoxFolders.SelectedItem.ToString();
      string fullPathName = Path.Combine(currentFolderPath, selectedString);
      DisplayFolderList(fullPathName);
   }
   catch(Exception ex)
   {
      MessageBox.Show(ex.Message);
   }
}
```

Finally, when the Up button is clicked, `DisplayFolderList` must also be called, except this time you need to obtain the path of the parent of the folder currently displayed. This is done with the `FileInfo` `.DirectoryName` property, which returns the parent folder path:

```
protected void OnUpButtonClick(object sender, EventArgs e)
{
   try
```

```
        {
            string folderPath = new FileInfo(currentFolderPath).DirectoryName;
            DisplayFolderList(folderPath);
        }
        catch(Exception ex)
        {
            MessageBox.Show(ex.Message);
        }
    }
```

MOVING, COPYING, AND DELETING FILES

As mentioned earlier, moving and deleting files or folders is done by the `MoveTo` and `Delete` methods of the `FileInfo` and `DirectoryInfo` classes. The equivalent methods on the `File` and `Directory` classes are `Move` and `Delete`. The `FileInfo` and `File` classes also implement the methods `CopyTo` and `Copy`, respectively. However, no methods exist to copy complete folders—you need to do that by copying each file in the folder.

Using all of these methods is quite intuitive—you can find detailed descriptions in the SDK documentation. This section illustrates their use for the particular cases of calling the static `Move`, `Copy`, and `Delete` methods on the `File` class. To do this, you will build on the previous `FileProperties` example and call its iteration `FilePropertiesAndMovement`. This example has the extra feature that whenever the properties of a file are displayed, the application gives you the options to delete that file or move or copy the file to another location.

FilePropertiesAndMovement Sample

Figure 24-4 shows the user interface of the new sample application.

As you can see, `FilePropertiesAndMovement` is similar in appearance to `FileProperties`, except for the group of three buttons and a text box at the bottom of the window. These controls are enabled only when the example is actually displaying the properties of a file; at all other times, they are disabled. The existing controls are also squashed a bit to stop the main form from getting too big. When the properties of a selected file are displayed, `FilePropertiesAndMovement` automatically places the full pathname of that file in the bottom text box for the user to edit. Users can then click any of the buttons to perform the appropriate operation. When they do, a message box is displayed that confirms the action taken by the user (see Figure 24-5).

FIGURE 24-4

When the user clicks the Yes button, the action is initiated. Some actions in the form that the user can take will cause the display to be incorrect. For instance, if the user moves or deletes a file, you obviously cannot continue to display the contents of that file in the same location. In addition, if you change the name of a file in the same folder, your display will also be out of date. In these cases, `FilePropertiesAndMovement` resets its controls to display only the folder where the file resides after the file operation.

FIGURE 24-5

Looking at the Code for FilePropertiesAndMovement

To code this process, you need to add the relevant controls, as well as their event handlers, to the code for the `FileProperties` sample. The new controls are given the names `buttonDelete`, `buttonCopyTo`, `buttonMoveTo`, and `textBoxNewPath`.

First, look at the event handler that is called when the user clicks the Delete button:

```
protected void OnDeleteButtonClick(object sender, EventArgs e)
{
    try
    {
        string filePath = Path.Combine(currentFolderPath,
                                     textBoxFileName.Text);
        string query = "Really delete the file\n" + filePath + "?";
        if (MessageBox.Show(query,
            "Delete File?", MessageBoxButtons.YesNo) == DialogResult.Yes)
        {
            File.Delete(filePath);
            DisplayFolderList(currentFolderPath);
        }
    }
    catch(Exception ex)
    {
        MessageBox.Show("Unable to delete file. The following exception"
                        + " occurred:\n" + ex.Message, "Failed");
    }
}
```

The code for this method is contained in a `try` block because of the obvious risk of an exception being thrown if, for example, the user doesn't have permission to delete the file, or the file is moved or locked by another process after it has been displayed but before the user presses the Delete button. You construct the path of the file to be deleted from the `CurrentParentPath` field, which contains the path of the parent folder, and the text in the `textBoxFileName` text box, which contains the name of the file.

The methods to move and copy the file are structured in a very similar manner:

```
protected void OnMoveButtonClick(object sender, EventArgs e)
{
    try
    {
        string filePath = Path.Combine(currentFolderPath,
                                     textBoxFileName.Text);
        string query = "Really move the file\n" + filePath + "\nto "
                        + textBoxNewPath.Text + "?";
        if (MessageBox.Show(query,
            "Move File?", MessageBoxButtons.YesNo) == DialogResult.Yes)
        {
            File.Move(filePath, textBoxNewPath.Text);
            DisplayFolderList(currentFolderPath);
        }
    }
    catch(Exception ex)
    {
        MessageBox.Show("Unable to move file. The following exception"
                        + " occurred:\n" + ex.Message, "Failed");
    }
}

protected void OnCopyButtonClick(object sender, EventArgs e)
{
    try
```

```
        {
            string filePath = Path.Combine(currentFolderPath,
                                           textBoxFileName.Text);
            string query = "Really copy the file\n" + filePath + "\nto "
                           + textBoxNewPath.Text + "?";
            if (MessageBox.Show(query,
               "Copy File?", MessageBoxButtons.YesNo) == DialogResult.Yes)
            {
                File.Copy(filePath, textBoxNewPath.Text);
                DisplayFolderList(currentFolderPath);
            }
        }
        catch(Exception ex)
        {
            MessageBox.Show("Unable to copy file. The following exception"
                            + " occurred:\n" + ex.Message, "Failed");
        }
    }
}
```

You are not quite done. You also need to ensure that the new buttons and text box are enabled and disabled at the appropriate times. To enable them when you are displaying the contents of a file, add the following code to `DisplayFileInfo`:

```
protected void DisplayFileInfo(string fileFullName)
{
    FileInfo theFile = new FileInfo(fileFullName);

    if (!theFile.Exists)
    {
        throw new FileNotFoundException("File not found: " + fileFullName);
    }

    textBoxFileName.Text = theFile.Name;
    textBoxCreationTime.Text = theFile.CreationTime.ToLongTimeString();
    textBoxLastAccessTime.Text = theFile.LastAccessTime.ToLongDateString();
    textBoxLastWriteTime.Text = theFile.LastWriteTime.ToLongDateString();
    textBoxFileSize.Text = theFile.Length.ToString() + " bytes";

    // enable move, copy, delete buttons
    textBoxNewPath.Text = theFile.FullName;
    textBoxNewPath.Enabled = true;
    buttonCopyTo.Enabled = true;
    buttonDelete.Enabled = true;
    buttonMoveTo.Enabled = true;
}
```

You also need to make one change to `DisplayFolderList`:

```
protected void DisplayFolderList(string folderFullName)
{
    DirectoryInfo theFolder = new DirectoryInfo(folderFullName);

    if (!theFolder.Exists)
    {
        throw new DirectoryNotFoundException("Folder not found: " + folderFullName);
    }

    ClearAllFields();
    DisableMoveFeatures();
    textBoxFolder.Text = theFolder.FullName;
    currentFolderPath = theFolder.FullName;

    // list all subfolders in folder
```

```
        foreach(DirectoryInfo nextFolder in theFolder.GetDirectories())
            listBoxFolders.Items.Add(NextFolder.Name);

        // list all files in folder
        foreach(FileInfo nextFile in theFolder.GetFiles())
            listBoxFiles.Items.Add(NextFile.Name);
    }
```

`DisableMoveFeatures` is a small utility function that disables the new controls:

```
        void DisableMoveFeatures()
        {
            textBoxNewPath.Text = "";
            textBoxNewPath.Enabled = false;
            buttonCopyTo.Enabled = false;
            buttonDelete.Enabled = false;
            buttonMoveTo.Enabled = false;
        }
```

Now add extra code to `ClearAllFields` to clear the extra text box:

```
        protected void ClearAllFields()
        {
            listBoxFolders.Items.Clear();
            listBoxFiles.Items.Clear();
            textBoxFolder.Text = "";
            textBoxFileName.Text = "";
            textBoxCreationTime.Text = "";
            textBoxLastAccessTime.Text = "";
            textBoxLastWriteTime.Text = "";
            textBoxFileSize.Text = "";
            textBoxNewPath.Text = "";
        }
```

READING AND WRITING TO FILES

Reading and writing to files is in principle very simple; however, it is not done through the `DirectoryInfo` or `FileInfo` objects. Instead, using .NET Framework 4.5, you can do it through the `File` object. Later in this chapter, you see how to accomplish this using a number of other classes that represent a generic concept called a *stream*.

Before .NET Framework 2.0, it took a bit of wrangling to read and write to files. It was possible using the available classes from the framework, but it was not straightforward. The .NET Framework 2.0 expanded the `File` class to make it as simple as just one line of code to read or write to a file. This same functionality is also available in version 4.5 of the .NET Framework.

Reading a File

For an example of reading a file, create a Windows Forms application that contains a regular text box, a button, and a multiline text box. When you are done, your form should appear similar to Figure 24-6.

FIGURE 24-6

The purpose of this form is to enable end users to enter the path of a specific file in the first text box and click the Read button. From there, the application will read the specified file and display the file's contents in the multiline text box. This is coded in the following example:

```
using System;
using System.IO;
using System.Windows.Forms;

namespace ReadingFiles
{
    public partial class Form1: Form
    {
        public Form1()
        {
            InitializeComponent();
        }

        private void button1_Click(object sender, EventArgs e)
        {
            textBox2.Text = File.ReadAllText(textBox1.Text);
        }
    }
}
```

In building this example, the first step is to add the using statement to bring in the System.IO namespace. From there, simply use the button1_Click event for the Send button on the form to populate the text box with what is returned from the file. You can now access the file's contents by using the File.ReadAllText method. As you can see, you can read files with a single statement. The ReadAllText method opens the specified file, reads the contents, and then closes the file. The return value of the ReadAllText method is a string containing the entire contents of the file specified. The result would be something similar to what is shown in Figure 24-7.

The File.ReadAllText signature shown in the preceding example is of the following construction:

```
File.ReadAllText(FilePath);
```

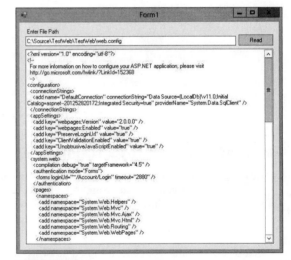

FIGURE 24-7

The other option is to also specify the encoding of the file being read:

```
File.ReadAllText(FilePath, Encoding);
```

Using this signature enables you to specify the encoding to use when opening and reading the contents of the file. Therefore, you could do something like the following:

```
File.ReadAllText(textBox1.Text, Encoding.ASCII);
```

Some of the other options for opening and working with files include using the ReadAllBytes and the ReadAllLines methods. The ReadAllBytes method enables you to open a binary file and read the contents into a byte array. The `ReadAllText` method shown earlier provides the entire contents of the specified file in a single string instance. If you are not interested in this, but instead would like to work with what comes back from the file in a line-by-line fashion, you should use the `ReadAllLines` method because it allows for this kind of functionality and will return a string array for you to work with.

Writing to a File

Besides making reading from files an extremely simple process under the .NET Framework umbrella, the base class library (BCL) has made writing to files just as easy. Just as the base class library gives you the `ReadAllText`, `ReadAllLines`, and `ReadAllBytes` methods to read files in a few different ways, it also provides the `WriteAllText`, `WriteAllBytes`, and `WriteAllLines` methods to write files.

For an example of how to write to a file, use the same Windows Forms application, but use the multiline text box in the form to input data into a file. The code for the `button1_Click` event handler should appear as shown here:

```
private void button1_Click(object sender, EventArgs e)
{
    File.WriteAllText(textBox1.Text, textBox2.Text);
}
```

Build and start the form, type **C:\Testing.txt** in the first text box, type some random content in the second text box, and then click the button. Nothing will happen visually, but if you look in your root C: drive, you will see the `Testing.txt` file with the content you specified.

The `WriteAllText` method went to the specified location, created a new text file, and provided the specified contents to the file before saving and closing the file. Not bad for just one line of code!

If you run the application again, and specify the same file (`Testing.txt`) but with some new content, pressing the button again will cause the application to perform the same task. This time, though, the new content is not added to the previous content you specified—instead, the new content completely overrides the previous content. In fact, `WriteAllText`, `WriteAllBytes`, and `WriteAllLines` all override any previous files, so be very careful when using these methods.

The `WriteAllText` method in the previous example uses the following signature:

```
File.WriteAllText(FilePath, Contents)
```

You can also specify the encoding of the new file:

```
File.WriteAllText(FilePath, Contents, Encoding)
```

The `WriteAllBytes` method enables you to write content to a file using a byte array, and the `WriteAllLines` method enables you to write a string array to a file. An example of this is illustrated in the following event handler:

```
private void button1_Click(object sender, EventArgs e)
{
    string[] movies =
        {"Grease",
         "Close Encounters of the Third Kind",
         "The Day After Tomorrow"};

    File.WriteAllLines(@"C:\Testing.txt", movies);
}
```

Now clicking the button for such an application will give you a `Testing.txt` file with the following contents:

```
Grease
Close Encounters of the Third Kind
The Day After Tomorrow
```

The `WriteAllLines` method writes out the string array with each array item occupying its own line in the file.

Because data may be written not only to disk but to other places as well (such as to named pipes or to memory), it is also important to understand how to deal with file I/O in .NET using streams as a means of moving file contents around. This is shown in the following section.

Streams

The idea of a stream has been around for a very long time. A stream is an object used to transfer data. The data can be transferred in one of two directions:

➤ If the data is being transferred from some outside source into your program, it is called *reading* from the stream.

➤ If the data is being transferred from your program to some outside source, it is called *writing* to the stream.

Very often, the outside source will be a file, but that is not always the case. Other possibilities include the following:

➤ Reading or writing data on the network using some network protocol, where the intention is for this data to be picked up by or sent from another computer

➤ Reading from or writing to a named pipe

➤ Reading from or writing to an area of memory

Of these examples, Microsoft has supplied a .NET base class for writing to or reading from memory, the `System.IO.MemoryStream` object. The `System.Net.Sockets.NetworkStream` object handles network data. There are no base stream classes for writing to or reading from pipes, but there is a generic stream class, `System.IO.Stream`, from which you would inherit if you wanted to write such a class. `Stream` does not make any assumptions about the nature of the external data source.

The outside source might even be a variable within your own code. This might sound paradoxical, but the technique of using streams to transmit data between variables can be a useful trick for converting data between data types. The C language used something similar—the `sprintf` function—to convert between integer data types and strings or to format strings.

The advantage of having a separate object for the transfer of data, rather than using the `FileInfo` or `DirectoryInfo` classes to do this, is that separating the concept of transferring data from the particular data source makes it easier to swap data sources. Stream objects themselves contain a lot of generic code that concerns the movement of data between outside sources and variables in your code. By keeping this code separate from any concept of a particular data source, you make it easier for this code to be reused (through inheritance) in different circumstances. For example, the `StringReader` and `StringWriter` classes are part of the same inheritance tree as two classes that you will be using later to read and write text files. The classes will almost certainly share a substantial amount of code behind the scenes. Figure 24-8 illustrates the actual hierarchy of stream-related classes in the `System.IO` namespace.

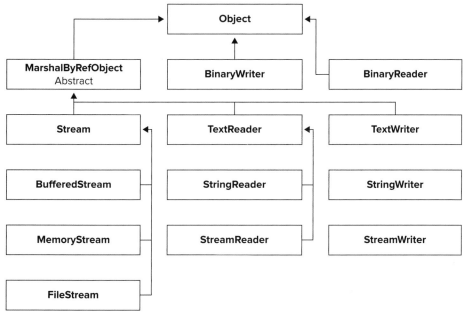

FIGURE 24-8

As far as reading and writing files, the classes that concern us most are as follows:

➤ `FileStream`—This class is intended for reading and writing binary data in a binary file. However, you can also use it to read from or write to any file.

➤ `StreamReader` and `StreamWriter`—These classes are designed specifically for reading from and writing to text files.

You might also find the `BinaryReader` and `BinaryWriter` classes useful, although they are not used in the examples here. These classes do not actually implement streams themselves, but they are able to provide wrappers around other stream objects. `BinaryReader` and `BinaryWriter` provide extra formatting of binary data, which enables you to directly read or write the contents of C# variables to or from the relevant stream. Think of the `BinaryReader` and `BinaryWriter` as sitting between the stream and your code, providing extra formatting (see Figure 24-9).

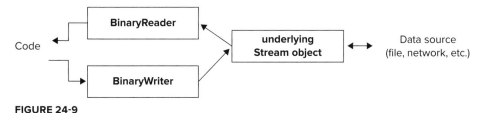

FIGURE 24-9

The difference between using these classes and directly using the underlying stream objects is that a basic stream works in bytes. For example, suppose that as part of the process of saving some document you want to write the contents of a variable of type `long` to a binary file. Each `long` occupies 8 bytes, and if you used an ordinary binary stream you would have to explicitly write each of those 8 bytes of memory.

In C# code, you would have to perform some bitwise operations to extract each of those 8 bytes from the `long` value. Using a `BinaryWriter` instance, you can encapsulate the entire operation in an overload of the `BinaryWriter.Write` method, which takes a `long` as a parameter, and which places those 8 bytes into the stream (and if the stream is directed to a file, into the file). A corresponding `BinaryReader.Read` method will extract 8 bytes from the stream and recover the value of the `long`. For more information on the `BinaryReader` and `BinaryWriter` classes, refer to the SDK documentation.

Buffered Streams

For performance reasons, when you read or write to or from a file, the output is buffered. This means that if your program asks for the next 2 bytes of a file stream, and the stream passes the request on to Windows, then Windows will not connect to the file system and then locate and read the file off the disk, just to get 2 bytes. Instead, Windows retrieves a large block of the file at one time and stores this block in an area of memory known as a *buffer*. Subsequent requests for data from the stream are satisfied from the buffer until the buffer runs out, at which point Windows grabs another block of data from the file.

Writing to files works in the same way. For files, this is done automatically by the operating system, but you might have to write a stream class to read from some other device that is not buffered. If so, you can derive your class from `BufferedStream`, which implements a buffer itself. (Note, however, that `BufferedStream` is not designed for the situation in which an application frequently alternates between reading and writing data.)

Reading and Writing to Binary Files Using FileStream

Reading and writing to and from binary files can be done using the `FileStream` class.

The FileStream Class

A `FileStream` instance is used to read or write data to or from a file. To construct a `FileStream`, you need four pieces of information:

1. The *file* you want to access.
2. The *mode,* which indicates how you want to open the file. For example, are you intending to create a new file or open an existing file? If you are opening an existing file, should any write operations be interpreted as overwriting the contents of the file or appending to the file?
3. The *access,* which indicates how you want to access the file. For example, do you want to read from or write to the file or do both?
4. The *share* access, which specifies whether you want exclusive access to the file. Alternately, are you willing to have other streams access the file simultaneously? If so, should other streams have access to read the file, to write to it, or to do both?

The first piece of information is usually represented by a string that contains the full pathname of the file, and this chapter considers only those constructors that require a string here. Besides those, however, some additional constructors take an old Windows-API–style Windows handle to a file instead. The remaining three pieces of information are represented by three .NET enumerations called `FileMode`, `FileAccess`, and `FileShare`. The values of these enumerations are listed in the following table and are self-explanatory:

ENUMERATION	VALUES
FileMode	Append, Create, CreateNew, Open, OpenOrCreate, or Truncate
FileAccess	Read, ReadWrite, or Write
FileShare	Delete, Inheritable, None, Read, ReadWrite, or Write

Note that in the case of `FileMode`, exceptions can be thrown if you request a mode that is inconsistent with the existing status of the file. `Append`, `Open`, and `Truncate` throw an exception if the file does not already exist, and `CreateNew` throws an exception if it does. `Create` and `OpenOrCreate` will cope with either scenario, but `Create` deletes any existing file to replace it with a new, initially empty, one. The `FileAccess` and `FileShare` enumerations are bitwise flags, so values can be combined with the C# bitwise `OR` operator, `|`.

There are a large number of constructors for the `FileStream`. The three simplest ones work as follows:

```
// creates file with read-write access and allows other streams read access
FileStream fs = new FileStream(@"C:\C# Projects\Project.doc",
                FileMode.Create);
// as above, but we only get write access to the file
FileStream fs2 = new FileStream(@"C:\C# Projects\Project2.doc",
                FileMode.Create, FileAccess.Write);
// as above but other streams don't get access to the file while
// fs3 is open
FileStream fs3 = new FileStream(@"C:\C# Projects\Project3.doc",
                FileMode.Create, FileAccess.Write, FileShare.None);
```

As this code reveals, the overloads of these constructors have the effect of providing default values of `FileAccess.ReadWrite` and `FileShare.Read` to the third and fourth parameters depending upon the `FileMode` value. It is also possible to create a file stream from a `FileInfo` instance in various ways:

```
FileInfo myFile4 = new FileInfo(@"C:\C# Projects\Project4.doc");
FileStream fs4 = myFile4.OpenRead();
FileInfo myFile5= new FileInfo(@"C:\C# Projects\Project5doc");
FileStream fs5 = myFile5.OpenWrite();
FileInfo myFile6= new FileInfo(@"C:\C# Projects\Project6doc");
FileStream fs6 = myFile6.Open(FileMode.Append, FileAccess.Write,
                FileShare.None);
FileInfo myFile7 = new FileInfo(@"C:\C# Projects\Project7.doc");
FileStream fs7 = myFile7.Create();
```

`FileInfo.OpenRead` supplies a stream that provides read-only access to an existing file, whereas `FileInfo.OpenWrite` provides read-write access. `FileInfo.Open` enables you to specify the mode, access, and file share parameters explicitly.

Of course, after finishing with a stream, you should close it:

```
fs.Close();
```

Closing the stream frees up the resources associated with it and allows other applications to set up streams to the same file. This action also flushes the buffer. In between opening and closing the stream, you should read data from it and/or write data to it. `FileStream` implements a number of methods to do this.

`ReadByte` is the simplest way to read data. It grabs 1 byte from the stream and casts the result to an `int` that has a value between 0 and 255. If you have reached the end of the stream, it returns -1:

```
int NextByte = fs.ReadByte();
```

If you prefer to read a number of bytes at a time, you can call the `Read` method, which reads a specified number of bytes into an array. `Read` returns the number of bytes actually read—if this value is 0, you know that you are at the end of the stream. The following example reads into a byte array called `ByteArray`:

```
int nBytesRead = fs.Read(ByteArray, 0, nBytes);
```

The second parameter to `Read` is an offset, which you can use to request that the `Read` operation start populating the array at some element other than the first. The third parameter is the number of bytes to read into the array.

If you want to write data to a file, two parallel methods are available, `WriteByte` and `Write`. `WriteByte` writes a single byte to the stream:

```
byte NextByte = 100;
fs.WriteByte(NextByte);
```

`Write`, however, writes out an array of bytes. For instance, if you initialized the `ByteArray` mentioned before with some values, you could use the following code to write out the first `nBytes` of the array:

```
fs.Write(ByteArray, 0, nBytes);
```

As with `Read`, the second parameter enables you to start writing from some point other than the beginning of the array. Both `WriteByte` and `Write` return `void`.

In addition to these methods, `FileStream` implements various other methods and properties related to bookkeeping tasks such as determining how many bytes are in the stream, locking the stream, or flushing the buffer. These other methods are not usually required for basic reading and writing, but if you need them, full details are in the SDK documentation.

BinaryFileReader Sample

The use of the `FileStream` class is illustrated by writing a sample, `BinaryFileReader`, that reads in and displays any file. Create the project in Visual Studio 2012 as a Windows application. It has one menu item,

which brings up a standard `OpenFileDialog` asking what file to read in and then displays the file as binary code. As you are reading in binary files, you need to be able to display nonprintable characters. You will do this by displaying each byte of the file individually, showing 16 bytes on each line of a multiline text box. If the byte represents a printable ASCII character, you will display that character; otherwise, you will display the value of the byte in a hexadecimal format. In either case, you pad the displayed text with spaces so that each byte displayed occupies four columns; this way, the bytes line up nicely under each other.

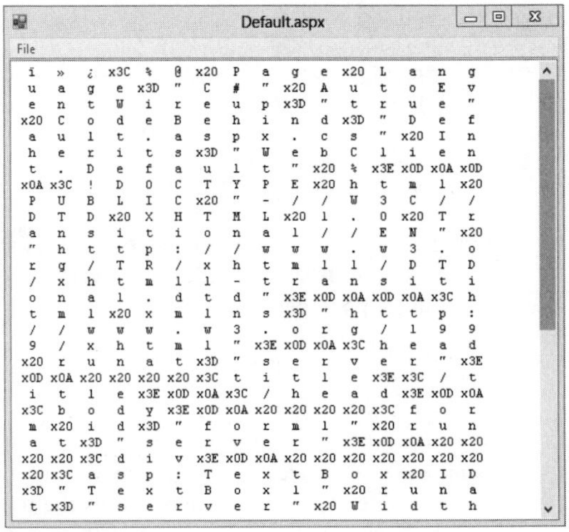

Figure 24-10 shows what the `BinaryFileReader` application looks like when viewing a text file. (Because `BinaryFileReader` can view any file, it can also be used on text files as well as binary files.) In this case, the application has read in a basic ASP.NET page (`.aspx`).

FIGURE 24-10

Clearly, this format is more suited for looking at the values of individual bytes than for displaying text! Later in this chapter, when you develop a sample that is specifically designed to read text files, you will see what this file really says. The advantage of this example is that you can look at the contents of any file.

This example does not demonstrate writing to files because you don't want to get bogged down in the complexities of trying to translate the contents of a text box such as the one shown in Figure 24-10 into a binary stream! You will see how to write to files later when you develop an example that can read or write only to and from text files.

Here is the code used to get these results. First, you need to ensure that you have brought in the `System.IO` namespace through the use of the `using` statement:

```
using System.IO;
```

Next, you add a couple of fields to the main form class—one representing the file dialog and a string that provides the path of the file currently being viewed:

```
partial class Form1: Form

{
   private readonly OpenFileDialog chooseOpenFileDialog =
      new OpenFileDialog();
   private string chosenFile;
}
```

You also need to add some standard Windows Forms code to deal with the handlers for the menu and the file dialog:

```
public Form1()
{
   InitializeComponent();
   menuFileOpen.Click += OnFileOpen;
   chooseOpenFileDialog.FileOk += OnOpenFileDialogOK;
}

void OnFileOpen(object Sender, EventArgs e)
{
   chooseOpenFileDialog.ShowDialog();
}

void OnOpenFileDialogOK(object Sender, CancelEventArgs e)
{
   chosenFile = chooseOpenFileDialog.FileName;
   this.Text = Path.GetFileName(chosenFile);
   DisplayFile();
}
```

As this code demonstrates, when the user clicks OK to select a file in the file dialog, you call the `DisplayFile` method, which does the work of reading in the selected file:

```
void DisplayFile()
{
   int nCols = 16;
   FileStream inStream = new FileStream(chosenFile, FileMode.Open,
                                                FileAccess.Read);
   long nBytesToRead = inStream.Length;
   if (nBytesToRead > 65536/4)
     nBytesToRead = 65536/4;

   int nLines = (int)(nBytesToRead/nCols) + 1;
   string [] lines = new string[nLines];
   int nBytesRead = 0;

   for (int i=0; i<nLines; i++)
   {
      StringBuilder nextLine = new StringBuilder();
      nextLine.Capacity = 4*nCols;

      for (int j = 0; j<nCols; j++)
      {
         int nextByte = inStream.ReadByte();
         nBytesRead++;
         if (nextByte < 0 || nBytesRead > 65536)
            break;
         char nextChar = (char)nextByte;
         if (nextChar < 16)
            nextLine.Append(" x0" + string.Format("{0,1:X}",
                                             (int)nextChar));
         else if
```

```
                    (char.IsLetterOrDigit(nextChar) ||
                                char.IsPunctuation(nextChar))
                nextLine.Append("  " + nextChar + " ");
            else
                nextLine.Append(" x" + string.Format("{0,2:X}",
                                (int)nextChar));
        }
        lines[i] = nextLine.ToString();
    }
    inStream.Close();
    this.textBoxContents.Lines = lines;
}
```

There is quite a lot going on in this method, so here is the breakdown. You instantiate a `FileStream` object for the selected file, which specifies that you want to open an existing file for reading. You then determine how many bytes need to be read in and how many lines should be displayed. The number of bytes will normally be the number of bytes in the file. This example limits the display of the contents in the text box control to a maximum of only 65,536 characters—with the chosen display format, you are displaying four characters for every byte in the file.

> **NOTE** *You might want to look up the* `RichTextBox` *class in the* `System.Windows` `.Forms` *namespace.* `RichTextBox` *is similar to a text box, but it has many more advanced formatting facilities.* `TextBox` *is used here to keep the example simple and focused on the process of reading in files.*

The bulk of the method is given to two nested `for` loops that construct each line of text to be displayed. You use a `StringBuilder` class to construct each line for performance reasons: You are appending suitable text for each byte to the string that represents each line 16 times. If on each occasion you allocated a new string and took a copy of the half-constructed line, you would not only spend a lot of time allocating strings but also waste a lot of memory on the heap. Notice that the definition of *printable* characters is anything that is a letter, digit, or punctuation, as indicated by the relevant static `System.Char` methods. You exclude any character with a value less than 16 from the printable list, however; this means that you will trap the carriage return (13) and line feed (10) as binary characters (a multiline text box isn't able to display these characters properly if they occur individually within a line).

Furthermore, using the Properties window, you change the `Font` property for the text box to a fixed-width font. In this case, you choose Courier New 9pt regular and set the text box to have vertical and horizontal scrollbars. Upon completion, you close the stream and set the contents of the text box to the array of strings that you have built.

Reading and Writing to Text Files

Theoretically, it is perfectly possible to use the `FileStream` class to read in and display text files. You have, after all, just done that. The format in which the `Default.aspx` file is displayed in the preceding sample is not particularly user-friendly, but that has nothing to do with any intrinsic problem with the `FileStream` class, only with how you choose to display the results in the text box.

Having said that, if you know that a particular file contains text, you will usually find it more convenient to read and write it using the `StreamReader` and `StreamWriter` classes instead of the `FileStream` class. That's because these classes work at a slightly higher level and are specifically geared to reading and writing text. The methods that they implement can automatically detect convenient points to stop reading text, based on the contents of the stream. In particular:

➤ These classes implement methods to read or write one line of text at a time, `StreamReader`
`.ReadLine` and `StreamWriter.WriteLine`. In the case of reading, this means that the stream
automatically determines where the next carriage return is and stops reading at that point. In the case
of writing, it means that the stream automatically appends the carriage return–line feed combination
to the text that it writes out.

➤ By using the `StreamReader` and `StreamWriter` classes, you don't need to worry about the encoding
(the text format) used in the file. Possible encodings include ASCII (1 byte for each character), or any
of the Unicode-based formats, Unicode, UTF7, UTF8, and UTF32. Text files on Windows 9*x* systems
are always in ASCII because Windows 9*x* does not support Unicode; however, because Windows NT,
2000, XP, 2003, Vista, Windows Server 2008, Windows 7, and Windows 8 all support Unicode, text
files might theoretically contain Unicode, UTF7, UTF8, or UTF32 data instead of ASCII data. The
convention is such that if the file is in ASCII format, it simply contains the text. If it is in any Unicode
format, this is indicated by the first 2 or 3 bytes of the file, which are set to particular combinations of
values to indicate the format used in the file.

These bytes are known as the *byte code markers*. When you open a file using any of the standard Windows
applications, such as Notepad or WordPad, you do not need to worry about this because these applications
are aware of the different encoding methods and automatically read the file correctly. This is also true for
the `StreamReader` class, which correctly reads in a file in any of these formats; and the `StreamWriter` class
is capable of formatting the text it writes out using whatever encoding technique you request. If you want to
read in and display a text file using the `FileStream` class, however, you need to handle this yourself.

The StreamReader Class

`StreamReader` is used to read text files. Constructing a `StreamReader` is in some ways easier than constructing a `FileStream` instance because some of the `FileStream` options are not required when using
`StreamReader`. In particular, the mode and access types are not relevant to `StreamReader` because the only
thing you can do with a `StreamReader` is read! Furthermore, there is no direct option to specify the sharing
permissions. However, there are a couple of new options:

➤ You need to specify what to do about the different encoding methods. You can instruct the
`StreamReader` to examine the byte code markers in the beginning of the file to determine the encoding method, or you can simply tell the `StreamReader` to assume that the file uses a specified encoding
method.

➤ Instead of supplying a filename to be read from, you can supply a reference to another stream.

This last option deserves a bit more discussion because it illustrates another advantage of basing the model
for reading and writing data on the concept of streams. Because the `StreamReader` works at a relatively
high level, you might find it useful when you have another stream that is there to read data from another
source but, you would like to use the facilities provided by `StreamReader` to process that other stream as
if it contained text. You can do so by simply passing the output from this stream to a `StreamReader`. In
this way, `StreamReader` can be used to read and process data from any data source—not only files. This is
essentially the situation discussed earlier with regard to the `BinaryReader` class. However, in this book you
only use `StreamReader` to connect directly to files.

The result of these possibilities is that `StreamReader` has a large number of constructors. Not only that,
but there is another `FileInfo` method that returns a `StreamReader` reference: `OpenText`. The following
examples illustrate just some of the constructors.

The simplest constructor takes only a filename. This `StreamReader` examines the byte order marks to determine the encoding:

```
StreamReader sr = new StreamReader(@"C:\My Documents\ReadMe.txt");
```

Alternatively, you can specify that UTF8 encoding should be assumed:

```
StreamReader sr = new StreamReader(@"C:\My Documents\ReadMe.txt",
                                   Encoding.UTF8);
```

You specify the encoding by using one of several properties on a class, `System.Text.Encoding`. This class is an abstract base class, from which a number of classes are derived and which implements methods that actually perform the text encoding. Each property returns an instance of the appropriate class, and the possible properties you can use are as follows:

➤ ASCII

➤ Unicode

➤ UTF7

➤ UTF8

➤ UTF32

➤ BigEndianUnicode

The following example demonstrates how to hook up a `StreamReader` to a `FileStream`. The advantage of this is that you can specify whether to create the file and the share permissions, which you cannot do if you directly attach a `StreamReader` to the file:

```
FileStream fs = new FileStream(@"C:\My Documents\ReadMe.txt",
                    FileMode.Open, FileAccess.Read, FileShare.None);
StreamReader sr = new StreamReader(fs);
```

For this example, you specify that the `StreamReader` will look for byte code markers to determine the encoding method used, as it will do in the following examples, in which the `StreamReader` is obtained from a `FileInfo` instance:

```
FileInfo myFile = new FileInfo(@"C:\My Documents\ReadMe.txt");
StreamReader sr = myFile.OpenText();
```

Just as with a `FileStream`, you should always close a `StreamReader` after use. Otherwise, the file will remain locked to other processes (unless you used a `FileStream` to construct the `StreamReader` and specified `FileShare.ShareReadWrite`):

```
sr.Close();
```

Now that you have gone to the trouble of instantiating a `StreamReader`, you can do something with it. As with the `FileStream`, the following examples demonstrate the various ways to read data; other, less commonly used `StreamReader` methods are left to the SDK documentation.

Possibly the easiest method to use is `ReadLine`, which keeps reading until it gets to the end of a line. It does not include the carriage return–line feed combination that marks the end of the line in the returned string:

```
string nextLine = sr.ReadLine();
```

Alternatively, you can grab the entire remainder of the file (or strictly, the remainder of the stream) in one string:

```
string restOfStream = sr.ReadToEnd();
```

You can read a single character as follows:

```
int nextChar = sr.Read();
```

This overload of `Read` casts the returned character to an `int`. This gives it the option of returning a value of -1 if the end of the stream has been reached.

Finally, you can read a given number of characters into an array, with an offset:

```
// to read 100 characters in.

int nChars = 100;
char [] charArray = new char[nChars];
int nCharsRead = sr.Read(charArray, 0, nChars);
```

`nCharsRead` will be less than `nChars` if you have requested to read more characters than remain in the file.

The StreamWriter Class

This works in the same way as the `StreamReader`, except that you can use `StreamWriter` only to write to a file (or to another stream). Possibilities for constructing a `StreamWriter` include the following:

```
StreamWriter sw = new StreamWriter(@"C:\My Documents\ReadMe.txt");
```

The preceding uses UTF8 encoding, which is regarded by .NET as the default encoding method. If you want, you can specify alternative encoding:

```
StreamWriter sw = new StreamWriter(@"C:\My Documents\ReadMe.txt", true,
    Encoding.ASCII);
```

In this constructor, the second parameter is a boolean that indicates whether the file should be opened for appending. There is, oddly, no constructor that takes only a filename and an encoding class.

Of course, you may want to hook up `StreamWriter` to a file stream to give you more control over the options for opening the file:

```
FileStream fs = new FileStream(@"C:\My Documents\ReadMe.txt",
    FileMode.CreateNew, FileAccess.Write, FileShare.Read);
StreamWriter sw = new StreamWriter(fs);
```

`FileStream` does not implement any methods that return a `StreamWriter` class.

Alternatively, if you want to create a new file and start writing data to it, you will find this sequence useful:

```
FileInfo myFile = new FileInfo(@"C:\My Documents\NewFile.txt");
StreamWriter sw = myFile.CreateText();
```

Just as with all other stream classes, it is important to close a `StreamWriter` class when you are finished with it:

```
sw.Close();
```

Writing to the stream is done using any of 17 overloads of `StreamWriter.Write`. The simplest writes out a string:

```
string nextLine = "Groovy Line";
sw.Write(nextLine);
```

It is also possible to write out a single character:

```
char nextChar = 'a';
sw.Write(nextChar);
```

And an array of characters:

```
char [] charArray = new char[100];

// initialize these characters

sw.Write(charArray);
```

It is even possible to write out a portion of an array of characters:

```
int nCharsToWrite = 50;
int startAtLocation = 25;
char [] charArray = new char[100];

// initialize these characters

sw.Write(charArray, startAtLocation, nCharsToWrite);
```

ReadWriteText Sample

The `ReadWriteText` sample displays the use of the `StreamReader` and `StreamWriter` classes. It is similar to the earlier `ReadBinaryFile` sample, but it assumes that the file to be read in is a text file and displays it as such. It is also capable of saving the file (with any modifications you have made to the text in the text box). It will save any file in Unicode format.

The screenshot in Figure 24-11 shows `ReadWriteText` displaying the same `Default.aspx` file that you used earlier. This time, however, you are able to read the contents a bit more easily!

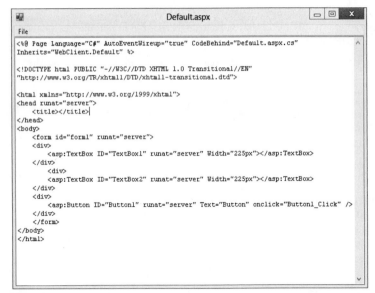

FIGURE 24-11

We don't cover the details of adding the event handlers for the Open File dialog, because they are basically the same as those in the earlier `BinaryFileReader` sample. As with that sample, opening a new file causes the `DisplayFile` method to be called. The only real difference between this sample and the previous one is the implementation of `DisplayFile`, and you now have the option to save a file. This is represented by another menu option, Save. The handler for this option calls another method you have added to the code, `SaveFile`. (Note that the new file always overwrites the original file; this sample does not have an option to write to a different file.)

You look at `SaveFile` first because it is the simplest function. You simply write each line of the text box, in turn, to a `StreamWriter` stream, relying on the `StreamReader.WriteLine` method to append the trailing carriage return and line feed to the end of each line:

```
void SaveFile()
{
    StreamWriter sw = new StreamWriter(chosenFile, false, Encoding.Unicode);

    foreach (string line in textBoxContents.Lines)
        sw.WriteLine(line);

    sw.Close();
}
```

chosenFile is a string field of the main form, which contains the name of the file you have read in (just as for the previous example). Notice that you specify Unicode encoding when you open the stream. If you want to write files in some other format, you simply need to change the value of this parameter. The second parameter to this constructor is set to true to append to a file, but you do not in this case. The encoding must be set at construction time for a StreamWriter. It is subsequently available as a read-only property, Encoding.

Now you examine how files are read in. The process of reading in is complicated by the fact that you don't know how many lines it will contain until you have read in the file. For example, you don't know how many (char)13(char)10 sequences are in the file because char(13)char(10) is the carriage return–line feed combination that occurs at the end of a line. You solve this problem by initially reading the file into an instance of the StringCollection class, which is in the System.Collections.Specialized namespace. This class is designed to hold a set of strings that can be dynamically expanded. It implements two methods that you will be interested in: Add, which adds a string to the collection, and CopyTo, which copies the string collection into a normal array (a System.Array instance). Each element of the StringCollection object holds one line of the file.

The DisplayFile method calls another method, ReadFileIntoStringCollection, which actually reads in the file. After doing this, you now know how many lines there are, so you are in a position to copy the StringCollection into a normal, fixed-size array and feed it into the text box. Because only the references to the strings, not the strings themselves, are copied when you actually make the copy, the process is reasonably efficient:

```
void DisplayFile()
{
    StringCollection linesCollection = ReadFileIntoStringCollection();
    string [] linesArray = new string[linesCollection.Count];
    linesCollection.CopyTo(linesArray, 0);
    this.textBoxContents.Lines = linesArray;
}
```

The second parameter of StringCollection.CopyTo indicates the index within the destination array where you want the collection to start.

The next example demonstrates the ReadFileIntoStringCollection method. You use a StreamReader to read in each line. The main complication here is the need to count the characters read in to ensure that you do not exceed the capacity of the text box:

```
StringCollection ReadFileIntoStringCollection()
{
    const int MaxBytes = 65536;
    StreamReader sr = new StreamReader(chosenFile);
    StringCollection result = new StringCollection();
    int nBytesRead = 0;
    string nextLine;
    while ( sr.Peek != 0 )
    {
        nextLine = sr.ReadLine()
```

```
            nBytesRead += nextLine.Length;
            if (nBytesRead > MaxBytes)
                break;
            result.Add(nextLine);
        }
        sr.Close();
        return result;
    }
```

That completes the code for this sample.

If you run `ReadWriteText`, read in the `Default.aspx` file, and then save it, the file will be in Unicode format. You would not be able to discern this from any of the usual Windows applications. Notepad, WordPad, and even the `ReadWriteText` example will still read the file in and display it correctly under most versions of Windows, but because Windows 9*x* doesn't support Unicode, applications like Notepad won't be able to understand the Unicode file on those platforms. (If you download the example from the Wrox Press website at `www.wrox.com`, you can try this!) However, if you try to display the file again using the earlier `BinaryFileReader` sample, you can see the difference immediately, as shown in Figure 24-12. The two initial bytes that indicate the file is in Unicode format are visible, and thereafter every character is represented by 2 bytes. This last fact is obvious because the high-order byte of every character in this particular file is zero, so every second byte in this file now displays x00.

MAPPED MEMORY FILES

If you have been working your entire coding life with only managed code, then mapped-memory files might be a brand-new concept. .NET Framework 4.5 supplies mapped-memory files as part of your toolkit for building applications with the `System .IO.MemoryMappedFiles` namespace.

It is always possible to use the concept of mapped-memory files by doing some P/Invokes to the underlying Windows APIs, but with of the `System .IO.MemoryMappedFiles` namespace, you can work with managed code rather than operate in the cumbersome P/Invoke world.

Mapped-memory files and the use of this namespace is ideal when your application requires frequent or random access to files. Using this approach enables you to load part or all of the file into a segment of virtual memory, which then appears to your application as if this file is contained within the primary memory for the application.

Interestingly, you can use this file in memory as a shared resource among more than one process. Prior

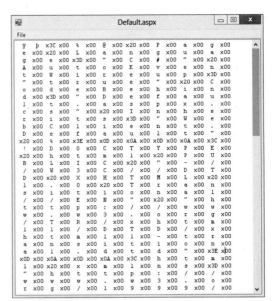

FIGURE 24-12

to this, you might have been using Windows Communication Foundation (WCF) or Named Pipes to communicate a shared resource between multiple processes, but now you can share a mapped-memory file between processes using a shared name.

To work with mapped-memory files, you have to work with a couple of objects. The first is a mapped-memory file instance that loads the file. The second is an accessor object. The following code writes to the mapped-memory file object and then reads from it. The write is also happening when the object is disposed:

```
using System;
using System.IO.MemoryMappedFiles;
using System.Text;

namespace MappedMemoryFiles
{
    class Program
    {
        static void Main(string[] args)
        {
            using (var mmFile = MemoryMappedFile.CreateFromFile(@"c:\users\bill\
                documents\visual studio 11\
                Projects\MappedMemoryFiles\MappedMemoryFiles\TextFile1.txt",
                System.IO.FileMode.Create, "fileHandle", 1024 * 1024))
            {
                string valueToWrite = "Written to the mapped-memory file on " +
                    DateTime.Now.ToString();
                var myAccessor = mmFile.CreateViewAccessor();

                myAccessor.WriteArray<byte>(0,
                    Encoding.ASCII.GetBytes(valueToWrite), 0,
                    valueToWrite.Length);

                var readOut = new byte[valueToWrite.Length];
                myAccessor.ReadArray<byte>(0, readOut, 0, readOut.Length);
                var finalValue = Encoding.ASCII.GetString(readOut);

                Console.WriteLine("Message: " + finalValue);
                Console.ReadLine();
            }
        }
    }
}
```

In this case, a mapped-memory file is created from a physical file using the `CreateFromFile` method. In addition to a mapped-memory file, you then need to create an accessor object to this mapping. That is done using the following:

```
var myAccessor = mmFile.CreateViewAccessor();
```

After the accessor is in place, you can write or read to this mapped-memory location as shown in the code example.

It is also possible to create multiple accessors to the same mapped-memory location as shown here:

```
var myAccessor1 = mmFile.CreateViewAccessor();
var myAccessor2 = mmFile.CreateViewAccessor();
```

READING DRIVE INFORMATION

In addition to working with files and directories, the .NET Framework includes the capability to read information from a specified drive. This is done using the `DriveInfo` class, which can perform a scan of a system to provide a list of available drives and then can dig in deeper, providing a large amount of detail about any of the drives.

To demonstrate using the `DriveInfo` class, the following example creates a simple Windows Form that will list all the available drives on a computer and then provide details on a user-selected drive. Your Windows Form will consist of a simple `ListBox` and should look like Figure 24-13.

When you have the form all set, the code consists of two events—one for when the form loads and another for when the end user makes a drive selection in the list box. The code for this form is shown here:

```csharp
using System;
using System.IO;
using System.Windows.Forms;

namespace DriveViewer
{
    public partial class Form1: Form
    {
        public Form1()
        {
            InitializeComponent();
        }

        private void Form1_Load(object sender, EventArgs e)
        {
            DriveInfo[] di = DriveInfo.GetDrives();

            foreach (DriveInfo itemDrive in di)
            {
                listBox1.Items.Add(itemDrive.Name);
            }
        }

        private void listBox1_SelectedIndexChanged(object sender, EventArgs e)
        {
            DriveInfo di = new DriveInfo(listBox1.SelectedItem.ToString());

            MessageBox.Show("Available Free Space: "
                + di.AvailableFreeSpace + "\n" +
                "Drive Format: " + di.DriveFormat + "\n" +
                "Drive Type: " + di.DriveType + "\n" +
                "Is Ready: " + di.IsReady + "\n" +
                "Name: " + di.Name + "\n" +
                "Root Directory: " + di.RootDirectory + "\n" +
                "ToString() Value: " + di + "\n" +
                "Total Free Space: " + di.TotalFreeSpace + "\n" +
                "Total Size: " + di.TotalSize + "\n" +
                "Volume Label: " + di.VolumeLabel, di.Name +
                " DRIVE INFO");
        }
    }
}
```

FIGURE 24-13

The first step is to bring in the `System.IO` namespace with the `using` keyword. Within the `Form1_Load` event, you use the `DriveInfo` class to get a list of all the available drives on the system. This is done using an array of `DriveInfo` objects and populating this array with the `DriveInfo.GetDrives` method. Then using a `foreach` loop, you are able to iterate through each drive found and populate the list box with the results. This produces something similar to what is shown in Figure 24-14.

This form enables the end user to select one of the drives in the list. After a drive is selected, a message box appears that contains details about that drive. Figure 29-14 shows a computer with four drives. Selecting a couple of these drives produces the message boxes collectively shown in Figure 24-15.

FIGURE 24-14

FIGURE 24-15

From here, you can see that these message boxes provide details about three entirely different drives. The first, drive C:\, is a hard drive, and the message box shows its drive type as Fixed. The second drive, drive D:\, is a CD/DVD drive. The third drive, drive E:\, is a USB pen and is labeled with a Removable drive type.

FILE SECURITY

When the .NET Framework 1.0/1.1 was first introduced, it didn't provide a way to easily access and work with access control lists (ACLs) for files, directories, and registry keys. To do such things at that time usually meant some work with COM interop, thus also requiring a more advanced programming knowledge of working with ACLs.

That changed considerably after the release of the .NET Framework 2.0, which made the process of working with ACLs much easier with a namespace—System.Security.AccessControl. With this namespace, it is possible to manipulate security settings for files, registry keys, network shares, Active Directory objects, and more.

Reading ACLs from a File

For an example of working with System.Security.AccessControl, this section looks at working with the ACLs for both files and directories. It starts by examining how you review the ACLs for a particular file. This example is accomplished in a console application and is illustrated here:

```
using System;
using System.IO;
using System.Security.AccessControl;
using System.Security.Principal;

namespace ReadingACLs
{
    internal class Program
    {
        private static string myFilePath;

        private static void Main()
        {
            Console.Write("Provide full file path: ");
            myFilePath = Console.ReadLine();

            try
            {
                using (FileStream myFile =
                    new FileStream(myFilePath, FileMode.Open, FileAccess.Read))
```

```
        {
            FileSecurity fileSec = myFile.GetAccessControl();

            foreach (FileSystemAccessRule fileRule in
                fileSec.GetAccessRules(true, true,
                    typeof (NTAccount)))
            {
                Console.WriteLine("{0} {1} {2} access for {3}",
                    myFilePath,
                    fileRule.AccessControlType ==
                    AccessControlType.Allow
                        ? "provides": "denies",
                        fileRule.FileSystemRights,
                        fileRule.IdentityReference);
            }
        }
    }
    catch
    {
        Console.WriteLine("Incorrect file path given!");
    }

    Console.ReadLine();
        }
    }
}
```

For this example to work, the first step is to refer to the `System.Security.AccessControl` namespace. This gives you access to the `FileSecurity` and `FileSystemAccessRule` classes later in the program.

After the specified file is retrieved and placed in a `FileStream` object, the ACLs of the file are grabbed using the `GetAccessControl` method now found on the `File` object. This information from the `GetAccessControl` method is then placed in a `FileSecurity` class, which has access rights to the referenced item. Each individual access right is then represented by a `FileSystemAccessRule` object. That is why a `foreach` loop is used to iterate through all the access rights found in the created `FileSecurity` object.

Running this example with a simple text file in the root directory produces something similar to the following results:

```
Provide full file path: C:\Sample.txt
C:\Sample.txt provides FullControl access for BUILTIN\Administrators
C:\Sample.txt provides FullControl access for NT AUTHORITY\SYSTEM
C:\Sample.txt provides ReadAndExecute, Synchronize access for BUILTIN\Users
C:\Sample.txt provides Modify, Sychronize access for
        NT AUTHORITY\Authenticated Users
```

Reading ACLs from a Directory

Reading ACL information about a directory instead of an actual file is not much different from the preceding example, as shown here:

```
using System;
using System.IO;
using System.Security.AccessControl;
using System.Security.Principal;

namespace ConsoleApplication1
```

```
{
    internal class Program
    {
        private static string mentionedDir;

        private static void Main()
        {
            Console.Write("Provide full directory path: ");
            mentionedDir = Console.ReadLine();

            try
            {
                DirectoryInfo myDir = new DirectoryInfo(mentionedDir);

                if (myDir.Exists)
                {
                    DirectorySecurity myDirSec = myDir.GetAccessControl();

                    foreach (FileSystemAccessRule fileRule in
                        myDirSec.GetAccessRules(true, true,
                                                typeof (NTAccount)))
                    {
                        Console.WriteLine("{0} {1} {2} access for {3}",
                            mentionedDir, fileRule.AccessControlType ==
                                AccessControlType.Allow
                                ? "provides": "denies",
                                fileRule.FileSystemRights,
                                fileRule.IdentityReference);
                    }
                }
            }
            catch
            {
                Console.WriteLine("Incorrect directory provided!");
            }

            Console.ReadLine();
        }
    }
}
```

The big difference with this example is that it uses the DirectoryInfo class, which now also includes the GetAccessControl method to pull information about the directory's ACLs. Running this example produces the following results when using Windows 8:

```
Provide full directory path: C:\Test
C:\Test provides FullControl access for BUILTIN\Administrators
C:\Test provides 268435456 access for BUILTIN\Administrators
C:\Test provides FullControl access for NT AUTHORITY\SYSTEM
C:\Test provides 268435456 access for NT AUTHORITY\SYSTEM
C:\Test provides ReadAndExecute, Synchronize access for BUILTIN\Users
C:\Test provides Modify, Synchronize access for
        NT AUTHORITY\Authenticated Users
C:\Test provides -536805376 access for NT AUTHORITY\Authenticated Users
```

The final thing you will look at when working with ACLs is using the new System.Security
.AccessControl namespace to add and remove items to and from a file's ACL.

Adding and Removing ACLs from a File

It is also possible to manipulate the ACLs of a resource using the same objects that were used in earlier examples. The following code changes a previous code example in which a file's ACL information was read. Here, the ACLs are read for a specified file, changed, and then read again:

```
try
{
    using (FileStream myFile = new FileStream(myFilePath,
        FileMode.Open, FileAccess.ReadWrite))
    {
        FileSecurity fileSec = myFile.GetAccessControl();

        Console.WriteLine("ACL list before modification:");

        foreach (FileSystemAccessRule fileRule in
            fileSec.GetAccessRules(true, true,
              typeof(System.Security.Principal.NTAccount)))
        {
            Console.WriteLine("{0} {1} {2} access for {3}", myFilePath,
                fileRule.AccessControlType == AccessControlType.Allow ?
                "provides": "denies",
                fileRule.FileSystemRights,
                fileRule.IdentityReference);
        }

        Console.WriteLine();
        Console.WriteLine("ACL list after modification:");

        FileSystemAccessRule newRule = new FileSystemAccessRule(
            new System.Security.Principal.NTAccount(@"PUSHKIN\Tuija"),
            FileSystemRights.FullControl,
            AccessControlType.Allow);

        fileSec.AddAccessRule(newRule);
        File.SetAccessControl(myFilePath, fileSec);

        foreach (FileSystemAccessRule fileRule in
            fileSec.GetAccessRules(true, true,
            typeof(System.Security.Principal.NTAccount)))
        {
            Console.WriteLine("{0} {1} {2} access for {3}", myFilePath,
                fileRule.AccessControlType == AccessControlType.Allow ?
                "provides": "denies",
                fileRule.FileSystemRights,
                fileRule.IdentityReference);
        }
    }
}
```

In this case, a new access rule is added to the file's ACL. This is done by using the `FileSystemAccessRule` object. The `FileSystemAccessRule` class is an abstraction access control entry (ACE) instance. The ACE defines the user account to use, the type of access to which user account applies, and whether this access is allowed or denied. In creating a new instance of this object, a new `NTAccount` is created and given `Full Control` to the file. Even though a new `NTAccount` is created, it must still reference an existing user. Then the `AddAccessRule` method of the `FileSecurity` class is used to assign the new rule. From there, the `FileSecurity` object reference is used to set the access control to the file in question using the `SetAccessControl` method of the `File` class.

Next, the file's ACL is listed again. The following is an example of what the preceding code could produce:

```
Provide full file path: C:\Users\Bill\Sample.txt
ACL list before modification:
C:\Sample.txt provides FullControl access for NT AUTHORITY\SYSTEM
C:\Sample.txt provides FullControl access for BUILTIN\Administrators
C:\Sample.txt provides FullControl access for PUSHKIN\Bill

ACL list after modification:
C:\Sample.txt provides FullControl access for PUSHKIN\Tuija
C:\Sample.txt provides FullControl access for NT AUTHORITY\SYSTEM
C:\Sample.txt provides FullControl access for BUILTIN\Administrators
C:\Sample.txt provides FullControl access for PUSHKIN\Bill
```

To remove a rule from the ACL list, not much needs to be done to the code. In the previous code example, you simply need to change the line

```
fileSec.AddAccessRule(newRule);
```

to the following to remove the rule that was just added:

```
fileSec.RemoveAccessRule(newRule);
```

READING AND WRITING TO THE REGISTRY

In all versions of Windows since Windows 95, the registry has been the central repository for all configuration information relating to Windows setup, user preferences, and installed software and devices. Almost all commercial software these days uses the registry to store information about itself, and any COM component must place information about itself in the registry in order to be called by clients. The .NET Framework and its accompanying concept of zero-impact installation has slightly reduced the significance of the registry for applications in the sense that assemblies are entirely self-contained; no information about particular assemblies needs to be placed in the registry, even for shared assemblies. In addition, the .NET Framework uses the concept of isolated storage—applications can store information that is particular to each user in files; and it ensures that data is stored separately for each user registered on a machine.

The fact that applications can now be installed using the Windows Installer also frees developers from some of the direct manipulation of the registry that used to be involved in installing applications. However, despite this, the possibility exists that if you distribute any complete application, the application will use the registry to store information about its configuration. For instance, if you want your application to appear in the Add/Remove Programs dialog in the control panel, that involves appropriate registry entries. You may also need to use the registry for backward compatibility with legacy code.

As you would expect from a library as comprehensive as the .NET library, it includes classes that give you access to the registry. Two classes are concerned with the registry, and both are in the `Microsoft.Win32` namespace: `Registry` and `RegistryKey`. Before examining these classes, the following section briefly reviews the registry's structure itself.

The Registry

The registry has a hierarchical structure much like that of the file system. The usual way to view or modify the contents of the registry is with one of two utilities: `regedit` or `regedt32`. Of these, `regedit` is standard with all versions of Windows since Windows 95. `regedt32` is included with Windows NT and Windows 2000; it is less user-friendly than `regedit` but allows access to security information that `regedit` is unable to view. Windows Server 2003 merged `regedit` and `regedt32` into a single new editor simply called `regedit`. The following example uses `regedit` from Windows 7, which you can launch by typing regedit in the Run dialog or at the command prompt.

Figure 24-16 shows the window that appears when you launch `regedit` for the first time.

`regedit` has a tree view/list view–style user interface similar to Windows Explorer, which matches the hierarchical structure of the registry itself. However, you will see some key differences shortly.

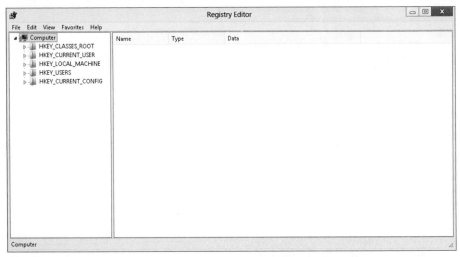

FIGURE 24-16

In a file system, the topmost-level nodes can be thought of as being the partitions on your disks, `C:\`, `D:\`, and so on. In the registry, the equivalent to a partition is the *registry hive*. It is not possible to change the existing hives—they are fixed, and there are seven of them, although only five are actually visible through `regedit`:

➤ `HKEY_CLASSES_ROOT` (HKCR) contains details of types of files on the system (`.txt`, `.doc`, and so on) and which applications are able to open files of each type. It also contains registration information for all COM components (this latter area is usually the largest single area of the registry because Windows now includes a huge number of COM components).

➤ `HKEY_CURRENT_USER` (HKCU) contains details of user preferences for the user currently logged on to the machine locally. These settings include desktop settings, environment variables, network and printer connections, and other settings that define the operating environment of the user.

➤ `HKEY_LOCAL_MACHINE` (HKLM) is a huge hive that contains details of all software and hardware installed on the machine. These settings are not user-specific but for all users that log on to the machine. This hive also includes the HKCR hive; HKCR is actually not an independent hive in its own right but simply a convenient mapping onto the registry key `HKLM/SOFTWARE/Classes`.

➤ `HKEY_USERS` (HKUSR) contains details of user preferences for all users. As you might guess, it also contains the HKCU hive, which is simply a mapping onto one of the keys in `HKEY_USERS`.

➤ `HKEY_CURRENT_CONFIG` (HKCF) contains details of hardware on the machine.

The remaining two keys contain information that is temporary and changes frequently:

➤ `HKEY_DYN_DATA` is a general container for any volatile data that needs to be stored somewhere in the registry.

➤ `HKEY_PERFORMANCE_DATA` contains information concerning the performance of running applications.

Within the hives is a tree structure of registry *keys*. Each key is in many ways analogous to a folder or file on the file system. However, there is one very important difference: The file system distinguishes between files (which are there to contain data) and folders (which are primarily there to contain other files or folders), but in the registry there are only keys. A key may contain both data and other keys.

If a key contains data, it will be presented as a series of values. Each value has an associated name, data type, and data. In addition, a key can have a default value, which is unnamed.

You can see this structure by using `regedit` to examine registry keys. Figure 24-17 shows the contents of the key `HKCU\Control Panel\Appearance`, which contains details about the chosen color scheme of the currently logged-in user. `regedit` shows which key is being examined by displaying it with an open folder icon in the tree view.

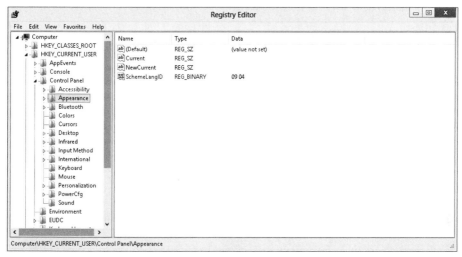

FIGURE 24-17

The `HKCU\Control Panel\Appearance` key has three named values set, although the default value does not contain any data. The column in the screenshot marked Type details the data type of each value. Registry entries can be formatted as one of three data types:

- ➤ `REG_SZ` (which roughly corresponds to a .NET string instance; the matching is not exact because the registry data types are not .NET data types)
- ➤ `REG_DWORD` (corresponds roughly to `uint`)
- ➤ `REG_BINARY` (array of bytes)

An application that stores data in the registry does so by creating a number of registry keys, usually under the key `HKLM\Software\<CompanyName>`. Note that it is not necessary for these keys to contain any data. Sometimes the very fact that a key exists provides the data that an application needs.

The .NET Registry Classes

Access to the registry is available through two classes in the `Microsoft.Win32` namespace: `Registry` and `RegistryKey`. A `RegistryKey` instance represents a registry key. This class implements methods to browse child keys, to create new keys, or to read or modify the values in the key—in other words, to do everything you would normally want to do with a registry key, including setting the security levels for the key. `RegistryKey` is the class you will likely use for much of your work with the registry. `Registry`, by contrast, is a class that enables singular access to registry keys for simple operations. Another role of the `Registry` class is simply to provide you with `RegistryKey` instances that represent the top-level keys, the different hives, to enable you to navigate the registry. `Registry` provides these instances through static properties, of which there are seven; they are called, respectively, `ClassesRoot`, `CurrentConfig`, `CurrentUser`, `DynData`, `LocalMachine`, `PerformanceData`, and `Users`. It should be obvious which property corresponds to which hive.

Therefore, for example, to obtain a `RegistryKey` instance that represents the `HKLM` key, you would use the following:

```
RegistryKey hklm = Registry.LocalMachine;
```

The process of obtaining a reference to a `RegistryKey` object is known as *opening the key*.

Although you might expect that the methods exposed by `RegistryKey` would be similar to those implemented by `DirectoryInfo`, given that the registry has a similar hierarchical structure to the file system, this actually isn't the case. Often, the way that you access the registry is different from the way that you would use files and folders, and `RegistryKey` implements methods that reflect this.

The most obvious difference is how you open a registry key at a given location in the registry. The `Registry` class does not have any public constructor that you can use, nor does it have any methods that provide direct access to a key, given its name. Instead, you are expected to browse down to that key from the top of the relevant hive. If you want to instantiate a `RegistryKey` object, the only way is to start off with the appropriate static property of `Registry`, and work down from there. For example, to read some data in the `HKLM/Software/Microsoft` key, you would get a reference to it like this:

```
RegistryKey hklm = Registry.LocalMachine;
RegistryKey hkSoftware = hklm.OpenSubKey("Software");
RegistryKey hkMicrosoft = hkSoftware.OpenSubKey("Microsoft");
```

A registry key accessed in this way gives you read-only access. If you want to write to the key (which includes writing to its values or creating or deleting direct children of it), you need to use another override to `OpenSubKey`, which takes a second parameter, of type `bool`, that indicates whether you want read-write access to the key. For example, in order to be able to modify the `Microsoft` key (and assuming that you are a system administrator with permission to do this), you would write this:

```
RegistryKey hklm = Registry.LocalMachine;
RegistryKey hkSoftware = hklm.OpenSubKey("Software");
RegistryKey hkMicrosoft = hkSoftware.OpenSubKey("Microsoft", true);
```

Incidentally, because this key contains information used by Microsoft's applications, in most cases you probably shouldn't be modifying this particular key.

The `OpenSubKey` method is the one you call if you are expecting the key to be present. If the key isn't there, it returns a `null` reference. If you want to create a key, you should use the `CreateSubKey` method (which automatically gives you read-write access to the key through the reference returned):

```
RegistryKey hklm = Registry.LocalMachine;
RegistryKey hkSoftware = hklm.OpenSubKey("Software");
RegistryKey hkMine = hkSoftware.CreateSubKey("MyOwnSoftware");
```

The way that `CreateSubKey` works is quite interesting. It creates the key if it does not already exist; but if it does exist, it quietly returns a `RegistryKey` instance that represents the existing key. The reason why the method behaves in this manner is related to how you normally use the registry. The registry, overall, contains long-term data such as configuration information for Windows and various applications. It is not very common, therefore, to find yourself in a situation where you need to explicitly create a key.

What is much more common is for your application to ensure that some data is present in the registry—in other words, create the relevant keys if they do not already exist, but do nothing when they do. `CreateSubKey` fills that need perfectly. Unlike the situation with `FileInfo.Open`, for example, there is no chance that `CreateSubKey` will accidentally remove any data. If deleting registry keys is your intention, you need to call the `RegistryKey.DeleteSubKey` method. This makes sense given the importance of the registry to Windows. The last thing you want is to completely break Windows accidentally by deleting a couple of important keys while you are debugging your C# registry calls!

After you have located the registry key you want to read or modify, you can use the `SetValue` or `GetValue` methods to set or get the data in it. Both methods take a string, giving the name of the value as a parameter, and `SetValue` requires an additional object reference containing details about the value. Because the parameter is defined as an object reference, it can actually be a reference to any class you want. `SetValue` determines from the type of class actually supplied whether to set the value as a REG_SZ, REG_DWORD, or a REG_BINARY value. For example, the following code sets the key with two values:

```
RegistryKey hkMine = HkSoftware.CreateSubKey("MyOwnSoftware");
hkMine.SetValue("MyStringValue", "Hello World");
hkMine.SetValue("MyIntValue", 20);
```

Here, MyStringValue will be of type REG_SZ, and MyIntValue will be of type REG_DWORD. These are the only two types you will consider here and use in the example presented later.

RegistryKey.GetValue works in much the same way. It is defined to return an object reference, which means that it is free to actually return a string reference if it detects the value is of type REG_SZ, and an int if that value is of type REG_DWORD:

```
string stringValue = (string)hkMine.GetValue("MyStringValue");
int intValue = (int)hkMine.GetValue("MyIntValue");
```

Finally, after you finish reading or modifying the data, close the key:

```
hkMine.Close();
```

RegistryKey implements a large number of methods and properties. The following table describes the most useful properties:

PROPERTY	DESCRIPTION
Name	Name of the key (read-only)
SubKeyCount	The number of children of this key
ValueCount	How many values the key contains

The following table describes the most useful methods:

METHOD	DESCRIPTION
Close()	Closes the key
CreateSubKey()	Creates a subkey of a given name (or opens it if it already exists)
DeleteSubKey()	Deletes a given subkey
DeleteSubKeyTree()	Recursively deletes a subkey and all its children
DeleteValue()	Removes a named value from a key
GetAccessControl()	Returns the ACL for a specified registry key. This method was added in .NET Framework 2.0
GetSubKeyNames()	Returns an array of strings containing the names of the subkeys
GetValue()	Returns a named value
GetValueKind()	Returns a named value whose registry data type is to be retrieved. This method was added in .NET Framework 2.0
GetValueNames()	Returns an array of strings containing the names of all the values of the key
OpenSubKey()	Returns a reference to a RegistryKey instance that represents a given subkey
SetAccessControl()	Allows you to apply an ACL to a specified registry key
SetValue()	Sets a named value

READING AND WRITING TO ISOLATED STORAGE

In addition to being able to read from and write to the registry, another option is reading and writing values to and from what is called *isolated storage*. If you are having issues writing to the registry or to disk in general, then isolated storage is where you should turn. You can use isolated storage to store application state or user settings quite easily.

Think of isolated storage as a virtual disk where you can save items that can be shared only by the application that created them, or with other application instances. There are two access types for isolated storage. The first is user and assembly.

When accessing isolated storage by user and assembly, there is a single storage location on the machine, which is accessible via multiple application instances. Access is guaranteed through the user identity and the application (or assembly) identity. This means that you can have multiple instances of the same application all working from the same store.

The second type of access for isolated storage is user, assembly, and domain. In this case, each application instance works off its own isolation store. In this case, the settings that each application instance records are related only to itself. This is a more fine-grained approach to isolated storage. For an example of using isolated storage from a Windows Forms application (although you can use this from an ASP.NET application just as well), you can use the ReadSettings and SaveSettings methods shown next to read and write values to isolated storage, rather than doing so directly in the registry.

> **NOTE** *The code shown here is only for the* ReadSettings *and* SaveSettings *methods. There is more code to the application, which you can see in the download code file in the sample titled* SelfPlacingWindow.

To start, you need to rework the SaveSettings method. In order for this next bit of code to work, you need to add the following using directives:

```
using System.IO;
using System.IO.IsolatedStorage;
using System.Text;
```

The SaveSettings method is detailed in the following example:

```
void SaveSettings()
{
    IsolatedStorageFile storFile = IsolatedStorageFile.GetUserStoreForDomain();
    IsolatedStorageFileStream storStream = new
        IsolatedStorageFileStream("SelfPlacingWindow.xml",

        FileMode.Create, FileAccess.Write);

    System.Xml.XmlTextWriter writer = new
        System.Xml.XmlTextWriter(storStream, Encoding.UTF8);
    writer.Formatting = System.Xml.Formatting.Indented;

    writer.WriteStartDocument();
    writer.WriteStartElement("Settings");

    writer.WriteStartElement("BackColor");
    writer.WriteValue(BackColor.ToKnownColor().ToString());
    writer.WriteEndElement();

    writer.WriteStartElement("Red");
```

```
        writer.WriteValue(BackColor.R);
        writer.WriteEndElement();

        writer.WriteStartElement("Green");
        writer.WriteValue(BackColor.G);
        writer.WriteEndElement();

        writer.WriteStartElement("Blue");
        writer.WriteValue(BackColor.B);
        writer.WriteEndElement();

        writer.WriteStartElement("Width");
        writer.WriteValue(Width);
        writer.WriteEndElement();

        writer.WriteStartElement("Height");
        writer.WriteValue(Height);
        writer.WriteEndElement();

        writer.WriteStartElement("X");
        writer.WriteValue(DesktopLocation.X);
        writer.WriteEndElement();

        writer.WriteStartElement("Y");
        writer.WriteValue(DesktopLocation.Y);
        writer.WriteEndElement();

        writer.WriteStartElement("WindowState");
        writer.WriteValue(WindowState.ToString());
        writer.WriteEndElement();

        writer.WriteEndElement();

        writer.Flush();
        writer.Close();

        storStream.Close();
        storFile.Close();
}
```

It is a bit more code than you might be used to when working with the registry, but that is mainly due to the code required to build the XML document placed in isolated storage. The first important thing happening with this code is presented here:

```
IsolatedStorageFile storFile = IsolatedStorageFile.GetUserStoreForDomain();
IsolatedStorageFileStream storStream = new
    IsolatedStorageFileStream("SelfPlacingWindow.xml",
    FileMode.Create, FileAccess.Write);
```

Here, an instance of an `IsolatedStorageFile` is created using a user, assembly, and domain type of access. A stream is created using the `IsolatedStorageFileStream` object, which creates the virtual `SelfPlacingWindow.xml` file.

From there, an `XmlTextWriter` object is created to build the XML document, and the XML contents are written to the `IsolatedStorageFileStream` object instance:

```
System.Xml.XmlTextWriter writer = new
    System.Xml.XmlTextWriter(storStream, Encoding.UTF8);
```

After the `XmlTextWriter` object is created, all the values are written to the XML document node by node. When everything is written to the XML document, everything is closed and stored in the isolated storage.

Reading from the storage is done through the `ReadSettings` method, shown here:

```
bool ReadSettings()
{
    IsolatedStorageFile storFile = IsolatedStorageFile.GetUserStoreForDomain();
    string[] userFiles = storFile.GetFileNames("SelfPlacingWindow.xml");

    foreach (string userFile in userFiles)
    {
        if(userFile == "SelfPlacingWindow.xml")
        {
            listBoxMessages.Items.Add("Successfully opened file " +
                                    userFile.ToString());

            StreamReader storStream =
                new StreamReader(new IsolatedStorageFileStream("SelfPlacingWindow.xml",
                FileMode.Open, storFile));
            System.Xml.XmlTextReader reader = new
                System.Xml.XmlTextReader(storStream);

            int redComponent = 0;
            int greenComponent = 0;
            int blueComponent = 0;

            int X = 0;
            int Y = 0;

            while (reader.Read())
            {
                switch (reader.Name)
                {
                    case "Red":
                        redComponent = int.Parse(reader.ReadString());
                        break;
                    case "Green":
                        greenComponent = int.Parse(reader.ReadString());
                        break;
                    case "Blue":
                        blueComponent = int.Parse(reader.ReadString());
                        break;
                    case "X":
                        X = int.Parse(reader.ReadString());
                        break;
                    case "Y":
                        Y = int.Parse(reader.ReadString());
                        break;
                    case "Width":
                        this.Width = int.Parse(reader.ReadString());
                        break;
                    case "Height":
                        this.Height = int.Parse(reader.ReadString());
                        break;
                    case "WindowState":
                        this.WindowState = (FormWindowState)FormWindowState.Parse
                            (WindowState.GetType(), reader.ReadString());
                        break;
                    default:
                        break;
                }
            }
        }

        this.BackColor =
```

```
            Color.FromArgb(redComponent, greenComponent, blueComponent);
            this.DesktopLocation = new Point(X, Y);

            listBoxMessages.Items.Add("Background color: " + BackColor.Name);
            listBoxMessages.Items.Add("Desktop location: " +
               DesktopLocation.ToString());
            listBoxMessages.Items.Add("Size: " + new Size(Width, Height).ToString());
            listBoxMessages.Items.Add("Window State: " + WindowState.ToString());

            storStream.Close();
            storFile.Close();
         }
      }
      return true;
   }
```

Using the `GetFileNames` method, the `SelfPlacingWindow.xml` document is pulled from the isolated storage and then placed into a stream and parsed using the `XmlTextReader` object:

```
IsolatedStorageFile storFile = IsolatedStorageFile.GetUserStoreForDomain();
string[] userFiles = storFile.GetFileNames("SelfPlacingWindow.xml");

foreach (string userFile in userFiles)
{
   if(userFile == "SelfPlacingWindow.xml")
   {
      listBoxMessages.Items.Add("Successfully opened file " +
                             userFile.ToString());

      StreamReader storStream =
         new StreamReader(new IsolatedStorageFileStream("SelfPlacingWindow.xml",
         FileMode.Open, storFile));
```

After the XML document is contained within the `IsolatedStorageFileStream` object, it is parsed using the `XmlTextReader` object:

```
System.Xml.XmlTextReader reader = new
   System.Xml.XmlTextReader(storStream);
```

It is pulled from the stream via the `XmlTextReader`, and the element values are then pushed back into the application. You will find—as accomplished in the `SelfPlacingWindow` sample that used the registry to record and retrieve application state values—that using isolated storage is just as effective as working with the registry. The application remembers the color, size, and position just as before.

SUMMARY

In this chapter, you examined how to use the .NET base classes to access the file system and registry from your C# code. You have seen that in both cases the base classes expose simple but powerful object models that make it very easy to perform almost any kind of action in these areas. For the file system, these actions are copying files; moving, creating, and deleting files and folders; and reading and writing both binary and text files. For the registry, these are creating, modifying, or reading keys.

This chapter also reviewed isolated storage and how to use it from your applications to store information in the application state.

This chapter assumed that you were running your code from an account that has sufficient access rights to do whatever the code needs to do. Obviously, the question of security is an important one, as discussed in detail in Chapter 22.

25

Transactions

WHAT'S IN THIS CHAPTER?

- ➤ Transaction phases and ACID properties
- ➤ Traditional transactions
- ➤ Committable transactions
- ➤ Transaction promotions
- ➤ Dependent transactions
- ➤ Ambient transactions
- ➤ Transaction isolation levels
- ➤ Custom resource managers
- ➤ Transactions with Windows 8 and Windows Server 2012

WROX.COM CODE DOWNLOADS FOR THIS CHAPTER

The wrox.com code downloads for this chapter are found at `http://www.wrox.com/remtitle .cgi?isbn=1118314425` on the Download Code tab. The code for this chapter is divided into the following major examples:

- ➤ Transaction Samples
- ➤ Multithreading Ambient Transactions
- ➤ Custom Resource
- ➤ Windows 8 Transactions

INTRODUCTION

All or nothing—this is the main characteristic of a transaction. When writing a few records, either all are written, or everything will be undone. If there is even one failure when writing one record, all the other things that are done within the transaction will be rolled back.

Transactions are commonly used with databases, but with classes from the namespace System .Transactions, you can also perform transactions on volatile or in-memory-based objects such as a list of objects. With a list that supports transactions, if an object is added or removed and the transaction fails, the list action is automatically undone. Writing to a memory-based list can be done in the same transaction as writing to a database.

Since Windows Vista, the file system and registry also have transactional support. Writing a file and making changes within the registry supports transactions.

OVERVIEW

In order to understand transactions, consider the ordering of a book from a web site. The book-ordering process removes the book you want to buy from stock and puts it in your shopping cart, and the cost of your book is charged to your credit card. With these two actions, either both actions should complete successfully or neither of these actions should happen. If there is a failure when getting the book from stock, the credit card should not be charged. Transactions address such scenarios.

The most common use of transactions is writing or updating data within the database. Transactions can also be performed when writing a message to a message queue, or writing data to a file or the registry. Multiple actions can be part of a single transaction.

> **NOTE** *The classes and architecture of Message Queuing and the* System.Messaging *namespace are discussed in Chapter 47.*

Figure 25-1 shows the main actors in a transaction. Transactions are managed and coordinated by the transaction manager, and a resource manager manages every resource that influences the outcome of the transaction. The transaction manager communicates with resource managers to define the outcome of the transaction.

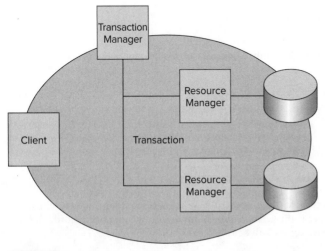

FIGURE 25-1

Transaction Phases

The timely phases of a transaction are the *active*, *preparing*, and *committing* phases:

➤ **Active phase**—During the active phase, the transaction is created. Resource managers that manage the transaction for resources can enlist with the transaction.

➤ **Preparing phase**—During the preparing phase, every resource manager can define the outcome of the transaction. This phase starts when the creator of the transaction sends a commit to end the transaction. The transaction manager sends a *Prepare* message to all resource managers. If the resource manager can produce the transaction outcome successfully, it sends a *Prepared* message to the transaction manager. Resource managers can abort the transaction if they fail to prepare by forcing a rollback with the transaction manager by sending a *Rollback* message. After the Prepared message is sent, the resource managers must guarantee to finish the work successfully in the committing phase. To make this possible, durable resource managers must write a log with the information from the prepared state, so that they can continue from there in case of, for example, a power failure between the prepared and committing phases.

➤ **Committing phase**—The committing phase begins when all resource managers have prepared successfully. This is when the *Prepared* message is received from all resource managers. Then the transaction manager can complete the work by sending a *Commit* message to all participants. The resource managers can now finish the work on the transaction and return a *Committed* message.

ACID Properties

A transaction has specific requirements; for example, a transaction must result in a valid state, even if the server has a power failure. The characteristics of transactions can be defined by the term ACID. *ACID* is a four-letter acronym for *atomicity*, *consistency*, *isolation*, and *durability*:

➤ **Atomicity**—Represents one unit of work. With a transaction, either the complete unit of work succeeds or nothing is changed.

➤ **Consistency**—The state before the transaction was started and after the transaction is completed must be valid. During the transaction, the state may have interim values.

➤ **Isolation**—Transactions that happen concurrently are isolated from the state, which is changed during a transaction. Transaction A cannot see the interim state of transaction B until the transaction is completed.

➤ **Durability**—After the transaction is completed, it must be stored in a durable way. This means that if the power goes down or the server crashes, the state must be recovered at reboot.

Not every transaction requires all four ACID properties. For example, a memory-based transaction (for example, writing an entry into a list) may not need to be durable; and complete isolation from the outside is not always required, as discussed later with transaction isolation levels.

> **NOTE** *Transactions and valid state can easily be explained with a wedding ceremony. A bridal couple is standing before a transaction coordinator. The transaction coordinator asks the first of the couple: "Do you want to marry this man on your side?" If the first one agrees, the second is asked: "Do you want to marry this woman?" If the second one denies, the first receives a rollback. A valid state with this transaction is only that both are married, or none are. If both agree, the transaction is committed and both are in the married state. If one denies, the transaction is aborted and both stay in the unmarried state. An invalid state is that one is married, and the other is not. The transaction guarantees that the result is never an invalid state.*

DATABASE AND ENTITY CLASSES

The sample database CourseManagement that is used with the transactions in this chapter is defined by the structure in Figure 25-2. The table Courses contains information about courses: course number and title. The table CourseDates contains the date of specific courses and is linked to the Courses table. The table Students contains information about persons attending a course. The table CourseAttendees is the link between Students and CourseDates. It defines which student is attending what course.

> **NOTE** *You can download the database along with the source code for this chapter from the Wrox web site.*

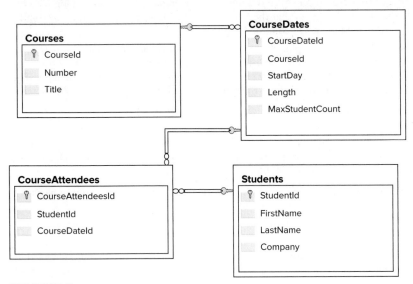

FIGURE 25-2

The sample applications in this chapter use a library with entity and data access classes. The class Student contains properties to define a student—for example, FirstName, LastName, and Company (code file DataLib/Student.cs):

```csharp
using System;

namespace Wrox.ProCSharp.Transactions
{
  [Serializable]
  public class Student
  {
    public string FirstName { get; set; }
    public string LastName { get; set; }
    public string Company { get; set; }
    public int Id { get; set; }

    public override string ToString()
    {
```

```
            return String.Format("{0} {1}", FirstName, LastName);
        }
    }
}
```

Adding student information to the database is done in the method `AddStudent` of the class `StudentData`. Here, an ADO.NET connection is created to connect to the SQL Server database, the `SqlCommand` object defines the SQL statement, and the command is executed by invoking `ExecuteNonQueryAsync` (code file `DataLib/StudentData.cs`):

```
using System.Data.SqlClient;
using System.Threading.Tasks;
using System.Transactions;

namespace Wrox.ProCSharp.Transactions
{
  public class StudentData
  {
    public async Task AddStudentAsync(Student student)
    {
      var connection = new SqlConnection(
          Properties.Settings.Default.CourseManagementConnectionString);
      await connection.OpenAsync();
      try
      {
        SqlCommand command = connection.CreateCommand();

        command.CommandText = "INSERT INTO Students " +
            "(FirstName, LastName, Company) VALUES " +
            "(@FirstName, @LastName, @Company)";
        command.Parameters.AddWithValue("@FirstName", student.FirstName);
        command.Parameters.AddWithValue("@LastName", student.LastName);
        command.Parameters.AddWithValue("@Company", student.Company);

        await command.ExecuteNonQueryAsync();
      }
      finally
      {
        connection.Close();
      }
    }
  }
}
```

> **NOTE** *ADO.NET is covered in detail in Chapter 32, "Core ADO.NET."*

TRADITIONAL TRANSACTIONS

Before `System.Transactions` was released, you could create transactions directly with ADO.NET, or you could do transactions with the help of components, attributes, and the COM+ runtime, which is covered in the namespace `System.EnterpriseServices`. Because COM+ usually is no longer used in new applications, it is not part of this book.

ADO.NET Transactions

Let's start with traditional ADO.NET transactions. If you don't create transactions manually, there is a single transaction with every SQL statement. If multiple statements need to participate with the same transaction, however, you must create a transaction manually to achieve this.

The following code segment shows how to work with ADO.NET transactions. The `SqlConnection` class defines the method `BeginTransaction`, which returns an object of type `SqlTransaction`. This transaction object must then be associated with every command that participates with the transaction. To associate a command with a transaction, set the `Transaction` property of the `SqlCommand` class to the `SqlTransaction` instance. For the transaction to be successful, you must invoke the `Commit` method of the `SqlTransaction` object. If there is an error, you must invoke the `Rollback` method, and every change is undone. You can check for an error with the help of a `try`/`catch` and do the rollback inside the `catch` (code file `DataLib/CourseData.cs`):

```
using System;
using System.Data.SqlClient;
using System.Diagnostics;
using System.Threading.Tasks;

namespace Wrox.ProCSharp.Transactions
{
  public class CourseData
  {
    public async Task AddCourseAsync(Course course)
    {
      var connection = new SqlConnection(
          Properties.Settings.Default.CourseManagementConnectionString);
      SqlCommand courseCommand = connection.CreateCommand();
      courseCommand.CommandText =
          "INSERT INTO Courses (Number, Title) VALUES (@Number, @Title)";
      await connection.OpenAsync();
      SqlTransaction tx = connection.BeginTransaction();

      try
      {
        courseCommand.Transaction = tx;

        courseCommand.Parameters.AddWithValue("@Number", course.Number);
        courseCommand.Parameters.AddWithValue("@Title", course.Title);
        await courseCommand.ExecuteNonQueryAsync();

        tx.Commit();
      }
      catch (Exception ex)
      {
        Trace.WriteLine("Error: " + ex.Message);
        tx.Rollback();
        throw;
      }
      finally
      {
        connection.Close();
      }
    }
  }
}
```

If multiple commands should run in the same transaction, every command must be associated with the transaction. Because the transaction is associated with a connection, every one of these commands must also be associated with the same connection instance. ADO.NET transactions do not support transactions across multiple connections; it is always a local transaction associated with one connection.

When you create an object persistence model using multiple objects—for example, classes `Course` and `CourseDate`—that should be persisted inside one transaction, it becomes very difficult using ADO.NET transactions. In this case, it is necessary to pass the transaction to all the objects participating in the same transaction.

> **NOTE** *ADO.NET transactions are not distributed transactions. In ADO.NET transactions, it is difficult to have multiple objects working on the same transaction.*

System.EnterpriseServices

Enterprise Services provides a lot of services free. One of them is automatic transactions. Enterprise Services today are mainly replaced by new technologies such as `System.Transactions`, WCF, and the Windows App Server. The transactional features of enterprise services influences the functionality of `System.Transactions`, and that's why Enterprise Services is covered here briefly.

Using transactions with `System.EnterpriseServices` has the advantage that it is not necessary to deal with transactions explicitly; transactions are automatically created by the runtime. You just have to add the attribute `[Transaction]` with the transactional requirements to the class. The `[AutoComplete]` attribute marks the method to automatically set the status bit for the transaction: if the method succeeds, the success bit is set, so the transaction can commit. If an exception happens, the transaction is aborted:

```
using System;
using System.Data.SqlClient;
using System.EnterpriseServices;
using System.Diagnostics;

namespace Wrox.ProCSharp.Transactions
{
  [Transaction(TransactionOption.Required)]
  public class CourseData: ServicedComponent
  {
    [AutoComplete]
    public void AddCourse(Course course)
    {
      var connection = new SqlConnection(
          Properties.Settings.Default.CourseManagementConnectionString);
      SqlCommand courseCommand = connection.CreateCommand();
      courseCommand.CommandText =
          "INSERT INTO Courses (Number, Title) VALUES (@Number, @Title)";
      connection.Open();
      try
      {
        courseCommand.Parameters.AddWithValue("@Number", course.Number);
        courseCommand.Parameters.AddWithValue("@Title", course.Title);
        courseCommand.ExecuteNonQuery();
      }
      finally
      {
        connection.Close();
      }
    }
  }
}
```

A big advantage of creating transactions with `System.EnterpriseServices` is that multiple objects can easily run within the same transaction, and transactions are automatically enlisted. The disadvantages are that it requires the COM+ hosting model, and the class using the features of this technology must be derived from the base class `ServicedComponent`.

SYSTEM.TRANSACTIONS

The namespace `System.Transactions` became available with .NET 2.0 and brought a modern transaction programming model to .NET applications.

This namespace offers a few dependent `TransactionXXX` classes. `Transaction` is the base class of all transaction classes and defines properties, methods, and events available with all transaction classes. `CommittableTransaction` is the only transaction class that supports committing. This class has a `Commit` method; all other transaction classes can perform only a rollback. The class `DependentTransaction` is used with transactions that are dependent on another transaction. A dependent transaction can depend on a transaction created from the committable transaction. Then the dependent transaction adds to the outcome of the committable transaction, whether or not it is successful. The class `SubordinateTransaction` is used in conjunction with the Distributed Transaction Coordinator (DTC). This class represents a transaction that is not a root transaction but can be managed by the DTC.

The following table describes the properties and methods of the `Transaction` class:

TRANSACTION CLASS MEMBER	DESCRIPTION
Current	The property `Current` is a static property that doesn't require an instance. `Transaction.Current` returns an ambient transaction if one exists. Ambient transactions are discussed later in this chapter.
IsolationLevel	The `IsolationLevel` property returns an object of type `IsolationLevel`. `IsolationLevel` is an enumeration that defines what access other transactions have to the interim results of the transaction. This reflects the "I" in ACID; not all transactions are isolated.
TransactionInformation	The `TransactionInformation` property returns a `TransactionInformation` object, which provides information about the current state of the transaction, the time when the transaction was created, and transaction identifiers.
EnlistVolatile EnlistDurable EnlistPromotableSinglePhase	With these enlist methods, you can enlist custom resource managers that participate with the transaction.
Rollback	With the `Rollback` method, you can abort a transaction and undo everything, setting all results to the state before the transaction.
DependentClone	With the `DependentClone` method, you can create a transaction that depends on the current transaction.
TransactionCompleted	`TransactionCompleted` is an event that is fired when the transaction is completed—either successfully or unsuccessfully. With an event handler object of type `TransactionCompletedEventHandler`, you can access the `Transaction` object and read its status.

To demonstrate the features of `System.Transactions`, the following example class `Utilities` inside a separate assembly offers some static methods. The method `AbortTx` returns `true` or `false` depending on the input from the user. The method `DisplayTransactionInformation` gets a `TransactionInformation` object as parameter and displays all the information from the transaction: creation time, status, local, and distributed identifiers (code file `Utilities/Utilities.cs`):

```
public static class Utilities
{
  public static bool AbortTx()
  {
    Console.Write("Abort the Transaction (y/n)?");
    return Console.ReadLine().ToLower().Equals("y");
  }

  public static void DisplayTransactionInformation(string title,
      TransactionInformation ti)
  {
    Contract.Requires<ArgumentNullException>(ti != null);

    Console.WriteLine(title);
    Console.WriteLine("Creation Time: {0:T}", ti.CreationTime);
    Console.WriteLine("Status: {0}", ti.Status);
    Console.WriteLine("Local ID: {0}", ti.LocalIdentifier);
    Console.WriteLine("Distributed ID: {0}", ti.DistributedIdentifier);
    Console.WriteLine();
  }
}
```

Committable Transactions

The `Transaction` class cannot be committed programmatically; it does not have a method to commit the transaction. The base class `Transaction` just supports aborting the transaction. The only transaction class that supports a commit is the class `CommittableTransaction`.

With ADO.NET, a transaction can be enlisted with the connection. To make this possible, an `AddStudentAsync` method is added to the class `StudentData` that accepts a `System.Transactions.Transaction` object as second parameter. The object `tx` is enlisted with the connection by calling the method `EnlistTransaction` of the `SqlConnection` class. This way, the ADO.NET connection is associated with the transaction (code file `DataLib/StudentData.cs`):

```
public async Task AddStudentAsync(Student student, Transaction tx)
{
  Contract.Requires<ArgumentNullException>(student != null);

  var connection = new SqlConnection(
      Properties.Settings.Default.CourseManagementConnectionString);
  await connection.OpenAsync();
  try
  {
    if (tx != null)
      connection.EnlistTransaction(tx);
    SqlCommand command = connection.CreateCommand();

    command.CommandText = "INSERT INTO Students (FirstName, " +
        "LastName, Company)" +
        "VALUES (@FirstName, @LastName, @Company)";
    command.Parameters.AddWithValue("@FirstName", student.FirstName);
    command.Parameters.AddWithValue("@LastName", student.LastName);
    command.Parameters.AddWithValue("@Company", student.Company);

    await command.ExecuteNonQueryAsync();
  }
  finally
```

```
        {
            connection.Close();
        }
    }
```

In the `CommittableTransaction` method of the console application TransactionSamples, first a transaction of type `CommittableTransaction` is created, and information is shown on the console. Then a `Student` object is created, which is written to the database from the `AddStudent` method. If you verify the record in the database from outside the transaction, you cannot see the student added until the transaction is completed. If the transaction fails, there is a rollback and the student is not written to the database.

After the `AddStudentAsync` method is invoked, the helper method `Utilities.AbortTx` is called to ask the user whether the transaction should be aborted. If the user aborts, an exception of type `ApplicationException` is thrown and, in the catch block, a rollback of the transaction is performed by calling the method `Rollback` of the `Transaction` class. The record is not written to the database. If the user does not abort, the `Commit` method commits the transaction, and the final state of the transaction is committed (code file `TransactionSamples/Program.cs`):

```csharp
static async Task CommittableTransactionAsync()
{
    var tx = new CommittableTransaction();
    Utilities.DisplayTransactionInformation("TX created",
        tx.TransactionInformation);

    try
    {
        var s1 = new Student
        {
            FirstName = "Stephanie",
            LastName = "Nagel",
            Company = "CN innovation"
        };
        var db = new StudentData();
        await db.AddStudentAsync(s1, tx);

        if (Utilities.AbortTx())
        {
            throw new ApplicationException("transaction abort");
        }

        tx.Commit();
    }
    catch (Exception ex)
    {
        Console.WriteLine(ex.Message);
        Console.WriteLine();
        tx.Rollback();
    }

    Utilities.DisplayTransactionInformation("TX completed",
        tx.TransactionInformation);

}
```

As shown in the following output of the application, the transaction is active and has a local identifier. In addition, the user has chosen to abort the transaction. After the transaction is finished, you can see the aborted state:

```
TX created
Creation Time: 7:30:49 PM
Status: Active
```

```
Local ID: bdcf1cdc-a67e-4ccc-9a5c-cbdfe0fe9177:1
Distributed ID: 00000000-0000-0000-0000-000000000000

Abort the Transaction (y/n)? y
Transaction abort

TX completed
Creation Time: 7:30:49 PM
Status: Aborted
Local ID: bdcf1cdc-a67e-4ccc-9a5c-cbdfe0fe9177:1
Distributed ID: 00000000-0000-0000-0000-000000000000
```

With the second output of the application that follows, the transaction is not aborted by the user. The transaction has the status committed, and the data is written to the database:

```
TX Created
Creation Time: 7:33:04 PM
Status: Active
Local ID: 708bda71-fa24-46a9-86b4-18b83120f6af:1
Distributed ID: 00000000-0000-0000-0000-000000000000

Abort the Transaction (y/n)? n

TX completed
Creation Time: 7:33:04 PM
Status: Committed
Local ID: 708bda71-fa24-46a9-86b4-18b83120f6af:1
Distributed ID: 00000000-0000-0000-0000-000000000000
```

Transaction Promotion

System.Transactions supports promotable transactions. Depending on the resources that participate with the transaction, either a local or a distributed transaction is created. SQL Server has supported promotable transactions since SQL Server 2005. So far, you have seen only local transactions. With all the previous examples, the distributed transaction ID was always set to 0, and only the local ID was assigned. With a resource that does not support promotable transactions, a distributed transaction is created. If multiple resources are added to the transaction, the transaction may start as a local transaction and be promoted to a distributed transaction as required. Such a promotion happens when multiple SQL Server database connections are added to the transaction. The transaction starts as a local transaction and then is promoted to a distributed transaction.

The console application is now changed to add a second student by using the same transaction object tx. Because every AddStudent method opens a new connection, two connections are associated with the transaction after the second student is added (code file TransactionSamples/Program.cs):

```
static void TransactionPromotion()
{
  var tx = new CommittableTransaction();
  Utilities.DisplayTransactionInformation("TX created",
      tx.TransactionInformation);

  try
  {
    var s1 = new Student
    {
      FirstName = "Matthias",
      LastName = "Nagel",
      Company = "CN innovation"
    };
```

```
        var db = new StudentData();
        db.AddStudent(s1, tx);

        var s2 = new Student
        {
            FirstName = "Stephanie",
            LastName = "Nagel",
            Company = "CN innovation"
        };
        db.AddStudent(s2, tx);

        Utilities.DisplayTransactionInformation(
            "2nd connection enlisted", tx.TransactionInformation);

        if (Utilities.AbortTx())
        {
            throw new ApplicationException("transaction abort");
        }

        tx.Commit();
    }
    catch (Exception ex)
    {
        Console.WriteLine(ex.Message);
        Console.WriteLine();
        tx.Rollback();
    }

    Utilities.DisplayTransactionInformation("TX finished",
        tx.TransactionInformation);
}
```

Running the application now, you can see that with the first student added the distributed identifier is 0, but with the second student added the transaction was promoted, so a distributed identifier is associated with the transaction:

```
TX created
Creation Time: 7:56:24 PM
Status: Active
Local ID: 0d2f5ada-32aa-40eb-b9d7-cc6aa9a2a554:1
Distributed ID: 00000000-0000-0000-0000-000000000000

2nd connection enlisted
Creation Time: 7:56:24 PM
Status: Active
Local ID: 0d2f5ada-32aa-40eb-b9d7-cc6aa9a2a554:1
Distributed ID: 501abd91-e512-47f3-95d5-f0488743293d

Abort the Transaction (y/n)?
```

Transaction promotion requires the DTC to be started. If promoting transactions fails with your system, verify that the DTC service is started. Starting the Component Services MMC snap-in, you can see the actual status of all DTC transactions running on your system.

By selecting Transaction List on the tree view, you can see all active transactions. Figure 25-3 shows a transaction active with the same distributed identifier that was shown in the console output earlier. If you verify the output on your system, ensure that the transaction has a timeout, and aborts if the timeout is reached. After the timeout, you cannot see the transaction in the transaction list anymore. You can also verify the transaction statistics with the same tool. Transaction Statistics shows the number of committed and aborted transactions.

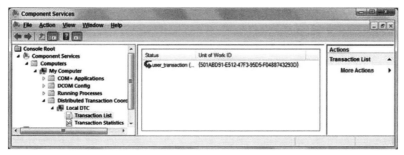

FIGURE 25-3

DEPENDENT TRANSACTIONS

With dependent transactions, you can influence one transaction among multiple tasks or threads. A dependent transaction depends on another transaction and influences the outcome of the transaction.

The sample application `DependentTransactions` creates a dependent transaction for a new task. `TxTask` is the method of the new task, in which a `DependentTransaction` object is passed as a parameter. Information about the dependent transaction is shown with the helper method `DisplayTransactionInformation`. Before the task exits, the `Complete` method of the dependent transaction is invoked to define the outcome of the transaction. A dependent transaction can define the outcome of the transaction by calling either the `Complete` or the `Rollback` method. The `Complete` method sets the success bit. If the root transaction finishes, and if all dependent transactions have set the success bit to `true`, the transaction commits. If any of the dependent transactions set the abort bit by invoking the `Rollback` method, then the entire transaction aborts:

```
static void TxTask(object obj)
{
  var tx = obj as DependentTransaction;
  Utilities.DisplayTransactionInformation("Dependent Transaction",
      tx.TransactionInformation);

  Thread.Sleep(3000);

  tx.Complete();

  Utilities.DisplayTransactionInformation("Dependent TX Complete",
      tx.TransactionInformation);
}
```

With the `DependentTransaction` method, first a root transaction is created by instantiating the class `CommittableTransaction`, and the transaction information is shown. Next, the method `tx.DependentClone` creates a dependent transaction. This dependent transaction is passed to the method `TxTask`, which is defined as the entry point of a new task.

The method `DependentClone` requires an argument of type `DependentCloneOption`, which is an enumeration with the values `BlockCommitUntilComplete` and `RollbackIfNotComplete`. This option is important if the root transaction completes before the dependent transaction. Setting the option to `RollbackIfNotComplete`, the transaction aborts if the dependent transaction didn't invoke the `Complete` method before the `Commit` method of the root transaction. Setting the option to `BlockCommitUntilComplete`, the method `Commit` waits until the outcome is defined by all dependent transactions.

Next, the `Commit` method of the `CommittableTransaction` class is invoked if the user does not abort the transaction:

> **NOTE** *Chapter 21, "Threads, Tasks, and Synchronization," covers threading.*

```
static void DependentTransaction()
{
  var tx = new CommittableTransaction();
  Utilities.DisplayTransactionInformation("Root TX created",
      tx.TransactionInformation);

  try
  {
    Task.Factory.StartNew(TxTask, tx.DependentClone(
        DependentCloneOption.BlockCommitUntilComplete));

    if (Utilities.AbortTx())
    {
      throw new ApplicationException("transaction abort");
    }

    tx.Commit();
  }
  catch (Exception ex)
  {
    Console.WriteLine(ex.Message);
    tx.Rollback();
  }

  Utilities.DisplayTransactionInformation("TX finished",
      tx.TransactionInformation);
}
```

The following output of the application shows the root transaction and its identifier. Because of the option `DependentCloneOption.BlockCommitUntilComplete`, the root transaction waits in the `Commit` method until the outcome of the dependent transaction is defined. As soon as the dependent transaction is finished, the transaction is committed:

```
Root TX created
Creation Time: 8:35:25 PM
Status: Active
Local ID: 50126e07-cd28-4e0f-a21f-a81a8e14a1a8:1
Distributed ID: 00000000-0000-0000-0000-0000000000

Abort the Transaction (y/n)? n

Dependent Transaction
Creation Time: 8:35:25 PM
Status: Active
Local ID: 50126e07-cd28-4e0f-a21f-a81a8e14a1a8:1
Distributed ID: 00000000-0000-0000-0000-0000000000

Dependent TX Complete
Root TX finished
Creation Time: 8:35:25 PM
```

```
Status: Committed
Local ID: 50126e07-cd28-4e0f-a21f-a81a8e14a1a8:1
Distributed ID: 00000000-0000-0000-0000-0000000000

Creation Time: 8:35:25 PM
Status: Committed
Local ID: 50126e07-cd28-4e0f-a21f-a81a8e14a1a8:1
Distributed ID: 00000000-0000-0000-0000-0000000000
```

Ambient Transactions

The biggest advantage of the classes in the System.Transactions namespace is the ambient transactions feature. With ambient transactions, there is no need to manually enlist a connection with a transaction; this is done automatically from the resources supporting ambient transactions.

An ambient transaction is associated with the current thread. You can get and set the ambient transaction with the static property Transaction.Current. APIs supporting ambient transactions check this property to get an ambient transaction and enlist with the transaction. ADO.NET connections support ambient transactions.

You can create a CommittableTransaction object and assign it to the property Transaction .Current to initialize the ambient transaction. Another way to create ambient transactions is with the TransactionScope class. The constructor of the TransactionScope creates an ambient transaction.

Important methods of the TransactionScope class are Complete and Dispose. The Complete method sets the happy bit for the scope, and the Dispose method finishes the scope and commits or rolls back the transaction if the scope is a root scope.

Because the TransactionScope class implements the IDisposable interface, you can define the scope with the using statement. The default constructor creates a new transaction. Immediately after creating the TransactionScope instance, the transaction is accessed with the get accessor of the property Transaction.Current to display the transaction information on the console.

To get the information when the transaction is completed, the method OnTransactionCompleted is set to the TransactionCompleted event of the ambient transaction.

Then a new Student object is created and written to the database by calling the StudentData.AddStudent method. With ambient transactions, it is not necessary to pass a Transaction object to this method because the SqlConnection class supports ambient transactions and automatically enlists it with the connection. Then the Complete method of the TransactionScope class sets the success bit. With the end of the using statement, the TransactionScope is disposed, and a commit is done. If the Complete method is not invoked, the Dispose method aborts the transaction:

> **NOTE** *If an ADO.NET connection should not enlist with an ambient transaction, you can set the value* Enlist=false *with the connection string.*

```
static void TransactionScope()
{
  using (var scope = new TransactionScope())
  {
    Transaction.Current.TransactionCompleted +=
        OnTransactionCompleted;

    Utilities.DisplayTransactionInformation("Ambient TX created",
```

```
                Transaction.Current.TransactionInformation);

        var s1 = new Student
        {
          FirstName = "Angela",
          LastName = "Nagel",
          Company = "Kantine M101"
        };
        var db = new StudentData();
        db.AddStudent(s1);

        if (!Utilities.AbortTx())
          scope.Complete();
        else
          Console.WriteLine("transaction will be aborted");

      } // scope.Dispose()
    }

    static void OnTransactionCompleted(object sender,
                                   TransactionEventArgs e)
    {
      Utilities.DisplayTransactionInformation("TX completed",
          e.Transaction.TransactionInformation);
    }
```

Running the application, you can see an active ambient transaction after an instance of the `TransactionScope` class is created. The last output of the application is the output from the `TransactionCompleted` event handler to display the finished transaction state:

```
Ambient TX created
Creation Time: 9:55:40 PM
Status: Active
Local ID: a06df6fb-7266-435e-b90e-f024f1d6966e:1
Distributed ID: 00000000-0000-0000-0000-0000000000000

Abort the Transaction (y/n)? n

TX completed
Creation Time: 9:55:40 PM
Status: Committed
Local ID: a06df6fb-7266-435e-b90e-f024f1d6966e:1
Distributed ID: 00000000-0000-0000-0000-0000000000000
```

Using Nested Scopes with Ambient Transactions

With the `TransactionScope` class you can also nest scopes. The nested scope can be directly inside the outer scope or within a method that is invoked from a scope. A nested scope can use the same transaction as the outer scope, suppress the transaction, or create a new transaction that is independent from the outer scope. The requirement for the scope is defined with a `TransactionScopeOption` enumeration that is passed to the constructor of the `TransactionScope` class.

The following table describes the values and corresponding functionality available with the `TransactionScopeOption` enumeration.

TRANSACTIONSCOPEOPTION MEMBER	DESCRIPTION
Required	`Required` defines that the scope requires a transaction. If the outer scope already contains an ambient transaction, the inner scope uses the existing transaction. If an ambient transaction does not exist, a new transaction is created. If both scopes share the same transaction, every scope influences the outcome of the transaction. Only if all scopes set the success bit can the transaction commit. If one scope does not invoke the `Complete` method before the root scope is disposed of, the transaction is aborted.
RequiresNew	RequiresNew always creates a new transaction. If the outer scope already defines a transaction, the transaction from the inner scope is completely independent. Both transactions can commit or abort independently.
Suppress	With `Suppress`, the scope does not contain an ambient transaction, whether or not the outer scope contains a transaction.

The next example defines two scopes. The inner scope is configured to require a new transaction with the option `TransactionScopeOption.RequiresNew`:

```
using (var scope = new TransactionScope())
{
  Transaction.Current.TransactionCompleted +=
      OnTransactionCompleted;

  Utilities.DisplayTransactionInformation("Ambient TX created",
      Transaction.Current.TransactionInformation);

  using (var scope2 =
      new TransactionScope(TransactionScopeOption.RequiresNew))
  {
    Transaction.Current.TransactionCompleted +=
        OnTransactionCompleted;

    Utilities.DisplayTransactionInformation(
        "Inner Transaction Scope",
        Transaction.Current.TransactionInformation);

    scope2.Complete();
  }
  scope.Complete();
}
```

Running the application, you can see from the following that both scopes have different transaction identifiers, although the same thread is used. With one thread but different ambient transaction identifiers, the transaction identifier just differs in the last number following the GUID.

NOTE *A GUID is a globally unique identifier consisting of a 128-bit unique value.*

```
Ambient TX created
Creation Time: 11:01:09 PM
Status: Active
Local ID: 54ac1276-5c2d-4159-84ab-36b0217c9c84:1
```

```
Distributed ID: 00000000-0000-0000-0000-0000000000

Inner Transaction Scope
Creation Time: 11:01:09 PM
Status: Active
Local ID: 54ac1276-5c2d-4159-84ab-36b0217c9c84:2
Distributed ID: 00000000-0000-0000-0000-0000000000

TX completed
Creation Time: 11:01:09 PM
Status: Committed
Local ID: 54ac1276-5c2d-4159-84ab-36b0217c9c84:2
Distributed ID: 00000000-0000-0000-0000-0000000000

TX completed
Creation Time: 11:01:09 PM
Status: Committed
Local ID: 54ac1276-5c2d-4159-84ab-36b0217c9c84:1
Distributed ID: 00000000-0000-0000-0000-0000000000
```

If you change the inner scope to the setting `TransactionScopeOption.Required`, you will find that both scopes use the same transaction, and both scopes influence the outcome of the transaction.

Multithreading with Ambient Transactions

If multiple threads should use the same ambient transaction, you need to do some extra work. An ambient transaction is bound to a thread, so if a new thread is created, it does not have the ambient transaction from the starter thread.

This behavior is demonstrated in the next example. In the `Main` method, a `TransactionScope` is created. Within this transaction scope, a new task is started. The main method of the new thread, `TaskMethod`, creates a new transaction scope. With the creation of the scope, no parameters are passed; therefore, the default option `TransactionScopeOption.Required` comes into play. If an ambient transaction exists, the existing transaction is used. Otherwise, a new transaction is created (code file `MultiThreadingAmbientTx/Program.cs`):

```csharp
using System;
using System.Threading.Tasks;
using System.Transactions;

namespace Wrox.ProCSharp.Transactions
{
  class Program
  {
    static void Main()
    {
      try
      {
        using (var scope = new TransactionScope())
        {
          Transaction.Current.TransactionCompleted +=
              TransactionCompleted;

          Utilities.DisplayTransactionInformation("Main task TX",
              Transaction.Current.TransactionInformation);

          Task.Factory.StartNew(TaskMethod);

          scope.Complete();
        }
      }
      catch (TransactionAbortedException ex)
```

```
          {
            Console.WriteLine("Main—Transaction was aborted, {0}",
                ex.Message);
          }
        }

        static void TransactionCompleted(object sender,
            TransactionEventArgs e)
        {
          Utilities.DisplayTransactionInformation("TX completed",
              e.Transaction.TransactionInformation);
        }

        static void TaskMethod()
        {
          try
          {
            using (var scope = new TransactionScope())
            {
              Transaction.Current.TransactionCompleted +=
                  TransactionCompleted;

              Utilities.DisplayTransactionInformation("Task TX",
                  Transaction.Current.TransactionInformation);
              scope.Complete();
            }
          }
          catch (TransactionAbortedException ex)
          {
            Console.WriteLine("TaskMethod—Transaction was aborted, {0}",
                ex.Message);
          }
        }
      }
    }
```

As shown in the following output, after starting the application, the transactions from the two threads are completely independent. The transaction from the new thread has a different transaction ID. The transaction ID differs by the number that is added to the GUID. You've seen this already with nested scopes:

```
Main task TX
Creation Time: 21:41:25
Status: Active
Local ID: f1e736ae-84ab-4540-b71e-3de272ffc476:1
Distributed ID: 00000000-0000-0000-0000-000000000000

TX completed
Creation Time: 21:41:25
Status: Committed
Local ID: f1e736ae-84ab-4540-b71e-3de272ffc476:1
Distributed ID: 00000000-0000-0000-0000-000000000000

Task TX
Creation Time: 21:41:25
Status: Active
Local ID: f1e736ae-84ab-4540-b71e-3de272ffc476:2
Distributed ID: 00000000-0000-0000-0000-000000000000

TX completed
Creation Time: 21:41:25
Status: Committed
Local ID: f1e736ae-84ab-4540-b71e-3de272ffc476:2
Distributed ID: 00000000-0000-0000-0000-000000000000
```

To use the same ambient transaction in another thread, you need the help of dependent transactions. In the next example, a dependent transaction is passed to the new task. The dependent transaction is created from the ambient transaction by calling the DependentClone method on the ambient transaction. With this method, the setting DependentCloneOption.BlockCommitUntilComplete is used so that the calling thread waits until the new task is completed before committing the transaction:

```csharp
class Program
{
  static void Main()
  {
    try
    {
      using (var scope = new TransactionScope())
      {
        Transaction.Current.TransactionCompleted +=
            TransactionCompleted;

        Utilities.DisplayTransactionInformation("Main thread TX",
            Transaction.Current.TransactionInformation);

        Task.Factory.StartNew(TaskMethod,
            Transaction.Current.DependentClone(
                DependentCloneOption.BlockCommitUntilComplete));

        scope.Complete();
      }
    }
    catch (TransactionAbortedException ex)
    {
      Console.WriteLine("Main-Transaction was aborted, {0}",
          ex.Message);
    }
  }
```

In the method of the thread, the dependent transaction that is passed is assigned to the ambient transaction by using the set accessor of the Transaction.Current property. Now the transaction scope is using the same transaction by using the dependent transaction. When you are finished using the dependent transaction, you need to invoke the Complete method of the DependentTransaction object:

```csharp
static void TaskMethod(object dependentTx)
{
  var dTx = dependentTx as DependentTransaction;

  try
  {
    Transaction.Current = dTx;

    using (var scope = new TransactionScope())
    {
      Transaction.Current.TransactionCompleted +=
          TransactionCompleted;

      Utilities.DisplayTransactionInformation("Task TX",
          Transaction.Current.TransactionInformation);
      scope.Complete();
    }
  }
  catch (TransactionAbortedException ex)
  {
    Console.WriteLine("TaskMethod-Transaction was aborted, {0}",
        ex.Message);
  }
```

```
      finally
      {
        if (dTx != null)
        {
          dTx.Complete();
        }
      }
    }

    static void TransactionCompleted(object sender,
        TransactionEventArgs e)
    {
      Utilities.DisplayTransactionInformation("TX completed",
          e.Transaction.TransactionInformation);
    }
  }
```

Running the application now, you can see that the main thread and the newly created thread are using, and influencing, the same transaction. The transaction listed by the threads has the same identifier. If with one thread the success bit is not set by calling the Complete method, the entire transaction aborts:

```
Main task TX
Creation Time: 23:00:57
Status: Active
Local ID: 2fb1b54d-61f5-4d4e-a55e-f4a9e04778be:1
Distributed ID: 00000000-0000-0000-0000-000000000000

Task TX
Creation Time: 23:00:57
Status: Active
Local ID: 2fb1b54d-61f5-4d4e-a55e-f4a9e04778be:1
Distributed ID: 00000000-0000-0000-0000-000000000000

TX completed
Creation Time: 23:00:57
Status: Committed
Local ID: 2fb1b54d-61f5-4d4e-a55e-f4a9e04778be:1
Distributed ID: 00000000-0000-0000-0000-000000000000

TX completed
Creation Time: 23:00:57
Status: Committed
Local ID: 2fb1b54d-61f5-4d4e-a55e-f4a9e04778be:1
Distributed ID: 00000000-0000-0000-0000-000000000000
```

ISOLATION LEVEL

The beginning of this chapter mentioned the ACID properties that describe successful transactions. The letter I (Isolation) in ACID is not always fully required. For performance reasons, you might reduce the isolation requirements, but you must be aware of the issues that you may encounter if you change the isolation level.

Problems that you can encounter if you don't completely isolate the scope outside the transaction can be divided into three categories:

➤ **Dirty reads**—Another transaction can read records that are changed within the transaction. Because the data that is changed within the transaction might roll back to its original state, reading this intermediate state from another transaction is considered "dirty"—the data has not been committed. You can avoid this by locking the records to be changed.

➤ **Nonrepeatable reads**—When data is read inside a transaction, and while the transaction is running, another transaction changes the same records. If the record is read once more inside the transaction, the result is different—nonrepeatable. You can avoid this by locking the read records.

➤ **Phantom reads**—When a range of data is read, for example, with a WHERE clause, another transaction can add a new record belonging to the range that is read within the transaction. A new read with the same WHERE clause returns a different number of rows. Phantom reads typically occur during an UPDATE of a range of rows. For example, UPDATE Addresses SET Zip=4711 WHERE (Zip=2315) updates the Zip code of all records from 2315 to 4711. After doing the update, there may still be records with a Zip code of 2315 if another user added a new record with Zip 2315 while the update was running. You can avoid this by doing a range lock.

When defining the isolation requirements, you can set the isolation level using an IsolationLevel enumeration that is configured when the transaction is created (either with the constructor of the CommittableTransaction class or with the constructor of the TransactionScope class). The IsolationLevel defines the locking behavior. The following table lists the values of the IsolationLevel enumeration.

ISOLATION LEVEL	DESCRIPTION
ReadUncommitted	Transactions are not isolated from each other. With this level, there is no wait for locked records from other transactions. This way, uncommitted data can be read from other transactions—dirty reads. This level is usually used only for reading records for which it does not matter if you read interim changes (e.g., reports).
ReadCommitted	Waits for records with a write-lock from other transactions. This way, a dirty read cannot happen. This level sets a read-lock for the current record read and a write-lock for the records being written until the transaction is completed. During the reading of a sequence of records, with every new record that is read, the prior record is unlocked. That's why nonrepeatable reads can happen.
RepeatableRead	Holds the lock for the records read until the transaction is completed. This way, the problem of nonrepeatable reads is avoided. Phantom reads can still occur.
Serializable	Holds a range lock. While the transaction is running, it is not possible to add a new record that belongs to the same range from which the data is being read.
Snapshot	With this level a snapshot is done from the actual data. This level reduces the locks as modified rows are copied. That way, other transactions can still read the old data without needing to wait for releasing of the lock.
Unspecified	Indicates that the provider is using an isolation level value that is different from the values defined by the IsolationLevel enumeration
Chaos	This level is similar to ReadUncommitted, but in addition to performing the actions of the ReadUncommitted value, Chaos does not lock updated records.

The following table summarizes the problems that can occur as a result of setting the most commonly used transaction isolation levels:

ISOLATION LEVEL	DIRTY READS	NONREPEATABLE READS	PHANTOM READS
Read Uncommitted	Y	Y	Y
Read Committed	N	Y	Y
Repeatable Read	N	N	Y
Serializable	N	N	N

The following code segment shows how the isolation level can be set with the TransactionScope class. With the constructor of TransactionScope, you can set the TransactionScopeOption that was discussed earlier and the TransactionOptions. The TransactionOptions class allows you to define the IsolationLevel and the Timeout.

```
var options = new TransactionOptions
{
  IsolationLevel = IsolationLevel.ReadUncommitted,
  Timeout = TimeSpan.FromSeconds(90)
};
using (var scope = new TransactionScope(
    TransactionScopeOption.Required, options))
{
  // Read data without waiting for locks from other transactions,
  // dirty reads are possible.
}
```

CUSTOM RESOURCE MANAGERS

One of the biggest advantages of the functionality offered by the classes in the `System.Transactions` namespace is that it is relatively easy to create custom resource managers that participate in the transaction. A resource manager can manage not only durable resources but volatile or in-memory resources—for example, a simple `int` and a generic list.

Figure 25-4 shows the relationship between a resource manager and transaction classes. The resource manager implements the interface `IEnlistmentNotification`, which defines the methods `Prepare`, `InDoubt`, `Commit`, and `Rollback`. This interface manages the transaction for a resource. To be part of a transaction, the resource manager must enlist with the `Transaction` class. Volatile resource managers invoke the method `EnlistVolatile`; durable resource managers invoke `EnlistDurable`. Depending on the transaction's outcome, the transaction manager invokes the methods from the interface `IEnlistmentNotification` with the resource manager.

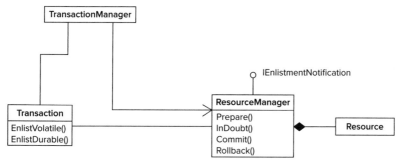

FIGURE 25-4

The next table explains the methods of the `IEnlistmentNotification` interface that you must implement with resource managers. As you review the table, recall the active, prepared, and committing phases explained earlier in this chapter in the "Transaction Phases" section.

IENLISTMENTNOTIFICATION MEMBER	DESCRIPTION
Prepare	The transaction manager invokes the `Prepare` method for preparation of the transaction. The resource manager completes the preparation by invoking the `Prepared` method of the `PreparingEnlistment` parameter, which is passed to the `Prepare` method. If the work cannot be done successfully, the resource manager informs the transaction manager by invoking the method `ForceRollback`. A durable resource manager must write a log so that it can finish the transaction successfully after the prepare phase.

(continues)

(continued)

IENLISTMENTNOTIFICATION MEMBER	DESCRIPTION
Commit	When all resource managers have successfully prepared for the transaction, the transaction manager invokes the Commit method. The resource manager can then complete the work to make it visible outside the transaction and invoke the Done method of the Enlistment parameter.
Rollback	If one of the resources could not successfully prepare for the transaction, the transaction manager invokes the Rollback method with all resource managers. After the state is returned to the state prior to the transaction, the resource manager invokes the Done method of the Enlistment parameter.
InDoubt	If there is a problem after the transaction manager invokes the Commit method (and the resources don't return completion information with the Done method), the transaction manager invokes the InDoubt method.

Transactional Resources

A transactional resource must keep the live value and a temporary value. The live value is read from outside the transaction and defines the valid state when the transaction rolls back. The temporary value defines the valid state of the transaction when the transaction commits.

To make nontransactional types transactional, the generic sample class Transactional<T> wraps a nongeneric type, so you can use it like this:

```
var txInt = new Transactional<int>();
var txString = new Transactional<string>();
```

The following example demonstrates implementation of the class Transactional<T>. The live value of the managed resource has the variable liveValue; the temporary value that is associated with a transaction is stored within the ResourceManager<T>. The variable enlistedTransaction is associated with the ambient transaction if there is one (code file CustomResource/Transactional.cs):

```
using System.Diagnostics;
using System.Transactions;

namespace Wrox.ProCSharp.Transactions
{
  public partial class Transactional<T>
  {
    private T liveValue;
    private ResourceManager<T> enlistment;
    private Transaction enlistedTransaction;
```

With the Transactional constructor, the live value is set to the variable liveValue. If the constructor is invoked from within an ambient transaction, the GetEnlistment helper method is invoked. It first checks whether there is an ambient transaction and asserts if there is none. If the transaction is not already enlisted, the ResourceManager<T> helper class is instantiated, and the resource manager is enlisted with the transaction by invoking the method EnlistVolatile. Also, the variable enlistedTransaction is set to the ambient transaction.

If the ambient transaction is different from the enlisted transaction, an exception is thrown. The implementation does not support changing the same value from within two different transactions. If you have this requirement, you can create a lock and wait for the lock to be released from one transaction before changing it within another transaction:

```
public Transactional(T value)
{
  if (Transaction.Current == null)
  {
    this.liveValue = value;
  }
  else
  {
    this.liveValue = default(T);
    GetEnlistment().Value = value;
  }
}

public Transactional()
    : this(default(T)) {}

private ResourceManager<T> GetEnlistment()
{
  Transaction tx = Transaction.Current;
  Trace.Assert(tx != null,
      "Must be invoked with ambient transaction");

  if (enlistedTransaction == null)
  {
    enlistment = new ResourceManager<T>(this, tx);
    tx.EnlistVolatile(enlistment, EnlistmentOptions.None);
    enlistedTransaction = tx;
    return enlistment;
  }
  else if (enlistedTransaction == Transaction.Current)
  {
    return enlistment;
  }
  else
  {
    throw new TransactionException(
        "This class only supports enlisting with one transaction");
  }
}
```

The property `Value` returns the value of the contained class and sets it. However, with transactions, you cannot just set and return the `liveValue` variable. This would be the case only if the object were outside a transaction. To make the code more readable, the property `Value` uses the methods `GetValue` and `SetValue` in the implementation:

```
public T Value
{
  get { return GetValue(); }
  set { SetValue(value); }
}
```

The method `GetValue` checks whether an ambient transaction exists. If one doesn't exist, the `liveValue` is returned. If there is an ambient transaction, the `GetEnlistment` method shown earlier returns the resource manager, and with the `Value` property, the temporary value for the contained object within the transaction is returned.

The method SetValue is very similar to GetValue; the difference is that it changes the live or temporary value:

```
protected virtual T GetValue()
{
  if (Transaction.Current == null)
  {
    return liveValue;
  }
  else
  {
    return GetEnlistment().Value;
  }
}

protected virtual void SetValue(T value)
{
  if (Transaction.Current == null)
  {
    liveValue = value;
  }
  else
  {
    GetEnlistment().Value = value;
  }
}
```

The Commit and Rollback methods that are implemented in the class Transactional<T> are invoked from the resource manager. The Commit method sets the live value from the temporary value received with the first argument and nullifies the variable enlistedTransaction as the transaction is completed. With the Rollback method, the transaction is completed as well, but here the temporary value is ignored, and the live value is kept in use:

```
internal void Commit(T value, Transaction tx)
{
  liveValue = value;
  enlistedTransaction = null;
}

internal void Rollback(Transaction tx)
{
  enlistedTransaction = null;
}
}
```

Because the resource manager that is used by the class Transactional<T> is used only within the Transactional<T> class itself, it is implemented as an inner class. With the constructor, the parent variable is set to have an association with the transactional wrapper class. The temporary value used within the transaction is copied from the live value. Remember the isolation requirements with transactions (code file CustomResource/ResourceManager.cs):

```
using System;
using System.Diagnostics;
using System.IO;
using System.Runtime.Serialization.Formatters.Binary;
using System.Transactions;

namespace Wrox.ProCSharp.Transactions
{
  public partial class Transactional<T>
  {
    internal class ResourceManager<T1>: IEnlistmentNotification
```

```
{
  private Transactional<T1> parent;
  private Transaction currentTransaction;

  internal ResourceManager(Transactional<T1> parent, Transaction tx)
  {
    this.parent = parent;
    Value = DeepCopy(parent.liveValue);
    currentTransaction = tx;
  }

  public T1 Value { get; set; }
```

Because the temporary value may change within the transaction, the live value of the wrapper class may not be changed within the transaction. When creating a copy with some classes, it is possible to invoke the Clone method that is defined with the ICloneable interface. However, as the Clone method is defined, it allows implementations to create either a shallow or a deep copy. If type T contains reference types and implements a shallow copy, changing the temporary value would also change the original value. This would be in conflict with the isolation and consistency features of transactions. Here, a deep copy is required.

To do a deep copy, the method DeepCopy serializes and deserializes the object to and from a stream. Because in C# 5 it is not possible to define a constraint to the type T, indicating that serialization is required, the static constructor of the class Transactional<T> checks whether the type is serializable by checking the property IsSerializable of the Type object:

```
static ResourceManager()
{
  Type t = typeof(T1);
  Trace.Assert(t.IsSerializable, "Type " + t.Name +
      " is not serializable");
}

private T1 DeepCopy(T1 value)
{
  using (var stream = new MemoryStream())
  {
    var formatter = new BinaryFormatter();
    formatter.Serialize(stream, value);
    stream.Flush();
    stream.Seek(0, SeekOrigin.Begin);

    return (T1)formatter.Deserialize(stream);
  }
}
```

The interface IEnlistmentNotification is implemented by the class ResourceManager<T>. This is the requirement for enlisting with transactions.

The implementation of the Prepare method answers by invoking Prepared with preparingEnlistment. There should not be a problem assigning the temporary value to the live value, so the Prepare method succeeds. With the implementation of the Commit method, the Commit method of the parent is invoked, where the variable liveValue is set to the value of the ResourceManager that is used within the transaction. The Rollback method just completes the work and leaves the live value where it was. With a volatile resource, there is not a lot you can do in the InDoubt method. Writing a log entry could be useful:

```
public void Prepare(PreparingEnlistment preparingEnlistment)
{
  preparingEnlistment.Prepared();
}

public void Commit(Enlistment enlistment)
```

```
      {
        parent.Commit(Value, currentTransaction);
        enlistment.Done();
      }

      public void Rollback(Enlistment enlistment)
      {
        parent.Rollback(currentTransaction);
        enlistment.Done();
      }

      public void InDoubt(Enlistment enlistment)
      {
        enlistment.Done();
      }
    }
  }
}
```

The class `Transactional<T>` can now be used to make nontransactional classes transactional—for example, `int` and `string` but also more complex classes such as `Student`—as long as the type is serializable (code file `CustomResource/Program.cs`):

```
using System;
using System.Transactions;

namespace Wrox.ProCSharp.Transactions
{
  class Program
  {
    static void Main()
    {
        var intVal = new Transactional<int>(1);
        var student1 = new Transactional<Student>(new Student());
        student1.Value.FirstName = "Andrew";
        student1.Value.LastName = "Wilson";

        Console.WriteLine("before the transaction, value: {0}",
            intVal.Value);
        Console.WriteLine("before the transaction, student: {0}",
            student1.Value);

        using (var scope = new TransactionScope())
        {
          intVal.Value = 2;
          Console.WriteLine("inside transaction, value: {0}",
              intVal.Value);

          student1.Value.FirstName = "Ten";
          student1.Value.LastName = "SixtyNine";

          if (!Utilities.AbortTx())
            scope.Complete();
        }
        Console.WriteLine("outside of transaction, value: {0}",
            intVal.Value);
        Console.WriteLine("outside of transaction, student: {0}",
            student1.Value);
    }
  }
}
```

The following console output shows a run of the application with a committed transaction:

```
before the transaction, value: 1
before the transaction: student: Andrew Wilson
inside transaction, value: 2

Abort the Transaction (y/n)? n

outside of transaction, value: 2
outside of transaction, student: Ten SixtyNine
```

FILE SYSTEM TRANSACTIONS

You can write a custom durable resource manager that works with the `File` and `Registry` classes. A file-based durable resource manager can copy the original file and write changes to the temporary file inside a temporary directory to make the changes persistent. When committing the transaction, the original file is replaced by the temporary file. Writing custom durable resource managers for files and the registry isn't necessary since Windows Vista and Windows Server 2008. With these and subsequent operating systems, native transactions with the file system and the registry are supported. For this, there are Windows API calls such as `CreateFileTransacted`, `CreateHardLinkTransacted`, `CreateSymbolicLinkTransacted`, `CopyFileTransacted`, and so on. What these API calls have in common is that they require a handle to a transaction passed as an argument; they do not support ambient transactions. The transactional API calls are not available from .NET 4.5, but you can create a custom wrapper by using `Platform Invoke`.

> **NOTE** *Platform Invoke is discussed in more detail in Chapter 23, "Interop."*

The sample application wraps the native method `CreateFileTransacted` for creating transactional file streams from .NET applications.

When invoking native methods, the parameters of the native methods must be mapped to .NET data types. Because of security issues, the base class `SafeHandle` is used to map a native `HANDLE` type. `SafeHandle` is an abstract type that wraps operating system handles and supports critical finalization of handle resources. Depending on the allowed values of a handle, the derived classes `SafeHandleMinusOneIsInvalid` and `SafeHandleZeroOrMinusOneIsInvalid` can be used to wrap native handles. `SafeFileHandle` itself derives from `SafeHandleZeroOrMinusOneIsInvalid`. To map a handle to a transaction, the class `SafeTransactionHandle` is defined (code file `FileSystemTransactions/SafeTransactionHandle.cs`):

```csharp
using System;
using System.Runtime.Versioning;
using System.Security.Permissions;
using Microsoft.Win32.SafeHandles;

namespace Wrox.ProCSharp.Transactions
{
  [SecurityCritical]
  internal sealed class SafeTransactionHandle:
      SafeHandleZeroOrMinusOneIsInvalid
  {
    private SafeTransactionHandle()
        : base(true) { }

    public SafeTransactionHandle(IntPtr preexistingHandle,
        bool ownsHandle)
        : base(ownsHandle)
```

```
          {
            SetHandle(preexistingHandle);
          }

          [ResourceExposure(ResourceScope.Machine)]
          [ResourceConsumption(ResourceScope.Machine)]
          protected override bool ReleaseHandle()
          {
            return NativeMethods.CloseHandle(handle);
          }
      }
  }
```

All native methods used from .NET are defined with the class `NativeMethods` shown here. With the
sample, the native APIs needed are `CreateFileTransacted` and `CloseHandle`, which are defined as static
members of the class. The methods are declared extern because there is no C# implementation. Instead,
the implementation is found in the native DLL as defined by the attribute `DllImport`. Both of these
methods can be found in the native DLL `Kernel32.dll`. With the method declaration, the parameters
defined with the Windows API call are mapped to .NET data types. The parameter `txHandle` represents
a handle to a transaction and is of the previously defined type `SafeTransactionHandle` (code file
`FileSystemTransactions/NativeMethods.cs`):

```csharp
using System;
using System.Runtime.ConstrainedExecution;
using System.Runtime.InteropServices;
using System.Runtime.Versioning;
using Microsoft.Win32.SafeHandles;

namespace Wrox.ProCSharp.Transactions
{
  internal static class NativeMethods
  {
    [DllImport("Kernel32.dll",
        CallingConvention = CallingConvention.StdCall,
        CharSet = CharSet.Unicode)]
    internal static extern SafeFileHandle CreateFileTransacted(
        String lpFileName,
        uint dwDesiredAccess,
        uint dwShareMode,
        IntPtr lpSecurityAttributes,
        uint dwCreationDisposition,
        int dwFlagsAndAttributes,
        IntPtr hTemplateFile,
        SafeTransactionHandle txHandle,
        IntPtr miniVersion,
        IntPtr extendedParameter);

    [DllImport("Kernel32.dll", SetLastError = true)]
    [ResourceExposure(ResourceScope.Machine)]
    [ReliabilityContract(Consistency.WillNotCorruptState, Cer.Success)]
    [return: MarshalAs(UnmanagedType.Bool)]
    internal static extern bool CloseHandle(IntPtr handle);

  }
}
```

The interface `IKernelTransaction` is used to get a transaction handle and pass it to the transacted
Windows API calls. This is a COM interface and must be wrapped to .NET by using COM interop
attributes as shown. The attribute `GUID` must have exactly the identifier as used here with the interface
definition, because this is the identifier used with the definition of the COM interface (code file
`FileSystemTransactions/IKernelTransaction.cs`):

```
using System;
using System.Runtime.InteropServices;

namespace Wrox.ProCSharp.Transactions
{
  [ComImport]
  [Guid("79427A2B-F895-40e0-BE79-B57DC82ED231")]
  [InterfaceType(ComInterfaceType.InterfaceIsIUnknown)]
  internal interface IKernelTransaction
  {
    void GetHandle(out SafeTransactionHandle ktmHandle);
  }
}
```

Finally, the class `TransactedFile` is the class that will be used by .NET applications. This class defines the method `GetTransactedFileStream`, which requires a filename as parameter and returns a `System.IO.FileStream`. The returned stream is a normal .NET stream; it just references a transacted file.

With the implementation, `TransactionInterop.GetDtcTransaction` creates an interface pointer of the `IKernelTransaction` to the ambient transaction that is passed as an argument to `GetDtcTransaction`. Using the interface `IKernelTransaction`, a handle of type `SafeTransactionHandle` is created. This handle is then passed to the wrapped API called `NativeMethods.CreateFileTransacted`. With the returned file handle, a new `FileStream` instance is created and returned to the caller (code file `FileSystemTransactions/TransactedFile.cs`):

```
using System;
using System.IO;
using System.Security.Permissions;
using System.Transactions;
using Microsoft.Win32.SafeHandles;

namespace Wrox.ProCSharp.Transactions
{
  public static class TransactedFile
  {
    internal const short FILE_ATTRIBUTE_NORMAL = 0x80;
    internal const short INVALID_HANDLE_VALUE = -1;
    internal const uint GENERIC_READ = 0x80000000;
    internal const uint GENERIC_WRITE = 0x40000000;
    internal const uint CREATE_NEW = 1;
    internal const uint CREATE_ALWAYS = 2;
    internal const uint OPEN_EXISTING = 3;

    [FileIOPermission(SecurityAction.Demand, Unrestricted=true)]
    public static FileStream GetTransactedFileStream(string fileName)
    {
      IKernelTransaction ktx = (IKernelTransaction)
          TransactionInterop.GetDtcTransaction(Transaction.Current);

      SafeTransactionHandle txHandle;
      ktx.GetHandle(out txHandle);

      SafeFileHandle fileHandle = NativeMethods.CreateFileTransacted(
          fileName, GENERIC_WRITE, 0,
          IntPtr.Zero, CREATE_ALWAYS, FILE_ATTRIBUTE_NORMAL,
          IntPtr.Zero,
          txHandle, IntPtr.Zero, IntPtr.Zero);

      return new FileStream(fileHandle, FileAccess.Write);
    }
  }
}
```

Now it is very easy to use the transactional API from .NET code. You can create an ambient transaction with the `TransactionScope` class and use the `TransactedFile` class within the context of the ambient transaction scope. If the transaction is aborted, the file is not written. If the transaction is committed, you can find the file in the temp directory (code file `Windows8Transactions/Program.cs`):

```
using System;
using System.IO;
using System.Transactions;

namespace Wrox.ProCSharp.Transactions
{
  class Program
  {
    static void Main()
    {
      using (var scope = new TransactionScope())
      {
        FileStream stream = TransactedFile.GetTransactedFileStream(
          "sample.txt");

        var writer = new StreamWriter(stream);
        writer.WriteLine("Write a transactional file");
        writer.Close();

        if (!Utilities.AbortTx())
            scope.Complete();
      }
    }
  }
}
```

Now you can use databases, volatile resources, and files within the same transaction.

SUMMARY

In this chapter, you learned the attributes of transactions and how you can create and manage transactions with the classes from the `System.Transactions` namespace.

Transactions are described with ACID properties: atomicity, consistency, isolation, and durability. Not all of these properties are always required, as you have seen with volatile resources that don't support durability but have isolation options.

The easiest way to deal with transactions is by creating ambient transactions and using the `TransactionScope` class. Ambient transactions are very useful for working with the ADO.NET data adapter and the ADO.NET Entity Framework, for which you usually do not open and close database connections explicitly. ADO.NET is covered in Chapter 32. The Entity Framework is explained in Chapter 33, "ADO.NET Entity Framework."

Using the same transaction across multiple threads, you can use the `DependentTransaction` class to create a dependency on another transaction. By enlisting a resource manager that implements the interface `IEnlistmentNotification`, you can create custom resources that participate with transactions.

Finally, you have seen how to use file system transactions with the .NET Framework and C#.

In the next chapter, you can learn how communication between different systems can be achieved with the `System.Net` namespace.

26

Networking

WROX.COM CODE DOWNLOADS FOR THIS CHAPTER

The wrox.com code downloads for this chapter are found at `http://www.wrox.com/remtitle .cgi?isbn=1118314425` on the Download Code tab. The code for this chapter is divided into the following major examples:

➤ BasicWebClient

➤ Browser

➤ DnsLookup

➤ SocketClient

➤ SocketServer

➤ TcpSend

➤ TcpReceive

➤ ViewHeaders

➤ WebSocketSample

NETWORKING

This chapter takes a fairly practical approach to networking, mixing examples with a discussion of the relevant theory and networking concepts as appropriate. This chapter is not a guide to computer networking but an introduction to using the .NET Framework for network communication.

You will learn how to use the `WebBrowser` control in a Windows Forms environment, and why it can make some specific Internet access tasks easier to accomplish. However, the chapter starts with the simplest case: sending a request to a server and storing the information sent back in the response.

This chapter covers facilities provided through the .NET base classes for using various network protocols, particularly HTTP and TCP, to access networks and the Internet as a client. It covers some of the lower-level means of getting at these protocols through the .NET Framework. You will also find other means of communicating via these items using technologies such as Windows Communication Foundation (WCF).

The two namespaces of most interest for networking are `System.Net` and `System.Net.Sockets`. The `System.Net` namespace is generally concerned with higher-level operations, such as downloading and uploading files, and making web requests using HTTP and other protocols, whereas `System.Net.Sockets` contains classes to perform lower-level operations. You will find these classes useful when you want to work directly with sockets or protocols, such as TCP/IP. The methods in these classes closely mimic the Windows socket (Winsock) API functions derived from the Berkeley sockets interface. You will also find that some of the objects that this chapter works with are found in the `System.IO` namespace.

Later chapters discuss how you can use C# to write powerful, efficient, and dynamic web pages using ASP.NET. For the most part, the clients accessing ASP.NET pages will be users running Internet Explorer or other web browsers such as Chrome, Opera, or Firefox. However, you might want to add web-browsing features to your own application, or you might need your applications to programmatically obtain information from a website. In this latter case, it is usually better for the site to implement a web service. However, when you are accessing public Internet sites, you might not have any control over how the site is implemented.

THE WEBCLIENT CLASS

If you only want to request a file from a particular URI (uniform resource identifier), then you will find that the easiest .NET class to use is `System.Net.WebClient`. This is an extremely high-level class designed to perform basic operations with only one or two commands. The .NET Framework currently supports URIs beginning with the `http:`, `https:`, and `file:` identifiers.

> **NOTE** *The term* URL (uniform resource locator) *is no longer in use in new technical specifications;* URI (uniform resource identifier) *is now preferred. URI has roughly the same meaning as URL, but it is a bit more general because URI does not imply you are using one of the familiar protocols, such as HTTP or FTP.*

Downloading Files

Two methods are available for downloading a file using `WebClient`. The method you choose depends on how you want to process the file's contents. If you simply want to save the file to disk, then you use the `DownloadFile` method. This method takes two parameters: the URI of the file and a location (path and filename) to save the requested data:

```
WebClient Client = new WebClient();
Client.DownloadFile("http://www.reuters.com/", "ReutersHomepage.htm");
```

More commonly, your application will want to process the data retrieved in response from the website. To do this, use the `OpenRead` method, which returns a `Stream` reference that you can then use to retrieve the data into memory:

```
WebClient Client = new WebClient();
Stream strm = Client.OpenRead("http://www.reuters.com/");
```

Basic WebClient Example

The first example demonstrates the `WebClient.OpenRead` method. You will display the contents of the downloaded page in a `ListBox` control. To begin, create a new project as a standard C# Windows Forms application and add a `ListBox` called `listBox1` with the docking property set to `DockStyle.Fill`. At the beginning of the file, you need to add the `System.Net` and `System.IO` namespaces references to your list of `using` directives. You then make the following changes to the constructor of the main form:

```csharp
public Form1()
{
    InitializeComponent();
    WebClient client = new WebClient();
    Stream strm = client.OpenRead("http://www.reuters.com");
    StreamReader sr = new StreamReader(strm);
    string line;

    while ( (line=sr.ReadLine()) != null )
    {
        listBox1.Items.Add(line);
    }

    strm.Close();
}
```

In this example, you connect a `StreamReader` class from the `System.IO` namespace to the network stream. This allows you to obtain data from the stream as text through the use of higher-level methods, such as `ReadLine`. This is an excellent example of the point made in Chapter 24, "Manipulating Files and the Registry," about the benefits of abstracting data movement into the concept of a stream.

Figure 26-1 shows the results of running this sample code.

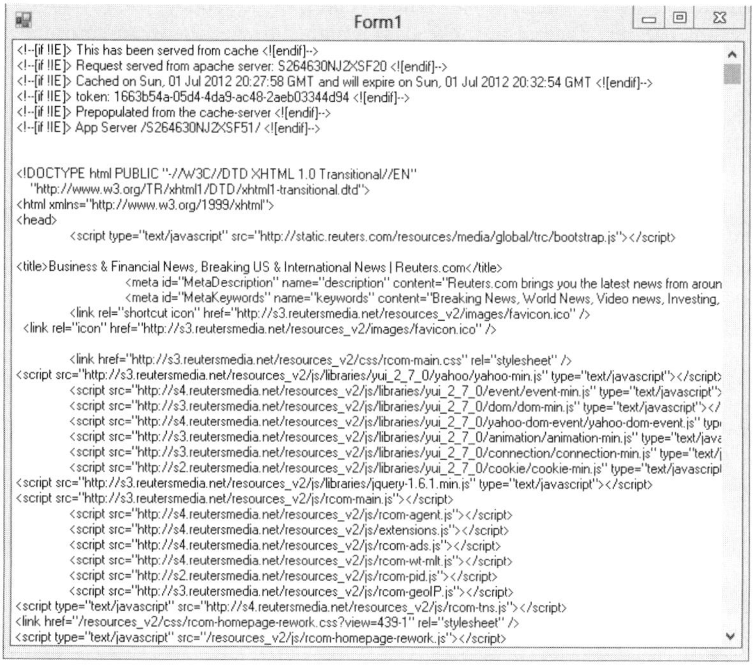

FIGURE 26-1

The WebClient class also has an OpenWrite method. This method returns a writable stream for sending data to a URI. You can also specify the method used to send the data to the host; the default method is POST. The following code snippet assumes a writable directory named accept on the local machine. The code creates a file in the directory with the name newfile.txt and the contents Hello World:

```
WebClient webClient = new WebClient();
Stream stream = webClient.OpenWrite("http://localhost/accept/newfile.txt", "PUT");
StreamWriter streamWriter = new StreamWriter(stream);
streamWriter.WriteLine("Hello World");
streamWriter.Close();
```

Uploading Files

The WebClient class also features UploadFile and UploadData methods. You use these methods when you need to post an HTML form or upload an entire file. UploadFile uploads a file to a specified location given the local filename, whereas UploadData uploads binary data supplied as an array of bytes to the specified URI (there is also a DownloadData method for retrieving an array of bytes from a URI):

```
WebClient client = new WebClient();
client.UploadFile("http://www.ourwebsite.com/NewFile.htm",
                  "C:\\WebSiteFiles\\NewFile.htm");
byte[] image;
// code to initialize image so it contains all the binary data for
// some jpg file
client.UploadData("http://www.ourwebsite.com/NewFile.jpg", image);
```

The WebClient class is very simple to use, but it has very limited features. In particular, you cannot use it to supply authentication credentials—a particular problem with uploading data is that not many sites accept uploaded files without authentication! It is possible to add header information to requests and to examine any headers in the response, but only in a very generic sense—there is no specific support for any one protocol. This is because WebClient is a very general-purpose class designed to work with any protocol for sending a request and receiving a response (such as HTTP or FTP). It cannot handle any features specific to any one protocol, such as cookies, which are specific to HTTP. To take advantage of these features, you need to use a family of classes based on two other classes in the System.Net namespace: WebRequest and WebResponse.

WEBREQUEST AND WEBRESPONSE CLASSES

The WebRequest class represents the request for information to send to a particular URI. The URI is passed as a parameter to the Create method. A WebResponse represents the data you retrieve from the server. By calling the WebRequest.GetResponse method, you actually send the request to the web server and create a WebResponse object to examine the return data. As with the WebClient object, you can obtain a stream to represent the data, but in this case you use the WebResponse.GetResponseStream method.

This section briefly discusses a few of the other areas supported by WebRequest, WebResponse, and other related classes. The first example downloads a web page using these classes, which is the same example as before but using WebRequest and WebResponse. In the process, you uncover the class hierarchy involved, and then see how to take advantage of extra HTTP features that are supported by this hierarchy.

The following code shows the modifications you need to make to the BasicWebClient sample to use the WebRequest and WebResponse classes:

```
public Form1()
{
    InitializeComponent();
```

```
WebRequest wrq = WebRequest.Create("http://www.reuters.com");
WebResponse wrs = wrq.GetResponse();
Stream strm = wrs.GetResponseStream();
StreamReader sr = new StreamReader(strm);
string line;

while ( (line = sr.ReadLine()) != null)
{
    listBox1.Items.Add(line);
}

strm.Close();
}
```

The preceding code begins by instantiating an object representing a web request. You don't do this using a constructor, but instead call the static method `WebRequest.Create`. As you learn in more detail later in this chapter (see the section "The Web Request and Web Response Hierarchy"), the `WebRequest` class is part of a hierarchy of classes supporting different network protocols. To receive a reference to the correct object for the request type, a factory mechanism is in place. The `WebRequest.Create` method creates the appropriate object for the given protocol.

An important part of the HTTP protocol is the capability to send extensive header information with both request and response streams. This information can include cookies and details about the particular browser sending the request (the user agent). As you would expect, the .NET Framework provides full support for accessing the most significant data. The `WebRequest` and `WebResponse` classes provide some support for reading the header information. However, two derived classes provide additional HTTP-specific information: `HttpWebRequest` and `HttpWebResponse`.

As shown in more detail later in the section "The WebRequest and WebResponse Classes Hierarchy," creating a `WebRequest` with an HTTP URI results in an `HttpWebRequest` object instance. Because `HttpWebRequest` is derived from `WebRequest`, you can use the new instance whenever a `WebRequest` is required. In addition, you can cast the instance to an `HttpWebRequest` reference and access properties specific to the HTTP protocol. Likewise, the `GetResponse` method call will actually return an `HttpWebResponse` instance as a `WebResponse` reference when dealing with HTTP. Again, you can perform a simple cast to access the HTTP-specific features.

To examine a few of the header properties, add the following code before the `GetResponse` method call:

```
WebRequest wrq = WebRequest.Create("http://www.reuters.com");
HttpWebRequest hwrq = (HttpWebRequest)wrq;
listBox1.Items.Add("Request Timeout (ms) = " + wrq.Timeout);
listBox1.Items.Add("Request Keep Alive = " + hwrq.KeepAlive);
listBox1.Items.Add("Request AllowAutoRedirect = " + hwrq.AllowAutoRedirect);
```

The `Timeout` property is specified in milliseconds, and the default value is `100,000`. You can set the `Timeout` property to control how long the `WebRequest` object will wait for the response before throwing a `WebException`. You can check the `WebException.Status` property to view the reason for an exception. This enumeration includes status codes for timeouts, connection failures, protocol errors, and more.

The `KeepAlive` property is a specific extension to the HTTP protocol, so you access this property through an `HttpWebRequest` reference. `KeepAlive` allows multiple requests to use the same connection, saving time in closing and reopening connections on subsequent requests. The default value for this property is `true`.

The `AllowAutoRedirect` property is also specific to the `HttpWebRequest` class. Use this property to control whether the web request should automatically follow redirection responses from the web server. Again, the default value is `true`. If you want to allow only a limited number of redirections, then set the `MaximumAutomaticRedirections` property of the `HttpWebRequest` to the desired number.

Although the request and response classes expose most of the important headers as properties, you can also use the `Headers` property itself to view the entire collection of headers. Add the following code after the `GetResponse` method call to place all the headers in the `ListBox` control:

```
WebRequest wrq = WebRequest.Create("http://www.reuters.com");
WebResponse wrs = wrq.GetResponse();
WebHeaderCollection whc = wrs.Headers;

for(int i = 0; i < whc.Count; i++)
{
    listBox1.Items.Add(string.Format("Header {0}: {1}",
        whc.GetKey(i), whc[i]));
}
```

This example code produces the list of headers shown in Figure 26-2.

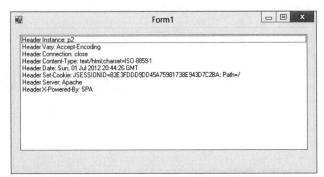

FIGURE 26-2

Authentication

Another property in the `WebRequest` class is the `Credentials` property. If you need authentication credentials to accompany your request, then you can create an instance of the `NetworkCredential` class (also from the `System.Net` namespace) with a username and password. You can place the following code *before* the call to `GetResponse`:

```
NetworkCredential myCred = new NetworkCredential("myusername", "mypassword");
wrq.Credentials = myCred;
```

Working with Proxies

Many enterprises must deal with a proxy server to make any type of HTTP or FTP request. Often, the proxy server, which routes all the organization's requests and responses, uses some form of security (usually a username and a password). For your applications that use the `WebClient` or the `WebRequest` objects, you might need to take these proxy servers into account. As with the preceding `NetworkCredential` object, you are going to want to use the `WebProxy` object *before* you make a call to make the actual request:

```
WebProxy wp = new WebProxy("192.168.1.100", true);
wp.Credentials = new NetworkCredential("user1", "user1Password");
WebRequest wrq = WebRequest.Create("http://www.reuters.com");
wrq.Proxy = wp;
WebResponse wrs = wrq.GetResponse();
```

If you require a designation of the user's domain in addition to its credentials, then you would use a different signature on the `NetworkCredential` instantiation:

```
WebProxy wp = new WebProxy("192.168.1.100", true);
wp.Credentials = new NetworkCredential("user1", "user1Password", "myDomain");
WebRequest wrq = WebRequest.Create("http://www.reuters.com");
wrq.Proxy = wp;
WebResponse wrs = wrq.GetResponse();
```

Asynchronous Page Requests

An additional feature of the `WebRequest` class is the ability to request pages asynchronously. This feature is significant because there can be quite a long delay between sending a request to a host and receiving the response. Methods such as `WebClient.DownloadData` and `WebRequest.GetResponse` will not return until the response from the server is complete. You might not want your application frozen due to a long period of inactivity, and in such scenarios it is better to use the `BeginGetResponse` and `EndGetResponse` methods. `BeginGetResponse` works asynchronously and returns almost immediately. Under the covers, the runtime asynchronously manages a background thread to retrieve the response from the server. Instead of returning a `WebResponse` object, `BeginGetResponse` returns an object implementing the `IAsyncResult` interface. With this interface, you can poll or wait for the response to become available and then invoke `EndGetResponse` to gather the results.

You can also pass a callback delegate into the `BeginGetResponse` method. The target of a callback delegate is a method returning `void` and accepting an `IAsyncResult` reference as a parameter. When the worker thread is finished gathering the response, the runtime invokes the callback delegate to inform you of the completed work. As shown in the following code, calling `EndGetResponse` in the callback method enables you to retrieve the `WebResponse` object:

```
public Form1()
{
    InitializeComponent();
    WebRequest wrq = WebRequest.Create("http://www.reuters.com");
    wrq.BeginGetResponse(new AsyncCallback(OnResponse), wrq);
}

protected static void OnResponse(IAsyncResult ar)
{
    WebRequest wrq = (WebRequest)ar.AsyncState;
    WebResponse wrs = wrq.EndGetResponse(ar);
    // read the response...
}
```

Notice that you can retrieve the original `WebRequest` object by passing the object as the second parameter to `BeginGetResponse`. The second parameter is an object reference known as the *state parameter*. During the callback method, you can retrieve the same state object using the `AsyncState` property of `IAsyncResult`.

DISPLAYING OUTPUT AS AN HTML PAGE

The examples so far in this chapter show how the .NET base classes make it very easy to download and process data from the Web. However, up until now you have displayed files only as plain text. Quite often, you will want to view an HTML file in an Internet Explorer–style interface in which the rendered HTML allows you to see what the web document actually looks like. Unfortunately, there is no .NET version of Microsoft's Internet Explorer, but you can still accomplish this task.

Before the release of the .NET Framework 2.0, you could make reference to a Component Object Model (COM) object that was an encapsulation of Internet Explorer and use the .NET-interop capabilities to have aspects of your application work as a browser. Beginning with the .NET Framework 2.0, you can use the built-in WebBrowser control available for your Windows Forms applications.

The WebBrowser control encapsulates the COM object even further for you, making tasks that were once more complicated even easier. In addition to the WebBrowser control, another option is to use the programmatic capability to call Internet Explorer instances from your code.

When not using the new WebBrowser control, you can programmatically start an Internet Explorer process and navigate to a web page using the Process class in the System.Diagnostics namespace:

```
Process myProcess = new Process();
myProcess.StartInfo.FileName = "iexplore.exe";
myProcess.StartInfo.Arguments = "http://www.wrox.com";
myProcess.Start();
```

However, the preceding code launches Internet Explorer as a separate window. Your application has no connection to the new window and therefore cannot control the browser.

Using the WebBrowser control, however, you can display and control the browser as an integrated part of your application. This control is quite sophisticated, featuring a large number of methods, properties, and events.

Allowing Simple Web Browsing from Your Applications

For the sake of simplicity, start by creating a Windows Forms application that simply has a TextBox control and a WebBrowser control. You will build the application so that the end user simply enters a URL into the text box and presses Enter, and the WebBrowser control does all the work of fetching the web page and displaying the resulting document.

In the Visual Studio 2012 designer, your application should look like Figure 26-3. With this application, when the end user types a URL and presses Enter, this key press registers with the application. Then the WebBrowser control will retrieve the requested page, subsequently displaying it in the control itself.

FIGURE 26-3

The code behind this application is shown here:

```
using System;
using System.Windows.Forms;

namespace Browser
{
```

```
partial class Form1: Form
{
    public Form1()
    {
        InitializeComponent();
    }

    private void textBox1_KeyPress(object sender, KeyPressEventArgs e)
    {
        if (e.KeyChar == (char)13)
        {
            webBrowser1.Navigate(textBox1.Text);
        }
    }
}
```

From this example, you can see that each key press made by the end user in the text box is captured by the textBox1_KeyPress event. If the character input is a carriage return (a press of the Enter key, which is (char)13), then you take action with the WebBrowser control. Using the WebBrowser control's Navigate method, you specify the URI (as a string) using the textBox1.Text property. The end result is shown in Figure 26-4.

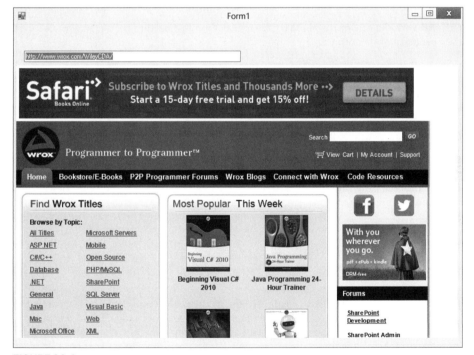

FIGURE 26-4

Launching Internet Explorer Instances

It might be that you are not interested in hosting a browser inside your application, as shown in the previous section, but instead are only interested in allowing the user to find your website in a typical browser (for example, by clicking a link inside your application). For an example of this task, create a Windows Forms application that has a LinkLabel control on it. For instance, you can have a form that has a LinkLabel control on it that states "Visit our company website!"

When you have this control in place, use the following code to launch your company's web site in an independent browser as opposed to being directly in the form of your application:

```
private void linkLabel1_LinkClicked(object sender, LinkLabelLinkClickedEventArgs e)
{
    WebBrowser wb = new WebBrowser();
    wb.Navigate("http://www.wrox.com", true);
}
```

In this example, when the LinkLabel control is clicked by the user, a new instance of the WebBrowser class is created. Then, using the WebBrowser class's Navigate method, the code specifies the location of the web page as well as a Boolean value that specifies whether this endpoint should be opened within the Windows Forms application (a false value) or from within an independent browser (using a true value). By default, this is set to false. With the preceding construct, when the end user clicks the link found in the Windows application, a browser instance is instantiated, and the Wrox web site at www.wrox.com is launched.

Giving Your Application More IE-Type Features

In the previous example, in which you used the WebBrowser control directly in the Windows Forms application, you may notice that when you click the links contained in the page, the text within the TextBox control is not updated to show the URL of the exact location where you are in the browsing process. You can fix this by listening for events coming from the WebBrowser control and adding handlers to the control.

Updating the form's title with the title of the HTML page is easy. You just need to use the Navigated event and update the Text property of the form:

```
private void webBrowser1_Navigated(object sender, EventArgs e)
{
    this.Text = webBrowser1.DocumentTitle.ToString();
}
```

In this case, when the WebBrowser control moves onto another page, the Navigated event fires, which causes the form's title to change to the title of the page being viewed. In some instances when working with pages on the Web, even though you have typed in a specific address, you are going to be redirected to another page altogether. You are most likely going to want to reflect this in the text box (address bar) of the form; to do this, you change the form's text box based on the complete URL of the page being viewed. To accomplish this task, you can use the WebBrowser control's Navigated event as well:

```
private void webBrowser1_Navigated(object sender, WebBrowserNavigatedEventArgs e)
{
    textBox1.Text = webBrowser1.Url.ToString();
    this.Text = webBrowser1.DocumentTitle.ToString();
}
```

Here, when the requested page has finished downloading in the WebBrowser control, the Navigated event is fired. In this case, you simply update the Text value of the textBox1 control to the URL of the page. This means that after a page is loaded in the WebBrowser control's HTML container, and if the URL changes in this process (for instance, there is a redirect), then the new URL will be shown in the text box. If you employ these steps and navigate to the Wrox web site (www.wrox.com), you will notice that the page's URL immediately changes to www.wrox.com/WileyCDA/. This process also means that if the end user clicks one of the links contained within the HTML view, then the URL of the newly requested page is also shown in the text box.

If you now run the application with the preceding changes in place, the form's title and address bar work as they do in Microsoft's Internet Explorer, as demonstrated in Figure 26-5.

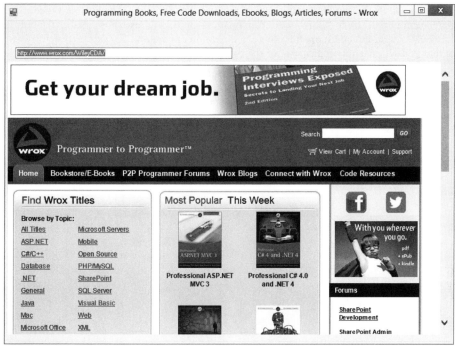

FIGURE 26-5

The next step is to create an IE-like toolbar that enables the end user to control the WebBrowser control a little better. This means incorporating buttons such as Back, Forward, Stop, Home, and Refresh.

Rather than use the ToolBar control, you will just add a set of Button controls at the top of the form where you currently have the address bar. Add five buttons to the top of the control, as illustrated in Figure 26-6.

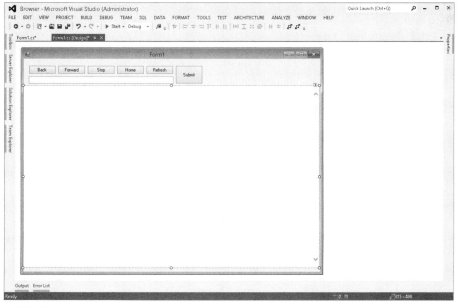

FIGURE 26-6

In this example, the text on the button face is changed to indicate the function of the button. Of course, you can even use a screen capture utility to "borrow" button images from IE and use those. Name the buttons buttonBack, buttonForward, buttonStop, buttonRefresh, and buttonHome. To get the resizing to work properly, ensure that you set the Anchor property of the three buttons on the right to Top, Right.

On startup, buttonBack, buttonForward, and buttonStop should be disabled because these buttons serve no purpose if no initial page is loaded in the WebBrowser control. You will later tell the application when to enable and disable the Back and Forward buttons yourself, depending on where the user is in the page stack. In addition, when a page is being loaded, you need to enable the Stop button—but you also need to disable the Stop button when the page has finished being loaded. Finally, a Submit button on the page will allow for the submission of the URL being requested.

First, however, add the functionality behind the buttons. The WebBrowser class itself has all the methods that you need, so this is all very straightforward:

```csharp
using System;
using System.Windows.Forms;

namespace Browser
{
    partial class Form1: Form
    {
        public Form1()
        {
            InitializeComponent();
        }

        private void textBox1_KeyPress(object sender, KeyPressEventArgs e)
        {
            if (e.KeyChar == (char)13)
            {
                webBrowser1.Navigate(textBox1.Text);
            }
        }

        private void webBrowser1_Navigated(object sender,
            WebBrowserNavigatedEventArgs e)
        {
            textBox1.Text = webBrowser1.Url.ToString();
            this.Text = webBrowser1.DocumentTitle.ToString();
        }

        private void Form1_Load(object sender, EventArgs e)
        {
            buttonBack.Enabled = false;
            buttonForward.Enabled = false;
            buttonStop.Enabled = false;

            this.webBrowser1.CanGoBackChanged +=
                new EventHandler(webBrowser1_CanGoBackChanged);
            this.webBrowser1.CanGoForwardChanged +=
                new EventHandler(webBrowser1_CanGoForwardChanged);
            this.webBrowser1.DocumentTitleChanged +=
                new EventHandler(webBrowser1_DocumentTitleChanged);
        }

        private void buttonBack_Click(object sender, EventArgs e)
        {
            webBrowser1.GoBack();
            textBox1.Text = webBrowser1.Url.ToString();
        }
```

```csharp
private void buttonForward_Click(object sender, EventArgs e)
{
    webBrowser1.GoForward();
    textBox1.Text = webBrowser1.Url.ToString();
}

private void buttonStop_Click(object sender, EventArgs e)
{
    webBrowser1.Stop();
}

private void buttonHome_Click(object sender, EventArgs e)
{
    webBrowser1.GoHome();
    textBox1.Text = webBrowser1.Url.ToString();
}

private void buttonRefresh_Click(object sender, EventArgs e)
{
    webBrowser1.Refresh();
}

private void buttonSubmit_Click(object sender, EventArgs e)
{
    webBrowser1.Navigate(textBox1.Text);
}

private void webBrowser1_Navigating(object sender,
    WebBrowserNavigatingEventArgs e)
{
    buttonStop.Enabled = true;
}

private void webBrowser1_DocumentCompleted(object sender,
    WebBrowserDocumentCompletedEventArgs e)
{
    buttonStop.Enabled = false;
    if (webBrowser1.CanGoBack)
    {
        buttonBack.Enabled = true;
    }
    else
    {
        buttonBack.Enabled = false;
    }
    if (webBrowser1.CanGoForward)
    {
        buttonForward.Enabled = true;
    }
    else
    {
        buttonForward.Enabled = false;
    }
}
}
}
```

Many different activities are occurring in this example because there are many options for the end user using this application. For each of the button-click events, a specific WebBrowser class method is assigned as the action to initiate. For instance, for the Back button on the form, you simply use the WebBrowser control's GoBack method; for the Forward button you have the GoForward method; and for the others, you have methods such as Stop, Refresh, and GoHome. This makes it fairly simple and straightforward to create a toolbar that provides actions similar to that of Microsoft's Internet Explorer.

When the form is first loaded, the Form1_Load event disables the appropriate buttons. From there, the end user can enter a URL into the text box and click the Submit button to have the application retrieve the desired page.

To manage the enabling and disabling of the buttons, you must key in to a couple of events. As mentioned before, whenever downloading begins, you need to enable the Stop button. For this, you simply added an event handler for the Navigating event to enable the Stop button:

```
private void webBrowser1_Navigating(object sender,
    WebBrowserNavigatingEventArgs e)
{
    buttonStop.Enabled = true;
}
```

Then, the Stop button is again disabled when the document has finished loading:

```
private void webBrowser1_DocumentCompleted(object sender,
    WebBrowserDocumentCompletedEventArgs e)
{
    buttonStop.Enabled = false;
}
```

Enabling and disabling the appropriate Back and Forward buttons depends on the capability to go backward or forward in the page stack. This is achieved by using both the CanGoForwardChanged and the CanGoBackChanged events:

```
private void webBrowser1_CanGoBackChanged(object sender, EventArgs e)
{
    if (webBrowser1.CanGoBack)
    {
        buttonBack.Enabled = true;
    }
    else
    {
        buttonBack.Enabled = false;
    }
}

private void webBrowser1_CanGoForwardChanged(object sender, EventArgs e)
{
    if (webBrowser1.CanGoForward)
    {
        buttonForward.Enabled = true;
    }
    else
    {
        buttonForward.Enabled = false;
    }
}
```

Run the project now, visit a web page, and click through a few links. You should also be able to use the toolbar to enhance your browsing experience. The end product is shown in Figure 26-7.

FIGURE 26-7

Printing Using the WebBrowser Control

Not only can users use the `WebBrowser` control to view pages and documents, they can also use the control to send these pages and documents to the printer for printing. To print the page or document being viewed in the control, simply use the following construct:

```
webBrowser1.Print();
```

As before, you do not need to view the page or document to print it. For instance, you can use the `WebBrowser` class to load an HTML document and print it without even displaying the loaded document. You can accomplish that as shown here:

```
WebBrowser wb = new WebBrowser();
wb.Navigate("http://www.wrox.com");
wb.Print();
```

Displaying the Code of a Requested Page

In the beginning of this chapter, you used the `WebRequest` and the `Stream` classes to access a remote page to display the code of the requested page. You used the following code to accomplish this task:

```
public Form1()
{
    InitializeComponent();
    System.Net.WebClient Client = new WebClient();
    Stream strm = Client.OpenRead("http://www.reuters.com");
    StreamReader sr = new StreamReader(strm);
    string line;
```

```
    while ( (line=sr.ReadLine()) != null )
    {
        listBox1.Items.Add(line);
    }

    strm.Close();
}
```

Using the `WebBrowser` control, it is quite easy to accomplish the same results. To do so, change the browser application that you have been working on thus far in this chapter by simply adding a single line to the `Document_Completed` event, as illustrated here:

```
private void webBrowser1_DocumentCompleted(object sender,
    WebBrowserDocumentCompletedEventArgs e)
{
    buttonStop.Enabled = false;
    textBox2.Text = webBrowser1.DocumentText;
}
```

In the application itself, add another `TextBox` control below the `WebBrowser` control. The idea is that when the end user requests a page, you display not only the visual aspect of the page but also the code for the page, in the `TextBox` control. The code of the page is displayed simply by using the `DocumentText` property of the `WebBrowser` control, which provides the entire page's content as a `String`. The other option is to get the contents of the page as a `Stream` using the `DocumentStream` property. The result of adding the second `TextBox` to display the contents of the page as a `String` is shown in Figure 26-8.

FIGURE 26-8

The WebRequest and WebResponse Classes Hierarchy

This section takes a closer look at the underlying architecture of the WebRequest and WebResponse classes. Figure 26-9 illustrates the inheritance hierarchy of the classes involved.

The hierarchy contains more than just the two classes you have used in your code. You should also know that the WebRequest and WebResponse classes are both abstract and cannot be instantiated. These base classes provide general functionality for dealing with web requests and responses independent of the protocol used for a given operation. Requests are made using a particular protocol (HTTP, FTP, SMTP, and so on), and a derived class written for the given protocol handles the request. Microsoft refers to this scheme as *pluggable protocols*.

In the code you examined earlier in the "WebRequest and WebResponse Classes" section, your variables are defined as references to the base classes. However, WebRequest .Create actually gives you an HttpWebRequest object, and the GetResponse method actually returns an HttpWebResponse object. This factory-based mechanism hides many of the details from the client code, allowing support for a wide variety of protocols from the same code base.

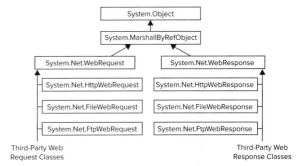

FIGURE 26-9

The fact that you need an object specifically capable of dealing with the HTTP protocol is clear from the URI that you supply to WebRequest.Create. WebRequest.Create examines the protocol specifier in the URI to instantiate and return an object of the appropriate class. This keeps your code free from having to know anything about the derived classes or specific protocol used. When you need to access specific features of a protocol, you might need the properties and methods of the derived class, in which case you can cast your WebRequest or WebResponse reference to the derived class.

With this architecture, you should be able to send requests using any of the common protocols. However, Microsoft currently provides derived classes to cover only the HTTP, HTTPS, FTP, and FILE protocols. The FTP option is the most recent option provided by the .NET Framework (available since the release of the .NET Framework 2.0). If you want to utilize other protocols, such as SMTP, then you need to use Windows Communication Foundation, revert to using the Windows API, or use the SmtpClient object.

UTILITY CLASSES

This section covers a couple of utility classes to make web programming easier when dealing with URIs and IP addresses.

URIs

Uri and UriBuilder are two classes in the System (not System.Net) namespace, and both are intended to represent a URI. UriBuilder enables you to build a URI given the strings for the component parts, and Uri enables you to parse, combine, and compare URIs.

For the Uri class, the constructor requires a complete URI string:

```
Uri MSPage = new

Uri("http://www.Microsoft.com/SomeFolder/SomeFile.htm?Order=true");
```

This class exposes a large number of read-only properties. A `Uri` object is not intended to be modified after it has been constructed:

```
string Query = MSPage.Query;                   // ?Order=true;
string AbsolutePath = MSPage.AbsolutePath;     // /SomeFolder/SomeFile.htm
string Scheme = MSPage.Scheme;                 // http
int Port = MSPage.Port;                        // 80 (the default for http)
string Host = MSPage.Host;                     // www.microsoft.com
bool IsDefaultPort = MSPage.IsDefaultPort;     // true since 80 is default
```

`UriBuilder`, however, implements fewer properties, just enough to enable you to build a complete URI. These properties are read-write.

You can supply the components to build a URI to the constructor:

```
UriBuilder MSPage = new
    UriBuilder("http", "www.microsoft.com", 80, "SomeFolder/SomeFile.htm");
```

Or, you can build the components by assigning values to the properties:

```
UriBuilder MSPage = new UriBuilder();
MSPage.Scheme ="http";
MSPage.Host = "www.microsoft.com";
MSPage.Port = 80;
MSPage.Path = "SomeFolder/SomeFile.htm";
```

After you have completed initializing the `UriBuilder`, you can obtain the corresponding `Uri` object with the `Uri` property:

```
Uri CompletedUri = MSPage.Uri;
```

IP Addresses and DNS Names

On the Internet, you identify servers as well as clients by IP address or host name (also referred to as a DNS name). Generally speaking, the host name is the human-friendly name that you type in a web browser window, such as `www.wrox.com` or `www.microsoft.com`. An IP address is the identifier that computers use to recognize each other. IP addresses are the identifiers used to ensure that web requests and responses reach the appropriate machines. It is even possible for a computer to have more than one IP address.

Today, IP addresses are typically a 32-bit value. An example of a 32-bit IP address is `192.168.1.100`. This format of IP address is referred to as Internet Protocol version 4. Because there are now so many computers and other devices vying for a spot on the Internet, a newer type of address was developed—Internet Protocol version 6. IPv6 provides a 64-bit IP address. IPv6 can potentially provide a maximum number of about 3×10^{28} unique addresses. The .NET Framework enables your applications to work with both IPv4 and IPv6.

For host names to work, you must first send a network request to translate the host name into an IP address, a task carried out by one or more DNS servers. A *DNS server* stores a table that maps host names to IP addresses for all the computers it knows about, as well as the IP addresses of other DNS servers to look up host names it does not know about. Your local computer should always know about at least one DNS server. Network administrators configure this information when a computer is set up.

Before sending out a request, your computer first asks the DNS server to give it the IP address corresponding to the host name you have typed in. When it is armed with the correct IP address, the computer can address the request and send it over the network. All this work normally happens behind the scenes while the user is browsing the web.

.NET Classes for IP Addresses

The .NET Framework supplies a number of classes that are able to assist with the process of looking up IP addresses and finding information about host computers.

IPAddress

IPAddress represents an IP address. The address itself is available as the GetAddressBytes property and may be converted to a dotted decimal format with the ToString method. IPAddress also implements a static Parse method that effectively performs the reverse conversion of ToString—converting from a dotted decimal string to an IPAddress:

```
IPAddress ipAddress = IPAddress.Parse("234.56.78.9");
byte[] address = ipAddress.GetAddressBytes();
string ipString = ipAddress.ToString();
```

In this example, the byte integer address is assigned a binary representation of the IP address, and the string ipString is assigned the text "234.56.78.9".

IPAddress also provides a number of constant static fields to return special addresses. For example, the Loopback address enables a machine to send messages to itself, whereas the Broadcast address enables multicasting to the local network:

```
// The following line will set loopback to "127.0.0.1".
// the loopback address indicates the local host.
string loopback = IPAddress.Loopback.ToString();

// The following line will set broadcast address to "255.255.255.255".
// the broadcast address is used to send a message to all machines on
// the local network.
string broadcast = IPAddress.Broadcast.ToString();
```

IPHostEntry

The IPHostEntry class encapsulates information related to a particular host computer. This class makes the host name available via the HostName property (which returns a string), and the AddressList property returns an array of IPAddress objects. You are going to use the IPHostEntry class in the next example: DNSLookupResolver.

Dns

The Dns class can communicate with your default DNS server to retrieve IP addresses. The two important (static) methods are Resolve, which uses the DNS server to obtain details about a host with a given host name, and GetHostByAddress, which also returns host details but this time using the IP address. Both methods return an IPHostEntry object:

```
IPHostEntry wroxHost = Dns.Resolve("www.wrox.com");
IPHostEntry wroxHostCopy = Dns.GetHostByAddress("208.215.179.178");
```

In this code, both IPHostEntry objects will contain details about the wrox.com servers.

The Dns class differs from the IPAddress and IPHostEntry classes in that it is capable of actually communicating with servers to obtain information. In contrast, IPAddress and IPHostEntry are more along the lines of simple data structures with convenient properties to allow access to the underlying data.

The DnsLookup Example

The DNS and IP-related classes are illustrated with an example that looks up DNS names: DnsLookup (see Figure 26-10). This sample application simply invites the user to type in a DNS name using the main text box. When the user clicks the Resolve button, the sample uses the Dns.Resolve method to retrieve an IPHostEntry reference and display the host name and IP addresses. Note that the host name displayed may be different from the name typed in. This can occur if one DNS name simply acts as a proxy for another DNS name.

The DnsLookup application is a standard C# Windows application. The controls are added as shown in Figure 26-10, giving them the names txtBoxInput, btnResolve, txtBoxHostName, and listBoxIPs, respectively. Then, you simply add the following method to the Form1 class as the event handler for the buttonResolve Click event:

```
void btnResolve_Click (object sender, EventArgs e)
{
    try
    {
        IPHostEntry iphost = Dns.GetHostEntry(txtBoxInput.Text);
        foreach (IPAddress ip in iphost.AddressList)
        {
            string ipaddress = ip.AddressFamily.ToString();
            listBoxIPs.Items.Add(ipaddress);
            listBoxIPs.Items.Add(" " + ip.ToString());
        }
        txtBoxHostName.Text = iphost.HostName;
    }
    catch(Exception ex)
    {
        MessageBox.Show("Unable to process the request because " +
            "the following problem occurred:\n" +
            ex.Message, "Exception occurred");
    }
}
```

Notice that this code is careful to trap any exceptions. An exception might occur if the user types an invalid DNS name or the network is down.

After retrieving the IPHostEntry instance, you use the AddressList property to obtain an array containing the IP addresses, which you then iterate through with a foreach loop. For each entry, you display the IP address as an integer and as a string, using the IPAddress .AddressFamily.ToString method.

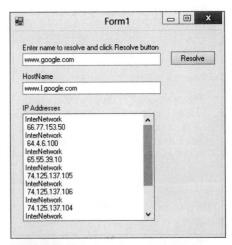

FIGURE 26-10

LOWER-LEVEL PROTOCOLS

This section briefly discusses some of the .NET classes used to communicate at a lower level. The System.Net.Sockets namespace contains the relevant classes. These classes, for example, enable you to directly send TCP network requests or listen to TCP network requests on a particular port. The following table describes the main classes:

CLASS	DESCRIPTION
Socket	Deals with managing connections. Classes such as `WebRequest`, `TcpClient`, and `UdpClient` use this class internally.
NetworkStream	Derived from `Stream`. Represents a stream of data from the network.
SmtpClient	Enables you to send messages (mail) through the Simple Mail Transfer Protocol.
TcpClient	Enables you to create and use TCP connections.
TcpListener	Enables you to listen for incoming TCP connection requests.
UdpClient	Enables you to create connections for UDP clients. (UDP is an alternative protocol to TCP but much less widely used, mostly on local networks.)

Network communications work on several different levels. The classes described in this chapter so far work at the highest level — the level at which specific commands are processed. It is probably easiest to understand this concept if you think of file transfer using FTP. Although today's GUI applications hide many of the FTP details, it was not so long ago that you executed FTP from a command-line prompt. In this environment, you explicitly typed commands to send to the server for downloading, uploading, and listing files.

FTP is not the only high-level protocol relying on textual commands. HTTP, SMTP, POP, and other protocols are based on a similar type of behavior. Again, many modern graphical tools hide the transmission of commands from the user, so you are generally not aware of them. For example, when you type a URL into a web browser, and the web request is sent to a server, the browser is actually sending a (plain text) GET command to the server, which fulfills a similar purpose as the FTP get command. It can also send a POST command, which indicates that the browser has attached other data to the request.

These protocols, however, are not sufficient by themselves to achieve communication between computers. Even if both the client and the server understand, for example, the HTTP protocol, it still won't be possible for them to understand each other unless there is also agreement about exactly how to transmit the characters — what binary format will be used? Moreover, getting down to the lowest level, what voltages will be used to represent 0s and 1s in the binary data? Because there are so many items to configure and agree upon, developers and hardware engineers in the networking field often refer to a *protocol stack*. When you list all the various protocols and mechanisms required for communication between two hosts, you create a protocol stack — with high-level protocols on the top and low-level protocols on the bottom. This approach results in a modular and layered approach to achieving efficient communication.

Luckily, for most development work, you do not need to go far down the stack or work with voltage levels. If you are writing code that requires efficient communication between computers, then it's not unusual to write code that works directly at the level of sending binary data packets between computers. This is the realm of protocols such as TCP, and Microsoft provides several classes that enable you to conveniently work with binary data at this level.

Using SmtpClient

The `SmtpClient` object enables you to send mail messages through the Simple Mail Transfer Protocol. A simple example of using the `SmtpClient` object is illustrated here:

```
SmtpClient sc = new SmtpClient("mail.mySmtpHost.com");
sc.Send("evjen@yahoo.com", "editor@wrox.com",
    "The latest chapter", "Here is the latest.");
```

In its most basic form, you work from an instance of the `SmtpClient` object. In this case, the instantiation also provided the host of the SMTP server that is used to send the mail messages over the Internet. You could have achieved the same task by using the `Host` property:

```
SmtpClient sc = new SmtpClient();
sc.Host = "mail.mySmtpHost.com";
sc.Send("evjen@yahoo.com", "editor@wrox.com",
    "The latest chapter", "Here is the latest.");
```

When you have the `SmtpClient` in place, it is simply a matter of calling the `Send` method and providing the From address, the To address, and the Subject, followed by the Body of the mail message.

In many cases you will have mail messages that are more complex than this. To handle this possibility, you can also pass a `MailMessage` object into the `Send` method:

```
SmtpClient sc = new SmtpClient();
sc.Host = "mail.mySmtpHost.com";
MailMessage mm = new MailMessage();
mm.Sender = new MailAddress("evjen@yahoo.com", "Bill Evjen");
mm.To.Add(new MailAddress("editor@wrox.com", "Paul Reese"));
mm.To.Add(new MailAddress("marketing@wrox.com", "Wrox Marketing"));
mm.CC.Add(new MailAddress("publisher@wrox.com", "Barry Pruett"));
mm.Subject = "The latest chapter";
mm.Body = "<b>Here you can put a long message</b>";
mm.IsBodyHtml = true;
mm.Priority = MailPriority.High;
sc.Send(mm);
```

Using `MailMessage` enables you to greatly fine-tune how you build your mail messages. You can send HTML messages, add as many To and CC recipients as you wish, change the message priority, work with the message encodings, and add attachments. The capability to add attachments is defined in the following code snippet:

```
SmtpClient sc = new SmtpClient();
sc.Host = "mail.mySmtpHost.com";
MailMessage mm = new MailMessage();
mm.Sender = new MailAddress("evjen@yahoo.com", "Bill Evjen");
mm.To.Add(new MailAddress("editor@wrox.com", "Paul Reese"));
mm.To.Add(new MailAddress("marketing@wrox.com", "Wrox Marketing"));
mm.CC.Add(new MailAddress("publisher@wrox.com", "Barry Pruett"));
mm.Subject = "The latest chapter";
mm.Body = "<b>Here you can put a long message</b>";
mm.IsBodyHtml = true;
mm.Priority = MailPriority.High;
Attachment att = new Attachment("myExcelResults.zip",
    MediaTypeNames.Application.Zip);
mm.Attachments.Add(att);
sc.Send(mm);
```

In this case, an `Attachment` object is created and added using the `Add` method to the `MailMessage` object before the `Send` method is called.

Using the TCP Classes

The Transmission Control Protocol (TCP) classes offer simple methods for connecting and sending data between two endpoints. An endpoint is the combination of an IP address and a port number. Existing protocols have well-defined port numbers—for example, HTTP uses port 80, whereas SMTP uses port 25. The Internet Assigned Numbers Authority, IANA (www.iana.org), assigns port numbers to these well-known services. Unless you are implementing a well-known service, you should select a port number higher than 1,024.

TCP traffic makes up the majority of traffic on the Internet today. It is often the protocol of choice because it offers guaranteed delivery, error correction, and buffering. The TcpClient class encapsulates a TCP connection and provides a number of properties to regulate the connection, including buffering, buffer size, and timeouts. Reading and writing is accomplished by requesting a NetworkStream object via the GetStream method.

The TcpListener class listens for incoming TCP connections with the Start method. When a connection request arrives, you can use the AcceptSocket method to return a socket for communication with the remote machine, or use the AcceptTcpClient method to use a higher-level TcpClient object for communication. The easiest way to see how the TcpListener and TcpClient classes work together is to go through an example.

The TcpSend and TcpReceive Examples

To demonstrate how these classes work, you need to build two applications. Figure 26-11 shows the first application, TcpSend. This application opens a TCP connection to a server and sends the C# source code for itself.

As before, create a C# Windows application. The form consists of two text boxes (txtHost and txtPort) for the host name and port, respectively, as well as a button (btnSend) to click and start a connection. First, you ensure that you include the relevant namespaces:

```
using System;
using System.IO;
using System.Net.Sockets;
using System.Windows.Forms;
```

The following code shows the event handler for the button's Click event:

```
private void btnSend_Click(object sender, System.EventArgs e)
{
    TcpClient tcpClient = new TcpClient(txtHost.Text, Int32.Parse(txtPort.Text));
    NetworkStream ns = tcpClient.GetStream();
    FileStream fs = File.Open("form1.cs", FileMode.Open);

    int data = fs.ReadByte();

    while(data != -1)
    {
        ns.WriteByte((byte)data);
        data = fs.ReadByte();
    }

    fs.Close();
    ns.Close();
    tcpClient.Close();
}
```

This example creates the TcpClient using a host name and a port number. Alternatively, if you have an instance of the IPEndPoint class, you can pass the instance to the TcpClient constructor. After retrieving an instance of the NetworkStream class, you open the source-code file and begin to read bytes. As with many of the binary streams, you need to check for the end of the stream by comparing the return value of the ReadByte method to -1. After your loop has

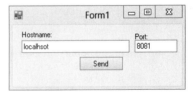

FIGURE 26-11

read all the bytes and sent them along to the network stream, you must close all the open files, connections, and streams.

On the other side of the connection, the `TcpReceive` application displays the received file after the transmission is finished (see Figure 26-12).

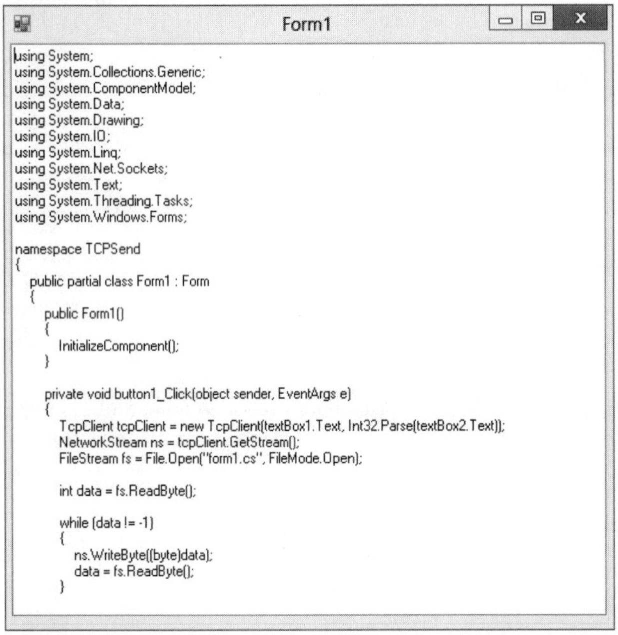

```csharp
using System;
using System.Collections.Generic;
using System.ComponentModel;
using System.Data;
using System.Drawing;
using System.IO;
using System.Linq;
using System.Net.Sockets;
using System.Text;
using System.Threading.Tasks;
using System.Windows.Forms;

namespace TCPSend
{
    public partial class Form1 : Form
    {
        public Form1()
        {
            InitializeComponent();
        }

        private void button1_Click(object sender, EventArgs e)
        {
            TcpClient tcpClient = new TcpClient(textBox1.Text, Int32.Parse(textBox2.Text));
            NetworkStream ns = tcpClient.GetStream();
            FileStream fs = File.Open("form1.cs", FileMode.Open);

            int data = fs.ReadByte();

            while (data != -1)
            {
                ns.WriteByte((byte)data);
                data = fs.ReadByte();
            }
```

FIGURE 26-12

The form consists of a single `TextBox` control named `txtDisplay`. The `TcpReceive` application uses a `TcpListener` to wait for the incoming connection. To prevent freezing the application interface, you use a background thread to wait for and then read from the connection. Thus, you need to include the `System .Threading` namespace as well these other namespaces:

```csharp
using System;
using System.IO;
using System.Net;
using System.Net.Sockets;
using System.Threading;
using System.Windows.Forms;
```

Inside the form's constructor, you spin up a background thread:

```csharp
public Form1()
{
    InitializeComponent();
    Thread thread = new Thread(new ThreadStart(Listen));
    thread.Start();
}
```

The remaining important code is as follows:

```csharp
public void Listen()
{
    IPAddress localAddr = IPAddress.Parse("127.0.0.1");
    Int32 port = 2112;
```

```
        TcpListener tcpListener = new TcpListener(localAddr, port);
        tcpListener.Start();

        TcpClient tcpClient = tcpListener.AcceptTcpClient();

        NetworkStream ns = tcpClient.GetStream();
        StreamReader sr = new StreamReader(ns);
        string result = sr.ReadToEnd();
        Invoke(new UpdateDisplayDelegate(UpdateDisplay),new object[] {result} );
        tcpClient.Close();
        tcpListener.Stop();
    }

    public void UpdateDisplay(string text)
    {
        txtDisplay.Text= text;
    }

    protected delegate void UpdateDisplayDelegate(string text);
```

The thread begins execution in the `Listen` method and allows you to make the blocking call to `AcceptTcpClient` without halting the interface. Notice that the IP address (`127.0.0.1`) and the port number (`2112`) are hard-coded into the application, so you need to enter the same port number from the client application.

You use the `TcpClient` object returned by `AcceptTcpClient` to open a new stream for reading. As in the earlier example, you create a `StreamReader` to convert the incoming network data into a string. Before closing the client and stopping the listener, you update the form's text box. You do not want to access the text box directly from your background thread, so you use the form's `Invoke` method with a delegate and pass the result string as the first element in an array of `object` parameters. `Invoke` ensures that your call is correctly marshalled into the thread that owns the control handles in the user interface.

TCP versus UDP

The other protocol covered in this section is UDP (User Datagram Protocol). UDP is a simple protocol with few features and little overhead. Developers often use UDP in applications for which the speed and performance requirements outweigh the reliability requirements—for example, video streaming. In contrast, TCP offers a number of features to confirm the delivery of data. TCP provides error correction and retransmission in the case of lost or corrupted packets. Last, but hardly least, TCP buffers incoming and outgoing data and guarantees that a sequence of packets scrambled in transmission is reassembled before delivery to the application. Even with the extra overhead, TCP is the most widely used protocol across the Internet because of its high reliability.

The UDP Class

As you might expect, the `UdpClient` class features a smaller and simpler interface than `TcpClient`. This reflects the relatively simpler nature of the protocol. Although both TCP and UDP classes use a socket beneath the covers, the `UdpClient` class does not contain a method to return a network stream for reading and writing. Instead, the member function `Send` accepts an array of bytes as a parameter, and the `Receive` function returns an array of bytes. Also, because UDP is a connectionless protocol, you can wait to specify the endpoint for the communication as a parameter to the `Send` and `Receive` methods, rather than specify it earlier in a constructor or `Connect` method. You can also change the endpoint on each subsequent send or receive.

The following code fragment uses the `UdpClient` class to send a message to an echo service. A server with an echo service running accepts TCP or UDP connections on port 7. The echo service simply echoes any data sent to the server back to the client. This service is useful for diagnostics and testing, although many system administrators disable echo services for security reasons:

```
using System;
using System.Text;
using System.Net;
using System.Net.Sockets;
namespace Wrox.ProCSharp.InternetAccess.UdpExample
{

    class Class1
    {
        [STAThread]
        static void Main(string[] args)
        {
            UdpClient udpClient = new UdpClient();
            string sendMsg = "Hello Echo Server";
            byte [] sendBytes = Encoding.ASCII.GetBytes(sendMsg);
            udpClient.Send(sendBytes, sendBytes.Length, "SomeEchoServer.net", 7);
            IPEndPoint endPoint = new IPEndPoint(0,0);
            byte [] rcvBytes = udpClient.Receive(ref endPoint);
            string rcvMessage = Encoding.ASCII.GetString(rcvBytes,
                                                         0,
                                                         rcvBytes.Length);
            // should print out "Hello Echo Server"
            Console.WriteLine(rcvMessage);
        }
    }
}
```

Here, you make heavy use of the `Encoding.ASCII` class to translate strings into arrays of `byte` and vice versa. Also note that you pass an `IPEndPoint` by reference into the `Receive` method. Because UDP is not a connection-oriented protocol, each call to `Receive` might pick up data from a different endpoint, so `Receive` populates this parameter with the IP address and port of the sending host. Both `UdpClient` and `TcpClient` offer a layer of abstraction over the lowest of the low-level classes: `Socket`.

The Socket Class

The `Socket` class offers the highest level of control in network programming. One of the easiest ways to demonstrate the class is to rewrite the `TcpReceive` application with the `Socket` class. The updated `Listen` method is shown in this example:

```
public void Listen()
{
    Socket listener = new Socket(AddressFamily.InterNetwork,
                                 SocketType.Stream,
                                 ProtocolType.Tcp);
    listener.Bind(new IPEndPoint(IPAddress.Any, 2112));
    listener.Listen(0);
    Socket socket = listener.Accept();
    Stream netStream = new NetworkStream(socket);
    StreamReader reader = new StreamReader(netStream);

    string result = reader.ReadToEnd();
    Invoke(new UpdateDisplayDelegate(UpdateDisplay),
           new object[] {result} );
    socket.Close();
    listener.Close();
}
```

The `Socket` class requires a few more lines of code to complete the same task. For starters, the constructor arguments need to specify an IP addressing scheme for a streaming socket with the TCP protocol. These arguments are just one of the many combinations available to the `Socket` class. The `TcpClient` class can configure these settings for you. You then bind the listener socket to a port and begin to listen for incoming connections. When an incoming request arrives, you can use the `Accept` method to create a new socket to handle the connection. You ultimately attach a `StreamReader` instance to the socket to read the incoming data, in much the same fashion as before.

The `Socket` class also contains a number of methods for asynchronously accepting, connecting, sending, and receiving. You can use these methods with callback delegates in the same way you used the asynchronous page requests with the `WebRequest` class. If you really need to dig into the internals of the socket, the `GetSocketOption` and `SetSocketOption` methods are available. These methods enable you to see and configure options, including timeout, time-to-live, and other low-level options.

Building a Server Console Application

Looking further into the `Socket` class, the following example creates a console application that acts as a server for incoming socket requests. A second example is created in parallel (another console application), which sends a message to the server console application.

The first application to build is the console application that acts as a server. This application will open a socket on a specific TCP port and listen for any incoming messages. The code for this console application is presented in its entirety here:

```
using System;
using System.Net;
using System.Net.Sockets;
using System.Text;

namespace SocketConsole
{
    class Program
    {
        static void Main()
        {
            Console.WriteLine("Starting: Creating Socket object");
            Socket listener = new Socket(AddressFamily.InterNetwork,
                                    SocketType.Stream,
                                    ProtocolType.Tcp);
            listener.Bind(new IPEndPoint(IPAddress.Any, 2112));
            listener.Listen(10);

            while (true)
            {
                Console.WriteLine("Waiting for connection on port 2112");
                Socket socket = listener.Accept();
                string receivedValue = string.Empty;

                while (true)
                {
                    byte[] receivedBytes = new byte[1024];
                    int numBytes = socket.Receive(receivedBytes);
                    Console.WriteLine("Receiving .");
                    receivedValue += Encoding.ASCII.GetString(receivedBytes,
                                        0, numBytes);
                    if (receivedValue.IndexOf("[FINAL]") > -1)
                    {
                        break;
                    }
                }
            }
```

```
                    Console.WriteLine("Received value: {0}", receivedValue);
                    string replyValue = "Message successfully received.";
                    byte[] replyMessage = Encoding.ASCII.GetBytes(replyValue);
                    socket.Send(replyMessage);
                    socket.Shutdown(SocketShutdown.Both);
                    socket.Close();
                }
                listener.Close();
            }
        }
    }
```

This example sets up a socket using the `Socket` class. The socket created uses the TCP protocol and is set up to receive incoming messages from any IP address using port 2112. Values received through the open socket are written to the console screen. This consuming application will continue to receive bytes until the `[FINAL]` string is received. This `[FINAL]` string signifies the end of the incoming message, which can then be interpreted.

After the end of the message is received from a client, a reply message is sent to the same client. From there, the socket is closed using the `Close` method, and the console application remains up until a new message is received.

Building the Client Application

The next step is to build a client application that will send a message to the first console application. The client will be able to send any message that it wants to the server console application as long as it follows some rules that were established by this application. The first of these rules is that the server console application is listening only on a particular protocol. In the case of this server application, it is listening using the TCP protocol. The next rule is that the server application is listening only on a particular port—in this case, port 2112. The last rule stipulates that for any message that is being sent, the last bits of the message need to end with the string `[FINAL]`.

The following client console application follows all these rules:

```
using System;
using System.Net;
using System.Net.Sockets;
using System.Text;

namespace SocketConsoleClient
{
    class Program
    {
        static void Main()
        {
            byte[] receivedBytes = new byte[1024];
            IPHostEntry ipHost = Dns.Resolve("127.0.0.1");
            IPAddress ipAddress = ipHost.AddressList[0];
            IPEndPoint ipEndPoint = new IPEndPoint(ipAddress, 2112);
            Console.WriteLine("Starting: Creating Socket object");

            Socket sender = new Socket(AddressFamily.InterNetwork,
                                       SocketType.Stream,
                                       ProtocolType.Tcp);
            sender.Connect(ipEndPoint);
            Console.WriteLine("Successfully connected to {0}",
                    sender.RemoteEndPoint);
            string sendingMessage = "Hello World Socket Test";
            Console.WriteLine("Creating message: Hello World Socket Test");
            byte[] forwardMessage = Encoding.ASCII.GetBytes(sendingMessage
```

```
                         + "[FINAL]");
                sender.Send(forwardMessage);
                int totalBytesReceived = sender.Receive(receivedBytes);
                Console.WriteLine("Message provided from server: {0}",
                               Encoding.ASCII.GetString(receivedBytes,
                               0, totalBytesReceived));
                sender.Shutdown(SocketShutdown.Both);
                sender.Close();
                Console.ReadLine();
        }
    }
}
```

In this example, an `IPEndPoint` object is created using the IP address of *localhost* as well as port 2112 as required by the server console application. In this case, a socket is created and the `Connect` method is called. After the socket is opened and connected to the server console application socket instance, a string of text is sent to the server application using the `Send` method. Because the server application is going to return a message, the `Receive` method is used to grab this message (placing it in a byte array). From there, the byte array is converted into a string and displayed in the console application before the socket is shut down.

Running this application produces the results shown in Figure 26-13.

FIGURE 26-13

Reviewing the two console applications in the figure, you can see that the server application opens and awaits incoming messages. The incoming message is sent from the client application, and the string sent is then displayed by the server application. The server application waits for other messages to come in, even after the first message is received and displayed. To confirm this, try shutting down the client application and rerunning the server application. You will see that the server application again displays the message received.

WebSockets

The WebSocket protocol is used for full duplex, bidirectional communication. Typically this communication would be between a browser and a web server, but just about any client could support the use of WebSockets. The WebSocket API is being standardized by the W3C and the protocol has been standardized by the IETF (Internet Engineering Task Force) in RFC 6455.

Unlike the request/response model that is used by browsers and web servers, websockets maintain an open connection. Whereas TCP sends a stream of bytes, websockets sends messages back and forth between the server and clients.

Not all browsers and web servers support the WebSocket protocol. Currently, Firefox 11.0 (MozWebSocket), Google Chrome 16, and Internet Explorer 10 provide such browser support. For servers, IIS 8 with ASP.NET 4.5 offers low-level WebSocket support.

Chat Example

The WebSocket endpoint can be created using any type of handler or module. The following example uses an .ashx handler as the endpoint. The example is a simple chat program using the browser and web server. Each client or user connects to the web server, supplies their name to "register" with the chat server, and can then send simple text messages to the other users registered with the server.

First, here's the code for the browser. This is a very simple HTML page using jQuery to set up the WebSocket. jQuery provides an easy way to handle the WebSocket events on the page.

```html
<!doctype html>
<head>
    <meta http-equiv="X-UA-Compatible" content="IE=edge" />
    <script src="Scripts/jquery-1.7.2.min.js" type="text/javascript"></script>
    <title>WroxChat</title>
    <script type="text/javascript">
        $(document).ready(function () {
            var name = prompt('what is your name?:');
            var url = 'ws://localhost/ws.ashx?name=' + name;
            ws = new WebSocket(url);
            ws.onopen = function () {
                $('#messages').prepend('Connected <br/>');
                $('#cmdSend').click(function () {
                    ws.send($('#txtMessage').val());
                    $('#txtMessage').val('');
                });
            };
            ws.onmessage = function (e) {
                $('#chatMessages').prepend(e.data + '<br/>');
            };
            $('#cmdLeave').click(function () {
                ws.close();
            });
            ws.onclose = function () {
                $('#chatMessages').prepend('Closed <br/>');
            };
            ws.onerror = function (e) {
                $('#chatMessages').prepend('Oops something went wrong <br/>');
            };
        });
    </script>
</head>
<body>
<input id="txtMessage" />
<input id="cmdSend" type="button" value="Send" />
<input id="cmdLeave" type="button" value="Leave" />
<br />
<div id="chatMessages" />
</body>
```

This example is hosted on localhost. The url variable can be changed to any valid URL that would be hosting the example.

The line ws = new WebSocket(url); establishes the connection between the browser and the server. When the onopen event is fired by the WebSocket class, the event handler for the cmdSend click event is defined. It calls the Send method of the WebSocket object.

The other WebSocket events handled in this example are onmessage, onclose, and onerror. onmessage is called when a message is sent to the browser, onclose is called when the WebSocket connection is terminated, and onerror is called if an exception happens.

On the server things are a little more complicated. For this example you need to create a simple ChatUser object. For each user who registers with the server, a ChatUser object is placed in an IList<ChatUser>. When a message is sent to the server, it is broadcasted to each user in the IList<ChatUser> list.

The IHttpHandler does this work. When the ProcessRequest method is handled it creates the new user and adds that user to the list. Finally, it calls the ChatUser's HandleWebSocket method. This finishes establishing the connection between the browser and the server.

First, here's the code in the ProcessRequest method of the IHttpHandler class ws.ashx:

```
public void ProcessRequest(HttpContext context)
{
    if (context.IsWebSocketRequest)
    {
        var chatuser = new ChatUser();
        chatuser.UserName = context.Request.QueryString["name"];
        ChatApp.AddUser(chatuser);
        context.AcceptWebSocketRequest(chatuser.HandleWebSocket);
    }
}
```

As shown here, the new ChatUser is created, the name is set from the query parameter sent in from the browser, the user is added to the list, and the HandleWebSocket method is called.

The HandleWebSocket method is where the messages are processed. Here is what the code looks like:

```
public async Task HandleWebSocket(WebSocketContext wsContext)
{
    _context = wsContext;
    const int maxMessageSize = 1024;
    byte[] receiveBuffer = new byte[maxMessageSize];
    WebSocket socket = _context.WebSocket;

    while (socket.State == WebSocketState.Open)
    {
        WebSocketReceiveResult receiveResult =
            await socket.ReceiveAsync(new ArraySegment<byte>(receiveBuffer),
                                      CancellationToken.None);

        if (receiveResult.MessageType == WebSocketMessageType.Close)
        {
            await socket.CloseAsync(WebSocketCloseStatus.NormalClosure,
                                    string.Empty,
                                    CancellationToken.None);
        }
        else if (receiveResult.MessageType == WebSocketMessageType.Binary)
        {
            await socket.CloseAsync(WebSocketCloseStatus.InvalidMessageType,
                                    "Cannot accept binary frame",
                                    CancellationToken.None);
        }
        else
        {
```

```
                    var receivedString = Encoding.UTF8.GetString(receiveBuffer,
                                                                 0,
                                                                 receiveResult.Count);
                    var echoString = string.Concat(UserName,
                                                   " said: ",
                                                   receivedString);
                    ArraySegment<byte> outputBuffer =
                        new ArraySegment<byte>(Encoding.UTF8.GetBytes(echoString));

                    ChatApp.BroadcastMessage(echoString);
                }
            }
        }
```

When the request arrives, you first need to ensure that the socket connection is open. You get the socket from the `WebSocketContext` object that's passed in and check the `State` property.

Next, the `ReceiveAsync` method is called, returning the `WebSocketReceiveResult` object. From this you can determine whether the message is a close message or a binary message. If a close message was sent, then the connection is closed—and in this example only text can be sent.

One of the parameters in the `ReceiveAsync` call is the `receiveBuffer`. This is a byte array that will be filled with the message data. In a more fully featured chat program, you want to ensure that the message doesn't exceed the maximum size limit.

Now it's time to handle the message. Because this is a byte array, you need to get the data into textual format. You do this by using the `Encoding.UTF8.GetString` method, which takes the byte array and returns a `string` of your message. You concatenate the name of the user who sent the message and the call the `Broadcast` method of the `ChatApp` class.

The `Broadcast` method iterates through all the `ChatUser` objects and calls the `SendMessage` method, which looks like this:

```
public async Task SendMessage(string message)
{
    if (_context != null && _context.WebSocket.State == WebSocketState.Open)
    {
        var outputBuffer = new ArraySegment<byte>(
                                    Encoding.UTF8.GetBytes(message));
        await _context.WebSocket.SendAsync(
                            outputBuffer,
                            WebSocketMessageType.Text,
                            true,
                            CancellationToken.None);
    }
}
```

The `SendMessage` method stakes the message string and puts it back into a byte array. This byte array is then sent as a parameter to the `SendAsync` method. The `_context` variable is the `WebSocketContext` created when the user first registered with the chat program, so the message is sent back on the active connection. Because the JavaScript in the page is listening to the `onMessage` event of the `WebSocket` object in the DOM, the message is received and displayed on the page.

SUMMARY

This chapter described the .NET Framework classes available in the `System.Net` namespace for communication across networks. You have seen some of the .NET base classes that deal with opening client connections on the network and Internet, and how to send requests to, and receive responses from, servers (the most obvious use of this being to receive HTML pages). By taking advantage of the `WebBrowser` control, you can easily make use of Internet Explorer from your desktop applications.

As a rule of thumb, when programming with classes in the `System.Net` namespace, you should always try to use the most generic class possible. For instance, using the `TcpClient` class instead of the `Socket` class isolates your code from many of the lower-level socket details. Moving one step higher, the `WebRequest` class enables you to take advantage of the pluggable protocol architecture of the .NET Framework. Your code will be ready to take advantage of new application-level protocols as Microsoft and other third-party developers introduce new functionality.

Finally, you learned how to use the asynchronous capabilities in the networking classes, which give a Windows Forms application the professional touch of a responsive user interface.

27

Windows Services

WROX.COM CODE DOWNLOADS FOR THIS CHAPTER

The wrox.com code downloads for this chapter are found at `http://www.wrox.com/remtitle .cgi?isbn=1118314425` on the Download Code tab. The code is in the chapter 27 download and individually named according to the names throughout the chapter.

➤ Quote Server

➤ Quote Client

➤ Quote Service

➤ Service Control

WHAT IS A WINDOWS SERVICE?

Windows Services are programs that can be started automatically at boot time without the need for anyone to log on to the machine. If you need to startup programs without user interaction or need to run under a different user than the interactive user, which can be a user with more privileges, you can create a Windows Service. Some examples could be a WCF host (if you can't use IIS for some reason), a program that caches data from a network server, or a program that re-organizes local disk data in the background.

This chapter starts with looking at the architecture of Windows Services, creates a Windows Service that hosts a networking server, and gives you information to start, monitor, control, and troubleshoot your Windows Services.

As previously mentioned, Windows Services are applications that can be automatically started when the operating system boots. These applications can run without having an interactive user logged on to the system, and can do some processing in the background.

For example, on a Windows Server, system networking services should be accessible from the client without a user logging on to the server; and on the client system, services enable you to do things such as get a new software version online or perform some file cleanup on the local disk.

You can configure a Windows Service to run from a specially configured user account or from the system user account — a user account that has even more privileges than that of the system administrator.

> **NOTE** *Unless otherwise noted, when we refer to a service, we are referring to a Windows Service.*

Here are a few examples of services:

➤ Simple TCP/IP Services is a service program that hosts some small TCP/IP servers: echo, daytime, quote, and others.

➤ World Wide Web Publishing Service is a service of Internet Information Services (IIS).

➤ Event Log is a service to log messages to the event log system.

➤ Windows Search is a service that creates indexes of data on the disk.

➤ SuperFetch is a service that preloads commonly used applications and libraries into memory, thus improving the startup time of these applications.

You can use the Services administration tool, shown in Figure 27-1, to see all the services on a system. This program can be found by selecting Administrative Tools from the control panel.

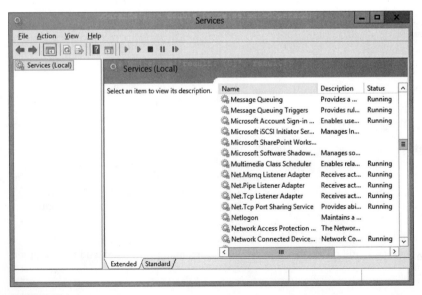

FIGURE 27-1

WINDOWS SERVICES ARCHITECTURE

Three program types are necessary to operate a Windows Service:

➤ A service program

➤ A service control program

➤ A service configuration program

The *service program* is the implementation of the service. With a *service control* program, it is possible to send control requests to a service, such as start, stop, pause, and continue. With a *service configuration* program, a service can be installed; it is copied to the file system, and information about the service needs to be written to the registry. This registry information is used by the `service control manager` (SCM) to start and stop the service. Although .NET components can be installed simply with an xcopy — because they don't need to write information to the registry — installation for services requires registry configuration. A service configuration program can also be used to change the configuration of that service at a later point. These three ingredients of a Windows Service are discussed in the following subsections.

Service Program

In order to put the .NET implementation of a service in perspective, this section takes a brief look at the Windows architecture of services in general, and the inner functionality of a service.

The service program implements the functionality of the service. It needs three parts:

➤ A main function

➤ A service-main function

➤ A handler

Before discussing these parts, however, it would be useful to digress for a moment for a short introduction to the service control manager (SCM), which plays an important role for services — sending requests to your service to start it and stop it.

Service Control Manager

The SCM is the part of the operating system that communicates with the service. Using a sequence diagram, Figure 27-2 illustrates how this communication works.

At boot time, each process for which a service is set to start automatically is started, and so the main function of this process is called. The service is responsible for registering the service-main function for each of its services. The main function is the entry point of the service program, and in this function the entry points for the service-main functions must be registered with the SCM.

Main Function, Service-Main, and Handlers

The main function of the service is the normal entry point of a program, the `Main` method. The main function of the service might register more than one service-main function. The *service-main* function contains the actual functionality

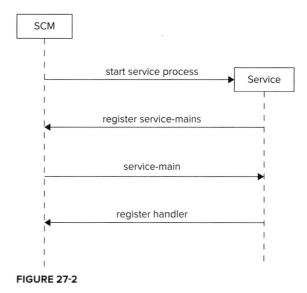

FIGURE 27-2

of the service, which must register a service-main function for each service it provides. A service program can provide a lot of services in a single program; for example, `<windows>\system32\services.exe` is the service program that includes Alerter, Application Management, Computer Browser, and DHCP Client, among other items.

The SCM calls the service-main function for each service that should be started. One important task of the service-main function is registering a handler with the SCM.

The *handler* function is the third part of a service program. The handler must respond to events from the SCM. Services can be stopped, suspended, and resumed, and the handler must react to these events.

After a handler has been registered with the SCM, the service control program can post requests to the SCM to stop, suspend, and resume the service. The service control program is independent of the SCM and the service itself. The operating system contains many service control programs, such as the MMC Services snap-in shown earlier. You can also write your own service control program; a good example of this is the SQL Server Configuration Manager shown in Figure 27-3.

FIGURE 27-3

Service Control Program

As the self-explanatory name suggests, with a service control program you can stop, suspend, and resume the service. To do so, you can send control codes to the service, and the handler should react to these events. It is also possible to ask the service about its actual status (if the service is running or suspended, or in some faulted state) and to implement a custom handler that responds to custom control codes.

Service Configuration Program

Because services must be configured in the registry, you can't use xcopy installation with services. The registry contains the startup type of the service, which can be set to automatic, manual, or disabled. You also need to configure the user of the service program and dependencies of the service — for example, any services that must be started before the current one can start. All these configurations are made within a service configuration program. The installation program can use the service configuration program to configure the service, but this program can also be used later to change service configuration parameters.

Classes for Windows Services

In the .NET Framework, you can find service classes in the `System.ServiceProcess` namespace that implement the three parts of a service:

> ➤ You must inherit from the `ServiceBase` class to implement a service. The `ServiceBase` class is used to register the service and to answer start and stop requests.
>
> ➤ The `ServiceController` class is used to implement a service control program. With this class, you can send requests to services.
>
> ➤ The `ServiceProcessInstaller` and `ServiceInstaller` classes are, as their names suggest, classes to install and configure service programs.

Now you are ready to create a new service.

CREATING A WINDOWS SERVICE PROGRAM

The service that you create in this chapter hosts a quote server. With every request that is made from a client, the quote server returns a random quote from a quote file. The first part of the solution uses three assemblies, one for the client and two for the server. Figure 27-4 provides an overview of the solution. The assembly `QuoteServer` holds the actual functionality. The service reads the quote file in a memory cache, and answers requests for quotes with the help of a socket server. The `QuoteClient` is a WPF rich–client application. This application creates a client socket to communicate with the `QuoteServer`. The third assembly is the actual service. The `QuoteService` starts and stops the `QuoteServer`; the service controls the server.

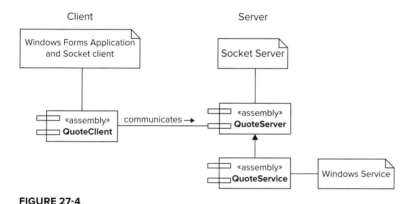

FIGURE 27-4

Before creating the service part of your program, create a simple socket server in an extra C# class library that will be used from your service process. How this can be done is discussed in the following section.

Creating Core Functionality for the Service

You can build any functionality in a Windows Service, such as scanning for files to do a backup or a virus check or starting a WCF server. However, all service programs share some similarities. The program must be able to start (and to return to the caller), stop, and suspend. This section looks at such an implementation using a socket server.

With Windows 8, the Simple TCP/IP Services can be installed as part of the Windows components. Part of the Simple TCP/IP Services is a "quote of the day," or qotd, TCP/IP server. This simple service listens to port 17 and answers every request with a random message from the file `<windows>\system32\drivers\etc\quotes`. With the sample service, a similar server will be built. The sample server returns a Unicode string, in contrast to the qotd server, which returns an ASCII string.

First, create a class library called `QuoteServer` and implement the code for the server. The following walks through the source code of your `QuoteServer` class in the file `QuoteServer.cs`:

```
using System;
using System.Collections.Generic;
using System.Diagnostics;
using System.IO;
using System.Linq;
using System.Net;
using System.Net.Sockets;
using System.Text;
using System.Threading.Tasks;

namespace Wrox.ProCSharp.WinServices
{
  public class QuoteServer
  {
    private TcpListener listener;
    private int port;
    private string filename;
    private List<string> quotes;
    private Random random;
    private Task listenerTask;
```

The constructor `QuoteServer` is overloaded so that a filename and a port can be passed to the call. The constructor where just the file name is passed uses the default port 7890 for the server. The default constructor defines the default filename for the quotes as `quotes.txt`:

```
    public QuoteServer()
        : this ("quotes.txt")
    {
    }
    public QuoteServer(string filename)
        : this(filename, 7890)
    {
    }
    public QuoteServer(string filename, int port)
    {
      Contract.Requires<ArgumentNullException>(filename != null);
      Contract.Requires<ArgumentException>(port >= IPEndpoint.MinPort &&
        port <= IPEndPoint.MaxPort);

      this.filename = filename;
      this.port = port;
    }
```

`ReadQuotes` is a helper method that reads all the quotes from a file that was specified in the constructor. All the quotes are added to the `List<string>` quotes. In addition, you are creating an instance of the `Random` class that will be used to return random quotes:

```
    protected void ReadQuotes()
    {
      try
```

```
    {
      quotes = File.ReadAllLines(filename).ToList();
      if (quotes.Count == 0)
      {
        throw new QuoteException("quotes file is empty");
      }
      random = new Random();
    }
    catch (IOException ex)
    {
      throw new QuoteException("I/O Error", ex);
    }
}
```

Another helper method is `GetRandomQuoteOfTheDay`. This method returns a random quote from the quotes collection:

```
protected string GetRandomQuoteOfTheDay()
{
  int index = random.Next(0, quotes.Count);
  return quotes[index];
}
```

In the `Start` method, the complete file containing the quotes is read in the `List<string>` quotes by using the helper method `ReadQuotes`. After this, a new thread is started, which immediately calls the `Listener` method — similarly to the `TcpReceive` example in Chapter 26, "Networking."

Here, a task is used because the `Start` method cannot block and wait for a client; it must return immediately to the caller (SCM). The SCM would assume that the start failed if the method didn't return to the caller in a timely fashion (30 seconds). The listener task is a long-running background thread. The application can exit without stopping this thread:

```
public void Start()
{
  ReadQuotes();

  listenerTask = Task.Factory.StartNew(Listener,
                    TaskCreationOptions.LongRunning);
}
```

The task function `Listener` creates a `TcpListener` instance. The `AcceptSocket` method waits for a client to connect. As soon as a client connects, `AcceptSocket` returns with a socket associated with the client. Next, `GetRandomQuoteOfTheDay` is called to send the returned random quote to the client using `socket.Send`:

```
protected void Listener()
{
  try
  {
    IPAddress ipAddress = IPAddress.Any;
    listener = new TcpListener(ipAddress, port);
    listener.Start();
    while (true)
    {
      Socket clientSocket = listener.AcceptSocket();
      string message = GetRandomQuoteOfTheDay();
      var encoder = new UnicodeEncoding();
      byte[] buffer = encoder.GetBytes(message);
      clientSocket.Send(buffer, buffer.Length, 0);
```

```
          clientSocket.Close();
        }
      }
    catch (SocketException ex)
    {
      Trace.TraceError(String.Format("QuoteServer {0}", ex.Message));
      throw new QuoteException("socket error", ex);
    }
  }
```

In addition to the `Start` method, the following methods, `Stop`, `Suspend`, and `Resume`, are needed to control the service:

```
public void Stop()
{
  listener.Stop();
}
public void Suspend()
{
  listener.Stop();
}
public void Resume()
{
  Start();
}
```

Another method that will be publicly available is `RefreshQuotes`. If the file containing the quotes changes, the file is reread with this method:

```
public void RefreshQuotes()
{
  ReadQuotes();
}
  }
}
```

Before building a service around the server, it is useful to build a test program that creates just an instance of the `QuoteServer` and calls `Start`. This way, you can test the functionality without the need to handle service-specific issues. This test server must be started manually, and you can easily walk through the code with a debugger.

The test program is a C# console application, `TestQuoteServer`. You need to reference the assembly of the `QuoteServer` class. The file containing the quotes must be copied to the directory `C:\ProCSharp\Services` (or you can change the argument in the constructor to specify where you have copied the file). After calling the constructor, the `Start` method of the `QuoteServer` instance is called. `Start` returns immediately after having created a thread, so the console application keeps running until `Return` is pressed (code file `TestQuoteServer/Program.cs`):

```
static void Main()
{
  var qs = new QuoteServer("quotes.txt", 4567);
  qs.Start();
  Console.WriteLine("Hit return to exit");
  Console.ReadLine();
  qs.Stop();
}
```

Note that `QuoteServer` will be running on port 4567 on localhost using this program — you will have to use these settings in the client later.

QuoteClient Example

The client is a simple WPF Windows application in which you can request quotes from the server. This application uses the `TcpClient` class to connect to the running server, and receives the returned message, displaying it in a text box. The user interface contains two controls: a `Button` and a `TextBlock`. Clicking the button requests the quote from the server, and the quote is displayed.

With the `Button` control, the `Click` event is assigned to the method `OnGetQuote`, which requests the quote from the server, and the `IsEnabled` property is bound to the `EnableRequest` method to disable the button while a request is active. With the `TextBlock` control, the `Text` property is bound to the `Quote` property to display the quote that is set:

```
<Button Margin="3" VerticalAlignment="Stretch" Grid.Row="0"
        IsEnabled="{Binding EnableRequest}" Click="OnGetQuote">
    Get Quote</Button>
<TextBlock Margin="6" Grid.Row="1" TextWrapping="Wrap"
        Text="{Binding Quote}" />
```

The information that is bound in the user interface, the properties `EnableRequest` and `Quote`, are defined within the class `QuoteInformation`. This class implements the interface `INotifyPropertyChanged` to enable WPF to receive changes in the property values:

```
using System.Collections.Generic;
using System.ComponentModel;
using System.Runtime.CompilerServices;

namespace Wrox.ProCSharp.WinServices
{
  public class QuoteInformation : INotifyPropertyChanged
  {
    public QuoteInformation()
    {
      EnableRequest = true;
    }
    private string quote;
    public string Quote
    {
      get
      {
        return quote;
      }
      internal set
      {
        SetProperty(ref quote, value);
      }
    }

    private bool enableRequest;
    public bool EnableRequest
    {
      get
      {
        return enableRequest;
      }
      internal set
      {
```

```
        SetProperty(ref enableRequest, value);
      }
    }

    private void SetProperty<T>(ref T field, T value,
                               [CallerMemberName] string propertyName = "")
    {
      if (!EqualityComparer<T>.Default.Equals(field, value))
      {
        field = value;
        var handler = PropertyChanged;
        if (handler != null)
        {
          handler(this, new PropertyChangedEventArgs(propertyName));
        }
      }
    }

    public event PropertyChangedEventHandler PropertyChanged;
  }
}
```

> **NOTE** *Implementation of the interface* `INotifyPropertyChanged` *makes use of the attribute* `CallerMemberNameAttribute`. *This attribute is explained in Chapter 16, "Errors and Exceptions."*

An instance of the class `QuoteInformation` is assigned to the `DataContext` of the Window class `QuoteClientWindow` to allow direct data binding to it (code file `QuoteClient/MainWindow.xaml.cs`):

```
using System;
using System.Net.Sockets;
using System.Text;
using System.Windows;
using System.Windows.Input;

namespace Wrox.ProCSharp.WinServices
{
  public partial class QuoteClientWindow : Window
  {
    private QuoteInformation quoteInfo = new QuoteInformation();

    public QuoteClientWindow()
    {
      InitializeComponent();
      this.DataContext = quoteInfo;
    }
```

You can configure server and port information to connect to the server from the Settings tab inside the properties of the project (see Figure 27-5). Here, you can define default values for the ServerName and PortNumber settings. With the Scope set to User, the settings can be placed in user-specific configuration files, so every user of the application can have different settings. This Settings feature of Visual Studio also creates a `Settings` class so that the settings can be read and written with a strongly typed class.

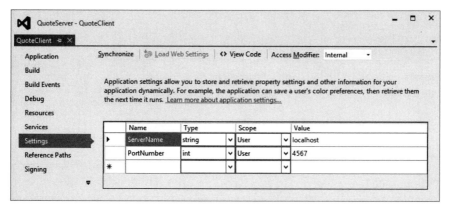

FIGURE 27-5

The major functionality of the client lies in the handler for the `Click` event of the Get Quote button:

```
protected async void OnGetQuote(object sender, RoutedEventArgs e)
{
  const int bufferSize = 1024;
  Cursor currentCursor = this.Cursor;
  this.Cursor = Cursors.Wait;
  quoteInfo.EnableRequest = false;

  string serverName = Properties.Settings.Default.ServerName;
  int port = Properties.Settings.Default.PortNumber;

  var client = new TcpClient();
  NetworkStream stream = null;
  try
  {
    await client.ConnectAsync(serverName, port);
    stream = client.GetStream();
    byte[] buffer = new byte[bufferSize];
    int received = await stream.ReadAsync(buffer, 0, bufferSize);
    if (received <= 0)
    {
      return;
    }
    quoteInfo.Quote = Encoding.Unicode.GetString(buffer).Trim('\0');
  }
  catch (SocketException ex)
  {
    MessageBox.Show(ex.Message, "Error Quote of the day",
        MessageBoxButton.OK, MessageBoxImage.Error);
  }
  finally
  {
    if (stream != null)
    {
      stream.Close();
    }

    if (client.Connected)
    {
      client.Close();
    }
```

```
        }
        this.Cursor = currentCursor;
        quoteInfo.EnableRequest = true;
    }
```

After starting the test server and this Windows application client, you can test the functionality. Figure 27-6 shows a successful run of this application.

At this point, you need to implement the service functionality in the server. The program is already running, so now you want to ensure that the server program starts automatically at boot time without anyone logged on to the system. You can do that by creating a service program, which is discussed next.

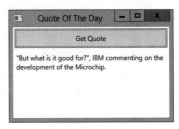

FIGURE 27-6

Windows Service Program

Using the C# Windows Service template from the Add New Project dialog, you can now create a Windows Service program. For the new service, use the name `QuoteService`.

After you click the OK button to create the Windows Service program, the designer surface appears but you can't insert any UI components because the application cannot directly display anything on the screen. The designer surface is used later in this chapter to add components such as installation objects, performance counters, and event logging.

Selecting the properties of this service opens the Properties dialog, where you can configure the following values:

➤ `AutoLog` — Specifies that events are automatically written to the event log for starting and stopping the service.

➤ `CanPauseAndContinue`, `CanShutdown`, and `CanStop` — Specify pause, continue, shut down, and stop requests.

➤ `ServiceName` — The name of the service written to the registry, and used to control the service.

➤ `CanHandleSessionChangeEvent` — Defines whether the service can handle change events from a terminal server session.

➤ `CanHandlePowerEvent` — This is a very useful option for services running on a laptop or mobile devices. If this option is enabled, the service can react to low-power events and change the behavior of the service accordingly. Examples of power events include battery low, power status change (because of a switch from or to A/C power), and change to suspend.

> **NOTE** *The default service name is* `Service1`, *regardless of what the project is called. You can install only one* `Service1` *service. If you get installation errors during your testing process, you might already have installed a* `Service1` *service. Therefore, ensure that you change the name of the service in the Properties dialog to a more suitable name at the beginning of the service's development.*

Changing these properties within the Properties dialog sets the values of your `ServiceBase`-derived class in the `InitalizeComponent` method. You already know this method from Windows Forms applications. It is used in a similar way with services.

A wizard generates the code but changes the filename to `QuoteService.cs`, the name of the namespace to `Wrox.ProCSharp.WinServices`, and the class name to `QuoteService`. The code of the service is discussed in detail shortly.

The ServiceBase Class

The ServiceBase class is the base class for all Windows Services developed with the .NET Framework. The class QuoteService is derived from ServiceBase; this class communicates with the SCM using an undocumented helper class, System.ServiceProcess.NativeMethods, which is just a wrapper class to the Windows API calls. The NativeMethods class is internal, so it cannot be used in your code.

The sequence diagram in Figure 27-7 shows the interaction of the SCM, the class QuoteService, and the classes from the System.ServiceProcess namespace. You can see the lifelines of objects vertically and the communication going on horizontally. The communication is time-ordered from top to bottom.

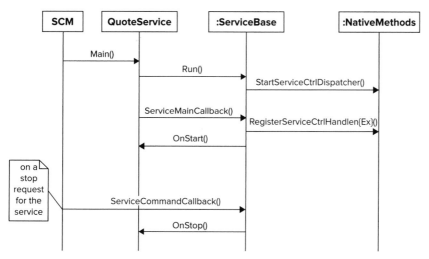

FIGURE 27-7

The SCM starts the process of a service that should be started. At startup, the Main method is called. In the Main method of the sample service, the Run method of the base class ServiceBase is called. Run registers the method ServiceMainCallback using NativeMethods.StartServiceCtrlDispatcher in the SCM and writes an entry to the event log.

Next, the SCM calls the registered method ServiceMainCallback in the service program. ServiceMainCallback itself registers the handler in the SCM using NativeMethods. RegisterServiceCtrlHandler[Ex] and sets the status of the service in the SCM. Then the OnStart method is called. In OnStart, you need to implement the startup code. If OnStart is successful, the string "Service started successfully" is written to the event log.

The handler is implemented in the ServiceCommandCallback method. The SCM calls this method when changes are requested from the service. The ServiceCommandCallback method routes the requests further to OnPause, OnContinue, OnStop, OnCustomCommand, and OnPowerEvent.

Main Function

This section looks into the application template–generated main function of the service process. In the main function, an array of ServiceBase classes, ServicesToRun, is declared. One instance of the QuoteService class is created and passed as the first element to the ServicesToRun array. If more than one service should run inside this service process, it is necessary to add more instances of the specific service classes to the array. This array is then passed to the static Run method of the ServiceBase class. With the Run method of ServiceBase, you are giving the SCM references to the entry points of your services. The main thread of your service process is now blocked and waits for the service to terminate.

Here is the automatically generated code (code file `QuoteService/Program.cs`):

```
/// <summary>
/// The main entry point for the application.
/// </summary>
static void Main()
{
    ServiceBase[] ServicesToRun;
    ServicesToRun = new ServiceBase[]
    {
        new QuoteService()
    };
    ServiceBase.Run(ServicesToRun);
}
```

If there is only a single service in the process, the array can be removed; the `Run` method accepts a single object derived from the class `ServiceBase`, so the `Main` method can be reduced to this:

```
ServiceBase.Run(new QuoteService());
```

The service program `Services.exe` includes multiple services. If you have a similar service, where more than one service is running in a single process in which you must initialize some shared state for multiple services, the shared initialization must be done before the `Run` method. With the `Run` method, the main thread is blocked until the service process is stopped, and any subsequent instructions are not reached before the end of the service.

The initialization shouldn't take longer than 30 seconds. If the initialization code were to take longer than this, the SCM would assume that the service startup failed. You need to take into account the slowest machines where this service should run within the 30-second limit. If the initialization takes longer, you could start the initialization in a different thread so that the main thread calls `Run` in time. An event object can then be used to signal that the thread has completed its work.

Service Start

At service start, the `OnStart` method is called. In this method, you can start the previously created socket server. You must reference the `QuoteServer` assembly for the use of the `QuoteService`. The thread calling `OnStart` cannot be blocked; this method must return to the caller, which is the `ServiceMainCallback` method of the `ServiceBase` class. The `ServiceBase` class registers the handler and informs the SCM that the service started successfully after calling `OnStart` (code file `QuoteService/QuoteService.cs`):

```
protected override void OnStart(string[] args)
{
    quoteServer = new QuoteServer(Path.Combine(
                    AppDomain.CurrentDomain.BaseDirectory, "quotes.txt"),
                    5678);
    quoteServer.Start();
}
```

The `quoteServer` variable is declared as a private member in the class:

```
namespace Wrox.ProCSharp.WinServices
{
    public partial class QuoteService: ServiceBase
    {
        private QuoteServer quoteServer;
```

Handler Methods

When the service is stopped, the OnStop method is called. You should stop the service functionality in this method:

```
protected override void OnStop()
{
  quoteServer.Stop();
}
```

In addition to OnStart and OnStop, you can override the following handlers in the service class:

➤ OnPause — Called when the service should be paused.

➤ OnContinue — Called when the service should return to normal operation after being paused. To make it possible for the overridden methods OnPause and OnContinue to be called, the CanPauseAndContinue property must be set to true.

➤ OnShutdown — Called when Windows is undergoing system shutdown. Normally, the behavior of this method should be similar to the OnStop implementation; if more time is needed for a shutdown, you can request more. Similarly to OnPause and OnContinue, a property must be set to enable this behavior: CanShutdown must be set to true.

➤ OnPowerEvent — Called when the power status of the system changes. Information about the change of the power status is in the argument of type PowerBroadcastStatus. PowerBroadcastStatus is an enumeration with values such as Battery Low and PowerStatusChange. Here, you will also get information if the system would like to suspend (QuerySuspend), which you can approve or deny. You can read more about power events later in this chapter.

➤ OnCustomCommand — This is a handler that can serve custom commands sent by a service control program. The method signature of OnCustomCommand has an int argument where you retrieve the custom command number. The value can be in the range from 128 to 256; values below 128 are system-reserved values. In your service, you are rereading the quotes file with the custom command 128:

```
protected override void OnPause()
{
  quoteServer.Suspend();
}

protected override void OnContinue()
{
  quoteServer.Resume();
}

public const int commandRefresh = 128;
protected override void OnCustomCommand(int command)
{
  switch (command)
  {
    case commandRefresh:
      quoteServer.RefreshQuotes();
      break;

    default:
      break;
  }
}
```

Threading and Services

As stated earlier in this chapter, the SCM assumes that the service failed if the initialization takes too long. To deal with this, you need to create a thread.

The OnStart method in your service class must return in time. If you call a blocking method such as AcceptSocket from the TcpListener class, you need to start a thread to do so. With a networking server that deals with multiple clients, a thread pool is also very useful. AcceptSocket should receive the call and hand the processing off to another thread from the pool. This way, no one waits for the execution of code and the system seems responsive.

Service Installation

Services must be configured in the registry. All services are found in HKEY_LOCAL_MACHINE\System\CurrentControlSet\Services. You can view the registry entries by using regedit. Found here are the type of the service, the display name, the path to the executable, the startup configuration, and so on. Figure 27-8 shows the registry configuration of the W3SVC service.

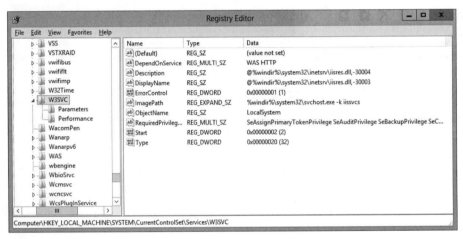

FIGURE 27-8

This configuration can be done by using the installer classes from the System.ServiceProcess namespace, as discussed in the following section.

Installation Program

You can add an installation program to the service by switching to the design view with Visual Studio and then selecting the Add Installer option from the context menu. With this option, a new ProjectInstaller class is created, along with a ServiceInstaller instance and a ServiceProcessInstaller instance.

Figure 27-9 shows the class diagram of the installer classes for services.

Keep this diagram in mind as we go through the source code in the file ProjectInstaller.cs that was created with the Add Installer option.

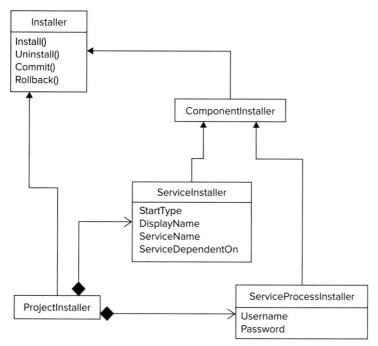

FIGURE 27-9

The Installer Class

The class `ProjectInstaller` is derived from `System.Configuration.Install.Installer`. This is the base class for all custom installers. With the `Installer` class, it is possible to build transaction-based installations. With a transaction-based installation, you can roll back to the previous state if the installation fails, and any changes made by this installation up to that point will be undone. As shown earlier in Figure 27-9, the `Installer` class has `Install`, `Uninstall`, `Commit`, and `Rollback` methods, and they are called from installation programs.

The attribute `[RunInstaller(true)]` means that the class `ProjectInstaller` should be invoked when installing an assembly. Custom action installers, as well as `installutil.exe` (which is used later in this chapter), check for this attribute.

`InitializeComponent` is called inside the constructor of the `ProjectInstaller` class:

```
using System.ComponentModel;
using System.Configuration.Install;

namespace Wrox.ProCSharp.WinServices
{
  [RunInstaller(true)]
  public partial class ProjectInstaller: Installer
  {
    public ProjectInstaller()
    {
      InitializeComponent();
    }
  }
}
```

Now let's move to the other installers of the installation program that are invoked by the project installer.

Process Installer and Service Installer

Within the implementation of InitializeComponent, instances of the ServiceProcessInstaller class and the ServiceInstaller class are created. Both of these classes derive from the ComponentInstaller class, which itself derives from Installer.

Classes derived from ComponentInstaller can be used with an installation process. Remember that a service process can include more than one service. The ServiceProcessInstaller class is used for the configuration of the process that defines values for all services in this process, and the ServiceInstaller class is for the configuration of the service, so one instance of ServiceInstaller is required for each service. If three services are inside the process, you need to add three ServiceInstaller objects:

```
partial class ProjectInstaller
{
  /// <summary>
  /// Required designer variable.
  /// </summary>
  private System.ComponentModel.IContainer components = null;

  /// <summary>
  /// Required method for Designer supportdo not modify
  /// the contents of this method with the code editor.
  /// </summary>
  private void InitializeComponent()
  {
    this.serviceProcessInstaller1 =
        new System.ServiceProcess.ServiceProcessInstaller();
    this.serviceInstaller1 =
        new System.ServiceProcess.ServiceInstaller();
    //
    // serviceProcessInstaller1
    //
    this.serviceProcessInstaller1.Password = null;
    this.serviceProcessInstaller1.Username = null;
    //
    // serviceInstaller1
    //
    this.serviceInstaller1.ServiceName = "QuoteService";
    //
    // ProjectInstaller
    //
    this.Installers.AddRange(
      new System.Configuration.Install.Installer[]
          {this.serviceProcessInstaller1,
           this.serviceInstaller1});
  }

  private System.ServiceProcess.ServiceProcessInstaller
      serviceProcessInstaller1;
  private System.ServiceProcess.ServiceInstaller serviceInstaller1;

}
```

ServiceProcessInstaller installs an executable that implements the class ServiceBase.Service ProcessInstaller has properties for the complete process. The following table describes the properties shared by all the services inside the process.

PROPERTY	DESCRIPTION
Username, Password	Indicates the user account under which the service runs if the Account property is set to ServiceAccount.User.
Account	With this property, you can specify the account type of the service.
HelpText	A read-only property that returns the help text for setting the username and password.

The process that is used to run the service can be specified with the Account property of the ServiceProcessInstaller class using the ServiceAccount enumeration. The following table describes the different values of the Account property.

VALUE	DESCRIPTION
LocalSystem	Setting this value specifies that the service uses a highly privileged user account on the local system, and acts as the computer on the network.
NetworkService	Similarly to LocalSystem, this value specifies that the computer's credentials are passed to remote servers; but unlike LocalSystem, such a service acts as a nonprivileged user on the local system. As the name implies, this account should be used only for services that need resources from the network.
LocalService	This account type presents anonymous credentials to any remote server and has the same privileges locally as NetworkService.
User	Setting the Account property to ServiceAccount.User means that you can define the account that should be used from the service.

ServiceInstaller is the class needed for every service; it has the following properties for each service inside a process: StartType, DisplayName, ServiceName, and ServicesDependentOn, as described in the following table.

PROPERTY	DESCRIPTION
StartTypev	The StartType property indicates whether the service is manually or automatically started. Possible values are ServiceStartMode.Automatic, ServiceStartMode.Manual, and ServiceStartMode.Disabled. With the last one, the service cannot be started. This option is useful for services that shouldn't be started on a system. You might want to set the option to Disabled if, for example, a required hardware controller is not available.
DelayedAutoStart	This property is ignored if the StartType is not set to Automatic. Here, you can specify that the service should not be started immediately when the system boots but afterward.

continues

(continued)

PROPERTY	DESCRIPTION
DisplayName	DisplayName is the friendly name of the service that is displayed to the user. This name is also used by management tools that control and monitor the service.
ServiceName	ServiceName is the name of the service. This value must be identical to the ServiceName property of the ServiceBase class in the service program. This name associates the configuration of the ServiceInstaller to the required service program.
ServicesDependentOn	Specifies an array of services that must be started before this service can be started. When the service is started, all these dependent services are started automatically, and then your service will start.

> **NOTE** *If you change the name of the service in the* ServiceBase-*derived class, be sure to also change the* ServiceName *property in the* ServiceInstaller *object!*

> **NOTE** *In the testing phases, set* StartType *to* Manual. *This way, if you can't stop the service (for example, when it has a bug), you still have the possibility to reboot the system; but if you have* StartType *set to* Automatic, *the service would be started automatically with the reboot! You can change this configuration later when you are sure that it works.*

The ServiceInstallerDialog Class

Another installer class in the System.ServiceProcess.Design namespace is ServiceInstallerDialog. This class can be used if you want the system administrator to enter the account that the service should use by assigning the username and password during the installation.

FIGURE 27-10

If you set the Account property of the class ServiceProcessInstaller to ServiceAccount.User and the Username and Password properties to null, you will see the Set Service Login dialog at installation time (see Figure 27-10). You can also cancel the installation at this point.

installutil

After adding the installer classes to the project, you can use the installutil.exe utility to install and uninstall the service. This utility can be used to install any assembly that has an Installer class. The installutil.exe utility calls the method Install of the class that derives from the Installer class for installation, and Uninstall for the uninstallation.

The command-line inputs for the installation and uninstallation of our example service are as follows:

```
installutil quoteservice.exe
installutil /u quoteservice.exe
```

> **NOTE** *If the installation fails, be sure to check the installation log files,* InstallUtil *.*InstallLog *and* <servicename>.InstallLog. *Often, you can find very useful information, such as* "The specified service already exists."

After the service has been successfully installed, you can start the service manually from the Services MMC (see the next section for details), and then you can start the client application.

MONITORING AND CONTROLLING WINDOWS SERVICES

To monitor and control Windows Services, you can use the Services Microsoft Management Console (MMC) snap-in that is part of the Computer Management administration tool. Every Windows system also has a command-line utility, net.exe, which enables you to control services. Another Windows command-line utility is sc.exe. This utility has much more functionality than net.exe. You can also control services directly from the Visual Studio Server Explorer. In this section, you also create a small Windows application that makes use of the System.ServiceProcess.ServiceController class to monitor and control services.

MMC Snap-in

Using the Services snap-in to the MMC, you can view the status of all services (see Figure 27-11). It is also possible to send control requests to services to stop, enable, or disable them, as well as to change their configuration. The Services snap-in is a service control program as well as a service configuration program.

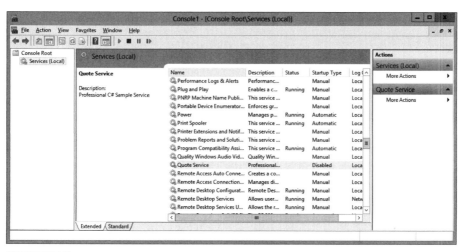

FIGURE 27-11

Double-click QuoteService to get the Properties dialog shown in Figure 27-12. From here you can view the service name, the description, the path to the executable, the startup type, and the status. The service is currently started. The account for the service process can be changed by selecting the Log On tab in this dialog.

FIGURE 27-12

net.exe Utility

The Services snap-in is easy to use, but system administrators cannot automate it because it is not usable within an administrative script. To control services with a tool that can be automated with a script, you can use the command-line utility `net.exe`. The `net start` command shows all running services, `net start servicename` starts a service, and `net stop servicename` sends a stop request to the service. It is also possible to pause and to continue a service with `net pause` and `net continue` (if the service allows it, of course).

sc.exe Utility

Another little-known utility delivered as part of the operating system is `sc.exe`. This is a great tool for working with services. Much more can be done with `sc.exe` than with the `net.exe` utility. With `sc.exe`, you can check the actual status of a service, or configure, remove, and add services. This tool also facilitates the uninstallation of the service if it fails to function correctly.

Visual Studio Server Explorer

To control services using the Server Explorer within Visual Studio, select Servers from the tree view, and then select your computer, then the Services element and the desired service. By selecting a service and opening the context menu, you can start or stop a service. This context menu can also be used to add a `ServiceController` class to the project.

To control a specific service in your application, drag-and-drop a service from the Server Explorer to the designer: a `ServiceController` instance is added to the application. The properties of this object are automatically set to access the selected service, and the assembly `System.ServiceProcess` is referenced. You can use this instance to control a service in the same way that you can with the application developed in the next section.

Writing a Custom Service Controller

In this section, you create a small Windows application that uses the `ServiceController` class to monitor and control Windows Services.

Create a WPF application with a user interface as shown in Figure 27-13. The main window of this application has a list box to display all services, four text boxes to show the display name, status, type, and name of the service, and six buttons. Four buttons are used to send control events, one button is used for a refresh of the list, and one button is used to exit the application.

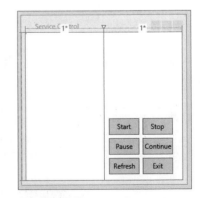

FIGURE 27-13

> **NOTE** *You can read more about WPF in Chapter 35, "Core WPF."*

Monitoring the Service

With the `ServiceController` class, you can get information about each service. The following table shows the properties of the `ServiceController` class:

PROPERTY	DESCRIPTION
CanPauseAndContinue	Returns `true` if pause and continue requests can be sent to the service.
CanShutdown	Returns `true` if the service has a handler for a system shutdown.
CanStop	Returns `true` if the service is stoppable.
DependentServices	Returns a collection of dependent services. If the service is stopped, then all dependent services are stopped beforehand.
ServicesDependentOn	Returns a collection of the services on which this service depends.
DisplayName	Specifies the name that should be displayed for this service.
MachineName	Specifies the name of the machine on which the service runs.
ServiceName	Specifies the name of the service.
ServiceType	Specifies the type of the service. The service can be run inside a shared process, whereby more than one service uses the same process (`Win32ShareProcess`), or run in such a way that there is just one service in a process (`Win32OwnProcess`). If the service can interact with the desktop, the type is `InteractiveProcess`.
Status	Specifies the service's status, which can be running, stopped, paused, or in some intermediate mode such as start pending, stop pending, and so on. The status values are defined in the enumeration `ServiceControllerStatus`.

In the sample application, the properties `DisplayName`, `ServiceName`, `ServiceType`, and `Status` are used to display the service information. `CanPauseAndContinue` and `CanStop` are used to enable or disable the Pause, Continue, and Stop buttons.

To get all the needed information for the user interface, the class `ServiceControllerInfo` is created. This class can be used for data binding and offers status information, the name of the service, the service type, and information about which buttons to control the service should be enabled or disabled.

> **NOTE** *Because the class* `System.ServiceProcess.ServiceController` *is used, you must reference the assembly* `System.ServiceProcess`.

`ServiceControllerInfo` contains an embedded `ServiceController` that is set with the constructor of the `ServiceControllerInfo` class. There is also a read-only property `Controller` to access the embedded `ServiceController` (code file `ServiceControl/ServiceControllerInfo.cs`):

```
public class ServiceControllerInfo
{
  private readonly ServiceController controller;

  public ServiceControllerInfo(ServiceController controller)
  {
    this.controller = controller;
  }

  public ServiceController Controller
  {
    get { return controller; }
  }
```

To display current information about the service, the `ServiceControllerInfo` class has the read-only properties `DisplayName`, `ServiceName`, `ServiceTypeName`, and `ServiceStatusName`. The implementation of the properties `DisplayName` and `ServiceName` just accesses the properties of those names of the underlying `ServiceController` class. With the implementation of the properties `ServiceTypeName` and `ServiceStatusName`, more work is needed — the status and type of the service cannot be returned that easily because a string should be displayed instead of a number, which is what the `ServiceController` class returns. The property `ServiceTypeName` returns a string that represents the type of the service. The `ServiceType` you get from the property `ServiceController.ServiceType` represents a set of flags that can be combined by using the bitwise `OR` operator. The `InteractiveProcess` bit can be set together with `Win32OwnProcess` and `Win32ShareProcess`. Therefore, the first check determines whether the `InteractiveProcess` bit is set before continuing to check for the other values. With services, the string returned will be `"Win32 Service Process"` or `"Win32 Shared Process"`:

```
public string ServiceTypeName
{
  get
  {
    ServiceType type = controller.ServiceType;
    string serviceTypeName = "";
    if ((type & ServiceType.InteractiveProcess) != 0)
    {
      serviceTypeName = "Interactive ";
      type -= ServiceType.InteractiveProcess;
    }
    switch (type)
    {
      case ServiceType.Adapter:
        serviceTypeName += "Adapter";
        break;

      case ServiceType.FileSystemDriver:
      case ServiceType.KernelDriver:
      case ServiceType.RecognizerDriver:
        serviceTypeName += "Driver";
        break;

      case ServiceType.Win32OwnProcess:
        serviceTypeName += "Win32 Service Process";
        break;

      case ServiceType.Win32ShareProcess:
```

```
            serviceTypeName += "Win32 Shared Process";
            break;

          default:
            serviceTypeName += "unknown type " + type.ToString();
            break;
      }
      return serviceTypeName;
    }
}

public string ServiceStatusName
{
  get
  {
    switch (controller.Status)
    {
      case ServiceControllerStatus.ContinuePending:
        return "Continue Pending";
      case ServiceControllerStatus.Paused:
        return "Paused";
      case ServiceControllerStatus.PausePending:
        return "Pause Pending";
      case ServiceControllerStatus.StartPending:
        return "Start Pending";
      case ServiceControllerStatus.Running:
        return "Running";
      case ServiceControllerStatus.Stopped:
        return "Stopped";
      case ServiceControllerStatus.StopPending:
        return "Stop Pending";
      default:
        return "Unknown status";
    }
  }
}

public string DisplayName
{
  get { return controller.DisplayName; }
}

public string ServiceName
{
  get { return controller.ServiceName; }
}
```

The ServiceControllerInfo class has some other properties to enable the Start, Stop, Pause, and Continue buttons: EnableStart, EnableStop, EnablePause, and EnableContinue. These properties return a Boolean value according to the current status of the service:

```
public bool EnableStart
{
  get
  {
    return controller.Status == ServiceControllerStatus.Stopped;
  }
}

public bool EnableStop
{
```

```
      get
      {
        return controller.Status == ServiceControllerStatus.Running;
      }
    }

    public bool EnablePause
    {
      get
      {
        return controller.Status == ServiceControllerStatus.Running &&
          controller.CanPauseAndContinue;
      }
    }

    public bool EnableContinue
    {
      get
      {
        return controller.Status == ServiceControllerStatus.Paused;
      }
    }
  }
```

In the `ServiceControlWindow` class, the method `RefreshServiceList` gets all the services using `ServiceController.GetServices` for display in the list box. The `GetServices` method returns an array of `ServiceController` instances representing all Windows Services installed on the operating system. The `ServiceController` class also has the static method `GetDevices` that returns a `ServiceController` array representing all device drivers. The returned array is sorted with the help of the extension method `OrderBy`. The sort is done by the `DisplayName` as defined with the Lambda expression that is passed to the `OrderBy` method. Using `Select`, the `ServiceController` instances are converted to the type `ServiceControllerInfo`. In the following code, a Lambda expression is passed that invokes the `ServiceControllerInfo` constructor for every `ServiceController` object. Last, the result is assigned to the `DataContext` property of the window for data binding (code file `ServiceControl/ServiceControlWindow.xaml.cs`):

```
    protected void RefreshServiceList()
    {
      this.DataContext = ServiceController.GetServices().
        OrderBy(sc => sc.DisplayName).
        Select(sc => new ServiceControllerInfo(sc));
    }
```

The method `RefreshServiceList`, to get all the services in the list box, is called within the constructor of the class `ServiceControlWindow`. The constructor also defines the event handler for the `Click` event of the buttons:

```
    public ServiceControlWindow()
    {
     InitializeComponent();

     RefreshServiceList();
    }
```

Now, you can define the XAML code to bind the information to the controls. First, a `DataTemplate` is defined for the information that is shown inside the `ListBox`. The `ListBox` will contain a `Label` in which the `Content` is bound to the `DisplayName` property of the data source. As you bind an array of

`ServiceControllerInfo` objects, the property `DisplayName` is defined with the `ServiceControllerInfo` class:

```
<Window.Resources>
  <DataTemplate x:Key="listTemplate">
    <Label Content="{Binding DisplayName}"/>
  </DataTemplate>
</Window.Resources>
```

The `ListBox` that is placed in the left side of the window sets the `ItemsSource` property to `{Binding}`. This way, the data that is shown in the list is received from the `DataContext` property that was set in the `RefreshServiceList` method. The `ItemTemplate` property references the resource `listTemplate` that is defined with the `DataTemplate` shown earlier. The property `IsSynchronizedWithCurrentItem` is set to `True` so that the `TextBox` and `Button` controls inside the same window are bound to the current item selected with the `ListBox`:

```
<ListBox Grid.Row="0" Grid.Column="0" HorizontalAlignment="Left"
  Name="listBoxServices" VerticalAlignment="Top"
  ItemsSource="{Binding}"
  ItemTemplate="{StaticResource listTemplate}"
  IsSynchronizedWithCurrentItem="True">
</ListBox>
```

To differentiate the `Button` controls to start/stop/pause/continue the service, the following enumeration is defined (code file `ServiceControl/ButtonState.cs`):

```
public enum ButtonState
{
  Start,
  Stop,
  Pause,
  Continue
}
```

With the `TextBlock` controls, the `Text` property is bound to the corresponding property of the `ServiceControllerInfo` instance. Whether the `Button` controls are enabled or disabled is also defined from the data binding by binding the `IsEnabled` property to the corresponding properties of the `ServiceControllerInfo` instance that return a Boolean value. The `Tag` property of the buttons is assigned to a value of the `ButtonState` enumeration defined earlier to differentiate the button within the same handler method `OnServiceCommand`:

```
<TextBlock Grid.Row="0" Grid.ColumnSpan="2"
  Text="{Binding /DisplayName, Mode=OneTime}" />
<TextBlock Grid.Row="1" Grid.ColumnSpan="2"
  Text="{Binding /ServiceStatusName, Mode=OneTime}" />
<TextBlock Grid.Row="2" Grid.ColumnSpan="2"
  Text="{Binding /ServiceTypeName, Mode=OneTime}" />
<TextBlock Grid.Row="3" Grid.ColumnSpan="2"
  Text="{Binding /ServiceName, Mode=OneTime}" />
<Button Grid.Row="4" Grid.Column="0" Content="Start"
  IsEnabled="{Binding /EnableStart, Mode=OneTime}"
  Tag="{x:Static local:ButtonState.Start}"
  Click="OnServiceCommand" />
<Button Grid.Row="4" Grid.Column="1" Name="buttonStop" Content="Stop"
  IsEnabled="{Binding /EnableStop, Mode=OneTime}"
  Tag="{x:Static local:ButtonState.Stop}"
  Click="OnServiceCommand" />
<Button Grid.Row="5" Grid.Column="0" Name="buttonPause" Content="Pause"
```

```
          IsEnabled="{Binding /EnablePause, Mode=OneTime}"
          Tag="{x:Static local:ButtonState.Pause}"
          Click="OnServiceCommand" />
      <Button Grid.Row="5" Grid.Column="1" Name="buttonContinue"
        Content="Continue"
        IsEnabled="{Binding /EnableContinue,
        Tag="{x:Static local:ButtonState.Continue}"
        Mode=OneTime}" Click="OnServiceCommand" />
      <Button Grid.Row="6" Grid.Column="0" Name="buttonRefresh"
        Content="Refresh"
        Click="OnRefresh" />
      <Button Grid.Row="6" Grid.Column="1" Name="buttonExit"
        Content="Exit" Click="OnExit" />
```

Controlling the Service

With the `ServiceController` class, you can also send control requests to the service. The following table describes the methods that can be applied:

METHOD	DESCRIPTION
Start	Tells the SCM that the service should be started. In the example service program, `OnStart` is called.
Stop	Calls `OnStop` in the example service program with the help of the SCM if the property `CanStop` is `true` in the service class.
Pause	Calls `OnPause` if the property `CanPauseAndContinue` is `true`.
Continue	Calls `OnContinue` if the property `CanPauseAndContinue` is `true`.
ExecuteCommand	Enables sending a custom command to the service.

The following code controls the services. Because the code for starting, stopping, suspending, and pausing is similar, only one handler is used for the four buttons:

```
protected void OnServiceCommand(object sender, RoutedEventArgs e)
{
  Cursor oldCursor = this.Cursor;
  try
  {
    this.Cursor = Cursors.Wait;
    ButtonState currentButtonState = (ButtonState)(sender as Button).Tag;

    var si = listBoxServices.SelectedItem as ServiceControllerInfo;
    if (currentButtonState == ButtonState.Start)
    {
      si.Controller.Start();
      si.Controller.WaitForStatus(ServiceControllerStatus.Running,
          TimeSpan.FromSeconds(10));
    }
    else if (currentButtonState == ButtonState.Stop)
    {
      si.Controller.Stop();
      si.Controller.WaitForStatus(ServiceControllerStatus.Stopped,
      TimeSpan.FromSeconds(10));
    }
```

```
            else if (currentButtonState == ButtonState.Pause)
            {
              si.Controller.Pause();
              si.Controller.WaitForStatus(ServiceControllerStatus.Paused,
                  TimeSpan.FromSeconds(10));
            }
            else if (currentButtonState == ButtonState.Continue)
            {
              si.Controller.Continue();
              si.Controller.WaitForStatus(ServiceControllerStatus.Running,
                  TimeSpan.FromSeconds(10));
            }
            int index = listBoxServices.SelectedIndex;
            RefreshServiceList();
            listBoxServices.SelectedIndex = index;
          }
          catch (System.ServiceProcess.TimeoutException ex)
          {
            MessageBox.Show(ex.Message, "Timout Service Controller",
            MessageBoxButton.OK, MessageBoxImage.Error);
          }
          catch (InvalidOperationException ex)
          {
            MessageBox.Show(String.Format("{0} {1}", ex.Message,
              ex.InnerException != null ? ex.InnerException.Message :
                String.Empty), MessageBoxButton.OK, MessageBoxImage.Error);
          }
          finally
          {
            this.Cursor = oldCursor;
          }
        }

        protected void OnExit(object sender, RoutedEventArgs e)
        {
          Application.Current.Shutdown();
        }

        protected void OnRefresh_Click(object sender, RoutedEventArgs e)
        {
          RefreshServiceList();
        }
```

Because the action of controlling the services can take some time, the cursor is switched to the wait cursor in the first statement. Then a `ServiceController` method is called depending on the pressed button. With the `WaitForStatus` method, you are waiting to confirm that the service changes the status to the requested value, but the wait maximum is only 10 seconds. After that, the information in the `ListBox` is refreshed, and the selected index is set to the same value as it was before. The new status of this service is then displayed.

Because the application requires administrative privileges, just as most services require that for starting and stopping, an application manifest with the `requestedExecutionLevel` set to `requireAdministrator` is added to the project (application manifest file `ServiceControl/app.manifest`):

```xml
<?xml version="1.0" encoding="utf-8"?>
<asmv1:assembly manifestVersion="1.0"
    xmlns="urn:schemas-microsoft-com:asm.v1"
    xmlns:asmv1="urn:schemas-microsoft-com:asm.v1"
    xmlns:asmv2="urn:schemas-microsoft-com:asm.v2"
    xmlns:xsi="http://www.w3.org/2001/XMLSchema-instance">
  <assemblyIdentity version="1.0.0.0" name="MyApplication.app"/>
```

```
<trustInfo xmlns="urn:schemas-microsoft-com:asm.v2">
  <security>
    <requestedPrivileges xmlns="urn:schemas-microsoft-com:asm.v3">
      <requestedExecutionLevel level="requireAdministrator"
          uiAccess="false" />
    </requestedPrivileges>
  </security>
</trustInfo>
</asmv1:assembly>
```

Figure 27-14 shows the completed, running application.

TROUBLESHOOTING AND EVENT LOGGING

Troubleshooting services is different from troubleshooting other types of applications. This section touches on some service issues, problems specific to interactive services, and event logging.

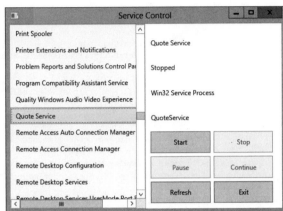

FIGURE 27-14

The best way to start building a service is to create an assembly with the functionality you want and a test client, before the service is actually created. Here, you can do normal debugging and error handling. As soon as the application is running, you can build a service by using this assembly. Of course, there might still be problems with the service:

➤ Don't display errors in a message box from the service (except for interactive services that are running on the client system). Instead, use the event logging service to write errors to the event log. Of course, in the client application that uses the service, you can display a message box to inform the user about errors.

➤ The service cannot be started from within a debugger, but a debugger can be attached to the running service process. Open the solution with the source code of the service and set breakpoints. From the Visual Studio Debug menu, select Processes and attach the running process of the service.

➤ Performance Monitor can be used to monitor the activity of services, and you can add your own performance objects to the service. This can add some useful information for debugging. For example, with the Quote service, you could set up an object to provide the total number of quotes returned, the time it takes to initialize, and so on.

Services can report errors and other information by adding events to the event log. A service class derived from `ServiceBase` automatically logs events when the `AutoLog` property is set to `true`. The `ServiceBase` class checks this property and writes a log entry at start, stop, pause, and continue requests.

Figure 27-15 shows an example of a log entry from a service.

FIGURE 27-15

> **NOTE** *You can read more about event logging and how to write custom events in Chapter 20, "Diagnostics."*

SUMMARY

In this chapter, you have seen the architecture of Windows Services and how you can create them with the .NET Framework. Applications can start automatically at boot time with Windows Services, and you can use a privileged system account as the user of the service. Windows Services are built from a main function, a service-main function, and a handler; and you looked at other relevant programs in regard to Windows Services, such as a service control program and a service installation program.

The .NET Framework has great support for Windows Services. All the plumbing code that is necessary for building, controlling, and installing services is built into the .NET Framework classes in the System.ServiceProcess namespace. By deriving a class from ServiceBase, you can override methods that are invoked when the service is paused, resumed, or stopped. For installation of services, the classes ServiceProcessInstaller and ServiceInstaller deal with all registry configurations needed for services. You can also control and monitor services by using ServiceController.

In the next chapter you can read about globalization and localization features of .NET, which are useful if your applications are used in different regions and with different languages.

28

Localization?

WROX.COM CODE DOWNLOADS FOR THIS CHAPTER

The wrox.com code downloads for this chapter are found at http://www.wrox.com/remtitle
.cgi?isbn=1118314425 on the Download Code tab. The code for this chapter is divided into the
following major examples:

➤ NumberAndDateFormatting

➤ CreateResource

➤ CultureDemo

➤ BookOfTheDay

➤ DatabaseResourceReader

➤ CustomCultures

GLOBAL MARKETS

NASA's Mars Climate Orbiter was lost on September 23, 1999, at a cost of $125 million, because
one engineering team used metric units while another one used inches for a key spacecraft operation.
When writing applications for international distribution, different cultures and regions must be kept
in mind.

Different cultures have diverging calendars and use different number and date formats; and sorting strings may lead to various results because the order of A–Z is defined differently based on the culture. To make usable applications for global markets, you have to globalize and localize them.

This chapter covers the globalization and localization of .NET applications. *Globalization* is about internationalizing applications: preparing applications for international markets. With globalization, the application supports number and date formats that vary according to culture, calendars, and so on. *Localization* is about translating applications for specific cultures. For translations of strings, you can use resources such as .NET resources or WPF resource dictionaries.

.NET supports the globalization and localization of Windows and web applications. To globalize an application, you can use classes from the namespace System.Globalization; to localize an application, you can use resources supported by the namespace System.Resources.

NAMESPACE SYSTEM.GLOBALIZATION

The System.Globalization namespace holds all the culture and region classes necessary to support different date formats, different number formats, and even different calendars that are represented in classes such as GregorianCalendar, HebrewCalendar, JapaneseCalendar, and so on. By using these classes, you can display different representations according to the user's locale.

This section looks at the following issues and considerations when using the System.Globalization namespace:

➤ Unicode issues

➤ Cultures and regions

➤ An example showing all cultures and their characteristics

➤ Sorting

Unicode Issues

A Unicode character has 16 bits, so there is room for 65,536 characters. Is this enough for all languages currently used in information technology? In the case of the Chinese language, for example, more than 80,000 characters are needed. Fortunately, Unicode has been designed to deal with this issue. With Unicode you have to differentiate between base characters and combining characters. You can add multiple combining characters to a base character to build a single display character or a text element.

Take, for example, the Icelandic character Ogonek. Ogonek can be combined by using the base character 0x006F (Latin small letter o) and the combining characters 0x0328 (combining Ogonek) and 0x0304 (combining Macron), as shown in Figure 28-1. Combining characters are defined within ranges from 0x0300 to 0x0345. For American and European markets, predefined characters exist to facilitate dealing with special characters. The character Ogonek is also defined by the predefined character 0x01ED.

FIGURE 28-1

For Asian markets, where more than 80,000 characters are necessary for Chinese alone, such predefined characters do not exist. In Asian languages, you always have to deal with combining characters. The problem is getting the right number of display characters or text elements, and getting to the base characters instead of the combined characters. The namespace System.Globalization offers the class StringInfo, which you can use to deal with this issue.

The following table lists the static methods of the class StringInfo that help in dealing with combined characters.

METHOD	DESCRIPTION
GetNextTextElement	Returns the first text element (base character and all combining characters) of a specified string
GetTextElementEnumerator	Returns a TextElementEnumerator object that allows iterating all text elements of a string
ParseCombiningCharacters	Returns an integer array referencing all base characters of a string

> **NOTE** *A single display character can contain multiple Unicode characters. To address this issue, when you write applications that support international markets, don't use the data type* char; *use* string *instead. A* string *can hold a text element that contains both base characters and combining characters, whereas a* char *cannot.*

Cultures and Regions

The world is divided into multiple cultures and regions, and applications have to be aware of these cultural and regional differences. A culture is a set of preferences based on a user's language and cultural habits. RFC 1766 (http://www.ietf.org/rfc/rfc1766.txt) defines culture names that are used worldwide, depending on a language and a country or region. Some examples are en-AU, en-CA, en-GB, and en-US for the English language in Australia, Canada, the United Kingdom, and the United States, respectively.

Possibly the most important class in the System.Globalization namespace is CultureInfo. CultureInfo represents a culture and defines calendars, formatting of numbers and dates, and sorting strings used with the culture.

The class RegionInfo represents regional settings (such as the currency) and indicates whether the region uses the metric system. Some regions can use multiple languages. One example is the region of Spain, which has Basque (eu-ES), Catalan (ca-ES), Spanish (es-ES), and Galician (gl-ES) cultures. Similar to one region having multiple languages, one language can be spoken in different regions; for example, Spanish is spoken in Mexico, Spain, Guatemala, Argentina, and Peru, to name only a few countries.

Later in this chapter is a sample application that demonstrates these characteristics of cultures and regions.

Specific, Neutral, and Invariant Cultures

When using cultures in the .NET Framework, you have to differentiate between three types: *specific, neutral,* and *invariant* cultures. A specific culture is associated with a real, existing culture defined with RFC 1766, as described in the preceding section. A specific culture can be mapped to a neutral culture. For example, de is the neutral culture of the specific cultures de-AT, de-DE, de-CH, and others. de is shorthand for the German language (Deutsch); AT, DE, and CH are shorthand for the countries Austria, Germany, and Switzerland, respectively.

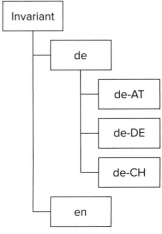

When translating applications, it is typically not necessary to do translations for every region; not much difference exists between the German language in the countries Austria and Germany. Instead of using specific cultures, you can use a neutral culture to localize applications.

The invariant culture is independent of a real culture. When storing formatted numbers or dates in files, or sending them across a network to a server, using a culture that is independent of any user settings is the best option.

Figure 28-2 shows how the culture types relate to each other.

FIGURE 28-2

CurrentCulture and CurrentUICulture

When you set cultures, you need to differentiate between a culture for the user interface and a culture for the number and date formats. Cultures are associated with a thread, and with these two culture types, two culture settings can be applied to a thread. The `Thread` class has the properties `CurrentCulture` and `CurrentUICulture`. The property `CurrentCulture` is for setting the culture that is used with formatting and sort options, whereas the property `CurrentUICulture` is used for the language of the user interface.

Users can change the default setting of the `CurrentCulture` by using the Region and Language options in the Windows control panel (see Figure 28-3). With this configuration, it is also possible to change the defaults for the number format, the time format, and the date format for the culture.

The `CurrentUICulture` does not depend on this configuration. The `CurrentUICulture` setting varies according to the language of the operating system. Other languages can be added from the Add Languages setting in the control panel, as shown in Figure 28-4.

FIGURE 28-3

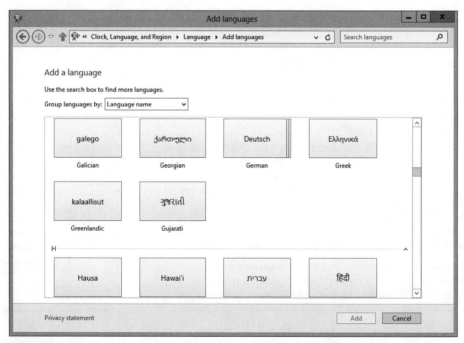

FIGURE 28-4

These settings provide a very good default, and in many cases you won't need to change the default behavior. If the culture should be changed, you can easily do this by changing both cultures of the thread to, say, the Spanish culture, as shown in this code snippet:

```
System.Globalization.CultureInfo ci = new
    System.Globalization.CultureInfo("es-ES");
System.Threading.Thread.CurrentThread.CurrentCulture = ci;
System.Threading.Thread.CurrentThread.CurrentUICulture = ci;
```

Now that you know how to set the culture, the following sections discuss number and date formatting, which are influenced by the CurrentCulture setting.

Number Formatting

The number structures Int16, Int32, Int64, and so on in the System namespace have an overloaded ToString method. This method can be used to create a different representation of the number, depending on the locale. For the Int32 structure, ToString is overloaded with the following four versions:

```
public string ToString();
public string ToString(IFormatProvider);
public string ToString(string);
public string ToString(string, IFormatProvider);
```

ToString without arguments returns a string without format options. You can also pass a string and a class that implements IFormatProvider.

The string specifies the format of the representation. The format can be a standard numeric formatting string or a picture numeric formatting string. For standard numeric formatting, strings are predefined in which C specifies the currency notation, D creates a decimal output, E creates scientific output, F creates fixed-point output, G creates general output, N creates number output, and X creates hexadecimal output. With a picture numeric formatting string, it is possible to specify the number of digits, section and group separators, percent notation, and so on. The picture numeric format string ###,### means two 3-digit blocks separated by a group separator.

The IFormatProvider interface is implemented by the NumberFormatInfo, DateTimeFormatInfo, and CultureInfo classes. This interface defines a single method, GetFormat, that returns a format object.

NumberFormatInfo can be used to define custom formats for numbers. With the default constructor of NumberFormatInfo, a culture-independent or invariant object is created. Using the properties of NumberFormatInfo, it is possible to change all the formatting options, such as a positive sign, a percent symbol, a number group separator, a currency symbol, and a lot more. A read-only, culture-independent NumberFormatInfo object is returned from the static property InvariantInfo. A NumberFormatInfo object in which the format values are based on the CultureInfo of the current thread is returned from the static property CurrentInfo.

To create the next example, you can start with a simple console project. In this code, the first example shows a number displayed in the format of the culture of the thread (here: English-US, the setting of the operating system). The second example uses the ToString method with the IFormatProvider argument. CultureInfo implements IFormatProvider, so create a CultureInfo object using the French culture. The third example changes the culture of the thread. The culture is changed to German by using the property CurrentCulture of the Thread instance (code file NumberAndDateFormatting\Program.cs):

```
using System;
using System.Globalization;
using System.Threading;

namespace NumberAndDateFormatting
{
```

```
class Program
{
  static void Main(string[] args)
  {
    NumberFormatDemo();
  }

  private static void NumberFormatDemo()
  {
    int val = 1234567890;

    // culture of the current thread
    Console.WriteLine(val.ToString("N"));

    // use IFormatProvider
    Console.WriteLine(val.ToString("N", new CultureInfo("fr-FR")));

    // change the culture of the thread
    Thread.CurrentThread.CurrentCulture = new CultureInfo("de-DE");
    Console.WriteLine(val.ToString("N"));
  }
}
```

You can compare the following different output for U.S. English, French, and German, respectively, shown here:

```
1,234,567,890.00
1 234 567 890,00
1.234.567.890,00
```

Date Formatting

The same support for numbers is available for dates. The `DateTime` structure has some methods for date-to-string conversions. The public instance methods `ToLongDateString`, `ToLongTimeString`, `ToShortDateString`, and `ToShortTimeString` create string representations using the current culture. You can use the `ToString` method to assign a different culture:

```
public string ToString();
public string ToString(IFormatProvider);
public string ToString(string);
public string ToString(string, IFormatProvider);
```

With the string argument of the `ToString` method, you can specify a predefined format character or a custom format string for converting the date to a string. The class `DateTimeFormatInfo` specifies the possible values. With `DateTimeFormatInfo`, the case of the format strings has a different meaning. D defines a long date format, d a short date format. Other examples of possible formats are ddd for the abbreviated day of the week, dddd for the full day of the week, yyyy for the year, T for a long time, and t for a short time format. With the `IFormatProvider` argument, you can specify the culture. Using an overloaded method without the `IFormatProvider` argument implies that the culture of the current thread is used:

```
DateTime d = new DateTime(2012, 06, 12);

// current culture
Console.WriteLine(d.ToLongDateString());

// use IFormatProvider
Console.WriteLine(d.ToString("D", new CultureInfo("fr-FR")));
```

```
                 // use culture of thread
                 CultureInfo ci = Thread.CurrentThread.CurrentCulture;
                 Console.WriteLine("{0}: {1}", ci.ToString(), d.ToString("D"));

                 ci = new CultureInfo("es-ES");
                 Thread.CurrentThread.CurrentCulture = ci;
                 Console.WriteLine("{0}: {1}", ci.ToString(), d.ToString("D"));
```

The output of this example program shows ToLongDateString with the current culture of the thread, a French version where a CultureInfo instance is passed to the ToString method, and a Spanish version where the CurrentCulture property of the thread is changed to es-ES:

```
Tuesday, June 12, 2012
mardi 12 juin 2012
en-US: Tuesday, June 12, 2012
es-ES: martes, 12 de junio de 2012
```

Cultures in Action

To see all cultures in action, you can use a sample Windows Presentation Foundation (WPF) application that lists all cultures and demonstrates different characteristics of culture properties. Figure 28-5 shows the user interface of the application in the Visual Studio 2012 WPF Designer.

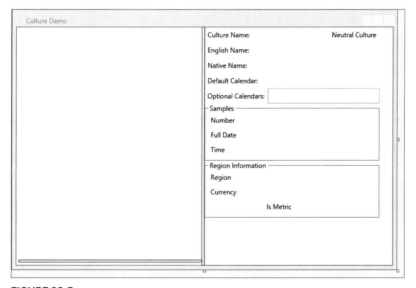

FIGURE 28-5

During initialization of the application, all available cultures are added to the TreeView control that is placed on the left side of the application. This initialization happens in the method SetupCultures, which is called in the constructor of the CultureDemoWindow class CultureDemoWindow (code file CultureDemo/MainWindow.xaml.cs):

```
                 public CultureDemoWindow()
                 {
                   InitializeComponent();

                   SetupCultures();
                 }
```

For the data that is shown in the user interface, the custom class `CultureData` is created. This class can be bound to a `TreeView` control, as it has a property `SubCultures` that contains a list of `CultureData`. Therefore, the `TreeView` control enables walking through this tree. Other than the subcultures, `CultureData` contains the `CultureInfo` type and sample values for a number, a date, and a time. The number returns a string in the number format for the specific culture, and the date and time return strings in the specific culture formats as well. `CultureData` contains a `RegionInfo` class to display regions. With some neutral cultures (e.g., English), creating a `RegionInfo` throws an exception, as there are regions only with specific cultures. However, with other neutral cultures (e.g., German), creating a `RegionInfo` succeeds and is mapped to a default region. The exception thrown here is handled:

```
public class CultureData
{
  public CultureInfo CultureInfo { get; set; }
  public List<CultureData> SubCultures { get; set; }

  double numberSample = 9876543.21;
  public string NumberSample
  {
    get { return numberSample.ToString("N", CultureInfo); }
  }

  public string DateSample
  {
    get { return DateTime.Today.ToString("D", CultureInfo); }
  }

  public string TimeSample
  {
    get { return DateTime.Now.ToString("T", CultureInfo); }
  }

  public RegionInfo RegionInfo
  {
    get
    {
      RegionInfo ri;
      try
      {
        ri = new RegionInfo(CultureInfo.Name);
      }
      catch (ArgumentException)
      {
        // with some neutral cultures regions are not available
        return null;
      }
      return ri;
    }
  }
}
```

In the method `SetupCultures`, you get all cultures from the static method `CultureInfo.GetCultures`. Passing `CultureTypes.AllCultures` to this method returns an unsorted array of all available cultures. The result is sorted by the name of the culture. With the result of the sorted cultures, a collection of `CultureData` objects is created and the `CultureInfo` and `SubCultures` properties are assigned. With the result of this, a dictionary is created to enable fast access to the culture name.

For the data that should be bound, a list of `CultureData` objects is created that contains all the root cultures for the tree view after the `foreach` statement is completed. Root cultures can be verified to determine whether they have the invariant culture as their parent. The invariant culture has the LCID 127. Root cultures are added to the `rootCultures` collection within the block of the `if` statement.

If the culture does not have a parent culture, it is added to the root nodes of the tree. To find parent cultures, all cultures are remembered inside a dictionary. (See Chapter 10, "Collections," for more information about dictionaries, and Chapter 8, "Delegates, Lambdas, and Events," for details about Lambda expressions.) If the culture iterated is not a root culture, it is added to the SubCultures collection of the parent culture. The parent culture can be quickly found by using the dictionary. In the last step, the root cultures are made available to the UI by assigning them to the DataContext of the Window:

```
private void SetupCultures()
{
  var cultureDataDict = CultureInfo.GetCultures(CultureTypes.AllCultures)
    .OrderBy(c => c.Name)
    .Select(c => new CultureData
    {
      CultureInfo = c,
      SubCultures = new List<CultureData>()
    })
    .ToDictionary(c => c.CultureInfo.Name);

  var rootCultures = new List<CultureData>();
  foreach (var cd in cultureDataDict.Values)
  {
    if (cd.CultureInfo.Parent.LCID == 127)
    {
      rootCultures.Add(cd);
    }
    else
    {
      CultureData parentCultureData;
      if (cultureDataDict.TryGetValue(cd.CultureInfo.Parent.Name,
        out parentCultureData))
      {
        parentCultureData.SubCultures.Add(cd);
      }
      else
      {
        throw new ParentCultureException(
          "unexpected error - parent culture not found");
      }

    }
  }
  this.DataContext = rootCultures.OrderBy(cd =>
    cd.CultureInfo.EnglishName);
}
```

When the user selects a node inside the tree, the handler of the SelectedItemChanged event of the TreeView is called. Here, the handler is implemented in the method treeCultures_SelectedItemChanged. Within this method, the DataContext of a Grid control is set to the selected CultureData object. In the XAML logical tree, this Grid is the parent of all controls that display information about the selected culture information:

```
private void treeCultures_SelectedItemChanged(object sender,
  RoutedPropertyChangedEventArgs<object> e)
{
  CultureData cd = e.NewValue as CultureData;
  if (cd != null)
  {
    itemGrid.DataContext = cd;
  }
}
```

Now let's get into the XAML code for the display. A `TreeView` is used to display all the cultures (code file `CultureDemo/MainWindow.xaml`). For the display of items inside the `TreeView`, an item template is used. This template uses a `TextBlock` that is bound to the `EnglishName` property of the `CultureInfo` class. For binding the items of the tree view, a `HierarchicalDataTemplate` is used to bind the property `SubCultures` of the `CultureData` type recursively:

```
<TreeView SelectedItemChanged="treeCultures_SelectedItemChanged" Margin="5"
  ItemsSource="{Binding}" >
  <TreeView.ItemTemplate>
    <HierarchicalDataTemplate DataType="{x:Type local:CultureData}"
      ItemsSource="{Binding SubCultures}">
      <TextBlock  Text="{Binding Path=CultureInfo.EnglishName}" />
    </HierarchicalDataTemplate>
  </TreeView.ItemTemplate>
</TreeView>
```

To display the values of the selected item, several `TextBlock` controls are used. These bind to the `CultureInfo` property of the `CultureData` class and in turn to properties of the `CultureInfo` type that is returned from `CultureInfo`, such as `Name`, `IsNeutralCulture`, `EnglishName`, `NativeName`, and so on. To convert a Boolean value, as returned from the `IsNeutralCulture` property, to a `Visibility` enumeration value, and to display calendar names, converters are used:

```
<TextBlock Grid.Row="0" Grid.Column="0" Text="Culture Name:" />
<TextBlock Grid.Row="0" Grid.Column="1" Text="{Binding CultureInfo.Name}"
  Width="100" />
<TextBlock Grid.Row="0" Grid.Column="2" Text="Neutral Culture"
  Visibility="{Binding CultureInfo.IsNeutralCulture,
  Converter={StaticResource boolToVisiblity}}" />

<TextBlock Grid.Row="1" Grid.Column="0" Text="English Name:" />
<TextBlock Grid.Row="1" Grid.Column="1" Grid.ColumnSpan="2"
  Text="{Binding CultureInfo.EnglishName}" />

<TextBlock Grid.Row="2" Grid.Column="0" Text="Native Name:" />
<TextBlock Grid.Row="2" Grid.Column="1" Grid.ColumnSpan="2"
  Text="{Binding CultureInfo.NativeName}" />

<TextBlock Grid.Row="3" Grid.Column="0" Text="Default Calendar:" />
<TextBlock Grid.Row="3" Grid.Column="1" Grid.ColumnSpan="2"
  Text="{Binding CultureInfo.Calendar,
  Converter={StaticResource calendarConverter}}" />

<TextBlock Grid.Row="4" Grid.Column="0" Text="Optional Calendars:" />
<ListBox Grid.Row="4" Grid.Column="1" Grid.ColumnSpan="2"

  ItemsSource="{Binding CultureInfo.OptionalCalendars}">
  <ListBox.ItemTemplate>
    <DataTemplate>
      <TextBlock Text="{Binding
        Converter={StaticResource calendarConverter}}" />
    </DataTemplate>
  </ListBox.ItemTemplate>
</ListBox>
```

The converter to convert a Boolean value to the `Visibility` enumeration is defined in the class `BooleanToVisibilityConverter` (code file `Converters\BooleanToVisiblityConverter.cs`):

```
using System;
using System.Globalization;
using System.Windows;
using System.Windows.Data;
```

```
namespace CultureDemo.Converters
{
  public class BooleanToVisibilityConverter : IValueConverter
  {

    public object Convert(object value, Type targetType, object parameter,
      CultureInfo culture)
    {
      bool b = (bool)value;
      if (b)
        return Visibility.Visible;
      else
        return Visibility.Collapsed;
    }

    public object ConvertBack(object value, Type targetType, object parameter,
      CultureInfo culture)
    {
      throw new NotImplementedException();
    }
  }
}
```

The converter for the calendar text to display is just a little bit more complex. Here is the implementation of the Convert method in the class CalendarTypeToCalendarInformationConverter. The implementation uses the class name and calendar type name to return a useful value for the calendar:

```
public object Convert(object value, Type targetType, object parameter,
  CultureInfo culture)
{
  Calendar c = value as Calendar;
  if (c == null) return null;
  StringBuilder calText = new StringBuilder(50);
  calText.Append(c.ToString());
  calText.Remove(0, 21); // remove the namespace
  calText.Replace("Calendar", "");

  GregorianCalendar gregCal = c as GregorianCalendar;
  if (gregCal != null)
  {
    calText.AppendFormat(" {0}", gregCal.CalendarType.ToString());
  }
  return calText.ToString();
}
```

The CultureData class contains properties to display sample information for number, date, and time formats. These properties are bound with the following TextBlock elements:

```
<TextBlock Grid.Row="0" Grid.Column="0" Text="Number" />
<TextBlock Grid.Row="0" Grid.Column="1"
  Text="{Binding NumberSample}" />

<TextBlock Grid.Row="1" Grid.Column="0" Text="Full Date" />
<TextBlock Grid.Row="1" Grid.Column="1"
  Text="{Binding DateSample}" />

<TextBlock Grid.Row="2" Grid.Column="0" Text="Time" />
<TextBlock Grid.Row="2" Grid.Column="1"
  Text="{Binding TimeSample}" />
```

The information about the region is shown with the last part of the XAML code. The complete `GroupBox` is hidden if the `RegionInfo` is not available. The `TextBlock` elements bind the `DisplayName`, `CurrencySymbol`, `ISOCurrencySymbol`, and `IsMetric` properties of the `RegionInfo` type:

```xml
<GroupBox x:Name="groupRegion" Header="Region Information" Grid.Row="6"
  Grid.Column="0" Grid.ColumnSpan="3" Visibility="{Binding RegionInfo,
  Converter={StaticResource nullToVisibility}}">
  <Grid>
    <Grid.RowDefinitions>
      <RowDefinition />
      <RowDefinition />
      <RowDefinition />
    </Grid.RowDefinitions>
    <Grid.ColumnDefinitions>
      <ColumnDefinition />
      <ColumnDefinition />
      <ColumnDefinition />
    </Grid.ColumnDefinitions>
    <TextBlock Grid.Row="0" Grid.Column="0" Text="Region" />
    <TextBlock Grid.Row="0" Grid.Column="1" Grid.ColumnSpan="2"
      Text="{Binding RegionInfo.DisplayName}" />

    <TextBlock Grid.Row="1" Grid.Column="0" Text="Currency" />
    <TextBlock Grid.Row="1" Grid.Column="1"
      Text="{Binding RegionInfo.CurrencySymbol}" />
    <TextBlock Grid.Row="1" Grid.Column="2"
      Text="{Binding RegionInfo.ISOCurrencySymbol}" />

    <TextBlock Grid.Row="2" Grid.Column="1" Text="Is Metric"
      Visibility="{Binding RegionInfo.IsMetric,
      Converter={StaticResource boolToVisiblity}}" />
  </Grid>
```

When you start the application, you can see all available cultures in the tree view, and selecting a culture lists its characteristics, as shown in Figure 28-6.

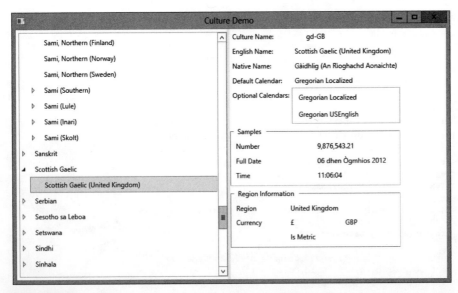

FIGURE 28-6

Sorting

Sorting strings varies according to the culture. The algorithms that compare strings for sorting by default are culture-specific. For example, in Finnish the characters V and W are treated the same. To demonstrate this behavior with a Finnish sort, the following code creates a small sample console application in which some U.S. states are stored unsorted inside an array. You are going to use classes from the namespaces System.Collections.Generic, System.Threading, and System.Globalization, so these namespaces must be declared. The method DisplayNames shown here is used to display all elements of an array or a collection on the console (code file SortingDemo/Program.cs):

```
static void DisplayNames(string title, IEnumerable<string> e)
{
  Console.WriteLine(title);
  foreach (string s in e)
    Console.Write(s + "-");
  Console.WriteLine();
  Console.WriteLine();
}
```

In the Main method, after creating the array with some of the U.S. states, the thread property CurrentCulture is set to the Finnish culture so that the following Array.Sort uses the Finnish sort order. Calling the method DisplayNames displays all the states on the console:

```
static void Main()
{
  string[] names = {"Alabama", "Texas", "Washington",
                    "Virginia", "Wisconsin", "Wyoming",
                    "Kentucky", "Missouri", "Utah", "Hawaii",
                    "Kansas", "Louisiana", "Alaska", "Arizona"};

  Thread.CurrentThread.CurrentCulture = new CultureInfo("fi-FI");

  Array.Sort(names);
  DisplayNames("Sorted using the Finnish culture", names);
```

After the first display of some U.S. states in the Finnish sort order, the array is sorted once again. If you want a sort that is independent of the users' culture, which would be useful when the sorted array is sent to a server or stored somewhere, you can use the invariant culture.

You can do this by passing a second argument to Array.Sort. The Sort method expects an object implementing IComparer with the second argument. The Comparer class from the System.Collections namespace implements IComparer. Comparer.DefaultInvariant returns a Comparer object that uses the invariant culture for comparing the array values for a culture-independent sort:

```
  // sort using the invariant culture
  Array.Sort(names, System.Collections.Comparer.DefaultInvariant);
  DisplayNames("Sorted using the invariant culture", names);
}
```

The program output shows different sort results with the Finnish and culture-independent cultures—Virginia is before Washington when using the invariant sort order, and vice versa when using Finnish:

```
Sorted using the Finnish culture
Alabama-Alaska-Arizona-Hawaii-Kansas-Kentucky-Louisiana-Missouri-Texas-Utah-
Washington-Virginia-Wisconsin-Wyoming -

Sorted using the invariant culture
Alabama-Alaska-Arizona-Hawaii-Kansas-Kentucky-Louisiana-Missouri-Texas-Utah-
Virginia-Washington-Wisconsin-Wyoming -
```

> **NOTE** *If sorting a collection should be independent of a culture, the collection must be sorted with the invariant culture. This can be particularly useful when sending the sort result to a server or storing it inside a file.*

In addition to a locale-dependent formatting and measurement system, text and pictures may differ depending on the culture. This is where resources come into play.

RESOURCES

Resources such as pictures or string tables can be put into resource files or satellite assemblies. Such resources can be very helpful when localizing applications, and .NET has built-in support to search for localized resources. Before you see how to use resources to localize applications, the following sections explain how resources can be created and read without looking at language aspects.

Creating Resource Files

Resource files can contain items such as pictures and string tables. A resource file is created by using either a normal text file or a `.resX` file that uses XML. This section starts with a simple text file.

A resource that embeds a string table can be created by using a normal text file. The text file just assigns strings to keys. The key is the name that can be used from a program to get the value. Spaces are allowed in both keys and values.

This example shows a simple string table in the file `Wrox.ProCSharp.Localization.MyResources.txt`:

```
Title = Professional C#
Chapter = Localization
Author = Christian Nagel
Publisher = Wrox Press
```

> **NOTE** *When saving text files with Unicode characters, you must save the file with the proper encoding. To select the Unicode encoding, use the Save dialog.*

Resource File Generator

The Resource File Generator (`Resgen.exe`) utility can be used to create a resource file out of `Wrox.ProCSharp.Localization.MyResources.txt`. **Typing** the line

```
resgen Wrox.ProCSharp.Localization.MyResources.txt
```

creates the file `Wrox.ProCSharp.Localization.MyResources.resources`. The resulting resource file can either be added to an assembly as an external file or embedded into the DLL or EXE. Resgen also supports the creation of XML-based `.resX` resource files. One easy way to build an XML file is by using Resgen itself:

```
resgen Wrox.ProCSharp.Localization.MyResources.txt
   Wrox.ProCSharp.Localization.MyResources.resX
```

This command creates the XML resource file `Wrox.ProCSharp.LocalizationMyResources.resX`. You'll see how to work with XML resource files in the section "Windows Forms Localization Using Visual Studio" later in this chapter.

Resgen supports strongly typed resources. A strongly typed resource is represented by a class that accesses the resource. The class can be created with the /str option of the Resgen utility:

```
resgen /str:C#,Wrox.ProCSharp.Localization,MyResources,MyResources.cs
Wrox.ProCSharp.Localization.MyResources.resX
```

With the /str option, the language, namespace, class name, and filename for the source code are defined, in that order.

The Resgen utility does not support adding pictures. The .NET Framework SDK includes a ResXGen sample with the tutorials. With ResXGen, it is possible to reference pictures in a .resX file. You can also add pictures programmatically by using the ResourceWriter or ResXResourceWriter classes, as shown next.

ResourceWriter

Instead of using the Resgen utility to build resource files, it's a simple task to write a program to create resources. The class ResourceWriter from the namespace System.Resources can be used to write binary resource files; ResXResourceWriter writes XML-based resource files. Both of these classes support pictures and any other object that is serializable. When you use the class ResXResourceWriter, the assembly System.Windows.Forms must be referenced.

In the following code example, you create a ResXResourceWriter object, rw, using a constructor with the filename Demo.resx. After creating an instance, you can add a number of resources up to 2GB in total size by using the AddResource method of the ResXResourceWriter class. The first argument of AddResource specifies the name of the resource, and the second argument specifies the value. A picture resource can be added using an instance of the Image class. To use the Image class, you have to reference the assembly System.Drawing. You also add the using directive to open the namespace System.Drawing.

Create an Image object by opening the file logo.gif. You have to copy the picture to the directory of the executable or specify the full path to the picture in the method argument of Image.ToFile. The using statement specifies that the image resource should automatically be disposed of at the end of the using block. Additional simple string resources are added to the ResXResourceWriter object. The Close method of the ResXResourceWriter class automatically calls ResXResourceWriter.Generate to write the resources to the file Demo.resx (code file CreateResource\Program.cs):

```csharp
using System;
using System.Resources;
using System.Drawing;

class Program
{
  static void Main()
  {
    var rw = new ResXResourceWriter("Demo.resx");
    using (Image image = Image.FromFile("logo.gif"))
    {
      rw.AddResource("WroxLogo", image);
      rw.AddResource("Title", "Professional C#");
      rw.AddResource("Chapter", "Localization");
      rw.AddResource("Author", "Christian Nagel");
      rw.AddResource("Publisher", "Wrox Press");
      rw.Close();
    }
  }
}
```

Starting this small program creates the resource file Demo.resx, which embeds the image logo.gif. In the next example, the resources are used with a Windows application.

Using Resource Files

You can add resource files to assemblies with the command-line C# compiler csc.exe by using the /resource option, or directly with Visual Studio. To see how resource files can be used with Visual Studio, create a console application and name it ResourceDemo.

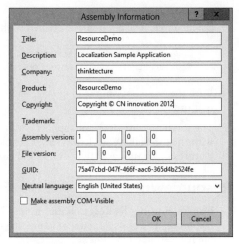

Use the context menu of Solution Explorer (Add ➪ Existing Item) to add the previously created resource file Demo.resx to this project. By default, the Build Action of this resource is set to Embedded Resource so that the resource is embedded into the output assembly.

In the project settings (Application ➪ Assembly information), set the Neutral Language setting of the application to the main language—for example, English (United States)—as shown in Figure 28-7. Changing this setting adds the attribute [NeutralResourceLanguageAttribute] to the file assemblyinfo.cs, as shown here:

FIGURE 28-7

```
[assembly: NeutralResourcesLanguageAttribute("en-US")]
```

Setting this option improves performance with the ResourceManager because it more quickly finds the resources for en-US that are also used as a default fallback. With this attribute, you can also specify the location of the default resource by using the second parameter with the constructor. With the enumeration UltimateResourceFallbackLocation, you can specify that the default resource is to be stored in the main assembly or in a satellite assembly (values MainAssembly and Satellite).

After building the project, you can check the generated assembly with ildasm to see the attribute .mresource in the manifest (see Figure 28-8). This attribute declares the name of the resource in the assembly. If .mresource is declared as public (as in the example), the resource is exported from the assembly and can be used from classes in other assemblies. .mresource private means that the resource is not exported and is available only within the assembly.

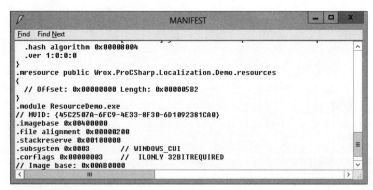

FIGURE 28-8

To access the embedded resource, use the ResourceManager class from the System.Resources namespace. You can pass the assembly that has the resources as an argument to the constructor of the ResourceManager class. In this example, the resources are embedded in the executing assembly, so pass the result of Assembly.GetExecutingAssembly as the second argument. The first argument is the root name of the resource. The root name consists of the namespace and the name of the resource file, but without the resources extension. As shown earlier, ildasm specifies the name. You only need to remove the file extension resources from the name shown. You can also get the name programmatically by using the GetManifestResourceNames method of the System.Reflection.Assembly class:

```
using System;
using System.Drawing;
using System.Reflection;
using System.Resources;

namespace Wrox.ProCSharp.Localization
{
  class Program
  {
    static void Main()
    {
      var rm = new ResourceManager("Wrox.ProCSharp.Localization.Demo",
                            Assembly.GetExecutingAssembly());
```

Using the ResourceManager instance rm, you can get all the resources by specifying the key to the methods GetObject and GetString:

```
      Console.WriteLine(rm.GetString("Title"));
      Console.WriteLine(rm.GetString("Chapter"));
      Console.WriteLine(rm.GetString("Author"));
      using (Image logo = (Image)rm.GetObject("WroxLogo"))
      {
        logo.Save("logo.bmp");
      }
    }
  }
}
```

With strongly typed resources, the code written earlier can be simplified; there is no need to instantiate the ResourceManager and access the resources using indexers. Instead, you can access the names of the resources with properties:

```
      private static void StronglyTypedResources()
      {
        Console.WriteLine(Demo.Title);
        Console.WriteLine(Demo.Chapter);
        Console.WriteLine(Demo.Author);
        using (Bitmap logo = Demo.WroxLogo)
        {
          logo.Save("logo.bmp");
        }
      }
```

To create a strongly typed resource with the Managed Resources Editor, reset the Access Modifier option from No Code Generation to Public or Internal. With Public, the generated class has a public access modifier and is available from other assemblies. With Internal, the generated class has an internal access modifier and can be accessed only from within the assembly.

When you set this option, the class Demo (it has the same name as the resource) is created. This class has static properties for all the resources to provide a strongly typed resource name. With the implementation of the static properties, a ResourceManager object is used, instantiated on first access and then cached (code file ResourceDemo\Demo.Designer.cs):

```
//------------------------------------------------------------------------------
// <auto-generated>
//     This code was generated by a tool.
//     Runtime Version:4.0.30319.17626
//
```

```
//      Changes to this file may cause incorrect behavior and will be lost if
//      the code is regenerated.
// </auto-generated>
//------------------------------------------------------------------------------

namespace Wrox.ProCSharp.Localization
{
  using System;


  /// <summary>
  ///    A strongly-typed resource class, for looking up localized strings, etc.
  /// </summary>
  // This class was auto-generated by the StronglyTypedResourceBuilder
  // class via a tool like ResGen or Visual Studio.
  // To add or remove a member, edit your .ResX file then rerun ResGen
  // with the /str option, or rebuild your VS project.
  [global::System.CodeDom.Compiler.GeneratedCodeAttribute(
    "System.Resources.Tools.StronglyTypedResourceBuilder", "4.0.0.0")]
  [global::System.Diagnostics.DebuggerNonUserCodeAttribute()]
  [global::System.Runtime.CompilerServices.CompilerGeneratedAttribute()]
  internal class Demo
  {
    private static global::System.Resources.ResourceManager resourceMan;

    private static global::System.Globalization.CultureInfo resourceCulture;

    [global::System.Diagnostics.CodeAnalysis.SuppressMessageAttribute(
      "Microsoft.Performance", "CA1811:AvoidUncalledPrivateCode")]
    internal Demo()
    {
    }

    /// <summary>
    ///    Returns the cached ResourceManager instance used by this class.
    /// </summary>
    [global::System.ComponentModel.EditorBrowsableAttribute(
      global::System.ComponentModel.EditorBrowsableState.Advanced)]
    internal static global::System.Resources.ResourceManager ResourceManager
    {
      get
      {
        if (object.ReferenceEquals(resourceMan, null))
        {
          global::System.Resources.ResourceManager temp =
            new global::System.Resources.ResourceManager(
            "Wrox.ProCSharp.Localization.Demo", typeof(Demo).Assembly);
          resourceMan = temp;
        }
        return resourceMan;
      }
    }

    /// <summary>
    ///    Overrides the current thread's CurrentUICulture property for all
    ///    resource lookups using this strongly typed resource class.
    /// </summary>
    [global::System.ComponentModel.EditorBrowsableAttribute(
      global::System.ComponentModel.EditorBrowsableState.Advanced)]
    internal static global::System.Globalization.CultureInfo Culture
    {
      get
      {
        return resourceCulture;
```

```
        }
        set
        {
          resourceCulture = value;
        }
      }

      /// <summary>
      ///    Looks up a localized string similar to Chapter.
      /// </summary>
      internal static string Chapter
      {
        get
        {
          return ResourceManager.GetString("Chapter", resourceCulture);
        }
      }

      //...

      internal static System.Drawing.Bitmap WroxLogo
      {
        get
        {
          object obj = ResourceManager.GetObject("WroxLogo", resourceCulture);
          return ((System.Drawing.Bitmap)(obj));
        }
      }
    }
  }
```

The System.Resources Namespace

Before moving on to the next example, this section concludes with a review of the classes contained in the `System.Resources` namespace that deal with resources:

- ➤ **ResourceManager**—Can be used to get resources for the current culture from assemblies or resource files. Using the `ResourceManager`, you can also get a `ResourceSet` for a particular culture.

- ➤ **ResourceSet**—Represents the resources for a particular culture. When a `ResourceSet` instance is created, it enumerates over a class, implementing the interface `IResourceReader`, and it stores all resources in a `Hashtable`.

- ➤ **IResourceReader**—This interface is used from the `ResourceSet` to enumerate resources. The class `ResourceReader` implements this interface.

- ➤ **ResourceWriter**—This class is used to create a resource file. `ResourceWriter` implements the interface `IResourceWriter`.

- ➤ **ResXResourceSet, ResXResourceReader, and ResXResourceWriter**—These are similar to `ResourceSet`, `ResourceReader`, and `ResourceWriter`, but they are used to create an XML-based resource file, `.resX`, instead of a binary file. You can use `ResXFileRef` to make a link to a resource instead of embedding it inside an XML file.

- ➤ **System.Resources.Tools**—This namespace contains the class `StronglyTypedResourceBuilder` to create a class from a resource.

WINDOWS FORMS LOCALIZATION USING VISUAL STUDIO

In this section, you create a simple Windows Forms application that demonstrates how to use Visual Studio 2012 for localization. This application does not use complex Windows Forms or have any real inner functionality because the key feature it is intended to demonstrate here is localization. In the automatically generated source code, change the namespace to `Wrox.ProCSharp` `.Localization` and the class name to `BookOfTheDayForm`. The namespace is changed not only in the source file `BookOfTheDayForm` `.cs` but also in the project settings, enabling all generated resource files to share this namespace, too. You can change the namespace for all new items that are created by selecting Common Properties from the Project ⇨ Properties menu.

To demonstrate various aspects of localization, this program has an image, some text, a date, and a number. The image shows a flag that is also localized. Figure 28-9 shows this form of the application as it appears in the Windows Forms Designer.

The following table lists the values for the `Name` and `Text` properties of the Windows Forms elements:

FIGURE 28-9

NAME	TEXT
`labelBookOfTheDay`	Book of the day
`labelItemsSold`	Books sold
`textDate`	Date
`textTitle`	Professional C# 2012
`textItemsSold`	30000
`pictureFlag`	

In addition to this form, you might want a message box that displays a welcome message; this message might vary according to the current time of day. The following example demonstrates that localization for dynamically created dialogs must be done differently. In the method `WelcomeMessage`, you display a message box using `MessageBox.Show`. Then you call the method `WelcomeMessage` in the constructor of the form class `BookOfTheDayForm`, before the call to `InitializeComponent`.

Here is the code for the method `WelcomeMessage`:

```
public void WelcomeMessage()
{
  DateTime now = DateTime.Now;
  string message;
  if (now.Hour <= 12)
  {
    message = "Good Morning";
  }
  else if (now.Hour <= 19)
  {
    message = "Good Afternoon";
  }
  else
  {
    message = "Good Evening";
  }
  MessageBox.Show(String.Format("{0}\nThis is a localization sample",
    message));
}
```

The number and date in the form should be set by using formatting options. The following adds a new method, `SetDateAndNumber`, to set the values with the format option. In a real application, these values could be received from a web service or a database, but this example focuses on localization. The date is formatted using the `D` option (to display the long-date name). The number is displayed using the picture number format string ###,###,###, where # represents a digit and ", " is the group separator (code file BookOfTheDay/BookOfTheDayForm.cs):

```
public void SetDateAndNumber()
{
  DateTime today = DateTime.Today;
  textDate.Text = today.ToString("D");
  int itemsSold = 327444;
  textItemsSold.Text = itemsSold.ToString("###,###,###");
}
```

In the constructor of the BookOfTheDayForm class, both the WelcomeMessage and SetDateAndNumber methods are called:

```
public BookOfTheDayForm()
{
  WelcomeMessage();

  InitializeComponent();

  SetDateAndNumber();
}
```

A magical feature of the Windows Forms Designer is started when you reset the Localizable property of the form from false to true. It results in the creation of an XML-based resource file for the dialog that stores all resource strings, properties (including the location and size of Windows Forms elements), embedded pictures, and so on. In addition, the implementation of the InitializeComponent method is changed; an instance of the class System.Resources.ResourceManager is created, and to get to the values and positions of the text fields and pictures, the GetObject method is used instead of writing the values directly into the code. GetObject uses the CurrentUICulture property of the current thread to find the correct localization of the resources.

Here is part of InitializeComponent from the file BookOfTheDayForm.Designer.cs before the Localizable property is set to true, where all properties of textboxTitle are set:

```
private void InitializeComponent()
{
  //...
  this.textTitle = new System.Windows.Forms.TextBox();
  //
  // textTitle
  //
  this.textTitle.Anchor = ((System.Windows.Forms.AnchorStyles)
    (((System.Windows.Forms.AnchorStyles.Top
    | System.Windows.Forms.AnchorStyles.Left)
    | System.Windows.Forms.AnchorStyles.Right)));
  this.textTitle.Location = new System.Drawing.Point(29, 164);
  this.textTitle.Name = "textTitle";
  this.textTitle.Size = new System.Drawing.Size(231, 20);
  this.textTitle.TabIndex = 3;
```

The code for the IntializeComponent method is automatically changed by setting the Localizable property to true:

```
private void InitializeComponent()
{
  System.ComponentModel.ComponentResourceManager resources =
    new System.ComponentModel.ComponentResourceManager(
      typeof(BookOfTheDayForm));
```

```
//...
this.textTitle = new System.Windows.Forms.TextBox();
//
// textTitle
//
resources.ApplyResources(this.textTitle, "textTitle");
this.textTitle.Name = "textTitle";
```

From where does the resource manager get the data? When the `Localizable` property is set to `true`, the resource file `BookOfTheDay.resX` is generated. In this file, you can find the scheme of the XML resource, followed by all elements in the form: `Type`, `Text`, `Location`, `TabIndex`, and so on.

The class `ComponentResourceManager` is derived from `ResourceManager` and offers the method `ApplyResources`. With `ApplyResources`, the resources defined with the second argument are applied to the object in the first argument.

The following XML segment shows a few of the properties of `textBoxTitle`: the `Location` property has a value of `29, 164`; the `Size` property has a value of `231, 20`; the `Text` property is set to `Professional C# 2012`; and so on. For every value, the type of the value is stored as well. For example, the `Location` property is of type `System.Drawing.Point`, and this class can be found in the assembly `System.Drawing`.

Why are the locations and sizes stored in this XML file? With translations, many strings have completely different sizes and no longer fit into the original positions. When the locations and sizes are all stored inside the resource file, everything needed for localization is stored in this file, separate from the C# code (code file `BookOfTheDay/BookOfTheDayForm.resX`):

```xml
<data name="textTitle.Anchor" type=
    "System.Windows.Forms.AnchorStyles, System.Windows.Forms">
  <value>Top, Left, Right</value>
</data>
<data name="textTitle.Location" type="System.Drawing.Point, System.Drawing">
  <value>29, 164</value>
</data>
<data name="textTitle.Size" type="System.Drawing.Size, System.Drawing">
  <value>231, 20</value>
</data>
<data name="textTitle.TabIndex" type="System.Int32, mscorlib">
  <value>3</value>
</data>
<data name="textTitle.Text" xml:space="preserve">
  <value>Professional C# 2012</value>
</data>
<data name="&gt;&gt;textTitle.Name" xml:space="preserve">
  <value>textTitle</value>
</data>
<data name="&gt;&gt;textTitle.Type" xml:space="preserve">
  <value>System.Windows.Forms.TextBox, System.Windows.Forms, Version=4.0.0.0,
        Culture=neutral, PublicKeyToken=b77a5c561934e089</value>
</data>
<data name="&gt;&gt;textTitle.Parent" xml:space="preserve">
  <value>$this</value>
</data>
<data name="&gt;&gt;textTitle.ZOrder" xml:space="preserve">
  <value>2</value>
</data>
```

When changing some of these resource values, it is not necessary to work directly with the XML code. You can change these resources right in the Visual Studio Designer. Whenever you change the `Language` property of the form and the properties of some form elements, a new resource file is generated for the specified language. Create a German version of the form by setting the `Language` property to German, and a French version by setting it to French, and so on. For each language, you get a resource file with the changed properties: in this case, `BookOfTheDayForm.de.resX` and `BookOfTheDayForm.fr.resX`.

The following table shows the changes needed for the German version:

GERMAN NAME	VALUE
`$this.Text` (title of the form)	Buch des Tages
`labelItemsSold.Text`	Bücher verkauft:
`labelBookOfTheDay.Text`	Buch des Tages:

The next table shows the changes for the French version:

FRENCH NAME	VALUE
`$this.Text` (title of the form)	Le livre du jour
`labelItemsSold.Text`	Des livres vendus:
`labelBookOfTheDay.Text`	Le livre du jour:

By default, images are not moved to satellite assemblies. However, in the sample application, the flag should vary according to the country. To achieve this, you have to add the image of the American flag to the file `Resources.resx`. You can find this file in the Properties section of the Visual Studio Solution Explorer. With the resource editor, select the Images category, as shown in Figure 28-10, and add the file `americanflag.bmp`. To make localization with images possible, the image must have the same name in all languages. Here, the image in the file `Resources.resx` has the name "Flag." You can rename the image in the properties editor. Within the properties editor, you can also specify whether the image should be linked or embedded.

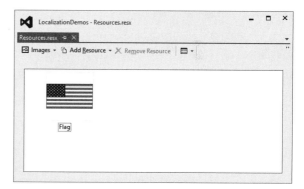

FIGURE 28-10

For best performance with resources, images are linked by default. With linked images, the image file must be delivered together with the application. If you want to embed the image within the assembly, you can change the `Persistence` property to `Embedded`.

You can add the localized versions of the flags by copying the file `Resource.resx` to `Resource.de.resx` and `Resource.fr.resx` and replacing the flags with `GermanFlag.bmp` and `FranceFlag.bmp`. Because a strongly typed resource class is needed only with the neutral resource, the property `CustomTool` can be cleared with the resource files of all specific languages.

Compiling the project now creates a *satellite assembly* for each language. Inside the `debug` directory (or the `release`, depending on your active configuration), language subdirectories such as `de` and `fr` are created. In such a subdirectory, you will find the file `BookOfTheDay.resources.dll`. Such a file is a satellite assembly that includes only localized resources. Opening this assembly with `ildasm`, you'll see a manifest with the embedded resources and a defined locale. For example, the assembly has the locale `de` in the assembly attributes, so it can be found in the `de` subdirectory. You can also see the name of the resource with `.mresource`; it is prefixed with the namespace `Wrox.ProCSharp.Localization`, followed by the class name `BookOfTheDayForm` and the language code `de`.

Changing the Culture Programmatically

After translating the resources and building the satellite assemblies, you will get the correct translations according to the configured culture for the user. The welcome message is not translated at this time. This needs to be done in a different way, as you'll see shortly.

In addition to the system configuration, it should be possible to send the language code as a command-line argument to your application for testing purposes. In the following example, the `BookOfTheDayForm` constructor (in the code file `BookOfTheDay\BookOfTheDayForm.cs`) is changed to enable the passing of a culture string, and the setting of the culture according to this string. A `CultureInfo` instance is created to pass it to the `CurrentCulture` and `CurrentUICulture` properties of the current thread. Remember that the `CurrentCulture` is used for formatting, and the `CurrentUICulture` is used for loading resources:

```csharp
public BookOfTheDayForm(string culture)
{
  if (!String.IsNullOrEmpty(culture))
  {
    var ci = new CultureInfo(culture);
    // set culture for formatting
    Thread.CurrentThread.CurrentCulture = ci;
    // set culture for resources
    Thread.CurrentThread.CurrentUICulture = ci;
  }

  WelcomeMessage();

  InitializeComponent();
  SetDateAndNumber();
}
```

The `BookOfTheDayForm` is instantiated in the `Main` method, which can be found in the file `Program.cs`. In this method, you pass the culture string to the `BookOfTheDayForm` constructor:

```csharp
[STAThread]
static void Main(string[] args)
{
  string culture = String.Empty;
  if (args.Length == 1)
  {
    culture = args[0];
  }

  Application.EnableVisualStyles();
  Application.SetCompatibleTextRenderingDefault(false);
  Application.Run(new BookOfTheDayForm(culture));
}
```

Now you can start the application by using command-line options. Running the application, you can see the formatting options and the resources that were generated from the Windows Forms Designer. Figures 28-11 and 28-12 show the two localizations in which the application is started with the command-line options `de-DE` and `fr-FR`, respectively.

FIGURE 28-11   **FIGURE 28-12**

There is still a problem with the welcome message box: the strings are hard-coded inside the program. Because these strings are not properties of elements inside the form, the Forms Designer does not extract XML resources as it does from the properties for Windows controls when changing the `Localizable` property of the form. You have to change this code yourself.

Using Custom Resource Messages

For the welcome message, you have to translate the hard-coded strings. The following table shows the translations for German and French. You can write custom resource messages directly in the file `Resources .resx` and the language-specific derivations. Of course, you can also create a new resource file.

NAME	ENGLISH	GERMAN	FRENCH
GoodMorning	Good Morning	Guten Morgen	Bonjour
GoodAfternoon	Good Afternoon	Guten Tag	Bonjour
GoodEvening	Good Evening	Guten Abend	Bonsoir
Message1	This is a localization sample.	Das ist ein Beispiel mit Lokalisierung.	C'est un exemple avec la localisation.

The source code of the method `WelcomeMessage` must also be changed to use the resources. With strongly typed resources, it isn't necessary to instantiate the `ResourceManager` class. Instead, the properties of the strongly typed resource can be used:

```
public static void WelcomeMessage()
{
  DateTime now = DateTime.Now;
  string message;
  if (now.Hour <= 12)
  {
    message = Properties.Resources.GoodMorning;
  }
  else if (now.Hour <= 19)
  {
    message = Properties.Resources.GoodAfternoon;
  }
  else
  {
    message = Properties.Resources.GoodEvening;
  }
  MessageBox.Show(String.Format("{0}\n{1}", message,
      Properties.Resources.Message1);
}
```

When the program is started using English, German, or French, a message box with the appropriate language will appear.

Automatic Fallback for Resources

For the French and German versions in the example, all the resources are located inside the satellite assemblies. If you are not using these versions, then all the values of labels or text boxes are changed; this is not a problem at all. You must have only the values that change in the satellite assembly; the other values are taken from the parent assembly. For example, for de-AT (Austria), you could change the value for the *Good Afternoon* resource to *Grüß Gott* while leaving the other values intact. During runtime, when looking for the value of the resource *Good Morning*, which is not located in the de-at satellite assembly, the parent assembly would be searched. The parent for de-AT is de. In cases where the de assembly does not have this resource either, the value would be searched for in the parent assembly of de, the neutral assembly. The neutral assembly does not have a culture code.

> **NOTE** *Keep in mind that the culture code of the main assembly shouldn't define any culture!*

Outsourcing Translations

It is an easy task to outsource translations using resource files. It is not necessary to install Visual Studio to translate these files; a simple XML editor will suffice. The disadvantage of using an XML editor is that it doesn't provide a way to rearrange Windows Forms elements and change their size if the translated text does not fit into the original borders of a label or button. Using a Windows Forms Designer to do translations is a natural choice.

Microsoft provides a tool as part of the .NET Framework SDK that fulfills all these requirements: the Windows Resource Localization Editor, `winres.exe` (see Figure 28-13). Users working with this tool do not need access to the C# source files; only binary or XML-based resource files are needed for translations. After these translations are completed, you can import the resource files to the Visual Studio project to build satellite assemblies.

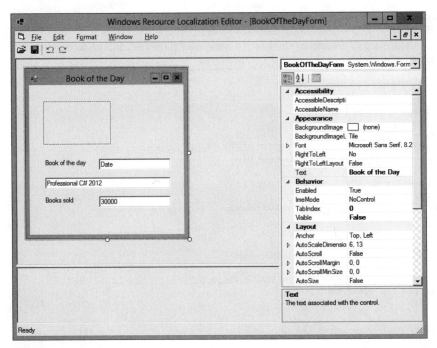

FIGURE 28-13

If you don't want your translation bureau to change the size and location of labels and buttons, and they cannot deal with XML files, you can send a simple text-based file. With the command-line utility `resgen .exe`, you can create a text file from an XML file:

```
resgen myresource.resX myresource.txt
```

After you have received the translation from the translation bureau, you can create an XML file from the returned text file. Remember to add the culture name to the filename:

```
resgen myresource.es.txt myresource.es.resX
```

LOCALIZATION WITH ASP.NET WEB FORMS

With ASP.NET Web Forms applications, localization happens in a similar way to Windows applications. Chapter 40, "ASP.NET Web Forms," discusses the functionality of ASP.NET Web Forms applications; this section discusses the localization of ASP.NET applications. ASP.NET 4.5 and Visual Studio 2012 have many features to support localization. The basic concepts of localization and globalization are the same as discussed before, but some specific issues are associated with ASP.NET.

As you have already learned, you have to differentiate between the user interface culture and the culture used for formatting. This is the same with ASP.NET. Both of these cultures can be defined at the web and page level, as well as programmatically.

To be independent of the web server's operating system, the culture and user interface culture can be defined with the <globalization> element in the configuration file web.config:

```
<configuration>
  <system.web>
    <globalization culture="en-US" uiCulture="en-US" />
  </system.web>
</configuration>
```

If the configuration should be different for specific web pages, the Page directive enables you to assign the culture:

```
<%Page Language="C#" Culture="en-US" UICulture="en-US" %>
```

Users can configure the language with the browser. With Internet Explorer 10 and Windows 8, this setting is taken from the operating system. The configuration within IE takes you to the Language settings, as shown in Figure 28-14.

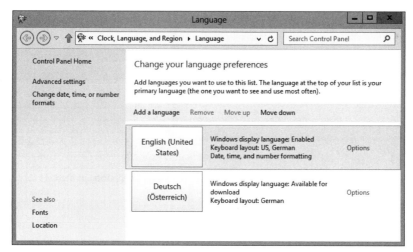

FIGURE 28-14

If the page language should be set according to the language setting of the client, the culture of the thread can be set programmatically to the language setting received from the client. ASP.NET has an automatic setting that does just that. Setting the culture to the value Auto sets the culture of the thread according to the client's settings:

```
<%Page Language="C#" Culture="Auto" UICulture="Auto" %>
```

In dealing with resources, ASP.NET differentiates between resources that are used for the complete web site and resources that are needed only within a page.

To create a resource used within a page, select Tools ⇨ Generate Local Resource from the Visual Studio menu in the design view. This creates the subdirectory `App_LocalResources`, where a resource file for every page is stored. These resources can be localized similarly to how they are localized in Windows applications. The association between the web controls and the local resource files is achieved by using a `meta:resourcekey` attribute, as shown in the following example with the ASP.NET `Label` control. `Label1Resource1` is the name of the resource that can be changed in the local resource file:

```
<asp:Label ID="Label1" Runat="server" Text="English Text"
    meta:resourcekey="Label1Resource1"></asp:Label>
```

For resources that should be shared between multiple pages, you have to create an ASP.NET folder, `Appl_GlobalResources`. Here you can add resource files, such as `Messages.resx` and its resources. To associate the web controls with these resources, you can use Expressions in the property editor. To do so, click the Expressions button to open the Expressions dialog (see Figure 28-15). Here, select the expression type Resources, set the name of the `ClassKey` (which is the name of the resource file—in this case, a strongly typed resource file is generated), and the name of the `ResourceKey`, which is the name of the resource.

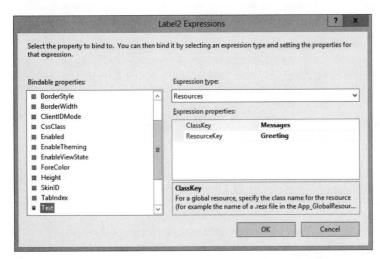

FIGURE 28-15

In the ASPX file, you can see the association to the resource with the binding expressions syntax `<%$`:

```
<asp:Label ID="Label2" Runat="server"
    Text="<%$ Resources:Messages, String1 %>">
</asp:Label>
```

LOCALIZATION WITH WPF

Visual Studio 2012 does not have great support for the localization of WPF applications, but you still can localize your WPF application. WPF has built-in localization support. With WPF, you can either use .NET resources, similar to what you've seen with Windows Forms and ASP.NET applications, or use an XAML (XML for Applications Markup Language) resource dictionary.

These options are discussed next. You can read more about WPF and XAML in Chapter 35, "Core WPF," and Chapter 36, "Business Applications with WPF." To demonstrate the use of resources with a WPF application, create a simple WPF application containing just one button, as shown in Figure 28-16.

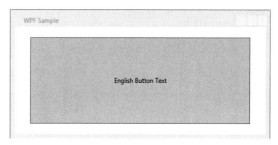

The XAML code for this application is shown here (code file WPFApplicationUsingResources\ MainWindow.xaml):

FIGURE 28-16

```xaml
<Window x:Class="Wrox.ProCSharp.Localization.MainWindow"
    xmlns="http://schemas.microsoft.com/winfx/2006/xaml/presentation"
    xmlns:x="http://schemas.microsoft.com/winfx/2006/xaml"
    Title="WPF Sample" Height="240" Width="500">
  <Grid>
    <Button Name="button1" Margin="30,20,30,20" Click="Button_Click"
        Content="English Button" />
  </Grid>
</Window>
```

With the handler code for the Click event of the button, only a message box containing a sample message pops up (code file WPFApplicationUsingResources\MainWindow.xaml.cs):

```csharp
private void Button_Click(object sender, RoutedEventArgs e)
{
    MessageBox.Show("English Message");
}
```

.NET Resources with WPF

You add .NET resources to a WPF application similarly to how you do so with other applications. Define the resources named Button1Text and Button1Message in the file Resources.resx. By default, this resource file has an Internal access modifier to create the Resources class. To use it from within XAML, you must change this to Public within the Managed Resources Editor.

To use the generated resource class, you need to change the XAML code. Add an XML namespace alias to reference the .NET namespace Wrox.ProCSharp.Localization.Properties as shown in the following code. Here, the alias is set to the value props. From XAML elements, properties of this class can be used with the x:Static markup extension. The Content property of the Button is set to the Button1Text property of the Resources class (code file WPFApplicationUsingResources\MainWindow .xaml):

```xaml
<Window x:Class="Wrox.ProCSharp.Localization.Window1"
    xmlns="http://schemas.microsoft.com/winfx/2006/xaml/presentation"
    xmlns:x="http://schemas.microsoft.com/winfx/2006/xaml"
    xmlns:props="clr-namespace:Wrox.ProCSharp.Localization.Properties"
    Title="WPF Sample" Height="300" Width="300">
  <Grid>
    <Button Name="button1" Margin="30,20,30,20" Click="Button_Click"
        Content="{x:Static props:Resources.Button1Text}" />
  </Grid>
</Window>
```

To use the .NET resource from code-behind, just access the `Button1Message` property directly, in the same way you do with Windows Forms applications (code file `WPFApplicationUsingResources\MainWindow.xaml.cs`):

```
private void Button_Click(object sender, RoutedEventArgs e)
{
    MessageBox.Show(Properties.Resources.Button1Message);
}
```

Now the resources can be localized as before.

Using .NET resources for localization of WPF applications offers two main advantages:

➤ .NET resources can be easily managed.

➤ `x:Static` bindings are checked by the compiler.

Of course, there are also disadvantages:

➤ You need to add the `x:Static` bindings to the XAML file, and there's no designer support for this.

➤ Binding is done to the generated resource classes that use the `ResourceManager`. You need to do some additional plumbing to support other resource managers, such as the `DatabaseResourceManager`, discussed later in this chapter.

➤ There's no type-converter support that can be used with other XAML elements.

XAML Resource Dictionaries

Instead of using .NET resources for localization of WPF applications, you can work directly with XAML to create localized content. This has its own advantages and disadvantages. The steps for a localization process can be described by these actions:

1. Create a satellite assembly from the main content.
2. Use resource dictionaries for localizable content.
3. Add `x:Uid` attributes to elements that should be localized.
4. Extract localization content from an assembly.
5. Translate the content.
6. Create satellite assemblies for every language.

These steps are described in the following sections.

Creating Satellite Assemblies

When compiling a WPF application, the XAML code is compiled to a binary format, BAML, that is stored into an assembly. To move the BAML code from the main assembly to a separate satellite assembly, you can change the `.csproj` build file by adding a `<UICulture>` element as a child to the `<PropertyGroup>` element, as shown in the following example. The culture, here en-US, defines the default culture of the project. Building the project with this build setting creates a subdirectory en-US and a satellite assembly containing BAML code for the default language (project file `WPFApplicationUsingXAMLDictionaries/WPFApplicationUsingXAMLDictionaries.csproj`):

```
<UICulture>en-US</UICulture>
```

> **NOTE** *The easiest way to modify project settings that are not available from the UI is to unload the project. To do so, select the project in Solution Explorer, select Unload Project from the context menu, and click Edit Project-File from the context menu. After the project file is changed, the project can be loaded again.*

When separating the BAML into a satellite assembly, you should also apply the NeutralResourcesLanguage attribute and supply the resource fallback location to a satellite assembly. If you decide to keep BAML in the main assembly (by not defining the <UICulture> to the .csproj file), the UltimateResourceFallbackLocation should be set to MainAssembly (code file WPFApplicationUsingXAMLDictionaries/AssemblyInfo.cs):

```
[assembly: NeutralResourcesLanguage("en-US",
UltimateResourceFallbackLocation.Satellite)]
```

Adding a Resource Dictionary

For code-behind content that needs to be localized, a resource dictionary can be added. Using XAML, you can define resources within the <ResourceDictionary> element, as shown in the following code. With Visual Studio, you can create a new resource dictionary by adding a new resource dictionary item and defining the filename. In the example here, the resource dictionary contains one string item. To get access to the String type from the System namespace, an XML namespace alias needs to be defined. Here, the alias system is set to the clr-namespace System in the assembly mscorlib. The string that is defined can be accessed with the key message1. This resource dictionary is defined in the file LocalizedStrings.xaml:

```
<ResourceDictionary
    xmlns="http://schemas.microsoft.com/winfx/2006/xaml/presentation"
    xmlns:x="http://schemas.microsoft.com/winfx/2006/xaml"
    xmlns:system="clr-namespace:System;assembly=mscorlib">
  <system:String x:Key="Message1">English Message</system:String>
</ResourceDictionary>
```

To make the resource dictionary available with the application, it must be added to the resources. If the resource dictionary is required only within a window or a specific WPF element, it can be added to the resources collection of the specific window or WPF element. If the same resource dictionary is needed by multiple windows, it can be added to the file App.xaml within the <Application> element, making it available to the complete application. Here, the resource dictionary is added within the resources of the main window (code file WPFApplicationUsingXAMLDictionaries/MainWindow.xaml):

```
<Window.Resources>
  <ResourceDictionary>
    <ResourceDictionary.MergedDictionaries>
      <ResourceDictionary Source="LocalizationStrings.xaml" />
    </ResourceDictionary.MergedDictionaries>
  </ResourceDictionary>
</Window.Resources>
```

To use the XAML resource dictionary from code-behind, you can use the indexer of the Resources property, the FindResource method, or the TryFindResource method. Because the resource is defined with the window, the indexer of the Resources property of the Window class can be used to access the resource. FindResource does a hierarchical search for a resource. If you use the FindResource method of the Button and it is not found with the Button resources, then resources are searched in the Grid. If the resource is not there, a lookup to the Window resources is done before the Application resources are consulted (code file WPFApplicationUsingXAMLDictionaries/MainWindow.xaml.cs):

```
private void Button_Click(object sender, RoutedEventArgs e)
{
    MessageBox.Show(this.Resources["Message1"] as string);
    MessageBox.Show(this.FindResource("Message1") as string);
}
```

Uid Attributes for Localization

With the custom resource dictionary file, you can reference the text from the code that should be localized. To localize XAML code with WPF elements, the x:Uid attribute is used as a unique identifier for the elements that need localization. You don't have to apply this attribute manually to the XAML content; instead, you can use the msbuild command with this option:

```
msbuild /t:updateuid
```

When you call this command in the directory where the project file is located, the XAML files of the project are modified to add an x:Uid attribute with a unique identifier to every element. If the control already has a Name or x:Name attribute applied, the x:Uid has the same value; otherwise, a new value is generated. The same XAML shown earlier now has the new attributes applied:

```
<Window x:Uid="Window_1"
        x:Class="WPFApplicationUsingXAMLDictionaries.MainWindow"
        xmlns="http://schemas.microsoft.com/winfx/2006/xaml/presentation"
        xmlns:x="http://schemas.microsoft.com/winfx/2006/xaml"
        Title="Main Window" Height="240" Width="500">
  <Window.Resources>
    <ResourceDictionary x:Uid="ResourceDictionary_1">
      <ResourceDictionary.MergedDictionaries>
        <ResourceDictionary x:Uid="ResourceDictionary_2"
                            Source="LocalizationStrings.xaml" />
      </ResourceDictionary.MergedDictionaries>
    </ResourceDictionary>
  </Window.Resources>
  <Grid x:Uid="Grid_1">
    <Button x:Uid="button1" Name="button1" Margin="30,20,30,20"
        Click="Button_Click" Content="English Button" />
  </Grid>
</Window>
```

If you change the XAML file after x:Uid attributes have been added, you can verify the correctness of the x:Uid attributes with the option /t:checkuid. Now you can compile the project to create BAML code containing the x:Uid attributes and use a tool to extract this information.

Using the LocBaml Tool for Localization

Compiling the project creates a satellite assembly containing the BAML code. From this satellite assembly, you can extract the content that needs to be localized with classes from the System.Windows.Markup .Localizer namespace. Included with the Windows SDK is the sample program LocBaml, a tool that can be used to extract localization content from BAML. You need to copy the executable, the satellite assembly with the default content, and LocBaml.exe to one directory and start the sample program to produce a .csv file with the localization content:

```
LocBaml /parse WPFApplicationUsingXAMLDictionaries.resources.dll /out: trans.csv
```

> **NOTE** *To use the LocBaml tool with a WPF application that is built with .NET 4.5, the tool also must be built with .NET 4 or a newer version. If you have an old version of the LocBaml tool that was built with .NET 2.0, it cannot load the .NET 4 assemblies. The Windows SDK contains the source of the tool, so you can rebuild it with the newest version of .NET.*

You can use Microsoft Excel to open the `.csv` file and translate its content. An extract from the `.csv` file that lists the content of the button and the message from the resource dictionary is shown here:

```
WPFandXAMLResources.g.en-US.resources:localizationstrings.baml,
system:String_1:System.String.$Content,None,True,True,,English Message
WPFandXAMLResources.g.en-US.resources:window1.baml,
button1:System.Windows.Controls.ContentControl.Content,Button,True,True,,
English Button
```

This file contains the following fields:

- ➤ The name of the BAML
- ➤ The identifier of the resource
- ➤ The category of the resource that provides the type of the content
- ➤ A Boolean value if the resource is visible for translation (readable)
- ➤ A Boolean value if the resource can be modified for the translation (modifiable)
- ➤ Localization comments
- ➤ The value of the resource

After localization of the resource, you can create a new directory for the new language (for example, `de` for German). The directory structure follows the same convention that was shown earlier in this chapter with satellite assemblies. With the LocBaml tool, you can create satellite assemblies with the translated content:

```
LocBaml /generate WPFandXAMLResources.resources.dll /trans:trans_de.csv
    /out: ./de /cul:de-DE
```

Now, the same rules for setting the culture of the thread and finding satellite assemblies that were shown with Windows Forms applications apply here.

As you've seen, it's quite a chore to perform the localization with XAML dictionaries. This is one of the disadvantages. Luckily, it's not necessary to do this on a daily basis. What are the advantages?

- ➤ You can delay the localization process within the XAML file until the application is completed. There's no special markup or resource-mapping syntax needed. The localization process can be separated from the development process.
- ➤ Using XAML resource dictionaries is very efficient at runtime.
- ➤ Localization can be done easily with a CSV editor.

The disadvantages are as follows:

- ➤ LocBaml is an unsupported tool found in the samples of the SDK.
- ➤ Localization is a one-time process. It's hard to make changes to the configured localization.

A CUSTOM RESOURCE READER

Using the resource readers that are part of .NET Framework 4.5, you can read resources from resource files and satellite assemblies. If you want to put the resources into a different store (such as a database), you can use a custom resource reader to read these resources.

To use a custom resource reader, you also need to create a custom resource set and a custom resource manager. Doing this is not a difficult task, however, because you can derive the custom classes from existing classes.

For the sample application, you need to create a simple database with just one table for storing messages; it should have one column for every supported language. The following table lists the columns and their corresponding values:

KEY	DEFAULT	DE	ES	FR	IT
Welcome	Welcome	Willkommen	Bienvenido	Bienvenue	Benvenuto
GoodMorning	Good morning	Guten Morgen	Buenos díaz	Bonjour	Buona mattina
GoodEvening	Good evening	Guten Abend	Buenos noches	Bonsoir	Buona sera
ThankYou	Thank you	Danke	Gracias	Merci	Grazie
Goodbye	Goodbye	Auf Wiedersehen	Adiós	Au revoir	Arrivederci

For the custom resource reader, you will create a component library with three classes: `DatabaseResourceReader`, `DatabaseResourceSet`, and `DatabaseResourceManager`.

Creating a DatabaseResourceReader

With the class `DatabaseResourceReader`, you define two fields: the connection string that is needed to access the database and the language that should be returned by the reader. These fields are filled inside the constructor of this class. The field `language` is set to the name of the culture that is passed with the `CultureInfo` object to the constructor (code file `DatabaseResourceReader\ DatabaseResourceReader.cs`):

```
public class DatabaseResourceReader: IResourceReader
{
  private string connectionString;
  private string language;

  public DatabaseResourceReader(string connectionString,
    CultureInfo culture)
  {
    this.connectionString = connectionString;
    this.language = culture.Name;
  }
}
```

A resource reader has to implement the interface `IResourceReader`. This interface defines the methods `Close` and `GetEnumerator` to return an `IDictionaryEnumerator` that returns keys and values for the resources. In the implementation of `GetEnumerator`, you create a `Hashtable` where all keys and values for a specific language are stored. Next, you can use the `SqlConnection` class in the namespace `System.Data .SqlClient` to access the database in SQL Server. `Connection.CreateCommand` creates a `SqlCommand` object that you use to specify the SQL `SELECT` statement to access the data in the database. If the language is set to de, the `SELECT` statement is `SELECT [key], [de] FROM Messages`. Then you use a `SqlDataReader` object to read all values from the database and put them into a `Hashtable`. Finally, the enumerator of the `Hashtable` is returned:

> **NOTE** *For more information about accessing data with ADO.NET, see Chapter 32, "Core ADO.NET."*

```csharp
public System.Collections.IDictionaryEnumerator GetEnumerator()
{
  Dictionary<string, string> dict = new Dictionary<string, string>();

  SqlConnection connection = new SqlConnection(connectionString);
  SqlCommand command = connection.CreateCommand();
  if (String.IsNullOrEmpty(language))
    language = "Default";

  command.CommandText = "SELECT [key], [" + language + "] " +
                        "FROM Messages";

  try
  {
    connection.Open();

    SqlDataReader reader = command.ExecuteReader();
    while (reader.Read())
    {
      if (reader.GetValue(1) != System.DBNull.Value)
      {
        dict.Add(reader.GetString(0).Trim(), reader.GetString(1));
      }
    }

    reader.Close();
  }
  catch (SqlException ex)
  {
    if (ex.Number != 207)  // ignore missing columns in the database
      throw;               // rethrow all other exceptions
  }
  finally
  {
    connection.Close();
  }
  return dict.GetEnumerator();
}

public void Close()
{
}
```

Because the interface IResourceReader is derived from IEnumerable and IDisposable, the methods GetEnumerator, which returns an IEnumerator interface, and Dispose must be implemented, too:

```csharp
IEnumerator IEnumerable.GetEnumerator()
{
  return this.GetEnumerator();
}

void IDisposable.Dispose()
{
}
}
```

Creating a DatabaseResourceSet

The class DatabaseResourceSet can use nearly all implementations of the base class ResourceSet. You just need a different constructor that initializes the base class with your own resource reader, DatabaseResourceReader. The constructor of ResourceSet allows passing an object by implementing `IResourceReader`; this requirement is fulfilled by `DatabaseResourceReader` (code file `DatabaseResourceReader\DatabaseResourceSet.cs`):

```
public class DatabaseResourceSet: ResourceSet
{
  internal DatabaseResourceSet(string connectionString, CultureInfo culture)
    : base(new DatabaseResourceReader(connectionString, culture))
  {
  }

  public override Type GetDefaultReader()
  {
    return typeof(DatabaseResourceReader);
  }
}
```

Creating a DatabaseResourceManager

The third class you have to create is the custom resource manager. `DatabaseResourceManager` is derived from the class `ResourceManager`, and you only have to implement a new constructor and override the method `InternalGetResourceSet`.

In the constructor, create a new `Dictionary<string, DatabaseResourceSet>` to store all queried resource sets and set it in the field `ResourceSets` defined by the base class (code file `DatabaseResourceReader/DatabaseResoureManager.cs`):

```
public class DatabaseResourceManager: ResourceManager
{
  private string connectionString;
  private Dictionary<string, DatabaseResourceSet> resourceSets;

  public DatabaseResourceManager(string connectionString)
  {
    this.connectionString = connectionString;
    resourceSets = new Dictionary<string, DatabaseResourceSet>();
  }
```

The methods of the `ResourceManager` class that you can use to access resources (such as `GetString` and `GetObject`) invoke the method `InternalGetResourceSet` to access a resource set where the appropriate values can be returned.

In the implementation of `InternalGetResourceSet`, you first check whether the resource set for the culture queried for a resource is already in the hash table; if so, you return it to the caller. If the resource set is not available, you create a new `DatabaseResourceSet` object with the queried culture, add it to the dictionary, and return it to the caller:

```
protected override ResourceSet InternalGetResourceSet(
    CultureInfo culture, bool createIfNotExists, bool tryParents)
{
  DatabaseResourceSet rs = null;

  if (resourceSets.ContainsKey(culture.Name))
  {
    rs = resourceSets[culture.Name];
  }
  else
  {
    rs = new DatabaseResourceSet(connectionString, culture);
    resourceSets.Add(culture.Name, rs);
```

```
        }
        return rs;
    }
}
```

Client Application for DatabaseResourceReader

The way in which the class `ResourceManager` is used from the client application here does not differ much from the earlier use of the `ResourceManager` class. The only difference is that the custom class `DatabaseResourceManager` is used instead of the class `ResourceManager`. The following code snippet demonstrates how you can use your own resource manager.

A new `DatabaseResourceManager` object is created by passing the database connection string to the constructor. Then, you can invoke the `GetString` method that is implemented in the base class as you did earlier, passing the key and an optional object of type `CultureInfo` to specify a culture. In turn, you get a resource value from the database because this resource manager is using the classes `DatabaseResourceSet` and `DatabaseResourceReader` (code file `DatabaseResourceReaderClient\Program.cs`):

```
var rm = new DatabaseResourceManager(
            @"server=(local)\sqlexpress;database=LocalizationDemo;" +
            "trusted_connection=true");

string spanishWelcome = rm.GetString("Welcome", new CultureInfo("es-ES"));
string italianThankyou = rm.GetString("ThankYou", new CultureInfo("it"));
string threadDefaultGoodMorning = rm.GetString("GoodMorning");
```

CREATING CUSTOM CULTURES

Over time, more and more languages have become supported by the .NET Framework. However, not all languages of the world are available with .NET, and for these you can create a custom culture. For example, creating a custom culture can be useful to support a minority within a region or to create subcultures for different dialects.

Custom cultures and regions can be created with the class `CultureAndRegionInfoBuilder` in the namespace `System.Globalization`. This class is located in the assembly `sysglobl`.

With the constructor of the class `CultureAndRegionInfoBuilder`, you can pass the culture's name. The second argument of the constructor requires an enumeration of type `CultureAndRegionModifiers`. This enumeration allows one of three values: `Neutral` for a neutral culture, `Replacement` if an existing Framework culture should be replaced, or `None`.

After the `CultureAndRegionInfoBuilder` object is instantiated, you can configure the culture by setting properties. With the properties of this class, you can define all the cultural and regional information, such as name, calendar, number format, metric information, and so on. If the culture should be based on existing cultures and regions, you can set the properties of the instance using the methods `LoadDataFromCultureInfo` and `LoadDataFromRegionInfo`, changing the values that are different by setting the properties afterward.

Calling the method `Register` registers the new culture with the operating system. Indeed, you can find the file that describes the culture in the directory `<windows>\Globalization`. Look for files with the extension `.nlp` (code file `CustomCultures\Program.cs`).

```
using System;
using System.Globalization;

namespace CustomCultures
{
  class Program
```

```
    {
      static void Main()
      {
        try
        {
          // Create a Styria culture
          var styria = new CultureAndRegionInfoBuilder("de-AT-ST",
            CultureAndRegionModifiers.None);
          var cultureParent = new CultureInfo("de-AT");
          styria.LoadDataFromCultureInfo(cultureParent);
          styria.LoadDataFromRegionInfo(new RegionInfo("AT"));
          styria.Parent = cultureParent;
          styria.RegionNativeName = "Steiermark";
          styria.RegionEnglishName = "Styria";
          styria.CultureEnglishName = "Styria (Austria)";
          styria.CultureNativeName = "Steirisch";

          styria.Register();
        }
        catch (UnauthorizedAccessException ex)
        {
          Console.WriteLine(ex.Message);
        }
      }
    }
}
```

Because registering custom languages on the system requires administrative privileges, an application manifest file is required that specifies the requested execution rights. In the project properties, the manifest file needs to be set in the Application settings.

```
<?xml version="1.0" encoding="utf-8"?>
<asmv1:assembly manifestVersion="1.0" xmlns="urn:schemas-microsoft-com:asm.v1"
xmlsn:asmv1="urn:schemas-microsoft-com:asm.v1" xmlns:asmv2="urn:schemas-microsoft-
com:asm.v2" xmlns:xsi="http://www.w3.org/2001/XMLSchema-instance">
  <assemblyIdentity version="1.0.0.0" name="MyApplication.app"/>
  <trustInfo xmlns="urn:schemas-microsoft-com:asm.v2">
    <security>
      <requestedPrivileges xmlns="urn:schemas-microsoft-com:asm.v3">
        <requestedExecutionLevel level="requireAdministrator"
          uiAccess="false" />
      </requestedPrivileges>
    </security>
  </trustInfo>
</asmv1:assembly>
```

The newly created culture can now be used like other cultures:

```
var ci = new CultureInfo("de-AT-ST");
Thread.CurrentThread.CurrentCulture = ci;
Thread.CurrentThread.CurrentUICulture = ci;
```

You can use the culture for formatting and for resources. If you start the Cultures In Action application that was written earlier in this chapter again, you can see the custom culture as well.

LOCALIZATION WITH WINDOWS STORE APPS

Localization with Windows Store apps is based on the concepts you've learned so far but brings some fresh ideas, as you will see here. For the best experience, you need to install the Multilingual App Toolkit for Visual Studio 2012 (http://msdn.microsoft.com/en-us/windows/apps/hh848309.aspx).

The concepts of cultures, regions, and resources are the same, but because Windows Store apps can be written with C# and XAML, C++ and XAML, and JavaScript and HTML, these concepts need to be available with all languages. Only the Windows Runtime is available with all these programming languages and Windows 8 apps. Therefore, new namespaces for globalization and resources are available with the Windows Runtime: `Windows.Globalization` and `Windows.ApplicationModel.Resources`. With the globalization namespaces you can find a `Calendar`, `GeographicRegion` (compare with the .NET `RegionInfo`) and a `Language` class. With subnamespaces, there are also classes for number and date formatting that vary according to the language. With C# and Windows Store apps you can still use the .NET classes for cultures and regions.

Let's get into an example so you can see localization with Windows Store apps in action. Create a small application using the Blank App (XAML) Visual Studio project template. Add two `TextBlock` and one `TextBox` controls to the page.

Within the `OnNavigatedTo` method of the code file you can assign a date with the current format to the `Text` property of the `text1` control. The `DateTime` structure can be used in a way very similar to before. Just note that a few methods are not available with Windows Store apps—for example, you cannot use the method `ToLongDateString`, but `ToString` with the same format is available:

```
protected override void OnNavigatedTo(NavigationEventArgs e)
{
    text1.Text = DateTime.Today.ToString("D");
}
```

Using Resources

With Windows Store apps you can create resource files with the file extension `resw` instead of `resx`. Behind the scenes, the same XML format is used with `resw` files, and you can use the same Visual Studio resource editor to create and modify these files. The following example uses the structure shown in Figure 28-17. The subfolder `Messages` contains a subdirectory, `en-us`, in which two resource files `Errors.resw` and `Messages.resw` are created. In the folder `Strings\en-us`, the resource file `Resources.resw` is created.

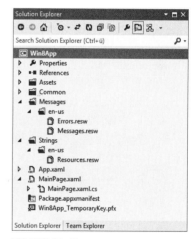

FIGURE 28-17

The `Messages.resw` file contains some English text resources, `Hello` with a value of `Hello World`, and resources named `GoodDay`, `GoodEvening`, and `GoodMorning`. The file `Resources.resw` contains the resources `Text3.Text` and `Text3.Width`, with the values `"This is a sample message for Text 4"` and a value of `"300"`.

With the code, resources can be accessed with the help of the `ResourceLoader` class from the namespace `Windows.ApplicationModel.Resources`. Here we use the string `"Messages"` with the constructor parameter. Thus, the resource file `Messages.resw` is being used. Invoking the method `GetString` retrieves the resource with the key `"Hello"`:

```
var resourceLoader = new ResourceLoader("Messages");
text2.Text = resourceLoader.GetString("Hello");
```

With Windows Store apps it is also easy to use the resources directly from XAML code. With the following `TextBox`, the `x:Uid` attribute is assigned the value `Text3`. This way, a resource named `Text3` with extensions is searched for in the resource file `Resources.resw`. This resource file contains value for the keys `Text3.Text` and `Text3.Width`. The values are retrieved, and both the `Text` and `Width` properties are set:

```
<TextBox x:Uid="Text3" HorizontalAlignment="Left" Margin="219,343,0,0"
    TextWrapping="Wrap" Text="TextBox" VerticalAlignment="Top"/>
```

Localization with the Multilingual App Toolkit

To localize Windows Store apps you can download the previously mentioned Multilingual App Toolkit. This toolkit integrates with Visual Studio 2012. After installing the toolkit you can enable it with the Windows Store apps via Tools ⇨ Enable Multilingual Toolkit. This adds a build command to the project file and adds one more options to the context menu in Solution Explorer. Select the option Add Translation Languages... to invoke the dialog shown in Figure 28-18, where you can choose which languages should be translated. The sample uses Pseudo Language, French, German, and Spanish. For these languages, a Microsoft Translator is available. This tool now creates a `MultilingualResources` subdirectory that contains .xlf files for the selected languages. The .xlf files are defined with the XLIFF (XML Localisation Interchange File Format) standard, a Microsoft-independent standard for localization.

FIGURE 28-18

The next time you start the build process for the project, the XLIFF files are filled with content from all the resources. Selecting the XLIFF files in Solution Explorer, you can send these directly to translation. To do so, select Send For Translation..., which opens e-mail and attaches the XLIFF files.

Because you have the Multilingual Toolkit on the system, you can also start the translation process by opening the Multilingual Editor, shown in Figure 28-19. Clicking the Translate button makes use of the Microsoft Translation Service to translate all the resource values automatically.

FIGURE 28-19

Don't use the translation without a manual review. The tool shows a status for every resource that is translated. After the automatic translation, the status is set to Needs Review. You have probably seen applications with automatic translations that are incorrect and sometimes really funny.

SUMMARY

This chapter demonstrated how to globalize and localize .NET applications. For the globalization of applications, you learned about using the namespace `System.Globalization` to format culture-dependent numbers and dates. Furthermore, you learned that sorting strings by default varies according to the culture, and you looked at using the invariant culture for a culture-independent sort. Using the `CultureAndRegionInfoBuilder` class, you've learned how to create a custom culture.

Localizing an application is accomplished by using resources, which you can pack into files, satellite assemblies, or a custom store such as a database. The classes used with localization are in the namespace `System.Resources`. To read resources from other places, such as satellite assemblies or resource files, you can create a custom resource reader.

You also learned how to localize Windows Forms, WPF, ASP.NET, and Windows Store apps, and some important vocabulary in different languages.

The next chapter provides information about XAML. XAML is used with WPF, Silverlight, XPS, Windows Workflow Foundation, and Windows Store apps, so it provides a foundation for many technologies.

29

Core XAML

WHAT'S IN THIS CHAPTER?

➤ XAML syntax
➤ Dependency properties
➤ Attached properties
➤ Markup extensions
➤ Loading XAML dynamically

WROX.COM CODE DOWNLOADS FOR THIS CHAPTER

The wrox.com code downloads for this chapter are found at `http://www.wrox.com/remtitle .cgi?isbn=1118314425` on the Download Code tab. The code for this chapter is divided into the following major examples:

➤ Code Intro
➤ XAML Intro
➤ XAML Syntax
➤ Dependency Objects
➤ Bubble Demo
➤ Attached Properties
➤ Markup Extensions

USES OF XAML

When writing a .NET application, usually C# is not the only syntax you need to know. If you write Windows Presentation Foundation (WPF) applications, use Windows Workflow Foundation (WF), create XPS documents, or write Silverlight or Windows 8 applications, you also need XAML. XAML (eXtensible Application Markup Language) is a declarative XML syntax that's usually needed with these applications. This chapter describes the syntax of XAML and the extensibility mechanisms that are available with this markup language.

XAML FOUNDATION

XAML code is declared using textual XML. You can use designers to create XAML code or write XAML code by hand. Visual Studio contains designers to write XAML code for WPF, Silverlight, WF, or Windows 8 apps. Other tools are also available to create XAML, such as Microsoft Expression Design and Microsoft Expression Blend.

XAML is used with several technologies, but there are differences among the various technologies. With the XML namespace `http://schemas.microsoft.com/winfx/2006/xaml/presentation`, which is mapped as the default with WPF and Windows 8 applications, WPF extensions to XAML are defined. WPF makes use of dependency properties, attached properties, and several WPF-specific markup extensions. WF 4 uses the XML namespace `http://schemas.microsoft.com/netfx/2009/xaml/activities` for the definition of the workflow activities. The XML namespace `http://schemas.microsoft.com/winfx/2006/xaml` usually is mapped to the x prefix and defines features that are common to all XAML vocabularies.

With WPF applications, a XAML element maps to a .NET class. That's not a strict requirement for XAML. With Silverlight 1.0, .NET was not available with the plugin and the XAML code was interpreted and could be accessed programmatically just with JavaScript. This changed with Silverlight 2.0, in which a smaller version of the .NET Framework is part of the Silverlight plugin. With WPF, every XAML element has a class behind it. That's also the case with Windows Workflow Foundation—for example, the `DoWhile` XAML element is a looping activity backed by the `DoWhile` class in the namespace `System.Activities` `.Statements`. The `Button` XAML element is the same as the `Button` class in the `System.Windows` `.Controls` namespace. With Windows 8 applications, every XAML element maps to either a .NET class or a Windows Runtime class.

It's also possible to use custom .NET classes within XML by mapping the .NET namespace to an XML alias, which is explained in the section Using Custom .NET Classes. With .NET 4, XAML's syntax was enhanced, and the newer version is known as XAML 2009. (The first version of XAML is XAML 2006, defined in the XML namespace `http://schemas.microsoft.com/winfx/2006/xaml`). The newest version of XAML supports enhancements, like generics within XAML code. However, the WPF, WF, and Windows 8 apps designers available with the release of Visual Studio 2012 are still based on XAML 2006. You can use XAML 2009 by using it directly from within your applications to load XAML. This chapter gives you the information on changes of XAML 2009.

What happens with XAML code on a build process? To compile a WPF project, MSBuild tasks are defined in the assembly `PresentationBuildTasks` named `MarkupCompilePass1` and `MarkupCompilePass2`. These MSBuild tasks create a binary representation of the markup code named BAML (Binary Application Markup Language) that is added to the .NET resources of an assembly. During runtime the binary representation is used.

You can read and write XAML and BAML with readers and writers. In the namespace `System.Xaml`, classes for core XAML features are available, such as abstract `XamlReader` and `XamlWriter` classes, and concrete implementations to read and write objects and XAML XML formats. The namespace `System.Windows.Markup` also contains some features that are available for all technologies using XAML from the assembly `System.Xaml`. Classes from this namespace but that are found in the assembly `PresentationFramework` are WPF-specific extensions. For example, there you can find other `XamlReader` and `XamlWriter` classes that are optimized for WPF features.

How Elements Map to .NET Objects

As mentioned earlier, usually a XAML element maps to a .NET class. In this section you'll begin by creating a `Button` object inside a `Window` programmatically with a C# console project. To compile the following code, whereby a `Button` object is instantiated with the `Content` property set to a string, a `Window` is defined with `Title` and `Content` properties set, and the assemblies `PresentationFramework`, `PresentationCore`, `WindowsBase`, and `System.Xaml` need to be referenced (code file `CodeIntro/Program.cs`).

```
using System;
using System.Windows;
using System.Windows.Controls;
namespace Wrox.ProCSharp.XAML
{
  class Program
  {
    [STAThread]
    static void Main()
    {
      var b = new Button
      {
        Content = "Click Me!"
      };
      var w = new Window
      {
        Title = "Code Demo",
        Content = b
      };

      var app = new Application();
      app.Run(w);
    }
  }
}
```

A similar UI can be created by using XAML code. As before, a `Window` element is created that contains a `Button` element. The `Window` element has the `Title` attribute set in addition to its content (XAML file XAMLIntro/MainWindow.xaml):

```xaml
<Window x:Class="Wrox.ProCSharp.XAML.MainWindow"
        xmlns="http://schemas.microsoft.com/winfx/2006/xaml/presentation"
        xmlns:x="http://schemas.microsoft.com/winfx/2006/xaml"
        Title="XAML Demo" Height="350" Width="525">
  <Button Content="Click Me!" />
</Window>
```

Of course, the `Application` instance in the last code example is missing. This can be defined with XAML as well. In the `Application` element, the `StartupUri` attribute is set, which links to the XAML file that contains the main window (XAML file XAMLIntro/App.xaml):

```xaml
<Application x:Class="Wrox.ProCSharp.XAML.App"
             xmlns="http://schemas.microsoft.com/winfx/2006/xaml/presentation"
             xmlns:x="http://schemas.microsoft.com/winfx/2006/xaml"
             StartupUri="MainWindow.xaml">
  <Application.Resources>
  </Application.Resources>
</Application>
```

Using Custom .NET Classes

To use custom .NET classes within XAML code, only the .NET namespace needs to be declared within XAML, and an XML alias must be defined. To demonstrate this, a simple `Person` class with the `FirstName` and `LastName` properties is defined as shown here (code file DemoLib/Person.cs):

```csharp
namespace Wrox.ProCSharp.XAML
{
  public class Person
  {
```

```
      public string FirstName { get; set; }
      public string LastName { get; set; }
      public override string ToString()
      {
        return string.Format("{0} {1}", FirstName, LastName);
      }
    }
  }
```

In XAML, an XML namespace alias named `local` is defined that maps to the .NET namespace `Wrox.ProCSharp.XAML`. Now it's possible to use all classes from this namespace with the alias. With WPF, the `clr-namespace` keyword maps to a .NET namespace, whereas with Windows 8 apps the `using` keyword is used to map to either a .NET or a Windows Runtime namespace.

In the XAML code, a `ListBox` is added that contains items of type `Person`. Using XAML attributes, the values of the properties `FirstName` and `LastName` are set. When you run the application, the output of the `ToString` method is shown inside the `ListBox` (XAML file `XAMLIntro/MainWindow.xaml`):

```
<Window x:Class="Wrox.ProCSharp.XAML.MainWindow"
        xmlns="http://schemas.microsoft.com/winfx/2006/xaml/presentation"
        xmlns:x="http://schemas.microsoft.com/winfx/2006/xaml"
        xmlns:local="clr-namespace:Wrox.ProCSharp.XAML"
        Title="XAML Demo" Height="350" Width="525">
  <StackPanel>
    <Button Content="Click Me!" />
    <ListBox>
      <local:Person FirstName="Stephanie" LastName="Nagel" />
      <local:Person FirstName="Matthias" LastName="Nagel" />
    </ListBox>
  </StackPanel>
</Window>
```

> **NOTE** *If the .NET namespace is not in the same assembly as the XAML code, the assembly name must also be included with the XML namespace alias—for example,* `xmlns:local="clr-namespace:Wrox.ProCSharp.XAML;assembly=XAMLIntro"`. *Both private and shared assemblies can be used with the reference here. With a shared assembly the full name, including the version number, culture, and key token of the assembly, needs to be specified here. More information about shared assemblies is found in Chapter 19, "Assemblies".*

To map a .NET namespace to an XML namespace, you can use the assembly attribute `XmlnsDefinition`. One argument of this attribute defines the XML namespace, the other the .NET namespace. Using this attribute, it is also possible to map multiple .NET namespaces to a single XML namespace (code file `DemoLib/AssemblyInfo.cs`):

```
[assembly: XmlnsDefinition("http://www.wrox.com/Schemas/2010", "Wrox.ProCSharp.XAML")]
```

With this attribute in place, the namespace declaration in the XAML code can be changed to map to the XML namespace (XAML file `XAMLIntro/MainWindow.xaml`):

```
<Window x:Class="Wrox.ProCSharp.XAML.MainWindow"
        xmlns="http://schemas.microsoft.com/winfx/2006/xaml/presentation"
        xmlns:x="http://schemas.microsoft.com/winfx/2006/xaml"
        xmlns:local="http://www.wrox.com/Schemas/2010"
        Title="XAML Demo" Height="350" Width="525">
  <StackPanel>
    <Button Content="Click Me!" />
    <ListBox>
      <local:Person FirstName="Stephanie" LastName="Nagel" />
```

```
        <local:Person FirstName="Matthias" LastName="Nagel" />
      </ListBox>
    </StackPanel>
  </Window>
```

Properties as Attributes

You can set properties as attributes as long as the property type can be represented as a string or there is a conversion from a string to the property type. The following code snippet sets the Content and Background properties of the Button element with attributes. The Content property is of type object and thus accepts a string. The Background property is of type Brush. The Brush type defines the BrushConverter class as a converter type with the attribute TypeConverter, with which the class is annotated. BrushConverter uses a list of colors to return a SolidColorBrush from the ConvertFromString method:

```
<Button Content="Click Me!" Background="LightGoldenrodYellow" />
```

> **NOTE** *A type converter derives from the base class* TypeConverter *in the* System .ComponentModel *namespace. The type of the class that needs conversion defines the type converter with the* TypeConverter *attribute. WPF uses many type converters to convert XML attributes to a specific type, including* ColorConverter, FontFamilyConverter, PathFigureCollectionConverter, ThicknessConverter, *and* GeometryConverter, *to name just a few.*

Properties as Elements

It's always also possible to use the element syntax to supply the value for properties. The Background property of the Button class can be set with the child element Button.Background. This way, more complex brushes can be applied to this property, such as a LinearGradientBrush, as shown in the example.

When setting the content in the sample, neither the Content attribute nor a Button.Content element is used to write the content; instead, the content is written directly as a child value to the Button element. That's possible because with a base class of the Button class (ContentControl), the ContentProperty attribute is applied, which marks the Content property as a ContentProperty: [ContentProperty("Content")]. With such a marked property, the value of the property can be written as a child element (XAML file XAMLSyntax/MainWindow.xaml):

```
<Button>
  Click Me!
  <Button.Background>
    <LinearGradientBrush StartPoint="0.5,0.0" EndPoint="0.5, 1.0">
      <GradientStop Offset="0" Color="Yellow" />
      <GradientStop Offset="0.3" Color="Orange" />
      <GradientStop Offset="0.7" Color="Red" />
      <GradientStop Offset="1" Color="DarkRed" />
    </LinearGradientBrush>
  </Button.Background>
</Button>
```

Essential .NET Types

In XAML 2006, core .NET types need to be referenced from an XML namespace like all other .NET classes—for example, with the String with the sys alias as shown here:

```
<sys:String xmlns:sys="clr-namespace:System;assembly=mscorlib>Simple String</sys:String>
```

XAML 2009 defines types such as `String`, `Boolean`, `Object`, `Decimal`, `Double`, `Int32` and others with the x alias:

```
<x:String>Simple String</x:String>
```

Using Collections with XAML

In the `ListBox` that contains `Person` elements, you've already seen a collection within XAML. In the `ListBox`, the items have been directly defined as child elements. In addition, the `LinearGradientBrush` contained a collection of `GradientStop` elements. This is possible because the base class `ItemsControl` has the attribute `ContentProperty` set to the `Items` property of the class, and the `GradientBrush` base class sets the attribute `ContentProperty` to `GradientStops`.

The following example shows a longer version that defines the background by directly setting the `GradientStops` property and defining the `GradientStopCollection` element as its child:

```
<Button Click="OnButtonClick">
    Click Me!
  <Button.Background>
    <LinearGradientBrush StartPoint="0.5,0.0" EndPoint="0.5, 1.0">
      <LinearGradientBrush.GradientStops>
        <GradientStopCollection>
          <GradientStop Offset="0" Color="Yellow" />
          <GradientStop Offset="0.3" Color="Orange" />
          <GradientStop Offset="0.7" Color="Red" />
          <GradientStop Offset="1" Color="DarkRed" />
        </GradientStopCollection>
      </LinearGradientBrush.GradientStops>
    </LinearGradientBrush>
  </Button.Background>
</Button>
```

To define an array, the `x:Array` extension can be used. The `x:Array` extension has a `Type` property that enables you to specify the type of the array's items:

```
<x:Array Type="local:Person">
  <local:Person FirstName="Stephanie" LastName="Nagel" />
  <local:Person FirstName="Matthias" LastName="Nagel" />
</x:Array>
```

> **NOTE** The `x:Array` extension is not supported with Windows 8 apps.

XAML 2006 does not support generics, so to use a generic collection class from XAML you need to define a nongeneric class that derives from the generic class and use that instead. In XAML 2009, generics are directly supported in XAML with the `x:TypeArguments` attribute to define the generic type, as shown here with `ObservableCollection<T>`:

```
<ObservableCollection x:TypeArguments="local:Person">
  <local:Person FirstName="Stephanie" LastName="Nagel" />
  <local:Person FirstName="Matthias" LastName="Nagel" />
</ObservableCollection>
```

Calling Constructors with XAML Code

If a class doesn't have a default constructor it cannot be used with XAML 2006. With XAML 2009 you can use `x:Arguments` to invoke a constructor with parameters. Here is the `Person` class instantiated with a constructor that requires two `String` arguments:

```
<local:Person>
  <x:Arguments>
    <x:String>Stephanie</x:String>
    <x:String>Nagel</x:String>
  </x:Arguments>
</local:Person>
```

DEPENDENCY PROPERTIES

WPF uses dependency properties for data binding, animations, property change notification, styling, and so forth. For data binding, the property of the UI element that is bound to the source of a .NET property must be a dependency property.

From the outside, a dependency property looks like a normal .NET property. However, with a normal .NET property you usually also define the data member that is accessed by the get and set accessors of the property:

```
private int val;
public int Value
{
  get
  {
    return val;
  }
  set
  {
    val = value;
  }
}
```

That's not the case with dependency properties. A dependency property usually has a get and set accessor of a property as well. This is common with normal properties. However, with the implementation of the get and set accessors, the methods GetValue and SetValue are invoked. GetValue and SetValue are members of the base class DependencyObject, which also stipulates a requirement for dependency objects—that they must be implemented in a class that derives from DependencyObject.

With a dependency property, the data member is kept inside an internal collection that is managed by the base class and only allocates data if the value changes. With unchanged values the data can be shared between different instances or base classes. The GetValue and SetValue methods require a DependencyProperty argument. This argument is defined by a static member of the class that has the same name as the property appended to the term Property. With the property Value, the static member has the name ValueProperty. DependencyProperty.Register is a helper method that registers the property in the dependency property system. In the following code snippet, the Register method is used with three arguments to define the name of the property, the type of the property, and the type of the owner—that is, the class MyDependencyObject (code file DependencyObjectDemo/MyDependencyObject.cs):

```
public int Value
{
  get { return (int)GetValue(ValueProperty); }
  set { SetValue(ValueProperty, value); }
}
public static readonly DependencyProperty ValueProperty =
    DependencyProperty.Register("Value", typeof(int), typeof(MyDependencyObject));
```

Creating a Dependency Property

This section looks at an example that defines not one but three dependency properties. The class MyDependencyObject defines the dependency properties Value, Minimum, and Maximum. All of these properties are dependency properties that are registered with the method DependencyProperty.Register. The methods GetValue and SetValue are members of the base class DependencyObject. For the Minimum and Maximum properties, default values are defined that can be set with the DependencyProperty .Register method and a fourth argument to set the PropertyMetadata. Using a constructor with one parameter, PropertyMetadata, the Minimum property is set to 0, and the Maximum property is set to 100:

```
using System;
using System.Windows;
namespace Wrox.ProCSharp.XAML
{
  class MyDependencyObject : DependencyObject
  {
    public int Value
    {
      get { return (int)GetValue(ValueProperty); }
      set { SetValue(ValueProperty, value); }
    }
    public static readonly DependencyProperty ValueProperty =
        DependencyProperty.Register("Value", typeof(int), typeof(MyDependencyObject));
    public int Minimum
    {
      get { return (int)GetValue(MinimumProperty); }
      set { SetValue(MinimumProperty, value); }
    }
    public static readonly DependencyProperty MinimumProperty =
        DependencyProperty.Register("Minimum", typeof(int), typeof(MyDependencyObject),
                            new PropertyMetadata(0));
    public int Maximum
    {
      get { return (int)GetValue(MaximumProperty); }
      set { SetValue(MaximumProperty, value); }
    }
    public static readonly DependencyProperty MaximumProperty =
        DependencyProperty.Register("Maximum", typeof(int), typeof(MyDependencyObject),
                            new PropertyMetadata(100));
  }
}
```

> **NOTE** *Within the implementation of the* get *and* set *property accessors, you should not do anything other than invoke the* GetValue *and* SetValue *methods. Using the dependency properties, the property values can be accessed from the outside with the* GetValue *and* SetValue *methods, which is also done from WPF; therefore, the strongly typed property accessors might not be invoked at all. They are just here for convenience, so you can use the normal property syntax from your custom code.*

Coerce Value Callback

Dependency properties support coercion. Using coercion, the value of a property can be checked to see if it is valid—for example, that it falls within a valid range. That's why the Minimum and Maximum properties are included in the sample. Now the registration of the Value property is changed to pass the event handler method CoerceValue to the constructor of PropertyMetadata, which is passed as an argument to the DependencyProperty.Register method. The CoerceValue method is invoked with every change of the property value from the implementation of the SetValue method. Within CoerceValue(), the set value is checked to determine whether it falls within the specified minimum and maximum range; if not, the value is set accordingly (code file DependencyObjectDemo/MyDependencyObject.cs).

```
using System;
using System.Windows;
namespace Wrox.ProCSharp.XAML
{
  class MyDependencyObject : DependencyObject
  {
    public int Value
    {
      get { return (int)GetValue(ValueProperty); }
      set { SetValue(ValueProperty, value); }
    }
    public static readonly DependencyProperty ValueProperty =
        DependencyProperty.Register("Value", typeof(int), typeof(MyDependencyObject));
        new PropertyMetadata(0, null, CoerceValue));
    public int Minimum
    {
      get { return (int)GetValue(MinimumProperty); }
      set { SetValue(MinimumProperty, value); }
    }
    public static readonly DependencyProperty MinimumProperty =
        DependencyProperty.Register("Minimum", typeof(int), typeof(MyDependencyObject),
                                 new PropertyMetadata(0));
    public int Maximum
    {
      get { return (int)GetValue(MaximumProperty); }
      set { SetValue(MaximumProperty, value); }
    }
    public static readonly DependencyProperty MaximumProperty =
        DependencyProperty.Register("Maximum", typeof(int), typeof(MyDependencyObject),
                                 new PropertyMetadata(100));
    private static object CoerceValue(DependencyObject element, object value)
    {
      int newValue = (int)value;
      MyDependencyObject control = (MyDependencyObject)element;

      newValue = Math.Max(control.Minimum, Math.Min(control.Maximum, newValue));
      return newValue;
    }
  }
}
```

Value Changed Callbacks and Events

To get some information on value changes, dependency properties also support value change callbacks. You can add a DependencyPropertyChanged event handler to the DependencyProperty.Register method that is invoked when the property value changes. In the sample code, the handler method OnValueChanged is assigned to the PropertyChangedCallback of the PropertyMetadata object. In the OnValueChanged method, you can access the old and new values of the property with the DependencyPropertyChangedEventArgs argument:

```
using System;
using System.Windows;
namespace Wrox.ProCSharp.XAML
{
  class MyDependencyObject : DependencyObject
  {
    public int Value
    {
      get { return (int)GetValue(ValueProperty); }
      set { SetValue(ValueProperty, value); }
    }
```

```
      public static readonly DependencyProperty ValueProperty =
          DependencyProperty.Register("Value", typeof(int), typeof(MyDependencyObject),
          new PropertyMetadata(0, OnValueChanged, CoerceValue));
      //...
      private static void OnValueChanged(DependencyObject obj,
                                         DependencyPropertyChangedEventArgs args)
      {
        int oldValue = (int)args.OldValue;
        int newValue = (int)args.NewValue;
        //...
      }
    }
  }
}
```

BUBBLING AND TUNNELING EVENTS

Elements can be contained in other elements. With XAML and WPF, you can define that a `Button` contains a `ListBox`; and the `ListBox` can contain items that are `Button` controls. When you click on an inner `Button` control, the `Click` event should go all the way up to the controls that contain the inner control. The `Click` event is a bubbling event. The `PreviewMouseMove` event is a tunneling event that tunnels from the outside to the inside. First the outer controls receive the event followed by the inner controls. The `MouseMove` event follows the `PreviewMouseMove` event and is a bubbling event that bubbles from the inside to the outside. WPF supports these bubbling and tunneling events, which are often used in pairs.

> **NOTE** *Core information about .NET events is explained in Chapter 8, "Delegates, Lambdas, and Events."*

To demonstrate bubbling, the following XAML code contains four `Button` controls whereby the surrounding `StackPanel` defines an event handler for the `Button.Click` event named `OnOuterButtonClick`. `button2` contains a `ListBox` that has two `Button` controls as its children and the `Click` event handler `OnButton2`. Both of the inner buttons also have an event handler associated with the `Click` event (XAML file `BubbleDemo/MainWindow.xaml`):

```
<Window x:Class=" Wrox.ProCSharp.XAML.MainWindow"
        xmlns="http://schemas.microsoft.com/winfx/2006/xaml/presentation"
        xmlns:x="http://schemas.microsoft.com/winfx/2006/xaml"
        Title="MainWindow" Height="350" Width="525">
  <StackPanel x:Name="stackPanel1" Button.Click="OnOuterButtonClick">
    <Button x:Name="button1" Content="Button 1" Margin="5" />
    <Button x:Name="button2" Margin="5" Click="OnButton2" >
      <ListBox x:Name="listBox1">
        <Button x:Name="innerButton1" Content="Inner Button 1" Margin="4" Padding="4"
                Click="OnInner1" />
        <Button x:Name="innerButton2" Content="Inner Button 2" Margin="4" Padding="4"
                Click="OnInner2" />
      </ListBox>
    </Button>
    <ListBox ItemsSource="{Binding}" />
  </StackPanel>
</Window>
```

The event handler methods are implemented in the code-behind. The second argument of the handler methods is of type `RoutedEventArgs`, which provides information about the `Source` of the event and the `OriginalSource`. When you click `button1`, the handler method `OnOuterButtonClick` is invoked, although there's no `Click` event directly associated with this button; the event is bubbled to the container element. In that case both `Source` and `OriginalSource` properties are set to `button1`. If you click `button2` first, the event handler OnButton2 is invoked, followed by OnOuterButtonClick. The handler OnButton2 changes the Source property, so with OnOuterButtonClick you see a different Source in the handler than before. The Source property of an event can be changed; the OriginalSource is readonly. Clicking the button innerButton1 invokes the OnInner1 event handler followed by OnButton2 and OnOuterButtonClick. The event bubbles. When you click innerButton2 only the handler OnInner2 is invoked because the Handled property there is set to true. Bubbling stops here (code file BubbleDemo/MainWindow.xaml.cs):

```
using System;
using System.Collections.ObjectModel;
using System.Windows;
namespace BubbleDemo
{
  public partial class MainWindow : Window
  {
    private ObservableCollection<string> messages = new ObservableCollection<string>();
    public MainWindow()
    {
      InitializeComponent();
      this.DataContext = messages;
    }
    private void AddMessage(string message, object sender, RoutedEventArgs e)
    {
      messages.Add(String.Format("{0}, sender: {1}; source: {2}; original source: {3}",
          message, (sender as FrameworkElement).Name,
          (e.Source as FrameworkElement).Name,
          (e.OriginalSource as FrameworkElement).Name));
    }
    private void OnOuterButtonClick(object sender, RoutedEventArgs e)
    {
      AddMessage("outer event", sender, e);
    }
    private void OnInner1(object sender, RoutedEventArgs e)
    {
      AddMessage("inner1", sender, e);
    }
    private void OnInner2(object sender, RoutedEventArgs e)
    {
      AddMessage("inner2", sender, e);
      e.Handled = true;
    }
    private void OnButton2(object sender, RoutedEventArgs e)
    {
      AddMessage("button2", sender, e);
      e.Source = sender;
    }
  }
}
```

> **NOTE** *Changing both the source and the event type is very common. For example, the* Button *class reacts to the mouse down and up events, handles these, and creates a button* Click *event instead.*

> **NOTE** *If the implementation of different handlers is very similar (for example, multiple buttons in a container), writing just one event handler in a container control and reacting to bubbling events is very beneficial. In the implementation, you just need to differentiate the sender or source.*

To define bubbling and tunneling events in custom classes, the MyDependencyObject is changed to support an event on a value change. For bubbling and tunneling event support, the class must derive from UIElement instead of DependencyObject because this class defines AddHandler and RemoveHandler methods for events.

To enable the caller of the MyDependencyObject to receive information about value changes, the class defines the ValueChanged event. The event is declared with explicit add and remove handlers, where the AddHandler and RemoveHandler methods of the base class are invoked. These methods require a type RoutedEvent and the delegate as parameters. The routed event named ValueChangedEvent is declared very similarly to a dependency property. It is declared as a static member and registered by calling the method EventManager.RegisterRoutedEvent. This method requires the name of the event, the routing strategy (which can be Bubble, Tunnel, or Direct), the type of the handler, and the type of the owner class. The EventManager class also enables you to register static events and get information about the events registered (code file DependecnyObjectDemo/MyDependencyObject.cs):

```
using System;
using System.Windows;
namespace Wrox.ProCSharp.XAML
{
  class MyDependencyObject : UIElement
  {
    public int Value
    {
      get { return (int)GetValue(ValueProperty); }
      set { SetValue(ValueProperty, value); }
    }
    public static readonly DependencyProperty ValueProperty =
        DependencyProperty.Register("Value", typeof(int), typeof(MyDependencyObject),
          new PropertyMetadata(0, OnValueChanged, CoerceValue));
    //...
    private static void OnValueChanged(DependencyObject obj,
                                  DependencyPropertyChangedEventArgs args)
    {
      MyDependencyObject control = (MyDependencyObject)obj;
      var e = new RoutedPropertyChangedEventArgs<int>((int)args.OldValue,
          (int)args.NewValue, ValueChangedEvent);
      control.OnValueChanged(e);
    }
    public static readonly RoutedEvent ValueChangedEvent =
        EventManager.RegisterRoutedEvent("ValueChanged", RoutingStrategy.Bubble,
            typeof(RoutedPropertyChangedEventHandler<int>), typeof(MyDependencyObject));
    public event RoutedPropertyChangedEventHandler<int> ValueChanged
    {
      add
      {
        AddHandler(ValueChangedEvent, value);
      }
      remove
      {
        RemoveHandler(ValueChangedEvent, value);
      }
    }
    protected virtual void OnValueChanged(RoutedPropertyChangedEventArgs<int> args)
    {
      RaiseEvent(args);
    }
  }
}
```

Now you can use this with bubbling functionality in the same way that you've seen it used before with the button Click event.

ATTACHED PROPERTIES

Whereas dependency properties are properties available with a specific type, with an attached property you can define properties for other types. Some container controls define attached properties for their children; for example, if the DockPanel control is used, a Dock property is available for its children. The Grid control defines Row and Column properties.

The following code snippet demonstrates how this looks in XAML. The Button class doesn't have the property Dock, but it's attached from the DockPanel:

```
<DockPanel>
  <Button Content="Top" DockPanel.Dock="Top" Background="Yellow" />
  <Button Content="Left" DockPanel.Dock="Left" Background="Blue" />
</DockPanel>
```

Attached properties are defined very similarly to dependency properties, as shown in the next example. The class that defines the attached properties must derive from the base class DependencyObject and defines a normal property, where the get and set accessors invoke the methods GetValue and SetValue of the base class. This is where the similarities end. Instead of invoking the method Register with the DependencyProperty class, now RegisterAttached is invoked, which registers an attached property that is now available with every element (code file AttachedPropertyDemo/MyAttachedProperyProvider.cs):

```
using System.Windows;
namespace Wrox.ProCSharp.XAML
{
  class MyAttachedPropertyProvider : DependencyObject
  {
    public int MyProperty
    {
      get { return (int)GetValue(MyPropertyProperty); }
      set { SetValue(MyPropertyProperty, value); }
    }
    public static readonly DependencyProperty MyPropertyProperty =
        DependencyProperty.RegisterAttached("MyProperty", typeof(int),
            typeof(MyAttachedPropertyProvider));
    public static void SetMyProperty(UIElement element, int value)
    {
      element.SetValue(MyPropertyProperty, value);
    }
    public static int GetMyProperty(UIElement element)
    {
      return (int)element.GetValue(MyPropertyProperty);
    }
  }
}
```

> **NOTE** *You might assume that* DockPanel.Dock *can only be added to elements within a* DockPanel. *In reality, attached properties can be added to any element. However, no one would use this property value. The* DockPanel *is aware of this property and reads it from its children elements to arrange them.*

In the XAML code, the attached property can now be attached to any elements. The second Button control, named button2, has the property MyAttachedPropertyProvider.MyProperty attached to it and the value 5 assigned (XAML file AttachedPropertyDemo/MainWindow.xaml):

```
<Window x:Class="Wrox.ProCSharp.XAML.MainWindow"
        xmlns="http://schemas.microsoft.com/winfx/2006/xaml/presentation"
```

```
      xmlns:x="http://schemas.microsoft.com/winfx/2006/xaml"
      xmlns:local="clr-namespace:Wrox.ProCSharp.XAML"
      Title="MainWindow" Height="350" Width="525">
  <Grid x:Name="grid1">
    <Grid.RowDefinitions>
      <RowDefinition Height="Auto" />
      <RowDefinition Height="Auto" />
      <RowDefinition Height="*" />
    </Grid.RowDefinitions>
    <Button Grid.Row="0" x:Name="button1" Content="Button 1" />
    <Button Grid.Row="1" x:Name="button2" Content="Button 2"
            local:MyAttachedPropertyProvider.MyProperty="5" />
    <ListBox Grid.Row="2" x:Name="list1"  />
  </Grid>
</Window>
```

Doing the same in code-behind it is necessary to invoke the static method SetMyProperty of the class MyAttachedPropertyProvider. It's not possible to extend the class Button with a property. The method SetProperty gets a UIElement instance that should be extended by the property and the value. In the following code snippet, the property is attached to button1 and the value is set to 44.

The foreach loop that follows the property setting retrieves the values from the attached properties from all child elements of the Grid element grid1. The values are retrieved with the GetProperty method of the class MyAttachedPropertyProvider. This is done from the DockPanel and the Grid control to retrieve the settings from its children in order to arrange them (code file AttachedPropertyDemo/MainWindow .xaml.cs):

```
using System;
using System.Windows;
namespace Wrox.ProCSharp.XAML
{
  public partial class MainWindow : Window
  {
    public MainWindow()
    {
      InitializeComponent();
      MyAttachedPropertyProvider.SetMyProperty(button1, 44);
      foreach (object item in LogicalTreeHelper.GetChildren(grid1))
      {
        FrameworkElement e = item as FrameworkElement;
        if (e != null)
          list1.Items.Add(String.Format("{0}: {1}", e.Name,
              MyAttachedPropertyProvider.GetMyProperty(e)));
      }
    }
  }
}
```

> **NOTE** *Some mechanisms are available to extend classes later. Extension methods can be used to extend any class with methods. Extension methods only support extending classes with methods, not properties. They are explained in Chapter 3, "Objects and Types." The* ExpandoObject *class allows the extension of types with methods and properties. To use this feature, the class must derive from* ExpandoObject .ExpandoObject; *dynamic types are explained in Chapter 12, "Dynamic Language Extensions."*

> **NOTE** *Chapters 35, "Core WPF," and 36, "Business Applications with WPF," show many different attached properties in action—for example, attached properties from container controls such as* Canvas, DockPanel, Grid, *but also the* ErrorTemplate *property from the* Validation *class.*

MARKUP EXTENSIONS

With markup extensions you can extend XAML, with either element or attribute syntax. If an XML attribute contains curly brackets, that's a sign of a markup extension. Often markup extensions with attributes are used as shorthand notation instead of using elements.

One example of such a markup extension is StaticResourceExtension, which finds resources. Here's a resource of a linear gradient brush with the key gradientBrush1 (XAML file MarkupExtensionDemo/MainWindow.xaml):

```
<Window.Resources>
  <LinearGradientBrush x:Key="gradientBrush1" StartPoint="0.5,0.0" EndPoint="0.5, 1.0">
    <GradientStop Offset="0" Color="Yellow" />
    <GradientStop Offset="0.3" Color="Orange" />
    <GradientStop Offset="0.7" Color="Red" />
    <GradientStop Offset="1" Color="DarkRed" />
  </LinearGradientBrush>
</Window.Resources>
```

This resource can be referenced by using the StaticResourceExtension with attribute syntax to set the Background property of a TextBlock. Attribute syntax is defined by curly brackets and the name of the extension class without the Extension suffix:

```
<TextBlock Text="Test" Background="{StaticResource gradientBrush1}" />
```

The longer form of the attribute shorthand notation uses element syntax, as the next code snippet demonstrates. StaticResourceExtension is defined as a child element of the TextBlock.Background element. The property ResourceKey is set with an attribute to gradientBrush1. In the previous example, the resource key is not set with the property ResourceKey (which would be possible as well) but with a constructor overload where the resource key can be set:

```
<TextBlock Text="Test">
  <TextBlock.Background>
    <StaticResourceExtension ResourceKey="gradientBrush1" />
  </TextBlock.Background>
</TextBlock>
```

Creating Custom Markup Extensions

A markup extension is created by defining a class that derives from the base class MarkupExtension. Most markup extensions have the Extension suffix (this naming convention is similar to the Attribute suffix with attributes, which you can read about in Chapter 15, "Reflection"). With a custom markup extension, you only need to override the method ProvideValue, which returns the value from the extension. The type that is returned is annotated to the class with the attribute MarkupExtensionReturnType. With the method ProvideValue, an IServiceProvider object is passed. With this interface you can query for different services, such as IProvideValueTarget or IXamlTypeResolver. IProvideValueTarget can be used to access the control and property to which the markup extension is applied with the TargetObject and TargetProperty properties. IXamlTypeResolver can be used to resolve XAML element names to CLR objects. The custom markup extension class CalculatorExtension defines the properties X and Y of type `double` and an `Operation` property that is defined by an enumeration. Depending on the value of the `Operation` property, different calculations are done on the X and Y input properties, and a string is returned (code file MarkupExtensionDemo/CalculatorExtension.cs):

```
using System;
using System.Windows;
using System.Windows.Markup;
namespace Wrox.ProCSharp.XAML
{
  public enum Operation
  {
    Add,
    Subtract,
    Multiply,
    Divide
  }
  [MarkupExtensionReturnType(typeof(string))]
  public class CalculatorExtension : MarkupExtension
  {
    public CalculatorExtension()
    {
    }
    public double X { get; set; }
    public double Y { get; set; }
    public Operation Operation { get; set; }
    public override object ProvideValue(IServiceProvider serviceProvider)
    {
      IProvideValueTarget provideValue =
          serviceProvider.GetService(typeof(IProvideValueTarget))
          as IProvideValueTarget;
      if (provideValue != null)
      {
        var host = provideValue.TargetObject as FrameworkElement;
        var prop = provideValue.TargetProperty as DependencyProperty;
      }
      double result = 0;
      switch (Operation)
      {
        case Operation.Add:
          result = X + Y;
          break;
        case Operation.Subtract:
          result = X - Y;
          break;
        case Operation.Multiply:
          result = X * Y;
          break;
        case Operation.Divide:
          result = X / Y;
          break;
        default:
          throw new ArgumentException("invalid operation");
      }
      return result.ToString();
    }
  }
}
```

The markup extension can now be used with an attribute syntax in the first `TextBlock` to add the values 3 and 4, or with the element syntax with the second `TextBlock` (XAML file MarkupExtensionDemo/MainWindow.xaml).

```
<Window x:Class="Wrox.ProCSharp.XAML.MainWindow"
        xmlns="http://schemas.microsoft.com/winfx/2006/xaml/presentation"
        xmlns:x="http://schemas.microsoft.com/winfx/2006/xaml"
        xmlns:local="clr-namespace:Wrox.ProCSharp.XAML"
        Title="MainWindow" Height="350" Width="525">
  <StackPanel>
    <TextBlock Text="{local:Calculator Operation=Add, X=3, Y=4}" />
    <TextBlock>
      <TextBlock.Text>
        <local:CalculatorExtension>
          <local:CalculatorExtension.Operation>
            <local:Operation>Multiply</local:Operation>
          </local:CalculatorExtension.Operation>
          <local:CalculatorExtension.X>7</local:CalculatorExtension.X>
          <local:CalculatorExtension.Y>11</local:CalculatorExtension.Y>
        </local:CalculatorExtension>
      </TextBlock.Text>
    </TextBlock>
  </StackPanel>
</Window>
```

XAML-Defined Markup Extensions

Markup extensions provide a lot of capabilities, and indeed XAML-defined markup extensions have already been used in this chapter. x:Array, which was shown in the "Collections" section, is defined as the markup extension class ArrayExtension. With this markup extension, using the attribute syntax is not possible because it would be difficult to define a list of elements.

Other markup extensions that are defined with XAML are the TypeExtension (x:Type), which returns the type based on string input; NullExtension (x:Null), which can be used to set values to null in XAML; and StaticExtension (x:Static), which is used to invoke static members of a class.

WPF, WF, and WCF define markup extensions that are specific to these technologies. WPF uses markup extensions to access resources, for data binding, and for color conversion; WF uses markup extensions with activities; and WCF defines markup extensions for endpoint definitions.

READING AND WRITING XAML

Several APIs exist for reading and writing XAML. There are high-level APIs that are easy to use but have less functionality, and low-level APIs with more features. Technology-specific APIs that make use of specific WPF or WF features are also available. XAML can be read from a textual XML form, from BAML, or from object trees, and written to XML or object trees.

Generic high-level APIs are available in the namespace System.Xaml. The class XamlServices allows loading, parsing, saving, and transforming XAML. XamlServices.Load can load XAML code from a file, a stream, or a reader, or by using a XamlReader object. XamlReader (in the namespace System.Xaml) is an abstract base class that has several concrete implementations. XamlObjectReader reads an object tree, XamlXmlReader reads XAML from an XML file, and Baml2006Reader reads the binary form of XAML. XamlDebuggerXmlReader, from the namespace System.Activities.Debugger, is a special reader for WF with special debugging support.

When passing XAML code in a string to XamlServices, the Parse method can be used. XamlServices.Save can be used to save XAML code. With the Save method you can use data sources similar to those used with the Load method. The object passed can be saved to a string, a stream, a TextWriter, a XamlWriter, or an XmlWriter. XamlWriter is an abstract base class. Classes that derive from XamlWriter are XamlObjectWriter and XamlXmlWriter. With the release of .NET 4.5, there's no writer for BAML code, but it is expected to have a BAML writer available at a later time.

When converting XAML from one format in another, you can use XamlServices.Transform. With the Transform method, you pass a XamlReader and a XamlWriter so that you can convert any format that is supported by specific readers and writers.

Instead of using the high-level API XamlServices class, you can use generic low-level APIs directly, which means using specific XamlReader and XamlWriter classes. With a reader, you can read node by node from a XAML tree with the Read method.

The generic XamlServices class doesn't support specific WPF features such as dependency properties or freezable objects. To read and write WPF XAML, you can use the classes XamlReader and XamlWriter from the namespace System.Windows.Markup that is defined in the assembly PresentationFramework, and thus has access to the WPF features. The names of these classes might be confusing, as the same class names are used with classes from different namespaces. System.Xaml.XamlReader is the abstract base class for readers; System.Windows.Markup.XamlReader is the WPF class to read XAML. This can be even more confusing when using the Load method of the WPF XamlReader class that accepts a System.Xaml.XamlReader as argument.

An optimized version to read XAML for WF is WorkflowXamlServices in the namespace System.Activities. This class is used to create dynamic activities during runtime.

> **NOTE** *Dynamic activities and Windows Workflow Foundation are explained in Chapter 45, "Windows Workflow Foundation."*

The following simple example loads XAML dynamically from a file to create an object tree and to attach the object tree to a container element, such as a StackPanel:

```
FileStream stream = File.OpenRead("Demo1.xaml");
object tree = System.Windows.Markup.XamlReader.Load(stream);
container1.Children.Add(tree as UIElement);
```

SUMMARY

In this chapter, you've seen the core functionality of XAML and some specific characteristics such as dependency properties, attached properties, bubbling and tunneling events, and markup extensions. With these features, you've not only seen the foundation of XAML based technologies, but also ways how C# and .NET features like properties and events can be adapted to extended use cases. Properties have been enhanced to support change notification and validation (dependency properties), and ways on adding properties to controls that don't really offer such properties (attached properties). Events have been enhanced with bubbling and tunneling functionality.

All these features facilitate the foundation for different XAML technologies, such as WPF, WF, and Windows 8 applications.

You can read more about XAML and see XAML in action in a lot of chapters in this book. In particular, you should read Chapters 35 and 36 for WPF, Chapter 37 for XPS, Chapter 38 for Windows 8 apps and Chapter 45 for Windows Workflow Foundation.

The next chapter is about the Managed Extensibility Framework (MEF).

30

Managed Extensibility Framework

WHAT'S IN THIS CHAPTER?

➤ Architecture of the Managed Extensibility Framework

➤ MEF using Attributes

➤ Convention-based Registration

➤ Contracts

➤ Exports and imports of parts

➤ Containers used by hosting applications

➤ Catalogs for finding parts

WROX.COM CODE DOWNLOADS FOR THIS CHAPTER

The wrox.com code downloads for this chapter are found at `http://www.wrox.com/remtitle .cgi?isbn=1118314425` on the Download Code tab. The code for this chapter is divided into the following major examples:

➤ Attribute-Based Sample

➤ Convention-Based Sample

➤ WPFCalculator

INTRODUCTION

Add-ins (or plugins) enable you to add functionality to an existing application. You can create a hosting application that gains more and more functionality over time—such functionality might be written by your team of developers, but different vendors can also extend your application by creating add-ins.

Today, add-ins are used with many different applications, such as Internet Explorer and Visual Studio. Internet Explorer is a hosting application that offers an add-in framework that is used by many companies to provide extensions when viewing web pages. The Shockwave Flash Object enables you to view web pages with Flash content. The Google toolbar offers specific Google features that can be accessed quickly from Internet Explorer. Visual Studio also has an add-in model that enables you to extend Visual Studio with different levels of extensions.

For your custom applications, it has always been possible to create an add-in model to dynamically load and use functionality from assemblies. However, all the issues associated with finding and using add-ins need to be resolved. You can accomplish that automatically using the Managed Extensibility Framework (MEF). The MEF can also be used on a smaller scale. For creating boundaries, MEF helps remove dependencies between parts and the clients or callers that make use of the parts. Such dependencies can also be removed just by using interfaces or delegates. However, MEF also helps in finding the parts by using catalogs, and connecting callers and parts in turn.

The major namespace covered in this chapter is System.ComponentModel.Composition.

MEF ARCHITECTURE

The .NET 4.5 Framework offers two technologies for writing flexible applications that load add-ins dynamically. One is the Managed Extensibility Framework (MEF), which is covered in this chapter. Another technology that has been available since .NET 3.5 is the Managed Add-in Framework (MAF). MAF uses a pipeline for communication between the add-in and the host application that makes the development process more complex but offers separation of add-ins via app-domains or even different processes. In that regard, MEF is the simpler of these two technologies. MAF and MEF can be combined to get the advantage of each, but it doubles the work.

MEF is built with parts and containers, as shown in Figure 30-1. A container finds parts from a catalog; and the catalog finds parts within an assembly or a directory. The container connects imports to exports, thereby making parts available to the hosting application.

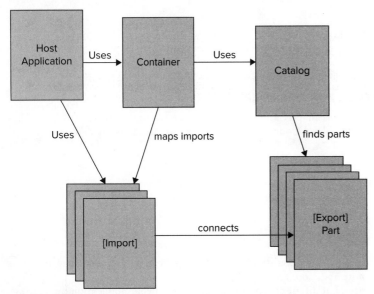

FIGURE 30-1

Here's the full picture of how parts are loaded. As mentioned, parts are found within a catalog. The catalog uses exports to find its parts. An export provider accesses the catalog to offer the exports from the catalog. Multiple export providers can be connected in chains for customizing exports—for example, with a custom export provider to only allow parts for specific users or roles. The container uses export providers to connect imports to exports and is itself an export provider.

MEF consists of three large categories: classes for hosting, primitives, and classes for the attribute-based mechanism. Hosting classes include catalogs and containers. Primitive classes can be used as base classes to extend the MEF architecture to use other techniques to connect exports and imports. Of course, the classes that make up the implementation of the attribute-based mechanism with reflection, such as the `Export` and `Import` attributes, and classes that offer extension methods that make it easier to work with attribute-based parts are also part of MEF.

> **NOTE** *The MEF implementation is based on attributes that specify what parts should be exported and then map these to the imports. However, the technology is flexible and allows for other mechanisms to be implemented by using the abstract base class* `ComposablePart` *and extension methods with reflection-based mechanisms from the class* `ReflectionModelServices`.

MEF Using Attributes

Let's start with a simple example to demonstrate the MEF architecture. The hosting application can dynamically load add-ins. With MEF, an add-in is referred to as a *part*. Parts are defined as *exports* and are loaded into a container that *imports* parts. The container finds parts by using a catalog; and the catalog lists parts.

In this example, a simple console application is created to host calculator add-ins from a library. To create independence from the host and the calculator add-in, three assemblies are required. One assembly, `CalculatorContract`, holds the contracts that are used by both the add-in assembly and the hosting executable. The add-in assembly `SimpleCalculator` implements the contract defined by the contract assembly. The host uses the contract assembly to invoke the add-in.

The contracts in the assembly `CalculatorContract` are defined by two interfaces, `ICalculator` and `IOperation`. The `ICalculator` interface defines the methods `GetOperations` and `Operate`. The `GetOperations` method returns a list of all operations that the add-in calculator supports, and with the `Operate` method an operation is invoked. This interface is flexible in that the calculator can support different operations. If the interface defined `Add` and `Subtract` methods instead of the flexible `Operate` method, a new version of the interface would be required to support `Divide` and `Multiply` methods. With the `ICalculator` interface as it is defined in this example, however, the calculator can offer any number of operations with any number of operands (code file `AttributeBasedSample/CalculatorContract/ICalculator.cs`):

```
using System.Collections.Generic;
namespace Wrox.ProCSharp.MEF
{
  public interface ICalculator
  {
    IList<IOperation> GetOperations();
    double Operate(IOperation operation, double[] operands);
  }
}
```

The `ICalculator` interface uses the `IOperation` interface to return the list of operations and to invoke an operation. The `IOperation` interface defines the read-only properties `Name` and `NumberOperands` (code file `AttributeBasedSample/CalculatorContract/IOperation.cs`):

```
namespace Wrox.ProCSharp.MEF
{
  public interface IOperation
```

```
    {
      string Name { get; }
      int NumberOperands { get; }
    }
  }
```

The `CalculatorContract` assembly doesn't require any reference to MEF assemblies. Only simple .NET interfaces are contained within it.

The add-in assembly `SimpleCalculator` contains classes that implement the interfaces defined by the contracts. The class `Operation` implements the interface `IOperation`. This class contains just two properties as defined by the interface. The interface defines `get` accessors of the properties; internal `set` accessors are used to set the properties from within the assembly (code file `AttributeBasedSample/SimpleCalculator/Operation.cs`):

```
namespace Wrox.ProCSharp.MEF
{
  public class Operation : IOperation
  {
    public string Name { get; internal set; }
    public int NumberOperands { get; internal set; }
  }
}
```

The `Calculator` class provides the functionality of this add-in by implementing the `ICalculator` interface. The `Calculator` class is exported as a part as defined by the `Export` attribute. This attribute is defined in the `System.ComponentModel.Composition` namespace in the `System.ComponentModel.Composition` assembly (code file `AttributeBasedSample/SimpleCalculator/Calculator.cs`):

```
using System;
using System.Collections.Generic;
using System.ComponentModel.Composition;
namespace Wrox.ProCSharp.MEF
{
  [Export(typeof(ICalculator))]
  public class Calculator : ICalculator
  {
    public IList<IOperation> GetOperations()
    {
      return new List<IOperation>()
      {
        new Operation { Name="+", NumberOperands=2},
        new Operation { Name="-", NumberOperands=2},
        new Operation { Name="/", NumberOperands=2},
        new Operation { Name="*", NumberOperands=2}
      };
    }
    public double Operate(IOperation operation, double[] operands)
    {
      double result = 0;
      switch (operation.Name)
      {
        case "+":
          result = operands[0] + operands[1];
          break;
        case "-":
          result = operands[0] - operands[1];
          break;
        case "/":
          result = operands[0] / operands[1];
```

```
              break;
           case "*":
              result = operands[0] * operands[1];
              break;
           default:
              throw new InvalidOperationException(String.Format(
                 "invalid operation {0}", operation.Name));
        }
        return result;
      }
    }
  }
```

The hosting application is a simple console application. The add-in uses an `Export` attribute to define what is exported; with the hosting application, the `Import` attribute defines what is used. Here, the `Import` attribute annotates the `Calculator` property that sets and gets an object implementing `ICalculator`. Therefore, any calculator add-in that implements this interface can be used here (code file `AttributeBasedSample/SimpleHost/Program.cs`):

```
using System;
using System.Collections.Generic;
using System.ComponentModel.Composition;
using System.ComponentModel.Composition.Hosting;
using Wrox.ProCSharp.MEF.Properties;
namespace Wrox.ProCSharp.MEF
{
  class Program
  {
    [Import]
    public ICalculator Calculator { get; set; }
```

In the entry method `Main` of the console application, a new instance of the `Program` class is created, and then the `Run` method invoked. In the `Run` method, a `DirectoryCatalog` is created that is initialized with the `AddInDirectory`, which is configured in the application configuration file. `Settings.Default.AddInDirectory` makes use of the project property `Settings` to use a strongly typed class to access a custom configuration.

The `CompositionContainer` class is a repository of parts. This container is initialized with the `DirectoryCatalog` to get the parts from the directory that is served by this catalog. `ComposeParts` is an extension method that extends the class `CompositionContainer` and is defined with the class `AttributedModelServices`. This method requires parts with an `Import` attribute passed with the arguments. Because the `Program` class has an `Import` attribute with the property `Calculator`, the instance of the `Program` class can be passed to this method. With the implementation for the imports, exports are searched and mapped. After a successful call of this method, exports mapped to the imports can be used. If not all imports can be mapped to exports, an exception of type `ChangeRejectedException` is thrown, which is caught to write the error message and to exit from the `Run` method:

```
static void Main()
{
  var p = new Program();
  p.Run();
}
public void Run()
{
  var catalog = new DirectoryCatalog(Settings.Default.AddInDirectory);
  var container = new CompositionContainer(catalog);
  try
  {
    container.ComposeParts(this);
  }
```

```
            catch (ChangeRejectedException ex)
            {
              Console.WriteLine(ex.Message);
              return;
            }
```

With the `Calculator` property, the methods from the interface `ICalculator` can be used. `GetOperations` invokes the methods of the previously created add-in, which returns four operations. After asking the user what operation should be invoked and requesting the operand values, the add-in method `Operate` is called:

```
          var operations = Calculator.GetOperations();
          var operationsDict = new SortedList<string, IOperation>();
          foreach (var item in operations)
          {
            Console.WriteLine("Name: {0}, number operands: {1}", item.Name,
                item.NumberOperands);
            operationsDict.Add(item.Name, item);
          }
          Console.WriteLine();
          string selectedOp = null;
          do
          {
            try
            {
              Console.Write("Operation? ");
              selectedOp = Console.ReadLine();
              if (selectedOp.ToLower() == "exit" || !operationsDict.ContainsKey(selectedOp))
                continue;
              var operation = operationsDict[selectedOp];
              double[] operands = new double[operation.NumberOperands];
              for (int i = 0; i < operation.NumberOperands; i++)
              {
                Console.Write("\t operand {0}? ", i + 1);
                string selectedOperand = Console.ReadLine();
                operands[i] = double.Parse(selectedOperand);
              }
              Console.WriteLine("calling calculator");
              double result = Calculator.Operate(operation, operands);
              Console.WriteLine("result: {0}", result);
            }
            catch (FormatException ex)
            {
              Console.WriteLine(ex.Message);
              Console.WriteLine();
              continue;
            }
          } while (selectedOp != "exit");
        }
      }
    }
```

The output of one sample run of the application is shown here:

```
Name: +, number operands: 2
Name: -, number operands: 2
Name: /, number operands: 2
Name: *, number operands: 2
Operation? +
        operand 1? 3
        operand 2? 5
calling calculator
```

```
result: 8
Operation? -
          operand 1? 7
          operand 2? 2
calling calculator
result: 5
Operation? exit
```

Without recompiling the host application, it is possible to use a completely different add-in library. The assembly AdvCalculator defines a different implementation for the Calculator class to offer more operations. This calculator can be used in place of the other one by copying the assembly to the directory that is specified by the DirectoryCatalog in the hosting application (code file AttributeBasedSample/SimpleCalculator/Calculator.cs):

```csharp
using System;
using System.Collections.Generic;
using System.ComponentModel.Composition;
namespace Wrox.ProCSharp.MEF
{
  [Export(typeof(ICalculator))]
  public class Calculator : ICalculator
  {
    public IList<IOperation> GetOperations()
    {
      return new List<IOperation>()
      {
        new Operation { Name="+", NumberOperands=2},
        new Operation { Name="-", NumberOperands=2},
        new Operation { Name="/", NumberOperands=2},
        new Operation { Name="*", NumberOperands=2},
        new Operation { Name="%", NumberOperands=2},
        new Operation { Name="++", NumberOperands=1},
        new Operation { Name="--", NumberOperands=1}
      };
    }
        public double Operate(IOperation operation, double[] operands)
        {
            double result = 0;
            switch (operation.Name)
            {
                case "+":
                    result = operands[0] + operands[1];
                    break;
                case "-":
                    result = operands[0] - operands[1];
                    break;
                case "/":
                    result = operands[0] / operands[1];
                    break;
                case "*":
                    result = operands[0] * operands[1];
                    break;
                case "%":
                    result = operands[0] % operands[1];
                    break;
                case "++":
                    result = ++operands[0];
                    break;
                case "--":
                    result = --operands[0];
                    break;
```

```
                    default:
                        throw new InvalidOperationException(
                            String.Format("invalid operation {0}", operation.Name));
                }
                return result;
            }
        }
    }
```

Now you've seen imports, exports, and catalogs from the MEF architecture. The next section takes a look at a new feature of .NET 4.5: convention-based part registration.

Convention-Based Part Registration

A new feature of MEF with .NET 4.5 is *convention-based part registration*. It's no longer required to use attributes with the exported parts. One scenario in which this is useful is when you don't have access to the source code of classes that should be used as parts to add attributes. Another scenario is when you want to remove the need for a user of your library to deal with attributes for imports. ASP.NET MVC 4 makes use of MEF with convention-based registration. This technology is based on the Model View Controller (MVC) pattern, and uses controller classes with the suffix Controller, which is a naming convention to find controllers.

> **NOTE** *ASP.NET MVC is discussed in Chapter 41, "ASP.NET MVC."*

> **NOTE** *Convention-based part registration requires an additional reference to the assembly* System.ComponentModel.Composition.Registration.

This introduction to convention-based part registration builds the same example code shown previously using attributes, but attributes are no longer needed; therefore, the same code is not repeated here. The same contract interfaces ICalculator and IOperation are implemented, and nearly the same part with the class Calculator. The difference with the Calculator class is that it doesn't have the Export attribute applied to it.

Creating the host application, all this becomes more interesting. Similar to before, a property of type ICalculator is created as shown in the following code snippet—it just doesn't have an Import attribute applied to it. In the Main method, a new instance of Program is created because the Calculator property is an instance property of the Program class (code file ConventionBasedSample/SimpleHost/Program.cs):

```
using System;
using System.Collections.Generic;
using System.ComponentModel.Composition;
using System.ComponentModel.Composition.Hosting;
using System.ComponentModel.Composition.Registration;

namespace Wrox.ProCSharp.MEF
{
  public class Program
  {
    public ICalculator Calculator { get; set; }
```

```
static void Main()
{
  var p = new Program();
  p.Run();
}
```

Within the Run method, a new RegistrationBuilder instance is created. This type is needed to define conventions for export and import. With the sample code, an export is defined for all the types that derive from the interface type ICalculator, and the export is of type ICalculator by calling the method conventions.ForTypesDerivedFrom<ICalculator>.Export<ICalculator>. This is similar to applying the attribute Export[typeof(ICalculator)] to all types that implement the interface ICalculator. For mapping the exported type to the Calculator property, ForType<Program> specifies a convention for the type Program, and the ImportProperty<ICalculator> method maps an import to the specified property. Similar to the previous sample, a DirectoryCatalog is created to find the parts in a specific directory. The constructor of the DirectoryCatalog allows passing the RegistrationBuilder to provide information about the conventions. The search in the directory starts by invoking the SatisfyImportOnce method of the CompositionSerivce. With this method invocation, the property Calculator is assigned, and now the methods of the Calculator can be invoked:

```
public void Run()
{
  var conventions = new RegistrationBuilder();
  conventions.ForTypesDerivedFrom<ICalculator>().Export<ICalculator>();
  conventions.ForType<Program>().ImportProperty<ICalculator>(p => p.Calculator);

  var catalog = new DirectoryCatalog(
      Properties.Settings.Default.AddInDirectory, conventions);

  using (CompositionService service = catalog.CreateCompositionService())
  {
    service.SatisfyImportsOnce(this, conventions);
  }

  CalculatorLoop();
}
```

As you've seen, the RegistrationBuilder is the heart of convention-based part registration and MEF. It uses a fluent API and offers all the flexibility you'll see with attributes as well. Conventions can be applied to a specific type with ForType; or for types that derive from a base class or implement an interface, ForTypesDerivedFrom. ForTypesMatching enables specifying a flexible predicate. For example, ForTypesMatching(t => t.Name.EndsWith("Controller")) applies a convention to all types that end with the name Controller.

The methods to select the type return a PartBuilder. With the PartBuilder, exports and imports can be defined, as well as metadata applied. The PartBuilder offers several methods to define exports: Export to export a specific type, ExportInterfaces to export a list of interfaces, and ExportProperties to export properties. Using the export methods to export multiple interfaces or properties, a predicate can be applied to further define a selection. The same applies to importing properties or constructors with ImportProperty, ImportProperties, and SelectConstructors.

Having briefly looked at the two ways of using MEF with attributes and conventions, the next section digs into the details by using a WPF application to host add-ins.

DEFINING CONTRACTS

The following sample application extends the first one. The hosting application is a WPF application that loads calculator add-ins for calculation functionality, and other add-ins that bring their own user interface into the host.

> **NOTE** *For more information about writing WPF applications, see Chapter 35, "Core WPF," and Chapter 36, "Business Applications with WPF."*

For the calculation, the same contracts that were defined earlier are used: ICalculator and IOperation. Added to this example is another contract, ICalculatorExtension. This interface defines the UI property that can be used by the hosting application. The get accessor of this property returns a FrameworkElement. This enables the add-in to return any WPF element that derives from FrameworkElement to be shown as the user interface within the host application (code file WPFCalculator/CalculatorContract/ICalculator.cs):

```
using System.Windows;
namespace Wrox.ProCSharp.MEF
{
  public interface ICalculatorExtension
  {
    FrameworkElement UI { get; }
  }
}
```

.NET interfaces are used to remove the dependency between one that implements the interface and one that uses it. This way, a .NET interface is also a good contract for MEF to remove a dependency between the hosting application and the add-in. If the interface is defined in a separate assembly, as with the CalculatorContract assembly, the hosting application and the add-in don't have a direct dependency. Instead, the hosting application and the add-in just reference the contract assembly.

From a MEF standpoint, an interface contract is not required at all. The contract can be a simple string. To avoid conflicts with other contracts, the name of the string should contain a namespace name—for example, Wrox.ProCSharp.MEF.SampleContract, as shown in the following code snippet. Here, the class Foo is exported by using the Export attribute, and a string passed to the attribute instead of the interface:

```
[Export("Wrox.ProCSharp.MEF.SampleContract")]
public class Foo
{
  public string Bar()
  {
    return "Foo.Bar";
  }
}
```

The problem with using a contract as a string is that the methods, properties, and events provided by the type are not strongly defined. Either the caller needs a reference to the type Foo to use it, or .NET reflection can be used to access its members. The C# 4 dynamic keyword makes reflection easier to use and can be very helpful in such scenarios.

The hosting application can use the dynamic type to import a contract with the name Wrox.ProCSharp .MEF.SampleContract:

```
[Import("Wrox.ProCSharp.MEF.SampleContract")]
public dynamic Foo { get; set; }
```

With the dynamic keyword, the Foo property can now be used to access the Bar method directly. The call to this method is resolved during runtime:

```
string s = Foo.Bar();
```

Contract names and interfaces can also be used in conjunction to define that the contract is used only if both the interface and the contract name are the same. This way, you can use the same interface for different contracts.

> **NOTE** *The dynamic type is explained in Chapter 12, "Dynamic Language Extensions."*

EXPORTING PARTS

The previous example showed the part `SimpleCalculator`, which exports the type `Calculator` with all its methods and properties. The following example contains the `SimpleCalculator` as well, with the same implementation that was shown previously; and two more parts, `TemperatureConversion` and `FuelEconomy`, are exported. These parts offer a UI for the hosting application.

Creating Parts

The WPF User Control library named `TemperatureConversion` defines a user interface as shown in Figure 30-2. This control provides conversion between Celsius, Fahrenheit, and Kelvin scales. With the first and second combo box, the conversion source and target can be selected. The `Calculate` button starts the calculation to do the conversion.

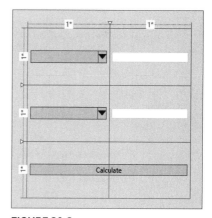

The user control has a simple implementation for temperature conversion. The enumeration `TempConversionType` defines the different conversions that are possible with that control. The enumeration values are shown in the two combo boxes by setting the `DataContext` property of the user control in the constructor. The method `ToCelsiusFrom` converts the argument *t* from its original value to Celsius. The temperature source type is defined with the second argument, `TempConversionType`. The method `FromCelsiusTo` converts a Celsius value to the selected temperature scale. The method `OnCalculate` is the handler of the `Button.Click` event and invokes the `ToCelsiusFrom` and

FIGURE 30-2

`FromCelsiusTo` methods to do the conversion according to the user's selected conversion type (code file `WPFCalculator/TemperatureConversion/TemperatureConversion.xaml.cs`):

```
using System;
using System.Windows;
using System.Windows.Controls;
namespace Wrox.ProCSharp.MEF
{
  public enum TempConversionType
  {
    Celsius,
    Fahrenheit,
    Kelvin
  }
  public partial class TemperatureConversion : UserControl
  {
    public TemperatureConversion()
    {
      InitializeComponent();
      this.DataContext = Enum.GetNames(typeof(TempConversionType));
    }
```

```
    private double ToCelsiusFrom(double t, TempConversionType conv)
    {
      switch (conv)
      {
        case TempConversionType.Celsius:
          return t;
        case TempConversionType.Fahrenheit:
          return (t - 32) / 1.8;
        case TempConversionType.Kelvin:
          return (t - 273.15);
        default:
          throw new ArgumentException("invalid enumeration value");
      }
    }
    private double FromCelsiusTo(double t, TempConversionType conv)
    {
      switch (conv)
      {
        case TempConversionType.Celsius:
          return t;
        case TempConversionType.Fahrenheit:
          return (t * 1.8) + 32;
        case TempConversionType.Kelvin:
          return t + 273.15;
        default:
          throw new ArgumentException("invalid enumeration value");
      }
    }
    private void OnCalculate(object sender, System.Windows.RoutedEventArgs e)
    {
      try
      {
        TempConversionType from;
        TempConversionType to;
        if (Enum.TryParse<TempConversionType>(
          (string)comboFrom.SelectedValue, out from) &&
              Enum.TryParse<TempConversionType>(
                  (string)comboTo.SelectedValue, out to))
        {
          double result = FromCelsiusTo(
              ToCelsiusFrom(double.Parse(textInput.Text), from), to);
          textOutput.Text = result.ToString();
        }
      }
      catch (FormatException ex)
      {
        MessageBox.Show(ex.Message);
      }
    }
  }
}
```

So far, this control is just a simple WPF user control. To create a MEF part, the class
`TemperatureCalculatorExtension` is exported by using the `Export` attribute. The class implements the
interface `ICalculatorExtension` to return the user control `TemperatureConversion` from the `UI`
property (code file `WPFCalculator/TemperatureConversion/TemperatureCalculatorExtension.cs`):

```
using System.ComponentModel.Composition;
using System.Windows;
namespace Wrox.ProCSharp.MEF
```

```
    {
      [Export(typeof(ICalculatorExtension))]
      public class TemperatureCalculatorExtension : ICalculatorExtension
      {
        private TemperatureConversion control;
        public FrameworkElement UI
        {
          get
          {
            return control ?? (control = new TemperatureConversion());
          }
        }
      }
    }
```

The second user control that implements the interface
ICalculatorExtension is FuelEconomy. With this control,
either miles per gallon or liters per 100 km can be calculated.
The user interface is shown in Figure 30-3.

The next code snippet shows the class FuelEconomyViewModel,
which defines several properties that are bound from the user
interface, such as a list of FuelEcoTypes that enables the user to
select between miles and kilometers, and the Fuel and Distance
properties, which are filled by the user:

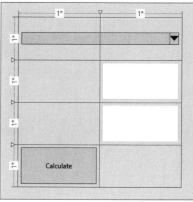

FIGURE 30-3

```
using System.Collections.Generic;

namespace Wrox.ProCSharp.MEF
{
  public class FuelEconomyViewModel : BindableBase
  {
    public FuelEconomyViewModel()
    {
      InitializeFuelEcoTypes();
    }

    private List<FuelEconomyType> fuelEcoTypes;
    public List<FuelEconomyType> FuelEcoTypes
    {
      get
      {
        return fuelEcoTypes;
      }
    }

    private void InitializeFuelEcoTypes()
    {
      var t1 = new FuelEconomyType
      {
        Id = "lpk",
        Text = "L/100 km",
        DistanceText = "Distance (kilometers)",
        FuelText = "Fuel used (liters)"
      };
      var t2 = new FuelEconomyType
      {
        Id = "mpg",
        Text = "Miles per gallon",
```

```
      DistanceText = "Distance (miles)",
      FuelText = "Fuel used (gallons)"
    };
    fuelEcoTypes = new List<FuelEconomyType>() { t1, t2 };
  }

  private FuelEconomyType selectedFuelEcoType;

  public FuelEconomyType SelectedFuelEcoType
  {
    get { return selectedFuelEcoType; }
    set { SetProperty(ref selectedFuelEcoType, value); }
  }

  private string fuel;
  public string Fuel
  {
    get { return fuel; }
    set { SetProperty(ref fuel, value); }
  }

  private string distance;
  public string Distance
  {
    get { return distance; }
    set { SetProperty(ref distance, value); }
  }

  private string result;
  public string Result
  {
    get { return result; }
    set { SetProperty(ref result, value); }
  }
  }
}
```

> **NOTE** *The base class* `BindableBase` *that is used with the sample code just offers an implementation of the interface* `INotifyPropertyChanged`. *This class is found in the* `CalculatorUtils` *assembly.*

The calculation is within the OnCalculate method. OnCalculate is the handler for the Click event of the Calculate button (code file `WPFCalculator/FuelEconomy/FuelEconomyUC.xaml.cs`):

```
    private void OnCalculate(object sender, RoutedEventArgs e)
    {
      double fuel = double.Parse(viewModel.Fuel);
      double distance = double.Parse(viewModel.Distance);
      FuelEconomyType ecoType = viewModel.SelectedFuelEcoType;
      double result = 0;
      switch (ecoType.Id)
      {
        case "lpk":
          result = fuel / (distance / 100);
          break;
        case "mpg":
          result = distance / fuel;
          break;
```

```
      default:
        break;
    }
    viewModel.Result = result.ToString();
  }
```

Again, the interface `ICalculatorExtension` is implemented and exported with the `Export` attribute (code file `WPFCalculator/FuelEconomy/FuelCalculatorExtension.cs`):

```csharp
using System.ComponentModel.Composition;
using System.Windows;

namespace Wrox.ProCSharp.MEF
{
  [Export(typeof(ICalculatorExtension))]
  public class FuelCalculatorExtension : ICalculatorExtension
  {
    private FrameworkElement control;
    public FrameworkElement UI
    {
      get
      {
        return control ?? (control = new FuelEconomyUC());
      }
    }
  }
}
```

Before continuing the WPF calculator example to import the user controls, let's take a look at what other options you have with exports. With exports, you can export not only complete types, but also properties and methods, and you can add metadata information to the exports.

Exporting Properties and Methods

Instead of exporting complete classes with properties, methods, and events, it is possible to export just properties or methods. Exporting properties makes it possible to use classes where you can't change the source code by adding the `Export` attribute to them (for example, classes from the .NET Framework or third-party libraries). For this, you just have to define a property of the specific type and export the property.

Exporting methods provides a finer degree of control than using types. The caller doesn't need to know about the type. Methods are exported with the help of delegates. The following code snippet defines the `Add` and `Subtract` methods with exports. The type of the export is the delegate `Func<double, double, double>`, which is a delegate that accepts two double parameters and a double return type. For methods without return types, the `Action<T>` delegate can be used (code file `WPFCalculator/Operations/Operations.cs`):

```csharp
using System;
using System.ComponentModel.Composition;
namespace Wrox.ProCSharp.MEF
{
  public class Operations
  {
    [Export("Add", typeof(Func<double, double, double>))]
    public double Add(double x, double y)
    {
      return x + y;
    }
    [Export("Subtract", typeof(Func<double, double, double>))]
    public double Subtract(double x, double y)
```

```
    {
      return x - y;
    }
  }
}
```

> **NOTE** *You can read about the* Func<T> *and* Action<T> *delegates in Chapter 8,* *"Delegates, Lambdas, and Events."*

The exported methods are imported from the SimpleCalculator add-in. A part itself can use other parts. To use the exported methods, delegates are declared with the attribute Import. This attribute contains the same name and delegate type that was declared with the export (code file WPFCalculator/ SimpleCalculator/Calculator.cs):

> **NOTE** SimpleCalculator *itself is a part that exports the* ICalculator *interface and consists of parts that are imported.*

```
[Export(typeof(ICalculator))]
public class Calculator : ICalculator
{
  [Import("Add", typeof(Func<double, double, double>))]
  public Func<double, double, double> Add { get; set; }

  [Import("Subtract", typeof(Func<double, double, double>))]
  public Func<double, double, double> Subtract { get; set; }
```

The imported methods that are represented by the Add and Subtract delegates are invoked via these delegates in the Operate method:

```
public double Operate(IOperation operation, double[] operands)
{
  double result = 0;
  switch (operation.Name)
  {
    case "+":
      result = Add(operands[0], operands[1]);
      break;
    case "-":
      result = Subtract(operands[0], operands[1]);
      break;
    case "/":
      result = operands[0] / operands[1];
      break;
    case "*":
      result = operands[0] * operands[1];
      break;
    default:
      throw new InvalidOperationException(
          String.Format("invalid operation {0}", operation.Name));
  }
  return result;
}
```

Exporting Metadata

With exports, you can also attach metadata information. Metadata enables you to provide information in addition to a name and a type. This can be used to add capability information and to determine, on the import side, which of the exports should be used.

The exported `Add` method is now changed to add speed capabilities with the attribute `ExportMetadata` (code file `WPFCalculator/Operations/Operation.cs`):

```
[Export("Add", typeof(Func<double, double, double>))]
[ExportMetadata("speed", "fast")]
public double Add(double x, double y)
{
  return x + y;
}
```

To have the option to choose from another implementation of the `Add` method, another method with different speed capabilities but the same delegate type and name is implemented (code file `WPFCalculator/Operations/Operation2.cs`):

```
public class Operations2
{
  [Export("Add", typeof(Func<double, double, double>))]
  [ExportMetadata("speed", "slow")]
  public double Add(double x, double y)
  {
    Thread.Sleep(3000);
    return x + y;
  }
}
```

Because more than one exported `Add` method is available, the import definition must be changed. The attribute `ImportMany` is used if more than one export of the same name and type is available. This attribute is applied to an array or `IEnumeration<T>` interface. `ImportMany` is explained with more detail in the next section. For accessing metadata, an array of `Lazy<T, TMetadata>` can be used. The class `Lazy<T>` is used to support lazy initialization of types on first use. `Lazy<T, TMetadata>` derives from `Lazy<T>` and supports, in addition to the base class, access to metadata information with the `Metadata` property. In the example, the method is referenced by the delegate `Func<double, double, double>`, which is the first generic parameter of `Lazy<T, TMetadata>`. The second generic parameter is `IDictionary<string, object>` for the metadata collection. The `ExportMetadata` attribute can be used multiple times to add more than one capability, and it always consists of a key of type `string` and a value of type `object` (code file `WPFCalculator/SimpleCalculator/Calculator.cs`):

```
[ImportMany("Add", typeof(Func<double, double, double>))]
public Lazy<Func<double, double, double>, IDictionary<string, object>>[]
    AddMethods { get; set; }
//[Import("Add", typeof(Func<double, double, double>))]
//public Func<double, double, double> Add { get; set; }
```

The call to the `Add` method is now changed to iterate through the collection of `Lazy<Func<double, double, double>, IDictionary<string, object>>` elements. With the `Metadata` property, the key for the capability is checked; if the speed capability has the value `fast`, the operation is invoked by using the `Value` property of `Lazy<T>` to get to the delegate:

```
case "+":
  // result = Add(operands[0], operands[1]);
  foreach (var addMethod in AddMethods)
```

```
      {
        if (addMethod.Metadata.ContainsKey("speed") &&
            (string)addMethod.Metadata["speed"] == "fast")
          result = addMethod.Value(operands[0], operands[1]);
      }
      // result = operands[0] + operands[1];
      break;
```

Instead of using the attribute `ExportMetadata`, you can create a custom export attribute class that derives from `ExportAttribute`. The class `SpeedExportAttribute` defines an additional `Speed` property that is of type `Speed` (code file WPFCalculator/CalculatorUtils/SpeedExportAttribute.cs):

```
using System;
using System.ComponentModel.Composition;
namespace Wrox.ProCSharp.MEF
{
  public enum Speed
  {
    Fast,
    Slow
  }
  [MetadataAttribute]
  [AttributeUsage(AttributeTargets.Method | AttributeTargets.Class)]
  public class SpeedExportAttribute : ExportAttribute
  {
    public SpeedExportAttribute(string contractName, Type contractType)
        : base(contractName, contractType) { }
    public Speed Speed { get; set; }
  }
}
```

> **NOTE** *For more information about how to create custom attributes, read Chapter 15, "Reflection."*

With the exported `Add` method, now the `SpeedExport` attribute can be used instead of the `Export` and `ExportMetadata` attributes (code file WPFCalculator/Operations/Operations.cs):

```
[SpeedExport("Add", typeof(Func<double, double, double>), Speed=Speed.Fast)]
public double Add(double x, double y)
{
  return x + y;
}
```

For the import, an interface with all the metadata is required. This makes it possible to access the strongly typed capabilities. The attribute `SpeedExport` just defines a single capability: speed. The interface `ISpeedCapabilities` defines the property `Speed` by using the same enumeration type `Speed` that was used with the `SpeedExport` attribute (code file WPFCalculator/CalculatorUtils/ISpeedCapabilities.cs):

```
namespace Wrox.ProCSharp.MEF
{
  public interface ISpeedCapabilities
  {
    Speed Speed { get; }
  }
}
```

Now it's possible to change the definition of the import by using the interface `ISpeedCapabilities` instead of the dictionary defined earlier (code file `WPFCalculator/SimpleCalculator/Calculator.cs`):

```
[ImportMany("Add", typeof(Func<double, double, double>))]
public Lazy<Func<double, double, double>, ISpeedCapabilities>[]
    AddMethods { get; set; }
```

Using the imports, the `Speed` property of the interface, `ISpeedCapabilities` can now be used directly:

```
foreach (var addMethod in AddMethods)
{
  if (addMethod.Metadata.Speed == Speed.Fast)
    result = addMethod.Value(operands[0], operands[1]);
}
```

Using Metadata for Lazy Loading

MEF metadata is not only useful for selecting parts based on metadata information. Another great use is providing information to the host application about the part before the part is instantiated.

The following example is implemented to offer a title, a description, and a link to an image for the calculator extensions `FuelEconomy` and `TemperatureConversion` (code file `WPFCalculator/CalculatorContract/ICalculatorExtensionMetadata.cs`):

```
public interface ICalculatorExtensionMetadata
{
  string Title { get; }
  string Description { get; }

  string ImageUri { get; }
}
```

For easy usage, an export attribute named `CalculatorExtensionExport` is created, as shown in the following code snippet. The implementation is very similar to the `SpeedExport` attribute shown earlier (code file `WPFCalculator/CalculatorUtils/CalculatorExtensionAttribute.cs`):

```
using System;
using System.ComponentModel.Composition;

namespace Wrox.ProCSharp.MEF
{
  [MetadataAttribute]
  [AttributeUsage(AttributeTargets.Method | AttributeTargets.Class)]
  public class CalculatorExtensionExportAttribute : ExportAttribute
  {
    public CalculatorExtensionExportAttribute(Type contractType)
      : base(contractType) { }

    public string Title { get; set; }
    public string Description { get; set; }

    public string ImageUri { get; set; }
  }
}
```

The exports of the parts can now be changed. In the next two code snippets the `CalculatorExtensionExport` attribute is applied with the parts `FuelEconomy` and `TemperatureConversion`. These two parts also use two images, `Fuel.png` and `Temperature.png`, which are copied to the add-in directory during the build process. These images can be used from the host application as well to display information before the parts are instantiated (code files WPFCalculator/FuelEconomy/ FuelCalculatorExtension.cs and TemperatureConversionExtension.cs):

```
[CalculatorExtensionExport(typeof(ICalculatorExtension),
  Title = "Fuel Economy",
  Description = "Calculate fuel economy",
  ImageUri = "Fuel.png")]
public class FuelCalculatorExtension : ICalculatorExtension
[CalculatorExtensionExport(typeof(ICalculatorExtension),
  Title = "Temperature Conversion",
  Description="Convert Celsius to Fahrenheit and Fahrenheit to Celsius",
  ImageUri = "Temperature.png")]
public class TemperatureCalculatorExtension : ICalculatorExtension
```

IMPORTING PARTS

Now let's take a look at using the WPF user controls with a WPF hosting application. The design view of the hosting application is shown in Figure 30-4. The application Calculator is a WPF application that loads the functional calculator add-in, which implements the interfaces ICalculator and IOperation, and add-ins with user interfaces that implement the interface ICalculatorExtension. To connect to the exports of the parts, you need imports.

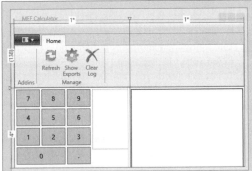

FIGURE 30-4

The calculator host application uses the class CalculatorViewModel to bind input and result data to the user interface. The property CalcExtensions contains a list of all available extension add-ins; the property ActivatedExtensions contains a list of the extensions that are loaded (code file WPFCalculator/ Calculator/CalculatorViewModel.cs):

```
using System;
using System.Collections.ObjectModel;

namespace Wrox.ProCSharp.MEF
{
  public class CalculatorViewModel : BindableBase
  {
    private string status;

    public string Status
    {
      get { return status; }
      set { SetProperty(ref status, value); }
    }

    private string input;
    public string Input
    {
      get { return input; }
      set { SetProperty(ref input, value); }
    }

    private string result;
```

```csharp
public string Result
{
  get { return result; }
  set { SetProperty(ref result, value); }
}

private string fullInputText;
public string FullInputText
{
  get { return fullInputText; }
  set { fullInputText = value; }
}

private readonly ObservableCollection<IOperation> calcAddInOperators =
    new ObservableCollection<IOperation>();
public object syncCalcAddInOperators = new object();
public ObservableCollection<IOperation> CalcAddInOperators
{
  get
  {
    return calcAddInOperators;
  }
}

private readonly ObservableCollection<Lazy<ICalculatorExtension>>
    calcExtensions = new ObservableCollection<Lazy<ICalculatorExtension>>();
public ObservableCollection<Lazy<ICalculatorExtension>> CalcExtensions
{
  get
  {
    return calcExtensions;
  }
}

private readonly ObservableCollection<Lazy<ICalculatorExtension>>
  activatedExtensions = new ObservableCollection<Lazy<ICalculatorExtension>>();
public object syncActivatedExtensions = new object();
public ObservableCollection<Lazy<ICalculatorExtension>> ActivatedExtensions
{
  get
  {
    return activatedExtensions;
  }
}
  }
}
```

Importing Collections

An import connects to an export. When using exported parts, an import is needed to make the connection. With the `Import` attribute, it's possible to connect to a single export. If more than one add-in should be loaded, the `ImportMany` attribute is required and needs to be defined as an array type or `IEnumerable<T>`. Because the hosting calculator application allows many calculator extensions that implement the interface `ICalculatorExtension` to be loaded, the class `CalculatorExtensionImport` defines the property `CalculatorExtensions` of type `IEnumerable<ICalculatorExtension>` to access all the calculator extension parts (code file `WPFCalculator/Calculator/CalculatorExtensionImport.cs`):

```csharp
using System.Collections.Generic;
using System.ComponentModel.Composition;
namespace Wrox.ProCSharp.MEF
```

```
  {
    public class CalculatorExtensionImport
    {
      [ImportMany(AllowRecomposition=true)]
      public IEnumerable<ICalculatorExtension> CalculatorExtensions { get; set; }
    }
  }
```

The `Import` and `ImportMany` attributes enable the use of `ContractName` and `ContractType` to map the import to an export. Other properties that can be set with these attributes are `AllowRecomposition` and `RequiredCreationPolicy`. `AllowRecomposition` enables dynamic mapping to new exports while the application is running, and the unloading of exports. With `RequiredCreationPolicy`, you can specify whether the parts should be shared (`CreationPolicy.Shared`) or not shared (`CreationPolicy.NonShared`) between requestors, or whether the policy should be defined by the container (`CreationPolicy.Any`).

You can get a confirmation that all imports are successful (or errors in case they are not), you can implement the interface `IPartImportsSatisfiedNotification`. This interface just defines a single method, `OnImportsSatifsifed`, which is called when all imports of the class are successful. In the `CalculatorImport` class, the method fires an `ImportsSatisfied` event (code file `WPFCalculator/Calculator/CalculatorImport.cs`):

```
using System;
using System.ComponentModel.Composition;
using System.Windows.Controls;
namespace Wrox.ProCSharp.MEF
{
  public class CalculatorImport : IPartImportsSatisfiedNotification
  {
    public event EventHandler<ImportEventArgs> ImportsSatisfied;
    [Import(typeof(ICalculator))]
    public ICalculator Calculator { get; set; }

    public void OnImportsSatisfied()
    {
      if (ImportsSatisfied != null)
        ImportsSatisfied(this, new ImportEventArgs {
            StatusMessage = "ICalculator import successful" });
    }
  }
}
```

The event of the `CalculatorImport` is connected to an event handler on creation of the `CalculatorImport` to write a message to a `Status` property that is bound in the UI for displaying status information (code file `WPFCalculator/CalculatorManager/MainWindow.xaml.cs`):

```
public sealed class CalculatorManager : IDisposable
{
  private DirectoryCatalog catalog;
  private CompositionContainer container;
  private CalculatorImport calcImport;
  private CalculatorExtensionImport calcExtensionImport;
  private CalculatorViewModel vm;

  public CalculatorManager(CalculatorViewModel vm)
  {
    this.vm = vm;
  }

  public async void InitializeContainer()
```

```
    {
        catalog = new DirectoryCatalog(Properties.Settings.Default.AddInDirectory);
        container = new CompositionContainer(catalog);

        calcImport = new CalculatorImport();

        calcImport.ImportsSatisfied += (sender, e) =>
        {
            vm.Status += string.Format("{0}\n", e.StatusMessage);
        };

        await Task.Run(() =>
            {
                container.ComposeParts(calcImport);
            });

        await InitializeOperationsAsync();
    }
```

Lazy Loading of Parts

By default, parts are loaded from the container—for example, by calling the extension method ComposeParts on the CompositionContainer. With the help of the Lazy<T> class, the parts can be loaded on first access. The type Lazy<T> enables the late instantiation of any type T and defines the properties IsValueCreated and Value. IsValueCreated is a Boolean that returns the information if the contained type T is already instantiated. Value initializes the contained type T on first access and returns the instance.

The import of an add-in can be declared to be of type Lazy<T>, as shown in the Lazy<ICalculator> example (code file WPFCalculator/Calculator/CalculatorImport.cs):

```
[Import(typeof(ICalculator))]
public Lazy<ICalculator> Calculator { get; set; }
```

Calling the imported property also requires some changes to access the Value property of the Lazy<T> type. calcImport is a variable of type CalculatorImport. The Calculator property returns Lazy<ICalculator>. The Value property instantiates the imported type lazily and returns the ICalculator interface, enabling the GetOperations method to be invoked in order to get all supported operations from the calculator add-in (code file WPFCalculator/Calculator/CalculatorManager.cs):

```
public Task InitializeOperationsAsync()
{
    Contract.Requires(calcImport != null);
    Contract.Requires(calcImport.Calculator != null);
    return Task.Run(() =>
        {
            var operators = calcImport.Calculator.Value.GetOperations();
            lock (vm.syncCalcAddInOperators)
            {
                vm.CalcAddInOperators.Clear();

                foreach (var op in operators)
                {
                    vm.CalcAddInOperators.Add(op);
                }
            }
        });
}
```

Reading Metadata with Lazily Instantiated Parts

The parts FuelEconomy and TemperatureConversion—all the parts that implement the interface ICalculatorExtension—are lazy loaded as well. As you've seen earlier, a collection can be imported with a property of IEnumerable<T>. Instantiating the parts lazily, the property can be of type IEnumerable<Lazy<T>>. Information about these parts is needed before instantiation in order to display information to the user about what can be expected with these parts. These parts offer additional information using metadata, as shown earlier. Metadata information can be accessed using a Lazy type with two generic type parameters. Using Lazy<ICalculatorExtension, ICalculatorExtensionMetadata>, the first generic parameter, ICalculatorExtension, is used to access the members of the instantiated type; the second generic parameter, ICalculatorExtensionMetadata, is used to access metadata information (code file WPFCalculator/Calculator/CalculatorExtensionImport.cs):

```
public class CalculatorExtensionImport : IPartImportsSatisfiedNotification
{
  public event EventHandler<ImportEventArgs> ImportsSatisfied;

  [ImportMany(AllowRecomposition = true)]
  public IEnumerable<Lazy<ICalculatorExtension, ICalculatorExtensionMetadata>>
      CalculatorExtensions { get; set; }

  public void OnImportsSatisfied()
  {
    if (ImportsSatisfied != null)
      ImportsSatisfied(this, new ImportEventArgs
      { StatusMessage = "ICalculatorExtension imports successful" });
  }
}
```

The method RefreshExtensions imports the calculator extension parts based on their Lazy type and adds the lazy types to the collection CalcExtensions shown earlier (code file WPFCalculator/Calculator/CalculatorManager.cs):

```
public void RefreshExensions()
{
  catalog.Refresh();
  calcExtensionImport = new CalculatorExtensionImport();
  calcExtensionImport.ImportsSatisfied += (sender, e) =>
  {
    vm.Status += String.Format("{0}\n", e.StatusMessage);
  };

  container.ComposeParts(calcExtensionImport);
  vm.CalcExtensions.Clear();
  foreach (var extension in calcExtensionImport.CalculatorExtensions)
  {
    vm.CalcExtensions.Add(extension);
  }
}
```

Within the XAML code, metadata information is bound. The Lazy type has a Metadata property that returns ICalculatorExtensionMetadata. This way, Description, Title, and ImageUri can be accessed for data binding without instantiating the add-ins (XAML file WPFCalculator/Calculator/MainWindow.xaml):

```
<RibbonGroup Header="Addins" ItemsSource="{Binding CalcExtensions}">
  <RibbonGroup.ItemTemplate>
    <DataTemplate>
      <RibbonButton ToolTip="{Binding Metadata.Description}"
          Label="{Binding Metadata.Title}" Tag="{Binding}"
```

```
LargeImageSource="{Binding Metadata.ImageUri,
    Converter={StaticResource bitmapConverter}}"
Command="local:CalculatorCommands.ActivateExtension" />
    </DataTemplate>
  </RibbonGroup.ItemTemplate>
</RibbonGroup>
```

To get an image from the link that is returned from the `ImageUri` property, a value converter is implemented that returns a `BitmapImage` (code file `WPFCalculator/Calculator/UriToBitmapConverter.cs`):

```csharp
public class UriToBitmapConverter : IValueConverter
{
  public object Convert(object value, Type targetType, object parameter,
      CultureInfo culture)
  {
    BitmapImage image = null;
    string uri = value.ToString();
    if (!string.IsNullOrEmpty(uri))
    {
      var stream = File.OpenRead(Path.Combine(
          Properties.Settings.Default.AddInDirectory, uri));
      image = new BitmapImage();
      image.BeginInit();
      image.StreamSource = stream;
      image.EndInit();
      return image;
    }
    else
    {
      return null;
    }
  }

  public object ConvertBack(object value, Type targetType, object parameter,
      CultureInfo culture)
  {
    throw new NotImplementedException();
  }
}
```

> **NOTE** *WPF value converters are discussed in Chapter 36, "Business Applications with WPF."*

Figure 30-5 shows the running application where metadata from the calculator extensions is read—it includes the image, the title, and the description.

CONTAINERS AND EXPORT PROVIDERS

The import of parts is facilitated with the help of a container. The types for hosting parts are defined in the namespace `System.ComponentModel.Composition.Hosting`. The class `CompositionContainer` is the container for parts. In the constructor of this class, multiple `ExportProvider` objects can be assigned, as well as

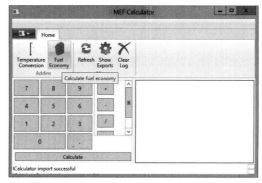

FIGURE 30-5

a `ComposablePartCatalog`. Catalogs are sources of parts and are discussed in the next section. Export providers enable you to access all exports programmatically with overloaded `GetExport<T>` methods. An export provider is used to access the catalog, and the `CompositionContainer` itself is an export provider. This makes it possible to nest containers in other containers.

Parts are loaded when the `Compose` method is invoked (if they are not lazy loaded). So far, the examples have used the `ComposeParts` method, as shown in the `InitializeContainer` method (code file `WPFCalculator/Calculator/CalculatorManager.cs`):

```
public async void InitializeContainer()
{
    catalog = new DirectoryCatalog(
                    Properties.Settings.Default.AddInDirectory);
    container = new CompositionContainer(catalog);
    calcImport = new CalculatorImport();
    calcImport.ImportsSatisfied += (sender, e) =>
        {
            textStatus.Text += String.Format("{0}\n", e.StatusMessage);
        };
    await Task.Run(() =>
      {
        container.ComposeParts(calcImport);
      });
    await InitializeOperationsAsync();
}
```

`ComposeParts` is an extension method defined with the class `AttributedModelServices`, which provides methods that use attributes and .NET reflection to access part information and add parts to the container. Instead of using this extension method, you can use the `Compose` method of `CompositionContainer`. The `Compose` method works with the class `CompositionBatch`. A `CompositionBatch` can be used to define which parts should be added or removed from the container. The methods `AddPart` and `RemovePart` have overloads whereby either an attributed part can be added (`calcImport` is an instance of the `CalculatorImport` class and contains `Import` attributes) or a part that derives from the base class `ComposablePart`:

```
var batch = new CompositionBatch();
batch.AddPart(calcImport);
container.Compose(batch);
```

Both kinds of parts used with the Calculator hosting application are searched in the same way. The part that implements the interface `ICalculator` is instantiated immediately when the application is launched. The `ICalculatorExtension` parts are instantiated only when the user clicks the part information in the ribbon control. Clicking on the buttons of the ribbon controls invokes the `OnActivateExtension` handler method. Within the implementation of this method, the selected `ICalculatorExtension` part is instantiated by using the `Value` property of the `Lazy<T>` type. A reference is then added to the `ActivatedExtensions` collection (code file `WPFCalculator/Calculator/MainWindow.xaml.cs`):

```
private void OnActivateExtension(object sender, ExecutedRoutedEventArgs e)
{
  var button = e.OriginalSource as RibbonButton;
  if (button != null)
  {
    Lazy<ICalculatorExtension> control = button.Tag as
      Lazy<ICalculatorExtension>;
    FrameworkElement el = control.Value.UI;
    viewModel.ActivatedExtensions.Add(control);
  }
}
```

All the activated `ICalculatorExtension` parts are shown as `TabItem` within the `TabControl` element, as the `TabControl` is bound to the `ActivatedExtensions` property. For the `TabItem` controls, both an `ItemTemplate` and a `ContentTemplate` are defined. The `ItemTemplate` defines a header to show the title and a button to close the part; the `ContentTemplate` accesses the user interface of the part by using the `UI` property (XAML file `WPFCalculator/Calculator/MainWindow.xaml`):

```
<TabControl Grid.Row="1" Grid.Column="1" Margin="2"
    ItemsSource="{Binding ActivatedExtensions}">
  <TabControl.ContentTemplate>
    <DataTemplate>
      <ContentPresenter Content="{Binding Value.UI}" />
    </DataTemplate>
  </TabControl.ContentTemplate>
  <TabControl.ItemTemplate>
    <DataTemplate>
      <StackPanel Orientation="Horizontal" Margin="0">
        <TextBlock Text="{Binding Metadata.Title}" Margin="0" />
        <Button Content="X" Margin="5,1"
          Command="local:CalculatorCommands.CloseExtension"
          Tag="{Binding}" />
      </StackPanel>
    </DataTemplate>
  </TabControl.ItemTemplate>
</TabControl>
```

The close button within the `ItemTemplate` activates the `CloseExtension` command. This invokes the `OnCloseExtension` handler method whereby the part is removed from the `ActivatedExtensions` collection (code file `WPFCalculator/Calculator/MainWindow.xaml.cs`):

```
private void OnCloseExtension(object sender, ExecutedRoutedEventArgs e)
{
  Button b = e.OriginalSource as Button;
  if (b != null)
  {
    Lazy<ICalculatorExtension> ext = b.Tag as Lazy<ICalculatorExtension>;
    if (ext != null)
    {
      viewModel.ActivatedExtensions.Remove(ext);
    }
  }
}
```

With an export provider, you can get information on exports added and removed by implementing a handler to the `ExportsChanged` event. The parameter e of type `ExportsChangedEventArgs` contains a list of added exports and removed exports that are written to a `Status` property (code file `WPFCalculator/Calculator/CalculatorManager.cs`):

```
container = new CompositionContainer(catalog);
container.ExportsChanged += (sender, e) =>
{
  var sb = new StringBuilder();

  foreach (var item in e.AddedExports)
  {
    sb.AppendFormat("added export {0}\n", item.ContractName);
  }
  foreach (var item in e.RemovedExports)
```

```
      {
        sb.AppendFormat("removed export {0}\n", item.ContractName);
      }
      vm.Status += sb.ToString();
    };
```

CATALOGS

A catalog defines where MEF searches for requested parts. The sample application uses a
DirectoryCatalog to load the assemblies with parts from a specified directory. With the
DirectoryCatalog, you can get change information with the Changed event and iterate through all added
and removed definitions. The DirectoryCatalog does not itself register to file system changes. Instead,
you need to invoke the Refresh method of the DirectoryCatalog; and if changes were made since the
last read, the Changing and Changed events are fired (code file WPFCalculator/Calculator/
CalculatorManager.cs):

```
public async void InitializeContainer()
{
    catalog = new DirectoryCatalog(Properties.Settings.Default.AddInDirectory);

    catalog.Changed += (sender, e) =>
    {
      var sb = new StringBuilder();

      foreach (var definition in e.AddedDefinitions)
      {
        foreach (var metadata in definition.Metadata)
        {
          sb.AppendFormat("added definition with metadata - key: {0}, " +
              "value: {1}\n", metadata.Key, metadata.Value);
        }
      }

      foreach (var definition in e.RemovedDefinitions)
      {
        foreach (var metadata in definition.Metadata)
        {
          sb.AppendFormat("removed definition with metadata - key: {0}, " +
              "value: {1}\n", metadata.Key, metadata.Value);
        }
      }

      vm.Status += sb.ToString();
    };

    container = new CompositionContainer(catalog);

    //...

}
```

> **NOTE** *To get immediate notification of new add-ins loaded to a directory, you can use
> the* System.IO.FileSystemWatcher *to register for changes to the add-in directory,
> and invoke the* Refresh *method of the* DirectoryCatalog *with the* Changed *event of
> the* FileSystemWatcher.

The `CompositionContainer` just needs a `ComposablePartCatalog` to find parts. `DirectoryCatalog` derives from `ComposablePartCatalog`. Other catalogs are `AssemblyCatalog`, `TypeCatalog`, and `AggregateCatalog`. Here's a brief description of these catalogs:

➤   `DirectoryCatalog` — Searches parts within a directory.

➤   The `AssemblyCatalog` — Searches for parts directly within a referenced assembly. Unlike the `DirectoryCatalog`, whereby assemblies might change in the directory during runtime, the `AssemblyCatalog` is immutable and parts cannot change.

➤   The `TypeCatalog` — Searches for imports within a list of types. `IEnumerable<Type>` can be passed to the constructor of this catalog.

➤   The `AggregateCatalog` — A catalog of catalogs. This catalog can be created from multiple `ComposablePartCatalog` objects, and it searches in all these catalogs. For example, you can create an `AssemblyCatalog` to search for imports within an assembly, two `DirectoryCatalog` objects to search in two different directories, and an `AggregateCatalog` that combines the three catalogs for import searches.

When running the sample application (see Figure 30-6), the `SimpleCalculator` add-in is loaded, and you can do some calculations with operations supported by the add-in. From the AddIns menu, you can start add-ins that implement the interface `ICalculatorExtension` and see the user interface from these add-ins in the tab control. Information about exports and changes in the directory catalog is shown with the status information at the bottom. You can also remove an `ICalculatorExtension` add-in from the add-in directory (while the application is not running), copy the add-in to the directory while the application is running, and do a refresh of the add-ins to see the new add-ins during runtime.

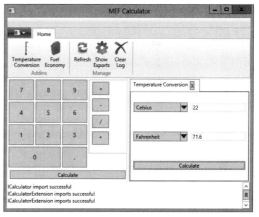

FIGURE 30-6

SUMMARY

In this chapter, you learned about the parts, containers, and catalogs of the Managed Extensibility Framework (MEF). You've learned how an application can be built up with complete independency of its parts and dynamically load parts that can come from different catalogs such as an assembly or directory catalog.

The MEF implementation uses attributes or conventions to find and connect add-ins. You've seen the new convention-based parts registration that allows exporting parts without the need of attributes. This allows using parts where you can't change the source code to add attributes, and also gives the option to create a framework based on MEF that doesn't require the user of your framework to add attributes for importing the parts.

You've also learned how parts can be lazy loaded to instantiate them only when they are needed. Parts can offer metadata that can give enough information for the client to decide if the part should be instantiated or not.

The next chapter covers the basics of the Windows Runtime to create Windows 8 applications.

31

Windows Runtime

WROX.COM CODE DOWNLOADS FOR THIS CHAPTER

The wrox.com code downloads for this chapter are found at `http://www.wrox.com/remtitle .cgi?isbn=1118314425` on the Download Code tab. The code for this chapter is divided into the following major examples:

- ➤ Language Projections
- ➤ Lifecycle Management
- ➤ App Settings
- ➤ Capabilities

OVERVIEW

Starting with Windows 8, Microsoft offers a new runtime for writing Windows applications with the new style: the Windows Runtime (WinRT). It contains classes with properties, methods, and events, and it uses delegates—so it looks like .NET but it's a native library. This chapter explains the core fundamentals of the Windows Runtime, demonstrating how it differs from .NET and how you can integrate the two to begin writing Windows 8 applications.

The Windows Runtime is easily accessible from C#, C++, and JavaScript. Although .NET has previously enabled other languages to use the framework, it required the languages to adapt. If you are familiar with JScript.NET, then you know that this is a JavaScript language for programming with .NET. In this case, JavaScript code can be used to directly access methods and properties from .NET classes.

Conversely, the Windows Runtime adapts to different languages, enabling developers to work within an environment with which they are familiar, whether it is C#, JavaScript, or C++. Using the

Windows Runtime from .NET languages like C# and Visual Basic, the Windows Runtime looks like .NET. Using it from C++, it contains methods that conform to the methods of the C++ Standard Library. Using the Windows Runtime from JavaScript, the methods have names and cases shared with JavaScript libraries.

The Windows Runtime primarily is a replacement for the Windows API. The .NET Framework is in large part a wrapper to the Windows API. It provides managed classes that can be used from C# to access operating system features. The Windows Runtime is a native API. It's just as easy to use as the .NET Framework classes. The .NET Framework is independent of the operating system. You can use .NET 4.5 on Windows Vista, Windows 7, and Windows 8. It is bound to a specific version of the operating system.

The first version of the Windows Runtime is available only with Windows 8. The next version is expected to be available with Windows 9, and this future version is not expected to run on Windows 8. This is very similar to the Windows API. You can also expect compatibility with future versions. Applications written with the Windows Runtime for Windows 8 will run on Windows 9 as well. This is not to be expected in the other direction. If applications are written using Windows 9, it can invoke methods that are not available with Windows 8, and thus the the application will not run on Windows 8.

Comparing .NET and Windows Runtime

With C# Windows 8 applications you can use both the Windows Runtime as well as the .NET Framework. However, not all classes and namespaces are available from the .NET Framework, and sometimes only some methods of classes are available. The Windows Runtime is a sandboxed API that wraps new UI classes and parts of the Windows API.

Namespaces unavailable with the .NET subset for Windows 8 apps are replaced by a corresponding WinRT namespace, as shown in the following table:

.NET NAMESPACE	WINRT NAMESPACE
System.Net.Sockets	Windows.Networking.Sockets
System.Net.WebClient	Windows.Networking.BackgroundTransfer and System.Net.HttpClient
System.Resources	Windows.ApplicationModel.Resources
System.Security.IsolatedStorage	Windows.Storage
System.Windows	Windows.UI.Xaml

Namespaces

The best way to see what's offered by the Windows Runtime is to look at the namespaces. The classes from the Windows Runtime are grouped within namespaces, similarly to the .NET Framework. Whereas the .NET Framework starts with the System namespace, the Windows Runtime starts with the Windows namespace. In addition, whereas a part of the .NET Framework is a public standard and can be implemented for other platforms (see Mono at http://www.go-mono.org), the Windows Runtime is meant for use only with Windows.

Some of the major namespaces are shown in Figure 31-1. An explanation is given in the following table:

WINDOWS RUNTIME NAMESPACE	DESCRIPTION
Windows.System	The Windows.System namespace and it subnamespaces contain a Launcher class for launching applications, classes with information about a remote desktop, a ThreadPool and ThreadPoolTimer for working with background tasks, and more.
Windows.Foundation	The Windows.Foundation namespace contains subnamespaces for collections, diagnostics, and metadata.

WINDOWS RUNTIME NAMESPACE	DESCRIPTION
Windows.ApplicationModel	Windows.ApplicationModel has subnamespaces to manage licensing with the store, to open the search with the Charms bar, to share data with other apps, to work with contacts, and to create background tasks.
Windows.Globalization	Windows.Globalization defines calendars, regions, languages, date, and number formats.
Windows.Graphics	Windows.Graphics is for images and printing.
Windows.Media	Windows.Media enables accessing audio and video, using the camera, and making use of the PlayTo standard to play videos to other devices.
Windows.Data	Windows.Data contains classes for XML, HTML, and JSON.
Windows.Devices	Windows.Devices enables interacting with devices and sensors, e.g., using Accelerometer, Compass, Gyrometer, Inclinometer, LightSensor, OrientationSensor, sending SMS, and using geo-location (of course, only if the device supports these options).
Windows.Storage	For reading and writing files, the Windows.Storage namespace contains classes such as StorageFile and StorageFolder, but also streams and file pickers, and classes for compression and decompression with the algorithms Mszip, Lzms, Xpress, and XpressHuff.
Windows.Security	This namespace contains subnamespaces for security with authentication, credentials, and cryptography.
Windows.Networking	Windows.Networking is for client socket programming. There's also a way to start a background transfer that continues when the application goes out of scope for the user.

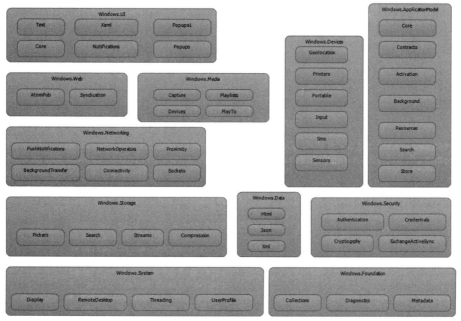

FIGURE 31-1

For XAML there's the subnamespace `Windows`
`.UI.Xaml`, which contains several other namespaces,
as shown in Figure 31-2. Here you find shapes
(`Shapes` namespace); XAML documents (`Documents`);
data binding (`Data`); bitmaps, brushes, paths,
transformations (`Media`); touch, mouse, and keyboard
input (`Input`); a XAML reader (`Markup`); printing of
XAML elements (`Printing`); and more.

Clearly, the namespaces for the Windows Runtime offer
a lot of possibilities. Of course, the .NET Framework is
huge compared to the Windows Runtime, but the latter

FIGURE 31-2

is primarily meant for Windows 8 apps; therefore, some parts of the .NET Framework are not required.

You can use a subset of the .NET Framework together with the Windows Runtime, although some categories of
classes are not offered for Windows 8 apps. For example, server-side code is not required for Windows 8 apps.
There's no ASP.NET and no hosting part of WCF. The client-side part for WCF is available with Windows 8
apps. Doing communication with a WCF service running on a server is possible with WCF client classes.

Other categories where classes are not available in the subset are *removing duplicates*, and doing some *clean
ups*. Classes that are available with the Windows Runtime are not duplicated with the .NET Framework for
Window 8 apps. The Windows Runtime already contains an `XmlDocument` class that deals with the DOM
of XML in the namespace `Windows.Data.Xml.Dom`, so there's no need for another one in the namespace
`System.Xml`. Clean ups are done with obsolete and unsafe APIs. These are not available anymore, and also
classes that directly access the Windows API are missing. That's the role of the Windows Runtime.

Metadata

Accessing metadata information is possible in the same way with .NET applications as it is with the Windows
Runtime. The metadata format is the same. The metadata information defined for .NET is specified by an
ECMA standard (ECMA 335), and the same standard has been used with the Windows Runtime.

You can use ildasm to read the metadata of the Windows Runtime libraries with the file extension
`.winmd`. You can find the metadata information for the Windows Runtime in the directory `<windows>\`
`system32\WinMetadata`. There you will find the files that can be opened using ildasm to read metadata
information. However, it's easier to use the Visual Studio Object Browser (see Figure 31-3), which makes use
of the metadata information as well.

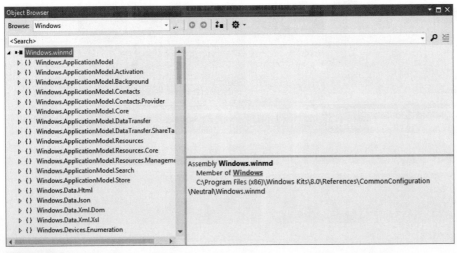

FIGURE 31-3

Using the Object Browser it's easy to look at the classes from the Windows Runtime by selecting Windows as the browsing scope, and the subset of .NET classes available by selecting .NET for Windows 8 apps as the browsing scope. Windows uses the `Windows.winmd` file from the directory `<Program Files (x86)>\ Windows Kits\8.0\References\CommonConfiguration\Neutral`, and the .NET subset can be found at `<Program Files (x86)>\Reference Assemblies\Microsoft\Framework\.NETCore\v4.5`. These files contain only metadata information that defines what is available.

Language Projections

The metadata information is used to create different projections that vary according to the programming language. The Windows Runtime looks different when using it from C++, C#, and JavaScript. This section creates two sample Windows 8 apps to demonstrate the differences between JavaScript and C#. The applications contain a button and an image. Clicking the button starts a file picker that enables the user to select an image, which is then displayed.

The first application built uses JavaScript. To begin, select the JavaScript Windows Store Blank App template. The generated HTML file, `default.html`, is modified to contain `button` and `img` elements as shown in the following code snippet (code file `ProjectionWithJavaScript/default.html`):

```
<button id="selectImageButton">Select an Image</button>
<p />
<img alt="Some Image" src="Images/logo.png" id="image1" />
```

The JavaScript file, `default.js`, is also created from the Visual Studio template. This file contains an event handler that is added to the `onactivated` event of the app. As the name suggests, this event handler is invoked when the application is activated. You just add functionality after the call to `setPromise`. Promise objects (one is returned from `setPromise`) and the `then` and `done` functions are the JavaScript variants of asynchronous programming. With C#, the `async` and `await` keywords are used instead. The `WinJS.UI.processAll` function processes all elements of the page and manages binding. This example focuses on the code that happens after that—the `done` function invokes the function that is passed as a parameter as soon as processing is completed. With the implementation of this function, a `click` event handler is added to the `selectImageButton`. The function that is passed to the `addEventListener` function is invoked as soon as the button is clicked.

Now we are getting into the Windows Runtime code. A `FileOpenPicker` from the namespace `Windows.Storage.Pickers` is instantiated. This picker requests a file from the user. To specify a preferred directory, the `suggestedStartLocation` is set to `Windows.Storage.Pickers.PickerLocationId .picturesLibrary`. Then file extensions are added to the file type filter list. `fileTypeFilter` is a property from the `FileOpenPicker`. This property returns an `IVector<string>` collection; and with JavaScript, to add items to the collection the `append` function is invoked. Calling the function `pickSingleFileAsync` the user is asked for a file to open. As soon as the result is retrieved, the `then` function defines what should be done next. The `file` argument is used to create a BLOB object that is assigned to the `src` attribute of the `image` element, enabling the selected image file to be shown in the UI. The following code shows how to accomplish all this (code file `ProjectionWithJavaScript/js/default.js`):

```
(function () {
  "use strict";

  var app = WinJS.Application;
  var activation = Windows.ApplicationModel.Activation;
  WinJS.strictProcessing();

  app.onactivated = function (args) {
    if (args.detail.kind === activation.ActivationKind.launch) {
      if (args.detail.previousExecutionState !==
        activation.ApplicationExecutionState.terminated) {
```

```
            // TODO: This application has been newly launched. Initialize
            // your application here.


        } else {
            // TODO: This application has been reactivated from suspension.
            // Restore application state here.
        }

        args.setPromise(WinJS.UI.processAll().done(function () {
          document.getElementById("selectImageButton").addEventListener(
            "click", function () {
            var picker = new Windows.Storage.Pickers.FileOpenPicker();
            picker.suggestedStartLocation =
              Windows.Storage.Pickers.PickerLocationId.picturesLibrary;
            picker.fileTypeFilter.append(".jpg");
            picker.fileTypeFilter.append(".png");
            picker.pickSingleFileAsync().then(function (file) {
              if (file) {
                var imageBlob = URL.createObjectURL(file);
                document.getElementById("image1").src = imageBlob;
              }
              else {

              }
            });
          });
        }));
      }
    };
```

Now, let's do the same with XAML and C#. This project makes use of the Windows Store Blank App
(XAML) template. As before, a `Button` element and an `Image` element are created, but this time XAML
code is used instead of HTML (code file `ProjectionWithCSharp/MainPage.xaml`):

```
<Grid Background="{StaticResource ApplicationPageBackgroundThemeBrush}">
  <Grid.RowDefinitions>
    <RowDefinition Height="Auto" />
    <RowDefinition Height="*" />
  </Grid.RowDefinitions>
  <Button Grid.Row="0" Click="OnOpenImage">Select an Image</Button>
  <Image Grid.Row="1" x:Name="image1" />
</Grid>
```

It's after the `OnOpenImage` handler method is assigned to the `Click` event of the button that things get
interesting. Similar to before, a `FileOpenPicker` object is created. However, immediately after that,
in the next line, an interesting difference can be seen. `SuggestedStartLocation` is of the type of the
`PickerLocationId` enumeration. The enumeration values are written with uppercase notation as you're
used to with C#. The `FileTypeFilter` does not return `IVector<string>`, but instead `IList<string>`.
With this the `Add` method is invoked to pass a few file extensions. Working with JavaScript, it's more
common to use an `append` function instead of the `Add` method. Using the `await` keyword, you can wait until
the `StorageFile` is returned. Finally, a `BitmapImage` object is assigned to the XAML `Image` element. The
`BitmapImage` itself receives a random access stream to load the image (code file `ProjectionWithCSharp/
MainPage.xaml.cs`):

```
private async void OnOpenImage(object sender, RoutedEventArgs e)
{
  var picker = new FileOpenPicker();
  picker.SuggestedStartLocation = PickerLocationId.PicturesLibrary;
  picker.FileTypeFilter.Add(".jpg");
```

```
                picker.FileTypeFilter.Add(".png");
                StorageFile file = await picker.PickSingleFileAsync();

                BitmapImage image = new BitmapImage();
                image.SetSource(await file.OpenReadAsync());

                image1.Source = image;
            }
```

The same classes have been used with these two examples, but the methods look different depending on the programming language used. With .NET, the convention is to use *PascalCase* with types, methods, properties, and events. With JavaScript, the convention is to use PascalCase for the types, *camelCase* with methods and properties, and *lowercase* with events. This conversion for the languages is handled by language projection, which changes not only uppercase and lowercase, but also data types and method names. More details about this are provided in subsequent sections.

Windows Runtime Types

This section looks at the Windows Runtime types, including how they are categorized and how they compare to .NET types. An important aspect of the types defined by the Windows Runtime is their interaction with various languages. For example, when passing a .NET string to a Windows Runtime method, it shouldn't necessary to create a new string with every method call just because there are two different technologies. Passing data here is known as marshalling, which is discussed in more detail in Chapter 23, "Interop". Understanding the Windows Runtime types is important not only when using classes and methods from the runtime, but also when creating types with C# that should be used from other languages, such as C++ and JavaScript.

Let's look at categories of Windows Runtime types:

➤ **Strings**—With the Windows Runtime, strings are defined as handles, HSTRING. A handle is a reference to a string that just references the first character of the string The HSTRING is added to the buffer of the .NET String type to address the rest of the string inside. With .NET, strings are immutable and cannot be changed. WinRT always assumes that the string buffer is immutable and null-terminated which is the case with .NET strings. A .NET String type simply maps to HSTRING.

➤ **Basic data types**—These types, such as Int16, Int32, Int64, Single, and Double, map directly to .NET representatives. The WinRT DateTime maps to a .NET DateTimeOffset.

➤ **Arrays**—Simple arrays such as Int32[] can be used for basic collections.

➤ **Enums**—These map easily to the C# enum. It's also possible to use flag and non-flag enums.

➤ **Structs**—These are available with WinRT as well, but they are different from .NET struct types. A struct can contain only basic data types and strings. Whereas a .NET struct can implement interfaces, this is not possible with WinRT; a struct is just a simple data holder.

➤ **Interfaces**—These are the heart of the Windows Runtime. Chapter 23 discusses COM interfaces such as IUnknown. The classes offered by the Windows Runtime are COM objects, the new generation. In addition to IUnknown, they also implement the interface IInspectible. Unlike IUnknown, IInspectible provides information about the implemented interfaces and the name of a class.

➤ **Generic interfaces**—The Windows Runtime supports these as well. IIterable<T> enables you to enumerate a collection, and IVector<T> represents a random-access collection of elements. These interfaces map to IEnumerable<T> and IList<T>, respectively.

➤ **Runtime classes**—This includes classes such as Windows.Storage.StorageFile. Runtime classes implement interfaces; for example, StorageFile implements IStorageFile, IStorageFileItem, IRandomAccessStreamReference, IInputStreamReference, and IStorageItemProperties (in addition to IUnknown and IInspectible). With .NET applications you typically work only with the runtime classes, not with the interfaces directly.

WINDOWS RUNTIME COMPONENTS

Although you have seen that there are differences between the Windows Runtime and .NET in terms of types, many of them map easily. For example, the HSTRING directly maps to a String. The differences are extremely important if you create Windows Runtime components with .NET. Visual Studio offers a Windows Runtime Component template with the application templates. Using this, you can create a component that is available for other languages using the Windows Runtime, such as C++ and JavaScript. This differs from the Portable class library whereby you can create classes that are available with other .NET variants, such as applications using the full .NET Framework, Silverlight, or Windows Runtime with C#.

When creating Windows Runtime components, the public classes offered must be sealed. Only sealed types are supported—with the exception of UI components, for which sealing is not that strict. The following sections take a closer look at both the automatic mappings and the sometimes not so automatic mappings.

Collections

The Windows Runtime defines collection interfaces that automatically map to .NET collection interfaces as shown in the following table:

WINDOWS RUNTIME	.NET
IIterable<T>	IEnumerable<T>
IIterator<T>	IEnumerator<T>
IVector<T>	IList<T>
IVectorView<T>	IReadOnlyList<T>
IMap<K, V>	IDictionary<K, V>
IMapView<K, V>	IReadOnlyDictionary<K, V>

When creating a Windows Runtime component, you need to return an interface, such as IList<string> shown in the following code snippet. Returning List<string> directly is not possible. IList<string> automatically maps to IVector<T>. Similarly, you can use IList<T> as a parameter with methods.

```
public IList<string> GetStringList()
{
  return new List<string> { "one", "two" };
}
```

Streams

Streams differ from collections. The foundation for working with Windows Runtime streams are, of course, interfaces. The Windows.Storage.Streams namespace also offers concrete stream classes such as FileInputStream, FileOutputStream, and RandomAccessStream, and reader and writer classes using streams such as DataReader and DataWriter. All these classes are based on the interfaces. .NET doesn't use interfaces for streams. Public signatures of Windows Runtime components always require interfaces for streams such as IInputStream, IOutputStream, and IRandomAccessStream. Mapping these interfaces to .NET types and vice versa is done with extension methods defined within the WindowsRuntimeStreamExtensions class. As shown in the following code snippet, AsStreamForRead creates a Stream object from an IInputStream:

```
public void StreamSample(IInputStream inputStream)
{
  var reader = new StreamReader(inputStream.AsStreamForRead());
  //...
}
```

Other extension methods defined are `AsStreamForWrite` to create a `Stream` object from an `IOutputStream` and `AsStream` to create a `Stream` from an `IRandomAccessStream`. To create a Windows Runtime stream from a .NET stream, the method `AsInputStream` can be used to create an `IInputStream` from a `Stream`, and `AsOutputStream` can be used to create an `IOuputStream` from a `Stream`.

The following code shows one example using only Windows Runtime classes. First, a `StorageFolder` object is created that references the local folder to which the application is allowed to write. `ApplicationData` `.Current` returns the current instance of the `ApplicationData` class, which defines properties for local, roaming, and temporary folders to read and write data. The content of the roaming folder is copied to the different systems into which the user logs in to. The roaming folder has size limitations (quotas). At the time of this writing the size is limited to 100 kB per application. With the sample code, in the local folder a new file is created. The method `CreateFileAsync` returns a `StorageFile` object. `StorageFile` is a Windows Runtime object and thus returns an object implementing the `IRandomAccessStream` interface on calling `OpenAsync`. The `IRandomAccessStream` can be passed to the constructor of the Windows Runtime `DataWriter` class, which is used to write a string to the file:

```
StorageFolder folder = ApplicationData.Current.LocalFolder;
StorageFile file = await folder.CreateFileAsync("demo1.txt");
IRandomAccessStream stream = await file.OpenAsync(FileAccessMode.ReadWrite);
using (var writer = new DataWriter(stream))
{
  writer.WriteString("Hello, WinRT");
  await writer.FlushAsync();
}
```

The preceding example is purely Windows Runtime code. Now let's look at a mixed variant with the Windows Runtime and .NET. As before, the `StorageFolder` is created. With the `StorageFolder`, the extension method `OpenStreamForWriteAsync` is used. `OpenStreamForWriteAsync` is an extension method defined with the `WindowsRuntimeStorageExtensions` class that returns a .NET `Stream` object. This enables all the .NET classes using streams to write to the file, such as the `StreamWriter` class. `WindowsRuntimeStorageExtension` is defined in the .NET assembly `System.Runtime.WindowsRuntime` in the namespace `System.IO`:

```
StorageFolder folder = ApplicationData.Current.LocalFolder;
Stream stream = await folder.OpenStreamForWriteAsync("demo2.text",
    CreationCollisionOption.ReplaceExisting);
using (var writer = new StreamWriter(stream))
{
  await writer.WriteLineAsync("Hello, .NET");
  await writer.FlushAsync();
}
```

With streams, `byte[]` often comes into play as well. For a `byte[]`, Windows Runtime defines the interface `IBuffer`. With byte arrays, there's a similar mix-and-match just like streams. With the `Create` method of the `WindowsRuntimeBuffer` class (namespace `System.Runtime.InteropServices.WindowsRuntime`), an object implementing `IBuffer` is returned from a `byte[]`. The `WindowsRuntimeBufferExtensions` class offers methods to get `IBuffer` from `byte[]` (`AsBuffer` method), to copy `byte[]` to `IBuffer` or vice versa (`CopyTo`), and to create a `byte[]` from `IBuffer` (`ToArray`).

Delegates and Events

Programming delegates and events looks very similar from .NET and the Windows Runtime, but behind the scenes the implementation is different. Windows Runtime events can only be of a Windows Runtime delegate type (or a type that matches a Windows Runtime delegate type). An event cannot be of type `EventHandler`, but using the type `EventHandler<object>` is OK.

For the Windows Runtime implementation of events, the `WindowsRuntimeMarshal` class is used. This class offers the methods `AddEventHandler` and `RemoveEventHandler` to add or remove handlers from events.

Async

For async operations with .NET, `Task` objects are used. An async method that does not have a return value returns `Task`, and an async method with a return value returns `Task<T>`. Async methods with the Windows Runtime are based on the interfaces `IAsyncAction` and `IAsyncOperation<T>`.

Async Windows Runtime methods can be used in the same way as async .NET methods, with the keywords `async` and `await`. The following code snippet makes use of the Windows Runtime `XmlDocument` class from the namespace `Windows.Data.Xml.Dom`. The method `LoadFromUriAsync` returns `IAsyncOperation<XmlDocument>`. This can be used in the same way as a method that returns `Task<XmlDocument>`:

```
private async Task<string> XmlDemo()
{
  Uri uri = new Uri("http://www.cninnovation.com/downloads/Racers.xml");
  XmlDocument doc = await XmlDocument.LoadFromUriAsync(uri);
  return doc.GetXml();
}

private async void OnXml(object sender, RoutedEventArgs e)
{
  text1.Text = await XmlDemo();
}
```

If you create a Windows Runtime component, a public async method cannot return `Task`. Such a method needs to be written as shown in the following two code snippets. If the method does not return a value, it needs to return `IAsyncAction`. A `Task` is converted to `IAsyncAction` with the extension method `AsAsyncAction`. The extension methods for tasks are defined in the `WindowsRuntimeSystem Extensions` class.

```
public IAsyncAction TaskSample()
{
  return Task.Run(async () =>
    {
      await Task.Delay(3000);
    }).AsAsyncAction();
}
```

With an async method that returns a value, `IAsyncOperation<T>` needs to be returned. The extension method `AsAsyncOperation` converts a `Task<T>` to `IAsyncOperation<T>`:

```
public IAsyncOperation<int> TaskWithReturn(int x, int y)
{
  return Task<int>.Run<int>(async () =>
    {
      await Task.Delay(3000);
      return x + y;
    }).AsAsyncOperation();
}
```

WINDOWS 8 APPS

Visual Studio offers several templates for creating Windows 8 apps, as shown in Figure 31-4. The Blank App template is the most rudimentary, containing just a single empty page. The Grid App template contains three pages that display grouped grid information, and the Split App template contains two pages to navigate with an item list. A Class Library template is a .NET library that you can reuse with different Windows 8 projects created with C# or Visual Basic. A Windows Runtime Component Library template creates a library that can be reused with various Windows 8 projects from other languages, such as C++ and JavaScript. The Windows Runtime Component Library template restricts you to define public signatures of methods that must match to the Windows Runtime types as explained in the previous section.

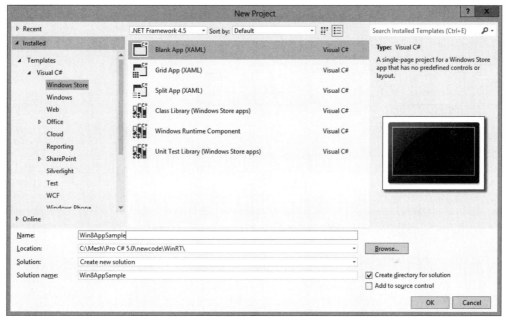

FIGURE 31-4

For the sample application, the Blank App template is used. With a Windows Store project, in addition to the usual project settings, there's also a configuration for the deployment package. The deployment package can be configured by clicking the file `Package.appxmanifest` in Solution Explorer. Clicking this file opens the Manifest Designer, shown in Figure 31-5. Using this designer you can configure application settings such as which images are used for the logo, names, rotation information, and colors. The second tab, Capabilities, enables you to define which capabilities are included with the application, and what it needs permissions to access (e.g., directories such as the documents library or the music library, and devices such as the microphone or webcam). The Declarations tab defines what the application needs to access (e.g., camera settings, registering a file type association, availability as a share target). The Packaging tab enables you to define the application logo, a certificate and version number, and other options that describe your deployed app.

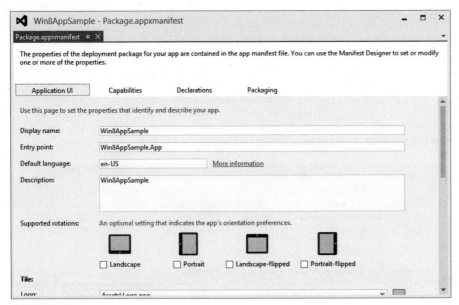

FIGURE 31-5

The Manifest Designer creates an XML file like the one shown here containing all the configured values:

```xml
<?xml version="1.0" encoding="utf-8"?>
<Package xmlns="http://schemas.microsoft.com/appx/2010/manifest">
  <Identity Name="920e63ef-9344-4925-a408-86f056314f31" Publisher="CN=Christian"
    Version="1.0.0.0" />
  <Properties>
    <DisplayName>Win8AppSample</DisplayName>
    <PublisherDisplayName>CN innovation</PublisherDisplayName>
    <Logo>Assets\StoreLogo.png</Logo>
  </Properties>
  <Prerequisites>
    <OSMinVersion>6.2.1</OSMinVersion>
    <OSMaxVersionTested>6.2.1</OSMaxVersionTested>
  </Prerequisites>
  <Resources>
    <Resource Language="x-generate" />
  </Resources>
  <Applications>
    <Application Id="App" Executable="$targetnametoken$.exe"
      EntryPoint="Win8AppSample.App">
      <VisualElements DisplayName="Win8AppSample" Logo="Assets\Logo.png"
        SmallLogo="Assets\SmallLogo.png" Description="Win8AppSample"
        ForegroundText="light" BackgroundColor="#464646">
        <DefaultTile ShowName="allLogos" />
        <SplashScreen Image="Assets\SplashScreen.png" />
      </VisualElements>
    </Application>
  </Applications>
  <Capabilities>
    <Capability Name="internetClient" />
  </Capabilities>
</Package>
```

Building the project with Visual Studio and starting it automatically deploys it on the system. You can also create an app package for deployment in the Windows Store or for the sideloading of business applications.

> **NOTE** *The deployment of Windows 8 app packages is discussed in Chapter 18, "Deployment."*

THE LIFE CYCLE OF APPLICATIONS

The life cycle of desktop applications is different from the life cycle of Windows 8 apps. With desktop applications, the user is in control of starting and stopping the application. Sometimes the Task Manager is needed to kill a hanging application, but usually the user decides how many applications should run concurrently. For example, it wouldn't be unusual to keep multiple instances of Visual Studio, Outlook, several Internet Explorer windows, and some tools open at the same time. On the contrary, other users start and end one application before opening the next. This is completely different to the new way Windows 8 apps work.

With Windows 8 apps, the user typically does not stop the application. The usual way to start an application is by clicking on its tile. Of course, this is very similar to desktop applications. The big differences are just following. When the user starts an application it is in *running mode*. As soon as another application is started and the previous application is no longer visible, it changes to suspended mode. In *suspended mode*, battery consumption is reduced if applicable. The application stays in memory but is no longer allowed to consume CPU, disk, or network resources. All threads are suspended. Before the application moves to the suspended mode, the application gets a chance to react. Here, the application should save the state.

When the user switches back to the first application it is instantly resumed from suspend (as it is still stored in memory) and brought to the foreground. The mode is now running again. Switching from suspended to running usually requires no action on behalf of the application, as all application data is still in memory; therefore, the application only needs reactivation.

In case memory resources are low, Windows can terminate suspended applications. To terminate applications the process is killed. No information is sent to the application, so it cannot react to this event. That's why an application should act on the suspended event and save its state there. Upon termination it is too late.

Application Execution States

States of the application are defined with the `ApplicationExecutionState` enumeration. This enumeration defines the states `NotRunning`, `Running`, `Suspended`, `Terminated`, and `ClosedByUser`. The application needs to be aware of and store its state, as users returning to the application expect to continue where they left it previously.

With the `OnLaunched` method in the `App` class, you can get the previous execution state of the application with the `PreviousExecutionState` property of the `LauchActivatedEventArgs` argument. The previous execution state is `NotRunning` if the application is being started for the first time after installing it, or after a reboot, or when the user stopped the process from the Task Manager. The application is in the `Running` state if it was already running when the user activated it from a second tile or it's activated by one of the activation contracts. The `PreviousExecutionState` property returns `Suspended` when the application was suspended previously. Usually there's no need to do anything special in that case.

> **NOTE** *The application can implement one or more* activation contracts *and can then be activated with one of these. A few examples of these contracts are* search *and* share. *Without starting the application first, the user can search for some terms in the application. This is when the application is started. Also, the user can share some data from another application, and start a Windows 8 app by using it as a share target. Application contracts are discussed in Chapter 38, "Windows 8 Apps."*

The sample application to demonstrate the life cycle of Windows 8 apps (LifecycleSample) is started with the Blank App template. After creation of the project, a new Basic Page named `MainPage` is added to replace the originally created `MainPage` from the project. The Visual Studio item template Basic Page adds several files to the `Common` directory. One of these files is `SuspensionManager.cs`, which contains the class `SuspensionManager`. This class greatly assists with state management.

To demonstrate navigation state, the application contains the basic pages `Page1` and `Page2` in addition to the `MainPage`. Each of these pages contains a button for navigation. The button of the `MainPage` has a `Click` event handler that navigates to `Page2`, as shown in the following code snippet (file `MainPage.xaml.cs`):

```
private void OnGotoPage2(object sender, RoutedEventArgs e)
{
    Frame.Navigate(typeof(Page2));
}
```

The other handlers are similar. The goal is to enable users to return to the page they had open in case the application was terminated in between.

Suspension Manager

The `SuspensionManager` class (code file `LifecycleSample/Common/SuspensionManager.cs`) contains a `SaveAsync` method that saves both frame navigation state and session state. For navigation state, the method sets it with all registered frames in the method `SaveFrameNavigationState`. In the following example, the frame state is added to the session state to save them together. Session state first is written to a `MemoryStream` with the help of the `DataContractSerializer`, and afterward is written to the XML file `_sessionState.xml`:

```
private static Dictionary<string, object> _sessionState =
    new Dictionary<string, object>();
private static List<Type> _knownTypes = new List<Type>();
private static const string sessionStateFilename = "_sessionState.xml";

public static async Task SaveAsync()
{
    // Save the navigation state for all registered frames
    foreach (var weakFrameReference in _registeredFrames)
    {
        Frame frame;
        if (weakFrameReference.TryGetTarget(out frame))
        {
            SaveFrameNavigationState(frame);
        }
    }

    // Serialize the session state synchronously to avoid asynchronous access
    // to shared state
    MemoryStream sessionData = new MemoryStream();
    DataContractSerializer serializer =
        new DataContractSerializer(typeof(Dictionary<string, object>), _knownTypes);
    serializer.WriteObject(sessionData, _sessionState);

    // Get an output stream for the SessionState file and write the
    // state asynchronously
    StorageFile file = await ApplicationData.Current.LocalFolder.CreateFileAsync(
        sessionStateFilename, CreationCollisionOption.ReplaceExisting);
    using (Stream fileStream = await file.OpenStreamForWriteAsync())
    {
        sessionData.Seek(0, SeekOrigin.Begin);
        await sessionData.CopyToAsync(fileStream);
        await fileStream.FlushAsync();
    }
```

```
    }

    private static void SaveFrameNavigationState(Frame frame)
    {
      var frameState = SessionStateForFrame(frame);
      frameState["Navigation"] = frame.GetNavigationState();
    }
```

For a restore of the data, the method `RestoreAsync` is available. This method opens a `StorageFile` and reads data using the `DataContractSerializer`:

```
public static async Task RestoreAsync()
{
  _sessionState = new Dictionary<String, Object>();

  // Get the input stream for the SessionState file
  StorageFile file = await ApplicationData.Current.LocalFolder.GetFileAsync(
    sessionStateFilename);
  using (IInputStream inStream = await file.OpenSequentialReadAsync())
  {
    // Deserialize the Session State
    DataContractSerializer serializer = new DataContractSerializer(
      typeof(Dictionary<string, object>), _knownTypes);
    _sessionState = (Dictionary<string, object>)serializer.ReadObject(
      inStream.AsStreamForRead());
  }

  // Restore any registered frames to their saved state
  foreach (var weakFrameReference in _registeredFrames)
  {
    Frame frame;
    if (weakFrameReference.TryGetTarget(out frame))
    {
      frame.ClearValue(FrameSessionStateProperty);
      RestoreFrameNavigationState(frame);
    }
  }
}
```

In the next section you'll add some code to make use of the `SuspensionManager` to save the navigation state.

Navigation State

To save state on suspending of the application, the `Suspending` event of the `App` class is set the `OnSuspending` event handler. The event is fired when the application moves into suspended mode. With the argument `SuspendingEventArgs`, the `SuspendingOperation` object can be accessed with the `SuspendingOperation` property. The `GetDeferral` property enables suspension of the application to be delayed, giving it some time to finish before it is suspended. `GetDeferral` returns a `SuspendingDeferral` that is used to inform the runtime of completion of the suspending state by invoking the `Complete` method. The maximum amount of time that can be used is defined by the `Deadline` property of `SuspendingOperation`. This property provides information about the time remaining before the application is suspended. After getting the `SuspendingDeferral`, the `SaveAsync` method of the `SuspensionManager` is invoked to save the application state:

```
private async void OnSuspending(object sender, SuspendingEventArgs e)
{
  var deferral = e.SuspendingOperation.GetDeferral();
  await SuspensionManager.SaveAsync();
  deferral.Complete();
}
```

To remember navigation information, the frame needs to be registered with the `SuspensionManager`. The `OnLaunched` method of the `Application` class is overridden, and after the `Frame` object is created it is registered with the `SuspensionManager` class. This way, the frame navigation information is saved on suspension, and the variable is filled when its state is restored. If the application was launched again after it was terminated previously (which is checked with the `PreviousExecutionState` property), the `RestoreAsync` method of the `SuspensionManager` is invoked to retrieve the navigation data from the frame. Before navigation to the `MainPage`, the `Content` property of the frame is checked to confirm that it is not null. If that's the case, the content is already filled from the restore. If a restore was not done, then navigation to the `MainPage` is initiated (code file `LifecycleSample/App.xaml.cs`):

```
protected async override void OnLaunched(LaunchActivatedEventArgs args)
{
  // Do not repeat app initialization when already running, just ensure that
  // the window is active
  if (args.PreviousExecutionState == ApplicationExecutionState.Running)
  {
    Window.Current.Activate();
    return;
  }

  var rootFrame = new Frame();

  SuspensionManager.RegisterFrame(rootFrame, "AppFrame");

  if (args.PreviousExecutionState == ApplicationExecutionState.Terminated)
  {
    await SuspensionManager.RestoreAsync();
  }

  // Create a Frame to act navigation context and navigate to the first page
  if (rootFrame.Content == null)
  {
    if (!rootFrame.Navigate(typeof(MainPage)))
    {
      throw new Exception("Failed to create initial page");
    }
  }
}
```

Testing Suspension

Now you can start the application, navigate to another page, and then open other applications to wait until the application is terminated. With the Task Manager, you can see the suspended applications with the More details view if the Status Values option is set to "Show suspended status." This is not an easy way to test suspension (because it can take a long time before the termination happens), however, and it would be nice to debug the different states.

Using the debugger, everything works differently. If the application would be suspended as soon as it doesn't have a focus, it would be suspended every time a breakpoint is reached. That's why suspension is disabled while running under the debugger. So the normal suspension mechanism doesn't apply. However, it's easy to simulate. If you open the Debug Location toolbar, there are three buttons for Suspend, Resume, and Suspend And Shutdown. If you select Suspend And Shutdown, and then start the application again, it continues from the previous state of `ApplicationExecutionState.Terminated`, and thus opens the page the user opened previously.

Page State

Any data that was input by the user should be restored as well. For this demonstration, on page 2 an input field is created. The data representation of this input field is a simple `Page2Data` class with a

Data property, as shown in the following code snippet (code file LifecycleSample/DataModel/ Page2Data.cs):

```
public class Page2Data : BindableBase
{
  private string data;
  public string Data
  {
    get { return data; }
    set { SetProperty(ref data, value); }
  }
}
```

The data is bound to a TextBox element (file Page2.xaml):

```
<StackPanel Grid.Row="1" DataContext="{Binding Page2Data}">
  <TextBox Text="{Binding Data, Mode=TwoWay}" />
  <Button Content="Goto Page 3" Click="OnGotoPage3" />
</StackPanel>
```

In the Page2 class, a variable of the Page2Data is defined to bind it to the UI element:

```
public sealed partial class Page2 : LayoutAwarePage
{
  private Page2Data data;
```

Assigning the variable data to bind it to the UI can be done within the LoadState method. The LoadState method is overridden from the base class LayoutAwarePage, which invokes the LoadState method within the OnNavigatedTo method. With the implementation, the pageState is used to verify whether the dictionary already contains the key for the data specific to Page2. If so, the value is accessed and assigned to the data variable. If the data is not yet there, a new Page2Data object is created:

```
protected override void LoadState(Object navigationParameter,
  Dictionary<String, Object> pageState)
{
  if (pageState != null && pageState.ContainsKey("Page2"))
  {
    data = pageState["Page2"] as Page2Data;
  }
  else
  {
    data = new Page2Data() { Data = "initital data" };
  }
  this.DefaultViewModel["Page2Data"] = data;
}
```

On leaving the page, the method SaveState is invoked. As before, SaveState is invoked by the base class LayoutAwarePage. This time it's invoked only from within the OnNavigatedFrom method, the method that is invoked on navigating away from the page. The implementation just needs to add the page state:

```
protected override void SaveState(Dictionary<String, Object> pageState)
{
  pageState.Add("Page2", data);
}
```

Run the application once more to test suspension and termination. The state of the input field will be set to the value from the previous session.

APPLICATION SETTINGS

Windows 8 application settings should not be handled by adding controls directly to a page and allowing the user to change their values. Instead, Windows 8 has a predefined area for application settings. These settings can be opened from the *Charms bar.* You can open the Charms bar with touch by swiping from right, or with the mouse by moving it to the top-right corner. In the Charms bar, selecting the Settings command (see Figure 31-6) opens the settings specific to the application.

All you need to do with the application to register with the settings is add a command handler to the `CommandsRequested` event with the `SettingsPane` class, as shown in the following code snippet (code file `MainPage.xaml.cs`):

```
protected override void LoadState(Object navigationParameter,
  Dictionary<String, Object> pageState)
{
  SettingsPane.GetForCurrentView().CommandsRequested +=
    MainPage_CommandsRequested;
}
```

The `SettingsPane` class also offers a static `Show` method that enables opening the settings directly controlled by the application. Opening the Settings pane is a good option if the application needs some initial configuration when the user starts it for the first time.

The command handler `MainPage_CommandsRequests` is invoked as soon as the user opens the settings. The handler just needs to add commands to the `SettingsPaneCommandRequest` object. This object is accessed with the `Request` property of the `SettingsPaneCommandsRequestEventArgs` argument. `ApplicationCommands` returns an `IList` of `SettingsCommand` that enables adding commands, including defining an ID, a label that is shown in the UI, and an event handler. The event handler is invoked when the user clicks the command. The following code creates two commands and adds these to the Settings pane:

FIGURE 31-6

```
void MainPage_CommandsRequested(SettingsPane sender,
  SettingsPaneCommandsRequestedEventArgs args)
{
  SettingsCommand command1 = new SettingsCommand("command1", "Command 1",
    new UICommandInvokedHandler(Command1));
  args.Request.ApplicationCommands.Add(command1);
  SettingsCommand command2 = new SettingsCommand("command2", "Command 2",
    new UICommandInvokedHandler(Command2));
  args.Request.ApplicationCommands.Add(command2);
}
```

When the user clicks Settings, the commands shown in Figure 31-7 are displayed. In addition to these commands, the Permissions command is available with all Windows 8 apps. This command displays all permissions requested by the application with respect to its capabilities.

Clicking on a command invokes the event handler of the application, enabling you to react to and adjust settings as needed.

If more information is needed from the user, a pop-up window can be shown in the event handler. The following code snippet shows the XAML code to define some input controls (code file `SettingsDemo/SampleSettingsPane.xaml`) within a user control:

```
<UserControl
    x:Class="SettingsDemo.SampleSettingsPane"
    xmlns="http://schemas.microsoft.com/winfx/2006/xaml/presentation"
    xmlns:x="http://schemas.microsoft.com/winfx/2006/xaml"
    xmlns:local="using:SettingsDemo"
    xmlns:d="http://schemas.microsoft.com/expression/blend/2008"
```

```
        xmlns:mc="http://schemas.openxmlformats.org/markup-
        compatibility/2006"
        mc:Ignorable="d"
        d:DesignHeight="300"
        d:DesignWidth="400">
    <Grid>
      <Grid.RowDefinitions>
        <RowDefinition Height="Auto" />
        <RowDefinition Height="Auto" />
        <RowDefinition Height="*" />
      </Grid.RowDefinitions>
      <Grid.ColumnDefinitions>
        <ColumnDefinition />
        <ColumnDefinition />
      </Grid.ColumnDefinitions>
      <TextBlock Text="Text1" Grid.Row="0" Grid.Column="0" />
      <TextBlock Text="Text2" Grid.Row="1" Grid.Column="0" />
      <TextBox Text="{Binding Text1}" Grid.Row="0" Grid.Column="1" />
      <TextBox Text="{Binding Text2}" Grid.Row="1" Grid.Column="1" />
    </Grid>
  </UserControl>
```

FIGURE 31-7

The pop-up window is opened from the Command2 event handler. The Child property is set to the instantiated user control SampleSettingsPane. Setting the property IsLightDismissedEnabled enables dismissing the pop-up by clicking on any position outside of the pop-up window. By default, the pop-up window is displayed in the top-left position. To change this to a top-right position with the Charms bar, the Canvas.LeftProperty and Canvas.TopProperty is set with the pop-up (code file SettingsDemo/MainPage.xaml.cs):

```
  void Command2(IUICommand command)
  {
    Window.Current.Activated += Window_Activated;
    SampleSettingsPane myPane = new SampleSettingsPane();
    myPane.Width = this.settingsWidth;
    myPane.Height = this.windowBounds.Height;
    settingsPopup = new Popup();
    settingsPopup.Closed += SettingsPopup_Closed;
    settingsPopup.Child = myPane;
    settingsPopup.IsLightDismissEnabled = true;
    settingsPopup.SetValue(Canvas.LeftProperty, windowBounds.Width - settingsWidth);
    settingsPopup.SetValue(Canvas.TopProperty, 0);

    settingsPopup.IsOpen = true;

  }

  void SettingsPopup_Closed(object sender, object e)
  {
    Window.Current.Activated -= Window_Activated;
  }

  private void Window_Activated(object sender, WindowActivatedEventArgs e)
  {
    if (e.WindowActivationState == CoreWindowActivationState.Deactivated)
    {
      settingsPopup.IsOpen = false;
    }
  }

  void MainPage_SizeChanged(object sender, SizeChangedEventArgs e)
```

```
  {
    windowBounds = Window.Current.Bounds;
  }
```

WEBCAM CAPABILITIES

A Windows 8 application that needs sensors or devices such as a microphone or a webcam needs to have permissions from the user to use these. The sample application that demonstrates how this can be done invokes the webcam on startup to take a picture, and shows the picture within an `Image` control of the UI.

The application for using the webcam is created from the Blank App (XAML) template. Not a lot of changes are required. In the XAML code, only an `Image` control is added, with the name `image1`. In the code-behind file `MainWindow.xaml.cs`, the `OnNavigatedTo` method is implemented to use the `CameraCaptureUI` to capture an image. `CameraCaptureUI` is defined in the namespace `Windows.Media.Capture` and enables capturing pictures and videos. You can change photo and video settings with the properties `PhotoSettings` and `VideoSettings`, and the photo or video is captured by invoking the method `CaptureFileAsync`. The sample application captures a photo by using the default settings. Camera settings are not changed, and the mode with `CaptureFileAsync` is set to `CameraCaptureUIMode.Photo`. If the user does not click Cancel and captures a video, a temporary file is created that is returned from the method and referenced from the `StorageFile` variable `file`. The `StorageFile` is used to create a `BitmapImage`, and the `BitmapImage` is assigned to the UI `Image` control to display:

```
protected async override void OnNavigatedTo(NavigationEventArgs e)
{
  var cam = new CameraCaptureUI();
  StorageFile file = await cam.CaptureFileAsync(CameraCaptureUIMode.Photo);
  if (file != null)
  {
    var image = new BitmapImage(new Uri(file.Path));
    image1.Source = image;
  }
}
```

By default, the application doesn't have permission to use the camera. To change this, you must enable the webcam capability in the package manifest, as shown in Figure 31-8.

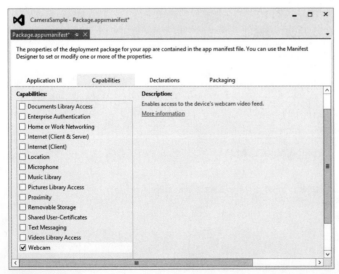

FIGURE 31-8

When running the application for the first time, the user is asked to allow permissions to use the camera (see Figure 31-9). If the application doesn't obtain permission, it cannot use the Webcam API.

FIGURE 31-9

With permission, the user can take a picture to which the application can have access. The application can display the picture in the image control, as shown in Figure 31-10.

FIGURE 31-10

After allowing permissions for an application, the user can later deny them with the application settings discussed earlier.

SUMMARY

In this chapter, you've seen the core features of the Windows Runtime and how it differs from .NET applications. Language projection enables an application to use the Windows Runtime in a way that's compatible with the programming language used. With language projection you've seen how the native API can be used easily writing .NET code.

You saw how interfaces are used with Windows Runtime components, how the interfaces map automatically to .NET interfaces (collections), and when it is necessary to work with different types and convert these by using extension methods.

With the Windows Runtime you've been introduced to core concepts on writing Windows 8 apps, including their life cycle and application settings, as well as defining and using capabilities.

For more information on writing Windows 8 applications, see Chapter 38, which covers the user interface aspects of writing these applications with XAML, including features such as the App bar. Having covered the core functionality of .NET and now the Windows Runtime, the next chapter begins our look at data access. Regarding Windows 8 apps, you cannot use ADO.NET directly from these apps, but ADO.NET is important with services—and of course Windows 8 apps communicate with services. The next chapter is also important for Windows 8 desktop applications.

PART IV
Data

32

Core ADO.NET

WROX.COM CODE DOWNLOADS FOR THIS CHAPTER

The wrox.com code downloads for this chapter are found at http://www.wrox.com/remtitle .cgi?isbn=1118314425 on the Download Code tab. The code for this chapter is divided into the following major examples:

ADO.NET OVERVIEW

This chapter discusses how to access data from your C# programs using ADO.NET. It shows you how to use the SqlConnection and OleDbConnection classes to connect to and disconnect from the database. You learn the various command object options and see how commands can be used for each of the options presented by the Sql and OleDB classes; how to call stored procedures with command objects; and how the results of those stored procedures can be integrated into the data cached on the client.

The ADO.NET object model is significantly different from the objects available with ADO. This chapter covers the `DataSet`, `DataTable`, `DataRow`, and `DataColumn` classes as well as the relationships between tables and constraints that are part of `DataSet`. The class hierarchy has changed significantly since the release of the .NET Framework 2.0, and some of these changes are also described. Finally, you examine the XML framework on which ADO.NET is built.

The chapter begins with a brief tour of ADO.NET.

ADO.NET is more than just a thin veneer over an existing API. The similarity to ADO is fairly minimal—the classes and methods for accessing data are quite a bit different.

ADO (ActiveX Data Objects) is a library of COM components that has had many incarnations over the past few years. ADO consists primarily of the `Connection`, `Command`, `Recordset`, and `Field` objects. Using ADO, a connection is opened to the database and data is selected and placed into a record set consisting of fields; that data is then manipulated and updated on the database server, and the connection is closed. ADO also introduced what is termed a disconnected record set, which is used when keeping the connection open for long periods of time is not desirable.

There were several problems that ADO did not address satisfactorily, most notably the unwieldiness (in physical size) of a disconnected record set. Support for disconnected scenarios was more necessary than ever with the evolution of web-centric computing, so a fresh approach was required. Migrating to ADO.NET from ADO should not be too difficult because there are some similarities between the two. Moreover, if you are using SQL Server, there is a fantastic set of managed classes that are tuned to squeeze maximum performance out of the database. This alone should be reason enough to migrate to ADO.NET.

ADO.NET ships with three database client namespaces: one for SQL Server, another for Open Database Connectivity (ODBC) data sources, and a third for any database exposed through OLE DB. If your database of choice is not SQL Server, search online for a dedicated .NET provider, and if one cannot be found use the OLE DB route unless you have no other choice than to use ODBC. If you are using Oracle as your database, you can visit the Oracle .NET Developer site and get their .NET provider, ODP.NET, at `http://www` `.oracle.com/technetwork/topics/dotnet/whatsnew/index.html`.

Namespaces

All the examples in this chapter access data in one way or another. The namespaces in the following table expose the classes and interfaces used in .NET data access.

NAMESPACE	BRIEF DESCRIPTION
`System.Data`	All generic data access classes
`System.Data.Common`	Classes shared (or overridden) by individual data providers
`System.Data.EntityClient`	Entity Framework classes
`System.Data.Linq.SqlClient`	LINQ to SQL provider classes
`System.Data.Odbc`	ODBC provider classes
`System.Data.OleDb`	OLE DB provider classes
`System.Data.ProviderBase`	New base classes and connection factory classes
`System.Data.Sql`	New generic interfaces and classes for SQL Server data access
`System.Data.SqlClient`	SQL Server provider classes
`System.Data.SqlTypes`	SQL Server data types

The main classes in ADO.NET are listed in the following subsections.

Shared Classes

ADO.NET contains a number of classes that are used regardless of whether you are using the SQL Server classes or the OLE DB classes. The following table lists the classes contained in the System.Data namespace:

CLASS	DESCRIPTION
DataSet	This object is designed for disconnected use and can contain a set of DataTables and relationships between these tables.
DataTable	A container of data that consists of one or more DataColumns and, when populated, will have one or more DataRows containing data.
DataRow	A number of values, akin to a row from a database table or a row from a spreadsheet.
DataColumn	This object contains the definition of a column, such as the name and data type.
DataRelation	A link between two DataTable classes within a DataSet class; used for foreign key and master/detail relationships.
Constraint	This class defines a rule for a DataColumn class (or set of data columns), such as unique values.
DataColumnMapping	Maps the name of a column from the database to the name of a column within a DataTable.
DataTableMapping	Maps a table name from the database to a DataTable within a DataSet.

Database-Specific Classes

In addition to the shared classes introduced in the previous section, ADO.NET contains a number of database-specific classes. These classes implement a set of standard interfaces defined within the System .Data namespace, enabling the classes to be used in a generic manner if necessary. For example, both the SqlConnection and OleDbConnection classes derive from the DbConnection class, which implements the IDbConnection interface. The following table lists the database-specific classes:

CLASSES	DESCRIPTION
SqlCommand, OleDbCommand, and ODBCCommand	Used as wrappers for SQL statements or stored procedure calls. Examples for the SqlCommand class are shown later in the chapter.
SqlCommandBuilder, OleDbCommandBuilder, and ODBCCommandBuilder	Used to generate SQL commands (such as INSERT, UPDATE, and DELETE statements) from a SELECT statement.
SqlConnection, OleDbConnection, and ODBCConnection	Used to connect to the database, this is similar to an ADO connection. Examples are shown later in the chapter.
SqlDataAdapter, OleDbDataAdapter, and ODBCDataAdapter	Used to hold select, insert, update, and delete commands, which are then used to populate a DataSet and update the database. Examples of the SqlDataAdapter are presented in this chapter.
SqlDataReader, OleDbDataReader, and ODBCDataReader	Used as a forward-only connected data reader. Some examples of the SqlDataReader are shown in this chapter.
SqlParameter, OleDbParameter, and ODBCParameter	Used to define a parameter to a stored procedure. Examples of how to use the SqlParameter class are shown in this chapter.
SqlTransaction, OleDbTransaction, and ODBCTransaction	Used for a database transaction, wrapped in an object.

The most important feature of the ADO.NET classes is that they are designed to work in a disconnected manner, which is important in today's highly web-centric world. It is now common practice to design a service (such as an online bookshop) to connect to a server, retrieve some data, and then work on that data on the client before reconnecting and passing the data back for processing. The disconnected nature of ADO.NET enables this type of behavior.

Classic ADO 2.1 introduced the *disconnected record set*, which permits data to be retrieved from a database, passed to the client for processing, and then reattached to the server. This used to be cumbersome to use because disconnected behavior was not part of the original design. The ADO.NET classes are different—in all but one case (the [provider]DataReader), they are designed for use offline from the database.

> **NOTE** *The classes and interfaces used for data access in the .NET Framework are introduced in the course of this chapter. The focus is mainly on the SQL Server classes used when connecting to the database because the Framework SDK samples install a SQL Server Express database (SQL Server). In most cases, the OLE DB and ODBC classes mimic the SQL Server code exactly.*

USING DATABASE CONNECTIONS

To access the database, you need to provide connection parameters, such as the machine on which the database is running and possibly your login credentials. Anyone who has worked with ADO will be familiar with the .NET connection classes: OleDbConnection and SqlConnection. Figure 32-1 shows two of the connection classes and includes the class hierarchy.

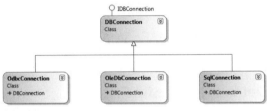

FIGURE 32-1

The examples in this chapter use the Northwind database, which you can find online by searching for **Northwind and pubs Sample Databases for SQL Server.** The following code snippet illustrates how to create, open, and close a connection to the Northwind database:

```
using System.Data.SqlClient;

string source = "server=(local);" +
                "integrated security=SSPI;" +
                "database=Northwind";
SqlConnection conn = new SqlConnection(source);
conn.Open();

// Do something useful

conn.Close();
```

The connection string should be very familiar to you if you have used ADO or OLE DB before—indeed, you should be able to cut and paste from your old code if you use the OleDb provider. In the example connection string, the parameters used are as follows (the parameters are delimited by a semicolon in the connection string):

➤ server=(local) — This denotes the database server to connect to. SQL Server permits a number of separate database server instances to be running on the same machine. Here, you are connecting to the default SQL Server instance. If you are using SQL Express, change the server part to server=./ sqlexpress.

➤ `integrated security=SSPI` — This uses Windows Authentication to connect to the database, which is highly recommended over using a username and password within the source code.

➤ `database=Northwind` — This describes the database instance to connect to; each SQL Server process can expose several database instances.

> **NOTE** *In case you forget the format of database connection strings (as many of us do now and then), the following URL is very handy:* `http://www.connectionstrings.com`.

The Northwind example opens a database connection using the defined connection string and then closes that connection. Once the connection has been opened, you can issue commands against the data source; and when you are finished, the connection can be closed.

SQL Server has another mode of authentication: It can use Windows integrated security, so that the credentials supplied at logon are passed to SQL Server. This is accomplished by removing the `uid` and `pwd` portions of the connection string and adding `Integrated Security=SSPI`.

In the download code available for this chapter is the file `login.cs`, which simplifies the examples in this chapter. It is linked to all the sample code and includes database connection information used for the examples; you can alter this to supply your own server name, user, and password as appropriate. This, by default, uses Windows integrated security; however, you can change the username and password as appropriate.

Managing Connection Strings

In the initial release of .NET, it was up to the developer to manage the database connection strings, which was often done by storing a connection string in the application configuration file or, more commonly, hard-coding it somewhere within the application itself.

Beginning with .NET 2.0, you have a predefined way to store connection strings and even use database connections in a type-agnostic manner—for example, you can write an application and then plug in various database providers, all without altering the main application.

To define a database connection string, you should use the `<connectionStrings>` section of the configuration file. Here, you can specify a name for the connection and the actual database connection string parameters; in addition, you can specify the provider for the connection type. Here is an example:

```
<configuration>
  ...
  <connectionStrings>
    <add name="Northwind"
         providerName="System.Data.SqlClient"
         connectionString="server=(local);integrated security=SSPI;database=Northwind" />
  </connectionStrings>
</configuration>
```

You use this same connection string in the other examples in this chapter.

Once the database connection information has been defined within the configuration file, you need to utilize it within the application. You will most likely want to create a method such as the following to retrieve a database connection based on the name of the connection:

```
private DbConnection GetDatabaseConnection ( string name )
{
  ConnectionStringSettings settings =
    ConfigurationManager.ConnectionStrings[name];
```

```
DbProviderFactory factory = DbProviderFactories.GetFactory
  ( settings.ProviderName );

DbConnection conn = factory.CreateConnection ( );
conn.ConnectionString = settings.ConnectionString;

return conn;
}
```

This code reads the named connection string section (using the `ConnectionStringSettings` class), and then requests a provider factory from the base `DbProviderFactories` class. This uses the `ProviderName` property, which was set to `"System.Data.SqlClient"` in the application configuration file. You might be wondering how this maps to the actual factory class used to generate a database connection for SQL Server—in this case, it should utilize the `SqlClientFactory` class from `System.Data.SqlClient`. You need to add a reference to the `System.Configuration` assembly in order to resolve the `ConfigurationManager` class used in the preceding code.

This may seem like a lot of unnecessary work to obtain a database connection, and indeed it is if your application is never going to run on any database other than the one for which it was designed. If, however, you use the preceding factory method and also use the generic Db* classes (such as `DbConnection`, `DbCommand`, and `DbDataReader`), you will future-proof the application, ensuring that any move later to another database system will be fairly simple.

Using Connections Efficiently

In general, when using scarce resources in .NET such as database connections, windows, or graphics objects, it is good practice to ensure that each resource is closed after use. Although the designers of .NET have implemented automatic garbage collection which will tidy up eventually, it is necessary to release resources as early as possible to avoid resource starvation.

This is all too apparent when writing code that accesses a database because keeping a connection open for slightly longer than necessary can affect other sessions. In extreme circumstances, not closing a connection can lock other users out of an entire set of tables, hurting application performance considerably. Closing database connections should be considered mandatory, so this section shows how to structure your code to minimize the risk of leaving a resource open. You have two main ways to ensure that database connections and the like are released after use, as described in the following sections.

Option One: try . . . catch . . . finally

The first option to ensure that resources are cleaned up is to use `try...catch...finally` blocks, closing any open connections within the `finally` block. Here is a short example:

```
try
{
   // Open the connection
   conn.Open();
   // Do something useful
}
catch ( SqlException ex )
{
   // Log the exception
}
finally
{
   // Ensure that the connection is freed
   conn.Close ( );
}
```

Within the `finally` block, you can release any resources you have used. The only trouble with this method is that you have to ensure that you close the connection—it is all too easy to forget to add the `finally` clause, so something less prone to vagaries in coding style might be worthwhile.

In addition, you might open a number of resources (for example, two database connections and a file) within a given method, so the cascade of `try...catch...finally` blocks can sometimes become less easy to read. There is, however, another way to guarantee resource cleanup: the `using` statement.

Option Two: The using Block Statement

During development of C#, the debate about how .NET uses nondeterministic destruction became very heated. In C++, as soon as an object goes out of scope, its destructor is automatically called. This was great news for designers of resource-based classes because the destructor was the ideal place to close the resource if the user had forgotten to do so. A C++ destructor is called whenever an object goes out of scope—so, for instance, if an exception were raised and not caught, all destructors would be called.

With C# and the other managed languages, there is no concept of automatic, deterministic destruction. Instead, there is the garbage collector, which disposes of resources at some point in the future. What makes this nondeterministic is that you have little say over when this process actually happens. Forgetting to close a database connection could cause all sorts of problems for a .NET executable. Luckily, help is on hand. The following code demonstrates how to use the `using` clause to ensure that objects that implement the `IDisposable` interface (see Chapter 14, "Memory Management and Pointers") are cleared up immediately after the block exits:

```
string source = "server=(local);" +
                "integrated security=SSPI;" +
                "database=Northwind";

using ( SqlConnection conn = new SqlConnection ( source ) )
{
   // Open the connection
   conn.Open ( );

   // Do something useful
}
```

In this instance, the `using` clause ensures that the database connection is closed, regardless of how the block is exited.

Looking at the IL code for the `Dispose` method of the connection classes, you can see that all of them check the current state of the connection object; if it is open, the `Close` method is called. A great tool for browsing .NET assemblies is Reflector (available at `http://www.reflector.net`). This tool enables you to view the IL code for any .NET method and will also reverse-engineer the IL into C# source code, so you can easily see what a given method is doing.

When programming, you should use at least one of these methods, and probably both. Wherever you acquire resources, it is good practice to use the `using` statement; even though we all mean to write the `Close` statement, sometimes we forget, and in the case of mistakes the `using` clause does the right thing. There is no substitute for good exception handling either, so in most cases it is best to use both methods together, as in the following example:

```
try
{
   using (SqlConnection conn = new SqlConnection ( source ))
   {
      // Open the connection
      conn.Open ( );

      // Do something useful
```

```
            // Close it myself
            conn.Close ( );
        }
    }
    catch (SqlException e)
    {
        // Log the exception & rethrow
         throw;
    }
```

Note that this example called `Close`, which is not strictly necessary, because the `using` clause handles that anyway. However, you should ensure that any resources such as this are released as soon as possible—you might have more code in the rest of the block, so there is no point locking a resource unnecessarily.

In addition, if an exception is raised within the `using` block, the `IDisposable.Dispose` method will be called on the resource guarded by the `using` clause, which, in this example, ensures that the database connection is always closed. This produces easier-to-read code, rather than ensuring you close a connection within an exception clause. Note also that the exception is defined as a `SqlException`, rather than the catch-all `Exception` type—always try to catch as specific an exception as possible, and let all others that are not explicitly handled rise up the execution stack. You really should catch this exception only if your specific data class can handle the error and do something with it.

In conclusion, if you are writing a class that wraps a resource, whatever that resource may be, always implement the `IDisposable` interface to close the resource. That way, anyone coding with your class can use the `using()` statement and guarantee that the resource will be cleared up.

Transactions

Often, when more than one update needs to be made to the database, these updates must be performed within the scope of a transaction. It is common in code to find a transaction object being passed around to many methods that update the database; however, since the release of .NET Framework 2.0, the `TransactionScope` class has been available. This class, found within the `System.Transactions` assembly, vastly simplifies writing transactional code because you can compose several transactional methods within a transaction scope and the transaction will flow to each of these methods as necessary.

The following sequence of code initiates a transaction on a SQL Server connection:

```
string source = "server=(local);" +
                "integrated security=SSPI;" +
                "database=Northwind";

using (TransactionScope scope = new
    TransactionScope(TransactionScopeOption.Required))
{
    using (SqlConnection conn = new SqlConnection(source))
    {
        // Do something in SQL
        .

        // Then mark complete
        scope.Complete();
    }
}
```

Here, the transaction is explicitly marked as complete by using the `scope.Complete` method. In the absence of this call, the transaction will be rolled back so that no changes are made to the database.

When you use a transaction scope, you can choose the isolation level for commands executed within that transaction. The level determines how changes made in one database session are viewed by another. Not all database engines support all of the four levels described in the following table:

ISOLATION LEVEL	DESCRIPTION
ReadCommitted	This is the default for SQL Server. This level ensures that data written by one transaction will be accessible in a second transaction only after the first transaction is committed.
ReadUncommitted	This permits your transaction to read data within the database, even data that has not yet been committed by another transaction. For example, if two users were accessing the same database and the first inserted some data without concluding the transaction (by means of a Commit or Rollback), the second user with an isolation level set to ReadUncommitted could read the data.
RepeatableRead	This level, which extends the ReadCommitted level, ensures that if the same statement is issued within the transaction, regardless of other potential updates made to the database, the same data will always be returned. This level requires extra locks to be held on the data, which could adversely affect performance. This level guarantees that for each row in the initial query, no changes can be made to that data. It does, however, permit "phantom" rows to show up—these are completely new rows that another transaction might have inserted while your transaction was running.
Serializable	This is the most "exclusive" transaction level, which, in effect, serializes access to data within the database. With this isolation level, phantom rows can never appear, so a SQL statement issued within a serializable transaction always retrieves the same data. The negative performance impact of a Serializable transaction should not be underestimated—if you don't absolutely need to use this level of isolation, avoid it.

The SQL Server default isolation level, ReadCommitted, is a good compromise between data coherence and data availability because fewer locks are required on data than in RepeatableRead or Serializable modes. However, in some situations the isolation level should be increased, and so within .NET you can begin a transaction with a level other than the default. There are no fixed rules as to which levels to pick—that comes with experience.

> **WARNING** *If you are currently using a database that does not support transactions, it is well worth changing to a database that does. One of the authors worked as a trusted employee with complete access to the bug database. He thought he typed* delete from bug where id=99999, *but in fact had typed a < rather than an =, thereby deleting the entire database of bugs (except for the desired one!). Luckily, the IS team backed up the database on a nightly basis and could restore this, but a rollback command would have been much easier.*

COMMANDS

The "Using Database Connections" section briefly touched on the idea of issuing commands against a database. A command is, in its simplest form, a string of text containing SQL statements to be issued to the database. A command could also be a stored procedure or the name of a table that will return all columns and all rows from that table (in other words, a SELECT *-style clause).

A command can be constructed by passing the SQL clause as a parameter to the constructor of the Command class, as shown in this example:

```
string source = "server=(local);" +
                "integrated security=SSPI;" +
                "database=Northwind";
```

```
string select = "SELECT ContactName,CompanyName FROM Customers";
SqlConnection conn = new SqlConnection(source);
conn.Open();
SqlCommand cmd = new SqlCommand(select, conn);
```

The `<provider>`Command classes have a property called `CommandType`, which is used to define whether the command is a SQL clause, a call to a stored procedure, or a full table statement (which simply selects all columns and rows from a given table). The following table summarizes the `CommandType` enumeration:

COMMANDTYPE	EXAMPLE
Text (default)	String select = "SELECT ContactName FROM Customers";SqlCommand cmd = new SqlCommand(select, conn);
StoredProcedure	SqlCommand cmd = new SqlCommand("CustOrderHist", conn); cmd.CommandType = CommandType.StoredProcedure;cmd.Parameters .AddWithValue("@CustomerID", "QUICK");
TableDirect	OleDbCommand cmd = new OleDbCommand("Categories", conn); cmd.CommandType = CommandType.TableDirect;

When executing a stored procedure, it might be necessary to pass parameters to that procedure. The previous example sets the `@CustomerID` parameter directly although there are other methods to set the parameter value. Note that since .NET 2.0, the `AddWithValue` method is included in the command parameters collection, and the `Add(name, value)` member was attributed as `Obsolete`. If you have used this original method of constructing parameters for calling a stored procedure, you will receive compiler warnings when you recompile your code. We suggest altering your code now because Microsoft will most likely remove the older method in a subsequent release of .NET.

> **NOTE** The `TableDirect` command type is valid only for the `OleDb` provider; other providers throw an exception if you attempt to use this command type with them.

Executing Commands

After you have defined the command, you need to execute it. There are several ways to issue the statement, depending on what, if anything, you expect to be returned from that command. The `<provider>`Command classes provide the following execute methods:

➤ `ExecuteNonQuery` — Executes the command but does not return any output

➤ `ExecuteReader` — Executes the command and returns a typed `IDataReader`

➤ `ExecuteScalar` — Executes the command and returns the value from the first column of the first row of any result set

In addition to these methods, the `SqlCommand` class exposes the following method:

➤ `ExecuteXmlReader` — Executes the command and returns an `XmlReader` object, which can be used to traverse the XML fragment returned from the database

ExecuteNonQuery()

The `ExecuteNonQuery` method is commonly used for UPDATE, INSERT, or DELETE statements, for which the only returned value is the number of records affected. This method can, however, return results if you call a stored procedure that has output parameters:

```
static void ExecuteNonQuery()
{
    string select = "UPDATE Customers " +
                    "SET ContactName = 'Bob' " +
                    "WHERE ContactName = 'Bill'";
    SqlConnection conn = new SqlConnection(GetDatabaseConnection());
    conn.Open();
    SqlCommand cmd = new SqlCommand(select, conn);
    int rowsReturned = cmd.ExecuteNonQuery();
    Console.WriteLine("{0} rows returned.", rowsReturned);
    conn.Close();
}
```

ExecuteNonQuery returns the number of rows affected by the command as an int.

ExecuteReader()

The ExecuteReader method executes the command and returns a typed data reader object, depending on the provider in use. The object returned can be used to iterate through the record(s) returned, as shown in the following code:

```
static void ExecuteReader()
{
    string select = "SELECT ContactName,CompanyName FROM Customers";
    SqlConnection conn = new SqlConnection(GetDatabaseConnection());
    conn.Open();
    SqlCommand cmd = new SqlCommand(select, conn);
    SqlDataReader reader = cmd.ExecuteReader();
    while (reader.Read())
    {
        Console.WriteLine("Contact: {0,-20} Company: {1}",
                          reader[0], reader[1]);
    }
}
```

Figure 32-2 shows the output of this code.

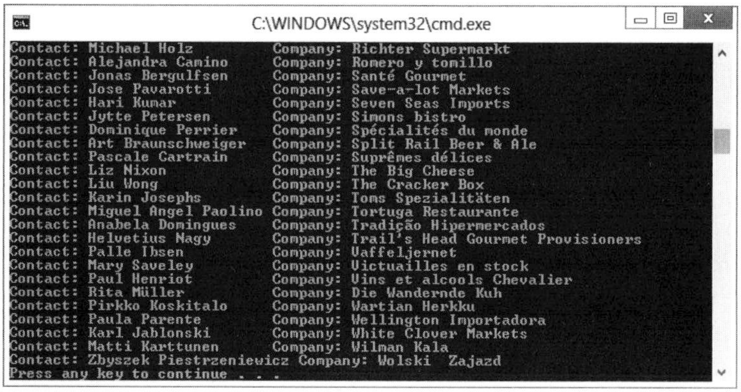

FIGURE 32-2

The <provider>DataReader objects are discussed in the section entitled "Fast Data Access: The Data Reader."

ExecuteScalar()

On many occasions it is necessary to return a single result from a SQL statement, such as the count of records in a given table or the current date/time on the server. The ExecuteScalar method can be used in such situations:

```
static void ExecuteScalar()
{
    string select = "SELECT COUNT(*) FROM Customers";
    SqlConnection conn = new SqlConnection(GetDatabaseConnection());
    conn.Open();
    SqlCommand cmd = new SqlCommand(select, conn);
    object o = cmd.ExecuteScalar();
    Console.WriteLine(o);
}
```

The method returns an object, which you can cast to the appropriate type if required. If the SQL you are calling returns only one column, it is preferable to use ExecuteScalar over any other method of retrieving that column. That also applies to stored procedures that return a single value.

ExecuteXmlReader() (SqlClient Provider Only)

As its name implies, the ExecuteXmlReader method executes a SQL statement and returns an XmlReader object to the caller. SQL Server permits a SQL SELECT statement to be extended with a FOR XML clause. This clause can include one of three options:

➤ FOR XML AUTO — Builds a tree based on the tables in the FROM clause

➤ FOR XML RAW — Maps result set rows to elements with columns mapped to attributes

➤ FOR XML EXPLICIT — Requires that you specify the shape of the XML tree to be returned

This example uses AUTO:

```
static void ExecuteXmlReader()
{
    string select = "SELECT ContactName,CompanyName " +
                    "FROM Customers FOR XML AUTO";
    SqlConnection conn = new SqlConnection(GetDatabaseConnection());
    conn.Open();
    SqlCommand cmd = new SqlCommand(select, conn);
    XmlReader xr = cmd.ExecuteXmlReader();
    xr.Read();
    string data;
    do
    {
        data = xr.ReadOuterXml();
        if (!string.IsNullOrEmpty(data))
            Console.WriteLine(data);
    } while (!string.IsNullOrEmpty(data));
    conn.Close();

}
```

Note that you have to import the System.Xml namespace in order to output the returned XML. This namespace and other XML capabilities of the .NET Framework are explored in more detail in Chapter 34, "Manipulating XML." Here, you include the FOR XML AUTO clause in the SQL statement, then call the ExecuteXmlReader method. Figure 32-3 shows the output of this code.

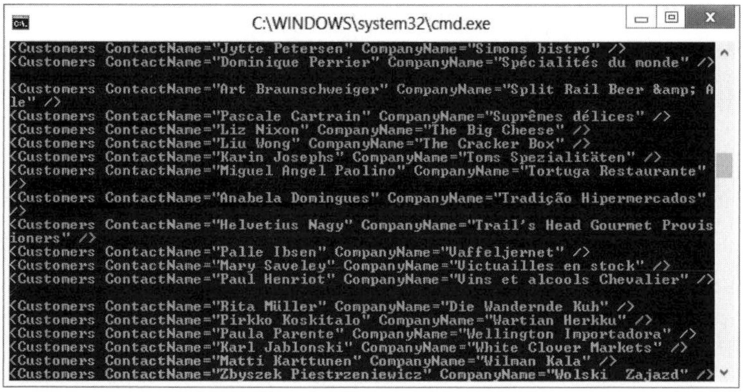

FIGURE 32-3

The SQL clause specified `FROM Customers`, so an element of type `Customers` is shown in the output. To this are added attributes, one for each column selected from the database. This builds an XML fragment for each row selected from the database.

Calling Stored Procedures

Calling a stored procedure with a command object is just a matter of defining the name of the stored procedure, adding a definition for each parameter of the procedure, and then executing the command with one of the methods presented in the previous section.

To make the examples in this section more useful, a set of stored procedures has been defined that can be used to insert, update, and delete records from the `Region` table in the Northwind sample database. Despite its small size, the `Region` table is a good candidate for an example because it can be used to define examples for each of the types of stored procedures you will commonly write.

Calling a Stored Procedure That Returns Nothing

The simplest examples of calling a stored procedure are ones that do not need to return anything to the caller. Two such procedures are defined in the following subsections: one for updating a preexisting `Region` record and one for deleting a given `Region` record.

Record Update

Updating a `Region` record is fairly trivial because only one column can be modified (assuming primary keys cannot be updated). The stored procedures used in this example are inserted into the database by the code, an example being the `RegionUpdate` procedure shown next. The stored procedures are defined as a string resource, which can be found in the `Strings.resx` file of the `02_StoredProcs` project.

```
CREATE PROCEDURE RegionUpdate (@RegionID INTEGER,
                               @RegionDescription NCHAR(50)) AS
    SET NOCOUNT OFF
    UPDATE Region
       SET RegionDescription = @RegionDescription
       WHERE RegionID = @RegionID
    GO
```

An update command on a real-world table might need to reselect and return the updated record in its entirety. This stored procedure takes two input parameters (`@RegionID` and `@RegionDescription`), and issues an `UPDATE` statement against the database.

To run this stored procedure from within .NET code, you need to define a SQL command and execute it:

```
SqlCommand cmd = new SqlCommand("RegionUpdate", conn);

cmd.CommandType = CommandType.StoredProcedure;
cmd.Parameters.AddWithValue ( "@RegionID", 23 );
cmd.Parameters.AddWithValue ( "@RegionDescription", "Something" );
```

This code creates a new `SqlCommand` object named `aCommand` and defines it as a stored procedure. You then add each parameter in turn using the `AddWithValue` method. This constructs a parameter and sets its value—you can also manually construct `SqlParameter` instances and add these to the `Parameters` collection if appropriate.

The stored procedure takes two parameters: the unique primary key of the `Region` record being updated and the new description to be given to this record. After the command has been created, you can execute it by issuing the following command:

```
cmd.ExecuteNonQuery();
```

Because the procedure returns nothing, `ExecuteNonQuery` will suffice. Command parameters can be set directly, using the `AddWithValue` method, or by constructing `SqlParameter` instances. Note that the parameter collection is indexable by position or parameter name.

Record Deletion

The next stored procedure required is one that can be used to delete a `Region` record from the database:

```
CREATE PROCEDURE RegionDelete (@RegionID INTEGER) AS
    SET NOCOUNT OFF
    DELETE FROM Region
    WHERE        RegionID = @RegionID
GO
```

This procedure requires only the primary key value of the record. The code uses a `SqlCommand` object to call this stored procedure as follows:

```
SqlCommand cmd = new SqlCommand("RegionDelete", conn);
cmd.CommandType = CommandType.StoredProcedure;
cmd.Parameters.Add(new SqlParameter("@RegionID", SqlDbType.Int, 0,
                                     "RegionID"));
cmd.UpdatedRowSource = UpdateRowSource.None;
```

This command accepts only a single parameter, as shown in the following code, which executes the `RegionDelete` stored procedure; here, you see an example of setting the parameter by name. If you have many similar calls to make to the same stored procedure, constructing `SqlParameter` instances and setting the values as shown in the following code may lead to better performance than reconstructing the entire `SqlCommand` for each call:

```
cmd.Parameters["@RegionID"].Value= 999;
cmd.ExecuteNonQuery();
```

Calling a Stored Procedure That Returns Output Parameters

Both of the previous examples execute stored procedures that return nothing. If a stored procedure includes output parameters, they need to be defined within the .NET client so that they can be filled when the procedure returns. The following example shows how to insert a record into the database and return the primary key of that record to the caller.

The `Region` table consists of only a primary key (`RegionID`) and a description field (`RegionDescription`). To insert a record, this numeric primary key must be generated and then a new row needs to be inserted into the database. The primary key generation in this example has been simplified by creating a key within the stored procedure. The method used is exceedingly crude, which is why there is a section on key generation later in this chapter. For now, this primitive example will suffice:

```
CREATE PROCEDURE RegionInsert(@RegionDescription NCHAR(50),
                             @RegionID INTEGER OUTPUT)AS

    SET NOCOUNT OFF
    SELECT @RegionID = MAX(RegionID)+ 1
    FROM Region
    INSERT INTO Region(RegionID, RegionDescription)
    VALUES(@RegionID, @RegionDescription)
GO
```

The insert procedure creates a new `Region` record. Because the primary key value is generated by the database itself, this value is returned as an output parameter from the procedure (`@RegionID`). This is sufficient for this simple example; for a more complex table (especially one with default values), it is more common not to use output parameters and instead to select the entire inserted row and return this to the caller. The .NET classes can handle either scenario. The code below shows how we would call the `RegionInsert` stored procedure:

```
SqlCommand  cmd = new SqlCommand("RegionInsert", conn);
cmd.CommandType = CommandType.StoredProcedure;
cmd.Parameters.Add(new SqlParameter("@RegionDescription",
                                    SqlDbType.NChar,
                                    50,
                                    "RegionDescription"));
cmd.Parameters.Add(new SqlParameter("@RegionID",
                                    SqlDbType.Int,
                                    0,
                                    ParameterDirection.Output,
                                    false,
                                    0,
                                    0,
                                    "RegionID",
                                    DataRowVersion.Default,
                                    null));
cmd.UpdatedRowSource = UpdateRowSource.OutputParameters;
```

Here, the definition of the parameters is much more complex. The second parameter, `@RegionID`, is defined to include its parameter direction, which in this example is `Output`. In addition to this direction flag, on the last line of the code the `UpdateRowSource` enumeration is used to indicate that data will be returned from this stored procedure via output parameters. This parameter is mainly used when issuing stored procedure calls from a `DataTable`.

Calling this stored procedure is similar to the previous examples, except in this instance the output parameter is read after executing the procedure:

```
cmd.Parameters.AddWithValue("@RegionDescription","South West");
cmd.ExecuteNonQuery();
int newRegionID = (int) cmd.Parameters["@RegionID"].Value;
```

After executing the command, the value of the `@RegionID` parameter is read and cast to an integer. A shorthand version of the preceding is the `ExecuteScalar` method, which will return (as an object) the first value returned from the stored procedure.

You might be wondering what to do if the stored procedure you call returns output parameters and a set of rows. In that case, define the parameters as appropriate and, rather than call `ExecuteNonQuery`, call one of the other methods (such as `ExecuteReader`) that permit you to traverse any record(s) returned.

FAST DATA ACCESS: THE DATA READER

A data reader is the simplest and fastest way to select data from a data source, but it is also the least capable. You cannot directly instantiate a data reader object—an instance is returned from the appropriate database's command object (such as `SqlCommand`) after having called the `ExecuteReader` method.

The following code demonstrates how to select data from the `Customers` table in the Northwind database. The example connects to the database, selects a number of records, loops through these selected records, and outputs them to the console.

This example uses the OLE DB provider, as a brief respite from the SQL provider. In most cases, the classes have a one-to-one correspondence with their `SqlClient` cousins; for example, the `OleDbConnection` object is similar to the `SqlConnection` object used in the previous examples.

To execute commands against an OLE DB data source, the `OleDbCommand` class is used. The following code shows an example of executing a simple SQL statement and reading the records by returning an `OleDbDataReader` object. Note the second `using` directive, which makes the `OleDb` classes available.

```
using System;
using System.Data.OleDb;
```

Most of the data providers currently available are shipped within the same assembly, so it is only necessary to reference the `System.Data.dll` assembly to import all classes used in this section.

The following code includes many familiar aspects of C# already covered in this chapter:

```
public class DataReaderExample
{
    public static void Main(string[] args)
    {
        string source = "Provider=SQLOLEDB;" +
                        "server=(local);" +
                        "integrated security=SSPI;" +
                        "database=northwind";
        string select = "SELECT ContactName,CompanyName FROM Customers";
        OleDbConnection conn = new OleDbConnection(source);
        conn.Open();
        OleDbCommand cmd = new OleDbCommand(select, conn);
        OleDbDataReader aReader = cmd.ExecuteReader();
        while(aReader.Read())
            Console.WriteLine("'{0}' from {1}",
                              aReader.GetString(0), aReader.GetString(1));
        aReader.Close();
        conn.Close();
    }
}
```

These three lines from the example create a new OLE DB .NET database connection, based on the source connection string:

```
OleDbConnection conn = new OleDbConnection(source);
conn.Open();
OleDbCommand cmd = new OleDbCommand(select, conn);
```

The third line in the previous code creates a new `OleDbCommand` object based on a particular SELECT statement and the database connection to be used when the command is executed. When you have a valid command, you need to execute it, which returns an initialized `OleDbDataReader`:

```
OleDbDataReader aReader = cmd.ExecuteReader();
```

An `OleDbDataReader` is a forward-only "connected" reader. That is, you can traverse the records returned in one direction only and the database connection used is kept open until the data reader is closed.

> **NOTE** An `OleDbDataReader` *keeps the database connection open until it is explicitly closed.*

The `OleDbDataReader` class cannot be instantiated directly—it is always returned by a call to the `ExecuteReader` method of the `OleDbCommand` class. Once you have an open data reader, there are various ways to access the data contained within it.

When the `OleDbDataReader` object is closed (via an explicit call to `Close` or the object being garbage collected), the underlying connection may also be closed, depending on which of the `ExecuteReader` methods is called. If you call `ExecuteReader` and pass `CommandBehavior.CloseConnection`, you can force the connection to be closed when the reader is closed.

The `OleDbDataReader` class has an indexer that permits access (although not type-safe access) to any field using the familiar array style syntax:

```
object o = aReader[0];
```
or
```
object o = aReader["CategoryID"];
```

Assuming that the `CategoryID` field was the first in the SELECT statement used to populate the reader, these two lines are functionally equivalent, although the second is slower than the first; to verify this, a test application was written that performs one million iterations of accessing the same column from an open data reader, just to get some numbers that were big enough to read. You probably don't read the same column one million times in a tight loop, but every (micro) second counts, so you should write code that is as optimal as possible.

There is one other option when accessing data from a `DataReader` — you can use the type-safe `GetInt32`, `GetDouble`, or other similar methods. When the first edition of this book was written, `GetInt32` was the fastest way to read an integer from an open data reader object. On a six-core AMD box, the figures are now as follows:

ACCESS METHOD	TIME FOR 1 MILLION ITERATIONS
Numeric indexer – `reader[0]`	23ms
String indexer – `reader["field"]`	109ms
Method call – `reader.GetInt32)`	177ms

These figures are surprising. In previous versions of this code (on older framework versions), `GetInt32` has always beaten the other versions hands down (by a factor of nearly 10).

In the current version, however, Microsoft has definitely made some optimizations, as now it's the slowest of the three methods—most probably due to better JIT compilation, function inlining, and better optimizations by the x64 processor. Even if you spent a good deal of time looking at the IL code emitted in each case to see if you could spot an obvious reason for this about-face, you probably couldn't find one.

The following example is almost the same as the previous one, except that in this instance the OLE DB provider and all references to OLE DB classes have been replaced with their SQL counterparts. The example is located in the `04_DataReaderSql` project on this book's website:

```
using System;
using System.Data.SqlClient;

public class DataReaderSql
{
```

```
public static int Main(string[] args)
{
    string source = "server=(local);" +
                    "integrated security=SSPI;" +
                    "database=northwind";
    string select = "SELECT ContactName,CompanyName FROM Customers";
    SqlConnection conn = new SqlConnection(source);
    conn.Open();
    SqlCommand cmd = new SqlCommand(select, conn);
    SqlDataReader aReader = cmd.ExecuteReader();
    while(aReader.Read())
        Console.WriteLine("'{0}' from {1}", aReader.GetString(0),
                          aReader.GetString(1));
    aReader.Close();
    conn.Close();
    return 0;
}
}
```

Notice the difference? If you're typing this, do a global replace on `OleDb` with `Sql`, change the data source string, and recompile. It's that easy!

The same performance tests were run on the indexers for the SQL provider, and this time `GetInt32` was the fastest method—the results are shown in the following table:

ACCESS METHOD	TIME TO COMPLETE 1 MILLION ITERATIONS
Numeric indexer — `reader[0]`	59 ms
String indexer — `reader["field"]`	153 ms
Method call — `reader.GetInt32)`	38 ms

This suggests that you should use the type-safe `GetXXX` methods when using a `SqlDataReader` and the numeric indexer when using an `OleDbDataReader`.

ASYNCHRONOUS DATA ACCESS: USING TASK AND AWAIT

Now that you've seen the most performant methods for accessing individual parts of a data reader, it's time to move on to tuning another aspect of the data access—making it asynchronous.

When accessing data you are almost always going out of process for that data, and most of the time you'll be accessing data on another machine, so it makes sense to limit the amount of data being passed across these boundaries; and, to provide the illusion that the system is responsive, you'll probably want to make data access asynchronous, too.

The primary way you can asynchronously request data is by using the `SqlCommand` (or `OleDbCommand`) classes, as these classes contain methods that use the Asynchronous Programming Model (APM), which exposes methods such as `BeginExecuteReader` and `EndExecuteReader`, and that use the `IAsyncResult` interface. These methods have been available in .NET since version 1.0, but with .NET 4.0 Microsoft added the `Task` class and updated the APIs for many of the inbuilt classes. Using the `Task` class makes accessing data asynchronously much easier than before.

To use the `Task` class to access data, you'll typically write code as shown in the following example function:

```
public static Task<int> GetEmployeeCount()
{
    using (SqlConnection conn = new SqlConnection(GetDatabaseConnection()))
    {
```

```
        SqlCommand cmd = new SqlCommand("WAITFOR DELAY '0:0:02';select count(*) from
          employees", conn);
        conn.Open();

        return cmd.ExecuteScalarAsync().ContinueWith(t => Convert.ToInt32(t.Result));
    }
}
```

This code creates a `Task` object that can then be waited upon by a caller; and, you could, for example, construct tasks that read data from different tables and execute these as separate tasks. The syntax here may seem strange at first but it shows some of the power of the `Task` class. After creating a `SqlCommand` that runs slowly (by using a 2-second delay in the SQL code), it uses `ExecuteScalarAsync` to call this command. This returns an object, so `ContinueWith` is used to convert the return value of the first task to an integer. Therefore, the code now contains two tasks: one selecting an object and the second one converting that object to an integer.

While this pattern may seem odd at first it comes into its own when using a method such as `ExecuteReaderAsync` which returns a `SqlDataReader` object, as in the continuation task you can convert this to a list of object instances constructed from the data returned from the data reader.

A fairly common use for asynchronous tasks is *fork and join*, which *forks* the flow off to a set of asynchronous tasks, and then *joins* back together at the end of all the tasks. In .NET, this is accomplished using the `Task` class. You can fork calls off to several methods, like in the preceding example, which return tasks; then join the results together by calling `Task.WaitAll` and passing the set of tasks to the method. The example code for this section can be found in the `06_AsyncDataReaders` project on this book's website.

```
var t1 = GetEmployeeCount();
var t2 = GetOrderCount();

Task.WaitAll(t1, t2);
```

Added to C# in .NET version 4.5 are the `async` and `await` keywords, which can be used to simplify executing tasks asynchronously. You can update the preceding example by adding the `async` modifier on the function declaration and adding `await` to the code, like this:

```
public async static Task<int> GetEmployeeCount()
{
    using (SqlConnection conn = new SqlConnection(GetDatabaseConnection()))
    {
        SqlCommand cmd = new SqlCommand("WAITFOR DELAY '0:0:02';select count(*) from
          employees", conn);
        conn.Open();

        return await cmd.ExecuteScalarAsync().ContinueWith(t => Convert.ToInt32(t.Result));
    }
}
```

In the calling code you can now simply write the following in order to call the `async` methods:

```
public async static Task GetEmployeesAndOrders()
{
    int employees = await GetEmployeeCount();
    int orders = await GetOrderCount();

    Console.WriteLine("Number of employes: {0}, Number of orders: {1}", employees, orders);
}
```

You must indicate that this is an asynchronous method (one that uses `await`) by adding the `async` keyword to the method declaration. Then you can call the other asynchronous methods using `await`; the code looks like you're calling simple methods but the compiler is constructing all of the asynchronous coordination code for you.

Note in the preceding example that the two `await` calls will effectively run the two tasks after each other, so if you want to truly asynchronously call these methods, you will need to drop down a level and use the `Task` class directly.

MANAGING DATA AND RELATIONSHIPS: THE DATASET CLASS

The `DataSet` class has been designed as an offline container of data. It has no notion of database connections. In fact, the data held within a `DataSet` does not necessarily need to have come from a database—it could just as easily be records from a CSV file, an XML file, or points read from a measuring device.

A `DataSet` class consists of a set of data tables, each of which has a set of data columns and data rows (see Figure 32-4). In addition to defining the data, you can also define links between tables within the `DataSet` class. One common scenario is defining a parent-child relationship (commonly known as master/detail). One record in a table (say `Order`) links to many records in another table (say `Order_Details`). This relationship can be defined and navigated within the `DataSet`.

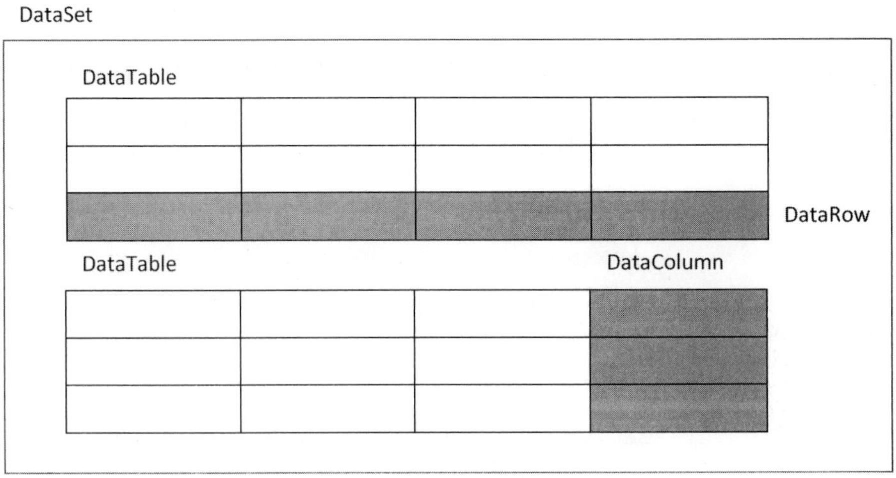

FIGURE 32-4

It is important to remember that, basically, the `DataSet` class is an in-memory database that includes all the tables, relationships, and constraints. The following sections describe the classes that are used with a `DataSet` class.

> **NOTE** The `DataSet` and related classes have largely been replaced with the Entity Framework. The classes are presented here for background only.

Data Tables

A data table is very similar to a physical database table. It consists of a set of columns with particular properties and might have zero or more rows of data. A data table might also define a primary key, which can be one or more columns, and it might contain constraints on columns. The generic term for this information used throughout the rest of the chapter is *schema*.

Several ways exist to define the schema for a particular data table (and indeed the `DataSet` class as a whole). These are discussed after introducing data columns and data rows. Figure 32-5 shows some of the objects that are accessible through the data table.

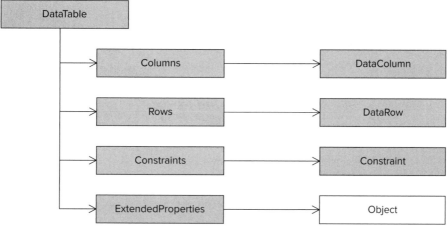

FIGURE 32-5

A `DataTable` (or `DataColumn`) object has an arbitrary number of extended properties associated with it. This collection can be populated with any user-defined information pertaining to the object. For example, a given column might have an input mask used to validate the contents of that column; a typical example is the U.S. Social Security number. Extended properties are especially useful when the data is constructed within a middle tier and returned to the client for processing. You could, for example, store validation criteria (such as `min` and `max`) for numeric columns in extended properties and use this in the UI tier when validating user input.

When a data table has been populated — by selecting data from a database, reading data from a file, or manually populating it within code — the `Rows` collection will contain this retrieved data.

The `Columns` collection contains `DataColumn` instances that have been added to this table. These define the schema of the data, such as the data type, nullability, default values, and so on. The `Constraints` collection can be populated with either unique or primary key constraints.

One example of when the schema information for a data table is used is when displaying that data in a `DataGrid`. The `DataGrid` control uses properties such as the data type of the column to determine which control to use for each column. A bit field within the database will be displayed as a check box within the `DataGrid`. If a column is defined within the database schema as `NOT NULL`, this fact is stored within the `DataColumn` so that it can be tested when the user attempts to move off a row.

Data Columns

A `DataColumn` object defines properties of a column within the `DataTable`, such as the data type of that column, whether the column is read-only, and various other facts. A column can be created in code or it can be automatically generated at runtime.

When creating a column, it is useful to give it a name; otherwise, the runtime generates a name for you in the form `Column`n, where n is an incrementing number.

The data type of the column can be set either by supplying it in the constructor or by setting the `DataType` property. Once you have loaded data into a data table, you cannot alter the type of a column — doing so will result in an `ArgumentException`.

Data columns can be created to hold the following .NET Framework data types:

Boolean	Decimal
Int64	TimeSpan
Byte	Double
Sbyte	UInt16
Char	Int16
Single	UInt32
DateTime	Int32
String	UInt64

Once a `DataColumn` object is created, the next thing to do with it is set up other properties, such as the nullability of the column or the default value. The following code fragment shows a few of the more common options that can be set on a `DataColumn` object:

```
DataColumn customerID = new DataColumn("CustomerID", typeof(int));
customerID.AllowDBNull = false;
customerID.ReadOnly = false;
customerID.AutoIncrement = true;
customerID.AutoIncrementSeed = 1000;
DataColumn name = new DataColumn("Name", typeof(string));
name.AllowDBNull = false;
name.Unique = true;
```

The following table describes the properties that can be set on a `DataColumn` object:

PROPERTY	DESCRIPTION
AllowDBNull	If `true`, permits the column to be set to `DBNull`
AutoIncrement	Indicates that the column value is automatically generated as an incrementing number
AutoIncrementSeed	Defines the initial seed value for an `AutoIncrement` column
AutoIncrementStep	Defines the step between automatically generated column values, with a default of one
Caption	Can be used for displaying the name of the column onscreen
ColumnMapping	Defines how a column is mapped into XML when a `DataSet` class is saved by calling `DataSet.WriteXml`
ColumnName	The name of the column; auto-generated by the runtime if not set in the constructor
DataType	Defines the `System.Type` value of the column
DefaultValue	Can define a default value for a column
Expression	Defines the expression to be used in a computed column

Data Rows

This class makes up the other part of the `DataTable` class. The columns within a data table are defined in terms of the `DataColumn` class. The actual data within the table is accessed by using the `DataRow` object. The following example shows how to access rows within a data table. First, the connection details:

```
string source = "server=(local);" +
                " integrated security=SSPI;" +
                "database=northwind";
string select = "SELECT ContactName,CompanyName FROM Customers";
SqlConnection  conn = new SqlConnection(source);
```

The following code introduces the `SqlDataAdapter` class, which is used to place data into a `DataSet` class. `SqlDataAdapter` issues the SQL clause and fills a table in the `DataSet` class called `Customers` with the output of the following query. (For more details on the `SqlDataAdapter` class, see the section "Populating a DataSet" later in this chapter.)

```
SqlDataAdapter da = new SqlDataAdapter(select, conn);
DataSet ds = new DataSet();
da.Fill(ds, "Customers");
```

In the following code, you might notice the use of the `DataRow` indexer to access values from within that row. The value for a given column can be retrieved by using one of the several overloaded indexers. These permit you to retrieve a value knowing the column number, name, or `DataColumn`:

```
foreach(DataRow row in ds.Tables["Customers"].Rows)
    Console.WriteLine("'{0}' from {1}", row[0],row[1]);
```

One of the most appealing aspects of `DataRow` is that it is versioned. This enables you to receive various values for a given column in a particular row. These versions are described in the following table:

DATAROW VERSION VALUE	DESCRIPTION
Current	The value existing at present within the column. If no edit has occurred, this will be the same as the original value. If an edit (or edits) has occurred, the value will be the last valid value entered.
Default	The default value (in other words, any default set up for the column).
Original	The value of the column when originally selected from the database. If the `DataRow`'s `AcceptChanges` method is called, this value will update to the `Current` value.
Proposed	When changes are in progress for a row, it is possible to retrieve this modified value. If you call `BeginEdit` on the row and make changes, each column will have a proposed value until either `EndEdit` or `CancelEdit` is called.

The version of a given column could be used in many ways. One example is when updating rows within the database, in which case it is common to issue a SQL statement such as the following:

```
UPDATE Products
SET    Name = Column.Current
WHERE  ProductID = xxx
AND    Name = Column.Original;
```

Obviously, this code would never compile, but it shows one use for original and current values of a column within a row.

To retrieve a versioned value from the `DataRow` indexer, use one of the indexer methods that accepts a `DataRowVersion` value as a parameter. The following snippet shows how to obtain all values of each column in a `DataTable` object:

```
foreach (DataRow row in ds.Tables["Customers"].Rows )
{
  foreach ( DataColumn dc in ds.Tables["Customers"].Columns )
  {
    Console.WriteLine ("{0} Current  = {1}", dc.ColumnName,
                                    row[dc,DataRowVersion.Current]);
```

```
            Console.WriteLine ("    Default  = {0}", row[dc,DataRowVersion.Default]);
            Console.WriteLine ("    Original = {0}",
                            row[dc,DataRowVersion.Original]);
    }
}
```

The whole row has a state flag called `RowState`, which can be used to determine what operation is needed on the row when it is persisted back to the database. The `RowState` property is set to keep track of all changes made to the `DataTable`, such as adding new rows, deleting existing rows, and changing columns within the table. When the data is reconciled with the database, the row state flag is used to determine what SQL operations should occur. The following table provides an overview of the flags that are defined by the `DataRowState` enumeration:

DATAROWSTATE VALUE	DESCRIPTION
Added	Indicates that the row has been newly added to a `DataTable`'s `Rows` collection. All rows created on the client are set to this value and will ultimately issue SQL INSERT statements when reconciled with the database.
Deleted	Indicates that the row has been marked as deleted from the `DataTable` by means of the `DataRow.Delete` method. The row still exists within the `DataTable` but will not normally be viewable onscreen (unless a `DataView` has been explicitly set up). Rows marked as deleted in the `DataTable` are deleted from the database when reconciled.
Detached	Indicates that a row is in this state immediately after it is created, and can also be returned to this state by calling `DataRow.Remove`. A detached row is not considered to be part of any data table, thus, no SQL for rows in this state will be issued.
Modified	Indicates that a row will be `Modified` if the value in any column has been changed.
Unchanged	Indicates that the row has not been changed since the last call to `AcceptChanges`.

The state of the row also depends on what methods have been called on the row. The `AcceptChanges` method is generally called after successfully updating the data source—that is, after persisting changes to the database.

The most common way to alter data in a `DataRow` is to use the indexer; however, if you have a number of changes to make, you should also consider the `BeginEdit` and `EndEdit` methods.

When an alteration is made to a column within a `DataRow`, the `ColumnChanging` event is raised on the row's `DataTable`. That enables you to override the `ProposedValue` property of the `DataColumnChangeEventArgs` class and change it as required. This is one way of performing some data validation on column values. If you call `BeginEdit` before making changes, the `ColumnChanging` event will not be raised, enabling you to make multiple changes and then call `EndEdit` to persist those changes. If you want to revert to the original values, call `CancelEdit`.

A `DataRow` can be linked in some way to other rows of data. This enables the creation of navigable links between rows, which is common in master/detail scenarios. The `DataRow` contains a `GetChildRows` method that will return an array of associated rows from another table in the same `DataSet` as the current row. These are discussed in the "Data Relationships" section later in this chapter.

Schema Generation

You can create the schema for a `DataTable` in three ways:

➤ Let the runtime do it for you.

➤ Write code to create the table(s).

➤ Use the XML schema generator.

The following sections describe these three alternatives.

Runtime Schema Generation

The `DataRow` example shown earlier presented the following code for selecting data from a database and populating a `DataSet` class:

```
SqlDataAdapter da = new SqlDataAdapter(select, conn);
DataSet ds = new DataSet();
da.Fill(ds, "Customers");
```

This is easy to use but has a few drawbacks. For example, you have to make do with the default column names, which might work for you; but in certain instances, you might want to rename a physical database column (for example, PKID) to something more user-friendly. To work around this, you could alias columns within your SQL clause, as in SELECT PID AS PersonID FROM PersonTable; it's best to not rename columns within SQL, though, because a column only really needs to have a "pretty" name onscreen.

Another potential problem with automated `DataTable`/`DataColumn` generation is that you have no control over the column types that the runtime chooses for your data. It does a fairly good job of deciding the correct data type for you but, as usual, there are scenarios in which you need more control. For example, you might have defined an enumerated type for a given column to simplify user code written against your class. If you accept the default column types that the runtime generates, the column will likely be an integer with a 32-bit range, as opposed to an `enum` with your predefined options.

The last, and probably most problematic, drawback is that when using automated table generation, you have no type-safe access to the data within the `DataTable`—you are at the mercy of indexers, which return instances of `object` rather than derived data types. If you like sprinkling your code with typecast expressions, skip the following sections.

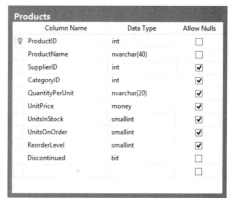

Hand-Coded Schema

Generating the code to create a `DataTable`, replete with associated `DataColumns`, is fairly easy. The examples in this section access the `Products` table, shown in Figure 32-6, from the Northwind database.

FIGURE 32-6

The following code manufactures a `DataTable` that corresponds to the schema shown in Figure 32-6 (but does not cover the nullability of columns):

```
public static void ManufactureProductDataTable(DataSet ds)
{
    DataTable    products = new DataTable("Products");
    products.Columns.Add(new DataColumn("ProductID", typeof(int)));
    products.Columns.Add(new DataColumn("ProductName", typeof(string)));
    products.Columns.Add(new DataColumn("SupplierID", typeof(int)));
    products.Columns.Add(new DataColumn("CategoryID", typeof(int)));
    products.Columns.Add(new DataColumn("QuantityPerUnit", typeof(string)));
    products.Columns.Add(new DataColumn("UnitPrice", typeof(decimal)));
    products.Columns.Add(new DataColumn("UnitsInStock", typeof(short)));
    products.Columns.Add(new DataColumn("UnitsOnOrder", typeof(short)));
    products.Columns.Add(new DataColumn("ReorderLevel", typeof(short)));
    products.Columns.Add(new DataColumn("Discontinued", typeof(bool)));
    ds.Tables.Add(products);
}
```

You can alter the code in the `DataRow` example to use this newly generated table definition as follows:

```
string source = "server=(local);" +
                "integrated security=sspi;" +
                "database=Northwind";
```

```
string select = "SELECT * FROM Products";
SqlConnection conn = new SqlConnection(source);
SqlDataAdapter cmd = new SqlDataAdapter(select, conn);
DataSet ds = new DataSet();
ManufactureProductDataTable(ds);
cmd.Fill(ds, "Products");
foreach(DataRow row in ds.Tables["Products"].Rows)
   Console.WriteLine("'{0}' from {1}", row[0], row[1]);
```

The `ManufactureProductDataTable` method creates a new `DataTable`, adds each column in turn, and appends the table to the list of tables within the `DataSet`. The `DataSet` has an indexer that takes the name of the table and returns that `DataTable` to the caller.

The previous example is still not type-safe because indexers are being used on columns to retrieve the data. What would be better is a class (or set of classes) derived from `DataSet`, `DataTable`, and `DataRow` that defines type-safe accessors for tables, rows, and columns. You can generate this code yourself; it is not particularly tedious and you end up with type-safe data access classes.

If you don't like generating these type-safe classes yourself, help is at hand. The .NET Framework includes support for the third method listed at the start of this section: using XML schemas to define a `DataSet` class, a `DataTable` class, and the other classes that we have described here. (For more details on this method, see the section "XML Schemas: Generating Code with XSD" later in this chapter.)

Data Relationships

When writing an application, it is often necessary to obtain and cache various tables of information. The `DataSet` class is the container for this information. With regular OLE DB, it was necessary to provide a strange SQL dialect to enforce hierarchical data relationships, and the provider itself was not without its own subtle quirks.

The `DataSet` class, however, has been designed from the start to easily establish relationships between data tables. The code in this section shows how to generate data manually and populate two tables with data. Therefore, if you don't have access to SQL Server or the Northwind database, you can run this example anyway:

```
DataSet ds = new DataSet("Relationships");
ds.Tables.Add(CreateBuildingTable());
ds.Tables.Add(CreateRoomTable());
ds.Relations.Add("Rooms",
                ds.Tables["Building"].Columns["BuildingID"],
                ds.Tables["Room"].Columns["BuildingID"]);
```

The tables used in this example are shown in Figure 32-7. They contain a primary key and a name field, with the `Room` table having `BuildingID` as a foreign key.

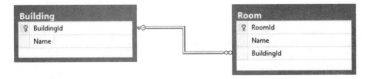

FIGURE 32-7

These tables have been kept simple deliberately. The following code shows how to iterate through the rows in the `Building` table and traverse the relationship to list all the child rows from the `Room` table:

```
foreach(DataRow theBuilding in ds.Tables["Building"].Rows)
{
    DataRow[] children = theBuilding.GetChildRows("Rooms");
    int roomCount = children.Length;
    Console.WriteLine("Building {0} contains {1} room{2}",
```

```
                        theBuilding["Name"],
                        roomCount,
                        roomCount > 1 ? "s": "");
    // Loop through the rooms
    foreach(DataRow theRoom in children)
        Console.WriteLine("Room: {0}", theRoom["Name"]);
}
```

The key difference between the `DataSet` class and the old-style hierarchical `Recordset` object is the way the relationship is presented. In a hierarchical `Recordset` object, the relationship was presented as a pseudo-column within the row. This column itself was a `Recordset` object that could be iterated through. Under ADO.NET, however, a relationship is traversed simply by calling the `GetChildRows` method:

```
DataRow[] children = theBuilding.GetChildRows("Rooms");
```

This method has a number of forms but the preceding simple example uses just the name of the relationship to traverse between parent and child rows. It returns an array of rows that can be updated as appropriate by using the indexers, as shown in earlier examples.

What's more interesting with data relationships is that they can be traversed both ways. Not only can you go from a parent to the child rows, but you can also find a parent row (or rows) from a child record simply by using the `ParentRelations` property on the `DataTable` class. This property returns a `DataRelationCollection`, which can be indexed by using the `[]` array syntax (for example, `ParentRelations["Rooms"]`); or, alternatively, the `GetParentRows` method can be called, as shown here:

```
foreach(DataRow theRoom in ds.Tables["Room"].Rows)
{
    DataRow[] parents = theRoom.GetParentRows("Rooms");
    foreach(DataRow theBuilding in parents)
        Console.WriteLine("Room {0} is contained in building {1}",
                          theRoom["Name"],
                          theBuilding["Name"]);
}
```

Two methods with various overrides are available for retrieving the parent row(s): `GetParentRows` (which returns an array of zero or more rows) and `GetParentRow` (which retrieves a single parent row, given a relationship).

Data Constraints

Changing the data type of columns created on the client is not the only thing for which a `DataTable` is well suited. ADO.NET enables you to create a set of constraints on a column (or columns), which are then used to enforce rules within the data.

The following table lists the constraint types that are currently supported by the runtime, embodied as classes in the `System.Data` namespace.

CONSTRAINT	DESCRIPTION
ForeignKeyConstraint	Enforces a link between two `DataTables` within a `DataSet`
UniqueConstraint	Ensures that entries in a given column are unique

Setting a Primary Key

As is common with a table in a relational database, you can supply a primary key, which can be based on one or more columns from the `DataTable`.

The following code creates a primary key for the `Products` table, whose schema was constructed by hand earlier. Note that a primary key on a table is just one form of constraint. When a primary key is added to a

`DataTable`, the runtime also generates a unique constraint over the key column(s). This is because there isn't actually a constraint type of `PrimaryKey`—a primary key is simply a unique constraint over one or more columns.

```
public static void ManufacturePrimaryKey(DataTable dt)
{
    DataColumn[] pk = new DataColumn[1];
    pk[0] = dt.Columns["ProductID"];
    dt.PrimaryKey = pk;
}
```

Because a primary key can contain several columns, it is typed as an array of `DataColumns`. A table's primary key can be set to those columns simply by assigning an array of columns to the property.

To check the constraints for a table, you can iterate through the `ConstraintCollection`. For the auto-generated constraint produced by the preceding code, the name of the constraint is `Constraint1`. That's not a very useful name, so to avoid this problem it is always best to create the constraint in code first, then define which column(s) make up the primary key.

The following code names the constraint before creating the primary key:

```
DataColumn[] pk = new DataColumn[1];
pk[0] = dt.Columns["ProductID"];
dt.Constraints.Add(new UniqueConstraint("PK_Products", pk[0]));
dt.PrimaryKey = pk;
```

Unique constraints can be applied to as many columns as you want.

Setting a Foreign Key

In addition to unique constraints, a `DataTable` class can also contain foreign key constraints. These are primarily used to enforce master/detail relationships but can also be used to replicate columns between tables if you set up the constraint correctly. A *master/detail* relationship is one in which there is commonly one parent record (an order, for example) and many child records (order lines), linked by the primary key of the parent record.

A foreign key constraint can operate only over tables within the same `DataSet`, so the following example uses the `Categories` table from the Northwind database (as shown in Figure 32-8), and assigns a constraint between it and the `Products` table.

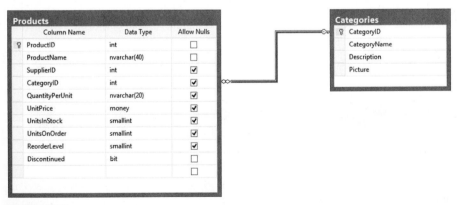

FIGURE 32-8

The first step is to generate a new data table for the `Categories` table:

```
DataTable categories = new DataTable("Categories");
categories.Columns.Add(new DataColumn("CategoryID", typeof(int)));
categories.Columns.Add(new DataColumn("CategoryName", typeof(string)));
categories.Columns.Add(new DataColumn("Description", typeof(string)));
categories.Constraints.Add(new UniqueConstraint("PK_Categories",
                            categories.Columns["CategoryID"]));
categories.PrimaryKey = new DataColumn[1]
                            {categories.Columns["CategoryID"]};
```

The last line of this code creates the primary key for the `Categories` table. The primary key in this instance is a single column; however, it is possible to generate a key over multiple columns using the array syntax shown.

Now the constraint can be created between the two tables:

```
DataColumn parent = ds.Tables["Categories"].Columns["CategoryID"];
DataColumn child = ds.Tables["Products"].Columns["CategoryID"];
ForeignKeyConstraint fk =
    new ForeignKeyConstraint("FK_Product_CategoryID", parent, child);
fk.UpdateRule = Rule.Cascade;
fk.DeleteRule = Rule.SetNull;
ds.Tables["Products"].Constraints.Add(fk);
```

This constraint applies to the link between `Categories.CategoryID` and `Products.CategoryID`. There are four different `ForeignKeyConstraints`—use a constructor that permits you to name the constraint.

Setting Update and Delete Constraints

In addition to defining that there is some type of constraint between parent and child tables, you can define what should happen when a column in the constraint is updated.

The previous example sets the update rule and the delete rule. These rules are used when an action occurs to a column (or row) within the parent table, and the rule is used to determine what should happen to the row(s) within the child table that could be affected. Four different rules can be applied through the `Rule` enumeration:

➤ `Cascade` — If the parent key has been updated, it copies the new key value to all child records. If the parent record has been deleted, it also deletes the child records. This is the default option.

➤ `None` — Takes no action whatsoever. This option leaves orphaned rows within the child data table.

➤ `SetDefault`—Each child record affected has the foreign key column(s) set to its default value, if one has been defined.

➤ `SetNull` — All child rows have the key column(s) set to `DBNull`. (Following the naming convention that Microsoft uses, this should really be `SetDBNull`.)

> **NOTE** *Constraints are enforced within a* `DataSet` *class only if the* `EnforceConstraints` *property of the* `DataSet` *is* true.

This section has covered the main classes that make up the constituent parts of the `DataSet` class and has shown how to manually generate each of these classes in code. You can also define a `DataTable`, `DataRow`, `DataColumn`, `DataRelation`, and `Constraint` using the XML schema file(s) and the XSD tool that ships with .NET. The following section describes how to set up a simple schema and generate type-safe classes to access your data.

XML SCHEMAS: GENERATING CODE WITH XSD

XML is firmly entrenched in ADO.NET—indeed, the remoting format for passing data between objects is now XML. With the .NET runtime, it is possible to describe a `DataTable` class within an XML schema definition (XSD) file. What's more, you can define an entire `DataSet` class, with a number of `DataTable` classes, and a set of relationships between these tables; and you can include various other details to fully describe the data.

When you have defined an XSD file, there is a tool in the runtime that will convert this schema to the corresponding data access class(es), such as the type-safe product `DataTable` class shown earlier. The following example starts with a simple XSD file (`Products.xsd`) that describes the same information as the `Products` sample discussed earlier, and then extends it to include some extra functionality:

```xml
<?xml version="1.0" encoding="utf-8" ?>
<xs:schema id="Products" targetNamespace="http://tempuri.org/XMLSchema1.xsd"
 xmlns:mstns="http://tempuri.org/XMLSchema1.xsd"
  xmlns:xs="http://www.w3.org/2001/XMLSchema"
  xmlns:msdata="urn:schemas-microsoft-com:xml-msdata">
  <xs:element name="Product">
    <xs:complexType>
      <xs:sequence>
        <xs:element name="ProductID" msdata:ReadOnly="true"
          msdata:AutoIncrement="true" type="xs:int" />
        <xs:element name="ProductName" type="xs:string" />
        <xs:element name="SupplierID" type="xs:int" minOccurs="0" />
        <xs:element name="CategoryID" type="xs:int" minOccurs="0" />
        <xs:element name="QuantityPerUnit" type="xs:string" minOccurs="0" />
        <xs:element name="UnitPrice" type="xs:decimal" minOccurs="0" />
        <xs:element name="UnitsInStock" type="xs:short" minOccurs="0" />
        <xs:element name="UnitsOnOrder" type="xs:short" minOccurs="0" />
        <xs:element name="ReorderLevel" type="xs:short" minOccurs="0" />
        <xs:element name="Discontinued" type="xs:boolean" />
      </xs:sequence>
    </xs:complexType>
  </xs:element>
</xs:schema>
```

These options are covered in detail in Chapter 34; for now, this file basically defines a schema with the `id` attribute set to `Products`. A complex type called `Product` is defined, which contains a number of elements, one for each of the fields within the `Products` table.

These items map to data classes as follows:

➤ The `Products` schema maps to a class derived from `DataSet`.

➤ The `Product` complex type maps to a class derived from `DataTable`.

➤ Each sub-element maps to a class derived from `DataColumn`.

➤ The collection of all columns maps to a class derived from `DataRow`.

Thankfully, a tool within the .NET Framework produces the code for these classes with the help of the input XSD file. Because its sole job is to perform various functions on XSD files, the tool itself is called `XSD.EXE`.

Assuming that you saved the preceding file as `Product.xsd`, you would convert the file into code by issuing the following command in a command prompt:

```
xsd Product.xsd /d
```

This creates the file `Product.cs`.

Various switches can be used with XSD to alter the output generated. Some of the more commonly used switches are described in the following table:

SWITCH	DESCRIPTION
/dataset (/d)	Enables you to generate classes derived from DataSet, DataTable, and DataRow.
/language:<language>	Enables you to choose the language in which the output file will be written. C# is the default, but you can choose VB for a Visual Basic .NET file.
/namespace:<namespace>	Enables you to define the namespace that the generated code should reside within. The default is no namespace.

The following is an abridged version of the output from XSD for the Products schema. The output has been altered slightly to fit into a format appropriate for this book. To see the complete output, run XSD.EXE on the Products schema (or another schema of your own making) and look at the .cs file generated. The example includes the entire source code plus the Product.xsd file:

```
//------------------------------------------------------------------------------
// <auto-generated>
//     This code was generated by a tool.
//     Runtime Version:2.0.50727.5456
//
//     Changes to this file may cause incorrect behavior and will be lost if
//     the code is regenerated.
// </auto-generated>
//------------------------------------------------------------------------------

//
// This source code was auto-generated by xsd, Version=2.0.50727.3238.
//


/// <summary>
///Represents a strongly typed in-memory cache of data.
///</summary>
[global::System.CodeDom.Compiler.GeneratedCodeAttribute("System.Data.Design.
TypedDataSetGenerator", "2.0.0.0")]
[global::System.Serializable()]
[global::System.ComponentModel.DesignerCategoryAttribute("code")]
[global::System.ComponentModel.ToolboxItem(true)]
[global::System.Xml.Serialization.XmlSchemaProviderAttribute("GetTypedDataSetSchema")]
[global::System.Xml.Serialization.XmlRootAttribute("Products")]
[global::System.ComponentModel.Design.HelpKeywordAttribute("vs.data.DataSet")]
public partial class Products : global::System.Data.DataSet {

    private ProductDataTable tableProduct;

    private global::System.Data.SchemaSerializationMode _schemaSerializationMode =
global::System.Data.SchemaSerializationMode.IncludeSchema;

    [global::System.Diagnostics.DebuggerNonUserCodeAttribute()]
    public Products() {
        this.BeginInit();
        this.InitClass();
        global::System.ComponentModel.CollectionChangeEventHandler schemaChangedHandler = new
global::System.ComponentModel.CollectionChangeEventHandler(this.SchemaChanged);
        base.Tables.CollectionChanged += schemaChangedHandler;
        base.Relations.CollectionChanged += schemaChangedHandler;
        this.EndInit();
    }
```

All private and protected members have been removed in order to concentrate on the public interface. The `ProductDataTable` and `ProductRow` definitions show the positions of two nested classes, which will be implemented next. You review the code for these classes after a brief explanation of the `DataSet`-derived class.

The `Products` constructor calls a private method, `InitClass`, which constructs an instance of the `DataTable`-derived class `ProductDataTable`, and adds the table to the `Tables` collection of the `DataSet` class. The `Products` data table can be accessed by the following code:

```
DataSet ds = new Products();
DataTable products = ds.Tables["Products"];
```

Alternatively, you can simply use the property `Product`, available on the derived `DataSet` object:

```
DataTable products = ds.Product;
```

Because the `Product` property is strongly typed, you could use `ProductDataTable` rather than the `DataTable` reference shown in the previous code.

The `ProductDataTable` class includes far more code (note that this is an abridged version):

```
[global::System.CodeDom.Compiler.GeneratedCodeAttribute("System.Data.Design.
TypedDataSetGenerator", "2.0.0.0")]
[global::System.Serializable()]
[global::System.Xml.Serialization.XmlSchemaProviderAttribute("GetTypedTableSchema")]
public partial class ProductDataTable : global::System.Data.DataTable, global::System.
Collections.IEnumerable {

    private global::System.Data.DataColumn columnProductID;

    private global::System.Data.DataColumn columnProductName;

    private global::System.Data.DataColumn columnSupplierID;

    private global::System.Data.DataColumn columnCategoryID;

    private global::System.Data.DataColumn columnQuantityPerUnit;

    private global::System.Data.DataColumn columnUnitPrice;

    private global::System.Data.DataColumn columnUnitsInStock;

    private global::System.Data.DataColumn columnUnitsOnOrder;

    private global::System.Data.DataColumn columnReorderLevel;

    private global::System.Data.DataColumn columnDiscontinued;

    [global::System.Diagnostics.DebuggerNonUserCodeAttribute()]
    public ProductDataTable() {
        this.TableName = "Product";
        this.BeginInit();
        this.InitClass();
        this.EndInit();
    }
```

The `ProductDataTable` class, derived from `DataTable` and implementing the `IEnumerable` interface, defines a private `DataColumn` instance for each of the columns within the table. These are initialized again from the constructor by calling the private `InitClass` member. Each column is used by the `DataRow` class (which is described shortly):

```
[global::System.Diagnostics.DebuggerNonUserCodeAttribute()]
[global::System.ComponentModel.Browsable(false)]
public int Count {
```

```
    get {
        return this.Rows.Count;
    }
}

// Other row accessors removed for clarity — there is one for each column
```

Adding rows to the table is handled by the two overloaded (and significantly different) `AddProductRow` methods. The first takes an already-constructed `DataRow` and returns a void. The second takes a set of values, one for each of the columns in the `DataTable`, constructs a new row, sets the values within this new row, adds the row to the `DataTable` object, and returns the row to the caller. Such widely different functions shouldn't really have the same name!

```
[global::System.Diagnostics.DebuggerNonUserCodeAttribute()]
public ProductRow AddProductRow(string ProductName, int SupplierID, int CategoryID, string
QuantityPerUnit, decimal UnitPrice, short UnitsInStock, short UnitsOnOrder, short ReorderLevel,
bool Discontinued) {
    ProductRow rowProductRow = ((ProductRow)(this.NewRow()));
    object[] columnValuesArray = new object[] {
            null,
            ProductName,
            SupplierID,
            CategoryID,
            QuantityPerUnit,
            UnitPrice,
            UnitsInStock,
            UnitsOnOrder,
            ReorderLevel,
            Discontinued};
    rowProductRow.ItemArray = columnValuesArray;
    this.Rows.Add(rowProductRow);
    return rowProductRow;
}
```

Just like the `InitClass` member in the `DataSet`-derived class, which added the table to the `DataSet` class, the `InitClass` member in `ProductDataTable` adds columns to the `DataTable` class. Each column's properties are set as appropriate, and the column is then appended to the columns collection:

```
[global::System.Diagnostics.DebuggerNonUserCodeAttribute()]
private void InitClass() {
    this.columnProductID = new global::System.Data.DataColumn("ProductID", typeof(int), null,
global::System.Data.MappingType.Element);
    base.Columns.Add(this.columnProductID);
    this.columnProductName = new global::System.Data.DataColumn("ProductName", typeof(string),
null, global::System.Data.MappingType.Element);
    base.Columns.Add(this.columnProductName);
    this.columnSupplierID = new global::System.Data.DataColumn("SupplierID", typeof(int), null,
global::System.Data.MappingType.Element);
    base.Columns.Add(this.columnSupplierID);
    this.columnCategoryID = new global::System.Data.DataColumn("CategoryID", typeof(int), null,
global::System.Data.MappingType.Element);
    base.Columns.Add(this.columnCategoryID);
    this.columnQuantityPerUnit = new global::System.Data.DataColumn("QuantityPerUnit",
typeof(string), null, global::System.Data.MappingType.Element);
    base.Columns.Add(this.columnQuantityPerUnit);
    this.columnUnitPrice = new global::System.Data.DataColumn("UnitPrice", typeof(decimal),
null, global::System.Data.MappingType.Element);
    base.Columns.Add(this.columnUnitPrice);
    this.columnUnitsInStock = new global::System.Data.DataColumn("UnitsInStock", typeof(short),
null, global::System.Data.MappingType.Element);
    base.Columns.Add(this.columnUnitsInStock);
    this.columnUnitsOnOrder = new global::System.Data.DataColumn("UnitsOnOrder", typeof(short),
null, global::System.Data.MappingType.Element);
```

```
      base.Columns.Add(this.columnUnitsOnOrder);
      this.columnReorderLevel = new global::System.Data.DataColumn("ReorderLevel", typeof(short),
null, global::System.Data.MappingType.Element);
      base.Columns.Add(this.columnReorderLevel);
      this.columnDiscontinued = new global::System.Data.DataColumn("Discontinued", typeof(bool),
null, global::System.Data.MappingType.Element);
      base.Columns.Add(this.columnDiscontinued);
      this.columnProductID.AutoIncrement = true;
      this.columnProductID.AllowDBNull = false;
      this.columnProductID.ReadOnly = true;
      this.columnProductName.AllowDBNull = false;
      this.columnDiscontinued.AllowDBNull = false;
   }
```

`NewRowFromBuilder` is called internally from the `DataTable` class's `NewRow` method. Here, it creates a new strongly typed row. The `DataRowBuilder` instance is created by the `DataTable` class, and its members are accessible only within the `System.Data` assembly:

```
[global::System.Diagnostics.DebuggerNonUserCodeAttribute()]
protected override global::System.Data.DataRow NewRowFromBuilder(global::System.Data.
DataRowBuilder builder) {
    return new ProductRow(builder);
}
```

The last class to discuss is the `ProductRow` class, derived from `DataRow`. This class is used to provide type-safe access to all fields in the data table. It wraps the storage for a particular row, and provides members to read (and write) each of the fields in the table.

In addition, for each nullable field, there are functions to set the field to `null` and to check if the field is `null`. The following example shows the functions for the `SupplierID` column:

```
[global::System.CodeDom.Compiler.GeneratedCodeAttribute("System.Data.Design.
TypedDataSetGenerator", "2.0.0.0")]
public partial class ProductRow : global::System.Data.DataRow {

    private ProductDataTable tableProduct;

    [global::System.Diagnostics.DebuggerNonUserCodeAttribute()]
    internal ProductRow(global::System.Data.DataRowBuilder rb) :
            base(rb) {
        this.tableProduct = ((ProductDataTable)(this.Table));
    }

    [global::System.Diagnostics.DebuggerNonUserCodeAttribute()]
    public int ProductID {
        get {
            return ((int)(this[this.tableProduct.ProductIDColumn]));
        }
        set {
            this[this.tableProduct.ProductIDColumn] = value;
        }
    }
}
```

The following code uses this class's output from the XSD tool to retrieve data from the `Products` table and display that data to the console:

```
using System;
using System.Data.SqlClient;

namespace _10_XSDDataset
{
    class Program
    {
        static void Main(string[] args)
        {
```

```
string select = "SELECT * FROM Products";

using (SqlConnection conn = new SqlConnection(GetDatabaseConnection()))
{
    SqlDataAdapter da = new SqlDataAdapter(select, conn);

    Products ds = new Products();

    da.Fill(ds, "Product");

    foreach (Products.ProductRow row in ds.Product)
        Console.WriteLine("'{0}' from {1}",
            row.ProductID,
            row.ProductName);

    conn.Close();
    }
}

private static string GetDatabaseConnection()
{
    return "server=(local);" +
        "integrated security=SSPI;" +
        "database=Northwind";
}
}
}
```

The output of the XSD file contains a class derived from DataSet called Products, which is created and then filled using the data adapter. The foreach statement uses the strongly typed ProductRow and the Product property, which returns the Product data table.

To compile the .XSD used in this example, issue the following command in a Visual Studio command prompt:

```
xsd product.xsd /d
```

This converts the .XSD to code so that it can be accessed more easily within Visual Studio.

POPULATING A DATASET

After defining the schema of your data set (replete with DataTable and DataColumn), Constraint classes, and whatever else is necessary, you need to be able to populate the DataSet class with information. You have two main methods of reading data from an external source and inserting it into the DataSet class:

➤   Use a data adapter
➤   Read XML into the DataSet class

The following sections discuss both of these methods.

Populating a DataSet Class with a Data Adapter

The section on data rows briefly introduced the SqlDataAdapter class, as shown in the following code:

```
string select = "SELECT ContactName,CompanyName FROM Customers";
SqlConnection conn = new SqlConnection(source);
SqlDataAdapter da = new SqlDataAdapter(select, conn);
DataSet ds = new DataSet();
da.Fill(ds, "Customers");
```

The bold line shows the SqlDataAdapter class in use; the other data adapter classes are again virtually identical in functionality to the SQL Server equivalent.

To retrieve data into a DataSet, it is necessary to execute a command to select that data. The command in question could be a SQL SELECT statement, a call to a stored procedure, or, for the OLE DB provider, a TableDirect command. The preceding example uses one of the constructors available on SqlDataAdapter that converts the passed SQL SELECT statement into a SqlCommand, and issues this select statement when the Fill method is called on the adapter.

The stored procedures example earlier in this chapter, defined the INSERT, UPDATE, and DELETE procedures but did not cover the SELECT procedure. That knowledge gap is covered in the next section, which also covers how to call a stored procedure from a SqlDataAdapter class to populate data in a DataSet class.

Using a Stored Procedure in a Data Adapter

The first step in this example is to define the stored procedure. The stored procedure to SELECT data is as follows:

```
CREATE PROCEDURE RegionSelect AS
   SET NOCOUNT OFF
   SELECT * FROM Region
GO
```

This stored procedure is created within the database by the InitialiseDatabase method in the code.

Next, you need to define the SqlCommand that executes this stored procedure. Again, the code is very simple, and most of it was presented presented earlier:

```
private static SqlCommand GenerateSelectCommand(SqlConnection conn)
{
    SqlCommand  aCommand = new SqlCommand("RegionSelect", conn);
    aCommand.CommandType = CommandType.StoredProcedure;
    aCommand.UpdatedRowSource = UpdateRowSource.None;
    return aCommand;
}
```

This method generates the SqlCommand that calls the RegionSelect procedure when executed. All that remains is to hook this command up to a SqlDataAdapter class and call the Fill method:

```
DataSet ds = new DataSet();
// Create a data adapter to fill the DataSet
SqlDataAdapter da = new SqlDataAdapter();
// Set the data adapter's select command
da.SelectCommand = GenerateSelectCommand (conn);
da.Fill(ds, "Region");
```

Here, the SqlDataAdapter class is created and the generated SqlCommand is assigned to the SelectCommand property of the data adapter. Subsequently, Fill is called, which executes the stored procedure and inserts all rows returned into the Region DataTable (which, in this instance, is generated by the runtime).

There is more to a data adapter than just selecting data by issuing a command, as discussed shortly in the "Persisting DataSet Changes" section.

Populating a DataSet from XML

In addition to generating the schema for a given DataSet, associated tables, and so on, a DataSet class can read and write data in native XML, such as files on a disk, a stream, or a text reader.

To load XML into a DataSet class, simply call one of the ReadXML methods to read data from a disk file, as shown in this example:

```
DataSet ds = new DataSet();
ds.ReadXml(".\\MyData.xml");
```

The ReadXml method attempts to load any inline schema information from the input XML. If a schema is found, the method uses this schema in the validation of any data loaded from that file. If no inline schema is found, the `DataSet` will extend its internal structure as data is loaded. This is similar to the behavior of `Fill` in the previous example, which retrieves the data and constructs a `DataTable` based on the data selected.

PERSISTING DATASET CHANGES

After editing data within a `DataSet`, it is usually necessary to persist these changes. The most common example is selecting data from a database, displaying it to the user, and returning those updates to the database.

In a less "connected" application, changes might be persisted to an XML file, transported to a middle-tier application server, and then processed to update several data sources.

You can use a `DataSet` class for either of these examples; it's easy to do.

Updating with Data Adapters

In addition to the `SelectCommand` that a `SqlDataAdapter` most likely includes, you can also define an `InsertCommand`, `UpdateCommand`, and `DeleteCommand`. As the names imply, these objects are instances of the command object appropriate for your provider, such as `SqlCommand` and `OleDbCommand`.

With this level of flexibility, you are free to tune the application by judicious use of stored procedures for frequently used commands (such as `SELECT` and `INSERT`), and use straight SQL code for less commonly used commands (such as `DELETE`). In general, it is recommended to provide stored procedures for all database interaction because they are faster and easier to tune.

This example uses the stored procedure code from the "Calling Stored Procedures" section for inserting, updating, and deleting `Region` records, as well as using the `RegionSelect` procedure written previously in the section on Using a Stored Procedure in a Data Adaptor, which produces an example that uses each of these commands to retrieve and update data in a `DataSet` class. The main body of the code for this task is shown in the following section.

Inserting a New Row

You can add a new row to a `DataTable` in one of two ways. The first way is to call the `NewRow` method, which returns a blank row that you then populate and add to the `Rows` collection, as follows:

```
DataRow r = ds.Tables["Region"].NewRow();
r["RegionID"]=999;
r["RegionDescription"]="North West";
ds.Tables["Region"].Rows.Add(r);
```

The second way to add a new row is to pass an array of data to the `Rows.Add` method as shown in the following code:

```
DataRow r = ds.Tables["Region"].Rows.Add
              (new object [] { 999, "North West" });
```

Each new row within the `DataTable` will have its `RowState` set to `Added`. The example dumps out the records before each change is made to the database, so after adding a row to the `DataTable` (using either method), the rows will look something like the following. Note that the column on the right shows the row's state:

```
New row pending inserting into database
    1   Eastern                              Unchanged
    2   Western                              Unchanged
    3   Northern                             Unchanged
    4   Southern                             Unchanged
    999 North West                           Added
```

To update the database from the `DataAdapter`, call one of the `Update` methods as shown here:

```
da.Update(ds, "Region");
```

For the new row within the `DataTable`, this executes the stored procedure (in this instance `RegionInsert`). The example then dumps the state of the data, so you can see that changes have been made to the database:

```
New row updated and new RegionID assigned by database
    1    Eastern                               Unchanged
    2    Western                               Unchanged
    3    Northern                              Unchanged
    4    Southern                              Unchanged
    5    North West                            Unchanged
```

Note the last row in the `DataTable`. The `RegionID` had been set in code to 999, but after executing the `RegionInsert` stored procedure, the value has been changed to 5. This is intentional—the database often generates primary keys for you and the updated data in the `DataTable` appears because the `SqlCommand` definition within the source code has the `UpdatedRowSource` property set to `UpdateRowSource` `.OutputParameters`:

```
SqlCommand aCommand = new SqlCommand("RegionInsert", conn);

aCommand.CommandType = CommandType.StoredProcedure;
aCommand.Parameters.Add(new SqlParameter("@RegionDescription",
                        SqlDbType.NChar,
                        50,
                        "RegionDescription"));
aCommand.Parameters.Add(new SqlParameter("@RegionID",
                        SqlDbType.Int,
                        0,
                        ParameterDirection.Output,
                        false,
                        0,
                        0,
                        "RegionID",    // Defines the SOURCE column
                        DataRowVersion.Default,
                        null));
aCommand.UpdatedRowSource = UpdateRowSource.OutputParameters;
```

This means that whenever a data adapter issues this command, the output parameters should be mapped to the source of the row, which in this instance was a row in a `DataTable`. The flag specifies what data should be updated—in this case, the stored procedure has an output parameter that is mapped to the `DataRow`. The column it applies to is `RegionID`; this is defined within the command definition.

The following table describes the values for `UpdateRowSource`:

UPDATEROWSOURCE VALUE	DESCRIPTION
`Both`	This indicates that a stored procedure has returned both output parameters and a complete database record. Both of these data sources are used to update the source row.
`FirstReturnedRecord`	This indicates that the command returns a single record and that the contents of that record should be merged into the original source `DataRow`. This is useful where a given table has a number of default (or computed) columns, because after an `INSERT` statement these need to be synchronized with the `DataRow` on the client. An example might be "`INSERT` (*columns*) `INTO` (*table*) `WITH` (*primarykey*)," then "`SELECT` (*columns*) `FROM` (*table*) `WHERE` (*primarykey*)." The returned record would then be merged into the original row.
`None`	All data returned from the command is discarded.
`OutputParameters`	Any output parameters from the command are mapped onto the appropriate column(s) in the `DataRow`.

Updating an Existing Row

Updating an existing row within the `DataTable` is just a case of using the `DataRow` class's indexer with either a column name or a column number, as shown in the following code:

```
r["RegionDescription"]="North West England";
r[1] = "North West England";
```

Both of the preceding statements are equivalent (in this example):

```
Changed RegionID 5 description
   1   Eastern                        Unchanged
   2   Western                        Unchanged
   3   Northern                       Unchanged
   4   Southern                       Unchanged
   5   North West England             Modified
```

Prior to updating the database, the row you are updating has its state set to `Modified`, as shown above. When the changes are persisted to the database this state will then revert to `Unchanged`.

Deleting a Row

Deleting a row is a matter of calling the `Delete` method:

```
r.Delete();
```

A deleted row has its row state set to `Deleted`, but you cannot read columns from the deleted `DataRow` because they are no longer valid. When the adapter's `Update` method is called, all deleted rows will use the `DeleteCommand`, which in this instance executes the `RegionDelete` stored procedure.

Writing XML Output

As you have seen already, the `DataSet` class provides great support for defining its schema in XML; and, just as you can read data from an XML document, you can also write data to an XML document.

The `DataSet.WriteXml` method enables you to output various parts of the data stored within the `DataSet`. You can elect to output just the data or to include the data and the schema. The following code demonstrates an example of both for the `Region` example shown earlier:

```
ds.WriteXml(".\\WithoutSchema.xml");
ds.WriteXml(".\\WithSchema.xml", XmlWriteMode.WriteSchema);
```

The first file, `WithoutSchema.xml`, is shown here:

```
<?xml version="1.0" standalone="yes"?>
<NewDataSet>
  <Region>
     <RegionID>1</RegionID>
     <RegionDescription>Eastern</RegionDescription>
  </Region>
  <Region>
     <RegionID>2</RegionID>
     <RegionDescription>Western</RegionDescription>
  </Region>
  <Region>
     <RegionID>3</RegionID>
     <RegionDescription>Northern</RegionDescription>
  </Region>
  <Region>
     <RegionID>4</RegionID>
     <RegionDescription>Southern</RegionDescription>
  </Region>
</NewDataSet>
```

The closing tag on `RegionDescription` is over to the right of the page because the database column is defined as `NCHAR(50)`, which is a 50-character string padded with spaces.

The output produced in the `WithSchema.xml` file includes the XML schema for the `DataSet` as well as the data itself:

```
<?xml version="1.0" standalone="yes"?>
<NewDataSet>
  <xs:schema id="NewDataSet" xmlns="" xmlns:xs="http://www.w3.org/2001/XMLSchema"
    xmlns:msdata="urn:schemas-microsoft-com:xml-msdata">
    <xs:element name="NewDataSet" msdata:IsDataSet="true"
      msdata:UseCurrentLocale="true">
      <xs:complexType>
        <xs:choice minOccurs="0" maxOccurs="unbounded">
          <xs:element name="Region">
            <xs:complexType>
              <xs:sequence>
                <xs:element name="RegionID" msdata:AutoIncrement="true"
                  msdata:AutoIncrementSeed="1" type="xs:int" />
                <xs:element name="RegionDescription" type="xs:string" />
              </xs:sequence>
            </xs:complexType>
          </xs:element>
        </xs:choice>
      </xs:complexType>
    </xs:element>
  </xs:schema>
  <Region>
    <RegionID>1</RegionID>
    <RegionDescription>Eastern</RegionDescription>
  </Region>
  <Region>
    <RegionID>2</RegionID>
    <RegionDescription>Western</RegionDescription>
  </Region>
  <Region>
    <RegionID>3</RegionID>
    <RegionDescription>Northern</RegionDescription>
  </Region>
  <Region>
    <RegionID>4</RegionID>
    <RegionDescription>Southern</RegionDescription>
  </Region>
</NewDataSet>
```

Note the use of the `msdata` schema in this file, which defines extra attributes for columns within a `DataSet`, such as `AutoIncrement` and `AutoIncrementSeed`—these attributes correspond directly to the properties definable on a `DataColumn` class.

WORKING WITH ADO.NET

This section addresses some common scenarios when developing data access applications with ADO.NET such as how to use ADO.NET in an application that is delivered using multiple tiers, and how to generate SQL Keys efficiently. The topics covered here don't naturally fit into other sections of this chapter.

Tiered Development

Producing an application that interacts with data is often done by splitting up the application into tiers. A common model is to have an application tier (the front end), a data services tier, and the database itself (the back end).

One of the difficulties with this model is deciding what data to transport between your tiers, as well as figuring out the format in which the data should be transported. With ADO.NET, these wrinkles have been ironed out and support for this style of architecture is part of the design.

One of the things that are much better in ADO.NET than OLE DB is ADO.NET's support for copying an entire record set. In .NET, it is easy to copy a `DataSet`; simply use the following code:

```
DataSet source = {some dataset};
DataSet dest = source.Copy();
```

This creates an exact copy of the source `DataSet`. Each `DataTable`, `DataColumn`, `DataRow`, and `Relation` will be copied and all the data will be in exactly the same state as it was in the source. If the only part you want to copy is the schema of the `DataSet`, you can use the following code:

```
DataSet source = {some dataset};
DataSet dest = source.Clone();
```

This copies all tables, relations, and so on, but each copied `DataTable` will be empty. This process really could not be more straightforward.

A common requirement when writing a tiered system, whether based on a Windows client application or on the web, is to be able to ship as little data as possible between tiers. This reduces the amount of resources consumed in transmitting the data set.

To handle this requirement, the `DataSet` class uses the `GetChanges` method. This simple method performs a huge amount of work and returns a `DataSet` with only the changed rows from the source data set. This is ideal for passing data between tiers because it only passes the essential set of data along.

The following example shows how to generate a `DataSet` consisting of just the changes:

```
DataSet source = {some dataset};
DataSet dest = source.GetChanges();
```

Again, this is trivial, but if you delve deeper you'll find things that are a little more interesting.

There are two overloads of the `GetChanges` method. One overload takes a value of the `DataRowState` enumeration and returns only rows that correspond to that state (or states). `GetChanges` simply calls `GetChanges(Deleted | Modified | Added)` and ensures that there really are changes by calling `HasChanges`. If no changes have been made, `null` is returned to the requestor immediately.

The next operation is to clone the current `DataSet`. Once this is done, the new `DataSet` is set up to ignore constraint violations (`EnforceConstraints = false`), and then each changed row for every table is copied into the new `DataSet`.

When you have a `DataSet` that contains just changes, you can then move these off to the data services tier for processing. After the data has been updated in the database, the "changes" `DataSet` can be returned to the requestor; for example, there might be some output parameters from the stored procedures that have updated values in the columns. These changes can then be merged into the original `DataSet` using the `Merge` method. Figure 32-9 depicts this sequence of operations.

FIGURE 32-9

Key Generation with SQL Server

The `RegionInsert` stored procedure presented earlier in this chapter is one example of generating a primary key value on insertion into the database. The method for generating the key in that particular example is fairly crude and wouldn't scale well, so for a real application you should use some other strategy for generating keys.

Your first instinct might be to define an identity column and return the `@@IDENTITY` value from the stored procedure. The following stored procedure shows how this might be defined for the `Categories` table in the Northwind example database from earlier in this chapter. Type this stored procedure into the SQL Query Analyzer or run the `StoredProcs.sql` file that is part of the code download for this chapter:

```
CREATE PROCEDURE CategoryInsert(@CategoryName NVARCHAR(15),
                                @Description NTEXT,
                                @CategoryID INTEGER OUTPUT) AS
    SET NOCOUNT OFF
    INSERT INTO Categories (CategoryName, Description)
        VALUES(@CategoryName, @Description)
    SELECT @CategoryID = @@IDENTITY
GO
```

This inserts a new row into the `Category` table and returns the generated primary key (the value of the `CategoryID` column) to the caller. You can test the procedure by typing the following in the SQL Query Analyzer:

```
DECLARE @CatID int;
EXECUTE CategoryInsert 'Pasties', 'Heaven Sent Food', @CatID OUTPUT;
PRINT @CatID;
```

When executed as a batch of commands, this inserts a new row into the `Categories` table and returns the identity of the new record, which is then displayed to the user.

Suppose that some months down the line, someone decides to add a simple audit trail which will record all insertions and modifications made to the category name. In that case, you need to define a table similar to the one shown in Figure 32-10, which will record the old and new values of the category.

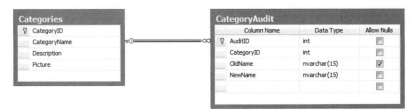

FIGURE 32-10

The script for this table is included in the `StoredProcs.sql` file on this book's website. The `AuditID` column is defined as an `IDENTITY` column. You then construct a couple of database triggers that will record changes to the `CategoryName` field using the following code:

```
CREATE TRIGGER CategoryInsertTrigger
    ON Categories
    AFTER UPDATE
AS
    INSERT INTO CategoryAudit(CategoryID, OldName, NewName )
        SELECT old.CategoryID, old.CategoryName, new.CategoryName
        FROM Deleted AS old,
             Categories AS new
        WHERE old.CategoryID = new.CategoryID;
GO
```

> **NOTE** *If you are used to Oracle stored procedures, you should remember that SQL Server doesn't exactly have the concept of* OLD *and* NEW *rows; instead, for an insert trigger there is an in-memory table called* Inserted, *and for deletes and updates the old rows are available within the* Deleted *table.*

The insert trigger is an in-memory table called Inserted, and for deletes and updates the old rows are available within the Deleted table. The CategoryInsertTrigger retrieves the CategoryID of the record(s) affected and stores this information together with the old and new value of the CategoryName column.

When you call your original stored procedure to insert a new CategoryID, you receive an identity value; however, this is no longer the identity value from the row inserted into the Categories table—it is now the new value generated for the row in the CategoryAudit table.

To view the problem firsthand, open a copy of SQL Server Enterprise Manager and look at the contents of the Categories table (see Figure 32-11). This lists all the categories in the Northwind database.

	CategoryID	CategoryName	Description	Picture
1	1	Beverages	Soft drinks, coffees, teas, beers, and ales	0x151C2F00020000000D000E0014002100FFFFFFFF4269746...
2	2	Condiments	Sweet and savory sauces, relishes, spreads, and ...	0x151C2F00020000000D000E0014002100FFFFFFFF4269746...
3	3	Confections	Desserts, candies, and sweet breads	0x151C2F00020000000D000E0014002100FFFFFFFF4269746...
4	4	Dairy Products	Cheeses	0x151C2F00020000000D000E0014002100FFFFFFFF4269746...
5	5	Grains/Cereals	Breads, crackers, pasta, and cereal	0x151C2F00020000000D000E0014002100FFFFFFFF4269746...
6	6	Meat/Poultry	Prepared meats	0x151C2F00020000000D000E0014002100FFFFFFFF4269746...
7	7	Produce	Dried fruit and bean curd	0x151C2F00020000000D000E0014002100FFFFFFFF4269746...
8	8	Seafood	Seaweed and fish	0x151C2F00020000000D000E0014002100FFFFFFFF4269746...

FIGURE 32-11

The next identity value for the Categories table should be 9, so a new row can be inserted by executing the following code, to see what ID is returned:

```
DECLARE @CatID int;
EXECUTE CategoryInsert 'Pasties', 'Heaven Sent Food', @CatID OUTPUT;
PRINT @CatID;
```

The output value of this on a test PC was 1. If you look at the CategoryAudit table shown in Figure 32-12, you will find that this is the identity of the newly inserted audit record, not the identity of the category record created.

	AuditID	CategoryID	OldName	NewName
1	1	9	NULL	Pasties

FIGURE 32-12

The problem lies in the way that @@IDENTITY actually works. It returns the LAST identity value created by your session so, as shown in Figure 32-12, it isn't completely reliable.

Two other identity functions can be used instead of @@IDENTITY, but neither is free from problems. The first, SCOPE_IDENTITY, returns the last identity value created within the current scope. SQL Server defines *scope* as a stored procedure, trigger, or function. This may work most of the time, but if for, some reason, someone adds another INSERT statement to the stored procedure, you can receive this other value rather than the one you expected.

The other identity function, IDENT_CURRENT, returns the last identity value generated for a given table in any scope. For example, if two users were accessing SQL Server at exactly the same time, it might be possible to receive the other user's generated identity value.

As you might imagine, tracking down a problem of this nature is not easy. The moral of the story is to beware when using IDENTITY columns in SQL Server.

Naming Conventions

The following tips and conventions are not directly .NET-related, but they are worth sharing and following, especially when naming constraints. Feel free to skip this section if you already have your own views on this subject.

Conventions for Database Tables

➤ **Use singular, rather than plural, names** — For example, use `Product` rather than `Products`. This recommendation stems from explaining a database schema to customers; it is much better grammatically to say, "the `Product` table contains products" than "the `Products` table contains products." Check out the Northwind database to see an example of how *not* to do this.

➤ **Adopt some form of naming convention for the fields of a table** — An obvious one is `<Table>_Id` for the primary key of a table (assuming that the primary key is a single column), `Name` for the field considered to be the user-friendly name of the record, and `Description` for any textual information about the record itself. Having a good table convention means that you can look at virtually any table in the database and easily understand what the fields are used for.

Conventions for Database Columns

➤ **Use singular, rather than plural, names** — See the explanation in the previous section.

➤ **Any columns that link to another table should be given the same name as the primary key of that table** — For example, a link to the `Product` table would be `Product_Id`, and one to the `Sample` table `Sample_Id`. This is not always possible, however, especially if one table has multiple references to another. In that case, use your own judgment.

➤ **Date fields should have a suffix of `_On`** — Examples include `Modified_On` and `Created_On`. This makes it easy to read SQL output and infer what a column means just by its name.

➤ **Fields that record activities from the user should have a suffix of `_By`** — Examples include `Modified_By` and `Created_By`. This promotes comprehension.

Conventions for Constraints

➤ **If possible, include the name of the constraint, the table, and column name** — One example would be `CK_<Table>_<Field>`. You would then use `CK_Person_Sex` for a check constraint on the `Sex` column of the `Person` table. A foreign key example would be `FK_Product_Supplier_Id`, for the foreign key relationship between product and supplier.

➤ **Show the type of constraint with a prefix** — For example, use `CK` for a check constraint or `FK` for a foreign key constraint. Feel free to be more specific, as in `CK_Person_Age_GT0` for a constraint on the age column indicating that the age should be greater than zero.

➤ **If you have to trim the length of the constraint, do so on the table name part rather than the column name** — When you get a constraint violation, it is usually easy to infer which table was in error, but sometimes it's not so easy to check which column caused the problem. Oracle has a 30-character limit on names, which is easy to surpass.

Stored Procedures

Just like the obsession many have developed over the past few years with putting a `C` in front of each and every class they declare (you know you have!), many SQL Server developers feel compelled to prefix every stored procedure with `sp_` or something similar. This is not a good idea.

SQL Server uses the `sp_` prefix for nearly all system stored procedures. Therefore, you risk confusing users into thinking that `sp_widget` is something included as standard with SQL Server. In addition, when looking for a stored procedure, SQL Server treats procedures with the `sp_` prefix differently from those without it.

If you use this prefix and do not qualify the database/owner of the stored procedure, SQL Server looks in the current scope and then jumps into the master database to search for the stored procedure there. Without the sp_ prefix, your users would get an error a little earlier. Even worse is creating a local stored procedure (one within your database) that has the same name and parameters as a system stored procedure. Avoid this at all costs. When in doubt, do not prefix.

When calling stored procedures, always prefix them with the owner of the procedure, as in dbo .selectWidgets. This is slightly faster than not using the prefix, because SQL Server has less work to do to find the stored procedure. Something like this is not likely to have a huge impact on the execution speed of your application, but it is a free tuning trick.

Above all, when naming entities, whether within the database or within code, *be consistent.*

SUMMARY

Data access is an extensive subject—especially in .NET, which has an abundance of material to cover. This chapter has provided an outline of the main classes in the ADO.NET namespaces and has demonstrated how to use the classes when manipulating data from a data source.

You first looked at the Connection object using both SqlConnection (SQL Server–specific) and OleDbConnection (for any OLE DB data sources). The programming model for these two classes is so similar that one can normally be substituted for the other and the code will continue to run.

This chapter also explained how to use connections properly so that they can be closed as early as possible, preserving valuable resources. All the connection classes implement the IDisposable interface, called when the object is placed within a using clause. If there is one thing you should take away from this chapter, it is the importance of closing database connections as early as possible.

In addition, this chapter discussed database commands using both examples that executed with no returned data and examples that called stored procedures with input and output parameters. It described various execute methods, including the ExecuteXmlReader method available only on the SQL Server provider. This vastly simplifies the selection and manipulation of XML-based data.

The generic classes within the System.Data namespace were described in detail, from the DataSet class through DataTable, DataColumn, DataRow, including relationships and constraints. The DataSet class is an excellent data container and various methods make it ideal for cross-tier data flow. The data within a DataSet is represented in XML for transport and methods are available that pass a minimal amount of data between tiers. The capability to have many tables of data within a single DataSet can greatly increase its usability.

Having the schema stored within a DataSet is useful, but .NET also includes the data adapter that, along with various Command objects, can be used to select data for a DataSet and subsequently update data in the data store. One of the beneficial aspects of a data adapter is that a distinct command can be defined for each of the four actions: SELECT, INSERT, UPDATE, and DELETE. The system can create a default set of commands based on database schema information and a SELECT statement. For the best performance, however, a set of stored procedures can be used that have the DataAdapter's commands defined appropriately to pass only the necessary information to these stored procedures.

The XSD tool (XSD.EXE) was also described, using an example that showed how to work with classes based on an XML schema from within .NET. The classes produced using this tool are ready to be used within an application and their automatic generation can save many hours of laborious typing.

Finally, this chapter discussed some best practices and naming conventions for database development. Further information about accessing SQL Server databases is provided in Chapter 33 "ADO.NET Entity Framework."

33

ADO.NET Entity Framework

WHAT'S IN THIS CHAPTER?

- ➤ Programming Models
- ➤ Mapping
- ➤ Entity classes
- ➤ Object contexts
- ➤ Relationships
- ➤ Querying data
- ➤ Updates
- ➤ Using POCOs
- ➤ Code First

WROX.COM CODE DOWNLOADS FOR THIS CHAPTER

The wrox.com code downloads for this chapter are found at http://www.wrox.com/remtitle .cgi?isbn=1118314425 on the Download Code tab. The code for this chapter is divided into the following major examples:

- ➤ Books Demo
- ➤ Formula 1 Demo
- ➤ Payments Demo
- ➤ Query Demo
- ➤ POCO Demo
- ➤ Code First Demo

PROGRAMMING WITH THE ENTITY FRAMEWORK

The ADO.NET Entity Framework is an object-relational mapping framework that offers an abstraction of ADO.NET to get an object model based on the referential databases. You can use different programming models with the Entity Framework: Model First, Database First, and Code First. Both Model First and Database First provide mapping information with a mapping file. Using Code

First, mapping information is all done via C# code. This chapter provides information about all these programming models.

You will learn about the mappings between the database and the entity classes using the Conceptual Schema Definition Language (CSDL), the Storage Schema Definition Language (SSDL), and the Mapping Schema Language (MSL). Different relationships between entities are covered, such as one table per hierarchy of objects, one table per type, and n-to-n relationships.

This chapter also describes different ways to access the database from the code directly with the EntityClient provider, using Entity SQL or helper methods that create Entity SQL, and using LINQ to Entities. Also described are object tracking and how the data context holds change information for updating data. Finally, you'll learn how POCO (Plain Old CLR Objects) can be used with the Entity Framework, and how to use the Code First programming model.

> **NOTE** *This chapter uses the Books and Formula1 databases. These databases are included with the download of the code samples at* http://www.wrox.com.

The ADO.NET Entity Framework provides a mapping from the relational database schema to objects. Relational databases and object-oriented languages define associations differently. For example, the sample database Formula1 contains the Racers and RaceResults tables. To access all the RaceResults rows for a racer, you need to do a SQL join statement. With object-oriented languages, it is more common to define a `Racer` class and a `RaceResult` class and access the race results of a racer by using a `RaceResults` property from the `Racer` class.

For object-relational mapping since .NET 1.0, it has been possible to use the `DataSet` class and typed data sets. Data sets are very similar to the structure of a database containing `DataTable`, `DataRow`, `DataColumn`, and `DataRelation` classes instead of offering object-support. The ADO.NET Entity Framework supports directly defining entity classes that are completely independent of a database structure and mapping them to tables and associations of the database. Using objects with the application, the application is shielded from changes in the database.

The ADO.NET Entity Framework offers Entity SQL to define entity-based queries to the store (an extension to T-SQL). LINQ to Entities makes it possible to use the LINQ syntax to query data. An object context acts as a bridge regarding entities that are changed, retaining information for when the entities should be written back to the store.

The namespaces that contain classes from the ADO.NET Entity Framework are listed in the following table:

NAMESPACE	DESCRIPTION
`System.Data`	A main namespace for ADO.NET. With the ADO.NET Entity Framework, this namespace contains exception classes related to entities—for example, `MappingException` and `QueryException`.
`System.Data.Common`	Contains classes shared by .NET data providers. The class `DbProviderServices` is an abstract base class that must be implemented by an ADO.NET Entity Framework provider.
`System.Data.Common.CommandTrees`	Contains classes to build an expression tree.
`System.Data.Entity`	Contains classes for the Code First development model.
`System.Data.Entity.Design`	Contains classes used by the designer to create Entity Data Model (EDM) files.

NAMESPACE	DESCRIPTION
`System.Data.EntityClient`	Specifies classes for the .NET Framework Data Provider to access the Entity Framework. `EntityConnection`, `EntityCommand`, and `EntityDataReader` can be used to access the Entity Framework.
`System.Data.Objects`	Contains classes to query and update databases. The class `ObjectContext` encapsulates the connection to the database and serves as a gateway for create, read, update, and delete methods. The class `ObjectQuery` represents a query against the store. `CompiledQuery` is a cached query.
`System.Data.Objects.DataClasses`	Contains classes and interfaces required for entities.

ENTITY FRAMEWORK MAPPING

With Model First and Database First, the ADO.NET Entity Framework offers several layers to map database tables to objects. With Database First you can start with a database schema and use a Visual Studio item template to create the complete mapping. You can also start designing entity classes with the designer (Model First) and map it to the database such that the tables and the associations between the tables can have a very different structure.

The layers that need to be defined are as follows:

➤ **Logical** — Defines the relational data.

➤ **Conceptual** — Defines the .NET entity classes.

➤ **Mapping** — Defines the mapping from .NET classes to relational tables and associations.

Figure 33-1 shows a simple database schema, with the tables `Books` and `Authors`, and an association table `BookAuthors` that maps the authors to books.

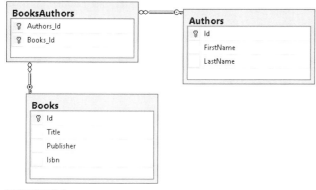

FIGURE 33-1

> **NOTE** *Code First uses programmatically mapping that is discussed later in section "Using the Code First Programming Model."*

Logical Layer

The logical layer is defined by the Store Schema Definition Language (SSDL) and describes the structure of the database tables and their relationships.

The following code uses SSDL to describe the three tables: `Books`, `Authors`, and `BooksAuthors`. The `EntityContainer` element describes all the tables with `EntitySet` elements, and associations with `AssociationSet` elements. The parts of a table are defined with the `EntityType` element. With `EntityType` `Books` you can see the columns `Id`, `Title`, `Publisher`, and `ISBN` defined by the `Property` element. The `Property` element contains XML attributes to define the data type. The `Key` element defines the primary key of the table: You can find the following code in the code file `BooksDemo/BooksModel.edmx`:

```
<edmx:StorageModels>
  <Schema Namespace="BooksModel.Store" Alias="Self"
      Provider="System.Data.SqlClient"
      ProviderManifestToken="2008"
      xmlns:store=
      "http://schemas.microsoft.com/ado/2007/12/edm/EntityStoreSchemaGenerator"
      xmlns="http://schemas.microsoft.com/ado/2009/02/edm/ssdl">
    <EntityContainer Name="BooksModelStoreContainer">
      <EntitySet Name="Authors" EntityType="BooksModel.Store.Authors"
          store:Type="Tables" Schema="dbo" />
      <EntitySet Name="Books" EntityType="BooksModel.Store.Books"
          store:Type="Tables" Schema="dbo" />
      <EntitySet Name="BooksAuthors" EntityType="BooksModel.Store.BooksAuthors"
          store:Type="Tables" Schema="dbo" />
      <AssociationSet Name="FK_BooksAuthors_Authors"
          Association="BooksModel.Store.FK_BooksAuthors_Authors">
        <End Role="Authors" EntitySet="Authors" />
        <End Role="BooksAuthors" EntitySet="BooksAuthors" />
      </AssociationSet>
      <AssociationSet Name="FK_BooksAuthors_Books"
          Association="BooksModel.Store.FK_BooksAuthors_Books">
        <End Role="Books" EntitySet="Books" />
        <End Role="BooksAuthors" EntitySet="BooksAuthors" />
      </AssociationSet>
    </EntityContainer>
    <EntityType Name="Authors">
      <Key>
        <PropertyRef Name="Id" />
      </Key>
      <Property Name="Id" Type="int" Nullable="false"
          StoreGeneratedPattern="Identity" />
      <Property Name="FirstName" Type="nvarchar" Nullable="false"
          MaxLength="50" />
      <Property Name="LastName" Type="nvarchar" Nullable="false"
          MaxLength="50" />
    </EntityType>
    <EntityType Name="Books">
      <Key>
        <PropertyRef Name="Id" />
      </Key>
      <Property Name="Id" Type="int" Nullable="false"
          StoreGeneratedPattern="Identity" />
      <Property Name="Title" Type="nvarchar" Nullable="false" MaxLength="50" />
      <Property Name="Publisher" Type="nvarchar" Nullable="false"
          MaxLength="50" />
      <Property Name="Isbn" Type="nchar" MaxLength="18" />
    </EntityType>
    <EntityType Name="BooksAuthors">
      <Key>
        <PropertyRef Name="BookId" />
        <PropertyRef Name="AuthorId" />
      </Key>
      <Property Name="BookId" Type="int" Nullable="false" />
      <Property Name="AuthorId" Type="int" Nullable="false" />
```

```
          </EntityType>
          <Association Name="FK_BooksAuthors_Authors">
            <End Role="Authors" Type="BooksModel.Store.Authors" Multiplicity="1" />
            <End Role="BooksAuthors" Type="BooksModel.Store.BooksAuthors"
                Multiplicity="*" />
            <ReferentialConstraint>
              <Principal Role="Authors">
                <PropertyRef Name="Id" />
              </Principal>
              <Dependent Role="BooksAuthors">
                <PropertyRef Name="AuthorId" />
              </Dependent>
            </ReferentialConstraint>
          </Association>
          <Association Name="FK_BooksAuthors_Books">
            <End Role="Books" Type="BooksModel.Store.Books" Multiplicity="1" />
            <End Role="BooksAuthors" Type="BooksModel.Store.BooksAuthors"
                Multiplicity="*" />
            <ReferentialConstraint>
              <Principal Role="Books">
                <PropertyRef Name="Id" />
              </Principal>
              <Dependent Role="BooksAuthors">
                <PropertyRef Name="BookId" />
              </Dependent>
            </ReferentialConstraint>
          </Association>
        </Schema>
      </edmx:StorageModels>
```

> **NOTE** *The file* `BooksModel.edmx` *contains SSDL, CSDL, and MSL. You can open this file with an XML editor to see its contents.*

Conceptual Layer

The conceptual layer defines .NET entity classes. This layer is created with the Conceptual Schema Definition Language (CSDL).

Figure 33-2 shows the entities Author and Book defined with the ADO.NET Entity Data Model Designer.

The following code (found in code file BooksDemo/BooksModel .edmx) is the CSDL content that defines the entity types Book and Author. This was created from the Books database:

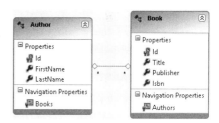

FIGURE 33-2

```
      <edmx:ConceptualModels>
        <Schema Namespace="BooksModel" Alias="Self" xmlns:annotation=
            "http://schemas.microsoft.com/ado/2009/02/edm/annotation"
            xmlns="http://schemas.microsoft.com/ado/2008/09/edm">
          <EntityContainer Name="BooksEntities" annotation:LazyLoadingEnabled="true">
            <EntitySet Name="Authors" EntityType="BooksModel.Author" />
            <EntitySet Name="Books" EntityType="BooksModel.Book" />
            <AssociationSet Name="BooksAuthors" Association="BooksModel.BooksAuthors">
              <End Role="Authors" EntitySet="Authors" />
              <End Role="Books" EntitySet="Books" />
            </AssociationSet>
          </EntityContainer>
```

```
<EntityType Name="Author">
  <Key>
    <PropertyRef Name="Id" />
  </Key>
  <Property Name="Id" Type="Int32" Nullable="false"
      annotation:StoreGeneratedPattern="Identity" />
  <Property Name="FirstName" Type="String" Nullable="false" MaxLength="50"
      Unicode="true" FixedLength="false" />
  <Property Name="LastName" Type="String" Nullable="false" MaxLength="50"
      Unicode="true" FixedLength="false" />
  <NavigationProperty Name="Books" Relationship="BooksModel.BooksAuthors"
      FromRole="Authors" ToRole="Books" />
</EntityType>
<EntityType Name="Book">
  <Key>
    <PropertyRef Name="Id" />
  </Key>
  <Property Name="Id" Type="Int32" Nullable="false"
      annotation:StoreGeneratedPattern="Identity" />
  <Property Name="Title" Type="String" Nullable="false" MaxLength="50"
      Unicode="true" FixedLength="false" />
  <Property Name="Publisher" Type="String" Nullable="false" MaxLength="50"
      Unicode="true" FixedLength="false" />
  <Property Name="Isbn" Type="String" MaxLength="18" Unicode="true"
      FixedLength="true" />
  <NavigationProperty Name="Authors" Relationship="BooksModel.BooksAuthors"
      FromRole="Books" ToRole="Authors" />
</EntityType>
<Association Name="BooksAuthors">
  <End Role="Authors" Type="BooksModel.Author" Multiplicity="*" />
  <End Role="Books" Type="BooksModel.Book" Multiplicity="*" />
</Association>
  </Schema>
</edmx:ConceptualModels>
```

The entity is defined by an `EntityType` element, which contains Key, Property, and `NavigationProperty` elements to describe the properties of the created class. The `Property` element contains attributes to describe the name and type of the .NET properties of the classes generated by the designer. The `Association` element connects the types `Author` and `Book`. `Multiplicity="*"` means that one `Author` can write multiple `Books`, and one `Book` can be written by multiple `Authors`.

Mapping Layer

The mapping layer maps the entity type definition from the CSDL to the SSDL using the Mapping Specification Language (MSL). The following specification (code file `BooksDemo/BooksModel.edmx`) includes a `Mapping` element that contains the `EntityTypeMapping` element to reference the `Book` type of the CSDL and it defines the `MappingFragment` to reference the `Authors` table from the SSDL. The `ScalarProperty` maps the property of the .NET class with the `Name` attribute to the column of the database table with the `ColumnName` attribute:

```
<edmx:Mappings>
  <Mapping Space="C-S"
      xmlns="http://schemas.microsoft.com/ado/2008/09/mapping/cs">
    <EntityContainerMapping StorageEntityContainer="BooksModelStoreContainer"
        CdmEntityContainer="BooksEntities">
      <EntitySetMapping Name="Authors">
        <EntityTypeMapping TypeName="BooksModel.Author">
          <MappingFragment StoreEntitySet="Authors">
            <ScalarProperty Name="Id" ColumnName="Id" />
```

```
            <ScalarProperty Name="FirstName" ColumnName="FirstName" />
            <ScalarProperty Name="LastName" ColumnName="LastName" />
          </MappingFragment>
        </EntityTypeMapping>
      </EntitySetMapping>
      <EntitySetMapping Name="Books">
        <EntityTypeMapping TypeName="BooksModel.Book">
          <MappingFragment StoreEntitySet="Books">
            <ScalarProperty Name="Id" ColumnName="Id" />
            <ScalarProperty Name="Title" ColumnName="Title" />
            <ScalarProperty Name="Publisher" ColumnName="Publisher" />
            <ScalarProperty Name="Isbn" ColumnName="Isbn" />
          </MappingFragment>
        </EntityTypeMapping>
      </EntitySetMapping>
      <AssociationSetMapping Name="BooksAuthors" TypeName=
          "BooksModel.BooksAuthors" StoreEntitySet="BooksAuthors">
        <EndProperty Name="Authors">
          <ScalarProperty Name="Id" ColumnName="AuthorId" />
        </EndProperty>
        <EndProperty Name="Books">
          <ScalarProperty Name="Id" ColumnName="BookId" />
        </EndProperty>
      </AssociationSetMapping>
    </EntityContainerMapping>
  </Mapping>
</edmx:Mappings>
```

Connection String

Using the designer, the connection string is stored in the configuration file. The connection string is required for EDM and is different from the normal ADO.NET connection string because mapping information is required. The mapping is defined with the keyword `metadata`. The connection string requires three parts:

➤ A `metadata` keyword with delimited list of mapping files

➤ A `provider` for the invariant provider name to access the data source

➤ A `provider connection string` to assign the provider-dependent connection string

The following code snippet shows a sample connection string. With the `metadata` keyword, the delimited list of mapping files references the files `BooksModel.csdl`, `BooksModel.ssdl`, and `BooksModel.msl`, which are contained within resources in the assembly as defined with the `res:` prefix. In Visual Studio, the designer uses just one file, `BooksModel.edmx`, which contains CSDL, SSDL, and MSL. Setting the property `Custom Tool` to `EntityModelCodeGenerator` creates three files that are contained in resources.

Within the `provider connection string` setting you can find the connection string to the database with the connection string setting. This part is the same as a simple ADO.NET connection string discussed in Chapter 32, Core "ADO.NET," and varies according to the provider that is set with the `provider` setting:

```
<connectionStrings>
  <add name="BooksEntities"
    connectionString="metadata=res://*/BooksModel.csdl|res://*/BooksModel.ssdl|
      res://*/BooksModel.msl;provider=System.Data.SqlClient;
      provider connection string=&quot;Data Source=(local);
      Initial Catalog=Books;Integrated Security=True;Pooling=False;
      MultipleActiveResultSets=True&quot;"
    providerName="System.Data.EntityClient" />
</connectionStrings>
```

> **NOTE** *With the connection string, you can also specify CSDL, SSDL, and MSL files that are not contained as a resource in the assembly. This is useful if you want to change the content of these files after deployment of the project.*

ENTITIES

Entity classes that are created with the designer and CSDL typically derive from the base class EntityObject, as shown with the Book class in the code that follows (code file BooksDemo/BooksModel .Designer.cs).

The Book class derives from the base class EntityObject and defines properties for its data such as Title and Publisher. The set accessors of these properties fire change information in two different ways:

➤ By invoking the methods **ReportPropertyChanging** and **ReportPropertyChanged** of the base class **EntityObject.** Invoking these methods uses the INotifyPropertyChanging and INotifyPropertyChanged interfaces to inform every client that registers with the events about these interfaces.

➤ By using partial methods such as **OnTitleChanging** and **OnTitleChanged.** By default, these have no implementation but can be implemented in custom extensions of this class.

The Authors property uses the RelationshipManager class to return the Books for an author:

```
[EdmEntityTypeAttribute(NamespaceName = "BooksModel", Name = "Book")]
[Serializable()]
[DataContractAttribute(IsReference = true)]
public partial class Book : EntityObject
{
  public static Book CreateBook(int id, string title, string publisher)
  {
    Book book = new Book();
    book.Id = id;
    book.Title = title;
    book.Publisher = publisher;
    return book;
  }

  [EdmScalarPropertyAttribute(EntityKeyProperty = true, IsNullable = false)]
  [DataMemberAttribute()]
  public int Id
  {
    get
    {
      return _Id;
    }
    set
    {
      if (_Id != value)
      {
        OnIdChanging(value);
        ReportPropertyChanging("Id");
        _Id = StructuralObject.SetValidValue(value);
        ReportPropertyChanged("Id");
        OnIdChanged();
      }
    }
  }
  private int _Id;
```

```
partial void OnIdChanging(int value);
partial void OnIdChanged();

[EdmScalarPropertyAttribute(EntityKeyProperty = false, IsNullable = false)]
[DataMemberAttribute()]
public string Title
{
  get
  {
    return _Title;
  }
  set
  {
    OnTitleChanging(value);
    ReportPropertyChanging("Title");
    _Title = StructuralObject.SetValidValue(value, false);
    ReportPropertyChanged("Title");
    OnTitleChanged();
  }
}
private string _Title;
partial void OnTitleChanging(string value);
partial void OnTitleChanged();

[EdmScalarPropertyAttribute(EntityKeyProperty = false, IsNullable = false)]
[DataMemberAttribute()]
public string Publisher
{
  get
  {
    return _Publisher;
  }
  set
  {
    OnPublisherChanging(value);
    ReportPropertyChanging("Publisher");
    _Publisher = StructuralObject.SetValidValue(value, false);
    ReportPropertyChanged("Publisher");
    OnPublisherChanged();
  }
}
private string _Publisher;
partial void OnPublisherChanging(string value);
partial void OnPublisherChanged();

[EdmScalarPropertyAttribute(EntityKeyProperty = false, IsNullable = true)]
[DataMemberAttribute()]
public string Isbn
{
  get
  {
    return _Isbn;
  }
  set
  {
    OnIsbnChanging(value);
    ReportPropertyChanging("Isbn");
    _Isbn = StructuralObject.SetValidValue(value, true);
    ReportPropertyChanged("Isbn");
    OnIsbnChanged();
  }
}
private string _Isbn;
```

```
      partial void OnIsbnChanging(string value);
      partial void OnIsbnChanged();

      [XmlIgnoreAttribute()]
      [SoapIgnoreAttribute()]
      [DataMemberAttribute()]
      [EdmRelationshipNavigationPropertyAttribute("BooksModel", "BooksAuthors",
          "Authors")]
      public EntityCollection<Author> Authors
      {
        get
        {
          return ((IEntityWithRelationships)this).RelationshipManager.
              GetRelatedCollection<Author>("BooksModel.BooksAuthors", "Authors");
        }
        set
        {
          if ((value != null))
          {
            ((IEntityWithRelationships)this).RelationshipManager.
                InitializeRelatedCollection<Author>("BooksModel.BooksAuthors",
                "Authors", value);
          }
        }
      }
    }
  }
```

The classes and interfaces that are important to entity classes are explained in the following table. With the exception of INotifyPropertyChanging and INotifyPropertyChanged, the types are defined in the namespace System.Data.Objects.DataClasses.

CLASS OR INTERFACE	DESCRIPTION
StructuralObject	The base class of the classes EntityObject and ComplexObject. This class implements the interfaces INotifyPropertyChanging and INotifyPropertyChanged.
INotifyPropertyChanging INotifyPropertyChanged	These interfaces define the PropertyChanging and PropertyChanged events to enable subscribing to information when the state of the object changes. Unlike the other classes and interfaces here, these interfaces are defined in the namespace System.ComponentModel.
EntityObject	This class derives from StructuralObject and implements the interfaces IEntityWithKey, IEntityWithChangeTracker, and IEntityWithRelationships. EntityObject is a commonly used base class for objects mapped to database tables that contain a primary key and relationships to other objects.
ComplexObject	You can use this class as a base class for entity objects that do not have a primary key. It derives from StructuralObject but does not implement other interfaces as the EntityObject class does.
IEntityWithKey	This interface defines an EntityKey property that enables fast access to the object.
IEntityWithChangeTracker	This interface defines the method SetChangeTracker whereby a change tracker that implements the interface IChangeTracker can be assigned to get information about state change from the object.
IEntityWithRelationships	This interface defines the read-only property RelationshipManager, which returns a RelationshipManager object that can be used to navigate between objects.

> **NOTE** *For an entity class, it's not necessary to derive from the base classes* `EntityObject` *or* `ComplexObject`. *An entity class can implement the required interfaces, and POCO objects, discussed later in the section "Using POCO Objects," are supported as well.*

The `Book` entity class can easily be accessed by using the object context class `BooksEntities`. The `Books` property returns a collection of `Book` objects that can be iterated (code file `BooksDemo/Program.cs`)

```
using (var data = new BooksEntities())
{
  foreach (var book in data.Books)
  {
    Console.WriteLine("{0}, {1}", book.Title, book.Publisher);
  }
}
```

OBJECT CONTEXT

To retrieve data from the database, the `ObjectContext` class is needed. This class defines the mapping from the entity objects to the database. With core ADO.NET, you can compare this class to the data adapter that fills a `DataSet`.

The `BooksEntities` class created by the designer derives from the base class `ObjectContext`. This class adds constructors to pass a connection string. With the default constructor, the connection string is read from the configuration file. It is also possible to pass an already opened connection to the constructor in the form of an `EntityConnection` instance. If you pass a connection to the constructor that is not opened, the object context opens and closes the connection; if you pass an opened connection, you also need to close it.

The created class defines `Books` and `Authors` properties, which return an `ObjectSet<TEntity>`. `ObjectSet<TEntity>` derives from `ObjectQuery<TEntity>` (code file `BooksDemo/BooksModel.Designer.cs`):

```
public partial class BooksEntities : ObjectContext
{
  public BooksEntities() : base("name=BooksEntities", "BooksEntities")
  {
    this.ContextOptions.LazyLoadingEnabled = true;
    OnContextCreated();
  }
  public BooksEntities(string connectionString)
    : base(connectionString, "BooksEntities")
  {
    this.ContextOptions.LazyLoadingEnabled = true;
    OnContextCreated();
  }
  public BooksEntities(EntityConnection connection)
    : base(connection, "BooksEntities")
  {
    this.ContextOptions.LazyLoadingEnabled = true;
    OnContextCreated();
  }

  partial void OnContextCreated();

  public ObjectSet<Author> Authors
  {
```

```
      get
      {
        if ((_Authors == null))
        {
          _Authors = base.CreateObjectSet<Author>("Authors");
        }
        return _Authors;
      }
    }
    private ObjectSet<Author> _Authors;

    public ObjectSet<Book> Books
    {
      get
      {
        if ((_Books == null))
        {
          _Books = base.CreateObjectSet<Book>("Books");
        }
        return _Books;
      }
    }
    private ObjectSet<Book> _Books;
  }
```

The `ObjectContext` class provides several services to the caller:

➤ It keeps track of entity objects that are already retrieved. If the object is queried again, it is taken from the object context.

➤ It keeps state information about the entities. You can get information about added, modified, and deleted objects.

➤ You can update the entities from the object context to write the changes to the underlying store.

Methods and properties of the `ObjectContext` class are listed in the following table:

METHOD OR PROPERTY	DESCRIPTION
Connection	This property returns a `DbConnection` object that is associated with the object context.
MetadataWorkspace	This property returns a `MetadataWorkspace` object that can be used to read the metadata and mapping information.
QueryTimeout	With this property you can get and set the timeout value for the queries of the object context.
ObjectStateManager	This property returns an `ObjectStateManager`. The `ObjectStateManager` keeps track of entity objects retrieved and object changes in the object context.
CreateQuery()	This method returns an `ObjectQuery` to get data from the store. The `Books` and `Authors` properties shown earlier use this method to return an `ObjectQuery`.
GetObjectByKey() TryGetObjectByKey()	These methods return the object by the primary key either from the object state manager or the underlying store. `GetObjectByKey` throws an exception of type `ObjectNotFoundException` if the primary key does not exist. `TryGetObjectByKey` returns `false`.
AddObject()	This method adds a new entity object to the object context.
DeleteObject()	This method deletes an object from the object context.

METHOD OR PROPERTY	DESCRIPTION
Detach()	This method detaches an entity object from the object context, so it is no longer tracked if changes occur.
Attach() AttachTo()	The Attach method attaches a detached object to the store. Attaching objects back to the object context requires that the entity object implements the interface IEntityWithKey. The AttachTo method does not have the requirement for a key with the object, but it requires the entity set name to which the entity object needs to be attached.
ApplyPropertyChanges()	If an object was detached from the object context, then the detached object is modified, and afterward the changes should be applied to the object within the object context, you can invoke the ApplyPropertyChanges method to apply the changes. This is useful in a scenario where a detached object was returned from a web service, changed by a client, and passed to the web service in a modified way.
Refresh()	The data in the store can change while entity objects are stored inside the object context. To make a refresh from the store, the Refresh method can be used. With this method you can pass a RefreshMode enumeration value. If the values for the objects are not the same between the store and the object context, passing the value ClientWins changes the data in the store. The value StoreWins changes the data in the object context.
SaveChanges()	Adding, modifying, and deleting objects from the object context does not change the object from the underlying store. Use the SaveChanges method to persist the changes to the store.
AcceptAllChanges()	This method changes the state of the objects in the context to unmodified. SaveChanges invokes this method implicitly.

RELATIONSHIPS

The entity types Book and Author are related to each other. A book can be written by one or more authors, and an author can write one or more books. Relationships are based on the count of types they relate and the multiplicity. The ADO.NET Entity Framework supports several kinds of relationships, some of which are described here, including table-per-hierarchy (TPH) and table-per-type (TPT). Multiplicity can be one-to-one, one-to-many, or many-to-many.

Table per Hierarchy

With TPH, there's one table in the database that corresponds to a hierarchy of entity classes. For example, the database table Payments shown in Figure 33-3 contains columns for a hierarchy of entity types. Some of the columns are common to all entities in the hierarchy, such as Id and Amount. The Number column is used only by a credit card payment and a check payment.

The entity classes that all map to the same Payments table are shown in Figure 33-4. Payment is an abstract base class to contain properties common to all types in the hierarchy. Concrete classes that derive from Payment are CreditCardPayment, CashPayment, and CheckPayment. CreditCardPayment has a CreditCard property in addition to the properties of the base class; ChequePayment has BankName and BankAccount properties.

FIGURE 33-3

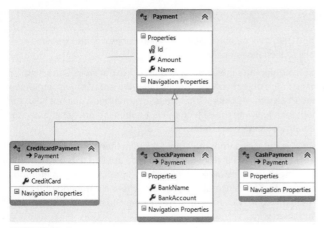

FIGURE 33-4

This mapping can be defined with the designer. The mapping details can be configured with the Mapping Details dialog shown in Figure 33-5. Selection of the concrete class type is done based on a `Condition` element as defined with the option Maps to Payments When Type = CREDITCARD. The type is selected based on the value of the `Type` column. Other options to select the type are also possible; for example, you can verify whether a column is not null.

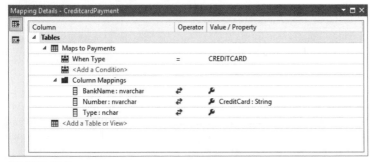

FIGURE 33-5

Now it's possible to iterate the data from the `Payments` table, and different types are returned based on the mapping (code file `PaymentsDemo/Program.cs`):

```
using (var data = new PaymentsEntities())
{
  foreach (var p in data.Payments)
  {
    Console.WriteLine("{0}, {1} - {2:C}", p.GetType().Name, p.Name,
        p.Amount);
  }
}
```

Running the application returns two `CashPayment` and one `CreditCardPayment` objects from the database:

```
CreditCardPayment, Gladstone - $22.00
CashPayment, Donald - $0.50
CashPayment, Scrooge - $80,000.00
```

Using the OfType method offers an easy way to get the result from a specific type:

```
foreach (var p in data.Payments.OfType<CreditcardPayment>())
{
    Console.WriteLine("{0} {1} {2}", p.Name, p.Amount, p.CreditCard);
}
```

The T-SQL statement that's generated from this query is very efficient to filter the type with the WHERE clause because it is defined from the model:

```
SELECT
'0X0X' AS [C1],
[Extent1].[Id] AS [Id],
[Extent1].[Amount] AS [Amount],
[Extent1].[Name] AS [Name],
[Extent1].[Number] AS [Number]
FROM [dbo].[Payments] AS [Extent1]
WHERE [Extent1].[Type] = N'CREDITCARD'
```

Table per Type

With TPT, one table maps to one type. The Formula1 database has a schema with the tables Racers, RaceResults, Races, and Circuits. The RaceResults table has a relationship with the Racers table with the foreign key RacerId; the Races table relates to the Circuits table with the foreign key CircuitId.

Figure 33-6 shows the entity types Racer, RaceResult, Race, and Circuit. There are several one-to-many relationships.

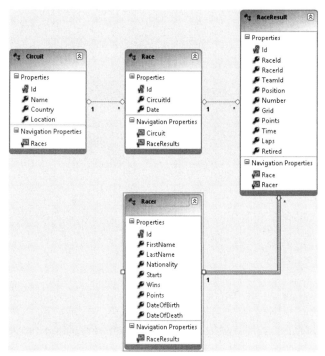

FIGURE 33-6

You access the customers and their orders with two iterations shown in the next code block (Formula1Demo/Program.cs). First, the Racer objects are accessed, and the values of the FirstName and LastName properties are written to the console. Then all race results are accessed by using the RaceResults property of the Racer class. The related orders are lazy loaded to access the property because with the ObjectContext, the ContextOptions.LazyLoadingEnabled property is set to true:

```
using (var data = new Formula1Entities())
{
  foreach (var racer in data.Racers)
  {
    Console.WriteLine("{0} {1}", racer.FirstName, racer.LastName);
    foreach (var raceResult in racer.RaceResults)
    {
      Console.WriteLine("\t{0} {1:d} {2}", raceResult.Race.Circuit.Name,
        raceResult.Race.Date,  raceResult.Position);
    }
  }
}
```

Behind the scenes, the RelationshipManager class is used to access the relationship. The RelationShipManager instance can be accessed by casting the entity object to the interface IEntityWithRelationships as you can see in the designer-generated property Orders from the class Customer (code file Formula1Demo/Formula1Model.Designer.cs). This interface is explicitly implemented by the class EntityObject. The RelationshipManager property returns a RelationshipManager that is associated with the entity object at one end. The other end is defined by invoking the method GetRelatedCollection. The first parameter Formula1Model.FK_RaceResults_Racers is the name of the relationship: the second parameter RaceResults defines the name of the target role:

```
public EntityCollection<RaceResult> RaceResults
{
  get
  {
    return ((IEntityWithRelationships)this).RelationshipManager
        .GetRelatedCollection<RaceResult>(
        "Formula1Model.FK_RaceResults_Racers", "RaceResults");
  }
  set
  {
    if ((value != null))
    {
      ((IEntityWithRelationships)this).RelationshipManager
          .InitializeRelatedCollection<RaceResult>(
          "Formula1Model.FK_RaceResults_Racers", "RaceResults", value);
    }
  }
}
```

Lazy, Delayed, and Eager Loading

With the designer's default setting, relationships are lazy loaded on request. The designer sets the property LazyLoadingEnabled from the ContextOptions to true. You have other options as well. Relationships can also be *eager loaded* or *delayed loaded*.

Eager loading means that the relationship is loaded at the same time the parent objects are loaded. The race results, the associated race with the race result, and the associated circuit with the race are loaded immediately after adding a call to the Include method. The Include method is available with ObjectSet<TEntity> types (the Racers property is of type ObjectSet<Racer>), and receives the relationship name. Accessing the `RaceResults` property in the `foreach` loop you can see that all the information up to the circuit information is shown:

```
foreach (var racer in data.Racers.Include("RaceResults.Race.Circuit"))
{
  Console.WriteLine("{0} {1}", racer.FirstName, racer.LastName);
  foreach (var raceResult in racer.RaceResults)
  {
    Console.WriteLine("\t{0} {1:d} {2}", raceResult.Race.Circuit.Name,
        raceResult.Race.Date,  raceResult.Position);
  }
}
```

Eager loading has the advantage that if all related objects are needed, then fewer requests to the database are made. Of course, if not all related objects are needed, lazy or delayed loading is preferred.

Delayed loading needs an explicit call to the `Load` method of the `EntityCollection<T>` class. Using this method, the option `LazyLoadingEnabled` can be set to `false`. With the following code snippet, the orders are loaded with the `Load` method if they are not loaded with the `IsLoaded` property:

```
if (!racer.RaceResults.IsLoaded)
    racer.RaceResult.Load();
```

One overload of the `Load` method accepts a `MergeOption` enumeration. The possible values are explained in the following table:

MERGEOPTION VALUE	DESCRIPTION
`AppendOnly`	This is the default value. New entities are appended; existing entities in the object context are not modified.
`NoTracking`	The `ObjectStateManager` that tracks changes to entity objects is not modified.
`OverwriteChanges`	The current values of the entity objects are replaced with the values from the store.
`PreserveChanges`	The original values of the entity objects in the object context are replaced with the values from the store.

QUERYING DATA

The Entity Framework offers several ways to query the data: Entity SQL, which is an extension to T-SQL; using helper methods to create Entity SQL; and LINQ. All of these variants are discussed in this section.

Entity SQL

Entity SQL enhances T-SQL by adding types. This syntax doesn't require joins because associations of entities can be used instead. You can use EntityClient, a low-level API to access the Entity Framework. This API is implemented as an ADO.NET provider. EntityClient offers `EntityConnection`, `EntityCommand`, `EntityParameter`, and `EntityDataReader` classes that derive from the base classes `DbConnection`, `DbCommand`, `DbParameter`, and `DbDataReader`.

You can use these classes in the same way that you would use the ADO.NET classes described in Chapter 32, except that a special connection string is required and Entity SQL is used instead of T-SQL to access the EDM.

The connection to the database is done with the `EntityConnection`, which requires an entity connection string. This string is read from the configuration file with the help of the `ConfigurationManager` class from the `System.Configuration` namespace. The `CreateCommand` method of the `EntityConnection` class returns an `EntityCommand`. The command text for the `EntityCommand` is assigned with the `CommandText` property and requires Entity SQL syntax. `Formula1Entities.Racers` is defined within the `EntityContainer` element in the `Formula1Entities` CSDL definition, and the `Racers EntitySet` gets all racers from the Racers table. `Command.ExecuteReader` returns a data reader that reads row by row (code file `QueryDemo/Program.cs`):

```
string connectionString =
    ConfigurationManager.ConnectionStrings["Formula1Entities"]
    .ConnectionString;
var connection = new EntityConnection(connectionString);
await connection.OpenAsync();
EntityCommand command = connection.CreateCommand();
command.CommandText = "[Formula1Entities].[Racers]";
DbDataReader reader = await command.ExecuteReaderAsync(
    CommandBehavior.SequentialAccess | CommandBehavior.CloseConnection);
while (await reader.ReadAsync())
{
    Console.WriteLine("{0} {1}", reader["FirstName"], reader["LastName"]);
}
reader.Close();
```

Let's look at a few more Entity SQL syntax options. Here, just a few are shown to help you get started with Entity SQL. In the MSDN documentation you can find the complete reference.

The preceding example showed how Entity SQL uses definitions from the CSDL in the `EntityContainer` and `EntitySet`—for example, `Formula1Entities.Racers` to get all the racers from the table Racers.

Instead of retrieving all columns, you can also use the `Property` elements of an `EntityType`. This might look very similar to the T-SQL queries used in the previous chapter:

```
EntityCommand command = connection.CreateCommand();
command.CommandText =
    "SELECT Racers.FirstName, Racers.LastName FROM Formula1Entities.Racers";
DbDataReader reader = await command.ExecuteReaderAsync(
    CommandBehavior.SequentialAccess | CommandBehavior.CloseConnection);
while (await reader.ReadAsync())
{
    Console.WriteLine("{0} {1}", reader.GetString(0), reader.GetString(1));
}
reader.Close();
```

There's no `SELECT *` with Entity SQL. All the columns were retrieved earlier by requesting the `EntitySet`. Using `SELECT VALUE` you can also get all the columns, as shown in the next snippet. This code uses a filter with `WHERE` to retrieve only specific publishers with the query. Note that the `CommandText` specifies the parameter with the `@` character—however, the parameter that is added to the `Parameters` collection does not use the `@` character to write a value to the same parameter:

```
EntityCommand command = connection.CreateCommand();
command.CommandText =
    "SELECT VALUE it FROM [Formula1Entities].[Racers] AS it " +
    "WHERE it.Nationality = @Country";
command.Parameters.AddWithValue("Country", "Austria");
```

Now let's change to the object context and the mapping functionality but stay with Entity SQL. Entity SQL can be created a lot easier with the help of query builder methods, as discussed next.

Object Query

You can define queries with the `ObjectQuery<T>` class, or the class that derives from it: `ObjectSet<T>`. The following example (code file `Formula1Demo/Program.cs`) demonstrates a simple query to access all `Racer` entities. The `Racers` property of the generated `Formula1Entities` class returns an `ObjectSet<Racer>`:

```
using (Formula1Entities data = new Formula1Entities())
{
  ObjectSet<Racer> racers = data.Racers;
  Console.WriteLine(racers.CommandText);
  Console.WriteLine(racers.ToTraceString());
}
```

The Entity SQL statement that is returned from the `CommandText` property is shown here:

```
[Formula1Entities].[Racers]
```

This was exactly the statement that you used earlier with the `EntityCommand` object. What about the T-SQL statement that is sent to the database? This is shown by the `ToTraceString` method:

```
SELECT
[Extent1].[Id] AS [Id],
[Extent1].[FirstName] AS [FirstName],
[Extent1].[LastName] AS [LastName],
[Extent1].[Nationality] AS [Nationality],
[Extent1].[Starts] AS [Starts],
[Extent1].[Wins] AS [Wins],
[Extent1].[Points] AS [Points],
[Extent1].[DateOfBirth] AS [DateOfBirth],
[Extent1].[DateOfDeath] AS [DateOfDeath]
```

Instead of accessing the `Racers` property from the object context, you can also create a query with the `CreateQuery` method:

```
ObjectQuery<Racer> racers =
    data.CreateQuery<Racer>("[Formula1Entities].[Racers]");
```

This is similar to using the `Racers` property.

Now it would be interesting to filter the racers based on a condition. This can be done by using the `Where` method of the `ObjectQuery<T>` class. `Where` is one of the query builder methods that creates Entity SQL. This method requires a predicate as a string, and optional parameters of type `ObjectParameter`. The predicate shown in the following example specifies that only racers from Brazil should be returned. The `it` specifies the item of the result and `Country` is the column `Country`. The first parameter of the `ObjectParameter` constructor references the `@Country` parameter of the predicate but doesn't list the @ sign:

```
string country = "Brazil";
ObjectQuery<Racer> racers = data.Racers.Where("it.Country = @Country",
  new ObjectParameter("Country", country));
```

The magic behind `it` can be seen immediately by accessing the `CommandText` property of the query. With Entity SQL, `SELECT VALUE it` declares `it` as the variable to access the columns:

```
SELECT VALUE it
FROM (
[Formula1Entities].[Racers]
) AS it
WHERE
it.Nationality = @Country
```

The method `ToTraceString` shows the generated SQL statement:

```
SELECT
[Extent1].[Id] AS [Id],
[Extent1].[FirstName] AS [FirstName],
[Extent1].[LastName] AS [LastName],
[Extent1].[Nationality] AS [Nationality],
[Extent1].[Starts] AS [Starts],
[Extent1].[Wins] AS [Wins],
[Extent1].[Points] AS [Points],
[Extent1].[DateOfBirth] AS [DateOfBirth],
[Extent1].[DateOfDeath] AS [DateOfDeath]
FROM [dbo].[Racers] AS [Extent1]
WHERE [Extent1].[Nationality] = @Country
```

Of course, you can also specify the complete Entity SQL:

```
string country = "Brazil";
ObjectQuery<Racer> racers = data.CreateQuery<Racer>(
  "SELECT VALUE it FROM ([Formula1Entities].[Racers]) AS it " +
  "WHERE it.Nationality = @Country",
  new ObjectParameter("Country", country));
```

The class `ObjectQuery<T>` offers several query builder methods, as described in the following table. Many of these methods are very similar to the LINQ extension methods covered in Chapter 11, "Language Integrated Query." An important difference with the methods here is that instead of parameters of type `delegate` or `Expression<T>`, the parameter type with `ObjectQuery<T>` is usually of type `string`.

OBJECTQUERY<T> QUERY BUILDER METHOD	DESCRIPTION
`Where`	Enables you to filter the results based on a condition.
`Distinct`	Creates a query with unique results.
`Except`	Returns the result without the items that meet the condition with the `except` filter.
`GroupBy`	Creates a new query to group entities based on a specified criterion.
`Include`	With relations, you saw earlier that related items are delay loaded. It is required to invoke the `Load` method of the `EntityCollection<T>` class to get related entities into the object context. Instead of using the `Load` method, you can specify a query with the `Include` method to eager fetch-related entities.
`OfType`	Specifies returning only those entities of a specific type. This is very helpful with TPH relations.
`OrderBy`	Defines the sort order of the entities.
`Select` `SelectValue`	These methods return a projection of the results. `Select` returns the result items in the form of a `DbDataRecord`; `SelectValue` returns the values as scalars or complex types as defined by the generic parameter `TResultType`.
`Skip` `Top`	These methods are useful for paging. Skip a number of items with the `Skip` method, and take a specified number as defined by the `Top` method.
`Intersect` `Union` `UnionAll`	These methods are used to combine two queries. `Intersect` returns a query containing only the results that are available in both of the queries. `Union` combines the queries and returns the complete result without duplicates. `UnionAll` also includes duplicates.

The following example (code file `QueryDemo/Program.cs`) demonstrates how to use these query builder methods. Here, the racers are filtered with the `Where` method to return only racers from the USA; the `OrderBy` method specifies descending sort order, first based on the number of wins and next on the number of starts. Finally, using the `Top` method, only the first three racers are returned in the result:

```
using (var data = new Formula1Entities())
{
  string country = "USA";
  ObjectQuery<Racer> racers = data.Racers.Where("it.Nationality = @Country",
      new ObjectParameter("Country", country))
      .OrderBy("it.Wins DESC, it.Starts DESC")
      .Top("3");
  foreach (var racer in racers)
  {
    Console.WriteLine("{0} {1}, wins: {2}, starts: {3}",
        racer.FirstName, racer.LastName, racer.Wins, racer.Starts);
  }
}
```

This is the result from the preceding query:

```
Mario Andretti, wins: 12, starts: 128
Dan Gurney, wins: 4, starts: 87
Phil Hill, wins: 3, starts: 48
```

LINQ to Entities

In several chapters of this book, you've seen LINQ to Query objects, databases, and XML. Of course, LINQ is also available to query entities. With LINQ to Entities, the source for the LINQ query is `ObjectQuery<T>`. Because `ObjectQuery<T>` implements the interface `IQueryable`, the extension methods selected for the query are defined with the class `Queryable` from the namespace `System.Linq`. The extension methods defined with this class have a parameter `Expression<T>`; that's why the compiler writes an expression tree to the assembly. You can read more about expression trees in Chapter 11. The expression tree is then resolved from the `ObjectQuery<T>` class to the SQL query.

As shown in the following example (code file `QueryDemo/Program.cs`), you can use a simple LINQ query to return the racers who won more than 40 races:

```
using (var data = new Formula1Entities())
{
  var racers = from r in data.Racers
               where r.Wins > 40
               orderby r.Wins descending
               select r;
  foreach (Racer r in racers)
  {
    Console.WriteLine("{0} {1}", r.FirstName, r.LastName);
  }
}
```

This is the result of accessing the Formula1 database:

```
Michael Schumacher
Alain Prost
Ayrton Senna
```

You can also define a LINQ query to access relationships, as shown in the next example. Variable `r` references racers, variable `rr` references all race results. The filter is defined with the `where` clause to retrieve only racers from Switzerland who had a race position on the podium. To get the podium finishes, the result is grouped, and the podium count calculated. Sorting is done based on the podium finishes:

```
using (var data = new Formula1Entities())
{
    var query = from r in data.Racers
                from rr in r.RaceResults
                where rr.Position <= 3 && rr.Position >= 1 &&
                      r.Nationality == "Switzerland"
                group r by r.Id into g
                let podium = g.Count()
                orderby podium descending
                select new
                {
                    Racer = g.FirstOrDefault(),
                    Podiums = podium
                };
    foreach (var r in query)
    {
        Console.WriteLine("{0} {1} {2}", r.Racer.FirstName, r.Racer.LastName,
                          r.Podiums);
    }
}
```

The names of three racers from Switzerland are returned when you run the application:

```
Clay Regazzoni 28
Jo Siffert 6
Rudi Fischer 2
```

WRITING DATA TO THE DATABASE

Reading, searching, and filtering data from the store are just one part of the work that usually needs to be done with data-intensive applications. Writing changed data back to the store is the other part you need to know. This section covers object tracking, a service and foundation of the object context, how the object context knows about changes of the objects, how to attach and detach objects from the context, and how the object context makes use of the state of objects to save entity objects.

Object Tracking

To enable data read from the store to be modified and saved, the entities must be tracked after they are loaded. This also requires that the object context be aware of whether an entity has already been loaded from the store. If multiple queries are accessing the same records, the object context needs to return already loaded entities. The `ObjectStateManager` is used by the object context to keep track of entities that are loaded into the context.

The following example demonstrates that indeed if two different queries return the same record from the database, the state manager is aware of that and does not create a new entity. Instead, the same entity is returned. The `ObjectStateManager` instance that is associated with the object context can be accessed with the `ObjectStateManager` property. The `ObjectStateManager` class defines an event named `ObjectStateManagerChanged` that is invoked every time a new object is added or removed from the object context. Here, the method `ObjectStateManager_ObjectStateManagerChanged` is assigned to the event to get information about changes.

Two different queries are used to return an entity object. The first query gets the first racer from the country Austria with the last name Lauda. The second query asks for the racers from Austria, sorts the racers by the number of races won, and gets the first result. As a matter of fact, that's the same racer. To verify that the same entity object is returned, the method `Object.ReferenceEquals` is used to verify whether the two object references indeed reference the same instance (code file `QueryDemo/Program.cs`):

```
private static void TrackingDemo()
{
  using (var data = new Formula1Entities())
  {
    data.ObjectStateManager.ObjectStateManagerChanged +=
      ObjectStateManager_ObjectStateManagerChanged;

    Racer niki1 = (from r in data.Racers
                   where r.Nationality == "Austria" && r.LastName == "Lauda"
                   select r).First();

    Racer niki2 = (from r in data.Racers
                   where r.Nationality == "Austria"
                   orderby r.Wins descending
                   select r).First();

    if (Object.ReferenceEquals(niki1, niki2))
    {
      Console.WriteLine("the same object");
    }
  }
}

private static void ObjectStateManager_ObjectStateManagerChanged(
    object sender, CollectionChangeEventArgs e)
{
  Console.WriteLine("Object State change — action: {0}", e.Action);
  Racer r = e.Element as Racer;
  if (r != null)
    Console.WriteLine("Racer {0}", r.LastName);
}
```

Running the application, you can see that the event of the `ObjectStateManagerChanged` of the `ObjectStateManager` occurs only once, and the references `niki1` and `niki2` are indeed the same:

```
Object State change — action: Add
Racer Lauda
The same object
```

Change Information

The object context is also aware of changes with the entities. The following example adds and modifies a racer from the object context and gets information about the change. First, a new racer is added with the `AddObject` method of the `ObjectSet<T>` class. This method adds a new entity with the `EntityState .Added` information. Next, a racer with the `Lastname` Alonso is queried. With this entity class, the `Starts` property is incremented and thus the entity is marked with the information `EntityState.Modified`. Behind the scenes, the `ObjectStateManager` is informed about a state change in the object based on the interface implementation's `INotifyPropertyChanged`. This interface is implemented in the entity base class `StructuralObject`. The `ObjectStateManager` is attached to the `PropertyChanged` event, and this event is fired with every property change.

To get all added or modified entity objects, you can invoke the GetObjectStateEntries method of the ObjectStateManager and pass an EntityState enumeration value as it is done here. This method returns a collection of ObjectStateEntry objects that keeps information about the entities. The helper method DisplayState iterates through this collection to provide detail information.

You can also get state information about a single entity by passing the EntityKey to the GetObjectStateEntry method. The EntityKey property is available with entity objects implementing the interface IEntityWithKey, which is the case with the base class EntityObject. The ObjectStateEntry object returned offers the method GetModifiedProperties for reading all property values that have been changed, and you can access the original and the current information about the properties with the OriginalValues and CurrentValues indexers (code file Formula1Demo/Program.cs):

```csharp
private static void ChangeInformation()
{
  using (var data = new Formula1Entities())
  {
    var jean = new Racer
    {
      FirstName = "Jean-Eric",
      LastName = "Vergne",
      Nationality = "France",
      Starts = 0
    };
    data.Racers.AddObject(jean);
    Racer fernando = data.Racers.Where("it.Lastname='Alonso'").First();
    fernando.Starts++;
    DisplayState(EntityState.Added.ToString(),
        data.ObjectStateManager.GetObjectStateEntries(EntityState.Added));
    DisplayState(EntityState.Modified.ToString(),
        data.ObjectStateManager.GetObjectStateEntries(EntityState.Modified));
    ObjectStateEntry stateOfFernando =
        data.ObjectStateManager.GetObjectStateEntry(fernando.EntityKey);
    Console.WriteLine("state of Fernando: {0}",
                stateOfFernando.State.ToString());
    foreach (string modifiedProp in stateOfFernando.GetModifiedProperties())
    {
      Console.WriteLine("modified: {0}", modifiedProp);
      Console.WriteLine("original: {0}",
                      stateOfFernando.OriginalValues[modifiedProp]);
      Console.WriteLine("current: {0}",
                      stateOfFernando.CurrentValues[modifiedProp]);
    }
  }
}

static void DisplayState(string state, IEnumerable<ObjectStateEntry> entries)
{
  foreach (var entry in entries)
  {
    var r = entry.Entity as Racer;
    if (r != null)
    {
      Console.WriteLine("{0}: {1}", state, r.Lastname);
    }
  }
}
```

When you run the application, the added and modified racers are displayed, and the changed properties are shown with their original and current values:

```
Added: Vergne
Modified: Alonso
state of Fernando: Modified
modified: Starts
original: 181
current: 182
```

Attaching and Detaching Entities

When returning entity data to the caller, it might be important to detach the objects from the object context. This is necessary, for example, if an entity object is returned from a web service. In this case, if the entity object is changed on the client, the object context is not aware of the change.

With the sample code, the `Detach` method of the `ObjectContext` detaches the entity named `fernando` and thus the object context is not aware of any change to this entity. If a changed entity object is passed from the client application to the service, it can be attached again. Just attaching it to the object context might not be enough, however, because it doesn't indicate that the object was modified. Instead, the original object must be available inside the object context. The original object can be accessed from the store by using the key with the method `GetObjectByKey` or `TryGetObjectByKey`. If the entity object is already inside the object context, the existing one is used; otherwise it is fetched newly from the database. Invoking the method `ApplyCurrentValues` passes the modified entity object to the object context; if there are changes, then the changes are made within the existing entity with the same key inside the object context, and the `EntityState` is set to `EntityState.Modified`. Remember that the method `ApplyCurrentValues` requires the object to exist within the object context; otherwise the new entity object is added with `EntityState.Added` (code file `Formula1Demo/Program.cs`):

```
using (var data = new Formula1Entities())
{
  data.ObjectStateManager.ObjectStateManagerChanged +=
      ObjectStateManager_ObjectStateManagerChanged;
  ObjectQuery<Racer> racers = data.Racers.Where("it.Lastname='Alonso'");
  Racer fernando = racers.First();
  EntityKey key = fernando.EntityKey;
  data.Racers.Detach(fernando);
  // Racer is now detached and can be changed independent of the
  // object context
  fernando.Starts++;
  Racer originalObject = data.GetObjectByKey(key) as Racer;
  data.Racers.ApplyCurrentValues(fernando);
}
```

Storing Entity Changes

Based on all the change information provided with the help of the `ObjectStateManager`, the added, deleted, and modified entity objects can be written to the store with the `SaveChanges` method of the `ObjectContext` class. To verify changes within the object context, you can assign a handler method to the `SavingChanges` event of the `ObjectContext` class. This event is fired before the data is written to the store, so you can add some verification logic to determine whether the changes should be done. `SaveChanges` returns the number of entity objects that have been written.

What happens if the records in the database that are represented by the entity classes have been changed after reading the record? The answer depends on the `ConcurrencyMode` property that is set with the model. With every property of an entity object, you can configure the `ConcurrencyMode` to `Fixed` or

None. The value `Fixed` means that the property is validated at write time to confirm that the value was not changed in the meantime. `None`, which is the default, ignores any change. If some properties are configured to the `Fixed` mode, and data changed between reading and writing the entity objects, an `OptimisticConcurrencyException` occurs.

You can deal with this exception by invoking the `Refresh` method to read the actual information from the database into the object context. This method accepts two refresh modes configured by a `RefreshMode` enumeration value: `ClientWins` or `StoreWins`. `StoreWins` means that the actual information is taken from the database and set to the current values of the entity objects. `ClientWins` means that the database information is set to the original values of the entity objects, and thus the database values will be over-written with the next `SaveChanges`. The second parameter of the `Refresh` method is either a collection of entity objects or a single entity object. You can specify the refresh behavior entity by entity (code file `Formula1Demo/Program.cs`):

```
private static void ChangeInformation()
{
    //...
        int changes = 0;
        try
        {
            changes += data.SaveChanges();
        }
        catch (OptimisticConcurrencyException ex)
        {
            data.Refresh(RefreshMode.ClientWins, ex.StateEntries);
            changes += data.SaveChanges();
        }
        Console.WriteLine("{0} entities changed", changes);
        //...
```

USING POCO OBJECTS

If you do not want to derive the entity classes from the base class `EntityObject`—for example, if you have an existing library with your own POCO (Plain Old CLR Objects) classes—you can use these classes as well. Another scenario for using POCO objects is if you want to send the objects directly across a WCF service.

The sample application that makes use of POCO objects is the same database used previously, which includes the `Books`, `Authors`, and `BooksAuthors` tables. The EDM is created as before. However, now the designer property Code Generation Strategy is changed from `Default` to `None`. This way, instead of creating entity objects that derive from the `EntityObject` base class, no code is generated at all.

Defining Entity Types

Now entity objects can be created manually as shown in the following code snippet (code file `POCODemo/Book.cs`). The entity objects just need simple properties to map scalar properties from the CSDL definition. To map navigation properties, properties of `ICollection<T>` are used. The object behind the navigation property is of type `HashSet<T>`:

```
public class Book
{
    public Book()
    {
        this.Authors = new HashSet<Author>();
    }

    public int Id { get; set; }
```

```
public string Title { get; set; }
public string Publisher { get; set; }
public string Isbn { get; set; }

public virtual ICollection<Author> Authors { get; set; }
}
```

> **NOTE** A `HashSet<T>` *contains a list of distinct elements that is unordered.*
> *The* `HashSet<T>` *class is covered in Chapter 10, "Collections."*

The `Author` type is implemented similarly to the `Book` type (code file `POCODemo/Author.cs`):

```
public class Author
{
  public Author()
  {
    this.Books = new HashSet<Book>();
  }

  public int Id { get; set; }
  public string FirstName { get; set; }
  public string LastName { get; set; }

  public virtual ICollection<Book> Books { get; set; }
}
```

The navigation properties are implemented as virtual properties. This way, the `DbContext` creates a proxy that derives from the entity type to be used, instead of directly using the entity types. This makes features, such as lazy loading of navigation properties, possible. If the navigation properties are not declared virtual, a proxy type is not created, and the entity types are used directly.

> **NOTE** *If you have existing entity objects that should be used, and the property names don't match the column names in the database, you just need to change the CSDL information with the mapping.*

Creating the Data Context

Creating POCO objects manually, the context is not created automatically as well. However, it's an easy task to do. `BooksEntities` derives from the base class `DbContext` and defines properties for all the mapped types of type `DbSet<T>`. In earlier examples we've just used `ObjectContext` and `ObjectSet<T>` instead of `DbContext` and `DbSet<T>`. `DbContext` and `DbSet<T>` are wrappers of the other types and make dealing with context and set easier (code file `POCODemo/BooksEntities.cs`):

```
public class BooksEntities : DbContext
{
  public BooksEntities()
    : base("name=BooksEntities")
  {
  }

  public DbSet<Author> Authors { get; set; }
  public DbSet<Book> Books { get; set; }
}
```

> **NOTE** *Rather than create entity types and the data context manually, you can use a T4 template to generate the code. Meanwhile, code-generation items exist for various scenarios. You just have to select the context menu Add Code Generation Item… from the EDM designer and select between Entity Objects, Self-Tracking Entities, and the* `DbContext` *generator.*

Queries and Updates

Now you can use the context and entity types in the same way as before. LINQ queries can be used to retrieve data; properties of entity objects are filled by the name; and it's also possible to make some changes and save them to the database (code file `POCODemo/Program.cs`):

```
using (BooksEntities data = new BooksEntities())
{
  var books = data.Books.Include("Authors");
  foreach (var b in books)
  {
    Console.WriteLine("{0} {1}", b.Title, b.Publisher);
    foreach (var a in b.Authors)
    {
      Console.WriteLine("\t{0} {1}", a.FirstName, a.LastName);
    }
  }
}
```

> **NOTE** *Using a proxy to your generated entity types, you should create objects by using the* `Create` *method of the* `DbSet<T>`*. This way, a proxy is created that derives from your class, and a reference to the proxy is returned. Otherwise, injection of a proxy wouldn't be possible.*

USING THE CODE FIRST PROGRAMMING MODEL

The Entity Framework 5.0 offers another scenario to map objects to the database. With Code First there's no mapping definition consisting of CSDL, SSDL, and MSL at all. A convention-based mapping can be used. Code First uses convention based programming similar to ASP.NET MVC. With convention-based programming, conventions are used before configuration. For example, instead of using attributes or a configuration file to define a primary key, a property just needs to be named with `Id`, or the name needs to end with `Id`, e.g. `BooksId`. Such a property automatically maps to a primary key.

This section discusses defining entity types for Code First, creating an object context, and customizing the created database mapping.

Defining Entity Types

For this example, two entity types are defined, `Menu` and `MenuCard` as shown in Figure 33-7. A `Menu` is associated with one `MenuCard`, and a `MenuCard` contains references to all `Menus` within the card.

The definition of the `Menu` class is shown in the following code snippet (code file `CodeFirst/Menu.cs`). There's no specific mapping to database keys or any other

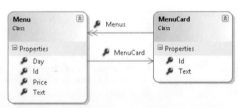

FIGURE 33-7

database-specific definition. It's just a convention. Because one property has the name Id, a primary key is created from this property. Naming the property MenuId would work as well. The MenuCard property is of type MenuCard. This is going to be a relationship.

```
public class Menu
{
  public int Id { get; set; }
  public string Text { get; set; }
  public decimal Price { get; set; }
  public DateTime? Day { get; set; }
  public MenuCard MenuCard { get; set; }
}
```

The MenuCard class looks very similar and has a Menus property that enables access to Menu objects associated with the MenuCard (code file CodeFirst/MenuCard.cs):

```
public class MenuCard
{
  public int Id { get; set; }
  public string Text { get; set; }
  public virtual ICollection<Menu> Menus { get; set; }
}
```

Creating the Data Context

Now a data context is needed. The MenuContext derives from the base class DbContext and defines properties for the tables in the same way shown earlier with POCO objects (code file CodeFirst/ MenuContext.cs):

```
public class MenuContext : DbContext
{
  public MenuContext()
  {
  }

  public DbSet<Menu> Menus { get; set; }
  public DbSet<MenuCard> MenuCards { get; set; }
}
```

Creating the Database and Storing Entities

Now, the data context can be used. The following example code (code file CodeFirst/Program.cs) adds objects: one MenuCard and two menu entries. Then the SaveChanges method of the DbContext is called to write the entries to the database:

```
using (var data = new MenuContext())
{
  MenuCard card = data.MenuCards.Create();
  card.Text = "Soups";
  data.MenuCards.Add(card);

  Menu m = data.Menus.Create();
  m.Text = "Baked Potato Soup";
  m.Price = 4.80M;
  m.Day = new DateTime(2012, 9, 20);
  m.MenuCard = card;
  data.Menus.Add(m);

  Menu m2 = data.Menus.Create();
```

```
                m2.Text = "Cheddar Broccoli Soup";
                m2.Price = 4.50M;
                m2.Day = new DateTime(2012, 9, 21);
                m2.MenuCard = card;
                data.Menus.Add(m2);

                try
                {
                    data.SaveChanges();
                }
                catch (Exception ex)
                {
                    Console.WriteLine(ex.Message);
                }
            }
        }
```

> **NOTE** *For the previous code, a connection string was never specified, nor was a database created. If the database doesn't exist, it is created.*

The Database

If the database doesn't exist, it is created. By default, the database is created with the server name—for example, in SQL Express, it would be `(local)\sqlexpress`. The database is assigned the name of the data context, including the namespace. With the sample application the database has the name `CodeFirstDemo.MenuContext`. The created tables, with their properties and relationships, are shown in Figure 33-8. For the "*-to-1" relationship between `Menus` and `MenuCards`, a foreign key `MenuCard_Id` is created in the Menus table. The `Day` column in the Menus table is defined to allow nulls because the entity type `Menu` defines this property to be nullable. The `Text` column is created with `nvarchar(max)` and allows null, as string is a reference type. The `Price` is a database float type and doesn't allow null. Value types are required, just if nullable value types are used, they are optional.

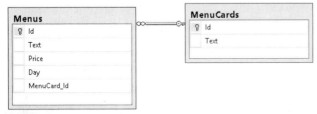

FIGURE 33-8

Query Data

The following example (code file `CodeFirst/Program.cs`) demonstrates reading the data from the database. After the context is created, menu cards are accessed in the outer `foreach` loop, and the inner `foreach` loop queries menus. Of course, you can also access the data using LINQ queries, which are translated to T-SQL by the context:

```
using (var data = new MenuContext())
{
    foreach (var card in data.MenuCards)
    {
        Console.WriteLine("{0}", card.Text);
```

```
                    foreach (var menu in card.Menus)
                    {
                      Console.WriteLine("\t{0} {1:d}", menu.Text, menu.Day);
                    }
                  }
                }
```

The `DbContext` has lazy loading enabled by default. Thus, first the menu cards are queried; and then with every request for the menus of the menu card, the `SELECT` statement to retrieve the menus is created. Similar to what you've seen before, you can do eager loading as well:

```
            data.Configuration.LazyLoadingEnabled = false;
            foreach (var card in data.MenuCards.Include("Menus"))
            {
              Console.WriteLine("{0}", card.Text);
              foreach (var menu in card.Menus)
              {
                Console.WriteLine("\t{0} {1:d}", menu.Text, menu.Day);
              }
            }
```

Customizing Database Generation

You can perform some simple customizations to generate the database, such as defining the database connection string. In the following code (code file `CodeFirst/MenuContext.cs`), the database connection string is assigned in the `MenuContext` class to a constructor of the base class `DbContext`. To define a connection string, the database with the specified name is created:

```
      public class MenuContext : DbContext
      {
        private const string connectionString =
            @"server=(local)\sqlexpress;database=WroxMenus;" +
            "trusted_connection=true";
        public MenuContext()
          : base(connectionString){ }
```

Data Annotations

To customize the generated tables, some attributes from the namespace `System.ComponentModel` `.DataAnnotations` can be used. The following example code (code file `CodeFirst/Menu.cs`) makes use of the `StringLengthAttribute` type. This way, the generated column type is `nvarchar(50)` instead of `nvarchar(max)`:

```
      public class Menu
      {
        public int Id { get; set; }
        [StringLength(50)] public string Text { get; set; }
        public double Price { get; set; }
        public DateTime? Day { get; set; }
        public MenuCard MenuCard { get; set; }
      }
```

Other attributes that can be used to customize entities are `Key`, to define other columns that don't have the `Id` in their name, `Timestamp`, to define the property as a row-version column, `ConcurrencyCheck`, to use the property for optimistic concurrency, and `Association`, to mark the property for a relationship.

Model Builder

Using only attributes to customize the generated tables and columns, you fast reach the limitations. There's a much more flexible option: using the model builder. The model builder offers a fluid API to customize tables, columns, and relationships.

Using the Code First development model you can get access to the model builder features with the `DbModelBuilder` class. With a context class deriving from `DbContext` you can override the method `OnModelCreating`. The method is invoked on creation of the database model. With this method, a model builder of type `DbModelBuilder` is received. With the model builder you can rename properties, change property types, define constraints, build relations, and do a lot more customization.

In the following code snippet (code file `CodeFirst/MenuContext.cs`), for the Menus table the `Price` column is changed to be of type `money`, the `Day` column of type `date`. The `Text` column is changed to have a maximum string length of 40, and it is set to required. The model builder uses a fluent API. The method `Entity` returns a `EntityTypeConfiguration`. Using the result of the `Entity` method, other methods of the `EntityTypeConfiguration` can be used. Using the `Price` property as a result of the Lambda expression with the `Property` method, this method returns a `DecimalPropertyConfiguration`. Using this, you can invoke the `HasColumnType` method, which sets the type for the database column to `money`. The `HasColumnType` method again returns a `DecimalPropertyConfiguration`, and it would be possible to continue there and invoke other methods for configuring the column.

As shown earlier for the `MenuCard` property in the `Menu` class, by default a foreign key named `MenuCard_Id` was created. Now the `Menu` class is extended by adding the property `MenuCardId` of type `int`. To use this property as a foreign key, the `HasForeignKey` method is used to assign the foreign key to the `MenuCardId` property. The last statement in the method `OnModelCreating` sets a cascading delete on the MenuCards table. If a row in the MenuCards table is deleted, all the menus with this ID should be deleted:

```
protected override void OnModelCreating(DbModelBuilder modelBuilder)
{
  modelBuilder.Entity<Menu>().Property(m => m.Price).HasColumnType("money");
  modelBuilder.Entity<Menu>().Property(m => m.Day).HasColumnType("date");
  modelBuilder.Entity<Menu>().Property(m => m.Text).HasMaxLength(40)
    .IsRequired();
  modelBuilder.Entity<Menu>().HasRequired(m => m.MenuCard)
    .WithMany(c => c.Menus).HasForeignKey(m => m.MenuCardId);
  modelBuilder.Entity<MenuCard>().Property(c => c.Text).HasMaxLength(30)
    .IsRequired();
  modelBuilder.Entity<MenuCard>().HasMany(c => c.Menus).WithRequired()
    .WillCascadeOnDelete();
}
```

SUMMARY

This chapter introduced you to the features of the ADO.NET Entity Framework, which is based on mapping that is defined by CSDL, MSL, and SSDL—XML information that describes the entities, the mapping, and the database schema. Using this mapping technique, you can create different relation types to map entity classes to database tables.

You've learned how the object context keeps knowledge about entities retrieved and updated, and how changes can be written to the store. You've also seen how using POCO objects enables you to use an existing object library to map the objects to the database, and how Code First enables a database to be created on the fly, with mapping information based on conventions.

LINQ to Entities is a facet of the ADO.NET Entity Framework that enables you to use the new query syntax to access entities.

The next chapter is on using XML as data source, creating and querying XML with LINQ to XML.

34

Manipulating XML

WROX.COM CODE DOWNLOADS FOR THIS CHAPTER

The wrox.com code downloads for this chapter are found at `http://www.wrox.com/remtitle .cgi?isbn=1118314425` on the Download Code tab. The code for this chapter is divided into the following major examples:

➤ XmlReaderSample

➤ ConsoleApplication1

➤ XmlSample

➤ XmlSample01

XML

XML plays a significant role in the .NET Framework. Not only does the .NET Framework allow you to use XML in your application, the .NET Framework itself uses XML for configuration files and source code documentation, as do SOAP, web services, and ADO.NET, to name just a few.

To accommodate this extensive use of XML, the .NET Framework includes the `System.Xml` namespace. This namespace is loaded with classes that can be used for the processing of XML, and many of these classes are discussed in this chapter.

This chapter discusses how to use the XmlDocument class, which is the implementation of the Document Object Model (DOM), as well as what .NET offers as a replacement for SAX (the XmlReader and XmlWriter classes). It also discusses the class implementations of XPath and XSLT and demonstrates how XML and ADO.NET work together, as well as how easy it is to transform one to the other. You also learn how you can serialize your objects to XML and create an object from (or deserialize) an XML document by using classes in the System.Xml.Serialization namespace. More to the point, you learn how you can incorporate XML into your C# applications.

Note that the XML namespace enables you to get similar results in a number of different ways. It is impossible to include all these variations in one chapter, so while exploring one possible way to do something, we'll try our best to mention alternatives that will yield the same or similar results.

Because it's beyond the scope of this book to teach you XML from scratch, we assume that you are already somewhat familiar with it. For example, you should be familiar with elements, attributes, and nodes, and you should understand what is meant by a *well-formed* document. Similarly, you should be familiar with SAX and DOM.

> **NOTE** *If you want to learn more about XML, Wrox's* Professional XML *(Wiley, 2007) is a great place to start.*

In addition to general XML usage, the .NET Framework also includes the capability to work with XML by using LINQ to XML. This can be a good alternative to using XPath for searching in an XML document.

The discussion begins with a brief overview of the current status of XML standards.

XML STANDARDS SUPPORT IN .NET

The World Wide Web Consortium (W3C) has developed a set of standards that give XML its power and potential. Without these standards, XML would not have the impact on the development world that it does. The W3C website (www.w3.org) is a valuable source for all things XML.

The .NET Framework supports the following W3C standards:

- ➤ XML 1.0 (www.w3.org/TR/1998/REC-xml-19980210), including DTD support
- ➤ XML namespaces (www.w3.org/TR/REC-xml-names), both stream level and DOM
- ➤ XML schemas (www.w3.org/2001/XMLSchema)
- ➤ XPath expressions (www.w3.org/TR/xpath)
- ➤ XSLT transformations (www.w3.org/TR/xslt)
- ➤ DOM Level 1 Core (www.w3.org/TR/REC-DOM-Level-1)
- ➤ DOM Level 2 Core (www.w3.org/TR/DOM-Level-2-Core)
- ➤ SOAP 1.1 (www.w3.org/TR/SOAP)

The level of standards support will change as the framework matures and the W3C updates the recommended standards. Therefore, you need to make sure that you stay up to date with the standards and the level of support provided by Microsoft.

INTRODUCING THE SYSTEM.XML NAMESPACE

Support for processing XML is provided by the classes in the System.Xml namespace in .NET. This section looks (in no particular order) at some of the more important classes that the System.Xml namespace provides. The following table lists the main XML reader and writer classes.

CLASS NAME	DESCRIPTION
XmlReader	An abstract reader class that provides fast, noncached XML data. XmlReader is forward-only, like the SAX parser.
XmlWriter	An abstract writer class that provides fast, noncached XML data in stream or file format
XmlTextReader	Extends XmlReader and provides fast forward-only stream access to XML data
XmlTextWriter	Extends XmlWriter and provides fast forward-only generation of XML streams.

The following table lists some other useful classes for handling XML.

CLASS NAME	DESCRIPTION
XmlNode	An abstract class that represents a single node in an XML document. It is the base class for several classes in the XML namespace.
XmlDocument	Extends XmlNode. This is the W3C DOM implementation. It provides a tree representation in memory of an XML document, enabling navigation and editing.
XmlDataDocument	Extends XmlDocument. This is a document that can be loaded from XML data or from relational data in an ADO.NET DataSet. It enables the mixing of XML and relational data in the same view.
XmlResolver	An abstract class that resolves external XML-based resources such as DTD and schema references. Also used to process <xsl:include> and <xsl:import> elements.
XmlNodeList	A list of XmlNodes that can be iterated through
XmlUrlResolver	Extends XmlResolver. Resolves external resources named by a uniform resource identifier (URI).

Many of the classes in the System.Xml namespace provide a means to manage XML documents and streams, whereas others (such as the XmlDataDocument class) provide a bridge between XML data stores and the relational data stored in DataSets.

> **NOTE** *The XML namespace is available to any language that is part of the .NET family. This means that all the examples in this chapter could also be written in Visual Basic .NET, managed C++, and so on.*

USING SYSTEM.XML CLASSES

The following examples use books.xml as the source of data. You can download this file and the other code samples for this chapter from the Wrox website (www.wrox.com), but it is also included in several examples in the .NET SDK. The books.xml file is a book catalog for an imaginary bookstore. It includes book information such as genre, author name, price, and ISBN number.

This is what the books.xml file looks like:

```
<?xml version='1.0'?>
<!--This file represents a fragment of a book store inventory database-->
<bookstore>
    <book genre="autobiography" publicationdate="1991" ISBN="1-861003-11-0">
        <title>The Autobiography of Benjamin Franklin</title>
        <author>
          <first-name>Benjamin</first-name>
```

```
            <last-name>Franklin</last-name>
        </author>
        <price>8.99</price>
    </book>
    <book genre="novel" publicationdate="1967" ISBN="0-201-63361-2">
        <title>The Confidence Man</title>
        <author>
            <first-name>Herman</first-name>
            <last-name>Melville</last-name>
        </author>
        <price>11.99</price>
    </book>
    <book genre="philosophy" publicationdate="1991" ISBN="1-861001-57-6">
        <title>The Gorgias</title>
        <author>
            <name>Plato</name>
        </author>
        <price>9.99</price>
    </book>
</bookstore>
```

READING AND WRITING STREAMED XML

The XmlReader and XmlWriter classes will feel familiar if you have ever used SAX. XmlReader-based classes provide a very fast, forward-only, read-only cursor that streams the XML data for processing. Because it is a streaming model, the memory requirements are not very demanding. However, you don't have the navigation flexibility and the read or write capabilities that would be available from a DOM-based model. XmlWriter-based classes produce an XML document that conforms to the W3C's XML 1.0 Namespace Recommendations.

XmlReader and XmlWriter are both abstract classes. The following classes are derived from XmlReader:

- ➤ XmlNodeReader
- ➤ XmlTextReader
- ➤ XmlValidatingReader

The following classes are derived from XmlWriter:

- ➤ XmlTextWriter
- ➤ XmlQueryOutput

XmlTextReader and XmlTextWriter work with either a stream-based object from the System.IO namespace or TextReader/TextWriter objects. XmlNodeReader uses an XmlNode as its source, rather than a stream. The XmlValidatingReader adds DTD and schema validation and therefore offers data validation. You look at these a bit more closely later in this chapter.

Using the XmlReader Class

XmlReader is a lot like SAX in the MSXML SDK. One of the biggest differences, however, is that whereas SAX is a *push* type of model (that is, it pushes data out to the application, and the developer has to be ready to accept it), the XmlReader is a *pull* model, whereby data is pulled into an application requesting it. This provides an easier and more intuitive programming model. Another advantage to this is that a pull model can be selective about the data that is sent to the application: it isn't necessary to process any data you don't need. In a push model, all the XML data has to be processed by the application, whether it is needed or not.

The following is a very simple example of reading XML data; later you will take a closer look at the XmlReader class. You'll find the code in the XmlReaderSample folder. Here is the code for reading in the books.xml document. As each node is read, the NodeType property is checked. If the node is a text node, the value is appended to the text box (code file XMLReaderSample.sln):

```
using System.Xml;

private void button3_Click(object sender, EventArgs e)
{
  richTextBox1.Clear();
  XmlReader rdr = XmlReader.Create("books.xml");
  while (rdr.Read())
  {
    if (rdr.NodeType == XmlNodeType.Text)
      richTextBox1.AppendText(rdr.Value + "\r\n");
  }
}
```

As previously discussed, XmlReader is an abstract class. Therefore, in order to use the XmlReader class directly, a Create static method has been added. The Create method returns an XmlReader object. The overload list for the Create method contains nine entries. In the preceding example, a string that represents the filename of the XmlDocument is passed in as a parameter. Stream-based objects and TextReader-based objects can also be passed in.

An XmlReaderSettings object can also be used. XmlReaderSettings specifies the features of the reader. For example, a schema can be used to validate the stream. Set the Schemas property to a valid XmlSchemaSet object, which is a cache of XSD schemas. Then the XsdValidate property on the XmlReaderSettings object can be set to true.

You can use several Ignore properties to control the way the reader processes certain nodes and values. These properties include IgnoreComments, IgnoreIdentityConstraints, IgnoreInlineSchema, IgnoreProcessingInstructions, IgnoreSchemaLocation, and IgnoreWhitespace. You can use these properties to strip certain items from the document.

Read Methods

Several ways exist to move through the document. As shown in the previous example, Read takes you to the next node. You can then verify whether the node has a value (HasValue) or, as you will see shortly, whether the node has any attributes (HasAttributes). You can also use the ReadStartElement method, which verifies whether the current node is the start element and then positions you on the next node. If you are not on the start element, an XmlException is raised. Calling this method is the same as calling the IsStartElement method followed by a Read method.

ReadElementString is similar to ReadString, except that you can optionally pass in the name of an element. If the next content node is not a start tag, or if the Name parameter does not match the current node Name, an exception is raised.

Here is an example showing how ReadElementString can be used. Notice that it uses FileStreams, so you need to ensure that you include the System.IO namespace via a using statement (code file XMLReaderSample.sln):

```
private void button6_Click(object sender, EventArgs e)
{
  richTextBox1.Clear();
      XmlReader rdr = XmlReader.Create("books.xml");
  while (!rdr.EOF)
  {
    //if we hit an element type, try and load it in the listbox
    if (rdr.MoveToContent() == XmlNodeType.Element && rdr.Name == "title")
    {
      richTextBox1.AppendText(rdr.ReadElementString() + "\r\n");
    }
    else
    {
      //otherwise move on
```

```
        rdr.Read();
    }
  }
}
```

In the while loop, you use MoveToContent to find each node of type XmlNodeType.Element with the name title. You use the EOF property of the XmlTextReader as the loop condition. If the node is not of type Element or not named title, the else clause will issue a Read method to move to the next node. When you find a node that matches the criteria, you add the result of a ReadElementString to the list box. This should leave you with just the book titles in the list box. Note that you don't have to issue a Read call after a successful ReadElementString because ReadElementString consumes the entire Element and positions you on the next node.

If you remove && rdr.Name=="title" from the if clause, you have to catch the XmlException when it is thrown. Looking at the data file, the first element that MoveToContent will find is the <bookstore> element. Because it is an element, it will pass the check in the if statement. However, because it does not contain a simple text type, it will cause ReadElementString to raise an XmlException. One way to work around this is to put the ReadElementString call in a function of its own. Then, if the call to ReadElementString fails inside this function, you can deal with the error and return to the calling function.

Go ahead and do that; call this new method LoadTextBox and pass in the XmlTextReader as a parameter. This is what the LoadTextBox method looks like with these changes:

```
private void LoadTextBox(XmlReader reader)
{
    try
    {
        richTextBox1.AppendText (reader.ReadElementString() + "\r\n");
    }
    // if an XmlException is raised, ignore it.
    catch(XmlException er){}
}
```

The following section from the previous example,

```
if (tr.MoveToContent() == XmlNodeType.Element && tr.Name == "title")
{
    richTextBox1.AppendText(tr.ReadElementString() + "\r\n");
}
else
{
    //otherwise move on
    tr.Read();
}
```

will have to be changed to this:

```
if (tr.MoveToContent() == XmlNodeType.Element)
{
    LoadTextBox(tr);
}
else
{
    //otherwise move on
    tr.Read();
}
```

After running this example, the results should be the same as before. What this demonstrates is that there is more than one way to accomplish the same goal. This is where the flexibility of the classes in the System.Xml namespace starts to become apparent.

The `XmlReader` can also read strongly typed data. There are several `ReadElementContentAs` methods, such as `ReadElementContentAsDouble`, `ReadElementContentAsBoolean`, and so on. The following example shows how to read in the values as a decimal and do some math on the value. In this case, the value from the price element is increased by 25 percent:

```
private void button5_Click(object sender, EventArgs e)
{
  richTextBox1.Clear();
  XmlReader rdr = XmlReader.Create("books.xml");
  while (rdr.Read())
  {
    if (rdr.NodeType == XmlNodeType.Element)
    {
      if (rdr.Name == "price")
      {
        decimal price = rdr.ReadElementContentAsDecimal();
        richTextBox1.AppendText("Current Price = " + price + "\r\n");
        price += price * (decimal).25;
        richTextBox1.AppendText("New Price = " + price + "\r\n\r\n");
      }
      else if(rdr.Name== "title")
        richTextBox1.AppendText(rdr.ReadElementContentAsString() + "\r\n");
    }
  }
}
```

If the value cannot be converted to a decimal value, a `FormatException` is raised. This is a much more efficient method than reading the value as a string and casting it to the proper data type.

Retrieving Attribute Data

As you play with the sample code, you might notice that when the nodes are read in, you don't see any attributes. This is because attributes are not considered part of a document's structure. When you are on an element node, you can check for the existence of attributes and optionally retrieve the attribute values.

For example, the `HasAttributes` property returns `true` if there are any attributes; otherwise, it returns `false`. The `AttributeCount` property tells you how many attributes there are, and the `GetAttribute` method gets an attribute by name or by index. If you want to iterate through the attributes one at a time, you can use the `MoveToFirstAttribute` and `MoveToNextAttribute` methods.

The following example iterates through the attributes of the `books.xml` document:

```
private void button7_Click(object sender, EventArgs e)
{
  richTextBox1.Clear();
  XmlReader tr = XmlReader.Create("books.xml");
  //Read in node at a time
  while (tr.Read())
  {
    //check to see if it's a NodeType element
    if (tr.NodeType == XmlNodeType.Element)
    {
      //if it's an element, then let's look at the attributes.
      for (int i = 0; i < tr.AttributeCount; i++)
      {
        richTextBox1.AppendText(tr.GetAttribute(i) + "\r\n");
      }
    }
  }
}
```

This time you are looking for element nodes. When you find one, you loop through all the attributes and, using the `GetAttribute` method, load the value of the attribute into the list box. In the preceding example, those attributes would be `genre`, `publicationdate`, and `ISBN`.

Validating with XmlReader

Sometimes it's important to know not only that the document is well formed but also that it is valid. An `XmlReader` can validate the XML according to an XSD schema by using the `XmlReaderSettings` class. The XSD schema is added to the `XmlSchemaSet` that is exposed through the `Schemas` property. The `XsdValidate` property must also be set to `true`; the default for this property is `false`.

The following example demonstrates the use of the `XmlReaderSettings` class. It is the XSD schema that will be used to validate the `books.xml` document (code file `books.xsd`):

```xml
<?xml version="1.0" encoding="utf-8"?>
<xs:schema attributeFormDefault="unqualified"
        elementFormDefault="qualified" xmlns:xs="http://www.w3.org/2001/XMLSchema">
  <xs:element name="bookstore">
    <xs:complexType>
      <xs:sequence>
        <xs:element maxOccurs="unbounded" name="book">
          <xs:complexType>
            <xs:sequence>
              <xs:element name="title" type="xs:string" />
              <xs:element name="author">
                <xs:complexType>
                  <xs:sequence>
                    <xs:element minOccurs="0" name="name"
                                              type="xs:string" />
                    <xs:element minOccurs="0" name="first-name"
                                              type="xs:string" />
                    <xs:element minOccurs="0" name="last-name"
                                              type="xs:string" />
                  </xs:sequence>
                </xs:complexType>
              </xs:element>
              <xs:element name="price" type="xs:decimal" />
            </xs:sequence>
            <xs:attribute name="genre" type="xs:string" use="required" />
            <!--<xs:attribute name="publicationdate"
                          type="xs:unsignedShort" use="required" />-->
            <xs:attribute name="ISBN" type="xs:string" use="required" />
          </xs:complexType>
        </xs:element>
      </xs:sequence>
    </xs:complexType>
  </xs:element>
</xs:schema>
```

This schema was generated from `books.xml` in Visual Studio. Notice that the `publicationdate` attribute has been commented out. This will cause the validation to fail.

The following code uses the schema to validate the `books.xml` document: (Code file `XMLReaderSample.sln`)

```csharp
private void button8_Click(object sender, EventArgs e)
{

  richTextBox1.Clear();
  XmlReaderSettings settings = new XmlReaderSettings();
  settings.Schemas.Add(null, "books.xsd");
```

```
      settings.ValidationType = ValidationType.Schema;
      settings.ValidationEventHandler +=
        new System.Xml.Schema.ValidationEventHandler(settings_ValidationEventHandler);
      XmlReader rdr = XmlReader.Create("books.xml", settings);
      while (rdr.Read())
      {
        if (rdr.NodeType == XmlNodeType.Text)
          richTextBox1.AppendText(rdr.Value + "\r\n");
      }
    }
```

After the `XmlReaderSettings` object setting is created, the schema `books.xsd` is added to the `XmlSchemaSet` object. The `Add` method for `XmlSchemaSet` has four overloads. One takes an `XmlSchema` object. The `XmlSchema` object can be used to create a schema on the fly, without having to create the schema file on disk. Another overload takes another `XmlSchemaSet` object as a parameter. The third overload takes two string values: the target namespace and the URL for the XSD document. If the target namespace parameter is null, the `targetNamespace` of the schema will be used. The last overload takes the `targetNamespace` as the first parameter as well, but it uses an `XmlReader`-based object to read in the schema. The `XmlSchemaSet` preprocesses the schema before the document to be validated is processed.

After the schema is referenced, the `XsdValidate` property is set to one of the `ValidationType` enumeration values. These valid values are `DTD`, `Schema`, or `None`. If the value selected is set to `None`, then no validation will occur.

Because the `XmlReader` object is being used, if there is a validation problem with the document, it will not be found until that attribute or element is read by the reader. When the validation failure does occur, an `XmlSchemaValidationException` is raised. This exception can be handled in a `catch` block; however, handling exceptions can make controlling the flow of the data difficult. To help with this, a `ValidationEvent` is available in the `XmlReaderSettings` class. This way, the validation failure can be handled without your having to use exception handling. The event is also raised by validation warnings, which do not raise an exception. The `ValidationEvent` passes in a `ValidationEventArgs` object that contains a `Severity` property. This property determines whether the event was raised by an error or a warning. If the event was raised by an error, the exception that caused the event to be raised is passed in as well. There is also a message property. In the example, the message is displayed in a `MessageBox`.

Using the XmlWriter Class

The `XmlWriter` class allows you to write XML to a stream, a file, a `StringBuilder`, a `TextWriter`, or another `XmlWriter` object. Like `XmlTextReader`, it does so in a forward-only, noncached manner. `XmlWriter` is highly configurable, enabling you to specify such things as whether or not to indent content, the amount to indent, what quote character to use in attribute values, and whether namespaces are supported. Like the `XmlReader`, this configuration is done using an `XmlWriterSettings` object.

Here's a simple example that shows how the `XmlTextWriter` class can be used:

```
    private void button9_Click(object sender, EventArgs e)
    {
      XmlWriterSettings settings = new XmlWriterSettings();
      settings.Indent = true;
      settings.NewLineOnAttributes = true;
      XmlWriter writer = XmlWriter.Create("newbook.xml", settings);
      writer.WriteStartDocument();
      //Start creating elements and attributes
      writer.WriteStartElement("book");
      writer.WriteAttributeString("genre", "Mystery");
      writer.WriteAttributeString("publicationdate", "2001");
      writer.WriteAttributeString("ISBN", "123456789");
      writer.WriteElementString("title", "Case of the Missing Cookie");
```

```
        writer.WriteStartElement("author");
        writer.WriteElementString("name", "Cookie Monster");
        writer.WriteEndElement();
        writer.WriteElementString("price", "9.99");
        writer.WriteEndElement();
        writer.WriteEndDocument();
        //clean up
        writer.Flush();
        writer.Close();
    }
```

Here, you are writing to a new XML file called `newbook.xml`, adding the data for a new book. Note that `XmlWriter` overwrites an existing file with a new one. You will look at inserting a new element or node into an existing document later in this chapter. You are instantiating the `XmlWriter` object by using the `Create` static method. In this example, a string representing a filename is passed as a parameter, along with an instance of an `XmlWriterSetting` class.

The `XmlWriterSettings` class has properties that control how the XML is generated. The `CheckedCharacters` property is a Boolean that raises an exception if a character in the XML does not conform to the W3C XML 1.0 recommendation. The `Encoding` class sets the encoding used for the XML being generated; the default is Encoding.UTF8. The `Indent` property is a Boolean value that determines whether elements should be indented. The `IndentChars` property is set to the character string that it is used to indent. The default is two spaces. The `NewLine` property is used to determine the characters for line breaks. In the preceding example, the `NewLineOnAttribute` is set to true. This will put each attribute in a separate line, which can make the XML generated a little easier to read.

`WriteStartDocument` adds the document declaration. Now you start writing data. First is the `book` element; next, you add the `genre`, `publicationdate`, and `ISBN` attributes. Then you write the `title`, `author`, and `price` elements. Note that the `author` element has a child element name.

When you click the button, you produce the `booknew.xml` file, which looks like this:

```
        <?xml version="1.0" encoding="utf-8"?>
        <book
          genre="Mystery"
          publicationdate="2001"
          ISBN="123456789">
          <title>Case of the Missing Cookie</title>
          <author>
            <name>Cookie Monster</name>
          </author>
          <price>9.99</price>
        </book>
```

The nesting of elements is controlled by paying attention to when you start and finish writing elements and attributes. You can see this when you add the `name` child element to the `authors` element. Note how the `WriteStartElement` and `WriteEndElement` method calls are arranged and how that arrangement produces the nested elements in the output file.

Along with the `WriteElementString` and `WriteAttributeString` methods, there are several other specialized write methods. `WriteCData` outputs a CData section (`<!CDATA[.]]>`), writing out the text it takes as a parameter. `WriteComment` writes out a comment in proper XML format. `WriteChars` writes out the contents of a char buffer. This works in a similar fashion to the `ReadChars` method shown earlier; they both use the same type of parameters. `WriteChars` needs a buffer (an array of characters), the starting position for writing (an integer), and the number of characters to write (an integer).

Reading and writing XML using the `XmlReader`- and `XmlWriter`-based classes are surprisingly flexible and simple to do. Next, you'll learn how the DOM is implemented in the `System.Xml` namespace through the `XmlDocument` and `XmlNode` classes.

USING THE DOM IN .NET

The DOM implementation in .NET supports the W3C DOM Level 1 and Core DOM Level 2 specifications. The DOM is implemented through the XmlNode class, which is an abstract class that represents a node of an XML document.

There is also an XmlNodeList class, which is an ordered list of nodes. This is a live list of nodes, and any changes to any node are immediately reflected in the list. XmlNodeList supports indexed access or iterative access.

The XmlNode and XmlNodeList classes make up the core of the DOM implementation in the .NET Framework. The following table lists some of the classes that are based on XmlNode.

CLASS NAME	DESCRIPTION
XmlLinkedNode	Returns the node immediately before or after the current node. Adds NextSibling and PreviousSibling properties to XmlNode.
XmlDocument	Represents the entire document. Implements the DOM Level 1 and Level 2 specifications.
XmlDocumentFragment	Represents a fragment of the document tree
XmlAttribute	Represents an attribute object of an XmlElement object
XmlEntity	Represents a parsed or unparsed entity node
XmlNotation	Contains a notation declared in a DTD or schema

The following table lists classes that extend XmlCharacterData.

CLASS NAME	DESCRIPTION
XmlCDataSection	Represents a CData section of a document
XmlComment	Represents an XML comment object
XmlSignificantWhitespace	Represents a node with whitespace. Nodes are created only if the PreserveWhiteSpace flag is true.
XmlWhitespace	Represents whitespace in element content. Nodes are created only if the PreserveWhiteSpace flag is true.
XmlText	Represents the textual content of an element or attribute

The following table lists classes that extend the XmlLinkedNode.

CLASS NAME	DESCRIPTION
XmlDeclaration	Represents the declaration node (e.g., <?xml version='1.0'.>)
XmlDocumentType	Represents data relating to the document type declaration
XmlElement	Represents an XML element object
XmlEntityReferenceNode	Represents an entity reference node
XmlProcessingInstruction	Contains an XML processing instruction

As you can see, .NET makes available a class to fit just about any XML type that you might encounter, which means you end up with a very flexible and powerful tool set. This section can't look at every class in detail, but you will see several examples to give you an idea of what you can accomplish.

Using the XmlDocument Class

XmlDocument and its derived class XmlDataDocument (discussed later in this chapter) are the classes that you will be using to represent the DOM in .NET. Unlike XmlReader and XmlWriter, XmlDocument provides read and write capabilities as well as random access to the DOM tree. XmlDocument resembles the DOM implementation in MSXML. If you have experience programming with MSXML, you will feel comfortable using XmlDocument.

This example introduced in this section creates an XmlDocument object, loads a document from disk, and loads a text box with data from the title elements. This is similar to one of the examples that you constructed in the section, "Using the XmlReader Class." The difference here is that you will be selecting the nodes you want to work with, instead of going through the entire document as in the XmlReader-based example.

Here is the code to create an XmlDocument object. Note how simple it looks in comparison to the XmlReader example (code file frmXMLDOM.cs):

```
private void button1_Click(object sender, System.EventArgs e)
{
      //doc is declared at the module level
      //change path to match your path structure
      _doc.Load("books.xml");
      //get only the nodes that we want.
      XmlNodeList nodeLst = _doc.GetElementsByTagName("title");
      //iterate through the XmlNodeList
      textBox1.Text = "";
      foreach (XmlNode node in nodeLst)
      {
          textBox1.Text += node.OuterXml + "\r\n";
      }
}
```

You also add the following declaration at the module level for the examples in this section:

```
private XmlDocument doc=new XmlDocument();
```

If this is all that you wanted to do, using the XmlReader would have been a much more efficient way to load the text box, because you just go through the document once and then you are finished with it. This is exactly the type of work that XmlReader was designed for. However, if you want to revisit a node, using XmlDocument is a better way.

Here is an example of using the XPath syntax to retrieve a set of nodes from the document:

```
private void button2_Click(object sender, EventArgs e)
{
  //doc is declared at the module level
  //change path to match your path structure
  doc.Load("books.xml");
  //get only the nodes that we want.
  XmlNodeList nodeLst = _doc.SelectNodes("/bookstore/book/title");
  textBox1.Text = "";
  //iterate through the XmlNodeList
  foreach (XmlNode node in nodeLst)
  {
      textBox1.Text += node.OuterXml + "\r\n";
  }
}
```

SelectNodes returns a NodeList, or a collection of XmlNodes. The list contains only nodes that match the XPath statement passed in as the parameter SelectNodes. In this example, all you want to see are the title nodes. If you had made the call to SelectSingleNode, then you would have received a single node object that contained the first node in the XmlDocument that matched the XPath criteria.

A quick comment regarding the `SelectSingleNode` method: this is an XPath implementation in the `XmlDocument` class. Both the `SelectSingleNode` and `SelectNodes` methods are defined in `XmlNode`, which `XmlDocument` is based on. `SelectSingleNode` returns an `XmlNode`, and `SelectNodes` returns an `XmlNodeList`. However, the `System.Xml.XPath` namespace contains a richer XPath implementation, which you will look at later in the chapter.

Inserting Nodes

Earlier, you looked at an example using `XmlTextWriter` that created a new document. The limitation was that it would not insert a node into a current document. With the `XmlDocument` class, you can do just that. Change the `button1_Click` event handler from the last example to the following:

```
private void button4_Click(object sender, System.EventArgs e)
{
        //change path to match your structure
        _doc.Load("books.xml");
        //create a new 'book' element
        XmlElement newBook = _doc.CreateElement("book");
        //set some attributes
        newBook.SetAttribute("genre", "Mystery");
        newBook.SetAttribute("publicationdate", "2001");
        newBook.SetAttribute("ISBN", "123456789");
        //create a new 'title' element
        XmlElement newTitle = _doc.CreateElement("title");
        newTitle.InnerText = "Case of the Missing Cookie";
        newBook.AppendChild(newTitle);
        //create new author element
        XmlElement newAuthor = _doc.CreateElement("author");
        newBook.AppendChild(newAuthor);
        //create new name element
        XmlElement newName = _doc.CreateElement("name");
        newName.InnerText = "Cookie Monster";
        newAuthor.AppendChild(newName);
        //create new price element
        XmlElement newPrice = _doc.CreateElement("price");
        newPrice.InnerText = "9.95";
        newBook.AppendChild(newPrice);
        //add to the current document
        _doc.DocumentElement.AppendChild(newBook);
        //write out the doc to disk
        XmlTextWriter tr = new XmlTextWriter("booksEdit.xml", null);
        tr.Formatting = Formatting.Indented;
        _doc.WriteContentTo(tr);
        tr.Close();
        //load listBox1 with all of the titles, including new one
        XmlNodeList nodeLst = _doc.GetElementsByTagName("title");
        textBox1.Text = "";
        foreach (XmlNode node in nodeLst)
        {
            textBox1.Text += node.OuterXml + "\r\n";
        }
}
```

After executing this code, you end up with the same functionality as in the previous example, but there is one additional book in the text box, *The Case of the Missing Cookie* (a soon-to-be classic). If you look closely at the code, you can see that this is actually a fairly simple process. The first thing that you do is create a new `book` element:

```
XmlElement newBook = doc.CreateElement("book");
```

`CreateElement` has three overloads that enable you to specify the following:

➤ The element name

➤ The name and namespace URI

➤ The prefix, localname, and namespace

Once the element is created, you need to add attributes:

```
newBook.SetAttribute("genre","Mystery");
newBook.SetAttribute("publicationdate","2001");
newBook.SetAttribute("ISBN","123456789");
```

Now that you have the attributes created, you need to add the other elements of a book:

```
XmlElement newTitle = doc.CreateElement("title");
newTitle.InnerText = "The Case of the Missing Cookie";
newBook.AppendChild(newTitle);
```

Again, you create a new `XmlElement`-based object (`newTitle`). Then you set the `InnerText` property to the title of our new classic and append the element as a child to the `book` element. You repeat this for the rest of the elements in this `book` element. Note that you add the `name` element as a child to the `author` element. This will give you the proper nesting relationship, as in the other `book` elements.

Finally, you append the `newBook` element to the `doc.DocumentElement` node. This is the same level as all of the other `book` elements. You have now updated an existing document with a new element.

The last thing to do is write the new XML document to disk. In this example, you create a new `XmlTextWriter` and pass it to the `WriteContentTo` method. `WriteContentTo` and `WriteTo` both take an `XmlTextWriter` as a parameter. `WriteContentTo` saves the current node and all of its children to the `XmlTextWriter`, whereas `WriteTo` just saves the current node. Because `doc` is an `XmlDocument`-based object, it represents the entire document, so that is what is saved. You could also use the `Save` method. It will always save the entire document. `Save` has four overloads. You can specify a string with the filename and path, a `Stream`-based object, a `TextWriter`-based object, or an `XmlWriter`-based object.

You also call the `Close` method on `XmlTextWriter` to flush the internal buffers and close the file. Figure 34-1 shows what you get when you run this example. Notice the new entry at the bottom of the list.

Earlier in the chapter, you saw how to create a document using the `XmlTextWriter` class. You can also use `XmlDocument`. Why would you use one in preference to the other? If the data that you want streamed to XML is available and ready to write, then the `XmlTextWriter` class is the best choice. However, if you need to build the XML document a little at a time, inserting nodes into various places, then creating the document with `XmlDocument` might be the better choice. You can accomplish this by changing the line,

FIGURE 34-1

```
doc.Load("books.xml");
```

to the following:

```
//create the declaration section
XmlDeclaration newDec = doc.CreateXmlDeclaration("1.0",null,null);
doc.AppendChild(newDec);
//create the new root element
XmlElement newRoot = doc.CreateElement("newBookstore");
doc.AppendChild(newRoot);
```

First, you create a new XmlDeclaration. The parameters are the version (always 1.0 for now), the encoding, and the standalone flag. The encoding parameter should be set to a string that is part of the System.Text.Encoding class if null is not used (null defaults to UTF-8). The standalone flag can be either yes, no, or null. If it is null, the attribute is not used and will not be included in the document.

The next element that is created will become the DocumentElement. In this case, it is called newBookstore so that you can see the difference. The rest of the code is the same as in the previous example and works in the same way. This is booksEdit.xml, which is generated from the following code:

```
<?xml version="1.0"?>
<newBookstore>
    <book genre="Mystery" publicationdate="2001" ISBN="123456789">
        <title>The Case of the Missing Cookie</title>
        <author>
            <name>C. Monster</name>
        </author>
        <price>9.95</price>
    </book>
</newBookstore>
```

You should use the XmlDocument class when you want to have random access to the document. Use the XmlReader-based classes when you want a streaming-type model instead. Remember that there is a cost for the flexibility of the XmlNode-based XmlDocument class—memory requirements are higher and the performance of reading the document is not as good as when using XmlReader. There is another way to traverse an XML document: the XPathNavigator.

USING XPATHNAVIGATORS

An XPathNavigator is used to select, iterate through, and sometimes edit data from an XML document. An XPathNavigator can be created from an XmlDocument to allow editing capabilities or from an XPathDocument for read-only use. Because the XPathDocument is read-only, it performs very well. Unlike the XmlReader, the XPathNavigator is not a streaming model, so the document is read and parsed only once.

The XPathNavigaor is part of the System.Xml.XPath namespace. XPath is a query language used to select specific nodes or elements from an XML document for processing.

The System.Xml.XPath Namespace

The System.Xml.XPath namespace is built for speed. It provides a read-only view of your XML documents, so there are no editing capabilities. Classes in this namespace are built for fast iteration and selections on the XML document in a cursory fashion.

The following table lists the key classes in System.Xml.XPath and gives a short description of the purpose of each class.

CLASS NAME	DESCRIPTION
XPathDocument	Provides a view of the entire XML document. Read-only.
XPathNavigator	Provides the navigational capabilities to an XPathDocument
XPathNodeIterator	Provides iteration capabilities to a node set
XPathExpression	Represents a compiled XPath expression. Used by SelectNodes, SelectSingle Nodes, Evaluate, and Matches.
XPathException	An XPath exception class

XPathDocument

XPathDocument does not offer any of the functionality of the XmlDocument class. Its sole purpose is to create XPathNavigators. In fact, that is the only method available on the XPathDocument class (other than those provided by Object).

You can create an XPathDocument in a number of different ways. You can pass in an XmlReader, a filename of an XML document, or a Stream-based object to the constructor. This provides a great deal of flexibility. For example, you can use the XmlValidatingReader to validate the XML and then use that same object to create the XPathDocument.

XPathNavigator

XPathNavigator contains all the methods for moving and selecting elements that you need. The following table lists some of the "move" methods defined in this class.

METHOD NAME	DESCRIPTION
MoveTo()	Takes XPathNavigator as a parameter. Moves the current position to be the same as that passed in to XPathNavigator.
MoveToAttribute()	Moves to the named attribute. Takes the attribute name and namespace as parameters.
MoveToFirstAttribute()	Moves to the first attribute in the current element. Returns true if successful.
MoveToNextAttribute()	Moves to the next attribute in the current element. Returns true if successful.
MoveToFirst()	Moves to the first sibling in the current node. Returns true if successful.
MoveToLast()	Moves to the last sibling in the current node. Returns true if successful.
MoveToNext()	Moves to the next sibling in the current node. Returns true if successful.
MoveToPrevious()	Moves to the previous sibling in the current node. Returns true if successful.
MoveToFirstChild()	Moves to the first child of the current element. Returns true if successful.
MoveToId()	Moves to the element with the ID supplied as a parameter. There must be a schema for the document, and the data type for the element must be of type ID.
MoveToParent()	Moves to the parent of the current node. Returns true if successful.
MoveToRoot()	Moves to the root node of the document

To select a subset of the document, you can use one of the Select methods listed in the following table.

METHOD NAME	DESCRIPTION
Select()	Selects a node set using an XPath expression
SelectAncestors()	Selects all the ancestors of the current node based on an XPath expression
SelectChildren()	Selects all the children of the current node based on an XPath expression
SelectDescendants()	Selects all the descendants of the current node based on an XPath expression
SelectSingleNode()	Selects one node based on an XPath expression

If the XPathNavigator was created from an XPathDocument, it is read-only. If it is created from an XmlDocument, the XPathNavigator can be used to edit the document. This can be verified by checking the CanEdit property. If it is true, you can use one of the Insert methods. InsertBefore and InsertAfter will create a new node either before or after the current node, respectively. The source of the new node can be an XmlReader or a string. Optionally, an XmlWriter can be returned and used to write the new node information.

Strongly typed values can be read from the nodes by using the ValueAs properties. Notice that this is different from XmlReader, which uses ReadValue methods.

XPathNodeIterator

XPathNodeIterator can be thought of as the equivalent of a NodeList or a NodeSet in XPath. This object has two properties and three methods:

➤ Clone() — Creates a new copy of itself

➤ Count — Specifies the number of nodes in the XPathNodeIterator object

➤ Current — Returns an XPathNavigator pointing to the current node

➤ CurrentPosition() — Returns an integer with the current position

➤ MoveNext() — Moves to the next node that matches the XPath expression that created the XPathNodeIterator

The XPathNodeIterator is returned by the XPathNavigator Select methods. You use it to iterate over the set of nodes returned by a Select method of the XPathNavigator. Using the MoveNext method of the XPathNodeIterator does not change the location of the XPathNavigator that created it.

Using Classes from the XPath Namespace

The best way to see how these classes are used is to look at some code that iterates through the books.xml document. This will enable you to see how the navigation works. In order to use the examples, first add a reference to the System.Xml.Xsl and System.Xml.XPath namespaces:

```
using System.Xml.XPath;
using System.Xml.Xsl;
```

For this example, you use the file booksxpath.xml. It is similar to the books.xml file that you have been using, except that a couple of extra books are added. Here's the form code, which is part of the XmlSample project (code file frmNavigator.cs):

```
private void button1_Click(object sender, EventArgs e)
{
  //modify to match your path structure
  XPathDocument doc = new XPathDocument("books.xml");
  //create the XPath navigator
  XPathNavigator nav = ((IXPathNavigable)doc).CreateNavigator();
  //create the XPathNodeIterator of book nodes
  // that have genre attribute value of novel
  XPathNodeIterator iter = nav.Select("/bookstore/book[@genre='novel']");
  textBox1.Text = "";
  while (iter.MoveNext())
  {
    XPathNodeIterator newIter =
      iter.Current.SelectDescendants(XPathNodeType.Element, false);
    while (newIter.MoveNext())
    {
      textBox1.Text += newIter.Current.Name + ": " +
          newIter.Current.Value + "\r\n";
    }
  }
}
```

The first thing you do in the button1_Click method is create the XPathDocument (called doc), passing in the file and path string of the document you want opened. The next line creates the XPathNavigator:

```
XPathNavigator nav = doc.CreateNavigator();
```

In this example, you use the Select method to retrieve a set of nodes that all have novel as the value of the genre attribute. You then use the MoveNext method to iterate through all the novels in the book list.

To load the data into the list box, you use the `XPathNodeIterator.Current` property. This creates a new `XPathNavigator` object based on just the node to which the `XPathNodeIterator` is pointing. In this case, you are creating an `XPathNavigator` for one `book` node in the document.

The next loop takes this `XPathNavigator` and creates another `XPathNodeIterator` by issuing another type of select method, the `SelectDescendants` method. This gives you an `XPathNodeIterator` of all of the child nodes and children of the child nodes of the `book` node.

Then, you do another `MoveNext` loop on the `XPathNodeIterator` and load the text box with the element names and element values. Figure 34-2 shows what the screen looks like after running the code. Note that the novel is the only book listed.

What if you wanted to add up the cost of these books? `XPathNavigator` includes the `Evaluate` method for just this reason. `Evaluate` has three overloads. The first one contains a string that is the `XPath` function call. The second overload uses the `XPathExpression` object as a parameter, and the third uses `XPathExpression` and an `XPathNodeIterator` as parameters. The following code is similar to the previous example, except that this time all the nodes in the document are iterated through. The `Evaluate` method call at the end totals the cost of all the books:

```csharp
private void button2_Click(object sender, EventArgs e)
{
  //modify to match your path structure
  XPathDocument doc = new XPathDocument("books.xml");
  //create the XPath navigator
  XPathNavigator nav = ((IXPathNavigable)doc).CreateNavigator();
  //create the XPathNodeIterator of book nodes
  XPathNodeIterator iter = nav.Select("/bookstore/book");
  textBox1.Text = "";
  while (iter.MoveNext())
  {
    XPathNodeIterator newIter =
        iter.Current.SelectDescendants(XPathNodeType.Element, false);
    while (newIter.MoveNext())
    {
      textBox1.Text += newIter.Current.Name + ": " + newIter.Current.Value +
        "\r\n";
    }
  }
  textBox1.Text += "=========================" + "\r\n";
  textBox1.Text += "Total Cost = " + nav.Evaluate("sum(/bookstore/book/price)");
}
```

This time, you see the total cost of the books evaluated in the text box (see Figure 34-3).

Now let's say that you need to add a node for discount. You can use the `InsertAfter` method to do this fairly easily. Here is the code:

```csharp
private void button3_Click(object sender, EventArgs e)
{
  XmlDocument doc = new XmlDocument();
  doc.Load("books.xml");
  XPathNavigator nav = doc.CreateNavigator();

  if (nav.CanEdit)
  {
    XPathNodeIterator iter = nav.Select("/bookstore/book/price");
    while (iter.MoveNext())
    {
```

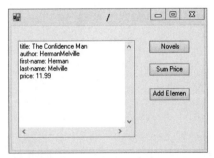

FIGURE 34-2

```
            iter.Current.InsertAfter("<disc>5</disc>");
      }
   }
   doc.Save("newbooks.xml");
}
```

Here, you have added the `<disc>5</disc>` element after the price elements. First, all the price nodes are selected. The `XPathNodeIterator` is used to iterate over the nodes, and the new node is inserted. The modified document is saved with a new name, `newbooks.xml`. The new version looks as follows:

```
<?xml version="1.0"?>
<!--This file represents a fragment of a book store inventory database-->
<bookstore>
   <book genre="autobiography" publicationdate="1991" ISBN="1-861003-11-0">
      <title>The Autobiography of Benjamin Franklin</title>
      <author>
        <first-name>Benjamin</first-name>
        <last-name>Franklin</last-name>
      </author>
      <price>8.99</price>
      <disc>5</disc>
   </book>
   <book genre="novel" publicationdate="1967" ISBN="0-201-63361-2">
      <title>The Confidence Man</title>
      <author>
        <first-name>Herman</first-name>
        <last-name>Melville</last-name>
      </author>
      <price>11.99</price>
      <disc>5</disc>
   </book>
   <book genre="philosophy" publicationdate="1991" ISBN="1-861001-57-6">
      <title>The Gorgias</title>
      <author>
        <name>Plato</name>
      </author>
      <price>9.99</price>
      <disc>5</disc>
   </book>
</bookstore>
```

Nodes can be inserted before or after a selected node. Nodes can also be changed and deleted. If you need to change a large numbers of nodes, using the `XPathNavigator` created from an `XmlDocument` may be your best choice.

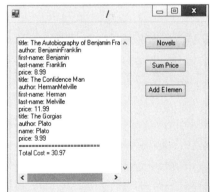

FIGURE 34-3

The System.Xml.Xsl Namespace

The `System.Xml.Xsl` namespace contains the classes that the .NET Framework uses to support XSL transforms. The contents of this namespace are available to any store whose classes implement the `IXPathNavigable` interface. In the .NET Framework, that would currently include `XmlDocument`, `XmlDataDocument`, and `XPathDocument`. As with XPath, use the store that makes the most sense. If you plan to create a custom store, such as one using the file system, and you want to be able to do transforms, be sure to implement the `IXPathNavigable` interface in your class.

XSLT is based on a streaming pull model. Therefore, you can chain several transforms together. You could even apply a custom reader between transforms if needed. This provides a great deal of design flexibility.

Transforming XML

The first example you will look at takes the `books.xml` document and transforms it into a simple HTML document for display, using the XSLT file `books.xsl`. (This code is in the `XSLSample01` folder.) You need to add the following `using` statements:

```
using System.IO;
using System.Xml.Xsl;
using System.Xml.XPath;
```

Here is the code to perform the transform (code file `XslSample01.sln`):

```
private void button1_Click(object sender, EventArgs e)
{
  XslCompiledTransform trans = new XslCompiledTransform();
  trans.Load("books.xsl");
  trans.Transform("books.xml", "out.html");
  webBrowser1.Navigate(AppDomain.CurrentDomain.BaseDirectory + "out.html");
}
```

A transform doesn't get any simpler than this. First, a new `XmlCompiledTransform` object is created. It loads the `books.xsl` transform document and then performs the transform. In this example, a string with the filename is used as the input. The output is `out.html`. This file is then loaded into the web browser control used on the form. Instead of using the filename `books.xml` as the input document, you can use an `IXPathNavigable`-based object. This would be any object that can create an `XPathNavigator`.

After the `XmlCompiledTransform` object is created and the stylesheet is loaded, the transform is performed. The `Transform` method can take just about any combination of `IXPathNavigable` objects, `Streams`, `TextWriters`, `XmlWriters`, and URIs as parameters. This gives you a great deal of flexibility for transform flow. You can pass the output of one transform as the input to the next transform.

`XsltArgumentLists` and `XmlResolver` objects are also included in the parameter options. You will look at the `XsltArgumentList` object in the next section. `XmlResolver`-based objects are used to resolve items that are external to the current document. This could include schemas, credentials, or, of course, stylesheets.

The `books.xsl` document is a fairly straightforward stylesheet. It looks like this:

```
<xsl:stylesheet version="1.0"
 xmlns:xsl="http://www.w3.org/1999/XSL/Transform">
<xsl:template match="/">
   <html>
      <head>
         <title>Price List</title>
      </head>
      <body>
         <table>
            <xsl:apply-templates/>
         </table>
      </body>
   </html>
    </xsl:template>
   <xsl:template match="bookstore">
      <xsl:apply-templates select="book"/>
   </xsl:template>
   <xsl:template match="book">
      <tr><td>
         <xsl:value-of select="title"/>
      </td><td>
         <xsl:value-of select="price"/>
      </td></tr>
   </xsl:template>
</xsl:stylesheet>
```

Using XsltArgumentList

XsltArgumentList provides a way to bind an object with methods to a namespace. Once this is done, you can invoke the methods during the transform. Here is an example:

```csharp
private void button3_Click(object sender, EventArgs e)
{
  //new XPathDocument
  XPathDocument doc = new XPathDocument("books.xml");
  //new XslTransform
  XslCompiledTransform trans = new XslCompiledTransform();
  trans.Load("booksarg.xsl");
  //new XmlTextWriter since we are creating a new xml document
  XmlWriter xw = new XmlTextWriter("argSample.xml", null);
  //create the XsltArgumentList and new BookUtils object
  XsltArgumentList argBook = new XsltArgumentList();
  BookUtils bu = new BookUtils();
  //this tells the argumentlist about BookUtils
  argBook.AddExtensionObject("urn:XslSample", bu);
  //new XPathNavigator
  XPathNavigator nav = doc.CreateNavigator();
  //do the transform
  trans.Transform(nav, argBook, xw);
  xw.Close();
  webBrowser1.Navigate(AppDomain.CurrentDomain.BaseDirectory + "argSample.xml");
}
```

The following is the code for the BooksUtils class, which is the class that will be called from the transform (code file BookUtils.cs):

```csharp
class BookUtils
{
  public BookUtils() { }

  public string ShowText()
  {
    return "This came from the ShowText method!";
  }
}
```

Here is the output of the transform, formatted for easier viewing (code file argSample.xml):

```xml
<books>
   <discbook>
      <booktitle>The Autobiography of Benjamin Franklin</booktitle>
      <showtext>This came from the ShowText method!</showtext>
   </discbook>
   <discbook>
      <booktitle>The Confidence Man</booktitle>
      <showtext>This came from the ShowText method!</showtext>
   </discbook>
   <discbook>
      <booktitle>The Gorgias</booktitle>
      <showtext>This came from the ShowText method!</showtext>
   </discbook>
   <discbook>
      <booktitle>The Great Cookie Caper</booktitle>
      <showtext>This came from the ShowText method!</showtext>
   </discbook>
   <discbook>
```

```
        <booktitle>A Really Great Book</booktitle>
        <showtext>This came from the ShowText method!</showtext>
    </discbook>
</books>
```

In this example, you define a new class, `BookUtils`, which has one rather useless method that returns the string `This came from the ShowText method!` In the `button3_Click` event, you create the `XPathDocument` and `XslTransform` objects. In a previous example, you loaded the XML document and the transform document directly into the `XslCompiledTransform` object. This time, you use the `XPathNavigator` to load the documents.

Next, you need to write the following:

```
XsltArgumentList argBook=new XsltArgumentList();
BookUtils bu=new BookUtils();
argBook.AddExtensionObject("urn:XslSample",bu);
```

This is where you create the `XsltArgumentList` object. You create an instance of the `BookUtils` object, and when you call the `AddExtensionObject` method, you pass in a namespace for your extension and the object from which you want to be able to call methods. When you make the `Transform` call, you pass in the `XsltArgumentList` (argBook), along with the `XPathNavigator` and the `XmlWriter` object you made.

The following is the `booksarg.xsl` document (based on `books.xsl`):

```
<xsl:stylesheet version="1.0" xmlns:xsl="http://www.w3.org/1999/XSL/Transform"
    xmlns:bookUtil="urn:XslSample">
<xsl:output method="xml" indent="yes"/>
<xsl:template match="/">
    <xsl:element name="books">
        <xsl:apply-templates/>
    </xsl:element>
</xsl:template>
<xsl:template match="bookstore">
    <xsl:apply-templates select="book"/>
</xsl:template>
<xsl:template match="book">
    <xsl:element name="discbook">
        <xsl:element name="booktitle">
            <xsl:value-of select="title"/>
        </xsl:element>
        <xsl:element name="showtext">
            <xsl:value-of select="bookUtil:ShowText()"/>
        </xsl:element>
    </xsl:element>
</xsl:template>
</xsl:stylesheet>
```

The two important new lines are highlighted. First, you add the namespace that you created when you added the object to `XsltArgumentList`. Then, when you want to make the method call, you use standard XSLT namespace-prefixing syntax and make the method call.

Another way you could have accomplished this is with XSLT scripting. You can include C#, Visual Basic, and JavaScript code in the stylesheet. The great thing about this is that unlike current non-.NET implementations, the script is compiled at the `XslTransform.Load` call; this way, you are executing already compiled scripts.

Go ahead and modify the previous XSLT file in this way. First, you add the script to the stylesheet. You can see the following changes in `booksscript.xsl`:

```
<xsl:stylesheet version="1.0" xmlns:xsl="http://www.w3.org/1999/XSL/Transform"
                              xmlns:msxsl="urn:schemas-microsoft-com:xslt"
                              xmlns:user="http://wrox.com">
   <msxsl:script language="C#" implements-prefix="user">
      string ShowText()
         {
             return "This came from the ShowText method!";
         }
   </msxsl:script>
   <xsl:output method="xml" indent="yes"/>
      <xsl:template match="/">
   <xsl:element name="books">
      <xsl:apply-templates/>
   </xsl:element>
      </xsl:template>
   <xsl:template match="bookstore">
      <xsl:apply-templates select="book"/>
   </xsl:template>
      <xsl:template match="book">
      <xsl:element name="discbook">
      <xsl:element name="booktitle">
         <xsl:value-of select="title"/>
      </xsl:element>
      <xsl:element name="showtext">
         <xsl:value-of select="user:ShowText()"/>
      </xsl:element>
     </xsl:element>
     </xsl:template>
</xsl:stylesheet>
```

As before, the changes are highlighted. You set the scripting namespace, add the code (which was copied and pasted in from the Visual Studio .NET IDE), and make the call in the stylesheet. The output is the same as that of the previous example.

Debugging XSLT

Visual Studio 2012 has the capability to debug transforms. You can actually step through a transform line by line, inspect variables, access the call stack, and set breakpoints just as if you were debugging C# source code. You can debug a transform in two ways: by just using the stylesheet and input XML file or by running the application to which the transform belongs.

Debugging without the Application

When you first start creating the transforms, sometimes you don't want to run through the entire application. You may just want to get a stylesheet working. Visual Studio 2012 enables you to do this using the XSLT editor.

Load the books.xsl stylesheet into the Visual Studio 2012 XSLT editor. Set a breakpoint on the following line:

```
<xsl:value-of select="title"/>
```

Next, select the XML menu and then Debug XSLT. You will be asked for the input XML document. This is the XML that you want transformed. Under the default configuration, the next thing you will see is shown in Figure 34-4.

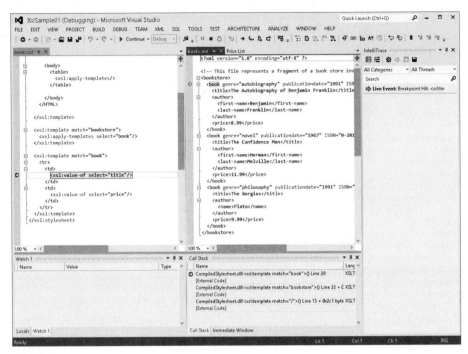

FIGURE 34-4

Now that the transform has been paused, you can explore almost all the same debug information you can when debugging source code. Notice that the debugger is displaying the XSLT, the input document with the current element highlighted, and the output of the transform. Now you can step through the transform line by line. If your XSLT had any scripting, you could also set breakpoints in the scripts and have the same debugging experience.

Debugging with the Application

If you want to debug a transform and the application at the same time, then you have to make one small change when you create the `XslCompiledTransform` object. The constructor has an overload that takes a Boolean as a parameter. This parameter is `enableDebug`. The default is `false`, which means that even if you have a break-point set in the transform, if you run the application code that calls the transform, it will not break. If you set the parameter to `true`, the debug information for the XSLT is generated and the breakpoint will be hit. Therefore, in the previous example, the line of code that created the `XslCompiledTransform` would change to this:

```
XslCompiledTransform trans = new XslCompiledTransform(true);
```

Now when the application is run in debug mode, even the XSLT will have debug information and you again have the full Visual Studio debugging experience in your stylesheets.

To summarize, the key thing to keep in mind when performing transforms is to remember to use the proper XML data store. Use `XPathDocument` if you do not need editing capabilities, `XmlDataDocument` if you are getting your data from ADO.NET, and `XmlDocument` if you need to be able to edit the data. In each case, you are dealing with the same process.

XML AND ADO.NET

XML is the glue that binds ADO.NET to the rest of the world. ADO.NET was designed from the ground up to work within the XML environment. XML is used to transfer the data to and from the data store and the application or web page. Because ADO.NET uses XML as the transport in remoting scenarios, data can be exchanged with applications and systems that are not even aware of ADO.NET. Because of the importance of XML in ADO.NET, some powerful features in ADO.NET allow the reading and writing of XML documents. The `System.Xml` namespace also contains classes that can consume or utilize ADO.NET relational data.

The database used for the examples is from the AdventureWorksLT sample application. The sample database can be downloaded from `codeplex.com/SqlServerSamples`. Note that there are several versions of the AdventureWorks database. Most will work, but the LT version is simplified and more than adequate for the purposes of this chapter.

Converting ADO.NET Data to XML

The first example uses ADO.NET, streams, and XML to pull some data from the database into a `DataSet`, load an `XmlDocument` object with the XML from the `DataSet`, and load the XML into a text box. To run the next few examples, you need to add the following `using` statements:

```
using System.Data;
using System.Xml;
using System.Data.SqlClient;
using System.IO;
```

The connection string is defined as a module-level variable:

```
string _connectString = "Server=.\\SQLExpress;
                         Database=adventureworkslt;Trusted_Connection=Yes";
```

The ADO.NET samples have a `DataGrid` object added to the forms. This enables you to see the data in the ADO.NET `DataSet` because it is bound to the grid, as well as the data from the generated XML documents that you load in the text box. The code for the first example follows. The first step in the examples is to create the standard ADO.NET objects to produce a `DataSet` object. After the data set has been created, it is bound to the grid (`frmADOXML.cs`):

```
private void button1_Click(object sender, EventArgs e)
{
  XmlDocument doc = new XmlDocument();
  DataSet ds = new DataSet("XMLProducts");
  SqlConnection conn = new SqlConnection(_connectString);
  SqlDataAdapter da = new SqlDataAdapter
                      ("SELECT Name, StandardCost FROM SalesLT.Product", conn);
  //fill the dataset
  da.Fill(ds, "Products");
  //load data into grid
  dataGridView1.DataSource = ds.Tables["Products"];
```

After you create the ADO.NET objects and bind to the grid, you instantiate a `MemoryStream` object, a `StreamReader` object, and a `StreamWriter` object. The `StreamReader` and `StreamWriter` objects will use the `MemoryStream` to move the XML around:

```
MemoryStream memStrm=new MemoryStream();
StreamReader strmRead=new StreamReader(memStrm);
StreamWriter strmWrite=new StreamWriter(memStrm);
```

You use a `MemoryStream` so that you don't have to write anything to disk; however, you could have used any object that was based on the `Stream` class, such as `FileStream`.

This next step is where the XML is generated. You call the `WriteXml` method from the `DataSet` class. This method generates an XML document. `WriteXml` has two overloads: one takes a string with the file path and name, and the other adds a mode parameter. This mode is an enumeration, with the following possible values:

➤ IgnoreSchema

➤ WriteSchema

➤ DiffGram

IgnoreSchema is used if you do not want WriteXml to write an inline schema at the start of your XML file; use the WriteSchema parameter if you do want one. A DiffGram shows the data before and after an edit in a DataSet.

```
//write the xml from the dataset to the memory stream
  ds.WriteXml(strmWrite, XmlWriteMode.IgnoreSchema);
  memStrm.Seek(0, SeekOrigin.Begin);
  //read from the memory stream to a XmlDocument object
  doc.Load(strmRead);
  //get all of the products elements
  XmlNodeList nodeLst = doc.SelectNodes("//XMLProducts/Products");
  textBox1.Text = "";

  foreach (XmlNode node in nodeLst)
  {
    textBox1.Text += node.InnerXml + "\r\n";
  }
```

Figure 34-5 shows the data in the list as well as the bound data grid.

Had you wanted only the schema, you could have called WriteXmlSchema instead of WriteXml. This method has four overloads. One takes a string, which is the path and filename of the location to which the XML document is written. The second overload uses an object that is based on the XmlWriter class. The third overload uses an object based on the TextWriter class. The fourth overload is derived from the Stream class.

In addition, if you wanted to persist the XML document to disk, you would have used something like this:

```
string file = "c:\\test\\product.xml";
ds.WriteXml(file);
```

This would give you a well-formed XML document on disk that could be read in by another stream or by a DataSet or used

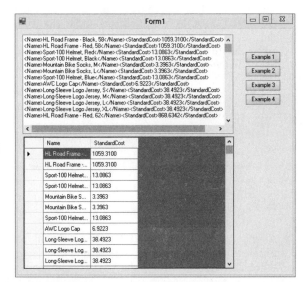

FIGURE 34-5

by another application or website. Because no XmlMode parameter is specified, this XmlDocument would include the schema. In this example, you use the stream as a parameter to the XmlDocument.Load method.

You now have two views of the data, but more important, you can manipulate the data using two different models. You can use the System.Data namespace to use the data, or you can use the System.Xml namespace on the data. This enables very flexible designs in your applications, because now you are not tied to programming with just one object model. This is the real power of the ADO.NET and System.Xml combination. You have multiple views of the same data and multiple ways to access the data.

The following example simplifies the process by eliminating the three streams and using some of the ADO capabilities built into the `System.Xml` namespace. You need to change the module-level line of code,

```
private XmlDocument doc = new XmlDocument();
```

to:

```
private XmlDataDocument doc;
```

You need this because you are now using the `XmlDataDocument`. Here is the code:

```
private void button3_Click(object sender, EventArgs e)
{
  XmlDataDocument doc;
  //create a dataset
  DataSet ds = new DataSet("XMLProducts");
  //connect to the northwind database and
  //select all of the rows from products table
  SqlConnection conn = new SqlConnection(_connectString);
  SqlDataAdapter da = new SqlDataAdapter
                      ("SELECT Name, StandardCost FROM SalesLT.Product", conn);
  //fill the dataset
  da.Fill(ds, "Products");
  ds.WriteXml("sample.xml", XmlWriteMode.WriteSchema);
  //load data into grid
  dataGridView1.DataSource = ds.Tables[0];
  doc = new XmlDataDocument(ds);
  //get all of the products elements
  XmlNodeList nodeLst = doc.GetElementsByTagName("Products");
  textBox1.Text = "";
  foreach (XmlNode node in nodeLst)
  {
    textBox1.Text += node.InnerXml + "\r\n";
  }
}
```

As you can see, the code to load the `DataSet` object into the XML document has been simplified. Instead of using the `XmlDocument` class, you are using the `XmlDataDocument` class. This class was built specifically for using data with a `DataSet` object.

The `XmlDataDocument` is based on the `XmlDocument` class, so it has all the functionality of the `XmlDocument` class. One of the main differences is the overloaded constructor of `XmlDataDocument`. Note the line of code that instantiates `XmlDataDocument` (`doc`):

```
doc = new XmlDataDocument(ds);
```

It passes in the `DataSet` object that you created, `ds`, as a parameter. This creates the XML document from the `DataSet`, and you do not have to use the `Load` method. In fact, if you instantiate a new `XmlDataDocument` object without passing in a `DataSet` as the parameter, it will contain a `DataSet` with the name `NewDataSet` that has no `DataTables` in the `tables` collection. There is also a `DataSet` property, which you can set after an `XmlDataDocument`-based object is created.

Suppose that you add the following line of code after the `DataSet.Fill` call:

```
ds.WriteXml("c:\\test\\sample.xml", XmlWriteMode.WriteSchema);
```

In this case, the following XML file, `sample.xml`, is produced in the folder `c:\test`:

```
<?xml version="1.0" standalone="yes"?>
<XMLProducts>
  <xs:schema id="XMLProducts" xmlns="" xmlns:xs="http://www.w3.org/2001/XMLSchema"
   xmlns:msdata="urn:schemas-microsoft-com:xml-msdata">
```

```
        <xs:element name="XMLProducts" msdata:IsDataSet="true"
         msdata:UseCurrentLocale="true">
          <xs:complexType>
            <xs:choice minOccurs="0" maxOccurs="unbounded">
              <xs:element name="Products">
                <xs:complexType>
                  <xs:sequence>
                    <xs:element name="Name" type="xs:string" minOccurs="0" />
                    <xs:element name="StandardCost" type="xs:decimal" minOccurs="0" />
                  </xs:sequence>
                </xs:complexType>
              </xs:element>
            </xs:choice>
          </xs:complexType>
        </xs:element>
    </xs:schema>
    <Products>
      <Name>HL Road Frame-Black, 58</Name>
      <StandardCost>1059.3100</StandardCost>
    </Products>
    <Products>
      <Name>HL Road Frame-Red, 58</Name>
      <StandardCost>1059.3100</StandardCost>
    </Products>
    <Products>
      <Name>Sport-100 Helmet, Red</Name>
      <StandardCost>13.0863</StandardCost>
    </Products>
  </XMLProducts>
```

Only the first couple of `Products` elements are shown. The actual XML file would contain all the products in the `Products` table of the `Northwind` database.

Converting Relational Data

That looks simple enough for a single table, but what about relational data, such as multiple `DataTables` and `Relations` in the `DataSet`? It all still works the same way. Here is an example using two related tables (code file `frmADOXML.cs`):

```
private void button5_Click(object sender, EventArgs e)
{
  XmlDocument doc = new XmlDocument();
  DataSet ds = new DataSet("XMLProducts");
  SqlConnection conn = new SqlConnection(_connectString);
  SqlDataAdapter daProduct = new SqlDataAdapter
  ("SELECT Name, StandardCost, ProductCategoryID FROM SalesLT.Product", conn);
  SqlDataAdapter daCategory = new SqlDataAdapter
        ("SELECT ProductCategoryID, Name from SalesLT.ProductCategory", conn);
  //Fill DataSet from both SqlAdapters
  daProduct.Fill(ds, "Products");
  daCategory.Fill(ds, "Categories");
  //Add the relation
  ds.Relations.Add(ds.Tables["Categories"].Columns["ProductCategoryID"],
  ds.Tables["Products"].Columns["ProductCategoryID"]);
  //Write the Xml to a file so we can look at it later
  ds.WriteXml("Products.xml", XmlWriteMode.WriteSchema);
  //load data into grid
  dataGridView1.DataSource = ds.Tables[0];
  //create the XmlDataDocument
  doc = new XmlDataDocument(ds);
  //Select the productname elements and load them in the grid
```

```
    XmlNodeList nodeLst = doc.SelectNodes("//XMLProducts/Products");
    textBox1.Text = "";
    foreach (XmlNode node in nodeLst)
    {
      textBox1.Text += node.InnerXml + "\r\n";
    }
  }
```

In the sample you are creating, there are two `DataTables` in the `XMLProducts DataSet`: `Products` and `Categories`. You create a new relation on the `ProductCategoryID` column in both tables.

By using the same `WriteXml` method call that you did in the previous example, you get the following XML file (code file `SuppProd.xml`):

```xml
<?xml version="1.0" standalone="yes"?>
<XMLProducts>
  <xs:schema id="XMLProducts" xmlns="" xmlns:xs="http://www.w3.org/2001/XMLSchema"
   xmlns:msdata="urn:schemas-microsoft-com:xml-msdata">
    <xs:element name="XMLProducts" msdata:IsDataSet="true"
     msdata:UseCurrentLocale="true">
      <xs:complexType>
        <xs:choice minOccurs="0" maxOccurs="unbounded">
          <xs:element name="Products">
            <xs:complexType>
              <xs:sequence>
                <xs:element name="Name" type="xs:string" minOccurs="0" />
                <xs:element name="StandardCost" type="xs:decimal" minOccurs="0" />
                <xs:element name="ProductCategoryID" type="xs:int" minOccurs="0" />
              </xs:sequence>
            </xs:complexType>
          </xs:element>
          <xs:element name="Categories">
            <xs:complexType>
              <xs:sequence>
                <xs:element name="ProductCategoryID" type="xs:int" minOccurs="0" />
                <xs:element name="Name" type="xs:string" minOccurs="0" />
              </xs:sequence>
            </xs:complexType>
          </xs:element>
        </xs:choice>
      </xs:complexType>
      <xs:unique name="Constraint1">
        <xs:selector xpath=".//Categories" />
        <xs:field xpath="ProductCategoryID" />
      </xs:unique>
      <xs:keyref name="Relation1" refer="Constraint1">
        <xs:selector xpath=".//Products" />
        <xs:field xpath="ProductCategoryID" />
      </xs:keyref>
    </xs:element>
  </xs:schema>
  <Products>
    <Name>HL Road Frame-Black, 58</Name>
    <StandardCost>1059.3100</StandardCost>
    <ProductCategoryID>18</ProductCategoryID>
  </Products>
  <Products>
    <Name>HL Road Frame-Red, 58</Name>
    <StandardCost>1059.3100</StandardCost>
    <ProductCategoryID>18</ProductCategoryID>
  </Products>
</XMLProducts>
```

The schema includes both DataTables that were in the DataSet. In addition, the data includes all the data from both tables. For the sake of brevity, only the first Products and ProductCategory records are shown here. As before, you could have saved just the schema or just the data by passing in the correct XmlWriteMode parameter.

Converting XML to ADO.NET Data

Suppose that you have an XML document that you would like to convert into an ADO.NET DataSet. You might want to do this so that you could load the XML into a database, or perhaps bind the data to a .NET data control such as a DataGrid. This way, you could actually use the XML document as your data store and eliminate the overhead of the database altogether. If your data is reasonably small, this is an attractive possibility. Here is some code to get you started:

```
private void button7_Click(object sender, EventArgs e)
{
    //create the DataSet
    DataSet ds = new DataSet("XMLProducts");

    //read in the xml document
    ds.ReadXml("Products.xml");

    //load data into grid
    dataGridView1.DataSource = ds.Tables[0];

    textBox1.Text = "";

    foreach (DataTable dt in ds.Tables)
    {
        textBox1.Text += dt.TableName + "\r\n";
        foreach (DataColumn col in dt.Columns)
        {
            textBox1.Text += "\t" + col.ColumnName + "-" + col.DataType.FullName +
                "\r\n";
        }
    }
}
```

It's that easy. In this example, you instantiate a new DataSet object. From there, you call the ReadXml method and you have XML in a DataTable in your DataSet. As with the WriteXml methods, ReadXml has an XmlReadMode parameter. ReadXml has a few more options in the XmlReadMode, as shown in the following table.

VALUE	DESCRIPTION
Auto	Sets the XmlReadMode to the most appropriate setting. If the data is in DiffGram format, DiffGram is selected. If a schema has already been read, or an inline schema is detected, then ReadSchema is selected. If no schema has been assigned to the DataSet and none is detected inline, then IgnoreSchema is selected.
DiffGram	Reads in the DiffGram and applies the changes to the DataSet.
Fragment	Reads documents that contain XDR schema fragments, such as the type created by SQL Server.
IgnoreSchema	Ignores any inline schema that may be found. Reads data into the current DataSet schema. If data does not match DataSet schema, it is discarded.
InferSchema	Ignores any inline schema. Creates the schema based on data in the XML document. If a schema exists in the DataSet, that schema is used, and extended with additional columns and tables if needed. An exception is thrown if a column exists but is of a different data type.
ReadSchema	Reads the inline schema and loads the data. Will not overwrite a schema in the DataSet but will throw an exception if a table in the inline schema already exists in the DataSet.

There is also a `ReadXmlSchema` method. This reads in a standalone schema and creates the tables, columns, and relations. You use this if your schema is not inline with your data. `ReadXmlSchema` has the same four overloads: a string with filename and pathname, a `Stream`-based object, a `TextReader`-based object, and an `XmlReader`-based object.

To confirm that the data tables are being created properly, you can iterate through the tables and columns and display the names in the text box, and then compare this to the database to verify that all is well. The last `foreach` loops perform this task. Figure 34-6 shows the output.

Looking at the list box, you can confirm that in the data tables that were created, all the columns have the correct names and data types.

Something else you might want to note is that, because the previous two examples did not transfer any data to or from a database, no `SqlDataAdapter` or `SqlConnection` was

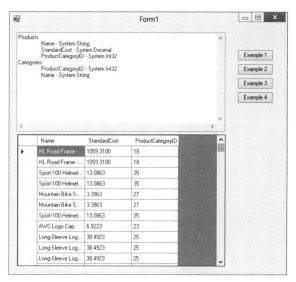

FIGURE 34-6

defined. This shows the real flexibility of both the `System.Xml` namespace and ADO.NET: you can look at the same data in multiple formats. Whether you need to do a transform and show the data in HTML format, or whether you need to bind the data to a grid, you can take the same data and, with just a method call, have it in the required format.

SERIALIZING OBJECTS IN XML

Serializing is the process of persisting an object to disk. Another part of your application, or even a separate application, can deserialize the object, and it will be in the same state it was in prior to serialization. The .NET Framework includes a couple of ways to do this.

This section looks at the `System.Xml.Serialization` namespace, which contains classes used to serialize objects into XML documents or streams. This means that an object's public properties and public fields are converted into XML elements, attributes, or both.

The most important class in the `System.Xml.Serialization` namespace is `XmlSerializer`. To serialize an object, you first need to instantiate an `XmlSerializer` object, specifying the type of the object to serialize. Then you need to instantiate a stream/writer object to write the file to a stream/document. The final step is to call the `Serialize` method on the `XMLSerializer`, passing it the stream/writer object and the object to serialize.

Data that can be serialized can be primitive types, fields, arrays, and embedded XML in the form of `XmlElement` and `XmlAttribute` objects. To deserialize an object from an XML document, you reverse the process in the previous example. You create a stream/reader and an `XmlSerializer` object and then pass the stream/reader to the `Deserialize` method. This method returns the deserialized object, although it needs to be cast to the correct type.

> **NOTE** *The XML serializer cannot convert private data, only public data, and it cannot serialize object graphs. However, these are not serious limitations; by carefully designing your classes, you should be able to easily avoid these issues. If you do need to be able to serialize public and private data as well as an object graph containing many nested objects, use the* `System.Runtime.Serialization.Formatters.Binary` *namespace.*

Some of the other tasks that you can accomplish with `System.Xml.Serialization` classes are as follows:

➤ Determine whether the data should be an attribute or element

➤ Specify the namespace

➤ Change the attribute or element name

The links between your object and the XML document are the custom C# attributes that annotate your classes. These attributes are what are used to determine how the serializer writes out the data. The `xsd.exe` tool, which is included with the .NET Framework, can help create these attributes for you. `xsd.exe` can do the following:

➤ Generate an XML schema from an XDR schema file

➤ Generate an XML schema from an XML file

➤ Generate `DataSet` classes from an XSD schema file

➤ Generate runtime classes that have the custom attributes for `XmlSerialization`

➤ Generate an XSD file from classes that you have already developed

➤ Limit which elements are created in code

➤ Determine the programming language of the generated code (C#, Visual Basic .NET, or JScript .NET)

➤ Create schemas from types in compiled assemblies

See the .NET Framework documentation for details about command-line options for `xsd.exe`.

Despite these capabilities, you don't *have* to use `xsd.exe` to create the classes for serialization. The process is quite simple. The following is a simple application that serializes a class. At the beginning of the example, you have very simple code that creates a new `Product` object, `pd`, and fills it with some data (code file `frmSerial.cs`):

```
private void button1_Click(object sender, EventArgs e)
{
  //new products object
  Product pd = new Product();
  //set some properties
  pd.ProductID = 200;
  pd.CategoryID = 100;
  pd.Discontinued = false;
  pd.ProductName = "Serialize Objects";
  pd.QuantityPerUnit = "6";
  pd.ReorderLevel = 1;
  pd.SupplierID = 1;
  pd.UnitPrice = 1000;
  pd.UnitsInStock = 10;
  pd.UnitsOnOrder = 0;

}
```

The `Serialize` method of the `XmlSerializer` class actually performs the serialization, and it has nine overloads. One of the parameters required is a stream to which the data should be written. It can be a `Stream`, a `TextWriter`, or an `XmlWriter` parameter. In the example, you create a `TextWriter`-based object, `tr`. Next, you create the `XmlSerializer`-based object, `sr`. The `XmlSerializer` needs to know type information for the object that it is serializing, so you use the `typeof` keyword with the type that is to be serialized. After the `sr` object is created, you call the `Serialize` method, passing in the `tr` (`Stream`-based object) and the object that you want serialized, in this case `pd`. Be sure to close the stream when you are finished with it:

```
//new TextWriter and XmlSerializer
TextWriter tr = new StreamWriter("serialprod.xml");
XmlSerializer sr = new XmlSerializer(typeof(Product));
```

```
//serialize object
sr.Serialize(tr, pd);
tr.Close();
webBrowser1.Navigate(AppDomain.CurrentDomain.BaseDirectory + "serialprod.xml");
```

Next is the `Product` class, the class to be serialized. The only differences between this and any other class that you may write are the C# attributes that have been added. The `XmlRootAttribute` and `XmlElementAttribute` classes in the attributes inherit from the `System.Attribute` class. Don't confuse these attributes with the attributes in an XML document. A C# attribute is simply some declarative information that can be retrieved at runtime by the CLR. In this case, the attributes describe how the object should be serialized:

```
//class that will be serialized.
//attributes determine how object is serialized
[System.Xml.Serialization.XmlRootAttribute()]
  public class Product {
    private int prodId;
    private string prodName;
    private int suppId;
    private int catId;
    private string qtyPerUnit;
    private Decimal unitPrice;
    private short unitsInStock;
    private short unitsOnOrder;
    private short reorderLvl;
    private bool discont;
    private int disc;
    //added the Discount attribute
    [XmlAttributeAttribute(AttributeName="Discount")]
    public int Discount {
      get {return disc;}
      set {disc=value;}
    }
    [XmlElementAttribute()]
    public int  ProductID {
      get {return prodId;}
      set {prodId=value;}
    }
    [XmlElementAttribute()]
    public string ProductName {
      get {return prodName;}
      set {prodName=value;}
    }
    [XmlElementAttribute()]
    public int SupplierID {
      get {return suppId;}
      set {suppId=value;}
    }
    [XmlElementAttribute()]
    public int CategoryID {
      get {return catId;}
      set {catId=value;}
    }
    [XmlElementAttribute()]
    public string QuantityPerUnit {
      get {return qtyPerUnit;}
      set {qtyPerUnit=value;}
    }
    [XmlElementAttribute()]
    public Decimal UnitPrice {
      get {return unitPrice;}
```

```
      set {unitPrice=value;}
   }
   [XmlElementAttribute()]
   public short UnitsInStock {
     get {return unitsInStock;}
     set {unitsInStock=value;}
   }
   [XmlElementAttribute()]
   public short UnitsOnOrder {
     get {return unitsOnOrder;}
     set {unitsOnOrder=value;}
   }
   [XmlElementAttribute()]
   public short ReorderLevel {
     get {return reorderLvl;}
     set {reorderLvl=value;}
   }
   [XmlElementAttribute()]
   public bool Discontinued {
     get {return discont;}
     set {discont=value;}
   }
   public override string ToString()
   {
     StringBuilder outText = new StringBuilder();
     outText.Append(prodId);
     outText.Append(" ");
     outText.Append(prodName);
     outText.Append(" ");
     outText.Append(unitPrice);
     return outText.ToString();
   }
}
```

The `XmlRootAttribute` invocation in the attribute above the `Products` class definition identifies this class as a root element (in the XML file produced upon serialization). The attribute containing `XmlElementAttribute` indicates that the member below the attribute represents an XML element.

Notice that the `ToString` method has been overridden. This provides the string that the message box will show when you run the deserialize example.

If you look at the XML document created during serialization, you will see that it looks like any other XML document that you might have created, which is the point of the exercise:

```xml
<?xml version="1.0" encoding="utf-8"?>
<Products xmlns:xsi=http://www.w3.org/2001/XMLSchema-instance
  xmlns:xsd="http://www.w3.org/2001/XMLSchema"
  Discount="0">
  <ProductID>200</ProductID>
  <ProductName>Serialize Objects</ProductName>
  <SupplierID>1</SupplierID>
  <CategoryID>100</CategoryID>
  <QuantityPerUnit>6</QuantityPerUnit>
  <UnitPrice>1000</UnitPrice>
  <UnitsInStock>10</UnitsInStock>
  <UnitsOnOrder>0</UnitsOnOrder>
  <ReorderLevel>1</ReorderLevel>
  <Discontinued>false</Discontinued>
</Products>
```

There is nothing out of the ordinary here. You could use this any way that you would use an XML document—transform it and display it as HTML, load it into a `DataSet` using ADO.NET, load an

XmlDocument with it, or, as shown in the example, deserialize it and create an object in the same state that pd was in prior to serializing it (which is exactly what you're doing with the second button).

Next, you add another button event handler to deserialize a new Products-based object, newPd. This time you use a FileStream object to read in the XML:

```
private void button2_Click(object sender, EventArgs e)
    {
        //create a reference to product type
        Product newPd;
        //new filestream to open serialized object
        FileStream f = new FileStream("serialprod.xml", FileMode.Open);
```

Again, you create a new XmlSerializer, passing in the type information of Product. You can then make the call to the Deserialize method. Note that you still need to do an explicit cast when you create the newPd object. At this point, newPd is in exactly the same state that pd was:

```
//new serializer
        XmlSerializer newSr = new XmlSerializer(typeof(Product));
        //deserialize the object
        newPd = (Product)newSr.Deserialize(f);
        f.Close();
        MessageBox.Show(newPd.ToString());
    }
```

The message box should display the product ID, the product name, and the unit price of the object you just deserialized. This results from the ToString override that you implemented in the Product class.

What about situations in which you have derived classes and possibly properties that return an array? XmlSerializer has that covered as well. Here's a slightly more complex example that deals with these issues.

First, you define three new classes, Product, BookProduct (derived from Product), and Inventory (which contains both of the other classes). Notice that again you have overridden the ToString method. This time you're just going to list the items in the Inventory class:

```
public class BookProduct: Product
{
    private string isbnNum;
    public BookProduct() {}
    public string ISBN
    {
        get {return isbnNum;}
        set {isbnNum=value;}
    }
}

public class Inventory
{
    private Product[] stuff;
    public Inventory() {}
    //need to have an attribute entry for each data type
    [XmlArrayItem("Prod",typeof(Product)),
    XmlArrayItem("Book",typeof(BookProduct))]
    public Product[] InventoryItems
    {
        get {return stuff;}
        set {stuff=value;}
    }
    public override string ToString()
```

```
      {
        StringBuilder outText = new StringBuilder();
        foreach (Product prod in stuff)
        {
          outText.Append(prod.ProductName);
          outText.Append("\r\n");
        }
        return outText.ToString();
      }
  }
```

The `Inventory` class is the one of interest here. To serialize this class, you need to insert an attribute containing `XmlArrayItem` constructors for each type that can be added to the array. Note that `XmlArrayItem` is the name of the .NET attribute represented by the `XmlArrayItemAttribute` class.

The first parameter supplied to these constructors is what you would like the element name to be in the XML document that is created during serialization. If you omit the `ElementName` parameter, the elements will be given the same name as the object type (`Product` and `BookProduct` in this case). The second parameter that must be specified is the type of the object.

There is also an `XmlArrayAttribute` class that you would use if the property were returning an array of objects or primitive types. Because you are returning different types in the array, you use `XmlArrayItemAttribute`, which enables the higher level of control.

In the `button4_Click` event handler, you create a new `Product` object and a new `BookProduct` object (`newProd` and `newBook`). You add data to the various properties of each object, and add the objects to a `Product` array. You next create a new `Inventory` object and pass in the array as a parameter. You can then serialize the `Inventory` object to re-create it later:

```
private void button4_Click(object sender, EventArgs e)
{
  //create the XmlAttributes object
  XmlAttributes attrs = new XmlAttributes();
  //add the types of the objects that will be serialized
  attrs.XmlElements.Add(new XmlElementAttribute("Book", typeof(BookProduct)));
  attrs.XmlElements.Add(new XmlElementAttribute("Product", typeof(Product)));
  XmlAttributeOverrides attrOver = new XmlAttributeOverrides();
  //add to the attributes collection
  attrOver.Add(typeof(Inventory), "InventoryItems", attrs);
  //create the Product and Book objects
  Product newProd = new Product();
  BookProduct newBook = new BookProduct();
  newProd.ProductID = 100;
  newProd.ProductName = "Product Thing";
  newProd.SupplierID = 10;
  newBook.ProductID = 101;
  newBook.ProductName = "How to Use Your New Product Thing";
  newBook.SupplierID = 10;
  newBook.ISBN = "123456789";
  Product[] addProd ={ newProd, newBook };
  Inventory inv = new Inventory();
  inv.InventoryItems = addProd;
  TextWriter tr = new StreamWriter("inventory.xml");
  XmlSerializer sr = new XmlSerializer(typeof(Inventory), attrOver);
  sr.Serialize(tr, inv);
  tr.Close();
  webBrowser1.Navigate(AppDomain.CurrentDomain.BaseDirectory + "inventory.xml");
}
```

The XML document looks like this:

```xml
<?xml version="1.0" encoding="utf-8"?>
<Inventory xmlns:xsi="http://www.w3.org/2001/XMLSchema-instance"
 xmlns:xsd="http://www.w3.org/2001/XMLSchema">
  <Product Discount="0">
    <ProductID>100</ProductID>
    <ProductName>Product Thing</ProductName>
    <SupplierID>10</SupplierID>
    <CategoryID>0</CategoryID>
    <UnitPrice>0</UnitPrice>
    <UnitsInStock>0</UnitsInStock>
    <UnitsOnOrder>0</UnitsOnOrder>
    <ReorderLevel>0</ReorderLevel>
    <Discontinued>false</Discontinued>
  </Product>
  <Book Discount="0">
    <ProductID>101</ProductID>
    <ProductName>How to Use Your New Product Thing</ProductName>
    <SupplierID>10</SupplierID>
    <CategoryID>0</CategoryID>
    <UnitPrice>0</UnitPrice>
    <UnitsInStock>0</UnitsInStock>
    <UnitsOnOrder>0</UnitsOnOrder>
    <ReorderLevel>0</ReorderLevel>
    <Discontinued>false</Discontinued>
    <ISBN>123456789</ISBN>
  </Book>
</Inventory>
```

The `button2_Click` event handler implements deserialization of the `Inventory` object. Note that you iterate through the array in the newly created `newInv` object to show that it is the same data:

```csharp
private void button2_Click(object sender, System.EventArgs e)
{
    Inventory newInv;
    FileStream f=new FileStream("order.xml",FileMode.Open);
    XmlSerializer newSr=new XmlSerializer(typeof(Inventory));
    newInv=(Inventory)newSr.Deserialize(f);
    foreach(Product prod in newInv.InventoryItems)
        listBox1.Items.Add(prod.ProductName);
    f.Close();
}
```

Serialization without Source Code Access

Well, this all works great, but what if you don't have access to the source code for the types that are being serialized? You can't add the attribute if you don't have the source. There is another way: You can use the `XmlAttributes` class and the `XmlAttributeOverrides` class. Together these classes enable you to accomplish exactly what you just did, but without adding the attributes. This section demonstrates how this works.

For this example, imagine that the `Inventory`, `Product`, and derived `BookProduct` classes are in a separate DLL and that you do not have the source. The `Product` and `BookProduct` classes are the same as in the previous example, but note that now no attributes are added to the `Inventory` class:

```csharp
public class Inventory
{
    private Product[] stuff;
    public Inventory() {}
    public Product[] InventoryItems
    {
```

```
        get {return stuff;}
        set {stuff=value;}
    }
}
```

Next, you deal with the serialization in the `button1_Click` event handler:

```
private void button1_Click(object sender, System.EventArgs e)
{
```

The first step in the serialization process is to create an `XmlAttributes` object and an `XmlElementAttribute` object for each data type that you will be overriding:

```
    XmlAttributes attrs=new XmlAttributes();
    attrs.XmlElements.Add(new XmlElementAttribute("Book",typeof(BookProduct)));
    attrs.XmlElements.Add(new XmlElementAttribute("Product",typeof(Product)));
```

Here you can see that you are adding new `XmlElementAttribute` objects to the `XmlElements` collection of the `XmlAttributes` class. The `XmlAttributes` class has properties that correspond to the attributes that can be applied; `XmlArray` and `XmlArrayItems`, which you looked at in the previous example, are just a couple of these. You now have an `XmlAttributes` object with two `XmlElementAttribute`-based objects added to the `XmlElements` collection.

Now you create an `XmlAttributeOverrides` object:

```
    XmlAttributeOverrides attrOver=new XmlAttributeOverrides();
    attrOver.Add(typeof(Inventory),"InventoryItems",attrs);
```

The `Add` method of this class has two overloads. The first one takes the type information of the object to override and the `XmlAttributes` object that you created earlier. The other overload, which is the one you are using, also takes a string value that is the member in the overridden object. In this case, you want to override the `InventoryItems` member in the `Inventory` class.

When you create the `XmlSerializer` object, you add the `XmlAttributeOverrides` object as a parameter. Now the `XmlSerializer` knows which types you want to override and what you need to return for those types:

```
//create the Product and Book objects
    Product newProd=new Product();
    BookProduct newBook=new BookProduct();
    newProd.ProductID=100;
    newProd.ProductName="Product Thing";
    newProd.SupplierID=10;
    newBook.ProductID=101;
    newBook.ProductName="How to Use Your New Product Thing";
    newBook.SupplierID=10;
    newBook.ISBN="123456789";
    Product[] addProd={newProd,newBook};

    Inventory inv=new Inventory();
    inv.InventoryItems=addProd;
    TextWriter tr=new StreamWriter("inventory.xml");
    XmlSerializer sr=new XmlSerializer(typeof(Inventory),attrOver);
    sr.Serialize(tr,inv);
    tr.Close();
}
```

If you execute the `Serialize` method, you get the following XML output:

```xml
<?xml version="1.0" encoding="utf-8"?>
<Inventory xmlns:xsi="http://www.w3.org/2001/XMLSchema-instance"
 xmlns:xsd="http://www.w3.org/2001/XMLSchema">
  <Product Discount="0">
    <ProductID>100</ProductID>
    <ProductName>Product Thing</ProductName>
    <SupplierID>10</SupplierID>
    <CategoryID>0</CategoryID>
    <UnitPrice>0</UnitPrice>
    <UnitsInStock>0</UnitsInStock>
    <UnitsOnOrder>0</UnitsOnOrder>
    <ReorderLevel>0</ReorderLevel>
    <Discontinued>false</Discontinued>
  </Product>
  <Book Discount="0">
    <ProductID>101</ProductID>
    <ProductName>How to Use Your New Product Thing</ProductName>
    <SupplierID>10</SupplierID>
    <CategoryID>0</CategoryID>
    <UnitPrice>0</UnitPrice>
    <UnitsInStock>0</UnitsInStock>
    <UnitsOnOrder>0</UnitsOnOrder>
    <ReorderLevel>0</ReorderLevel>
    <Discontinued>false</Discontinued>
    <ISBN>123456789</ISBN>
  </Book>
</Inventory>
```

As you can see, you get the same XML you did with the earlier example. To deserialize this object and re-create the `Inventory`-based object that you started out with, you need to create all the same `XmlAttributes`, `XmlElementAttribute`, and `XmlAttributeOverrides` objects that you created when you serialized the object. After you do that, you can read in the XML and re-create the `Inventory` object just as you did before. Here is the code to deserialize the `Inventory` object:

```csharp
private void button2_Click(object sender, System.EventArgs e)
{
   //create the new XmlAttributes collection
   XmlAttributes attrs=new XmlAttributes();
   //add the type information to the elements collection
   attrs.XmlElements.Add(new XmlElementAttribute("Book",typeof(BookProduct)));
   attrs.XmlElements.Add(new XmlElementAttribute("Product",typeof(Product)));

   XmlAttributeOverrides attrOver=new XmlAttributeOverrides();
   //add to the Attributes collection
   attrOver.Add(typeof(Inventory),"InventoryItems",attrs);

   //need a new Inventory object to deserialize to
   Inventory newInv;

   //deserialize and load data into the listbox from deserialized object
   FileStream f=new FileStream(".\\.\\.\\inventory.xml",FileMode.Open);
   XmlSerializer newSr=new XmlSerializer(typeof(Inventory),attrOver);

   newInv=(Inventory)newSr.Deserialize(f);
   if(newInv!=null)
   {
      foreach(Product prod in newInv.InventoryItems)
      {
         listBox1.Items.Add(prod.ProductName);
      }
   }
   f.Close();
}
```

Note that the first few lines of code are identical to the code you used to serialize the object.

The `System.Xml.XmlSerialization` namespace provides a very powerful toolset for serializing objects to XML. By serializing and deserializing objects to XML instead of to binary format, you have the option to do something else with this XML, greatly adding to the flexibility of your designs.

LINQ TO XML AND .NET

With the introduction of LINQ to the .NET Framework, the focus was on easy access to the data that you want to use in your applications. One of the main data stores in the application space is XML, so it was a natural evolution to create the LINQ to XML implementation.

Prior to the LINQ to XML release, working with XML using `System.Xml` was not an easy task. With the inclusion of `System.Xml.Linq`, you now have a set of capabilities that make the process of working with XML in your code much easier.

Many developers previously turned to the `XmlDocument` object to create XML within their application code. This object enables you to create XML documents that allow you to append elements, attributes, and other items in a hierarchical fashion. With LINQ to XML and the inclusion of the `System.Xml.Linq` namespace, you have the tools that make the creation of XML documents a much simpler process.

WORKING WITH DIFFERENT XML OBJECTS

In addition to the LINQ querying ability included in .NET 4.5, the .NET Framework includes XML objects that work so well they can stand on their own outside of LINQ. You can use these objects in place of working directly with the DOM. The `System.Xml.Linq` namespace includes a series of LINQ to XML helper objects that make working with an XML document in memory much easier.

The following sections describe the objects that are available within this namespace.

> **NOTE** *Many of the examples in this chapter use a file called* `Hamlet.xml`, *which you can find at* `http://metalab.unc.edu/bosak/xml/eg/shaks200.zip`. *It includes all of Shakespeare's plays as XML files.*

XDocument

The `XDocument` is a replacement for the `XmlDocument` object from the pre-.NET 3.5 world; it is easier to work with in dealing with XML documents. The `XDocument` object works with the other new objects in this space, such as the `XNamespace`, `XComment`, `XElement`, and `XAttribute` objects.

One of the more important members of the `XDocument` object is the `Load` method:

```
XDocument xdoc = XDocument.Load(@"C:\Hamlet.xml");
```

This operation loads the `Hamlet.xml` contents as an in-memory `XDocument` object. You can also pass a `TextReader` or `XmlReader` object into the `Load` method. From here, you can programmatically work with the XML (code file `ConsoleApplication1.sln`):

```
XDocument xdoc = XDocument.Load(@"C:\Hamlet.xml");
Console.WriteLine(xdoc.Root.Name.ToString());
Console.WriteLine(xdoc.Root.HasAttributes.ToString());
```

This produces the following results:

```
PLAY
False
```

Another important member to be aware of is the `Save` method, which, like the `Load` method, allows you to save to a physical disk location or to a `TextWriter` or `XmlWriter` object:

```
XDocument xdoc = XDocument.Load(@"C:\Hamlet.xml");

xdoc.Save(@"C:\CopyOfHamlet.xml");
```

XElement

One object that you will work with frequently is the `XElement` object. With `XElement` objects, you can easily create single-element objects that are XML documents themselves, as well as fragments of XML. For instance, here is an example of writing an XML element with a corresponding value:

```
XElement xe = new XElement("Company", "Lipper");
Console.WriteLine(xe.ToString());
```

In the creation of a `XElement` object, you can define the name of the element as well as the value used in the element. In this case, the name of the element will be `<Company>`, and the value of the `<Company>` element will be `Lipper`. Running this in a console application with a `System.Xml.Linq` reference produces the following result:

```
<Company>Lipper</Company>
```

You can create an even more complete XML document using multiple `XElement` objects, as shown in the following example:

```
using System;
using System.Linq;
using System.Xml.Linq;

namespace ConsoleApplication1
{
    class Class1
    {
        static void Main()
        {
            XElement xe = new XElement("Company",
                new XElement("CompanyName", "Lipper"),
                new XElement("CompanyAddress",
                    new XElement("Address", "123 Main Street"),
                    new XElement("City", "St. Louis"),
                    new XElement("State", "MO"),
                    new XElement("Country", "USA")));

            Console.WriteLine(xe.ToString());

            Console.ReadLine();
        }
    }
}
```

Running this application produces the results shown in Figure 34-7.

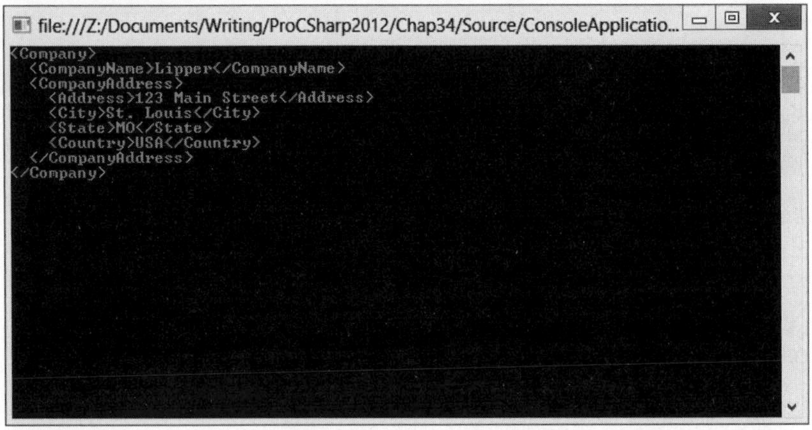

FIGURE 34-7

XNamespace

The XNamespace is an object that represents an XML namespace, and it is easily applied to elements within your document. For instance, you can take the previous example and easily apply a namespace to the root element:

```
using System;
using System.Linq;
using System.Xml.Linq;

namespace ConsoleApplication1
{
    class Class1
    {
        static void Main()
        {
            XNamespace ns = "http://www.lipperweb.com/ns/1";

            XElement xe = new XElement(ns + "Company",
                new XElement("CompanyName", "Lipper"),
                new XElement("CompanyAddress",
                    new XElement("Address", "123 Main Street"),
                    new XElement("City", "St. Louis"),
                    new XElement("State", "MO"),
                    new XElement("Country", "USA")));

            Console.WriteLine(xe.ToString());

            Console.ReadLine();
        }
    }
}
```

In this case, an XNamespace object is created by assigning it a value of http://www.lipperweb.com/ns/1. From there, it is actually used in the root element <Company> with the instantiation of the XElement object:

```
XElement xe = new XElement(ns + "Company", // .
```

This produces the results shown in Figure 34-8.

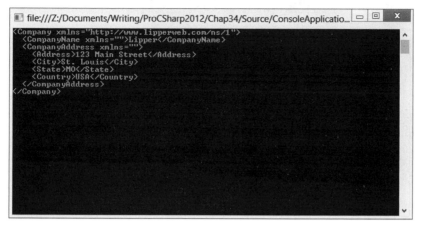

FIGURE 34-8

In addition to dealing with only the root element, you can also apply namespaces to all your elements, as shown in the following example:

```csharp
using System;
using System.Linq;
using System.Xml.Linq;

namespace ConsoleApplication1
{
    class Class1
    {
        static void Main()
        {
            XNamespace ns1 = "http://www.lipperweb.com/ns/root";
            XNamespace ns2 = "http://www.lipperweb.com/ns/sub";

            XElement xe = new XElement(ns1 + "Company",
                new XElement(ns2 + "CompanyName", "Lipper"),
                new XElement(ns2 + "CompanyAddress",
                    new XElement(ns2 + "Address", "123 Main Street"),
                    new XElement(ns2 + "City", "St. Louis"),
                    new XElement(ns2 + "State", "MO"),
                    new XElement(ns2 + "Country", "USA")));

            Console.WriteLine(xe.ToString());

            Console.ReadLine();
        }
    }
}
```

This produces the results shown in Figure 34-9.

FIGURE 34-9

In this case, you can see that the subnamespace was applied to everything you specified except for the `<Address>`, `<City>`, `<State>`, and the `<Country>` elements because they inherit from their parent, `<CompanyAddress>`, which has the namespace declaration.

XComment

The `XComment` object enables you to easily add XML comments to your XML documents. The following example shows the addition of a comment to the top of the document:

```csharp
using System;
using System.Linq;
using System.Xml.Linq;

namespace ConsoleApplication1
{
    class Class1
    {
        static void Main(string[] args)
        {
            XDocument xdoc = new XDocument();

            XComment xc = new XComment("Here is a comment.");
            xdoc.Add(xc);

            XElement xe = new XElement("Company",
                new XElement("CompanyName", "Lipper"),
                new XElement("CompanyAddress",
                    new XComment("Here is another comment."),
                    new XElement("Address", "123 Main Street"),
                    new XElement("City", "St. Louis"),
                    new XElement("State", "MO"),
                    new XElement("Country", "USA")));
            xdoc.Add(xe);

            Console.WriteLine(xdoc.ToString());

            Console.ReadLine();
        }
    }
}
```

Here, an XDocument object that contains two XML comments is written to the console, one at the top of the document and another within the <CompanyAddress> element. The output of this is presented in Figure 34-10.

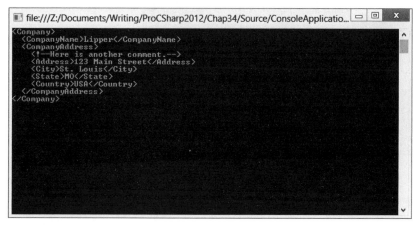

FIGURE 34-10

XAttribute

In addition to elements, another important factor of XML is attributes. Adding and working with attributes is done through the use of the XAttribute object. The following example shows the addition of an attribute to the root <Company> node:

```csharp
using System;
using System.Linq;
using System.Xml.Linq;

namespace ConsoleApplication1
{
    class Class1
    {
        static void Main()
        {
            XElement xe = new XElement("Company",
                new XAttribute("MyAttribute", "MyAttributeValue"),
                new XElement("CompanyName", "Lipper"),
                new XElement("CompanyAddress",
                    new XElement("Address", "123 Main Street"),
                    new XElement("City", "St. Louis"),
                    new XElement("State", "MO"),
                    new XElement("Country", "USA")));

            Console.WriteLine(xe.ToString());

            Console.ReadLine();
        }
    }
}
```

Here, the attribute MyAttribute with a value of MyAttributeValue is added to the root element of the XML document, producing the results shown in Figure 34-11.

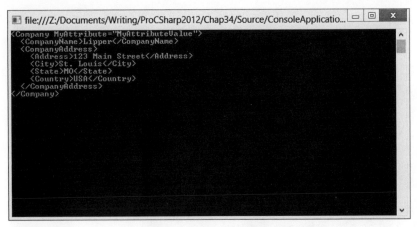

FIGURE 34-11

USING LINQ TO QUERY XML DOCUMENTS

Now that you can get your XML documents into an XDocument object and work with the various parts of this document, you can also use LINQ to XML to query your XML documents and work with the results.

Querying Static XML Documents

You will notice that querying a static XML document using LINQ to XML takes almost no work at all. The following example makes use of the hamlet.xml file and queries to get all the players (actors) who appear in the play. Each of these players is defined in the XML document with the <PERSONA> element:

```
using System;
using System.Linq;
using System.Xml.Linq;

namespace ConsoleApplication1
{
    class Class1
    {
        static void Main(string[] args)
        {
            XDocument xdoc = XDocument.Load(@"C:\hamlet.xml");

            var query = from people in xdoc.Descendants("PERSONA")
                        select people.Value;

            Console.WriteLine("{0} Players Found", query.Count());
            Console.WriteLine();

            foreach (var item in query)
            {
                Console.WriteLine(item);
            }

            Console.ReadLine();
        }
    }
}
```

In this case, an XDocument object loads up a physical XML file (hamlet.xml) and then performs a LINQ query over the contents of the document:

```
var query = from people in xdoc.Descendants("PERSONA")
            select people.Value;
```

The `people` object is a representation of all the `<PERSONA>` elements found in the document. Then the `select` statement gets the values of these elements. From there, a `Console.WriteLine` method is used to write out a count of all the players found using `query.Count`. Next, each of the items is written to the screen in a `foreach` loop. The results you should see are presented here:

```
26 Players Found

CLAUDIUS, king of Denmark.
HAMLET, son to the late king, and nephew to the present king.
POLONIUS, lord chamberlain.
HORATIO, friend to Hamlet.
LAERTES, son to Polonius.
LUCIANUS, nephew to the king.
VOLTIMAND
CORNELIUS
ROSENCRANTZ
GUILDENSTERN
OSRIC
A Gentleman
A Priest.
MARCELLUS
BERNARDO
FRANCISCO, a soldier.
REYNALDO, servant to Polonius.
Players.
Two Clowns, grave-diggers.
FORTINBRAS, prince of Norway.
A Captain.
English Ambassadors.
GERTRUDE, queen of Denmark, and mother to Hamlet.
OPHELIA, daughter to Polonius.
Lords, Ladies, Officers, Soldiers, Sailors, Messengers, and other Attendants.
Ghost of Hamlet's Father.
```

Querying Dynamic XML Documents

A lot of dynamic XML documents are available online these days. You will find blog feeds, podcast feeds, and more that provide an XML document by sending a request to a specific URL endpoint. These feeds can be viewed either in the browser, through an RSS-aggregator, or as pure XML. This example demonstrates how to work with an RSS feed directly from your code:

```
using System;
using System.Linq;
using System.Xml.Linq;

namespace ConsoleApplication1
{
    class Class1
    {
        static void Main()
        {
            XDocument xdoc =
                XDocument.Load(@"http://geekswithblogs.net/evjen/Rss.aspx");

            var query = from rssFeed in xdoc.Descendants("channel")
                        select new
                        {
```

```
                         Title = rssFeed.Element("title").Value,
                         Description = rssFeed.Element("description").Value,
                         Link = rssFeed.Element("link").Value,
                     };

            foreach (var item in query)
            {
               Console.WriteLine("TITLE: " + item.Title);
                Console.WriteLine("DESCRIPTION: " + item.Description);
                Console.WriteLine("LINK: " + item.Link);
            }

            Console.WriteLine();

            var queryPosts = from myPosts in xdoc.Descendants("item")
                             select new
                             {
                                 Title = myPosts.Element("title").Value,
                                 Published =
                                    DateTime.Parse(
                                       myPosts.Element("pubDate").Value),
                                 Description =
                                    myPosts.Element("description").Value,
                                 Url = myPosts.Element("link").Value,
                                 Comments = myPosts.Element("comments").Value
                             };

            foreach (var item in queryPosts)
            {
                Console.WriteLine(item.Title);
            }

            Console.ReadLine();
        }
    }
}
```

Here, you can see that the Load method of the XDocument object points to a URL where the XML is retrieved. The first query pulls out all the main sub-elements of the <channel> element in the feed and creates new objects called Title, Description, and Link to get the values of these sub-elements. From there, a foreach statement is run to iterate through all the items found in the query.

The results are as follows:

```
TITLE: Bill Evjen's Blog
DESCRIPTION: Code, Life and Community
LINK: http://geekswithblogs.net/evjen/Default.aspx
```

The second query works through all the <item> elements and the various sub-elements it finds (these are all the blog entries found in the blog). Although a lot of the items found are rolled up into properties, in the foreach loop, only the Title property is used. You will see something similar to the following results from this query:

```
AJAX Control Toolkit Controls Grayed Out-HOW TO FIX
Welcome .NET 4.5!
Visual Studio
IIS 7.0 Rocks the House!
Word Issue-Couldn't Select Text
Microsoft Releases XML Schema Designer CTP1
Silverlight Book
```

```
Microsoft Tafiti as a beta
ReSharper on Visual Studio
Windows Vista Updates for Performance and Reliability Issues
First Review of Professional XML
Go to MIX07 for free!
Microsoft Surface and the Future of Home Computing?
Alas my friends-I'm *not* TechEd bound
```

MORE QUERY TECHNIQUES FOR XML DOCUMENTS

If you have been working with the XML document `hamlet.xml`, you will notice that it is quite large. So far, you've seen a couple of ways to query into the XML document in this chapter; this section takes a look at reading and writing to the XML document.

Reading from an XML Document

Earlier you saw just how easy it is to query into an XML document using the LINQ query statements, as shown here:

```
var query = from people in xdoc.Descendants("PERSONA")
            select people.Value;
```

This query returns all the players found in the document. Using the `Element` method of the `XDocument` object, you can also access specific values of the XML document that you are working with. For instance, the following XML fragment shows you how the title is represented in the `hamlet.xml` document:

```xml
<?xml version="1.0"?>

<PLAY>
    <TITLE>The Tragedy of Hamlet, Prince of Denmark</TITLE>

    <!-XML removed for clarity->

</PLAY>
```

As you can see, the `<TITLE>` element is a nested element of the `<PLAY>` element. You can easily get the title by using the following bit of code in your console application:

```
XDocument xdoc = XDocument.Load(@"C:\hamlet.xml");

Console.WriteLine(xdoc.Element("PLAY").Element("TITLE").Value);
```

This bit of code will output the title, *The Tragedy of Hamlet, Prince of Denmark*, to the console screen. In the code, you were able to work down the hierarchy of the XML document by using two `Element` method calls—first calling the `<PLAY>` element and then the `<TITLE>` element found nested within the `<PLAY>` element.

Looking again at the `hamlet.xml` document, you will see a large list of players who are defined with the use of the `<PERSONA>` element:

```xml
<?xml version="1.0"?>

<PLAY>
    <TITLE>The Tragedy of Hamlet, Prince of Denmark</TITLE>

    <!--XML removed for clarity-->

    <PERSONAE>
```

```
      <TITLE>Dramatis Personae</TITLE>

      <PERSONA>CLAUDIUS, king of Denmark.</PERSONA>
      <PERSONA>HAMLET, son to the late king,
       and nephew to the present king.</PERSONA>
      <PERSONA>POLONIUS, lord chamberlain.</PERSONA>
      <PERSONA>HORATIO, friend to Hamlet.</PERSONA>
      <PERSONA>LAERTES, son to Polonius.</PERSONA>
      <PERSONA>LUCIANUS, nephew to the king.</PERSONA>

      <!--XML removed for clarity-->

   </PERSONAE>

 </PLAY>
```

Now look at this C# query:

```
XDocument xdoc = XDocument.Load(@"C:\hamlet.xml");

Console.WriteLine(
    xdoc.Element("PLAY").Element("PERSONAE").Element("PERSONA").Value);
```

This bit of code starts at <PLAY>, works down to the <PERSONAE> element, and then makes use of the <PERSONA> element. However, using this produces the following results:

```
CLAUDIUS, king of Denmark
```

The reason for this is that although there is a collection of <PERSONA> elements, you are dealing only with the first one that is encountered using the Element().Value call.

Writing to an XML Document

In addition to reading from an XML document, you can write to the document just as easily. For instance, if you wanted to change the name of the first player of the Hamlet play file, you could use the following code:

```
using System;
using System.Linq;
using System.Xml.Linq;

namespace ConsoleApplication1
{
    class Class1
    {
        static void Main()
        {
            XDocument xdoc = XDocument.Load(@"C:\hamlet.xml");

            xdoc.Element("PLAY").Element("PERSONAE").
                Element("PERSONA").SetValue("Bill Evjen, king of Denmark");

            Console.WriteLine(xdoc.Element("PLAY").
                Element("PERSONAE").Element("PERSONA").Value);

            Console.ReadLine();
        }
    }
}
```

In this case, the first instance of the <PERSONA> element is overwritten with the value of Bill Evjen, king of Denmark using the SetValue method of the Element object. After the SetValue is called and the value is applied to the XML document, the value is then retrieved using the same approach as before. When you run this bit of code, you can indeed see that the value of the first <PERSONA> element has been changed.

Another way to change the document, by adding items to it in this example, is to create the elements you want as XElement objects and then add them to the document:

```
using System;
using System.Linq;
using System.Xml.Linq;

namespace ConsoleApplication1
{
    class Class1
    {
        static void Main()
        {
            XDocument xdoc = XDocument.Load(@"C:\hamlet.xml");

            XElement xe = new XElement("PERSONA",
                "Bill Evjen, king of Denmark");

            xdoc.Element("PLAY").Element("PERSONAE").Add(xe);

            var query = from people in xdoc.Descendants("PERSONA")
                        select people.Value;

            Console.WriteLine("{0} Players Found", query.Count());
            Console.WriteLine();

            foreach (var item in query)
            {
                Console.WriteLine(item);
            }

            Console.ReadLine();
        }
    }
}
```

In this case, an XElement document is created called xe. The construction of xe will produce the following XML output:

```
<PERSONA>Bill Evjen, king of Denmark</PERSONA>
```

Then using the Element().Add method from the XDocument object, you are able to add the created element:

```
xdoc.Element("PLAY").Element("PERSONAE").Add(xe);
```

Now when you query all the players, you will find that instead of 26 as before, you now have 27, with the new one at the bottom of the list. In addition to Add, you can also use AddFirst, which does just that—adds it to the beginning of the list instead of the end (which is the default).

SUMMARY

This chapter explored many aspects of the `System.Xml` namespace of the .NET Framework. You looked at how to read and write XML documents using the very fast `XmlReader`- and `XmlWriter`-based classes. You saw how the DOM is implemented in .NET and how to use the power of DOM, and you saw that XML and ADO.NET are indeed very closely related. A `DataSet` and an XML document are just two different views of the same underlying architecture. In addition, you visited XPath, XSL transforms, and the debugging features added to Visual Studio. Finally, you serialized objects to XML and were able to bring them back with just a couple of method calls.

XML will be an important part of your application development for years to come. The .NET Framework has made available a very rich and powerful toolset for working with XML.

This chapter also focused on using LINQ to XML and some of the options available to you in reading and writing from XML files and XML sources, whether the source is static or dynamic.

Using LINQ to XML, you can have a strongly typed set of operations for performing CRUD operations against your XML files and sources. However, you can still use your `XmlReader` and `XmlWriter` code along with the LINQ to XML capabilities.

This chapter also introduced the LINQ to XML helper objects `XDocument`, `XElement`, `XNamespace`, `XAttribute`, and `XComment`. You will find these to be outstanding objects that make working with XML easier than ever before.

PART V
Presentation

35

Core WPF

WHAT'S IN THIS CHAPTER?

➤ Shapes and geometry as the base drawing elements

➤ Scaling, rotating, and skewing with transformations

➤ Brushes to fill backgrounds

➤ WPF controls and their features

➤ Defining a layout with WPF panels

➤ Styles, templates, and resources

➤ Triggers and the Visual State Manager

➤ Animations

➤ 3-D

WROX.COM CODE DOWNLOADS FOR THIS CHAPTER

The wrox.com code downloads for this chapter are found at `http://www.wrox.com/remtitle.cgi?isbn=1118314425` on the Download Code tab. The code for this chapter is divided into the following major examples:

➤ Shapes Demo

➤ Geometry Demo

➤ Transformation Demo

➤ Brushes Demo

➤ Decorations Demo

➤ Layout Demo

➤ Styles and Resources

➤ Trigger Demo

➤ Template Demo

➤ Animation Demo

➤ Visual State Demo

➤ 3D Demo

UNDERSTANDING WPF

Windows Presentation Foundation (WPF) is a library to create the UI for smart client applications. This chapter gives you broad information on the important concepts of WPF. It covers a large number of different controls and their categories, including how to arrange the controls with panels, customize the appearance using styles, resources, and templates, add some dynamic behavior with triggers and animations, and create 3-D with WPF.

One of the main advantages of WPF is that work can be easily separated between designers and developers. The outcome from the designer's work can directly be used by the developer. To make this possible, you need to understand *eXtensible Application Markup Language*, or *XAML*. Readers unfamiliar with XAML can read Chapter 29, "Core XAML," for information about its syntax.

The first topic of this chapter provides an overview of the class hierarchy and categories of classes that are used with WPF, including additional information to understand the principles of XAML. WPF consists of several assemblies containing thousands of classes. To help you navigate within this vast number of classes and find what you need, this section explains the class hierarchy and namespaces in WPF.

Namespaces

Classes from Windows Forms and WPF can easily be confused. The Windows Forms classes are located in the `System.Windows.Forms` namespace, and the WPF classes are located inside the namespace `System .Windows` and subnamespaces thereof, with the exception of `System.Windows.Forms`. For example, the `Button` class for Windows Forms has the full name `System.Windows.Forms.Button`, and the `Button` class for WPF has the full name `System.Windows.Controls.Button`.

Namespaces and their functionality within WPF are described in the following table.

NAMESPACE	DESCRIPTION
System.Windows	The core namespace of WPF. Here you can find core classes from WPF such as the `Application` class; classes for dependency objects, `DependencyObject` and `DependencyProperty`; and the base class for all WPF elements, `FrameworkElement`.
System.Windows .Annotations	Classes from this namespace are used for user-created annotations and notes on application data that are stored separately from the document. The namespace `System.Windows.Annotations.Storage` contains classes for storing annotations.
System.Windows .Automation	This namespace can be used for automation of WPF applications. Several sub-namespaces are available. `System.Windows.Automation .Peers` exposes WPF elements to automation — for example, `ButtonAutomationPeer` and `CheckBoxAutomationPeer`. The namespace `System.Windows .Automation.Provider` is needed if you create a custom automation provider.
System.Windows .Baml2006	This namespace contains the `Baml2006Reader` class, which is used to read binary markup language and produces XAML.
System.Windows .Controls	This namespace contains all the WPF controls, such as `Button`, `Border`, `Canvas`, `ComboBox`, `Expander`, `Slider`, `ToolTip`, `TreeView`, and the like. In the namespace `System.Windows .Controls.Primitives`, you can find classes to be used within complex controls, such as `Popup`, `ScrollBar`, `StatusBar`, `TabPanel`, and so on.

System.Windows.Converters	This namespace contains classes for data conversion. Don't expect to find all converter classes in this namespace; core converter classes are defined in the namespace System.Windows.
System.Windows.Data	This namespace is used by WPF data binding. An important class in this namespace is the Binding class, which is used to define the binding between a WPF target element and a CLR source. Data binding is covered in Chapter 36, "Business Applications with WPF."
System.Windows.Documents	When working with documents, you can find many helpful classes in this namespace. FixedDocument and FlowDocument are content elements that can contain other elements from this namespace. With classes from the namespace System.Windows.Documents.Serialization you can write documents to disk. The classes from this namespace are explained in Chapter 37, "Creating Documents with WPF."
System.Windows.Ink	With the increasingly popular Windows Tablet PC and Ultra Mobile PCs, ink can be used for user input. The namespace System.Windows.Ink contains classes to deal with ink input.
System.Windows.Input	Contains several classes for command handling, keyboard inputs, working with a stylus, and so on
System.Windows.Interop	For integration of WPF with native Window handles from the Windows API and Windows Forms, you can find classes in this namespace.
System.Windows.Markup	Helper classes for XAML markup code are located in this namespace.
System.Windows.Media	To work with images, audio, and video content, you can use classes in this namespace.
System.Windows.Navigation	Contains classes for navigation between windows
System.Windows.Resources	Contains supporting classes for resources
System.Windows.Shapes	Core classes for the UI are located in this namespace: Line, Ellipse, Rectangle, and the like.
System.Windows.Threading	WPF elements are bound to a single thread. In this namespace, you can find classes to deal with multiple threads—for example, the Dispatcher class belongs to this namespace.
System.Windows.Xps	XML Paper Specification (XPS) is a document specification that is also supported by Microsoft Word. In the namespaces System .Windows.Xps, System .Windows.Xps.Packaging and System.Windows.Xps.Serialization, you can find classes to create and stream XPS documents.

Class Hierarchy

WPF consists of thousands of classes within a deep hierarchy. For an overview of the relationships between the classes, see Figure 35-1. Some classes and their functionality are described in the following table.

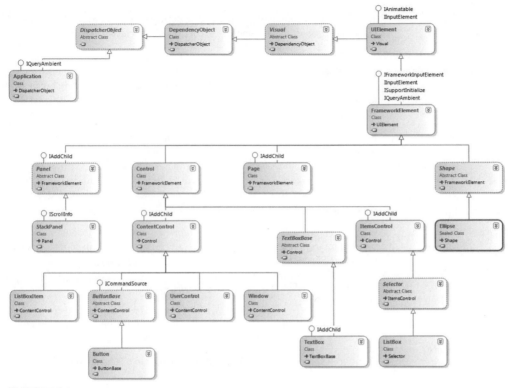

FIGURE 35-1

CLASS	DESCRIPTION
DispatcherObject	An abstract base class for classes that are bound to one thread. WPF controls require that methods and properties be invoked only from the creator thread. Classes derived from DispatcherObject have an associated Dispatcher object that can be used to switch the thread.
Application	In a WPF application, one instance of the Application class is created. This class implements a singleton pattern for access to the application windows, resources, and properties.
DependencyObject	This is the base class for all classes that support dependency properties. Dependency properties are discussed in Chapter 29, "Core XAML."
Visual	The base class for all visual elements. This class includes features for hit testing and transformation.
UIElement	The abstract base class for all WPF elements that need basic presentation features. This class provides tunneling and bubbling events for mouse moves, drag and drop, and key clicks. It exposes virtual methods for rendering that can be overridden by derived classes, and it provides methods for layout. As WPF does not use Window handles, you can consider this class equivalent to Window handles.

CLASS	DESCRIPTION
FrameworkElement	FrameworkElement is derived from the base class UIElement and implements the default behavior of the methods defined by the base class.
Shape	Base class for all shape elements, such as Line, Ellipse, Polygon, and Rectangle
Control	Control derives from FrameworkElement and is the base class for all user-interactive elements.
ContentControl	Base class for all controls that have a single content (for example, Label, Button). The default style of a content control may be limited, but it is possible to change the look by using templates.
ItemsControl	Base class for all controls that contain a collection of items as content (for example, ListBox, ComboBox)
Panel	This class derives from FrameworkElement and is the abstract base class for all panels. Panel has a Children property for all UI elements within the panel and defines methods for arranging the child controls. Classes derived from Panel define different behavior regarding how the children are organized—for example, WrapPanel, StackPanel, Canvas, and Grid.

As this brief introduction demonstrates, WPF classes have a deep hierarchy. This chapter and the next few chapters cover their core functionality, but it is not possible to provide comprehensive coverage all the WPF features in this book.

SHAPES

Shapes are the core elements of WPF. With shapes you can draw two-dimensional graphics using rectangles, lines, ellipses, paths, polygons, and polylines that are represented by classes derived from the abstract base class Shape. Shapes are defined in the namespace System.Windows.Shapes.

The following XAML example (code file ShapesDemo/MainWindow.xaml) draws a yellow face consisting of an ellipse for the face, two ellipses for the eyes, two ellipses for the pupils in the eyes, and a path for the mouth:

```
<Window x:Class="ShapesDemo.MainWindow"
        xmlns="http://schemas.microsoft.com/winfx/2006/xaml/presentation"
        xmlns:x="http://schemas.microsoft.com/winfx/2006/xaml"
        Title="MainWindow" Height="300" Width="300">
  <Canvas>
    <Ellipse Canvas.Left="10" Canvas.Top="10" Width="100" Height="100"
       Stroke="Blue" StrokeThickness="4" Fill="Yellow" />
    <Ellipse Canvas.Left="30" Canvas.Top="12" Width="60" Height="30">
      <Ellipse.Fill>
        <LinearGradientBrush StartPoint="0.5,0" EndPoint="0.5, 1">
          <GradientStop Offset="0.1" Color="DarkGreen" />
          <GradientStop Offset="0.7" Color="Transparent" />
        </LinearGradientBrush>
      </Ellipse.Fill>
    </Ellipse>
    <Ellipse Canvas.Left="30" Canvas.Top="35" Width="25" Height="20" Stroke="Blue"
       StrokeThickness="3" Fill="White" />
    <Ellipse Canvas.Left="40" Canvas.Top="43" Width="6" Height="5" Fill="Black" />
```

```
        <Ellipse Canvas.Left="65" Canvas.Top="35" Width="25" Height="20" Stroke="Blue"
            StrokeThickness="3" Fill="White" />
        <Ellipse Canvas.Left="75" Canvas.Top="43" Width="6" Height="5" Fill="Black" />
        <Path Name="mouth" Stroke="Blue" StrokeThickness="4"
            Data="M 40,74 Q 57,95 80,74 " />
    </Canvas>

  </Window>
```

Figure 35-2 shows the result of the XAML code.

FIGURE 35-2

All these WPF elements can be accessed programmatically, even if they are buttons or shapes, such as lines or rectangles. Setting the Name or x:Name property with the Path element to mouth enables you to access this element programmatically with the variable name mouth:

```
        <Path Name="mouth" Stroke="Blue" StrokeThickness="4"
            Data="M 40,74 Q 57,95 80,74 " />
```

In the code-behind Data property of the Path element (code file ShapesDemo/MainWindow .xaml.cs), mouth is set to a new geometry. For setting the path, the Path class supports PathGeometry with path markup syntax. The letter M defines the starting point for the path; the letter Q specifies a control point and an endpoint for a quadratic Bézier curve. Running the application results in the image shown in Figure 35-3.

FIGURE 35-3

```
        public MainWindow()
        {
          InitializeComponent();
          mouth.Data = Geometry.Parse("M 40,92 Q 57,75 80,92");
        }
```

The following table describes the shapes available in the namespace System.Windows.Shapes.

SHAPE CLASS	DESCRIPTION
Line	You can draw a line from the coordinates X1.Y1 to X2.Y2.
Rectangle	Enables drawing a rectangle by specifying Width and Height
Ellipse	With the Ellipse class, you can draw an ellipse.
Path	You can use the Path class to draw a series of lines and curves. The Data property is a Geometry type. You can do the drawing by using classes that derive from the base class Geometry, or you can use the path markup syntax to define geometry.
Polygon	Enables drawing a closed shape formed by connected lines with the Polygon class. The polygon is defined by a series of Point objects assigned to the Points property.
Polyline	Similar to the Polygon class, you can draw connected lines with Polyline. The difference is that the polyline does not need to be a closed shape.

GEOMETRY

One of the shapes, Path, uses Geometry for its drawing. Geometry elements can also be used in other places, such as with a DrawingBrush.

In some ways, geometry elements are very similar to shapes. Just as there are `Line`, `Ellipse`, and `Rectangle` shapes, there are also geometry elements for these drawings: `LineGeometry`, `EllipseGeometry`, and `RectangleGeometry`. There are also big differences between shapes and geometries. A `Shape` is a `FrameworkElement` and can be used with any class that supports `UIElement` as its children. `FrameworkElement` derives from `UIElement`. Shapes participate with the layout system and render themselves. The `Geometry` class can't render itself and has fewer features and less overhead than `Shape`. The `Geometry` class derives from the `Freezable` base class and can be shared from multiple threads.

The `Path` class uses `Geometry` for its drawing. The geometry can be set with the `Data` property of the `Path`. Simple geometry elements that can be set are `EllipseGeometry` for drawing an ellipse, `LineGeometry` for drawing a line, and `RectangleGeometry` for drawing a rectangle. Combining multiple geometries, as demonstrated in the next example, can be done with `CombinedGeometry`.

`CombinedGeometry` has the properties `Geometry1` and `Geometry2` and allows them to combine with `GeometryCombineMode` to form a `Union`, `Intersect`, `Xor`, and `Exclude`. `Union` merges the two geometries. With `Intersect`, only the area that is covered with both geometries is visible. `Xor` contrasts with `Intersect` by showing the area that is covered by one of the geometries but not showing the area covered by both. `Exclude` shows the area of the first geometry minus the area of the second geometry.

The following example (code file `GeometryDemo/MainWindow.xaml`) combines an `EllipseGeometry` and a `RectangleGeometry` to form a union, as shown in Figure 35-4.

FIGURE 35-4

```
<Path Canvas.Top="0" Canvas.Left="250" Fill="Blue" Stroke="Black" >
  <Path.Data>
    <CombinedGeometry GeometryCombineMode="Union">
      <CombinedGeometry.Geometry1>
        <EllipseGeometry Center="80,60" RadiusX="80" RadiusY="40" />
      </CombinedGeometry.Geometry1>
      <CombinedGeometry.Geometry2>
        <RectangleGeometry Rect="30,60 105 50" />
      </CombinedGeometry.Geometry2>
    </CombinedGeometry>
  </Path.Data>
</Path>
```

Geometries can also be created by using segments. The geometry class `PathGeometry` uses segments for its drawing. The following code segment uses the `BezierSegment` and `LineSegment` elements to build one red and one green figure, as shown in Figure 35-5. The first `BezierSegment` draws a Bézier curve between the points 70,40, which is the starting point of the figure, and 150,63 with control points 90,37 and 130,46. The following `LineSegment` uses the ending point of the Bézier curve and draws a line to 120,110:

```
<Path Canvas.Left="0" Canvas.Top="0" Fill="Red" Stroke="Blue"
      StrokeThickness="2.5">
  <Path.Data>
    <GeometryGroup>
      <PathGeometry>
        <PathGeometry.Figures>
          <PathFigure StartPoint="70,40" IsClosed="True">
            <PathFigure.Segments>
              <BezierSegment Point1="90,37" Point2="130,46" Point3="150,63" />
              <LineSegment Point="120,110" />
              <BezierSegment Point1="100,95" Point2="70,90" Point3="45,91" />
            </PathFigure.Segments>
          </PathFigure>
        </PathGeometry.Figures>
```

```
            </PathGeometry>
          </GeometryGroup>
        </Path.Data>
      </Path>

      <Path Canvas.Left="0" Canvas.Top="0" Fill="Green" Stroke="Blue"
          StrokeThickness="2.5">
        <Path.Data>
          <GeometryGroup>
            <PathGeometry>
              <PathGeometry.Figures>
                <PathFigure StartPoint="160,70">
                  <PathFigure.Segments>
                    <BezierSegment Point1="175,85" Point2="200,99"
                               Point3="215,100" />
                    <LineSegment Point="195,148" />
                    <BezierSegment Point1="174,150" Point2="142,140"
                               Point3="129,115" />
                    <LineSegment Point="160,70" />
                  </PathFigure.Segments>
                </PathFigure>
              </PathGeometry.Figures>
            </PathGeometry>
          </GeometryGroup>
        </Path.Data>
      </Path>
```

FIGURE 35-5

Other than the `BezierSegment` and `LineSegment` elements, you can use `ArcSegment` to draw an elliptical arc between two points. With `PolyLineSegment` you can define a set of lines: `PolyBezierSegment` consists of multiple Bézier curves, `QuadraticBezierSegment` creates a quadratic Bézier curve, and `PolyQuadraticBezierSegment` consists of multiple quadratic Bézier curves.

A speedy drawing can be created with `StreamGeometry`. Programmatically, the figure can be defined by creating lines, Bézier curves, and arcs with members of the `StreamGeometryContext` class. With XAML, path markup syntax can be used. You can use path markup syntax with the `Data` property of the `Path` class to define `StreamGeometry`. Special characters define how the points are connected. In the following example, `M` marks the start point, `L` is a line command to the point specified, and `Z` is the Close command to close the figure. Figure 35-6 shows the result. The path markup syntax allows more commands such as horizontal lines (`H`), vertical lines (`V`), cubic Bézier curves (`C`), quadratic Bézier curves (`Q`), smooth cubic Bézier curves (`S`), smooth quadratic Bézier curves (`T`), and elliptical arcs (`A`):

FIGURE 35-6

```
      <Path Canvas.Left="0" Canvas.Top="200" Fill="Yellow" Stroke="Blue"
          StrokeThickness="2.5"
          Data="M 120,5 L 128,80 L 220,50 L 160,130 L 190,220 L 100,150
              L 80,230 L 60,140 L0,110 L70,80 Z" StrokeLineJoin="Round">
      </Path>
```

TRANSFORMATION

Because WPF is vector-based, you can resize every element. In the next example, the vector-based graphics are now scaled, rotated, and skewed. Hit testing (for example, with mouse moves and mouse clicks) still works but without the need for manual position calculation.

Adding the `ScaleTransform` element to the `LayoutTransform` property of the `Canvas` element, as shown here (code file `TransformationDemo/MainWindow.xaml`), resizes the content of the complete canvas by 1.5 in the x and y axes:

```
<Canvas.LayoutTransform>
  <ScaleTransform ScaleX="1.5" ScaleY="1.5" />
</Canvas.LayoutTransform>
```

Rotation can be done in a similar way as scaling. Using the `RotateTransform` element you can define the `Angle` for the rotation:

```
<Canvas.LayoutTransform>
  <RotateTransform Angle="40" />
</Canvas.LayoutTransform>
```

For skewing, you can use the `SkewTransform` element. With skewing you can assign angles for the x and y axes:

```
<Canvas.LayoutTransform>
  <SkewTransform AngleX="20" AngleY="25" />
</Canvas.LayoutTransform>
```

To rotate and skew together, it is possible to define a `TransformGroup` that contains both `RotateTransform` and `SkewTransform`. You can also define a `MatrixTransform` whereby the `Matrix` element specifies the properties `M11` and `M22` for stretch and `M12` and `M21` for skew:

```
<Canvas.LayoutTransform>
  <MatrixTransform>
    <MatrixTransform.Matrix>
      <Matrix M11="0.8" M22="1.6" M12="1.3" M21="0.4" />
    </MatrixTransform.Matrix>
  </MatrixTransform>
</Canvas.LayoutTransform>
```

Figure 35-7 shows the result of all these transformations. The figures are placed inside a `StackPanel`. Starting from the left, the first image is resized, the second image is rotated, the third image is skewed, and the fourth image uses a matrix for its transformation. To highlight the differences between these four images, the `Background` property of the `Canvas` elements is set to different colors.

FIGURE 35-7

> **NOTE** *In addition to* LayerTransform *there's also a* RenderTransform.
> LayerTransform *happens before the layout phase and* RenderTransform *happens after.*

BRUSHES

This section demonstrates how to use the brushes that WPF offers for drawing backgrounds and foregrounds. The examples in this section reference Figure 35-8, which shows the effects of using various brushes within a Path and the Background of Button elements.

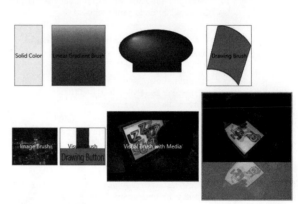

FIGURE 35-8

SolidColorBrush

The first button in Figure 35-8 uses the SolidColorBrush, which, as the name suggests, uses a solid color. The complete area is drawn with the same color.

You can define a solid color just by setting the Background attribute to a string that defines a solid color. The string is converted to a SolidColorBrush element with the help of the BrushValueSerializer:

```
<Button Height="30" Background="PapayaWhip">Solid Color</Button>
```

Of course, you will get the same effect by setting the Background child element and adding a SolidColorBrush element as its content (code file BrushesDemo/MainWindow.xaml). The first button in the application is using PapayaWhip as the solid background color:

```
<Button Content="Solid Color" Margin="10">
  <Button.Background>
    <SolidColorBrush Color="PapayaWhip" />
  </Button.Background>
</Button>
```

LinearGradientBrush

For a smooth color change, you can use the LinearGradientBrush, as the second button shows. This brush defines the StartPoint and EndPoint properties. With this, you can assign two-dimensional coordinates for the linear gradient. The default gradient is diagonal linear from 0,0 to 1,1. By defining different values, the gradient can take different directions. For example, with a StartPoint of 0,0 and an EndPoint of 0,1, you get a vertical gradient. The StartPoint and EndPoint value of 1,0 creates a horizontal gradient.

With the content of this brush, you can define the color values at the specified offsets with the GradientStop element. Between the stops, the colors are smoothed (code file BrushesDemo/MainWindow .xaml):

```
<Button Content="Linear Gradient Brush" Margin="10">
  <Button.Background>
    <LinearGradientBrush StartPoint="0,0" EndPoint="0,1">
      <GradientStop Offset="0" Color="LightGreen" />
      <GradientStop Offset="0.4" Color="Green" />
      <GradientStop Offset="1" Color="DarkGreen" />
```

```
        </LinearGradientBrush>
      </Button.Background>
    </Button>
```

RadialGradientBrush

With the `RadialGradientBrush` you can smooth the color in a radial way. In Figure 35-8, the third element is a `Path` that uses `RadialGradientBrush`. This brush defines the color start with the `GradientOrigin` point (code file `BrushesDemo/MainWindow.xaml`):

```
<Canvas Width="200" Height="150">
  <Path Canvas.Top="0" Canvas.Left="20" Stroke="Black" >
    <Path.Fill>
      <RadialGradientBrush GradientOrigin="0.2,0.2">
        <GradientStop Offset="0" Color="LightBlue" />
        <GradientStop Offset="0.6" Color="Blue" />
        <GradientStop Offset="1.0" Color="DarkBlue" />
      </RadialGradientBrush>
    </Path.Fill>
    <Path.Data>
      <CombinedGeometry GeometryCombineMode="Union">
        <CombinedGeometry.Geometry1>
          <EllipseGeometry Center="80,60" RadiusX="80" RadiusY="40" />
        </CombinedGeometry.Geometry1>
        <CombinedGeometry.Geometry2>
          <RectangleGeometry Rect="30,60 105 50" />
        </CombinedGeometry.Geometry2>
      </CombinedGeometry>
    </Path.Data>
  </Path>
</Canvas>
```

DrawingBrush

The `DrawingBrush` enables you to define a drawing that is created with the brush. The drawing that is shown with the brush is defined within a `GeometryDrawing` element. The `GeometryGroup`, which you can see within the `Geometry` property, consists of the `Geometry` elements discussed earlier in this chapter (code file `BrushesDemo/MainWindow.xaml`):

```
<Button Content="Drawing Brush" Margin="10" Padding="10">
  <Button.Background>
    <DrawingBrush>
      <DrawingBrush.Drawing>
        <GeometryDrawing Brush="Red">
          <GeometryDrawing.Pen>
            <Pen>
              <Pen.Brush>
                <SolidColorBrush>Blue</SolidColorBrush>
              </Pen.Brush>
            </Pen>
          </GeometryDrawing.Pen>
          <GeometryDrawing.Geometry>
            <PathGeometry>
              <PathGeometry.Figures>
                <PathFigure StartPoint="70,40">
                  <PathFigure.Segments>
                    <BezierSegment Point1="90,37" Point2="130,46"
                                   Point3="150,63" />
                    <LineSegment Point="120,110" />
                    <BezierSegment Point1="100,95" Point2="70,90"
                                   Point3="45,91" />
                    <LineSegment Point="70,40" />
```

```
                </PathFigure.Segments>
              </PathFigure>
            </PathGeometry.Figures>
          </PathGeometry>
        </GeometryDrawing.Geometry>
      </GeometryDrawing>
    </DrawingBrush.Drawing>
  </DrawingBrush>
</Button.Background>
</Button>
```

ImageBrush

To load an image into a brush, you can use the `ImageBrush` element. With this element, the image defined by the `ImageSource` property is displayed. The image can be accessed from the file system or from a resource within the assembly. In the example (code file `BrushesDemo/MainWindow.xaml`), the image is added as a resource to the assembly and referenced with the assembly and resource names:

```
<Button Content="Image Brush" Width="100" Height="80" Margin="5"
        Foreground="White">
  <Button.Background>
    <ImageBrush ImageSource="/BrushesDemo;component/Budapest.jpg" />
  </Button.Background>
</Button>
```

VisualBrush

The `VisualBrush` enables you to use other WPF elements in a brush. The following example (code file `BrushesDemo/MainWindow.xaml`) adds a WPF element to the `Visual` property. The sixth element in Figure 35-8 contains a `Rectangle` and a `Button`:

```
<Button Content="Visual Brush" Width="100" Height="80">
  <Button.Background>
    <VisualBrush>
      <VisualBrush.Visual>
        <StackPanel Background="White">
          <Rectangle Width="25" Height="25" Fill="Blue" />
          <Button Content="Drawing Button" Background="Red" />
        </StackPanel>
      </VisualBrush.Visual>
    </VisualBrush>
  </Button.Background>
</Button>
```

You can add any `UIElement` to the `VisualBrush`. For example, you can play a video by using the `MediaElement`:

```
<Button Content="Visual Brush with Media" Width="200" Height="150"
    Foreground="White">
  <Button.Background>
    <VisualBrush>
      <VisualBrush.Visual>
        <MediaElement Source="./Stephanie.wmv" />
      </VisualBrush.Visual>
    </VisualBrush>
  </Button.Background>
</Button>
```

You can also use the `VisualBrush` to create interesting effects such as reflection. The button coded in the following example contains a `StackPanel` that itself contains a `MediaElement` playing a video and a `Border`. The `Border` contains a `Rectangle` that is filled with a `VisualBrush`. This brush defines an opacity value and a transformation. The `Visual` property is bound to the `Border` element. The transformation is achieved by setting the `RelativeTransform` property of the `VisualBrush`. This transformation uses relative coordinates. By setting `ScaleY` to -1, a reflection in the y axis is done. `TranslateTransform` moves the transformation in the y axis so that the reflection is below the original object. You can see the result in the eighth element in Figure 35-8.

> **NOTE** *Data binding and the* `Binding` *element used here are explained in detail in Chapter 36, "Business Applications with WPF."*

```
<Button Width="200" Height="200" Foreground="White">
  <StackPanel>
    <MediaElement x:Name="reflected" Source="./Stephanie.wmv" />
    <Border Height="100">
      <Rectangle>
        <Rectangle.Fill>
          <VisualBrush Opacity="0.35" Stretch="None"
              Visual="{Binding ElementName=reflected}">
            <VisualBrush.RelativeTransform>
              <TransformGroup>
                <ScaleTransform ScaleX="1" ScaleY="-1" />
                <TranslateTransform Y="1" />
              </TransformGroup>
            </VisualBrush.RelativeTransform>
          </VisualBrush>
        </Rectangle.Fill>
      </Rectangle>
    </Border>
  </StackPanel>
</Button>
```

CONTROLS

Because you can use hundreds of controls with WPF, they are categorized into the following groups, each of which is described in the following sections.

Simple Controls

Simple controls are controls that don't have a `Content` property. With the `Button` class, you have seen that the `Button` can contain any shape, or any element you like. This is not possible with simple controls. The following table describes the simple controls.

SIMPLE CONTROL	DESCRIPTION
PasswordBox	This control is used to enter a password and has specific properties for password input, such as `PasswordChar`, to define the character that should be displayed as the user enters the password, or `Password`, to access the password entered. The `PasswordChanged` event is invoked as soon as the password is changed.
ScrollBar	This control contains a `Thumb` that enables the user to select a value. A scrollbar can be used, for example, if a document doesn't fit on the screen. Some controls contain scrollbars that are displayed if the content is too big.

continues

continued

ProgressBar	Indicates the progress of a lengthy operation.
Slider	Enables users to select a range of values by moving a Thumb. ScrollBar, ProgressBar, and Slider are derived from the same base class, RangeBase.
TextBox	Used to display simple, unformatted text
RichTextBox	Supports rich text with the help of the FlowDocument class. RichTextBox and TextBox are derived from the same base class, TextBoxBase.
Calendar	Displays a month, year, or decade. The user can select a date or range of dates.
DatePicker	Opens a calendar onscreen for date selection by the user

> **NOTE** *Although simple controls do not have a* Content *property, you can completely customize the look of a control by defining a template. Templates are discussed later in this chapter in the section Templates.*

Content Controls

A ContentControl has a Content property, with which you can add any content to the control. The Button class derives from the base class ContentControl, so you can add any content to this control. In a previous example, you saw a Canvas control within the Button. Content controls are described in the following table.

CONTENTCONTROL CONTROLS	DESCRIPTION
ButtonRepeat ButtonToggle ButtonCheckBox RadioButton	The classes Button, RepeatButton, ToggleButton, and GridViewColumnHeader are derived from the same base class, ButtonBase. All buttons react to the Click event. The RepeatButton raises the Click event repeatedly until the button is released. ToggleButton is the base class for CheckBox and RadioButton. These buttons have an on and off state. The CheckBox can be selected and cleared by the user; the RadioButton can be selected by the user. Clearing the RadioButton must be done programmatically.
Label	The Label class represents the text label for a control. This class also has support for access keys—for example, a menu command.
Frame	The Frame control supports navigation. You can navigate to a page's content with the Navigate method. If the content is a web page, then the WebBrowser control is used for display.
ListBoxItem	An item inside a ListBox control
StatusBarItem	An item inside a StatusBar control
ScrollViewer	A content control that includes scrollbars. You can put any content in this control; the scrollbars are displayed as needed.
ToolTip	Creates a pop-up window to display additional information for a control.

CONTENTCONTROL CONTROLS	DESCRIPTION
UserControl	Using this class as a base class provides a simple way to create custom controls. However, the UserControl base class does not support templates.
Window	This class enables you to create windows and dialogs. It includes a frame with minimize/maximize/close buttons and a system menu. When showing a dialog, you can use the ShowDialog method; the Show method opens a window.
NavigationWindow	This class derives from the Window class and supports content navigation.

Only a Frame control is contained within the Window of the following XAML code (code file FrameDemo/ MainWindow.xaml). The Source property is set to http://www.cninnovation.com, so the Frame control navigates to this website, as shown in Figure 35-9.

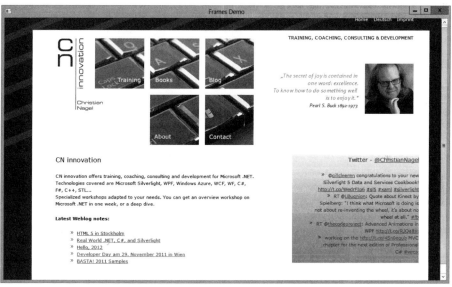

FIGURE 35-9

```
<Window x:Class="FrameDemo.MainWindow"
        xmlns="http://schemas.microsoft.com/winfx/2006/xaml/presentation"
        xmlns:x="http://schemas.microsoft.com/winfx/2006/xaml"
        Title="Frames Demo" Height="240" Width="500">
    <Frame Source="http://www.cninnovation.com" />
</Window>
```

Headered Content Controls

Content controls with a header are derived from the base class HeaderedContentControl, which itself is derived from the base class ContentControl. The HeaderedContentControl class has a property Header to define the content of the header and HeaderTemplate for complete customization of the header. The controls derived from the base class HeaderedContentControl are listed in the following table.

HEADEREDCONTENTCONTROL	DESCRIPTION
Expander	This control enables you to create an "advanced" mode with a dialog that, by default, does not show all information but can be expanded by the user for additional details. In the unexpanded mode, header information is shown. In expanded mode, the content is visible.
GroupBox	Provides a border and a header to group controls
TabItem	These controls are items within the class TabControl. The Header property of the TabItem defines the content of the header shown with the tabs of the TabControl.

A simple use of the Expander control is shown in the next example. The Expander control has the property Header set to Click for more. This text is displayed for expansion. The content of this control is shown only if the control is expanded. Figure 35-10 shows the application with a collapsed Expander control, and Figure 35-11 shows the same application with an expanded Expander control. The code (code file ExpanderDemo/MainWindow.xaml) is as follows:

```
<Window x:Class="ExpanderDemo.MainWindow"
        xmlns="http://schemas.microsoft.com/winfx/2006/xaml/presentation"
        xmlns:x="http://schemas.microsoft.com/winfx/2006/xaml"
        Title="Expander Demo" Height="240" Width="500">
  <StackPanel>
    <TextBlock>Short information</TextBlock>
    <Expander Header="Additional Information">
      <Border Height="200" Width="200" Background="Yellow">
        <TextBlock HorizontalAlignment="Center" VerticalAlignment="Center">
          More information here!
        </TextBlock>
      </Border>
    </Expander>
  </StackPanel>

</Window>
```

> **NOTE** *To make the header text of the* Expander *control change when the control is expanded, you can create a trigger. Triggers are explained later in this chapter in the section Triggers.*

FIGURE 35-10   **FIGURE 35-11**

Items Controls

The ItemsControl class contains a list of items that can be accessed with the Items property. Classes derived from ItemsControl are shown in the following table.

ITEMSCONTROL	DESCRIPTION
Menu and ContextMenu	These classes are derived from the abstract base class MenuBase. You can offer menus to the user by placing MenuItem elements in the items list and associating commands.
StatusBar	This control is usually shown at the bottom of an application to give status information to the user. You can put StatusBarItem elements inside a StatusBar list.
TreeView	Use this control for a hierarchical display of items.
ListBox ComboBox TabControl	These have the same abstract base class, Selector. This base class makes it possible to select items from a list. The ListBox displays the items from a list. The ComboBox has an additional Button control to display the items only if the button is clicked. With TabControl, content can be arranged in tabular form.
DataGrid	This control is a customizable grid that displays data. It is discussed in detail in the next chapter.

Headered Items Controls

HeaderedItemsControl is the base class of controls that include items but also have a header. The class HeaderedItemsControl is derived from ItemsControl.

Classes derived from HeaderedItemsControl are listed in the following table.

HEADEREDITEMSCONTROL	DESCRIPTION
MenuItem	The menu classes Menu and ContextMenu include items of the MenuItem type. Menu items can be connected to commands, as the MenuItem class implements the interface ICommandSource.
TreeViewItem	This class can include items of type TreeViewItem.
ToolBar	This control is a container for a group of controls, usually Button and Separator elements. You can place the ToolBar inside a ToolBarTray that handles the rearranging of ToolBar controls.

Decoration

You can add decorations to a single element with the Decorator class. Decorator is a base class that has derivations such as Border, Viewbox, and BulletDecorator. Theme elements such as ButtonChrome and ListBoxChrome are also decorators.

The following example (code file DecorationsDemo/MainWindow.xaml) demonstrates a Border, Viewbox, and BulletDecorator, as shown in Figure 35-12. The Border class decorates the Children element by adding a border around it. You can define a brush and the thickness of the border, the background, the radius of the corner, and the padding of its children:

```
<Border BorderBrush="Violet" BorderThickness="5.5">
  <Label>Label with a border</Label>
</Border>
```

FIGURE 35-12

The Viewbox stretches and scales its child to the available space. The StretchDirection and Stretch properties are specific to the functionality of the Viewbox. These properties enable specifying whether the child is stretched in both directions, and whether the aspect ratio is preserved:

```
<Viewbox StretchDirection="Both" Stretch="Uniform">
  <Label>Label with a viewbox</Label>
</Viewbox>
```

The BulletDecorator class decorates its child with a bullet. The child can be any element (in this example, a TextBlock). Similarly, the bullet can also be any element. The example uses an Image, but you can use any UIElement:

```
<BulletDecorator>
  <BulletDecorator.Bullet>
    <Image Width="25" Height="25" Margin="5" HorizontalAlignment="Center"
           VerticalAlignment="Center"
           Source="/DecorationsDemo;component/images/apple1.jpg" />
  </BulletDecorator.Bullet>
  <BulletDecorator.Child>
    <TextBlock VerticalAlignment="Center" Padding="8">Granny Smith</TextBlock>
  </BulletDecorator.Child>
</BulletDecorator>
```

LAYOUT

To define the layout of the application, you can use a class that derives from the Panel base class. A layout container needs to do two main tasks: measure and arrange. With *measuring*, the container asks its children for the preferred sizes. Because the full size requested by the controls might not be available, the container determines the available sizes and *arranges* the positions of its children accordingly. This section discusses several available layout containers.

StackPanel

The Window can contain just a single element as content, but if you want more than one element inside it, you can use a StackPanel as a child of the Window, and add elements to the content of the StackPanel. The StackPanel is a simple container control that just shows one element after the other. The orientation of the StackPanel can be horizontal or vertical. The class ToolBarPanel is derived from StackPanel (code file LayoutDemo/StackPanelWindow.xaml):

```
<Window x:Class="LayoutDemo.StackPanelWindow"
        xmlns="http://schemas.microsoft.com/winfx/2006/xaml/presentation"
        xmlns:x="http://schemas.microsoft.com/winfx/2006/xaml"
        Title="StackPanelWindow" Height="300" Width="300">
  <StackPanel Orientation="Vertical">
    <Label>Label</Label>
    <TextBox>TextBox</TextBox>
    <CheckBox>CheckBox</CheckBox>
    <CheckBox>CheckBox</CheckBox>
    <ListBox>
      <ListBoxItem>ListBoxItem One</ListBoxItem>
      <ListBoxItem>ListBoxItem Two</ListBoxItem>
    </ListBox>
    <Button>Button</Button>
  </StackPanel>
</Window>
```

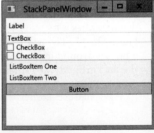

FIGURE 35-13

Figure 35-13 shows the child controls of the StackPanel organized vertically.

WrapPanel

The `WrapPanel` positions the children from left to right, one after the other, as long as they fit into the line, and then continues with the next line. The panel's orientation can be horizontal or vertical (code file `LayoutDemo/WrapPanelWindow.xaml`):

```xml
<Window x:Class="LayoutDemo.WrapPanelWindow"
        xmlns="http://schemas.microsoft.com/winfx/2006/xaml/presentation"
        xmlns:x="http://schemas.microsoft.com/winfx/2006/xaml"
        Title="WrapPanelWindow" Height="300" Width="300">
  <WrapPanel>
    <Button Width="100" Margin="5">Button</Button>
    <Button Width="100" Margin="5">Button</Button>
    <Button Width="100" Margin="5">Button</Button>
    <Button Width="100" Margin="5">Button</Button>
    <Button Width="100" Margin="5">Button</Button>
    <Button Width="100" Margin="5">Button</Button>
    <Button Width="100" Margin="5">Button</Button>
    <Button Width="100" Margin="5">Button</Button>
  </WrapPanel>
</Window>
```

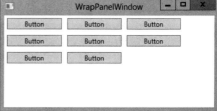

Figure 35-14 shows the output of the panel. If you resize the application, the buttons will be rearranged accordingly so that they fit into a line.

FIGURE 35-14

Canvas

`Canvas` is a panel that enables you to explicitly position controls. `Canvas` defines the attached properties `Left`, `Right`, `Top`, and `Bottom` that can be used by the children for positioning within the panel (code file `LayoutDemo/CanvasWindow.xaml`):

```xml
<Window x:Class="LayoutDemo.CanvasWindow"
        xmlns="http://schemas.microsoft.com/winfx/2006/xaml/presentation"
        xmlns:x="http://schemas.microsoft.com/winfx/2006/xaml"
        Title="CanvasWindow" Height="300" Width="300">
  <Canvas Background="LightBlue">
    <Label Canvas.Top="30" Canvas.Left="20">Enter here:</Label>
    <TextBox Canvas.Top="30" Canvas.Left="120" Width="100" />
    <Button Canvas.Top="70" Canvas.Left="130" Content="Click Me!" Padding="5" />
  </Canvas>
</Window>
```

Figure 35-15 shows the output of the `Canvas` panel with the positioned children `Label`, `TextBox`, and `Button`.

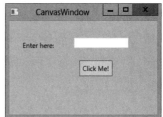

DockPanel

The `DockPanel` is very similar to the Windows Forms docking functionality. Here, you can specify the area in which child controls should be arranged. `DockPanel` defines the attached property `Dock`, which you can set in the children of the controls to the values `Left`, `Right`, `Top`, and `Bottom`. Figure 35-16 shows the outcome of text blocks with borders that are arranged in the dock

FIGURE 35-15

panel. For easier differentiation, different colors are specified for the various areas (code file `LayoutDemo/DockPanelWindow.xaml`):

```xml
<Window x:Class="LayoutDemo.DockPanelWindow"
        xmlns="http://schemas.microsoft.com/winfx/2006/xaml/presentation"
        xmlns:x="http://schemas.microsoft.com/winfx/2006/xaml"
        Title="DockPanelWindow" Height="300" Width="300">
  <DockPanel>
    <Border Height="25" Background="AliceBlue" DockPanel.Dock="Top">
      <TextBlock>Menu</TextBlock>
    </Border>
    <Border Height="25" Background="Aqua" DockPanel.Dock="Top">
      <TextBlock>Ribbon</TextBlock>
    </Border>
    <Border Height="30" Background="LightSteelBlue" DockPanel.Dock="Bottom">
      <TextBlock>Status</TextBlock>
    </Border>
    <Border Height="80" Background="Azure" DockPanel.Dock="Left">
      <TextBlock>Left Side</TextBlock>
    </Border>
    <Border Background="HotPink">
      <TextBlock>Remaining Part</TextBlock>
    </Border>
  </DockPanel>
</Window>
```

Grid

Using the `Grid`, you can arrange your controls with rows and columns. For every column, you can specify a `ColumnDefinition`. For every row, you can specify a `RowDefinition`. The following example code (code file `LayoutDemo/GridWindow.xaml`) lists two columns and three rows. With each column and row, you can specify the width or height. `ColumnDefinition` has a `Width` dependency property; `RowDefinition` has a `Height` dependency property. You can define the height and width in pixels, centimeters, inches, or points, or set it to `Auto` to determine

FIGURE 35-16

the size depending on the content. The grid also allows *star sizing*, whereby the space for the rows and columns is calculated according to the available space and relative to other rows and columns. When providing the available space for a column, you can set the `Width` property to `*`. To have the size doubled for another column, you specify `2*`. The sample code, which defines two columns and three rows, doesn't define additional settings with the column and row definitions; the default is the star sizing.

The grid contains several `Label` and `TextBox` controls. Because the parent of these controls is a grid, you can set the attached properties `Column`, `ColumnSpan`, `Row`, and `RowSpan`:

```xml
<Window x:Class="LayoutDemo.GridWindow"
        xmlns="http://schemas.microsoft.com/winfx/2006/xaml/presentation"
        xmlns:x="http://schemas.microsoft.com/winfx/2006/xaml"
        Title="GridWindow" Height="300" Width="300">
  <Grid ShowGridLines="True">
    <Grid.ColumnDefinitions>
      <ColumnDefinition />
      <ColumnDefinition />
    </Grid.ColumnDefinitions>
    <Grid.RowDefinitions>
      <RowDefinition />
```

```
      <RowDefinition />
      <RowDefinition />
    </Grid.RowDefinitions>
    <Label Grid.Column="0" Grid.ColumnSpan="2" Grid.Row="0"
        VerticalAlignment="Center" HorizontalAlignment="Center" Content="Title"
    />
    <Label Grid.Column="0" Grid.Row="1" VerticalAlignment="Center"
        Content="Firstname:" Margin="10" />
    <TextBox Grid.Column="1" Grid.Row="1" Width="100" Height="30" />
    <Label Grid.Column="0" Grid.Row="2" VerticalAlignment="Center"
        Content="Lastname:" Margin="10" />
    <TextBox Grid.Column="1" Grid.Row="2" Width="100" Height="30" />
  </Grid>
</Window>
```

The outcome of arranging controls in a grid is shown in Figure 35-17. For easier viewing of the columns and rows, the property `ShowGridLines` is set to `true`.

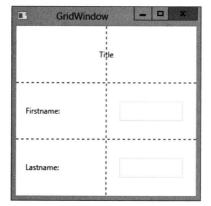

FIGURE 35-17

> **NOTE** *For a grid in which every cell is the same size, you can use the* `UniformGrid` *class.*

STYLES AND RESOURCES

You can define the look and feel of the WPF elements by setting properties, such as `FontSize` and `Background`, with the `Button` element (code file `StylesAndResources/MainWindow.xaml`):

```
<Button Width="150" FontSize="12" Background="AliceBlue" Content="Click Me!" />
```

Instead of defining the look and feel with every element, you can define styles that are stored with resources. To completely customize the look of controls, you can use templates and add them to resources.

Styles

The `Style` property of a control can be assigned to a `Style` element that has setters associated with it. A `Setter` element defines the `Property` and `Value` properties and sets a specified property to a value. In the following example (code file `StylesAndResources/MainWindow.xaml`), the `Background`, `FontSize`, and `FontWeight` properties are set. The `Style` is set to the `TargetType` Button, so that the properties of the `Button` can be directly accessed. If the `TargetType` of the style is not set, the properties can be accessed via `Button.Background`, `Button.FontSize`. This is especially important if you need to set properties of different element types:

```
<Button Width="150" Content="Click Me!">
  <Button.Style>
    <Style TargetType="Button">
      <Setter Property="Background" Value="Yellow" />
      <Setter Property="FontSize" Value="14" />
      <Setter Property="FontWeight" Value="Bold" />
    </Style>
  </Button.Style>
</Button>
```

Setting the `Style` directly with the `Button` element doesn't really help a lot in regard to style sharing. Styles can be put into resources. Within the resources you can assign styles to specific elements, assign a style to all elements of a type, or use a key for the style. To assign a style to all elements of a type, use the `TargetType` property of the `Style` and assign it to a `Button` by specifying the `x:Type` markup extension `{x:Type Button}`. To define a style that needs to be referenced, `x:Key` must be set:

```
<Window.Resources>
  <Style TargetType="{x:Type Button}">
    <Setter Property="Background" Value="LemonChiffon" />
    <Setter Property="FontSize" Value="18" />
  </Style>
  <Style x:Key="ButtonStyle">
    <Setter Property="Button.Background" Value="Red" />
    <Setter Property="Button.Foreground" Value="White" />
    <Setter Property="Button.FontSize" Value="18" />
  </Style>
</Window.Resources>
```

In the following XAML code the first button—which doesn't have a style defined with the element properties—gets the style that is defined for the `Button` type. With the next button, the `Style` property is set with the `StaticResource` markup extension to `{StaticResource ButtonStyle}`, whereas `ButtonStyle` specifies the key value of the style resource defined earlier, so this button has a red background and a white foreground:

```
<Button Width="200" Content="Uses named style"
        Style="{StaticResource ButtonStyle}" Margin="3" />
```

Rather than set the `Background` of a button to just a single value, you can also do more. You can set the `Background` property to a `LinearGradientBrush` with a gradient color definition:

```
<Style x:Key="FancyButtonStyle">
  <Setter Property="Button.FontSize" Value="22" />
  <Setter Property="Button.Foreground" Value="White" />
  <Setter Property="Button.Background">
    <Setter.Value>
      <LinearGradientBrush StartPoint="0,0" EndPoint="0,1">
        <GradientStop Offset="0.0" Color="LightCyan" />
        <GradientStop Offset="0.14" Color="Cyan" />
```

```
            <GradientStop Offset="0.7" Color="DarkCyan" />
          </LinearGradientBrush>
        </Setter.Value>
      </Setter>
    </Style>
```

The next button in this example has a fancy style with cyan applied as the linear gradient:

```
<Button Width="200" Content="Fancy button style"
    Style="{StaticResource FancyButtonStyle}" Margin="3" />
```

Styles offer a kind of inheritance. One style can be based on another one. The style AnotherButtonStyle is based on the style FancyButtonStyle. It uses all the settings defined by the base style (referenced by the BasedOn property), except the Foreground property—which is set to LinearGradientBrush:

```
<Style x:Key="AnotherButtonStyle" BasedOn="{StaticResource FancyButtonStyle}"
    TargetType="Button">
  <Setter Property="Foreground">
    <Setter.Value>
      <LinearGradientBrush>
        <GradientStop Offset="0.2" Color="White" />
        <GradientStop Offset="0.5" Color="LightYellow" />
        <GradientStop Offset="0.9" Color="Orange" />
      </LinearGradientBrush>
    </Setter.Value>
  </Setter>
</Style>
```

The last button has the AnotherButtonStyle applied:

```
<Button Width="200" Content="Style inheritance"
    Style="{StaticResource AnotherButtonStyle}" Margin="3" />
```

The result of all these buttons after styling is shown in Figure 35-18.

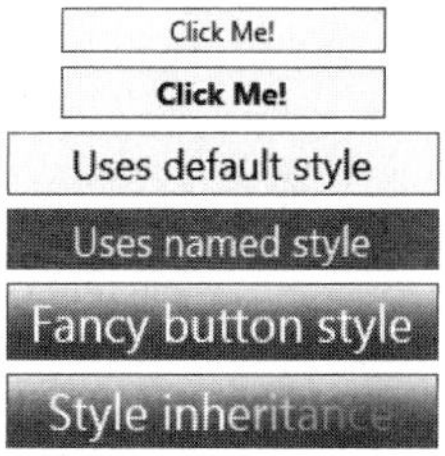

FIGURE 35-18

Resources

As you have seen with the styles sample, usually styles are stored within resources. You can define any freezable element within a resource. For example, the brush created earlier for the background style of the button can itself be defined as a resource, so you can use it everywhere a brush is required.

The following example (code file StylesAndResources/ResourceDemo.xaml) defines a LinearGradientBrush with the key name MyGradientBrush inside the StackPanel resources. button1 assigns the Background property by using a StaticResource markup extension to the resource MyGradientBrush. Figure 35-19 shows the output from this XAML code:

```
<StackPanel x:Name="myContainer">
  <StackPanel.Resources>
    <LinearGradientBrush x:Key="MyGradientBrush" StartPoint="0,0"
        EndPoint="0.3,1">
      <GradientStop Offset="0.0" Color="LightCyan" />
      <GradientStop Offset="0.14" Color="Cyan" />
      <GradientStop Offset="0.7" Color="DarkCyan" />
    </LinearGradientBrush>
  </StackPanel.Resources>
  <Button Width="200" Height="50" Foreground="White" Margin="5"
      Background="{StaticResource MyGradientBrush}" Content="Click Me!" />
</StackPanel>
```

FIGURE 35-19

Here, the resources have been defined with the `StackPanel`. In the previous example, the resources were defined with the `Window` element. The base class `FrameworkElement` defines the property `Resources` of type `ResourceDictionary`. That's why resources can be defined with every class that is derived from the `FrameworkElement`—any WPF element.

Resources are searched hierarchically. If you define the resource with the `Window`, it applies to every child element of the `Window`. If the `Window` contains a `Grid`, and the `Grid` contains a `StackPanel`, and you define the resource with the `StackPanel`, then the resource applies to every control within the `StackPanel`. If the `StackPanel` contains a `Button`, and you define the resource just with the `Button`, then this style is valid only for the `Button`.

> **NOTE** *In regard to hierarchies, you need to pay attention if you use the* `TargetType` *without a* `Key` *for styles. If you define a resource with the* `Canvas` *element and set the* `TargetType` *for the style to apply to* `TextBox` *elements, then the style applies to all* `TextBox` *elements within the* `Canvas`. *The style even applies to* `TextBox` *elements that are contained in a* `ListBox` *when the* `ListBox` *is in the* `Canvas`.

If you need the same style for more than one window, then you can define the style with the application. In a Visual Studio WPF project, the file `App.xaml` is created for defining global resources of the application. The application styles are valid for every window of the application. Every element can access resources that are defined with the application. If resources are not found with the parent window, then the search for resources continues with the `Application` (code file `StylesAndResources/App.xaml`):

```
<Application x:Class="StylesAndResources.App"
            xmlns="http://schemas.microsoft.com/winfx/2006/xaml/presentation"
            xmlns:x="http://schemas.microsoft.com/winfx/2006/xaml"
            StartupUri="MainWindow.xaml">
    <Application.Resources>

    </Application.Resources>
</Application>
```

System Resources

Some system-wide resources for colors and fonts are available for all applications. These resources are defined with the classes `SystemColors`, `SystemFonts`, and `SystemParameters`:

➤   `SystemColors`—Provides the color settings for borders, controls, the desktop, and windows, such as `ActiveBorderColor`, `ControlBrush`, `DesktopColor`, `WindowColor`, `WindowBrush`, and so on.

➤   `SystemFonts`—Returns the settings for the fonts of the menu, status bar, and message box. These include `CaptionFont`, `DialogFont`, `MenuFont`, `MessageBoxFont`, `StatusFont`, and so on.

➤   `SystemParameters`—Provides settings for sizes of menu buttons, cursors, icons, borders, captions, timing information, and keyboard settings, such as `BorderWidth`, `CaptionHeight`, `CaptionWidth`, `MenuButtonWidth`, `MenuPopupAnimation`, `MenuShowDelay`, `SmallIconHeight`, `SmallIconWidth`, and so on.

Accessing Resources from Code

To access resources from code-behind, the base class `FrameworkElement` implements the method `FindResource`, so you can invoke this method with every WPF object. To do this, `button1` doesn't have a background specified, but the `Click` event is assigned to the method `button1_Click` (code file `StylesAndResources/ResourceDemo.xaml`):

```
<Button Name="button1" Width="220" Height="50" Margin="5"
    Click="button1_Click" Content="Apply Resource Programmatically" />
```

With the implementation of button1_Click, the FindResource method is used on the Button that was clicked. Then a search for the resource MyGradientBrush happens hierarchically, and the brush is applied to the Background property of the control. The resource MyGradientBrush was created previously in the resources of the StackPanel (code file StylesAndResources/ResourceDemo.xaml.cs):

```
public void button1_Click(object sender, RoutedEventArgs e)
{
    Control ctrl = sender as Control;
    ctrl.Background = ctrl.FindResource("MyGradientBrush") as Brush;
}
```

> **NOTE** If FindResource does not find the resource key, then an exception is thrown. If you aren't certain whether the resource is available, then you can instead use the method TryFindResource, which returns null if the resource is not found.

Dynamic Resources

With the StaticResource markup extension, resources are searched at load time. If the resource changes while the program is running, then you should use the DynamicResource markup extension instead.

The next example (code file StylesAndResources/ResourceDemo.xaml) is using the same resource defined previously. The earlier example used StaticResource. This button uses DynamicResource with the DynamicResource markup extension. The event handler of this button changes the resource programmatically. The handler method button2_Click is assigned to the Click event handler:

```
<Button Name="button2" Width="200" Height="50" Foreground="White" Margin="5"
    Background="{DynamicResource MyGradientBrush}" Content="Change Resource"
    Click="button2_Click" />
```

The implementation of button2_Click clears the resources of the StackPanel and adds a new resource with the same name, MyGradientBrush. This new resource is very similar to the resource defined in XAML code; it just defines different colors (code file StylesAndResources/ResourceDemo.xaml.cs):

```
private void button2_Click(object sender, RoutedEventArgs e)
{
  myContainer.Resources.Clear();
  var brush = new LinearGradientBrush
  {
    StartPoint = new Point(0, 0),
    EndPoint = new Point(0, 1)
  };

  brush.GradientStops = new GradientStopCollection()
  {
    new GradientStop(Colors.White, 0.0),
    new GradientStop(Colors.Yellow, 0.14),
    new GradientStop(Colors.YellowGreen, 0.7)
  };
  myContainer.Resources.Add("MyGradientBrush", brush);
}
```

When running the application, the resource changes dynamically by clicking the Change Resource button. Using the button with `DynamicResource` gets the dynamically created resource; the button with `StaticResource` looks the same as before.

Resource Dictionaries

If the same resources are used with different applications, it's useful to put the resource in a resource dictionary. Using resource dictionaries, the files can be shared between multiple applications, or the resource dictionary can be put into an assembly and shared by the applications.

To share a resource dictionary in an assembly, create a library. A resource dictionary file, here `Dictionary1.xaml`, can be added to the assembly. The build action for this file must be set to `Resource` so that it is added as a resource to the assembly.

`Dictionary1.xaml` defines two resources: `LinearGradientBrush` with the `CyanGradientBrush` key, and a style for a `Button` that can be referenced with the `PinkButtonStyle` key (code file download ResourcesLib/Dictionary1.xaml):

```xml
<ResourceDictionary
    xmlns="http://schemas.microsoft.com/winfx/2006/xaml/presentation"
    xmlns:x="http://schemas.microsoft.com/winfx/2006/xaml">
  <LinearGradientBrush x:Key="CyanGradientBrush" StartPoint="0,0"
      EndPoint="0.3,1">
    <GradientStop Offset="0.0" Color="LightCyan" />
    <GradientStop Offset="0.14" Color="Cyan" />
    <GradientStop Offset="0.7" Color="DarkCyan" />
  </LinearGradientBrush>

  <Style x:Key="PinkButtonStyle" TargetType="Button">
    <Setter Property="FontSize" Value="22" />
    <Setter Property="Foreground" Value="White" />
    <Setter Property="Background">
      <Setter.Value>
        <LinearGradientBrush StartPoint="0,0" EndPoint="0,1">
          <GradientStop Offset="0.0" Color="Pink" />
          <GradientStop Offset="0.3" Color="DeepPink" />
          <GradientStop Offset="0.9" Color="DarkOrchid" />
        </LinearGradientBrush>
      </Setter.Value>
    </Setter>
  </Style>
</ResourceDictionary>
```

With the target project, the library needs to be referenced, and the resource dictionary added to the dictionaries. You can use multiple resource dictionary files that can be added with the `Merged Dictionaries` property of the `ResourceDictionary`. A list of resource dictionaries can be added to the merged dictionaries. With the `Source` property of `ResourceDictionary`, a dictionary can be referenced. For the reference, the pack URI syntax is used. The pack URI can be assigned as *absolute*, whereby the URI begins with `pack://`, or as *relative*, as it is used in this example. With relative syntax, the referenced assembly `ResourceLib`, which includes the dictionary, is first after the `/` followed by `;component`. `.Component` means that the dictionary is included as a resource in the assembly. After that, the name of the dictionary file `Dictionary1.xaml` is added. If the dictionary is added into a subfolder, the folder name must be declared as well (code file StylesAndResources/App.xaml):

```xml
<Application x:Class="StylesAndResources.App"
             xmlns="http://schemas.microsoft.com/winfx/2006/xaml/presentation"
             xmlns:x="http://schemas.microsoft.com/winfx/2006/xaml"
             StartupUri="MainWindow.xaml">
```

```
  <Application.Resources>
    <ResourceDictionary>
      <ResourceDictionary.MergedDictionaries>
        <ResourceDictionary Source="/ResourceLib;component/Dictionary1.xaml" />
      </ResourceDictionary.MergedDictionaries>
    </ResourceDictionary>
  </Application.Resources>
</Application>
```

Now it is possible to use the resources from the referenced assembly in the same way as local resources (code file StylesAndResources/ResourceDemo.xaml):

```
<Button Width="300" Height="50" Style="{StaticResource PinkButtonStyle}"
    Content="Referenced Resource" />
```

TRIGGERS

With triggers you can change the look and feel of your controls dynamically based on certain events or property value changes. For example, when the user moves the mouse over a button, the button can change its look. Usually, you need to do this with the C# code. With WPF, you can also do this with XAML, as long as only the UI is influenced.

There are several triggers with XAML. Property triggers are activated as soon as a property value changes. Multi-triggers are based on multiple property values. Event triggers fire when an event occurs. Data triggers happen when data that is bound is changed. This section discusses property triggers, multi-triggers, and data triggers. Event triggers are explained later with animations.

Property Triggers

The Style class has a Triggers property whereby you can assign property triggers. The following example (code file TriggerDemo/PropertyTriggerWindow.xaml) includes a Button element inside a Grid panel. With the Window resources, a default style for Button elements is defined. This style specifies that the Background is set to LightBlue and the FontSize to 17. This is the style of the Button elements when the application is started. Using triggers, the style of the controls change. The triggers are defined within the Style.Triggers element, using the Trigger element. One trigger is assigned to the property IsMouseOver; the other trigger is assigned to the property IsPressed. Both of these properties are defined with the Button class to which the style applies. If IsMouseOver has a value of true, then the trigger fires and sets the Foreground property to Red and the FontSize property to 22. If the Button is pressed, then the property IsPressed is true, and the second trigger fires and sets the Foreground property of the TextBox to Yellow:

> **NOTE** *If the* IsPressed *property is set to* true, *the* IsMouseOver *property will be* true *as well. Pressing the button also requires the mouse to be over the button. Pressing the button triggers it to fire and changes the properties accordingly. Here, the order of triggers is important. If the* IsPressed *property trigger is moved before the* IsMouseOver *property trigger, the* IsMouseOver *property trigger overwrites the values that the first trigger set.*

```
<Window x:Class="TriggerDemo.PropertyTriggerWindow"
        xmlns="http://schemas.microsoft.com/winfx/2006/xaml/presentation"
        xmlns:x="http://schemas.microsoft.com/winfx/2006/xaml"
        Title="PropertyTriggerWindow" Height="300" Width="300">
  <Window.Resources>
```

```
        <Style TargetType="Button">
          <Setter Property="Background" Value="LightBlue" />
          <Setter Property="FontSize" Value="17" />
          <Style.Triggers>
            <Trigger Property="IsMouseOver" Value="True">
              <Setter Property="Foreground" Value="Red" />
              <Setter Property="FontSize" Value="22" />
            </Trigger>
            <Trigger Property="IsPressed" Value="True">
              <Setter Property="Foreground" Value="Yellow" />
              <Setter Property="FontSize" Value="22" />
            </Trigger>
          </Style.Triggers>
        </Style>
      </Window.Resources>
      <Grid>
        <Button Width="200" Height="30" Content="Click me!" />
      </Grid>
    </Window>
```

You don't need to reset the property values to the original values when the reason for the trigger is not valid anymore. For example, you don't need to define a trigger for IsMouseOver=true and IsMouseOver=false. As soon as the reason for the trigger is no longer valid, the changes made by the trigger action are reset to the original values automatically.

Figure 35-20 shows the trigger sample application in which the foreground and font size of the button are changed from their original values when the button has the focus.

Click me!

FIGURE 35-20

> **NOTE** *When using property triggers, it is extremely easy to change the look of controls, fonts, colors, opacity, and the like. When the mouse moves over them, the keyboard sets the focus—not a single line of programming code is required.*

The Trigger class defines the following properties to specify the trigger action.

TRIGGER PROPERTY	DESCRIPTION
Property Value	With property triggers, the Property and Value properties are used to specify when the trigger should fire—for example, Property="IsMouseOver" Value="True".
Setters	As soon as the trigger fires, you can use Setters to define a collection of Setter elements to change values for properties. The Setter class defines the properties Property, TargetName, and Value for the object properties to change.
EnterActions ExitActions	Instead of defining setters, you can define EnterActions and ExitActions. With both of these properties, you can define a collection of TriggerAction elements. EnterActions fires when the trigger starts (with a property trigger, when the Property/Value combination applies); ExitActions fires before it ends (just at the moment when the Property/Value combination no longer applies).Trigger actions that you can specify with these actions are derived from the base class TriggerAction, such as, SoundPlayerAction and BeginStoryboard. With SoundPlayerAction, you can start the playing of sound. BeginStoryboard is used with animation, discussed later in this chapter.

MultiTrigger

A property trigger fires when a value of a property changes. If you need to set a trigger because two or more properties have a specific value, you can use MultiTrigger.

MultiTrigger has a Conditions property whereby valid values of properties can be specified. It also has a Setters property that enables you to specify the properties that need to be set. In the following example (code file TriggerDemo/MultiTriggerWindow.xaml), a style is defined for TextBox elements such that the trigger applies if the IsEnabled property is True and the Text property has the value Test. If both apply, the Foreground property of the TextBox is set to Red:

```
<Window x:Class="TriggerDemo.MultiTriggerWindow"
    xmlns="http://schemas.microsoft.com/winfx/2006/xaml/presentation"
    xmlns:x="http://schemas.microsoft.com/winfx/2006/xaml"
    Title="MultiTriggerWindow" Height="300" Width="300">
  <Window.Resources>
    <Style TargetType="TextBox">
      <Style.Triggers>
        <MultiTrigger>
          <MultiTrigger.Conditions>
            <Condition Property="IsEnabled" Value="True" />
            <Condition Property="Text" Value="Test" />
          </MultiTrigger.Conditions>
          <MultiTrigger.Setters>
            <Setter Property="Foreground" Value="Red" />
          </MultiTrigger.Setters>
        </MultiTrigger>
      </Style.Triggers>
    </Style>
  </Window.Resources>
  <Grid>
    <TextBox />
  </Grid>
</Window>
```

Data Triggers

Data triggers fire if bound data to a control fulfills specific conditions. In the following example (code file TriggerDemo/Book.cs), a Book class is used that has different displays depending on the publisher of the book.

The Book class defines the properties Title and Publisher and has an overload of the ToString method:

```
public class Book
{
  public string Title { get; set; }
  public string Publisher { get; set; }

  public override string ToString()
  {
    return Title;
  }
}
```

In the XAML code, a style is defined for ListBoxItem elements. The style contains DataTrigger elements that are bound to the Publisher property of the class that is used with the items. If the value of the Publisher property is Wrox Press, the Background is set to Red. With the publishers Dummies and Wiley, the Background is set to Yellow and DarkGray, respectively (code file TriggerDemo/DataTriggerWindow .xaml):

```xaml
<Window x:Class="TriggerDemo.DataTriggerWindow"
    xmlns="http://schemas.microsoft.com/winfx/2006/xaml/presentation"
    xmlns:x="http://schemas.microsoft.com/winfx/2006/xaml"
    Title="Data Trigger Window" Height="300" Width="300">
  <Window.Resources>
    <Style TargetType="ListBoxItem">
      <Style.Triggers>
        <DataTrigger Binding="{Binding Publisher}" Value="Wrox Press">
          <Setter Property="Background" Value="Red" />
        </DataTrigger>
        <DataTrigger Binding="{Binding Publisher}" Value="Dummies">
          <Setter Property="Background" Value="Yellow" />
        </DataTrigger>
        <DataTrigger Binding="{Binding Publisher}" Value="Wiley">
          <Setter Property="Background" Value="DarkGray" />
        </DataTrigger>
      </Style.Triggers>
    </Style>
  </Window.Resources>
  <Grid>
    <ListBox x:Name="list1" />
  </Grid>
</Window>
```

In the code-behind (code file `TriggerDemo/DataTriggerWindow.xaml.cs`), the list with the name `list1` is initialized to contain several `Book` objects:

```csharp
public DataTriggerWindow()
{
  InitializeComponent();
  list1.Items.Add(new Book
  {
    Title = "Professional C# 4.0 and .NET 4",
    Publisher = "Wrox Press"
  });
  list1.Items.Add(new Book
  {
    Title = "C# 2010 for Dummies",
    Publisher = "For Dummies"
  });
  list1.Items.Add(new Book
  {
    Title = "HTML and CSS: Design and Build Websites",
    Publisher = "Wiley"
  });
}
```

Running the application, you can see in Figure 35-21 the `ListBoxItem` elements that are formatted according to the publisher value.

With `DataTrigger`, multiple properties must be set for `MultiDataTrigger` (similar to `Trigger` and `MultiTrigger`).

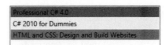

FIGURE 35-21

TEMPLATES

In this chapter, you have already seen that a `Button` control can contain any content. The content can be simple text, but you can also add a `Canvas` element, which can contain shapes; a `Grid`; or a video. In fact, you can do even more than that with a button!

In WPF, the functionality of controls is completely separate from their look and feel. A button has a default look, but you can completely customize that look as you like with templates.

WPF provides several template types that derive from the base class `FrameworkTemplate`.

TEMPLATE TYPE	DESCRIPTION
ControlTemplate	Enables you to specify the visual structure of a control and override its look
ItemsPanelTemplate	For an `ItemsControl` you can specify the layout of its items by assigning an `ItemsPanelTemplate`. Each `ItemsControl` has a default `ItemsPanelTemplate`. For the `MenuItem`, it is a `WrapPanel`. The `StatusBar` uses a `DockPanel`, and the `ListBox` uses a `VirtualizingStackPanel`.
DataTemplate	These are very useful for graphical representations of objects. When styling a `ListBox`, by default the items of the `ListBox` are shown according to the output of the `ToString` method. By applying a `DataTemplate` you can override this behavior and define a custom presentation of the items.
HierarchicalDataTemplate	Used for arranging a tree of objects. This control supports `HeaderedItemsControls`, such as `TreeViewItem` and `MenuItem`.

Control Templates

Previously in this chapter you've seen how the properties of a control can be styled. If setting simple properties of the controls doesn't give you the look you want, you can change the `Template` property. With the `Template` property, you can customize the complete look of the control. The next example demonstrates customizing buttons; and later in the following sections ("Data Templates," "Styling a ListBox," "ItemTemplate," and "Control Templates for ListBox Elements"), list boxes are customized step by step, so you can see the intermediate results of the changes.

You customize the `Button` type in a separate resource dictionary file, `Styles.xaml`. Here, a style with the key name `RoundedGelButton` is defined. The style `GelButton` sets the properties `Background`, `Height`, `Foreground`, and `Margin`, and the `Template`. The `Template` is the most interesting aspect with this style. The `Template` specifies a `Grid` with just one row and one column.

Inside this cell, you can find an ellipse with the name `GelBackground`. This ellipse has a linear gradient brush for the stroke. The stroke that surrounds the rectangle is very thin because the `StrokeThickness` is set to 0.5.

The second ellipse, `GelShine`, is a small ellipse whose size is defined by the `Margin` property and so is visible within the first ellipse. The stroke is transparent, so there is no line surrounding the ellipse. This ellipse uses a linear gradient fill brush, which transitions from a light, partly transparent color to full transparency. This gives the ellipse a shimmering effect (code file `TemplateDemo/Styles.xaml`):

```xml
<ResourceDictionary
    xmlns="http://schemas.microsoft.com/winfx/2006/xaml/presentation"
    xmlns:x="http://schemas.microsoft.com/winfx/2006/xaml">
  <Style x:Key="RoundedGelButton" TargetType="Button">
    <Setter Property="Width" Value="100" />
    <Setter Property="Height" Value="100" />
    <Setter Property="Foreground" Value="White" />
```

```
              <Setter Property="Template">
                <Setter.Value>
                  <ControlTemplate TargetType="{x:Type Button}">
                    <Grid>
                      <Ellipse Name="GelBackground" StrokeThickness="0.5" Fill="Black">
                        <Ellipse.Stroke>
                          <LinearGradientBrush StartPoint="0,0" EndPoint="0,1">
                            <GradientStop Offset="0" Color="#ff7e7e7e" />
                            <GradientStop Offset="1" Color="Black" />
                          </LinearGradientBrush>
                        </Ellipse.Stroke>
                      </Ellipse>
                      <Ellipse Margin="15,5,15,50">
                        <Ellipse.Fill>
                          <LinearGradientBrush StartPoint="0,0" EndPoint="0,1">
                            <GradientStop Offset="0" Color="#aaffffff" />
                            <GradientStop Offset="1" Color="Transparent" />
                          </LinearGradientBrush>
                        </Ellipse.Fill>
                      </Ellipse>
                    </Grid>
                  </ControlTemplate>
                </Setter.Value>
              </Setter>
            </Style>
          </ResourceDictionary>
```

From the `app.xaml` file, the resource dictionary is referenced as shown here (code file `TemplateDemo/App.xaml`):

```
<Application x:Class="TemplateDemo.App"
    xmlns="http://schemas.microsoft.com/winfx/2006/xaml/presentation"
    xmlns:x="http://schemas.microsoft.com/winfx/2006/xaml"
    StartupUri="MainWindow.xaml">
  <Application.Resources>
    <ResourceDictionary Source="Styles.xaml" />
  </Application.Resources>
</Application>
```

Now a `Button` control can be associated with the style. The new look of the button is shown in Figure 35-22 and uses code file `TemplateDemo/StyledButtonWindow.xaml`:

FIGURE 35-22

```
      <Button Style="{StaticResource RoundedGelButton}" Content="Click Me!" />
```

The button now has a completely different look. However, the content that is defined with the button itself is missing. The template created previously must be extended to get the content of the `Button` into the new look. What needs to be added is a `ContentPresenter`. The `ContentPresenter` is the placeholder for the control's content, and it defines the place where the content should be positioned. In the code that follows (code file `TemplateDemo/StyledButtonWindow.xaml`), the content is placed in the first row of the `Grid`, as are the `Ellipse` elements. The `Content` property of the `ContentPresenter` defines what the content should be. The content is set to a `TemplateBinding` markup expression. `TemplateBinding` binds the template parent, which is the `Button` element in this case. `{TemplateBinding Content}` specifies that the value of the `Content` property of the `Button` control should be placed inside the placeholder as content. Figure 35-23 shows the result with the content shown in the here:

```
              <Setter Property="Template">
                <Setter.Value>
                  <ControlTemplate TargetType="{x:Type Button}">
```

```
<Grid>
  <Ellipse Name="GelBackground" StrokeThickness="0.5" Fill="Black">
    <Ellipse.Stroke>
      <LinearGradientBrush StartPoint="0,0" EndPoint="0,1">
        <GradientStop Offset="0" Color="#ff7e7e7e" />
        <GradientStop Offset="1" Color="Black" />
      </LinearGradientBrush>
    </Ellipse.Stroke>
  </Ellipse>
  <Ellipse Margin="15,5,15,50">
    <Ellipse.Fill>
      <LinearGradientBrush StartPoint="0,0" EndPoint="0,1">
        <GradientStop Offset="0" Color="#aaffffff" />
        <GradientStop Offset="1" Color="Transparent" />
      </LinearGradientBrush>
    </Ellipse.Fill>
  </Ellipse>
  <ContentPresenter Name="GelButtonContent"
                    VerticalAlignment="Center"
                    HorizontalAlignment="Center"
                    Content="{TemplateBinding Content}" />
</Grid>
      </ControlTemplate>
    </Setter.Value>
```

FIGURE 35-23

Such a styled button now looks very fancy on the screen, but there's still a problem: There is no action if the mouse is clicked or the mouse moves over the button. This isn't the typical experience a user has with a button. This can be solved, however. With a template-styled button, you must have triggers that enable the button to look differently in response to mouse moves and mouse clicks.

Using property triggers (discussed previously), this can be done easily. The triggers just need to be added to the `Triggers` collection of the `ControlTemplate` as shown next. Here, two triggers are defined. One property trigger is active when the `IsMouseOver` property of the button is `true`. Then the `Fill` property of the `Ellipse` with the name `GelBackground` is changed to a `RadialGradientBrush` with values from `Lime` to `DarkGreen`. With the `IsPressed` property, other colors are specified for the `RadialGradientBrush`:

```
<ControlTemplate.Triggers>
  <Trigger Property="IsMouseOver" Value="True">
    <Setter Property="Ellipse.Fill" TargetName="GelBackground">
      <Setter.Value>
        <RadialGradientBrush>
          <GradientStop Offset="0" Color="Lime" />
          <GradientStop Offset="1" Color="DarkGreen" />
        </RadialGradientBrush>
      </Setter.Value>
    </Setter>
  </Trigger>
  <Trigger Property="IsPressed" Value="True">
    <Setter Property="Ellipse.Fill" TargetName="GelBackground">
      <Setter.Value>
        <RadialGradientBrush>
          <GradientStop Offset="0" Color="#ffcc34" />
          <GradientStop Offset="1" Color="#cc9900" />
        </RadialGradientBrush>
      </Setter.Value>
    </Setter>
  </Trigger>

</ControlTemplate.Triggers>
```

Now run the application and you should see visual feedback from the button as soon as the mouse hovers over it or the mouse is clicked.

Data Templates

The content of `ContentControl` elements can be any content—not only WPF elements but also .NET objects. For example, an object of the `Country` type can be assigned to the content of a `Button` class. In the following example (code file `TemplateDemo/Country.cs`), the `Country` class is created to represent the name and flag with a path to an image. This class defines the `Name` and `ImagePath` properties, and it has an overridden `ToString` method for a default string representation:

```
public class Country
{
  public string Name { get; set; }
  public string ImagePath { get; set; }

  public override string ToString()
  {
    return Name;
  }
}
```

How does this content look within a `Button` or any other `ContentControl`? By default, the `ToString` method is invoked, and the string representation of the object is shown. For a custom look you can also create a `DataTemplate` for the `Country` type.

Here, within the resources of the `Window`, a `DataTemplate` is created. This `DataTemplate` doesn't have a key assigned and thus is a default for the `Country`. `src` type—it is also the alias of the XML namespace referencing the .NET assembly and .NET namespace. Within the `DataTemplate` the main elements are a `TextBox` with the `Text` property bound to the `Name` property of the `Country`, and an `Image` with the `Source` property bound to the `ImagePath` property of the `Country`. The `Grid`, `Border`, and `Rectangle` elements define the layout and visual appearance (code file `TemplateDemo/StyledButtonWindow.xaml`):

```
<Window.Resources>
  <DataTemplate DataType="{x:Type src:Country}">
    <Grid>
      <Grid.ColumnDefinitions>
        <ColumnDefinition Width="Auto" />
        <ColumnDefinition Width="Auto" />
      </Grid.ColumnDefinitions>
    <Grid.RowDefinitions>
      <RowDefinition Height="60" />
    </Grid.RowDefinitions>
    <TextBlock FontSize="16" VerticalAlignment="Center" Margin="5"
        Text="{Binding Name}" FontWeight="Bold" Grid.Column="0" />
      <Border Margin="4,0" Grid.Column="1" BorderThickness="2"
          CornerRadius="4">
        <Border.BorderBrush>
          <LinearGradientBrush StartPoint="0,0" EndPoint="0,1">
            <GradientStop Offset="0" Color="#aaa" />
            <GradientStop Offset="1" Color="#222" />
          </LinearGradientBrush>
        </Border.BorderBrush>
        <Grid>
          <Rectangle>
            <Rectangle.Fill>
              <LinearGradientBrush StartPoint="0,0" EndPoint="0,1">
                <GradientStop Offset="0" Color="#444" />
                <GradientStop Offset="1" Color="#fff" />
```

```
            </LinearGradientBrush>
          </Rectangle.Fill>
        </Rectangle>
        <Image Width="48" Margin="2,2,2,1" Source="{Binding ImagePath}" />
      </Grid>
    </Border>
  </Grid>
  </DataTemplate>
</Window.Resources>
```

With the XAML code, a simple `Button` element with the name `button1` is defined:

```
<Button Grid.Row="1" x:Name="button1" Margin="10" />
```

Within the code-behind (code file `TemplateDemo/StyledButtonWindow.xaml.cs`), a new `Country` object is instantiated that is assigned to the `Content` property of `button1`:

```
public StyledButtonWindow()
{
    InitializeComponent();
    button1.Content = new Country
    {
        Name = "Austria",
        ImagePath = "images/Austria.bmp"
    };
}
```

After running the application, you can see that the `DataTemplate` is applied to the `Button` because the `Country` data type has a default template, shown in Figure 35-24.

Of course, you can also create a control template and use a data template from within.

FIGURE 35-24

Styling a ListBox

Changing a style of a button or a label is a simple task, such as changing the style of an element that contains a list of elements. For example, how about changing a `ListBox`? Again, a list box has behavior and a look. It can display a list of elements, and you can select one or more elements from the list. For the behavior, the `ListBox` class defines methods, properties, and events. The look of the `ListBox` is separate from its behavior. It has a default look, but you can change this look by creating a template.

With a `ListBox`, the `ControlTemplate` defines how the complete control looks, an `ItemTemplate` defines how an item looks, and a `DataTemplate` defines the type that might be within an item. To fill a `ListBox` with some items, the static class `Countries` returns a list of a few countries that will be displayed (code file `TemplateDemo/Countries.cs`):

```
public class Countries
{
    public static IEnumerable<Country> GetCountries()
    {
        return new List<Country>
        {
            new Country { Name = "Austria", ImagePath = "Images/Austria.bmp" },
            new Country { Name = "Germany", ImagePath = "Images/Germany.bmp" },
            new Country { Name = "Norway", ImagePath = "Images/Norway.bmp" },
            new Country { Name = "USA", ImagePath = "Images/USA.bmp" }
        };
    }
}
```

Inside the code-behind file (code file `TemplateDemo/StyledListBoxWindow1.xaml.cs`) in the constructor of the `StyledListBoxWindow1` class, the `DataContext` property of the `StyledListBoxWindow1` instance is set to the list of countries returned from the method `Countries.GetCountries`. (The `DataContext` property is a data binding feature discussed in the next chapter.)

```
public partial class StyledListBoxWindow1 : Window
{
  public StyledListBoxWindow1()
  {
    InitializeComponent();
    this.DataContext = Countries.GetCountries();
  }
}
```

Within the XAML code (code file `TemplateDemo/StyledListBoxWindow.xaml`), the `ListBox` named `countryList1` is defined. `countryList1` doesn't have a different style. It uses the default look from the `ListBox` element. The property `ItemsSource` is set to the `Binding` markup extension, which is used by data binding. From the code-behind, you have seen that the binding is done to an array of `Country` objects. Figure 35-25 shows the default look of the `ListBox`. By default, only the names of the countries returned by the `ToString` method are displayed in a simple list:

```
<Window x:Class="TemplateDemo.StyledListBoxWindow1"
    xmlns="http://schemas.microsoft.com/winfx/2006/xaml/presentation"
    xmlns:x="http://schemas.microsoft.com/winfx/2006/xaml"
    xmlns:src="clr-namespace:TemplateDemo"
    Title="StyledListBoxWindow1" Height="300" Width="300">
  <Grid>
    <ListBox ItemsSource="{Binding}" Margin="10" />
  </Grid>
</Window>
```

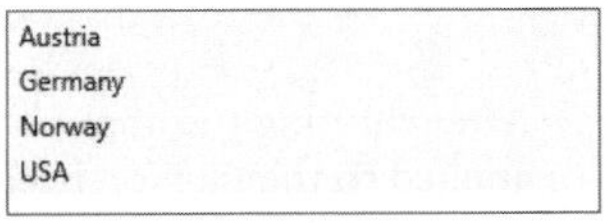

FIGURE 35-25

ItemTemplate

The `Country` objects contain both the name and the flag. Of course, you can display both values in the list box. To do this, you need to define a template.

The `ListBox` element contains `ListBoxItem` elements. You can define the content for an item with the `ItemTemplate`. The style `ListBoxStyle1` defines an `ItemTemplate` with a value of a `DataTemplate`. A `DataTemplate` is used to bind data to elements. You can use the `Binding` markup extension with `DataTemplate` elements.

The `DataTemplate` contains a grid with three columns. The first column contains the string `Country:` The second column contains the name of the country. The third column contains the flag for the country. Because the country names are of different lengths but the view should be the same size for every country name, the `SharedSizeGroup` property is set with the second column definition. This shared size information for the column is used only because the property `Grid.IsSharedSizeScope` is also set.

After the column and row definitions, you can see two `TextBlock` elements. The first `TextBlock` element contains the text `Country:`. The second `TextBlock` element binds to the `Name` property defined in the `Country` class.

The content for the third column is a `Border` element containing a `Grid`. The `Grid` contains a `Rectangle` with a linear gradient brush and an `Image` element that is bound to the `ImagePath` property of the `Country` class. Figure 35-26 shows the countries in a `ListBox` with completely different output than before (code file `TemplateDemo/Styles.xaml`):

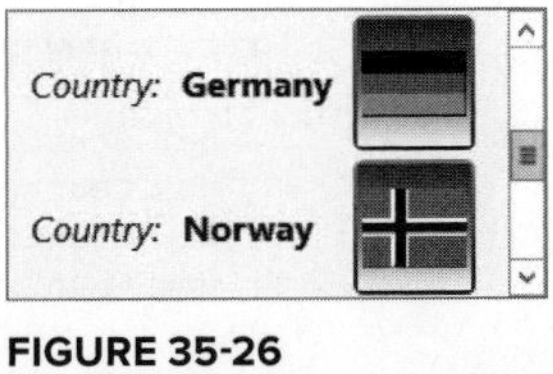

FIGURE 35-26

```xml
<Style x:Key="ListBoxStyle1" TargetType="{x:Type ListBox}" >
  <Setter Property="ItemTemplate">
    <Setter.Value>
      <DataTemplate>
        <Grid>
          <Grid.ColumnDefinitions>
            <ColumnDefinition Width="Auto" />
            <ColumnDefinition Width="*" SharedSizeGroup="MiddleColumn" />
            <ColumnDefinition Width="Auto" />
          </Grid.ColumnDefinitions>
          <Grid.RowDefinitions>
            <RowDefinition Height="60" />
          </Grid.RowDefinitions>
          <TextBlock FontSize="16" VerticalAlignment="Center" Margin="5"
                     FontStyle="Italic" Grid.Column="0" Text="Country:" />
          <TextBlock FontSize="16" VerticalAlignment="Center" Margin="5"
                     Text="{Binding Name}" FontWeight="Bold" Grid.Column="1" />
          <Border Margin="4,0" Grid.Column="2" BorderThickness="2"
                  CornerRadius="4">
            <Border.BorderBrush>
              <LinearGradientBrush StartPoint="0,0" EndPoint="0,1">
                <GradientStop Offset="0" Color="#aaa" />
                <GradientStop Offset="1" Color="#222" />
              </LinearGradientBrush>
            </Border.BorderBrush>
            <Grid>
              <Rectangle>
                <Rectangle.Fill>
                  <LinearGradientBrush StartPoint="0,0" EndPoint="0,1">
                    <GradientStop Offset="0" Color="#444" />
                    <GradientStop Offset="1" Color="#fff" />
                  </LinearGradientBrush>
                </Rectangle.Fill>
              </Rectangle>
              <Image Width="48" Margin="2,2,2,1" Source="{Binding ImagePath}" />
            </Grid>
          </Border>
        </Grid>
      </DataTemplate>
    </Setter.Value>
  </Setter>
  <Setter Property="Grid.IsSharedSizeScope" Value="True" />
</Style>
```

Control Templates for ListBox Elements

It is not necessary for a ListBox to have items that follow vertically, one after the other. You can give the user a different view with the same functionality. The next style, ListBoxStyle2, defines a template in which the items are shown horizontally with a scrollbar.

In the previous example, only an ItemTemplate was created to define how the items should look in the default ListBox. In the following code (code file TemplateDemo/Styles.xaml), a template is created to define a different ListBox. The template contains a ControlTemplate element to define the elements of the ListBox. The element is now a ScrollViewer—a view with a scrollbar—that contains a StackPanel. Because the items should now be listed horizontally, the Orientation of the StackPanel is set to Horizontal. The stack panel will contain the items defined with the ItemsTemplate. As a result, the IsItemsHost of the StackPanel element is set to true. IsItemsHost is a property that is available with every Panel element that can contain a list of items.

The `ItemTemplate` that defines the look for the items in the stack panel is taken from the style `ListBoxStyle1` where `ListBoxStyle2` is based.

Figure 35-27 shows the `ListBox` styled with `ListBoxStyle2`, whereby the scrollbar appears automatically when the view is too small to display all items in the list:

```
<Style x:Key="ListBoxStyle2" TargetType="{x:Type ListBox}"
    BasedOn="{StaticResource ListBoxStyle1}">
  <Setter Property="Template">
    <Setter.Value>
      <ControlTemplate TargetType="{x:Type ListBox}">
        <ScrollViewer HorizontalScrollBarVisibility="Auto">
          <StackPanel Name="StackPanel1" IsItemsHost="True"
              Orientation="Horizontal" />
        </ScrollViewer>
      </ControlTemplate>
    </Setter.Value>
  </Setter>
  <Setter Property="VerticalAlignment" Value="Center" />
</Style>
```

Certainly you see the advantages of separating the look of the controls from their behavior. You may already have many ideas about how you can display your items in a list that best fits the requirements of your application. Perhaps you just want to display as many items as will fit in the window, position them horizontally, and then continue to the next line vertically. That's where a `WrapPanel` comes in; and, of course, you can have a `WrapPanel` inside a template for a `ListBox`, as shown in `ListBoxStyle3`. Figure 35-28 shows the result of using the `WrapPanel`:

FIGURE 35-27

```
<Style x:Key="ListBoxStyle3" TargetType="{x:Type ListBox}">
  <Setter Property="Template">
    <Setter.Value>
      <ControlTemplate TargetType="{x:Type ListBox}">
        <ScrollViewer VerticalScrollBarVisibility="Auto"
            HorizontalScrollBarVisibility="Disabled">
          <WrapPanel IsItemsHost="True" />
        </ScrollViewer>
      </ControlTemplate>
    </Setter.Value>
  </Setter>
  <Setter Property="ItemTemplate">
    <Setter.Value>
      <DataTemplate>
        <Grid>
          <Grid.ColumnDefinitions>
            <ColumnDefinition Width="140" />
          </Grid.ColumnDefinitions>
          <Grid.RowDefinitions>
            <RowDefinition Height="60" />
            <RowDefinition Height="30" />
          </Grid.RowDefinitions>
          <Image Grid.Row="0" Width="48" Margin="2,2,2,1"
              Source="{Binding ImagePath}" />
          <TextBlock Grid.Row="1" FontSize="14"
              HorizontalAlignment="Center" Margin="5" Text="{Binding Name}" />
```

```
        </Grid>
      </DataTemplate>
    </Setter.Value>
  </Setter>
</Style>
```

FIGURE 35-28

ANIMATIONS

Using animations you can make a smooth transition between images by using moving elements, color changes, transforms, and so on. WPF makes it easy to create animations. You can animate the value of any dependency property. Different animation classes exist to animate the values of different properties, depending on their type.

The major elements of animations are as follows:

➤ **Timeline**—Defines how a value changes over time. Different kinds of timelines are available for changing different types of values. The base class for all timelines is `Timeline`. To animate a `double`, the class `DoubleAnimation` can be used. `Int32Animation` is the animation class for `int` values. `PointAnimation` is used to animate points, and `ColorAnimation` is used to animate colors.

➤ **Storyboard**—Used to combine animations. The `Storyboard` class itself is derived from the base class `TimelineGroup`, which derives from `Timeline`. With `DoubleAnimation` you can animate a double value; with `Storyboard` you combine all the animations that belong together.

➤ **Triggers**—Used to start and stop animations. You've seen property triggers previously, which fire when a property value changes. You can also create an event trigger. An event trigger fires when an event occurs.

> **NOTE** *The namespace for animation classes is* `System.Windows.Media.Animation`.

Timeline

A `Timeline` defines how a value changes over time. The following example animates the size of an ellipse. In the code that follows (code file `AnimationDemo/EllipseWindow.xaml`), a `DoubleAnimation` timeline changes to a double value. The `Triggers` property of the `Ellipse` class is set to an `EventTrigger`. The event trigger is fired when the ellipse is loaded as defined with the `RoutedEvent` property of the `EventTrigger`. `BeginStoryboard` is a trigger action that begins the storyboard. With the storyboard, a `DoubleAnimation` element is used to animate the `Width` property of the `Ellipse` class. The animation changes the width of the ellipse from 100 to 300 within three seconds, and reverses the animation after three seconds. The animation `ColorAnimation` animates the color from the `ellipseBrush` which is used to fill the ellipse:

```xml
<Ellipse Height="50" Width="100">
  <Ellipse.Fill>
    <SolidColorBrush x:Name="ellipseBrush" Color="Yellow" />
  </Ellipse.Fill>
  <Ellipse.Triggers>
    <EventTrigger RoutedEvent="Ellipse.Loaded" >
      <EventTrigger.Actions>
        <BeginStoryboard>
          <Storyboard Duration="00:00:06" RepeatBehavior="Forever">
            <DoubleAnimation Storyboard.TargetProperty="(Ellipse.Width)"
```

```
                      Duration="0:0:3" AutoReverse="True" FillBehavior="Stop"
                      RepeatBehavior="Forever" AccelerationRatio="0.9"
                      DecelerationRatio="0.1" From="100" To="300" />
                  <ColorAnimation Storyboard.TargetName="ellipseBrush"
                      Storyboard.TargetProperty="(SolidColorBrush.Color)"
                      Duration="0:0:3" AutoReverse="True"
                      FillBehavior="Stop" RepeatBehavior="Forever"
                      From="Yellow" To="Red" />
                </Storyboard>
              </BeginStoryboard>
            </EventTrigger.Actions>
          </EventTrigger>
        </Ellipse.Triggers>
      </Ellipse>
```

FIGURE 35-29

Figures 35-29 and 35-30 show two states from the animated ellipse.

Animations are far more than typical window-dressing animation that appears onscreen constantly and immediately. You can add animation to business applications that make the user interface more responsive.

FIGURE 35-30

The following example (code file `AnimationDemo/ButtonAnimationWindow.xaml`) demonstrates a decent animation and shows how the animation can be defined in a style. Within the `Window` resources you can see the style `AnimatedButtonStyle` for buttons. In the template, a rectangle-named outline is defined. This template has a thin stroke with the thickness set to 0.4.

The template defines a property trigger for the `IsMouseOver` property. The `EnterActions` property of this trigger applies as soon as the mouse is moved over the button. The action to start is `BeginStoryboard`, which is a trigger action that can contain and thus start `Storyboard` elements. The `Storyboard` element defines a `DoubleAnimation` to animate a double value. The property value that is changed in this animation is the `Rectangle.StrokeThickness` of the `Rectangle` element with the name `outline`. The value is changed in a smooth way by 1.2, as the `By` property specifies, for a time length of 0.3 seconds as specified by the `Duration` property. At the end of the animation, the stroke thickness is reset to its original value because `AutoReverse="True"`. To summarize: As soon as the mouse moves over the button, the thickness of the outline is incremented by 1.2 for 0.3 seconds. Figure 35-31 shows the button without animation, and Figure 35-32 shows the button 0.3 seconds after the mouse moved over it. (Unfortunately, it's not possible to show the intermediate appearance of the smooth animation in a print medium.)

FIGURE 35-31

FIGURE 35-32

```
<Window x:Class="AnimationDemo.ButtonAnimationWindow"
    xmlns="http://schemas.microsoft.com/winfx/2006/xaml/presentation"
    xmlns:x="http://schemas.microsoft.com/winfx/2006/xaml"
    Title="ButtonAnimationWindow" Height="300" Width="300">
  <Window.Resources>
    <Style x:Key="AnimatedButtonStyle" TargetType="{x:Type Button}">
      <Setter Property="Template">
        <Setter.Value>
          <ControlTemplate TargetType="{x:Type Button}">
            <Grid>
              <Rectangle Name="outline" RadiusX="9" RadiusY="9"
                  Stroke="Black" Fill="{TemplateBinding Background}"
                  StrokeThickness="1.6">
              </Rectangle>
              <ContentPresenter VerticalAlignment="Center"
                  HorizontalAlignment="Center" />
            </Grid>
            <ControlTemplate.Triggers>
```

```
                        <Trigger Property="IsMouseOver" Value="True">
                          <Trigger.EnterActions>
                            <BeginStoryboard>
                              <Storyboard>
                                <DoubleAnimation Duration="0:0:0.3" AutoReverse="True"
                                    Storyboard.TargetProperty="(Rectangle.StrokeThickness)"
                                    Storyboard.TargetName="outline" By="1.2" />
                              </Storyboard>
                            </BeginStoryboard>
                          </Trigger.EnterActions>
                        </Trigger>
                      </ControlTemplate.Triggers>
                    </ControlTemplate>
                  </Setter.Value>
                </Setter>
              </Style>
          </Window.Resources>
          <Grid>
            <Button Style="{StaticResource AnimatedButtonStyle}" Width="200"
                Height="100" Content="Click Me!" />
          </Grid>
        </Window>
```

The following table describes what you can do with a timeline.

TIMELINE PROPERTIES	DESCRIPTION
AutoReverse	Use this property to specify whether the value that is animated should return to its original value after the animation.
SpeedRatio	Use this property to transform the speed at which an animation moves. You can define the relation in regard to the parent. The default value is 1; setting the ratio to a smaller value makes the animation move slower; setting the value greater than 1 makes it move faster.
BeginTime	Use this to specify the time span from the start of the trigger event until the moment the animation starts. You can specify days, hours, minutes, seconds, and fractions of seconds. This might not be real time, depending on the speed ratio. For example, if the speed ratio is set to 2, and the beginning time is set to six seconds, the animation will start after three seconds.
AccelerationRatio DecelerationRatio	An animation's values need not be changed in a linear way. You can specify an AccelerationRatio and DecelerationRatio to define the impact of acceleration and deceleration. The sum of both values must not be greater than 1.
Duration	Use this property to specify the length of time for one iteration of the animation.
RepeatBehavior	Assigning a RepeatBehavior struct to the RepeatBehavior property enables you to define how many times or for how long the animation should be repeated.
FillBehavior	This property is important if the parent timeline has a different duration. For example, if the parent timeline is shorter than the duration of the actual animation, setting FillBehavior to Stop means that the actual animation stops. If the parent timeline is longer than the duration of the actual animation, HoldEnd keeps the actual animation active before resetting it to its original value (if AutoReverse is set).

Depending on the type of the Timeline class, more properties may be available. For example, with DoubleAnimation you can specify From and To properties for the start and end of the animation. An alternative is to specify the By property, whereby the animation starts with the current value of the Bound property and is incremented by the value specified by By.

Nonlinear Animations

One way to define nonlinear animations is by setting the speed of AccelerationRatio and DecelerationRatio animation at the beginning and at the end. .NET 4.5 has more flexible possibilities than that.

Several animation classes have an EasingFunction property. This property accepts an object that implements the interface IEasingFunction. With this interface, an easing function object can define how the value should be animated over time. Several easing functions are available to create a nonlinear animation. Examples include ExponentialEase, which uses an exponential formula for animations; QuadraticEase, CubicEase, QuarticEase, and QuinticEase, with powers of 2, 3, 4, or 5; and PowerEase, with a power level that is configurable. Of special interest are SineEase, which uses a sinusoid curve, BounceEase, which creates a bouncing effect, and ElasticEase, which resembles animation values of a spring oscillating back and forth.

Such an ease can be specified in XAML by adding the ease to the EasingFunction property of the animation as shown in the following code (code file AnimationDemo/EllipseWindow.xaml). Adding different ease functions results in very interesting animation effects:

```
<DoubleAnimation Storyboard.TargetProperty="(Ellipse.Width)"
                 Duration="0:0:3" AutoReverse="True"
                 FillBehavior=" RepeatBehavior="Forever"
                 From="100" To="300">
  <DoubleAnimation.EasingFunction>
    <BounceEase EasingMode="EaseInOut" />
  </DoubleAnimation.EasingFunction>
</DoubleAnimation>
```

Event Triggers

Instead of having a property trigger, you can define an event trigger to start the animation. The property trigger fires when a property changes its value; the event trigger fires when an event occurs. Examples of such events are the Load event from a control, the Click event from a Button, and the MouseMove event.

The next example creates an animation for the face that was created earlier with shapes. It is now animated so that the eye moves as soon as a Click event from a button is fired.

Inside the Window element, a DockPanel element is defined to arrange the face and buttons to control the animation. A StackPanel that contains three buttons is docked at the top. The Canvas element that contains the face gets the remaining part of the DockPanel.

The first button is used to start the animation of the eye; the second button stops the animation. A third button is used to start another animation to resize the face.

The animation is defined within the DockPanel.Triggers section. Instead of a property trigger, an event trigger is used. The first event trigger is fired as soon as the Click event occurs with the buttonBeginMove-Eyes button defined by the RoutedEvent and SourceName properties. The trigger action is defined by the BeginStoryboard element that starts the containing Storyboard. BeginStoryboard has a name defined because a name is needed to control the storyboard with pause, continue, and stop actions. The Storyboard element contains four animations. The first two animate the left eye; the last two animate the right eye. The first and third animation change the Canvas.Left position for the eyes, and the second and fourth animation change Canvas.Top. The animations in the x and y axes have different time values that make the eye movement very interesting using the defined repeated behavior.

The second event trigger is fired as soon as the Click event of the buttonStopMoveEyes button occurs. Here, the storyboard is stopped with the StopStoryboard element, which references the started storyboard beginMoveEye.

The third event trigger is fired by clicking the buttonResize button. With this animation, the transformation of the Canvas element is changed. Because this animation doesn't run endlessly, there's no stop. This storyboard also makes use of the EaseFunction explained previously (code file AnimationDemo/ EventTriggerWindow.xaml):

```xml
<Window x:Class="AnimationDemo.EventTriggerWindow"
    xmlns="http://schemas.microsoft.com/winfx/2006/xaml/presentation"
    xmlns:x="http://schemas.microsoft.com/winfx/2006/xaml"
    Title="EventTriggerWindow" Height="300" Width="300">
  <DockPanel>
    <DockPanel.Triggers>
      <EventTrigger RoutedEvent="Button.Click" SourceName="buttonBeginMoveEyes">
        <BeginStoryboard x:Name="beginMoveEyes">
          <Storyboard>
            <DoubleAnimation RepeatBehavior="Forever" DecelerationRatio=".8"
                AutoReverse="True" By="6" Duration="0:0:1"
                Storyboard.TargetName="eyeLeft"
                Storyboard.TargetProperty="(Canvas.Left)" />
            <DoubleAnimation RepeatBehavior="Forever" AutoReverse="True"
                By="6" Duration="0:0:5"
                Storyboard.TargetName="eyeLeft"
                Storyboard.TargetProperty="(Canvas.Top)" />
            <DoubleAnimation RepeatBehavior="Forever" DecelerationRatio=".8"
                AutoReverse="True" By="-6" Duration="0:0:3"
                Storyboard.TargetName="eyeRight"
                Storyboard.TargetProperty="(Canvas.Left)" />
            <DoubleAnimation RepeatBehavior="Forever" AutoReverse="True"
                By="6" Duration="0:0:6"
                Storyboard.TargetName="eyeRight"
                Storyboard.TargetProperty="(Canvas.Top)" />
          </Storyboard>
        </BeginStoryboard>
      </EventTrigger>
      <EventTrigger RoutedEvent="Button.Click" SourceName="buttonStopMoveEyes">
        <StopStoryboard BeginStoryboardName="beginMoveEyes" />
      </EventTrigger>
      <EventTrigger RoutedEvent="Button.Click" SourceName="buttonResize">
        <BeginStoryboard>
          <Storyboard>
            <DoubleAnimation RepeatBehavior="2" AutoReverse="True"
                Storyboard.TargetName="scale1"
                Storyboard.TargetProperty="(ScaleTransform.ScaleX)"
                From="0.1" To="3" Duration="0:0:5">
              <DoubleAnimation.EasingFunction>
                <ElasticEase />
              </DoubleAnimation.EasingFunction>
            </DoubleAnimation>
            <DoubleAnimation RepeatBehavior="2" AutoReverse="True"
                Storyboard.TargetName="scale1"
                Storyboard.TargetProperty="(ScaleTransform.ScaleY)"
                From="0.1" To="3" Duration="0:0:5">
              <DoubleAnimation.EasingFunction>
                <BounceEase />
              </DoubleAnimation.EasingFunction>
            </DoubleAnimation>
          </Storyboard>
        </BeginStoryboard>
```

```
        </EventTrigger>
      </DockPanel.Triggers>
      <StackPanel Orientation="Vertical" DockPanel.Dock="Top">
        <Button x:Name="buttonBeginMoveEyes" Content="Start Move Eyes" Margin="5" />
        <Button x:Name="buttonStopMoveEyes" Content="Stop Move Eyes" Margin="5" />
        <Button x:Name="buttonResize" Content="Resize" Margin="5" />
      </StackPanel>
      <Canvas>
        <Canvas.LayoutTransform>
          <ScaleTransform x:Name="scale1" ScaleX="1" ScaleY="1" />
        </Canvas.LayoutTransform>
        <Ellipse Canvas.Left="10" Canvas.Top="10" Width="100" Height="100"
            Stroke="Blue" StrokeThickness="4" Fill="Yellow" />
        <Ellipse Canvas.Left="30" Canvas.Top="12" Width="60" Height="30">
          <Ellipse.Fill>
            <LinearGradientBrush StartPoint="0.5,0" EndPoint="0.5, 1">
              <GradientStop Offset="0.1" Color="DarkGreen" />
              <GradientStop Offset="0.7" Color="Transparent" />
            </LinearGradientBrush>
          </Ellipse.Fill>
        </Ellipse>
        <Ellipse Canvas.Left="30" Canvas.Top="35" Width="25" Height="20"
            Stroke="Blue" StrokeThickness="3" Fill="White" />
        <Ellipse x:Name="eyeLeft" Canvas.Left="40" Canvas.Top="43" Width="6"
            Height="5" Fill="Black" />
        <Ellipse Canvas.Left="65" Canvas.Top="35" Width="25" Height="20"
            Stroke="Blue" StrokeThickness="3" Fill="White" />
        <Ellipse x:Name="eyeRight" Canvas.Left="75" Canvas.Top="43" Width="6"
            Height="5" Fill="Black" />
        <Path Name="mouth" Stroke="Blue" StrokeThickness="4"
            Data="M 40,74 Q 57,95 80,74 " />
      </Canvas>
    </DockPanel>
  </Window>
```

Figure 35-33 shows the output after running the application.

Rather than start and stop the animation directly from event triggers in XAML, you can easily control the animation from code-behind. You just need to assign a name to the Storyboard and invoke the Begin, Stop, Pause, and Resume methods.

Keyframe Animations

With acceleration and deceleration ratio as well as the ease functions, you've seen how animations can be built in a nonlinear fashion. If you need to specify several values for an animation, you can use *keyframe animations*. Like normal animations, keyframe animations are various animation types that exist to animate properties of different types.

FIGURE 35-33

DoubleAnimationUsingKeyFrames is the keyframe animation for double types. Other keyframe animation types are Int32AnimationUsingKeyFrames, PointAnimationUsingKeyFrames, ColorAnimationUsingKeyFrames, SizeAnimationUsingKeyFrames, and ObjectAnimationUsingKeyFrames.

The following example XAML code (code file `AnimationDemo/KeyFrameWindow.xaml`) animates the position of an ellipse by animating the X and Y values of a `TranslateTransform` element. The animation starts when the ellipse is loaded by defining an `EventTrigger` to the `RoutedEvent Ellipse.Loaded`. The event trigger starts a `Storyboard` with the `BeginStoryboard` element. The `Storyboard` contains two keyframe animations of type `DoubleAnimationUsingKeyFrame`. A keyframe animation consists of frame elements. The first keyframe animation uses a `LinearKeyFrame`, a `DiscreteDoubleKeyFrame`, and a `SplineDoubleKeyFrame`; the second animation is an `EasingDoubleKeyFrame`. The `LinearDoubleKeyFrame` makes a linear change of the value. The `KeyTime` property defines when in the animation the value of the `Value` property should be reached.

Here, the `LinearDoubleKeyFrame` has three seconds to move the property X to the value 30. `DiscreteDoubleKeyFrame` makes an immediate change to the new value after four seconds. `SplineDoubleKeyFrame` uses a Bézier curve whereby two control points are specified by the `KeySpline` property. `EasingDoubleKeyFrame` is a frame class that supports setting an easing function such as `BounceEase` to control the animation value:

```xml
<Canvas>
  <Ellipse Fill="Red" Canvas.Left="20" Canvas.Top="20" Width="25" Height="25">
    <Ellipse.RenderTransform>
      <TranslateTransform X="50" Y="50" x:Name="ellipseMove" />
    </Ellipse.RenderTransform>
    <Ellipse.Triggers>
      <EventTrigger RoutedEvent="Ellipse.Loaded">
        <BeginStoryboard>
          <Storyboard>
            <DoubleAnimationUsingKeyFrames Storyboard.TargetProperty="X"
                Storyboard.TargetName="ellipseMove">
              <LinearDoubleKeyFrame KeyTime="0:0:2" Value="30" />
              <DiscreteDoubleKeyFrame KeyTime="0:0:4" Value="80" />
              <SplineDoubleKeyFrame KeySpline="0.5,0.0 0.9,0.0"
                  KeyTime="0:0:10" Value="300" />
              <LinearDoubleKeyFrame KeyTime="0:0:20" Value="150" />
            </DoubleAnimationUsingKeyFrames>
            <DoubleAnimationUsingKeyFrames Storyboard.TargetProperty="Y"
                Storyboard.TargetName="ellipseMove">
              <SplineDoubleKeyFrame KeySpline="0.5,0.0 0.9,0.0"
                  KeyTime="0:0:2" Value="50" />
              <EasingDoubleKeyFrame KeyTime="0:0:20" Value="300">
                <EasingDoubleKeyFrame.EasingFunction>
                  <BounceEase />
                </EasingDoubleKeyFrame.EasingFunction>
              </EasingDoubleKeyFrame>
            </DoubleAnimationUsingKeyFrames>
          </Storyboard>
        </BeginStoryboard>
      </EventTrigger>
    </Ellipse.Triggers>
  </Ellipse>
</Canvas>
```

VISUAL STATE MANAGER

Beginning with .NET 4, Visual State Manager offers an alternative way to control animations. Controls can have specific states. The *state* defines a look that is applied to controls when the state is reached. A *state transition* defines what happens when one state changes to another one.

With a data grid you can use `Read`, `Selected`, and `Edit` states to define different looks for a row, depending on user selection. `MouseOver` and `IsPressed` are states that replace the triggers, which have been discussed earlier.

The following example (code file `VisualStateDemo/Style.xaml`) creates a custom template for the `Button` type whereby visual states are used instead of the triggers used earlier. The XAML code in this snippet defines a template for the `Button` type that consists of `Ellipse` elements with gradient brushes. As the code stands here, nothing happens when the user moves the mouse over a button or clicks it. This is going to be changed using visual states.

```xaml
<Style TargetType="Button">
  <Setter Property="Width" Value="100" />
  <Setter Property="Height" Value="100" />
  <Setter Property="Foreground" Value="White" />
  <Setter Property="Template">
    <Setter.Value>
      <ControlTemplate TargetType="{x:Type Button}">
        <Grid>
          <Ellipse Name="GelBackground" StrokeThickness="0.5">
            <Ellipse.Fill>
              <LinearGradientBrush StartPoint="0,0" EndPoint="0,1">
                <GradientStop Offset="0" Color="Black" />
                <GradientStop Offset="1" Color="Black" />
              </LinearGradientBrush>
            </Ellipse.Fill>
            <Ellipse.Stroke>
              <LinearGradientBrush StartPoint="0,0" EndPoint="0,1">
                <GradientStop Offset="0" Color="#ff7e7e7e" />
                <GradientStop Offset="1" Color="Black" />
              </LinearGradientBrush>
            </Ellipse.Stroke>
          </Ellipse>
          <Ellipse Margin="15,5,15,50">
            <Ellipse.Fill>
              <LinearGradientBrush StartPoint="0,0" EndPoint="0,1">
                <GradientStop Offset="0" Color="#aaffffff" />
                <GradientStop Offset="1" Color="Transparent" />
              </LinearGradientBrush>
            </Ellipse.Fill>
          </Ellipse>
          <ContentPresenter Name="GelButtonContent" VerticalAlignment="Center"
              HorizontalAlignment="Center"
              Content="{TemplateBinding Content}" />
        </Grid>
      </ControlTemplate>
    </Setter.Value>
  </Setter>
</Style>
```

Visual States

The `Button` type defines several state groups and states. The state group `CommonStates` defines the states `Normal`, `MouseOver`, and `Pressed`. The state group `FocusedStates` defines `Focused` and `Unfocused`. As shown in the following example (code file `VisualStateDemo/Style.xaml`), the implementation of the `Button` class changes the states using the `VisualStateManager`—you just have to define a look for these states.

For defining a different appearance for the controls using visual states, the attached property VisualStateManager.VisualStateGroups is defined within the template. The first group defined is `CommonStates`. Within this group, looks for the `MouseOver` and `Pressed` states are defined. Within the `MouseOver` state, a key frame color animation changes the fill color of the ellipse to a gradient color from lime to dark green. The `Pressed` state has a similar implementation: the fill color changes to a new range from `ffcc34` to `cc9900`:

```
<ContentPresenter Name="GelButtonContent" VerticalAlignment="Center"
    HorizontalAlignment="Center"
    Content="{TemplateBinding Content}" />
<VisualStateManager.VisualStateGroups>
  <VisualStateGroup Name="CommonStates">
    <VisualState Name="Normal" />
    <VisualState Name="MouseOver">
      <Storyboard>
        <ColorAnimationUsingKeyFrames
            Storyboard.TargetProperty=
            "(Shape.Fill).(GradientBrush.GradientStops)[0].
            (GradientStop.Color)"
            Storyboard.TargetName="GelBackground">
          <EasingColorKeyFrame KeyTime="0" Value="Lime"/>
        </ColorAnimationUsingKeyFrames>
        <ColorAnimationUsingKeyFrames
            Storyboard.TargetProperty=
            "(Shape.Fill).(GradientBrush.GradientStops)[1].
            (GradientStop.Color)"
            Storyboard.TargetName="GelBackground">
          <EasingColorKeyFrame KeyTime="0" Value="DarkGreen"/>
        </ColorAnimationUsingKeyFrames>
      </Storyboard>
    </VisualState>
    <VisualState Name="Pressed">
      <Storyboard>
        <ColorAnimationUsingKeyFrames
            Storyboard.TargetProperty=
            "(Shape.Fill).(GradientBrush.GradientStops)[0].
            (GradientStop.Color)"
            Storyboard.TargetName="GelBackground">
          <EasingColorKeyFrame KeyTime="0" Value="#ffcc34"/>
        </ColorAnimationUsingKeyFrames>
        <ColorAnimationUsingKeyFrames
            Storyboard.TargetProperty=
            "(Shape.Fill).(GradientBrush.GradientStops)[1].
            (GradientStop.Color)"
            Storyboard.TargetName="GelBackground">
          <EasingColorKeyFrame KeyTime="0" Value="#cc9900"/>
        </ColorAnimationUsingKeyFrames>
      </Storyboard>
    </VisualState>
  </VisualStateGroup>
  <VisualStateGroup Name="FocusedStates">
    <VisualState Name="Focused" />
    <VisualState Name="Unfocused" />
  </VisualStateGroup>

</VisualStateManager.VisualStateGroups>
```

The state change is already evident. Moving the mouse over a Button or clicking the Button changes its user interface. Next, an animation between state transitions is added.

Transitions

With state transitions you can define what should happen when a change into a state occurs. Transitions are added by using VisualStateGroup.Transitions. In the following example (code file VisualStateDemo/Style.xaml), the first transition is a global transition specifying that the state change should take 0.2 seconds, and a QuadraticEase function should be used for the animation. The second defined transition is specified if the state changes into the MouseOver state. With the implementation of this state transition, the thickness of the ellipse Gelbackground is changed by adding 2 within 0.5 seconds, and after the animation is completed it reverts to its original value:

```
<ContentPresenter Name="GelButtonContent" VerticalAlignment="Center"
    HorizontalAlignment="Center"
    Content="{TemplateBinding Content}" />
<VisualStateManager.VisualStateGroups>
  <VisualStateGroup Name="CommonStates">
    <!-- ... -->
    <VisualStateGroup.Transitions>
      <VisualTransition GeneratedDuration="0:0:0.2" >
        <VisualTransition.GeneratedEasingFunction>
          <QuadraticEase EasingMode="EaseOut" />
        </VisualTransition.GeneratedEasingFunction>
      </VisualTransition>
      <VisualTransition GeneratedDuration="0:0:0.5" To="MouseOver">
        <Storyboard>
          <DoubleAnimation By="2" Duration="0:0:0.5"
              AutoReverse="True"
              Storyboard.TargetProperty="(Shape.StrokeThickness)"
              Storyboard.TargetName="GelBackground" />
        </Storyboard>
      </VisualTransition>
    </VisualStateGroup.Transitions>
  </VisualStateGroup>
  <VisualStateGroup Name="FocusedStates">
    <VisualState Name="Focused" />
    <VisualState Name="Unfocused" />
  </VisualStateGroup>
</VisualStateManager.VisualStateGroups>
```

> **NOTE** *Using custom states, you can easily change the state with the* VisualState Manager *class, invoking the method* GoToElementState.

3-D

This last section of a long chapter introduces the 3-D features of WPF. Here you'll find the information you need to get started.

> **NOTE** *The namespace for 3-D with WPF is* System.Windows.Media.Media3D.

To understand 3-D with WPF it is important to know the difference between the coordinate systems. Figure 35-34 shows the WPF 3-D coordinate system. The origin is placed in the center. The x-axis has positive values to the right and negative values to the left. The y-axis is vertical with positive values up and negative values down. The z-axis defines positive values in direction to the viewer of the scene.

The most important concepts to understand in order to understand 3-D with WPF are that of model, camera, and lights. The model defines what is shown using triangles. The camera defines the point at which and how we look at the model, and without light the model is dark. The light defines how the complete scene is illuminated. The following sections provide details about how to define the model, camera, and light with WPF and what different options are available. Also covered is how the scene can be animated.

Model

This section creates a model that has the 3-D look of a book. A 3-D model is made up of triangles, so the simplest model is just one triangle. More complex models are made from multiple triangles. Rectangles can be made from two triangles, and balls are made from a multiplicity of triangles. The more triangles used, the rounder the ball.

With the book model, each side is a rectangle, which could be made from only two triangles. However, because the front cover has three different materials, six triangles are used.

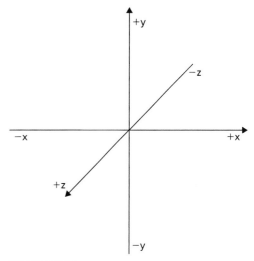

A triangle is defined by the Positions property of the MeshGeometry3D. This example uses just a part of the front side of the book. The MeshGeometry3D defines two triangles. You can count five coordinates for the points because the third point of the first triangle is also the first point of the second triangle. This can be done for optimization to reduce the size of the model.

FIGURE 35-34

All the points use the same z coordinate, 0, and x/y coordinates 0 0, 10 0, 0 10, 10 10, and 10 0. The property TriangleIndices indicates the order of the positions. The first triangle is defined clockwise, the second triangle counterclockwise. With this property you define which side of the triangle is visible. One side of the triangle shows the color defined with the Material property of the GeometryModel3D class, and the other side shows the BackMaterial property.

The rendering surface for 3-D is ModelVisual3D, which surrounds the models as shown (code file 3DDemo/ MainWindow.xaml):

```
<ModelVisual3D>
  <ModelVisual3D.Content>
    <Model3DGroup>

      <!-- front -->
      <GeometryModel3D>
        <GeometryModel3D.Geometry>
          <MeshGeometry3D
              Positions="0 0 0, 10 0 0, 0 10 0, 10 10 0, 10 0 0"
              TriangleIndices="0, 1, 2, 2, 4, 3" />
      </GeometryModel3D.Geometry>
```

The Material property of the GeometryModel defines what material is used by the model. Depending on the viewpoint, the Material or BackMaterial property is important.

WPF offers different material types: DiffuseMaterial, EmissiveMaterial, and SpecularMaterial. The material influences the look of the model, together with the light that is used to illuminate the scene. EmmisiveMaterial and the color applied to the brush of the material are part of the calculations to define the light to show the model. SpecularMaterial adds illuminated highlight reflections when specular highlight reflections occur. The example code makes use of DiffuseMaterial and references a brush from the resource named mainCover:

```
<GeometryModel3D.Material>
  <DiffuseMaterial Brush="{StaticResource mainCover}" />
</GeometryModel3D.Material>
</GeometryModel3D>
```

The brush for the main cover is a VisualBrush. The VisualBrush has a Border with a Grid that consists of two Label elements. One Label element defines the text "Professional C# 4" and is written to the cover:

```
<VisualBrush x:Key="mainCover">
  <VisualBrush.Visual>
    <Border Background="Red">
      <Grid>
        <Grid.RowDefinitions>
          <RowDefinition Height="30" />
          <RowDefinition Height="*" />
        </Grid.RowDefinitions>
        <Label Grid.Row="0" HorizontalAlignment="Center">
            Professional C# 5</Label>
        <Label Grid.Row="1"></Label>
      </Grid>
    </Border>
  </VisualBrush.Visual>
</VisualBrush>
```

Because a brush is defined by a 2-D coordinate system and the model has a 3-D coordinate system, a translation between them needs to be done. This translation is done by the TextureCoordinates property of the MeshGeometry3D. This property specifies every point of the triangle and shows how it maps to 2-D. The first point, 0 0 0, maps to 0 1, the second point, 10 0 0, maps to 1 1, and so on. Be aware that y has a different direction in the 3-D and 2-D coordinate systems. Figure 35-35 shows the coordinate system for 2-D:

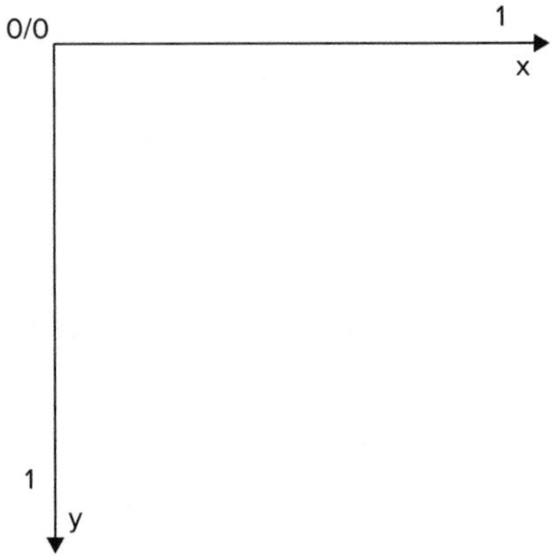

FIGURE 35-35

```
<MeshGeometry3D Positions="0 0 0, 10 0 0, 0 10 0, 10 10 0, 10 0 0"
      TriangleIndices="0, 1, 2, 2, 4, 3"
      TextureCoordinates="0 1, 1 1, 0 0, 1 0, 1 1" />
```

Cameras

A camera is needed with a 3-D model in order to see something. The following example (code file 3DDemo/MainWindow.xaml) uses the PerspectiveCamera, which has a position and a direction. Changing the camera position to the left moves the model to the right and vice versa. Changing the y position of the camera, the model appears larger or smaller. With this camera, the further away the model is, the smaller it becomes:

```
<Viewport3D.Camera>
  <PerspectiveCamera Position="0,0,25" LookDirection="15,6,-50" />
</Viewport3D.Camera>
```

WPF also has an OrtographicCamera that doesn't have a horizon on the scene, so the size of the element doesn't change if it is further away. With MatrixCamera, the behavior of the camera can be exactly specified.

Lights

Without any light specified it is dark. A 3-D scene requires a light source to make the model visible. Different lights can be used. The AmbientLight lights the scene uniformly. DirectionalLight is a light that shines in one direction, similar to sunlight. PointLight has a position in space and lights in all directions. SpotLight has a position as well but uses a cone for its lighting.

The following example code uses a SpotLight with a position, a direction, and cone angles:

```
<ModelVisual3D>
  <ModelVisual3D.Content>
    <SpotLight Color="White" InnerConeAngle="20" OuterConeAngle="60"
            Direction="15,6,-50" Position="0,0,25" />
  </ModelVisual3D.Content>
</ModelVisual3D>
```

Rotation

To get a 3-D look from the model, it should be able to be rotated. For rotation, the `RotateTransform3D` element is used to define the center of the rotation and the rotation angle:

```
<Model3DGroup.Transform>
  <RotateTransform3D CenterX="0" CenterY="0" CenterZ="0">
    <RotateTransform3D.Rotation>
      <AxisAngleRotation3D x:Name="angle" Axis="-1,-1,-1" Angle="70" />
    </RotateTransform3D.Rotation>
  </RotateTransform3D>
</Model3DGroup.Transform>
```

To run a rotation from the completed model, an animation is started by an event trigger. The animation changes the `Angle` property of the `AxisAngleRotation3D` element continuously:

```
<Window.Triggers>
  <EventTrigger RoutedEvent=f"Window.Loaded">
    <BeginStoryboard>
      <Storyboard>
        <DoubleAnimation From="0" To="360" Duration="00:00:10"
            Storyboard.TargetName="angle"
            Storyboard.TargetProperty="Angle"
            RepeatBehavior="Forever" />
      </Storyboard>
    </BeginStoryboard>
  </EventTrigger>
</Window.Triggers>
```

Running the application results in the output shown in Figure 35-36.

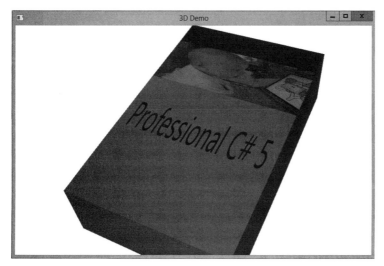

FIGURE 35-36

SUMMARY

In this chapter you have taken a brief tour through many of the features of WPF. WPF makes it easy to separate the work of developers and designers. All UI features can be created with XAML, and the functionality can be created by using code-behind.

You have seen many controls and containers, all of which are based on vector-based graphics. Vector-based graphics enable WPF elements to be scaled, sheared, and rotated. Because content controls offer great content flexibility, the event-handling mechanism is based on bubbling and tunneling events.

Different kinds of brushes are available to paint the background and foreground of elements. You can use not only solid brushes, and linear or radial gradient brushes, but also visual brushes to do reflections or show videos.

Styling and templates enable you to customize the look of controls; and triggers enable you to change properties of WPF elements dynamically. Animations can be done easily by animating a property value from a WPF control. The next chapter continues with WPF, covering data binding, commands, navigation, and several more features.

36

Business Applications with WPF

WROX.COM CODE DOWNLOADS FOR THIS CHAPTER

The wrox.com code downloads for this chapter are found at `http://www.wrox.com/remtitle .cgi?isbn=1118314425` on the Download Code tab. The code for this chapter is divided into the following major examples:

INTRODUCTION

In the previous chapter you read about some of the core functionality of WPF. This chapter continues the journey through WPF. Here you read about important aspects for creating complete applications, such as data binding and command handling, and about the `DataGrid` control. Data binding is an important concept for bringing data from .NET classes into the user interface, and allowing the user to change data. WPF not only allows binding to simple entities or lists, but also offers binding of one

UI property to multiple properties of possible different types with multi binding and priority binding that you'll learn here as well. Along with data binding it is also important to validate data entered by a user. Here, you can read about different ways for validation including the interface `INotifyDataErrorInfo` that is new with .NET 4.5. Also covered in this chapter is commanding, which enables mapping events from the UI to code. In contrast to the event model, this provides a better separation between XAML and code. You will learn about using predefined commands and creating custom commands.

The `TreeView` and `DataGrid` controls are UI controls to display bound data. You will see the `TreeView` control to display data in the tree where data is loaded dynamically depending on the selection of the user. With the `DataGrid` control you will learn how to using filtering, sorting, and grouping, as well as one new .NET 4.5 feature named *live shaping* that allows changing sorting or filtering options to change in real time.

To begin let's start with the `Menu` and the `Ribbon` controls. The `Ribbon` control made it into the release of .NET 4.5.

MENU AND RIBBON CONTROLS

Many data-driven applications contain menus and toolbars or ribbon controls to enable users to control actions. With WPF 4.5, ribbon controls are now available as well, so both menu and ribbon controls are covered here.

In this section, you create a new WPF application named BooksDemo to use throughout this chapter—not only with menu and ribbon controls but also with commanding and data binding. This application displays a single book, a list of books, and a grid of books. Actions are started from menu or ribbon controls to which commands associated.

Menu Controls

Menus can easily be created with WPF using the `Menu` and `MenuItem` elements, as shown in the following code snippet containing two main menu items, File and Edit, and a list of submenu entries. The _ in front of the characters marks the special character that can be used to access the menu item easily without using the mouse. Using the Alt key makes these characters visible and enables access to the menu with this character. Some of these menu items have a command assigned, as discussed in the next section (XAML file `BooksDemo/MainWindow.xaml`):

```
<Window x:Class="Wrox.ProCSharp.WPF.MainWindow"
        xmlns="http://schemas.microsoft.com/winfx/2006/xaml/presentation"
        xmlns:x="http://schemas.microsoft.com/winfx/2006/xaml"
        xmlns:local="clr-namespace:Wrox.ProCSharp.WPF"
        Title="Books Demo App" Height="400" Width="600">
  <DockPanel>
    <Menu DockPanel.Dock="Top">
      <MenuItem Header="_File">
        <MenuItem Header="Show _Book" />
        <MenuItem Header="Show Book_s" />
        <Separator />
        <MenuItem Header="E_xit" />
      </MenuItem>
      <MenuItem Header="_Edit">
        <MenuItem Header="Undo" Command="Undo" />
        <Separator />
        <MenuItem Header="Cut" Command="Cut" />
        <MenuItem Header="Copy" Command="Copy" />
        <MenuItem Header="Paste" Command="Paste" />
      </MenuItem>
    </Menu>
  </DockPanel>
</Window>
```

Running the application results in the menus shown in Figure 36-1. The menus are not active yet because commands are not active.

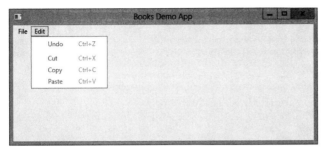

FIGURE 36-1

Ribbon Controls

Microsoft Office was the first application released with Microsoft's newly invented ribbon control. Shortly after its introduction, many users of previous versions of Office complained that they could not find the actions they wanted with the new UI. New Office users who had no experience with the previous user interface had a better experience with the new UI, easily finding actions that users of previous versions found hard to detect.

Of course, nowadays the ribbon control is very common in many applications. With Windows 8, the ribbon can be found in tools delivered with the operating system, e.g., Windows Explorer, Paint, and WordPad.

The WPF ribbon control is in the namespace `System.Windows.Controls.Ribbon` and requires referencing the assembly `system.windows.controls.ribbon`.

Figure 36-2 shows the ribbon control of the sample application. In the topmost line left of the title is the quick access toolbar. The leftmost item in the second line is the application menu, followed by two ribbon tabs: Home and Ribbon Controls. The Home tab, which is selected, shows two groups: Clipboard and Show. Both of these groups contain some button controls.

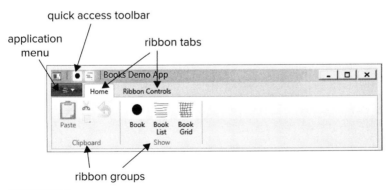

FIGURE 36-2

The `Ribbon` control is defined in the following code snippet. The first children of the `Ribbon` element are defined by the `QuickAccessToolBar` property. This toolbar contains two `RibbonButton` controls with small images referenced. These buttons provide users with direct access to quickly and easily fulfill actions:

```
<Ribbon DockPanel.Dock="Top">
  <Ribbon.QuickAccessToolBar>
    <RibbonQuickAccessToolBar>
      <RibbonButton SmallImageSource="Images/one.png" />
      <RibbonButton SmallImageSource="Images/list.png" />
    </RibbonQuickAccessToolBar>
  </Ribbon.QuickAccessToolBar>
```

To get these buttons from the quick access toolbar directly to the chrome of the Window, the base class needs to be changed to the `RibbonWindow` class instead of the `Window` class (code file `BooksDemo/MainWindow.xaml.cs`):

```
public partial class MainWindow : RibbonWindow
{
```

Changing the base class with the code-behind also requires a change in the XAML code to use the `RibbonWindow` element:

```
<RibbonWindow x:Class="Wrox.ProCSharp.WPF.MainWindow"
        xmlns="http://schemas.microsoft.com/winfx/2006/xaml/presentation"
        xmlns:x="http://schemas.microsoft.com/winfx/2006/xaml"
        xmlns:local="clr-namespace:Wrox.ProCSharp.WPF"
        Title="Books Demo App" Height="400" Width="600">
```

The application menu is defined by using the `ApplicationMenu` property. The application menu defines two menu entries—the first one to show a book, the second one to close the application:

```
<Ribbon.ApplicationMenu>
  <RibbonApplicationMenu SmallImageSource="Images/books.png" >
    <RibbonApplicationMenuItem Header="Show _Book" />
    <RibbonSeparator />
    <RibbonApplicationMenuItem Header="Exit" Command="Close" />
  </RibbonApplicationMenu>
</Ribbon.ApplicationMenu>
```

After the application menu, the content of the `Ribbon` control is defined by using `RibbonTab` elements. The title of the tab is defined with the `Header` property. The `RibbonTab` contains two `RibbonGroup` elements. Each of the `RibbonGroup` elements contains `RibbonButton` elements. With the buttons, a `Label` can be set to display a text and either `SmallImageSource` or `LargeImageSource` properties for displaying an image:

```
<RibbonTab Header="Home">
  <RibbonGroup Header="Clipboard">
    <RibbonButton Command="Paste" Label="Paste"
        LargeImageSource="Images/paste.png" />
    <RibbonButton Command="Cut" SmallImageSource="Images/cut.png" />
    <RibbonButton Command="Copy" SmallImageSource="Images/copy.png" />
    <RibbonButton Command="Undo" LargeImageSource="Images/undo.png" />
  </RibbonGroup>
  <RibbonGroup Header="Show">
    <RibbonButton LargeImageSource="Images/one.png" Label="Book" />
    <RibbonButton LargeImageSource="Images/list.png" Label="Book List" />
    <RibbonButton LargeImageSource="Images/grid.png" Label="Book Grid" />
  </RibbonGroup>
</RibbonTab>
```

The second `RibbonTab` is just used to demonstrate different controls that can be used within a ribbon control, for example, text box, check box, combo box, split button, and gallery elements. Figure 36-3 shows this tab open.

```xml
<RibbonTab Header="Ribbon Controls">
  <RibbonGroup Header="Sample">
    <RibbonButton Label="Button" />
    <RibbonCheckBox Label="Checkbox" />
    <RibbonComboBox Label="Combo1">
      <Label>One</Label>
      <Label>Two</Label>
    </RibbonComboBox>
    <RibbonTextBox>Text Box </RibbonTextBox>
    <RibbonSplitButton Label="Split Button">
      <RibbonMenuItem Header="One" />
      <RibbonMenuItem Header="Two" />
    </RibbonSplitButton>
    <RibbonComboBox Label="Combo2" IsEditable="False">
      <RibbonGallery SelectedValuePath="Content" MaxColumnCount="1"
          SelectedValue="Green">
        <RibbonGalleryCategory>
          <RibbonGalleryItem Content="Red" Foreground="Red" />
          <RibbonGalleryItem Content="Green" Foreground="Green" />
          <RibbonGalleryItem Content="Blue" Foreground="Blue" />
        </RibbonGalleryCategory>
      </RibbonGallery>
    </RibbonComboBox>
  </RibbonGroup>
</RibbonTab>
```

FIGURE 36-3

> **NOTE** *For additional information about the* `Ribbon` *control, read Chapter 30,* *"Managed Extensibility Framework," in which ribbon items are built dynamically.*

COMMANDING

Commanding is a WPF concept that creates a loose coupling between the source of an action (for example, a button) and the target that does the work (for example, a handler method). This concept is based on the *Command* pattern from the Gang of Four. Events are strongly coupled (at least with XAML 2006). Compiling the XAML code that includes references to events requires that the code-behind have a handler implemented and available at compile time. With commands, the coupling is loose.

The action that is executed is defined by a command object. Commands implement the interface `ICommand`. Command classes that are used by WPF are `RoutedCommand` and a class that derives from it, `RoutedUICommand`. `RoutedUICommand` defines an additional `Text` property that is not defined by `ICommand`. This property can be used as textual information in the UI. `ICommand` defines the methods `Execute` and `CanExecute`, which are executed on a target object.

The *command source* is an object that invokes the command. Command sources implement the interface `ICommandSource`. Examples of such command sources are button classes that derive from `ButtonBase`, `Hyperlink`, and `InputBinding`. `KeyBinding` and `MouseBinding` are examples of `InputBinding` derived classes. Command sources have a `Command` property whereby a command object implementing `ICommand` can be assigned. This fires the command when the control is used, such as with the click of a button.

The *command target* is an object that implements a handler to perform the action. With command binding, a mapping is defined to map the handler to a command. Command bindings define what handler is invoked on a command. Command bindings are defined by the `CommandBinding` property that is implemented in the `UIElement` class. Thus, every class that derives from `UIElement` has the `CommandBinding` property.

This makes finding the mapped handler a hierarchical process. For example, a button that is defined within a `StackPanel` that is inside a `ListBox`—which itself is inside a `Grid`—can fire a command. The handler is specified with command bindings somewhere up the tree—such as with command bindings of a `Window`. The next section changes the implementation of the BooksDemo project to use commands.

Defining Commands

.NET gives you classes that return predefined commands. The `ApplicationCommands` class defines the static properties `New`, `Open`, `Close`, `Print`, `Cut`, `Copy`, `Paste`, and others. These properties return `RoutedUICommand` objects that can be used for a specific purpose. Other classes offering commands are `NavigationCommands` and `MediaCommands`. `NavigationCommands` is self-explanatory, providing commands that are common for navigation such as `GoToPage`, `NextPage`, and `PreviousPage`. `MediaCommands` are useful for running a media player, with `Play`, `Pause`, `Stop`, `Rewind`, and `Record`.

It's not hard to define custom commands that fulfill application domain–specific actions. For this, the `BooksCommands` class is created, which returns `RoutedUICommands` with the `ShowBook` and `ShowBooksList` properties. You can also assign an input gesture to a command, such as `KeyGesture` or `MouseGesture`. In the following example, a `KeyGesture` is assigned that defines the key B with the `Alt` modifier. An input gesture is a command source, so clicking the Alt+B combination invokes the command (code file `BooksDemo/BooksCommands.cs`):

```
public static class BooksCommands
{
  private static RoutedUICommand showBook;
  public static ICommand ShowBook
  {
    get
    {
      return showBook ?? (showBook = new RoutedUICommand("Show Book",
          "ShowBook", typeof(BooksCommands)));
    }
  }

  private static RoutedUICommand showBooksList;
  public static ICommand ShowBooksList
  {
    get
    {
      if (showBooksList == null)
      {
        showBooksList = new RoutedUICommand("Show Books", "ShowBooks",
            typeof(BooksCommands));
        showBook.InputGestures.Add(new KeyGesture(Key.B, ModifierKeys.Alt));
      }
      return showBooksList;
    }
  }
}
```

Defining Command Sources

Every class that implements the `ICommandSource` interface can be a source of commands, such as `Button` and `MenuItem`. Inside the `Ribbon` control created earlier, the `Command` property is assigned to several `RibbonButton` elements, e.g., in the quick access toolbar, as shown in the following code snippet (XAML file `BooksDemo/MainWindow.xaml`):

```
<Ribbon.QuickAccessToolBar>
  <RibbonQuickAccessToolBar>
    <RibbonButton SmallImageSource="Images/one.png"
```

```
        Command="local:BooksCommands.ShowBook" />
      <RibbonButton SmallImageSource="Images/list.png"
        Command="local:BooksCommands.ShowBooksList" />
    </RibbonQuickAccessToolBar>
  </Ribbon.QuickAccessToolBar>
```

Predefined commands such as `ApplicationCommands.Cut`, `Copy`, and `Paste` are assigned to the `Command` property of `RibbonButton` elements as well. With the predefined commands the shorthand notation is used:

```
<RibbonGroup Header="Clipboard">
  <RibbonButton Command="Paste" Label="Paste"
    LargeImageSource="Images/paste.png" />
  <RibbonButton Command="Cut" SmallImageSource="Images/cut.png" />
  <RibbonButton Command="Copy" SmallImageSource="Images/copy.png" />
  <RibbonButton Command="Undo" LargeImageSource="Images/undo.png" />
</RibbonGroup>
```

Command Bindings

Command bindings need to be added to connect them to handler methods. In the following example, the command bindings are defined within the `Window` element so these bindings are available to all elements within the window. When the command `ApplicationCommands.Close` is executed, the `OnClose` method is invoked. When the command `BooksCommands.ShowBooks` is executed, the `OnShowBooks` method is called:

```
<Window.CommandBindings>
  <CommandBinding Command="Close" Executed="OnClose" />
  <CommandBinding Command="local:BooksCommands.ShowBooksList"
    Executed="OnShowBooksList" />
</Window.CommandBindings>
```

With command binding you can also specify the `CanExecute` property, whereby a method is invoked to verify whether the command is available. For example, if a file is not changed, the `ApplicationCommands` `.Save` command could be unavailable.

The handler needs to be defined with an object parameter, for the sender, and `ExecutedRoutedEventArgs`, where information about the command can be accessed (code file `BooksDemo/MainWindow.xaml.cs`):

```
private void OnClose(object sender, ExecutedRoutedEventArgs e)
{
  Application.Current.Shutdown();
}
```

> **NOTE** *You can also pass parameters with a command. You can do this by specifying the* `CommandParameter` *property with a command source, such as the* `MenuItem`. *To access the parameter, use the* `Parameter` *property of* `ExecutedRoutedEventArgs`.

Command bindings can also be defined by controls. The `TextBox` control defines bindings for `ApplicationCommands.Cut`, `ApplicationCommands.Copy`, `ApplicationCommands.Paste`, and `ApplicationCommands.Undo`. This way, you only need to specify the command source and use the existing functionality within the `TextBox` control.

DATA BINDING

WPF data binding takes another huge step forward compared with previous technologies. Data binding gets data from .NET objects for the UI or the other way around. Simple objects can be bound to UI elements, lists of objects, and XAML elements themselves. With WPF data binding, the target can be any dependency property of a WPF element, and every property of a CLR object can be the source. Because a WPF element is implemented as a .NET class, every WPF element can be the source as well. Figure 36-4 shows the connection between the source and the target. The `Binding` object defines the connection.

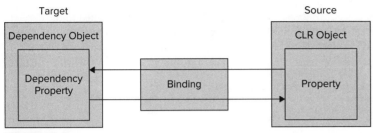

FIGURE 36-4

Binding supports several binding modes between the target and source. With *one-way* binding, the source information goes to the target but if the user changes information in the user interface, the source is not updated. For updates to the source, *two-way* binding is required.

The following table shows the binding modes and their requirements.

BINDING MODE	DESCRIPTION
One-time	Binding goes from the source to the target and occurs only once when the application is started or the data context changes. Here, you get a snapshot of the data.
One-way	Binding goes from the source to the target. This is useful for read-only data, because it is not possible to change the data from the user interface. To get updates to the user interface, the source must implement the interface `INotifyPropertyChanged`.
Two-way	With two-way binding, the user can make changes to the data from the UI. Binding occurs in both directions—from the source to the target and from the target to the source. The source needs to implement read/write properties so that changes can be updated from the UI to the source.
One-way-to-source	With one-way-to-source binding, if the target property changes, the source object is updated.

WPF data binding involves many facets besides the binding modes. This section provides details on binding to XAML elements, binding to simple .NET objects, and binding to lists. Using change notifications, the UI is updated with changes in the bound objects. The material presented here discusses getting the data from object data providers and directly from the code. Multibinding and priority binding demonstrate different binding possibilities other than the default binding. This section also describes dynamically selecting data templates, and validation of binding values.

Let's start with the BooksDemo sample application.

BooksDemo Application Content

In the previous sections, a ribbon and commands have been defined with the BooksDemo application. Now content is added. Change the XAML file `MainWindow.xaml` by adding a `ListBox`, a `Hyperlink`, and a `TabControl` (XAML file `BooksDemo/MainWindow.xaml`):

```
<ListBox DockPanel.Dock="Left" Margin="5" MinWidth="120">
  <Hyperlink Click="OnShowBook">Show Book</Hyperlink>
</ListBox>
<TabControl Margin="5" x:Name="tabControl1">
</TabControl>
```

Now add a WPF user control named `BookUC`. This user control contains a `DockPanel`, a `Grid` with several rows and columns, a `Label`, and `TextBox` controls (XAML file `BooksDemo/BookUC.xaml`):

```
<UserControl x:Class="Wrox.ProCSharp.WPF.BookUC"
    xmlns="http://schemas.microsoft.com/winfx/2006/xaml/presentation"
    xmlns:x="http://schemas.microsoft.com/winfx/2006/xaml"
    xmlns:mc="http://schemas.openxmlformats.org/markup-compatibility/2006"
    xmlns:d="http://schemas.microsoft.com/expression/blend/2008"
    mc:Ignorable="d"
    d:DesignHeight="300" d:DesignWidth="300">
  <DockPanel>
    <Grid>
      <Grid.RowDefinitions>
        <RowDefinition />
        <RowDefinition />
        <RowDefinition />
        <RowDefinition />
      </Grid.RowDefinitions>
      <Grid.ColumnDefinitions>
        <ColumnDefinition Width="Auto" />
        <ColumnDefinition Width="*" />
      </Grid.ColumnDefinitions>
      <Label Content="Title" Grid.Row="0" Grid.Column="0" Margin="10,0,5,0"
          HorizontalAlignment="Left" VerticalAlignment="Center" />
      <Label Content="Publisher" Grid.Row="1" Grid.Column="0"
          Margin="10,0,5,0" HorizontalAlignment="Left"
          VerticalAlignment="Center" />
      <Label Content="Isbn" Grid.Row="2" Grid.Column="0"
          Margin="10,0,5,0" HorizontalAlignment="Left"
          VerticalAlignment="Center" />
      <TextBox Grid.Row="0" Grid.Column="1" Margin="5" />
      <TextBox Grid.Row="1" Grid.Column="1" Margin="5" />
      <TextBox Grid.Row="2" Grid.Column="1" Margin="5" />
      <StackPanel Grid.Row="3" Grid.Column="0" Grid.ColumnSpan="2">
        <Button Content="Show Book" Margin="5" Click="OnShowBook" />
      </StackPanel>
    </Grid>
  </DockPanel>
</UserControl>
```

Within the `OnShowBook` handler in the `MainWindow.xaml.cs`, create a new instance of the user control `BookUC` and add a new `TabItem` to the `TabControl`. Then change the `SelectedIndex` property of the `TabControl` to open the new tab (code file `BooksDemo/MainWindow.xaml.cs`):

```
private void OnShowBook(object sender, ExecutedRoutedEventArgs e)
{
  var bookUI = new BookUC();
  this.tabControl1.SelectedIndex = this.tabControl1.Items.Add(
      new TabItem { Header = "Book", Content = bookUI });
}
```

After building the project you can start the application and open the user control within the `TabControl` by clicking the hyperlink.

Binding with XAML

In addition to being the target for data binding, a WPF element can also be the source. You can bind the source property of one WPF element to the target of another WPF element.

In the following code example, data binding is used to resize the controls within the user control with a slider. You add a `StackPanel` control to the user control `BookUC`, which contains a `Label` and a `Slider` control. The `Slider` control defines `Minimum` and `Maximum` values that define the scale, and an initial value of 1 is assigned to the `Value` property (XAML file `BooksDemo/BooksUC.xaml`):

```
<DockPanel>
  <StackPanel DockPanel.Dock="Bottom" Orientation="Horizontal"
      HorizontalAlignment="Right">
    <Label Content="Resize" />
    <Slider x:Name="slider1" Value="1" Minimum="0.4" Maximum="3"
        Width="150" HorizontalAlignment="Right" />
  </StackPanel>
```

Now you set the `LayoutTransform` property of the `Grid` control and add a `ScaleTransform` element. With the `ScaleTransform` element, the `ScaleX` and `ScaleY` properties are data bound. Both properties are set with the `Binding` markup extension. In the `Binding` markup extension, the `ElementName` is set to `slider1` to reference the previously created `Slider` control. The `Path` property is set to the `Value` property to get the value of the slider:

```
<Grid>
  <Grid.LayoutTransform>
    <ScaleTransform x:Name="scale1"
        ScaleX="{Binding Path=Value, ElementName=slider1}"
        ScaleY="{Binding Path=Value, ElementName=slider1}" />
  </Grid.LayoutTransform>
```

When running the application, you can move the slider and thus resize the controls within the `Grid`, as shown in Figures 36-5 and 36-6.

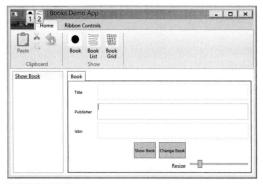

FIGURE 36-5

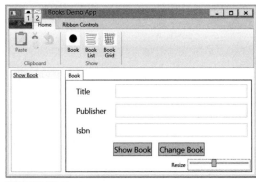

FIGURE 36-6

Rather than define the binding information with XAML code, as shown in the preceding code with the `Binding` metadata extension, you can do it with code-behind. With code-behind you have to create a new `Binding` object and set the `Path` and `Source` properties. The `Source` property must be set to the source object; here, it is the WPF object `slider1`. The `Path` is set to a `PropertyPath` instance that is initialized with the name of the property of the source object, `Value`. With controls that derive from `FrameworkElement`, you can invoke the method `SetBinding` to define the binding. However, `ScaleTransform` does not derive from `FrameworkElement` but from the `Freezable` base class instead. Use the helper class `BindingOperations` to bind such controls. The `SetBinding` method of the `BindingOperations` class requires a `DependencyObject`—which is the `ScaleTransform` instance in the example. With the second and third argument, the `SetBinding` method requires the `dependency` property of the target (which should be bound), and the `Binding` object:

```
var binding = new Binding
{
  Path = new PropertyPath("Value"),
  Source = slider1
```

```
    };
    BindingOperations.SetBinding(scale1, ScaleTransform.ScaleXProperty,
        binding);
    BindingOperations.SetBinding(scale1, ScaleTransform.ScaleYProperty,
        binding);
```

> **NOTE** *Remember that all classes that derive from* DependencyObject *can have dependency properties. You can learn more about dependency properties in Chapter 29, "Core XAML."*

You can configure a number of binding options with the Binding class, as described in the following table:

BINDING CLASS MEMBERS	DESCRIPTION
Source	Use this property to define the source object for data binding.
RelativeSource	Specify the source in relation to the target object. This is useful to display error messages when the source of the error comes from the same control.
ElementName	If the source is a WPF element, you can specify the source with the ElementName property.
Path	Use this property to specify the path to the source object. This can be the property of the source object, but indexers and properties of child elements are also supported.
XPath	With an XML data source, you can define an XPath query expression to get the data for binding.
Mode	The mode defines the direction for the binding. The Mode property is of type BindingMode. BindingMode is an enumeration with the following values: Default, OneTime, OneWay, TwoWay, and OneWayToSource. The default mode depends on the target: with a TextBox, two-way binding is the default; with a Label that is read-only, the default is one-way. OneTime means that the data is only init loaded from the source; OneWay updates from the source to the target. With TwoWay binding, changes from the WPF elements are written back to the source. OneWayToSource means that the data is never read but always written from the target to the source.
Converter	Use this property to specify a converter class that converts the data for the UI and back. The converter class must implement the interface IValueConverter, which defines the methods Convert and ConvertBack. You can pass parameters to the converter methods with the ConverterParameter property. The converter can be culture-sensitive; and the culture can be set with the ConverterCulture property.
FallbackValue	Use this property to define a default value that is used if binding doesn't return a value.
ValidationRules	Using this property, you can define a collection of ValidationRule objects that are checked before the source is updated from the WPF target elements. The class ExceptionValidationRule is derived from the class ValidationRule and checks for exceptions.
Delay	This property is new with WPF 4.5. It enables you to specify an amount of time to wait before the binding source is updated. This can be used in scenarios where you want to give the user some time to enter more characters before starting a validation.

Simple Object Binding

To bind to CLR objects, with the .NET classes you just have to define properties, as shown in the Book class example and the properties Title, Publisher, Isbn, and Authors. This class is in the Data folder of the BooksDemo project (code file BooksDemo/Data/Book.cs).

```
using System.Collections.Generic;

namespace Wrox.ProCSharp.WPF.Data
{
  public class Book
  {
    public Book(string title, string publisher, string isbn,
                params string[] authors)
    {
      this.Title = title;
      this.Publisher = publisher;
      this.Isbn = isbn;
      this.authors.AddRange(authors);
    }
    public Book()
      : this("unknown", "unknown", "unknown")
    {
    }
    public string Title { get; set; }
    public string Publisher { get; set; }
    public string Isbn { get; set; }

    private readonly List<string> authors = new List<string>();
    public string[] Authors
    {
      get
      {
        return authors.ToArray();
      }
    }

    public override string ToString()
    {
      return Title;
    }
  }
}
```

In the XAML code of the user control BookUC, several labels and TextBox controls are defined to display book information. Using Binding markup extensions, the TextBox controls are bound to the properties of the Book class. With the Binding markup extension, nothing more than the Path property is defined to bind it to the property of the Book class. There's no need to define a source because the source is defined by assigning the DataContext, as shown in the code-behind that follows. The mode is defined by its default with the TextBox element, and this is two-way binding (XAML file BooksDemo/BookUC.xaml):

```
<TextBox Text="{Binding Title}" Grid.Row="0" Grid.Column="1" Margin="5" />
<TextBox Text="{Binding Publisher}" Grid.Row="1" Grid.Column="1" Margin="5" />
<TextBox Text="{Binding Isbn}" Grid.Row="2" Grid.Column="1" Margin="5" />
```

With the code-behind, a new Book object is created, and the book is assigned to the DataContext property of the user control. DataContext is a dependency property that is defined with the base class FrameworkElement. Assigning the DataContext with the user control means that every element in the user control has a default binding to the same data context (code file BooksDemo/MainWindow.xaml.cs):

```
private void OnShowBook(object sender, ExecutedRoutedEventArgs e)
{
  var bookUI = new BookUC();
  bookUI.DataContext = new Book
  {
    Title = "Professional C# 4 and .NET 4",
    Publisher = "Wrox Press",
    Isbn = "978-0-470-50225-9"
  };
  this.tabControl1.SelectedIndex =
    this.tabControl1.Items.Add(
      new TabItem { Header = "Book", Content = bookUI });
}
```

After starting the application, you can see the bound data, as shown in Figure 36-7.

To see two-way binding in action (changes to the input of the WPF element are reflected inside the CLR object), the Click event handler of the button in the user control, the OnShowBook method, is implemented. When implemented, a message box pops up to show the current title and ISBN number of the book1 object. Figure 36-8 shows the output from the message box after a change to the input was made during runtime (code file BooksDemo/BookUC .xaml.cs):

FIGURE 36-7

```
private void OnShowBook(object sender, RoutedEventArgs e)
{
  Book theBook = this.DataContext as Book;
  if (theBook != null)
    MessageBox.Show(theBook.Title, theBook.Isbn);
}
```

FIGURE 36-8

Change Notification

With the current two-way binding, the data is read from the object and written back. However, if data is not changed by the user, but is instead changed directly from the code, the UI does not receive the change information. You can easily verify this by adding a button to the user control and implementing the Click event handler OnChangeBook (XAML file BooksDemo/BookUC.xaml):

```
<StackPanel Grid.Row="3" Grid.Column="0" Grid.ColumnSpan="2"
            Orientation="Horizontal" HorizontalAlignment="Center">
    <Button Content="Show Book" Margin="5" Click="OnShowBook" />
    <Button Content="Change Book" Margin="5" Click="OnChangeBook" />
</StackPanel>
```

Within the implementation of the handler, the book inside the data context is changed but the user interface doesn't show the change (code file BooksDemo/BookUC.xaml.cs):

```
private void OnChangeBook(object sender, RoutedEventArgs e)
{
  Book theBook = this.DataContext as Book;
  if (theBook != null)
  {
    theBook.Title = "Professional C# 5";
    theBook.Isbn = "978-0-470-31442-5";
  }
}
```

To get change information to the user interface, the entity class must implement the interface INotifyPropertyChanged. Instead of having an implementation with every class that needs this interface, the abstract base class BindableObject is created. This base class implements the interface INotifyPropertyChanged. The interface defines the event PropertyChanged, which is fired from the OnPropertyChanged method. As a convenience for firing the event from the property setters from the derived classes, the method SetProperty makes the change of the property and invokes the method OnPropertyChanged to fire the event. This method makes use of the caller information feature from C# using the attribute CallerMemberName. Defining the parameter propertyName as an optional parameter with this attribute, the C# compiler passes the name of the property with this parameter, so it's not necessary to add a hard-coded string to the code (code file BooksDemo/Data/BindableObject.cs):

```csharp
using System.Collections.Generic;
using System.ComponentModel;
using System.Runtime.CompilerServices;

namespace Wrox.ProCSharp.WPF.Data
{
  public abstract class BindableObject : INotifyPropertyChanged
  {
    public event PropertyChangedEventHandler PropertyChanged;
    protected void OnPropertyChanged(string propertyName)
    {
      var propertyChanged = PropertyChanged;
      if (propertyChanged != null)
      {
        PropertyChanged(this, new PropertyChangedEventArgs(propertyName));
      }
    }

    protected void SetProperty<T>(ref T item, T value,
        [CallerMemberName] string propertyName = null)
    {
      if (!EqualityComparer<T>.Default.Equals(item, value))
      {
        item = value;
        OnPropertyChanged(propertyName);
      }
    }
  }
}
```

> **NOTE** *Caller information is covered in Chapter 16.*

The class Book is now changed to derive from the base class BindableObject in order to inherit the implementation of the interface INotifyPropertyChanged. The property setters are changed to invoke the SetProperty method, as shown here (code file BooksDemo/Data/Book.cs):

```csharp
using System.ComponentModel;
using System.Collections.Generic;

namespace Wrox.ProCSharp.WPF.Data
{
  public class Book : BindableObject
  {
    public Book(string title, string publisher, string isbn,
            params string[] authors)
```

```csharp
    {
      this.title = title;
      this.publisher = publisher;
      this.isbn = isbn;
      this.authors.AddRange(authors);
    }
    public Book()
      : this("unknown", "unknown", "unknown")
    {
    }

    private string title;
    public string Title {
      get
      {
        return title;
      }
      set
      {
        SetProperty(ref title, value);
      }
    }

    private string publisher;
    public string Publisher
    {
      get
      {
        return publisher;
      }
      set
      {
        SetProperty(ref publisher, value);
      }
    }
    private string isbn;
    public string Isbn
    {
      get
      {
        return isbn;
      }
      set
      {
        SetProperty(ref isbn, value);
      }
    }

    private readonly List<string> authors = new List<string>();
    public string[] Authors
    {
      get
      {
        return authors.ToArray();
      }
    }

    public override string ToString()
    {
      return this.title;
    }
  }
}
```

With this change, the application can be started again to verify that the user interface is updated following a change notification in the event handler.

Object Data Provider

Instead of instantiating the object in code-behind, you can do this with XAML. To reference a class from code-behind within XAML, you have to reference the namespace with the namespace declarations in the XML root element. The XML attribute `xmlns:local="clr-namespace:Wrox.ProCSharp.WPF"` assigns the .NET namespace `Wrox.ProCSharp.WPF` to the XML namespace alias `local`.

One object of the `Book` class is now defined with the `Book` element inside the `DockPanel` resources. By assigning values to the XML attributes `Title`, `Publisher`, and `Isbn`, you set the values of the properties from the `Book` class. `x:Key="theBook"` defines the identifier for the resource so that you can reference the book object (XAML file `BooksDemo/BookUC.xaml`):

```xml
<UserControl x:Class="Wrox.ProCSharp.WPF.BookUC"
    xmlns="http://schemas.microsoft.com/winfx/2006/xaml/presentation"
    xmlns:x="http://schemas.microsoft.com/winfx/2006/xaml"
    xmlns:mc="http://schemas.openxmlformats.org/markup-compatibility/2006"
    xmlns:d="http://schemas.microsoft.com/expression/blend/2008"
    xmlns:local="clr-namespace:Wrox.ProCSharp.WPF.Data"
    mc:Ignorable="d"
    d:DesignHeight="300" d:DesignWidth="300">
  <DockPanel>
    <DockPanel.Resources>
      <local:Book x:Key="theBook" Title="Professional C# 4 and .NET 4"
          Publisher="Wrox Press" Isbn="978-0-470-50225-9" />
    </DockPanel.Resources>
```

> **NOTE** *If the .NET namespace to reference is in a different assembly, you have to add the assembly to the XML declaration:*
>
> ```
> xmlsn:sys="clr-namespace:System;assembly=mscorlib"
> ```

In the `TextBox` element, the `Source` is defined with the `Binding` markup extension that references the `theBook` resource:

```xml
<TextBox Text="{Binding Path=Title, Source={StaticResource theBook}}"
    Grid.Row="0" Grid.Column="1" Margin="5" />
<TextBox Text="{Binding Path=Publisher, Source={StaticResource theBook}}"
    Grid.Row="1" Grid.Column="1" Margin="5" />
<TextBox Text="{Binding Path=Isbn, Source={StaticResource theBook}}"
    Grid.Row="2" Grid.Column="1" Margin="5" />
```

Because all these `TextBox` elements are contained within the same control, it is possible to assign the `DataContext` property with a parent control and set the `Path` property with the `TextBox` binding elements. Because the `Path` property is a default, you can also reduce the `Binding` markup extension to the following code:

```xml
<Grid x:Name="grid1" DataContext="{StaticResource theBook}">
  <!-- ... -->
  <TextBox Text="{Binding Title}" Grid.Row="0" Grid.Column="1"
      Margin="5" />
  <TextBox Text="{Binding Publisher}" Grid.Row="1" Grid.Column="1"
      Margin="5" />
  <TextBox Text="{Binding Isbn}" Grid.Row="2" Grid.Column="1"
      Margin="5" />
```

Instead of defining the object instance directly within XAML code, you can define an object data provider that references a class to invoke a method. For use by the ObjectDataProvider, it's best to create a factory class that returns the object to display, as shown with the BookFactory class (code file BooksDemo/Data/BookFactory.cs):

```
using System.Collections.Generic;

namespace Wrox.ProCSharp.WPF.Data
{
  public class BookFactory
  {
    private List<Book> books = new List<Book>();

    public BookFactory()
    {
      books.Add(new Book
      {
        Title = "Professional C# 4 and .NET 4",
        Publisher = "Wrox Press",
        Isbn = "978-0-470-50225-9"
      });
    }

    public Book GetTheBook()
    {
      return books[0];
    }
  }
}
```

The ObjectDataProvider element can be defined in the resources section. The XML attribute ObjectType defines the name of the class; with MethodName you specify the name of the method that is invoked to get the book object (XAML file BooksDemo/BookUC.xaml):

```
<DockPanel.Resources>
  <ObjectDataProvider x:Key="theBook" ObjectType="local:BookFactory"
      MethodName="GetTheBook" />
</DockPanel.Resources>
```

The properties you can specify with the ObjectDataProvider class are listed in the following table:

OBJECTDATAPROVIDER PROPERTY	DESCRIPTION
ObjectType	Defines the type to create an instance.
ConstructorParameters	Using the ConstructorParameters collection, you can add parameters to the class to create an instance.
MethodName	Defines the name of the method that is invoked by the object data provider.
MethodParameters	Using this property, you can assign parameters to the method defined with the MethodName property.
ObjectInstance	Using this property, you can get and set the object that is used by the ObjectDataProvider class. For example, you can assign an existing object programmatically rather than define the ObjectType so that an object is instantiated by ObjectDataProvider.
Data	Enables you to access the underlying object that is used for data binding. If the MethodName is defined, with the Data property you can access the object that is returned from the method defined.

List Binding

Binding to a list is more frequently done than binding to a simple object. Binding to a list is very similar to binding to a simple object. You can assign the complete list to the DataContext from code-behind, or you can use an ObjectDataProvider that accesses an object factory that returns a list. With elements that support binding to a list (for example, a ListBox), the complete list is bound. With elements that support binding to just one object (for example, a TextBox), the current item is bound.

With the BookFactory class, now a list of Book objects is returned (code file BooksDemo/Data/BookFactory.cs):

```
public class BookFactory
{
  private List<Book> books = new List<Book>();

  public BookFactory()
  {
    books.Add(new Book("Professional C# 4 with .NET 4", "Wrox Press",
                "978-0-470-50225-9", "Christian Nagel", "Bill Evjen",
                "Jay Glynn", "Karli Watson", "Morgan Skinner"));
    books.Add(new Book("Professional C# 2008", "Wrox Press",
                "978-0-470-19137-8", "Christian Nagel", "Bill Evjen",
                "Jay Glynn", "Karli Watson", "Morgan Skinner"));
    books.Add(new Book("Beginning Visual C# 2010", "Wrox Press",
                "978-0-470-50226-6", "Karli Watson", "Christian Nagel",
                "Jacob Hammer Pedersen", "Jon D. Reid",
                "Morgan Skinner", "Eric White"));
    books.Add(new Book("Windows 7 Secrets", "Wiley", "978-0-470-50841-1",
                "Paul Thurrott", "Rafael Rivera"));
    books.Add(new Book("C# 2008 for Dummies", "For Dummies",
                "978-0-470-19109-5", "Stephen Randy Davis",
                "Chuck Sphar"));
  }

  public IEnumerable<Book> GetBooks()
  {
    return books;
  }
}
```

To use the list, create a new BooksUC user control. The XAML code for this control contains Label and TextBox controls that display the values of a single book, as well as a ListBox control that displays a book list. The ObjectDataProvider invokes the GetBooks method of the BookFactory, and this provider is used to assign the DataContext of the DockPanel. The DockPanel has the bound ListBox and TextBox as its children (XAML file BooksDemo/BooksUC.xaml):

```
<UserControl x:Class="Wrox.ProCSharp.WPF.BooksUC"
    xmlns="http://schemas.microsoft.com/winfx/2006/xaml/presentation"
    xmlns:x="http://schemas.microsoft.com/winfx/2006/xaml"
    xmlns:mc="http://schemas.openxmlformats.org/markup-compatibility/2006"
    xmlns:d="http://schemas.microsoft.com/expression/blend/2008"
    xmlns:local="clr-namespace:Wrox.ProCSharp.WPF.Data"
    mc:Ignorable="d"
    d:DesignHeight="300" d:DesignWidth="300">
  <UserControl.Resources>
    <ObjectDataProvider x:Key="books" ObjectType="local:BookFactory"
                        MethodName="GetBooks" />
  </UserControl.Resources>
  <DockPanel DataContext="{StaticResource books}">
    <ListBox DockPanel.Dock="Left" ItemsSource="{Binding}" Margin="5"
        MinWidth="120" />
```

```
<Grid>
  <Grid.RowDefinitions>
    <RowDefinition />
    <RowDefinition />
    <RowDefinition />
    <RowDefinition />
  </Grid.RowDefinitions>
  <Grid.ColumnDefinitions>
    <ColumnDefinition Width="Auto" />
    <ColumnDefinition Width="*" />
  </Grid.ColumnDefinitions>
  <Label Content="Title" Grid.Row="0" Grid.Column="0" Margin="10,0,5,0"
      HorizontalAlignment="Left" VerticalAlignment="Center" />
  <Label Content="Publisher" Grid.Row="1" Grid.Column="0" Margin="10,0,5,0"
      HorizontalAlignment="Left" VerticalAlignment="Center" />
  <Label Content="Isbn" Grid.Row="2" Grid.Column="0" Margin="10,0,5,0"
      HorizontalAlignment="Left" VerticalAlignment="Center" />
  <TextBox Text="{Binding Title}" Grid.Row="0" Grid.Column="1" Margin="5" />
  <TextBox Text="{Binding Publisher}" Grid.Row="1" Grid.Column="1"
      Margin="5" />
  <TextBox Text="{Binding Isbn}" Grid.Row="2" Grid.Column="1" Margin="5" />
</Grid>
    </DockPanel>
  </UserControl>
```

The new user control is started by adding a `Hyperlink` to `MainWindow.xaml`. It uses the `Command` property to assign the `ShowBooks` command. The command binding must be specified as well to invoke the event handler `OnShowBooksList`. (XAML file `BooksDemo/BooksUC.xaml`):

```
<ListBox DockPanel.Dock="Left" Margin="5" MinWidth="120">
  <ListBoxItem>
    <Hyperlink Command="local:BooksCommands.ShowBook">Show Book</Hyperlink>
  </ListBoxItem>
  <ListBoxItem>
    <Hyperlink Command="local:ShowCommands.ShowBooksList">
        Show Books List</Hyperlink>
  </ListBoxItem>
</ListBox>
```

The implementation of the event handler adds a new `TabItem` control to the `TabControl`, assigns the `Content` to the user control `BooksUC` and sets the selection of the `TabControl` to the newly created `TabItem` (code file `BooksDemo/BooksUC.xaml.cs`):

```
private void OnShowBooks(object sender, ExecutedRoutedEventArgs e)
{
  var booksUI = new BooksUC();
  this.tabControl1.SelectedIndex =
    this.tabControl1.Items.Add(
      new TabItem { Header="Books List", Content=booksUI});
}
```

Because the `DockPanel` has the `Book` array assigned to the `DataContext`, and the `ListBox` is placed within the `DockPanel`, the `ListBox` shows all books with the default template, as illustrated in Figure 36-9.

For a more flexible layout of the `ListBox`, you have to define a template, as discussed in the previous chapter for `ListBox` styling. The `ItemTemplate` of the `ListBox` defines a `DataTemplate` with a `Label` element. The content of the label is bound to the `Title`. The item

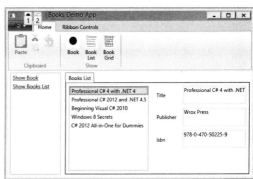

FIGURE 36-9

template is repeated for every item in the list. Of course, you can also add the item template to a style within resources (XAML file `BooksDemo/BooksUC.xaml`):

```xml
<ListBox DockPanel.Dock="Left" ItemsSource="{Binding}" Margin="5"
    MinWidth="120">
  <ListBox.ItemTemplate>
    <DataTemplate>
      <Label Content="{Binding Title}" />
    </DataTemplate>
  </ListBox.ItemTemplate>
</ListBox>
```

Master Details Binding

Instead of just showing all the elements inside a list, you might want or need to show detail information about the selected item. It doesn't require a lot of work to do this. The `Label` and `TextBox` controls are already defined; currently, they only show the first element in the list.

There's one important change you have to make to the `ListBox`. By default, the labels are bound to just the first element of the list. By setting the `ListBox` property `IsSynchronizedWithCurrentItem="True"`, the selection of the list box is set to the current item (XAML file `BooksDemo/BooksUC.xaml`):

```xml
<ListBox DockPanel.Dock="Left" ItemsSource="{Binding}" Margin="5"
        MinWidth="120" IsSynchronizedWithCurrentItem="True">
  <ListBox.ItemTemplate>
    <DataTemplate>
      <Label Content="{Binding Title}" />
    </DataTemplate>
  </ListBox.ItemTemplate>
</ListBox>
```

Figure 36-10 shows the result; details about the selected item are shown on the right.

MultiBinding

`Binding` is one of the classes that can be used for data binding. `BindingBase` is the abstract base class of all bindings and has different concrete implementations. Besides `Binding`, there's also `MultiBinding` and

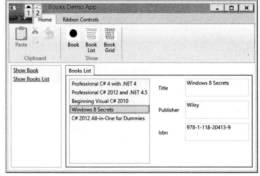

FIGURE 36-10

`PriorityBinding`. `MultiBinding` enables you to bind one WPF element to multiple sources. For example, with a `Person` class that has `LastName` and `FirstName` properties, it is interesting to bind both properties to a single WPF element (code file `MultiBindingDemo/Person.cs`):

```csharp
public class Person
{
  public string FirstName { get; set; }
  public string LastName { get; set; }
}
```

For `MultiBinding`, a markup extension is not available—therefore, the binding must be specified with XAML element syntax. The child elements of `MultiBinding` are `Binding` elements that specify the binding to the various properties. In the following example, the `FirstName` and `LastName` properties are used. The data context is set with the `Grid` element to reference the `person1` resource.

To connect the properties, `MultiBinding` uses a `Converter` to convert multiple values to one. This converter uses a parameter that allows for different conversions based on the parameter (XAML file `MultiBindingDemo/MainWindow.xaml`):

```xml
<Window x:Class="Wrox.ProCSharp.WPF.MainWindow"
        xmlns="http://schemas.microsoft.com/winfx/2006/xaml/presentation"
```

```
            xmlns:x="http://schemas.microsoft.com/winfx/2006/xaml"
            xmlns:system="clr-namespace:System;assembly=mscorlib"
            xmlns:local="clr-namespace:Wrox.ProCSharp.WPF"
            Title="MainWindow" Height="240" Width="500">
  <Window.Resources>
    <local:Person x:Key="person1" FirstName="Tom" LastName="Turbo" />
    <local:PersonNameConverter x:Key="personNameConverter" />
  </Window.Resources>
  <Grid DataContext="{StaticResource person1}">
    <TextBox>
      <TextBox.Text>
        <MultiBinding Converter="{StaticResource personNameConverter}" >
          <MultiBinding.ConverterParameter>
            <system:String>FirstLast</system:String>
          </MultiBinding.ConverterParameter>
          <Binding Path="FirstName" />
          <Binding Path="LastName" />
        </MultiBinding>
      </TextBox.Text>
    </TextBox>
  </Grid>
</Window>
```

The multi-value converter implements the interface `IMultiValueConverter`. This interface defines two methods, `Convert` and `ConvertBack`. `Convert` receives multiple values with the first argument from the data source and returns one value to the target. With the implementation, depending on whether the parameter has a value of `FirstLast` or `LastFirst`, the result varies (code file `MultiBindingDemo/PersonNameConverter.cs`):

```
using System;
using System.Globalization;
using System.Windows.Data;

namespace Wrox.ProCSharp.WPF
{
  public class PersonNameConverter : IMultiValueConverter
  {
    public object Convert(object[] values, Type targetType, object parameter,
                          CultureInfo culture)
    {
      switch (parameter as string)
      {
        case "FirstLast":
          return values[0] + " " + values[1];
        case "LastFirst":
          return values[1] + ", " + values[0];
        default:
          throw new ArgumentException(String.Format(
              "invalid argument {0}", parameter));
      }
    }

    public object[] ConvertBack(object value, Type[] targetTypes,
                                object parameter, CultureInfo culture)
    {
      throw new NotSupportedException();
    }
  }
}
```

In such simple scenarios, just combining some strings with a `MultiBinding` doesn't require an implementation of `IMultiValueConverter`. Instead, a definition for a format string is adequate, as shown in the following XAML code snippet. The string format defined with the `MultiBinding` first needs a `{}` prefix. With XAML the curly brackets usually define a markup expression. Using `{}` as a prefix escapes this and defines that no markup expression, but instead a normal string, follows. The sample specifies that both Binding elements are separated by a comma and a blank (XAML file `MultiBindingDemo/MainWindow.xaml`):

```xaml
<TextBox>
    <TextBox.Text>
        <MultiBinding StringFormat="{}{0}, {1}">
            <Binding Path="LastName" />
            <Binding Path="FirstName" />
        </MultiBinding>
    </TextBox.Text>
</TextBox>
```

Priority Binding

`PriorityBinding` makes it easy to bind to data that is not readily available. If you need time to get the result with `PriorityBinding`, you can inform users about the progress so they are aware of the wait.

To illustrate priority binding, use the `PriorityBindingDemo` project to create the `Data` class. Accessing the `ProcessSomeData` property requires some time, which is simulated by calling the `Thread.Sleep` method (code file `PriorityBindingDemo/Data.cs`):

```csharp
public class Data
{
  public string ProcessSomeData
  {
    get
    {
      Thread.Sleep(8000);
      return "the final result is here";
    }
  }
}
```

The `Information` class provides information to the user. The information from property `Info1` is returned immediately, whereas `Info2` returns information after five seconds. With a real implementation, this class could be associated with the processing class to get an estimated time frame for the user (code file `PriorityBindingDemo/Information.cs`):

```csharp
public class Information
{
  public string Info1
  {
    get
    {
      return "please wait...";
    }
  }
  public string Info2
  {
    get
    {
      Thread.Sleep(5000);
      return "please wait a little more";
    }
  }
}
```

In the `MainWindow.xaml` file, the `Data` and `Information` classes are referenced and initiated within the resources of the `Window` (XAML file `PriorityBindingDemo/MainWindow.xaml`):

```
<Window.Resources>
    <local:Data x:Key="data1" />
    <local:Information x:Key="info" />
</Window.Resources>
```

`PriorityBinding` is done in place of normal binding within the `Content` property of a `Label`. It consists of multiple `Binding` elements whereby all but the last one have the `IsAsync` property set to `True`. Because of this, if the first binding expression result is not immediately available, the binding process chooses the next one. The first binding references the `ProcessSomeData` property of the `Data` class, which needs some time. Because of this, the next binding comes into play and references the `Info2` property of the `Information` class. `Info2` does not return a result immediately; and because `IsAsync` is set, the binding process does not wait but continues to the next binding. The last binding uses the `Info1` property. If it doesn't immediately return a result, you would wait for the result because `IsAsync` is set to the default, `False`:

```
<Label>
  <Label.Content>
    <PriorityBinding>
      <Binding Path="ProcessSomeData" Source="{StaticResource data1}"
          IsAsync="True" />
      <Binding Path="Info2" Source="{StaticResource info}"
          IsAsync="True" />
      <Binding Path="Info1" Source="{StaticResource info}"
          IsAsync="False" />
    </PriorityBinding>
  </Label.Content>
</Label>
```

When the application starts, you can see the message "please wait…" in the user interface. After a few seconds the result from the `Info2` property is returned as "please wait a little more." It replaces the output from `Info1`. Finally, the result from `ProcessSomeData` replaces the output again.

Value Conversion

Returning to the BooksDemo application, the authors of the book are still missing in the user interface. If you bind the `Authors` property to a `Label` element, the `ToString` method of the `Array` class is invoked, which returns the name of the type. One solution to this is to bind the `Authors` property to a `ListBox`. For the `ListBox`, you can define a template for a specific view. Another solution is to convert the string array returned by the `Authors` property to a string and use the string for binding.

The class `StringArrayConverter` converts a string array to a string. WPF converter classes must implement the interface `IValueConverter` from the namespace `System.Windows.Data`. This interface defines the methods `Convert` and `ConvertBack`. With the `StringArrayConverter`, the `Convert` method converts the string array from the variable `value` to a string by using the `String.Join` method. The separator parameter of the `Join` is taken from the variable `parameter` received with the `Convert` method (code file `BooksDemo/Utilities/StringArrayConverter.cs`):

```
using System;
using System.Diagnostics.Contracts;
using System.Globalization;
using System.Windows.Data;

namespace Wrox.ProCSharp.WPF.Utilities

{
    [ValueConversion(typeof(string[]), typeof(string))]
    class StringArrayConverter : IValueConverter
```

```
    {
      public object Convert(object value, Type targetType, object parameter,
                            CultureInfo culture)
      {
        if (value == null) return null;

        string[] stringCollection = (string[])value;
        string separator = parameter == null;

        return String.Join(separator, stringCollection);
      }

      public object ConvertBack(object value, Type targetType, object parameter,
                                CultureInfo culture)
      {
        throw new NotImplementedException();
      }
    }
  }
}
```

> **NOTE** *You can read more about the methods of the* String *classes in Chapter 9,* *"Strings and Regular Expressions."*

In the XAML code, the StringArrayConverter class can be declared as a resource. This resource can be referenced from the Binding markup extension (XAML file BooksDemo/BooksUC.xaml):

```
<UserControl x:Class="Wrox.ProCSharp.WPF.BooksUC"
    xmlns="http://schemas.microsoft.com/winfx/2006/xaml/presentation"
    xmlns:x="http://schemas.microsoft.com/winfx/2006/xaml"
    xmlns:mc="http://schemas.openxmlformats.org/markup-compatibility/2006"
    xmlns:d="http://schemas.microsoft.com/expression/blend/2008"
    xmlns:local="clr-namespace:Wrox.ProCSharp.WPF.Data"
    xmlns:utils="clr-namespace:Wrox.ProCSharp.WPF.Utilities"
    mc:Ignorable="d"
    d:DesignHeight="300" d:DesignWidth="300">
  <UserControl.Resources>
    <utils:StringArrayConverter x:Key="stringArrayConverter" />
    <ObjectDataProvider x:Key="books" ObjectType="local:BookFactory"
                        MethodName="GetBooks" />
  </UserControl.Resources>
  <!-- -->
```

For multiline output, a TextBlock element is declared with the TextWrapping property set to Wrap to make it possible to display multiple authors. In the Binding markup extension, the Path is set to Authors, which is defined as a property returning a string array. The string array is converted from the resource stringArrayConverter as defined by the Converter property. The Convert method of the converter implementation receives the ConverterParameter=', ' as input to separate the authors:

```
<TextBlock Text="{Binding Authors,
           Converter={StaticResource stringArrayConverter},
           ConverterParameter=', '}"
           Grid.Row="3" Grid.Column="1" Margin="5"
               VerticalAlignment="Center" TextWrapping="Wrap" />
```

Figure 36-11 shows the book details, including authors.

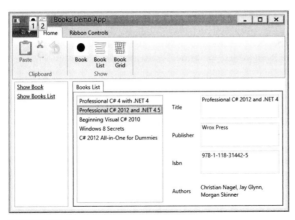

FIGURE 36-11

Adding List Items Dynamically

If list items are added dynamically, the WPF element must be notified of elements added to the list.

In the XAML code of the WPF application, a `Button` element is added inside a `StackPanel`. The `Click` event is assigned to the method `OnAddBook` (XAML file `BooksDemo/BooksUC.xaml`):

```
<StackPanel Orientation="Horizontal" DockPanel.Dock="Bottom"
            HorizontalAlignment="Center">
  <Button Margin="5" Padding="4" Content="Add Book" Click="OnAddBook" />
</StackPanel>
```

In the method `OnAddBook`, a new `Book` object is added to the list. If you test the application with the `BookFactory` as it is implemented now, there's no notification to the WPF elements that a new object has been added to the list (code file `BooksDemo/BooksUC.xaml.cs`):

```
private void OnAddBook(object sender, RoutedEventArgs e)
{
  ((this.FindResource("books") as ObjectDataProvider).Data as IList<Book>).
     Add(new Book("HTML and CSS: Design and Build Websites",
         "Wiley", "978-1118-00818-8"));
}
```

The object that is assigned to the `DataContext` must implement the interface `INotifyCollectionChanged`. This interface defines the `CollectionChanged` event that is used by the WPF application. Instead of implementing this interface on your own with a custom collection class, you can use the generic collection class `ObservableCollection<T>` that is defined with the namespace `System.Collections.ObjectModel` in the assembly `WindowsBase`. Now, as a new item is added to the collection, the new item immediately appears in the `ListBox` (code file `BooksDemo/Data/BookFactory.cs`):

```
public class BookFactory
{
  private ObservableCollection<Book> books = new ObservableCollection<Book>();
  // ...


  public IEnumerable<Book> GetBooks()
  {
    return books;
  }
}
```

Adding Tab Items Dynamically

Adding items dynamically to a list is in principle the same scenario as adding user controls to the tab control dynamically. Until now, the tab items have been added dynamically using the `Add` method of the `Items` property from the `TabControl` class. In the following example, the `TabControl` is directly referenced from code-behind. Using data binding instead, information about the tab item can be added to an `ObservableCollection<T>`.

The code from the BookSample application is now changed to use data binding with the `TabControl`. First, the class `UIControlInfo` is defined. This class contains properties that are used with data binding within the `TabControl`. The `Title` property is used to show heading information within tab items, and the `Content` property is used for the content of the tab items:

```
using System.Windows.Controls;

namespace Wrox.ProCSharp.WPF
{
  public class UIControlInfo
  {
    public string Title { get; set; }
    public UserControl Content { get; set; }
  }
}
```

Now an observable collection is needed to allow the tab control to refresh the information of its tab items. `userControls` is a member variable of the `MainWindow` class. The property `Controls`—used for data binding—returns the collection (code file BooksDemo/MainWindow.xaml.cs):

```
private ObservableCollection<UIControlInfo> userControls =
    new ObservableCollection<UIControlInfo>();
public IEnumerable<UIControlInfo> Controls
{
  get { return userControls; }
}
```

With the XAML code the `TabControl` is changed. The `ItemsSource` property is bound to the `Controls` property. Now, two templates need to be specified. One template, `ItemTemplate`, defines the heading of the item controls. The `DataTemplate` specified with the `ItemTemplate` just uses a `TextBlock` element to display the value from the `Text` property in the heading of the tab item. The other template is `ContentTemplate`. This template specifies using the `ContentPresenter` that binds to the `Content` property of the bound items (XAML file BooksDemo/MainWindow.xaml):

```
<TabControl Margin="5" x:Name="tabControl1" ItemsSource="{Binding Controls}">
  <TabControl.ContentTemplate>
    <DataTemplate>
      <ContentPresenter Content="{Binding Content}" />
    </DataTemplate>
  </TabControl.ContentTemplate>
  <TabControl.ItemTemplate>
    <DataTemplate>
      <StackPanel Margin="0">
        <TextBlock Text="{Binding Title}" Margin="0" />
      </StackPanel>
    </DataTemplate>
  </TabControl.ItemTemplate>
</TabControl>
```

Now the event handlers can be modified to create new `UIControlInfo` objects and add them to the observable collection instead of creating `TabItem` controls. Changing the item and content templates is a much easier way to customize the look, instead of doing this with code-behind.

```
private void OnShowBooksList(object sender, ExecutedRoutedEventArgs e)
{
  var booksUI = new BooksUC();
  userControls.Add(new UIControlInfo
  {
    Title = "Books List",
    Content = booksUI
  });
}
```

Data Template Selector

The previous chapter described how you can customize controls with templates. You also saw how to create a data template that defines a display for specific data types. A *data template selector* can create different data templates dynamically for the same data type. It is implemented in a class that derives from the base class DataTemplateSelector.

The following example implements a data template selector by selecting a different template based on the publisher. These templates are defined within the user control resources. One template can be accessed by the key name wroxTemplate; the other template has the key name dummiesTemplate, and the third one is bookTemplate (XAML file BooksDemo/BooksUC.xaml):

```
<DataTemplate x:Key="wroxTemplate" DataType="{x:Type local:Book}">
  <Border Background="Red" Margin="10" Padding="10">
    <StackPanel>
      <Label Content="{Binding Title}" />
      <Label Content="{Binding Publisher}" />
    </StackPanel>
  </Border>
</DataTemplate>

<DataTemplate x:Key="dummiesTemplate" DataType="{x:Type local:Book}">
  <Border Background="Yellow" Margin="10" Padding="10">
    <StackPanel>
      <Label Content="{Binding Title}" />
      <Label Content="{Binding Publisher}" />
    </StackPanel>
  </Border>
</DataTemplate>

<DataTemplate x:Key="bookTemplate" DataType="{x:Type local:Book}">
  <Border Background="LightBlue" Margin="10" Padding="10">
    <StackPanel>
      <Label Content="{Binding Title}" />
      <Label Content="{Binding Publisher}" />
    </StackPanel>
  </Border>
</DataTemplate>
```

For selecting the template, the class BookDataTemplateSelector overrides the method SelectTemplate from the base class DataTemplateSelector. The implementation selects the template based on the Publisher property from the Book class (code file BooksDemo/Utilities/BookTemplateSelector.cs):

```
using System.Windows;
using System.Windows.Controls;
using Wrox.ProCSharp.WPF.Data;

namespace Wrox.ProCSharp.WPF.Utilities
{
  public class BookTemplateSelector : DataTemplateSelector
  {
    public override DataTemplate SelectTemplate(object item,
```

```
                      DependencyObject container)
        {
          if (item != null && item is Book)
          {
            var book = item as Book;
            switch (book.Publisher)
            {
              case "Wrox Press":
                return (container as FrameworkElement).FindResource(
                    "wroxTemplate") as DataTemplate;
              case "For Dummies":
                return (container as FrameworkElement).FindResource(
                    "dummiesTemplate") as DataTemplate;
              default:
                return (container as FrameworkElement).FindResource(
                    "bookTemplate") as DataTemplate;
            }
          }
          return null;
        }
      }
    }
```

For accessing the class `BookDataTemplateSelector` from XAML code, the class is defined within the `Window` resources (XAML file `BooksDemo/BooksUC.xaml`):

```
        <src:BookDataTemplateSelector x:Key="bookTemplateSelector" />
```

Now the selector class can be assigned to the `ItemTemplateSelector` property of the `ListBox`:

```
    <ListBox DockPanel.Dock="Left" ItemsSource="{Binding}" Margin="5"
            MinWidth="120" IsSynchronizedWithCurrentItem="True"
            ItemTemplateSelector="{StaticResource bookTemplateSelector}">
```

Running the application, you can see different data templates based on the publisher, as shown in Figure 36-12.

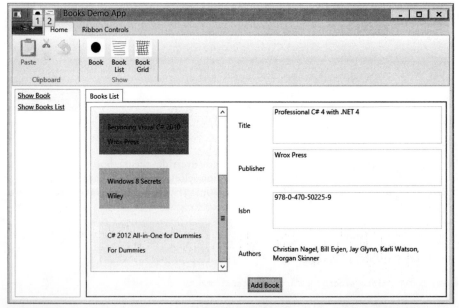

FIGURE 36-12

Binding to XML

WPF data binding has special support for binding to XML data. You can use `XmlDataProvider` as a data source and bind the elements by using XPath expressions. For a hierarchical display, you can use the `TreeView` control and create the view for the items by using the `HierarchicalDataTemplate`.

The following XML file containing `Book` elements is used as a source in the next examples (XML file `XmlBindingDemo/Books.xml`):

```xml
<?xml version="1.0" encoding="utf-8" ?>
<Books>
  <Book isbn="978-1-118-31442-5">
    <Title>Professional C# 2012</Title>
    <Publisher>Wrox Press</Publisher>
    <Author>Christian Nagel</Author>
    <Author>Jay Glynn</Author>
    <Author>Morgan Skinner</Author>
  </Book>
  <Book isbn="978-0-470-50226-6">
    <Title>Beginning Visual C# 2010</Title>
    <Publisher>Wrox Press</Publisher>
    <Author>Karli Watson</Author>
    <Author>Christian Nagel</Author>
    <Author>Jacob Hammer Pedersen</Author>
    <Author>John D. Reid</Author>
    <Author>Morgan Skinner</Author>
  </Book>
</Books>
```

Similarly to defining an object data provider, you can define an XML data provider. Both `ObjectDataProvider` and `XmlDataProvider` are derived from the same base class, `DataSourceProvider`. With the `XmlDataProvider` in the example, the `Source` property is set to reference the XML file `books.xml`. The `XPath` property defines an XPath expression to reference the XML root element `Books`. The `Grid` element references the XML data source with the `DataContext` property. With the data context for the grid, all `Book` elements are required for a list binding, so the XPath expression is set to `Book`. Inside the grid, you can find the `ListBox` element that binds to the default data context and uses the `DataTemplate` to include the title in `TextBlock` elements as items of the `ListBox`. You can also see three `Label` elements with data binding set to XPath expressions to display the title, publisher, and ISBN numbers:

```xml
<Window x:Class="XmlBindingDemo.MainWindow"
        xmlns="http://schemas.microsoft.com/winfx/2006/xaml/presentation"
        xmlns:x="http://schemas.microsoft.com/winfx/2006/xaml"
        Title="Main Window" Height="240" Width="500">
  <Window.Resources>
    <XmlDataProvider x:Key="books" Source="Books.xml" XPath="Books" />
    <DataTemplate x:Key="listTemplate">
      <TextBlock Text="{Binding XPath=Title}" />
    </DataTemplate>

    <Style x:Key="labelStyle" TargetType="{x:Type Label}">
      <Setter Property="Width" Value="190" />
      <Setter Property="Height" Value="40" />
      <Setter Property="Margin" Value="5" />
    </Style>
  </Window.Resources>

  <Grid DataContext="{Binding Source={StaticResource books}, XPath=Book}">
    <Grid.RowDefinitions>
      <RowDefinition />
      <RowDefinition />
      <RowDefinition />
      <RowDefinition />
    </Grid.RowDefinitions>
```

```
<Grid.ColumnDefinitions>
  <ColumnDefinition />
  <ColumnDefinition />
</Grid.ColumnDefinitions>
<ListBox IsSynchronizedWithCurrentItem="True" Margin="5"
    Grid.Column="0" Grid.RowSpan="4" ItemsSource="{Binding}"
    ItemTemplate="{StaticResource listTemplate}" />

  <Label Style="{StaticResource labelStyle}" Content="{Binding XPath=Title}"
      Grid.Row="0" Grid.Column="1" />
  <Label Style="{StaticResource labelStyle}"
      Content="{Binding XPath=Publisher}" Grid.Row="1" Grid.Column="1" />
  <Label Style="{StaticResource labelStyle}"
      Content="{Binding XPath=@isbn}" Grid.Row="2" Grid.Column="1" />
  </Grid>
</Window>
```

Figure 36-13 shows the result of the XML binding.

FIGURE 36-13

> **NOTE** *If XML data should be shown hierarchically, you can use the* `TreeView` *control.*

Binding Validation and Error Handling

Several options are available to validate data from the user before it is used with the .NET objects:

➤ Handling exceptions

➤ Handling data error information errors

➤ Handling notify data error information errors

➤ Defining custom validation rules

Handling Exceptions

The first option demonstrated here reflects the fact that the .NET class throws an exception if an invalid value is set, as shown in the class `SomeData`. The property `Value1` accepts values only larger than or equal to 5 and smaller than 12 (code file `ValidationDemo/SomeData.cs`):

```
public class SomeData
{
  private int value1;
  public int Value1 {
    get { return value1;  }
    set
```

```
    {
      if (value < 5 || value > 12)
      {
        throw new ArgumentException(
            "value must not be less than 5 or greater than 12");
      }
      value1 = value;
    }
  }
}
```

In the constructor of the `MainWindow` class, a new object of the class `SomeData` is initialized and passed to the `DataContext` for data binding (code file `ValidationDemo/MainWindow.xaml.cs`):

```
public partial class MainWindow: Window
{
  private SomeData p1 = new SomeData { Value1 = 11 };

  public MainWindow()
  {
    InitializeComponent();
    this.DataContext = p1;


  }
```

The event handler method `OnShowValue` displays a message box to show the actual value of the `SomeData` instance:

```
    private void OnShowValue(object sender, RoutedEventArgs e)
    {
      MessageBox.Show(p1.Value1.ToString());
    }
  }
```

With simple data binding, the following shows the `Text` property of a `TextBox` bound to the `Value1` property. If you run the application now and try to change the value to an invalid one, you can verify that the value never changed by clicking the Submit button. WPF catches and ignores the exception thrown by the set accessor of the property `Value1` (XAML file `ValidationDemo/MainWindow.xaml`):

```
<Label Margin="5" Grid.Row="0" Grid.Column="0" >Value1:</Label>
<TextBox Margin="5" Grid.Row="0" Grid.Column="1"
    Text="{Binding Path=Value1}" />
```

To display an error as soon as the context of the input field changes, you can set the `ValidatesOnException` property of the `Binding` markup extension to `True`. With an invalid value (as soon as the exception is thrown when the value should be set), the `TextBox` is surrounded by a red line. The application showing the error rectangle is shown in Figure 36-14.

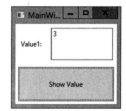

FIGURE 36-14

```
<Label Margin="5" Grid.Row="0" Grid.Column="0" >Value1:</Label>
<TextBox Margin="5" Grid.Row="0" Grid.Column="1"
    Text="{Binding Path=Value1, ValidatesOnExceptions=True}" />
```

To return the error information in a different way to the user, you can assign the attached property `ErrorTemplate` that is defined by the `Validation` class to a template defining the UI for errors. The new template to mark the error is shown as follows with the key `validationTemplate`. The `ControlTemplate` puts a red exclamation point in front of the existing control content:

```
<ControlTemplate x:Key="validationTemplate">
  <DockPanel>
    <TextBlock Foreground="Red" FontSize="40">!</TextBlock>
    <AdornedElementPlaceholder/>
  </DockPanel>
</ControlTemplate>
```

Setting the validationTemplate with the Validation.ErrorTemplate attached property activates the template with the TextBox:

```
<Label Margin="5" Grid.Row="0" Grid.Column="0" >Value1:</Label>
<TextBox Margin="5" Grid.Row="0" Grid.Column="1"
    Text="{Binding Path=Value1, ValidatesOnExceptions=True}"
    Validation.ErrorTemplate="{StaticResource validationTemplate}" />
```

The new look of the application is shown in Figure 36-15.

FIGURE 36-15

> **NOTE** *Another option for a custom error message is to register to the* Error *event of the* Validation *class. In this case, the property* NotifyOnValidationError *must be set to* true.

The error information itself can be accessed from the Errors collection of the Validation class. To display the error information in the ToolTip of the TextBox you can create a property trigger as shown next. The trigger is activated as soon as the HasError property of the Validation class is set to True. The trigger sets the ToolTip property of the TextBox:

```
<Style TargetType="{x:Type TextBox}">
  <Style.Triggers>
    <Trigger Property="Validation.HasError" Value="True">
      <Setter Property="ToolTip"
          Value="{Binding RelativeSource={x:Static RelativeSource.Self},
          Path=(Validation.Errors)[0].ErrorContent}" />
    </Trigger>
  </Style.Triggers>
</Style>
```

Data Error Information

Another way to deal with errors is when the .NET object implements the interface IDataErrorInfo. The class SomeData is now changed to implement this interface, which defines the property Error and an indexer with a string argument. With WPF validation during data binding, the indexer is called and the name of the property to validate is passed as the columnName argument. With the implementation, the value is verified as valid; if it isn't, an error string is passed. Here, the validation is done on the property Value2, which is implemented by using the C# automatic property notation (code file ValiationDemo/SomeData.cs):

```
public class SomeData: IDataErrorInfo
{
  //...

  public int Value2 { get; set; }

  string IDataErrorInfo.Error
  {
    get
    {
      return null;
    }
  }

  string IDataErrorInfo.this[string columnName]
```

```
    {
      get
      {
        if (columnName == "Value2")
        {
          if (this.Value2 < 0 || this.Value2 > 80)
              return "age must not be less than 0 or greater than 80";

        }
        return null;
      }
    }
  }
```

> **NOTE** *With a .NET object, it would not be clear what an indexer would return; for example, what would you expect from an object of type* Person *calling an indexer? That's why it is best to do an explicit implementation of the interface* IDataErrorInfo. *This way, the indexer can be accessed only by using the interface, and the .NET class could use a different implementation for other purposes.*

If you set the property ValidatesOnDataErrors of the Binding class to true, the interface IDataErrorInfo is used during binding. In the following code, when the TextBox is changed the binding mechanism invokes the indexer of the interface and passes Value2 to the columnName variable (XAML file ValidationDemo/MainWindow.xaml):

```
<Label Margin="5" Grid.Row="1" Grid.Column="0" >Value2:</Label>
<TextBox Margin="5" Grid.Row="1" Grid.Column="1"
    Text="{Binding Path=Value2, ValidatesOnDataErrors=True}" />
```

Notify Data Error Info

Besides supporting validation with exceptions and the IDataErrorInfo interface, WPF with .NET 4.5 supports validation with the interface INotifyDataErrorInfo as well. Unlike the interface IDataErrorInfo, whereby the indexer to a property can return one error, with INotifyDataErrorInfo multiple errors can be associated with a single property. These errors can be accessed using the GetErrors method. The HasErrors property returns true if the entity has any error. Another great feature of this interface is the notification of errors with the event ErrorsChanged. This way, errors can be retrieved asynchronously on the client—for example, a Web service can be invoked to verify the input from the user. In this case, the user can continue working with the input form while the result is retrieved, and can be informed asynchronously about any mismatch.

Let's get into an example in which validation is done using INotifyDataErrorInfo. The base class NotifyDataErrorInfoBase is defined, which implements the interface INotifyDataErrorInfo. This class derives from the base class BindableObject to get an implementation for the interface INotifyPropertyChanged that you've seen earlier in this chapter. NotifyDataErrorInfoBase uses a dictionary named errors that contains a list for every property to store error information. The property HasErrors returns true if any property has an error; the method GetErrors returns the error list for a single property; and the event ErrorsChanged is fired every time error information is changed. In addition to the members of the interface INotifyDataErrorInfo, the base class implements the methods SetError, ClearErrors, and ClearAllErrors to make it easier to deal with setting errors (code file ValidationDemo/NotifyDataErrorInfoBase.cs):

```
using System;
using System.Collections;
using System.Collections.Generic;
```

```csharp
using System.ComponentModel;
using System.Runtime.CompilerServices;

namespace ValidationDemo
{
  public abstract class NotifyDataErrorInfoBase : BindableObject,
      INotifyDataErrorInfo
  {
    public void SetError(string errorMessage,
        [CallerMemberName] string propertyName = null)
    {
      List<string> errorList;
      if (errors.TryGetValue(propertyName, out errorList))
      {
        errorList.Add(errorMessage);
      }
      else
      {
        errorList = new List<string> { errorMessage };
        errors.Add(propertyName, errorList);
      }
      HasErrors = true;
      OnErrorsChanged(propertyName);
    }

    public void ClearErrors([CallerMemberName] string propertyName = null)
    {
      if (hasErrors)
      {
        List<string> errorList;
        if (errors.TryGetValue(propertyName, out errorList))
        {
          errors.Remove(propertyName);
        }
        if (errors.Count == 0)
        {
          HasErrors = false;
        }
        OnErrorsChanged(propertyName);
      }
    }

    public void ClearAllErrors()
    {
      if (HasErrors)
      {
        errors.Clear();
        HasErrors = false;
        OnErrorsChanged(null);
      }
    }

    public event EventHandler<DataErrorsChangedEventArgs> ErrorsChanged;

    private Dictionary<string, List<string>> errors =
        new Dictionary<string, List<string>>();
    public IEnumerable GetErrors(string propertyName)
    {
      List<string> errorsForProperty;
      bool err = errors.TryGetValue(propertyName, out errorsForProperty);
      if (!err) return null;
```

```
        return errorsForProperty;
      }

      private bool hasErrors = false;
      public bool HasErrors
      {
        get { return hasErrors; }
        protected set {
          if (SetProperty(ref hasErrors, value))
          {
            OnErrorsChanged(propertyName: null);
          }
        }
      }

      protected void OnErrorsChanged([CallerMemberName] string propertyName = null)
      {
        var errorsChanged = ErrorsChanged;
        if (errorsChanged != null)
        {
          errorsChanged(this, new DataErrorsChangedEventArgs(propertyName));
        }
      }
    }
  }
```

The class `SomeDataWithNotifications` is the data object that is bound to the XAML code. This class derives from the base class `NotifyDataErrorInfoBase` to inherit the implementation of the interface `INotifyDataErrorInfo`. The property `Val1` is validated asynchronously. For the validation, the method `CheckVal1` is invoked after the property is set. This method makes an asynchronous call to the method `ValidationSimulator.Validate`. After invoking the method, the UI thread can return to handle other events; and as soon as the result is returned, the `SetError` method of the base class is invoked if an error was returned. You can easily change the async invocation to call a Web service or perform another async activity (code file `ValidationDemo/SomeDataWithNotifications.cs`):

```
using System.Runtime.CompilerServices;
using System.Threading.Tasks;

namespace ValidationDemo
{
  public class SomeDataWithNotifications : NotifyDataErrorInfoBase
  {
    private int val1;
    public int Val1
    {
      get { return val1; }
      set
      {
        SetProperty(ref val1, value);
        CheckVal1(val1, value);
      }
    }

    private async void CheckVal1(int oldValue, int newValue,
        [CallerMemberName] string propertyName = null)
    {
      ClearErrors(propertyName);

      string result = await ValidationSimulator.Validate(newValue, propertyName);
      if (result != null)
```

```
            {
                SetError(result, propertyName);
            }
        }
    }
}
```

The `Validate` method of the `ValidationSimilator` has a delay of three seconds before checking the value, and returns an error message if the value is larger than 50:

```
public static class ValidationSimulator
{
    public static Task<string> Validate(int val,
        [CallerMemberName] string propertyName = null)
    {
        return Task<string>.Run(async () =>
            {
                await Task.Delay(3000);
                if (val > 50) return "bad value";
                else return null;
            });
    }
}
```

With data binding, just the `ValidatesOnNotifyDataErrors` property must be set to `True` to make use of the async validation of the interface `INotifyDataErrorInfo` (XAML file `ValidationDemo/NotificationWindow.xaml`):

```
<TextBox Grid.Row="0" Grid.Column="1"
    Text="{Binding Val1, ValidatesOnNotifyDataErrors=True}" Margin="8" />
```

Running the application, you can see the text box surrounded by the default red rectangle three seconds after wrong input was entered. Showing error information in a different way can be done in the same way you've seen it before—with error templates and triggers accessing validation errors.

Custom Validation Rules

To get more control of the validation you can implement a custom validation rule. A class implementing a custom validation rule needs to derive from the base class `ValidationRule`. In the previous two examples, validation rules have been used as well. Two classes that derive from the abstract base class `ValidationRule` are `DataErrorValidationRule` and `ExceptionValidationRule`. `DataErrorValidationRule` is activated by setting the property `ValidatesOnDataErrors` and uses the interface `IDataErrorInfo`; `ExceptionValidationRule` deals with exceptions and is activated by setting the property `ValidatesOnException`.

In the following example, a validation rule is implemented to verify a regular expression. The class `RegularExpressionValidationRule` derives from the base class `ValidationRule` and overrides the abstract method `Validate` that is defined by the base class. With the implementation, the `RegEx` class from the namespace `System.Text.RegularExpressions` is used to validate the expression defined by the `Expression` property:

```
public class RegularExpressionValidationRule : ValidationRule
{
    public string Expression { get; set; }
    public string ErrorMessage { get; set; }

    public override ValidationResult Validate(object value,
        CultureInfo cultureInfo)
    {
        ValidationResult result = null;
        if (value != null)
        {
```

```
        var regEx = new Regex(Expression);
        bool isMatch = regEx.IsMatch(value.ToString());
        result = new ValidationResult(isMatch, isMatch ?
            null: ErrorMessage);
    }
    return result;
  }
}
```

> **NOTE** *Regular expressions are explained in Chapter 9, "Strings and Regular Expressions."*

Instead of using the `Binding` markup extension, now the binding is done as a child of the `TextBox.Text` element. The bound object defines an `Email` property that is implemented with the simple property syntax. The `UpdateSourceTrigger` property defines when the source should be updated. Possible options for updating the source are as follows:

➤ When the property value changes, which is every character typed by the user

➤ When the focus is lost

➤ Explicitly

`ValidationRules` is a property of the `Binding` class that contains `ValidationRule` elements. Here, the validation rule used is the custom class `RegularExpressionValidationRule`, where the `Expression` property is set to a regular expression that verifies whether the input is a valid e-mail address; and the `ErrorMessage` property, which outputs the error message if the data entered in the `TextBox` is invalid:

```
<Label Margin="5" Grid.Row="2" Grid.Column="0">Email:</Label>
<TextBox Margin="5" Grid.Row="2" Grid.Column="1">
  <TextBox.Text>
    <Binding Path="Email" UpdateSourceTrigger="LostFocus">
      <Binding.ValidationRules>
        <src:RegularExpressionValidationRule
            Expression="^([\w-\.]+)@((\[[0-9]{1,3}\.[0-9]{1,3}\.
                       [0-9]{1,3}\.)|(([\w-]+\.)+))([a-zA-Z]{2,4}|
                       [0-9]{1,3})(\]?)$"
            ErrorMessage="Email is not valid" />
      </Binding.ValidationRules>
    </Binding>
  </TextBox.Text>
</TextBox>
```

TREEVIEW

The `TreeView` control is used to display hierarchical data. Binding to a `TreeView` is very similar to the binding you've seen with the `ListBox`. What's different is the hierarchical data display—a `HierarchicalDataTemplate` can be used.

The next example uses hierarchical displays and the `DataGrid` control. The `Formula1` sample database is accessed with the ADO.NET Entity Framework. The mapping used is shown in Figure 36-16. The `Race` class contains information about the date of the race and is associated with the `Circuit` class. The `Circuit` class has information about the `Country` and the name of the race circuit. `Race` also has an association with `RaceResult`. A `RaceResult` contains information about the `Racer` and the `Team`.

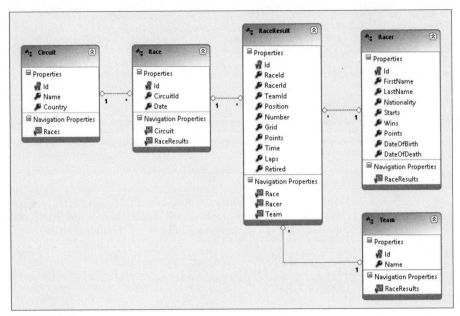

FIGURE 36-16

> **NOTE** *The ADO.NET Entity Framework is covered in Chapter 33, "ADO.NET Entity Framework."*

With the XAML code a `TreeView` is declared. `TreeView` derives from the base class `ItemsControl`, where binding to a list can be done with the `ItemsSource` property. `ItemsSource` is bound to the data context. The data context is assigned in the code-behind, as you will see next. Of course, this could also be done with an `ObjectDataProvider`. To define a custom display for the hierarchical data, `HierarchicalDataTemplate` elements are defined. The data templates here are defined for specific data types with the `DataType` property. The first `HierarchicalDataTemplate` is the template for the `Championship` class and binds the `Year` property of this class to the `Text` property of a `TextBlock`. The `ItemsSource` property defines the binding for the data template itself to specify the next level in the data hierarchy. If the `Races` property of the `Championship` class returns a collection, you bind the `ItemsSource` property directly to `Races`. However, because this property returns a `Lazy<T>` object, binding is done to `Races.Value`. The advantages of the `Lazy<T>` class are discussed later in this chapter.

The second `HierarchicalDataTemplate` element defines the template for the `F1Race` class and binds the `Country` and `Date` properties of this class. With the `Date` property a `StringFormat` is defined with the binding. The next level of the hierarchy is defined binding the `ItemsSource` to `Results.Value`.

The class `F1RaceResult` doesn't have a children collection, so the hierarchy stops here. For this data type, a normal `DataTemplate` is defined to bind the `Position`, `Racer`, and `Car` properties (XAML file `Formula1Demo/TreeUC.xaml`):

```
<UserControl x:Class="Formula1Demo.TreeUC"
             xmlns="http://schemas.microsoft.com/winfx/2006/xaml/presentation"
             xmlns:x="http://schemas.microsoft.com/winfx/2006/xaml"
             xmlns:mc="http://schemas.openxmlformats.org/markup-compatibility/2006"
```

```
                  xmlns:d="http://schemas.microsoft.com/expression/blend/2008"
                  xmlns:local="clr-namespace:Formula1Demo"
                  mc:Ignorable="d"
                  d:DesignHeight="300" d:DesignWidth="300">
  <Grid>
    <TreeView ItemsSource="{Binding}" >
      <TreeView.Resources>
        <HierarchicalDataTemplate DataType="{x:Type local:Championship}"
                                  ItemsSource="{Binding Races.Value}">
          <TextBlock Text="{Binding Year}" />
        </HierarchicalDataTemplate>

        <HierarchicalDataTemplate DataType="{x:Type local:F1Race}"
                                  ItemsSource="{Binding Results.Value}">
          <StackPanel Orientation="Horizontal">
            <TextBlock Text="{Binding Country}" Margin="5,0,5,0" />
            <TextBlock Text="{Binding Date, StringFormat=d}" Margin="5,0,5,0" />
          </StackPanel>
        </HierarchicalDataTemplate>

        <DataTemplate DataType="{x:Type local:F1RaceResult}">
          <StackPanel Orientation="Horizontal">
            <TextBlock Text="{Binding Position}" Margin="5,0,5,0" />
            <TextBlock Text="{Binding Racer}" Margin="5,0,0,0" />
            <TextBlock Text=", " />
            <TextBlock Text="{Binding Car}" />
          </StackPanel>
        </DataTemplate>
      </TreeView.Resources>
    </TreeView>
  </Grid>
</UserControl>
```

Now for the code that fills the hierarchical control. In the code-behind file of the XAML code,
DataContext is assigned to the Years property. The Years property uses a LINQ query, instead of the
ADO.NET Entity Framework data context, to get all the years of the Formula-1 races in the database and
to create a new Championship object for every year. With the instance of the Championship class, the Year
property is set. This class also has a Races property to return the races of the year, but this information is
not yet filled in (code file Formula1Demo/TreeUC.xaml.cs):

> **NOTE** *LINQ is discussed in Chapter 11, "Language Integrated Query," and Chapter 33.*

```
using System.Collections.Generic;
using System.Linq;
using System.Windows.Controls;

namespace Formula1Demo
{
  public partial class TreeUC : UserControl
  {
    private Formula1Entities data = new Formula1Entities();

    public TreeUC()
    {
      InitializeComponent();
```

```
      this.DataContext = Years;
    }

    public IEnumerable<Championship> Years
    {
      get
      {
        F1DataContext.Data = data;
        return data.Races.Select(r => new Championship
        {
          Year = r.Date.Year
        }).Distinct().OrderBy(c => c.Year);
      }
    }
  }
}
```

The Championship class has a simple automatic property for the year. The Races property is of type
Lazy<IEnumerable<F1Race>>. The Lazy<T> class was introduced with .NET 4 for lazy initialization. With
a TreeView control, this class comes in very handy. If the data behind the tree is large and you do not want
to load the full tree in advance, but only when a user makes a selection, lazy loading can be used. With the
constructor of the Lazy<T> class, a delegate Func<IEnumerable<F1Race>> is used. With this delegate,
IEnumerable<F1Race> needs to be returned. The implementation of the Lambda expression, assigned to
the delegate, uses a LINQ query to create a list of F1Race objects that have the Date and Country property
assigned (code file Formula1Demo/Championship.cs):

```
public class Championship
{
  public int Year { get; set; }
  public Lazy<IEnumerable<F1Race>> Races
  {
    get
    {
      return new Lazy<IEnumerable<F1Race>>(() =>
      {
        return from r in F1DataContext.Data.Races
               where r.Date.Year == Year
               orderby r.Date
               select new F1Race
               {
                 Date = r.Date,
                 Country = r.Circuit.Country
               };
      });
    }
  }
}
```

The F1Race class again defines the Results property that uses the Lazy<T> type to return a list of
F1RaceResult objects (code file Formula1Demo/F1Race.cs):

```
public class F1Race
{
  public string Country { get; set; }
  public DateTime Date { get; set; }
  public Lazy<IEnumerable<F1RaceResult>> Results
  {
    get
    {
      return new Lazy<IEnumerable<F1RaceResult>>(() =>
      {
        return from rr in F1DataContext.Data.RaceResults
```

```
                where rr.Race.Date == this.Date
                select new F1RaceResult
                {
                  rr.Position,
                  Racer = rr.Racer.FirstName + " " + rr.Racer.LastName,
                  Car = rr.Team.Name
                };
        });
      }
    }
  }
```

The final class of the hierarchy is `F1RaceResult`, which is a simple data holder for `Position`, `Racer`, and `Car` (code file `Formula1Demo/Championship.cs`):

```
public class F1RaceResult
{
  public int Position { get; set; }
  public string Racer { get; set; }
  public string Car { get; set; }
}
```

When you run the application, you can see at first all the years of the championships in the tree view. Because of binding, the next level is already accessed—every `Championship` object already has the `F1Race` objects associated. The user doesn't need to wait for the first level after the year or an open year with the default appearance of a small triangle. As shown in Figure 36-17, the year 1984 is open. As soon as the user clicks a year to see the second-level binding, the third level is done and the race results are retrieved.

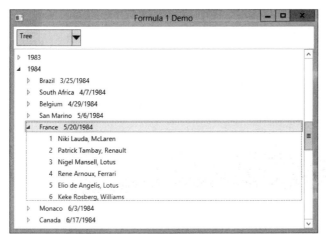

FIGURE 36-17

Of course, you can also customize the `TreeView` control and define different styles for the complete template or the items in the view.

DATAGRID

To display and edit data using rows and columns, the `DataGrid` control can be used. The `DataGrid` control is an `ItemsControl` and defines the `ItemsSource` property that is bound to a collection. The XAML code of this user interface also defines two `RepeatButton` controls that are used for paging functionality. Instead of loading all the race information at once, paging is used so users can step through pages. In a simple scenario, only the `ItemsSource` property of the `DataGrid` needs to be assigned. By default, the `DataGrid` creates columns based on the properties of the bound data (XAML file `Formula1Demo/GridUC.xaml`):

```
<UserControl x:Class="Formula1Demo.GridUC"
    xmlns="http://schemas.microsoft.com/winfx/2006/xaml/presentation"
    xmlns:x="http://schemas.microsoft.com/winfx/2006/xaml"
    xmlns:mc="http://schemas.openxmlformats.org/markup-compatibility/2006"
    xmlns:d="http://schemas.microsoft.com/expression/blend/2008"
    mc:Ignorable="d"
    d:DesignHeight="300" d:DesignWidth="300">
  <Grid>
    <Grid.RowDefinitions>
      <RepeatButton Margin="5" Click="OnPrevious">Previous</RepeatButton>
      <RepeatButton Margin="5" Click="OnNext">Next</RepeatButton>
    </Grid.RowDefinitions>
    <StackPanel Orientation="Horizontal" Grid.Row="0">
      <Button Click="OnPrevious">Previous</Button>
      <Button Click="OnNext">Next</Button>
    </StackPanel>
    <DataGrid Grid.Row="1" ItemsSource="{Binding}" />
  </Grid>
</UserControl>
```

The code-behind uses the same `Formula1` database as the previous `TreeView` example. The `DataContext` of the `UserControl` is set to the `Races` property. This property returns `IEnumerable<object>`. Instead of assigning a strongly typed enumeration, an `object` is used to make it possible to create an anonymous class with the LINQ query. The LINQ query creates the anonymous class with `Year`, `Country`, `Position`, `Racer`, and `Car` properties and uses a compound to access `Races` and `RaceResults`. It also accesses other associations of `Races` to get country, racer, and team information. With the `Skip` and `Take` methods, paging functionality is implemented. The size of a page is fixed to 50 items, and the current page changes with the `OnNext` and `OnPrevious` handlers (code file `Formula1Demo/GridUC.xaml.cs`):

```
using System.Collections.Generic;
using System.Linq;
using System.Windows;
using System.Windows.Controls;

namespace Formula1Demo
{
  public partial class GridUC : UserControl
  {
    private int currentPage = 0;
    private int pageSize = 50;
    private Formula1Entities data = new Formula1Entities();
    public GridUC()
    {
      InitializeComponent();
      this.DataContext = Races;
    }

    public IEnumerable<object> Races
    {
      get
      {
        return (from r in data.Races
                from rr in r.RaceResults
                orderby r.Date ascending
                select new
                {
                  r.Date.Year,
                  r.Circuit.Country,
                  rr.Position,
```

```
                    Racer = rr.Racer.FirstName + " " + rr.Racer.LastName,
                    Car = rr.Team.Name
                }).Skip(currentPage * pageSize).Take(pageSize);
        }
    }

    private void OnPrevious(object sender, RoutedEventArgs e)
    {
        if (currentPage > 0)
        {
            currentPage--;
            this.DataContext = Races;
        }
    }

    private void OnNext(object sender, RoutedEventArgs e)
    {
        currentPage++;
        this.DataContext = Races;
    }
}
```

Figure 36-18 shows the running application with the default grid styles and headers.

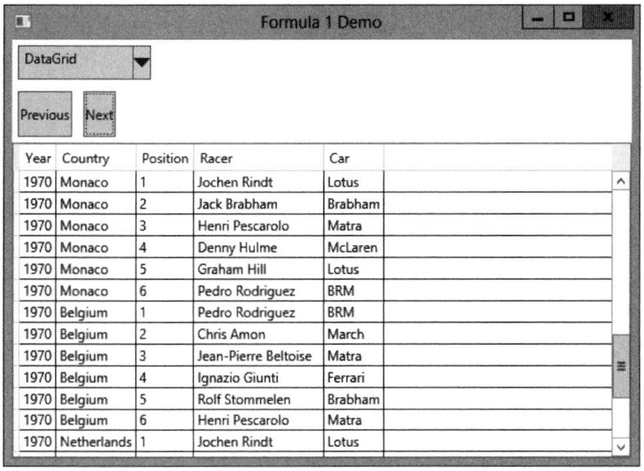

FIGURE 36-18

In the next DataGrid example, the grid is customized with custom columns and grouping.

Custom Columns

Setting the property AutoGenerateColumns of the DataGrid to False doesn't generate default columns. You can create custom columns with the Columns property. You can also specify elements that derive from DataGridColumn. You can use predefined classes, and DataGridTextColumn can be used to read and edit text. DataGridHyperlinkColumn is for displaying hyperlinks. DataGridCheckBoxColumn displays a check box for Boolean data. For a list of items in a column, you can use the DataGridComboBoxColumn. More DataGridColumn types will be available in the future, but if you need a different representation now, you can use the DataGridTemplateColumn to define and bind any elements you want.

The example code uses DataGridTextColumn elements that are bound to the Position and Racer properties. The Header property is set to a string for display. Of course, you can also use a template to define a complete custom header for the column (XAML file Formula1Demo/GridUC.xaml.cs):

```xaml
<DataGrid ItemsSource="{Binding}" AutoGenerateColumns="False">
  <DataGrid.Columns>
    <DataGridTextColumn Binding="{Binding Position, Mode=OneWay}"
                        Header="Position" />
    <DataGridTextColumn Binding="{Binding Racer, Mode=OneWay}"
                        Header="Racer" />
  </DataGrid.Columns>
```

Row Details

When a row is selected, the DataGrid can display additional information for the row. This is done by specifying a RowDetailsTemplate with the DataGrid. A DataTemplate is assigned to the RowDetailsTemplate, which contains several TextBlock elements that display the car and points (XAML file Formula1Demo/GridUC.xaml.cs):

```xaml
<DataGrid.RowDetailsTemplate>
  <DataTemplate>
    <StackPanel Orientation="Horizontal">
      <TextBlock Text="Car:" Margin="5,0,0,0" />
      <TextBlock Text="{Binding Car}" Margin="5,0,0,0" />
      <TextBlock Text="Points:" Margin="5,0,0,0" />
      <TextBlock Text="{Binding Points}" />
    </StackPanel>
  </DataTemplate>
</DataGrid.RowDetailsTemplate>
```

Grouping with the DataGrid

The Formula-1 races have several rows that contain the same information, such as the year and the country. For such data, grouping can be helpful to organize the information for the user.

For grouping, the CollectionViewSource can be used in XAML code. It also supports sorting and filtering. With code-behind you can also use the ListCollectionView class, which is used only by the CollectionViewSource.

CollectionViewSource is defined within a Resources collection. The source of CollectionViewSource is the result from an ObjectDataProvider. The ObjectDataProvider invokes the GetRaces method of the F1Races type. This method has two int parameters that are assigned from the MethodParameters collection. The CollectionViewSource uses two descriptions for grouping—first by the Year property and then by the Country property (XAML file Formula1Demo/GridGroupingUC.xaml):

```xaml
<Grid.Resources>
  <ObjectDataProvider x:Key="races" ObjectType="{x:Type local:F1Races}"
                      MethodName="GetRaces">
    <ObjectDataProvider.MethodParameters>
      <sys:Int32>0</sys:Int32>
      <sys:Int32>20</sys:Int32>
    </ObjectDataProvider.MethodParameters>
  </ObjectDataProvider>
  <CollectionViewSource x:Key="viewSource"
                        Source="{StaticResource races}">
    <CollectionViewSource.GroupDescriptions>
      <PropertyGroupDescription PropertyName="Year" />
      <PropertyGroupDescription PropertyName="Country" />
    </CollectionViewSource.GroupDescriptions>
  </CollectionViewSource>
</Grid.Resources>
```

How the group is displayed is defined with the DataGrid GroupStyle property. With the GroupStyle element you need to customize the ContainerStyle as well as the HeaderTemplate and the complete panel. To dynamically select the GroupStyle and HeaderStyle, you can also write a container style selector and a header template selector. It is very similar in functionality to the data template selector described earlier.

The GroupStyle in the example sets the ContainerStyle property of the GroupStyle. With this style, the GroupItem is customized with a template. The GroupItem appears as the root element of a group when grouping is used. Displayed within the group is the name, using the Name property, and the number of items, using the ItemCount property. The third column of the Grid contains all the normal items using the ItemsPresenter. If the rows are grouped by country, the labels of the Name property would all have a different width, which doesn't look good. Therefore, the SharedSizeGroup property is set with the second column of the grid to ensure all items are the same size. The shared size scope needs to be set for all elements that have the same size. This is done in the DataGrid setting Grid.IsSharedSizeScope="True":

```xml
<DataGrid.GroupStyle>
  <GroupStyle>
    <GroupStyle.ContainerStyle>
      <Style TargetType="{x:Type GroupItem}">
        <Setter Property="Template">
          <Setter.Value>
            <ControlTemplate >
              <StackPanel Orientation="Horizontal" >
                <Grid>
                  <Grid.ColumnDefinitions>
                    <ColumnDefinition SharedSizeGroup="LeftColumn" />
                    <ColumnDefinition />
                    <ColumnDefinition />
                  </Grid.ColumnDefinitions>
                  <Label Grid.Column="0" Background="Yellow"
                      Content="{Binding Name}" />
                  <Label Grid.Column="1" Content="{Binding ItemCount}" />
                  <Grid Grid.Column="2" HorizontalAlignment="Center"
                      VerticalAlignment="Center">
                    <ItemsPresenter/>
                  </Grid>
                </Grid>
              </StackPanel>
            </ControlTemplate>
          </Setter.Value>
        </Setter>
      </Style>
    </GroupStyle.ContainerStyle>
  </GroupStyle>
</DataGrid.GroupStyle>
```

The class F1Races that is used by the ObjectDataProvider uses LINQ to access the Formula1 database and returns a list of anonymous types with Year, Country, Position, Racer, Car, and Points properties. The Skip and Take methods are used to access part of the data (code file Formula1Demo/F1Races.cs):

```csharp
using System.Collections.Generic;
using System.Linq;

namespace Formula1Demo
{
  public class F1Races
  {
    private int lastpageSearched = -1;
    private IEnumerable<object> cache = null;
    private Formula1Entities data = new Formula1Entities();

    public IEnumerable<object> GetRaces(int page, int pageSize)
```

```
        {
          if (lastpageSearched == page)
            return cache;
          lastpageSearched = page;

          var q = (from r in data.Races
                   from rr in r.RaceResults
                   orderby r.Date ascending
                   select new
                   {
                     Year = r.Date.Year,
                     Country = r.Circuit.Country,
                     Position = rr.Position,
                     Racer = rr.Racer.Firstname + " " + rr.Racer.Lastname,
                     Car = rr.Team.Name,
                     Points = rr.Points
                   }).Skip(page * pageSize).Take(pageSize);
          cache = q;
          return cache;
        }
      }
    }
```

Now all that's left is for the user to set the page number and change the parameter of the `ObjectDataProvider`. In the user interface, a `TextBox` and a `Button` are defined (XAML file `Formula1Demo/GridGroupingUC.xaml`):

```xml
<StackPanel Orientation="Horizontal" Grid.Row="0">
  <TextBlock Margin="5" Padding="4" VerticalAlignment="Center">
    Page:
  </TextBlock>
  <TextBox Margin="5" Padding="4" VerticalAlignment="Center"
      x:Name="textPageNumber" Text="0" />
  <Button Click="OnGetPage">Get Page</Button>
</StackPanel>
```

The `OnGetPage` handler of the button in the code-behind accesses the `ObjectDataProvider` and changes the first parameter of the method. It then invokes the `Refresh` method so the `ObjectDataProvider` requests the new page (code file `Formula1Demo/GridGroupingUC.xaml.cs`):

```csharp
private void OnGetPage(object sender, RoutedEventArgs e)
{
  int page = int.Parse(textPageNumber.Text);
  var odp = (sender as FrameworkElement).FindResource("races")
            as ObjectDataProvider;
  odp.MethodParameters[0] = page;
  odp.Refresh();
}
```

Running the application, you can see grouping and row detail information, as shown in Figure 36-19.

Live Shaping

A new feature with WPF 4.5 is *live shaping*. You've seen the collection view source with its support for sorting, filtering, and grouping. However, if the collection changes over time in that sorting, filtering, or grouping returns different results, the `CollectionViewSource` didn't help—until now. For live shaping, a new interface, `ICollectionViewLiveShaping`, is

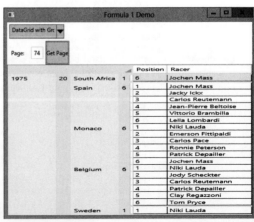

FIGURE 36-19

used. This interface defines the properties CanChangeLiveFiltering, CanChangeLiveGrouping, and CanChangeLiveSorting to check the data source if these live shaping features are available. The properties IsLiveFiltering, IsLiveGrouping, and IsLiveSorting enable turning on the live shaping features—if available. With LiveFilteringProperties, LiveGroupingProperties, and LiveSortingProperties, you can define the properties of the source that should be used for live filtering, grouping, and sorting.

The sample application shows how the results of a Formula 1 race—this time the race from Barcelona in 2012—change lap by lap.

A racer is represented by the Racer class. This type has the simple properties Name, Team, and Number. These properties are implemented using auto properties, as the values of this type don't change when the application is run (code file LiveShaping/Racer.cs):

```
public class Racer
{
  public string Name { get; set; }
  public string Team { get; set; }
  public int Number { get; set; }

  public override string ToString()
  {
    return Name;
  }
}
```

The class Formula1 returns a list of all racers who competed at the Barcelona race 2012 (code file LiveShaping/Formula1.cs):

```
public class Formula1
{
  private List<Racer> racers;
  public IEnumerable<Racer> Racers
  {
    get
    {
      return racers ?? (racers = GetRacers());
    }
  }

  private List<Racer> GetRacers()
  {
    return new List<Racer>()
    {
      new Racer { Name="Sebastian Vettel", Team="Red Bull Racing", Number=1 },
      new Racer { Name="Mark Webber", Team="Red Bull Racing", Number=2 },
      new Racer { Name="Jenson Button", Team="McLaren", Number=3 },
      new Racer { Name="Lewis Hamilton", Team="McLaren", Number=4 },
      new Racer { Name="Fernando Alonso", Team="Ferrari", Number=5 },
      new Racer { Name="Felipe Massa", Team="Ferrari", Number=6 },
      new Racer { Name="Michael Schumacher", Team="Mercedes", Number=7 },
      new Racer { Name="Nico Rosberg", Team="Mercedes", Number=8 },
      new Racer { Name="Kimi Raikkonen", Team="Lotus", Number=9 },
      new Racer { Name="Romain Grosjean", Team="Lotus", Number=10 },
      new Racer { Name="Paul di Resta", Team="Force India", Number=11 },
      new Racer { Name="Nico Hülkenberg", Team="Force India", Number=12 },
      new Racer { Name="Kamui Kobayashi", Team="Sauber", Number=14 },
      new Racer { Name="Sergio Perez", Team="Sauber", Number=15 },
      new Racer { Name="Daniel Riccardio", Team="Toro Rosso", Number=16 },
      new Racer { Name="Jean-Eric Vergne", Team="Toro Rosso", Number=17 },
```

```
            new Racer { Name="Pastor Maldonado", Team="Williams", Number=18 },

        //... more racers in the source code download
        };
    }
}
```

Now it gets more interesting. The `LapRacerInfo` class is the type that is shown in the `DataGrid` control. The class derives from the base class `BindableObject` to get an implementation of `INotifyPropertyChanged` as you've seen earlier. The properties `Lap`, `Position`, and `PositionChange` change over time. `Lap` gives the current lap number, `Position` gives the position in the race in the specified lap, and `PositionChange` provides information about how the position changed from the previous lap. If the position did not change, the state is `None`; if the position is lower than in the previous lap, it is `Up`; if it is higher, then it is `Down`; and if the racer is out of the race, the `PositionChange` is `Out`. This information can be used within the UI for a different representation (code file `LiveShaping/LapRacerInfo.cs`):

```
public enum PositionChange
{
  None,
  Up,
  Down,
  Out
}

public class LapRacerInfo : BindableObject
{
  public Racer Racer { get; set; }
  private int lap;
  public int Lap
  {
    get { return lap; }
    set { SetProperty(ref lap, value); }
  }
  private int position;
  public int Position
  {
    get { return position; }
    set { SetProperty(ref position, value); }
  }
  private PositionChange positionChange;
  public PositionChange PositionChange
  {
    get { return positionChange; }
    set { SetProperty(ref positionChange, value); }
  }
}
```

The class `LapChart` contains all the information about all laps and racers. This class could be changed to access a live Web service to retrieve this information, and then the application could show the current live results from an active race.

The method `SetLapInfoForStart` creates the initial list of `LapRacerInfo` items and fills the position to the grid position. The grid position is the first number of the `List<int>` collection that is added to the positions dictionary. Then, with every invocation of the `NextLap` method, the items inside the `lapInfo` collection change to a new position and set the `PositionChange` state information (code file `LiveShaping/LapChart.cs`):

```
public class LapChart
{
  private Formula1 f1 = new Formula1();
  private List<LapRacerInfo> lapInfo;
  private int currentLap = 0;
```

```
      private const int PostionOut = 999;
      private int maxLaps;
      public LapChart()
      {
        FillPositions();
        SetLapInfoForStart();
      }

      private Dictionary<int, List<int>> positions =
          new Dictionary<int, List<int>>();
      private void FillPositions()
      {
        positions.Add(18, new List<int> { 1, 2, 2, 2, 2, 2, 2, 2, 2, 2, 1, 1, 2, 2,
            2, 2, 2, 2, 2, 2, 2, 2, 2, 3, 3, 1, 1, 1, 1, 1, 1, 1, 1, 1, 1, 1,
            1, 1, 1, 1, 3, 3, 3, 2, 2, 1, 1, 1, 1, 1, 1, 1, 1, 1, 1, 1, 1, 1,
            1, 1, 1, 1, 1 });
        positions.Add(5, new List<int> { 2, 1, 1, 1, 1, 1, 1, 1, 1, 1, 2, 3, 1, 1,
            1, 1, 1, 1, 1, 1, 1, 1, 1, 1, 1, 3, 2, 2, 2, 2, 2, 2, 2, 2, 2, 2,
            2, 2, 2, 1, 1, 1, 3, 3, 3, 2, 2, 2, 2, 2, 2, 2, 2, 2, 2, 2, 2, 2,
            2, 2, 2, 2, 2 });
        positions.Add(10, new List<int> { 3, 5, 5, 5, 5, 5, 5, 5, 5, 4, 4, 9, 7, 6,
            6, 5, 4, 4, 4, 4, 4, 4, 4, 4, 4, 4, 4, 5, 4, 4, 4, 4, 4, 4, 4, 4, 4,
            4, 4, 4, 4, 4, 4, 4, 4, 4, 4, 3, 3, 4, 4, 4, 4, 4, 4, 4, 4, 4, 4,
            4, 4, 4, 4, 4 });
        // more position information with the code download

        maxLaps = positions.Select(p => p.Value.Count).Max() - 1;
      }

      private void SetLapInfoForStart()
      {
        lapInfo = positions.Select(x => new LapRacerInfo
        {
          Racer = f1.Racers.Where(r => r.Number == x.Key).Single(),
          Lap = 0,
          Position = x.Value.First(),
          PositionChange = PositionChange.None
        }).ToList();
      }

      public IEnumerable<LapRacerInfo> GetLapInfo()
      {
        return lapInfo;
      }

      public bool NextLap()
      {
        currentLap++;
        if (currentLap > maxLaps) return false;

        foreach (var info in lapInfo)
        {
          int lastPosition = info.Position;
          var racerInfo = positions.Where(x => x.Key == info.Racer.Number).Single();

          if (racerInfo.Value.Count > currentLap)
          {
            info.Position = racerInfo.Value[currentLap];
          }
          else
          {
            info.Position = lastPosition;
```

```
        }
        info.PositionChange = GetPositionChange(lastPosition, info.Position);

        info.Lap = currentLap;
      }
      return true;
    }

    private PositionChange GetPositionChange(int oldPosition, int newPosition)
    {
      if (oldPosition == PositionOut ||| newPosition == PositionOut)
        return PositionChange.Out;
      else if (oldPosition == newPosition)
        return PositionChange.None;
      else if (oldPosition < newPosition)
        return PositionChange.Down;
      else
        return PositionChange.Up;
    }
  }
```

In the main window, the DataGrid is specified and contains some DataGridTextColumn elements that are bound to properties of the LapRacerInfo class that is returned from the collection shown previously. DataTrigger elements are used to define a different background color for the row depending on whether the racer has a better or worse position compared to the previous lap by using the enumeration value from the PositionChange property (XAML file LiveShaping/MainWindow.xaml):

```xml
<DataGrid IsReadOnly="True" ItemsSource="{Binding}"
    DataContext="{StaticResource cvs}" AutoGenerateColumns="False">
  <DataGrid.CellStyle>
    <Style TargetType="DataGridCell">
      <Style.Triggers>
        <Trigger Property="IsSelected" Value="True">
          <Setter Property="Background" Value="{x:Null}" />
          <Setter Property="BorderBrush" Value="{x:Null}" />
        </Trigger>
      </Style.Triggers>
    </Style>
  </DataGrid.CellStyle>
  <DataGrid.RowStyle>
    <Style TargetType="DataGridRow">
      <Style.Triggers>
        <Trigger Property="IsSelected" Value="True">
          <Setter Property="Background" Value="{x:Null}" />
          <Setter Property="BorderBrush" Value="{x:Null}" />
        </Trigger>
        <DataTrigger Binding="{Binding PositionChange}" Value="None">
          <Setter Property="Background" Value="LightGray" />
        </DataTrigger>
        <DataTrigger Binding="{Binding PositionChange}" Value="Up">
          <Setter Property="Background" Value="LightGreen" />
        </DataTrigger>
        <DataTrigger Binding="{Binding PositionChange}" Value="Down">
          <Setter Property="Background" Value="Yellow" />
        </DataTrigger>
        <DataTrigger Binding="{Binding PositionChange}" Value="Out">
          <Setter Property="Background" Value="Red" />
        </DataTrigger>
      </Style.Triggers>
    </Style>
  </DataGrid.RowStyle>
  <DataGrid.Columns>
```

```
    <DataGridTextColumn Binding="{Binding Position}" />
    <DataGridTextColumn Binding="{Binding Racer.Number}" />
    <DataGridTextColumn Binding="{Binding Racer.Name}" />
    <DataGridTextColumn Binding="{Binding Racer.Team}" />
    <DataGridTextColumn Binding="{Binding Lap}" />
  </DataGrid.Columns>
</DataGrid>
```

> **NOTE** *Data triggers are explained in Chapter 35, "Core WPF."*

The data context specified with the `DataGrid` control is found in the resources of the window with the `CollectionViewSource`. The collection view source is bound to the data context that you'll see soon is specified with the code-behind. The important property set here is `IsLiveSortingRequested`. The value is set to `true` to change the order of the elements in the user interface. The property used for sorting is `Position`. As the position changes, the items are reordered in real time:

```
<Window.Resources>
  <CollectionViewSource x:Key="cvs" Source="{Binding}"
      IsLiveSortingRequested="True">
    <CollectionViewSource.SortDescriptions>
      <scm:SortDescription PropertyName="Position" />
    </CollectionViewSource.SortDescriptions>
  </CollectionViewSource>
</Window.Resources>
```

Now, you just need to get to the code-behind source code where the data context is set and the live values are changed dynamically. In the constructor of the main window, the `DataContext` property is set to the initial collection of type `LapRacerInfo`. Next, a background task invokes the `NextLap` method every three seconds to change the values in the UI with the new positions. The background task makes use of an async Lambda expression. The implementation could be changed to get live data from a Web service (code file `LiveShaping/MainWindow.xaml.cs`).

```
public partial class MainWindow : Window
{
  private LapChart lapChart = new LapChart();
  public MainWindow()
  {
    InitializeComponent();
    this.DataContext = lapChart.GetLapInfo();

    Task.Run(async () =>
      {
        bool raceContinues = true;
        while (raceContinues)
        {
          await Task.Delay(3000);
          raceContinues = lapChart.NextLap();
        }
      });
  }
}
```

Figure 36-20 shows a run of the application while in lap 14, with a leading Fernando Alonso driving a Ferrari.

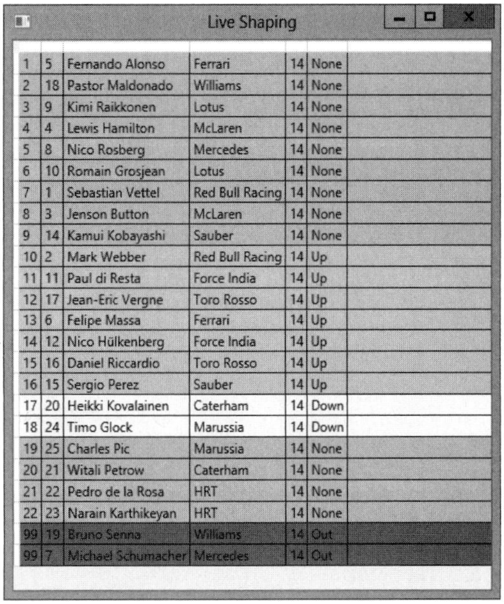

FIGURE 36-20

SUMMARY

This chapter covered some features of WPF that are extremely important for business applications. For clear and easy interaction with data, WPF data binding provides a leap forward. You can bind any property of a .NET class to a property of a WPF element. The binding mode defines the direction of the binding. You can bind .NET objects and lists, and define a data template to create a default look for a .NET class.

Command binding makes it possible to map handler code to menus and toolbars. You've also seen how easy it is to copy and paste with WPF because a command handler for this technology is already included in the `TextBox` control. You've also seen many more WPF features, such as using a `DataGrid`, the `CollectionViewSource` for sorting and grouping, and all this with live shaping as well.

The next chapter goes into another facet of WPF: working with documents.

37

Creating Documents with WPF

WHAT'S IN THIS CHAPTER?

- ➤ Creating flow documents
- ➤ Creating fixed documents
- ➤ Creating XPS documents
- ➤ Printing documents

WROX.COM CODE DOWNLOADS FOR THIS CHAPTER

The wrox.com code downloads for this chapter are found at `http://www.wrox.com/remtitle .cgi?isbn=1118314425` on the Download Code tab. The code for this chapter is divided into the following major examples:

- ➤ Show Fonts
- ➤ Text Effects
- ➤ Table
- ➤ Flow Documents
- ➤ Create XPS
- ➤ Printing

INTRODUCTION

Creating documents is a large part of WPF. The namespace `System.Windows.Documents` supports creating both flow documents and fixed documents. This namespace contains elements with which you can have a rich Word-like experience with flow documents, and create WYSIWYG fixed documents.

Flow documents are geared toward screen reading; the content of the document is arranged based on the size of the window and the flow of the document changes if the window is resized. *Fixed documents* are mainly used for printing and page-oriented content and the content is always arranged in the same way.

This chapter teaches you how to create and print flow documents and fixed documents, and covers the namespaces `System.Windows.Documents`, `System.Windows.Xps`, and `System.IO.Packaging`.

TEXT ELEMENTS

To build the content of documents, you need document elements. The base class of these elements is `TextElement`. This class defines common properties for font settings, foreground and background, and text effects. `TextElement` is the base class for the classes `Block` and `Inline`, whose functionality is explored in the following sections.

Fonts

An important aspect of text is how it looks, and thus the importance of the font. With the `TextElement`, the font can be specified with the properties `FontWeight`, `FontStyle`, `FontStretch`, `FontSize`, and `FontFamily`:

➤ `FontWeight` — Predefined values are specified by the `FontWeights` class, which offers values such as `UltraLight`, `Light`, `Medium`, `Normal`, `Bold`, `UltraBold`, and `Heavy`.

➤ `FontStyle` — Values are defined by the `FontStyles` class, which offers `Normal`, `Italic`, and `Oblique`.

➤ `FontStretch` — Enables you to specify the degrees to stretch the font compared to the normal aspect ratio. `FrontStretch` defines predefined stretches that range from 50% (`UltraCondensed`) to 200% (`UltraExpanded`). Predefined values in between the range are `ExtraCondensed` (62.5%), `Condensed` (75%), `SemiCondensed` (87.5%), `Normal` (100%), `SemiExpanded` (112.5%), `Expanded` (125%), and `ExtraExpanded` (150%).

➤ `FontSize` — This is of type `double` and enables you to specify the size of the font in device-independent units, inches, centimeters, and points.

➤ `FontFamily` — Use this to define the name of the preferred font-family, e.g., Arial or Times New Roman. With this property you can specify a list of font family names so if one font is not available, the next one in the list is used. (If neither the selected font nor the alternate font are available, a flow document falls back to the default `MessageFontFamily`.) You can also reference a font family from a resource or use a URI to reference a font from a server. With fixed documents there's no fallback on a font not available because the font is available with the document.

To give you a feel for the look of different fonts, the following sample WPF application includes a `ListBox`. The `ListBox` defines an `ItemTemplate` for every item in the list. This template uses four `TextBlock` elements whereby the `FontFamily` is bound to the `Source` property of a `FontFamily` object. With different `TextBlock` elements, `FontWeight` and `FontStyle` are set (XAML file ShowFonts/ShowFontsWindow .xaml):

```
<ListBox ItemsSource="{Binding}">
  <ListBox.ItemTemplate>
    <DataTemplate>
      <StackPanel Orientation="Horizontal" >
        <TextBlock Margin="3, 0, 3, 0" FontFamily="{Binding Path=Source}"
          FontSize="18" Text="{Binding Path=Source}" />
        <TextBlock Margin="3, 0, 3, 0" FontFamily="{Binding Path=Source}"
          FontSize="18" FontStyle="Italic" Text="Italic" />
        <TextBlock Margin="3, 0, 3, 0" FontFamily="{Binding Path=Source}"
          FontSize="18" FontWeight="UltraBold" Text="UltraBold" />
        <TextBlock Margin="3, 0, 3, 0" FontFamily="{Binding Path=Source}"
          FontSize="18" FontWeight="UltraLight" Text="UltraLight" />
      </StackPanel>
    </DataTemplate>
  </ListBox.ItemTemplate>
</ListBox>
```

In the code-behind, the data context is set to the result of the `SystemFontFamilies` property of the `System.Windows.Media.Font` class. This returns all the available fonts (code file ShowFonts/ ShowFontsWindow.xaml.cs):

```
public partial class ShowFontsWindow : Window
{
  public ShowFontsWindow()
  {
    InitializeComponent();

    this.DataContext = Fonts.SystemFontFamilies;
  }
}
```

Running the application, you get a large list of system font families with italic, bold, ultrabold, and ultralight characteristics, as shown in Figure 37-1.

TextEffect

Now let's have a look into `TextEffect`, as it is also common to all document elements. `TextEffect` is defined in the namespace `System.Windows.Media` and derives from the base class `Animatable`, which enables the animation of text.

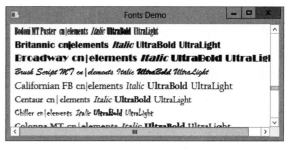

FIGURE 37-1

`TextEffect` enables you to animate a clipping region, the foreground brush, and a transformation. With the properties `PositionStart` and `PositionCount` you specify the position in the text to which the animation applies.

For applying the text effects, the `TextEffects` property of a `Run` element is set. The `TextEffect` element specified within the property defines a foreground and a transformation. For the foreground, a `SolidColorBrush` with the name `brush1` is used that is animated with a `ColorAnimation` element. The transformation makes use of a `ScaleTransformation` with the name `scale1`, which is animated from two `DoubleAnimation` elements (XAML file `TextEffectsDemo/MainWindow.xaml`):

```
<TextBlock>
  <TextBlock.Triggers>
    <EventTrigger RoutedEvent="TextBlock.Loaded">
      <BeginStoryboard>
        <Storyboard>
          <ColorAnimation AutoReverse="True" RepeatBehavior="Forever"
              From="Blue" To="Red" Duration="0:0:16"
              Storyboard.TargetName="brush1"
              Storyboard.TargetProperty="Color" />
          <DoubleAnimation AutoReverse="True"
              RepeatBehavior="Forever"
              From="0.2" To="12" Duration="0:0:16"
              Storyboard.TargetName="scale1"
              Storyboard.TargetProperty="ScaleX" />
          <DoubleAnimation AutoReverse="True"
              RepeatBehavior="Forever"
              From="0.2" To="12" Duration="0:0:16"
              Storyboard.TargetName="scale1"
              Storyboard.TargetProperty="ScaleY" />
        </Storyboard>
      </BeginStoryboard>
    </EventTrigger>
  </TextBlock.Triggers>
  <Run FontFamily="Segoe UI">
      cn|elements
```

```
          <Run.TextEffects>
            <TextEffect PositionStart="0" PositionCount="30">
              <TextEffect.Foreground>
                <SolidColorBrush x:Name="brush1" Color="Blue" />
              </TextEffect.Foreground>
              <TextEffect.Transform>
                <ScaleTransform x:Name="scale1" ScaleX="3" ScaleY="3" />
              </TextEffect.Transform>
            </TextEffect>
          </Run.TextEffects>
        </Run>
      </TextBlock>
```

Running the application, you can see the changes in size and color as shown in Figures 37-2 and 37-3.

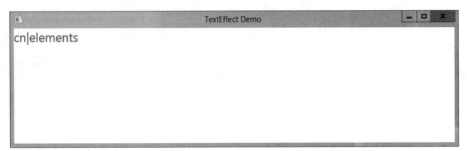

FIGURE 37-2

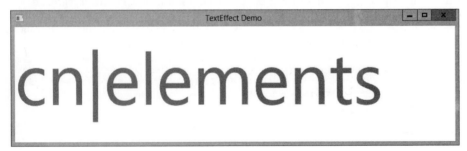

FIGURE 37-3

Inline

The base class for all inline flow content elements is Inline. You can use Inline elements within a paragraph of a flow document. Because within a paragraph one Inline element can follow another, the Inline class provides the PreviousInline and NextInline properties to navigate from one element to another. You can also get a collection of all peer inlines with SiblingInlines.

The Run element that was used earlier to write some text is an Inline element for formatted or unformatted text, but there are many more. A new line after a Run element can be done with the LineBreak element.

The Span element derives from the Inline class and enables the grouping of Inline elements. Only Inline elements are allowed within the content of Span. The self-explanatory Bold, Hyperlink, Italic, and Underline classes all derive from Span and thus have the same functionality to enable Inline elements as its content, but to act on these elements differently. The following XAML code demonstrates using

Bold, Italic, Underline, and LineBreak, as shown in Figure 37-4 (XAML file FlowDocumentsDemo/
FlowDocument1.xaml):

```
<Paragraph FontWeight="Normal">
  <Span>
    <Span>Normal</Span>
    <Bold>Bold</Bold>
    <Italic>Italic</Italic>
    <LineBreak />
    <Underline>Underline</Underline>
  </Span>
</Paragraph>
```

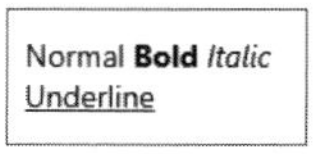

AnchoredBlock is an abstract class that derives from Inline and is used to anchor
Block elements to flow content. Figure and Floater are concrete classes that derive
from AnchoredBlock. Because these two inline elements become interesting in relation to
blocks, these elements are discussed later in this chapter.

Normal **Bold** *Italic*
Underline

FIGURE 37-4

Another Inline element that maps UI elements that have been used in previous chapters is InlineUIContainer. InlineUIContainer enables adding all UIElement objects (for example, a Button) to the document. The following code segment adds an InlineUIContainer with ComboBox, RadioButton, and TextBox elements to the document (the result is shown in Figure 37-5) (XAML file FlowDocumentsDemo/FlowDocument2.xaml):

> **NOTE** *Of course, you can also style the UI elements as shown in Chapter 35, "Core WPF."*

```
<Paragraph TextAlignment="Center">
  <Span FontSize="36">
    <Italic>cn|elements</Italic>
  </Span>
  <LineBreak />
  <LineBreak />
  <InlineUIContainer>
    <Grid>
      <Grid.RowDefinitions>
        <RowDefinition />
        <RowDefinition />
      </Grid.RowDefinitions>
      <Grid.ColumnDefinitions>
        <ColumnDefinition />
        <ColumnDefinition />
      </Grid.ColumnDefinitions>
      <ComboBox Width="40"  Margin="3"  Grid.Row="0">
        <ComboBoxItem>Filet Mignon</ComboBoxItem>
        <ComboBoxItem>Rib Eye</ComboBoxItem>
        <ComboBoxItem>Sirloin</ComboBoxItem>
      </ComboBox>
      <StackPanel Grid.Row="0" Grid.RowSpan="2" Grid.Column="1">
        <RadioButton>Raw</RadioButton>
        <RadioButton>Medium</RadioButton>
        <RadioButton>Well done</RadioButton>
      </StackPanel>
      <TextBox Grid.Row="1" Grid.Column="0" Width="140"></TextBox>
    </Grid>
  </InlineUIContainer>
</Paragraph>
```

Block

Block is an abstract base class for block-level elements. Blocks enable grouping elements contained to specific views. Common to all blocks are the properties PreviousBlock, NextBlock, and SiblingBlocks that enable you to navigate from block to block. Setting BreakPageBefore and BreakColumnBefore page and column breaks are done before the block starts. A Block also defines a border with the BorderBrush and BorderThickness properties.

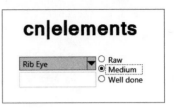

FIGURE 37-5

Classes that derive from Block are Paragraph, Section, List, Table, and BlockUIContainer. BlockUIContainer is similar to InlineUIContainer in that you can add elements that derive from UIElement.

Paragraph and Section are simple blocks; Paragraph contains inline elements, and Section is used to group other Block elements. With the Paragraph block you can determine whether a page or column break is allowed within the paragraph or between paragraphs. KeepTogether can be used to disallow breaking within the paragraph; KeepWithNext tries to keep one paragraph and the next together. If a paragraph is broken by a page or column break, MinWidowLines defines the minimum number of lines that are placed after the break; MinOrphanLines defines the minimum number of lines before the break.

The Paragraph block also enables decorating the text within the paragraph with TextDecoration elements. Predefined text decorations are defined by TextDecorations: Baseline, Overline, Strikethrough, and Underline.

The following XAML code shows multiple Paragraph elements. One Paragraph element with a title follows another with the content belonging to this title. These two paragraphs are connected with the attribute KeepWithNext. It's also assured that the paragraph with the content is not broken by setting KeepTogether to True (XAML file FlowDocumentsDemo/ParagraphDemo.xaml):

```xml
<FlowDocument xmlns="http://schemas.microsoft.com/winfx/2006/xaml/presentation"
              ColumnWidth="300" FontSize="16" FontFamily="Georgia">
  <Paragraph FontSize="36">
    <Run>Lyrics</Run>
  </Paragraph>
  <Paragraph TextIndent="10" FontSize="24" KeepWithNext="True">
    <Bold>
      <Run>Mary had a little lamb</Run>
    </Bold>
  </Paragraph>
  <Paragraph KeepTogether="True">
    <Run>Mary had a little lamb,</Run>
    <LineBreak />
    <Run>little lamb, little lamb,</Run>
    <LineBreak />
    <Run>Mary had a little lamb,</Run>
    <LineBreak />
    <Run>whose fleece was white as snow.</Run>
    <LineBreak />
    <Run>And everywhere that Mary went,</Run>
    <LineBreak />
    <Run>Mary went, Mary went,</Run>
    <LineBreak />
    <Run>and everywhere that Mary went,</Run>
    <LineBreak />
    <Run>the lamb was sure to go.</Run>
  </Paragraph>
  <Paragraph TextIndent="10" FontSize="24" KeepWithNext="True">
    <Bold>
      <Run>Humpty Dumpty</Run>
```

```
      </Bold>
    </Paragraph>
    <Paragraph KeepTogether="True">
      <Run>Humpty dumpty sat on a wall</Run>
      <LineBreak />
      <Run>Humpty dumpty had a great fall</Run>
      <LineBreak />
      <Run>All the King's horses</Run>
      <LineBreak />
      <Run>And all the King's men</Run>
      <LineBreak />
      <Run>Couldn't put Humpty together again</Run>
    </Paragraph>
  </FlowDocument>
```

The result is shown in Figure 37-6.

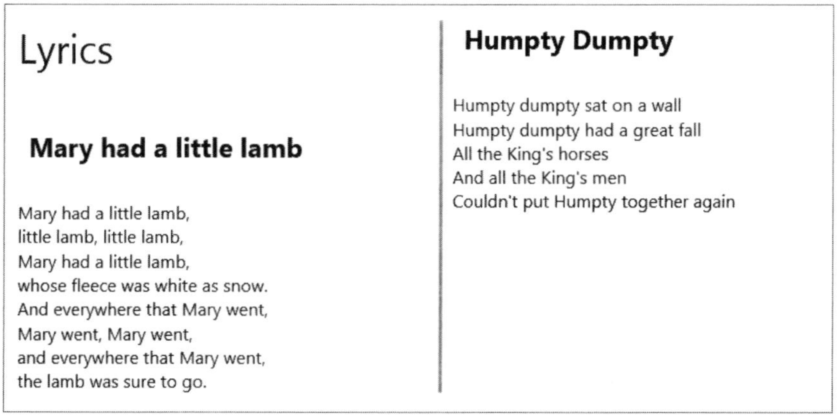

FIGURE 37-6

Lists

The `List` class is used to create textual unordered or ordered lists. `List` defines the bullet style of its items by setting the `MarkerStyle` property. `MarkerStyle` is of type `TextMarkerStyle` and can be a number (`Decimal`), a letter (`LowerLatin` and `UpperLatin`), a roman numeral (`LowerRoman` and `UpperRoman`), or a graphic (`Disc`, `Circle`, `Square`, `Box`). `List` can only contain `ListItem` elements, which in turn can only contain `Block` elements.

Defining the following list with XAML results in the output shown in Figure 37-7 (XAML file `FlowDocumentsDemo/ListDemo.xaml`):

```
    <List MarkerStyle="Square">
      <ListItem>
        <Paragraph>Monday</Paragraph>
      </ListItem>
      <ListItem>
        <Paragraph>Tuesday</Paragraph>
      </ListItem>
      <ListItem>
        <Paragraph>Wednesday</Paragraph>
      </ListItem>
    </List>
```

Tables

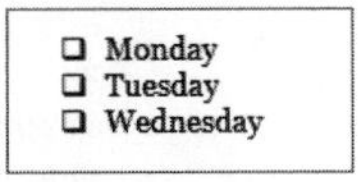

The Table class is very similar to the Grid class presented in Chapter 35 to define rows and columns. The following example demonstrates creating a FlowDocument with a Table. To create tables you can add TableColumn objects to the Columns property. With TableColumn you can specify the width and background.

FIGURE 37-7

The Table also contains TableRowGroup objects. The TableRowGroup has a Rows property whereby TableRow objects can be added. The TableRow class defines a Cells property that enables adding TableCell objects. TableCell objects can contain any Block element. Here, a Paragraph is used that contains the Inline element Run (code file TableDemo/MainWindow.xaml.cs):

```csharp
var doc = new FlowDocument();
var t1 = new Table();
t1.Columns.Add(new TableColumn
{ Width = new GridLength(50, GridUnitType.Pixel) });
t1.Columns.Add(new TableColumn
{ Width = new GridLength(1, GridUnitType.Auto) });
t1.Columns.Add(new TableColumn
{ Width = new GridLength(1, GridUnitType.Auto) });

var titleRow = new TableRow { Background = Brushes.LightBlue };
var titleCell = new TableCell
{ ColumnSpan = 3, TextAlignment = TextAlignment.Center };
titleCell.Blocks.Add(
    new Paragraph(new Run("Formula 1 Championship 2011")
    { FontSize=24, FontWeight = FontWeights.Bold }));
titleRow.Cells.Add(titleCell);

var headerRow = new TableRow
{ Background = Brushes.LightGoldenrodYellow };
headerRow.Cells.Add(new TableCell(new Paragraph(new Run("Pos"))
{ FontSize = 14, FontWeight=FontWeights.Bold}));
headerRow.Cells.Add(new TableCell(new Paragraph(new Run("Name"))
{ FontSize = 14, FontWeight = FontWeights.Bold }));
headerRow.Cells.Add(new TableCell(new Paragraph(new Run("Points"))
{ FontSize = 14, FontWeight = FontWeights.Bold }));

var rowGroup = new TableRowGroup();
rowGroup.Rows.Add(titleRow);
rowGroup.Rows.Add(headerRow);

string[][] results = new string[][]
{
  new string[] { "1.", "Sebastian Vettel", "392" },
  new string[] { "2.", "Jenson Button", "270" },
  new string[] { "3.", "Mark Webber", "258" },
  new string[] { "4.", "Fernando Alonso", "257" },
  new string[] { "5.", "Lewis Hamilton", "227"}
};

List<TableRow> rows = results.Select(row =>
  {
    var tr = new TableRow();
    foreach (var cell in row)
    {
      tr.Cells.Add(new TableCell(new Paragraph(new Run(cell))));
    }
    return tr;
  }).ToList();
```

```
rows.ForEach(r => rowGroup.Rows.Add(r));

t1.RowGroups.Add(rowGroup);
doc.Blocks.Add(t1);

reader.Document = doc;
```

Running the application, you can see the nicely formatted table as shown in Figure 37-8.

Anchor to Blocks

Now that you've learned about the Inline and Block elements, you can combine the two by using the Inline elements of type AnchoredBlock. AnchoredBlock is an abstract base class with two concrete implementations, Figure and Floater.

The Floater displays its content parallel to the main content with the properties HorizontalAlignment and Width.

Starting with the earlier example, a new paragraph is added that contains a Floater. This Floater is aligned to the left and has a width of 120. As shown in Figure 37-9, the next paragraph flows around it (XAML file FlowDocumentsDemo/ParagraphKeepTogether.xaml):

Formula 1 Championship 2011		
Pos	**Name**	**Points**
1.	Sebastian Vettel	392
2.	Jenson Button	270
3.	Mark Webber	258
4.	Fernando Alonso	257
5.	Lewis Hamilton	227

FIGURE 37-8

Mary had a little lamb

Sarah Josepha Hale   Mary had a little lamb, little lamb, little lamb,
Mary had a little lamb,
whose fleece was white as snow.
And everywhere that Mary went,
Mary went, Mary went,
and everywhere that Mary went,
the lamb was sure to go.

FIGURE 37-9

```xml
<Paragraph TextIndent="10" FontSize="24" KeepWithNext="True">
  <Bold>
    <Run>Mary had a little lamb</Run>
  </Bold>
</Paragraph>
<Paragraph>
  <Floater HorizontalAlignment="Left" Width="120">
    <Paragraph Background="LightGray">
      <Run>Sarah Josepha Hale</Run>
    </Paragraph>
  </Floater>
</Paragraph>
<Paragraph KeepTogether="True">
  <Run>Mary had a little lamb</Run>
  <LineBreak />
  <!-- ... -->
</Paragraph>
```

A Figure aligns horizontally and vertically and can be anchored to the page, content, a column, or a paragraph. The Figure in the following code is anchored to the page center but with a horizontal and vertical offset. The WrapDirection is set so that both left and right columns wrap around the figure. Figure 37-10 shows the result of the wrap (XAML file FlowDocumentsDemo/FigureAlignment.xaml):

```xml
<Paragraph>
  <Figure HorizontalAnchor="PageCenter" HorizontalOffset="20"
    VerticalAnchor="PageCenter" VerticalOffset="20" WrapDirection="Both" >
    <Paragraph Background="LightGray" FontSize="24">
      <Run>Lyrics Samples</Run>
    </Paragraph>
  </Figure>
</Paragraph>
```

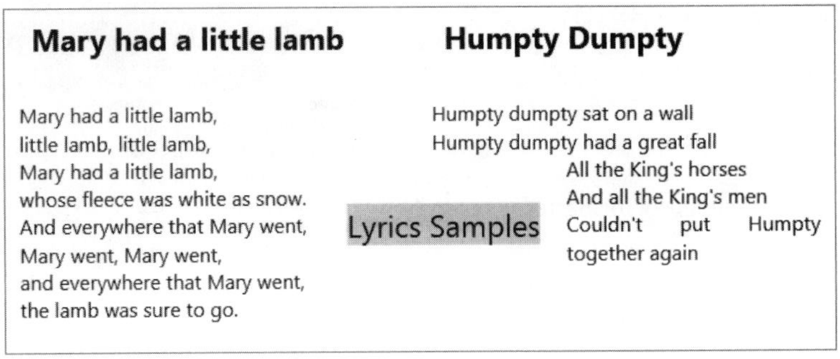

FIGURE 37-10

`Floater` and `Figure` are both used to add content that is not in the main flow. Although these two features seem similar, the characteristics of these elements are quite different. The following table explains the differences between `Floater` and `Figure`:

CHARACTERISTIC	FLOATER	FIGURE
Position	A floater cannot be positioned. It is rendered where space is available.	A figure can be positioned with horizontal and vertical anchors. It can be docked relative to the page, content, column, or paragraph.
Width	A floater can be placed only within one column. If the width is set larger than the column's size, it is ignored.	A figure can be sized across multiple columns. The width of a figure can be set to 0.5 pages or two columns.
Pagination	If a floater is larger than a column's height, the floater breaks and paginates to the next column or page.	If a figure is larger than a column's height, only the part of the figure that fits in the column is rendered; the other content is lost.

FLOW DOCUMENTS

With all the `Inline` and `Block` elements, now you know what should be put into a flow document. The class `FlowDocument` can contain `Block` elements, and the `Block` elements can contain `Block` or `Inline` elements, depending on the type of the `Block`.

A major functionality of the `FlowDocument` class is that it is used to break up the flow into multiple pages. This is done via the `IDocumentPaginatorSource` interface, which is implemented by `FlowDocument`.

Other options with a `FlowDocument` are to set up the default font and foreground and background brushes, and to configure the page and column sizes.

The following XAML code for the `FlowDocument` defines a default font and font size, a column width, and a ruler between columns:

```
<FlowDocument xmlns="http://schemas.microsoft.com/winfx/2006/xaml/presentation"
    ColumnWidth="300" FontSize="16" FontFamily="Georgia"
    ColumnRuleWidth="3" ColumnRuleBrush="Violet">
```

Now you just need a way to view the documents. The following list describes several viewers:

➤ RichTextBox — A simple viewer that also allows editing (as long as the IsReadOnly property is not set to true). The RichTextBox doesn't display the document with multiple columns but instead in scroll mode. This is similar to the Web layout in Microsoft Word. The scrollbar can be enabled by setting the HorizontalScrollbarVisibility to ScrollbarVisibility.Auto.

➤ FlowDocumentScrollViewer — A reader that is meant only to read but not edit documents. This reader enables zooming into the document. There's also a toolbar with a slider for zooming that can be enabled with the property IsToolbarEnabled. Settings such as CanIncreaseZoom, CanDecreaseZoom, MinZoom, and MaxZoom enable setting the zoom features.

➤ FlowDocumentPageViewer — A viewer that paginates the document. With this viewer you not only have a toolbar to zoom into the document, you can also switch from page to page.

➤ FlowDocumentReader — A viewer that combines the functionality of FlowDocumentScrollViewer and FlowDocumentPageViewer. This viewer supports different viewing modes that can be set from the toolbar or with the property ViewingMode that is of type FlowDocumentReaderViewingMode. This enumeration has the possible values Page, TwoPage, and Scroll. The viewing modes can also be disabled according to your needs.

The sample application to demonstrate flow documents defines several readers such that one reader can be chosen dynamically. Within the Grid element you can find the FlowDocumentReader, RichTextBox, FlowDocumentScrollViewer, and FlowDocumentPageViewer. With all the readers the Visibility property is set to Collapsed, so on startup none of the readers appear. The ComboBox that is the first child element within the grid enables the user to select the active reader. The ItemsSource property of the ComboBox is bound to the Readers property to display the list of readers. On selection of a reader, the method OnReaderSelectionChanged is invoked (XAML file FlowDocumentsDemo/MainWindow.xaml):

```xaml
<Grid x:Name="grid1">
  <Grid.RowDefinitions>
    <RowDefinition Height="Auto" />
    <RowDefinition Height="*" />
  </Grid.RowDefinitions>
  <Grid.ColumnDefinitions>
    <ColumnDefinition Width="*" />
    <ColumnDefinition Width="Auto" />
  </Grid.ColumnDefinitions>
  <ComboBox ItemsSource="{Binding Readers}" Grid.Row="0" Grid.Column="0"
      Margin="4" SelectionChanged="OnReaderSelectionChanged"
    SelectedIndex="0">
    <ComboBox.ItemTemplate>
      <DataTemplate>
        <StackPanel>
          <TextBlock Text="{Binding Name}" />
        </StackPanel>
      </DataTemplate>
    </ComboBox.ItemTemplate>
  </ComboBox>
  <Button Grid.Column="1" Margin="4" Padding="3" Click="OnOpenDocument">
    Open Document</Button>
  <FlowDocumentReader ViewingMode="TwoPage" Grid.Row="1"
      Visibility="Collapsed" Grid.ColumnSpan="2" />
  <RichTextBox IsDocumentEnabled="True" HorizontalScrollBarVisibility="Auto"
      VerticalScrollBarVisibility="Auto" Visibility="Collapsed"
      Grid.Row="1" Grid.ColumnSpan="2" />
  <FlowDocumentScrollViewer Visibility="Collapsed" Grid.Row="1"
      Grid.ColumnSpan="2" />
  <FlowDocumentPageViewer Visibility="Collapsed" Grid.Row="1"
      Grid.ColumnSpan="2" />
</Grid>
```

The Readers property of the MainWindow class invokes the GetReaders method to return to return the readers to the ComboBox data binding. The GetReaders method returns the list assigned to the variable documentReaders. In case documentReaders was not yet assigned, the LogicalTreeHelper class is used to get all the flow document readers within the grid `grid1`. As there is not a base class for a flow document reader nor an interface implemented by all readers, the `LogialTreeHelper` looks for all elements of type `FrameworkElement` that have a property `Document`. The `Document` property is common to all flow document readers. With every reader a new anonymous object is created with the properties `Name` and `Instance`. The `Name` property is used to appear in the `ComboBox` to enable the user to select the active reader, and the `Instance` property holds a reference to the reader to show the reader if it should be active (code file `FlowDocumentsDemo/MainWindow.xaml.cs`):

```
public IEnumerable<object> Readers
{
  get
  {
    return GetReaders();
  }
}

private List<object> documentReaders = null;
private IEnumerable<object> GetReaders()
{
  return documentReaders ?? (documentReaders =
    LogicalTreeHelper.GetChildren(grid1).OfType<FrameworkElement>()
      .Where(el => el.GetType().GetProperties()
          .Where(pi => pi.Name == "Document").Count() > 0)
      .Select(el => new
      {
        Name = el.GetType().Name,
        Instance = el
      }).Cast<object>().ToList());
}
```

When the user selects a flow document reader, the method `OnReaderSelectionChanged` is invoked. The XAML code that references this method was shown earlier. Within this method the previously selected flow document reader is made invisible by setting it to collapsed, and the variable `activeDocumentReader` is set to the selected reader:

```
private void OnReaderSelectionChanged(object sender,
                                      SelectionChangedEventArgs e)
{
  dynamic item = (sender as ComboBox).SelectedItem;

  if (activedocumentReader != null)
  {
    activedocumentReader.Visibility = Visibility.Collapsed;
  }
  activedocumentReader = item.Instance;
}

private dynamic activedocumentReader = null;
```

> **NOTE** *The sample code makes use of the* dynamic *keyword—the variable* activeDocumentReader *is declared as* dynamic *type. The* dynamic *keyword is used because the* SelectedItem *from the* ComboBox *either returns a* FlowDocumentReader, *a* FlowDocumentScrollViewer, *a* FlowDocumentPageViewer, *or a* RichTextBox. *All these types are flow document readers that offer a* Document *property of type* FlowDocument. *However, there's no common base class or interface defining this property. The* dynamic *keyword allows accessing these different types from the same variable and using the* Document *property. The* dynamic *keyword is explained in detail in Chapter 12, "Dynamic Language Extensions."*

When the user clicks the button to open a document, the method `OnOpenDocument` is invoked. With this method the `XamlReader` class is used to load the selected XAML file. If the reader returns a `FlowDocument` (which is the case when the root element of the XAML is the `FlowDocument` element), the `Document` property of the `activeDocumentReader` is assigned, and the `Visibility` is set to visible:

```
private void OnOpenDocument(object sender, RoutedEventArgs e)
{
  try
  {
    var dlg = new OpenFileDialog();
    dlg.DefaultExt = "*.xaml";
    dlg.InitialDirectory = Environment.CurrentDirectory;
    if (dlg.ShowDialog() == true)
    {
      using (FileStream xamlFile = File.OpenRead(dlg.FileName))
      {
        var doc = XamlReader.Load(xamlFile) as FlowDocument;
        if (doc != null)
        {
          activedocumentReader.Document = doc;
          activedocumentReader.Visibility = Visibility.Visible;
        }
      }
    }
  }
  catch (XamlParseException ex)
  {
    MessageBox.Show(string.Format("Check content for a Flow document, {0}",
        ex.Message));
  }
}
```

The running application is shown in Figure 37-11. This figure shows a flow document with the `FlowDocumentReader` in `TwoPage` mode.

FIGURE 37-11

FIXED DOCUMENTS

Fixed documents always define the same look, the same pagination, and use the same fonts—no matter where the document is copied or used. WPF defines the class `FixedDocument` to create fixed documents, and the class `DocumentViewer` to view fixed documents.

This section uses a sample application to create a fixed document programmatically by requesting user input for a menu plan. The data for the menu plan is the content of the fixed document. Figure 37-12 shows the main user interface of this application, where the user can select a day with the `DatePicker` class, enter menus for a week in a `DataGrid`, and click the Create Doc button to create a new `FixedDocument`. This application uses `Page` objects that are navigated within a `NavigationWindow`. Clicking the Create Doc button navigates to a new page that contains the fixed document.

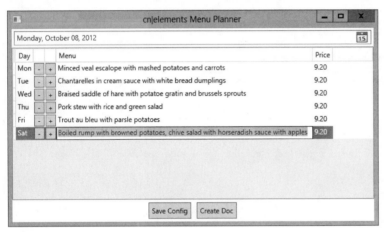

FIGURE 37-12

The event handler for the Create Doc button, `OnCreateDoc`, navigates to a new page. To do this, the handler instantiates the new page, `DocumentPage`. This page includes a handler, `NavigationService_LoadCompleted`, that is assigned to the `LoadCompleted` event of the `NavigationService`. Within this handler the new page can access the content that is passed to the page. Then the navigation is done by invoking the `Navigate` method to page2. The new page receives the object `menus` that contains all the menu information needed to build the fixed page. `menus` is a readonly variable of type `ObservableCollection<MenuEntry>` (code file `CreateXps/MenuPlannerPage.xaml.cs`):

```
private void OnCreateDoc(object sender, RoutedEventArgs e)
{
  if (menus.Count == 0)
  {
    MessageBox.Show("Select a date first", "Menu Planner",
        MessageBoxButton.OK);
    return;
  }
  var page2 = new DocumentPage();
  NavigationService.LoadCompleted +=
      page2.NavigationService_LoadCompleted;
  NavigationService.Navigate(page2, menus);
}
```

Within the `DocumentPage`, a `DocumentViewer` is used to provide read access to the fixed document. The fixed document is created in the method `NavigationService_LoadCompleted`. With the event handler, the data that is passed from the first page is received with the `ExtraData` property of `NavigationEventArgs`.

The received `ObservableCollection<MenuEntry>` is assigned to a `menus` variable that is used to build the fixed page (code file `CreateXps/DocumentPage.xaml.cs`):

```
internal void NavigationService_LoadCompleted(object sender,
    NavigationEventArgs e)
{
  menus = e.ExtraData as ObservableCollection<MenuEntry>;
  fixedDocument = new FixedDocument();
  var pageContent1 = new PageContent();
  fixedDocument.Pages.Add(pageContent1);
  var page1 = new FixedPage();
  pageContent1.Child = page1;
  page1.Children.Add(GetHeaderContent());
  page1.Children.Add(GetLogoContent());
  page1.Children.Add(GetDateContent());
  page1.Children.Add(GetMenuContent());
  viewer.Document = fixedDocument;
  NavigationService.LoadCompleted -= NavigationService_LoadCompleted;
}
```

Fixed documents are created with the `FixedDocument` class. The `FixedDocument` element only contains `PageContent` elements that are accessible via the `Pages` property. The `PageContent` elements must be added to the document in the order in which they should appear on the page. `PageContent` defines the content of a single page.

`PageContent` has a `Child` property such that a `FixedPage` can be associated with it. To the `FixedPage` you can add elements of type `UIElement` to the `Children` collection. This is where you can add all the elements you've learned about in the last two chapters, including a `TextBlock` element that itself can contain `Inline` and `Block` elements.

In the sample code, the children to the `FixedPage` are created with helper methods `GetHeaderContent`, `GetLogoContent`, `GetDateContent`, and `GetMenuContent`.

The method `GetHeaderContent` creates a `TextBlock` that is returned. The `TextBlock` has the `Inline` element `Bold` added, which in turn has the `Run` element added. The `Run` element then contains the header text for the document. With `FixedPage.SetLeft` and `FixedPage.SetTop` the position of the `TextBox` within the fixed page is defined:

```
private static UIElement GetHeaderContent()
{
  var text1 = new TextBlock
  {
    FontFamily = new FontFamily("Segoe UI"),
    FontSize = 34,
    HorizontalAlignment = HorizontalAlignment.Center
  };
  text1.Inlines.Add(new Bold(new Run("cn|elements")));
  FixedPage.SetLeft(text1, 170);
  FixedPage.SetTop(text1, 40);
  return text1;
}
```

The method `GetLogoContent` adds a logo in the form of an `Ellipse` with a `RadialGradientBrush` to the fixed document:

```
private static UIElement GetLogoContent()
{
  var ellipse = new Ellipse
  {
    Width = 90,
    Height = 40,
    Fill = new RadialGradientBrush(Colors.Yellow, Colors.DarkRed)
  };
  FixedPage.SetLeft(ellipse, 500);
  FixedPage.SetTop(ellipse, 50);
  return ellipse;
}
```

The method `GetDateContent` accesses the `menus` collection to add a date range to the document:

```
private UIElement GetDateContent()
{
  Contract.Requires(menus != null);
  Contract.Requires(menus.Count > 0);

  string dateString = String.Format("{0:d} to {1:d}",
      menus[0].Day, menus[menus.Count - 1].Day);
  var text1 = new TextBlock
  {
    FontSize = 24,
    HorizontalAlignment = HorizontalAlignment.Center
  };
  text1.Inlines.Add(new Bold(new Run(dateString)));
  FixedPage.SetLeft(text1, 130);
  FixedPage.SetTop(text1, 90);
  return text1;
}
```

Finally, the method `GetMenuContent` creates and returns a `Grid` control. This grid contains columns and rows that contain the date, menu, and price information:

```
private UIElement GetMenuContent()
{
  var grid1 = new Grid { ShowGridLines = true };

  grid1.ColumnDefinitions.Add(new ColumnDefinition
  { Width= new GridLength(50)});
  grid1.ColumnDefinitions.Add(new ColumnDefinition
  { Width = new GridLength(300)});
  grid1.ColumnDefinitions.Add(new ColumnDefinition
  { Width = new GridLength(70) });
  for (int i = 0; i < menus.Count; i++)
  {
    grid1.RowDefinitions.Add(new RowDefinition
    { Height = new GridLength(40) });
    var t1 = new TextBlock(new Run(String.Format(
                            "{0:ddd}", menus[i].Day)));
    var t2 = new TextBlock(new Run(menus[i].Menu));
    var t3 = new TextBlock(new Run(menus[i].Price.ToString()));
    var textBlocks = new TextBlock[] { t1, t2, t3 };

    for (int column = 0; column < textBlocks.Length; column++)
```

```
        {
          textBlocks[column].VerticalAlignment = VerticalAlignment.Center;
          textBlocks[column].Margin = new Thickness(5, 2, 5, 2);
          Grid.SetColumn(textBlocks[column], column);
          Grid.SetRow(textBlocks[column], i);
          grid1.Children.Add(textBlocks[column]);
        }
      }
      FixedPage.SetLeft(grid1, 100);
      FixedPage.SetTop(grid1, 140);
      return grid1;
    }
```

Run the application to see the created fixed document shown in Figure 37-13.

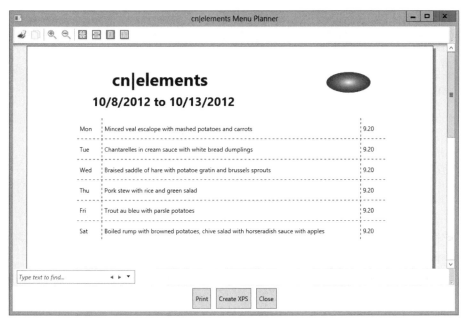

FIGURE 37-13

XPS DOCUMENTS

With Microsoft Word you can save a document as a PDF or a XPS file. XPS is the *XML Paper Specification*, a subset of WPF. Windows includes an XPS reader.

.NET includes classes and interfaces to read and write XPS documents with the namespaces `System .Windows.Xps`, `System.Windows.Xps.Packaging`, and `System.IO.Packaging`.

XPS is packaged in the zip file format, so you can easily analyze an XPS document by renaming a file with an `.xps` extension to `.zip` and opening the archive.

An XPS file requires a specific structure in the zipped document that is defined by the XML Paper Specifications (which you can download from http://www.microsoft.com/whdc/xps/xpsspec.mspx). The structure is based on the Open Packaging Convention (OPC) that Word documents (OOXML or Office Open XML) are based on as well. Within such a file you can find different folders for metadata, resources (such as fonts and pictures), and the document itself. Within the document folder of an XPS document is the XAML code representing the XPS subset of XAML.

To create an XPS document, you use the `XpsDocument` class from the namespace `System.Windows.Xps.Packaging`. To use this class, you need to reference the assembly `ReachFramework` as well. With this class you can add a thumbnail (`AddThumbnail`) and fixed document sequences (`AddFixedDocumentSequence`) to the document, as well as digitally sign the document. A fixed document sequence is written by using the interface `IXpsFixedDocumentSequenceWriter`, which in turn uses an `IXpsFixedDocumentWriter` to write the document within the sequence.

If a `FixedDocument` already exists, there's an easier way to write the XPS document. Instead of adding every resource and every document page, you can use the class `XpsDocumentWriter` from the namespace `System.Windows.Xps`. For this class the assembly `System.Printing` must be referenced.

With the following code snippet you can see the handler to create the XPS document. First, a filename for the menu plan is created that uses a week number in addition to the name `menuplan`. The week number is calculated with the help of the `GregorianCalendar` class. Then the `SaveFileDialog` is opened to enable the user overwrite the created filename and select the directory where the file should be stored. The `SaveFileDialog` class is defined in the namespace `Microsoft.Win32` and wraps the native file dialog. Then a new `XpsDocument` is created whose filename is passed to the constructor. Recall that the XPS file uses a .zip format to compress the content. With the `CompressionOption` you can specify whether the compression should be optimized for time or space.

Next, an `XpsDocumentWriter` is created with the help of the static method `XpsDocument.CreateXpsDocumentWriter`. The `Write` method of the `XpsDocumentWriter` is overloaded to accept different content or content parts to write the document. Examples of acceptable options with the `Write` method are `FixedDocumentSequence`, `FixedDocument`, `FixedPage`, `string`, and a `DocumentPaginator`. In the sample code, only the `fixedDocument` that was created earlier is passed:

```
private void OnCreateXPS(object sender, RoutedEventArgs e)
{
  var c = new GregorianCalendar();
  int weekNumber = c.GetWeekOfYear(menus[0].Day,
      CalendarWeekRule.FirstFourDayWeek, DayOfWeek.Monday);
  string fileName = String.Format("menuplan{0}", weekNumber);
  var dlg = new SaveFileDialog
  {
    FileName = fileName,
    DefaultExt = "xps",
    Filter = "XPS Documents|*.xps|All Files|*.*",
    AddExtension = true
  };
  if (dlg.ShowDialog() == true)
  {
    var doc = new XpsDocument(dlg.FileName, FileAccess.Write,
                             CompressionOption.Fast);
    XpsDocumentWriter writer = XpsDocument.CreateXpsDocumentWriter(doc);
    writer.Write(fixedDocument);
    doc.Close();
  }
}
```

By running the application to store the XPS document, you can view the document with an XPS viewer, as shown in Figure 37-14.

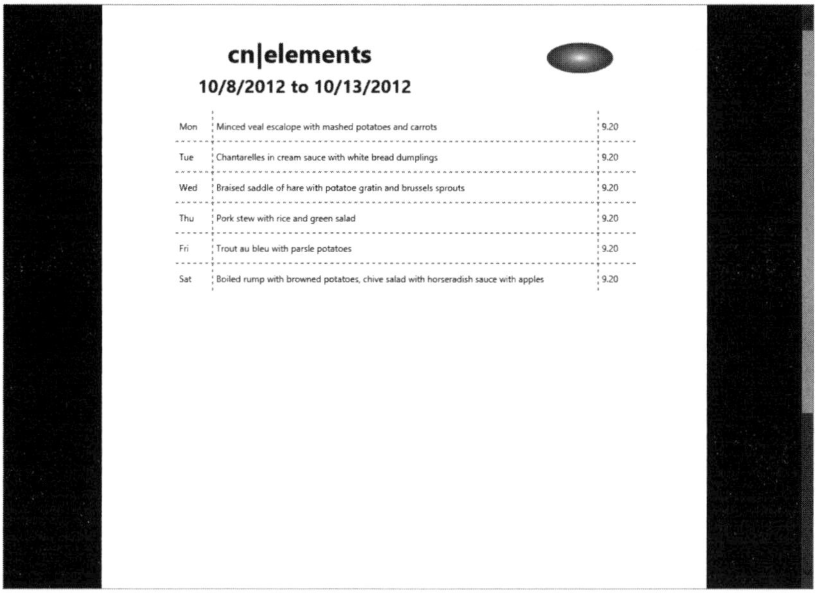

cn|elements

10/8/2012 to 10/13/2012

Mon	Minced veal escalope with mashed potatoes and carrots	9.20
Tue	Chantarelles in cream sauce with white bread dumplings	9.20
Wed	Braised saddle of hare with potatoe gratin and brussels sprouts	9.20
Thu	Pork stew with rice and green salad	9.20
Fri	Trout au bleu with parsle potatoes	9.20
Sat	Boiled rump with browned potatoes, chive salad with horseradish sauce with apples	9.20

FIGURE 37-14

To one overload of the `Write` method of the `XpsDocumentWriter` you can also pass a `Visual`, which is the base class of `UIElement`, and thus you can pass any `UIElement` to the writer to create an XPS document easily. This functionality is used in the following printing example.

PRINTING

The simplest way to print a `FixedDocument` that is shown onscreen with the `DocumentViewer` is to invoke the `Print` method of the `DocumentViewer` with which the document is associated. This is all that needs to be done with the menu planner application in an `OnPrint` handler. The `Print` method of the `DocumentViewer` opens the `PrintDialog` and sends the associated `FixedDocument` to the selected printer (code file `CreateXPS/DocumentPage.xaml.cs`):

```
private void OnPrint(object sender, RoutedEventArgs e)
{
  viewer.Print();
}
```

Printing with the PrintDialog

If you want more control over the printing process, the `PrintDialog` can be instantiated, and the document printed with the `PrintDocument` method. The `PrintDocument` method requires a `DocumentPaginator` with the first argument. The `FixedDocument` returns a `DocumentPaginator` object with the `DocumentPaginator` property. The second argument defines the string that appears with the current printer and in the printer dialogs for the print job:

```
var dlg = new PrintDialog();
if (dlg.ShowDialog() == true)
{
  dlg.PrintDocument(fixedDocument.DocumentPaginator, "Menu Plan");
}
```

Printing Visuals

It's also simple to create `UIElement` objects. The following XAML code defines an `Ellipse`, a `Rectangle`, and a `Button` that is visually represented with two `Ellipse` elements. With the `Button`, there's a `Click` handler `OnPrint` that starts the print job of the visual elements (XAML file `PrintingDemo/MainWindow .xaml`):

```
<Canvas x:Name="canvas1">
  <Ellipse Canvas.Left="10" Canvas.Top="20" Width="180" Height="60"
      Stroke="Red" StrokeThickness="3" >
    <Ellipse.Fill>
      <RadialGradientBrush>
        <GradientStop Offset="0" Color="LightBlue" />
        <GradientStop Offset="1" Color="DarkBlue" />
      </RadialGradientBrush>
    </Ellipse.Fill>
  </Ellipse>
  <Rectangle Width="180" Height="90" Canvas.Left="50" Canvas.Top="50">
    <Rectangle.LayoutTransform>
      <RotateTransform Angle="30" />
    </Rectangle.LayoutTransform>
    <Rectangle.Fill>
      <LinearGradientBrush>
        <GradientStop Offset="0" Color="Aquamarine" />
        <GradientStop Offset="1" Color="ForestGreen" />
      </LinearGradientBrush>
    </Rectangle.Fill>
    <Rectangle.Stroke>
      <LinearGradientBrush>
        <GradientStop Offset="0" Color="LawnGreen" />
        <GradientStop Offset="1" Color="SeaGreen" />
      </LinearGradientBrush>
    </Rectangle.Stroke>
  </Rectangle>
  <Button Canvas.Left="90" Canvas.Top="190" Content="Print" Click="OnPrint">
    <Button.Template>
      <ControlTemplate TargetType="Button">
        <Grid>
          <Grid.RowDefinitions>
            <RowDefinition />
            <RowDefinition />
          </Grid.RowDefinitions>
          <Ellipse Grid.Row="0" Grid.RowSpan="2" Width="60"
              Height="40" Fill="Yellow" />
          <Ellipse Grid.Row="0" Width="52" Height="20"
              HorizontalAlignment="Center">
            <Ellipse.Fill>
              <LinearGradientBrush StartPoint="0.5,0" EndPoint="0.5,1">
                <GradientStop Color="White" Offset="0" />
                <GradientStop Color="Transparent" Offset="0.9" />
              </LinearGradientBrush>
            </Ellipse.Fill>
          </Ellipse>
          <ContentPresenter Grid.Row="0" Grid.RowSpan="2"
              HorizontalAlignment="Center"
              VerticalAlignment="Center" />
        </Grid>
      </ControlTemplate>
    </Button.Template>
  </Button>
</Canvas>
```

In the `OnPrint` handler, the print job can be started by invoking the `PrintVisual` method of the `PrintDialog`. `PrintVisual` accepts any object that derives from the base class `Visual` (code file `PrintingDemo/MainWindow.xaml.cs`):

```
private void OnPrint(object sender, RoutedEventArgs e)
{
    var dlg = new PrintDialog();
    if (dlg.ShowDialog() == true)
    {
        dlg.PrintVisual(canvas1, "Print Demo");

    }
}
```

To programmatically print without user intervention, the `PrintDialog` classes from the namespace `System.Printing` can be used to create a print job and adjust print settings. The class `LocalPrintServer` provides information about print queues and returns the default `PrintQueue` with the `DefaultPrintQueue` property. You can configure the print job with a `PrintTicket`. `PrintQueue.DefaultPrintTicket` returns a default `PrintTicket` that is associated with the queue. The `PrintQueue` method `GetPrintCapabilities` returns the capabilities of a printer, and depending on those you can configure the `PrintTicket` as shown in the following code segment. After configuration of the print ticket is complete, the static method `PrintQueue.CreateXpsDocumentWriter` returns an `XpsDocumentWriter` object. The `XpsDocumentWriter` class was used previously to create an XPS document. You can also use it to start a print job. The `Write` method of the `XpsDocumentWriter` accepts not only a `Visual` or `FixedDocument` as the first argument but also a `PrintTicket` as the second argument. If a `PrintTicket` is passed with the second argument, the target of the writer is the printer associated with the ticket and thus the writer sends the print job to the printer:

```
var printServer = new LocalPrintServer();
PrintQueue queue = printServer.DefaultPrintQueue;
PrintTicket ticket = queue.DefaultPrintTicket;
PrintCapabilities capabilities =
    queue.GetPrintCapabilities(ticket);
if (capabilities.DuplexingCapability.Contains(
    Duplexing.TwoSidedLongEdge))
  ticket.Duplexing = Duplexing.TwoSidedLongEdge;
if (capabilities.InputBinCapability.Contains(InputBin.AutoSelect))
  ticket.InputBin = InputBin.AutoSelect;
if (capabilities.MaxCopyCount > 3)
  ticket.CopyCount = 3;
if (capabilities.PageOrientationCapability.Contains(
    PageOrientation.Landscape))
  ticket.PageOrientation = PageOrientation.Landscape;
if (capabilities.PagesPerSheetCapability.Contains(2))
  ticket.PagesPerSheet = 2;
if (capabilities.StaplingCapability.Contains(Stapling.StapleBottomLeft))
  ticket.Stapling = Stapling.StapleBottomLeft;
XpsDocumentWriter writer = PrintQueue.CreateXpsDocumentWriter(queue);
writer.Write(canvas1, ticket);
```

SUMMARY

In this chapter you learned how WPF capabilities can be used with documents, how to create flow documents that adjust automatically depending on the screen sizes, and fixed documents that always look the same. You've also seen how to print documents and how to send visual elements to the printer.

The next chapter continues with XAML, showing how it can be used with Windows 8 applications.

38

Windows 8 Apps

WHAT'S IN THIS CHAPTER?

➤ How Windows 8 apps differ from Windows desktop apps

➤ Defining app bars

➤ Navigating between pages

➤ Reacting to layout changes

➤ Using storage and pickers

➤ Using sharing contracts

➤ Creating tiles

WROX.COM CODE DOWNLOADS FOR THIS CHAPTER

The wrox.com code downloads for this chapter are found at http://www.wrox.com/remtitle .cgi?isbn=1118314425 on the Download Code tab. The code for this chapter just contains one big sample that shows the various aspects of this chapter:

➤ Menu Card

OVERVIEW

If you read Chapter 31, then you are now familiar with the foundations of Windows 8 apps and how the Windows Runtime relates to .NET. Knowing the basics covered in Chapter 31 will enable you to begin writing Windows 8 apps. This chapter covers the design principles and special XAML features that are not available with WPF, and demonstrates several aspects of working with Windows 8 apps, such as reacting to layout changes, reading and writing files with the Windows Runtime storage API and file pickers, and using contracts to communicate with other applications.

In addition to Chapter 31, you should also be familiar with the basic information about XAML already covered in Chapters 29, 35, and 36. Only those features specific to Windows 8 apps are covered here.

WINDOWS 8 MODERN UI DESIGN

One of the first things you notice about Windows 8 apps is that they look different to desktop applications. There's a big emphasis on the UI design, based on the belief that users should feel comfortable with and enjoy working with the application. This focus on design in Windows 8 apps is derived from some principles that are not new. One is Swiss graphic design, developed in the 1950s, which emphasizes cleanliness (lack of clutter) and readability. For example, signs in airports and train stations are based on this concept, enabling users to process information as quickly as possible.

Another foundation of the modern UI design is the famous Bauhaus school in Germany, which was extremely influential between 1919 and 1933. The objective of this school was to unify arts, crafts, and technology, with design based on functionality, not decoration—no unnecessary squiggles if it doesn't serve the functionality.

The third foundation is motion as defined by cinematography. Animation is an important tool for bringing your application to life. Windows 8 frameworks provide a rich set of animation features to provide users with a realistic experience that both conveys information and makes it enjoyable to use your application.

Content, Not Chrome

The guiding principle of designing Windows 8 applications is focusing on the content, which means presenting users with only the information they need at any given moment, and not distracting them with anything they don't need—that is, the chrome (menus, toolbar, and so on. When users open Internet Explorer, the content gets the complete view. Menus are hidden unless they are explicitly enabled by the user.

For example, web pages occupy the entire screen, enabling users to quickly zero in on the content they need, without the clutter of various menus and toolbars. Figure 38-1 shows the main view of a weather application. Note how the large graphics make it easy to quickly focus on the desired information.

FIGURE 38-1

Of course, users can also change settings and use commands from within the application. To modify settings, the new *Charms bar* comes into play. Users can activate the Charm bars by swiping from the right edge of the screen, invoking the controls needed to change application settings.

Commands, which are placed in an *app bar* at the top or the bottom edge of the screen, are similarly activated by the user, who can open them by swiping from the bottom edge or top edge of the screen. Figure 38-2 shows the Windows Store command bar. In this case, the commands are located on top.

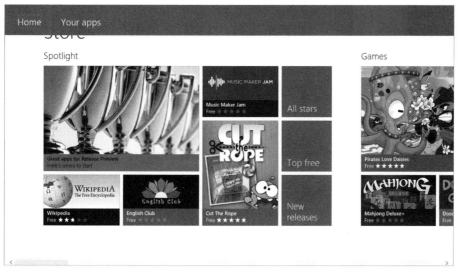

FIGURE 38-2

The Wikipedia application, shown in Figure 38-3, has the commands on bottom (as most applications do).

FIGURE 38-3

Fast and Fluid

Fast and fluid is another important principle with Windows 8 apps. When using the mouse with a traditional user interface, users are accustomed to a slight delay. Similarly, when clicking a button or moving some objects around the screen, we are used to some delay. Such a delay is unacceptable with touch. If something doesn't happen immediately, or if the UI blocks, the user experience is very poor.

The new Windows Runtime specifies that if a method might take longer than 50 ms, it is only available asynchronously. With the .NET framework many API calls are both available synchronously and asynchronously. Because synchronous programming has been easier to create compared to async, typically the synchronous version of the API was used. Using the new async features from C# 5, with the `async` and `await` keywords, the async API calls are very easy to use. Chapter 13 has all the details about these new keywords. Besides using async APIs, you should also create async APIs with your application for tasks that can take a long time.

Async programming is just one part of fast and fluid. As previously mentioned, animations are also strongly supported in Windows 8, as they tie the user experience together in a natural, realistic way, but without causing distractions. The built-in controls already have animation, enabling you to program smooth transitions, rather than jarring changes. Using these built-in controls, it's not necessary to define custom animations, although you can also do that if desired.

Readability

Readability is critical to any application, and Windows 8 provides a comprehensive set of style application guidelines. These guidelines cover all typographic aspects of the user's experience, including readable fonts, color, and letter spacing. For example, the Segoe UI font should be used for UI elements (buttons, date pickers), Calibri for text that the user reads and writes, and Cambria for larger text blocks.

SAMPLE APPLICATION CORE FUNCTIONALITY

The example Windows 8 application developed in this section is used to create menu cards. The menus and pictures you will see are from my wife's restaurant in the center of Vienna, http://www.kantine.at. You're welcome to visit this restaurant.

With the application, a restaurant can create menu cards e.g., a breakfast and a dinner card, a soup card, and so on. With this functionality, the application makes use of XAML with C# to get information from the user to write data, deal with images for the menu cards, and any other tasks associated with the application.

Creating the sample app starts with the Blank App (XAML) template from the Windows Store category, as shown in Figure 38-4.

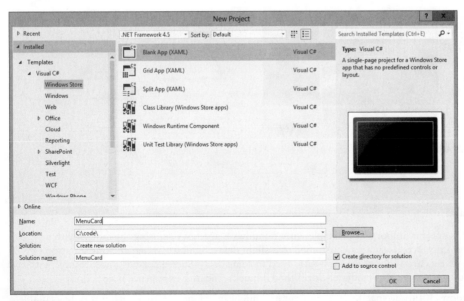

FIGURE 38-4

Files and Directories

With the project created from the template, the solution consists of a few directories and some files. The `Assets` directory contains images for the logo of the application and a splash screen. The `Common` directory is for standard styles and utility classes used and created from templates. With the Blank App (XAML) template, the `Common` directory just contains styles (filename `StandardStyles.xaml`). Feature classes will be added when other features using item templates are added to the project. The most important files with the project are `App.xaml` with its code-file `App.xaml.cs`, and `MainPage.xaml` with its code-file `MainPage.xaml.cs`, and `Package.appxmanifest`. The XAML and code-file are very similar to the structure you've seen with WPF in Chapter 35.

`Package.appxmanifest` is an XML file that describes packaging and capabilities of the application. Opening this file with Visual Studio opens the Manifest Designer, shown in Figure 38-5. Here, the name of the application and images for the logo and splash screen are defined. The pixel sizes required for the images are shown in this editor. The logo needs to be 150×150 pixels; and if the application supports a wide logo as well (which can be selected from the user), the wide logo needs to be 310×150 pixels. The splash screen needs 620×300 pixels. You can add either PNG or JPG files.

The entry point of the application is the `App` class. From there the main page is instantiated. Other than the definition of the UI, capabilities and declarations can also be specified with this package. From the Capabilities tab, the application specifies whether it wants access to devices such as the microphone or the webcam. Upon installation of the application from the Windows Store, the user is informed about the application's requirements. The application cannot use these devices if it doesn't declare its use. From the Declarations tab, the application declares features it supports; for example, whether it is available for searching from the system, or whether it offers a share target that allows other applications to offer some data to it.

FIGURE 38-5

Let's add some pages to the application.

Application Data

For the data that is used from the UI, the application defines a few types in the subdirectory DataModel.

The class MenuCard (code file MenuCard/DataModel/MenuCard.cs) represents a menu card that contains the major data of the application. This class defines the properties Title, Description, and Image to be used for display. Like all the classes used for data binding, it derives from the base class BindingBase. BindingBase offers an implementation of INotifyPropertyChanged. The method SetProperty that is invoked with the set accessors of the properties is implemented by this base class for change notification. This base class does not yet exist but will be created in the next section with a Visual Studio item template:

```csharp
using System;
using System.Collections.Generic;
using System.Collections.ObjectModel;
using System.IO;
using System.Linq;
using System.Text;
using System.Xml.Linq;
using Windows.UI.Xaml.Media;
using Windows.UI.Xaml.Media.Imaging;
using Wrox.Win8.Common;

namespace Wrox.Win8.DataModel
{
  public class MenuCard : BindableBase
  {
    private string title;
    public string Titled
    {
      get { return title; }
      set
      {
        SetProperty(ref title, value);
        SetDirty();
      }
    }

    private string description;
    public string Description
    {
      get { return description; }
      set
      {
        SetProperty(ref description, value);
        SetDirty();
      }
    }

    private ImageSource image;
    public ImageSource Image
    {
      get { return image; }
      set { SetProperty(ref image, value); }
    }

    private string imagePath;
    public string ImagePath
    {
      get { return imagePath; }
      set { imagePath = value; }
    }
```

```
        public void SetDirty()
        {
            IsDirty = true;
        }
        public void ClearDirty()
        {
          IsDirty = false;
        }
        public bool IsDirty { get; private set; }

        private readonly ICollection<MenuItem> menuItems =
            new ObservableCollection<MenuItem>();
        public ICollection<MenuItem> MenuItems
        {
          get { return menuItems; }
        }

        public void RestoreReferences()
        {
          foreach (var menuItem in MenuItems)
          {
            menuItem.MenuCard = this;
          }
        }

        public override string ToString()
        {
          return Title;
        }
    }
}
```

The class `MenuItem` (code file `MenuCard/DataModel/MenuItem.cs`) that is contained within `MenuCard` defines simple properties with change notification as well:

```
using Wrox.Win8.Common;

namespace Wrox.Win8.DataModel
{
  public class MenuItem : BindableBase
  {
    private string text;
    public string Text
    {
      get { return text; }
      set
      {
        SetProperty(ref text, value);
        SetDirty();
      }
    }

    private void SetDirty()
    {
      if (MenuCard != null)
      {
        MenuCard.SetDirty();
      }
    }
```

```
      private double price;
      public double Price
      {
        get { return price; }
        set
        {
          SetProperty(ref price, value);
          SetDirty();
        }
      }

      public MenuCard MenuCard { get; set; }

    }
  }
```

The class `AddMenuCardInfo` (code file `MenuCard/DataModel/AddMenuCardInfo.cs`) will be used to create new menu cards. This class is also a simple type used for data binding:

```
using Windows.UI.Xaml.Media;
using Wrox.Win8.Common;

namespace Wrox.Win8.DataModel
{
  public class AddMenuCardInfo : BindableBase
  {
    private string title;
    public string Title
    {
      get { return title; }
      set { SetProperty(ref title, value); }
    }

    private string description;
    public string Description
    {
      get { return description; }
      set { SetProperty(ref description, value); }
    }

    private ImageSource image;
    public ImageSource Image
    {
      get { return image; }
      set { SetProperty(ref image, value); }
    }

    private string imageFileName;
    public string ImageFileName
    {
      get { return imageFileName; }
      set { SetProperty(ref imageFileName, value); }
    }
  }
}
```

The class `MenuCardFactory` (in the code file `MenuCard/DataModel/MenuCardFactory.cs`) acts as singleton to return a list of menu cards. The method `InitMenuCards` is used to initialize the collection and assign an `ObservableCollection<MenuCard>` to the `cards` variable:

```csharp
using System;
using System.Collections.Generic;
using System.Collections.ObjectModel;

namespace Wrox.Win8.DataModel
{
  public class MenuCardFactory
  {
    private ICollection<MenuCard> cards;
    public ICollection<MenuCard> Cards
    {
      get
      {
        return cards;
      }
    }

    public void InitMenuCards(IEnumerable<MenuCard> menuCards)
    {
      cards = new ObservableCollection<MenuCard>(menuCards);
    }

    private static MenuCardFactory instance = null;
    public static MenuCardFactory Instance
    {
      get
      {
        return instance ?? (instance = new MenuCardFactory());
      }
    }
  }
}
```

> **NOTE** *The class* `ObservableCollection<T>` *is used to bind collections to the UI as it implements the interface* `INotifyCollectionChanged`. *This class is explained in Chapter 10.*

Although the application will be used to create menu cards, when it is started for the first time it would be nice to show some initial menu cards to the user. To create the sample data, the method `GetSampleMenuCards` in the class `MenuCardDataFactory` returns a list of menu cards filled with some menus. Images for the sample menu cards are stored in the `Assets` folder and referenced from there, as shown with `Breakfast.jpg`:

```csharp
public static ObservableCollection<MenuCard> GetSampleMenuCards()
{
  Uri baseUri = new Uri("ms-appx:///");

  var cards = new ObservableCollection<MenuCard>();
  MenuCard card1 = new MenuCard
  {
    Title = "Breakfast"
  };
  card1.MenuItems.Add(new MenuItem
  {
    Text = "Spezialfrühstück",
    Price = 5.4,
    MenuCard = card1
  });
```

```
card1.MenuItems.Add(new MenuItem
{
  Text = "Wiener Frühstück",
  Price = 4.4,
  MenuCard = card1
});
card1.MenuItems.Add(new MenuItem
{
  Text = "Schinken mit 3 Eiern",
  Price = 4.4,
  MenuCard = card1
});
card1.ImagePath = string.Format("{0}{1}", baseUri, "Assets/Breakfast.jpg");
cards.Add(card1);

//... more menu cards in the code download
```

Application Pages

Now let's add some UI pages to the application. The first page that is added from the template is `MainPage`
`.xaml`. With the Blank App (XAML) template, the page doesn't offer any structure, and content can be
completely customized. If you don't create a Windows 8 game or some other application that needs a
specific layout, it's best to make use of a standard format and style, and put the application name in an
exactly defined position by the Windows 8 style guidelines. As you begin to run different Windows 8
applications, you'll find many similarities. Rather than recreate the wheel, you can directly use predefined
styles by using a Visual Studio item template, as shown in Figure 38-6.

FIGURE 38-6

With the sample application, the main page created previously is replaced with an Items Page template.
Other pages that are created with the application are a Basic Page named `AddMenuCardPage` and an Items
Page named `MenuItemsPage`.

The Basic Page offers a layout to put the application name in the top-most position where users are
accustomed to seeing it. A Split Page divides a page in two, with a list in one half and details in the other.

An Items Page contains a `GridView` control to display a list of items within a grid. For using groups of items, the templates Grouped Items Page, Group Detail Page, and Item Detail Page can be used. The Grouped Items Page is used to show the different groups of items and uses a `ListView` with `GroupStyle` settings, as well as a `CollectionViewSource` with grouping. The Group Detail Page shows a single group with detail information and uses a `GridView` for this task. The Item Detail Page displays the details of one item by using a `RichTextBlock` and allows switching between items with a `FlipView`.

> **NOTE** *Of course, you can always start with a Blank Page and add controls and define the layout as needed. However, using the predefined templates and then adapting the XAML code to your needs saves a lot of time and effort.*

Using these template adds some more classes to the `Common` directory in the project: `BindableBase` can be used as a base class for some data classes as it implements the interface `INotifyPropertyChanged`; `LayoutAwarePage` is a new base class for the custom pages that is aware of rotation changes and offers visual states for rotation. `BooleanNegationConverter` and `BooleanToVisibilityConverter` are converters for XAML implementing `IValueConverter`. `RichTextColumns` is a class that can be used with `RichTextBlock` controls for text overflow. Finally, the `SuspensionManager` is used to store and load state for the application when it is suspended.

> **NOTE** *The Visual State Manager and value converters are explained in Chapter 35, "Core WPF".*

Main Page

The main page of the application is shown in Figure 38-7. It shows the title of each menu card as well as an image.

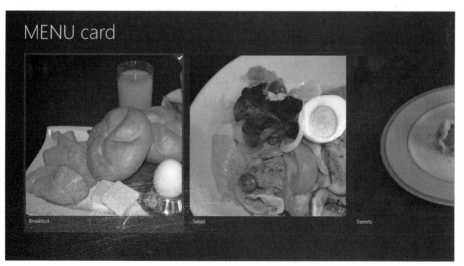

FIGURE 38-7

To achieve this, only some small adjustments to the XAML code (code file `MainPage.xaml`) are required, as shown in the following code snippet. From the Items Page template, the XAML code contains a `GridView` as a child element. What has changed is the item template from the default `Standard250x250ItemTemplate` to the `MenuCardItemTemplate`, and an `ItemClick` event handler to act when items are clicked:

```
<GridView x:Name="itemGridView"
          AutomationProperties.AutomationId="ItemsGridView"
          AutomationProperties.Name="Items"
          TabIndex="1"
          Grid.Row="1"
          Margin="0,-4,0,0"
          Padding="116,0,116,46"
          ItemsSource="{Binding Source={StaticResource itemsViewSource}}"
          ItemTemplate="{StaticResource MenuCardItemTemplate}"
          IsItemClickEnabled="True"
          ItemClick="OnMenuCardClick"/>
```

> **NOTE** *XAML templates and item templates are explained in Chapters 35 and 36.*

The source for the `GridView` is defined with the `ItemsSource` property, which references a static resource named `itemsViewSource`. `itemsViewSource` is a simple `CollectionViewSource` specified within the page resources that just binds to the `Items` property:

```
<CollectionViewSource
    x:Name="itemsViewSource"
    Source="{Binding Items}"/>
```

The `MenuCardItemTemplate` is defined in the custom styles file `Styles\MenuCardStyles.xaml`. Unlike the default template, where an item is built using two columns, here the items are made from two rows. The size is larger, and it binds to the `Image` and `Title` properties. Remember that the `MenuCard` class defined earlier implements these properties:

```
<DataTemplate x:Key="MenuCardItemTemplate">
  <Grid Margin="6">
    <Grid.RowDefinitions>
      <RowDefinition Height="*" />
      <RowDefinition Height="Auto" />
    </Grid.RowDefinitions>
    <Border Background="{StaticResource
        ListViewItemPlaceholderBackgroundThemeBrush}" Width="450" Height="450">
      <Image Source="{Binding Image}" Stretch="UniformToFill"/>
    </Border>
    <StackPanel Grid.Column="1" Margin="10,0,0,0">
      <TextBlock Text="{Binding Title}" Style="{StaticResource ItemTextStyle}"
          MaxHeight="40"/>
    </StackPanel>
  </Grid>
</DataTemplate>
```

The collection view source defined earlier binds to the `Items` collection. The value for the `Items` collection is assigned in the `LoadState` method of the `MainPage` class (code file `MenuCard/MainPage .xaml.cs`). The implementation of the `LoadState` method assigns the `DefaultViewModel` property of the base class `LayoutAwarePage`. This property returns `IObservableMap<string, object>`, where any data object can be assigned to a key name. The key name is used within XAML to reference data.

```
protected override async void LoadState(Object navigationParameter,
    Dictionary<String, Object> pageState)
{
```

```
    var storage = new MenuCardStorage();
    MenuCardFactory.Instance.InitMenuCards(new ObservableCollection<MenuCard>(
        await storage.ReadMenuCardsAsync()));
    this.DefaultViewModel["Items"] = MenuCardFactory.Instance.Cards;
}
```

> **NOTE** *The code makes use of a custom* MenuCardStorage *class that is used to read data from, and write data to, the roaming storage. This class is shown later in the chapter.*

Add Menu Card Page

For adding new menu cards, AddMenuCardPage has been added. The template used here was just the Basic Page template. However, there's not a lot to define here. The user just needs to assign a title, a description, and an image to a menu card. The UI is shown in Figure 38-8. Only two TextBox, one Button, and one Image controls are needed.

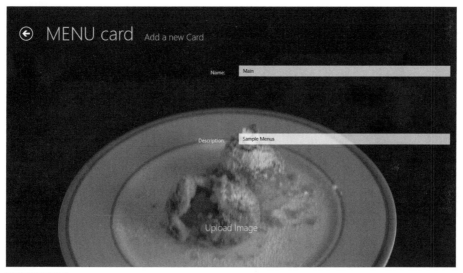

FIGURE 38-8

The XAML code to define the main controls from the file AddMenuCard.xaml is shown in the following code snippet. Note two important points here: Controls bind to Image, Title, and Description properties, and the data context assigned to a parent control (the Grid) is set to the Item property:

```
<Grid Grid.Row="1" DataContext="{Binding Item}">
  <Grid.RowDefinitions>
    <RowDefinition Height="100" />
    <RowDefinition Height="300" />
    <RowDefinition Height="*" />
  </Grid.RowDefinitions>
  <Grid.ColumnDefinitions>
    <ColumnDefinition />
    <ColumnDefinition />
  </Grid.ColumnDefinitions>
  <Border Grid.Row="0" Grid.RowSpan="3" Grid.Column="0" Grid.ColumnSpan="2">
    <Image Source="{Binding Image, Mode=OneWay}" Stretch="UniformToFill" />
  </Border>
```

```xml
<TextBlock Text="Name:" Style="{StaticResource TitleTextStyle}" Margin="20"
  VerticalAlignment="Center" HorizontalAlignment="Right" />
<TextBox Grid.Column="1" Text="{Binding Title, Mode=TwoWay}" Margin="20"
  VerticalAlignment="Center" />
<TextBlock Grid.Row="1" Text="Description:"
  Style="{StaticResource TitleTextStyle}" Margin="20"
  VerticalAlignment="Center"
  HorizontalAlignment="Right" />
<TextBox Grid.Row="1" Grid.Column="1"
  Text="{Binding Description, Mode=TwoWay}"
  Margin="20" MaxHeight="100" VerticalAlignment="Center" />
<Button HorizontalAlignment="Center" VerticalAlignment="Center"
  Visibility="{Binding ImageUploaded,
  Converter={StaticResource visibilityConverter}}" Content="Upload Image"
  Grid.Row="2" Grid.Column="0" Grid.ColumnSpan="2"
  Style="{StaticResource TextButtonStyle}" Click="OnUploadImage"
  Padding="10" Margin="20" />
</Grid>
```

In the code file, the `Item` property is assigned to an object of type `AddMenuCardInfo` (which contains the properties bound to in the XAML code) in the `LoadState` method (code file `AddMenuCardPage.xaml.cs`):

```csharp
private AddMenuCardInfo info = new AddMenuCardInfo();

protected override void LoadState(Object navigationParameter,
  Dictionary<String, Object> pageState)
{
  this.DefaultViewModel["Item"] = info;
}
```

Menu Items Page

The third page of the application is the `MenuItemsPage`, shown in Figure 38-9. This page displays the menu items of one menu card and allows for changing the data.

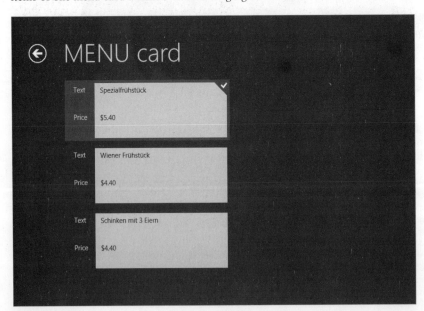

FIGURE 38-9

This page again is based on the Items Page template and binds to a list of menu items within the LoadState method (code file MenuItemsPage.xaml.cs):

```
protected override void LoadState(Object navigationParameter,
  Dictionary<String, Object> pageState)
{
  card = navigationParameter as MenuCard;
  if (card != null)
  {
    this.DefaultViewModel["Items"] = card.MenuItems;
  }
}
```

Now that three pages exist, you are ready to get into navigating with Windows 8 apps.

APP BARS

Although putting content before chrome is an important design aspect of Windows 8 applications, obviously users need a way to interact with the UI. This is now provided by the new *app bar*. Unlike previous versions of Windows, which display commands by default, users can choose when they want to view application commands.

Using touch, the app bar shows up when the user swipes from the bottom or top edge of the screen. Using a mouse, the app bar is invoked by clicking the right mouse button. Using a keyboard, users can click the context menu button.

You can define the app bar within the BottomAppBar and the TopAppBar properties of the page. Most applications have an app bar on the bottom. If your application uses app bars at both the top and the bottom, they are both displayed with the same gesture, at the same time.

The following code snippet (code file MainPage.xaml) defines an AppBar element within the BottomAppBar property of the page. Within the AppBar, any XAML elements can be used to define the content and layout of the app bar. In this case, two Button controls are added that make use of a predefined style and add handlers to the Click event:

```
<Page.BottomAppBar>
  <AppBar>
    <Grid>
      <Grid.ColumnDefinitions>
        <ColumnDefinition Width="50*"/>
        <ColumnDefinition Width="50*"/>
      </Grid.ColumnDefinitions>
      <StackPanel x:Name="LeftCommands" Orientation="Horizontal" Grid.Column="0"
        HorizontalAlignment="Left">
        <Button Style="{StaticResource AddAppBarButtonStyle}"
          HorizontalAlignment="Left" Tag="Add" Click="OnAddMenuCard" />
        <Button Style="{StaticResource DeleteAppBarButtonStyle}"
          HorizontalAlignment="Left" Tag="Delete" Click="OnDeleteMenuCard" />
      </StackPanel>
      <StackPanel x:Name="RightCommands" Orientation="Horizontal" Grid.Column="1"
        HorizontalAlignment="Right">
      </StackPanel>
    </Grid>
  </AppBar>
</Page.BottomAppBar>
```

In the style file generated by the Visual Studio template, some predefined buttons for the app bar exist. Following is the style named AddAppBarButtonStyle that is used with the sample code. This style just defines the value for a character with the Segoe UI Symbol font family to show the plus symbol. Other than that, an outline glyph and a `TextBlock` to show the text for the button are defined with the base style `AppBarButtonStyle`:

```
<Style x:Key="AddAppBarButtonStyle" TargetType="Button"
  BasedOn="{StaticResource AppBarButtonStyle}">
  <Setter Property="AutomationProperties.AutomationId" Value="AddAppBarButton"/>
  <Setter Property="AutomationProperties.Name" Value="Add"/>
  <Setter Property="Content" Value="&#xE109;"/>
</Style>
```

Figure 38-10 shows the application with the app bar displayed.

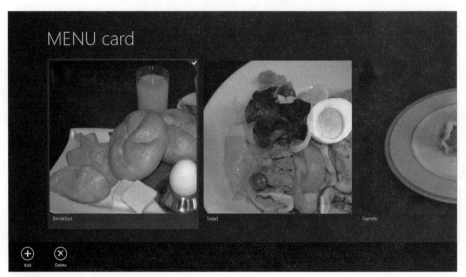

FIGURE 38-10

LAUNCHING AND NAVIGATION

To enable navigation between the pages, first the `MainPage` is shown. The `MainPage` is activated within the `App` class in the `OnLaunched` method (code file `App.xaml.cs`):

```
protected override async void OnLaunched(LaunchActivatedEventArgs args)
{
  // Do not repeat app initialization when already running, just ensure that
  // the window is active
  if (args.PreviousExecutionState == ApplicationExecutionState.Running)
  {
    Window.Current.Activate();
    return;
  }

  if (args.PreviousExecutionState == ApplicationExecutionState.Terminated)
  {
    //TODO: Load state from previously suspended application
  }

  // Create a Frame to act navigation context and navigate to the first page
  var rootFrame = new Frame();
  if (!rootFrame.Navigate(typeof(MainPage)))
```

```
        {
            throw new Exception("Failed to create initial page");
        }

        // Place the frame in the current Window and ensure that it is active
        Window.Current.Content = rootFrame;
        Window.Current.Activate();
    }
```

`OnLaunched` is invoked at different times when the application is launched. For example, the application could have been suspended previously, or it may be invoked for sharing data from another application. The `LaunchActivatedEventArgs` argument provides details about the reason for the launch and the previous state of the application. `LaunchActivatedEventArgs` defines a `Kind` property of type `ActivationKind` whereby you can read the reason for the launch. Some examples of the enumeration values that you can use here are `Launch` (a normal start of the application by clicking on a tile), `Search` (starting the application by using search from Windows), `File`, `FileOpenPicker`, and `FileSavePicker` (starting the application by selecting a file). The tile that started the application can be read with the `TileId` property of `LaunchActivatedEventArgs`. Applications can offer multiple tiles as a starting action for cases in which different information or behaviour is offered. For example, weather applications make use of this feature to enable users to add different tiles to show the weather for different cities. With the `LaunchActivatedEventArgs` argument, the application can then show the weather for a specific city in the main page. Previous execution state is read with the `PreviousExecutionState` property of type `ApplicationExecutionState`. Possible values are `NotRunning`, `Running`, `Suspended`, `Terminated`, and `ClosedByUser`.

> **NOTE** *How suspension can be dealt with is explained in Chapter 31, "Windows Runtime".*

With the `OnLaunched` method, a new `Frame` is created that acts as navigation context. This class defines the properties `CanGoBack` and `CanGoForward`, which can be used to show or hide controls:

```
        var rootFrame = new Frame();
        if (!rootFrame.Navigate(typeof(MainPage)))
        {
            throw new Exception("Failed to create initial page");
        }
```

The `MainPage.xaml` contains a Go Back button that makes use of the `CanGoBack` property of the `Frame` and sets the `IsEnabled` property accordingly:

```
        <Button x:Name="backButton" Click="GoBack"
            IsEnabled="{Binding Frame.CanGoBack, ElementName=pageRoot}"
            Style="{StaticResource BackButtonStyle}"/>
```

The `Frame` class also offers events that enable you to add handlers for when the navigation starts (`Navigating`), is completed (`Navigated`), failed (`NavigationFailed`), or stopped (`NavigationStopped`). The stopped event occurs when another navigation event is started before the current one is completed.

Navigation starts by calling the `Navigate` method. The first argument of the `Navigate` method defines the type of the page where the navigation should terminate. With a second argument it is possible to send some data to the navigated page. In the sample code (code file `MenuCard/App.xaml.cs`), no data is sent to the `MainPage`. Instead, the `MainPage` gets the menu card data on its own request.

One way to navigate away from the main page is by clicking the Add button in the app bar. This button has the `Click` event associated with the `OnAddMenuCard` handler method (code file `MainPage.xaml.cs`) where a simple navigation to the `AddMenuCardPage` is done:

```
private void OnAddMenuCard(object sender, RoutedEventArgs e)
{
   this.Frame.Navigate(typeof(AddMenuCardPage));
}
```

The pages usually have a back button (refer to Figure 38-9). The XAML code for this button is shown in the following code snippet (code file `MainPage.xaml`). This button has the `Click` event associated with the `GoBack` method. The default generated code does not contain the method in the code-behind file; instead, it is implemented in the base class `LayoutAwarePage`. The `IsEnabled` property is bound to the `CanGoBack` property of the `Frame`. The look of the button is defined by the `BackButtonStyle`:

```
<Button x:Name="backButton" Click="GoBack"
   IsEnabled="{Binding Frame.CanGoBack, ElementName=pageRoot}"
   Style="{StaticResource BackButtonStyle}"/>
```

Usually one would expect to have the button disabled when `CanGoBack` is set to `false`. However, the button is not visible at all because of how it is defined by the style (code file `Common\StandardStyles.xaml`). With the `BackButtonStyle`, a visual state is defined that changes the `Visibility` property of the outer element of the button (`RootGrid`) to `Collapsed`, making the button invisible if it is not enabled:

```
<VisualState x:Name="Disabled">
  <Storyboard>
    <ObjectAnimationUsingKeyFrames Storyboard.TargetName="RootGrid"
      Storyboard.TargetProperty="Visibility">
      <DiscreteObjectKeyFrame KeyTime="0" Value="Collapsed"/>
    </ObjectAnimationUsingKeyFrames>
  </Storyboard>
</VisualState>
```

With the implementation of the `GoBack` method (code file `MenuCard/Common/LayoutAwarePage.cs`) only the `GoBack` method of the `Frame` is invoked—if `GoBack` is allowed:

```
protected virtual void GoBack(object sender, RoutedEventArgs e)
{
   // Use the navigation frame to return to the previous page
   if (this.Frame != null && this.Frame.CanGoBack) this.Frame.GoBack();
}
```

Another way to navigate away from the `MainPage` can occur by clicking within an item of the `GridView` control. Here, the `ItemClick` event is assigned to the handler method `OnMenuCardClick`, which is shown in the following code snippet (code file `MainPage.xaml.cs`). Navigation is sent to the `MenuItemsPage`. Data is passed with the second parameter of the `Navigate` method. `e.ClickedItem` represents a `MenuCard` instance that is bound to the `GridView`:

```
private void OnMenuCardClick(object sender, ItemClickEventArgs e)
{
   Frame.Navigate(typeof(MenuItemsPage), e.ClickedItem);
}
```

LAYOUT CHANGES

A Windows 8 app must support different sizes and layouts. An application can occupy the full screen with a horizontal or vertical display, or it can occupy just a part of the screen. Windows 8 also supports a split-screen mode where one app is snapped. Users can select a snapped mode by swiping from the left edge of the screen, snapping the application to a limited part of the available space.

The minimum resolution for Windows 8 devices is 1024 × 768. To use snapped mode, the minimum resolution is 1366 × 768. Other values are supported, and you can test the look of your application without the need to have monitors supporting all the highest resolution.

Using the Visual Studio simulator you can easily check the look of the application with different resolutions. Figure 38-11 shows the application with a resolution setting of 2560 × 1440 pixels. Here, the grid switches to two rows instead of one.

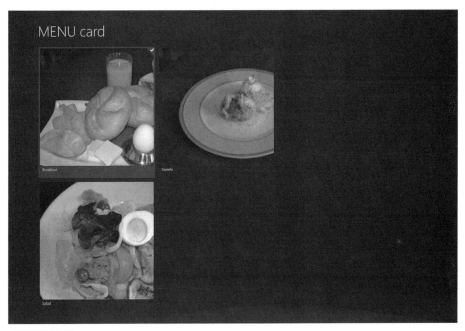

FIGURE 38-11

You can read the current layout with the static property `ApplicationView.Value`. This property returns a value of an `ApplicationViewState` enumeration. The possible values are `FullScreenLandscape`, `Filled`, `Snapped`, and `FullScreenPortrait`.

The base class `LayoutAwarePage` offers support for different layouts. With the `LayoutAwarePage` class (code file `MenuCard/Common/LayoutAwarePage.cs`), the method `StartLayoutUpdates` is added to the `Loaded` event of the page and thus invoked on loading of the page. With the implementation, the sender is added to the `_layoutAwareControls` collection (by default it's just page), and sets the visual state to the value returned from the `ApplicationViewState` enumeration. The method `DetermineVisualState` just returns a string representation of the enumeration:

```
public void StartLayoutUpdates(object sender, RoutedEventArgs e)
{
  var control = sender as Control;
  if (control == null) return;
  if (this._layoutAwareControls == null)
```

```
    {
      // Start listening to view state changes when there are controls
      // interested in updates
      Window.Current.SizeChanged += this.WindowSizeChanged;
      this._layoutAwareControls = new List<Control>();
    }
    this._layoutAwareControls.Add(control);

    // Set the initial visual state of the control
    VisualStateManager.GoToState(control, DetermineVisualState(
      ApplicationView.Value), false);
  }
```

After attaching the `WindowSizeChanged` method (code file `MenuCard/Common/LayoutAware Page.cs`) to the `SizeChanged` event, every time the layout changes the method is invoked. This method in turn invokes the `InvalidateVisualState` method, where the state of the control is changed using the `VisualStateManager`:

```
private void WindowSizeChanged(object sender, WindowSizeChangedEventArgs e)
{
  this.InvalidateVisualState();
}

public void InvalidateVisualState()
{
  if (this._layoutAwareControls != null)
  {
    string visualState = DetermineVisualState(ApplicationView.Value);
    foreach (var layoutAwareControl in this._layoutAwareControls)
    {
      VisualStateManager.GoToState(layoutAwareControl, visualState, false);
    }
  }
}
```

Now just two different looks need to be defined. The `MainPage` (code file `MainPage.xaml`) defines a `GridView` and a `ListView`. The `GridView` is used with most layout modes, the `ListView` only in snapped mode. The `ListView` has the `Visibility` property set to `Collapsed` by default. This property changes dynamically with the snapped mode. The item templates that are used by these controls are different. The `GridView` uses the item template with the resource key `MenuCardItemTemplate`, whereas the `ListView` uses `MenuCardItemSnappedTemplate`. Otherwise, the settings are similar. Both controls bind to the same data and invoke the same event handler on clicking of the items:

```
<GridView x:Name="itemGridView"
          AutomationProperties.AutomationId="ItemsGridView"
          AutomationProperties.Name="Items"
          TabIndex="1"
          Grid.Row="1"
          Margin="0,-4,0,0"
          Padding="116,0,116,46"
          ItemsSource="{Binding Source={StaticResource itemsViewSource}}"
          ItemTemplate="{StaticResource MenuCardItemTemplate}"
          IsItemClickEnabled="True"
          ItemClick="OnMenuCardClick"/>

<ListView x:Name="itemListView"
          AutomationProperties.AutomationId="ItemsListView"
          AutomationProperties.Name="Items"
          TabIndex="1"
```

```
        Grid.Row="1"
        Visibility="Collapsed"
        Margin="0,-10,0,0"
        Padding="10,0,0,60"
        ItemsSource="{Binding Source={StaticResource itemsViewSource}}"
        ItemTemplate="{StaticResource MenuCardItemSnappedTemplate}"
        IsItemClickEnabled="True"
        ItemClick="OnMenuCardClick"/>
```

The last necessary change to the layout is modifying the Visibility properties of the ListView and the
GridView controls. This is done with the VisualState definitions in the XAML code (code file MainPage
.xaml). For the view states named FullScreenLandscape and Filled, only the default settings are used.
In portrait mode with FullScreenPortrait, the Padding property of the itemGridView is changed.
With the snapped mode, the Visibility property of the itemListView is set to Visible, and with the
itemGridView it is set to Collapsed:

```
<VisualStateManager.VisualStateGroups>
  <!-- Visual states reflect the application's view state -->
  <VisualStateGroup x:Name="ApplicationViewStates">
    <VisualState x:Name="FullScreenLandscape"/>
    <VisualState x:Name="Filled"/>

    <!-- The entire page respects the narrower 100-pixel margin convention
         for portrait -->
    <VisualState x:Name="FullScreenPortrait">
      <Storyboard>
        <ObjectAnimationUsingKeyFrames Storyboard.TargetName="backButton"
          Storyboard.TargetProperty="Style">
          <DiscreteObjectKeyFrame KeyTime="0"
            Value="{StaticResource PortraitBackButtonStyle}"/>
        </ObjectAnimationUsingKeyFrames>
        <ObjectAnimationUsingKeyFrames Storyboard.TargetName="itemGridView"
          Storyboard.TargetProperty="Padding">
          <DiscreteObjectKeyFrame KeyTime="0" Value="96,0,86,56"/>
        </ObjectAnimationUsingKeyFrames>
      </Storyboard>
    </VisualState>

    <!-- The back button and title have different styles when snapped, and the
         list representation is substituted for the grid displayed in all other
         view states -->
    <VisualState x:Name="Snapped">
      <Storyboard>
        <ObjectAnimationUsingKeyFrames Storyboard.TargetName="backButton"
          Storyboard.TargetProperty="Style">
          <DiscreteObjectKeyFrame KeyTime="0"
            Value="{StaticResource SnappedBackButtonStyle}"/>
        </ObjectAnimationUsingKeyFrames>
        <ObjectAnimationUsingKeyFrames Storyboard.TargetName="pageTitle"
          Storyboard.TargetProperty="Style">
          <DiscreteObjectKeyFrame KeyTime="0"
            Value="{StaticResource SnappedPageHeaderTextStyle}"/>
        </ObjectAnimationUsingKeyFrames>

        <ObjectAnimationUsingKeyFrames Storyboard.TargetName="itemListView"
          Storyboard.TargetProperty="Visibility">
          <DiscreteObjectKeyFrame KeyTime="0" Value="Visible"/>
        </ObjectAnimationUsingKeyFrames>
        <ObjectAnimationUsingKeyFrames Storyboard.TargetName="itemGridView"
          Storyboard.TargetProperty="Visibility">
          <DiscreteObjectKeyFrame KeyTime="0" Value="Collapsed"/>
```

```
      </ObjectAnimationUsingKeyFrames>
    </Storyboard>
  </VisualState>
</VisualStateGroup>
</VisualStateManager.VisualStateGroups>
```

Now the application can be snapped. The result is shown in Figure 38-12.

STORAGE

Let's get into the storage API, reading and writing files. Typical
Windows 8 apps don't have access to the full file system without user
interaction. However, there are some specific directories from which
the application can read data and to which data can be written, and
there's also the option to ask the user for a file. Asking users for files is
done using pickers, which are discussed in the section "Pickers." First,
however, this section takes a look at the file system what and how to
program with it.

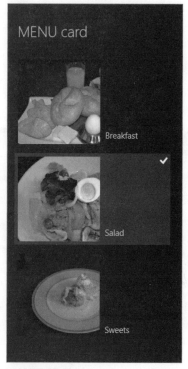

FIGURE 38-12

The sample application needs to read and write menu cards, including
both items and images. The functionality to store the textual information for the menus and the images is separated, to enable the option to
later store images with blogs inside Windows Azure Storage, and the
textual information inside either SQL Azure or Windows Azure
Table Storage. However, here just local storage is used. With a cloud
solution, local storage could be used for caching.

Defining a Data Contract

The data that should be stored is defined in separate classes within the
Storage folder. This enables defining attributes needed for serialization independent of the classes that are used to bind them to the UI
elements. For serialization of objects, both the XML Serializer and
the data contract serializer are available with Windows 8 applications. In this chapter, serialization is done using the data contract,
so the `DataContract` and `DataMember` attributes are applied to the
`MenuCardData` class (code file `MenuCard/Storage/MenuCardData`
`.cs`). With this class, only simple properties like `Title`, `Description`,
and `ImagePath` are defined for serialization, as well as a collection of
`MenuItemData`. The class also enables easy conversion from and to the `MenuCard` class by implementing a
constructor that accepts a `MenuCard` as an argument, and a `ToMenuCard` method that returns a `MenuCard`:

```csharp
using System.Collections.Generic;
using System.Runtime.Serialization;
using Wrox.Win8.DataModel;

namespace Wrox.Win8.Storage
{
  [DataContract(Name="MenuCard")]
  public class MenuCardData
  {
    public MenuCardData() { }
    public MenuCardData(MenuCard menuCard)
    {
      this.Title = menuCard.Title;
      this.Description = menuCard.Description;
```

```
        this.ImagePath = menuCard.ImagePath;
        MenuItems = new List<MenuItemData>();
        foreach (var item in menuCard.MenuItems)
        {
          MenuItems.Add(new MenuItemData(item));
        }
      }
      public MenuCard ToMenuCard()
      {
        var menuCard = new MenuCard
        {
          Title = this.Title,
          Description = this.Description,
          ImagePath = this.ImagePath
        };
        foreach (MenuItemData item in this.MenuItems)
        {
          menuCard.MenuItems.Add(item.ToMenuItem());
        }
        menuCard.ClearDirty();
        return menuCard;
      }

      [DataMember]
      public string Title { get; set; }
      [DataMember]
      public string Description { get; set; }
      [DataMember]
      public string ImagePath { get; set; }
      [DataMember]
      public List<MenuItemData> MenuItems { get; set; }
    }
  }
```

The class `MenuItemData` (code file `MenuCard/Storage/MenuItemData.cs`) represents menu items within a menu card and requires data contract attributes as well:

```
using System.Runtime.Serialization;
using Wrox.Win8.DataModel;

namespace Wrox.Win8.Storage
{
  [DataContract(Name="MenuItem")]
  public class MenuItemData
  {
    public MenuItemData() { }
    public MenuItemData(MenuItem item)
    {
      if (item != null)
      {
        this.Text = item.Text;
        this.Price = item.Price;
      }
    }

    public MenuItem ToMenuItem()
    {
      return new MenuItem
      {
        Text = this.Text,
        Price = this.Price
```

```
      };
    }
    [DataMember]
    public string Text { get; set; }
    [DataMember]
    public double Price { get; set; }
  }
}
```

Writing Roaming Data

Now you can create a method to write a `MenuCard` object. There are some predefined folders to which the application can write its data. The folders can be accessed with the `ApplicationData` class. `ApplicationData.Current` returns an instance of the `ApplicationData` singleton object. From there you can access the `LocalFolder` and `RoamingFolder`. With the `LocalFolder` property an application-specific folder that is only available on the local system is returned; `RoamingFolder` returns a folder where (after the data is written locally) the data is written to a cloud service, enabling users to access this data with every system on which they use the same live account.

The sample application makes use of the roaming folder so that users have the data available with all their Windows 8 systems. The method `WriteMenuCardAsync` (code file `Storage\MenuCardStorage`) receives a `MenuCard` with the parameter `menuCard` and accesses the roaming folder in the first line. Next, it is determined whether the `MenuCard` object contains any changes since it was last written. The `MenuCard` has a dirty flag that is changed with every property change. A file is created by invoking the `CreateFileAsync` method on the `StorageFolder`. The name for the file contains the title of the menu card. With the second argument on the `CreateFileAsync` method, it can be specified what should happen if the file already exists. Possible options are to throw an exception or open the existing file. Here the existing file is just overwritten. The opened file and the menu card are then passed to the method `WriteMenuCardToFileAsync`:

```
public async Task WriteMenuCardAsync(MenuCard menuCard)
{
  StorageFolder folder = ApplicationData.Current.RoamingFolder;

  if (menuCard.IsDirty)
  {
    StorageFile storageFile = await folder.CreateFileAsync(
      string.Format("MenuCards{0}.xml", menuCard.Title),
      CreationCollisionOption.ReplaceExisting);
    await WriteMenuCardToFileAsync(menuCard, storageFile);
    menuCard.ClearDirty();
  }
}
```

The method `WriteMenuCardToFileAsync` finally writes the data with the help of the data contract serializer. The `StorageFile` class offers several methods that return streams to read and write data—for example, `OpenAsync` returns an `IRandomAccessStream`, `OpenTransactedWriteAsync` returns a `StorageStreamTransaction`. These streams are all Windows Runtime streams. For the data contract serialization, a .NET stream is required. The extension method `OpenStreamForWriteAsync` that is defined within the class `WindowsRuntimeStorageExtensions` directly returns a .NET `Stream`. The stream returned from this method gets a copy of the `MemoryStream` that is filled earlier with the `DataContractSerializer`:

```
public async Task WriteMenuCardToFileAsync(MenuCard menuCard,
  StorageFile storageFile)
{
  var menuCardData = new MenuCardData(menuCard);
  var knownTypes = new Type[]
```

```
        {
          typeof(MenuItemData)
        };
  var cardStream = new MemoryStream();
  var serializer = new DataContractSerializer(typeof(MenuCardData), knownTypes);
  serializer.WriteObject(cardStream, menuCardData);

  using (Stream fileStream = await storageFile.OpenStreamForWriteAsync())
  {
    cardStream.Seek(0, SeekOrigin.Begin);
    await cardStream.CopyToAsync(fileStream);
    await fileStream.FlushAsync();
  }
}
```

> **NOTE** *Reading and writing .NET streams with Windows 8 applications is not
> different from other applications. See Chapter 24 for more information on .NET
> files and streams.*

Now you just need to connect the code to save the menu card with the UI. One point at which saving
takes place is when a new menu card is created in the AddMenuCardPage. Upon leaving the page (e.g.,
clicking the back button), the SaveState method (code file MenuCard/AddMenuCardPage.xaml.cs) is
invoked. SaveState is invoked by the base class LayoutAwarePage upon leaving the page within the
OnNavigatedFrom method. With the implementation here, a new MenuCard is created from the
information that is bound to the UI, and then WriteMenuCardsAsync is invoked to write all dirty menu
cards to the roaming storage:

```
protected async override void SaveState(Dictionary<String, Object> pageState)
{
  var mc = new MenuCard
  {
    Title = info.Title,
    Description = info.Description,
    Image = info.Image,
    ImagePath = info.ImageFileName
  };
  mc.SetDirty();
  MenuCardFactory.Instance.Cards.Add(mc);

  var storage = new MenuCardStorage();
  await storage.WriteMenuCardsAsync(MenuCardFactory.Instance.Cards.ToList());
}
```

After writing data to the storage, the next step is to read it again.

Reading Data

To read the menu cards, the method ReadMenuCardsAsync (code file MenuCard/Storage/
MenuCardsStorage.cs) reads all menu card files from the roaming application folder, fills MenuCard
objects, and returns a list. Before reading all the files, a list of XML files from the roaming folder is created.
The method CreateFileQuery from the StorageFolder class enables defining a query to search files. The
query defined here specifies to not use the indexer, to just read this directory and not subdirectories, and to
search for XML files. With the QueryOptions class it is also possible to use the Advanced Query Syntax
(AQS) to search for files by using keywords and properties. The files returned from the query are read by

using a .NET stream that is returned from the extension method `OpenStreamForReadAsync`. Next, the deserialization is performed using the data contract serializer:

```csharp
public async Task<IEnumerable<MenuCard>> ReadMenuCardsAsync()
{
  List<MenuCard> varmenuCards = new List<MenuCard>();
  StorageFolder folder = ApplicationData.Current.RoamingFolder;

  StorageFileQueryResult result = folder.CreateFileQuery();
  var queryOptions = new QueryOptions();
  queryOptions.IndexerOption = IndexerOption.DoNotUseIndexer;
  queryOptions.FolderDepth = FolderDepth.Shallow;
  queryOptions.FileTypeFilter.Add(".xml");
  result.ApplyNewQueryOptions(queryOptions);
  IReadOnlyList<StorageFile> files = await result.GetFilesAsync();

  foreach (var file in files)
  {
    using (Stream stream = await file.OpenStreamForReadAsync())
    {
      try
      {
        var serializer = new DataContractSerializer(typeof(MenuCardData));
        object data = await Task<object>.Run(() => serializer.ReadObject(stream));

        MenuCard menuCard = (data as MenuCardData).ToMenuCard();
        menuCard.RestoreReferences();
        menuCards.Add(menuCard);
      }
      catch (Exception )
      {
        // log exception
      }
    }
  }
  return menuCards;
}
```

Whereas the `StoreState` method can be used to write application state, the `LoadState` method is used to read application state. The following code snippet shows the `LoadState` method from the `MainPage`. This method is invoked upon navigating to the page. Here, the method `ReadMenuCardsAsync` is invoked to get a collection of `MenuCard` objects. This collection is put into an `ObservableCollection`, and then put into the view model to use the menu cards for data binding with the UI:

```csharp
protected override async void LoadState(Object navigationParameter,
  Dictionary<String, Object> pageState)
{
  var storage = new MenuCardStorage();
  MenuCardFactory.Instance.InitMenuCards(
    new ObservableCollection<MenuCard>(await storage.ReadMenuCardsAsync()));
  this.DefaultViewModel["Items"] = MenuCardFactory.Instance.Cards;
}
```

Reading and writing menu cards is now implemented, but the images are not saved yet.

Writing Images

Writing images needs some special handling. With the sample application, the user can upload images to be used with the menu cards. With images and videos, you need to pay attention to their size. Users can upload images with huge pixel densities that are not really needed when they are just being displayed on the screen. The issue here is that the roaming folder used can have some quotas associated with it; and for data stored in the cloud, charges are based on data sizes stored, and transferring larger images across the network takes more time. With this in mind, you want to store only the image size required.

With the Windows Runtime, resizing images is already part of the framework. The BitmapDecoder class can deal with image resizing, as demonstrated in the following example in the method WriteImageAsync (code file Storage\MenuCardImageStorage.cs). An image is received with the IRandomAccessStream argument. The BitmapDecoder accesses the received image stream and here the pixel height and width can be read. When resizing the image, some calculations are performed to maintain the ratio, the new width and height are passed to the BitmapTransform object, and this is then used upon saving the image with the help of the StorageFile object:

```
public async Task WriteImageAsync(IRandomAccessStream sourceStream,
  string filename)
{
  BitmapDecoder decoder = await BitmapDecoder.CreateAsync(sourceStream);
  uint scaledWidth = 0;
  uint scaledHeight = 0;
  if (decoder.PixelWidth > decoder.PixelHeight)
  {
    scaledWidth = 600;
    double relation = (double)decoder.PixelHeight / decoder.PixelWidth;
    scaledHeight = Convert.ToUInt32(relation * scaledWidth);
  }
  else
  {
    scaledHeight = 600;
    double relation = decoder.PixelWidth / decoder.PixelHeight;
    scaledWidth = Convert.ToUInt32(relation * scaledHeight);
  }
  var transform = new BitmapTransform()
  { ScaledWidth = scaledWidth, ScaledHeight = scaledHeight };
  PixelDataProvider pixelData = await decoder.GetPixelDataAsync(
      BitmapPixelFormat.Rgba8,
      BitmapAlphaMode.Straight,
      transform,
      ExifOrientationMode.RespectExifOrientation,
      ColorManagementMode.DoNotColorManage);

  var folder = ApplicationData.Current.RoamingFolder;
  StorageFile destinationFile = await folder.CreateFileAsync(filename);

  using (var destinationStream = await destinationFile.OpenAsync(
    FileAccessMode.ReadWrite))
  {
    BitmapEncoder encoder = await BitmapEncoder.CreateAsync(
      BitmapEncoder.PngEncoderId, destinationStream);
    encoder.SetPixelData(BitmapPixelFormat.Rgba8,
      BitmapAlphaMode.Premultiplied,
      scaledWidth, scaledHeight, 96, 96, pixelData.DetachPixelData());
    await encoder.FlushAsync();
  }
}
```

As discussed earlier in the chapter, the application includes some sample data. This provides the user with a good starting point and helps to demonstrate how the application can be used. The predefined text content for the menus was created with code to fill the menu cards. The images are stored in the Assets folder alongside the logos needed by the application. When first starting the application, it is useful to write the menu cards and the images to the roaming folder, which enables dealing with them in the same way as the content that created by the user.

The implementation for the first start of the application is defined in the App class within the method InitSampleDataAsync (code file App.xaml.cs). This method itself is invoked from the OnLaunched handler method in the same class. The method first verifies whether the roaming folder is empty. If it is not empty, the menu cards have been written already. The method GetSampleMenuCards returns menu cards that are filled with sample data, including links to the images from the Assets folder. These images can be retrieved using RandomAccessStreamReference, and creating such an object can be achieved with the CreateFromUri method. CreateFromFile and CreateFromStream are other options used to create RandomAccessStreamReference objects. With the RandomAccessStreamReference object, the method OpenReadAsync is invoked to get a Windows Runtime stream. This is the stream type needed to write the image with the WriteImageAsync method:

```
private static async Task InitSampleDataAsync()
{
  var storage = new MenuCardStorage();
  var imageStorage = new MenuCardImageStorage();
  if (await storage.IsRoamingFolderEmpty())
  {
    List<MenuCard> menuCards = MenuCardFactory.GetSampleMenuCards().ToList();

    foreach (var card in menuCards)
    {
      RandomAccessStreamReference streamRef =
        RandomAccessStreamReference.CreateFromUri(new Uri(card.ImagePath));
      using (IRandomAccessStreamWithContentType stream =
        await streamRef.OpenReadAsync())
      {
        card.ImagePath = string.Format("{0}.png", Guid.NewGuid());
        await imageStorage.WriteImageAsync(stream, card.ImagePath);
      }
    }

    await storage.WriteMenuCardsAsync(menuCards);
  }
}
```

Reading Images

Compared to writing images, reading images is the simpler task. Within the method ReadImageAsync (code file MenuCard/Storage/MenuCardImageStorage.cs), first a file is opened to create an IRandomAccessStreamWithContentType, and this stream is passed to the BitmapImage. The image is returned before reading of the image is completed, as this all happens asynchronously. To get success or failure information, you can add event handlers to the ImageOpened and ImageFailed events. In case the path to the image is not correct or another failure happens, these two events are very helpful:

```
public async Task<ImageSource> ReadImageAsync(string filename)
{
  StorageFolder folder = ApplicationData.Current.RoamingFolder;

  StorageFile file = await folder.CreateFileAsync(filename,
    CreationCollisionOption.OpenIfExists);

  var image = new BitmapImage();
  image.SetSource(await file.OpenReadAsync());

  image.ImageOpened += (sender1, e1) =>
```

```
            {
            };
            image.ImageFailed += (sender1, e1) =>
            {
            };

            return image;
        }
```

PICKERS

For security reasons, a Windows 8 application cannot read from or write to any location without user interaction. For such tasks, pickers can be used. With storage, the FileOpenPicker can be used to open a single or multiple files; the FileSavePicker is used to select a filename, folder, and file extension for saving a file; and the FolderPicker is used to select a folder.

The method OnUploadImage from the class AddMenuCardPage (code file MenuCard/AddMenuCardPage .xaml.cs) makes use of the FileOpenPicker to enable users to select a file for upload. The PickSingleFileAsync method returns a single file. If the user should select multiple files, PickMultipleFilesAsync can be used instead. The picker is configured by defining the start location (here the pictures library) and which file extensions can be selected. The StorageFile that is returned from the picker is then read to write the image to the menu card. Earlier, in the discussion on writing images, you saw how the BitmapDecoder can be used to resize images. With the BitmapImage it is also possible—and easier—to define the decoding as shown in the ImageOpened event handler that is implemented as a lambda expression:

```csharp
private async void OnUploadImage(object sender, RoutedEventArgs e)
{
    var filePicker = new FileOpenPicker();
    filePicker.SuggestedStartLocation = PickerLocationId.PicturesLibrary;
    filePicker.FileTypeFilter.Add(".jpg");
    filePicker.FileTypeFilter.Add(".png");
    StorageFile file = await filePicker.PickSingleFileAsync();
    if (file == null) return;

    var stream = await file.OpenAsync(FileAccessMode.Read);

    var image = new BitmapImage();

    image.SetSource(stream);
    image.ImageOpened += async (sender1, e1) =>
    {
      if (image.PixelHeight > image.PixelWidth)
      {
        image.DecodePixelHeight = 900;
      }
      else
      {
        image.DecodePixelWidth = 900;
      }
      stream.Seek(0);
      MenuCardImageStorage imageStorage = new MenuCardImageStorage();
      MenuCardStorage storage = new MenuCardStorage();
      info.ImageFileName = string.Format("{0}.jpg", Guid.NewGuid().ToString());

      await imageStorage.WriteImageAsync(stream, info.ImageFileName);
    };
    image.ImageFailed += (sender1, e1) =>
```

```
        {
          // log error
        };

        info.Image = image;
    }
```

The `FileOpenPicker` is shown in Figure 38-13. This picker provides a preview of images from the selected folder.

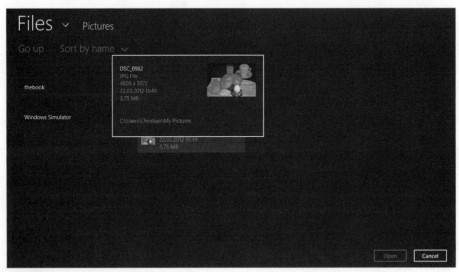

FIGURE 38-13

SHARING CONTRACT

Your application is more useful when it offers interaction with other applications. Instead of doing copy and paste, as you've done previously, the menu card application could offer data that is directly used with e-mail or an application that posts the information to a website. The application could also receive some information from other applications—for example, pictures for the menu card.

Such communication is done with Windows 8 applications by using a *contract*. The following sections first turn the sample application into a sharing source, and then a sharing target as well.

Sharing Source

The first consideration in terms of sharing is determining what data should be shared in what format. It's possible to share simple text, rich text, HTML, and images, but also a custom type. Of course, all these types must be known and used from other applications, the sharing targets. Sharing custom types can only be done with other applications that know the type and are a share target for the type. The sample application only offers HTML code for a menu card.

The HTML code for the menu card is created from the `GetHtmlContent` method in the class `MenuCard` (code file `DataModel\MenuCard.cs`). Here, LINQ to XML is used to create HTML content from the `Text` and `Price` properties of the `MenuItem` objects contained within the menu card:

```
    public string GetHtmlContent()
    {
      return
        new XElement("table",
```

```
        new XElement("thead",
          new XElement("td", "Text"),
          new XElement("td", "Price"),
          MenuItems.Select(mi =>
            new XElement("tr",
              new XElement("td", mi.Text),
              new XElement("td", mi.Price.ToString("C")))))).ToString();

    }
```

> **NOTE** *LINQ to XML is covered in Chapter 34.*

Sharing will be offered from the Menu Card when the Menu items page is opened—to share a single menu card. For better reuse, the sharing code is put into the class SharingContract (code file Contracts\ SharingContract.cs). The heart of sharing data is the DataTransferManager. In the constructor of the SharingContract the DataTransferManager for the current view is remembered with the manager variable, and an event handler to the DataRequested event is added. Sharing is possible as soon as an event handler is added to the DataTransferManager. When the user requests sharing, the event is fired, thereby invoking the method OnMenuRequested. With the implementation of this method, the DataPackage is filled with data used for sharing. Finally, HTML data is shared by invoking the method SetHtmlFormat. This makes HTML code available for other applications. With HTML, the sharing facility requires some header information with size information. This can be easily created with the HtmlFormatHelper class, as shown here. Calling other methods like SetBitmap, SetRtf, and SetUri enable offering other data.

```
using System;
using Windows.ApplicationModel.DataTransfer;
using Windows.Storage.Streams;
using Wrox.Win8.DataModel;

namespace Wrox.Win8.Contracts
{
  public class SharingContract : IDisposable
  {
    private MenuCard card;
    DataTransferManager manager;

    public void ShareMenuCard(MenuCard card)
    {
      this.card = card;
      manager = DataTransferManager.GetForCurrentView();
      manager.DataRequested += OnMenuCardRequested;
    }

    private void OnMenuCardRequested(DataTransferManager sender,
      DataRequestedEventArgs args)
    {
      Uri baseUri = new Uri("ms-appx:///");
      DataPackage package = args.Request.Data;
      package.Properties.Title = string.Format("MENU card {0}", card.Title);
      if (card.Description != null)
        package.Properties.Description = card.Description;
      package.Properties.Thumbnail = RandomAccessStreamReference.CreateFromUri(
        new Uri(baseUri, "Assets/Logo.png"));
      package.SetHtmlFormat(HtmlFormatHelper.CreateHtmlFormat(
        card.GetHtmlContent()));
    }
```

```
      public void Dispose()
      {
        if (manager != null)
          manager.DataRequested -= OnMenuCardRequested;
      }
    }
  }
```

In case you need the information when the sharing operating is completed—for example, to remove the data from the source application—the `DataPackage` class fires `OperationCompleted` and `Destroyed` events.

Sharing of a menu card is offered when the `MenuItemsPage` is opened. Within the `OnNavigatedTo` method, the previously defined `SharingContract` is instantiated, and the method `ShareMenuCard` is called:

```
public sealed partial class MenuItemsPage : Wrox.Win8.Common.LayoutAwarePage
{
  private MenuCard card;
  private SharingContract sharing;

  //...
  protected override void OnNavigatedTo(NavigationEventArgs e)
  {
    base.OnNavigatedTo(e);
    if (card != null)
    {
      sharing = new SharingContract();
      sharing.ShareMenuCard(card);
    }
  }
```

Figure 38-14 shows the activation of sharing from the Charms bar. Here, the Mail application is the only sharing target that accepts HTML content.

Selecting the Mail application, the `DataRequested` event is fired and the Menu card application passes menu card information to the `DataPackage`, which in turn is received from the Mail application. Figure 38-15 shows how the Mail application formats the received HTML content, and here it is possible to send the data directly by e-mail.

Sharing Target

Now let's have a look at the recipient of sharing. If an application should receive information from a sharing source, it needs to be declared as a share target. Figure 38-16 shows the Manifest Designer's Declarations page within Visual Studio, where you can define share targets. Here is where you add the Share Target declaration, which must include at least one data format. Possible data formats are Text. URI, Bitmap, HTML, StorageItems, or RTF. You can also specify which file types should be supported by adding the appropriate file extensions.

FIGURE 38-14

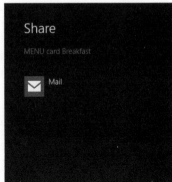

FIGURE 38-15

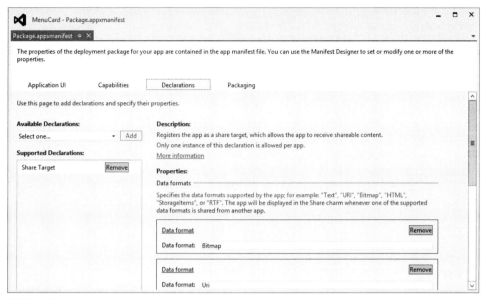

FIGURE 38-16

The information in the package manifest is used upon registration of the application. This tells Windows which applications are available as a share target. Users can configure this information from the Share dialog of the PC settings (see Figure 38-17).

FIGURE 38-17

You can use a Visual Studio item template Share Target Contract to create the code foundation needed for share targets. When a share source offers data to share, and the available share target is selected by the user, the method OnShareTargetActivated is invoked in the App class. On activation of the share target, it is not the OnLaunched method we've used until now that is invoked but rather OnShareTargetActivated.

With the implementation, the page that should be shown for the sharing request is activated. This page is displayed by the Charms bar for sharing.

```
protected override void OnShareTargetActivated(ShareTargetActivatedEventArgs args)
{
  var shareTargetPage = new ShareTargetApp.ShareTargetPage1();
  shareTargetPage.Activate(args);
}
```

The `Activate` method within the `ShareTargetPage1` class receives activation information with the `ShareTargetActivatedEventArgs` object. The `ShareOperation` property returns a `ShareOperation` object that contains a `DataPackageView`. This view information gives information about the available data. The available data can be retrieved with the `AvailableFormats` property, and the data can be accessed with appropriate methods depending on the format, e.g., `GetTextAsync` and `GetBitmapAsync`:

```
public async void Activate(ShareTargetActivatedEventArgs args)
{
  this._shareOperation = args.ShareOperation;

  // Communicate metadata about the shared content through the view model
  var shareProperties = this._shareOperation.Data.Properties;
  if (sharedProperties == null) return;

  var thumbnailImage = new BitmapImage();
  this.DefaultViewModel["Title"] = shareProperties.Title;
  this.DefaultViewModel["Description"] = shareProperties.Description;
  this.DefaultViewModel["Image"] = thumbnailImage;
  this.DefaultViewModel["Sharing"] = false;
  this.DefaultViewModel["ShowImage"] = false;
  this.DefaultViewModel["Comment"] = String.Empty;
  this.DefaultViewModel["SupportsComment"] = true;
  Window.Current.Content = this;
  Window.Current.Activate();

  // Update the shared content's thumbnail image in the background
  if (shareProperties.Thumbnail != null)
  {
    var stream = await shareProperties.Thumbnail.OpenReadAsync();
    thumbnailImage.SetSource(stream);
    this.DefaultViewModel["ShowImage"] = true;
  }
}
```

When data is retrieved, this must be communicated with the `ReportStarted` and `ReportCompleted` methods:

```
private void ShareButton_Click(object sender, RoutedEventArgs e)
{
  this.DefaultViewModel["Sharing"] = true;
  this._shareOperation.ReportStarted();

  // TODO: Perform work appropriate to your sharing scenario using
  //       this._shareOperation.Data, typically with additional information
  //       captured through custom user interface elements added to this page
  //       such as this.DefaultViewModel["Comment"]

  this._shareOperation.ReportCompleted();
}
```

TILES

Because tiles are the first entry point of the application, they should be designed to catch the user's attention. Using the Manifest Designer (see Figure 38-18) you can specify two sizes for logo tiles: one with a size of 150 × 150 pixels, and a wide logo of 310 × 150 pixels. The tile can display a name in addition to the image. If the name should be shown, it can be configured independently for the normal and wide logos, and the foreground and background color can be specified as well.

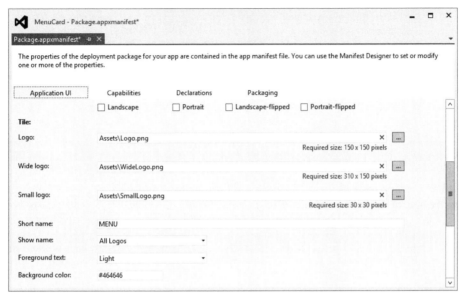

FIGURE 38-18

The tile can also be changed dynamically within the application. Some sample code to update the tile is shown in the following code snippet with the method `UpdateTile` (code file `Notification/Tile Update.cs`). To update the tile, an XML definition needs to be created that defines the tile and an optional notification that defines the expiration time of the tile, and then the tile is updated by using the `TileUpdater` class:

```
public static void UpdateTile()
{
  TileTemplateType tileTemplate = TileTemplateType.TileWideImageAndText01;
  XmlDocument tileXml = TileUpdateManager.GetTemplateContent(tileTemplate);
  XmlNodeList tileImageAttributes = tileXml.GetElementsByTagName("image");
  ((XmlElement)tileImageAttributes[0]).SetAttribute("src",
    "ms-appx:///Assets/breakfast400.jpg");
  ((XmlElement)tileImageAttributes[0]).SetAttribute("alt", "Breakfast");

  var textElements = tileXml.GetElementsByTagName("text");
  ((XmlElement)textElements[0]).InnerText = "MENU card";

  TileNotification notification = new TileNotification(tileXml);
  notification.ExpirationTime = DateTimeOffset.Now.AddMinutes(60);

  TileUpdater tileUpdater = TileUpdateManager.CreateTileUpdaterForApplication();

  tileUpdater.Update(notification);
}
```

Let's look at this in more detail. If you've noticed that many tiles of different applications look very similar, there's a good reason. The `TileTemplateType` defines several templates for tiles that can be customized. The template that is used in the sample is `TileWideImageAndText01`. As the name suggests, this template shows a wide tile with image and text. Other templates can be used for text only or images only, square blocks, or a collection of images. `TileWideImageAndText01` contains an image and text whereby the text may be wrapped, `TileWideImageAndText02` contains an image and text whereby the text is not wrapped. Using XML classes from the namespace `Windows.Data.Xml.Dom`, the XML content is modified to add an image from the `Assets` folder and some text. The final XML code for the tile is shown here:

```
<tile>
  <visual>
    <binding template="TileWideImageAndText01">
      <image id="1" src="ms-appx:///Assets/breakfast400.jpg" alt="Breakfast"/>
      <text id="1">MENU card</text>
    </binding>
  </visual>
</tile>
```

With the XML content, a `TileNotification` is created. The `ExpirationTime` defines that the tile is reset after 60 minutes. Last, with the `TileUpdater`, the update is done. The `TileUpdater` is created from the `CreateTileUpdaterForApplication` method. Because an application can have multiple tiles, other tiles can be updated with `CreateTileUpdaterForSecondaryTile`.

Instead of doing the update just once, it is also possible to specify periodic updates. The `StartPeriodicUpdate` method enables specifying an URL to a server that is invoked repeatedly with a time interval. The time interval is specified with an enumeration that defines values ranging from every half hour to daily. The server needs to return the XML code for the tile. The periodic update runs without the application being active. Starting the `TileUpdater` instructs Windows to perform the tile update.

SUMMARY

This chapter provided an introduction to many different aspects of programming Windows 8 applications. You've seen how XAML is very similar to programming WPF applications as described in previous chapters. Data binding has been used with content controls and items controls. The Visual State Manager was shown in action for dealing with different layout changes. You've also seen the Windows Runtime in action for accessing storage to read and write data and images, using roaming storage. Using the `FileOpenPicker`, files were uploaded with interaction from the user. Also covered was the sharing contract, which defines both the sharing source that offers some data and the sharing target that receives some data. Finally, you looked at tiles, the important first entry point of the application to the user.

Of course, there's a lot more to know when designing Windows 8 applications. Also available are more pickers (for example, a contact picker); contracts to offer the application for the file open picker; enhanced search capabilities that enable the application to give information to users using toasts; and much more. Unfortunately, space doesn't allow comprehensive coverage of all these topics. Nonetheless, you now have enough knowledge to get started.

The next chapter is the first of four chapters covering how to write web applications and provides you with a foundation for working with ASP.NET.

39

Core ASP.NET

WROX.COM CODE DOWNLOADS FOR THIS CHAPTER

The wrox.com code downloads for this chapter are found at `http://www.wrox.com/remtitle .cgi?isbn=1118314425` on the Download Code tab. The code for this chapter is divided into the following major examples:

➤ Handlers and Modules

➤ State Management

➤ Membership and Roles

.NET FRAMEWORKS FOR WEB APPLICATIONS

Part of the .NET Framework, ASP.NET is a technology that enables the dynamic creation of documents on a web server when they are requested via HTTP. Unlike WPF, which requires the .NET Framework on the client, an ASP.NET client only needs a browser. Here, .NET code is running on the server, and thus the Framework is required on the server. The client just needs support for HTML and JavaScript.

With the .NET Framework and Visual Studio 2012 you've different frameworks for creating Web applications. ASP.NET Web Forms is the older of these technologies, ASP.NET MVC the newer one. Every one of these technologies has its use and advantages and disadvantages.

This chapter takes a detailed look at the foundation of ASP.NET, including how it works, what you can do with it, and what ASP.NET Web Forms and ASP.NET MVC share in common.

ASP.NET offers different frameworks to create web applications: ASP.NET Web Forms, ASP.NET Web Pages, and ASP.NET MVC. ASP.NET Web Forms is the oldest of these technologies, available since .NET 1.0. The other technologies are newer and based on newer concepts. The following sections look at these options for returning HTML to the client.

ASP.NET Web Forms

ASP.NET Web Forms, which has been in existence since 2002 with the inception of .NET, is now available in version 4.5. The goal of ASP.NET Web Forms is that Windows Forms developers should feel at home. This framework offers server-side controls that have properties and methods very similar to Windows Forms controls. The developer using this framework doesn't need to know HTML and JavaScript because as the controls themselves create HTML and JavaScript to be returned to the client.

It's very easy to use this framework without any knowledge of HTML, JavaScript, or HTTP requests that are sent across the network. However, it's always useful to know something about these technologies otherwise you run the risk of sending unnecessary data across the network within a view state. The view state is used by the server-side controls to make event handling on the server side possible. Chapter 40, "ASP.NET Web Forms," provides more details on the view state as it is used with ASP.NET server-side controls. Sometimes the generated HTML code is not the code wanted. Server-side controls often provide an option to define the HTML code with a custom template.

For small websites, ASP.NET Web Forms is extremely easy to use, with results quickly achieved. With bigger and more complex websites, it's important to pay attention to the postbacks that are done from the client to the server and the view state that is sent across the network; otherwise, the application could easily become slow. ASP.NET Web Forms provides numerous options to effect this, making it fast and fluent, but this cancels out the advantage of using Web Forms and other frameworks might lead to better results. Making Web Forms fast and fluid means not using some of the available controls and writing custom code instead. So the advantage of not writing custom code with Web Forms is gone.

ASP.NET Web Pages

ASP.NET Web Pages is a new technology for those new to Microsoft .NET. This technology offers easier control of HTML and JavaScript. Indeed, in developing with this technology it's necessary to write HTML and JavaScript. .NET code can be added to the same pages as HTML code. Rendering code and functionality is mixed within the same file. This actually has a big disadvantage when writing unit tests, but it provides HTML and JavaScript developers with an easier way to start using .NET.

ASP.NET Web Pages provide helper classes that enable using specific functionality with just a few lines of code, such as reading data from the database, as the following code snippet demonstrates:

```
@{
  var db = Database.OpenConnectionString(
    "server=(local)\sqlexpress;database=Formula1;trusted_connection=true");
}
//...
  @foreach (row in db.Query("SELECT * FROM Racers") {
  //...
```

> **NOTE** *For creating ASP.NET Web Pages you can use the free tool WebMatrix, which can be downloaded from Microsoft:* http://www.microsoft.com/web/webmatrix/. *This tool offers several templates for predefined web pages and numerous features for writing web applications with ASP.NET Web Pages.*

The `Database` class is part of the WebMatrix assembly. It enables querying the database with just a few lines of code. With this, database code and UI code are mixed within the same file. While this is not a recommended practice for maintainable code, it does offer a good way to begin programming simple websites.

After starting with ASP.NET Web Pages, users can easily move to ASP.NET MVC from there. Creating websites is simple with both ASP.NET MVC and ASP.NET Web Pages, and it's easy to move code from within the page to the controller that's used with ASP.NET MVC.

Because this book is targeted for professional programmers, this chapter does not discuss ASP.NET Web Pages. Instead, it focuses on ASP.NET Web Forms and ASP.NET MVC.

ASP.NET MVC

ASP.NET MVC is based on the MVC pattern: Model-View-Controller. Shown in Figure 39-1, this standard pattern (a pattern documented in the Design Patterns book by the GOF) defines a *model* that implements data entities and data access, a *view* that represents the information shown to the user, and a *controller* that makes use of the model and sends data to the view. The controller receives a request from the browser and returns a response. To build the response, the controller can make use of a model to provide some data, and a view to define the HTML that is returned.

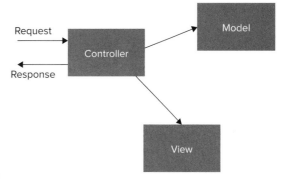

FIGURE 39-1

With ASP.NET MVC, the controller and model are typically created with C# and .NET code that is all run server-side. The view is HTML code with JavaScript and just a little C# code to access server-side information.

The big advantage of this separation with the MVC pattern is that unit tests can easily test the functionality. The controller just contains methods with parameters and return values that can be covered easily with unit tests.

> **NOTE** *You can read more about unit tests in Chapter 17, "Visual Studio." ASP.NET MVC is covered in Chapters 41, "ASP.NET MVC."*

WEB TECHNOLOGIES

Before getting into the foundations of ASP.NET, this section describes core web technologies that are important to know when creating web applications: HTML, CSS, JavaScript, and jQuery.

HTML

HTML is the markup language that is interpreted by web browsers. It defines elements to display various headings, tables, lists, and input elements such as text and combo boxes.

The W3C recommendations for HTML 4.01 were released in December 1999. HTML5, still in draft at the time of this writing (2012), is already in use. By using a restricted subset of HTML5, it can be used in older browsers. It is also increasingly adopted because several new features make it unnecessary to use Flash and Silverlight, so browser add-ins are not required. Some browsers, such as Internet Explorer in Windows 8 or Safari on the iPad, don't support add-ins.

HTML5 adds new semantic elements that can better be used by search engines to analyze the site. A `canvas` element enables the dynamic use of 2-D shapes and images, and `video` and `audio` elements make the `object` element obsolete.

HTML5 also defines APIs for drag-and-drop, storage, web sockets, and much more.

With ASP.NET Web Forms, server-side controls generate HTML. With ASP.NET MVC, the programmer has more responsibility to write HTML code.

CSS

Whereas HTML defines the content of web pages, CSS defines the look. In the earlier days of HTML, for example, the list item tag `<li>` defined whether list elements should be displayed with a circle, a disc, or a square. Nowadays such information is completely removed from HTML and is instead put into a cascading stylesheet (CSS).

With CSS styles, HTML elements can be selected using flexible selectors, and styles can be defined for these elements. An element can be selected via its id or its name, and you can define CSS classes that can be referenced from within the HTML code. With newer versions of CSS, quite complex rules can be defined to select specific HTML elements.

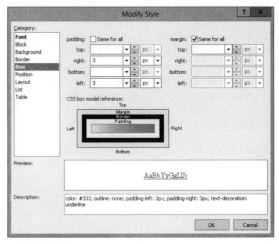

Figure 39-2 shows the Modify Style dialog of the CSS editor that is part of Visual Studio 2012, which can be used with all web applications to define stylesheets.

FIGURE 39-2

JavaScript and jQuery

Not all platforms and browsers can use .NET code, but nearly every browser understands JavaScript. One common misconception about JavaScript is that it has something to do with Java. In fact, only the name is similar because it uses some of the same naming conventions, and both Java and JavaScript have the same roots (the C programming language), which is also true for C#. JavaScript is a functional programming language that is not object-oriented, although object-oriented capabilities have been added to it.

JavaScript enables accessing the DOM from the HTML page and thus it is possible to change elements dynamically on the client. In addition to JavaScript, Internet Explorer enables the use of VBScript for accessing the DOM. However, as other browsers don't support VBScript, JavaScript is the only real option to write client-side code that should run everywhere.

Supporting web pages with JavaScript across different browsers is still a nightmare, as many implementations are handled differently, not only between different browser vendors but also from a single vendor but using different browser versions. One solution for this is a JavaScript library, such as jQuery (http://www.jquery.org). Using just a few lines of code, jQuery makes it easy to do things that required a lot of JavaScript code, and it assumes the responsibility for dealing with different browser engines, abstracting this work away from the JavaScript programmer.

ASP.NET Web Projects include the jQuery library, and Visual Studio 2012 also supports IntelliSense and debugging JavaScript code.

> **NOTE** *Styling web applications and writing JavaScript code is not part of this book. You can read more about HTML and styles in* HTML and CSS: Design and Build Websites *by John Ducket (Wiley, 2011); and get up to speed with JavaScript with* Professional JavaScript for Web Developers *by Nicholas C. Zakas (Wrox, 2005).*

HOSTING AND CONFIGURATION

A web application needs a host on which it can run. Usually, Internet Information Services (IIS) is the host used for production sites. On the developer system it's not necessary to install IIS. Visual Studio 2012 includes Visual Studio Development Server and IIS Express.

Visual Studio Development Server is a simple server that hosts the ASP.NET runtime. This server runs in a different security context than IIS. Using IIS Express is a new option that is very similar to the full IIS.

Configure the server for your web project from the Web tab in the project settings, as shown in Figure 39-3.

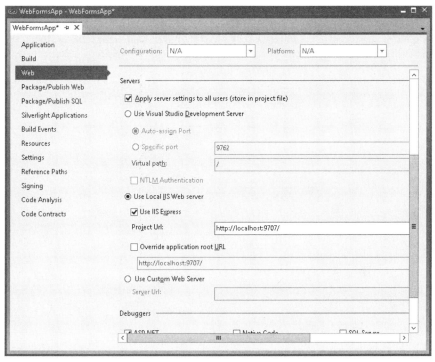

FIGURE 39-3

To configure web applications, application configuration files come into play. The first configuration file that is used by all .NET applications (not only web applications) is the file machine.config, which can be found in the directory <windir>\Microsoft.NET\Framework\v4.0.30319. For web applications, configuration is necessary for membership and role providers. These providers can also be used from other .NET applications, so it is useful to have this configuration within machine.config.

The web.config file in the same directory is used for specific ASP.NET configurations. The configurations here are exclusively for web applications. You will find default settings for trust levels and fully trusted assemblies (see Chapter 22, "Security" for more information on permissions for assemblies), compiler configurations that are used for compilation of C# code on first use of a website, referenced assemblies, health monitoring, event log and profile providers, HTTP handlers and modules, configured protocols for WCF, site maps, and Web Part configurations.

Other configuration files to define browser-specific capabilities are found in the subdirectory Browsers. Here you can find the files Default.browser, ie.browser, opera.browser, and iphone.browser, firefox.browser, among others, that define all the capabilities of the specified browser. These capabilities can be used—and are used—from server-side controls to influence the HTML and JavaScript code returned, depending on the capabilities of the caller.

> **NOTE** *Browser capabilities are based on a browser identifier string that is sent from the browser. The browser can lie and send a wrong string for identification, e.g., the Opera browser to send Internet Explorer as its identification string. Some browsers allow the user to define the identifier string that should be used. Because of this, many web applications nowadays use JavaScript to verify whether a capability is truly available. One JavaScript library to check for browser capabilities is Modernizr. This library can be installed by using the NuGet packages.*

Running the web application with Internet Information Services (IIS), the next configuration file is in the directory `inetpub\wwwroot`, if settings from the global `Web.config` file are overridden. Every web application and even subdirectories create other `Web.config` files that override parent settings. Using the Internet Information Services (IIS) Manager tool, you can change a configuration using a graphical UI, as shown in Figure 39-4.

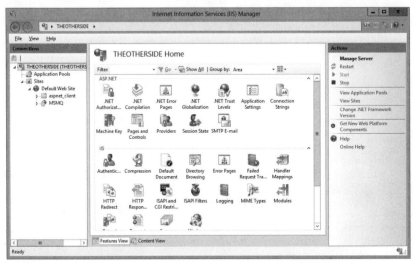

FIGURE 39-4

Another tool for changing the configuration of the `Web.config` file is the ASP.NET Web Site Administration Tool, shown in Figure 39-5. This tool is available both directly from within Visual Studio (select Project ⇨ ASP.NET Configuration) and when the application is not hosted within IIS. However, this tool provides very limited configuration options.

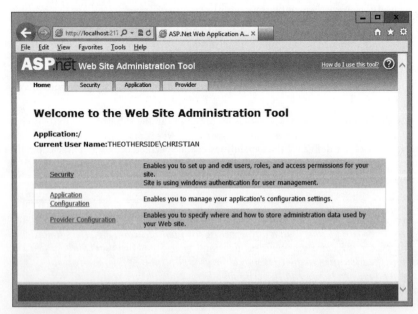

FIGURE 39-5

HANDLERS AND MODULES

This section examines what happens when the client makes a request to the web server. First, the web server tries to find a handler suitable for the request type. IIS includes a large number of handlers, as shown in Figure 39-6, such as a handler for .aspx files that instantiates a page class through a `PageHandlerFactory`, or a handler for .svc files that is used by WCF.

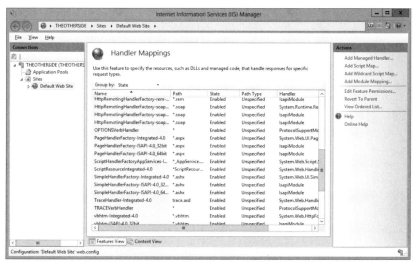

FIGURE 39-6

> **NOTE** *WCF is covered in Chapter 43, "Windows Communication Foundation."*

With each handler that is invoked, several modules come into play. There's a module to deal with security, to authenticate the user, to handle authorization, to create the session state, and so on. Figure 39-7 shows the Modules dialog and how they can be configured with IIS.

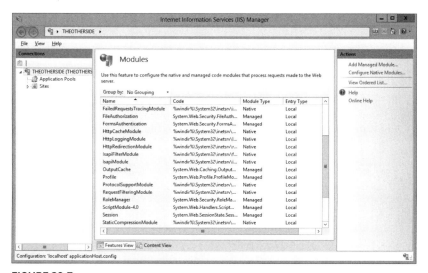

FIGURE 39-7

Creating a Custom Handler

A custom handler can be created by creating a class that implements the interface `IHttpHandler`. The following example (code file `HandlerSample/SampleHandler.cs`) creates a library that references the `System.Web` assembly and defines the class `SampleHandler`, which implements the interface `IHttpHandler`. This interface defines a property `IsReusable` and a method `ProcessRequest`. `IsReusable` returns `true` if the handler instance can be reused across different requests. The `ProcessRequest` method receives an `HttpContext` with the argument. The `HttpContext` enables receiving request information from the caller and sends a response back. The sample code defines an HTML string that is returned. From the `HttpRequest` object, the `UserAgent` property is used to send the result from this property back with the response:

```
using System.Web;

namespace Wrox.ProCSharp.ASPNETCore
{
  public class SampleHandler : IHttpHandler
  {
    private string responseString = @"
<!DOCTYPE HTML>
<html>
<head>
  <meta charset=""UTF-8"">
  <title>Sample Handler</title>
</head>
<body>
  <h1>Hello from the custom handler</h1>
  <div>{0}</div>
</body>
</html>";

    public bool IsReusable
    {
      get { return true; }
    }

    public void ProcessRequest(HttpContext context)
    {
      HttpRequest request = context.Request;
      HttpResponse response = context.Response;
      response.ContentType = "text/html";
      response.Write(string.Format(responseString, request.UserAgent));
    }
  }
}
```

With a web application, the assembly from the handler is referenced, and the handler is added to the `handlers` section in the `Web.config` file. A handler is defined by specifying a `name` that can be used to reference it programmatically, a `verb` that specifies the HTTP method (`GET`, `POST`, `HEAD`, etc.), a `path` that specifies the link that is used by the user, and the `type` identifying the class implementing `IHttpHandler`. The path also enables specifying file extensions, e.g., `*.aspx` to invoke the handler with every request to an aspx file.

```
<system.webServer>
  <handlers>
    <add name="SampleHandler" verb="*" path="CallSampleHandler"
      type="Wrox.ProCSharp.ASPNETCore.SampleHandler, HandlerSample" />
  </handlers>
</system.webServer>
```

Requesting the link `/CallSampleHandler`, the handler is invoked to return the user agent string from the client. The user agent information from Internet Explorer 10 is shown in Figure 39-8.

FIGURE 39-8

ASP.NET Handlers

For ASP.NET Web Forms applications, a handler named `PageHandlerFactory` is configured for the file extension `aspx`. The type responsible for this handler is `System.Web.UI.PageHandlerFactory`. This type implements the interface `IHttpHandlerFactory`, which is a factory for `IHttpHandler` objects. This interface defines `GetHandler` and `ReleaseHandler` methods to return and release Web Form pages, respectively. The Web Form base class `Page` implements the interface `IHttpHandler` and serves as a handler.

For files that shouldn't be served to the user (e.g., files with the extension `.cshtml`), the type `HttpForbiddenHandler` answers the request with HTTP 403 errors to deny access.

For ASP.NET MVC, an `ExtensionlessUrlHandler` is configured for the path `*`. The type dealing with these requests is `System.Web.Handlers.TransferRequestHandler`. For using routes as they are used by ASP.NET MVC, the `UrlRoutingModule` class takes action to transfer the request `MvcRouteHandler`. This handler creates an `MvcHandler` for a specific route. The `MvcHandler` searches for a controller to take the request.

With a web application it's possible to create generic handlers. A generic handler has the file extension `ashx` and is indirectly invoked from the `SimpleHandlerFactory` type. Generic handlers implement the interface `IHttpHandler` in the same way as shown earlier, but it's not necessary to configure them. Because of the file extension, the `SimpleHandlerFactory` is invoked, which searches for the requested file to transfer the handler request.

Creating a Custom Module

To create a custom module, the class needs to implement the interface `IHttpModule`. This interface defines `Init` and `Dispose` methods.

The following code snippet (code file `WebApp/ModuleSample/SampleModule.cs`) shows a module that verifies whether the request is coming from a predefined list of IP addresses, denying access if not. The `Init` method is invoked with the start of the web application. The parameter is of type `HttpContext`. However, not a lot can be done in this method because many of the `HttpContext` parameters are not filled yet, as the method is invoked before the first request is created. It is possible to add event handlers to events such as `BeginRequest`, `EndRequest`, `AuthorizeRequest`, `AuthenticateRequest`, `PreRequestHandlerExecute`, and so on. The sample code adds event handlers to the `BeginRequest` and `PreRequestHandlerExecute` events. With the `BeginRequest` method, a file is loaded to a list collection that contains all allowed IP addresses. The `PreRequestExecute` method verifies whether the IP address of the caller is in the list of allowed IP addresses by using the `UserHostAddress` property of the `HttpRequest` object. If it isn't, it throws an exception of type `HttpException` with an HTTP error code 403:

```
using System;
using System.Collections.Generic;
using System.IO;
using System.Linq;
```

```
using System.Web;

namespace Wrox.ProCSharp.ASPNETCore
{
  public class SampleModule : IHttpModule
  {
    private const string allowedAddressesFile = "AllowedAddresses.txt";
    private List<string> allowedAddresses;

    public void Dispose()
    {
    }

    public void Init(HttpApplication context)
    {
      context.LogRequest += new EventHandler(OnLogRequest);
      context.BeginRequest += BeginRequest;
      context.PreRequestHandlerExecute += PreRequestHandlerExecute;
    }

    private void BeginRequest(object sender, EventArgs e)
    {
      LoadAddresses((sender as HttpApplication).Context);
    }

    private void LoadAddresses(HttpContext context)
    {
      if (allowedAddresses == null)
      {
        string path = context.Server.MapPath(allowedAddressesFile);
        allowedAddresses = File.ReadAllLines(path).ToList();
      }
    }

    private void PreRequestHandlerExecute(object sender, EventArgs e)
    {
      HttpApplication app = sender as HttpApplication;
      HttpRequest req = app.Context.Request;
      if (!allowedAddresses.Contains(req.UserHostAddress))
      {
        throw new HttpException(403, "IP address denied");
      }
    }

    public void OnLogRequest(Object source, EventArgs e)
    {
      //custom logging logic can go here
    }
  }
}
```

The file `AllowedAddresses.txt` contains a list of allowed IP addresses. In case you're using IPv6, you should also add an IPv6 address to allow communication between the client and the server, as shown here:

```
127.0.0.1
10.0.0.22
::1
```

The module is configured in the section `system.webServer` in the file `Web.config`. The configuration is similar to the handlers; only here it needs to be within `modules`:

```
<system.webServer>
  <modules>
```

```
      <add name="SampleModule"
        type="Wrox.ProCSharp.ASPNETCore.SampleModule, ModuleSample" />
    </modules>
  </system.webServer>
```

Common Modules

With every request, several modules are invoked. The following code snippet is from the `InfoHandler.cs` file of the `HandlerSample` project. It shows the loaded modules. `HttpContext.ApplicationInstance` returns the `HttpApplication`, and this type defines a `Modules` property, which returns a collection of all the loaded modules:

```
public void ProcessRequest(HttpContext context)
{
  var sb = new StringBuilder();
  sb.Append("<ul>");
  foreach (var module in context.ApplicationInstance.Modules)
  {
    sb.AppendFormat("<li>{0}</li>", module);
  }
  sb.Append("</ul>");
  context.Response.ContentType = "text/html";
  context.Response.Write(string.Format(responseString, sb.ToString()));
}
```

Figure 39-9 shows the output of the configured handler. Common modules include `OutputCache`, to cache responses; `Session`, which deals with remembering memory state for a client; various authentication and authorization modules such as `WindowsAuthentication`, `FormsAuthentication`, `FileAuthorization`, and `UrlAuthorization`; `Profile`, for persistence user-based storage; and `ServiceModule`, for WCF.

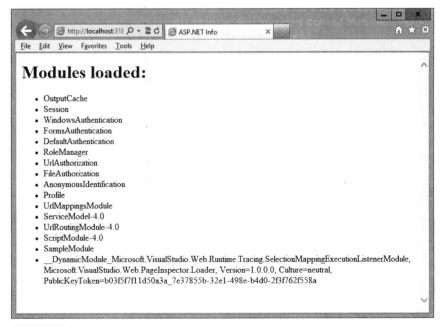

FIGURE 39-9

In addition to dealing with common functionality globally by using handlers and modules, another way is to use the global application class, discussed next.

GLOBAL APPLICATION CLASS

The *global application class* is available globally for the web application to deal with events independent of the pages. Here you can add initialization code for the web application, and code that is invoked with every request. An Application object is created when an application is started for the first time, which is when the first HTTP request arrives. Also at this time, the Application_Start event is triggered, and a pool of HttpApplication instances is created. Each incoming request receives one of these instances, which performs request processing. Note that this means HttpApplication objects do not need to cope with concurrent access, unlike the global Application object. When all HttpApplication instances finish their work, the Application_End event fires and the application terminates, destroying the Application object.

The event handlers for the events mentioned earlier (along with handlers for all other events discussed in this chapter) can be defined in a global.asax file, which you can add to any website project (it is listed as Global Application Class in the templates that appear when you add a new item to a web application). The generated file contains blanks for you to fill in, as shown in this example:

```
void Application_Start(Object sender, EventArgs e)
{
    // Code that runs on application startup
}
```

When an individual user accesses the web application, a *session* is started. Similar to the application, this involves the creation of a user-specific Session object, along with the triggering of a Session_Start event. Within a session, individual *requests* trigger Application_BeginRequest and Application_EndRequest events. These can occur several times during the scope of a session as different resources within the application are accessed. Individual sessions can be terminated manually or they will time out if no further requests are received. Session termination triggers a Session_End event and the destruction of the Session object.

Against the background of this process, you can do several things to streamline your application. If all instances of your application use a single, resource-heavy object, for example, then you might consider instantiating it at the application level. This can improve performance and reduce memory usage with multiple users because, in most requests, no such instantiation will be required.

Another technique you can use is to store session-level information for use by individual users across requests. This might include user-specific information that is extracted from a data store when the user first connects (in the Session_Start event handler), and which is made available until the session is terminated (through a timeout or user request).

> **WARNING** *Be aware that the* HttpContext *is not available with* Session_End *and* Application_End *events. Nor can you be sure that* Application_End *is called. This event might not be fired when the worker process needs to be fired immediately.*

REQUEST AND RESPONSE

In the handler example shown earlier, you saw how a request from a client is answered with a response. Information from the request can be directly accessed by using an HttpRequest object, and defining what to return is wrapped with an HttpResponse. The following sections examine these objects.

Using the HttpRequest Object

The `HttpRequest` object can be accessed by using the `Request` property of the class or the `HttpContext`. One feature of the `HttpRequest` is to receive browser information including the capabilities of the browser. The `Browser` property of `HttpRequest` returns an `HttpBrowserCapabilities` object that provides access to the capabilities of the browser. With this object you can check the JavaScript version, whether the browser supports cookies and frames, and so on.

The following code snippet uses the `Browser` property of the `HttpRequest` object to get information about the browser capabilities. You can use strongly typed access to check for various features, e.g., `CanInitiateVoiceCall` to check whether voice calls can be made, or `CanSendMail` to check whether e-mail can be sent. The following code snippet directly accesses a dictionary by using the `Capabilities` property:

```
HttpBrowserCapabilities browserCapabilities = Request.Browser;
Response.Write("<ul>");
foreach (var key in browserCapabilities.Capabilities.Keys)
{
  Response.Write("<li>");
  Response.Write(string.Format("{0}: {1}", key,
    browserCapabilities.Capabilities[key]));
  Response.Write("</li>");
}
Response.Write("</ul>");
```

Figure 39-10 shows the capabilities as returned from IE10.

All the capabilities information is taken from the browser configuration files, as discussed earlier in the configuration section. The `Browsers` property of the `HttpBrowserCapabilities` object provides information about how the capabilities are retrieved. IE10 returns `default`, `mozilla`, `ie`, `ie6plus`, and `ie10plus` with this property, which specifies exactly from what configurations the capabilities are created.

The `Headers` property of the `HttpRequest` object returns all HTTP header information. The following code snippet gets all header information from the browser. The result is shown in Figure 39-11.

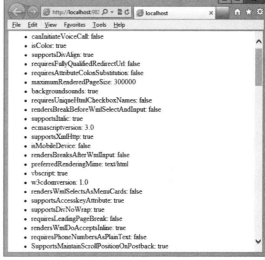

FIGURE 39-10

```
NameValueCollection headers = Request.Headers;
Response.Write("<ul>");
foreach (var key in headers.Keys)
{
  foreach (var value in headers.GetValues(key.ToString()))
  {
    Response.Write("<li>");
    Response.Write(string.Format("{0}: {1}", key, value));
    Response.Write("</li>");
  }
}
Response.Write("</ul>");
```

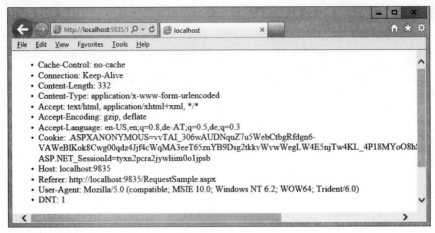

FIGURE 39-11

The HTTP header includes cookies sent from the client. However, to retrieve cookies, an easier form of access than using the `Headers` property is to use the `Cookies` property. This is discussed later in the section "Cookies." User information and the data that is sent from the client within the HTML Form can also be accessed using the request object.

Using the HttpResponse Object

The `HttpResponse` object enables sending data back to the client. The `Response` property of the `Page` (and the `HttpContext`) returns the current `HttpResponse` object.

You've already seen how the `HttpResponse` object was used to return data back to the client (with the `Write` method). Just as HTTP headers and cookie information can be accessed with the `HttpRequest` object, the header and cookies returned to the client are influenced by the `HttpResponse` object. `HttpResponse` defines `Headers` and `Cookies` properties as well.

Instead of sending content to the client, the response object can also send a redirect. `Redirect` sends a HTTP 302 status code with the information to the client that it should use another URL instead. `RedirectPermanent` sends a HTTP 301 status code instructing the caller to use the new URL permanently. `RedirectToRoute` uses the route table to find a matching route for building a redirect request to the client.

STATE MANAGEMENT

The HTTP protocol is stateless. Every new page request can be a new connection. However, it's often necessary to remember user information. State can be remembered on either the client or the server. This section discusses the different options to do that and how to program them. The samples make use of ASP.NET Web Form pages and use simple `TextBox`, `Label`, and `Button` controls with equally simple event handlers to demonstrate the different state features. Properties of the `Page` class are used to access features for state management, e.g., the `HttpSessionState` object can be directly accessed from the `Page` class with the `Session` property. Outside of the `Page` class, the same can be achieved using the `HttpContext`. `HttpContext.Current` returns the active `HttpContext` object, and this class has a `Session` property as well to return the `HttpSessionState`. In other words, all the state management features can be easily achieved both from ASP.NET Web Forms and from ASP.NET MVC.

To keep state on the client, ASP.NET gives different options: view state, cookies, and parameters. Because of security issues there are some restrictions with this state. Keeping state on the server is done with session objects, global application state, cache, and user profiles. All these different options are covered in the following subsections.

View State

View state is valid only within a page. As long as the user stays on the same page, view state can be used. View state creates a hidden HTML field in the page that is sent to the server because it is within the `<form>` tag.

View state can be accessed by using the `ViewState` property of the `Page`. The `ViewState` property returns a `StateBag` object. Passing a key value to the indexer, data can be read and written with the view state. The following example reads data from the view state with the key `state1`, and writes the value from the `Text` property of `TextBox1` to the same view state object:

```
protected void Button1_Click(object sender, EventArgs e)
{
  Label1.Text = string.Format("TextBox1.Text: {0}", TextBox1.Text);
  Label2.Text = string.Format("ViewState[\"state1\"] {0}",
    ViewState["state1"]);
  ViewState["state1"] = TextBox1.Text;
}
```

Opening the sample page `ViewState1.aspx` for the first time, the `Button1_Click` method was not yet invoked, and thus both labels show the initial value `Label`.

If you write **one** to the text box control and click the button, a postback to the server is done and the `Button1_Click` method invoked for the first time. Here the `TextBox1.Text` property returns the entered data, and thus the `Text` property of the first label is filled with this data. The second label only shows the first part of the message, the `ViewState["state1"]` returns null. In the last line of the method, view state is initialized to the value from the text box.

Writing **two** to the text box and clicking the button for the second time, another postback to the server is done. `ViewState["state1"]` now returns the previous entered data one, and `TextBox1.Text` returns the new string two.

View state is stored with a hidden field in the page:

```
<input type="hidden" name="__VIEWSTATE" id="__VIEWSTATE" value=
"XSLM3n7Gl3EVtL9CN4jAYfe3T5x/Lr26ORPT4+MEsapcFdvlu0Ooc9uiyOGku2IKOyEgv3WyR0
0iUNUKM0kBaVN1nMVm/W8c8I1x2cyeHO+zVbzAfZCYVUPD1gIIlup2ZLW9fpfYZ+d8S+uBM/Vg
WbCmsYBHW5RGaINY2QsSxep2kMfeoueD4YHND36J29XcRMV9K86Bzw4/OcX9uc7WwA==" />
```

Using a hidden field has the advantage that there's no timeout. As long as the user keeps the page open, the hidden field is there and sent to the server the next time. If the user closes the page, the state is gone. The state is also gone if the user switches to a different page. Two disadvantages of view state is that the state must be represented in a string, and all the view state data is always sent across the network. This can involve transfer of large amount of data, slowing performance.

> **NOTE** *ASP.NET server-side controls make use of view state. The server-side event model is based on this state model. When sending form content to the server, the form contains the previous value from the text box in the view state and the current value in the text box. This way, the event mechanism can determine whether the change event should be fired, and the corresponding handler methods invoked.*

Cookies

Cookies are stored on the client, either just in the memory of the browser (session cookie) or on disk (persistent cookie). They are part of the HTTP protocol and sent within the HTTP header. Every time a user visits a website, the cookies from this site are sent to the server. If a path is set with the cookie, they are sent only if the path is the same.

With ASP.NET, cookies can be sent to the client with the `HttpResponse` class (`Response` property of the `Page`). `HttpResponse` has a `SetCookie` method (code file `StateSample/CookieWrite.aspx.cs`) to pass an

`HttpCookie`. The constructor of the `HttpCookie` enables setting the name and value of the cookie. Other than that, the `HttpCookie` class defines the properties `Domain` and `Path` to associate and send the cookie to the server only if files within a specific directory are requested. The sample code sends a single value with the cookie named `cookieState`. A single cookie can also contain a list of values that can be assigned with the `Values` property. If the `Expires` property is set to a date, the cookie is a persistent cookie; otherwise, it's just a temporary cookie that is lost as soon as the browser is closed. The following code creates a persistent cookie if a check box is selected. Setting the `Secure` property of the cookie to `true` sends the cookie only if the HTTPS protocol is used:

```
protected void Button1_Click(object sender, EventArgs e)
{
  var cookie = new HttpCookie("cookieState", TextBox1.Text);
  if (CheckBox1.Checked)
  {
    cookie.Expires = DateTime.Now.AddYears(1);
  }
  Response.SetCookie(cookie);
}
```

The browser sends the cookies to the server. Of course the browser does not send all cookies to all servers, but only cookies to the server with the same domain name and path (if the path was specified). Retrieving the cookie is done with the `Cookies` property of the `HttpRequest` object. Just pass in the name to the indexer, and the `HttpCookie` is retrieved (code file `StateSample/CookieRead.aspx.cs`):

```
protected void Page_Load(object sender, EventArgs e)
{
  HttpCookie cookie = Request.Cookies["cookieState"];
  if (cookie != null)
  {
    Label1.Text = cookie.Value;
  }
}
```

Using the developer tools from Internet Explorer (press the F12 key), cookies that are sent across can be easily seen when network profiling is done. Figure 39-12 shows the cookies information with the sample page `CookieWrite.aspx`.

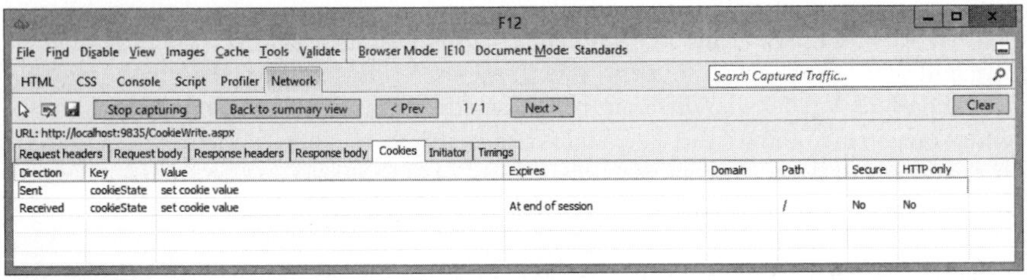

FIGURE 39-12

Cookies have some limitations. The user can turn off persistent cookies with browser settings, so there's no guarantee that they work at all. You should always expect that cookies might be deleted on the client. Some users delete cookies from time to time. The browser itself can also delete cookies. There's a limit to the size of the cookie (4,096 bytes), the number of cookies the browser stores by the domain (50 cookies), and a limited number of cookies the browser stores overall (3,000 cookies). If the limit is reached, the cookies can be deleted by the browser without user interaction. Browsers must support the specified cookie numbers at least, but could also use higher limits instead. With the limitations in mind, cookies are usually used just to set some identifier on the client that is used to map it to the real user data on the server.

Session

You can remember state for a user session by using the `HttpSessionState` object that is returned from the `Session` property of the `Page`. It's simple to write an object using a key to the session that is remembered on the server (code file `StateSample/SessionWrite.aspx.cs`). Any serializable object can be added to the session state:

```
protected void Button1_Click(object sender, EventArgs e)
{
    Session["state1"] = TextBox1.Text;
}
```

For reading the data, the get accessor of the indexer can be used. You should always check whether the indexer did return anything:

```
protected void Page_Load(object sender, EventArgs e)
{
    object state1 = Session["state1"];
    if (state1 != null)
    {
        Label1.Text = state1.ToString();
    }
}
```

Sessions are started when the user opens a page on the server and a session didn't exist previously. As the user browses different files from the same website, the same session is used. The session ends with a timeout (when the user does not request another page before the timeout occurs), or if the session is prematurely ended by invoking the `Abandon` method of the `HttpSessionState`. To globally handle session start and session end events, the `Global.asax.cs` file defines a `Session_Start` and a `Session_End` event handler:

```
protected void Session_Start(object sender, EventArgs e)
{
}

protected void Session_End(object sender, EventArgs e)
{
}
```

The user can use multiple windows of IE to use the same session. Selecting File ➪ New Window in IE opens a new window that uses the same session. Selecting File ➪ New Session creates a new session. This enables two sessions to the same website from two different windows.

Session Identifiers

With session state on the server, the client needs to be identified somehow to map the session to the client. By default, this is done using a temporary cookie named `ASP.NET_SessionId`, as shown in Figure 39-13.

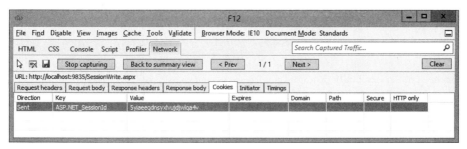

FIGURE 39-13

Session state can be configured in various ways. URLs can also be used to identify sessions if cookies are not used. This can be done by defining the `sessionState` within the `system.web` configuration, and setting the `cookieless` attribute to `UseUri`:

```
<sessionState cookieless="UseUri" />
```

Figure 39-14 shows a session identifier with the URL string, as created with the `UseUri` configuration. Using the URL with identifiers in the link is not as nice as omitting them, but it has the advantage that sessions work without cookies.

FIGURE 39-14

The `cookieless` attribute enables settings of `UseCookies` (which is the default), `UseUri`, `UseDeviceProfile`, and `AutoDetect`. With `UseDeviceProfile` the capabilities of the browser are taken from the configuration files; and if the browser supports cookies, cookies are used. This setting doesn't detect whether the user turns cookies off with the browser. Automatic detection is done by the setting `AutoDetect`. Automatic detection sends a detection cookie to the client, which uses any detected cookies returned for the session; otherwise URIs are used.

Session Storage

By default, session information is just stored in memory within the ASP.NET process. This is not practical in a web farm when the user might reach different servers on different requests, and session state is lost when the ASP.NET process is recycled. Storing session state in different places than the process is just a matter of configuration.

Using the `StateServer` mode, sessions can be stored in a separate process. The ASP.NET State Service is installed on every system running ASP.NET. It just needs to be started with the local services. With the session configuration, the `mode` needs to be set to `StateServer`, and the `stateConnectionString` to the server name and port of the state service. By default, that's port 42424:

```
<sessionState mode="StateServer"
    stateConnectionString="tcpip=127.0.0.1:42424"
    cookieless="UseCookies"
    timeout="20" />
```

Using the state server is greatly helpful with the recycling of ASP.NET processes, but it doesn't help in a web farm scenario. If the web farm is used for reliability issues to serve the clients with answers even if one system from the web farm breaks, the reliability from the complete web farm does not help in case the state service is not accessible. Here, it helps if the session state is stored in a SQL Server database cluster. The mode needs to be set to `SQLServer`:

```
<sessionState mode="SQLServer"
    sqlConnectionString="Integrated Security=SSPI;database=StateServer;" />
```

The database for the state service can be configured with the aspnet_regsql tool.

Session state can also be stored in custom state providers. Custom session state providers need to derive from the base class `SessionStateProviderBase` and implement the abstract methods accordingly. The configuration of a custom state provider is shown here to use the `DistributedCacheSessionStateStoreProvider`, which makes use of distributed memory with Windows Azure:

```
<sessionState mode="Custom" customProvider="DistributedSessionProvider">
    <providers>
        <add name="DistributedSessionProvider"
          type=
"Microsoft.Web.DistributedCache.DistributedCacheSessionStateStoreProvider,
Microsoft.Web.DistributedCache" cacheName="default"
        applicationName="AzureSampleApp"
```

```
        useBlobMode="true" />
      </providers>
    </sessionState>
```

> **NOTE** *With all the different providers, programming session state is always the same. Just be aware that when using in-process session state, any objects can be passed to the session. With other providers, the types put into the session must be serializable. It's best to ensure that all the objects put into the session are serializable, even if you're just using in-process session state.*

Application

Session state is a per-user, server-side state. Application state is a global server-side state; it is shared among all users.

In the following code snippet (code file StateSample/Global.asax.cs), the Application property returns an HttpApplicationState object. This can be used very similarly to the HttpSessionState object. However, as application state is shared among all users, it needs to be locked before changing values. Using Application.Lock and Application.UnLock, care must be taken to perform the unlock. To be on the safe side, a try/finally is used. The amount of time between locking and unlocking should be very short—you should only use memory access within this timespan—as long locking periods can degrade performance because only one thread can hold the lock; all others have to wait until it is released, with the Lock method:

```
    {
      Application["UserCount"] = 0;
    }

    protected void Session_Start(object sender, EventArgs e)
    {
      try
      {
        Application.Lock();
        int userCount = (int)Application["UserCount"];
        Application["UserCount"] = ++userCount;
      }
      finally
      {
        Application.UnLock();
      }
    }
```

With the code file StateSample/ApplicationStateRead.aspx.cs the application state is read:

```
    protected void Page_Load(object sender, EventArgs e)
    {
      int userCount = (int)Application["UserCount"];
      Label1.Text = userCount.ToString();
    }
```

Cache

Cache is very similar to application state in that it is shared among multiple users, but more control can be exercised over the lifetime of the cache object. The following code snippet (code file StateSample/CacheWrite.aspx.cs) shows how an object can be added to the cache. Cache is a property of the Page class, which returns a Cache object from the System.Web.Caching namespace:

```
    protected void Button1_Click(object sender, EventArgs e)
    {
      Cache.Add(key: "cache1", value: TextBox1.Text, dependencies: null,
```

```
            absoluteExpiration: Cache.NoAbsoluteExpiration,
            slidingExpiration: TimeSpan.FromMinutes(30),
            priority: CacheItemPriority.Normal, onRemoveCallback: null);
    }
```

The `Add` method of the `Cache` class enables flexible control of the cache object added. The first and second parameters define the key and the value of the object.

Cache Dependency

The third parameter is of type `CacheDependency`. The dependency can define when the cache object is invalidated. Besides passing a `CacheDependency`, any type that derives from the class `CacheDependency` can be added, such as `SqlCacheDependency` and `AggregateCacheDependency`. With such a dependency, it is possible to load the content of a file to the cache and create a dependency on the file—when the file changes, the cache object is invalidated.

Time

The fourth and fifth parameter define when the cache should be invalidated. With the `absoluteExpiration` parameter, a `DateTime` can be specified that indicates an absolute time when the cache should be invalidated. The `slidingExpiration` parameter allows a `TimeSpan`. Only one of these two values can be set. If the `slidingExpiration` is used, the absolute time must be set to `Cache.NoAbsoluteExpiration`. Conversely, if the `absoluteExpiration` is used, the `TimeSpan` must be set to `Cache.NoSlidingExpiration`.

Priority

Another parameter enables you to specify the priority of an object. When there's not enough memory available for the web application, the ASP.NET runtime removes cache objects. Cache objects with a lower priority are removed before objects with a higher priority. The priority is defined with an enumeration of type `CacheItemPriority`. The values are `Low`, `BelowNormal`, `Normal`, `AboveNormal`, `High`, and `NotRemovable`.

Callback Method

With the last parameter, a callback method of type `CacheItemRemovedCallback` can be defined. This method is invoked when the cache item is removed. The reason for removing the cache item is found in the `CachItemRemovedReason` enumeration. `DependencyChanged`, `Expired`, `Removed`, and `Underused` are the possible values. With the callback handler you can decide—for example, if the cache consists of file content loaded—to reload the cache if the dependency changed. Of course, the cache item shouldn't be recreated immediately if the reason for removing the cache item is low memory.

Profiles

If you've ever done any shopping online, then you are familiar with websites whose shopping-cart functionality fails to hold the selected items during the session. This creates a very bad user experience. When users take a break during their online shopping and a timeout occurs, they should not lose the items already selected. Otherwise, users must waste time retracing their steps and filling their baskets again. Companies who design their site this way can expect to lose sales. Instead, shopping cart items should be put into a database. ASP.NET profiles make this an easy task.

Profile Provider

The Profile API is based on a provider model. Providers are used with many features of ASP.NET—for example, you've already seen providers for session state. A provider derives from the base class `ProviderBase` in the namespace `System.Configuration.Provider`. Profile providers derive from the base class `ProfileProvider`, which itself derives from `SettingsProvider`. The one profile provider that is included with the .NET Framework is `SqlProfileProvider`. This provider stores profile information in the SQL Server database. The default provider is configured with `machine.config` and uses the SQL Server database defined with the connection string `LocalSqlServer` as shown:

```
<profile>
  <providers>
    <add name="AspNetSqlProfileProvider"
      connectionStringName="LocalSqlServer" applicationName="/"
      type="System.Web.Profile.SqlProfileProvider, System.Web,
      Version=4.0.0.0, Culture=neutral, PublicKeyToken=b03f5f7f11d50a3a" />
  </providers>
</profile>
```

Creating the Database

The database can be created on the fly. The first time the Profile API is used (or the Membership API that is discussed later), a new database is created. This is because the `machine.config` file contains the `LocalSqlServer` connection string that references an `aspnetdb.mdf` database file in the `DataDirectory` (App_data). The connection string named `LocalSqlServer` is by default used by the profile provider:

```
<connectionStrings>
  <add name="LocalSqlServer" connectionString="data source=.\SQLEXPRESS;
    Integrated Security=SSPI;AttachDBFilename=|DataDirectory|aspnetdb.mdf;
    User Instance=true" providerName="System.Data.SqlClient" />
</connectionStrings>
```

With Visual Studio 2012, the connection string could be changed to use `LocalDb` instead, as shown in the `Web.config` file:

```
<connectionStrings>
  <clear/>
  <add name="LocalSqlServer" connectionString="data source=(localdb)\v11.0;
    Integrated Security=SSPI;AttachDBFilename=|DataDirectory|aspnetdb.mdf;"
    providerName="System.Data.SqlClient" />
</connectionStrings>
```

Instead of automatically creating a database on the first request, with the sample application a database is created in advance. You can create an ASP.NET SQL Server database that includes all the tables needed for the different ASP.NET services using the aspnet_regsql tool (located in the directory of the .NET Runtime). Starting aspnet_regsql without options starts the ASP.NET SQL Server Setup Wizard, shown in Figure 39-15.

When configuring the database, you can define the database name or use the default (aspnetdb) (see Figure 39-16).

Running the wizard creates a database with all tables needed for profiles, membership, roles, personalization, and so on. If you need only a subset of the ASP.NET features and want a database with

FIGURE 39-15   **FIGURE 39-16**

fewer tables, you can use the command-line version of the aspnet_reqsql tool and create tables with only selected features.

The `Web.config` file now references the newly created database:

```
<connectionStrings>
  <clear/>
  <add name="LocalSqlServer" connectionString=
    "data source=(local);Database=aspnetdb;Integrated Security=SSPI;"
    providerName="System.Data.SqlClient" />
</connectionStrings>
```

Profile Settings

With the default profile provider, profile information can be defined with `Web.config` within the `system.web` element. You can save profile information for both users logged on to the system and anonymous users. If the user is not logged in, with anonymous identification enabled, an anonymous user ID is created. To map the user to the anonymous user in subsequent sessions, a persistent cookie is used. This way, the settings are always mapped to the same anonymous user. All the properties that should be stored for anonymous users must be marked with the `allowAnonymous` attribute. Profile properties are defined within the `profile/properties`. To add properties, use the `add` element. Profile properties are described by a `name` and a `type`. The `type` is used to hold the value for the property. How the type is serialized in the database is defined by the `serializeAs` attribute. Serialization can be handled as a string, using the binary or XML serializer, or with a custom class that handles serialization. To group profile state information, properties can be put into `group` elements:

```
<anonymousIdentification enabled="true" />
<profile>
  <properties>
    <add allowAnonymous="true" name="Color" type="System.String"
      serializeAs="Xml" />
    <add allowAnonymous="true" name="ShoppingCart"
      type="StateSample.ShoppingCart" serializeAs="Binary" />
    <group name="UserInfo">
      <add name="Name" type="String" serializeAs="Binary" />
    </group>
  </properties>
</profile>
```

Using Custom Types

The sample profile makes use of the `ShoppingCart` type, which is defined to be binary serialized. This type (code file `StateSample/ShoppingCart.cs`) contains a list of items that are serialized:

```
[Serializable]
public class ShoppingCart
{
  private List<Item> items = new List<Item>();
  public IList<Item> Items
  {
    get
    {
      return items;
    }
  }

  public decimal TotalCost
  {
    get
    {
      return items.Sum(item => item.Cost);
```

```
      }
    }
  }

  [Serializable]
  public class Item
  {
    public string Description { get; set; }
    public decimal Cost { get; set; }
  }
```

Writing Profile Data

With this setup it's easy to write user profile data. The `HttpContext` defines a `Profile` property that returns `ProfileBase`. With `ProfileBase`, the indexer can be used to write and read profile properties. The configuration done earlier defines a profile property named `Color`; it is used here with the indexer:

```
        this.Context.Profile["Color"] = "Blue";
        this.Context.Profile.Save();
```

In case you're using Visual Studio websites instead of web projects, the `Page` class defines a `Profile` property that returns a dynamically created `ProfileCommon` class. `ProfileCommon` derives from the base class `ProfileBase` and offers the properties defined with the configuration type as properties for strongly typed access. With web projects, the `Profile` property of the `Page` is not available. The `ProfileCommon` class is created in a similar way. Using the `dynamic` keyword, programming code looks better than using the indexer (code file `StateSample/ProfileWrite.aspx.cs`). The `Save` method writes the property names and values to the database:

```
        dynamic p = this.Context.Profile;
        p.Color = "Red";
        p.UserInfo.Name = "Christian";

        var cart = new ShoppingCart();
        cart.Items.Add(new Item { Description = "Sample1", Cost = 20.30M });
        cart.Items.Add(new Item { Description = "Sample2", Cost = 14.30M });

        p.ShoppingCart = cart;
        p.Save();
```

> **NOTE** *The* `dynamic` *keyword is explained in Chapter 12, "Dynamic Language Extensions."*

After saving the profile, you can see a new row in the aspnet_Profile table, with the property names and values shown in Figure 39-17. If the user were an anonymous user, a new user with a unique user ID would be created as well.

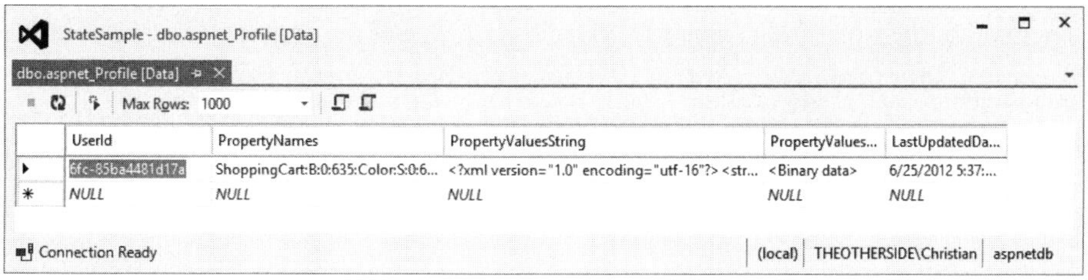

FIGURE 39-17

Reading Profile Data

Reading profile data can be done in a similar way to access the `Profile` property from the `HttpContext`. The following example code accesses the `Color` profile property as well as the profile property that is defined within the group `UserInfo`, and the custom type `ShoppingCart` (code file `StateSample/ProfileRead.aspx.cs`):

```
dynamic profile = Context.Profile;
Response.Write(string.Format("Color: {0}", profile.Color));
Response.Write("<br />");
Response.Write(string.Format("Name: {0}", profile.UserInfo.Name));
Response.Write("<br />");
ShoppingCart shoppingCart = profile.ShoppingCart;
foreach (var item in shoppingCart.Items)
{
  Response.Write(string.Format("{0} {1}", item.Description, item.Cost));
  Response.Write("<br />");
}
Response.Write(shoppingCart.TotalCost);
Response.Write("<br />");
```

Profile Manager

When profile state is used with anonymous users, over time "debris" accumulates. If an anonymous user deletes his cookies, next time another user with a new anonymous user ID is created. The old one cannot be mapped to the original user anymore.

There's an API available that can manage all the profiles. The `ProfileManager` from the `System.Web .Profile` namespace offers simple methods to retrieve all the profiles (`GetAllProfiles`), including the inactive profiles (`GetAllInactiveProfiles`). The following code snippet returns all profiles from anonymous users that have been inactive over the last year:

```
var inactiveProfiles = ProfileManager.GetAllInactiveProfiles(
    ProfileAuthenticationOption.Anonymous, DateTime.Now.AddYears(-1));
```

Inactive profiles can also be directly deleted with the method `DeleteInactiveProfiles`.

MEMBERSHIP AND ROLES

Authentication and authorization are important aspects of web applications. If a website or parts of it should not be public, users must be authorized. For authentication of users, the .NET Framework offers the Membership API. For the mapping of users to roles, the Roles API is available.

The Membership API can use the same database as the Profiles API used earlier. The Membership API is based on a provider that derives from the base class `MembershipProvider` (from the namespace `System.Web.Security`). Two membership providers are part of ASP.NET: `SqlMembershipProvider` and `ActiveDirectoryMembershipProvider`. The `SqlMembershipProvider` uses the SQL Server database to store username, password, and other security-related user information. The `ActiveDirectoryMembershipProvider` makes use of the Active Directory.

For mapping users to roles, the Roles API can be used. The Roles API uses the abstract `RoleProvider`. Existing concrete types are `SqlRoleProvider` and `WindowsTokenRoleProvider`. `SqlRoleProvider` accesses roles from the database; `WindowsTokenRoleProvider` uses Windows groups.

It's also possible to mix different membership and role providers. For example, the users could be taken from the Active Directory with the `ActiveDirectoryMembershipProvider`, and roles from the SQL Server database with `SqlRoleProvider`.

Configuring Membership

To configure membership for user authentication, the `authentication` element within `system.web` needs to be set to `Forms` authentication. The default setting is Windows Authentication, and then IIS authenticates users before they arrive with ASP.NET. The `forms` child element of `authentication` can define the login page to which users should be redirected if they are not authenticated. With the `forms` element you can also configure whether authentication cookies should be used, whether identifiers should be sent with the URL string, and whether HTTPS is a requirement:

```
<authentication mode="Forms">
  <forms defaultUrl="login.aspx" />
</authentication>
```

Configuring the authentication mode does not automatically mean that anonymous users are not allowed to access the website. The following `authorization` element defines that anonymous users are not allowed:

```
<authorization>
  <deny users="?" />
</authorization>
```

You can configure authentication and authorization either directly with the `Web.config` file and an XML editor or by using the ASP.NET Website Administration Tool, as shown in Figure 39-18.

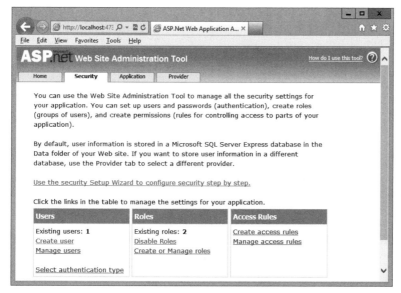

FIGURE 39-18

With this configuration, users are automatically redirected to the `login.aspx` page if they are not authenticated.

The subdirectory `AnonymousAllowed` has a separate `Web.config` file that overrides the `authorization` section from the parent directory to allow anonymous users:

```
<?xml version="1.0" encoding="utf-8"?>
<configuration>
  <system.web>
    <authorization>
      <allow users="?" />
    </authorization>
  </system.web>
</configuration>
```

The default membership provider is defined with the `machine.config` file as shown in the following example. The `AspNetSqlMembershipProvider` offers many options for configuration. With the default configuration, it uses the same connection string name as the profile provider earlier, and thus the same aspnetdb database is used. You can also adjust password requirements. For example, the `passwordStrengthRegularExpression` enables specifying a regular expression requiring the user to enter a very strong password. In this example, the password requirement specifies a minimum of seven characters with `minRequiredPasswordLength`, and consisting of at least one non-alphanumeric character with `minRequiredNonalphanumericCharacters`. In the database, the password is not stored in clear text. The password format is hashed as defined by the `passwordFormat` attribute. If a user forgot the password, it can be reset using a question and answer. Question and answer is required upon creation of the user as defined by the `requiresQuestionAndAnswer` configuration:

```xml
<membership>
  <providers>
    <add name="AspNetSqlMembershipProvider"
      type="System.Web.Security.SqlMembershipProvider, System.Web,
      Version=4.0.0.0, Culture=neutral, PublicKeyToken=b03f5f7f11d50a3a"
      connectionStringName="LocalSqlServer" enablePasswordRetrieval="false"
      enablePasswordReset="true" requiresQuestionAndAnswer="true"
      applicationName="/" requiresUniqueEmail="false" passwordFormat="Hashed"
      maxInvalidPasswordAttempts="5" minRequiredPasswordLength="7"
      minRequiredNonalphanumericCharacters="1" passwordAttemptWindow="10"
      passwordStrengthRegularExpression="" />
  </providers>
</membership>
```

Configurations can be changed within the `Web.config` file as shown earlier with the profile provider.

Using the Membership API

The Membership API enables creating, finding, and deleting users, and validating the user password. The following code creates a new user (code file `MembershipSample/AnonymousAllowed/CreateUser.aspx.cs`) with the `CreateUser` method of the `Membership` class. This example creates a user with username, password, and other parameters such as question and answer. The output parameter `MembershipCreateStatus` returns information indicating whether the user was created successfully; and if not, what failure happened. Some of the possible failures are `InvalidUserName`, `InvalidPassword`, `InvalidEmail`, `DuplicateUserName`, and `DuplicateEmail`. These failures vary according to the configuration of the membership provider:

```csharp
MembershipCreateStatus status;
MembershipUser user = Membership.CreateUser("Christian", "Pa$$w0rd",
    "christian@christiannagel.com", "was wann wo warum", "keine ahnung",
    true, out status);
```

The `CreateUser` method is overloaded to offer a version whereby only username and password are provided. However, if the membership provider is configured to require Q&A, this overload throws an exception.

Login of the user is done in the page `Login.aspx`. `Membership.ValidateUser` verifies whether the username and password match the database. If so, with `FormsAuthentication.RedirectFromLoginPage` the user is redirected to the page from which he or she came. The first parameter of this method specifies the username that can be retrieved in all the pages with the identity information. The second parameter specifies whether a permanent or temporary cookie should be used. Passing `false` uses a temporary memory-based cookie, meaning the user needs to log in again when the browser is closed:

```csharp
string userName = TextBox1.Text;
string password = TextBox2.Text;
if (Membership.ValidateUser(userName, password))
{
    FormsAuthentication.RedirectFromLoginPage(userName, false);
}
else
{
    Label1.Text = "invalid username or password";
}
```

After the user is authenticated, user information can be accessed. The code file `MembershipSample/default.aspx.cs` uses the `User` property of the `Page` to retrieve the username and write it to a label:

```
this.Label1.Text = string.Format("Hello, {0}", User.Identity.Name);
```

Enabling the Roles API

If user groups should be used to allow or deny features of the website, the role manager for the Roles API needs to be enabled. `Web.config` is changed to enable roles with the `roleManager` element. You can also configure which roles are allowed to use folders or files from the web application. In the following example, the role Developers is granted authorization to use the site; all other users are denied access:

```
<roleManager enabled="true" />
<authorization>
  <allow roles="Developers" />
  <deny users="*" />
</authorization>
```

The `Roles` class enables management of roles with the methods `AddUser(s)ToRole(s)`, `RemoveUser(s)FromRole(s)`, `CreateRole`, and `DeleteRole`. `GetRolesForUser` returns all the roles of a user. `IsUserInRole` returns `true` or `false` depending on whether the user is in the queried role. The last method can be used to allow or deny access programmatically.

> **NOTE** *You can also use attributes with methods to allow or deny users access. This is discussed in Chapter 22.*

> **NOTE** *More information on the Membership API is found in the next two chapters. Chapter 40 describes how this API can be used with the help of server-side controls, and Chapter 41 explains how to create and map models for this API with ASP.NET MVC.*

SUMMARY

This chapter provided you with core information about ASP.NET, including the parts of ASP.NET that are shared with ASP.NET Web Forms and ASP.NET MVC. You looked behind the scenes at handlers and modules, which can also be used to create specific functionality that is invoked with every request. This chapter also covered requests and responses with web applications, state management, as well as some providers such as membership and roles.

You've learned how to create handlers and modules as well as the foundation of both ASP.NET Web Forms and ASP.NET MVC. You can create custom handlers and modules even if you're creating web applications with non .NET technologies.

You've seen the different variants of state management, dealing with state on the client and state on the server. Client-side state view state is bound to single pages; cookies can be temporary as long as the browser session is alive, or persistent. With server-side state, you've seen different options with session, application, cache, and profiles. Session state is based on user sessions that can be configured to be stored in-process, in a state server, or in the database. Application state is shared between all users, and you need to pay attention to locking issues. Cache is stored just in memory mainly for reference data to not consult the database with every request. Profiles you've seen to act as a persistent store to keep user data.

The next chapter is on ASP.NET Web Forms, the ASP.NET technology in existence since .NET 1.0.

40

ASP.NET Web Forms

WHAT'S IN THIS CHAPTER?

- ➤ Server-side controls
- ➤ Master pages
- ➤ Site navigation
- ➤ Validating user input
- ➤ Data access
- ➤ Security
- ➤ ASP.NET AJAX

WROX.COM CODE DOWNLOADS FOR THIS CHAPTER

The wrox.com code downloads for this chapter are found at http://www.wrox.com/remtitle .cgi?isbn=1118314425 on the Download Code tab. The code for this chapter is divided into the following major examples:

- ➤ ProCSharpSample
- ➤ ProCSharpAjaxSample

OVERVIEW

In this chapter you look at some of the techniques that ASP.NET Web Forms supplies to enhance your web applications. These techniques make it easier for you to create websites and applications, make it possible for you to add advanced functionality, and improve the user experience.

You start by looking into the page model from ASP.NET Web Forms, checking the page events and postbacks, and then take a detailed look at the <% syntax variants for encoding, data binding, and expressions.

The chapter also covers master pages, a technique that enables you to provide templates for your websites. Using master pages you can implement complex layouts on web pages throughout a website with a great deal of code reuse. You also see how you can use the navigation web server controls in combination with a master page to provide consistent navigation across a website.

Site navigation can be made user-specific, such that only certain users (those who are registered with the site, or site administrators, for example) can access certain sections. You also look at site security and how to log in to web applications—something that is made extremely easy via the login web server controls.

Finally, you look at ASP.NET AJAX, a powerful set of technologies that provides a way to enhance the user experience. It enables websites and applications to become more responsive by updating sections of a page independently, and streamlines the process of adding client-side functionality.

ASPX PAGE MODEL

When the client makes an HTTP request to a Web Forms application, a page is instantiated and creates the response. To see the page and its model in action, create an ASP.NET Empty Web Application named `ProCSharpSample`, and add a Web Form named `ShowMeetingRooms.aspx`.

The first line of the ASPX page contains a `Page` directive, as shown in the following code snippet (code file `ProCSharpWeb/PageModel/ShowMeetingRooms.aspx`). This directive defines attributes for the ASP.NET page parser and compiler, as well as for Visual Studio. The Language attribute is used by the compiler during runtime to compile the statements within the ASPX page. The ASPX statements are surrounded with `<% %>`. The `AutoEventWireup` attribute is set to `true`, which means that the event handlers for the page events are automatically wired. It's only necessary to define the methods with the correct name and signature to activate the event handlers for the page. The `CodeBehind` attribute is not used during runtime; this informs Visual Studio that the file `ShowMeetingRooms.aspx.cs` belongs to the `ShowMeetingRooms.aspx` page and thus they will be displayed in relation to each other within Solution Explorer. What's important for the ASPX engine is the `Inherits` attribute. From the ASPX page, a class is created that derives from the base class as defined by the `Inherits` attribute:

```
<%@ Page Language="C#" AutoEventWireup="true"
   CodeBehind="ShowMeetingRooms.aspx.cs"
   Inherits="ProCSharpSample.ShowMeetingRooms" %>
```

The file `ShowMeetingRooms.aspx.cs` contains the code-behind. By default, just the handler method `Page_Load` for the `Load` event of the `Page` is implemented. Mapping to this handler is done because of the `AutoEventWireup` attribute:

```
using System;
using System.Collections.Generic;
using System.Linq;
using System.Web;
using System.Web.UI;
using System.Web.UI.WebControls;

namespace ProCSharpSample
{
  public partial class ShowMeetingRooms : System.Web.UI.Page
  {
    protected void Page_Load(object sender, EventArgs e)
    {

    }
  }
}
```

Adding Controls

Controls are added to the page by dropping them from the toolbox to either the designer or the source code view in the editor. The first page of the application will show a drop-down for selecting a meeting room. For this, the page contains a `DropDownList`, a `Label`, and a `Button` control. In the designer view, clicking the smart tag of the `DropDownList` control opens the `DropDownList` tasks, which includes the menu entry Edit Items. Selecting this opens the ListItem Collection Editor shown in Figure 40-1.

This editor can be used to add some meeting room names to the `DropDownList` control. The resulting code from the page `ShowMeetingRooms.aspx` is as follows:

FIGURE 40-1

```
<body>
  <form id="form1" runat="server">
  <div>
    <asp:DropDownList ID="DropDownListMeetingRooms" runat="server" Width="165px">
      <asp:ListItem>Sacher</asp:ListItem>
      <asp:ListItem>Hawelka</asp:ListItem>
      <asp:ListItem>Hummel</asp:ListItem>
      <asp:ListItem>Prückel</asp:ListItem>
      <asp:ListItem>Landtmann</asp:ListItem>
      <asp:ListItem>Sperl</asp:ListItem>
      <asp:ListItem>Alt Wien</asp:ListItem>
      <asp:ListItem>Eiles</asp:ListItem>
    </asp:DropDownList>
    <br />
    <br />
    <asp:Label ID="LabelSelectedRoom" runat="server" Text=""></asp:Label>
    <br />
    <br />
    <asp:Button ID="Button1" runat="server" Text="Submit" />
  </div>
  </form>
</body>
```

`DropDownList`, `Label`, and `Button` are server-side controls, as indicated by the `runat="server"` attribute. These controls are programmable with server-side C# code and return HTML and JavaScript code to the client. The code-behind file is a partial class. The designer creates another partial class file for the same type that contains only member variables of the server-side controls named within the ASPX file. This way, it's possible to access all the controls from the code-behind file, as the code-behind file is the same class.

Using Events

Now you'll add an event handler to the controls. With ASPX, event handlers can be added directly from within the ASPX code editor or from the Properties window. For the `DropDownList` control in the sample page, the `OnRoomSelection` method is assigned to the event `OnSelectedIndexChanged`. If the user changes the selection, server-side code should take over:

```
protected void OnRoomSelection(object sender, EventArgs e)
{
  this.LabelSelectedRoom.Text = DropDownListMeetingRooms.SelectedItem.Value;
}
```

Working with Postbacks

You can try that out by starting the page from Visual Studio. The drop-down list contains all the meeting rooms, and the generated HTML code is shown in the following code snippet. This code does not contain any server-side code. The attribute `runat="server"` is also stripped out.

```
<!DOCTYPE html>
<html xmlns="http://www.w3.org/1999/xhtml">
<head><title>
</title></head>
<body>
  <form method="post" action="ShowMeetingRooms.aspx" id="form1">
    <div class="aspNetHidden">
      <input type="hidden" name="__VIEWSTATE" id="__VIEWSTATE"
        value="ulPYwDLRsU6bWhjWCNAUuO+9ETPHK9DCpZyJxKTHikrAh/ghb3nUb81ZP06x2
        sDPdBHpJ4ObOMGKB8reZ2yNJqg42ep+xM6cgmks2irc7+ZrY5bnMtGj22CfjGOW5otD" />
    </div>
    <div class="aspNetHidden">
      <input type="hidden" name="__EVENTVALIDATION" id="__EVENTVALIDATION"
        value="AIZNlXgDjsO7fINvnNT9WSFZZfkci1pv28cSbIIvwKCAGjBtX9ZDzL+NL4+S
        LcTF2t7XXvjezChHhEHzRI08UHIfPpQ1AfRlc81+s3If0l9+FPdZg4d8ByuVtUu9nIL
        0mZEaiwn3Ab8KrkuYaHm6KaXqksh4/BJrp4SV5BjetsYgC/F5+JFdFi70Uy/yORSlzr
        8XJGOmHEmjxXf3XILwf1MEkBifAF9KAc/05a9h7Ih5HSFh6/8nODcbHCsywcvpWnoW1
        kCCe3DeAD74aIoert/JOR+9cjwqBcvS+uRE7Vs=" />
    </div>
    <div>
      <select name="DropDownListMeetingRooms" id="DropDownListMeetingRooms"
        style="width:165px;">
      <option selected="selected" value="Sacher">Sacher</option>
      <option value="Hawelka">Hawelka</option>
      <option value="Hummel">Hummel</option>
      <option value="Prückel">Prückel</option>
      <option value="Landtmann">Landtmann</option>
      <option value="Sperl">Sperl</option>
      <option value="Alt&#32;Wien">Alt Wien</option>
      <option value="Eiles">Eiles</option>
      </select>
      <br />
      <br />
      <span id="LabelSelectedRoom"></span>
      <br />
      <br />
      <input type="submit" name="Button1" value="Submit" id="Button1" />
    </div>
  </form>
</body>
</html>
```

There's an issue, however: The event handler is not invoked when the selection is changed. Only when the Submit button is clicked is the event handler invoked on the server side. The ASPX page model is based on postbacks. As the C# compiled code is running on the server, the client needs to send a request to the server to call the event handler. This happens upon clicking the Submit button, sending all the state information from the controls within the `form` element with the HTTP POST request to the server. This also includes the view state information. ASPX controls make use of view state to manage event handling functions. When sending the page to the client, the view state contains information about the actual control state, e.g., what is selected with the `DropDownList` control. This state information remains unchanged when the user changes a value in the `DropDownList` control. When posting the data to the server, the view state still contains the original information, and the state that is passed with the `DropDownList` within the view contains the current information. On the server side, now a change can be detected between the original state information and the current state, which fires the event `OnSelectedIndexChanged` and therefore invokes the event handler.

Using Auto-Postbacks

Sometimes it's necessary to do a postback to the server immediately following a change to the `DropDownList` control. Because of the selection some other parts of the page might be necessary to change. You can do this by setting the `AutoPostBack="true"` property with the `DropDownList` control. With HTML, this cannot be achieved without JavaScript code, but the `DropDownList` control automatically creates the JavaScript code that does a form postback on the `onchange` event of the `select` element.

Doing Postbacks to Other Pages

Until now you've seen postbacks that always request the same page. In case a different page needs to be returned to the client after the postback is done, there are several ways to do this. Invoking the `Response .Redirect` method, the client receives an HTTP redirect request to request another page. This method requires an extra round-trip to the server. Invoking the `Server.Transfer` method, another page is invoked on the server side. This doesn't require another roundtrip, but the URL that is seen by the client is just the original page and not the new page. ASPX supports another way: cross-page postbacks.

Now a second page named `MeetingRoomInformation.aspx` is created. This page includes a `Label` control that should display the selected meeting room.

In the page `ShowMeetingRooms.aspx`, the Submit button is modified to set the `PostBackUrl` property to the new page. With this information, the HTML code generated contains a JavaScript `onclick` event to the `Button` control, which changes the postback of the form to the new page:

```
<asp:Button ID="Button1" runat="server" Text="Submit"
  PostBackUrl="~/MeetingRoomInformation.aspx" />
```

The `Page_Load` event handler of the `MeetingRoomInformation.aspx` page can access page values from the previous page. The `PreviousPage` property contains the information from the previous page in case of a cross-page postback. To handle that behavior, the previous page has the `IsCrossPagePostback` property set to `true`. With the previous page, all the controls and their state that are set, and the values passed from the client can be accessed. The controls can be found with the `FindControl` method of the page, passing the name. In the following code snippet, the selected value from the `DropDownList` control is assigned to the `Text` property of the `Label` within the current page:

```
protected void Page_Load(object sender, EventArgs e)
{
  if (this.PreviousPage != null)
  {
    DropDownList meetingRoomSelection = this.PreviousPage.FindControl(
      "DropDownListMeetingRooms") as DropDownList;
    if (meetingRoomSelection != null)
    {
      this.Label1.Text = meetingRoomSelection.SelectedItem.Value;
    }
  }
}
```

To test this, open the `ShowMeetingRooms.aspx` page in the browser now and click the Submit button. This should result in a cross-page postback and open the second page.

Defining Strongly Typed Cross-Page Postbacks

ASPX also offers strongly typed access to a previous page. To take advantage of this, a read-only property `SelectedMeetingRoom` is added to the `MeetingRooms` class. This property accesses the selected value from the `DropDownList` control:

```
public string SelectedMeetingRoom
{
  get
  {
    return DropDownListMeetingRooms.SelectedItem.Value;
  }
}
```

In the `MeetingRoomInformation.aspx` file, the `PreviousPageType` directive is added following the `Page` directive. The previous page is specified with the `VirtualPath` attribute:

```
<%@ Page Language="C#" AutoEventWireup="true"
  CodeBehind="MeetingRoomInformation.aspx.cs"
  Inherits="Meetingroom.MeetingRoomInformation" %>
<%@ PreviousPageType VirtualPath="~/ShowMeetingRooms.aspx" %>
```

> **NOTE** *In the example code, the previous page is always* `ShowMeetingRooms.aspx`. *In case more than one page should be used as a previous page, a class that derives from the* `Page` *class can be created that itself is the* `Page` *class for all the previous page types. Then you can specify the* `TypeName` *attribute with the* `PreviousPageType` *directive instead of the* `VirtualPath` *attribute.*

Now you can simplify the implementation of the `Page_Load` method to directly access the `SelectedMeetingRoom` property:

```
protected void Page_Load(object sender, EventArgs e)
{
  if (this.PreviousPage != null)
  {
    this.Label1.Text = this.PreviousPage.SelectedMeetingRoom;
  }
}
```

Using Page Events

With the `ShowMeetingRooms.aspx` page, you've seen load and change events of the page. There are many more page events. Before the page is rendered, these `Page` events are fired on a first request: `PreInit`, `Init`, `InitComplete`, `PreLoad`, `Load`, `LoadComplete`, `PreRender`, `Render`, and `RenderComplete`. Many of these events are defined with three steps: Pre*XX*, *XX*, and *XX*Complete. In the case of a postback to a page, some additional events are fired to take care of the view state and the HTTP POST data to fill the values of the controls and to fire change and action events.

The first step in the life cycle of the `Page` is initialization. The `PreInit` event is fired before the initialization takes place. Here it's possible to change the master page, and themes. After this event, these properties cannot be set again. It's also possible to create controls dynamically with this event. The `Init` event is fired after all controls of the page have been initialized. Initialization values for the controls in the page can be set with the `Page_Init` event handler. The `InitComplete` event is fired after the initialization of the page and all controls has been completed.

After the initialization stage, the loading stage takes place. `PreLoad` is fired after the view state is loaded for the page and its controls, and postback data of the form is assigned to the controls of the page. When the `Load` event is fired, the page has been restored and all the controls are set to their previous state (based on the view state). Validation can be done here, as well as dynamically creating new controls that are not based on view state initialization from postbacks. Change and action events are fired in this state—such as the `OnSelectedIndexChanged` event of the `DropDownList` control, and the `OnClick` event of a `Button` control. Change events are fired before action events. The end of the loading stage is marked with the `LoadComplete` event.

After the loading stage, the rendering stage takes place. With a handler on the `PreRender` event, some final changes to the page or its controls can be done. This event is fired before any view state is saved. This is the last point in time when property values can be changed before the information goes to the view state. `SaveStateComplete` is fired next when the view state is saved. Then you are ready for rendering the content and generating HTML and JavaScript for the client. The `Render` method is called here. After the rendering is completed, the page is unloaded, and the `UnLoad` event is fired. Cleanup can be done here to release all the resources needed to build the page.

To analyze the page events and to see what happens when, it's a good idea to turn on ASP.NET web tracing. Tracing can be enabled in the `web.config` file with the `trace` element. This element is defined as a child of `system.web`. The example configuration in the next code snippet enables tracing and defines some trace configurations. The trace information should not be shown in the requested page itself (`pageOutput`), but the `trace.axd` URL can be used instead. `requestLimit` specifies that only the 10 most recent requests should be remembered, with older ones discarded. Setting `mostRecent` to `true` specifies that the request limit should apply to the most recent pages, and not the first requested pages since the application was started. The `localOnly` attribute specifies that trace information should be shown only from a client on the same system as the server. This is restricted for security reasons. The `traceMode` is set to sort the traces by time. Sorting by category is the alternate option.

```
<trace enabled="true" pageOutput="false" mostRecent="true"
    requestLimit="10" localOnly="true" traceMode="SortByTime"/>
```

Starting the application after tracing has been enabled, the traces are filled and can be viewed by opening `trace.axd` from within the browser. The output is shown in Figure 40-2. With this application trace, `ShowMeetingRooms.aspx` was opened with a `GET` request, an item in the `DropDownList` was selected that caused a `POST` request to the same page, then the Submit button was clicked which resulted in a `POST` request to the page `MeetingRoomInformation.aspx`.

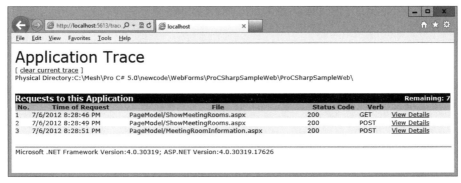

FIGURE 40-2

Clicking a View Details link on the page provides a plethora of additional information. Figure 40-3 shows request details for the session identifier, and trace information about what events occurred on the page, including timing information. Here you can easily see how much time an event handler needed, so you might find code that needs some tweaking for better performance. You can write your own custom messages to this trace information by invoking the `Write` and `Warn` methods of the `TraceContext` class. This class can be accessed by using the `Trace` property from the page, or the `Trace` property from `HttpContext.Current`.

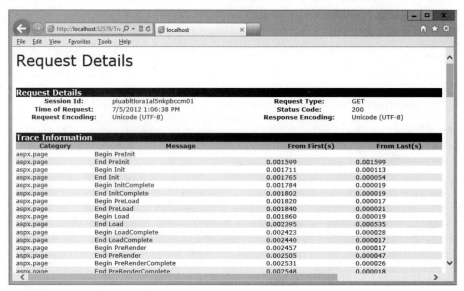

FIGURE 40-3

ASPX Code

Server-side controls can be accessed from the code-behind code by using the ID of the variable. A code file with a partial class that is hidden by default contains all the members of the page that are defined with the ASPX file. The following sections look at the different options for accessing code from within ASPX.

Writing to the Response Stream

Using the syntax `<% %>` defines a code block within the ASPX page. Multiple statements can be used within this code block, and each of them must end with the semicolon. The following code snippet does some calculation and writes the result to the response using `Response.Write`:

```
<div>
  <%
    int a = 3;
    int b = 4;
    int c = a + b;
    Response.Write(c);
  %>
</div>
```

Getting Results

To get the result of a method or property directly to the response stream, `<%=` can be used. The following code snippet invokes the method `GetText1` from the page and writes the result directly to the content of the `div` element:

```
<div>
  <%= GetText1() %>
</div>
```

The GetText1 method just returns a simple string to be called from the ASPX page:

```
public string GetText1()
{
  return "Hello from the Page";
}
```

Encoding

Using <%= can be potentially dangerous, in particular if the content that is written to the UI comes from users without any validation of their input. To see how this could happen, a simple script is added to the return string of the GetText2 method. Calling this method as shown previously, the script is invoked in the browser. The alert function just opens a message box on the client, but it would be possible to access the complete DOM model, and redirect the user to other pages:

```
public string GetText2()
{
  return @"<script>alert(""Hello"");</script>";
}
```

To avoid such scripting attacks, output should be encoded. Server.HtmlEncode encodes the input string and returns an HTML encoded string that enables the browser to display the script as text:

```
<div>
  <%= Server.HtmlEncode(GetText2()) %>
</div>
```

Because encoding should be used in so many places, a nice shorthand notation for Server.HtmlEncode and <%= is available.

```
<div>
  <%: GetText2() %>
</div>
```

Data Binding

To bind the result of methods or properties, <%# is used. The following code snippet binds the result of the GetText1 method to the Text property of the Button control:

```
<asp:Button ID="Button1" runat="server" Text="<%# GetText1() %>" />
```

Merely defining the binding does not mean something happens. The DataBind method must be invoked. Here it's done in the Page_Load event handler method:

```
protected void Page_Load(object sender, EventArgs e)
{
  this.Button1.DataBind();
}
```

Instead of invoking DataBind on the control, the DataBind method can also be invoked on the Page. This in turn invokes DataBind on all the controls associated with the Page.

Expressions

<%$ is the syntax for using an expression builder. The following code snippet uses the *resources expression* to access the result from the resource named SampleResources, and the key Message1:

```
<asp:Button ID="Button2" runat="server"
  Text="<%$ Resources:SampleResources, Message1 %>" />
```

A resources expression starts with <%$ Resources:. Resources are covered in detail in Chapter 28, "Localization."

ASP.NET comes with several expression types. AppSettings expressions read application configuration values from the configuration file, ConnectionString expressions read connection strings from the configuration file, and RouteUrl and RouteValue expressions use the URL link to get values from the route.

To edit expressions of the various types, select the Properties window from the design editor, and then open the Expressions editor, shown in Figure 40-4.

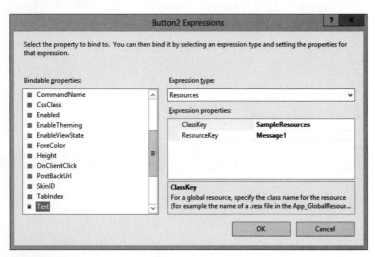

FIGURE 40-4

Server-Side Controls

So far, you have seen two web server controls: DropDownList and Button. There are many more, of course, and they are grouped in the toolbar within categories. Most of these categories are covered in this chapter.

The Standard category in the toolbar contains not only simple controls such as Button, Label, DropDownList, CheckBox, and ListBox, which are easily represented in HTML, but also controls with more complex HTML, such as Table, Calendar, MultiView, and Wizard. MultiView enables defining different views that can be selected based on different options (e.g., different views depending on whether the user is logged in), and the Wizard enables the user to complete a process step by step.

The Data category contains controls to both display data (Repeater, FormView, GridView) and access data (EntityDataSource, ObjectDataSource, SiteMapDataSource).

The Validation category contains validator controls that enable checking user input for both client-side and server-side code. The RequiredFieldValidator requires user input, the RangeValidator checks user information from a specified range of values, and the CompareValidator not only checks whether a newly entered password matches the one in another field, but also verifies whether the input conforms to a date or a currency value. With the RegularExpressionValidator, regular expressions can be specified to validate user input.

The Navigation category contains Menu, SiteMapPath, and Tree controls that enable creating a navigation structure for the user.

The Login category contains controls for security-related tasks. The Login control enables entering the username and password, and makes use of the Membership API. A user can register with the CreateUser Wizard control, change and recover the password with ChangePassword and PasswordRecovery, and display the state of authentication with LoginName, LoginStatus, and LoginView controls.

The WebParts category contains controls for building dynamic web applications. With controls from this category, users can select what Web parts should be displayed, and move Web parts between different zones.

The AJAX Extensions category contains controls that make it easy, with the server-side controls model of ASP.NET Web Forms, to use AJAX features without the need to write JavaScript code. ScriptManager, UpdatePanel, and Timer controls belong to this category.

Finally, the HTML category contains controls that by default do not have any server-side functionality. Simple HTML controls are in this category such as Input (Button), Input (Text), and Textarea. There's also a way to use these controls from server-side code by applying the attribute runat="server". With server-side functionality, the types for these controls are defined in the namespace System.Web.UI.HtmlControls. Unlike the web server controls (namespace System.Web.UI.WebControls), these controls have server-side properties and names that conform to the functions of client-side scripting code accessing the HTML DOM.

MASTER PAGES

Many web applications contain some parts that are shared across all of the pages. With ASP.NET Web Forms, *master pages* can be used to handle this behavior. Using master pages, the content pages do not return the complete HTML code. Content pages only define the parts of the page that should be placed within the master page. A master page defines the places where a content page should dock into using content placeholders. With these content placeholders, the master page can also define defaults if the content page doesn't supply content.

Creating a Master Page

This section adds a master page named Company.Master to the sample web application. The Visual Studio 2012 template creates a master page with one ContentPlaceHolder control in the head section, and one ContentPlaceHolder control in the body section. The content placeholder in the head section enables the content page to add scripting code or stylesheets to the page. With the code snippet shown next, multiple ContentPlaceHolder controls are added to the body section, along with some HTML code.

Looking at the code of the master page in the example, note that a master page starts with the Master directive. This is very similar to the Page directive used with web pages. However, master pages with the .Master file extension are never requested by the client. Indeed, a forbidden handler is defined with the handler mappings if a master file is requested. Instead, the client requests an ASPX page, and the ASPX page handler uses a master page to generate the HTML code for the client. The <html> root element, including head, body, and form, are defined within the master page, not with content pages that use a master page. You can add HTML and web server controls to master pages in the same way that you do with web pages.

What's special about the content of master pages are the ContentPlaceHolder controls. The example code defines ContentPlaceHolder controls with the IDs topContent, leftContent, and mainContent. These are the parts that can be replaced by content pages. The master page can also supply default content. This is shown with the ContentPlaceHolder control named leftContent. Here, a nav element is defined with a list of navigation items. This list is shown in content pages if the content page doesn't add its own content for this content placeholder.

```
<%@ Master Language="C#" AutoEventWireup="true" CodeBehind="Company.master.cs"
   Inherits="Meetingroom.Company" %>

<!DOCTYPE html>
<html>
<head runat="server">
  <link rel="stylesheet" type="text/css" href="Company.css" />
  <title></title>
  <asp:ContentPlaceHolder ID="head" runat="server">
  </asp:ContentPlaceHolder>
</head>
```

```
<body>
  <form id="form1" runat="server">
  <div class="top">
    <h1>Professional C# 2012 Demo Web Application</h1>
  </div>
  <div class="top2">
    <asp:ContentPlaceHolder ID="topContent" runat="server">
    </asp:ContentPlaceHolder>
  </div>
  <div class="left">
    <!-- Navigation Controls -->
    <asp:ContentPlaceHolder ID="leftContent" runat="server">
      <nav>
        <ul>
          <li>Home
          <ul>
            <li>Reserve Room</li>
            <li>Show Rooms</li>
          </ul>
          </li>
          <li>About</li>
        </ul>
      </nav>
    </asp:ContentPlaceHolder>
  </div>
  <div class="main">
    <asp:ContentPlaceHolder ID="mainContent" runat="server">
    </asp:ContentPlaceHolder>
  </div>
  <div class="bottom">
    <div>CN innovation</div>
    <div>http://www.cninnovation.com</div>
  </div>
  </form>
</body>
</html>
```

As shown in Figure 40-5, the design view of Visual Studio shows the look of the page, along with the CSS file that is applied to the master page.

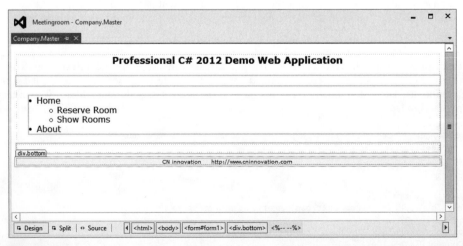

FIGURE 40-5

Using Master Pages

To use a master page, Visual Studio 2012 includes the template Web Form Using Master Page. With this item template, a master page can be selected upon creating the page. The Page directive of the generated page just defines the additional attribute MasterPageFile to reference the selected master page. Other than the Page directive, the page only contains Content controls. The Content controls define what is replaced from the master page. With the ContentPlaceHolderId property, the Content control references the ContentPlaceHolder control to define the content to replace:

```
<%@ Page Title="" Language="C#" MasterPageFile="~/Company.Master"
    AutoEventWireup="true" CodeBehind="ReserveRoom.aspx.cs"
    Inherits="Meetingroom.ReserveRoom" %>
<asp:Content ID="Content1" ContentPlaceHolderID="head" runat="server">
</asp:Content>
<asp:Content ID="Content2" runat="server" contentplaceholderid="topContent">
</asp:Content>
<asp:Content ID="Content3" runat="server" contentplaceholderid="mainContent">
</asp:Content>
```

> **NOTE** *The sample page uses the master page by applying the* MasterPageFile *attribute with the* Page *directive. Other options to reference a master page include defining it globally in the configuration file, or programmatically within a page event. In the* web .config *configuration file, the* page *element uses the* MasterPageFile *attribute to indicate where a master page can be set globally. This setting can be overridden with the* Page *directive in the page, or using code-behind. Using code-behind, a master page can be set in the* Page_PreLoad *event handler (this is the latest point at which the* MasterPageFile *property can be set). Applying this setting programmatically, it is possible to use different master page files depending on some requirements, such as different partners and different contracts, or offering a different master page for mobile devices.*

By default, Content controls are created for all these placeholders where the master page doesn't create default content. To replace the default content, you can access the design view of the web page to use the smart tags from the controls to replace content.

With the sample web page, the content of the mainContent is replaced with a DropDownList as it has been used in a previous example:

```
<asp:Content ID="Content3" runat="server" contentplaceholderid="mainContent">
  <div>
    <asp:DropDownList ID="DropDownListMeetingRooms" runat="server"
      OnSelectedIndexChanged="OnRoomSelection" Width="165px" AutoPostBack="True">
      <asp:ListItem>Sacher</asp:ListItem>
      <asp:ListItem>Hawelka</asp:ListItem>
      <asp:ListItem>Hummel</asp:ListItem>
      <asp:ListItem>Prückel</asp:ListItem>
      <asp:ListItem>Landtmann</asp:ListItem>
      <asp:ListItem>Sperl</asp:ListItem>
      <asp:ListItem>Alt Wien</asp:ListItem>
      <asp:ListItem>Eiles</asp:ListItem>
    </asp:DropDownList>
    <br />
    <br />
    <asp:Label ID="LabelSelectedRoom" runat="server" Text=""></asp:Label>
    <br />
    <br />
    <asp:Button ID="Button1" runat="server" Text="Submit" />
  </div>
</asp:Content>
```

Running the application, the HTML code is merged with the master and content pages, as shown in Figure 40-6.

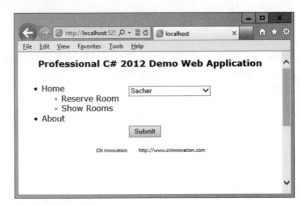

Defining Master Page Content from Content Pages

Using placeholders and content controls to define the content for pages is a very powerful option. However, sometimes you only need to replace a few items in the master page, or change some content. You can access a master page from a content page by using the `Master` property of the `page` object.

FIGURE 40-6

The following code snippet accesses the `Label` control named `LabelBottom` from the master page by using the `Master` property of the `Page`, which returns a `MasterPage` object, and then the `FindControl` method to determine where the content should be set:

```
protected void Page_Load(object sender, EventArgs e)
{
    Label label = Master.FindControl("LabelBottom") as Label;
    if (label != null)
    {
        label.Text = "Hello from the content page";
    }
}
```

Similar to what you've seen with strongly typed access to cross-page postback, strongly typed access to master pages is also possible. Next, with the master page code-behind file `Company.Master.cs`, the property `LabelBottomText` is defined to allow read/write access to the `Text` property of the `LabelBottom` control:

```
public string LabelBottomText
{
    get
    {
        return LabelBottom.Text;
    }
    set
    {
        LabelBottom.Text = value;
    }
}
```

To define a strongly typed master page, the `MasterType` directive can be applied with the content page:

```
<%@ Page Title="" Language="C#" MasterPageFile="~/Company.Master"
    AutoEventWireup="true" CodeBehind="ReserveRoom.aspx.cs"
    Inherits="Meetingroom.ReserveRoom" %>
<%@ MasterType VirtualPath="~/Company.Master" %>
```

Now the code accessing the master page can be simplified to directly use the property defined:

```
protected void Page_Load(object sender, EventArgs e)
{
    Master.LabelBottomText = "Hello from the content page";
}
```

> **NOTE** *If multiple master pages should be used with a content page, strongly typed access to the master page is also possible. For this, a custom base class that derives from the* MasterPage *class can define the properties needed from the content pages. With the* MasterType *directive to reference the master page for strongly typed access, the* TypeName *attribute can be used instead of* VirtualPath.

NAVIGATION

Let's add some navigation content to navigate within different pages of the web application. ASP.NET offers a site map that can be used with Menu and MenuPath controls.

Site Map

The structure of the web application can be described in a site map file. To create site maps, Visual Studio 2012 offers a Site Map item template that creates a file with the name Web.sitemap. A sample site map file is shown in the following code. siteMap is the root element, which can contain a hierarchy of siteMapNode elements. A siteMapNode defines attributes for the url that it accesses, a title that is displayed with menus, and a description that is used with a tooltip:

```xml
<?xml version="1.0" encoding="utf-8" ?>
<siteMap xmlns="http://schemas.microsoft.com/AspNet/SiteMap-File-1.0" >
  <siteMapNode url="~/Default.aspx" title="Home"
    description="Professional C# 2012 Demo Web Application">
    <siteMapNode url="MeetingRooms.aspx" title="Meeting Rooms" description="" >
      <siteMapNode url="~/ReserveRoom.aspx" title="Reserve a Room" />
      <siteMapNode url="~/CancelRoom.aspx" title="Cancel a Room" />
    </siteMapNode>
    <siteMapNode url="~/Accounts.aspx" title="Accounts">
      <siteMapNode url="~/RegisterUser.aspx" title="Register User"
        description="" />
    </siteMapNode>
  </siteMapNode>
</siteMap>
```

Other than the attributes used with the example, the siteMapNode also offers localization and support for roles. For localization, a resourceKey is used to specify resources to be used for menu titles and tooltips. The roles attributed is used to specify access only to users who belong to the specified roles.

> **NOTE** *Resources for localization are explained in Chapter 28.*

> **NOTE** *The ASP.NET site map is different from the XML site map that is used by crawlers to find links of a website. The ASP.NET site map is a data source used by navigation controls, and it fits well with some features of ASP.NET like data binding. It cannot be directly accessed from the client. Conversely, the XML site map is accessible from the client, and it uses a different syntax for crawlers that is explained at* http://www.sitemaps.org.

Menu Control

The web site map is used by a Menu control. All you need to do to fill the content for the Menu control is add a SiteMapDataSource. By default, the SiteMapDataSource uses the site map file named Web.sitemap. The Menu control references the data source with the DataSourceID property (code file Company.Master):

```
<div class="left">
  <asp:ContentPlaceHolder ID="leftContent" runat="server">
    <asp:Menu ID="Menu1" runat="server" DataSourceID="SiteMapDataSource1" >
    </asp:Menu>
    <asp:SiteMapDataSource ID="SiteMapDataSource1" runat="server" />
  </asp:ContentPlaceHolder>
</div>
```

> **NOTE** *The site map is provider-based, similar to Membership, Roles, and Profiles. You can also create a custom provider that derives from the base class* SiteMapProvider. XmlSiteMapProvider *is the only concrete site map provider that is part of the .NET Framework.* XmlSiteMapProvider *derives from the base class* StaticSiteMapProvider, *which in turn derives from* SiteMapProvider. *You can read more about the provider-based model with ASP.NET in Chapter 39, "Core ASP.NET."*

The Menu control is shown in Figure 40-7. By default, the control creates HTML list content with ul, li, and a elements. The outcome is completely customizable. The RenderingMode property can be set to List or Table to create list or table elements, respectively; items can be displayed statically or dynamically; horizontal or vertical displays can be configured with the Orientation property; and colors, styles, and CSS classes can be set.

Home
Meeting Rooms
Accounts

FIGURE 40-7

Menu Path

The SiteMapPath control is a breadcrumb control that indicates its current position, along with information about how to go back in the tree:

```
<div class="top2">
  <asp:ContentPlaceHolder ID="topContent" runat="server">
    <asp:SiteMapPath ID="SiteMapPath1" runat="server"></asp:SiteMapPath>
  </asp:ContentPlaceHolder>
</div>
```

Figure 40-8 shows the SiteMapPath control on the web page Reserve a Room.

Home > Meeting Rooms > Reserve a Room

FIGURE 40-8

VALIDATING USER INPUT

ASP.NET Web Forms contains several validation controls that offer validation on both the client and the server. Validating input on the client is just done for convenience of the user, as he sees the validation result faster without the need to send data to the server. However, you can never trust input from the client, and you need to verify the data on the server again.

Using Validation Controls

To show validation in action, this section creates the ValidationDemo.aspx page. At first, this page contains two Labelcontrols, two TextBox controls (named textName and textEmail), and a Button control. Users are required to enter their name and e-mail address, and the latter should be validated. Validation controls that can be used for this scenario are the RequiredFieldValidator and the RegularExpressionValidator.

All the validator controls derive from the base class `BaseValidator` and thus have the properties `ControlToValidate`, which needs to be set to the `TextBox` control that is covered by the validation control; and `ErrorMessage`, which defines the text that is displayed in case of invalid input. The following code snippets show the validator controls connected to the `TextBox` controls, and the `ErrorMessage` properties set. The `TextBox` control named `TextEmail` has two validation controls: a `RequiredFieldValidator` and an associated `RegularExpressionValidator`. With the `RegularExpressionValidator`, the `ValidationExpression` property is set, to verify that the e-mail address is valid. The Regular Expression Editor, shown in Figure 40-9, contains a list of predefined regular expressions, one of which is the Internet e-mail address. Of course, you can also add a custom regular expression.

```
<table class="auto-style1">
  <tr>
    <td>Name:</td>
    <td>
      <asp:TextBox ID="TextName" runat="server"></asp:TextBox>
      <asp:RequiredFieldValidator ID="RequiredFieldValidator1"
        runat="server" ControlToValidate="TextName"
        ErrorMessage="Name required"></asp:RequiredFieldValidator>
    </td>
  </tr>
  <tr>
    <td>Email:</td>
    <td>
      <asp:TextBox ID="TextEmail" runat="server"></asp:TextBox>
      <asp:RequiredFieldValidator ID="RequiredFieldValidator2"
        runat="server" ControlToValidate="TextEmail" Display="Dynamic"
        ErrorMessage="Email required"></asp:RequiredFieldValidator>
      <asp:RegularExpressionValidator ID="RegularExpressionValidator1"
        runat="server" ControlToValidate="TextEmail" Display="Dynamic"
        ErrorMessage="Please enter an email"
        ValidationExpression="\w+([-+.']\w+)*@\w+([-.]\w+)*\.\w+([-.]\w+)*">
      </asp:RegularExpressionValidator>
    </td>
  </tr>
  <tr>
    <td>
      <asp:Button ID="Button1" runat="server" Text="Register" />
    </td>
    <td> </td>
  </tr>
</table>
```

In Figure 40-10, the name is not entered and the e-mail address is invalid. Therefore, two validation controls apply: the `RequiredFieldValidator` with the `TextName` control and the `RegularExpressionValidator` with the `TextEmail` control. The error messages from these two validation controls are shown. With the `RequiredFieldValidator` that is connected to the `TextEmail` control, the `Display` property is set to `Dynamic`. This is necessary to arrange the error message from the `RequiredFieldValidator` in the position of the `RequiredFieldValidator`. Otherwise the space would be empty.

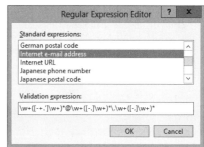

FIGURE 40-9

Using a Validation Summary

If error messages shouldn't be displayed with the input controls but instead with summary information on the page, all you need to do is add

FIGURE 40-10

a `ValidationSummary` control; and with the validation controls, the `Text` property should be set to a string that is shown in case of an error. With the sample page, the `Text` properties are set to `*`, and the `ErrorMessage` properties keep the value from the previous code snippet.

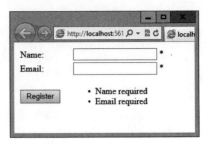

The result is shown in Figure 40-11. Here, both `RequiredFieldValidator` validation controls apply, and thus the values for the `ErrorMessage` properties are shown in the `ValidationSummary` control. With each of the failing validation controls, the value of the `Text` property is displayed.

FIGURE 40-11

Validation Groups

If the page contains multiple submit-type buttons with different areas of validation, validation groups can be assigned. If validation groups are not used, with every postback all the controls are verified to be correct. With the page shown in Figure 40-12, if the user clicks the Register button, only the controls that belong to this part should be validated; and if the user clicks the Submit button, only these controls should be validated. This issue is solved by setting the `ValidationGroup` property of the first group of validation controls as well as the `Button` control to `"Register"`, and the second group of validation controls to `"Event"`. Clicking the button belonging to the `ValidationGroup` `"Event"` validates only the validation controls from the same group.

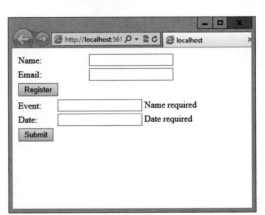

FIGURE 40-12

ACCESSING DATA

Data access can be very simple using data controls from ASP.NET. A lot is possible without writing a single line of C# code. Controls in the category Data belong to two different groups: data sources and UI controls. Data sources are used to access data, such as by using the ADO.NET Entity Framework or `DataSets`. UI controls define different looks, such as the `GridView` and the `DetailsView`.

The following table describes the data source controls.

DATA SOURCE CONTROL	DESCRIPTION
`AccessDataSource`	Used to access Microsoft Access databases.
`EntityDataSource`	Makes use of the ADO.NET Entity Framework to read and write data.
`LinqDataSource`	Used to access LINQ to SQL. This mapping tool has been mostly replaced by the ADO.NET Entity Framework.
`ObjectDataSource`	This can be used to access custom objects with static or instance members to return list of objects, and offers methods to add and update objects.
`SiteMapDataSource`	Reads the `Web.sitemap` file and is used for navigation. This data source was shown previously in the chapter.
`SqlDataSource`	Makes use of either a `DataReader` or a `DataSet`. These types are explained in Chapter 32, "Core ADO.NET."
`XmlDataSource`	Used to access XML data, either from a file or an XML object. XML manipulation is explained in Chapter 34, "Manipulating XML."

The next table contains information about controls for the UI.

WEB SERVER DATA CONTROL	DESCRIPTION
ListView	A powerful control for showing data in a grid style. It enables selecting, sorting, deleting, editing, and inserting records. The UI is customized with templates.
DataList	This control can be bound to a data source to show data in a grid-style format. The UI can be customized with templates. This control also supports selecting and editing data.
DataPager	This can be used in conjunction with another control (e.g., the ListView) to add paging functionality.
GridView	Uses a table to show bound data. Selecting, sorting, and editing are possible.
Repeater	Unlike the other UI controls, the Repeater requires a custom layout using templates in order to have useful output. Many other controls can use templates, but without them there is already output.
DetailsView	Shows a single record and allows editing, deleting, and inserting records.
FormView	Like the DetailsView, the FormView is used to display a single record. FormView requires a user-defined template, and enables more customization than the DetailsView.

Clearly, many controls can be used to display grids. Over the years, ASP.NET Web Forms has continued to add grid controls with more features. Usually a good option is to use the ListView control. This control is only available since .NET 3.5 and offers features found in the other controls and more. GridView has been available since .NET 2.0, and DataList since .NET 1.1. Knowing the availability of these controls helps deciding which one to use, which one offers more "modern" features.

Using the Entity Framework

Although the ADO.NET Entity Framework is covered in detail in Chapter 33, "ADO.NET Entity Framework," this section describes how to define access code using it.

The sample database contains two tables, Reservations and MeetingRooms, and these tables are mapped to the types MeetingRoom and Reservation as shown in Figure 40-13. The model can be created easily by adding a new item of type ADO .NET Entity Data Model, and selecting the existing database. You can download the database along with the sample code.

The designer creates entity types MeetingRoom and Reservation that derive from the base class EntityObject and contain all the properties defined in the database schema. In addition to the entity objects, an object context named RoomReservationEntities is created. This context defines properties for every table to return ObjectSet<MeetingRoom> and ObjectSet<Reservation> objects. This class manages the connection to the database.

FIGURE 40-13

Using the Entity Data Source

With the first page, the meeting rooms should be shown in a DropDownList, and a GridView should display the reservations for a room. With a simple scenario, this can be done without writing a single line of C# code.

The first two controls on the page ShowReservations.aspx are a DropDownList and an EntityDataSource control. Using the smart tag, the data source can be configured to use the connection that was used to create the model. Selecting this connection finds the container name of the entities,

`RoomReservationEntities`. The second dialog, shown in Figure 40-14, requires the entity set `MeetingRooms`, with an `EntityTypeFilter`.

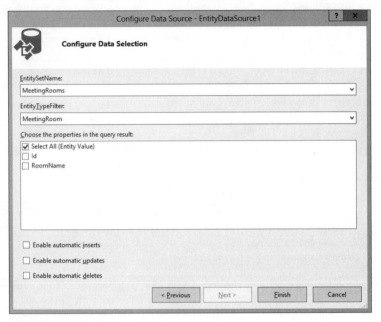

FIGURE 40-14

After configuring the data source, the UI control can be configured to reference the data source control. For this, you can use the Data Source Configuration Wizard, shown in Figure 40-15. For the display in the `DropDownList`, the `RoomName` property is used; for the identification of the data field, the `Id` property is used.

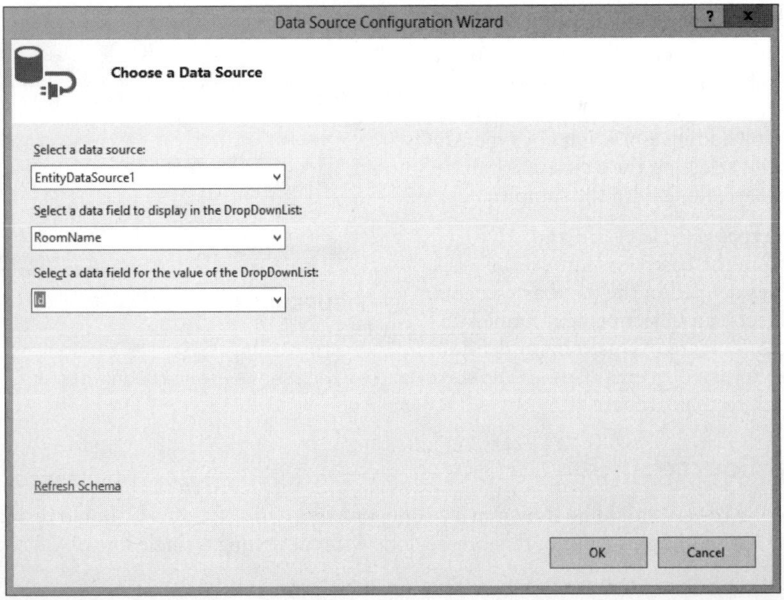

FIGURE 40-15

Opening the page, the rooms from the database are displayed. The next step is to display the reservations based on the selection. For this activity, a GridView and one more EntityDataSource control are added to the page. The second data source control is configured to access the Reservations EntitySetName, and automatic inserts, updates, and deletes are enabled.

After initial configuration of the data source, more options are available with the properties of this control. Grouping, ordering, and filtering can be configured. With the sample page, the Where property is set to a RoomId parameter, as shown in Figure 40-16. If the parameter has the same name as a property of the entity type, a WHERE expression is created based on the paramter. The value of the parameter is taken directly from the SelectedValue property of the DropDownList. This selection is directly available from the Expression Editor. One advanced property also needs to be set. Because the RoomId is of type int, the property type needs to be set to Int32. By default, it's a string.

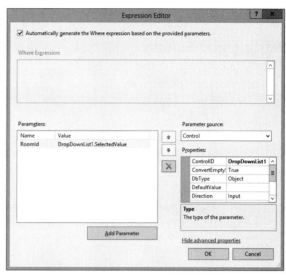

FIGURE 40-16

In the example code, the source of the parameter is the DropDownList control. With the Expression Editor you can also see other source types available. Cookie, Form, Profile, QueryString, Session, and RouteData are other parameter source options. There's really a lot that can be done just by configuration of some properties. With the GridView control, only the DataSourceId needs to be set to the second EntityDataSource control.

So far, the code-behind is empty, and the DropDownList, EntityDataSource, and GridView controls are configured as follows:

```
<asp:DropDownList ID="DropDownList1" runat="server" AutoPostBack="True"
  DataSourceID="EntityDataSource1" DataTextField="RoomName"
  DataValueField="Id" Height="22px" Width="150px">
</asp:DropDownList>
<br />
<asp:EntityDataSource ID="EntityDataSource1" runat="server"
  ConnectionString="name=RoomReservationEntities"
  DefaultContainerName="RoomReservationEntities" EnableFlattening="False"
  EntitySetName="MeetingRooms" EntityTypeFilter="MeetingRoom">
</asp:EntityDataSource>
<br />
<asp:GridView ID="GridView1" runat="server"
  DataSourceID="EntityDataSource2">
</asp:GridView>
<br />
<br />
<asp:EntityDataSource ID="EntityDataSource2" runat="server"
  AutoGenerateWhereClause="True"
  ConnectionString="name=RoomReservationEntities"
  DefaultContainerName="RoomReservationEntities" EnableDelete="True"
  EnableFlattening="False" EnableInsert="True" EnableUpdate="True"
  EntitySetName="Reservations" Where="">
  <WhereParameters>
    <asp:ControlParameter ControlID="DropDownList1" Name="RoomId"
      PropertyName="SelectedValue" Type="Int32" />
  </WhereParameters>
</asp:EntityDataSource>
```

The page can now be opened in the browser to select room reservations, as shown in Figure 40-17.

Sorting and Editing

Out of the box, the GridView supports sorting, paging, end editing, depending on the capabilities of the data source. For example, earlier in the chapter, Figure 40-14 shows the editing features of the EntityDataSource: automatic inserts, updates, and deletes. When this is selected, editing and deleting can be enabled with the GridView (see Figure 40-18).

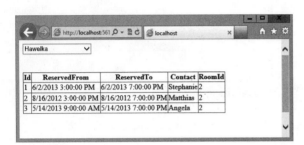

FIGURE 40-17   **FIGURE 40-18**

Setting these options with the GridView sets the properties AllowPaging and AllowSorting, and adds a CommandField column with Delete, Edit, and Select buttons:

```
<asp:GridView ID="GridView1" runat="server" DataSourceID="EntityDataSource2"
  AllowPaging="True" AllowSorting="True">
  <Columns>
    <asp:CommandField ShowDeleteButton="True" ShowEditButton="True"
      ShowSelectButton="True" />
  </Columns>
</asp:GridView>
```

The GridView just uses the name of the properties in the heading (Id, ReservedFrom, ReservedTo, Contact), and uses Label controls in read mode, and TextBox controls in edit mode, as shown in Figure 40-19. When the Edit button is clicked, the row changes to edit mode. In edit mode, TextBox controls are bound to the data. Changing the values there also changes the entities in the Entity Framework object context. Clicking Update invokes the SaveChanges method of the object context and writes the changes to the database.

	Id	ReservedFrom	ReservedTo	Contact	RoomId
Edit Delete Select	1	6/2/2013 3:00:00 PM	6/2/2013 7:00:00 PM	Stephanie	2
Update Cancel	2	8/16/2012 3:00:00 PM	8/16/2012 7:00:00 PM	Matthias	2
Edit Delete Select	3	5/14/2013 9:00:00 AM	5/14/2013 7:00:00 PM	Angela	2

FIGURE 40-19

Customizing Columns

By default all the properties are shown. At least the heading should be changed, and the Id column should remain read-only in edit mode. Such customization is easy by opening the Fields editor, shown in Figure 40-20.

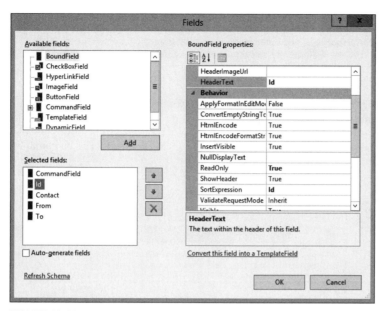

FIGURE 40-20

Instead of auto-generating fields, you can select the fields that should be displayed. You can configure many aspects of these fields, including heading information and images for the headings, footer text, a default display for null values, a format string, and styles for the control, header, footer, and item elements. The content of the `GridView` is now changed to `BoundField` objects, as shown in the following code snippet:

```
<asp:GridView ID="GridView1" runat="server" DataSourceID="EntityDataSource2"
  AllowPaging="True" AllowSorting="True" AutoGenerateColumns="False">
  <Columns>
    <asp:CommandField ShowDeleteButton="True" ShowEditButton="True"
      ShowSelectButton="True" />
    <asp:BoundField DataField="Id" HeaderText="Id" ReadOnly="True"
      SortExpression="Id"></asp:BoundField>
    <asp:BoundField DataField="Contact" HeaderText="Contact"
      SortExpression="Contact"></asp:BoundField>
    <asp:BoundField DataField="ReservedFrom" HeaderText="From"
      SortExpression="ReservedFrom"></asp:BoundField>
    <asp:BoundField DataField="ReservedTo" HeaderText="To"
      SortExpression="ReservedTo"></asp:BoundField>
  </Columns>
</asp:GridView>
```

Using Templates with the Grid

For more customization, you can use templates. With the Fields editor, columns can be converted to templates. Changing the Contact field to templates, now a `TemplateField` instead of a `BoundField` is used, as shown in the following code snippet. With template fields, you can create different user interfaces, such as `ItemTemplate`, `EditItemTemplate`, `AlternatingItemTemplate`, `HeaderTemplate`, `FooterTemplate`, and more. The default `ItemTemplate` makes use of a `Label`, and the `EditItemTemplate` uses a `TextBox`. With both of these, the `Text` property is bound to the `Contact` property of the bound object:

```
<asp:TemplateField HeaderText="Contact" SortExpression="Contact">
  <EditItemTemplate>
    <asp:TextBox ID="TextBox2" runat="server"
      Text='<%# Bind("Contact") %>'></asp:TextBox>
```

```
    </EditItemTemplate>
    <ItemTemplate>
      <asp:Label ID="Label2" runat="server"
        Text='<%# Bind("Contact") %>'></asp:Label>
    </ItemTemplate>
  </asp:TemplateField>
```

Using the Template Editor (see Figure 40-21), any ASP.NET controls can be added to the different template modes. The sample adds a template for the MeetingRoom column, and replaces a TextBox in edit mode by a DropDownList control. With the DropDownList control, the data source is selected to be the first entity data source control that returns the meeting rooms. Properties of the DropDownList control can be bound by using the DataBindings editor, shown in Figure 40-22.

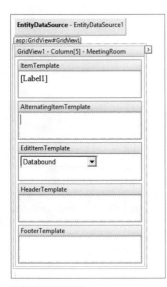

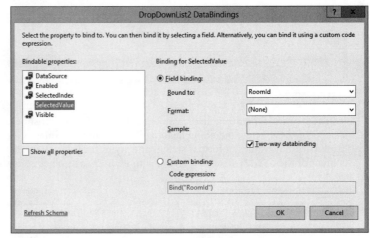

FIGURE 40-21   **FIGURE 40-22**

The resulting ASPX code now uses a DropDownList in the EditItemTemplate, and a Label in the ItemTemplate:

```
<asp:TemplateField HeaderText="MeetingRoom" SortExpression="MeetingRoom">
  <EditItemTemplate>
    <asp:DropDownList ID="DropDownList2" runat="server"
      DataTextField="RoomName" DataValueField="Id"
      Width="146px" Height="16px" SelectedValue='<%# Bind("RoomId") %>'
      DataSourceID="EntityDataSource1">
    </asp:DropDownList>
  </EditItemTemplate>
  <ItemTemplate>
    <asp:Label ID="Label1" runat="server" Text='<%#
      Bind("MeetingRoom.RoomName") %>'></asp:Label>
  </ItemTemplate>
</asp:TemplateField>
```

Figure 40-23 shows the opened page with the DropDownList in the edit mode. Meeting rooms are retrieved from the first data source, while the grid itself is bound to the second data source.

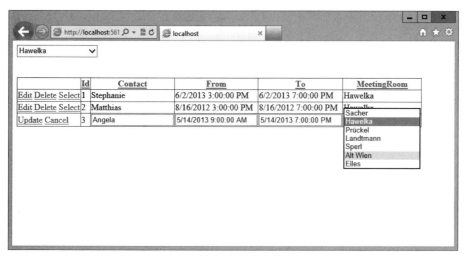

FIGURE 40-23

Customizing Object Context Creation

Displaying and editing with a grid covering multiple data sources is an easy task. So far, not a single line of code was added to the code-behind; everything was just set by using the properties of existing controls. However, as multiple EntityDataSource controls are used within the page, with every request multiple object context instances are created. You can tweak this behavior easily by adding the event handlers OnContextCreating and OnContextDisposing to the page. Within the OnContextCreating method, a new RoomReservationEntities object context is created if the method is called for the first time. This object context is assigned to the Context property of EntityDataSourceContextCreatingEventArgs. After assigning this context, the EntityDataSource control makes use of it instead of creating a new one:

```csharp
using System;
using System.Web.UI.WebControls;

namespace ProCSharpSampleWeb.DataAccess
{
  public partial class ShowReservations : System.Web.UI.Page
  {
    private RoomReservationEntities data;

    protected void Page_Load(object sender, EventArgs e)
    {
    }

    protected void OnContextCreating(object sender,
      EntityDataSourceContextCreatingEventArgs e)
    {
      if (data == null)
      {
        data = new RoomReservationEntities();
      }
      e.Context = data;
    }

    protected void OnContextDisposing(object sender,
      EntityDataSourceContextDisposingEventArgs e)
```

```
        {
          if (data != null)
          {
            data.Dispose();
            data = null;
          }
        }
      }
    }
```

With the two `EntityDataSource` objects, the `ContextCreating` and `ContextDisposing` events are set to the corresponding event handlers, and performance is improved.

> **NOTE** *Using the `EntityDataSource` control (or many of the other data source controls) offers the advantage of enabling you to build web applications very quickly. However, the disadvantage is that data access code is coupled in the UI. This doesn't help with unit testing and maintainability of the web application. The `ObjectDataSource` can solve this issue, separating data access code from the UI, as discussed next.*

Object Data Source

Whereas the `EntityDataSource` makes direct use of the ADO.NET Entity Framework, the `ObjectDataSource` can use a class with static or instance members and invoke these. This gives you a lot more flexibility to work with the data access code.

The `RoomReservationFactory` class implements the methods `MeetingRooms`, `GetReservationsByRoom`, and `UpdateReservation`:

```csharp
using System.Collections.Generic;
using System.Data;
using System.Linq;

namespace ProCSharpSampleWeb.DataAccess
{
  public class RoomReservationFactory
  {
    public IEnumerable<MeetingRoom> MeetingRooms()
    {
      IEnumerable<MeetingRoom> rooms;
      using (RoomReservationEntities data = new RoomReservationEntities())
      {
        rooms = data.MeetingRooms.ToList();
      }
      return rooms;
    }

    public IEnumerable<Reservation> GetReservationsByRoom(int roomId)
    {
      IEnumerable<Reservation> reservations;
      using (RoomReservationEntities data = new RoomReservationEntities())
      {
        reservations = data.Reservations.Where(r => r.RoomId == roomId).ToList();
      }
      return reservations;
    }
```

```
public void UpdateReservation(Reservation reservation)
{
  using (RoomReservationEntities data = new RoomReservationEntities())
  {
    data.Reservations.Attach(reservation);
    data.ObjectStateManager.ChangeObjectState(reservation,
      EntityState.Modified);
    data.SaveChanges();
  }
}
```

Using an `ObjectDataSource`, you can define methods to select, update, insert, and delete from the `RoomReservationFactory` class, as shown in Figure 40-24. Then the data source can be used similarly to the `EntityDataSource` as before.

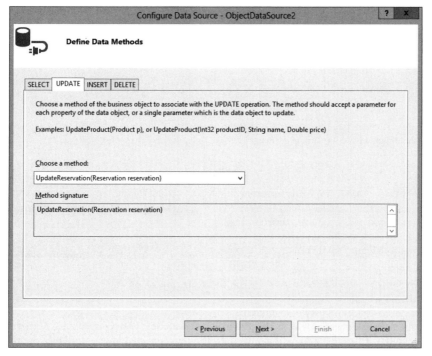

FIGURE 40-24

SECURITY

Another important aspect of ASP.NET web applications is using authentication and authorization. In the previous chapter, the `Membership` and `Roles` APIs have been discussed. This chapter covers calling these APIs with the help of available web server controls.

Enabling Forms Authentication

You can configure forms authentication by starting the ASP.NET Configuration Tool from within Visual Studio 2012. Starting this tool also creates the aspnetdb database as you can see with the configuration string in the web.config file:

```
<connectionStrings>
  <clear />
  <add name="LocalSqlServer" connectionString="data source=(localDB)\v11.0;
    Integrated Security=SSPI;AttachDBFilename=|DataDirectory|aspnetdb.mdf"
    providerName="System.Data.SqlClient"/>
  <!-- ... -->
</connectionStrings>
```

Using this tool to change to Internet authentication adds the authentication configuration with the mode attribute set to Forms. If only authorized users are allowed, by default the file login.aspx is requested if the user is not authenticated.

```
<authorization>
  <deny users="?" />
</authorization>
<authentication mode="Forms" />
```

Login Controls

Needed along with the login.aspx page are controls to enter username and password, and probably a check box to remember the password. All this is offered by the Login control:

```
<asp:Login ID="Login1" runat="server"></asp:Login>
```

This control makes use of several Label controls for user information, two TextBox controls for user input, a CheckBox to enable remembering the password, validator controls, and a Button to submit the login information that uses the predefined Elegant format (see Figure 40-25).

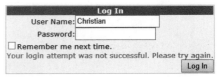

FIGURE 40-25

To customize the Login control, set its properties—for example, title text and the text that should be shown for the username and password, and whether a "remember me" check box should be displayed. Some predefined style schemes are available to provide different looks. Of course, you can also style the outcome with custom CSS. If these format settings are not enough, a LayoutTemplate can be used for complete customization. Only the IDs of the essential UI controls must stay the same.

When the Log In button is clicked, the events LoggingIn, LoggedIn, and LoginError are fired. If no event handlers are added, the Login control already uses the Membership.ValidateUser method to validate the user.

> **NOTE** *The Membership API is covered in Chapter 39 and Chapter 22, "Security."*

To allow registration of anonymous users with the sample application, a subdirectory named anonymous is created. This subdirectory contains a web.config file that allows anonymous users. This setting overrides the setting from the web.config file in the parent directory:

```xml
<?xml version="1.0" encoding="utf-8"?>
<configuration>
  <system.web>
    <authorization>
      <allow users="?" />
    </authorization>
  </system.web>
</configuration>
```

The subdirectory contains the ASP.NET page `RegisterUser.aspx`, which contains only the control `CreateUserWizard` within the form element. `CreateUserWizard` is a simple control for asking users all the information needed to create a new account. Figure 40-26 shows the default output of this control.

```xml
<asp:CreateUserWizard ID="CreateUserWizard1" runat="server">
  <WizardSteps>
    <asp:CreateUserWizardStep runat="server" />
    <asp:CompleteWizardStep runat="server" />
  </WizardSteps>
</asp:CreateUserWizard>
```

AJAX

Ajax enables you to enhance the user interfaces of web applications by means of asynchronous postbacks and dynamic client-side web page manipulation. The term Ajax was invented by Jesse James Garrett and is shorthand for *Asynchronous JavaScript and XML*.

FIGURE 40-26

> **NOTE** *Ajax is not an acronym, which is why it is not capitalized as AJAX. However, it is capitalized in the product name ASP.NET AJAX, which is Microsoft's implementation of Ajax, as described in the section "What is ASP.NET AJAX?"*

By definition, Ajax involves both JavaScript and XML. However, Ajax programming requires the use of other technologies as well, such as HTML, CSS, and the document object model (DOM). Nowadays, XML is not always used with Ajax for transferring data between the client and the server. Instead, JSON (JavaScript Object Notation) is used an alternative. It has less overhead compared to XML.

Of course, the most important part of Ajax is the `XMLHttpRequest`. Since Internet Explorer 5, IE has supported the `XMLHttpRequest` API as a means of performing asynchronous communication between the client and server. This was originally introduced by Microsoft as a technology to access e-mail stored in an Exchange server over the Internet, in a product known as Outlook Web Access. Since then, it has become the standard way to perform asynchronous communications in web applications, and it is a core technology of Ajax-enabled web applications. Microsoft's implementation of this API is known as XMLHTTP, which communicates over what is often called the XMLHTTP Protocol.

Ajax also requires server-side code to handle both partial-page postbacks and full-page postbacks. This can include both event handlers for server-control events and web services. Figure 40-27 shows how these technologies fit together in the Ajax web browser model, in contrast to the "traditional" web browser model.

Prior to Ajax, the first four technologies listed in the preceding table (HTML, CSS, the DOM, and JavaScript) were used to create what was known as Dynamic HTML (DHTML) web applications. These applications were notable for two reasons: they provided a much better user interface and they generally worked on only one type of web browser.

"Traditional" Web Browser Model

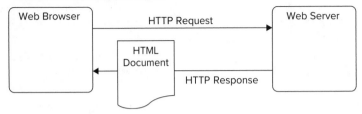

Ajax Web Browser Model

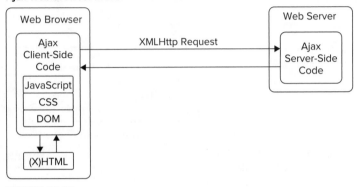

FIGURE 40-27

Since DHTML, standards have improved, along with the level of adherence to standards in web browsers. However, there are still differences, and an Ajax solution must take them into account. This has meant that most developers have been quite slow to implement Ajax solutions. Only with the advent of more abstracted Ajax frameworks (such as ASP.NET AJAX) has Ajax-enabled website creation become a viable option for enterprise-level development.

What Is ASP.NET AJAX?

ASP.NET AJAX is Microsoft's implementation of the Ajax framework, and it is specifically targeted at ASP .NET Web Forms developers. It is part of the core ASP.NET Web Forms functionality. The website dedicated to ASP.NET AJAX is `http://ajax.asp.net`, where you can find documentation, forums, and sample code that you may find useful for whichever version of ASP.NET you are using.

ASP.NET AJAX provides the following functionality:

➤ A server-side framework that enables ASP.NET web pages to respond to partial-page postback operations

➤ ASP.NET server controls that make the implementation of Ajax functionality easy

➤ An HTTP handler that enables ASP.NET web services to communicate with client-side code by using JSON serialization in partial-page postback operations

➤ Web services that enable client-side code to gain access to ASP.NET application services, including authentication and personalization services

➤ A website template for creating ASP.NET AJAX-enabled web applications

➤ A client-side JavaScript library that provides a number of enhancements to JavaScript syntax, as well as code to simplify the implementation of Ajax functionality

These server controls and the server-side framework that makes them possible are collectively known as the ASP.NET Extensions. The client-side part of ASP.NET AJAX is known as the AJAX Library. The ASP.NET

AJAX Control Toolkit is not part of the Visual Studio 2012 installation. This toolkit can be installed from a NuGet Package. At the time of this writing, the most current version is 4.1.60623, which is used with the examples. This toolkit contains a lot of server controls that are available as shared source.

Together these downloads provide a richly featured framework that you can use to add Ajax functionality to your ASP.NET web applications. In the following sections, you learn more about the various component parts of ASP.NET AJAX. Its core functionality is contained in two parts: the AJAX Extensions and the AJAX Library.

ASP.NET AJAX Extensions

ASP.NET AJAX extensions are contained in two assemblies that are installed in the GAC:

➤ System.Web.Extensions.dll—This assembly contains the ASP.NET AJAX functionality, including the AJAX Extensions and the AJAX Library JavaScript files, which are available through the ScriptManager component (described shortly).

➤ System.Web.Extensions.Design.dll—This assembly contains ASP.NET Designer components for the AJAX Extensions server controls. This is used by the ASP.NET Designer in Visual Studio or Visual Web Developer.

Much of the AJAX Extensions component of ASP.NET AJAX is concerned with enabling partial-page postbacks and JSON serialization for web services. This includes various HTTP handler components and extensions to the existing ASP.NET Framework. All this functionality can be configured through the web.config file for a site. There are also classes and attributes that you can use for additional configuration. However, most of this configuration is transparent, and you will rarely need to change the defaults.

Your main interaction with AJAX Extensions will be using server controls to add Ajax functionality to your web applications. There are several of these, which you can use to enhance your applications in various ways. The following table shows a selection of the server-side components. These components are demonstrated later in this chapter.

CONTROL	DESCRIPTION
ScriptManager	This control, central to ASP.NET AJAX functionality, is required on every page that uses partial-page postbacks. Its main purpose is to manage client-side references to the AJAX Library JavaScript files, which are served from the ASP.NET AJAX assembly. The AJAX Library is used extensively by the AJAX Extensions server controls, which all generate their own client-side code. This control is also responsible for the configuration of web services that you intend to access from client-side code. By supplying web service information to the ScriptManager control, you can generate client-side and server-side classes to manage asynchronous communication with web services transparently. You can also use the ScriptManager control to maintain references to your own JavaScript files.
UpdatePanel	This extremely useful control may be the ASP.NET AJAX control that you will use most often. It acts like a standard ASP.NET placeholder and can contain any other controls. More important, it also marks a section of a page as a region that can be updated independently of the rest of the page, in a partial-page postback. Any controls contained by an UpdatePanel control that cause a postback (a Button control, for example) will not cause full-page postbacks. Instead, they cause partial-page postbacks that update only the contents of the UpdatePanel. In many situations, this control is all you need to implement Ajax functionality. For example, you can place a GridView control in an UpdatePanel control, and any pagination, sorting, and other postback functionality of the control will take place in a partial-page postback.

continues

(continued)

CONTROL	DESCRIPTION
`UpdateProgress`	This control enables you to provide feedback to users when a partial-page postback is in progress. You can supply a template for this control that will be displayed when an `UpdatePanel` is updating. For example, you could use a floating `<div>` control to display a message such as "Updating..." so that the user is aware that the application is busy. Note that partial-page postbacks do not interfere with the rest of a web page, which will remain responsive.
`Timer`	The ASP.NET AJAX control provides a way to cause an `UpdatePanel` to update periodically. You can configure this control to trigger postbacks at regular intervals. If the `Timer` control is contained in an `UpdatePanel` control, then the `UpdatePanel` is updated every time the `Timer` control is triggered. This control also has an associated event so that you can carry out periodic server-side processing.
`AsyncPostBackTrigger`	You can use this control to trigger `UpdatePanel` updates from controls that aren't contained in the `UpdatePanel`. For example, you can enable a drop-down list elsewhere on a web page to cause an `UpdatePanel` containing a `GridView` control to update.

The AJAX Extensions also include the `ExtenderControl` abstract base class for extending existing ASP .NET server controls. This is used, for example, by various classes in the ASP.NET AJAX Control Toolkit, as you will see shortly.

AJAX Library

The AJAX Library consists of JavaScript files that are used by client-side code in ASP.NET AJAX-enabled web applications. A lot of functionality is included in these JavaScript files, some of which is general code that enhances the JavaScript language and some of which is specific to Ajax functionality. The AJAX Library contains layers of functionality that are built on top of each other, as described in the following table.

LAYER	DESCRIPTION
Browser compatibility	The lowest-level code in the AJAX Library consists of code that maps various JavaScript functionality according to the client web browser. This is necessary because browsers differ in terms of how they implement JavaScript. By providing this layer, JavaScript code in other layers does not have any browser compatibility issues, and you can write browser-neutral code that will work in all client environments.
Core services	This layer contains the enhancements to the JavaScript language, in particular OOP functionality. By using the code in this layer you can define namespaces, classes, derived classes, and interfaces using JavaScript script files. This is of particular interest to C# developers, because it makes writing JavaScript code much more like writing .NET code (by using C# and encouraging reusability).
Base class library	The client base class library (BCL) includes many JavaScript classes that provide low-level functionality to classes further down the AJAX Library hierarchy. Most of these classes are not intended to be used directly.
Networking	Classes in the networking layer enable client-side code to call server-side code asynchronously. This layer includes the basic framework for making a call to a URL and responding to the result in a callback function. For the most part, this is functionality that you will not use directly; instead, you will use classes that wrap this functionality. This layer also contains classes for JSON serialization and deserialization. You will find most of the networking classes on the client-side `Sys .Net` namespace.

LAYER	DESCRIPTION
User interface	This layer contains classes that abstract user interface elements such as HTML elements and DOM events. You can use the properties and methods of this layer to write language-neutral JavaScript code to manipulate web pages from the client. User interface classes are contained in the `Sys.UI` namespace.
Controls	The final layer of the AJAX Library contains the highest-level code, which provides Ajax behaviors and server control functionality. This includes dynamically generated code that you can use, for example, to call web services from client-side JavaScript code.

You can use the AJAX Library to extend and customize the behavior of ASP.NET AJAX-enabled web applications, but it is important to note that it isn't necessary. You can go a long way without using any additional JavaScript in your applications—it becomes a requirement only when you need more advanced functionality. If you do write additional client-side code, however, you will find that it is much easier using the functionality that the AJAX Library offers.

ASP.NET AJAX Control Toolkit

The AJAX Control Toolkit is a collection of additional server controls, including extender controls, that have been written by the ASP.NET AJAX community. Extender controls are controls that enable you to add functionality to an existing ASP.NET server control, typically by associating a client-side behavior with it. For example, one of the extenders in the AJAX Control Toolkit extends the `TextBox` control by placing "watermark" text in the `TextBox`, which appears when the user hasn't yet added any content to the text box. This extender control is implemented in a server control called `TextBoxWatermark`.

Using the AJAX Control Toolkit, you can add quite a lot more functionality to your sites beyond what is provided in the core download. These controls are also interesting simply to browse, and they will probably give you plenty of ideas about enhancing your web applications. However, because the AJAX Control Toolkit is separate from the core download, you should not expect the same level of support for these controls.

ASP.NET AJAX Website Example

Now that you have seen the component parts of ASP.NET AJAX, it is time to start looking at how to use them to enhance your websites. This section demonstrates how web applications that use ASP.NET AJAX work, and how to use the various aspects of functionality that ASP.NET AJAX includes. You start by examining a simple application, and then add functionality in subsequent sections.

The ASP.NET Web Site template includes all the ASP.NET AJAX core functionality. You can also use the AJAX Control Toolkit Web Site template (after it is installed) to include controls from the AJAX Control Toolkit. For the purposes of this example, you can create a new ASP.NET Emtpy Web Application template called `ProCSharpAjaxSample`.

Add a web form called `Default.aspx` and modify its code as follows:

```
<%@ Page Language="C#" AutoEventWireup="true" CodeBehind="Default.aspx.cs"
  Inherits="ProCSharpAjaxSample.Default" %>

<!DOCTYPE html>

<html>
<head runat="server">
  <title>Pro C# ASP.NET AJAX Sample</title>
</head>
<body>
  <form id="form1" runat="server">
  <asp:ScriptManager ID="ScriptManager1" runat="server" />
  <div>
```

```
<h1>Pro C# ASP.NET AJAX Sample</h1>
This sample obtains a list of primes up to a maximum value.
  <br />
Maximum:
  <asp:TextBox runat="server" ID="MaxValue" Text="2500" />
<br />
Result:
  <asp:UpdatePanel runat="server" ID="ResultPanel">
    <ContentTemplate>
      <asp:Button runat="server" ID="GoButton" Text="Calculate" />
      <br />
      <asp:Label runat="server" ID="ResultLabel" />
      <br />
      <small>Panel render time: <%= DateTime.Now.ToLongTimeString() %>
      </small>
    </ContentTemplate>
  </asp:UpdatePanel>
  <asp:UpdateProgress runat="server" ID="UpdateProgress1">
    <ProgressTemplate>
      <div style="position: absolute; left: 100px; top: 200px;
        padding: 40px 60px 40px 60px; background-color: lightyellow;
        border: black 1px solid; font-weight: bold; font-size: larger;
        filter: alpha(opacity=80);">
        Updating.
      </div>
    </ProgressTemplate>
  </asp:UpdateProgress>
  <small>Page render time: <%= DateTime.Now.ToLongTimeString() %></small>
  </div>
  </form>
</body>
</html>
```

Switch to design view (note that the ASP.NET AJAX controls such as UpdatePanel and UpdateProgress have visual designer components) and double-click the Calculate button to add an event handler. Modify the code as follows (code file ProCSharpAjaxSample/Default.aspx.cs):

```csharp
protected void GoButton_Click(object sender, EventArgs e)
{
  int maxValue = 0;
  var resultText = new StringBuilder();
  if (int.TryParse(MaxValue.Text, out maxValue))
  {
    for (int trial = 2; trial <= maxValue; trial++)
    {
      bool isPrime = true;
      for (int divisor = 2; divisor <= Math.Sqrt(trial); divisor++)
      {
        if (trial % divisor == 0)
        {
          isPrime = false;
          break;
        }
      }
      if (isPrime)
      {
        resultText.AppendFormat("{0} ", trial);
      }
    }
  }
  else
```

```
    {
      resultText.Append("Unable to parse maximum value.");
    }
    ResultLabel.Text = resultText.ToString();
  }
}
```

Save your modifications and press F5 to run the project. If prompted, enable debugging in `web.config`.

When the web page appears, as shown in Figure 40-28, note that the two render times shown are the same.

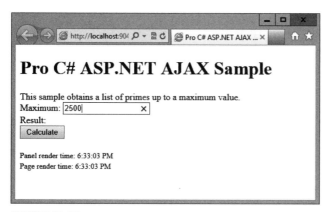

FIGURE 40-28

Click the Calculate button to display prime numbers less than or equal to 2500. Unless you are running on a slow machine, this should be almost instantaneous. Note that the render times are now different—only the one in the `UpdatePanel` has changed.

Finally, add some zeros to the maximum value to introduce a processing delay (about three more should be enough on a fast PC) and click the Calculate button again. This time, before the result is displayed, the `UpdateProgress` control displays a partially transparent feedback message, as shown in Figure 40-29.

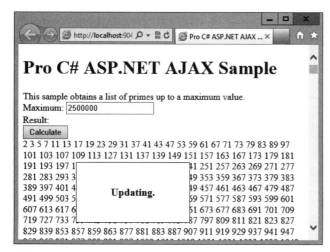

FIGURE 40-29

While the application updates, the page remains responsive. You can, for example, scroll through the page. Close the browser to return to Visual Studio.

> **NOTE** *When the update completes, the scroll position of the browser is set to the point it was at before Calculate was clicked. In most cases, when partial-page updates are quick to execute, this is great for usability.*

Close the browser to return to Visual Studio.

ASP.NET AJAX-Enabled Website Configuration

Most of the configuration required for ASP.NET AJAX is supplied for you by default; you only need to add to `web.config` if you want to change these defaults. For example, you can add a `<system.web .extensions>` section to provide additional configuration. Most of the configuration that you can add with this section concerns web services and is contained in an element called `<webServices>`, which in turn is placed in a `<scripting>` element. First, you can add a section to enable access to the ASP.NET authentication service through a web service (you can choose to enforce SSL here if you wish):

```
<system.web.extensions>
  <scripting>
    <webServices>
      <authenticationService enabled="true" requireSSL="true"/>
```

Next, you can enable and configure access to ASP.NET personalization functionality through the profile web service:

```
<profileService enabled="true"
  readAccessProperties="propertyname1,propertyname2"
  writeAccessProperties="propertyname1,propertyname2" />
```

The last setting related to web services is for enabling and configuring access to ASP.NET role functionality through the role web service:

```
<roleService enabled="true"/>
</webServices>
```

Finally, the `<system.web.extensions>` section can contain an element that enables you to configure compression and caching for asynchronous communications:

```
<scriptResourceHandler enableCompression="true" enableCaching="true" />
  </scripting>
</system.web.extensions>
```

Additional Configuration for the AJAX Control Toolkit

Installing the AJAX Control Toolkit using NuGet adds the following configuration to `web.config`:

```
<pages>
  <controls>
    <add tagPrefix="ajaxToolkit" assembly="AjaxControlToolkit"
      namespace="AjaxControlToolkit" />
  </controls>
</pages>
```

This maps the toolkit controls to the `ajaxToolkit` tag prefix. These controls are contained in the `AjaxControlToolkit.dll` assembly, which should be in the `/bin` directory for the web application.

Alternatively, you could register the controls individually on web pages using the `<%@ Register %>` directive:

```
<%@ Register Assembly="AjaxControlToolkit" Namespace="AjaxControlToolkit"
    TagPrefix="ajaxToolkit" %>
```

Adding ASP.NET AJAX Functionality

The first step in adding Ajax functionality to a website is to add a `ScriptManager` control to your web pages. Then you add server controls such as `UpdatePanel` controls to enable partial-page rendering, and dynamic controls such as those supplied in the AJAX Control Toolkit to add usability and glitz to your application. You may also add client-side code, and you can use the AJAX Library for further assistance in customizing and enhancing your application's functionality. This section describes the functionality you can add using server controls. Later in this chapter you look at client-side techniques.

The ScriptManager Control

As mentioned earlier in the chapter, the `ScriptManager` control must be included on all pages that use partial-page postbacks and several other aspects of ASP.NET AJAX functionality.

> **NOTE** *A great way to ensure that all the pages in your web application contain the* `ScriptManager` *control is to add this control to the master page (or master pages) that your application uses.*

As well as enabling ASP.NET AJAX functionality, you can also use properties to configure this control. The simplest of these properties is `EnablePartialRendering`, which is `true` by default. Setting this property to `false` disables all asynchronous postback processing, such as that provided by `UpdatePanel` controls. This can be useful, for example, if you want to compare your AJAX-enabled website with a traditional website—perhaps if you were giving a demonstration to a manager.

You can use the `ScriptManager` control for several reasons, including the following common scenarios:

➤ To determine whether server-side code is being called as a result of a partial-page postback

➤ To add references to additional client-side JavaScript files

➤ To reference web services

➤ To return error messages to the client

These configuration options are covered in the following sections.

Detecting Partial-Page Postbacks

The `ScriptManager` control includes a Boolean property called `IsInAsyncPostBack`. You can use this property in server-side code to detect whether a partial-page postback is in progress. Note that the `ScriptManager` for a page may actually be on a master page. Rather than access this control through the master page, you can obtain a reference to the current `ScriptManager` instance by using the static `GetCurrent` method, for example:

```
ScriptManager scriptManager = ScriptManager.GetCurrent(this);
if (scriptManager != null && scriptManager.IsInAsyncPostBack)
{
    // Code to execute for partial-page postbacks.
}
```

You must pass a reference to a `Page` control to the `GetCurrent` method. For example, if you use this method in a `Page_Load` event handler for an ASP.NET web page, you can use `this` as your `Page` reference. Also, remember to check for a `null` reference to avoid exceptions.

Client-Side JavaScript References

Rather than add code to the HTML page header, or in `<script>` elements on the page, you can use the `Scripts` property of the `ScriptManager` class. This centralizes your script references and makes it easier to maintain them. To do this declaratively, first add a child `<Scripts>` element to the `<UpdatePanel>` control element, and then add `<asp:ScriptReference>` child control elements to `<Scripts>`. You use the `Path` property of a `ScriptReference` control to reference a custom script.

The following example shows how to add references to a custom script file called `MyScript.js` in the root folder of the web application:

```
<asp:ScriptManager runat="server" ID="ScriptManager1">
  <Scripts>
    <asp:ScriptReference Path="~/MyScript.js" />
  </Scripts>
</asp:ScriptManager>
```

Web Service References

To access web services from client-side JavaScript code, ASP.NET AJAX must generate a proxy class. To control this behavior, you use the `Services` property of the `ScriptManager` class. As with `Scripts`, you can specify this property declaratively, this time with a `<Services>` element. You add `<asp:ServiceReference>` controls to this element. For each `ServiceReference` object in the `Services` property, you specify the path to the web service by using the `Path` property.

The `ServiceReference` class also has a property called `InlineScript`, which defaults to `false`. When this property is `false`, client-side code obtains a proxy class to call the web service by requesting it from the server. To enhance performance (particularly if you use a lot of web services on a page), you can set `InlineScript` to `true`. This causes the proxy class to be defined in the client-side script for the page.

ASP.NET web services use a file extension of `.asmx`. Without going into too much detail in this chapter, to add a reference to a web service called `MyService.asmx` in the root folder of a web application, you would use code as follows:

```
<asp:ScriptManager runat="server" ID="ScriptManager1">
  <Services>
    <asp:ServiceReference Path="~/MyService.asmx" />
  </Services>
</asp:ScriptManager>
```

You can add references only to local web services (that is, web services in the same web application as the calling code) in this way. You can call remote web services indirectly via local web methods.

Later in this chapter you will see how to make asynchronous web method calls from client-side JavaScript code that uses proxy classes generated in this way.

Client-Side Error Messages

If an exception is thrown as part of a partial-page postback, the default behavior is to place the error message contained in the exception into a client-side JavaScript alert message box. You can customize the message that is displayed by handling the `AsyncPostBackError` event of the `ScriptManager` instance. In the event handler, you can use the `AsyncPostBackErrorEventArgs.Exception` property to access the exception that is thrown and the `ScriptManager.AsyncPostBackErrorMessage` property to set the message that is displayed to the client. You might do this to hide the exception details from users.

To override the default behavior and display a message in a different way, you must handle the endRequest event of the client-side PageRequestManager object by using JavaScript. This is described later in this chapter.

Using UpdatePanel Controls

The UpdatePanel control is likely to be the control that you will use most often when you write ASP.NET AJAX-enabled web applications. This control, as you have seen in the simple example earlier in the chapter, enables you to wrap a portion of a web page so that it is capable of participating in a partial-page postback operation. To do this, you add an UpdatePanel control to the page and fill its child <ContentTemplate> element with the controls that you want it to contain:

```
<asp:UpdatePanel runat="Server" ID="UpdatePanel1">
  <ContentTemplate>
    ...
  </ContentTemplate>
</asp:UpdatePanel>
```

The contents of the <ContentTemplate> template are rendered in either a <div> or <span> element according to the value of the RenderMode property of the UpdatePanel. The default value of this property is Block, which results in a <div> element. To use a <span> element, set RenderMode to Inline.

Multiple UpdatePanel Controls on a Single Web Page

You can include any number of UpdatePanel controls on a page. If a postback is caused by a control that is contained in the <ContentTemplate> of any UpdatePanel on the page, a partial-page postback will occur instead of a full-page postback. This will cause all the UpdatePanel controls to update according to the value of their UpdateMode property. The default value of this property is Always, which means that the UpdatePanel will update for a partial-page postback operation on the page, even if this operation occurs in a different UpdatePanel control. If you set this property to Conditional, the UpdatePanel updates only when a control that it contains causes a partial-page postback or when a trigger that you have defined occurs. Triggers are covered shortly.

If you have set UpdateMode to Conditional, you can also set the ChildrenAsTriggers property to false to prevent controls that are contained by the UpdatePanel from triggering an update of the panel. Note, though, that in this case these controls still trigger a partial-page update, which may result in other UpdatePanel controls on the page being updated. For example, this would update controls that have an UpdateMode property value of Always. This is illustrated in the following code:

```
<asp:UpdatePanel runat="Server" ID="UpdatePanel1" UpdateMode="Conditional"
  ChildrenAsTriggers="false">
  <ContentTemplate>
    <asp:Button runat="Server" ID="Button1" Text="Click Me" />
    <small>Panel 1 render time: <%= DateTime.Now.ToLongTimeString() %></small>
  </ContentTemplate>
</asp:UpdatePanel>
<asp:UpdatePanel runat="Server" ID="UpdatePanel2">
  <ContentTemplate>
    <small>Panel 2 render time: <%= DateTime.Now.ToLongTimeString() %></small>
  </ContentTemplate>
</asp:UpdatePanel>
<small>Page render time: <%= DateTime.Now.ToLongTimeString() %></small>
```

In this code, the UpdatePanel2 control has an UpdateMode property of Always, the default value. When the button is clicked, it causes a partial-page postback, but only UpdatePanel2 will be updated. Visually, you will notice that only the "Panel 2 render time" label is updated.

Server-Side UpdatePanel Updates

Sometimes when you have multiple `UpdatePanel` controls on a page, you might decide not to update one of them unless certain conditions are met. In this case, you would configure the `UpdateMode` property of the panel to `Conditional` as shown in the previous section, and possibly also set the `ChildrenAsTriggers` property to `false`. Then, in your server-side event-handler code for one of the controls on the page that causes a partial-page update, you would (conditionally) call the `Update` method of the `UpdatePanel`. Here is an example:

```
protected void Button1_Click(object sender, EventArgs e)
{
  if (TestSomeCondition())
  {
    UpdatePanel1.Update();
  }
}
```

UpdatePanel Triggers

You can cause an `UpdatePanel` control to be updated by a control elsewhere on the web page by adding triggers to the `Triggers` property of the control. A trigger is an association between an event of a control elsewhere on the page and the `UpdatePanel` control. All controls have default events (for example, the default event of a `Button` control is `Click`), so specifying the name of an event is optional. Two types of triggers can be added, represented by the following two classes:

➤ `AsyncPostBackTrigger`—This class causes the `UpdatePanel` to update when the specified event of the specified control is triggered.

➤ `PostBackTrigger`—This class causes a full-page update to be triggered when the specified event of the specified control is triggered.

You will mostly use `AsyncPostBackTrigger`, but `PostBackTrigger` can be useful if you want a control inside an `UpdatePanel` to trigger a full-page postback.

Both of these trigger classes have two properties: `ControlID`, which specifies the control that causes the trigger by its identifier, and `EventName`, which specifies the name of the event for the control linked to the trigger.

To extend an earlier example, consider the following code:

```
<asp:UpdatePanel runat="Server" ID="UpdatePanel1" UpdateMode="Conditional"
  ChildrenAsTriggers="false">
  <Triggers>
    <asp:AsyncPostBackTrigger ControlID="Button2" />
  </Triggers>
  <ContentTemplate>
    <asp:Button runat="Server" ID="Button1" Text="Click Me" />
    <small>Panel 1 render time: <% =DateTime.Now.ToLongTimeString() %></small>
  </ContentTemplate>
</asp:UpdatePanel>
<asp:UpdatePanel runat="Server" ID="UpdatePanel2">
  <ContentTemplate>
    <asp:Button runat="Server" ID="Button2" Text="Click Me" />
    <small>Panel 2 render time: <% =DateTime.Now.ToLongTimeString() %></small>
  </ContentTemplate>
</asp:UpdatePanel>
<small>Page render time: <% =DateTime.Now.ToLongTimeString() %></small>
```

The new `Button` control, `Button2`, is specified as a trigger in the `UpdatePanel1`. When this button is clicked, both `UpdatePanel1` and `UpdatePanel2` will be updated: `UpdatePanel1` because of the trigger, and `UpdatePanel2` because it uses the default `UpdateMode` value of `Always`.

Using UpdateProgress

The UpdateProgress control, as shown in the earlier example, enables you to display a progress message to the user while a partial-page postback is in operation. You use the ProgressTemplate property to supply an ITemplate for the progress display. You will typically use the <ProgressTemplate> child element of the control to do this.

You can place multiple UpdateProgress controls on a page by using the AssociatedUpdatePanelID property to associate the control with a specific UpdatePanel. If this is not set (the default), the UpdateProgress template will be displayed for any partial-page postback, regardless of which UpdatePanel causes it.

When a partial-page postback occurs, there is a delay before the UpdateProgress template is displayed. This delay is configurable through the DisplayAfter property, which is an int that specifies the delay in milliseconds. The default is 500 milliseconds.

Finally, you can use the Boolean DynamicLayout property to specify whether space is allocated for the template before it is displayed. With the default value of true for this property, space on the page is dynamically allocated, which may result in other controls being moved out of the way for an inline progress template display. If you set this property to false, space will be allocated for the template before it is displayed, so the layout of other controls on the page will not change. You set this property according to the effect you want to achieve when displaying progress. For a progress template that is positioned by using absolute coordinates, as in the earlier example, you should leave this property set to the default value.

Using Extender Controls

The core ASP.NET AJAX download includes a class called ExtenderControl. The purpose of this control is to enable you to extend (that is, add functionality to) other ASP.NET server controls. This is used extensively in the AJAX Control Toolkit to great effect, and you can use the ASP.NET AJAX Server Control Extender project template to create your own extended controls. ExtenderControl controls all work similarly—you place them on a page, associate them with target controls, and add further configuration. The extender then emits client-side code to add functionality.

To see this in action in a simple example, create a new Web Form named ExtenderDemo.aspx, and then add the following code:

```
<%@ Page Language="C#" AutoEventWireup="true" CodeBehind="ExtenderDemo.aspx.cs"
  Inherits="ProCSharpAjaxSample.ExtenderDemo" %>

<!DOCTYPE html>

<html>
<head runat="server">
  <title>Color Selector</title>
</head>
<body>
  <form id="form1" runat="server">
  <asp:ScriptManager ID="ScriptManager1" runat="server" />
  <div>
    <asp:UpdatePanel runat="server" ID="updatePanel1">
      <ContentTemplate>
        <span style="display: inline-block; padding: 2px;">My favorite color is:
        </span>
        <asp:Label runat="server" ID="favoriteColorLabel" Text="green"
          Style="color: #00dd00; display: inline-block; padding: 2px;
            width: 70px; font-weight: bold;" />
        <ajaxToolkit:DropDownExtender runat="server" ID="dropDownExtender1"
          TargetControlID="favoriteColorLabel"
          DropDownControlID="colDropDown" />
        <asp:Panel ID="colDropDown" runat="server"
          Style="display: none; visibility: hidden; width: 60px;
            padding: 8px; border: double 4px black; background-color: #ffffdd;
```

```
                    font-weight: bold;">
          <asp:LinkButton runat="server" ID="OptionRed" Text="red"
            OnClick="OnSelect" Style="color: #ff0000;" /><br />
          <asp:LinkButton runat="server" ID="OptionOrange" Text="orange"
            OnClick="OnSelect" Style="color: #dd7700;" /><br />
          <asp:LinkButton runat="server" ID="OptionYellow" Text="yellow"
            OnClick="OnSelect" Style="color: #dddd00;" /><br />
          <asp:LinkButton runat="server" ID="OptionGreen" Text="green"
            OnClick="OnSelect" Style="color: #00dd00;" /><br />
          <asp:LinkButton runat="server" ID="OptionBlue" Text="blue"
            OnClick="OnSelect" Style="color: #0000dd;" /><br />
          <asp:LinkButton runat="server" ID="OptionPurple" Text="purple"
            OnClick="OnSelect" Style="color: #dd00ff;" />
        </asp:Panel>
      </ContentTemplate>
    </asp:UpdatePanel>
  </div>
  </form>
</body>
</html>
```

You also need to add the following event handler to the code-behind (code file `ProCSharpAjaxSample/ExtenderDemo.aspx.cs`):

```
protected void OnSelect(object sender, EventArgs e)
{
    favoriteColorLabel.Text = ((LinkButton)sender).Text;
    favoriteColorLabel.Style["color"] = ((LinkButton)sender).Style["color"];
}
```

As shown in Figure 40-30, not very much is visible in the browser at first, and the extender seems to have no effect.

However, when you hover over the text that reads "green," a drop-down dynamically appears. If you click this drop-down, a list appears, as shown in Figure 40-31.

When you click one of the links in the drop-down list, the text changes accordingly (after a partial-page postback operation).

Note two important points about this simple example:

➤ It was extremely easy to associate the extender with target controls.

➤ The drop-down list was styled using custom code—meaning you can place whatever content you like in the list. This simple extender is a great, and easy, way to add functionality to your web applications.

The extenders contained in the AJAX Control Toolkit are continually being added to and updated. If you have installed it using NuGet, you'll be automatically informed when a new version is available.

In addition to the extender controls that are supplied by the AJAX Control Toolkit, you can create your own. To create an effective extender, you must use the AJAX Library. However, a discussion of this scripting library is not part of this book.

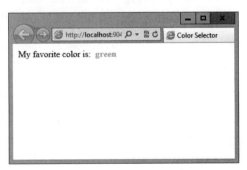

FIGURE 40-30

FIGURE 40-31

ASP.NET Application Services

ASP.NET AJAX includes three specialized web services that you can use to access ASP.NET application services. These services are accessed through the following client-side classes:

➤ `Sys.Services.AuthenticationService`—This service includes methods to log in or log out a user or determine whether a user is logged in.

➤ `Sys.Services.ProfileService`—This service enables you to get and set profile properties for the currently logged-on user. The profile properties are configured in the `web.config` file for the application.

➤ `Sys.Services.RoleService`—This service enables you to determine role membership for the currently logged-on user.

Used properly, these classes enable you to implement extremely responsive user interfaces that include authorization, profile, and membership functionality. A discussion of these services is beyond the scope of this chapter, but you should be aware of them—and they are well worth investigating.

SUMMARY

In this chapter you looked at several advanced techniques for creating ASP.NET pages and web applications. You've seen how you can use ASP.NET AJAX to enhance ASP.NET web applications. ASP.NET AJAX contains a wealth of functionality that makes websites far more responsive and dynamic and can provide a much better user experience.

First, you learned about the ASP.NET Web Forms page model, the event model, and how to find out about these events by using tracing. The page events are most important understanding ASP.NET Web Forms. You then looked at master pages, and how to provide a template for the pages of your website, which is another way to reuse code and simplify development.

You've seen validation using ASP.NET validation controls, and you took a brief look at security and how you can implement forms-based authentication on your websites with minimal effort based on the APIs shown in the previous chapter

Next, you investigated data controls and how easy it is to access the Entity Framework. Then, the `ObjectDataSource` illustrated some more flexible use. In the last part of this chapter, you learned about ASP.NET AJAX, Microsoft's implementation of Ajax.

The next chapter is about another ASP.NET framework: ASP.NET MVC. Unlike Web Forms, with ASP .NET MVC it's necessary to deal with HTML and JavaScript, and to use .NET for server-side functionality. Because of a clear separation between the UI, functionality, and data access, unit testing is easier with ASP .NET MVC.

41

ASP.NET MVC

WHAT'S IN THIS CHAPTER?

➤ Understanding ASP.NET MVC

➤ Creating Controllers

➤ Creating Views

➤ Validating User Inputs

➤ Using Filters

➤ Authentication and Authorization

➤ Working with the ASP.NET Web API

WROX.COM CODE DOWNLOADS FOR THIS CHAPTER

The wrox.com code downloads for this chapter are found at http://www.wrox.com/remtitle
.cgi?isbn=1118314425 on the Download Code tab. The code for this chapter is divided into the
following major examples:

➤ MVC Sample App

➤ Menu Planner

➤ Web API Sample

ASP.NET MVC OVERVIEW

In Chapter 39, "Core ASP.NET" you've learned the basics of web programming with ASP.NET, a
foundation both for ASP.NET Web Forms and ASP.NET MVC. Chapter 40, "ASP.NET Web Forms,"
discusses ASP.NET Web Forms, which is a framework that makes it easy to create web applications
just using server-side code, with server-side controls that create HTML and JavaScript code on
its own. This chapter is about the opposite—using a technology in which HTML and JavaScript
becomes more important. Server-side C# code is written for controllers and models, and with the
views HTML and JavaScript is the way to go along with just a little bit of C# code. With the release of
Visual Studio 2012 you use version 4 of ASP.NET MVC.

The major namespaces used in this chapter are System.Web.Mvc and its subnamespaces and
System.Web.Http.

In Chapter 39 you learned about the MVC pattern. Now get into code; start with a simple ASP.NET MVC project. Visual Studio 2012 offers several ASP.NET MVC 4 project templates, as shown in Figure 41-1:

➤ The *Empty template* creates the directory structure and sets up routing.

➤ The *Internet* and *Intranet templates* contain a few controllers and views; the Internet template configures security to Forms authentication; *the Intranet template* configures security to Windows authentication.

➤ The *Mobile Application template* contains JavaScript libraries for mobile clients and has some optimized views.

➤ Use the *Single Page Application template* if the user stays mainly on a single page, and JavaScript is used to get information from the server.

➤ The *Web API template* is a new way of REST communication. The Web API is covered later in the section "ASP.NET Web API."

> **NOTE** *Chapter 39 discusses the foundation of Internet and intranet security. Specific information relevant to ASP.NET MVC is discussed in the section Authentication and Authorization.*

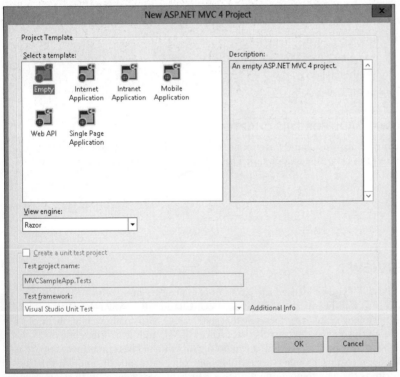

FIGURE 41-1

For the first sample application, the Empty template is used. The ASP.NET MVC project templates create a directory structure that shows the important aspects of an ASP.NET MVC application. Now get into the directories.

DIRECTORY	DESCRIPTION
App_Data	The App_Data folder is used to store database files or other data files such as XML files.
Content	The Content folder contains styles. The Empty template already contains a style sheet file Site.css with styles for basic forms and validation helpers. This makes it easier to adapt the styles for custom use. In addition to the style sheet file Site.css, the Content folder also contains a theme with styles for the jQuery.UI library.
Controllers	The Controllers folder contains—as the name clearly defines—controllers. Here you should add controller classes that react to user requests.
Models	The Models folder is used for data classes, for example, the ADO.NET Entity Framework.
Scripts	The Scripts folder contains the JavaScript libraries jQuery, jQuery.UI, Knockout, and Modernizr.
Views	The Views folder contains the views. Views are usually HTML code.

Now look at ASP.NET MVC from a different angle. Figure 41-2 shows all the parts of ASP.NET MVC that come into play when a user makes a HTTP request. As the *request* is received on the server, *routing* defines what controller should be invoked, and what action in the controller should be invoked. The *controller* is responsible to return a result. It can use a model for its work and finally returns a *view result*. Based on the view result, a *view engine* is selected, and this one searches for a view that fits. The result from the view is returned with the *response*.

Now let's explore the major steps starting with routing.

FIGURE 41-2

DEFINING ROUTES

The controller is selected based on a route. You can see the default routes defined in the method RegisterRoutes (code file MVCSampleApp/Global.asax.cs). This method is invoked from within the Application_Start method that is invoked on the start of the web application. The route named DefaultApi is for the Web API. The route named Default is the default route for ASP.NET MVC applications. The default route is defined with the URL {controller}/{action}/{id}. This route maps three segments of the URL. The first segment is mapped to the controller, the second segment to the action, and the third segment to a parameter named id. Now look at a sample URL with ASP.NET MVC, for example, http://localhost:Home/Index/demo. With this URL, the value for controller is Home, the value for action is Index, and the value for id is demo. With ASP.NET MVC applications, the controller and action are mandatory, but there can be defaults. The parameter of the MapRoute method that sets the defaults parameter defines defaults for controller and action, and specifies that the id parameter is optional. This way specifying the URL http://localhost defines the controller Home and the action Index.

```
public static void RegisterRoutes(RouteCollection routes)
{
  routes.IgnoreRoute("{resource}.axd/{*pathInfo}");

  routes.MapHttpRoute(
      name: "DefaultApi",
      routeTemplate: "api/{controller}/{id}",
      defaults: new { id = RouteParameter.Optional }
  );

  routes.MapRoute(
      name: "Default",
      url: "{controller}/{action}/{id}",
      defaults: new { controller = "Home", action = "Index",
                      id = UrlParameter.Optional }
  );
```

> **NOTE** *Chapter 39 explains the application events such as* `Application_Start`.

Adding Routes

There are several reasons to add or change routes. For example, routes can be modified to just use actions with the link and define the `Home` as the default controller, adding additional entries to the link, or using multiple parameters.

A route where the user can use links such as `http://<server>/About` to address the `About` action method in the `Home` controller without passing a controller name can be defined as shown in the following snippet. The controller is left out from the URL. It is mandatory, but it can be defined with the defaults:

```
routes.MapRoute(
    name: "Default",
    url: "{action}/{id}",
    defaults: new { controller = "Home", action = "Index",
                    id = UrlParameter.Optional }
);
```

Another scenario to change the route is shown here. With this code snippet a variable language is added to the route. This variable is set to the section within the URL that follows the server name and is placed before the controller, for example, `http://server/en/Home/About`. You can use this to specify a language:

```
routes.MapRoute(
    name: "Language",
    url: "{language}/{controller}/{action}/{id}",
    defaults: new { controller = "Home", action = "Index",
        id = UrlParameter.Optional }
);
```

Route Constraints

Mapping the route, constraints can be specified. This way other URLs than defined by the constraint are not possible. The following constraint defines that the `language` parameter can be only `en` or `de` by using the regular expression `(en)|(de)`. URLs like `http://<server>/en/Home/About` or `http://<server>/de/Home/About` are valid:

```
routes.MapRoute(
    name: "Language",
    url: "{language}/{controller}/{action}/{id}",
    defaults: new { controller = "Home", action = "Index",
        id = UrlParameter.Optional },
    constraints: new {language = @"(en)|(de)"}
);
```

If a link should enable only numbers (for example, to access products with a product number), the regular expression `\d+` matches any number of numerical digits but at least one:

```
routes.MapRoute(
    name: "Products",
    url: "{controller}/{action}/{productId}",
    defaults: new { controller = "Home", action = "Index",
        productId = UrlParameter.Optional },
    constraints: new { productId = @"\d+"}
);
```

Routing specifies the controller that is used and the action of the controller. So get into controllers next.

CREATING CONTROLLERS

A *controller* reacts to requests from the user and sends a response. A view is not required as you see next.

There are some conventions with ASP.NET MVC. With the architecture of ASP.NET MVC, conventions have been preferred to configuration. The same is true with controllers. You can find controllers in the directory `Controllers`, and the name of the controller class must be suffixed with the name `Controller`.

You can easily create a controller by selecting the `Controllers` directory in Solution Explorer, and using the menu Add ➪ Controller from the context menu. Figure 41-3 displays the dialog. Here the name of the controller can be set, and different scaffolding options can be configured. Currently, only the Empty controller template is used. Other templates will be shown later in this chapter in the sections Data-Driven Application and ASP.NET Web API. The first controller class created is the `HomeController`.

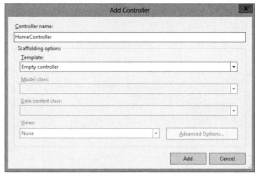

FIGURE 41-3

The generated code contains a `HomeController` class that derives from the base class `Controller`. This class also contains an `Index` method that corresponds to the `Index` action. Requesting an action as defined by the route, a method within the controller is invoked:

```
public class HomeController : Controller
{
  // GET: /Home/
  public ActionResult Index()
  {
    return View();
  }
}
```

Action Methods

A controller contains action methods. A simple action method is the `Hello` method from the following code snippet (code file `MVCSampleApp/Controllers/HomeController.cs`):

```
public string Hello()
{
  return "Hello, ASP.NET MVC";
}
```

The `Hello` action in the Home controller can be invoked with the link `http://localhost:41270/Home/Hello`. Of course, the port number depends on your settings and can be configured with the web properties in the project settings. Opening this link from the browser, the controller returns just the string `Hello, ASP.NET MVC`—no HTML, just a string. The browser displays the string.

An action can return anything, for example, the bytes of an image, a video, XML or JSON data, or of course HTML. Views are of great help for returning HTML. Before getting into views, look at more controller features.

Parameters

Action methods can be declared with parameters like in the following code snippet:

```
public string Greeting(string name)
{
  return HttpUtility.HtmlEncode("Hello, " + name);
}
```

With this declaration, the `Greeting` action method can be invoked requesting this URL passing a value with the `name` parameter in the URL: `http://localhost:41270/Home/Greeting?name=Stephanie`

To use links that can be better remembered, route information can be used to specify the parameters. With the default route configuration, the `Greeting2` action method is specified with the id parameter because the route specifies this parameter value:

```
public string Greeting2(string id)
{
    return HttpUtility.HtmlEncode("Hello, " + id);
}
```

Now this link can be used, and the id parameter contains the string `Matthias`: `http://localhost:41270/Home/Greeting2/Matthias`

Action methods can also be declared with any number of parameters. You can add the `Add` action method to the Home controller with two parameters:

```
public int Add(int x, int y)
{
    return x + y;
}
```

You can invoke this action with the URL `http://localhost:41270/Home/Add?x=4&y=5` to fill the x and y parameters.

With multiple parameters, you can also define a route to pass the values with a different link. The following code snippet shows an additional route defined in the route table to specify multiple parameters that fill the variables x and y (code file `MVCSampleApp/Global.asax.cs`):

```
routes.MapRoute(
  name: "MultipleParameters",
  url: "{controller}/{action}/{x}/{y}",
  defaults: new { controller = "Home", action = "Index" }
);
```

Now the same action as before can be invoked using this URL: `http://localhost:41270/Home/Add/7/2`.

Returning Data

So far you returned only string values from the controller. Usually, an `ActionResult` or a class that derives from `ActionResult` is returned.

Following are several examples with the `ResultController` class (code file `MVCSampleApp/Controllers/ResultController.cs`). The first code snippet uses of the `ContentResult` class to return simple text content. Instead of creating an instance of the `ContentResult` class and returning the instance, methods from the base class `Controller` can be used to return `ActionResults`. Here, the method `Content` is used to return text content. The `Content` method enables specifying the content, the MIME type, and encoding:

```
public ActionResult ContentDemo()
{
    return Content("Hello World", "text/plain");
}
```

With the `JavaScript` method, JavaScript code can be returned. The method automatically sets the MIME type to application/x-javascript with the sample code:

```
public ActionResult JavaScriptDemo()
{
    return JavaScript("<script>function foo { alert('foo'); }</script>");
}
```

To return JSON (which is the preferred from JavaScript), the `Json` method can be used. With the sample code, a `Menu` object is created. To allow a HTTP GET request from the client, `JsonRequestBehavior` `.AllowGet` must be specified with the `Json` method. A different way to use JSON would be to use it from within server-side code in a view where a GET request wouldn't be necessary:

```
public ActionResult JsonDemo()
{
  var m = new Menu
  {
    Id = 3,
    Text = "Grilled sausage with sauerkraut und potatoes",
    Price = 12.90,
    Category = "Main"
  };
  return Json(m, JsonRequestBehavior.AllowGet);
}
```

The `Menu` class is defined within the `Models` directory and defines a simple POCO class to contain some properties (code file `MVCSampleApp/Models/Menu.cs`):

```
public class Menu
{
  public int Id { get; set; }
  public string Text { get; set; }
  public double Price { get; set; }
  public string Category { get; set; }
}
```

The client sees this JSON data in the response body that can now easily be used as a JavaScript object:

```
{"Id":3,"Text":"Grilled sausage with sauerkraut und potatoes",
 "Price":12.9,"Category":"Main"}
```

Using the `Redirect` method of the `Controller` class, the client receives a HTTP redirect request. After receiving the redirect request, the browser requests the link it received. The `Redirect` method returns a `RedirectResult` (code file `MVCSampleApp/Controllers/ResultController.cs`):

```
public ActionResult RedirectDemo()
{
  return Redirect("http://www.cninnovation.com");
}
```

You can also build a redirect request to the client by specifying a redirect to another controller and action. `RedirectToRoute` returns a `RediretToRouteResult` that enables specifying route names, controllers, actions, and parameters. This builds a link that is returned to the client with an HTTP redirect request:

```
public ActionResult RedirectRouteDemo()
{
  return RedirectToRoute(new { controller = "Home", action="Hello" });
}
```

With the `File` method depending on different overloads of the method, `FilePathResult`, `FileContentResult`, and `FileStreamResult` can be returned. The different return types depend on the parameters used, for example, a string for a file path, a `Stream` for a stream result, and a `byte` array for a content result. The sample code returns a `FilePathResult` specifying a JPG filename that is also defined with the `contentType` parameter:

```
public ActionResult FileDemo()
{
  return File("~/Content/Images/Stephanie.jpg", "image/jpg");
}
```

The next section shows how to return different `ViewResult` variants.

CREATING VIEWS

The HTML code that is returned to the client is best specified with a view. For the samples in this section, the `ViewsDemoController` is created. The views are all defined within the `Views` folder. The views for the ViewsDemo controller need a `ViewsDemo` subdirectory. This is a convention for the views.

Another place in which views are searched is the `Shared` directory. You can put views that should be used from multiple controllers (and special partial views used by multiple views) into the `Shared` directory (code file `MVCSampleApp/Controllers/ViewDemoController.cs`):

FIGURE 41-4

```
public ActionResult Index()
{
    return View();
}
```

Selecting the `ViewsDemo` directory in the Solution Explorer, you can create a view by selecting Add ⇨ View from the context menu. The Add View dialog displays, as shown in Figure 41-4. To start just a simple view is created by deselecting the use of the layout or master page.

The action method `Index` uses the `View` method without parameters, and thus the view engine searches for a view file with the same name as the action name in the `ViewsDemo` directory. The `View` method has overloads that enable passing a different view name. In that case the view engine looks for a view with the name passed to the `View` method.

A view contains HTML code mixed with a little server-side code as shown. The following snippet contains the default generated HTML code (code file `MVCSampleApp/Views/ViewsDemo/Index.cshtml`):

```
@{
    Layout = null;
}

<!DOCTYPE html>

<html>
<head>
    <meta name="viewport" content="width=device-width" />
    <title>Index</title>
</head>
<body>
    <div>
    </div>
</body>
</html>
```

Server-side code is written using the @ sign: the Razor syntax. This syntax is discussed in the section Razor Syntax. Before getting into the details of the Razor syntax, the next section shows how to pass data from a controller to a view.

Passing Data to Views

The controller and view run in the same process. The view is directly created from within the controller. This makes it easy to pass data from the controller to the view. To pass data, a `ViewDataDictionary` can be used. This dictionary stores keys as string and enables object values. The `ViewDataDictionary` can be used with the `ViewData` property of the `Controller` class, for example, passing a string to the dictionary where the key value `MyData` is used: `ViewData["MyData"] = "Hello"`. An easier syntax is using the `ViewBag` property. `ViewBag` is a dynamic type that enables assigning any property name to pass data to the view (code file `MVCSampleApp/Controllers/SubmitDataController.cs`)

```
public ActionResult PassingData()
{
  ViewBag.MyData = "Hello from the controller";
  return View();
}
```

> **NOTE** *Using dynamic types has the advantage that there is no direct dependency from the view to the controller. Dynamic types are explained in detail in Chapter 12, "Dynamic Language Extensions."*

Accessing the data passed from the controller, the `ViewBag` can be used in a similar way. Similar to the `Controller` base class, the `ViewBag` property is defined in the base class of the view, `WebViewPage` (code file `MVCSampleApp/Views/ViewsDemo/PassingData.cshtml`).

```
<div>
  <div>@ViewBag.MyData</div>
</div>
```

Razor Syntax

As you've seen, the view contains both HTML and server-side code. With ASP.NET MVC you can use ASPX syntax or Razor syntax. Razor syntax is simpler and requires fewer key strokes. Razor uses the @ character as a transition character. Starting with @, C# code begins.

With ASPX syntax, both start and end characters are needed to mark the start and end of a code block; this is not required with Razor. Razor automatically detects the end when C# code finishes.

With Razor you need to differentiate statements that return a value and methods that don't. A value that is returned can be directly used. For example, `ViewBag.MyData` returns a string. This string is put directly between the HTML div tags:

```
<div>@ViewBag.MyData</div>
```

> **NOTE** *Comparing the Razor syntax to the ASPX syntax you've worked with in the previous chapter,* `<div>@ViewBag.MyData</div>` *is represented with ASPX syntax as* `<div><%:ViewBag.MyData %></div>`. *With Razor, HTML encoding is done by default.*

Invoking methods that return void, or specifying some other statements that don't return a value, a Razor code block is needed. The following code block defines a string variable:

```
@{
  string name = "Angela";
}
```

Using the variable can now be done with the simple syntax just using the transition character:

```
<div>@name</div>
```

With the Razor syntax the engine automatically detects the end of the code when a HTML element is found. There are some cases in which this cannot be seen automatically. Here parentheses can be used to mark a variable. Following that normal text continues:

```
<div>@(name), Stephanie</div>
```

A `foreach` statement defines a Razor code block as well:

```
@foreach(var item in list)
{
  <li>The item name is @item.</li>
}
```

> **NOTE** *Usually text content is automatically detected with Razor, for example, with opening an angle bracket or using parentheses with a variable. There are a few cases in which this does not work. Here, you can explicitly use `@:` to define the start of text.*

Strongly Typed Views

Using the `ViewBag` to pass data to views is one way. Another way is passing a model to the view. This allows you to create strongly typed views.

The `ViewsDemoController` is now extended with the action method `PassingAModel`. Here, a new list of `Menu` items is created, and this list is passed to the `View` method of the `Controller` base class (code file `MVCSampleApp/Controllers/SubmitDataController.cs`):

```
public ActionResult PassingAModel()
{
  var menus = new List<Menu>
  {
    new Menu { Id=1, Text="Schweinsbraten mit Knödel und Sauerkraut",
               Price=6.9, Category="Main" },
    new Menu { Id=2, Text="Erdäpfelgulasch mit Tofu und Gebäck",
               Price=6.9, Category="Vegetarian" },
    new Menu { Id=3,
               Text="Tiroler Bauerngröst'l mit Spiegelei und Krautsalat",
               Price=6.9, Category="Main" }
  };
  return View(menus);
}
```

The information from the action method can be used within the view as a model. The model can be defined in the view with the `model` keyword as shown in the following code snippet. The model is of type `IEnumerable<Menu>`. Because the `Menu` class is defined within the namespace `MVCSampleApp.Models`, this namespace is opened with the `using` keyword. After the model is defined, the `Model` property that is defined with the abstract base class `WebViewModel<TModel>` is of the type of the model (code file `MVCSampleApp/ViewsDemo/PassingAModel.cshtml`):

```
@using MVCSampleApp.Models
@model IEnumerable<Menu>
@{
  Layout = null;
}

<!DOCTYPE html>

<html>
<head>
  <meta name="viewport" content="width=device-width" />
  <title>PassingAModel</title>
</head>
<body>
  <div>
    <ul>
      @foreach (var item in Model)
      {
```

```
          <li>@item.Text</li>
        }
      </ul>
    </div>
  </body>
</html>
```

You can pass any object as the model, whatever you need with the view. For example, editing a single `Menu` object, the model would be of type `Menu`. Showing or editing a list, the model can be `IEnumerable<Menu>`.

Running the application showing the defined view, a list of menus is shown in the browser.

Layout

Usually many pages of web applications show partly the same content, for example, copyright information, a logo, and a main navigation structure. This is where layout pages come into play. With ASP.NET Web Forms in the previous chapter, you saw master pages that fulfilled the same functionality as layout pages with the Razor syntax.

Until now you didn't use layout pages, and all the views contained the complete HTML content. Not using a layout page needs to be explicitly specified by setting the `Layout` property to `null`:

```
@{
  Layout = null;
}
```

Using a Default Layout Page

You can set the Layout property to a specific layout page or remove the setting. Removing the setting there's a good default behavior. The `_ViewStart.cshtml` page contains default configuration for all views. The only setting that is defined by default is setting the Layout property to the shared layout page `_Layout .cshtml` (code file `MVCSampleApp/Views/_ViewStart.cshtml`):

```
@{
  Layout = "~/Views/Shared/_Layout.cshtml";
}
```

The layout page contains the HTML content that is common to all pages that make use of this layout page. Communication with the view and the controller can be done using `ViewBag`. The value for `ViewBag .Title` can be defined within a content page, and it is shown here within the HTML `title` element. The `RenderBody` method of the base class `WebPageBase` renders the content of the content page and thus defines the position in which the content should be placed (code file `MVCSampleApp/Views/Shared/_Layout .cshtml`):

```
@using Sytem.Web.Optimization
<!DOCTYPE html>
<html>
<head>
  <meta charset="utf-8" />
  <meta name="viewport" content="width=device-width" />
  <title>@ViewBag.Title</title>
  <link href="@BundleTable.Bundles.ResolveBundleUrl("~/Content/css")"
      rel="stylesheet" type="text/css" />
  <link href="@BundleTable.Bundles.ResolveBundleUrl(
      "~/Content/themes/base/css")" rel="stylesheet" type="text/css" />
  <script src="@BundleTable.Bundles.ResolveBundleUrl("~/Scripts/js")"></script>
</head>
<body>
  @RenderBody()
</body>
</html>
```

The _Layout.cshtml page is now changed to include header and footer information and a navigation structure for some main links. Html.ActionLink is a HTML Helper that creates an HTML a element to define a link. HTML Helpers are discussed in the section HTML Helpers:

```
<body>
  <header>
    <h1>ASP.NET MVC Sample App</h1>
  </header>
  <nav>
    <ul>
      <li>
        @Html.ActionLink("Layout Sample", "LayoutSample")
      </li>
      <li>
        @Html.ActionLink("Layout using Sections", "LayoutUsingSections")
      </li>
    </ul>
  </nav>
  <div>
    @RenderBody()
  </div>
  <footer>Sample code for Professional C#</footer>
</body>
```

A view is created for the action LayoutSample (code file MVCSampleApp/Views/ViewsDemo/LayoutSample .cshtml). This view doesn't set the Layout property and thus uses the default layout. The ViewBag.Title is set that is used within the HTML title element in the layout:

```
@{
  ViewBag.Title = "Layout Sample";
}
<h2>LayoutSample</h2>
<p>
  This content is merged with the layout page
</p>
```

Running the application now, the content from the layout and the view is merged, as is shown in Figure 41-5.

FIGURE 41-5

Using Sections

There are more ways than rendering the body and using the ViewBag for exchanging data between the layout and the view. With section areas you can define where the named content within a view should be placed. The following code snippet (code file MVCSampleApp/Views/Shared/_Layout.cshtml) makes use of a section named PageNavigation. Such sections are by default required, and loading the view fails if the section is not defined. Setting the required parameter to false, the section becomes optional:

```
<div>
  @RenderSection("PageNavigation", required: false)
</div>
<div>
  @RenderBody()
</div>
```

Within the view (code file MVCSampleApp/Views/ViewsDemo/LayoutUsingSections.cshtml), the section is defined with the section keyword. The position where the section is placed is completely independent from the other content. The section PageNavigation is positioned from the layout:

```
@{
    ViewBag.Title = "Layout Using Sections";
}


<h2>Layout Using Sections</h2>
Main content here

@section PageNavigation
{
  <div>Navigation defined from the view</div>
  <ul>
    <li>Nav1</li>
    <li>Nav2</li>
  </ul>
}
```

Running the application now, the content from the view and the layout is merged according to the positions defined by the layout, as shown in Figure 41-6.

FIGURE 41-6

> **NOTE** *Sections aren't used only to place some content within the body of a HTML page; they are also useful to allow the view to place something in the head, for example, metadata from the page.*

Partial Views

Although layouts give an overall definition for multiple pages from the web application, partial views can be used to define content within views. A partial view doesn't have a layout.

Other than that, partial views are similar to normal views. They can also have a model. Partial views use the same base class as normal views.

Following is an example of partial views. Here you start with a model that contains properties for independent collections, events, and menus as defined by the class EventsAndMenus (code file MVCSampleApp/Models/EventsAndMenus.cs):

```
public class EventsAndMenus
{
  private IEnumerable<Event> events = null;
  public IEnumerable<Event> Events
  {
    get
    {
      return events ?? (events = new List<Event>()
      {
        new Event { Id=1, Text="Formula 1 G.P. Abu Dhabi, Yas Marina",
            Day=new DateTime(2012, 11, 4) },
        new Event { Id=2, Text="Formula 1 G.P. USA, Austin",
            Day = new DateTime(2012, 11, 18) },
        new Event { Id=3, Text="Formula 1 G.P. Brasil, Sao Paulo",
            Day = new DateTime(2012, 11, 25) }
      });
    }
  }

  private List<Menu> menus = null;
  public IEnumerable<Menu> Menus
```

```
    {
      get
      {
        return menus ?? (menus = new List<Menu>()
        {
          new Menu { Id=1, Text="Baby Back Barbecue Ribs", Price=16.9,
              Category="Main" },
          new Menu { Id=2, Text="Chicken and Brown Rice Piaf", Price=12.9,
              Category="Main" },
          new Menu { Id=3, Text="Chicken Miso Soup with Shiitake Mushrooms",
              Price=6.9, Category="Soup" }
        });
      }
    }
  }
```

Using this model, you get into partial views loaded from server-side code followed by partial views that are requested from JavaScript code on the client.

Using Partial Views from Server-Side Code

In the `ViewsDemoController` (code file `MVCSampleApp/Controllsers/ViewsDemoController.cs`), the action method `UseAPartialView` passes an instance of `EventsAndMenus` to the view:

```
public ActionResult UseAPartialView1()
{
  return View(new EventsAndMenus());
}
```

The view is defined to use the model of type `EventsAndMenus` (code file `MVCSampleApp/Views/ViewsDemo/UseAPartialView1.cshtml`). A partial view can be shown by using the HTML Helper method `Html.Partial`. `Html.Partial` returns an `MvcHtmlString`. Using the Razor syntax, the string is written as content of the `div` element. The first parameter of the `Partial` method accepts the name of the partial view. With the second parameter, the `Partial` method enables passing a model. If no model is passed, the partial view has access to the same model as the view. Here, the view uses the model of type `EventsAndMenus`, and the partial view just uses a part of it with the type `IEnumerable<Event>`:

```
@model MVCSampleApp.Models.EventsAndMenus
@{
  ViewBag.Title = "Use a Partial View";
  ViewBag.EventsTitle = "Live Events";
}
<h2>Use a Partial View</h2>
<div>this is the main view</div>
<div>
  @Html.Partial("ShowEvents", Model.Events)
</div>
```

Another way to render a partial view within the view is to use the HTML Helper method `Html.RenderPartial`, which is defined to return `void`. This method directly writes the partial view content to the response stream. This way, `RenderPartial` can be used within a Razor code block.

The partial view is created in a similar way to a normal view. With the Add View dialog, there's a check box that you can check to create a partial view. Using this check box, a layout cannot be assigned because the layout is defined by the view where the partial view is loaded within. Other than that, the partial view can be created in a similar way to normal views. You have access to the model and also to the dictionary that is accessed by using the `ViewBag` property. A partial view receives a copy of the dictionary to receive the same dictionary data that can be used (code file `MVCSampleApp/Views/ViewsDemo/ShowEvents.cshtml`):

```
@using MVCSampleApp.Models
@model IEnumerable<Event>
```

```
<h2>
  @ViewBag.EventsTitle
</h2>
<table>
  @foreach (var item in Model)
  {
    <tr>
      <td>@item.Day.ToShortDateString()</td>
      <td>@item.Text</td>
    </tr>
  }
</table>
```

Running the application, the view, partial view, and layout is rendered, as shown in Figure 41-7.

Returning Partial Views from the Controller

FIGURE 41-7

So far the partial view was loaded directly without the interaction with a controller. Controllers can be used as well to return a partial view.

In the following code snippet (code file MVCSampleApp/Controllers/ViewDemoController.cs), two action methods are defined within the class ViewsDemoController. The first action method UsePartialView2 returns a normal view; the second action method ShowEvents returns a partial view with the Controller method PartialView. The partial view ShowEvents was already created and used previously, which is used here. With the method PartialView a model containing the event list is passed to the partial view:

```
public ActionResult UseAPartialView2()
{
  return View();
}

public ActionResult ShowEvents()
{
  ViewBag.EventsTitle = "Live Events";
  return PartialView(new EventsAndMenus().Events);
}
```

The view UsePartialView2 (code file MVCSampleApp/Views/ViewsDemo/UseAPartialView2.cshtml) invokes the controller by calling the HTML Helper method Html.Action. The action name is ShowEvents and uses the same controller as the view came from. Otherwise other controllers and parameters to the action method can be passed with the Action method:

```
@model MVCSampleApp.Models.EventsAndMenus
@{
  ViewBag.Title = "Use a Partial View";
}
<h2>UseAPartialView</h2>
<div>this is the main view</div>
<div>
  @Html.Action("ShowEvents")
</div>
```

Calling Partial Views from jQuery

Partial views can also be loaded directly from code on the client. In the following code snippet (code file MVCSampleApp/Views/ViewsDemo/UseAPartialView3.cshtml), an event handler is linked to the click event of a button. Inside the click event handler, a GET request is made to the server to request /ViewsDemo/ShowEvents. This request returns a partial view, and the result from the partial view is placed within the div element named events:

```
@model MVCSampleApp.Models.EventsAndMenus
@{
  ViewBag.Title = "Use a Partial View";
```

```
    }
    <script>
      $(function () {
        $("#getEvents").click(function () {
          $("#events").load("/ViewsDemo/ShowEvents");
        });
      });
    </script>
    <h2>Use a Partial View</h2>
    <div>this is the main view</div>
    <button id="getEvents">Get Events</button>
    <div id="events">
    </div>
```

SUBMITTING DATA FROM THE CLIENT

Until now you used only HTTP GET requests from the client to retrieve HTML code from the server. What about sending form data from the client?

> **NOTE** *Chapter 39 discusses behind-the-scenes information on HTTP GET, POST, PUT, and DELETE requests.*

To submit form data, the view `CreateMenu` for the controller `SubmitData` is created. This view (code file `MVCSampleApp/Views/SubmitData/CreateMenu.cshtml`) contains an HTML form element that defines what data should be sent to the server. The form method is declared as a HTTP POST request. The `input` elements that define the input fields all have names that correspond to the properties of the `Menu` type.

```
@{
    ViewBag.Title = "Create Menu";
}
<h2>Create Menu</h2>
<form action="/SubmitData/CreateMenu" method="post">
<fieldset>
    <legend>Menu</legend>
    <div>Id:</div>
    <input name="id" />
    <div>Text:</div>
    <input name="text" />
    <div>Price:</div>
    <input name="price" />
    <div>Category:</div>
    <input name="category" />
    <div></div>
    <button type="submit">Submit</button>
</fieldset>
</form>
```

FIGURE 41-8

Figure 41-8 shows the opened page within the browser.

Within the `SubmitData` controller (code file `MVCSampleApp/Controllers/SubmitDataController.cs`) two `CreateMenu` action methods are created: one for a HTTP GET request and another for a HTTP POST request. With C# having different methods with the same name, it's required that the parameter numbers or types are different. Of course, this requirement is the same with action methods. Action methods also need to differ with the HTTP request method. By default the request method is GET; applying the attribute `HttpPost`, the request method is POST. For reading HTTP POST data, information from the `Request` object could be used (refer to Chapter 39). However, it's much simpler to define the `CreateMenu` method with parameters. The parameters are matched with the name of the form fields:

```
public ActionResult CreateMenu()
{
  return View();
}

[HttpPost]
public ActionResult CreateMenu(int id, string text, double price,
    string category)
{
  var m = new Menu { Id = id, Text = text, Price = price };
  ViewBag.Info = string.Format(
      "menu created: {0}, Price: {1}, category: {2}", m.Text, m.Price,
      m.Category);
  return View("Index");
}
```

Model Binder

Instead of using multiple parameters with the action method, you can also use a type that contains properties that match with the incoming field names:

```
[HttpPost]
public ActionResult CreateMenu(Menu m)
{
  ViewBag.Info = string.Format(
      "menu created: {0}, Price: {1}, category: {2}", m.Text, m.Price,
      m.Category);
  return View("Index");
}
```

Submitting the data with the form, `CreateMenu` is invoked that shows the Index view with the submitted menu data, as shown in Figure 41-9.

A model binder is responsible to transfer the data from the HTTP POST request. A model binder implements the interface `IModelBinder`. By default the `DefaultModelBinder` class is used to bind the input fields to the model. This binder supports primitive types, model classes (such as the `Menu` type), and collections implementing `ICollection<T>`, `IList<T>`, and `IDictionary<TKey, TValue>`.

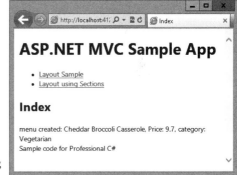

FIGURE 41-9

You can also pass the input data to the model using an action method without parameters as the next code snippet demonstrates. Here, a new instance of the `Menu` class is created, and this instance is passed to the `UpdateModel` method of the `Controller` class:

```
[HttpPost]
public ActionResult CreateMenu2()
{
  var m = new Menu();
  UpdateModel<Menu>(m);
  ViewBag.Info = string.Format(
      "menu created: {0}, Price: {1}, category: {2}", m.Text, m.Price,
      m.Category);
  return View("Index");
}
```

UpdateModel throws an InvalidOperationException if the updated model is not in a valid state after the update. You can use the TryUpdateModel method to avoid this exception.

> **WARNING** *If the model class has some properties that should not be updated, you shouldn't use the* UpdateModel *method. A malicious user could change the request from the browser to update these properties as well. With the* TryUpdateModel *method, you can pass a whitelist of properties that should be updated, or a blacklist of properties that should not be updated.*

Annotations and Validation

You can add some annotations to the model type that are used when updating the data for validation. The namespace System.ComponentModel.DataAnnotations contains attribute types that can be used to specify some information for data on the client, and be used for validation.

The Menu type is changed with these added attributes (code file MVCSampleApp/Models/Menu.cs):

```
public class Menu
{
  public int Id { get; set; }
  [Required, StringLength(50)] public string Text { get; set; }
  [DisplayName("Price"), DisplayFormat(DataFormatString="{0:C}")]
  public double Price { get; set; }
  [DataType(DataType.Date)] public DateTime Date { get; set; }
  [StringLength(10)] public string Category { get; set; }
}
```

Possible attribute types you can use for validation are CompareAttribute to compare different properties, CreditCardAttribute to verify a valid credit card number, EmailAddressAttribute to verify an email address, EnumDataTypeAttribute to compare the input to enumeration values, and PhoneAttribute to verify a phone number.

You can also use other attributes to get values for display and error messages, for example, DataTypeAttribute, DisplayFormatAttribute.

To use the validation attributes, you can verify the state of the model using ModelState.IsValid within an action method as shown here (code file MVCSampleApp/Controllers/SumitDataController.cs):

```
[HttpPost]
public ActionResult CreateMenu(Menu m)
{
  if (ModelState.IsValid)
  {
    ViewBag.Info = string.Format(
        "menu created: {0}, Price: {1}, category: {2}", m.Text, m.Price,
        m.Category);
  }
  else
  {
    ViewBag.Info = "not valid";
  }
  return View("Index");
}
```

If you use tool-generated model classes, it can be hard to add attributes to properties. As the tool-generated classes are defined as partial classes, the class can be extended by adding properties and methods, by implementing additional interfaces, and by implementing partial methods that are used by the tool-generated classes. You cannot add attributes to existing properties and methods. However, there's also help for such scenarios. Now assume the Menu class is a tool-generated partial class. Then a new class with a different name (for example, MenuMetadata) can define the same properties as the entity class and add the annotations:

```
public class MenuMetadata
{
  public int Id { get; set; }
  [Required, StringLength(25)] public string Text { get; set; }
  [DisplayName("Price"), DisplayFormat(DataFormatString="{0:C}")]
  public double Price { get; set; }
  [DataType(DataType.Date)] public DateTime Date { get; set; }
  [StringLength(10)] public string Category { get; set; }
}
```

The MenuMetadata class must be linked to the Menu class. With tool-generated partial classes, you can create another partial type in the same namespace to add the MetadataType attribute to the type definition that creates the connection:

```
[MetadataType(typeof(MenuMetadata))]
public partial class Menu
{
}
```

HTML Helpers (as shown next) can also make use of annotations to add information to the client.

HTML HELPERS

So far you've seen some HTML Helper methods such as Html.ActionLink and Html.Partial. There are a lot more that can help generate HTML content.

Html is a property of the view base class WebViewPage and is of type HtmlHelper. HTML Helper methods are implemented as extension methods to extend the HtmlHelper class.

The class InputExtensions defines HTML Helper methods to create check boxes, password controls, radio buttons, and textbox controls. The Action and RenderAction helpers are defined by the class ChildActionExtensions. Helper methods for display are defined by the class DisplayExtensions. Helper methods for HTML forms are defined by the class FormExtensions.

Now get into some examples using HTML helpers.

Simple Helpers

The following code snippet uses the HTML helper methods BeginForm, Label, and CheckBox. BeginForm starts a form element. There's also an EndForm for ending the form element. The sample makes use of the IDisposable interface implemented by the MvcForm returned from the BeginForm method. On disposing of the MvcForm, EndForm is invoked. This way the BeginForm method can be surrounded by a using statement to end the form at the closing curly brackets. The method DisplayName directly returns the content from the argument; the method CheckBox is an input element with the type attribute set to checkbox (code file MVCSampleApp/Views/HelperMethods/SimpleHelper.cshtml):

```
@using (Html.BeginForm()) {
  @Html.DisplayName("Check this (or not)")
  @Html.CheckBox("check1")
}
```

The resulting HTML code is shown here. The CheckBox method creates two input elements with the same name; one is set to hidden. The reason is if a check box has a value false, the browser does not pass this information to the server with the forms content. Only check box values of selected check boxes are passed to the server. This HTML characteristic creates a problem with automatic binding to the parameters of action methods. A simple solution is performed by the `CheckBox` helper method. This method creates a hidden `input` element with the same name that is set to `false`. If the check box is not selected, the hidden input element is passed to the server, and the false value can be bound. If the check box is selected, two input elements with the same name are sent to the server. The first one is set to `true`; the second one is set to `false`. With automatic binding just the first one is selected to bind:

```
<form action="/HelperMethods/Helper1" method="post">
  Check this (or not)
  <input id="check1" name="check1" type="checkbox" value="true" />
  <input name="check1" type="hidden" value="false" />
</form>
```

Using Model Data

Helper methods can be used with model data. This example creates a `Menu` object. This type was declared earlier in this chapter within the Models directory. and passes the menu as a model to the view (code file `MVCSampleApp/Controllers/HelperMethodsController.cs`):

```
public ActionResult HelperWithMenu()
{
  var menu = new Menu
  {
    Id = 1,
    Text = "Schweinsbraten mit Knödel und Sauerkraut",
    Price = 6.9,
    Date = new DateTime(2012, 10, 5),
    Category = "Main"
  };
  return View(menu);
}
```

The view has the model defined to be of type `Menu`. The `DisplayName` HTML helper just returns the text from the parameter as was already shown with the previous sample. The `Display` method uses an expression as the parameter where a property name can be passed in the string format. This way this property tries to find a property with this name and accesses the property accessor to return the value of the property (code file `MVCSampleApp/Views/HelperMethods/HelperWithMenu.cshtml`):

```
@model MVCSampleApp.Models.Menu

@{
    ViewBag.Title = "HelperWithMenu";
}

<h2>Helper with Menu</h2>

@Html.DisplayName("Text:")
@Html.Display("Text")
<br />
@Html.DisplayName("Category:")
@Html.Display("Category")
```

With the resulting HTML code, you can see this as output from calling the `DisplayName` and `Display` methods:

```
Text:
Schweinsbraten mit Kn&#246;del und Sauerkraut
<br />
Category:
Main
```

> **NOTE** *Helper methods also offer strongly typed variants to access members of the model as is shown in the section "Strongly Typed Helpers."*

Define HTML Attributes

Most HTML Helper methods have overloads in which you can pass any HTML attributes. For example, the following `TextBox` method creates an `input` element of type text. The first parameter defines the name; the second parameter defines the value that is set with the textbox. The third parameter of the `TextBox` method is of type object that enables passing an anonymous type where every property is changed to an attribute of the HTML element. Here, the result of the input element has the `required` attribute set to `required`, the `maxlength` attribute to 15, and the `class` attribute to `CSSDemo`. Because class is a C# keyword, it cannot be directly set as a property. Instead it is prefixed with @ to generate the class attribute for CSS styling:

```
@Html.TextBox("text1", "input text here",
    new { required="required", maxlength=15, @class="CSSDemo" });
```

The resulting HTML output is shown here:

```
<input class="Test" id="text1" maxlength="15" name="text1" required="required"
    type="text" value="input text here" />
```

Create Lists

For displaying lists, helper methods such as `DropDownList` and `ListBox` exist. These methods create the HTML select element.

Within the controller, first a dictionary is created that contains keys and values. The dictionary is then converted to a list of `SelectListItem` with the custom extension method `ToSelectListItems`. The `DropDownList` and `ListBox` methods make use of `SelectListItem` collections (code file `MVCSampleApp/Controllers/HelperMethodsController.cs`):

```
public ActionResult HelperList()
{
  var cars = new Dictionary<int, string>();
  cars.Add(1, "Red Bull Racing");
  cars.Add(2, "McLaren");
  cars.Add(3, "Lotus");
  cars.Add(4, "Ferrari");

  return View(cars.ToSelectListItems(4));
}
```

The custom extension method `ToSelectListItems` is defined within the class `SelectListItemsExtensions` that extends `IDictionary<int, string>`, the type from the cars collection. Within the implementation just a new `SelectListItem` object is returned for every item in the dictionary:

```
public static class SelectListItemsExtensions
{
  public static IEnumerable<SelectListItem> ToSelectListItems(
      this IDictionary<int, string> dict, int selectedId)
  {
    return dict.Select(item =>
      new SelectListItem
      {
        Selected = item.Key == selectedId,
        Text = item.Value,
        Value = item.Key.ToString()
      });
  }
}
```

With the view, the helper method `DropDownList` directly accesses the Model that is returned from the controller (code file `MVCSampleApp/Views/HelperMethods/HelperList.cshtml`):

```
@{
    ViewBag.Title = "Helper List";

}
@model IEnumerable<SelectListItem>

<h2>Helper2</h2>

@Html.DropDownList("carslist", Model)
```

The resulting HTML creates a `select` element with option child elements as created from the `SelectListItem` and defines the selected item as returned from the controller:

```
<select id="carslist" name="carslist">
  <option value="1">Red Bull Racing</option>
  <option value="2">McLaren</option>
  <option value="3">Lotus</option>
  <option selected="selected" value="4">Ferrari</option>
</select>
```

Strongly Typed Helpers

The HTML helper methods offer strongly typed methods to access the model passed from the controller. These methods are all suffixed with the name `For`. For example, instead of the `TextBox` method, here the `TextBoxFor` method can be used.

The next sample again makes use of a controller that returns a single entity (code file `MVCSampleApp/Controllers/HelperMethodsController.cs`):

```
        public ActionResult StronglyTypedMenu()
        {
          var menu = new Menu
          {
            Id = 1,
            Text = "Schweinsbraten mit Knödel und Sauerkraut",
            Price = 6.9,
            Date = new DateTime(2012, 10, 5),
            Category = "Main"
          };
          return View(menu);
        }
```

The view uses the `Menu` type as a model, and thus accessing the properties can be strongly typed with the `DisplayNameFor` and the `DisplayFor` methods. `DisplayNameFor` by default returns the name of the property (here it's the `Text` property), and `DisplayFor` returns the value of the property (code file `MVCSampleApp/Views/HelperMethods/StronglyTypedMenu.cshtml`):

```
@Html.DisplayNameFor(m => m.Text)
<br />
@Html.DisplayFor(m => m.Text)
```

Similar, you can use `Html.TextBoxFor(m => m.Text)`, which returns an input element that enables setting the `Text` property of the model. This method also makes use of the annotations added to the `Text` property of the `Menu` type. The `Text` property has the `Required` and `MaxStringLength` attributes added, which is why the `data-val-length`, `data-val-length-max`, and `data-val-required` attributes are returned from the `TextBoxFor` method:

```
<input data-val="true"
  data-val-length="The field Text must be a string with a maximum length of 50."
  data-val-length-max="50" data-val-required="The Text field is required."
  id="Text" name="Text" type="text"
  value="Schweinsbraten mit Knödel und Sauerkraut" />
```

Editor Extensions

Instead of using at least one helper method for every property, helper methods from the class `EditorExtensions` offer an editor all properties of a type.

Using the same `Menu` model as before, with the method `Html.EditorFor(m => m)` the complete UI for editing the menu is built. The result from this method invocation is shown in Figure 41-10.

Instead of using `Html.EditorFor(m => m)`, `Html.EditorForModel()` can be used. The method `EditorForModel` just makes use of the model of the view without the need to specify it explicitly. `EditorFor` has more flexibility in using other data sources (for example, just properties offered by the model), and `EditorForModel` needs less parameters to add.

| Id |
| 1 |
| Text |
| Schweinsbraten mit Knöd |
| Price |
| 6.9 |
| Date |
| 10/5/2012 |
| Category |
| Main |

FIGURE 41-10

Creating Custom Helpers

Razor has a specific syntax to create custom helpers. One way to create a helper method is to create an extension method that extends the type `HtmlHelper` or `HtmlHelper<TModel>`. This way the helper method can be used like all other HTML helpers using the `Html` property that returns an `HtmlHelper`.

Another way to create helpers is by using the Razor `helper` keyword. This creates a method that can be implemented and used in a Razor way. The helper method `DisplayDay` shown in the following code snippet receives a `DateTime` with the parameter and writes a `span` element if the passed date is before today. Mixing HTML and code works the same way as you're used to with Razor within the helper method implementation. The method is then used directly from within the view:

```
@helper DisplayDay(DateTime day)
{
  if (day < DateTime.Today)
  {
    <span>History day</span>
  }
  @String.Format("{0:d}", day);
}
@Html.DisplayFor(m => m.Text)
@Html.DisplayTextFor(m => m.Price)
@Html.TextBoxFor(m => m.Text)
@DisplayDay(Model.Date)
```

Templates

A great way to extend the outcome from HTML helpers is by using templates. A *template* is a simple view used by the HTML helper methods either implicitly or explicitly. Templates are stored within special folders. Display templates are stored within the `DisplayTemplates` folder that is in the view folder (for example, `Views/HelperMethods`), or in a shared folder (`Shared/DisplayTemplates`). The shared folder is used by all views; the specific view folder is used only by views within this folder. For editor templates the folder `EditorTemplates` is used.

Now get into an example (code file `MVCSampleApp/Models/Menu.cs`). With the `Menu` type, the `Date` property has the annotation `DataType` with a value of `DataType.Date`. Specifying this attribute the `DateTime` type by default does not show as date and time, but only with the short date format:

```
public class Menu
{
  public int Id { get; set; }
  [Required, StringLength(50)] public string Text { get; set; }
  [DisplayName("Price"), DisplayFormat(DataFormatString="{0:c}")]
    public double Price { get; set; }
  [DataType(DataType.Date)] public DateTime Date { get; set; }
  [StringLength(10)] public string Category { get; set; }
}
```

Now the template `Date.cshtml` is created within the directory `Views/HelperMethods/`
`DisplayTemplates`. Here the `Model` is returned using a long date string format `D` that is embedded within a
`div` tag that has the CSS class `markRed`:

```
<div class="markRed">
  @string.Format("{0:D}", Model)
</div>
```

The `markRed` CSS class is defined within the style sheet to set the color red (code file `MVCSampleApp/`
`Content/Site.css`):

```
.markRed {
  color: #f00;
}
```

Now a display HTML helper like the `DisplayForModel` can be used that makes use of the defined template.
The model is of type `Menu`, so the `DisplayForModel` method displays all properties of the `Menu` type. For
the `Date` it finds the template `Date.cshtml`, so this template is used to display the date in long date format
with the CSS style (code file `MVCSampleApp/Views/HelperMethods/Display.cshtml`):

```
@model MVCSampleApp.Models.Menu

@{
    ViewBag.Title = "Display";
}

<h2>Display</h2>

@Html.DisplayForModel()
```

If a single type should have different presentations in the same view, other names for the template file can be
used. Then the attribute `UIHint` specifying this template name can be used, or the template can be specified
with the template parameter of the helper method.

Next use a data-driven application that makes use of HTML helpers.

CREATING A DATA-DRIVEN APPLICATION

After discussing all the foundations of ASP.NET MVC, look into a data-driven application that uses the
ADO.NET Entity Framework. Here you can see features offered by ASP.NET MVC in combination with
data access.

> **NOTE** *The ADO.NET Entity Framework is covered in detail in Chapter 33, "ADO*
> *.NET Entity Framework."*

The sample application is used to maintain restaurant menu
entries in a database. Maintenance of the database entries should
be done only from an authenticated account. Browsing menus
should be possible for nonauthenticated users.

Defining a Model

Start with defining a model within the `Models` directory. Using
the ADO.NET Entity Model designer, the database Restaurant is
accessed to define entities, as shown in Figure 41-11.

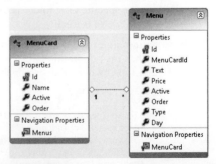

FIGURE 41-11

Creating Controllers and Views

After compiling the project, the classes from the model are available and can be selected to create the controllers and views. Create a new controller MenuAdmin, as shown in Figure 41-12, and select the template Controller with read/write actions and views using Entity Framework. With this template the model and data context classes can be selected. Based on this selection controller and view code is generated.

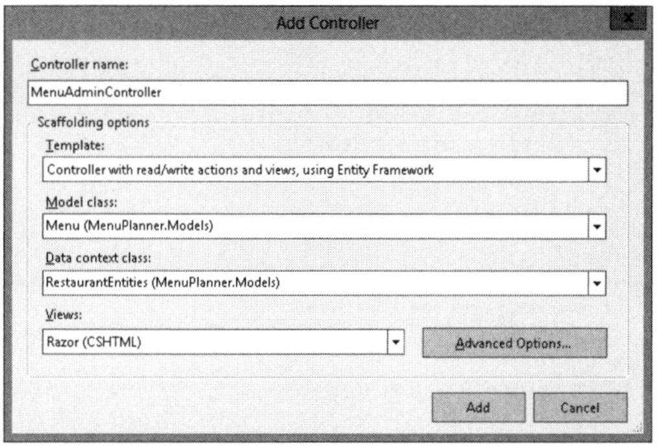

FIGURE 41-12

Controller

The generated controller class uses of the object context by creating RestaurantEntities on creation of the controller and offers action methods to view, edit, modify, and delete menu entries from the database. Just step into a few of these methods. The Index method is the default method that gets invoked when just the link of the controller is referenced. Here, all Menu items from the database are created and passed to the view as a List<Menu>.

When the user creates a new menu, the first Create method is invoked after an HTTP GET request from the client. With this method information the view is created with the help of a ViewBag. This ViewBag contains information about the menu cards because this is a relation to the menu, and the user can now select one menu card with the newly created menu. After the user fills out the form and submits the form with the new menu to the server, the second Create method is invoked from a HTTP POST request. This method uses model binding to pass the form data to the Menu object and adds the Menu object to the data context to write the newly created menu to the database (code file MenuPlanner/Controllers/MenuAdminController.cs):

```csharp
using System.Data;
using System.Linq;
using System.Web.Mvc;
using MenuPlanner.Models;

namespace MenuPlanner.Controllers
{
  public class MenuAdminController : Controller
  {
    private RestaurantEntities db = new RestaurantEntities();

    //
    // GET: /Admin/
    public ActionResult Index()
    {
      var menus = db.Menus.Include("MenuCard");
      return View(menus.ToList());
    }

    //
    // GET: /Admin/Details/5
    public ActionResult Details(int id = 0)
    {
      Menu menu = db.Menus.Single(m => m.Id == id);
      if (menu == null)
      {
        return HttpNotFound();
      }
      return View(menu);
    }

    //
```

```
// GET: /Admin/Create
public ActionResult Create()
{
  ViewBag.MenuCardId = new SelectList(db.MenuCards, "Id", "Name");
  return View();
}

//
// POST: /Admin/Create
[HttpPost]
public ActionResult Create(Menu menu)
{
  if (ModelState.IsValid)
  {
    db.Menus.AddObject(menu);
    db.SaveChanges();
    return RedirectToAction("Index");
  }

  ViewBag.MenuCardId = new SelectList(db.MenuCards,
      "Id", "Name", menu.MenuCardId);
  return View(menu);
}

//
// GET: /Admin/Edit/5
public ActionResult Edit(int id = 0)
{
  Menu menu = db.Menus.Single(m => m.Id == id);
  if (menu == null)
  {
    return HttpNotFound();
  }
  ViewBag.MenuCardId = new SelectList(db.MenuCards, "Id",
      "Name", menu.MenuCardId);
  return View(menu);
}

//
// POST: /Admin/Edit/5
[HttpPost]
public ActionResult Edit(Menu menu)
{
  if (ModelState.IsValid)
  {
    db.Menus.Attach(menu);
    db.ObjectStateManager.ChangeObjectState(menu, EntityState.Modified);
    db.SaveChanges();
    return RedirectToAction("Index");
  }
  ViewBag.MenuCardId = new SelectList(db.MenuCards, "Id",
      "Name", menu.MenuCardId);
  return View(menu);
}

//
// GET: /Admin/Delete/5
public ActionResult Delete(int id = 0)
{
  Menu menu = db.Menus.Single(m => m.Id == id);
  if (menu == null)
  {
    return HttpNotFound();
```

```
        }
        return View(menu);
    }

    //
    // POST: /Admin/Delete/5
    [HttpPost, ActionName("Delete")]
    public ActionResult DeleteConfirmed(int id)
    {
        Menu menu = db.Menus.Single(m => m.Id == id);
        db.Menus.DeleteObject(menu);
        db.SaveChanges();
        return RedirectToAction("Index");
    }

    protected override void Dispose(bool disposing)
    {
        db.Dispose();
        base.Dispose(disposing);
    }
  }
}
```

Views

Now explore some of the designer-generated views. The `Index` view has a `Menu` collection as its model and defines an HTML table. For the header elements of the table, the HTML helper `DisplayNameFor` is used to access property names for display. For displaying the items, the menu collection is iterated using `@foreach`, and every property value is accessed with `DisplayFor` (code file `MenuPlanner/Views/MenuPlanner/Index.cshtml`):

```
@model IEnumerable<MenuPlanner.Models.Menu>
@{
    ViewBag.Title = "Index";
}
<h2>Index</h2>
<p>
    @Html.ActionLink("Create New", "Create")
</p>
<table>
    <tr>
        <th>
            @Html.DisplayNameFor(model => model.MenuCard.Name)
        </th>
        <th>
            @Html.DisplayNameFor(model => model.Text)
        </th>
        <th>
            @Html.DisplayNameFor(model => model.Price)
        </th>
        <th>
            @Html.DisplayNameFor(model => model.Active)
        </th>
        <th>
            @Html.DisplayNameFor(model => model.Order)
        </th>
        <th>
            @Html.DisplayNameFor(model => model.Type)
        </th>
        <th>
            @Html.DisplayNameFor(model => model.Day)
        </th>
```

```
            <th></th>
        </tr>

@foreach (var item in Model) {
        <tr>
            <td>
                @Html.DisplayFor(modelItem => item.MenuCard.Name)
            </td>
            <td>
                @Html.DisplayFor(modelItem => item.Text)
            </td>
            <td>
                @Html.DisplayFor(modelItem => item.Price)
            </td>
            <td>
                @Html.DisplayFor(modelItem => item.Active)
            </td>
            <td>
                @Html.DisplayFor(modelItem => item.Order)
            </td>
            <td>
                @Html.DisplayFor(modelItem => item.Type)
            </td>
            <td>
                @Html.DisplayFor(modelItem => item.Day)
            </td>
            <td>
                @Html.ActionLink("Edit", "Edit", new { id=item.Id }) |
                @Html.ActionLink("Details", "Details", new { id=item.Id }) |
                @Html.ActionLink("Delete", "Delete", new { id=item.Id })
            </td>
        </tr>
}

    </table>
```

The second view for the `MenuAdmin` controller shown here is the `Create` view. An HTML form is created without arguments passed to the `BeginForm` method. This way the action method with the same name (`Create`) but with a POST request is requested on submitting the form. As you can see, the form content is built up using the helpers `DropDownList`, `ValidationMessageFor`, and `EditorFor` helper methods (code file `MenuPlanner/Views/MenuAdmin/Create.cshtml`):

```
@model MenuPlanner.Models.Menu

@{
    ViewBag.Title = "Create";
}

<h2>Create</h2>

<script src="@Url.Content("~/Scripts/jquery.validate.min.js")"></script>
<script src="@Url.Content("~/Scripts/jquery.validate.unobtrusive.min.js")">
    </script>

@using (Html.BeginForm()) {
  @Html.ValidationSummary(true)

    <fieldset>
      <legend>Menu</legend>

      <div class="editor-label">
        @Html.LabelFor(model => model.MenuCardId, "MenuCard")
      </div>
```

```
            <div class="editor-field">
              @Html.DropDownList("MenuCardId", String.Empty)
              @Html.ValidationMessageFor(model => model.MenuCardId)
            </div>

            <div class="editor-label">
              @Html.LabelFor(model => model.Text)
            </div>
            <div class="editor-field">
              @Html.EditorFor(model => model.Text)
              @Html.ValidationMessageFor(model => model.Text)
            </div>

            <div class="editor-label">
              @Html.LabelFor(model => model.Price)
            </div>
            <div class="editor-field">
              @Html.EditorFor(model => model.Price)
              @Html.ValidationMessageFor(model => model.Price)
            </div>

            <div class="editor-label">
              @Html.LabelFor(model => model.Active)
            </div>
            <div class="editor-field">
              @Html.EditorFor(model => model.Active)
              @Html.ValidationMessageFor(model => model.Active)
            </div>
            <div class="editor-label">
              @Html.LabelFor(model => model.Order)
            </div>
            <div class="editor-field">
              @Html.EditorFor(model => model.Order)
              @Html.ValidationMessageFor(model => model.Order)
            </div>
            <div class="editor-label">
              @Html.LabelFor(model => model.Type)
            </div>
            <div class="editor-field">
              @Html.EditorFor(model => model.Type)
              @Html.ValidationMessageFor(model => model.Type)
            </div>
            <div class="editor-label">
              @Html.LabelFor(model => model.Day)
            </div>
            <div class="editor-field">
              @Html.EditorFor(model => model.Day)
              @Html.ValidationMessageFor(model => model.Day)
            </div>

            <p>
              <input type="submit" value="Create" />
            </p>
        </fieldset>
    }

    <div>
      @Html.ActionLink("Back to List", "Index")
    </div>
```

The other views are created similar to the views shown here, so they are not covered in this book. Just consult the downloadable code or create the views with the Add Controller template as discussed.

ACTION FILTERS

ASP.NET MVC is extensible in many areas. A controller factory can be implemented to search and instantiate a controller (interface `IControllerFactory`). Controllers implement the `IController` interface. Finding action methods in a controller is resolved by using the `IActionInvoker` interface. The `ActionMethodSelectorAttribute` (...) can be used to define the HTTP methods allowed. The model binder that maps the HTTP request to parameters can be customized by implementing the `IModelBinder` interface. In the section "Model Binder," we've used the `DefaultModelBinder` type. Different view engines that implement the interface `IViewEngine` can be used. In this chapter, we've used the Razor view engine. Customization can also be done by using HTML Helpers (we've looked at this in some detail), and action filters. Most of the extension points are out of the scope of this book, but action filters are likely ones that you implement or use, and thus these are covered here.

Action filters are called before and after an action is executed. They are assigned to controllers or action methods of controllers using attributes. Action filters are implemented by creating a class that derives from the base class `ActionFilterAttribute`. With this class the base class members `OnActionExecuting`, `OnActionExecuted`, `OnResultExecuting`, and `OnResultExecuted` can be overridden. `OnActionExecuting` is called before the action method is invoked, and `OnActionExecuted` is called when the action method is completed. After that, before the result is returned, the method `OnResultExecuting` is invoked, and finally `OnResultExecuted`. Within these methods you can access the `Request` object to retrieve information of the caller and decide some actions depending on the browser, access routing information, change the view result dynamically, and so on. The code snippet accesses the variable language from routing information. To add this variable to the route, the route can be changed as was shown in the section Defining Routes . With an added `language` variable with the route information, the value supplied with the URL can be accessed using `RouteData.Values` as shown. You can use the retrieved value to change the culture for the user:

```
public class LanguageAttribute : ActionFilterAttribute
{
  private string language = null;

  public override void OnActionExecuting(ActionExecutingContext filterContext)
  {
    language = filterContext.RouteData.Values["language"] == null ?
      null : filterContext.RouteData.Values["language"].ToString();

    //...
  }

  public override void OnResultExecuting(ResultExecutingContext filterContext)
  {
  }
}
```

> **NOTE** *Globalization and localization, setting cultures, and other regional specifics are explained in Chapter 28, "Localization."*

With the created action filter attribute class, the attribute can be applied to a controller as shown. Using the attribute with the class, the members of the attribute class are invoked with every action method. Instead, the attribute can also be applied to an action method, so the members are invoked only when the action method is called.

```
[Language]
public class HomeController : Controller
{
```

ASP.NET MVC includes some predefined action filters. You can use the `OutputCacheAttribute` to define caching of the result. Some predefined filters derive from the base class `FilterAttribute`, which is the base class of `ActionFilterAttribute`. Using the base class `FilterAttribute` instead of `ActionFilterAttribute` allows only filtering action methods before they are invoked, but not afterward. Classes that derive from `FilterAttribute` are `HandleErrorAttribute`, `AuthorizeAttribute`, and `RequireHttpsAttribute`. `HandleError` enables reacting to exceptions and defining a view that should be shown in case of an error. The type of the exception can also be filtered, which enables specifying different views depending on the exception type. Specifying the `RequireHttpsAttribute` checks if the request is coming with HTTPS and denies invoking the action method otherwise.

Using the `AuthorizeAttribute` is covered in the next section.

AUTHENTICATION AND AUTHORIZATION

Chapter 39 laid the foundation for using the membership and role providers with ASP.NET. Chapter 40 showed how to use these with ASP.NET Web Forms. This chapter is based on the foundation of Chapter 39 to give you information how you can use these providers with ASP.NET MVC.

With the MenuPlanner sample application, Forms authentication should be used to allow only users from a specific role to change the menu entries. Here the `Membership` and `Roles` API can be used as with ASP.NET Web Forms; server-side controls are not available to deal with this.

Model for Login

For asking the user to log in, the `LoginModel` is created. This model defines `UserName`, `Password`, and `RememberMe` properties—all the information the user is asked with the login. This model has some annotations used with HTML helpers (code file `MVCSampleApp/Models/LoginModel.cs`):

```
public class LoginModel
{
  [Required]
  [Display(Name = "User name")]
  public string UserName { get; set; }

  [Required]
  [DataType(DataType.Password)]
  [Display(Name = "Password")]
  public string Password { get; set; }

  [Display(Name = "Remember me?")]
  public bool RememberMe { get; set; }
}
```

Controller for Login

The controller used for the login of the user is the `AccountController` (code file `MenuPlanner/Controllers/AccountController.cs`). This controller defines the `Login` action that can be requested with a HTTP GET request. This action just returns the Login view where the user can enter a username and password. From there an HTTP POST request is done to the second `Login` action where the `LoginModel` is used as an argument, and the values from the HTML form are assigned to the properties of the model. With the implementation, `Membership.ValidateUser` is invoked to pass the username and password to the configured membership provider. Next, the authentication cookie is set. Depending on the boolean member `RememberMe`, the cookie is set as a persistent or memory-based cookie:

```
using System.Web.Mvc;
using System.Web.Security;
```

```
using MenuPlanner.Models;

namespace MenuPlanner.Controllers
{
  [Authorize]
  public class AccountController : Controller
  {
    //
    // GET: /Account/Login
    [AllowAnonymous]
    public ActionResult Login()
    {
      return View();
    }

    [AllowAnonymous]
    [HttpPost]
    public ActionResult Login(LoginModel model, string returnUrl)
    {
      if (ModelState.IsValid)
      {
        if (Membership.ValidateUser(model.UserName, model.Password))
        {
          FormsAuthentication.SetAuthCookie(model.UserName, model.RememberMe);
          if (Url.IsLocalUrl(returnUrl))
          {
            return Redirect(returnUrl);
          }
          else
          {
            return RedirectToAction("Index", "Home");
          }
        }
        else
        {
          ModelState.AddModelError("",
              "The user name or password provided is incorrect.");
        }
      }

      // If we got this far, something failed, redisplay form
      return View(model);
    }

    //
    // GET: /Account/LogOff
    public ActionResult LogOff()
    {
      FormsAuthentication.SignOut();

      return RedirectToAction("Index", "Home");
    }
  }
}
```

To specify the Login action and in turn the view to be used, with the web.config file, the loginUrl is set to the Login method of the Account controller (code file MenuPlanner/web.config):

```
<authentication mode="Forms">
  <forms loginUrl="~/Account/Login" timeout="2880" />
</authentication>
```

Login View

The login view just defines a form that uses the Account controller and defines labels and input controls based on the model. This view is invoked the first time with a GET request on the Login action and in turn invokes the Login action with a POST request passing the model data (code file MenuPlanner/Views/ Account/Login.cshtml):

```
@model MenuPlanner.Models.LoginModel
@{
    ViewBag.Title = "Log in";
}

<hgroup class="title">
    <h1>@ViewBag.Title.</h1>
    <h2>Enter your user name and password below.</h2>
</hgroup>

@using (Html.BeginForm((string)ViewBag.FormAction, "Account")) {
    @Html.ValidationSummary(true,
        "Log in was unsuccessful. Please correct the errors and try again.")

    <fieldset>
        <legend>Log in Form</legend>
        <ol>
            <li>
                @Html.LabelFor(m => m.UserName)
                @Html.TextBoxFor(m => m.UserName)
                @Html.ValidationMessageFor(m => m.UserName)
            </li>
            <li>
                @Html.LabelFor(m => m.Password)
                @Html.PasswordFor(m => m.Password)
                @Html.ValidationMessageFor(m => m.Password)
            </li>
            <li>
                @Html.CheckBoxFor(m => m.RememberMe)
                @Html.LabelFor(m => m.RememberMe, new { @class = "checkbox" })
            </li>
        </ol>
        <input type="submit" value="Log in" />
    </fieldset>
}
```

Now you just need to make sure that a user who is not in the correct role is not allowed to access the methods. This can be done by applying the Authorize attribute to the MenuAdminController class (code file MenuPlanner/Controllers/MenuAdminController.cs) and specifying the roles that are allowed to use it:

```
[Authorize(Roles="Menu Admins")]
public class MenuAdminController : Controller
{
```

Applying this attribute to the class requires the role for every action method of the class. If there are different authorization requirements on different action methods, the Authorize attribute can also be applied to the action methods. With this attribute, it is verified if the caller is already authorized (by checking the authorization cookie). If the caller is not yet authorized, a 401 HTTP status code is returned with a redirect to the login action (which is defined in the web configuration file).

> **NOTE** *Chapter 39 explains how the membership provider can be configured. You can find more information on the Membership API in Chapter 22, "Security."*

ASP.NET WEB API

ASP.NET MVC 4 defines one great new feature that is independent of the UI but an easy way to do REST-based communication. For complex and advanced communication using SOAP and features such as discovery, transactions, and reliability, read Chapter 43, "Windows Communication Foundation." A simpler way to communicate with REST can easily be done with the ASP.NET Web API covered in this chapter.

The ASP.NET Web API is a communication technology that can be used from any client using the HTTP protocol (for example, Windows 8 Metro apps or jQuery) but is based on the same functionality you learned with this chapter: routing and controllers. Just views are not needed here.

Data Access Using Entity Framework Code-First

The ASP.NET Web API sample makes use of a database again. This time, Entity Framework Code-First is used to access the database. Chapter 33, "ADO.NET Entity Framework," explains Code-First.

The sample uses two entity types: `Menu` (code file `WebAPISample/Models/Menu.cs`) and `MenuCard` (code file `WebAPISample/Models/MenuCard.cs`). Both of these types have simple properties with one association. The `Menu` type is directly related to one `MenuCard`, and the `MenuCard` contains a collection of `Menu` objects:

```
public class Menu
{
  public int Id { get; set; }
  public string Text { get; set; }
  public decimal Price { get; set; }
  public bool Active { get; set; }
  public int Order { get; set; }
  public MenuCard MenuCard { get; set; }
}

public class MenuCard
{
  public int Id { get; set; }
  public string Name { get; set; }
  public bool Active { get; set; }
  public int Order { get; set; }
  public ICollection<Menu> Menus { get; set; }
}
```

The context is defined with the `MenuCardModel` type (code file `WebAPISample/Models/MenuCardModel.cs`). Using Code-First the only need with the context is to define properties of type `DbSet`:

```
public class MenuCardModel : DbContext
{
  public DbSet<Menu> Menus { get; set; }
  public DbSet<MenuCard> MenuCards { get; set; }
}
```

With Entity Framework Code-First, a database is automatically created if it doesn't already exist. Here, the created database is also filled with data. This can be done by creating a class that derives from `DropCreateDatabaseAlways`. Deriving from this base class, the database is created every time the application is started. Another base class that could be used here is `DropCreateDatabaseIfModelChanges`. Then the database would be created only if the model looks different, for example, with changed properties. To fill data, the `Seed` method is overridden (code file `WebAPISample/Models/MenuContextInitializer.cs`). The `Seed` method receives a `MenuCardModel` where new objects are added to the context, and then `SaveChanges` is invoked to write the objects to the database:

```
public class MenuContextInitializer : DropCreateDatabaseAlways<MenuCardModel>
{
  protected override void Seed(MenuCardModel context)
  {
```

```
var cards = new List<MenuCard>
{
  new MenuCard { Id = 1, Active = true, Name = "Soups", Order = 1 },
  new MenuCard { Id=2, Active = true, Name = "Main", Order = 2 }
};
cards.ForEach(c => context.MenuCards.Add(c));

new List<Menu>
{
  new Menu { Id=1, Active = true, Text = "Fritattensuppe", Order = 1,
             Price = 2.4M, MenuCard = cards[0] },
  new Menu { Id=2, Active = true, Text = "Wiener Schnitzel", Order = 2,
             Price= 6.9M, MenuCard=cards[1] }
}.ForEach(m => context.Menus.Add(m));
base.Seed(context);
    }
  }
```

To use the context initializer, the SetInitializer method of the Database class must be invoked to define the MenuContextInitializer. This code snippet (code file WebAPISample/Global.asax.cs) is from the global application class to set it every time the application starts:

```
protected void Application_Start()
{
  Database.SetInitializer(new MenuContextInitializer());
  //...
```

Now as the data access code is ready, you must understand the route to the Web API.

Defining Routes for ASP.NET Web API

Because the ASP.NET Web API is based on ASP.NET MVC, routes are an important aspect again. The default route created with an ASP.NET MVC project is shown here. Contrary to ASP.NET MVC where the route is defined with the MapRoute method, here the route is defined with the MapHttpRoute method. The route starts with api followed by the name of the controller, and then an optional parameter id. There's no action name as you've seen with the ASP.NET MVC route where action was mandatory. Instead, the methods within the controller are named Get, Post, Put, and Delete—corresponding to the HTTP request methods (code file WebAPISample/Global.asax.cs):

```
routes.MapHttpRoute(
    name: "DefaultApi",
    routeTemplate: "api/{controller}/{id}",
    defaults: new { id = RouteParameter.Optional }
);
```

Routes can also be changed and constraints added as you've seen earlier.

Controller Implementation

Now consider the implementation of the controller. The Web API controller derives from the base class ApiController. Contrary to the controllers that have been implemented previously, the method names of the API controller are based on the HTTP method. For a GET request, the method is named Get, for a POST request the method is named Post. The methods are implemented to access the MenuCardModel defined earlier. With one of the Get methods, a list of the menu objects is returned, with the second one a single menu is returned (code file WebAPISample/Controllers/MenuController.cs):

```
using System.Collections.Generic;
using System.Data;
using System.Linq;
using System.Web.Http;
```

```
using WebApiSample.Models;

namespace WebApiSample.Controllers
{
  public class MenusController : ApiController
  {
    private MenuCardModel data = new MenuCardModel();

    // GET /api/menus
    public IEnumerable<Menu> Get()
    {
      return data.Menus.Include("MenuCard").Where(m => m.Active).ToList();
    }

    // GET /api/menus/5
    public Menu Get(int id)
    {
      return data.Menus.Where(m => m.Id == id).Single();
    }

    // POST /api/menus
    public void Post(Menu m)
    {
      data.Menus.Add(m);
      data.SaveChanges();
    }

    // PUT /api/menus/5
    public void Put(int id, Menu m)
    {
      data.Menus.Attach(m);
      data.Entry(m).State = EntityState.Modified;
      data.SaveChanges();
    }

    // DELETE /api/menus/5
    public void Delete(int id)
    {
      var menu = data.Menus.Where(m => m.Id == id).Single();
      data.Menus.Remove(menu);
      data.SaveChanges();
    }

    protected override void Dispose(bool disposing)
    {
      if (disposing)
        data.Dispose();

      base.Dispose(disposing);
    }
  }
}
```

The controller can now be invoked by sending the requests to the server. GET requests can easily be initiated from a web browser. After the program starts, you can add api/menus following the server name and port to get some JSON data returned. The content returned looks similar to this code snippet:

```
[{"Active":true,"Id":1,
 "MenuCard":{"Active":true,"Id":1,"Name":"Soups","Order":1},
 "Order":1,"Price":2.40,"Text":"Fritattensuppe"},
{"Active":true,"Id":2,
 "MenuCard":{"Active":true,"Id":2,"Name":"Main","Order":2},
 "Order":2,"Price":6.90,"Text":"Wiener Schnitzel"}]
```

Client Application Using jQuery

Creating a client application, you can use the `HttpClient` class from the namespace `System.Net.Http` to send JSON or XML data and receive the answers from the service. The `HttpClient` class is covered in Chapter 26, "Networking." Here an HTML page is created by using jQuery to send the requests to the server hosting the ASP.NET Web API. This is a typical use for the Web API. However, since jQuery is not discussed in further detail in this book you should read another book for this scripting library.

The HTML page used to send requests to the server makes use of the jQuery JavaScript Library and the jQuery Template Plug-in. The jQuery JavaScript Library by default is included with the ASP.NET Web API project. The jQuery Template Plug-in needs to be installed with the NuGet Package Manager. NuGet is introduced in Chapter 17, "Visual Studio 2012."

The newly created view page `Menus.cshtml` doesn't use a layout page. The jQuery script libraries are referenced with a script tag:

```
<script src="@Url.Content("~/Scripts/jquery-1.6.2.js")"
    type="text/javascript"></script>
<script src="@Url.Content("~/Scripts/jQuery.tmpl.js")"
    type="text/javascript"></script>
```

The HTML content of the page contains an empty `ul` element with the id `menus` that will be filled with a HTTP GET request on loading of the page. The form element initially is hidden with the style `display: none`, and shown later to display elements where the user can add new menus and submit them with a POST request:

```
<body>
  <div>
    <ul id="menus">
    </ul>
    <form method="post" id="addMenu" style="display: none">
      <fieldset>
        <legend>Add New Menu</legend>
        <ol>
          <li>
            <label for="Text">Text</label>
            <input type="text" name="Text" />
          </li>
          <li>
            <label for="Price">Price</label>
            <input type="text" name="Price" />
          </li>
        </ol>
      </fieldset>
      <input type="submit" value="Add" />
    </form>
  </div>
</body>
```

On loading of the document, a GET request is made with the `$.getJSON` function. The first parameter defines the link to the API controller. The second parameter defines a function that is invoked when the result from the service is received. The `Get` method of the controller returns a list of menus that asynchronously finds its way to the `data` variable. This list is iterated with the `each` function, and every menu item from the list is appended to the element with the id `menus` (that's the `ul` element from the HTML code) by using the template with the id `menusTemplate`. After that the hidden form element is shown:

```
<script>
$(function () {
  $.getJSON(
    "http://localhost:15390/api/menus",
    function (data) {
```

```
    $.each(data,
      function (index, value) {
        $("#menusTemplate").tmpl(value).appendTo("#menus");
      }
      );
    $("#addMenu").show();
  });
```

The template is defined within a script element to define HTML li elements. This template contains placeholders using ${} where properties of the JavaScript objects returned are filled in. Text, Id, Price, and MenuCard are properties of the Menu class:

```
<script id="menusTemplate" type="text/html">
  <li>
    <h3> ${ Text } </h3>
    <span>${ Id }</span>
    <span>Price: ${ Price }</span>
    <span>Menu card: ${ MenuCard.Name }</span>
  </li>
</script>
```

Figure 41-13 shows the browser window after opening the page, the GET request sent, and the form shown dynamically.

FIGURE 41-13

Adding data to the form elements and clicking the Add button submits the form data by invoking the following submit method. Here, a HTTP POST request is performed using the post function. The data that is passed to the server is serialized from the form elements by using the serialize function. The data is now stored in the database:

```
$("#addMenu").submit(function () {
    $.post(
      "http://localhost:15390/api/menus",
      $("#addMenu").serialize(),
      function (value) {
        $("#menusTemplate").tmpl(value).appendTo("#menus");
      },
      "json"
      );

  });
});
</script>
```

SUMMARY

In this chapter, you explored the latest (and perhaps greatest) web technology to make use of ASP.NET, the ASP.NET MVC 4 framework. You saw how this provides you with a robust structure to work with, which is ideal for large-scale applications that require proper unit testing. You saw how easy it is to provide advanced capabilities with the minimum of effort, and how the logical structure and separation of functionality that this framework provides makes code easy to understand and easy to maintain.

You've also seen the new ASP.NET Web API that offers an easy way to create a REST-based service that can be accessed using JSON.

In the next chapter, you look at ASP.NET Dynamic Data, which makes use of technologies you've learned in the last few chapters to offer an automatic way to create HTML forms for accessing a database.

42

ASP.NET Dynamic Data

WHAT'S IN THIS CHAPTER?

➤ Creating Dynamic Data Web Applications
➤ Customizing Scaffolding
➤ Customizing Templates
➤ Configuring Routing for Dynamic Data

WROX.COM CODE DOWNLOADS FOR THIS CHAPTER

You can find the wrox.com code downloads for this chapter at `http://www.wrox.com/remtitle .cgi?isbn=1118314425` on the Download Code tab. The code for this chapter is contains this major examples covering all aspects of the chapter:

➤ Dynamic Data Sample

OVERVIEW

In the previous three chapters, you learned about how to use ASP.NET to create web applications and how to add advanced functionality to streamline those. In this chapter, you look at a framework that includes best-practice techniques to make data-driven web applications easy to create.

ASP.NET Dynamic Data enables you to build a website from preexisting data that you have in a database. The wizards that Visual Studio supplies make it possible to generate dynamic data websites quickly, which you can then customize to get the look and feel you want. Advanced template capabilities are included in dynamic data websites so that you can get up and running quickly. Dynamic data isn't suitable for all types of websites, but for many types—including e-commerce sites and data manipulation sites—it provides a perfect starting point for development.

If you think about data-driven websites (which these days includes most websites), you probably realize that a lot of their functionality is very similar. Such a website is likely to include one or more of the following concepts:

➤ Render HTML shaped dynamically based on data in an underlying data source (such as a database table or individual database row).

➤ Include pages in a site map that map directly or indirectly to entries in a data source (such as a database table).

➤ Have a structure that relates directly or indirectly to the structure of the underlying data source. (A section of the site may map to a database table, such as About or Products.)

➤ Allow modification to the underlying data source that will be reflected on pages.

If you want to build a data-driven site, you would probably use fairly standardized code to achieve the previous concepts. You might bind ASP.NET elements such as tables of data directly to a database table, or you might include an intermediate layer of data objects to represent data in the database and bind to those. You have seen a lot of the code you would use for that in earlier chapters.

However, because this situation is so common, there is an alternative. You could instead use a framework that provides a lot of the code for you to save a lot of tedious coding. ASP.NET Dynamic Data is just such a framework, and makes creating a data-driven website much easier. In addition to giving you the code previously outlined (referred to in dynamic data web applications as *scaffolding*), dynamic data web applications provide a lot of additional functionality, as you see shortly.

In this section, you can see how to create a dynamic data application and look at some of the features that it offers.

CREATING DYNAMIC DATA WEB APPLICATIONS

The best way to get a taste of what dynamic data websites have to offer is to build one in Visual Studio, which is a surprisingly simple thing to do.

To create a dynamic data website you need to have some source data. You can use whatever data you like, but if you want you can use the sample data that is included in the downloadable code for this chapter. This data is a SQL Server database with the database named MagicShop. Figure 42-1 shows the tables included in this database.

The MagicShop database represents a simple structure that you can use in an e-commerce website. The types of and relationships between data can illustrate how dynamic data sites work.

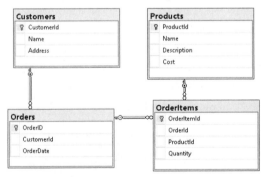

FIGURE 42-1

When you create a dynamic data site through the File ⇨ New Project ⇨ Web menu item, you can notice that there is one template available for dynamic data: ASP.NET Dynamic Data Entities Web Application.

> **NOTE** *Visual Studio 2010 included a template for LINQ to SQL as well. Now because the features of LINQ to SQL are now available with the Entity Framework, the LINQ to SQL template is no longer needed and not available with Visual Studio 2012.*

After you create a web application, the next thing to do is to add a data source. This means adding a new item to your project, ADO.NET Entity Model template. Before you do that, you may also want to add a local copy of your database to the `App_Data` directory of your website or use a SQL connection to the SQL Server database.

If you use the `MagicShop.mdf` database as a test, then—after adding the database to the `App_Data` directory—add an entity model called `MagicShop.edmx`, and in the Add New Item Wizard, use the default settings and add entities for all tables in the database as shown in Figure 42-2.

Configuring Scaffolding

There is one more step to perform before the initial build of your dynamic data website is complete. You must configure your data model for scaffolding in the `Global.asax` file for the website. Apart from differences in explanatory comments, this file is identical in both site template types. If you inspect the file, you can see that scaffolding for the website is configured through a model, which is defined at the application level as follows (code file `Global.asax.cs`):

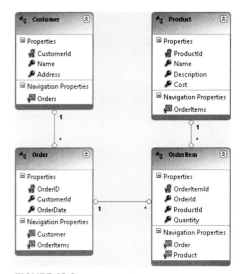

FIGURE 42-2

```
private static MetaModel s_defaultModel = new MetaModel();
public static MetaModel DefaultModel
{
  get
  {
    return s_defaultModel;
  }
}
```

The `Global.asax` file accesses this model in the `RegisterRoutes()` method, called in the `Application_Start()` handler. This method also configures dynamic data routing in the website, which you look at later in the section "Configuring Routing." The method contains the following commented-out line of code:

```
//DefaultModel.RegisterContext(typeof(YourDataContextType),
//   new ContextConfiguration() { ScaffoldAllTables = false });
```

Configuring the model simply requires you to uncomment this code and supply the appropriate data context type for your data model. You can also change the `ScaffoldAllTables` property to `true` initially to instruct the model to provide scaffolding for all available tables. Later, you may want to revert this change because you probably want a finer degree of control over exactly what scaffolding is created (including what data is visible in the site, what is editable, and so on), as you see in the section Controlling Scaffolding.

For the ADO.NET Entities version of this site, the code is as follows:

```
DefaultModel.RegisterContext(typeof(MagicShopEntities),
    new ContextConfiguration() { ScaffoldAllTables = true });
```

Exploring the Result

At this point, everything is in place to test the default dynamic data websites. The end result is identical regardless of which template you use. If you look at `Default.aspx` in a browser, the display appears, as shown in Figure 42-3.

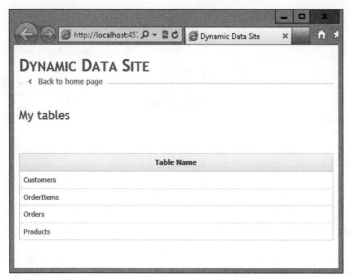

FIGURE 42-3

This page shows a list of links to each of the tables in the database along with some additional information, defined in the `Default.aspx` page as follows:

```
<%@ Page Language="C#" MasterPageFile="~/Site.master" CodeBehind="Default.aspx.cs"
        Inherits="DynamicDataSample._Default" %>

<asp:Content ID="headContent" ContentPlaceHolderID="head" Runat="Server">
</asp:Content>

<asp:Content ID="Content1" ContentPlaceHolderID="ContentPlaceHolder1"
  Runat="Server">
  <asp:ScriptManagerProxy ID="ScriptManagerProxy1" runat="server" />

  <h2 class="DDSubHeader">My tables</h2>

  <br /><br />

  <asp:GridView ID="Menu1" runat="server" AutoGenerateColumns="false"
    CssClass="DDGridView" RowStyle-CssClass="td" HeaderStyle-CssClass="th"
    CellPadding="6">
    <Columns>
      <asp:TemplateField HeaderText="Table Name" SortExpression="TableName">
        <ItemTemplate>
          <asp:DynamicHyperLink ID="HyperLink1" runat="server">
            <%# Eval("DisplayName") %>
          </asp:DynamicHyperLink>
        </ItemTemplate>
      </asp:TemplateField>
    </Columns>
  </asp:GridView>
</asp:Content>
```

A lot of the display code is contained in the master page and the CSS file for the website, which won't be listed here to save space. The important section of the preceding code is the `GridView` control, which contains a `DynamicHyperLink` control that renders the link to a table. Data is bound to the `GridView` control from code-behind as follows (code file `Default.aspx.cs`):

```
protected void Page_Load(object sender, EventArgs e)
{
    System.Collections.IList visibleTables =
        Global.DefaultModel.VisibleTables;
    if (visibleTables.Count == 0)
    {
        throw new InvalidOperationException(
            "There are no accessible tables. Make sure that at least one data"
            + " model is registered in Global.asax and scaffolding is enabled"
            + " or implement custom pages.");
    }
    Menu1.DataSource = visibleTables;
    Menu1.DataBind();
}
```

This extracts the list of visible tables from the model (in this case, all the tables because scaffolding is provided for all of them as discussed earlier), each of which is described by a `MetaTable` object. The `DynamicHyperLink` controls intelligently render links to pages for the tables based on properties of these objects. For example, the link for the Customers table is as follows:

```
http://localhost:45724/Customers/List.aspx
```

Obviously, the website has no such page defined; instead, routing is used as described in the first part of this chapter to generate content for this link. If you click the link, you see a listing page for the Customers table, as shown in Figure 42-4.

This page is generated from templates, which are stored in the code for the site and are discussed in the next section. You can use the links on this page to inspect, edit, insert, and delete records, as well as to traverse associations between tables. The View Orders link for each customer displays any orders for that particular customer—on a page that includes a drop-down list of customers that you can use to view orders for different customers if you want to.

FIGURE 42-4

If you click Edit for a customer, you see an edit customer view, as shown in Figure 42-5.

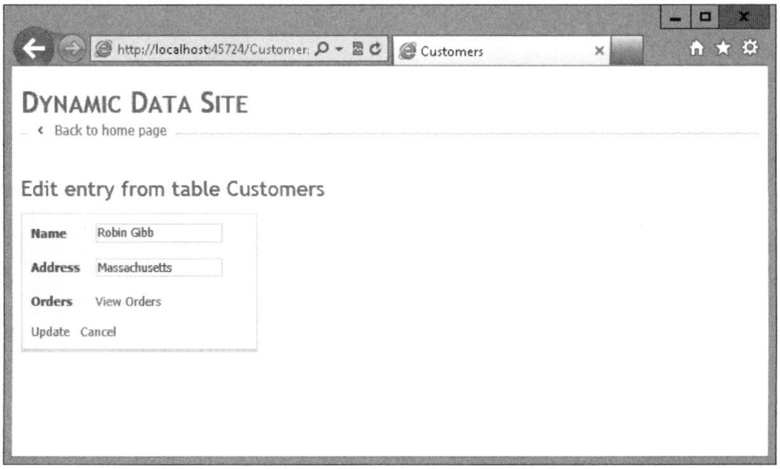

FIGURE 42-5

The template system used by a dynamic data website enables you to customize what is shown for each column in a table according to what data type it is. Or you can make further customizations that are unique to columns that you specify; you do have a lot of flexibility here.

What you have seen in this section is that even with the default settings, dynamic data can get you up and running quickly. Now, you may think that this ease of use comes at a cost, namely flexibility. This is not the case. Using some simple techniques, you can completely customize how dynamic data websites work, as you see in the next section.

CUSTOMIZING DYNAMIC DATA WEBSITES

There are a number of ways in which you can customize dynamic data websites to get exactly the effect you want. These range from simply modifying the HTML and CSS for the templates to customizing the way in which data is rendered though code and attribute modifications. In this section, you look at a few of these, starting with how to customize scaffolding—which, among other things, can affect the visibility of primary key values as noted in the previous section.

Controlling Scaffolding

In the sample dynamic data web application you have seen so far in this chapter, scaffolding was configured automatically for all tables (and all columns of those tables). This was achieved by setting the `ScaffoldAllTables` property of the `ContextConfiguration` for the sites to `true`, as shown in this code (code file `Global.asax.cs`):

If the value is changed to `false`, then the default behavior is not to provide any scaffolding for any tables or columns. To instruct the dynamic data framework to scaffold a table or column, you must provide metadata in your data model. This metadata is then read by the dynamic data runtime, and scaffolding is generated for you. Metadata can also provide information for other things—such as validation logic—as you see shortly.

Metadata is added using attributes. The attributes can be applied to types and properties to influence the UI. With designer-generated types, you can add attributes to the class. Because the designer-generated class is created as a partial class, another partial part of the class can be created to apply the attribute. However, you cannot add attributes to the designer-generated properties. If these would be done, all the modifications would be lost if the designer-generated code is regenerated. There's a solution—another way to do this. To add metadata to properties of an entity, a separate metadata class can be created that defines the same properties as the entity type, and the attributes can be applied there.

To supply metadata for a table, you must do two things:

➤ Create a metadata class definition for each table you want to supply metadata for, with members that map to columns.

➤ Associate the metadata classes with the data model table classes.

All data model items, the generated code items, are defined as partial class definitions. In the sample code, for example, there is a class called `Customer` (contained in the `MagicShopModel.Designer.cs` file) that is used for rows in the Customers table. To supply metadata for Customers rows, you might create a class called `CustomerMetadata`. After you have done that, you can supply a second partial class definition for `Customer` and use the `MetadataType` attribute to link the classes together.

In the .NET Framework, metadata is supported through *data annotations*. As such it should come as no surprise that the `MetadataType` attribute, along with other metadata attributes, is found in the `System.ComponentModel.DataAnnotations` namespace. The `MetadataType` attribute uses a `Type` parameter to specify the metadata type. The two attributes that control scaffolding are `ScaffoldTable` and `ScaffoldColumn`. Both of these attributes have a Boolean parameter to specify whether scaffolding will be generated for a table or column.

The following code shows an example of how this is achieved (code file `Customer.cs`):

```
using System.ComponentModel.DataAnnotations;

//...

[MetadataType(typeof(CustomerMetadata))]
public partial class Customer { }
```

And here is the metadata definition (code file `CustomerMetadata.cs`)

```
using System.ComponentModel.DataAnnotations;

//...

[ScaffoldTable(true)]
public class CustomerMetadata
{
    [ScaffoldColumn(false)]
    public string Address { get; set; }
}
```

Here, the `ScaffoldTable` attribute specifies that scaffolding will be generated for the Customer table, and the `ScaffoldColumn` attribute is used to ensure that the `Address` column will have no scaffolding. Note that columns are represented by `object` type properties, regardless of the type. You just have to ensure that the name of the property matches the name of the column.

The code shown here can be used with the example web applications introduced in the previous section to hide the addresses of customers.

You can apply other scaffolding configurations. When you set `Scaffolding` to `false` with the `ConfigurationContext`, then only the entity types that have the `ScaffoldTable` attribute applied are shown.

With the metadata type it can not only be configured if the table or columns should be used for scaffolding, but it is also possible to apply other annotations such as `StringLength`, as discussed in the next section.

Customizing Templates

As mentioned earlier in the chapter, dynamic data is generated through a system of templates. There are page templates used for laying out controls within different types of list and details pages, and field templates for displaying different data types in display, edit, and foreign key selection modes.

All the project templates are located in the DynamicData subfolder of a dynamic data website, which has the nested subfolders described in the following table.

DIRECTORY	DESCRIPTION
Content	This folder contains images used in other templates as well as the template for pagination (which is applied automatically when lists of data are long).
CustomPages	Use this directory if you want to supply custom pages.
EntityTemplates	This directory contains user control templates used for displaying a single row of data on a page, in either view, edit, or insert mode. The base class for templates in this category is `EntityTemplateUserControl`.
FieldTemplates	This directory contains user control templates used to display individual column data. Field templates derive from `FieldTemplateUserControl`.

continues

(continued)

DIRECTORY	DESCRIPTION
Filters	This directory contains user control templates used to display filters for foreign key relationships. In the default code, these are drop-down lists. For example, the list page for orders includes a filter to display only those orders associated with a particular user. The base class for filters is `QueryableFilterUserControl`.
PageTemplates	This directory contains the main templates used to display single or multiple rows of data in various modes of operation. The body of these pages uses the user control templates from the other directories to build its content. Page templates are complete pages and thus derive from the base class `Page`.

It is worth digging into these templates and their code-behind to see how everything fits together. For example, text columns display using two field templates in the FieldTemplates directory. The first of these, `Text.ascx`, is as follows (code file `DynamicData/FieldTemplates/Text.ascx`):

```
<asp:Literal runat="server" ID="Literal1" Text="<%# FieldValueString %>" />
```

This code is self-explanatory; it simply outputs the text value of a column in a `Literal` control. The code-behind (code file `DynamicData/FieldTemplates/Text.ascx.cs`) derives from the base class `FieldTemplateUserControl` and overrides the `FieldValueString` and `DataControl` properties. The `FieldValueString` property reduces the length of the string defined in the base class if the string is used within a list control. The `DataControl` property returns the `Literal` control defined with the ASPX code.

```csharp
using System.Web.DynamicData;
using System.Web.UI;

namespace DynamicDataSample
{
    public partial class TextField : FieldTemplateUserControl
    {
        private const int MAX_DISPLAYLENGTH_IN_LIST = 25;

        public override string FieldValueString
        {
            get
            {
                string value = base.FieldValueString;
                if (ContainerType == ContainerType.List)
                {
                    if (value != null && value.Length > MAX_DISPLAYLENGTH_IN_LIST)
                    {
                        value = value.Substring(0, MAX_DISPLAYLENGTH_IN_LIST - 3) + "...";
                    }
                }
                return value;
            }
        }

        public override Control DataControl
        {
            get
            {
                return Literal1;
```

```
          }
        }
      }
    }
```

If, though, the column is in an editable mode, `Text_Edit.ascx` is used instead. For the edit mode always `_Edit` is added to the control filename and the base type (code file `DynamicData/FieldTemplates/Text/Edit.ascx`):

```
<asp:TextBox ID="TextBox1" runat="server" Text='<%# FieldValueEditString %>'
  CssClass="DDTextBox"></asp:TextBox>

<asp:RequiredFieldValidator runat="server" ID="RequiredFieldValidator1"
  CssClass="DDControl" ControlToValidate="TextBox1" Display="Dynamic"
  Enabled="false" />
<asp:RegularExpressionValidator runat="server" ID="RegularExpressionValidator1"
  CssClass="DDControl" ControlToValidate="TextBox1" Display="Dynamic"
  Enabled="false" />
<asp:DynamicValidator runat="server" ID="DynamicValidator1" CssClass="DDControl"
  ControlToValidate="TextBox1" Display="Dynamic" />
```

A `TextBox` control is used here to render the control so that it is editable, and a combination of the three validation controls is used to provide validation functionality if required. Exactly how these validation controls work is determined by the data model and its associated metadata. Non-nullable columns, for example, result in the `RequiredFieldValidator` being active. The `DynamicValidator` control is used with metadata attributes, for example, `StringLength`, which you can use to set the maximum permitted length of a string.

The code from the code-behind file `Text_Edit.ascx.cs` is shown here.

```
using System;
using System.Collections.Specialized;
using System.Web.DynamicData;
using System.Web.UI;

namespace DynamicDataSample
{
  public partial class Text_EditField : FieldTemplateUserControl
  {
    protected void Page_Load(object sender, EventArgs e)
    {
      if (Column.MaxLength < 20)
      {
        TextBox1.Columns = Column.MaxLength;
      }
      TextBox1.ToolTip = Column.Description;

      SetUpValidator(RequiredFieldValidator1);
      SetUpValidator(RegularExpressionValidator1);
      SetUpValidator(DynamicValidator1);
    }

    protected override void OnDataBinding(EventArgs e)
    {
      base.OnDataBinding(e);
      if (Column.MaxLength > 0)
      {
        TextBox1.MaxLength = Math.Max(FieldValueEditString.Length,
          Column.MaxLength);
      }
    }
```

```
protected override void ExtractValues(IOrderedDictionary dictionary)
{
  dictionary[Column.Name] = ConvertEditedValue(TextBox1.Text);
}

public override Control DataControl
{
  get
  {
    return TextBox1;
  }
}
}
}
```

Now consider some examples for customizing templates and changing the template to use. Showing all orders, the OrderDate displays a date and time, as shown in Figure 42-6. However, just the date is set. With the table headings, the OrderDate and OrderItems titles should be changed to Order Date and Order Items.

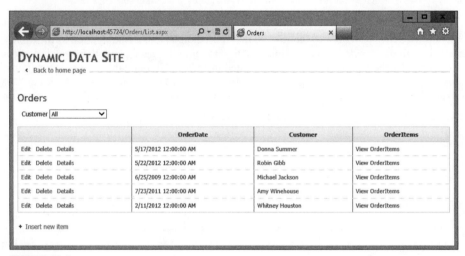

FIGURE 42-6

These requirements can be easily fulfilled by using metadata with the OrderMetadata class. Similar to mapping the CustomerMetadata to the Customer type as was done in the controlling scaffolding section, the mapping between Order and OrderMetadata is done in a similar way. With the following code snippet (code file OrderMetadata.cs), the OrderMetadata type now has some annotations to the OrderDate and OrderItems properties. With both of these properties, the DisplayName attribute is applied. This attribute is used when showing the titles. With OrderDate the additional annotation to define a DataType is applied. The DataType attribute changes the type to DataType.Date to show only the date both with display and edit modes (code file OrderMetadata.cs):

```
using System;
using System.ComponentModel;
using System.ComponentModel.DataAnnotations;
using System.Data.Objects.DataClasses;

namespace DynamicDataSample
{
  [ScaffoldTable(true)]
  public class OrderMetadata
  {
```

```
    [DisplayName("Order Date")]
    [DataType(DataType.Date)]
    public DateTime OrderDate { get; set; }

    [DisplayName("Order Items")]
    public EntityCollection<OrderItem> OrderItems { get; set; }
  }
}
```

DataType is an enumeration that defines Duration, EmailAddress, PhoneNumber, PostalCode, Url, and many other definitions to allow for different template selections.

Running the application again, the title and order date changes, as shown in Figure 42-7.

FIGURE 42-7

If the format of the date should be represented differently, for example, with a long date format, it's easy to create a custom field template. Although a template for the Date type (as defined by the DataType attribute) doesn't exist with the project as it was created, it's easy to do this just by naming the file Date.ascx within the FieldTemplates folder.

The following code snippet (code file Date.ascx) just contains a Literal control:

```
<%@ Control Language="C#" AutoEventWireup="true" CodeBehind="Date.ascx.cs"
  Inherits="DynamicDataSample.DynamicData.FieldTemplates.DateField" %>
<asp:Literal runat="server" ID="Literal1" Text="<%# FieldValueString %>" />
```

With the code-behind (code file Date.ascx.cs) the FieldValueString property is overridden to return a long date format string:

```
using System;
using System.Web.DynamicData;
using System.Web.UI;

namespace DynamicDataSample.DynamicData.FieldTemplates
{
  public partial class DateField : FieldTemplateUserControl
  {
    public override string FieldValueString
    {
      get
```

```
        {
            if (FieldValue == null) return null;

            DateTime date = (DateTime)FieldValue;
            return date.ToLongDateString();
        }
    }
    public override Control DataControl
    {
      get
      {
        return Literal1;
      }
    }
  }
}
```

Running the application once more, the custom template is selected based on its name that maps to the type.

For a single data type, multiple templates should be used; the `UIHint` attribute can be used to specify a template with a different name.

Configuring Routing

One of the most important concepts to grasp when dealing with dynamic data sites is that pages are generated according to *actions*. An action is a way to define what a page should do in response to, for example, the user clicking a particular link. There are four page actions defined for you by default: List, Details, Edit, and Insert.

Each of the page templates defined for a dynamic data site (which are also known as *views*) can function differently according to what action is currently performed. The routing configuration for the website associates actions with views, and each route can optionally be constrained by the tables that it should apply to. For example, you might create a new view intended for listing customers. That view might function differently from the default `List.aspx` view. To create the new view, you must configure routing so that the correct view will be used.

The default routing for a dynamic data website is configured in `Global.asax` as follows:

```
routes.Add(new DynamicDataRoute("{table}/{action}.aspx")
{
  Constraints = new RouteValueDictionary(
    new { action = "List|Details|Edit|Insert" }),
  Model = DefaultModel
});
```

This uses the routing framework described earlier in the chapter; although, here routes use the `DynamicDataRoute` type. This class derives from `Route` and provides specialized functionality for dealing with actions, views, and tables.

You can notice in this code that this route includes the name of a table and the name of an action—where the value of the action is constrained to the four predefined page action types. To take the example of using a different view for listing customers, you might add the following route (before the existing one, or that one would take precedence):

```
routes.Add(new DynamicDataRoute("Customers/List.aspx")
{
  Table = "Customers",
  Action = PageAction.List,
  ViewName = "ListCustomers",
  Model = DefaultModel
});
```

This route associates the `/Customers/List.aspx` URL with the view `ListCustomers.aspx`, so for this code to work, you must supply a file of this name in the PageTemplates directory. You can also see that the `Table` and `Action` properties are specified here because they are not available in the URL any more. The way the dynamic data routing works is that `{table}` and `{action}` routing parameters are used to populate the `Table` and `Action` properties, and in this URL these parameters are not present.

You can build up as complex a system of routing as you want in this manner, providing specialized pages for tables and actions as you see fit. You can also make use of the `ListDetails.aspx` view, which is a master-detail view of data that enables row selection and inline editing. To use this view, you can supply alternative routes, or simply uncomment the following routes that the dynamic data site template provides (code file `Global.asax.cs`):

```
routes.Add(new DynamicDataRoute("{table}/ListDetails.aspx")
{
  Action = PageAction.List,
  ViewName = "ListDetails",
  Model = DefaultModel
});

routes.Add(new DynamicDataRoute("{table}/ListDetails.aspx")
{
  Action = PageAction.Details,
  ViewName = "ListDetails",
  Model = DefaultModel
});
```

These routes can cause the `ListDetails.aspx` view to be used whenever the List or Details page actions are used. The Edit and Insert page actions are then not required because (as mentioned earlier) editing capabilities are provided inline. An example of this is shown in Figure 42-8.

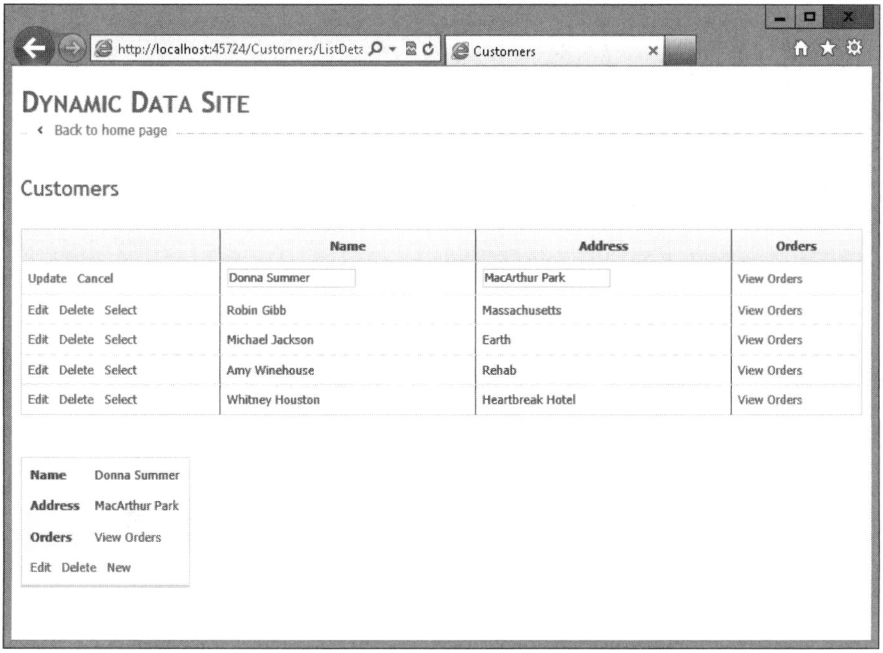

FIGURE 42-8

SUMMARY

In this chapter, you saw how to create dynamic data websites that provide seamless integration of your data with a powerful frontend ASP.NET UI. This technology provides so much code for you by default that at times it feels like your websites write themselves. You saw how to customize scaffolding, templates, and routing to make sites work just the way you want.

Having the framework like ASP.NET Dynamic Data in place can drastically reduce the work you must do to access data, while leaving you free to concentrate on the rest of your website.

In the next chapter, you look at Windows Communication Foundation, which enables you to make remote calls across application boundaries in a flexible, secure way. This underpins a lot of web development, because you often want to pull in data from disparate sources for your web applications rather than including in-place databases as you have been doing in this chapter.

PART VI
Communication

43

Windows Communication Foundation

WHAT'S IN THIS CHAPTER?

- ➤ WCF overview
- ➤ Creating a simple service and client
- ➤ Defining service, operation, data, and message contracts
- ➤ Implementing a service
- ➤ Using binding for communication
- ➤ Creating different hosts for services
- ➤ Creating clients with a service reference and programmatically
- ➤ Using duplex communication
- ➤ Using routing

WROX.COM CODE DOWNLOADS FOR THIS CHAPTER

You can find the wrox.com code downloads for this chapter at `http://www.wrox.com/remtitle.cgi?isbn=1118314425` on the Download Code tab. The code for this chapter is divided into the following major examples:

- ➤ Simple service and client
- ➤ WebSocket
- ➤ Duplex communication
- ➤ Routing

WCF OVERVIEW

Windows Communication Foundation (WCF) is the flexible communication technology of the .NET Framework. Previous to .NET 3.0, several communication technologies were required in a single enterprise solution. For platform-independent communication, ASP.NET Web services were used. For more advanced web services—technologies such as reliability, platform-independent security, and atomic transactions—Web Services Enhancements added a complexity layer to ASP.NET web services. If the communication needed to be faster, and both the client and service were .NET applications, .NET Remoting was the technology of choice. .NET Enterprise Services with its automatic transaction support, by default, used the DCOM protocol, which was even faster than .NET Remoting. DCOM was also the only protocol to allow the passing of transactions. All of these technologies have different programming models that require many skills from the developer.

.NET Framework 3.0 introduced a new communication technology that includes all the features from these predecessors and combines them into one programming model: Windows Communication Foundation (WCF).

The namespace covered in this chapter is `System.ServiceModel`.

WCF combines the functionality from ASP.NET Web services, .NET Remoting, Message Queuing, and Enterprise Services. You can get the following from WCF:

➤ **Hosting for components and services**—Just as you can use custom hosts with .NET Remoting and Web Service Enhancements (WSE), you can host a WCF service in the ASP.NET runtime, a Windows service, a COM+ process, or just a Windows Forms application for peer-to-peer computing.

➤ **Declarative behavior**—Instead of the requirement to derive from a base class (this requirement exists with .NET Remoting and Enterprise Services), attributes can be used to define the services. This is similar to web services developed with ASP.NET.

➤ **Communication channels**—Although .NET Remoting is flexible for changing the communication channel, WCF is a good alternative because it offers the same flexibility. WCF offers multiple channels to communicate using HTTP, TCP, or an IPC channel. Custom channels using different transport protocols can be created as well.

➤ **Security infrastructure**—For implementing platform-independent web services, a standardized security environment must be used. The proposed standards are implemented with WSE 3.0, and this continues with WCF.

➤ **Extensibility**—.NET Remoting has a rich extensibility story. It is not only possible to create custom channels, formatters, and proxies, but also to inject functionality inside the message flow on the client and on the server. WCF offers similar extensibilities; however, here the extensions are created by using SOAP headers.

➤ **Support of previous technologies**—Instead of rewriting a distributed solution completely to use WCF, WCF can be integrated with existing technologies. WCF offers a channel that can communicate with serviced components using DCOM. Web services that have been developed with ASP.NET can be integrated with WCF as well.

The final goal is to send and receive messages between a client and a service across processes or different systems, across a local network, or across the Internet. This should be done, if required, in a platform-independent way and as fast as possible. From a distant view, the service offers an endpoint that is described by a contract, a binding, and an address. The contract defines the operations offered by the service; binding gives information about the protocol and encoding; and the address is the location of the service. The client needs a compatible endpoint to access the service.

Figure 43-1 shows the components that participate with a WCF communication.

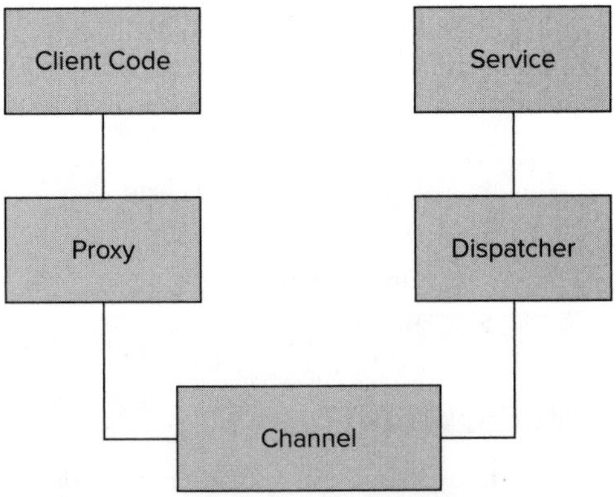

FIGURE 43-1

The client invokes a method on the proxy. The proxy offers methods as defined by the service but converts the method call to a message and transfers the message to the channel. The channel has a client-side part and a server-side part that communicate across a networking protocol. From the channel, the message is passed to the dispatcher, which converts the message to a method call invoked with the service.

WCF supports several communication protocols. For platform-independent communication, web services standards are supported. For communication between .NET applications, faster communication protocols with less overhead can be used.

The following sections look at the functionality of core services used for platform-independent communication:

> **SOAP**—A platform-independent protocol that is the foundation of several web service specifications to support security, transactions, reliability

> **Web Services Description Language (WSDL)**—Offers metadata to describe a service

> **Representational State Transfer (REST)**—Used with RESTful Web services to communicate across HTTP

> **JavaScript Object Notation (JSON)**—Enables easy use from within JavaScript clients

SOAP

For platform-independent communication, the SOAP protocol can be used and is directly supported from WCF. SOAP originally was shorthand for Simple Object Access Protocol (SOAP), but since SOAP 1.2 this is no longer the case. SOAP no longer is an object access protocol because instead messages are sent that can be defined by an XML schema.

A service receives a SOAP message from a client and returns a SOAP response message. A SOAP message consists of an envelope, which contains a header and a body:

```
<s:Envelope xmlns:s="http://schemas.xmlsoap.org/soap/envelope/">
  <s:Header>
  </s:Header>
  <s:Body>
    <ReserveRoom xmlns="http://www.cninnovation.com/RoomReservation/2012">
      <roomReservation
        xmlns:a=
          "http://schemas.datacontract.org/2004/07/Wrox.ProCSharp.WCF.Contracts"
        xmlns:i="http://www.w3.org/2001/XMLSchema-instance">
      <a:Contact>UEFA</a:Contact>
      <a:EndTime>2012-07-01T22:45:00</a:EndTime>
      <a:Id>0</a:Id>
      <a:RoomName>Kiew</d4p1:RoomName>
      <a:StartTime>2012-07-01T20:45:00</a:StartTime>
      <a:Text>Spain-Germany</a:Text>
      </roomReservation>
    </ReserveRoom>
  </s:Body>
</s:Envelope>
```

The header is optional and can contain information about addressing, security, and transactions. The body contains the message data.

WSDL

A Web Services Description Language (WSDL) document describes the operations and messages of the service. WSDL defines metadata of the service that can be used to create a proxy for the client application.

The WSDL contains this information:

> **Types** for the messages described using an XML schema.

> **Messages** sent to and from the service. Parts of the messages are the types defined with an XML schema.

> **Port types** map to service contracts and list operations defined with the service contract. Operations contain messages; for example, an input and an output message as used with a request and response sequence.

➤ **Binding** information that contains the operations listed with the port types and that defines the SOAP variant used.

➤ **Service** information that maps port types to endpoint addresses.

> **NOTE** *With WCF, WSDL information is offered by Metadata Exchange (MEX) endpoints.*

REST

WCF also offers communication by using REST. This is not actually a protocol but defines several principles for using services to access resources. A RESTful Web service is a simple service based on the HTTP protocol and REST principles. The principles are defined by three categories: a service can be accessed with a simple URI, supports MIME types, and uses different HTTP methods. With the support of MIME types, different data formats can be returned from the service such as plain XML, JSON, or AtomPub. The GET method of a HTTP request returns data from the service. Other methods that are used are PUT, POST, and DELETE. The PUT method is used to make an update on the service side, POST creates a new resource, and DELETE deletes a resource.

REST enables the sending of smaller requests to services than is possible with SOAP. If transactions, secure messages, (secure communication is still possible, for example via HTTPS), and the reliability offered by SOAP are not needed, a REST-architected service can reduce overhead.

With the REST architecture, the service is always stateless, and the response from the service can be cached.

JSON

Instead of sending SOAP messages, accessing services from JavaScript can best be done by using JSON. .NET includes a data contract serializer to create objects with the JSON notation.

JSON has less overhead than SOAP because it is not XML but is optimized for JavaScript clients. This makes it extremely useful from Ajax clients. Ajax is discussed in Chapter 40, "ASP.NET Web Forms." JSON does not provide the reliability, security, and transaction features that can be sent with the SOAP header, but these are features usually not needed by JavaScript clients.

CREATING A SIMPLE SERVICE AND CLIENT

Before going into the details of WCF, start with a simple service. The service is used to reserve meeting rooms.

For a backing store of room reservations, a simple SQL Server database with the table RoomReservations is used. You can download the database from www.wrox.com together with the sample code of this chapter.

Following are the next steps to create a service and a client:

1. Create service and data contracts.
2. Create a library to access the database using the ADO.NET Entity Framework.
3. Implement the service.
4. Use the WCF Service Host and WCF Test Client.
5. Create a custom service host.
6. Create a client application using metadata.
7. Create a client application using shared contracts.
8. Configure diagnostics.

Defining Service and Data Contracts

To start, create a new solution with the name **RoomReservation**. Add a new project of type Class Library to the solution, and name the project **RoomReservationContracts**. Create a new class named **RoomReservation** (code file RoomReservation/RoomReservationContracts/RoomReservation.cs). This class contains the properties Id, RoomName, StartTime, EndTime, Contact, and Text to define the data needed in the database and sent across the network. For sending the data across a WCF service, the class is annotated with the DataContract and the DataMember attributes. The attributes StringLength from the namespace System.ComponentModel.DataAnnotations can not only be used with validation on user input, but they can also define column schemas on creating the database table.

```
using System;
using System.Collections.Generic;
using System.ComponentModel;
using System.ComponentModel.DataAnnotations;
using System.Runtime.CompilerServices;
using System.Runtime.Serialization;

namespace Wrox.ProCSharp.WCF.Contracts
{
  [DataContract]
  public class RoomReservation : INotifyPropertyChanged
  {
    private int id;

    [DataMember]
    public int Id
    {
      get { return id; }
      set { SetProperty(ref id, value); }
    }

    private string roomName;

    [DataMember]
    [StringLength(30)]
    public string RoomName
    {
      get { return roomName; }
      set { SetProperty(ref roomName, value); }
    }

    private DateTime startTime;

    [DataMember]
    public DateTime StartTime
    {
      get { return startTime; }
      set { SetProperty(ref startTime, value); }
    }

    private DateTime endTime;

    [DataMember]
    public DateTime EndTime
    {
      get { return endTime; }
      set { SetProperty(ref endTime, value); }
    }

    private string contact;

    [DataMember]
```

```
      [StringLength(30)]
      public string Contact
      {
        get { return contact; }
        set { SetProperty(ref contact, value); }
      }

      private string text;

      [DataMember]
      [StringLength(50)]
      public string Text
      {
        get { return text; }
        set { SetProperty(ref text, value); }
      }

      protected virtual void OnNotifyPropertyChanged(string propertyName)
      {
        PropertyChangedEventHandler eventHandler = PropertyChanged;
        if (eventHandler != null)
        {
          eventHandler(this, new PropertyChangedEventArgs(propertyName));
        }
      }

      protected virtual void SetProperty<T>(ref T item, T value,
        [CallerMemberName] string propertyName = null)
      {
        if (!EqualityComparer<T>.Default.Equals(item, value))
        {
          item = value;
          OnNotifyPropertyChanged(propertyName);
        }
      }

      public event PropertyChangedEventHandler PropertyChanged;
    }
  }
```

Next, create the service contract. The operations offered by the service can be defined by an interface. The interface IRoomService defines the methods ReserveRoom and GetRoomReservations. The service contract is defined with the attribute ServiceContract. The operations defined by the service have the attribute OperationContract applied (code file RoomReservation/RoomReservationContracts/IRoomService.cs).

```
using System;
using System.ServiceModel;

namespace Wrox.ProCSharp.WCF.Contracts
{
  [ServiceContract(Namespace= "http://www.cninnovation.com/RoomReservation/2012")]
  public interface IRoomService
  {
    [OperationContract]
    bool ReserveRoom(RoomReservation roomReservation);

    [OperationContract]
    RoomReservation[] GetRoomReservations(DateTime fromTime, DateTime toTime);
  }
}
```

Data Access

Next, create a library used to access, read and write reservations to the database named RoomReservationData. This time use the Code First model with the ADO.NET Entity Framework. This way mapping information is not needed; everything can be defined using code. And you can also create a database on-the-fly during runtime. The class to define the entities was already defined with the RoomReservationContracts assembly, so this assembly needs to be referenced. Also the EntityFramework assembly is required. Now the RoomReservationContext class (code file RoomReservation/RoomReservationData/RoomReservationContext.cs) can be created. This class derives from the base class DbContext to act as a context for the ADO.NET Entity Framework and defines a property named RoomReservations to return a DbSet<RoomReservation>.

```
using System.Data.Entity;
using Wrox.ProCSharp.WCF.Contracts;

namespace Wrox.ProCSharp.WCF.Data
{
  public class RoomReservationContext : DbContext
  {

    public RoomReservationContext()
      : base("name=RoomReservation")
    {

    }
    public DbSet<RoomReservation> RoomReservations { get; set; }
  }
}
```

With the default constructor of the class, the base constructor is invoked to pass the name of an SQL connection string. This way on creation of the database a name is not automatically mapped from the name of the context. If the database does not exist before starting the application, it is automatically created on first use of the context. The hosting application than needs a connection string is configured as shown. The connection string makes use of the Microsoft SQL Server Express LocalDB database that is a new improved version of SQL Express and comes with the installation of Visual Studio 2012.

```
<connectionStrings>
  <add
    name="RoomReservation" providerName="System.Data.SqlClient"
    connectionString="Server=(localdb)\v11.0;Database=RoomReservation;
    Trusted_Connection=true;Integrated Security=True;
    MultipleActiveResultSets=True"/>
</connectionStrings>
```

Functionality that will be used by the service implementation is defined with the RoomReservationData class (code file RoomReservation/RoomReservationData/RoomReservationData.cs). The method ReserveRoom writes a new record to the database, and the method GetReservations returns a collection of RoomReservation for a specified time span.

```
using System;
using System.Linq;
using Wrox.ProCSharp.WCF.Contracts;

namespace Wrox.ProCSharp.WCF.Data
{
  public class RoomReservationData
  {
    public void ReserveRoom(RoomReservation roomReservation)
    {
      using (var data = new RoomReservationContext())
      {
```

```
        data.RoomReservations.Add(roomReservation);
        data.SaveChanges();
      }
    }

    public RoomReservation[] GetReservations(DateTime fromTime, DateTime toTime)
    {
      using (var data = new RoomReservationContext())
      {
        return (from r in data.RoomReservations
                where r.StartTime > fromTime && r.EndTime < toTime
                select r).ToArray();
      }
    }
  }
}
```

> **NOTE** *Chapter 33, "ADO.NET Entity Framework," gives you the details of the ADO .NET Entity Framework.*

Service Implementation

Now you can step into the implementation of the service. Create a WCF service library named RoomReservationService. By default, this library type contains both the service contract and the service implementation. If the client application just uses metadata information to create a proxy accessing the service, this model is okay to work with. However, if the client might use the contract types directly, it is a better idea to put the contracts in a separate assembly as it was done here. With the first client that is done, a proxy is created from metadata. Later you can see how to create a client to share the contract assembly. Splitting the contracts and implementation is a good preparation for this.

The service class RoomReservationService implements the interface IRoomService. The service is implemented just by invoking the appropriate methods of the RoomReservationData class (code file RoomReservation/RoomReservationService/RoomReservationService.cs):

```
using System;
using System.ServiceModel;
using Wrox.ProCSharp.WCF.Contracts;
using Wrox.ProCSharp.WCF.Data;

namespace Wrox.ProCSharp.WCF.Service
{
  [ServiceBehavior(InstanceContextMode = InstanceContextMode.PerCall)]
  public class RoomReservationService : IRoomService
  {
    public bool ReserveRoom(RoomReservation roomReservation)
    {
      var data = new RoomReservationData();
      data.ReserveRoom(roomReservation);
      return true;
    }

    public RoomReservation[] GetRoomReservations(DateTime fromTime,
        DateTime toTime)
    {
      var data = new RoomReservationData();
      return data.GetReservations(fromTime, toTime);
    }
  }
}
```

Figure 43-2 shows the assemblies created so far and their dependencies. The RoomReservationContracts assembly is used by both RoomReservationData and RoomReservationService.

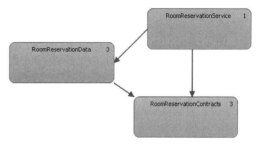

WCF Service Host and WCF Test Client

The WCF Service Library project template creates an application configuration file named App.config that you need to adapt to the new class and interface names. The service element references the service type RoomReservationService, including the namespace; the contract interface needs to be defined with the endpoint element (configuration file RoomReservation/RoomReservationService/app.config):

FIGURE 43-2

```xml
<?xml version="1.0" encoding="utf-8" ?>
<configuration>
  <system.web>
    <compilation debug="true" />
  </system.web>
  <system.serviceModel>
    <services>
      <service name="Wrox.ProCSharp.WCF.Service.RoomService">
        <endpoint address="" binding="basicHttpBinding"
            contract="Wrox.ProCSharp.WCF.Service.IRoomService">
          <identity>
            <dns value="localhost" />
          </identity>
        </endpoint>
        <endpoint address="mex" binding="mexHttpBinding"
            contract="IMetadataExchange" />
        <host>
          <baseAddresses>
          <add baseAddress=
"http://localhost:8733/Design_Time_Addresses/RoomReservationService/Service1/"
            />
          </baseAddresses>
        </host>
      </service>
    </services>
    <behaviors>
      <serviceBehaviors>
        <behavior>
          <serviceMetadata httpGetEnabled="True" httpsGetEnabled="True"/>
          <serviceDebug includeExceptionDetailInFaults="False" />
        </behavior>
      </serviceBehaviors>
    </behaviors>
  </system.serviceModel>
</configuration>
```

> **NOTE** *The service address* http://localhost:8733/Design_Time_Addresses *has an access control list (ACL) associated with it that enables the interactive user to create a listener port. By default, a nonadministrative user is not allowed to open ports in listening mode. You can view the ACLs with the command-line utility* netsh http show urlacl *and add new entries with* netsh http add urlacl url=http://+:8080/MyURI user=someUser.

Starting this library from Visual Studio 2012 starts the WCF Service Host, which appears as an icon in the notification area of the taskbar. Clicking this icon opens the WCF Service Host window (see Figure 43-3), where you can see the status of the service. The project properties of a WCF library application include the tab WCF options, where you can select whether the WCF service host should be started when running a project from the same solution. By default, this option is turned on. Also, with the Debug configuration of the project properties, you can find the command-line argument `/client: "WcfTestClient.exe"` defined. With this option, the WCF Service host starts the WCF Test Client (see Figure 43-4), which you can use to test the application. When you double-click an operation, input fields appear on the right side of the application that

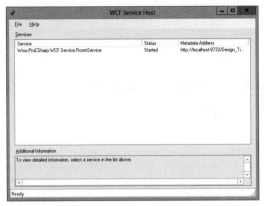

FIGURE 43-3

you can fill to send data to the service. When you click the XML tab, you can see the SOAP messages that have been sent and received.

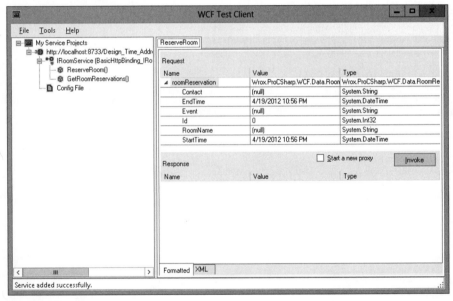

FIGURE 43-4

Custom Service Host

WCF enables services to run in any host. You can create a Windows Forms or Windows Presentation Foundation (WPF) application for peer-to-peer services. Or you can create a Windows service or host the service with Windows Activation Services (WAS) or Internet Information Services (IIS). A console application is also good to demonstrate a simple custom host.

With the service host, you must reference the library RoomReservationService in addition to the assembly System.ServiceModel. The service is started by instantiating and opening an object of type ServiceHost.

This class is defined in the namespace System.ServiceModel. The RoomReservationService class that implements the service is defined in the constructor. Invoking the Open() method starts the listener channel of the service—the service is ready to listen for requests. The Close() method stops the channel. The code snippet also adds a behavior of type ServiceMetadataBehavior. This behavior is added to allow creating a client application by using WSDL (code file RoomReservation/RoomReservationServiceHost/Program.cs).

```csharp
using System;
using System.ServiceModel;
using System.ServiceModel.Description;
using Wrox.ProCSharp.WCF.Service;

namespace Wrox.ProCSharp.WCF.Host
{
  class Program
  {
    internal static ServiceHost myServiceHost = null;

    internal static void StartService()
    {
      try
      {
        myServiceHost = new ServiceHost(typeof(RoomReservationService),
          new Uri("http://localhost:9000/RoomReservation"));
        myServiceHost.Description.Behaviors.Add(new ServiceMetadataBehavior
        { HttpGetEnabled = true });
        myServiceHost.Open();
      }
      catch (AddressAccessDeniedException)
      {
        Console.WriteLine("either start Visual Studio in elevated admin " +
            "mode or register the listener port with netsh.exe");
      }
    }

    internal static void StopService()
    {
      if (myServiceHost != null &&
          myServiceHost.State == CommunicationState.Opened)
      {
        myServiceHost.Close();
      }
    }

    static void Main()
    {
      StartService();

      Console.WriteLine("Server is running. Press return to exit");
      Console.ReadLine();

      StopService();
    }
  }
}
```

For the WCF configuration, you can copy the application configuration file created with the service library to the host application. You can edit this configuration file with the WCF Service Configuration Editor (see Figure 43-5).

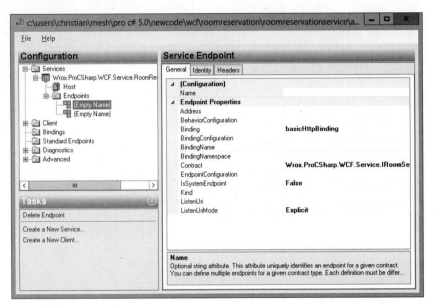

FIGURE 43-5

Instead of using the configuration file, you can configure everything programmatically and also use several defaults. The sample code for the host application doesn't need any configuration file. The second parameter of the `ServiceHost` constructor defines a base address for the service. With the protocol of this base address, a default binding is defined. The default for the HTTP is the `BasicHttpBinding`.

Using the custom service host, you can deselect the WCF option to start the WCF Service Host in the project settings of the WCF library.

WCF Client

For the client, WCF is flexible again in what application type can be used. The client can be a simple console application as well. However, for reserving rooms, create a simple WPF application with controls, as shown in Figure 43-6.

Because the service host is configured with the `ServiceMetadataBehavior`, it offers a MEX endpoint. After the service host is started, you can add a service reference from Visual Studio. Adding the service reference, the dialog shown in Figure 43-7 pops up. Enter the link to the service metadata with the URL `http://localhost:9000/RoomReservation?wsdl`, and set the namespace name to `RoomReservationService`. This defines the namespace of the generated proxy class.

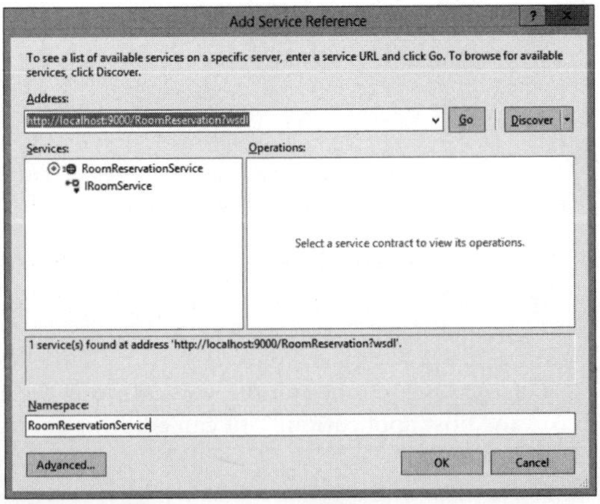

Adding a service reference adds references to the assemblies `System.Runtime.Serialization` and

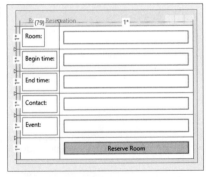

FIGURE 43-6

FIGURE 43-7

`System.ServiceModel` and a configuration file containing the binding information and the endpoint address to the service.

From the data contract the class `RoomReservation` is generated as a partial class. This class contains all `[DataMember]` elements of the contract. The class `RoomServiceClient` is the proxy for the client that contains methods that are defined by the operation contracts. Using this client, you can send a room reservation to the running service.

In the code file `RoomReservation/RoomReservationClient/MainWindow.xaml.cs`, the `OnReserveRoom` method is invoked with the `Click` event of the button. The `ReserveRoomAsync` is invoked with the service proxy. The `reservation` variable receives the data from the UI via data binding.

```
public partial class MainWindow : Window
{
  private RoomReservation reservation;
  public MainWindow()
  {
    InitializeComponent();
    reservation = new RoomReservation
    { StartTime = DateTime.Now, EndTime = DateTime.Now.AddHours(1) };
    this.DataContext = reservation;
  }

  private async void OnReserveRoom(object sender, RoutedEventArgs e)
  {
    var client = new RoomServiceClient();
    bool reserved = await client.ReserveRoomAsync(reservation);
    client.Close();

    if (reserved)
      MessageBox.Show("reservation ok");
  }
}
```

By running both the service and the client, the database is created, and you can add room reservations to the database. With the settings of the `RoomReservation` solution, you can configure multiple startup projects, which should be `RoomReservationClient` and `RoomReservationHost` in this case.

Diagnostics

When running a client and service application, it can be helpful to know what's happening behind the scenes. For this, WCF makes use of a trace source that just needs to be configured. You can configure tracing using the Service Configuration Editor, selecting Diagnostics, and enabling Tracing and Message Logging. Setting the trace level of the trace sources to Verbose produces detailed information. This configuration change adds trace sources and listeners to the application configuration file as shown here:

```
<?xml version="1.0" encoding="utf-8" ?>
<configuration>
  <connectionStrings>
    <add
      name="RoomReservation" providerName="System.Data.SqlClient"
      connectionString="Server=(localdb)\v11.0;Database=RoomReservation;
      Trusted_Connection=true;Integrated Security=True;
      MultipleActiveResultSets=True" />
  </connectionStrings>

  <system.diagnostics>
    <sources>
      <source name="System.ServiceModel.MessageLogging"
        switchValue="Verbose,ActivityTracing">
        <listeners>
```

```xml
              <add type="System.Diagnostics.DefaultTraceListener" name="Default">
                <filter type="" />
              </add>
              <add name="ServiceModelMessageLoggingListener">
                <filter type="" />
              </add>
            </listeners>
          </source>
          <source propagateActivity="true" name="System.ServiceModel"
            switchValue="Warning,ActivityTracing">
            <listeners>
              <add type="System.Diagnostics.DefaultTraceListener" name="Default">
                <filter type="" />
              </add>
              <add name="ServiceModelTraceListener">
                <filter type="" />
              </add>
            </listeners>
          </source>
        </sources>
        <sharedListeners>
          <add initializeData=
            "c:\code\wcf\roomreservation\roomreservationhost\app_messages.svclog"
            type="System.Diagnostics.XmlWriterTraceListener, System, Version=4.0.0.0,
            Culture=neutral, PublicKeyToken=b77a5c561934e089"
            name="ServiceModelMessageLoggingListener"
            traceOutputOptions="DateTime, Timestamp, ProcessId, ThreadId">
            <filter type="" />
          </add>
          <add initializeData=
            "c:\code\wcf\roomreservation\roomreservationhost\app_tracelog.svclog"
            type="System.Diagnostics.XmlWriterTraceListener, System, Version=4.0.0.0,
            Culture=neutral, PublicKeyToken=b77a5c561934e089"
            name="ServiceModelTraceListener"
            traceOutputOptions="DateTime, Timestamp, ProcessId, ThreadId">
            <filter type="" />
          </add>
        </sharedListeners>
      </system.diagnostics>
      <startup>
        <supportedRuntime version="v4.0" sku=".NETFramework,Version=v4.5" />
      </startup>

      <system.serviceModel>
        <diagnostics>
          <messageLogging logEntireMessage="true" logMalformedMessages="true"
            logMessagesAtTransportLevel="true" />
          <endToEndTracing propagateActivity="true" activityTracing="true"
            messageFlowTracing="true" />
        </diagnostics>
      </system.serviceModel>
    </configuration>
```

> **NOTE** *The implementation of the WCF classes uses the trace sources named* System
> .ServiceModel *and* System.ServiceModel.MessageLogging *for writing trace
> messages. You can read more about tracing and configuring trace sources and listeners
> in Chapter 20, "Diagnostics."*

When you start the application, the trace files soon get large with verbose trace settings. To analyze the information from the XML log file, the .NET SDK includes the Service Trace Viewer tool, svctraceviewer.exe. Figure 43-8 shows the client application with some data entered, and Figure 43-9 shows the view from the svctraceviewer.exe after selecting the trace and message log files. The BasicHttpBinding is light with the messages sent across. If you change the configuration to use the WsHttpBinding, you see many messages related to security. Depending on your security needs, you can choose other configuration options.

FIGURE 43-8

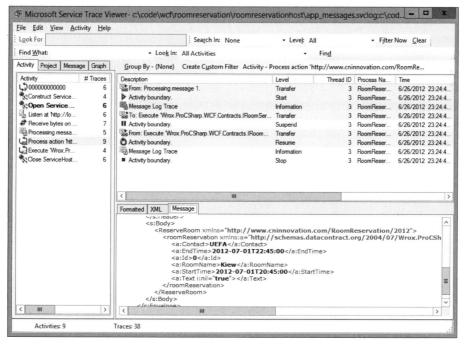

FIGURE 43-9

The following sections discuss the details and different options of WCF.

Sharing Contract Assemblies with the Client

With the previous WPF client application, a proxy class was created using the metadata, adding a service reference with Visual Studio. A client can also be created by using the shared contract assembly as is shown now. Using the contract interface, the ChannelFactory<TChannel> class is used to instantiate the channel to connect to the service.

The constructor of the class ChannelFactory<TChannel> accepts the binding configuration and endpoint address. The binding must be compatible with the binding defined with the service host, and the address defined with the EndpointAddress class references the URI of the running service. The CreateChannel method creates a channel to connect to the service. Then, you can invoke methods of the service.

```
using System;
using System.ServiceModel;
using System.Windows;
using Wrox.ProCSharp.WCF.Contracts;

namespace RoomReservationClientSharedAssembly
{
  /// <summary>
  /// Interaction logic for MainWindow.xaml
  /// </summary>
  public partial class MainWindow : Window
  {
    private RoomReservation roomReservation;
    public MainWindow()
    {
      InitializeComponent();
      roomReservation = new RoomReservation
      {
        StartTime = DateTime.Now,
        EndTime = DateTime.Now.AddHours(1)
      };
      this.DataContext = roomReservation;
    }

    private void OnReserveRoom(object sender, RoutedEventArgs e)
    {
      var binding = new BasicHttpBinding();
      var address = new EndpointAddress("http://localhost:9000/RoomReservation");

      var factory = new ChannelFactory<IRoomService>(binding, address);
      IRoomService channel = factory.CreateChannel();
      if (channel.ReserveRoom(roomReservation))
      {
        MessageBox.Show("success");
      }
    }
  }
}
```

CONTRACTS

A contract defines what functionality a service offers and what functionality can be used by the client. The contract can be completely independent of the implementation of the service.

The contracts defined by WCF can be grouped into four different contract types: Data, Service, Message, and Fault. The contracts can be specified by using .NET attributes:

➤   **Data contract**—The data contract defines the data received by and returned from the service. The classes used for sending and receiving messages have data contract attributes associated with them.

➤   **Service contract**—The service contract is used to define the WSDL that describes the service. This contract is defined with interfaces or classes.

➤   **Operation contract**—The operation contract defines the operation of the service and is defined within the service contract.

➤   **Message contract**—If complete control over the SOAP message is needed, a message contract can specify what data should go into the SOAP header and what belongs in the SOAP body.

➤   **Fault contract**—The fault contract defines the error messages that are sent to the client.

The following sections explore these contract types further and discuss versioning issues that should be thought about when defining the contracts.

Data Contract

With the data contract, CLR types are mapped to XML schemas. The data contract is different from other .NET serialization mechanisms: with runtime serialization, all fields are serialized (including private fields); with XML serialization, only the public fields and properties are serialized. The data contract requires explicit marking of the fields that should be serialized with the `DataMember` attribute. This attribute can be used regardless of whether the field is private or public, or if it is applied to a property.

```
[DataContract(Namespace="http://www.cninnovation.com/Services/20102")]
public class RoomReservation
{
    [DataMember] public string Room { get; set; }
    [DataMember] public DateTime StartTime { get; set; }
    [DataMember] public DateTime EndTime { get; set; }
    [DataMember] public string Contact { get; set; }
    [DataMember] public string Text { get; set; }
}
```

To be platform-independent, and provide the option to change data with new versions without breaking older clients and services, using data contracts is the best way to define which data should be sent. However, you can also use XML serialization and runtime serialization. XML serialization is the mechanism used by ASP.NET Web services; .NET Remoting uses runtime serialization.

With the attribute `DataMember`, you can specify the properties described in the following table.

DATAMEMBER PROPERTY	DESCRIPTION
Name	By default, the serialized element has the same name as the field or property where the `[DataMember]` attribute is applied. You can change the name with the `Name` property.
Order	The `Order` property defines the serialization order of the data members.
IsRequired	With the `IsRequired` property, you can specify that the element must be received with serialization. This property can be used for versioning. If you add members to an existing contract, the contract is not broken because, by default, the fields are optional (`IsRequired=false`). You can break an existing contract by setting `IsRequired` to true.
EmitDefaultValue	The property `EmitDefaultValue` defines whether the member should be serialized if it has the default value. If `EmitDefaultValue` is set to true, the member is not serialized if it has the default value for the type.

Versioning

When you create a new version of a data contract, pay attention to what kind of change it is and act accordingly if old and new clients and old and new services should be supported simultaneously.

When defining a contract, you should add XML namespace information with the `Namespace` property of the `DataContractAttribute`. This namespace should be changed if a new version of the data contract is created that breaks compatibility. If just optional members are added, the contract is not broken—this is a compatible change. Old clients can still send a message to the new service because the additional data is not needed. New clients can send messages to an old service because the old service just ignores the additional data.

Removing fields or adding required fields breaks the contract. Here, you should also change the XML namespace. The name of the namespace can include the year and the month, for example, `http://www .cninnovation.com/Services/2012/08`. Every time a breaking change is done, the namespace is changed; for example, by changing the year and month to the actual value.

Service and Operation Contracts

The service contract defines the operations the service can perform. The attribute `ServiceContract` is used with interfaces or classes to define a service contract. The methods that are offered by the service have the attribute `OperationContract` applied, as you can see with the interface `IRoomService`:

```
[ServiceContract]
public interface IRoomService
{
    [OperationContract]
    bool ReserveRoom(RoomReservation roomReservation);
}
```

The possible properties that you can set with the `ServiceContract` attribute are described in the following table.

SERVICECONTRACT PROPERTY	DESCRIPTION
`ConfigurationName`	This property defines the name of the service configuration in a configuration file.
`CallbackContract`	When the service is used for duplex messaging, the property `CallbackContract` defines the contract that is implemented in the client.
`Name`	The `Name` property defines the name for the `<portType>` element in the WSDL.
`Namespace`	The `Namespace` property defines the XML namespace for the `<portType>` element in the WSDL.
`SessionMode`	With the `SessionMode` property, you can define whether sessions are required for calling operations of this contract. The possible values `Allowed`, `NotAllowed`, and `Required` are defined with the `SessionMode` enumeration.
`ProtectionLevel`	The `ProtectionLevel` property defines whether the binding must support protecting the communication. Possible values defined by the `ProtectionLevel` enumeration are None, Sign, and EncryptAndSign.

With the `OperationContract`, you can specify properties, as shown in the following table.

OPERATIONCONTRACT PROPERTY	DESCRIPTION
`Action`	WCF uses the `Action` of the SOAP request to map it to the appropriate method. The default value for the `Action` is a combination of the contract XML namespace, the name of the contract, and the name of the operation. If the message is a response message, Response is added to the `Action` string. You can override the `Action` value by specifying the `Action` property. If you assign the value "*", the service operation handles all messages.
`ReplyAction`	Whereas `Action` sets the `Action` name of the incoming SOAP request, `ReplyAction` sets the `Action` name of the reply message.
`AsyncPattern`	If the operation is implemented by using an asynchronous pattern, set the `AsyncPattern` property to `true`. The async pattern is discussed in Chapter 21, "Threads, Tasks, and Synchronization."
`IsInitiating` `IsTerminating`	If the contract consists of a sequence of operations, the initiating operation should have the `IsInitiating` property assigned to it; the last operation of the sequence needs the `IsTerminating` property assigned. The initiating operation starts a new session; the server closes the session with the terminating operation.

OPERATIONCONTRACT PROPERTY	DESCRIPTION
IsOneWay	With the IsOneWay property set, the client does not wait for a reply message. Callers of a one-way operation have no direct way to detect a failure after sending the request message.
Name	The default name of the operation is the name of the method the operation contract is assigned to. You can change the name of the operation by applying the Name property.
ProtectionLevel	With the ProtectionLevel property, you define whether the message should be signed or encrypted and signed.

With the service contract, you can also define the requirements that the service has from the transport with the attribute [DeliveryRequirements]. The property RequireOrderedDelivery defines that the messages sent must arrive in the same order. With the property QueuedDeliveryRequirements, you can define that the message should be sent in a disconnected mode, for example, by using Message Queuing (covered in Chapter 47, "Message Queuing").

Message Contract

A message contract is used if complete control over the SOAP message is needed. With the message contract, you can specify what part of the message should go into the SOAP header and what belongs in the SOAP body. The following example shows a message contract for the class ProcessPersonRequestMessage. The message contract is specified with the attribute MessageContract. The header and body of the SOAP message are specified with the attributes MessageHeader and MessageBodyMember. By specifying the Position property, you can define the element order within the body. You can also specify the protection level for header and body fields.

```
[MessageContract]
public class ProcessPersonRequestMessage
{
  [MessageHeader]
  public int employeeId;

  [MessageBodyMember(Position=0)]
  public Person person;
}
```

The class ProcessPersonRequestMessage is used with the service contract defined with the interface IProcessPerson:

```
[ServiceContract]
public interface IProcessPerson
{
  [OperationContract]
  public PersonResponseMessage ProcessPerson(ProcessPersonRequestMessage message);
}
```

Another contract that is important for WCF services is the fault contract. This contract is discussed in the next section with Error Handling.

Fault Contract

By default, the detailed exception information that occurs in the service is not returned to the client application. The reason for this behavior is security. You wouldn't want to give detailed exception information to a third party by using your service. Instead, the exception should be logged on the service (which you can do with tracing and event logging), and an error with useful information should be returned to the caller.

You can return SOAP faults by throwing a `FaultException`. Throwing a `FaultException` creates an untyped SOAP fault. The preferred way to return errors is to generate a strongly typed SOAP fault.

The information that should be passed with a strongly typed SOAP fault is defined with a data contract, as shown with the `RoomReservationFault` class (code file `RoomReservation/RoomReservationContracts/RoomReservationFault.cs`):

```
[DataContract]
public class RoomReservationFault
{
  [DataMember]
  public string Message { get; set; }
}
```

The type of the SOAP fault must be defined by using the `FaultContractAttribute` with the operation contract:

```
[FaultContract(typeof(RoomReservationFault))]
[OperationContract]
bool ReserveRoom(RoomReservation roomReservation);
```

With the implementation, a `FaultException<TDetail>` is thrown. With the constructor, you can assign a new `TDetail` object, which is a `StateFault` in the example. In addition, error information within a `FaultReason` can be assigned to the constructor. `FaultReason` supports error information in multiple languages.

```
FaultReasonText[] text = new FaultReasonText[2];
text[0] = new FaultReasonText("Sample Error", new CultureInfo("en"));
text[1] = new FaultReasonText("Beispiel Fehler", new CultureInfo("de"));
FaultReason reason = new FaultReason(text);

throw new FaultException<RoomReservationFault>(
  new RoomReservationFault() { Message = m }, reason);
```

With the client application, exceptions of type `FaultException<RoomReservationFault>` can be caught. The reason for the exception is defined by the `Message` property; the `RoomReservationFault` is accessed with the `Detail` property:

```
try
{
  //...
}
catch (FaultException<RoomReservationFault> ex)
{
  Console.WriteLine(ex.Message);
  StateFault detail = ex.Detail;
  Console.WriteLine(detail.Message);
}
```

In addition to catching the strongly typed SOAP faults, the client application can also catch exceptions of the base class of `FaultException<Detail>`: `FaultException` and `CommunicationException`. By catching `CommunicationException`, you can also catch other exceptions related to the WCF communication.

> **NOTE** *During development you can return exceptions to the client. To enable exceptions propagated, you need to configure a service behavior configuration with the* serviceDebug *element. The* serviceDebug *element has the attribute* IncludeExceptionDetailInFaults *that can be set to true to return exception information.*

SERVICE BEHAVIORS

The implementation of the service can be marked with the attribute `ServiceBehavior`, as shown with the class `RoomReservationService`:

```
[ServiceBehavior]
public class RoomReservationService: IRoomService
{
  public bool ReserveRoom(RoomReservation roomReservation)
  {
    // implementation
  }
}
```

The attribute ServiceBehavior is used to describe behavior as is offered by WCF services to intercept the code for required functionality, as shown in the following table.

SERVICEBEHAVIOR PROPERTY	DESCRIPTION
TransactionAutoComplete OnSessionClose	When the current session is finished without error, the transaction is automatically committed. This is similar to the AutoComplete attribute used with Enterprise Services.
TransactionIsolationLevel	To define the isolation level of the transaction within the service, the property TransactionIsolationLevel can be set to one value of the IsolationLevel enumeration. You can read information about transaction information levels in Chapter 25, "Transactions."
ReleaseServiceInstanceOn TransactionComplete	When the transaction finishes, the instance of the service recycles.
AutomaticSessionShutdown	If the session should not be closed when the client closes the connection, you can set the property AutomaticSessionShutdown to false. By default, the session is closed.
InstanceContextMode	With the property InstanceContextMode, you can define whether stateful or stateless objects should be used. The default setting is InstanceContextMode.PerCall to create a new object with every method call. Other possible settings are PerSession and Single. With both of these settings, stateful objects are used. However, with PerSession a new object is created for every client. Single enables the same object to be shared with multiple clients.
ConcurrencyMode	Because stateful objects can be used by multiple clients (or multiple threads of a single client), you must pay attention to concurrency issues with such object types. If the property ConcurrencyMode is set to Multiple, multiple threads can access the object, and you must deal with synchronization. If you set the option to Single, only one thread accesses the object at a time. Here, you don't have to do synchronization; however, scalability problems can occur with a higher number of clients. The value Reentrant means that only a thread coming back from a callout might access the object. For stateless objects, this setting has no meaning because new objects are instantiated with every method call and thus no state is shared.
UseSynchronizationContext	With Windows Forms and WPF, members of controls can be invoked only from the creator thread. If the service is hosted in a Windows application, and the service methods invoke control members, set the UseSynchronizationContext to true. This way, the service runs in a thread defined by the SynchronizationContext.

continues

(continued)

SERVICEBEHAVIOR PROPERTY	DESCRIPTION
IncludeExceptionDetailInFaults	With .NET, errors show up as exceptions. SOAP defines that a SOAP fault is returned to the client in case the server has a problem. For security reasons, it's not a good idea to return details of server-side exceptions to the client. Thus, by default, exceptions are converted to unknown faults. To return specific faults, throw an exception of type FaultException. For debugging purposes, it can be helpful to return the real exception information. This is the case when changing the setting of IncludeExceptionDetailIn Faults to true. Here a FaultException<TDetail> is thrown where the original exception contains the detail information.
MaxItemsInObjectGraph	With the property MaxItemsInObjectGraph, you can limit the number of objects that are serialized. The default limitation might be too low if you serialize a tree of objects.
ValidateMustUnderstand	The property ValidateMustUnderstand set to true means that the SOAP headers must be understood (which is the default).

To demonstrate a service behavior, the interface IStateService defines a service contract with two operations to set and get state. With a stateful service contract, a session is needed. That's why the SessionMode property of the service contract is set to SessionMode.Required. The service contract also defines methods to initiate and close the session by applying the IsInitiating and IsTerminating properties to the operation contract:

```
[ServiceContract(SessionMode=SessionMode.Required)]
public interface IStateService
{
    [OperationContract(IsInitiating=true)]
    void Init(int i);

    [OperationContract]
    void SetState(int i);

    [OperationContract]
    int GetState();


    [OperationContract(IsTerminating=true)]
    void Close();
}
```

The service contract is implemented by the class StateService. The service implementation defines the InstanceContextMode.PerSession to keep state with the instance:

```
[ServiceBehavior(InstanceContextMode=InstanceContextMode.PerSession)]
public class StateService: IStateService
{
    int i = 0;

    public void Init(int i)
    {
        this.i = i;
    }

    public void SetState(int i)
    {
        this.i = i;
```

```
    }

    public int GetState()
    {
      return i;
    }

    public void Close()
    {
    }
  }
```

Now the binding to the address and protocol must be defined. Here, the `basicHttpBinding` is assigned to the endpoint of the service:

```xml
<?xml version="1.0" encoding="utf-8" ?>
<configuration>
  <system.serviceModel>
    <services>
      <service behaviorConfiguration="StateServiceSample.Service1Behavior"
        name="Wrox.ProCSharp.WCF.StateService">
        <endpoint address="" binding="basicHttpBinding"
            bindingConfiguration=""
            contract="Wrox.ProCSharp.WCF.IStateService">
        </endpoint>
        <endpoint address="mex" binding="mexHttpBinding"
            contract="IMetadataExchange" />
        <host>
          <baseAddresses>
            <add baseAddress="http://localhost:8731/Design_Time_Addresses/
                              StateServiceSample/Service1/" />
          </baseAddresses>
        </host>
      </service>
    </services>
    <behaviors>
      <serviceBehaviors>
        <behavior name="StateServiceSample.Service1Behavior">
          <serviceMetadata httpGetEnabled="True"/>
          <serviceDebug includeExceptionDetailInFaults="False" />
        </behavior>
      </serviceBehaviors>
    </behaviors>
  </system.serviceModel>
</configuration>
```

If you start the service host with the defined configuration, an exception of type `InvalidOperationException` is thrown. The error message with the exception gives this error message: Contract Requires Session, but Binding 'BasicHttpBinding' Doesn't Support It or Isn't Configured Properly to Support It.

Not all bindings support all services. Because the service contract requires a session with the attribute `[ServiceContract(SessionMode=SessionMode.Required)]`, the host fails because the configured binding does not support sessions.

As soon as you change the configuration to a binding that supports sessions (for example, the `wsHttpBinding`), the server starts successfully:

```xml
<endpoint address="" binding="wsHttpBinding"
    bindingConfiguration=""
    contract="Wrox.ProCSharp.WCF.IStateService">
</endpoint>
```

With the implementation of the service, you can apply the properties in the following table to the service methods, with the attribute `OperationBehavior`.

OPERATIONBEHAVIOR PROPERTY	DESCRIPTION
AutoDisposeParameters	By default, all disposable parameters are automatically disposed. If the parameters should not be disposed, you can set the property `AutoDisposeParameters` to false. Then the sender is responsible for disposing the parameters.
Impersonation	With the `Impersonation` property, the caller can be impersonated, and the method runs with the identity of the caller.
ReleaseInstanceMode	The `InstanceContextMode` defines the lifetime of the object instance with the service behavior setting. With the operation behavior setting, you can override the setting based on the operation. The `ReleaseInstanceMode` defines an instance release mode with the enumeration `ReleaseInstanceMode`. The value `None` uses the instance context mode setting. With the values `BeforeCall`, `AfterCall`, and `BeforeAndAfterCall`, you can define recycle times with the operation.
TransactionScopeRequired	With the property `TransactionScopeRequired`, you can specify if a transaction is required with the operation. If a transaction is required, and the caller already flows a transaction, the same transaction is used. If the caller doesn't flow a transaction, a new transaction is created.
TransactionAutoComplete	The `TransactionAutoComplete` property specifies whether the transaction should complete automatically. If the `TransactionAutoComplete` property is set to true, the transaction is aborted if an exception is thrown. The transaction is committed if it is the root transaction and no exception is thrown.

BINDING

A binding describes how a service wants to communicate. With binding, you can specify the following features:

- ➤ Transport protocol
- ➤ Security
- ➤ Encoding format
- ➤ Transaction flow
- ➤ Reliability
- ➤ Shape change
- ➤ Transport upgrade

Standard Bindings

A binding is composed of multiple binding elements that describe all binding requirements. You can create a custom binding or use one of the predefined bindings that are shown in the following table.

STANDARD BINDING	DESCRIPTION
`BasicHttpBinding`	`BasicHttpBinding` is the binding for the broadest interoperability, the first-generation web services. Transport protocols used are HTTP or HTTPS; security is available only from the transport protocol.
`WSHttpBinding`	`WSHttpBinding` is the binding for the next-generation web services, platforms that implement SOAP extensions for security, reliability, and transactions. The transports used are HTTP or HTTPS; for security the WS-Security specification is implemented; transactions are supported, as has been described, with the WS-Coordination, WS-AtomicTransaction, and WS-BusinessActivity specifications; reliable messaging is supported with an implementation of WS-ReliableMessaging. WS-Profile also supports Message Transmission Optimization Protocol (MTOM) encoding for sending attachments. You can find specifications for the WS-* standards at `http://www.oasis-open.org`.
`WS2007HttpBinding`	`WS2007HttpBinding` derives from the base class `WSHttpBinding` and supports security, reliability, and transaction specifications defined by Organization for the Advancement of Structured Information Standards (OASIS). This class offers newer SOAP standards.
`WSHttpContextBinding`	`WSHttpContextBinding` derives from the base class `WSHttpBinding` and adds support for a context without using cookies. This binding adds a `ContextBindingElement` to exchange context information. The context binding element was needed with Workflow Foundation 3.0.
`WebHttpBinding`	This binding is used for services that are exposed through HTTP requests instead of SOAP requests. This is useful for scripting clients—for example, ASP.NET AJAX.
`WSFederationHttpBinding`	`WSFederationHttpBinding` is a secure and interoperable binding that supports sharing identities across multiple systems for authentication and authorization.
`WSDualHttpBinding`	The binding `WSDualHttpBinding`, in contrast to `WSHttpBinding`, supports duplex messaging.
`NetTcpBinding`	All standard bindings prefixed with the name `Net` use a binary encoding used for communication between .NET applications. This encoding is faster than the text encoding with WSxxx bindings. The binding `NetTcpBinding` uses the TCP/IP protocol.
`NetTcpContextBinding`	Similar to `WSHttpContextBinding`, `NetTcpContextBinding` adds a `ContextBindingElement` to exchange context with the SOAP header.
`NetHttpBinding`	This is a new binding with .NET 4.5 to support the Web Socket transport protocol.
`NetPeerTcpBinding`	`NetPeerTcpBinding` provides a binding for peer-to-peer communication.
`NetNamedPipeBinding`	`NetNamedPipeBinding` is optimized for communication between different processes on the same system.
`NetMsmqBinding`	The binding `NetMsmqBinding` brings queued communication to WCF. Here, the messages are sent to the message queue.
`MsmqIntegrationBinding`	`MsmqIntegrationBinding` is the binding for existing applications that uses message queuing. In contrast, the binding `NetMsmqBinding` requires WCF applications both on the client and server.
`CustomBinding`	With a `CustomBinding` the transport protocol and security requirements can be completely customized.

Features of Standard Bindings

Depending on the binding, different features are supported. The bindings starting with WS are platform-independent, supporting web services specifications. Bindings that start with the name Net use binary formatting for high-performance communication between .NET applications. The new NetHttpBinding changes the naming conventions because it does not require .NET applications on both sides of the wire it's based on the Web Socket standard.

Other features are support of sessions, reliable sessions, transactions, and duplex communication; the following table lists the bindings supporting these features.

FEATURE	BINDING
Sessions	WSHttpBinding, WSDualHttpBinding, WsFederationHttpBinding, NetTcpBinding, NetNamedPipeBinding
Reliable Sessions	WSHttpBinding, WSDualHttpBinding, WsFederationHttpBinding, NetTcpBinding
Transactions	WSHttpBinding, WSDualHttpBinding, WSFederationHttpBinding, NetTcpBinding, NetNamedPipeBinding, NetMsmqBinding, MsmqIntegrationBinding
Duplex Communication	WsDualHttpBinding, NetTcpBinding, NetNamedPipeBinding, NetPeerTcpBinding

Along with defining the binding, the service must define an endpoint. The endpoint is dependent on the contract, the address of the service, and the binding. In the following code sample, a ServiceHost object is instantiated, and the address http://localhost:8080/RoomReservation, a WsHttpBinding instance, and the contract are added to an endpoint of the service:

```
static ServiceHost host;

static void StartService()
{
  var baseAddress = new Uri("http://localhost:8080/RoomReservation");
  host = new ServiceHost(typeof(RoomReservationService));

  var binding1 = new WSHttpBinding();
  host.AddServiceEndpoint(typeof(IRoomService), binding1, baseAddress);
  host.Open();
}
```

In addition to defining the binding programmatically, you can define it with the application configuration file. The configuration for WCF is placed inside the element <system.serviceModel>. The <service> element defines the services offered. Similarly, as you've seen in the code, the service needs an endpoint, and the endpoint contains address, binding, and contract information. The default binding configuration of wsHttpBinding is modified with the bindingConfiguration XML attribute that references the binding configuration wsHttpConfig1. This is the binding configuration you can find inside the <bindings> section, which is used to change the wsHttpBinding configuration to enable reliableSession.

```
<?xml version="1.0" encoding="utf-8" ?>
<configuration>
  <system.serviceModel>
    <services>
      <service name="Wrox.ProCSharp.WCF.RoomReservationService">
        <endpoint address=" http://localhost:8080/RoomReservation"
            contract="Wrox.ProCSharp.WCF.IRoomService"
            binding="wsHttpBinding" bindingConfiguration="wsHttpBinding" />
```

```
          </service>
        </services>
        <bindings>
          <wsHttpBinding>
            <binding name="wsHttpBinding">
              <reliableSession enabled="true" />
            </binding>
          </wsHttpBinding>
        </bindings>
      </system.serviceModel>
    </configuration>
```

Web Socket

WebSocket is a new communication protocol based on TCP. The HTTP protocol is stateless. With HTTP the server can close the connection every time it answers the request. If a client wants to receive ongoing information from the server, this always had some issues with the HTTP protocol.

Because the HTTP connection is kept, one way to deal with this would be to have a service running on the client, and the server connects to the client and sends responses. If a firewall is between the client and the server, this usually doesn't work because the firewall blocks incoming requests.

Another way to deal with this is to use another protocol than the HTTP protocol. The connection can stay alive. The issue with other protocols is that the port needs to be opened with the firewall. Firewalls are always an issue, but they are needed to keep the bad folks out.

The way such a scenario was usually done is by instantiating the request every time from the client. The client polls the server to ask if there's something new. This works but has the disadvantage that either the client asks too many times for news when there is none and thus increases the network traffic, or the client does get old information.

A new solution for this scenario is the WebSocket protocol. This protocol is defined by the W3C (`http://www.w3.org/TR/websockets`) and starts with an HTTP request. Starting with an HTTP request from the client, the firewall usually allows the request. The client starts with a GET request with `Upgrade: websocket Connection: Upgrade` in the HTTP header, along with the WebSocket version and security information. If the server supports the WebSocket protocol, the server answers with an upgrade and switches from HTTP to the WebSocket protocol.

With WCF the two bindings new with .NET 4.5 support the WebSocket protocol: `netHttpBinding`, and `netHttpsBinding`.

Now get into a sample to make use of the WebSocket protocol. Start with an empty web application used to host the service.

The default binding for the HTTP protocol is the `basicHttpBinding` as you've seen earlier. This can be changed defining the `protocolMapping` to specify the `netHttpBinding` as shown. This way it's not necessary to configure the service element to match the contract, binding, and address to an endpoint. With the configuration, `serviceMetadata` is enabled to allow the client referencing the service with the Add Service Reference dialog (configuration file `WebSocketsSample/web.config`).

```
<system.serviceModel>
  <protocolMapping>
    <remove scheme="http" />
    <add scheme="http" binding="netHttpBinding" />
    <remove scheme="https" />
    <add scheme="https" binding="netHttpsBinding" />
  </protocolMapping>
  <behaviors>
    <serviceBehaviors>
      <behavior name="">
```

```
          <serviceMetadata httpGetEnabled="true" httpsGetEnabled="true" />
          <serviceDebug includeExceptionDetailInFaults="false" />
        </behavior>
      </serviceBehaviors>
    </behaviors>
    <serviceHostingEnvironment aspNetCompatibilityEnabled="true"
        multipleSiteBindingsEnabled="true" />
  </system.serviceModel>
```

The service contract is defined by the interfaces IDemoServices and IDemoCallback (code file WebSocketsSample/IDemoService.cs). IDemoService is the service interface that defines the method StartSendingMessages. The client invokes the method StartSendingMessages to start the process that the service can return messages to the client. The client therefore needs to implement the interface IDemoCallback. This interface is invoked by the server and implemented by the client.

The methods of the interfaces are defined to return Task. With this the service can easily make use of asynchronous features, but this doesn't go through to the contract. Defining the methods asynchronously is independent of the WSDL generated.

```
using System.ServiceModel;
using System.Threading.Tasks;

namespace WebSocketsSample
{
  [ServiceContract]
  public interface IDemoCallback
  {
    [OperationContract(IsOneWay = true)]
    Task SendMessage(string message);
  }

  [ServiceContract(CallbackContract = typeof(IDemoCallback))]
  public interface IDemoService
  {
    [OperationContract]
    Task StartSendingMessages();
  }
}
```

The implementation of the service is done in the DemoService class (code file WebSocketsSample/DemoService.cs). Within StartSendindingMessages, the callback interface to go back to the client is retrieved with OperationContext.Current.GetCallbackChannel. When the client invokes the method, it returns immediately as soon as the first time the SendMessage method is invoked. The thread is not blocked until the SendMessage method completes. With await a thread just comes back to the StartSendingMessages when the SendMessage is completed. Then a delay of 1 second is done before the client receives another message. In case the communication channel is closed the while loop exits.

```
using System.ServiceModel;
using System.ServiceModel.Channels;
using System.Threading.Tasks;

namespace WebSocketsSample
{
  public class DemoService : IDemoService
  {
    public async Task StartSendingMessages()
    {
      IDemoCallback callback =
        OperationContext.Current.GetCallbackChannel<IDemoCallback>();
      int loop = 0;
      while ((callback as IChannel).State == CommunicationState.Opened)
```

```
        {
          await callback.SendMessage(string.Format(
            "Hello from the server {0}", loop++));
          await Task.Delay(1000);
        }
      }
    }
  }
```

The client application is created as a console application. Because metadata is available with the service, adding a service reference creates a proxy class that can be used to call the service and also to implement the callback interface. Adding the service reference not only creates the proxy class, but also adds the netHttpBinding to the configuration file:

```xml
<?xml version="1.0" encoding="utf-8" ?>
<configuration>
  <startup>
    <supportedRuntime version="v4.0" sku=".NETFramework,Version=v4.5" />
  </startup>
  <system.serviceModel>
    <bindings>
      <netHttpBinding>
        <binding name="NetHttpBinding_IDemoService">
          <webSocketSettings transportUsage="Always" />
        </binding>
      </netHttpBinding>
    </bindings>
    <client>
      <endpoint address="ws://localhost:20839/DemoService.svc"
        binding="netHttpBinding"
        bindingConfiguration="NetHttpBinding_IDemoService"
        contract="DemoService.IDemoService"
        name="NetHttpBinding_IDemoService" />
    </client>
  </system.serviceModel>
</configuration>
```

The implementation of the callback interface just writes a message to the console with the information received from the service. To start all the processing, a DemoServiceClient instance is created that receives an InstanceContext object. The InstanceContext object contains an instance to the CallbackHandler, a reference retrieved by the service to go back to the client.

```csharp
using System;
using System.ServiceModel;
using ClientApp.DemoService;

namespace ClientApp
{
  class Program
  {
    private class CallbackHandler : IDemoServiceCallback
    {
      public void SendMessage(string message)
      {
        Console.WriteLine("message from the server {0}", message);
      }
    }

    static void Main(string[] args)
    {
      Console.WriteLine("client... wait for the server");
      Console.ReadLine();
```

```
        StartSendRequest();
        Console.WriteLine("next return to exit");
        Console.ReadLine();
    }

    static async void StartSendRequest()
    {
      var callbackInstance = new InstanceContext(new CallbackHandler());
      var client = new DemoServiceClient(callbackInstance);
      await client.StartSendingMessagesAsync();
    }
  }
}
```

Running the application, the client requests the messages from the service, and the service responds independent of the client:

```
client... wait for the server

next return to exit
message from the server Hello from the server 0
message from the server Hello from the server 1
message from the server Hello from the server 2
message from the server Hello from the server 3
message from the server Hello from the server 4

Press any key to continue . . .
```

HOSTING

WCF is flexible when you are choosing a host to run the service. The host can be a Windows service, a COM+ application, WAS (Windows Activation Services) or IIS, a Windows application, or just a simple console application. When creating a custom host with Windows Forms or WPF, you can easily create a peer-to-peer solution.

Custom Hosting

Start with a custom host. The sample code shows hosting of a service within a console application; however, in other custom host types, such as Windows services or Windows applications, you can program the service in the same way.

In the Main method, a ServiceHost instance is created. After the ServiceHost instance is created, the application configuration file is read to define the bindings. You can also define the bindings programmatically, as shown earlier. Next, the Open method of the ServiceHost class is invoked, so the service accepts client calls. With a console application, you need to be careful not to close the main thread until the service should be closed. Here, the user is asked to press Return to exit the service. When the user does this, the Close method is called to actually end the service:

```
using System;
using System.ServiceModel;

public class Program
{
  public static void Main()
  {
    using (var serviceHost = new ServiceHost())
    {
      serviceHost.Open();

      Console.WriteLine("The service started. Press return to exit");
```

```
        Console.ReadLine();

        serviceHost.Close();
    }
  }
}
```

To abort the service host, you can invoke the `Abort` method of the `ServiceHost` class. To get the current state of the service, the `State` property returns a value defined by the `CommunicationState` enumeration. Possible values are `Created`, `Opening`, `Opened`, `Closing`, `Closed`, and `Faulted`.

> **NOTE** *If you start the service from within a Windows Forms or WPF application and the service code invokes methods of Windows controls, you must be sure that only the control's creator thread is allowed to access the methods and properties of the control. With WCF, this behavior can be achieved easily by setting the `UseSynchronizatonContext` property of the attribute* `[ServiceBehavior]`.

WAS Hosting

With Windows Activation Services (WAS) hosting, you get the features from the WAS worker process such as automatic activation of the service, health monitoring, and process recycling.

To use WAS hosting, you just need to create a website and a `.svc` file with the `ServiceHost` declaration that includes the language and the name of the service class. The code shown here is using the class `Service1`. In addition, you must specify the file that contains the service class. This class is implemented in the same way that you saw earlier when defining a WCF service library.

```
<%@ServiceHost language="C#" Service="Service1" CodeBehind="Service1.svc.cs" %>
```

If you use a WCF service library that should be available from WAS hosting, you can create a `.svc` file that just contains a reference to the class:

```
<%@ ServiceHost Service="Wrox.ProCSharp.WCF.Services.RoomReservationService" %>
```

Since the introduction of Windows Vista and Windows Server 2008, WAS enables defining .NET TCP and Message Queue bindings. If you use the previous edition, IIS 6 or IIS 5.1, which is available with Windows Server 2003 and Windows XP, activation from a `.svc` file can be done only with an HTTP binding.

Preconfigured Host Classes

To reduce the configuration necessities, WCF also offers some hosting classes with preconfigured bindings. One example is located in the assembly `System.ServiceModel.Web` in the namespace `System.ServiceModel.Web` with the class `WebServiceHost`. This class creates a default endpoint for HTTP and HTTPS base addresses if a default endpoint is not configured with the `WebHttpBinding`. Also, this class adds the `WebHttpBehavior` if another behavior is not defined. With this behavior, simple HTTP `GET` and `POST`, `PUT`, `DELETE` (with the `WebInvoke` attribute) operations can be done without additional setup (code file `RoomReservation/RoomReservationWebHost/Program.cs`).

```
using System;
using System.ServiceModel;
using System.ServiceModel.Web;
using Wrox.ProCSharp.WCF.Service;

namespace RoomReservationWebHost
{
  class Program
  {
```

```
static void Main()
{
  var baseAddress = new Uri("http://localhost:8000/RoomReservation");
  var host = new WebServiceHost(typeof(RoomReservationService), baseAddress);
  host.Open();

  Console.WriteLine("service running");
  Console.WriteLine("Press return to exit...");
  Console.ReadLine();

  if (host.State == CommunicationState.Opened)
    host.Close();

  }
 }
}
```

To use a simple HTTP GET request to receive the reservations, the method GetRoomReservation needs a WebGet attribute to map the method parameters to the input from the GET request. In the following code, a UriTemplate is defined that requires Reservations to be added to the base address followed by From and To parameters. The From and To parameters in turn are mapped to the fromTime and toTime variables (code file RoomReservationService/RoomReservationService.cs).

```
[WebGet(UriTemplate="Reservations?From={fromTime}&To={toTime}")]
public RoomReservation[] GetRoomReservations(DateTime fromTime,
  DateTime toTime)
{
  var data = new RoomReservationData();
  return data.GetReservations(fromTime, toTime);
}
```

Now the service can be invoked with a simple request as shown. All the reservations for the specified time frame are returned.

```
http://localhost:8000/RoomReservation/Reservations?From=2012/1/1&To=2012/8/1
```

> **NOTE** System.Data.Services.DataServiceHost *is another class with preconfigured features. This class derives itself from* WebServiceHost *and offers data services discussed in Chapter 44, "WCF Data Services."*

CLIENTS

A client application needs a proxy to access a service. There are three ways to create a proxy for the client:

➤ **Visual Studio Add Service Reference**—This utility creates a proxy class from the metadata of the service.

➤ **ServiceModel Metadata Utility tool (Svcutil.exe)**—You can create a proxy class with the Svcutil utility. This utility reads metadata from the service to create the proxy class.

➤ **ChannelFactory class**—This class is used by the proxy generated from Svcutil; however, it can also be used to create a proxy programmatically.

Using Metadata

Adding a service reference from Visual Studio requires accessing a WSDL document. The WSDL document is created by a MEX endpoint that needs to be configured with the service. With the following configuration, the endpoint with the relative address mex uses the mexHttpBinding and

implements the contract `IMetadataExchange`. To access the metadata with an HTTP GET request, the
`behaviorConfiguration MexServiceBehavior` is configured.

```xml
<?xml version="1.0" encoding="utf-8" ?>
<configuration>
  <system.serviceModel>
    <services>
      <service behaviorConfiguration=" MexServiceBehavior "
        name="Wrox.ProCSharp.WCF.RoomReservationService">
        <endpoint address="Test" binding="wsHttpBinding"
          contract="Wrox.ProCSharp.WCF.IRoomService" />
        <endpoint address="mex" binding="mexHttpBinding"
          contract="IMetadataExchange" />
        <host>
          <baseAddresses>
            <add baseAddress=
        "http://localhost:8733/Design_Time_Addresses/RoomReservationService/" />
          <baseAddresses>
        </host>
      </service>
    </services>
    <behaviors>
      <serviceBehaviors>
        <behavior name="MexServiceBehavior">
          <! - To avoid disclosing metadata information,
          set the value below to false and remove the metadata endpoint above
          before deployment - >
          <serviceMetadata httpGetEnabled="True"/>
        </behavior>
      </serviceBehaviors>
    </behaviors>
  </system.serviceModel>
</configuration>
```

Similar to the Add service reference from Visual Studio, the `Svcutil` utility needs metadata to create the
proxy class. The `Svcutil` utility can create a proxy from the MEX metadata endpoint, the metadata of the
assembly, or WSDL and XSD documentation:

```
svcutil http://localhost:8080/RoomReservation?wsdl /language:C# /out:proxy.cs
svcutil CourseRegistration.dll
svcutil CourseRegistration.wsdl CourseRegistration.xsd
```

After the proxy class is generated, it just needs to be instantiated from the client code, the methods need to
be called, and finally the `Close()` method must be invoked:

```
var client = new RoomServiceClient();
client.RegisterForCourse(roomReservation);
client.Close();
```

Sharing Types

The generated proxy class derives from the base class `ClientBase<TChannel>` that wraps the
`ChannelFactory<TChannel>` class. Instead of using a generated proxy class, you can use
the `ChannelFactory<TChannel>` class directly. The constructor requires the binding and endpoint address;
next, you can create the channel and invoke methods as defined by the service contract. Finally, the factory
must be closed:

```
var binding = new WsHttpBinding();
var address = new EndpointAddress("http://localhost:8080/RoomService");

var factory = new ChannelFactory<IStateService>(binding, address);

IRoomService channel = factory.CreateChannel();
```

```
channel.ReserveRoom(roomReservation);

//.
factory.Close();
```

The `ChannelFactory<TChannel>` class has several properties and methods, as shown in the following table.

CHANNELFACTORY MEMBERS	DESCRIPTION
Credentials	Credentials is a read-only property to access the ClientCredentials object assigned to the channel for authentication with the service. The credentials can be set with the endpoint.
Endpoint	Endpoint is a read-only property to access the ServiceEndpoint associated with the channel. The endpoint can be assigned in the constructor.
State	The State property is of type CommunicationState to return the current state of the channel. CommunicationState is an enumeration with the values Created, Opening, Opened, Closing, Closed, and Faulted.
Open()	The Open method is used to open the channel.
Close()	The Close method closes the channel.
Opening Opened Closing Closed Faulted	You can assign event handlers to get informed about state changes of the channel. Events are fired before and after the channel is opened, before and after the channel is closed, and in case of a fault.

DUPLEX COMMUNICATION

The next sample application shows how a duplex communication can be done between the client and the service. The client starts the connection to the service. After the client connects to the service, the service can call back into the client. Duplex communication was shown earlier with WebSocket protocol as well. Instead of using the WebSocket protocol (which are just supported with Windows 8 and Windows Server 2012), duplex communication can also be done with the `WsHttpBinding` and the `NetTcpBinding` as shown here.

Contract for Duplex Communication

For duplex communication, a contract must be specified that is implemented in the client. Here the contract for the client is defined by the interface `IMyMessageCallback`. The method implemented by the client is `OnCallback`. The operation has the operation contract setting `IsOneWay=true` applied. This way, the service doesn't wait until the method is successfully invoked on the client. By default, the service instance can be invoked from only one thread. (See the `ConcurrencyMode` property of the service behavior, which is, by default, set to `ConcurrencyMode.Single`.)

If the service implementation now does a callback to the client and waits to get an answer from the client, the thread getting the reply from the client must wait until it gets a lock to the service object. Because the service object is already locked by the request to the client, a deadlock occurs. WCF detects the deadlock and throws an exception. To avoid this situation, you can change the `ConcurrencyMode` property to the value `Multiple` or `Reentrant`. With the setting `Multiple`, multiple threads can access the instance concurrently. Here, you must implement locking on your own. With the setting `Reentrant`, the service instance stays single-threaded but enables answers from callback requests to reenter the context. Instead of changing the concurrency mode, you can specify the `IsOneWay` property with the operation contract. This way, the caller does not wait for a reply. Of course, this setting is possible only if return values are not expected.

The contract of the service is defined by the interface `IMyMessage`. The callback contract is mapped to the service contract with the `CallbackContract` property of the service contract definition (code file `DuplexCommunication/MessageService/IMyMessage.cs`):

```
public interface IMyMessageCallback
{
  [OperationContract(IsOneWay=true)]
  void OnCallback(string message);
}

[ServiceContract(CallbackContract=typeof(IMyMessageCallback))]
public interface IMyMessage
{
  [OperationContract]
  void MessageToServer(string message);
}
```

Service for Duplex Communication

The class MessageService implements the service contract IMyMessage. The service writes the message from the client to the console. To access the callback contract, you can use the OperationContext class. OperationContext.Current returns the OperationContext associated with the current request from the client. With the OperationContext, you can access session information, message headers and properties, and, in the case of a duplex communication, the callback channel. The generic method GetCallbackChannel returns the channel to the client instance. This channel can then be used to send a message to the client by invoking the method OnCallback, which is defined with the callback interface IMyMessageCallback. To demonstrate that it is also possible to use the callback channel from the service independently of the completion of the method, a new thread that receives the callback channel is created. The new thread sends messages to the client by using the callback channel (code file DuplexCommunication/MessageService/MessageService.cs).

```
public class MessageService: IMyMessage
{
  public void MessageToServer(string message)
  {
    Console.WriteLine("message from the client: {0}", message);
    IMyMessageCallback callback =
        OperationContext.Current.
            GetCallbackChannel<IMyMessageCallback>();

    callback.OnCallback("message from the server");

    Task.Factory.StartNew(new Action<object>(TaskCallback), callback);
  }

  private async void ThreadCallback(object callback)
  {
    IMyMessageCallback messageCallback = callback as IMyMessageCallback;
    for (int i = 0; i < 10; i++)
    {
      messageCallback.OnCallback("message " + i.ToString());
      await Task.Delay(1000);
    }
  }
}
```

Hosting the service is the same as it was with the previous samples, so it is not shown here. However, for duplex communication, you must configure a binding that supports a duplex channel. One of the bindings supporting a duplex channel is wsDualHttpBinding, which is configured in the application's configuration file:

```
<?xml version="1.0" encoding="utf-8" ?>
<configuration>
  <system.serviceModel>
    <services>
```

```
<service name="Wrox.ProCSharp.WCF.MessageService">
  <endpoint contract="Wrox.ProCSharp.WCF.IMyMessage"
      binding="wsDualHttpBinding"/>
  <host>
    <baseAddresses>
      <add baseAddress="http://localhost:8733/Service1" />
    </baseAddresses>
  </host>
</service>
</services>
</system.serviceModel>
</configuration>
```

Client Application for Duplex Communication

With the client application, the callback contract must be implemented as shown here with the class `ClientCallback` that implements the interface `IMyMessageCallback` (code file `DuplexCommunication/MessageClient/Program.cs`):

```
class ClientCallback: IMyMessageCallback
{
  public void OnCallback(string message)
  {
    Console.WriteLine("message from the server: {0}", message);
  }
}
```

With a duplex channel, you cannot use the `ChannelFactory` to initiate the connection to the service as was done previously. To create a duplex channel, you can use the `DuplexChannelFactory` class. This class has a constructor with one more parameter in addition to the binding and address configuration. This parameter specifies an `InstanceContext` that wraps one instance of the `ClientCallback` class. When passing this instance to the factory, the service can invoke the object across the channel. The client just needs to keep the connection open. If the connection is closed, the service cannot send messages across it.

```
private async static void DuplexSample()
{
  var binding = new WSDualHttpBinding();
  var address = new EndpointAddress("http://localhost:8733/Service1");

  var clientCallback = new ClientCallback();
  var context = new InstanceContext(clientCallback);

  var factory = new DuplexChannelFactory<IMyMessage>(context, binding,
                    address);

  IMyMessage messageChannel = factory.CreateChannel();

  await Task.Run(() => messageChannel.MessageToServer("From the client"));
}
```

Duplex communication is achieved by starting the service host and the client application.

ROUTING

Using the SOAP protocol has some advantages to HTTP GET requests with REST. One of the advanced features that can be done with SOAP is routing. With routing, the client does not directly address the service, but a router in between that forwards the request.

There are different scenarios to use this feature. One is for failover (see Figure 43-10). If the service cannot be reached or returns in an error, the router calls the service on a different host. This is abstracted from the client; the client just receives a result.

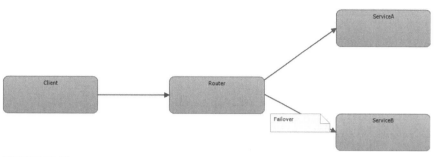

FIGURE 43-10

Routing can also be used to change the communication protocol (see Figure 43-11). The client can use the HTTP protocol to call a request and sends this to the router. The router acts as a client with the net.tcp protocol and calls a service forwarding the message.

FIGURE 43-11

Using routing for scalability is another scenario (see Figure 43-12). Depending on a field of the message header or also information from the message content, the router can decide to forward a request to one or the other server. Requests from customers that start with the letter A–F go to the first server, G–N to the second one, and O–Z to the third.

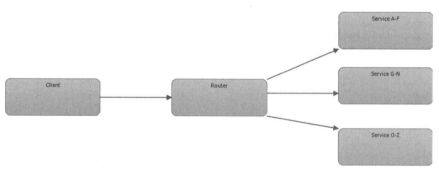

FIGURE 43-12

Sample Application

With the routing sample application, a simple service contract is defined where the caller can invoke the GetData operation from the IDemoService interface (code file RoutingSample/DemoService/IDemoService.cs):

```
using System.ServiceModel;

namespace Wrox.ProCSharp.WCF
{
  [ServiceContract(Namespace="http://www.cninnovation.com/Services/2012")]
  public interface IDemoService
  {
    [OperationContract]
    string GetData(string value);
  }
}
```

The implementation of the service (code file `RoutingSample/DemoService/DemoService.cs`) just returns a message with the `GetData` method. The message contains the information received along a server-side string that is initialized from the host. This way you can see the host that returned the call to the client.

```
using System;

namespace Wrox.ProCSharp.WCF
{
  public class DemoService : IDemoService
  {
    public static string Server { get; set; }

    public string GetData(string value)
    {
      string message = string.Format("Message from {0}, You entered: {1}",
        Server, value);
      Console.WriteLine(message);
      return message;
    }
  }
}
```

Two sample hosts just create a `ServiceHost` instance and open it to start the listener. Each of the hosts defined assigns a different value to the Server property of the `DemoService`.

Routing Interfaces

For routing, WCF defines the interfaces `ISimplexDataGramRouter`, `ISimplexSessionRouter`, `IRequestReplyRouter`, and `IDuplexSessionRouter`. Depending on the service contract, different interfaces can be used. `ISimplexDataGramRouter` can be used with operations that have the `OperationContract` with `IsOneWay` settings. With `ISimplexDatagramRouter`, sessions are optional. `ISimplexSessionRouter` can be used for one-way messages like `ISimlexDatagramRouter`, but here sessions are mandatory. `IRequestReplyRouter` is used for the most common scenario, messages with request and response. With duplex communications (for example, with the `WsDualHttpBinding` used earlier), the interface `IDuplexSessionRouter` is used.

Depending on the message pattern used, a custom router needs to implement the corresponding router interface.

WCF Routing Service

Instead of creating a custom router, the `RouterService` from the namespace `System.ServiceModel` `.Routing` can be used. This class implements all the routing interfaces and thus can be used with all the message patterns. It can be hosted just like any other service (code file `RoutingSample/Router/Program` `.cs`). In the `StartService` method, a new `ServiceHost` is instantiated passing the `RoutingService` type. This is just like the other hosts you've seen before.

```
using System;
using System.ServiceModel;
using System.ServiceModel.Routing;

namespace Router
{
  class Program
  {
    internal static ServiceHost routerHost = null;

    static void Main()
    {
      StartService();

      Console.WriteLine("Router is running. Press return to exit");
```

```
      Console.ReadLine();

      StopService();
    }

    internal static void StartService()
    {
      try
      {
        routerHost = new ServiceHost(typeof(RoutingService));
        routerHost.Faulted += myServiceHost_Faulted;
        routerHost.Open();
      }
      catch (AddressAccessDeniedException)
      {
        Console.WriteLine("either start Visual Studio in elevated admin " +
          "mode or register the listener port with netsh.exe");
      }
    }

    static void myServiceHost_Faulted(object sender, EventArgs e)
    {
      Console.WriteLine("router faulted");
    }

    internal static void StopService()
    {
      if (routerHost != null && routerHost.State == CommunicationState.Opened)
      {
        routerHost.Close();
      }
    }
  }
}
```

Using a Router for Failover

More interesting than the hosting code is the configuration (configuration file `Router/App.config`) of the
router. The router acts as a server to the client application and as a client to the service. So both parts need
to be configured. The configuration as shown here offers the `wsHttpBinding` as a server part and uses the
`wsHttpBinding` as a client to connect to the service. The service endpoint needs to specify the contract that
is used with the endpoint. With the request-reply operations offered by the service, the contract is defined by
the `IRequestReplyRouter` interface.

```xml
<system.serviceModel>
  <services>
    <service behaviorConfiguration="routingData"
      name="System.ServiceModel.Routing.RoutingService">
      <endpoint address="" binding="wsHttpBinding"
        name="reqReplyEndpoint"
        contract="System.ServiceModel.Routing.IRequestReplyRouter" />
      <endpoint address="mex" binding="mexHttpBinding"
        contract="IMetadataExchange" />
      <host>
        <baseAddresses>
          <add baseAddress="http://localhost:8000/RoutingDemo/router" />
        </baseAddresses>
      </host>
    </service>
  </services>
</system.serviceModel>
```

The client part of the router defines two endpoints for services. For testing the routing service, you can use one system. Of course, usually the hosts run on a different system. The contract can be set to * to allow all contracts to pass through to the services covered by these endpoints.

```
<client>
  <endpoint address="http://localhost:9001/RoutingDemo/HostA"
    binding="wsHttpBinding" contract="*" name="RoutingDemoService1" />
  <endpoint address="http://localhost:9001/RoutingDemo/HostB"
    binding="wsHttpBinding" contract="*" name="RoutingDemoService2" />
</client>
```

The behavior configuration for the service becomes important for routing. The behavior configuration named routingData is referenced with the service configuration you've seen earlier. For routing the routing element must be set with the behavior, and here a routing table is referenced using the attribute filterTableName.

```
<behaviors>
  <serviceBehaviors>
    <behavior name="routingData">
      <serviceMetadata httpGetEnabled="True"/>
      <routing filterTableName="routingTable1" />
      <serviceDebug includeExceptionDetailInFaults="true"/>
    </behavior>
  </serviceBehaviors>
</behaviors>
```

The filter table named routingTable1 contains a filter with the filterType MatchAll. This filter matches with every request. Now every request from the client is routed to the endpoint name RoutingDemoService1. If this service fails and cannot be reached, the backup list takes importance. The backup list named failOver1 defines the second endpoint used in case the first one fails.

```
<routing>
  <filters>
    <filter name="MatchAllFilter1" filterType="MatchAll" />
  </filters>
  <filterTables>
    <filterTable name="routingTable1">
      <add filterName="MatchAllFilter1" endpointName="RoutingDemoService1"
        backupList="failOver1" />
    </filterTable>
  </filterTables>
  <backupLists>
    <backupList name="failOver1">
      <add endpointName="RoutingDemoService2"/>
    </backupList>
  </backupLists>
</routing>
```

With the routing server and routing configuration in place, you can start the client that makes a call to a service via the router. If everything is fine, the client gets an answer from the service running in host 1. If you stop host 1, and another request from the client, host 2 takes responsibility and returns an answer.

Bridging for Protocol Changes

If the router should act to change the protocol, you can configure the host to use the netTcpBinding instead of the wsHttpBinding. With the router, the client configuration needs to be changed to reference the other endpoint.

```
<endpoint address="net.tcp://localhost:9010/RoutingDemo/HostA"
  binding="netTcpBinding" contract="*" name="RoutingDemoService1" />
```

That's all that needs to be done to change the scenario.

Filter Types

With the sample application, a match-all filter has been used. WCF offers more filter types.

FILTER TYPE	DESCRIPTION
Action	The Action filter enables filtering depending on the action of the message. See the Action property of the OperationContract.
Address	The Address filter enables filtering on the address that is in the To field of the SOAP header.
AddressPrefix	The AddressPrefix filter does not match on the complete address but on the best prefix match of the address.
MatchAll	The MatchAll filter is a filter that matches every request.
XPath	With the XPath message filter, an XPath expression can be defined to filter on the message header. You can add information to the SOAP header with a message contract.
Custom	If you need to route depending on the content of the message, a Custom filter type is required. With a custom filter type, you need to create a class that derives from the base class `MessageFilter`. Initialization of the filter is done with a constructor that takes a `string` parameter. This `string` can be passed from the configuration initialization.

If multiple filters apply to a request, priorities can be used with filters. However, it's best to avoid priorities as this decreases performance.

SUMMARY

In this chapter, you learned how to use Windows Communication Foundation for communication between a client and a server. WCF is platform-independent like ASP.NET Web services, but it offers features similar to .NET Remoting, Enterprise Services, and Message Queuing.

WCF has a heavy focus on contracts to make it easier to isolate developing clients and services, and to support platform independence. It defines three different contract types: service contracts, data contracts, and message contracts. You can use several attributes to define the behavior of the service and its operations.

You saw how to create clients from the metadata offered by the service and also by using the .NET interface contract. You learned the features of different binding options. WCF offers not only bindings for platform independence, but also bindings for fast communication between .NET applications. You've seen how to create custom hosts and also make use of the WAS host. You saw how duplex communication is achieved by defining a callback interface, applying a service contract, and implementing a callback contract in the client application.

The next few chapters continue with WCF features. In Chapter 44, "WCF Data Services", you learn about WCF Data Services, Chapter 45, "Windows Workflow Foundation", you learn about Windows Workflow Foundation and how WCF is used to communicate with workflow instances. Chapter 46, "Windows Communication Foundation", makes use of a WCF service with peer-to-peer communication. Chapter 47, "Message Queuing" explains how disconnected Message Queuing features can be used with WCF bindings.

44

WCF Data Services

WHAT'S IN THIS CHAPTER?

➤ Overview of WCF Data Services

➤ WCF Data Services hosting with CLR objects

➤ HTTP client access to WCF Data Services

➤ URL queries to WCF Data Services

➤ WCF Data Services with the ADO.NET Entity Framework

➤ Using the WCF Data Services Client Library

➤ Tracking, updates, and batching

WROX.COM CODE DOWNLOADS FOR THIS CHAPTER

The wrox.com code downloads for this chapter are found at http://www.wrox.com/remtitle
.cgi?isbn=1118314425 on the Download Code tab. The code for this chapter is divided into the
following major examples:

➤ Data Services Samples

    ➤ Data Services Host

    ➤ Web Request Client

➤ EDM Data Services Samples

    ➤ Restaurant Data Services Web

    ➤ Client App

OVERVIEW

WCF Data Services is based on WCF, which was covered in Chapter 43, "Windows Communication
Foundation," and it also makes a lot of use of the ADO.NET Entity Framework, that was covered in
Chapter 33, "ADO.NET Entity Framework." In that chapter, the ADO.NET Entity Framework was
used to easily create an object model to map to the database structures. The Entity Framework does
not provide a way to get the objects across different tiers; however, this is where WCF Data Services
come into play. WCF Data Services offers a WCF service to easily access data provided by an Entity
Data Model or by simple CLR objects implementing the IQueryable<T> interface.

The main namespace used with this chapter is `System.Data.Services`. A new technology that partly offers the same functionality as WCF Data Services but is not as mature as WCF Data Services is *ASP.NET Web API*. This technology is covered in Chapter 41, "ASP.NET MVC."

The ADO.NET Entity Framework offers mapping between objects and relational databases and creates entity classes. The data context of the Entity Framework stays informed about changes to data so that it knows what should be updated, but the Entity Framework does not help when creating solutions over multiple tiers.

Using WCF Data Services, you can use the Entity Framework (or a simple CLR object model) on the server side and send HTTP queries from the client to the service to retrieve and update data. Figure 44-1 shows a typical scenario with a Windows client or a Web page using HTML and JavaScript to send an HTTP request to the server.

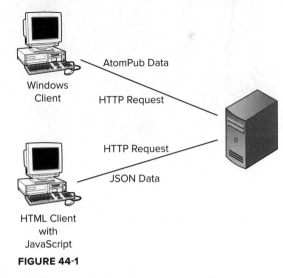

FIGURE 44-1

The returned information can be in AtomPub or JSON format. AtomPub is the Atom Publisher format based on XML. JSON (JavaScript Object Notation) is best accessed from JavaScript clients.

WCF Data Services makes use of WCF (Windows Communication Foundation) for the communication part and uses the `WebHttpBinding`.

With WCF Data Services you not only get features on the server and the capability to use HTTP Web requests with AtomPub or JSON, there is also a client-side part of WCF Data Services. For the client, there's a data service context and the possibility to create queries that are transformed in the AtomPub or JSON format. Whereas the HTTP protocol is stateless, the data service context for the client is stateful. With this context, the client can keep track of what entities are changed, added, or removed, and send a request with all the change information to the service. In the following section, we'll get into the details of WCF Data Services by first creating a simple service that is accessed from a client using HTTP Web requests.

CUSTOM HOSTING WITH CLR OBJECTS

The heart of WCF Data Services is the `DataService<T>` class, which enables implementation of a WCF service. `DataService<T>` implements the interface `IRequestHandler`, which is defined as follows. The attribute `WebInvoke` is specified to accept any URI parameters and any HTTP methods. With the parameter and return type, the method `ProcessRequestForMessage` is very flexible. It accepts any stream and returns a message. This is a requirement for the flexibility of data supported.

```
[ServiceContract]
public interface IRequestHandler
{
  [OperationContract]
  [WebInvoke(UriTemplate="*", Method="*")]
  Message ProcessRequestForMessage(Stream messageBody);
}
```

> **NOTE** *The WCF attributes* `ServiceContract`, `OperationContract`, *and* `WebInvoke` *are explained in Chapter 43, "Windows Communication Foundation."*

This section begins with a simple example by using a console application to host a service that offers a list of CLR objects. This service will then be used from a client application that directly sends HTTP requests to retrieve the data.

CLR Objects

The sample defines two entity classes: Category and Menu. These classes are simple data holders. The Menu class contains Name, Price, and a reference to the Category class. To make the different instances uniquely identifiable by Data Services, the attribute DataServiceKey must be added to reference the unique identifier. This attribute is defined in the namespace System.Data.Services.Common. Instead of defining a single property as the identity, it is also possible to assign a list of properties for unique identification. The Category class is defined in the code file DataServicesSamples/DataServicesHost/Category.cs:

```
[DataServiceKey("Id")]
public class Category
{
  public int Id { get; set; }
  public string Name { get; set; }

  public Category() { }
  public Category(int id, string name)
  {
    this.Id = id;
    this.Name = name;
  }
}
```

The Menu class is defined in the code file DataServicesSamples/DataServicesHost/Menu.cs:

```
[DataServiceKey("Id")]
public class Menu
{
  public int Id { get; set; }
  public string Name { get; set; }
  public decimal Price { get; set; }
  public Category Category { get; set; }

  public Menu() { }
  public Menu(int id, string name, decimal price, Category category)
  {
    this.Id = id;
    this.Name = name;
    this.Price = price;
    this.Category = category;
  }
}
```

The class MenuCard manages the collections of Menu and Category items. It contains a list of Menu and Category items that can be iterated from the public Menus and Categories properties. This class implements a singleton pattern, so only one list of each exists (code file DataServicesSamples/ DataServicesHost/MenuCard.cs):

```
using System;
using System.Collections.Generic;
using System.Linq;
using System.Text;
namespace Wrox.ProCSharp.DataServices
{
```

```
public class MenuCard
{
  private static object sync = new object();
  private static MenuCard menuCard;
  public static MenuCard Instance
  {
    get
    {
      lock (sync)
      {
        if (menuCard == null)
          menuCard = new MenuCard();
      }
      return menuCard;
    }
  }

  private readonly List<Category> categories;
  private readonly List<Menu> menus;

  private MenuCard()
  {
    categories = new List<Category>
    {
      new Category(1, "Main"),
      new Category(2, "Appetizer")
    };

    menus = new List<Menu>()
    {
      new Menu(1, "Roasted Chicken", 22, categories[0]),
      new Menu(2, "Rack of Lamb", 32, categories[0]),
      new Menu(3, "Pork Tenderloin", 23, categories[0]),
      new Menu(4, "Fried Calamari", 9, categories[1])
    };
  }

  public IEnumerable<Menu> Menus
  {
    get
    {
      return menus;
    }
  }

  public IEnumerable<Category> Categories
  {
    get
    {
      return categories;
    }
  }
}
```

Data Model

Now it gets really interesting with the class MenuCardDataModel. This class defines what entities are offered from the data service by specifying properties that return IQueryable<T>. IQueryable<T> is used by the DataService<T> class to pass expressions for querying in object lists (code file DataServicesSamples/ DataServicesHost/MenuCardDataModel.cs):

```
public class MenuCardDataModel
{
  public IQueryable<Menu> Menus
  {
    get
    {
      return MenuCard.Instance.Menus.AsQueryable();
    }
  }

  public IQueryable<Category> Categories
  {
    get
    {
      return MenuCard.Instance.Categories.AsQueryable();
    }
  }
}
```

Data Service

The implementation of the data service MenuDataService derives from the base class DataService<T>.
The generic parameter of the DataService<T> class is the class MenuCardDataModel, with the Menus and
Categories properties returning IQueryable<T>.

In the IntializeService method, you need to configure the entity and service operations access rules by using
the DataServiceConfiguration class. You can pass * for the entity and operations access rules to allow access
to every entity and operation. With the enumerations EntitySetRights and ServiceOperationsRights,
you can specify whether read and/or write access should be enabled. The MaxProtocolVersion property of the
DataServiceBehavior defines what version of the AtomPub protocol should be supported. Version 2 is
supported since .NET 4.0 and includes support for some additional features, such as getting the number of
items from a list (code file DataServicesSamples/DataServicesHost/MenuDataService.cs):

```
using System.Data.Services;
using System.Data.Services.Common;
using System.Linq;
using System.ServiceModel.Web;

namespace Wrox.ProCSharp.DataServices
{
  public class MenuDataService : DataService<MenuCardDataModel>
  {
    public static void InitializeService(DataServiceConfiguration config)
    {
      config.SetEntitySetAccessRule("Menus", EntitySetRights.AllRead);
      config.SetEntitySetAccessRule("*", EntitySetRights.AllRead);

      config.DataServiceBehavior.MaxProtocolVersion =
          DataServiceProtocolVersion.V2;
    }
  }
}
```

Hosting the Service

Finally, you need a process to host the application. Later in this chapter, a web application is used for
hosting. You can also host the service in any application type that's supported by WCF; this can be a simple
console application or a Windows Service. This sample uses a console application that you can easily change
to any other hosting type.

In the `Main` method of the console application, a `DataServiceHost` is instantiated. `DataServiceHost` derives from the base class `ServiceHost` to offer WCF functionality. You can also use the `DataServiceHostFactory` to create the `DataServiceHost`. Calling the `Open` method, `DataServiceHost` instantiates an instance from the `MenuDataService` class for offering the service functionality. The address of the service is defined with `http://localhost:9000/Samples` (code file `DataServicesSamples/DataServicesHost/Program.cs`):

```
using System;
using System.Data.Services;
using System.ServiceModel;

namespace Wrox.ProCSharp.DataServices
{
  class Program
  {
    static void Main()
    {
      DataServiceHost host = null;
      try
      {
        host = new DataServiceHost(typeof(MenuDataService),
          new Uri[] { new Uri("http://localhost:9000/Samples ") });

        host.Open();

        Console.WriteLine("service running");
        Console.WriteLine("Press return to exit");
        Console.ReadLine();
      }
      catch (CommunicationException ex)
      {
        Console.WriteLine(ex.Message);
      }
      finally
      {
        if (host.State == CommunicationState.Opened)
          host.Close();
      }
    }
  }
}
```

Now you can start the executable and request the service with the links `http://localhost:9000/Samples/Menus` and `http://localhost:9000/Samples/Categories` from within Internet Explorer. To use Internet Explorer to see the data returned from the service, you need to deselect the option "Turn on feed reading view."

> **NOTE** *To start a listener without elevated administrator rights, you need to configure the ACL for the port and the user as follows:*
>
> ```
> netsh http add urlacl url=http://+:9000/ Samples user=username
>     listen=yes
> ```
>
> *Of course, changing these administrative settings requires elevated administrator rights.*

Additional Service Operations

Instead of offering only the properties from the data model, you can add additional service operations to the data service. In the following sample code, you can see the method `GetMenusByName`, which gets a request parameter from the client and returns all menus starting with the requested string with an `IQueryable<Menu>` collection. Such operations need to be added to the service operation access rules in the `InitalizeService` method in case you do not offer all service operations using the * (code file `DataServicesSamples/DataServicesHost/MenuDataService.cs`):

```
public class MenuDataService : DataService<MenuCardDataModel>
{
  public static void InitializeService(DataServiceConfiguration config)
  {
    config.SetEntitySetAccessRule("Menus", EntitySetRights.AllRead);
    config.SetEntitySetAccessRule("Categories", EntitySetRights.AllRead);
    config.SetServiceOperationAccessRule("GetMenusByName",
        ServiceOperationRights.AllRead);

    config.DataServiceBehavior.MaxProtocolVersion =
        DataServiceProtocolVersion.V2;
  }

  [WebGet(UriTemplate="GetMenusByName?name={name}",
          BodyStyle=WebMessageBodyStyle.Bare)]
  public IQueryable<Menu> GetMenusByName(string name)
  {
    return (from m in CurrentDataSource.Menus
            where m.Name.StartsWith(name)
            select m).AsQueryable();
  }
}
```

HTTP CLIENT APPLICATION

The client application can be a simple application to just send HTTP requests to the service and receive AtomPub or JSON responses. The first client application example is a WPF application that makes use of the `HttpClient` class from the `System.Net` namespace.

FIGURE 44-2

Figure 44-2 shows the UI from the Visual Studio Designer, and Figure 44-3 provides details about the document outline. A `TextBox` control at the top of Figure 44-2 is used to enter the HTTP request. The `TextBlock` control receives the answer from the service. You can also see a `CheckBox` control, where the response can be requested in the JSON format. The Call Data Service button has the `Click` event associated with the `OnRequest` method.

The `TextBox`, `TextBlock`, and `CheckBox` XAML elements are bound to properties of the window, `Result`, `UrlRequest`, and `JsonRequest`. The window implements the interface `INotifyPropertyChanged` for data

FIGURE 44-3

binding as shown in the following code snippet (code file `DataServicesSample/WebRequestClient`
`.xaml.cs`):

```
private string result;
public string Result
{
  get { return result; }
  set {
    SetProperty(ref result, value);
  }
}

private string urlRequest;
public string UrlRequest
{
  get
  {
    return urlRequest;
  }
  set
  {
    SetProperty(ref urlRequest, value);
  }
}

private bool? jsonRequest;
public bool? JsonRequest
{
  get
  {
    return jsonRequest;
  }
  set
  {
    SetProperty(ref jsonRequest, value);
  }
}

private void OnPropertyChanged(string propertyName)
{
  var handler = PropertyChanged;
  if (handler != null)
  {
    handler(this, new PropertyChangedEventArgs(propertyName));
  }
}

private void SetProperty<T>(ref T field, T value,
    [CallerMemberName] string propertyName = "")
{
  if (!EqualityComparer<T>.Default.Equals(field, value))
  {
    field = value;
    OnPropertyChanged(propertyName);
  }
}
```

In the implementation of the `OnRequest` handler, an `HttpClient` object is instantiated. `HttpClient` is new
with .NET 4.5. The HTTP request that is sent is defined by the `UrlRequest` property. If the JSON check
box is selected, along with the HTTP headers that are sent to the service, the `Accept` header is set to
`application/json`. This way, the data service returns a JSON response instead of the default AtomPub

format. The HTTP GET request to the server is sent with the asynchronous method GetAsync. When a response from the service is received, the Result property is set:

```
private void OnRequest(object sender, RoutedEventArgs e)
{
  Cursor oldCursor = this.Cursor;
  try
  {
    Result = string.Empty;
    this.Cursor = Cursors.Wait;

    using (var client = new HttpClient())
    {
      if (JsonRequest == true)
      {
        client.DefaultRequestHeaders.Accept.Add(
            MediaTypeWithQualityHeaderValue.Parse("application/json"));
      }
      using (HttpResponseMessage response =
          await client.GetAsync(UrlRequest))
      {
        Result = await response.Content.ReadAsStringAsync();
      }
    }
  }
  catch (InvalidOperationException ex)
  {
    Result = ex.Message;
  }
  catch (HttpRequestException ex)
  {
    Result = ex.Message;
  }
  catch (UriFormatException ex)
  {
    Result = ex.Message;
  }
  finally
  {
    this.Cursor = oldCursor;
  }
}
```

Now you can use several HTTP requests to the service and see the data returned. The running application is shown in Figure 44-4.

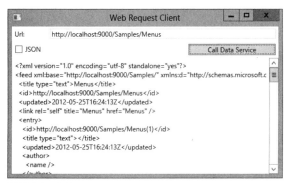

FIGURE 44-4

Using the request `http://localhost:9000/Samples/Menus(3)` to get the menu with the unique identifier 3, the following AtomPub information is received:

```xml
<?xml version="1.0" encoding="utf-8" standalone="yes"?>
<entry xml:base="http://localhost:9000/Samples/"
       xmlns:d="http://schemas.microsoft.com/ado/2007/08/dataservices"
       xmlns:m="http://schemas.microsoft.com/ado/2007/08/dataservices/metadata"
       xmlns="http://www.w3.org/2005/Atom">
  <id>http://localhost:9000/Samples/Menus(3)</id>
  <title type="text"></title>
  <updated>2012-02-03T15:49:49Z</updated>
  <author>
    <name />
  </author>
  <link rel="edit" title="Menu" href="Menus(3)" />
  <link rel=
    "http://schemas.microsoft.com/ado/2007/08/dataservices/related/Category"
    type="application/atom+xml;type=entry" title="Category"
    href="Menus(3)/Category" />
  <category term="Wrox.ProCSharp.DataServices.Menu"
    scheme="http://schemas.microsoft.com/ado/2007/08/dataservices/scheme" />
  <content type="application/xml">
    <m:properties>
      <d:Id m:type="Edm.Int32">3</d:Id>
      <d:Name>Pork Tenderloin</d:Name>
      <d:Description m:null="true" />
      <d:Price m:type="Edm.Decimal">23</d:Price>
    </m:properties>
  </content>
</entry>
```

If you select the JSON format, a response with the same information but a JSON representation that can be easily read from JavaScript is returned:

```
{ "d" :
  { "__metadata":
    { "uri": "http://localhost:9000/Samples/Menus(3)",
      "type": "Wrox.ProCSharp.DataServices.Menu"
    },
    "Id": 3, "Name": "Pork Tenderloin", "Price": "23",
    "Category":
      { "__deferred":
        { "uri": "http://localhost:9000/Samples/Menus(3)/Category"
        }
      }
  }
}
```

In the next section, you'll take a look at all the addressing options you have to build the query.

QUERIES WITH URLS

With the flexibility of the data services interface, you can request all objects from the service or get into specific objects and even values for specific properties.

> **NOTE** *For better readability, the following queries omit the address of the service,* `http://localhost:9000/Samples`. *This must be prefixed to all the queries.*

You've already seen that you can get a list of all entities in an entity set. The query:

```
Menus
```

returns all menu entities, while:

```
Categories
```

returns all category entities. According to the AtomPub protocol, the returned root element is <feed> and contains <entry> elements for every element. This query does not work across references; for example, getting all menus with Menus doesn't return the content of the category, only a reference to it. To get the category information within a menu, you can use the $expand query string:

```
Menus?$expand=Category
```

Passing the primary key value inside brackets returns just a single entity. In the next example, the menu with identifier 3 is accessed. This requires the definition of the DataServiceKey attribute used earlier:

```
Menus(3)
```

With a navigation property (using /), you can access a property of an entity:

```
Menus(3)/Price
```

The same syntax works for relations, accessing properties from related entities:

```
Menus(3)/Category/Name
```

To get just the value without the surrounding XML content of an entity, you can use the $value query function:

```
Menus(3)/Category/Name/$value
```

Getting back to complete lists, you can get the number of entities in a list with $count (note that $count is only available with V2 of the AtomPub protocol):

```
Menus/$count
```

Getting just the first entities of a list is done with the query string option $top:

```
Menus?$top=2
```

You can skip a number of entities with $skip (both $skip and $top can be combined for implementing paging functionality):

```
Menus?$skip=2
```

Filtering entities can be performed with the $filter query string option and by using the logical operators eq (equal), ne (not equal), gt (greater than), and ge (greater than or equal to):

```
Menus?$filter=Category/Name eq 'Appetizer'
```

You can sort the result with the $orderby query string option:

```
Menus?$filter=Category/Name eq 'Appetizer'&$orderby=Price desc
```

To only get a projection, a subset of the available properties, $select can be used to specify the properties that should be accessed:

```
Menus?$select=Name, Price
```

USING WCF DATA SERVICES WITH THE ADO.NET ENTITY FRAMEWORK

Now that you've learned the basic concept of Data Services, passing AtomPub or JSON data across simple HTTP requests, let's get into a more complex example, using the ADO.NET Entity Framework for the data model, a web application for hosting, and clients performing LINQ queries across a network that makes use of classes from the System.Data.Services.Client namespace.

ASP.NET Hosting and EDM

First you have to create a new project. This time a Web Application project named RestaurantDataServiceWeb is used to host the service. The new data model is created with the help of the ADO.NET Entity Data Model (EDM) template and uses the tables Menus and Categories from a Restaurant database, as shown in Figure 44-5, to create the entity classes Menu and Category.

> **NOTE** *Chapter 33, "ADO.NET Entity Framework," explains how to create and use ADO.NET Entity Data Models.*

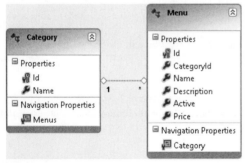

FIGURE 44-5

Now, use the Data Service template and create RestaurantDataService.svc. The .svc file contains the ASP. NET ServiceHost directive and uses the DataServiceHostFactory to instantiate the data service on request (markup file EDMDataServicesSamples/RestaurantDataServiceWeb/RestaurantDataService.svc):

```
<%@ ServiceHost Language="C#"
    Factory="System.Data.Services.DataServiceHostFactory,
        System.Data.Services, Version=4.0.0.0, Culture=neutral,
        PublicKeyToken=b77a5c561934e089"
    Service="Wrox.ProCSharp.DataServices.RestaurantDataService" %>
```

With the code-behind, you need to change the template parameter of the DataService<T> class to reference the previously created entity data service context class, and change the entity set access rule and service operations access rule to allow access (code file EDMDataServicesSamples/RestaurantDataServiceWeb/RestaurantDataService.svc.cs):

```
using System.Data.Services;
using System.Data.Services.Common;
```

```
namespace Wrox.ProCSharp.DataServices
{
  public class RestaurantDataService : DataService<RestaurantEntities>
  {
    // This method is called only once to initialize service-wide policies.
    public static void InitializeService(DataServiceConfiguration config)
    {
      config.SetEntitySetAccessRule("Menus", EntitySetRights.All);
      config.SetEntitySetAccessRule("Categories", EntitySetRights.All);
      config.DataServiceBehavior.MaxProtocolVersion =
          DataServiceProtocolVersion.V2;
    }
  }
}
```

Now, you can use a web browser to invoke queries as before to this data service; for example, you can use
`http://localhost:13617/RestaurantDataService.svc/Menus` to receive the AtomPub of all menus
from the database. Next, you create a client application that makes use of the client part of Data Services.

> **NOTE** *With a large database you shouldn't return all the items with a query. Of
> course, the client can restrict the query to request a specified limited number of items.
> However, can you trust the client? With configuration options you can restrict limits
> on the server. For example, by setting* `config.MaxResultsPerCollection` *you can
> restrict the number of items that are returned from a collection to a specified maximum.
> You can also configure the maximum batch count, the maximum number of objects
> on an insert, and the maximum depth of objects in the tree. Alternatively, to allow any
> query, you can define service operations as shown in the section "Additional Service
> Operations."*

Using the WCF Data Service Client Library

Earlier in this chapter, you read how a .NET client application can be created that simply sends HTTP
requests by using the `HttpClient` class. The client part of Data Services, with the namespace `System.Data`
`.Services.Client`, offers functionality for the client to build HTTP requests. The two most important
classes with this namespace are `DataServiceContext`
and `DataServiceQuery<TElement>`.
`DataServiceContext` represents the state that is
managed on the client. This state keeps track of objects
that are loaded from the server as well as all changes
made on the client. `DataServiceQuery<TElement>`
represents an HTTP query to a data service.

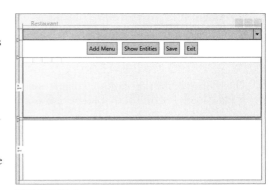

To call the data service, create a WPF application.
Figure 44-6 shows the design view of the WPF application. The top row contains a `ComboBox` control, which
is used to display all categories. The second row
contains a `StackPanel` with four `Button` controls. The
third row contains a `DataGrid` control to display the
menus, and the fourth row contains a `TextBlock`
element to display some status information.

FIGURE 44-6

To create a client proxy and entity classes to be used on the client, you need metadata information. The Data
Service offers metadata by using the `$metadata` query string:

```
http://localhost:13617/RestaurantDataService.svc/$metadata.
```

With this information a service reference can be added to the client application project to create a proxy class and entity classes. With the Restaurant data service, the class `RestaurantEntities` that derives from the base class `DataServiceContext` is created, which can be used as a proxy. Entity classes `Menu` and `Category` to keep the data are created as well. The entity classes implement the interface `INotifyPropertyChanged`, which makes it easy to be kept informed about changes from the UI.

Data Service Context

Now you can use the data service context `RestaurantEntities` to send a query to the data service. A variable of the service context is defined in the code-behind of the WPF window, in the class `MainWindow`. To avoid conflict with the `Menu` class that's generated for the data service and the `Menu` control from WPF, a namespace alias is defined with the alias name R, for *Restaurant*, to reference the generated classes from the service reference (code file EDMDataServicesSamples/ClientApp/MainWindow.xaml.cs):

```
using System;
using System.Collections.Generic;
using System.Data.Services.Client;
using System.Linq;
using System.Text;
using System.Windows;
using System.Windows.Controls;
using R = Wrox.ProCSharp.DataServices.RestaurantService;

namespace Wrox.ProCSharp.DataServices
{
  public partial class MainWindow : Window
  {
    private R.RestaurantEntities data;
    private DataServiceCollection<R.Menu> trackedMenus;
```

The instance of the `RestaurantEntities` is created in the constructor of the `MainWindow` class. The constructor of the data service context requires a link to the service root. This is defined within the application configuration file and accessed from the strongly typed settings:

```
    public MainWindow()
    {
      var serviceRoot = new Uri(Properties.Settings.Default.RestaurantServiceURL);
      data = new R.RestaurantEntities(serviceRoot);
      data.SendingRequest += data_SendingRequest;

      InitializeComponent();
      this.DataContext = this;
    }
```

The content of the application configuration file used to reference the data service is shown here (config file EDMDataServicesSamples/ClientApp/app.config):

```
<?xml version="1.0" encoding="utf-8" ?>
<configuration>
  <configSections>
    <sectionGroup name="applicationSettings"
        type="System.Configuration.ApplicationSettingsGroup, System,
            Version=4.0.0.0, Culture=neutral, PublicKeyToken=b77a5c561934e089" >
      <section name="Wrox.ProCSharp.DataServices.Properties.Settings"
          type="System.Configuration.ClientSettingsSection, System,
              Version=4.0.0.0, Culture=neutral, PublicKeyToken=b77a5c561934e089"
              requirePermission="false" />
    </sectionGroup>
  </configSections>
```

```
      <applicationSettings>
        <Wrox.ProCSharp.DataServices.Properties.Settings>
          <setting name="RestaurantServiceURL" serializeAs="String">
            <value>http://localhost:13617/RestaurantDataService.svc</value>
          </setting>
        </Wrox.ProCSharp.DataServices.Properties.Settings>
      </applicationSettings>
    </configuration>
```

With the `SendingRequest` event, the data service context invokes the handler every time a request is sent to the service. The method `data_sendingRequest` is associated with the `SendingRequest` event and receives information about the request in the `SendingRequestEventArgs` argument. With `SendingRequestEventArgs`, you can access request and header information. The request method and URI retrieved from the `Method` and `RequestUri` properties is written to the `textStatus` control in the UI (code file EDMDataServicesSamples/ClientApp/MainWindow.xaml.cs):

```
    void data_SendingRequest(object sender, SendingRequestEventArgs e)
    {
      var sb = new StringBuilder();
      sb.AppendFormat("Method: {0}\n", e.Request.Method);
      sb.AppendFormat("Uri: {0}\n", e.Request.RequestUri.ToString());
      this.textStatus.Text = sb.ToString();
    }
```

The data service context `RestaurantEntities` enables you to retrieve entities from the service; tracks the entities that have been retrieved; enables you to add, delete, and change entities inside the data context; and keeps the state of the changes for sending update requests.

LINQ Query

The data service context implements a LINQ provider to convert LINQ requests to HTTP requests. The `Categories` property of the `MainWindow` class defines a LINQ query by using the data context to return all categories:

```
    public IEnumerable<R.Category> Categories
    {
      get
      {
        return from c in data.Categories
               orderby c.Name
               select c;
      }
    }
```

The `ComboBox` in the XAML code defines a binding to this property to display all categories (XAML file EDMDataServicesSamples/ClientApp/MainWindow.xaml):

```
    <ComboBox x:Name="comboCategories" Grid.Row="0"
              ItemsSource="{Binding Path=Categories}" SelectedIndex="0"
              SelectionChanged="OnCategorySelection">
      <ComboBox.ItemTemplate>
        <DataTemplate>
          <TextBlock Text="{Binding Path=Name}" />
        </DataTemplate>
      </ComboBox.ItemTemplate>
    </ComboBox>
```

With the help of the `SendingRequest` event, the LINQ query to access all categories is converted to an HTTP `GET` request with the following URI:

```
Method: GET
Uri: http://localhost:13617/RestaurantDataService.svc/Categories()?$orderby=Name
```

The `Categories` property of the `RestaurantEntities` class returns a `DataServiceQuery<Category>`. `DataServiceQuery<T>` implements `IQueryable`, and thus the compiler creates expression trees from the LINQ query that are analyzed and converted to an HTTP `GET` request.

> **NOTE** *LINQ queries are covered in Chapter 11, "Language Integrated Query."*

You can also create a LINQ query to get only the menus from the category `Soups`:

```
var q = from m in data.Menus
        where m.Category.Name == "Soups"
        orderby m.Name
        select m;
```

This translates the following URI:

```
filter=Category/Name eq 'Soups'&$orderby=Name.
```

The query can be expanded by using Data Services query options. For example, to include the relationship and get all categories with the selected menus, add `AddQueryOption` with `$expand` and the parameter value `Category`:

```
var q = from m in data.Menus.AddQueryOption("$expand", "Category")
        where m.Category.Name == "Soups"
        orderby m.Name
        select m;
```

This modifies the query as follows:

```
Menus()?$filter=Category/Name eq 'Soups'&$orderby=Name&$expand=Category
```

The `DataServiceQuery<T>` class also offers the `Expand` method for this particular query option:

```
var q = from m in data.Menus.Expand("Category")
        where m.Category.Name == "Soups"
        orderby m.Name
        select m;
```

Observable Collections

To keep the user interface informed about collection changes, Data Services contains the collection class `DataServiceCollection<T>`. This collection class is based on `ObservableCollection<T>`, which implements the interface `INotifyCollectionChanged`. WPF controls register with the event of this interface to keep informed about changes in the collection so that the UI can be updated immediately.

The `Menus` property creates a new `DataServiceCollection<T>` if one was not already created, and fills the collection with menus from a selected category by using a LINQ query. The retrieved entities are associated with the data service context data as the context is passed with the constructor of the `DataServiceCollection<T>` (code file `EDMDataServicesSamples/ClientApp/MainWindow.xaml.cs`):

```
public IEnumerable<R.Menu> Menus
{
  get
  {
    if (trackedMenus == null)
    {
      trackedMenus = new DataServiceCollection<R.Menu>(data);

      trackedMenus.Load(
          from m in data.Menus
          where m.CategoryId ==
              (comboCategories.SelectedItem as R.Category).Id
              && m.Active
          select m);
    }
    return trackedMenus;
  }
}
```

The `DataGrid` from the XAML code maps to the `Menus` property with the `Binding` markup extension (XAML file `EDMDataServicesSamples/ClientApp/MainWindow.xaml`):

```
<DataGrid Grid.Row="2" ItemsSource="{Binding Path=Menus}"
          AutoGenerateColumns="False">
  <DataGrid.Columns>
    <DataGridTextColumn Binding="{Binding Path=Name}" />
    <DataGridTextColumn Binding="{Binding Path=Description}" />
    <DataGridTextColumn Binding="{Binding Path=Price}" />
    <DataGridTextColumn Binding="{Binding Path=CategoryId}" />
  </DataGrid.Columns>
</DataGrid>
```

Using the `SelectionChanged` event from the `ComboBox` to select a new category, the menus are retrieved again with the newly selected category in the handler method `OnCategorySelection` (code file `EDMDataServicesSamples/ClientApp/MainWindow.xaml.cs`):

```
private void OnCategorySelection(object sender, SelectionChangedEventArgs e)
{
  var selectedCategory = comboCategories.SelectedItem as R.Category;
  if (selectedCategory != null && trackedMenus != null)
  {
    trackedMenus.Clear();
    trackedMenus.Load(from m in data.Menus
                    where m.CategoryId == selectedCategory.Id
                    select m);
  }
}
```

> **NOTE** *For more information about observable collections and the class* `ObservableCollection<T>`, *please consult Chapter 10, "Collections."*

Object Tracking

The data service context keeps track of all the objects that have been retrieved. You can get information about the objects by iterating through the return of the `Entities` property. `Entities` returns a read-only collection of `EntityDescriptor` objects. The `EntityDescriptor` contains the entity itself, which can be accessed via the `Entity` property, and state information. The state of type `EntityStates` is an enumeration with the possible values `Added`, `Deleted`, `Detached`, `Modified`, or `Unchanged`. This information is used to keep track of changes and send a change request to the service.

To get information about the current entities associated with the data context, the handler method `OnShowEntities` is associated with the `Click` event of the Show Entities button. In the following code, the `State`, `Identity`, and `Entity` properties are used to write status information to the UI:

```csharp
private void OnShowEntities(object sender, RoutedEventArgs e)
{
  var sb = new StringBuilder();
  foreach (var entity in data.Entities)
  {
    sb.AppendFormat("state = {0}, Uri = {1}, Element = {2}\n",
                    entity.State, entity.Identity, entity.Entity);
  }
  this.textStatus.Text = sb.ToString();
}
```

Figure 44-7 shows the running application with information about the objects tracked.

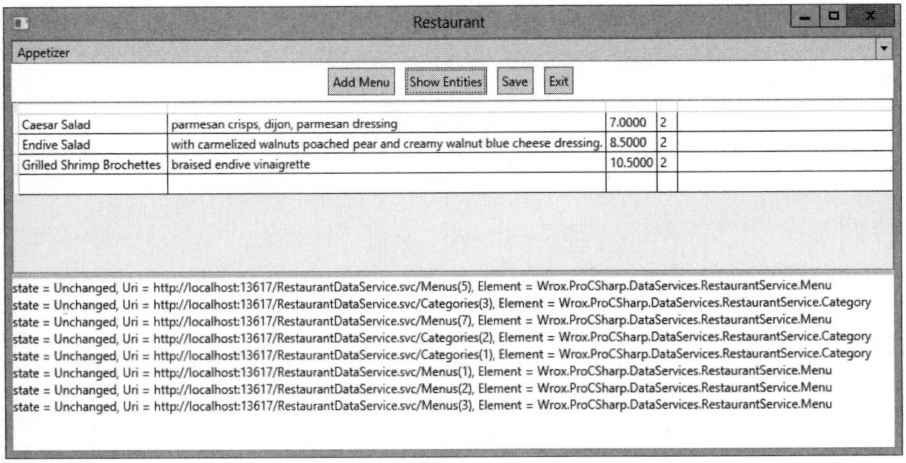

FIGURE 44-7

Adding, Modifying, and Deleting Entities

To add new entities to the data service context and thus send the new objects later to the data service, you can add entities to the data service context with the `AddObject` method, or strongly typed variants such as `AddToMenus` and `AddToCategories`. You just have to fill the mandatory properties; otherwise, saving the state will not succeed.

Adding new objects sets the state to `Added`. The `DeleteObject` method of the data service context sets the state of an object to `Deleted`. If properties of an object are modified, the state changes from `Unchanged` to `Modified`.

Now you can invoke the method `SaveChanges()`, which sends HTTP MERGE requests to update entities, HTTP DELETE requests to delete entities, and HTTP POST requests to add new entities. The following code snippet invokes the asynchronous version of `SaveChanges`, `BeginSaveChanges`, and `EndSaveChanges`. This client proxy implements the async pattern that is converted to the task-based async pattern with the help of the method `FromAsync`:

```
private async void OnSave(object sender, RoutedEventArgs e)
{
  try
  {
    DataServiceResponse response = await Task<DataServiceResponse>.
      Factory.FromAsync(data.BeginSaveChanges, data.EndSaveChanges);
  }
  catch (DataServiceRequestException ex)
  {
    textStatus.Text = ex.ToString();
  }
}
```

Operation Batching

Instead of sending DELETE and MODIFY requests for every entity in a collection, you can batch multiple change requests to a single network request. By default, every change is sent by using a single request when the BeginSaveChanges method is applied. Adding the parameter SaveChangesOptions.Batch to the BeginSaveChanges method combines all the change requests to a single network call with the $batch query option:

```
private async void OnSave(object sender, RoutedEventArgs e)
{
  try
  {
    DataServiceResponse response = await Task<DataServiceResponse>.Factory.
      FromAsync<SaveChangesOptions>(data.BeginSaveChanges,
      data.EndSaveChanges, SaveChangesOptions.Batch, null);
  }
  catch (DataServiceRequestException ex)
  {
    textStatus.Text = ex.ToString();
  }
}
```

As the transferred data demonstrates, multiple HTTP headers are combined inside a single HTTP POST request, and split again on the server side. With the following HTTP POST request, you can see that the DELETE and MERGE requests are combined. The DELETE request deletes the menu with id 4; the MERGE request contains AtomPub information to update the menu with id 2:

```
POST /RestaurantDataService.svc/$batch HTTP/1.1
User-Agent: Microsoft WCF Data Services
DataServiceVersion: 1.0;NetFx
MaxDataServiceVersion: 2.0;NetFx
Accept: application/atom+xml,application/xml
Accept-Charset: UTF-8
Content-Type: multipart/mixed; boundary=batch_24448a55-e96f-4e88-853b-cdb5c1ddc8bd
Host: 127.0.0.1.:13617
Content-Length: 1742
Expect: 100-continue

--batch_24448a55-e96f-4e88-853b-cdb5c1ddc8bd
Content-Type: multipart/mixed;
boundary=changeset_8bc1382a-aceb-400b-9d19-dc2eec0e33b7

--changeset_8bc1382a-aceb-400b-9d19-dc2eec0e33b7
Content-Type: application/http
Content-Transfer-Encoding: binary
```

```
DELETE http://127.0.0.1.:13617/RestaurantDataService.svc/Menus(4) HTTP/1.1
Host: 127.0.0.1.:13617
Content-ID: 18

--changeset_8bc1382a-aceb-400b-9d19-dc2eec0e33b7
Content-Type: application/http
Content-Transfer-Encoding: binary

MERGE http://127.0.0.1.:13617/RestaurantDataService.svc/Menus(2) HTTP/1.1
Host: 127.0.0.1.:13617
Content-ID: 19
Content-Type: application/atom+xml;type=entry
Content-Length: 965

<?xml version="1.0" encoding="utf-8" standalone="yes"?>
<entry xmlns:d="http://schemas.microsoft.com/ado/2007/08/dataservices"
xmlsn:m="http://schemas.microsoft.com/ado/2007/08/dataservices/metadata"
xmlsn="http://www.w3.org/2005/Atom">
  <category scheme="http://schemas.microsoft.com/ado/2007/08/dataservices/scheme"
           term="RestaurantModel.Menu" />
  <title />
  <author>
    <name />
  </author>
  <updated>2009-08-01T19:17:43.4741882Z</updated>
  <id>http://127.0.0.1.:13617/RestaurantDataService.svc/Menus(2)</id>
  <content type="application/xml">
    <m:properties>
      <d:Active m:type="Edm.Boolean">true</d:Active>
      <d:Description>Lean and tender 8 oz. sirloin seasoned perfectly
                    with our own special seasonings and topped with seasoned
                    butter.
      </d:Description>
      <d:Id m:type="Edm.Int32">2</d:Id>
      <d:Name>Sirloin Steak</d:Name>
      <d:Price m:type="Edm.Decimal">44.0</d:Price>
    </m:properties>
  </content>
</entry>
--changeset_8bc1382a-aceb-400b-9d19-dc2eec0e33b7--
--batch_24448a55-e96f-4e88-853b-cdb5c1ddc8bd--
```

SUMMARY

This chapter described the features of WCF Data Services, which brings the data model from the ADO.NET Entity Framework across multiple tiers. The technology that it is based on is WCF, by using connectionless, stateless communication sending AtomPub or JSON queries.

You've not only seen the server-side part of this technology but also the client-side part, where change information is tracked inside a data service context. The client-side part of WCF Data Services implements a LINQ provider, so you can create simple LINQ requests that are converted to HTTP GET/POST/PUT/DELETE requests.

The next chapter gives you information about Windows Workflow Foundation (WF), which allows graphically assigning different activities to form a workflow. Such workflows can describe a WCF service, and thus not only be used to host a workflow but also a WCF service.

45

Windows Workflow Foundation

WHAT'S IN THIS CHAPTER?

➤ Learning the different types of workflows that you can create

➤ Exploring descriptions of some of the built-in activities

➤ Creating custom activities

➤ Getting an overview of a workflow

WROX.COM CODE DOWNLOADS FOR THIS CHAPTER

The wrox.com code downloads for this chapter are found at `http://www.wrox.com/remtitle.cgi?isbn=1118314425` on the Download Code tab. The code for this chapter is divided into the following major examples:

➤ Hello World

➤ Parallel Execution

➤ Pick Demo

➤ Custom Activities

➤ Args and Vars

➤ Workflow Application

➤ Workflow as Services

➤ Dynamic Update

➤ Designer Hosting

A WORKFLOW OVERVIEW

This chapter presents an overview of the Windows Workflow Foundation 4.5 (referred to as WF and Workflow throughout the rest of this chapter), which provides a model to define and execute processes using a set of building blocks called *activities*. WF provides a Designer that, by default, is hosted within Visual Studio, which enables you to drag and drop activities from the toolbox onto the design surface to create a workflow template.

This template can then be executed in a number of different ways, as explained throughout the chapter. As a workflow executes, it may need to access the outside world, and there are a couple of methods typically used that enable you to do this. In addition, a workflow may need to save and restore its state, for example, when a long wait is needed.

A workflow is constructed from a number of activities, and these activities are executed at runtime. An activity might send an e-mail, update a row in a database, or execute a transaction on a back-end system. A number of built-in activities can be used for general-purpose work, and you can also create your own custom activities and plug these into the workflow as necessary.

With Visual Studio 2012, there are now effectively two versions of Workflow with different types—the 3.*x* version, which shipped with the .NET Framework 3 (namespace `System.Workflow` and its subnamespaces, which is also used by SharePoint 2010), and the 4.*x* version (namespace `System.Activities` and its subnamespaces), which ships since the .NET Framework 4. This chapter concentrates on the latest version of Workflow, and we'll begin with the canonical example that everyone uses when faced with a new technology—Hello World.

HELLO WORLD

Visual Studio 2012 contains built-in support to create workflow projects for both the 3.*x* and 4.*x* versions of the frameworks. When you open the New Project dialog, you see a list of workflow project types, as shown in Figure 45-1.

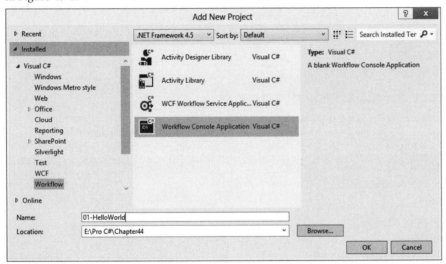

FIGURE 45-1

Ensure that you select .NET Framework 4 or 4.5 from the version combo box, and then choose Workflow Console Application from the available templates. This constructs a simple console application that includes a workflow template and also a main program, which executes this template.

Next, drag a `WriteLine` activity from the toolbox onto the design surface so that you have a workflow that looks like the one shown in Figure 45-2. The `WriteLine` activity is within the Primitives category of the toolbox.

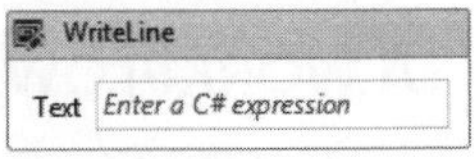

FIGURE 45-2

The `WriteLine` activity includes a `Text` property that you can set either on the design surface by simply entering text inline, or by displaying the property grid. Later in the section, "Custom Activities," you see how to define your custom activities to use this same behavior.

The `Text` property is not just a simple string—it's actually defined as an argument type that can use an expression as its source. Expressions are evaluated at runtime to yield a result, and it is this textual result that is used as the input to the `WriteLine` activity. To enter a simple text expression, you must use double quotation marks—so if you follow along with this in Visual Studio, type "Hello World" into the `Text` property. If you omit the quotation marks, you receive a compiler error because without quotation marks this is not a legal expression. The expression in 4.5 is a C# expression for C# projects—in version 4.0 the expression editor syntax was VB instead, which caused some confusion!

If you build and run the program, you see the output text on the console. When the program executes, an instance of the workflow is created in the `Main` method, which uses a static method of the `WorkflowInvoker` class to execute the instance. The code for this example is available in the `Chapter45` solution in the `01-HelloWorld` project.

The `WorkflowInvoker` class enables you to synchronously invoke a workflow. There are two other methods of workflow execution that execute workflows asynchronously, which you see later in the section "Workflow Application." Synchronous execution was possible in Workflow 3.*x* but was somewhat more difficult to set up, and there was a lot more overhead.

The synchronous nature of `WorkflowInvoker` makes it ideal for running short-lived workflows in response to some UI action—you could use a workflow here to enable or disable some elements of the UI.

ACTIVITIES

Everything in a workflow is an activity, including the workflow itself. The term *workflow* is actually a synonym for a collection of activities; there is no actual `Workflow` class in version 4.*x* (there was in 3.*x*). An activity is just a class that ultimately derives from the abstract `Activity` class.

The class hierarchy is somewhat deeper than that defined for WF 3.*x*, and the main classes are defined in Figure 45-3.

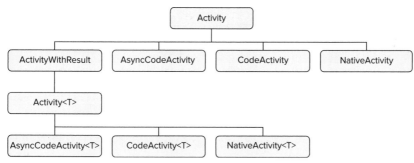

FIGURE 45-3

The `Activity` class is the root for all workflow activities, and typically you derive custom activities from the second tier. To create a simple activity like the `WriteLine` activity previously mentioned, you would derive from `CodeActivity` because this class has just enough functionality for your write line clone to function. Activities that execute and return some form of a result should derive from the `ActivityWithResult` class—you should use the generic `Activity<TResult>` class here because that provides a strongly typed `Result` property.

Deciding which base class to derive from can be the main battle when constructing custom activities, and you see examples in this chapter to assist with choosing the right base class.

For an activity to do something, it typically overrides the `Execute` method, which has a number of different signatures depending on the base class chosen. These signatures are shown in the following table.

BASE CLASS	EXECUTE METHOD
AsyncCodeActivity	IAsyncResult BeginExecute(AsyncCodeActivityContext, AsyncCallback, object) void EndExecute(AsyncCodeActivityContext, IAsyncResult)
CodeActivity	void Execute (CodeActivityContext)
NativeActivity	void Execute (NativeActivityContext)
AsyncCode Activity<TResult>	IAsyncResult BeginExecute(AsyncCodeActivityContext, AsyncCallback, object) TResult EndExecute(AsyncCodeActivityContext, IAsyncResult)
CodeActivity<TResult>	TResult Execute (CodeActivityContext)
NativeActivity<TResult>	void Execute (NativeActivityContext)

Here you may notice that the parameters passed into the `Execute` methods differ in that there are type-specific execution context parameters used. In WF 3.*x*, there was a single class used (the `ActivityExecutionContext`); however, in WF 4.*x* you can use different contexts for different classes of activity.

The main difference is that the `CodeActivityContext` (and by derivation the `AsyncCodeActivityContext`) has a limited set of functionality compared with the `NativeActivityContext`. This means that activities deriving from `CodeActivity` and `AsyncCodeActivity` can do far less with their container. For example, the `WriteLine` activity presented earlier needs to write only to the console. Therefore, it doesn't need access to its runtime environment. A more complex activity might need to schedule other child activities or communicate with other systems, in which case you must derive from `NativeActivity` to access the full runtime. You revisit this topic when you create your own custom activities.

Numerous standard activities are provided with WF, and the following sections provide examples of some of these together with scenarios in which you might use these activities. WF 4.*x* uses three main assemblies" `System.Activities.dll`, `System.Activities.Core.Presentation.dll`, and `System.Activities .Presentation.dll`.

If Activity

As its name implies, this activity acts like an `If-Else` statement in C#. When you drop an `If` onto the design surface, you see an activity, as shown in Figure 45-4. The `If` is a composite activity that contains two child activity placeholders, one for the Then part and one for the Else part.

The `If` activity (refer to Figure 45-4) also includes a glyph indicating that there is a validation error with the activity; in this instance it is saying that the

FIGURE 45-4

`Condition` property needs to be defined. This condition is evaluated when the activity is executed. If it returns `True`, the `Then` branch executes; otherwise the `Else` branch will be called.

The `Condition` property is an expression that evaluates to a Boolean value, so you can include any expression here that is valid.

An expression can reference any variables defined in the workflow and also access many static classes available in the .NET framework. So you could, for example, define an expression based on the `Environment.Is64BitOperatingSystem` value, if that were crucial to some part of your workflow. Naturally, you can define arguments that are passed into the workflow and that can then be evaluated by an expression inside an `If` activity. Arguments and variables are covered in the section, "Arguments and Variables."

InvokeMethod Activity

This is one of the most useful activities in the box because it enables you to execute code that already exists and effectively wrap that code within the execution semantics of a workflow. It's typical to have a lot of preexisting code, and this activity enables you to call that code directly from within a workflow.

There are two ways that you can use `InvokeMethod` to call code; which method you use depends on whether you want to call a static method or an instance method. If you call a static method, you need to define the `TargetType` and the `MethodName` parameters. However if you call an instance method, the `TargetObject` and `MethodName` properties are used. In this instance the `TargetObject` could be created inline, or it could be a variable defined somewhere within the workflow. The example code in the `02-ParallelExecution` sample shows both modes to use the `InvokeMethod` activity.

If you need to pass arguments to the method you're invoking, you can define these using the `Parameters` collection. The order of the parameters in the collection must match the order of the parameters to the method. In addition, there is a `Result` property set to the return value of the function call. You can bind this to a variable within the workflow to use the value as appropriate.

Parallel Activity

The `Parallel` activity is rather poorly named because, at first sight, you might think that on a multiprocessor machine this activity would schedule its children in true parallel; however, that isn't the case apart from some special circumstances.

After you drop a `Parallel` activity onto the design surface, you can then drop in other subordinate activities, as shown in Figure 45-5.

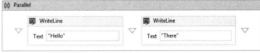

FIGURE 45-5

These child activities can be singular activities, as in Figure 45-5, or they can form a composite activity, such as a `Sequence` or another `Parallel` activity.

At runtime, the `Parallel` activity schedules each immediate child for execution. The underlying runtime execution engine then schedules these children in a first in, first out (FIFO) manner, thereby providing the illusion of parallel execution; however, they run only on a single thread.

To include true parallel execution, the activities you drop into the `Parallel` activity must be derived from the `AsyncCodeActivity` class. The sample code in `02_ParallelExecution` includes an example that shows how to asynchronously process code within two branches of a `Parallel` activity. Figure 45-6 shows the use of two `InvokeMethod` activities within a `Parallel` activity.

FIGURE 45-6

The `InvokeMethod` activities used here call two simple methods, `DoJob1` and `DoJob2`, which sleep for 2 and 3 seconds, respectively. To run these methods asynchronously, there is one final change needed. The `InvokeMethod` activity has a `Boolean RunAsynchronously` property that defaults to `False`. Setting this in the UI to `True` then calls the target method asynchronously, thereby enabling the `Parellel` activity to execute more than one activity at the same time. With a uniprocessor machine, two threads can execute, giving the illusion of simultaneous execution; however, on a multiprocessor machine, these threads may be scheduled on different cores, thereby providing true parallel execution. If you create your own activities, it is worthwhile creating these as asynchronous activities because then the end user can get the benefits of true parallel execution.

Delay Activity

Business processes often need to wait for a period before completing. Consider using a workflow for expense approval. Your workflow might send an e-mail to your immediate manager asking him to approve your expense claim. The workflow then enters a waiting state in which it waits for approval (or horror of horrors, rejection). But it would also be nice to define a timeout so that if no response is returned within, say, one day, the expense claim is then routed to the next manager up the chain of command.

The Delay activity can form part of this scenario. (The other part is the Pick activity defined in the next section.) Its job is to wait for a predefined time before continuing execution of the workflow.

The Delay activity contains a Duration property, which can be set to a discrete TimeSpan value, but because it is defined as an expression, this value could be linked to a variable within the workflow or computed from some other values as required.

When a workflow is executed, it enters an Idle state, in which it runs a Delay activity. Workflows that are idle are candidates for persistence—this is where the workflow instance data is stored within a persistent medium (such as an SQL Server database), and the workflow can then be unloaded from memory. This conserves system resources because only running workflows need to be in memory at any given time. Any workflows delayed will be persisted to disk.

Pick Activity

A common programming construct is to wait for one of a set of possible events—one example of this is the WaitAny method of the WaitHandle class in the System.Threading namespace. The Pick activity is the way to do this in a workflow because it can define any number of branches, and each branch can wait for a trigger action to occur before running. After a trigger has been fired, the other activities within that branch execute.

As a concrete example, consider the expense claims procedure outlined in the previous section. Here, you have a Pick activity with three branches: one to deal with accepted claims, one to deal with rejected claims, and a third to deal with a timeout.

The example is available in the 03_PickDemo code in the download. This contains a sample workflow consisting of a Pick activity and three branches. When it is run, you are prompted to accept or reject the claim. If 10 seconds or more elapses, it closes this prompt and runs the delay branch instead.

In the example, the DisplayPrompt activity is used as the first activity in the workflow. This calls a method defined on an interface that would prompt the manager for approval or rejection. Because this functionality is defined as an interface, the prompt could be an e-mail, an IM message, or any other manner of notifying your manager that an expense claim needs to be processed. The workflow then executes the Pick, which awaits input from this external interface (either an approval or a rejection) and also waits on a delay.

When the pick executes, it effectively queues a wait on the first activity in each branch, and when one event is triggered, this cancels all other waiting events and then processes the rest of the branch where the event was raised. So, in the instance in which the expense report is approved, the WaitForAccept activity completes, and then the next action is to write out a confirmation message. If, however, your manager rejects the claim, the WaitForReject activity completes, and in the example this then outputs a rejection message.

Lastly, if neither the WaitForAccept nor WaitForReject activities completes, the WaitForTimeout ultimately completes after its delay expires, and the expense report could then be routed to another manager—potentially looking up that person in Active Directory. In the example, a dialog displays to the user when the DisplayPrompt activity executes, so if the delay executes, you also need to close the dialog, which is the purpose of the activity named ClosePrompt in Figure 45-7.

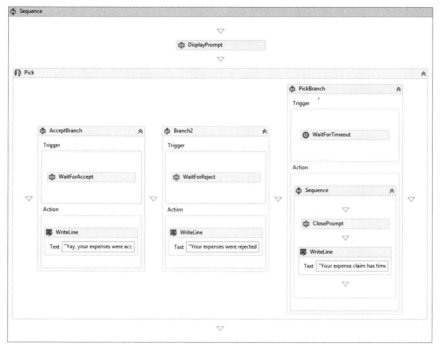

FIGURE 45-7

Some concepts used in that example have not been covered yet—such as how to write custom activities or waiting on external events; however, these topics are covered in the section, "Custom Activities."

CUSTOM ACTIVITIES

So far, you have used activities defined within the `System.Activities` namespace. In this section, you learn how to create custom activities and extend these activities to provide a good user experience at both design time and runtime.

To begin, you create a `DebugWrite` activity that can be used to output a line of text to the console in debug builds. Although this is a trivial example, it will be expanded to show the full gamut of options available for custom activities using this example. When creating custom activities, you can simply construct a class within a workflow project; however, it is preferable to construct your custom activities inside a separate assembly because then your activities will be reusable. For this reason, you should create a simple class library project to construct your custom activities within. The code for this example is available in the 04_ CustomActivities project.

A simple activity, such as the `DebugWrite` activity, will be derived directly from the `CodeActivity` base class. The following code shows a constructed activity class and defines a `Message` property that displays when the activity executes (code file `04_CustomActivities/Activities/DebugWrite.cs`):

```
using System;
using System.Activities;
using System.Diagnostics;
namespace Activities
{
  public class DebugWrite : CodeActivity
  {
    [Description("The message output to the debug stream")]
```

```
      public InArgument<string> Message { get; set; }
      protected override void Execute(CodeActivityContext context)
      {
        Debug.WriteLine(Message.Get(context));
      }
    }
  }
```

When a `CodeActivity` is scheduled for execution, its `Execute` method is called—this is where the activity actually needs to do something.

In the example, you defined the `Message` property, which looks like a regular .NET property; however, its usage inside the `Execute` method may be unfamiliar. One of the many changes made in WF 4 is where state data is stored. Within WF 3.*x*, it was common to use standard .NET properties and store activity data within the activity. The problem with that method was that this storage was effectively opaque to the workflow runtime engine. so to persist a workflow, you need to perform binary persistence on all constructed activities to faithfully restore their data.

With WF 4, all data is stored outside of the individual activities—so the model here is that to get the value of an argument, you ask the context for the value, and to set the value of an argument, you provide the new value to the context. In this way the workflow engine can track changes to state as the workflow executes and potentially store only the changes between persistence points rather than the entire workflow data.

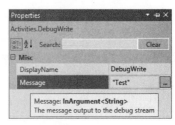

The `[Description]` attribute defined on the `Message` property is used within the property grid in Visual Studio to provide extra information about the property, as shown in Figure 45-8.

FIGURE 45-8

As it stands, the activity is perfectly usable; however, several areas should be addressed to make this more user-friendly. As you have seen with activities such as the `Pick` earlier in the chapter, an activity may have some mandatory properties that, when not defined, produce an error glyph on the design surface. To get the same behavior from your activity, you need to extend the code.

Activity Validation

When an activity is placed on the design surface, the Designer looks in two places for validation information. The simplest form of validation is to add a `[RequiredArgument]` attribute to the argument property. If the argument is not defined, the exclamation mark glyph is shown to the right of the activity name, as in Figure 45-9.

FIGURE 45-9

If you hover over the glyph, a tooltip displays that states Value for a Required Activity Argument "Message" Was Not Supplied. This is a compilation error, so you need to define a value for this argument before you can execute your application.

In the case where multiple properties may be related, you can override the `CacheMetadata` method to add on some extra validation code. This method is called prior to the activity being executed; within it you can check that mandatory arguments are defined and optionally add extra metadata to the passed argument. You can also add extra validation errors (or warnings) by calling one of the `AddValidationError` overrides on the `CodeActivityMetadata` object passed to the `CacheMetadata` method.

Now that you have completed the activity validation, the next thing to do is to change the rendering behavior of the activity because the current Designer experience is provided for you, and it could be made more interesting.

Designers

When an activity is rendered onscreen, it is typical to associate a designer with the activity. The job of the designer is to provide the onscreen representation of that activity, and in WF this representation is done in

XAML. If you haven't used XAML before to create user interfaces, look at Chapter 35, "Core WPF," before continuing.

The design-time experience for an activity is typically created in a separate assembly from the activity because this design experience is unnecessary at runtime. Visual Studio includes an Activity Designer Library project type that is an ideal starting point because when you create a project using this template, you're provided with a default activity designer that you can then alter as appropriate.

Within the XAML for your designer, you can provide anything you want—including animations. Less is usually more for user interfaces, so look at the preexisting activities to understand what is appropriate.

First, create a simple designer and associate this with the DebugWrite activity. The code that follows (code file 04_CustomActivities/Activities.Design/DebugWriteDesigner.xaml) shows the template created for you when you add an activity designer to your project (or when you construct a new activity designer library project):

```
<sap:ActivityDesigner x:Class="Activities.<Presentation.DebugWriteDesigner"
    xmlns="http://schemas.microsoft.com/winfx/2006/xaml/presentation"
    xmlns:x="http://schemas.microsoft.com/winfx/2006/xaml"
    xmlns:sap="clr-namespace:System.Activities.Presentation;
            assembly=System.Activities.Presentation"
    xmlns:sapv="clr-namespace:System.Activities.Presentation.View;
            assembly=System.Activities.Presentation">
  <Grid>
  </Grid>
</sap:ActivityDesigner>
```

The XAML created simply constructs a grid and also includes some imported namespaces, which may be needed by your activity. Obviously, there is little content within the template, so to begin add in a label and a text box that can define the message.

```
<Grid>
  <Grid.ColumnDefinitions>
    <ColumnDefinition Width="Auto"/>
    <ColumnDefinition Width="*"/>
  </Grid.ColumnDefinitions>
  <TextBlock Text="Message" Margin="0,0,5,0"/>
  <TextBox Text="{Binding Path=ModelItem.Message, Mode=TwoWay}"
    Grid.Column="1"/>
</Grid>
```

The XAML here constructs a binding between the Message property of the activity and the text box. Within the designer XAML, you can always reference the activity being designed by using the ModelItem reference.

To associate the designer previously defined with the DebugWrite activity, you also need to alter the activity and add on a Designer attribute. (You can also implement the IRegisterMetadata interface, which isn't covered further in this chapter.)

```
[Designer("Activities.Presentation.DebugWriteDesigner, Activities.Presentation")]
public class DebugWrite : CodeActivity
{
    . . .
}
```

Here, you used the [Designer] attribute to define the link between the designer and the activity. It's good practice to use the string version of this attribute because that ensures that there is no reference to the design assembly within the activity assembly.

Now when you use an instance of the DebugWrite activity within Visual Studio, you see something like Figure 45-10.

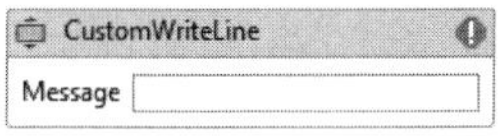

FIGURE 45-10

The problem with this, however, is the Message property. It's not showing the value defined within the property grid, and if you try to set a value by typing it into the text box, you receive an exception. The reason is that you're trying to bind a simple text value to an `InArgument<string>` type, and to do that, you need to use another couple built-in classes that come with WF: the `ExpressionTextBox` and the `ArgumentToExpressionConverter`. The full XAML for the designer is now as follows. You can see the lines that have been added or modified in boldface.

```xml
<sap:ActivityDesigner x:Class="Activities.Presentation.DebugWriteDesigner"
  xmlns="http://schemas.microsoft.com/winfx/2006/xaml/presentation"
  xmlns:x="http://schemas.microsoft.com/winfx/2006/xaml"
  xmlns:sap="clr-namespace:System.Activities.Presentation;
      assembly=System.Activities.Presentation"
  xmlns:sapv="clr-namespace:System.Activities.Presentation.View;
      assembly=System.Activities.Presentation"
  xmlns:sadc="clr-namespace:System.Activities.Presentation.Converters;
      assembly=System.Activities.Presentation">
  <sap:ActivityDesigner.Resources>
    <sadc:ArgumentToExpressionConverter x:Key="argConverter"/>
  </sap:ActivityDesigner.Resources>
  <Grid>
    <Grid.ColumnDefinitions>
      <ColumnDefinition Width="Auto"/>
      <ColumnDefinition Width="*"/>
    </Grid.ColumnDefinitions>
    <TextBlock Text="Message" Margin="0,0,5,0" />
    <sapv:ExpressionTextBox Grid.Column="1"
        Expression="{Binding Path=ModelItem.Message, Mode=TwoWay,
                    Converter={StaticResource argConverter},
                    ConverterParameter=In}"
        OwnerActivity="{Binding ModelItem}"/>
  </Grid>
</sap:ActivityDesigner>
```

You included a new namespace in the file: the `System.Activities.Presentation.View`. This includes the converter used to convert between an expression onscreen and the `Message` property of the activity. This is the `ArgumentToExpressionConverter`, which has been added to the resources of the XAML file.

Then replace the standard `TextBox` control with an `ExpressionTextBox`. This control enables the user to enter expressions and simple text, so the `DebugWrite` activity could include an expression combining many values from the running workflow, rather than just a simple text string. With those changes in place, the activity behaves more like the built-in activities.

If you upgrade a solution from .NET 4 to .NET 4.5, you might be surprised to see Enter a VB Expression in any expression text boxes that you have in your activities for existing workflows, and Enter a C# Expression in any new workflows you create. WF 4.5 has an attribute defined in the XAML that if absent shows the VB expression prompt. If you look at the XAML for a new workflow, you can see the following directive.

```
sap:2010:ExpressionActivityEditor.ExpressionActivityEditor="C#"
```

If this is omitted, the VB expression displays. Needless to say, working out this foible of WF 4.5 cost me a lot of time!

Custom Composite Activities

A common requirement with activities is to create a composite activity—that is, an activity that contains other child activities. You have already seen examples, such as the `Pick` activity and the `Parallel` activity. The execution of a composite activity is entirely up to the programmer—you could, for example, have a random activity that schedules only one of its children, or an activity that bypasses some children based on the current day of the week. The simplest execution pattern would be to execute all children, but as the developer you can decide how child activities are executed and also when your activity is complete.

This example creates a "retry" activity. It is quite common to try an operation, and if it fails, retry it a number of times before having it fail. The pseudo-code for this activity is as follows:

```
    int iterationCount = 0;
    bool looping = true;
    while ( looping )
    {
      try
      {
        // Execute the activity here
        looping = false;
      }
      catch (Exception ex)
      {
        iterationCount += 1;
        if ( iterationCount >= maxRetries )
          rethrow;
      }
    }
```

You need to replicate the preceding code as an activity and insert the activity you want to execute where the comment is placed. You might consider doing this all within the Execute method of a custom activity. However, there is another way: You can code the whole lot using other activities. Create a custom activity that contains a "hole" into which the end user can place the activity that will be retried, and then a maximum retry count property. The code that follows shows how to do this (code file 04_CustomActivities/Activities/Retry.cs):

```
    public class Retry : Activity
    {
      public Activity Body { get; set; }
      [RequiredArgument]
      public InArgument<int> NumberOfRetries { get; set; }
      public Retry()
      {
        Variable<int> iterationCount =
          new Variable<int> ( "iterationCount", 0 );
        Variable<bool> looping = new Variable<bool> ( "looping", true );
        this.Implementation = () =>
        {
          return new While
          {
            Variables = { iterationCount, looping },
            Condition = new VariableValue<bool> { Variable = looping },
            Body = new TryCatch
            {
              Try = new Sequence
              {
                Activities =
                {
                  this.Body,
                  new Assign
                  {
                    To = new OutArgument<bool> ( looping ),
                    Value = new InArgument<bool> { Expression = false }
                  }
                }
              },
              Catches =
              {
                new Catch<Exception>
                {
                  Action = new ActivityAction<Exception>
                  {
                    Handler = new Sequence
                    {
```

```
                            Activities =
                            {
                              new Assign
                              {
                                To = new OutArgument<int>(iterationCount),
                                Value = new InArgument<int>
                                  (ctx => iterationCount.Get(ctx) + 1)
                              },
                              new If
                              {
                                Condition = new InArgument<bool>
                                  (env=>iterationCount.Get(env) >=
                                    NumberOfRetries.Get(env)),
                                Then = new Rethrow()
                              }
                            }
                          }
                        }
                      }
                    }
                  }
                };
              };
            }
          }
```

Phew!

First, you defined a `Body` property of type `Activity`, which is the activity executed within the retry loop. Then define the `RetryCount` property, which is used to define the number of times the operation will be tried.

This custom activity derives directly from the `Activity` class and provides the implementation as a function. When a workflow is executed that contains this activity, it effectively executes the function, which provides a runtime execution path similar to the pseudo-code defined earlier. Within the constructor, create the local variables used by the activity and then construct a set of activities that matches the pseudo-code. The code for this example is also available in the `04_CustomActivities` solution.

From the preceding code, you can infer that you can create workflows without XAML—there is no design experience (that is, you can't drag and drop activities to generate code). However, if code is what you prefer, there's no reason not to use it instead of XAML.

Now that you have the custom composite activity, you also need to define a designer. What's needed here is an activity that has a placeholder into which you can drop another activity. If you look at other standard activities, there are several that exhibit a similar behavior, such as the `If` and `Pick` activities. Ideally, you would like the activity to work in a similar manner to the built-in activities, so it's time to look at their implementations.

If you use Reflector to poke around inside the workflow libraries, you'll find a distinct lack of any designer XAML. This is because it's been compiled into the assemblies as a set of resources. You can use Reflector to look at these resources, and the current version (v7.5) includes the capability to decompile BAML resources so that you can read them.

In Reflector, load up the `System.Activities.Presentation` assembly, and then navigate to the Resources node in the treeview and open out `System.Activites.Presentation.g.resources`. This presents you with a list of all the BAML resources in the currently loaded assemblies, and you can then look at an appropriate sample to see some sample XAML.

The author used this method to learn about the XAML that was used for the built-in activities, which helped to construct the example for the Retry activity shown in Figure 45-11.

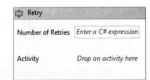

FIGURE 45-11

The key to this activity is the `WorkflowItemPresenter` class, which is used in the XAML to define the placeholder for the child activity. This is defined as follows:

```
<sap:WorkflowItemPresenter IsDefaultContainer="True"
    AllowedItemType="{x:Type sa:Activity}"
    HintText="Drop an activity here" MinWidth="100" MinHeight="60"
    Item="{Binding Path=ModelItem.Body, Mode=TwoWay}"
    Grid.Column="1" Grid.Row="1" Margin="2">
```

This control is bound to the `Body` property of the `Retry` activity, and the `HintText` defines the help text shown when no child activity has been added to the control. The XAML also includes some styles used to show the expanded or contracted version of the designer—this ensures that the activity works the same way as the built-in activities. All the code and XAML for this example is available in the `04_CustomActivities` solution.

WORKFLOWS

Up to this point, the chapter has concentrated on activities but has not discussed workflows. A *workflow* is simply a list of activities, and indeed a workflow is just another type of activity. Using this model simplifies the runtime engine because the engine needs to know how to execute one type of object—that being anything derived from the `Activity` class.

You've already seen the `WorkflowInvoker` class, which can execute a workflow synchronously, but as mentioned at the time this is only one of the ways that a workflow can be executed. There are three different options for executing workflows, and each has different capabilities. Before getting into the other methods to execute workflows, you must delve into arguments and variables.

Arguments and Variables

A workflow can be considered a program, and one of the facets of any programming language is the capability to create variables and pass arguments into and out of that program. Naturally, WF supports both constructs, and this section shows you how you can define both arguments and variables.

To begin, assume that the workflow processes an insurance policy, so a likely argument to pass to the workflow would be the policy ID. To define an argument to a workflow, you need to go into the Designer and click the Arguments button on the bottom left. This brings up a list of arguments defined for the workflow, as shown in Figure 45-12, and here you can also add your own.

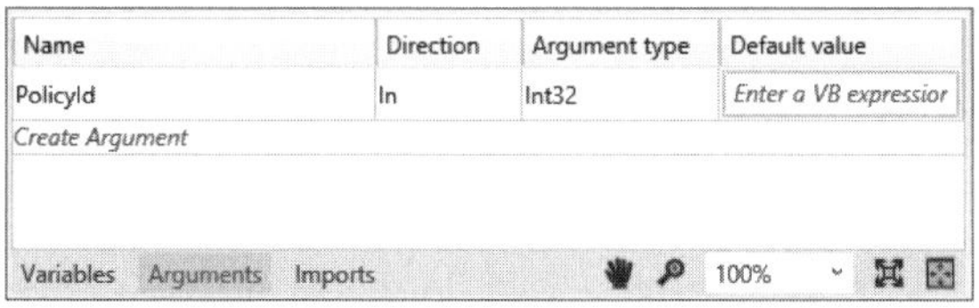

Name	Direction	Argument type	Default value
PolicyId	In	Int32	Enter a VB expression
Create Argument			

| Variables | Arguments | Imports | | | 100% | | |

FIGURE 45-12

To define an argument, you need to specify the Name, Direction (which can be `In`, `Out`, or `InOut`) and the data type for that argument. You can optionally specify a default value, which will be used if the argument is not provided.

The direction of the argument is used to define whether the argument is expected as an input to the workflow, as an output from the workflow, or in the case of the `InOut` direction, as both an input and output.

The first section of this chapter described using the `WorkflowInvoker` class to execute a workflow. You can use several overrides of the `Invoke` method to pass arguments into the workflow. They are passed as a dictionary of name/value pairs, where the name must match the argument's name exactly—this match is

case-sensitive. The following code passes a `PolicyId` value into a workflow (code file 05_ArgsAndVars/
Program.cs):

```
Dictionary<string, object> parms = new Dictionary<string, object>();
parms.Add("PolicyId", 123);
WorkflowInvoker.Invoke(new PolicyFlow(), parms);
```

This then invokes the workflow and passes the `PolicyId` from the dictionary to the named parameter. If
you supply a name in the dictionary for which an argument does not exist, then an `ArgumentException`
will be thrown. Conversely, if you don't supply the value for an `In` argument, no exception is thrown. This is
the wrong way around—you would expect an argument exception to be thrown for any `In` arguments that
were not defined and would prefer no exception to be thrown if you passed in too many arguments.

When a workflow completes, you may want to retrieve output arguments. To do this, there is a specific
override of the `WorkflowInvoker.Invoke` method that returns a dictionary. This dictionary contains just
the `Out` or `InOut` arguments.

Within the workflow, you may then want to define variables. This wasn't easy to do in XAML workflows in
WF 3.x; however, in WF 4 this has been addressed, and you can easily define parameters in the XAML.

As in any programming language, workflow variables have the notion of scope. You can define "globally"
scoped variables by defining them on the root activity of the workflow. These variables are available by all
activities within the workflow, and their lifetime is tied to that of the workflow.

You can also define variables on individual activities, and in this case these variables are only available to
the activity that the variable is defined on and also children of that activity. After an activity has completed,
its variables go out of scope and are no longer accessible.

WorkflowApplication

Although `WorkflowInvoker` is a useful class for synchronous execution of workflows, you might need to
have long-running workflows that may persist to a database and need to be rehydrated at some point in the
future. If that's the case then you might want to use the `WorkflowApplication` class.

The `WorkflowApplication` class is similar to the `WorkflowRuntime` class that existed in Workflow 3 in
that it enables you to run a workflow and also respond to events that occur on that workflow instance.
Probably the simplest program you can write to use the `WorkflowApplication` class is shown here:

```
WorkflowApplication app = new WorkflowApplication(new Workflow1());
ManualResetEvent finished = new ManualResetEvent(false);
app.Completed = (completedArgs) => { finished.Set(); };
app.Run();
finished.WaitOne();
```

This constructs a workflow application instance and then hooks up to the `Completed` delegate of that
instance to set a manual reset event. The `Run` method is called to start the workflow execution, and lastly
the code waits for the event to be triggered.

This shows one of the main differences between `WorkflowExecutor` and `WorkflowApplication`—the
latter is asynchronous. When you call `Run`, the system uses a thread pool thread to execute the workflow
rather than the calling thread. Thus, you need some form of synchronization to ensure that the application
hosting the workflow doesn't exit before the workflow completes.

A typical long-running workflow may have many periods when it is dormant—the execution behavior for
most workflows can best be described as periods of episodic execution. There is typically some work done
at the start of the workflow; then it waits on some input or a delay. After this input has been received, it
processes up to the next wait state.

So, when a workflow is dormant, it would be ideal to unload it from memory and only reload it when an
event triggers the workflow to continue. To do this, you need to add an `InstanceStore` object to the
`WorkflowApplication` and also make some other minor alterations to the preceding code. There is one
implementation of the abstract `InstanceStore` class in the framework—the `SqlWorkflowInstanceStore`.

To use this class, you first need a database, and the scripts for this can be found by default in the `C:\ Windows\Microsoft.NET\Framework64\v4.0.30319\SQL\en` directory. Note that the version number is subject to change.

You can find a number of SQL files in this directory, but the two you need are: `SqlWorkflowInstanceStoreSchema.sql` and `SqlWorkflowInstanceStoreLogic.sql`. You can run these against an existing database or create an entirely new database as appropriate, and you can use a full SQL server installation or an SQL Express installation.

After you have a database, you need to make some alterations to the hosting code. First, you need to construct an instance of the `SqlWorkflowInstanceStore` and then add this to the workflow application (code file `06_WorkflowApplication/Program.cs`)

```
SqlWorkflowInstanceStore store = new SqlWorkflowInstanceStore
  (ConfigurationManager.ConnectionStrings["db"].ConnectionString);
AutoResetEvent finished = new AutoResetEvent(false);
WorkflowApplication app = new WorkflowApplication(new Workflow1());
app.Completed = (e) => { finished.Set(); };
app.PersistableIdle = (e) => { return PersistableIdleAction.Unload; };
app.InstanceStore = store;
app.Run();
finished.WaitOne();
```

The bold lines are those added to the previous example. You can also notice that the addition of an event handler to the `PersistableIdle` delegate on the workflow application. When a workflow executes, it runs as many activities as it can, until there is no more work to do. At that point, it transitions to an `Idle` state, and an idle workflow is a candidate for persistence. The `PersistableIdle` delegate determines what should happen to an idle workflow. The default is to do nothing; however, you can also specify `PersistableIdleAction.Persist`, which can take a copy of the workflow and store that in the database but still leave the workflow in memory, or you can specify `PersistableIdleAction.Unload`, which persists and then unloads the workflow.

You can also request persistence of a workflow by using the `Persist` activity, and indeed as a custom activity writer, you can also request persistence if you have derived from `NativeActivity` by calling the `RequestPersist` method of the `NativeActivityContext`.

You now have a problem—you have the ability to unload a workflow from memory and store it in the persistence store, but as yet you haven't described how to retrieve it from the store and get it to execute again.

Bookmarks

The traditional use of a bookmark is to mark a page in a book, so you can resume reading from the same point. In the context of a workflow, a bookmark specifies a place in which you would like to resume running that workflow, and bookmarks are typically used when you're waiting for external input.

For example, you might write an application that deals with insurance quotes. An end user might go online to produce a quotation, and as you can imagine, there would be a workflow associated with that quotation. The quotation might be valid for only 30 days, so you would like to invalidate the quote after that point. Similarly, you might request proof of a no-claims discount and cancel the policy if that proof didn't arrive within a specified time. This workflow then has a number of periods of execution, and other times when it is dormant and could be unloaded from memory. Before being unloaded, however, you must define a point in the workflow where processing can be resumed, and this is where bookmarks are used.

To define a bookmark, you need a custom activity that derives from `NativeActivity` (code file `06_Workflow Application/CustomActivities/Task.cs`). You can then create a bookmark within the `Execute` method, and when the bookmark has been resumed, your code continues. The example activity defines a simplistic `Task` activity that creates a bookmark, and on resumption at the point of that bookmark, the activity completes.

```
public class Task : NativeActivity<Boolean>
{
  [RequiredArgument]
  public InArgument<string> TaskName { get; set; }
```

```
    protected override bool CanInduceIdle
    {
      get { return true; }
    }
    protected override void Execute(NativeActivityContext context)
    {
      context.CreateBookmark(TaskName.Get(context),
        new BookmarkCallback(OnTaskComplete));
    }
    private void OnTaskComplete(NativeActivityContext context,
        Bookmark bookmark, object state)
    {
      bool taskOK = Convert.ToBoolean(state);
      this.Result.Set(context, taskOK);
    }
  }
```

The call to `CreateBookmark` passes the name of the bookmark and also a callback function. This callback executes when the bookmark resumes. The callback is passed an arbitrary object, which in this case is a `Boolean` because you decided that each task should report success or failure, and you can then use this to decide on the next steps in the workflow. There's nothing to stop you from passing any object into the workflow—it could be a complex type with many fields.

So that's the activity written; you now need to alter the hosting code to resume at the point of the bookmarks. But there's another problem. How does the hosting code know that a workflow has created a bookmark? If it's the host's responsibility to resume from the bookmark, it needs to know that one exists.

The `Task` you created needs to do some more work—telling the outside world that a task has been created. In a production system, this would typically result in an entry being stored in a queue table, and this queue would be presented to the call center staff as a job list.

Communicating with the host is the subject of the next section.

Extensions

An extension is simply a class or interface added to the runtime context of a workflow application. In WF 3.*x* these were called Services; however, that clashed with WCF Services, so these have been renamed *extensions* in WF 4.

You typically define an interface for your extensions and then provide a runtime implementation of this interface. Your activities simply call the interface, and this allows the implementation to change as necessary. A good example of an extension is something that sends an e-mail. You could create a `SendEmail` activity that calls the extension within its `Execute` method, and then you can define an SMTP-based e-mail extension or an Exchange-based outlook extension to actually send the e-mail at runtime. Your activity wouldn't need to be changed to use any e-mail provider—you can just plug in a new one by altering the application configuration file.

For the task sample, you need an extension that will be notified when the `Task` activity is about to wait at its bookmark. This could write the name of the bookmark and other pertinent information into a database so that a task queue could then be presented to the user. Use the following interface to define this extension (code file `06_WorkflowApplication/SharedInterfaces/ITaskExtension.cs`):

```
public interface ITaskExtension
{
    void ExecuteTask(string taskName);
}
```

The task activity can then be updated to notify the task extension that it's executing by modifying the `Execute` method as follows (code file `06_WorkflowApplication/CustomActivities/Task.cs`):

```
protected override void Execute(NativeActivityContext context)
{
    context.CreateBookmark(TaskName.Get(context),
        new BookmarkCallback(OnTaskComplete));
```

```
context.GetExtension<ITaskExtension>().
    ExecuteTask(TaskName.Get(context));
}
```

The context object passed to the Execute method is queried for the ITaskExtension interface and then the code calls the ExecuteTask method. The WorkflowApplication maintains a collection of extensions, so you can create a class that implements this extension interface, which can then be used to maintain the list of tasks. You could then construct and execute a new workflow, and each task would then notify the extension when it was executed. Some other process might look at the task list and present this to the end user.

To keep things simple in the sample code, you created just one workflow instance. This instance contains a Task activity followed by an If, which outputs a message according to whether the user accepts or rejects the task.

Putting It All Together

Now you can run, persist, and unload a workflow, and also deliver events into that workflow via bookmarks; the last part reloads the workflow. When using WorkflowApplication, you can call Load and pass through the unique ID of the workflow. Every workflow has a unique ID that can be retrieved from the WorkflowApplication object by calling the Id property. So, in pseudo-code, the workflow-hosting application is as follows (code file 06_WorkflowApplication/Program.cs):

```
WorkflowApplication app = BuildApplication();
Guid id = app.Id;
app.Run();
// Wait for a while until a task is created, then reload the workflow
app = BuildApplication();
app.Load(id);
app.ResumeBookmark()
```

The sample code provided is more complex than the preceding because it also includes an implementation of the ITaskExtension interface, but the code follows the earlier pattern. You may notice two calls to the BuildApplication method. This is one used in the code to construct a WorkflowApplication instance and to set up all required properties, such as the InstanceStore and the delegates for Completed and PersistableIdle. After the first call, execute the Run method. This begins execution of a new instance of the workflow.

The second time the application is loaded is after a persistence point, so by that point the workflow has been unloaded; hence, the application instance is also essentially dead. Then construct a new WorkflowApplication instance, but instead of calling Run, call the Load method, which uses the persistence provider to load up an existing instance from the database. This instance is then resumed by calling the ResumeBookmark function.

If you run the example, you see a prompt onscreen. Although that prompt is there, the workflow is persisted and unloaded, and you can check this by running SQL Server Management Studio and executing the command, as shown in Figure 45-13.

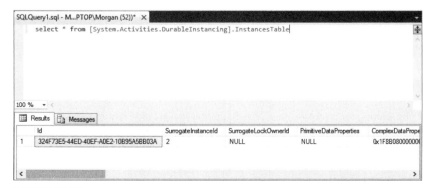

FIGURE 45-13

Workflow instances are stored within the `InstancesTable` of the `System.Activities` `.DurableInstancing` schema. The entry shown in Figure 45-13 is the persisted instance of the workflow running on the author's machine.

When you continue the workflow will eventually complete, and at that point the workflow will be deleted from the instances table because there's an option on the instance store exposed as the `InstanceCompletionAction`, which by default is set to be `DeleteAll`. This ensures that any data stored in the database for a given workflow instance will be deleted after that workflow completes. This is a sensible default because after a workflow completes, you would normally not expect any data to hang around. You can change this option when you define the instance store by setting the instance completion action to `DeleteNothing`.

If you now continue running the test application and then retry the SQL command from Figure 45-13, the workflow instance has been deleted.

Hosting WCF Workflows

As previously mentioned there were three ways to host workflows—the last is to use the `WorkflowServiceHost` class, which exposes a workflow through WCF. One of the major areas that Workflow is destined to be used for is as the backend to WCF services. If you think about what a typical WCF service does, it's usually a bunch of related methods typically called in some sort of order. The main problem here is that you could call these methods in any order, and usually you need to define the ordering so that, for example, the order details are not uploaded before the order.

With Workflow you can easily expose WCF services that also have a notion of method ordering. The main classes you use here are the `Receive` and the `Send` activities. In the code for this example (which is available in the `07_WorkflowsAsServices` solution), the scenario used is an estate agent (a Realtor if you're in the US) who wants to upload information about a property to a website.

You can host workflows using WCF in two ways: either explicitly in your code by constructing an instance of `WorkflowServiceHost` (much like the regular WCF `ServiceHost` class). But you can also construct a service as a `.xamlx` file in which case the workflow will most likely be exposed using IIS or WAS. This option is used in the sample, but it's worth knowing that you can do this all manually if you need to.

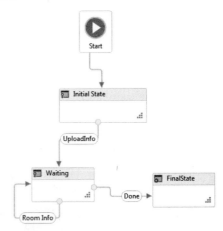

FIGURE 45-14

This example also showcases two new features of WF 4.5, the first is that you use a State Machine workflow, and the second is that the implementation of this workflow uses a WCF service contract that has been defined in a contract-first manner. The State Machine workflow type was missing in .NET 4 but has made a welcome return in the latest version of the framework, and it's a good fit for the example you write here. Figure 45-14 shows an overview of the state-machine that you create in this sample.

With a state-machine you have a start state, any number of intermediate states, and an optional end state. In addition to the states, there are also transitions, which await an event (typically an activity receiving some input) and then transition the state-machine to another state.

The state-machine works by waiting for a transition activity to complete. This then moves the state-machine into a new state. On entry to a state, you can call an activity, and on exit from a state, you can also execute an activity. The state-machine then waits for one of the transitions to complete and moves into the new state.

In the previous diagram the first state is marked as "Initial State". That has just one transition that waits for a message to come in over WCF. After this message has been received, the state-machine then moves to the "Waiting" state, which has two transitions. These map to the two operations that are then available on the WCF interface; either the user can send up details of a room, or they can indicate that the data upload is complete. The WCF service used in this example is modeled as follows (code file 07_WorkflowsAsServices/SharedInterfaces/IPropertyInformation.cs):

```
[ServiceContract(Namespace="http://www.morganskinner.com")]
public interface IPropertyInformation
{
    [OperationContract()]
    Guid UploadPropertyInformation(string ownerName, string address, float price);

    [OperationContract(IsOneWay=true)]
    void UploadRoomInformation(Guid propertyId, string roomName, float width,
      float length);

    [OperationContract(IsOneWay = true)]
    void DetailsComplete(Guid propertyId);
}
```

The UploadPropertyInformation call is the start of the state machine. This effectively creates a new workflow instance, transitions the state machine to the "Waiting" state and then awaits either a call to UploadRoomInformation or DetailsComplete.

To use an existing WCF service contract in WF, you need to display the context menu for a Workflow project and select the Import Service Contract item from the menu. This constructs activities for each operation in the service contract. If you want to see these activities, click the Show All Files toolbar button, and expand the ServiceContracts item for the current project in Visual Studio. This shows the service contract name (in the example, IPropertyInformation), and then show the activities that were automatically generated, as shown in Figure 45-15.

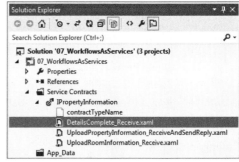

FIGURE 45-15

This shows that three activities have been created from the service contract, and these are subsequently used in the workflow to implement the service contract.

Correlation

The other important topic to understand with WCF workflows is how to make a call from the client and that call can find the right workflow instance on the server. If you look at the WCF service interface, you need to make a call to the server to initiate an upload using the UploadPropertyInformation operation.

This operation returns a unique ID, and this ID is passed back on the subsequent calls to UploadRoomInformation and DetailsComplete. To do this, Workflow has the concept of Correlation, which, simply put, enables you to use an arbitrary piece of information (or indeed, pieces of information) to route a call to the correct workflow instance. In the first call you return this ID, and as long as you use the same ID on the next call to the workflow, that is enough to find the correct workflow instance to route that message to.

To have correlation work you need two things: a CorrelationHandle and a correlation initializer. The handle is simply a variable that you defined with a suitable scope (that is, outside of all activities that need it). The correlation initializer defines what item(s) are used either in the incoming or outgoing messages to uniquely identify one workflow instance from another.

In the example there is a CorrelationHandle defined as a variable on the root activity in the workflow. Then in the UploadInfo transition, there is a Receive/Send pair. The Receive has its CanCreateInstance property set to True, which tells Workflow that when the client calls the server, it is this operation that is permitted to be first in the chain of execution of a workflow. The Receive activity can read any data from the parameters passed to the service call (and store these away for later in the workflow if appropriate).

The `Send` activity used here sets up the correlation to the unique ID created within the workflow. In this case it uses an XPath expression, as shown in Figure 45-16, to extract the Guid sent back to the user as the return value of the `UploadPropertyInformation` method.

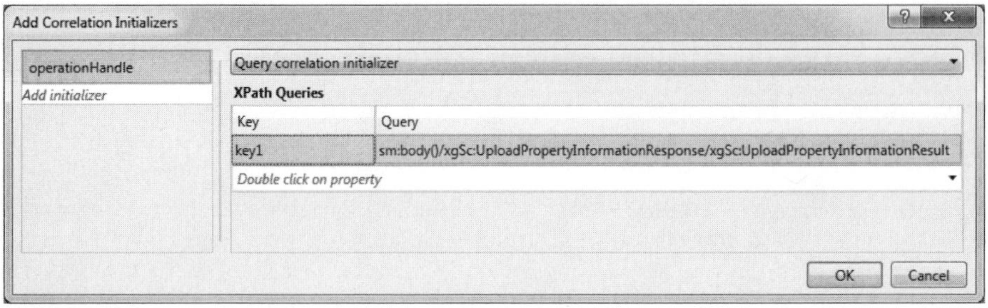

FIGURE 45-16

Now that you have effectively associated the workflow instance with this ID, you can use correlation again to allow subsequent calls to one of the other methods on the service contract, and these can find the right workflow instance as correlation is used here again, in this case to extract a value from the parameters passed to the operation(s) that process data on the server side. This is powerful; in Workflow 3.x you could use only the inbuilt Workflow Instance ID; however, in 4.x you can choose any unique parts of the data to allow a client call to find the right workflow instance.

Similarly, you can correlate on different data during the life of the workflow. So, you might return a Guid from the first call but then return a unique integer key from subsequent method invocations.

Calling Workflow Services

With a Workflow hosted as a `.xamlx` file, you need some way to call that workflow. This is the same as calling any standard WCF service in that you need to add a reference to that service. In this case the service is not addressed by a URL that ends in a `.svc` file, but instead it's a URL that ends with the `.xamlx` workflow definition.

The client can then interact with the service by making WCF calls. The only difference here is that a Workflow won't accept any call on that WCF interface at all times. The operation(s) that are valid at any specific time are dependent on the state of the workflow. When you initially call the workflow, you use the `UploadPropertyInformation` call, which due to the receiver of that call having its `CanCreateInstance` property set to true allows a new workflow instance to be created.

Then you can call either of the other methods on the interface because these are what the workflow instance is now awaiting.

The code download for this example includes a proxy class similar to that created with an add service reference. The author tends to create these in code because the process is more intuitive than using add service reference and also better to support a large development team, where a service interface can often change. Using the method here that change needs to be made only in one place, rather than regenerating multiple service references in multiple projects.

The code then creates an instance of this proxy class as follows:

```
PropertyInformationClient client = new PropertyInformationClient("state");
```

This uses an endpoint defined within the `app.config`:

```
<endpoint address="http://localhost:1353/StateService.xamlx"
          binding="basicHttpBinding"
          contract="SharedInterfaces.IPropertyInformation"
          name="state"/>
```

Here as you can see the address of the service ends with .xamlx, which indicates that the service is a Workflow rather than a standard WCF service.

Workflow Versioning

Because a workflow can be persisted and potentially run for a long time, you need a way to change a workflow. For example, consider a workflow that deals with insurance renewals. An instance of this workflow might run for every new policy taken out, and 10 months from the time the policy was taken out it might reactivate to then send out a renewal quotation, and, depending on the response from the customer, send out a reminder or two.

Now say that you implement a new customer contact mechanism that enables you to send text messages to inform customers of their renewal. What would you do with all the workflows already in the database?

Before WF 4.5 there were only two options and neither was particularly palatable. The first option was to ignore the change for any existing workflows and implement the change only in new workflow instances. The other was to cancel all existing instances and restart them. Neither of these options are what you would ideally like to do, and WF 4.5 adds a couple of new capabilities that can help in this area.

Dynamic Update

The Dynamic Update feature enables a persisted workflow instance to be changed to apply some new functionality to that workflow. There are several steps to undertake to update a workflow, which can be broken into two phases.

The first phase prepares to update your persisted workflows. Here you use the new `DynamicUpdateServices` class by calling the `PrepareForUpdate` method as shown in the following code. Then you alter the workflow as appropriate, such as adding new activities. The example has a new `WriteLine` activity and adds this to the end of the current workflow. After all changes have been made, you can then call the `CreateUpdateMap` method, which returns an instance of the `DynamicUpdateMap` class, which is used when loading existing instances to update them to the new workflow definition (code file `08_DynamicUpdate/Program.cs`):

```
Activity workflowDefinition = GetInitialWorkflow();
DynamicUpdateServices.PrepareForUpdate(workflowDefinition);

// Now update the workflow - add in a new activity
Sequence seq = workflowDefinition as Sequence;
seq.Activities.Add(new WriteLine { Text = "Second version of workflow" });

// And then after all the changes, create the map
return DynamicUpdateServices.CreateUpdateMap(workflowDefinition);
```

You can use an update map repeatedly to update workflow instances, which is why the author mentions there are two phases, the second being loading up existing workflows and upgrading them. The following snippet shows how you could load an existing workflow instance and use the upgrade map previously created to update that instance.

```
SqlWorkflowInstanceStore store = new SqlWorkflowInstanceStore(
  ConfigurationManager.ConnectionStrings["db"].ConnectionString);
WorkflowApplicationInstance instance = WorkflowApplication.GetInstance(id, store);
WorkflowApplication app = new WorkflowApplication(GetUpdatedWorkflow());
app.Load(instance, map);
app.Unload();
```

Here the `GetUpdatedWorkflow` method loads the new workflow definition, and the existing instance data is loaded into this new workflow definition using the `map` object to indicate how to move persistence data between the existing and new activities. As the workflow persistence data contains only the data and not the workflow definition, upgrading is merely an act to move persistence information between nodes in the workflow.

After a workflow has been upgraded, it must run against the new workflow definition. And to simplify the task to know what version a workflow is within the database, there is the new `WorkflowIdentity` class, which can be attached to a `WorkflowApplication` when the application is created. This information forms part of the persistence information of a workflow and can be accessed using the `DefinitionIdentity` property of the `WorkflowApplicationInstance` class. You could use this to iterate through all workflows in the persistence store to find which have been upgraded and which need to be altered.

Side-by-Side Workflows

When hosting workflows using the `WorkflowApplication` class, you can now include a `WorkflowIdentity` object, which allows you to associate version information with a workflow definition so that when that workflow is persisted to the database, the version information is also persisted. Then, when reading persisted workflow instances back from the database, you can find workflows of a given version so that you can map the runtime workflow definition in the persisted state of the workflow in the database.

To load and resume any workflow instance, the `WorkflowApplication` that hosts that workflow must have been initialized with the specific workflow definition used to create the workflow place. By reading the version information prior to resuming the workflow, you can use this to map to a specific workflow definition.

In addition, this versioning support has also been extended to workflows hosted using the `WorkflowServiceHost` class. When hosting versioned workflows with `WorkflowServiceHost`, you need to specify version information in the `DefinitionIdentity` property of the workflow service.

These additions make workflow a much better option than it was previously, especially for business processes that might span weeks or months. Over the longer term it is much more likely that changes will need to be made. Although making those changes is a nontrivial matter, at least you now have the option.

Hosting the Designer

Often people save the best until last. Keeping with that tradition, that's what is done in this chapter. The Workflow Designer used within Visual Studio can also be hosted within your own application, allowing your end users to create their own workflows without a copy of Visual Studio in sight. This is the best feature of WF 4 by far. Traditional application extension mechanisms always require some form of developer—either to write an extension DLL and plug it into the system somewhere, or by writing macros or scripts. Windows Workflow enables end users to customize an application simply by dragging and dropping activities onto a design surface.

Rehosting the designer in Workflow 3.*x* was not for the faint-hearted; however, in WF 4 it became almost trivial. The Designer is a WPF control, so you can use a WPF project as the main application. The code for this example is available in the `09_DesignerRehosting` project.

The first thing you need to do is to include the workflow assemblies, and then you need to define the main window XAML. Use the Model-View-ViewModel (MVVM) pattern when constructing WPF user interfaces because it simplifies the coding and also ensures that you can drape different XAML over the same view model if necessary. The XAML for the main window is as follows (code file `09_DesignerRehosting/MainWindow.xaml`):

```
<Window x:Class="HostApp.MainWindow"
        xmlns="http://schemas.microsoft.com/winfx/2006/xaml/presentation"
        xmlns:x="http://schemas.microsoft.com/winfx/2006/xaml"
        Title="MainWindow">
  <Grid>
    <Grid.RowDefinitions>
      <RowDefinition Height="Auto"/>
      <RowDefinition Height="*"/>
    </Grid.RowDefinitions>
    <Menu IsMainMenu="True">
      <MenuItem Header="_File">
```

```
            <MenuItem Header="_New" Command="{Binding New}"/>
            <MenuItem Header="_Open" Command="{Binding Open}"/>
            <MenuItem Header="_Save" Command="{Binding Save}"/>
            <Separator/>
            <MenuItem Header="_Exit" Command="{Binding Exit}"/>
          </MenuItem>
          <MenuItem Header="Workflow">
            <MenuItem Header="_Run" Command="{Binding Run}"/>
          </MenuItem>
        </Menu>
        <Grid Grid.Row="1">
          <Grid.ColumnDefinitions>
            <ColumnDefinition Width="*"/>
            <ColumnDefinition Width="4*"/>
            <ColumnDefinition Width="*"/>
          </Grid.ColumnDefinitions>
          <ContentControl Content="{Binding Toolbox}" />
          <ContentControl Content="{Binding DesignerView}"
            Grid.Column="1"/>
          <ContentControl Content="{Binding PropertyInspectorView}"
            Grid.Column="2"/>
        </Grid>
      </Grid>
    </Window>
```

It is a simple layout with a main menu and then a grid that defines placeholders for the toolbox, designer, and property grid. You can notice that everything is bound including the commands.

The `ViewModel` created consists of properties for each of the main UI elements: the Toolbox, Designer, and Property Grid. In addition to these properties, there are also properties for each command, such as New, Save, and Exit (code file `09_DesignerRehosting/ViewModel.cs`):

```
public class ViewModel : BaseViewModel
{
    public ViewModel()
    {
        // Ensure all designers are registered for inbuilt activities
        new DesignerMetadata().Register();
    }
    public void InitializeViewModel(Activity root)
    {
        _designer = new WorkflowDesigner();
        _designer.Load(root);
        this.OnPropertyChanged("DesignerView");
        this.OnPropertyChanged("PropertyInspectorView");
    }
    public UIElement DesignerView
    {
        get { return _designer.View; }
    }
    public UIElement PropertInspectorView
    {
        get { return _designer.PropertyInspectorView; }
    }
    private WorkflowDesigner _designer;
}
```

To begin, the `ViewModel` class derives from `BaseViewModel`. This base class is one that you use every time you construct a view model because it provides an implementation of `INotifyPropertyChanged`. It comes from a set of snippets written by Josh Twist and is available on `www.thejoyofcode.com`.

The constructor ensures that the metadata for all the built-in activities is registered. Without this call, none of the type specific designers show up on the user interface. Within the `InitializeViewModel` method, you then construct an instance of the Workflow Designer and load an activity into it. The `WorkflowDesigner` class is curious in that, after you load one workflow into it, you cannot load another. So here you re-create this class whenever a new workflow is created.

The last thing that the `InitializeViewModel` method does is to call the property change notification function to indicate to the user interface that both the `DesignerView` and `PropertyInspectorView` are updated. As the UI is bound to these properties, they will be requeried and will load the new values from the new Workflow Designer instance.

The next part of the user interface that needs to be created is the toolbox. In Workflow 3.*x* you had to construct this control yourself; however, in WF 4 there is a `ToolboxControl`, which is trivially easy to use (code file `09_DesignerRehosting/ViewModel.cs`):

```
public UIElement Toolbox
{
  get
  {
    if (null == _toolbox)
    {
      _toolbox = new ToolboxControl();
      ToolboxCategory cat = new ToolboxCategory
        ("Standard Activities");
      cat.Add(new ToolboxItemWrapper(typeof(Sequence),
        "Sequence"));
      cat.Add(new ToolboxItemWrapper(typeof(Assign), "Assign"));
      _toolbox.Categories.Add(cat);
      ToolboxCategory custom = new ToolboxCategory("Custom Activities");
      custom.Add(new ToolboxItemWrapper(typeof(Message), "MessageBox"));
      _toolbox.Categories.Add(custom);
    }
    return _toolbox;
  }
}
```

Here, you construct the toolbox control and then add two toolbox items to the first category and one toolbox item to a second category. The `ToolboxItemWrapper` class is used to simplify the code needed to add a given activity to the toolbox.

With that code in place, you have a functioning application—well almost. All you need to do now is wire up the `ViewModel` with the XAML. This is done in the constructor for the main window.

```
public MainWindow()
{
    InitializeComponent();
    ViewModel vm = new ViewModel();
    vm.InitializeViewModel(new Sequence());
    this.DataContext = vm;
}
```

Here, you construct the view model, and, by default, add in a `Sequence` activity so that something displays onscreen when the application runs.

The only part missing now is some commands. We use a `DelegateCommand` class to write `ICommand`-based commands for WPF because then you can find the code in the view model is easy to understand. The commands are fairly trivial to implement because is evident by the `New` command shown here:

```
public ICommand New
{
  get
  {
    return new DelegateCommand(unused =>
      {
```

```
            InitializeViewModel(new Sequence());
        });
    }
}
```

This command is bound to the New menu item, so when that is clicked, the delegate is executed, and in this instance that simply calls the `InitializeViewModel` method with a new `Sequence` activity. Because this method also raises the property change notification for the designer and the property grid, these are updated, too.

The `Open` command is a little more involved but not much:

```
public ICommand Open
{
    get
    {
        return new DelegateCommand(unused =>
        {
            OpenFileDialog ofn = new OpenFileDialog();
            ofn.Title = "Open Workflow";
            ofn.Filter = "Workflows (*.xaml)|*.xaml";
            ofn.CheckFileExists = true;
            ofn.CheckPathExists = true;
            if (true == ofn.ShowDialog())
                InitializeViewModel(ofn.FileName);
        });
    }
}
```

Here, you use another override of `InitializeViewModel`, which in this instance takes a filename rather than an activity. You've not seen this code, but it is available in the code download. This command displays an `OpenFileDialog`, and when one is chosen, it loads the workflow into the Designer. There is a corresponding `Save` command, which calls the `WorkflowDesigner.Save` method to store the workflow XAML on disk. If you run the application now, you see a window that looks like that in Figure 45-17.

FIGURE 45-17

The last section of code in the view model is the Run command. It wouldn't be much good designing workflows without executing them, so you can include this facility in the view model as well. It's fairly trivial—the Designer includes a `Text` property, which is the XAML representation of the activities within the workflow. All you need to do is convert this into an `Activity` and then execute that using the `WorkflowInvoker` class.

```
public ICommand Run
{
  get
  {
    return new DelegateCommand(unused =>
    {
      Activity root = _designer.Context.Services.
        GetService<ModelService>().Root.
        GetCurrentValue() as Activity;
      WorkflowInvoker.Invoke(root);
    },
    unused => { return !HasErrors; }
    );
  }
}

public bool HasErrors
{
  get { return (0 != _errorCount); }
}

public void ShowValidationErrors(IList<ValidationErrorInfo> errors)
{
  _errorCount = errors.Count;
  OnPropertyChanged("HasErrors");
}
private int _errorCount;
```

The author butchered the preceding code to fit it into the space on the page because the first line of the delegate command that retrieves the root activity from the designer is long, to say the least. All you then need to do is use the `WorkflowInvoker.Invoke` method to execute the workflow.

The command infrastructure within WPF includes a way to disable commands if they cannot be accessed, and that's the second Lambda function on the `DelegateCommand`. This function returns the value of `HasErrors`, a Boolean property that has been added to the view model. This property indicates whether any validation errors have been found within the workflow because the view model implements the `IValidationErrorService`, which is notified whenever the valid state of the workflow changes.

You could extend the sample to expose this list of validation errors on the user interface as necessary—and you probably want to add in some more activities to the toolbox because you won't get far with just three activities.

SUMMARY

Windows Workflow offers a radical change in the way that you construct applications. You can now surface complex parts of an application as activities and permit users to alter the processing of the system simply by dragging and dropping activities into a workflow.

You can apply workflow to almost all applications—from the simplest command-line tool to the most complex system containing many hundreds of modules. Before you might have needed a developer to write an extension module for a system, but now you can provide a simple and extensible customization mechanism that almost anyone can use. As an application vendor, you would have provided the custom activities that interacted with your system, and you would also have provided the code in the application that called the workflows, but you can now leave it up to your customers to define what they want to happen when an event occurs in the application.

WF 3.*x* has now been largely superseded by WF 4, and if you plan to use workflow for the first time, start with this version and bypass Workflow 3.*x* entirely.

46

Peer-to-Peer Networking

WHAT'S IN THIS CHAPTER?

➤ Learning about P2P

➤ Using the Microsoft Windows 8 P2P Networking platform

➤ Registering and Resolving Peer Names

➤ Sending and receiving messages across peers

➤ Building P2P applications with the .NET Framework

WROX.COM CODE DOWNLOADS FOR THIS CHAPTER

You can find the wrox.com code downloads for this chapter at `http://www.wrox.com/remtitle .cgi?isbn=1118314425` on the Download Code tab. The code for this chapter contains this major example:

➤ P2PSample

PEER-TO-PEER NETWORKING OVERVIEW

Peer-to-peer networking, often referred to as P2P, is perhaps one of the most useful and yet misunderstood technologies to emerge in recent years. When people think of P2P, they usually think of one thing: sharing music video, software, and other files, often illegally. This is because file-sharing applications such as BitTorrent have risen in popularity at a staggering rate, and these applications use P2P technology to work.

Although P2P is used in file-sharing applications, that doesn't mean it doesn't have other applications. Indeed, as you see in this chapter, you can use P2P for a vast array of applications, and it is becoming more important in the interconnected world in which you live. You learn about this in the first part of this chapter, when you look at an overview of P2P technologies.

Microsoft has not been oblivious to the emergence of P2P and has been developing its own tools and technologies to use it. You can use the Microsoft Windows Peer-to-Peer Networking platform as a communication framework for P2P applications. This platform includes the important component Peer Name Resolution Protocol (PNRP). The .NET Framework contains the namespace, `System .Net.PeerToPeer`, and several types and features that you can use to build P2P applications with minimal effort.

Peer-to-peer networking is an alternative approach to network communication. To understand how P2P differs from the "standard" approach to network communication, you need to take a step backward to look at client-server communications. Client-server communications are ubiquitous in networked applications today.

Client-Server Architecture

Traditionally, you interact with applications over a network (including the Internet) using a client-server architecture. Websites are a great example of this. When you look at a website, you send a request over the Internet to a web server, which then returns the information that you require. If you want to download a file, you do so directly from the web server.

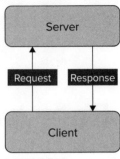

FIGURE 46-1

Similarly, desktop applications that include local or wide area network connectivity typically connect to a single server, for example, a database server or a server that hosts other services.

This simple form of client-server architecture is shown in Figure 46-1.

There is nothing inherently wrong with the client-server architecture, and indeed in many cases it is exactly what you want. However, there is a scalability problem. Figure 46-2 shows how the client-server architecture scales with additional clients.

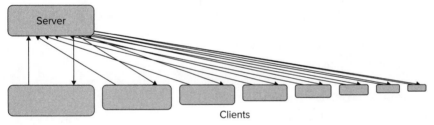

FIGURE 46-2

With every client added an increased load is placed on the server, which must communicate with each client. To return to the website example, this increased communication load is how websites collapse. When there is too much traffic, the server simply becomes unresponsive.

There are, of course, scaling options that you can implement to mitigate this situation. You can *scale up* by increasing the power and resources available to the server, or you can *scale out* by adding additional servers. Scaling up is limited by the technology available and the cost of better hardware. Scaling out is potentially more flexible but requires an additional infrastructure layer to ensure that clients either communicate with individual servers or maintain session state independent of the server with which they communicate. Plenty of solutions are available for this, such as web or server farm products.

P2P Architecture

The peer-to-peer approach is completely different from either the scaling up or scaling out approach. With P2P, instead of focusing on and attempting to streamline the communication between the server and its clients, you instead look at ways in which clients can communicate with each other.

Say, for example, that the website that clients communicate with is `www.wrox.com`. In your imaginary scenario, Wrox has announced that a new version of this book is to be released on the wrox.com website and will be free to download to anyone who wants it; however, it will be removed after one day. Before the book becomes available on the website you might imagine that many people will look at the website and refresh their browsers, waiting for the file to appear. When the file is available, everyone will try to download it at the same time, and more than likely the wrox.com web server will collapse under the strain.

You could use P2P technology to prevent this web server collapse. Instead of sending the file directly from the server to all the clients, you send the file to just a few clients. A few of the remaining clients then download the file from the clients that already have it; a few more clients download it from those second-level clients; and so on. This process is made even faster by splitting the file into chunks and dividing these chunks among clients, some of whom download it directly from the server, and some whom download chunks from other clients. This is how file-sharing technologies such as BitTorrent work, as shown in Figure 46-3.

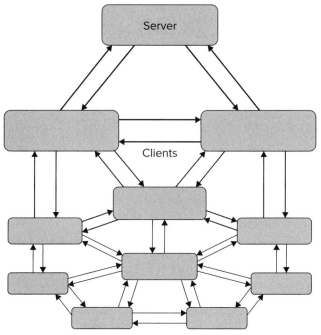

FIGURE 46-3

P2P Architectural Challenges

You still need to solve problems in the file-sharing architecture discussed here. For a start, how do clients detect that other clients exist, and how do they locate chunks of the file that other clients might have? Also, how can you ensure optimal communication between clients that may be separated by entire continents?

Every client participating in a P2P network application must perform the following operations to overcome these problems:

➤ It must *discover* other clients.

➤ It must *connect* to other clients.

➤ It must *communicate* with other clients.

The discovery problem has two obvious solutions. You can either keep a list of the clients on the server so that clients can obtain this list and contact other clients (known as *peers*), or you can use an infrastructure (for example PNRP, covered in the section "Peer Name Resolution Protocol") that enables clients to find each other directly. Most file-sharing systems use the "list on a server" solution by using servers known as *trackers*. Also, in file-sharing systems any client may act as a server, as shown in Figure 46-3, by declaring that it has a file available and registering it with a tracker. In fact, a pure P2P network doesn't need servers, just peers.

The connection problem is a more subtle one and concerns the overall structure of the networks used by a P2P application. If you have one group of clients, all of which can communicate with one another, the topology of the connections between these clients can become extremely complex. You can often improve performance by having more than one group of clients, each of which consists of connections between clients in that group, but not to clients in other groups. If you can make these groups locale-based, you can get an additional performance boost because clients can communicate with each other with fewer hops between networked computers.

Communication is perhaps a problem of lesser importance because communication protocols such as TCP/IP are well established and can be reused here. There is, however, scope for improvement in both high-level technologies (for example, you can use WCF services and therefore all the functionality that WCF offers) and low-level protocols (such as multicast protocols to send data to multiple endpoints simultaneously).

Discovery, connection, and communication are central to any P2P implementation. The implementation you look at in this chapter is to use the `System.Net.PeerToPeer` types with PNM for discovery and PNRP for connection. As you see in subsequent sections, these technologies cover all three operations.

P2P Terminology

In the previous sections you were introduced to the concept of a *peer,* which is how clients are referred to in a P2P network. The word *client* makes no sense in a P2P network because there is not necessarily a server to be a client of.

Groups of peers connected to each other are known by the interchangeable terms *meshes, clouds,* or *graphs.* A given group can be said to be *well connected* if at least one of the following statements applies:

➤ There is a connection path between every pair of peers so that every peer can connect to any other peer as required.

➤ There are a relatively small number of connections to traverse between any pair of peers.

➤ Removing a peer does not prevent other peers from connecting to each other.

This does not mean that every peer must connect to every other peer directly. If you analyze a network mathematically, you can find that peers need to connect only to a relatively small number of other peers for these conditions to be met.

Another P2P concept to be aware of is *flooding.* Flooding is the way in which a single piece of data may be propagated through a network to all peers, or querying other nodes in a network to locate a specific piece of data. In unstructured P2P networks this is a fairly random process to contact nearest neighbor peers, which in turn contact their nearest neighbors, and so on until every peer in the network is contacted. You can also create structured P2P networks so that there are well-defined pathways for queries and data flow among peers.

P2P Solutions

When you have an infrastructure for P2P, you can start to develop not only improved versions of client-server applications, but also entirely new applications. P2P is particularly suited to the following classes of applications:

➤ Content distribution applications, including the file-sharing applications discussed earlier

➤ Collaboration applications, such as desktop sharing and shared whiteboard applications

➤ Multi-user communication applications that enable users to communicate and exchange data directly rather than through a server

➤ Distributed processing applications, as an alternative to supercomputing applications that process enormous amounts of data

➤ Web 2.0 applications that combine some or all the preceding points in dynamic, next-generation web applications

PEER NAME RESOLUTION PROTOCOL (PNRP)

The Microsoft Windows Peer-to-Peer Networking platform is Microsoft's implementation of P2P technology. It is part of Windows since Windows XP SP2. You can use the Peer Name Resolution Protocol (PNRP) to publish and resolve peer addresses. In this section you learn about this protocol.

You can use any protocol at your disposal to implement a P2P application, but if you work in a Microsoft Windows 8 environment (and if you're reading this book you probably are) it makes sense to at least consider PNRP. In itself, PNRP doesn't give you everything you need to create a P2P application. Rather, it is one of the underlying technologies that you use to resolve peer addresses. PNRP enables a client to register an endpoint (known as a *peer name*) that is automatically circulated among peers in a cloud. This peer name is encapsulated in a PNRP ID. A peer that discovers the PNRP ID can use PNRP to resolve it to the actual peer name and can then communicate directly with the associated client.

For example, you might define a peer name that represents a WCF service endpoint. You could use PNRP to register this peer name in a cloud as a PNRP ID. A peer running a suitable client application that uses a discovery mechanism that can identify peer names for the service you are exposing might then discover this PNRP ID. When discovered, the peer would use PNRP to locate the endpoint of the WCF service and then use that service.

> **NOTE** *PNRP makes no assumptions about what a peer name actually represents. It is up to peers to decide how to use them when discovered. The information a peer receives from PNRP when resolving a PNRP ID includes the IPv6 (and usually also the IPv4) address of the publisher of the ID, along with a port number and optionally a small amount of additional data. Unless the peer knows what the peer name means, it is unlikely to do anything useful with this information.*

PNRP IDs

PNRP IDs are 256-bit identifiers. The low-order 128 bits can uniquely identify a particular peer, and the high-order 128 bits identify a peer name. The high-order 128 bits are a hashed combination of a hashed public key from the publishing peer and a string of up to 149 characters that identifies the peer name. The hashed public key (known as the *authority*) combined with this string (the *classifier*) are together referred to as the P2P ID. You can also use a value of 0 instead of a hashed public key, in which case the peer name is said to be *unsecured* (as opposed to *secured* peer names, which use a public key).

Figure 46-4 uses the structure of a PNRP ID.

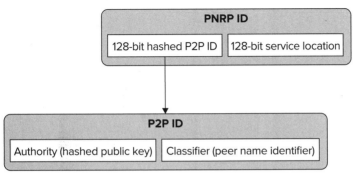

FIGURE 46-4

The PNRP service on a peer is responsible to maintain a list of PNRP IDs, including the ones that it publishes and a cached list of those it has obtained by PNRP service instances elsewhere in the cloud. When a peer attempts to resolve a PNRP ID, the PNRP service either uses a cached copy of the endpoint to resolve the peer that published the PNRP or it asks its neighbors if they can resolve it. Eventually a connection to the publishing peer is made, and the PNRP service can resolve the PNRP ID.

All this happens without you intervening in any way. All you must do is ensure that peers know what to do with peer names after they have resolved them using their local PNRP service.

Peers can use PNRP to locate PNRP IDs that match a particular P2P ID. You can use this to implement a basic form of discovery for unsecured peer names. This is because if several peers expose an unsecured peer name that uses the same classifier, the P2P ID will be the same. Of course, because any peer can use an unsecured peer name, you have no guarantee that the endpoint you connect to will be the sort of endpoint you expect, so this is only a viable solution for discovery over a local network.

PNRP Clouds

In the preceding discussion you learned how PNRP registers and resolves peer names in clouds. A cloud is maintained by a *seed server,* which can be any server running the PNRP service that maintains a record of at least one peer. Two types of clouds are available to the PNRP service:

➤ **Link local:** These clouds consist of the computers attached to a local network. A PC may connect to more than one link local cloud if it has multiple network adapters.

➤ **Global:** This cloud consists of computers connected to the Internet by default; although you can define a private global cloud. The difference is that Microsoft maintains the seed server for the global Internet cloud, whereas if you define a private global cloud you must use your own seed server. If you use your own seed server, you must ensure that all peers connect to it by configuring policy settings.

> **NOTE** *In previous versions of PNRP, a third type of cloud existed: site local. This is no longer used and is not covered in this chapter.*

You can discover what clouds you are connected to with the following command:

```
netsh p2p pnrp cloud show list
```

A typical result is shown here:

```
Scope  Id     Addr   State             Name
-----  -----  -----  ----------------  -----
    1      0      1   Virtual           Global_
    3     13      1   Virtual           LinkLocal_ff00::%13/8
    3     19      1   Virtual           LinkLocal_ff00::%19/8
```

The output shows that three clouds are available: one is a global and two are link local clouds. You can tell this from both the name and the Scope value, which is 3 for link local clouds and 1 for global clouds. To connect to a global cloud, you must have an IPv6 address.

Clouds may be in one of the following states:

➤ **Active:** If the state of a cloud is active, you can use it to publish and resolve peer names.

➤ **Alone:** If the peer you query the cloud from is not connected to any other peers, it has a state of alone.

➤ **No Net:** If the peer is not connected to a network, the cloud state may change from `active` to `no net`.

➤ **Synchronizing:** Clouds are in the `synchronizing` state when the peer connects to them. This state changes to another state extremely quickly because this connection does not take long, so you will probably never see a cloud in this state.

➤ **Virtual:** The PNRP service connects to clouds only as required by peer name registration and resolution. If a cloud connection has been inactive for more than 15 minutes, it may enter the `virtual` state.

> **NOTE** *If you experience network connectivity problems, you should check your firewall to see if it prevents local network traffic over the UDP ports 3540 or 1900. UDP port 3540 is used by PNRP, and UDP port 1900 is used by the Simple Service Discovery Protocol (SSDP), which in turn is used by the PNRP service (and UPnP devices).*

PNRP Since Windows 7

Since Windows 7, PNRP makes use of a component called the *Distributed Routing Table (DRT)*. This component is responsible to determine the structure of the keys used by PNRP; the default implementation of which is the PNRP ID previously described. By using the DRT API you can define an alternative key scheme, but the keys must be 256-bit integer values (just like PNRP IDs). This means that you can use any scheme you want, but you are then responsible for the generation and security of the keys. By using this component you can create new cloud topologies beyond the scope of PNRP, and indeed, beyond the scope of this chapter because this is an advanced technique.

Windows 7 also introduced a new way to connect to other users for the Remote Assistance application: Easy Connect. This connection option uses PNRP to locate users to connect to. After a session is created, through Easy Connect or by other means (for example an e-mail invitation), users can share their Desktops and assist each other through the Remote Assistance interface.

BUILDING P2P APPLICATIONS

Now that you have learned what P2P networking is and what technologies are available to .NET developers to implement P2P applications, it's time to look at how you can build them. From the preceding discussion you know that you will use PNRP to publish, distribute, and resolve peer names, so the first thing you look at here is how to achieve that using .NET. Next you look at how to use PNM as a framework for a P2P application. This can be advantageous because if you use PNM you do not need to implement your own discovery mechanisms.

To examine these subjects you need to learn about the classes in the `System.Net.PeerToPeer` namespace. For these classes you must have a reference to the `System.Net` assembly.

The classes in the `System.Net.PeerToPeer` namespace encapsulate the API for PNRP and enable you to interact with the PNRP service. You can use these classes for two main tasks:

➤ Registering peer names

➤ Resolving peer names

In the following sections, all the types referred to come from the `System.Net.PeerToPeer` namespace unless otherwise specified.

Registering Peer Names

To register a peer name follow these steps:

1. Create a secured or unsecured peer name with a specified classifier.

2. Configure a registration for the peer name, providing as much of the following optional information as you choose:

   ➤ A TCP port number.

   ➤ The cloud or clouds with which to register the peer name. (If unspecified, PNRP registers the peer name in all available clouds.)

   ➤ A comment of up to 39 characters.

   ➤ Up to 4,096 bytes of additional data.

   ➤ Whether to generate endpoints for the peer name automatically. (The default behavior, where endpoints will be generated from the IP address or addresses of the peer and, if specified, the port number.)

   ➤ A collection of endpoints.

3. Use the peer name registration to register the peer name with the local PNRP service.

After step 3, the peer name is available to all peers in the selected cloud (or clouds). Peer registration continues until it explicitly stops, or until the process that registers the peer name is terminated.

To create a peer name, you use the `PeerName` class. You create an instance of this class from a string representation of a P2P ID in the form `authority.classifier` or from a classifier string and a `PeerNameType`. You can use `PeerNameType.Secured` or `PeerNameType.Unsecured`, for example:

```
var pn = new PeerName("Peer classifier", PeerNameType.Secured);
```

Because an unsecured peer name uses an authority value of 0, the following lines of code are equivalent:

```
var pn = new PeerName("Peer classifier", PeerNameType.Unsecured);
```

```
var pn = new PeerName("0.Peer classifier");
```

After you have a `PeerName` instance, you can use it along with a port number to initialize a `PeerNameRegistration` object:

```
var pnr = new PeerNameRegistration(pn, 8080);
```

Alternatively, you can set the `PeerName` and (optionally) the `Port` properties on a `PeerNameRegistration` object created using its default parameter. You can also specify a `Cloud` instance as a third parameter of the `PeerNameRegistration` constructor, or through the `Cloud` property. You can obtain a `Cloud` instance from the cloud name or by using one of the following static members of `Cloud`:

➤ `Cloud.Global`: This static property obtains a reference to the global cloud. This may be a private global cloud depending on peer policy configuration.

➤ `Cloud.AllLinkLocal`: This static field gets a cloud that contains all the link local clouds available to the peer.

➤ `Cloud.Available`: This static field gets a cloud that contains all the clouds available to the peer, which includes link local clouds and (if available) the global cloud.

When created, you can set the `Comment` and `Data` properties if you want. Be aware of the limitations of these properties, though. You receive a `PeerToPeerException` if you try to set `Comment` to a string greater than 39 Unicode characters or an `ArgumentOutOfRangeException` if you try to set `Data` to a `byte[]`

greater than 4,096 bytes. You can also add endpoints by using the `EndPointCollection` property. This property is a `System.Net.IPEndPointCollection` collection of `System.Net.IPEndPoint` objects. If you use the `EndPointCollection` property you might also want to set the `UseAutoEndPointSelection` property to `false` to prevent automatic generation of endpoints.

When you are ready to register the peer name, you can call the `PeerNameRegistration.Start` method. To remove a peer name registration from the PNRP service, use the `PeerNameRegistration.Stop` method.

The following code registers a secured peer name with a comment:

```
var pn = new PeerName("Peer classifier", PeerNameType.Unsecured);
var pnr = new PeerNameRegistration(pn, 8080);
pnr.Comment = "Get pizza here";
pnr.Start();
```

Resolving Peer Names

To resolve a peer name you must carry out the following steps:

1. Generate a peer name from a known P2P ID or a P2P ID obtained through a discovery technique.

2. Use a resolver to resolve the peer name and obtain a collection of peer name records. You can limit the resolver to a particular cloud and a maximum number of results to return.

3. For any peer name records that you obtain, obtain peer name, endpoint, comment, and additional data information as required.

This process starts with a `PeerName` object similar to a peer name registration. The difference here is that you use a peer name registered by one or more remote peers. The simplest way to get a list of active peers in your link local cloud is for each peer to register an unsecured peer name with the same classifier and to use the same peer name in the resolving phase. However, this is not a recommended strategy for global clouds because unsecured peer names are easily spoofed.

To resolve peer names use the `PeerNameResolver` class. When you have an instance of this class, you can choose to resolve peer names synchronously by using the `Resolve` method or asynchronously using the `ResolveAsync` method.

You can call the `Resolve` method with a single `PeerName` parameter, but you can also pass an optional `Cloud` instance to resolve in, an `int` maximum number of peers to return, or both. This method returns a `PeerNameRecordCollection` instance, which is a collection of `PeerNameRecord` objects. For example, the following code resolves an unsecured peer name in all link local clouds and returns a maximum of five results:

```
var pn = new PeerName("0.Peer classifier");
var pnres = new PeerNameResolver();
PeerNameRecordCollection pnrc = pnres.Resolve(pn, Cloud.AllLinkLocal, 5);
```

The `ResolveAsync` method uses a standard asynchronous method call pattern. You pass a unique `userState` object to the method and listen for `ResolveProgressChanged` events for peers being found and the `ResolveCompleted` event when the method terminates. You can cancel a pending asynchronous request with the `ResolveAsyncCancel` method.

Event handlers for the `ResolveProgressChanged` event use the `ResolveProgressChangedEventArgs` event arguments parameter, which derives from the standard `System.ComponentModel.ProgressChangedEventArgs` class. You can use the `PeerNameRecord` property of the event argument object you receive in the event handler to get a reference to the peer name record that was found.

Similarly, the `ResolveCompleted` event requires an event handler that uses a parameter of type `ResolveCompletedEventArgs`, which derives from `AsyncCompletedEventArgs`. This type includes a

`PeerNameRecordCollection` parameter you can use to obtain a complete list of the peer name records that were found.

The following code shows an implementation of event handlers for these events:

```
private pnres_ResolveProgressChanged(object sender,
    ResolveProgressChangedEventArgs e)
{
  // Use e.ProgressPercentage (inherited from base event args)
  // Process PeerNameRecord from e.PeerNameRecord
}

private pnres_ResolveCompleted(object sender,
    ResolveCompletedEventArgs e)
{
  // Test for e.IsCancelled and e.Error (inherited from base event args)
  // Process PeerNameRecordCollection from e.PeerNameRecordCollection
}
```

After you have one or more `PeerNameRecord` objects you can proceed to process them. This `PeerNameRecord` class exposes `Comment` and `Data` properties to examine the comment and data set in the peer name registration (if any), a `PeerName` property to get the `PeerName` object for the peer name record, and, most important, an `EndPointCollection` property. As with `PeerNameRegistration`, this property is a `System.Net.IPEndPointCollection` collection of `System.Net.IPEndPoint` objects. You can use these objects to connect to endpoints exposed by the peer in any way you want.

Code Access Security in System.Net.PeerToPeer

The `System.Net.PeerToPeer` namespace also includes the following two classes that you can use with Code Access Security (CAS). See Chapter 22, "Security," for more details.

➤   `PnrpPermission`, which inherits from `CodeAccessPermission`

➤   `PnrpPermissionAttribute`, which inherits from `CodeAccessSecurityAttribute`

You can use these classes to provide permissions functionality for PNRP access in the usual CAS way.

Sample Application

The downloadable code for this chapter includes a sample P2P application (P2PSample) that uses the concepts and namespace introduced in this section. It is a WPF application that uses a WCF service for a peer endpoint.

The application is configured with an application configuration file, in which you can specify the name of the peer and a port to listen on as follows (code file `App.config`):

```
<?xml version="1.0" encoding="utf-8" ?>
<configuration>
  <appSettings>
    <add key="username" value="Christian" />
    <add key="port" value="8731" />
  </appSettings>
</configuration>
```

After you build the application, you can test it either by copying it to other computers in your local network and running all instances, or by running multiple instances on one computer. If you choose the latter option, you must remember to change the port used for each instance by changing individual config files. (Copy the contents of the `Debug` directory on your local computer and edit each config file in turn.) The results are clearer in both ways to test this application if you also change the username for each instance.

When the peer applications run, you can use the Refresh button to obtain a list of peers asynchronously. When you locate a peer, you can send a default message by clicking the Message button for the peer.

Figure 46-5 shows this application in action with three instances running on one machine. In the figure, one peer has just messaged another, which results in a dialog box.

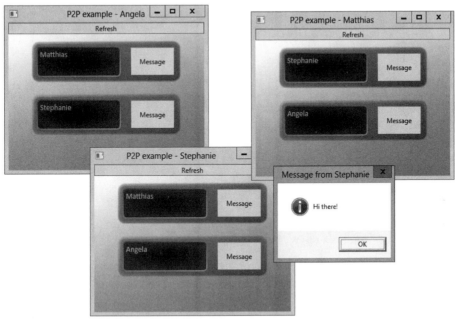

FIGURE 46-5

Now get into the code. With the field members of the class `MainWindow` (code file `MainWindow .xaml.cs`) an observable collection is defined that contains all the peers. In the constructor of the class, just one `PeerEntry` is added to the collection that gives information to the user to click the Refresh button to get all the peers.

```
public partial class MainWindow : Window
{
  private P2PService localService;
  private ServiceHost host;
  private PeerName peerName;
  private PeerNameRegistration peerNameRegistration;
  private ObservableCollection<PeerEntry> peerList =
    new ObservableCollection<PeerEntry>();
  private object peersLock = new object();

  public MainWindow()
  {
    InitializeComponent();
    this.DataContext = peerList;
    peerList.Add(
      new PeerEntry
      {
        DisplayString = "Refresh to look for peers.",
        ButtonsEnabled = false
      });
    BindingOperations.EnableCollectionSynchronization(peerList, peersLock);
  }
```

Most of the work in this application takes place in the `Window_Loaded` event handler for the `MainWindow` window. This method starts by loading configuration information and setting the window title with the username:

```
private void Window_Loaded(object sender, RoutedEventArgs e)
{
  // Get configuration from app.config
  string port = ConfigurationManager.AppSettings["port"];
  string username = ConfigurationManager.AppSettings["username"];
  string machineName = Environment.MachineName;
  string serviceUrl = null;

  // Set window title
  this.Title = string.Format("P2P example — {0}", username);
```

Next, the peer host address is used along with the configured port to determine the endpoint on which to host the WCF service. The service uses `NetTcpBinding` binding, so the URL of the endpoint uses the `net.tcp` protocol:

```
  // Get service url using IPv4 address and port from config file
  serviceUrl = Dns.GetHostAddresses(Dns.GetHostName())
    .Where(address => address.AddressFamily == AddressFamily.InterNetwork)
    .Select(address =>
      string.Format("net.tcp://{0}:{1}/P2PService", address, port))
    .FirstOrDefault();
```

The endpoint URL is validated, and then the WCF service is registered and started:

```
  // Check for null address
  if (serviceUrl == null)
  {
    // Display error and shutdown
    MessageBox.Show(this, "Unable to determine WCF endpoint.",
      "Networking Error", MessageBoxButton.OK, MessageBoxImage.Stop);
    Application.Current.Shutdown();
  }

  // Register and start WCF service.
  localService = new P2PService(this, username);
  host = new ServiceHost(localService, new Uri(serviceUrl));
  var binding = new NetTcpBinding();
  binding.Security.Mode = SecurityMode.None;
  host.AddServiceEndpoint(typeof(IP2PService), binding, serviceUrl);
  try
  {
    host.Open();
  }
  catch (AddressAlreadyInUseException)
  {
    // Display error and shutdown
    MessageBox.Show(this, "Cannot start listening, port in use.",
      "WCF Error", MessageBoxButton.OK, MessageBoxImage.Stop);
    Application.Current.Shutdown();
  }
```

A single instance of the service class enables easy communication between the host app and the service (for sending and receiving messages). Also, security is disabled in the binding configuration for simplicity.

Next, the `System.Net.PeerToPeer` namespace classes register a peer name:

```
  // Create peer name
  peerName = new PeerName("P2P Sample", PeerNameType.Unsecured);

  // Prepare peer name registration in link local clouds
```

```
    peerNameRegistration = new PeerNameRegistration(peerName, int.Parse(port));
    peerNameRegistration.Cloud = Cloud.AllLinkLocal;

    // Start registration
    peerNameRegistration.Start();
}
```

When the Refresh button is clicked, the `RefreshButton_Click` event handler uses `PeerNameResolver` `.ResolveAsync` to get peers asynchronously:

```
private async void RefreshButton_Click(object sender, RoutedEventArgs e)
{
    // Create resolver and add event handlers
    var resolver = new PeerNameResolver();
    resolver.ResolveProgressChanged +=
      new EventHandler<ResolveProgressChangedEventArgs>(
        resolver_ResolveProgressChanged);
    resolver.ResolveCompleted +=
      new EventHandler<ResolveCompletedEventArgs>(
        resolver_ResolveCompleted);

    // Prepare for new peers
    peerList.Clear();
    RefreshButton.IsEnabled = false;

    // Resolve unsecured peers asynchronously
    resolver.ResolveAsync(new PeerName("0.P2P Sample"), 1);
```

When peer information is received, the events `ResolveProgressChanged` and `ResolveCompleted` events are fired where the peer information is received. If case peers are not active yet, a timeout is defined to cancel the resolve process to fire the `ResolveCompleted`. The timeout is dealt with the `Task.Delay` method, and after the timeout `ResolveAsyncCancel` is invoked with the same user state value, that is passed to the `ResolveAsync` method. With the user state value, the same resolve task is mapped for cancellation.

```
    await Task.Delay(5000);
    resolver.ResolveAsyncCancel(1);
}
```

The remainder of the code is responsible to display and communicate with peers, and you can explore it at your leisure.

Exposing WCF endpoints through P2P clouds is a great way to locate services within an enterprise, as well as being an excellent way to communicate between peers, as in this example.

SUMMARY

This chapter demonstrated how to implement peer-to-peer functionality in your applications by using the P2P classes.

You have looked at the types of solutions that P2P makes possible and how these solutions are structured and how to use PNRP with the types in the `System.Net.PeerToPeer` namespaces. You also learned about the extremely useful technique to expose WCF services as P2P endpoints.

In the next chapter you look at Message Queuing, both with classes from the `System.Messaging` namespace and with WCF.

47

Message Queuing

WHAT'S IN THIS CHAPTER?

➤ Message Queuing architecture

➤ Using Message Queuing administrative tools

➤ Creating Message Queues programmatically

➤ Sending and receiving messages

➤ Course order sample application

➤ Using Message Queuing with WCF

WROX.COM CODE DOWNLOADS FOR THIS CHAPTER

You can find the wrox.com code downloads for this chapter `http://www.wrox.com/remtitle`
`.cgi?isbn=1118314425` on the Download Code tab.

➤ Working with Queues

    ➤ Create Message Queue

    ➤ Find Queues

    ➤ Open Queues

    ➤ Send Messages

    ➤ Receive Messages

➤ Course Order Sample

    ➤ Sender

    ➤ Receiver

➤ WCF Course Order Sample

    ➤ Sender

    ➤ Receiver

OVERVIEW

System.Messaging is a namespace that includes classes for reading and writing messages with the Message Queuing facility of the Windows operating system. You can use messaging in a disconnected scenario in which the client and server don't need to run at the same time.

This chapter gives you information about the architecture and usage scenarios of Message Queuing, and then you dive into the classes from the System.Messaging namespace to create queues, and send and receive messages. You see how to deal with getting answers from the server with acknowledgment and response queues, and also how to use message queuing with a WCF message queuing binding.

Before diving into programming Message Queuing, this section discusses the basic concepts of messaging and compares it to synchronous and asynchronous programming. With synchronous programming, when a method is invoked, the caller must wait until the method completes. With asynchronous programming, the calling thread starts the method that runs concurrently. Asynchronous programming can be done with delegates, class libraries that already support asynchronous methods (for example, web service proxies, System.Net, and System.IO classes), or by using custom threads and tasks (see Chapter 21, "Tasks, Threads, and Synchronization"). With both synchronous and asynchronous programming, the client and the server must run at the same time.

Although Message Queuing operates asynchronously, because the client (sender) does not wait for the server (receiver) to read the data sent to it, there is a crucial difference between Message Queuing and asynchronous programming: Message Queuing can be done in a disconnected environment. At the time data is sent, the receiver can be offline. Later, when the receiver goes online, it receives the data without intervention from the sending application.

You can compare connected and disconnected programming with talking to someone on the phone and sending an e-mail. When talking to someone on the phone, both participants must be connected at the same time; the communication is synchronous. With an e-mail, the sender isn't sure when the e-mail will be dealt with. People using this technology work in a disconnected mode. Of course the e-mail may never be dealt with—it may be ignored. That's in the nature of disconnected communication. To avoid this problem, you can ask for a reply to confirm that the e-mail has been read. If the answer doesn't arrive within a time limit, you may be required to deal with this "exception." This is also possible with Message Queuing.

You can think of Message Queuing as e-mail for application-to-application communication, instead of person-to-person communication. Message Queuing offers a lot of features not available with mailing services, such as guaranteed delivery, transactions, confirmations, express mode using memory, and so on. As you see in the next section, Message Queuing has a lot of features useful for communication between applications.

With Message Queuing, you can send, receive, and route messages in a connected or disconnected environment. Figure 47-1 shows a simple way to use messages. The sender sends messages to the message queue, and the receiver receives messages from the queue.

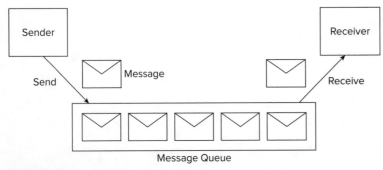

FIGURE 47-1

When to Use Message Queuing

One case in which Message Queuing is useful is when the client application is often disconnected from the network, for example, when a salesperson visits a customer onsite. The salesperson can enter order data directly at the customer's site. The application sends a message for each order to the message queue located on the client's system (see Figure 47-2). As soon as the salesperson is back in the office, the order is automatically transferred from the message queue of the client system to the message queue of the target system, where the message is processed.

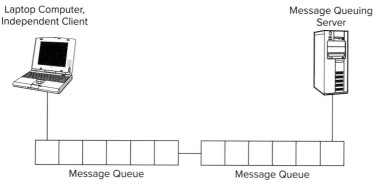

Laptop Computer,
Independent Client

Message Queuing
Server

Message Queue   Message Queue

FIGURE 47-2

In addition to using a laptop, the salesperson could use a smaller device where Message Queuing is available.

Message Queuing can also be useful in a connected environment. Imagine an e-commerce site (see Figure 47-3) where the server is fully loaded with order transactions at certain times, for example, early evening and weekends, but the load is low at nighttime. A solution would be to buy a faster server or to add additional servers to the system so that the peaks can be handled. But there's a cheaper solution: Flatten the peak loads by moving transactions from the times with higher loads to the times with lower loads. In this scheme, orders are sent to the message queue, and the receiving side reads the orders at the rates that are useful for the database system. The load of the system is now flattened over time so that the server dealing with the transactions can be less expensive than an upgrade of the database server(s).

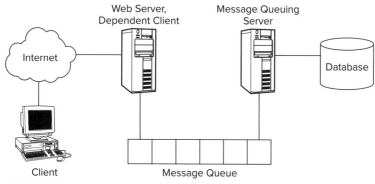

Web Server,
Dependent Client

Message Queuing
Server

Internet

Database

Client   Message Queue

FIGURE 47-3

Message Queuing Features

Message Queuing is part of the Windows 8 operating system. The main features of this service follow:

➤ Messages can be sent in a disconnected environment. It is not necessary for the sending and receiving applications to run at the same time.

➤ With express mode, messages can be sent quickly. Express-mode messages are just stored in memory.

➤ For a recoverable mechanism, messages can be sent using guaranteed delivery. Recoverable messages are stored within files and are delivered even in cases when the server reboots.

➤ Message queues can be secured with access-control lists to define which users can send or receive messages from a queue. Messages can also be encrypted to avoid network sniffers reading them. Messages can be sent with priorities so that high-priority items are handled faster.

➤ Message Queuing 3.0 supports sending multicast messages.

➤ Message Queuing 4.0 supports *poison messages*. A poison message is one that isn't getting resolved. You can define a *poison queue* where unresolved messages are moved. For example, if the job after reading the message from the normal queue were to insert it into the database, but the message did not get into the database and thus this job failed, it would get sent to the poison queue. It is someone's job to handle the poison queue—and that person should deal with the message in a way that resolves it.

➤ Message Queuing 5.0 supports more secure authentication algorithms and can handle a larger number of queues. (Message Queuing 4.0 had performance problems with several thousand queues.)

> **NOTE** *Because Message Queuing is part of the operating system, you cannot install Message Queuing 5.0 on a Windows Vista or Windows Server 2008 system. Message Queuing 5.0 is part of Windows 7 and 8, and Windows Server 2008 R2 and Windows Server 2012.*

The remainder of this chapter discusses how to use these features.

MESSAGE QUEUING PRODUCTS

Message Queuing 5.0 is part of Windows since Windows 7 and Windows Server 2008 R2. Windows 2000 was delivered with Message Queuing 2.0, which didn't have support for the HTTP protocol and multicast messages. Message Queuing 3.0 is part of Windows XP and Windows Server 2003. Message Queuing 4.0 is part of Windows Vista and Windows Server 2008.

When you use the link Turn Windows Features On or Off in Configuring Programs and Features of Windows 8, there is a separate section for Message Queuing options. With this section, you can select these components:

➤ **Microsoft Message Queue (MSMQ) Server Core:** Required for base functionality with Message Queuing.

➤ **Active Directory Domain Services Integration:** Message queue names are written to the Active Directory. With this option, you can find queues with the Active Directory integration and secure queues with Windows users and groups.

➤ **MSMQ HTTP Support:** Enables you to send and receive messages using the HTTP protocol.

➤ **Triggers:** Applications can be instantiated on the arrival of a new message.

➤ **Multicast Support:** A message can be sent to a group of servers.

➤ **MSMQ DCOM Proxy:** A system can connect to a remote server by using the DCOM API.

When Message Queuing is installed, the Message Queuing service (see Figure 47-4) must be started. This service reads and writes messages and communicates with other Message Queuing servers to route messages across the network.

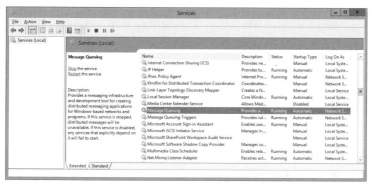

FIGURE 47-4

MESSAGE QUEUING ARCHITECTURE

With Message Queuing, messages are written to and read from a message queue. Messages and message queues have several attributes that must be further elaborated.

Messages

A message is sent to a message queue. The message includes a body containing the data that is sent and a label that is the title of the message. Any information can be put into the body of the message. With .NET, several formatters convert data to be put into the body. In addition to the label and the body, the message includes more information about the sender, timeout configuration, transaction ID, or priority.

Message queues have several types of messages:

A *normal message* is sent by an application.

An *acknowledgment message* reports the status of a normal message. Acknowledgment messages are sent to administration queues to report success or failure when sending normal messages.

Response messages are sent by receiving applications when the original sender requires some special answer.

A *report message* is generated by the Message Queuing system. Test messages and route-tracking messages belong to this category.

A message can have a priority that defines the order in which the messages will be read from the queue. The messages are sorted in the queue according to their priority, so the next message read in the queue is the one with the highest priority.

Messages have two delivery modes: *express* and *recoverable*. Express messages are delivered quickly because memory is used only for the message store. Recoverable messages are stored in files at every step along the route until the message is delivered. This way, delivery of the message is ensured, even with a computer reboot or network failure.

Transactional messages are a special version of recoverable messages. With transactional messaging, it is guaranteed that messages arrive only once and in the same order that they were sent. Priorities cannot be used with transactional messages.

Message Queue

A message queue is a storage bin for messages. You can find messages stored on disk in the `<windir>\system32\msmq\storage` directory.

Public or private queues are usually used for sending messages, but other queue types also exist:

A *public queue* is published in the Active Directory. Information about these queues is replicated across Active Directory domains. You can use browse and search features to get information about these queues.

A public queue can be accessed without knowing the name of the computer where it is placed. You can also move such a queue from one system to another without the client knowing it. You cannot create public queues in a Workgroup environment because the Active Directory is needed.

Private queues are not published in the Active Directory. You can only access these queues when the full pathname to the queue is known. You can use private queues in a Workgroup environment.

Journal queues keep copies of messages after they have been received or sent. Enabling journaling for a public or private queue automatically creates a journal queue. With journal queues, two different queue types are possible: source journaling and target journaling. *Source journaling* is turned on with the properties of a message; journal messages are stored with the source system. *Target journaling* is turned on with the properties of a queue; these messages are stored in the journal queue of the target system.

Dead-letter queues store messages if a message doesn't arrive at the target system before a specific timeout is reached. Contrary to synchronous programming where errors are immediately detected, errors must be dealt with differently using Message Queuing. The dead-letter queue can be checked for messages that didn't arrive.

Administration queues contain acknowledgments for messages sent. The sender can specify an administration queue from which it receives notification of whether the message was sent successfully.

A *response queue* is used if more than a simple acknowledgment is needed as an answer from the receiving side. The receiving application can send response messages back to the original sender.

A *report queue* is used for test messages. You can create report queues by changing the type (or category) of a public or private queue to the predefined ID {55EE8F33-CCE9-11CF-B108-0020AFD61CE9}. Report queues are useful as a testing tool to track messages on their route.

System queues are private and are used by the Message Queuing system. These queues are used for administrative messages, storing of notification messages, and to guarantee the correct order of transactional messages.

MESSAGE QUEUING ADMINISTRATIVE TOOLS

Before looking at how to deal with Message Queuing programmatically, this section looks at the administrative tools that are part of the Windows operating system to create and manage queues and messages.

> **NOTE** *The tools shown here are not used only with Message Queuing. The Message Queuing features of these tools are available only if Message Queuing is installed.*

Creating Message Queues

Message queues can be created with the Computer Management MMC snap-in. In the tree view pane, Message Queuing is located below the Services and Applications entry. By selecting Private Queues or Public Queues, new queues can be created from the Action menu (see Figure 47-5). Public queues are available only if Message Queuing is configured in Active Directory mode.

Message Queue Properties

After a queue is created, you can modify the queue's properties with the Computer Management snap-in by selecting the queue in the tree pane and selecting the Action Properties menu (see Figure 47-6).

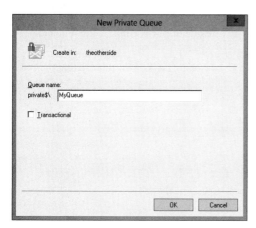

FIGURE 47-5

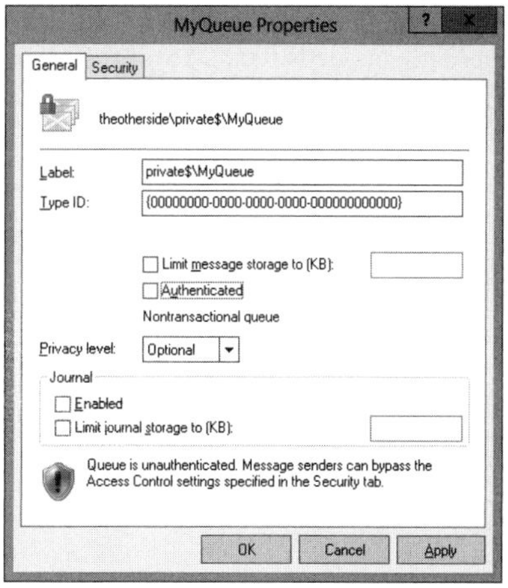

FIGURE 47-6

You can configure several options:

➤ The label is the name of the queue that can search for the queue.

➤ The type ID, which is by default, set to {00000000–0000–0000–0000–000000000000} to map multiple queues to a single category or type. Report queues use a specific type ID, as discussed earlier. A type ID is a universal unique ID (UUID) or GUID.

> **NOTE** *Custom type identifiers can be created with the* uuidgen.exe *or* guidgen.exe *utilities.* uuidgen.exe *is a command-line utility that can create unique IDs, and* guidgen.exe *is a graphical version that creates UUIDs.*

➤ The maximum size of all messages of a queue can be limited to avoid filling up the disk.

➤ When checked, the Authenticated option enables only authenticated users to write and read messages to and from the queue.

➤ With the Privacy Level option, the content of the message can be encrypted. The possible values to set are None, Optional, or Body. None means that no encrypted messages are accepted; Body accepts only encrypted messages; and the default Optional value accepts both.

➤ Target journaling can be configured with the Journal settings. With this option, copies of the messages received are stored in the journal. The maximum size of disk space occupied can be configured for the journal messages of a queue. When the maximum size is reached, target journaling ceases.

➤ With the configuration option Multicast, you can define a multicast IP address for the queue. The same multicast IP address can be used with different nodes in the network so that a message sent to a single address is received with multiple queues.

PROGRAMMING MESSAGE QUEUING

Now that you understand the architecture of Message Queuing, you can look into the programming. In the next sections, you see how to create and control queues, and how to send and receive messages.

You also build a small course order application that consists of a sending and a receiving part.

Creating a Message Queue

You've already seen how to create message queues with the Computer Management utility. Message queues can be created programmatically with the Create method of the MessageQueue class.

With the `Create` method, the path of the new queue must be passed. The path consists of the host name where the queue is located and the name of the queue. In the following example, the queue `MyNewPublicQueue` is created on the local host. To create a private queue, the pathname must include `Private$`; for example, `\Private$\MyNewPrivateQueue`.

After the `Create` method is invoked, properties of the queue can be changed. For example, using the `Label` property, the label of the queue is set to `Demo Queue`. The sample program writes the path of the queue and the format name to the console. The format name is automatically created with a UUID that can access the queue without the name of the server (code file `WorkingWithQueues/CreateMessageQueue/Program.cs`):

```
using System;
using System.Messaging;

namespace Wrox.ProCSharp.Messaging
{
  class Program
  {
    static void Main()
    {
      using (var queue = MessageQueue.Create(@".\MyNewPublicQueue"))
      {
        queue.Label = "Demo Queue";
        Console.WriteLine("Queue created:");
        Console.WriteLine("Path: {0}", queue.Path);
        Console.WriteLine("FormatName: {0}", queue.FormatName);
      }
    }
  }
}
```

> **NOTE** *Administrative privileges are required to create a queue. Usually, you cannot expect the user of your application to have administrative privileges. That's why queues usually are created with installation programs. In the section Message Queue Installation, you see how message queues can be created with the* `MessageQueueInstaller` *class.*

Finding a Queue

You can use the pathname and the format name to identify queues. To find queues, you must differentiate between public and private queues. Public queues are published in the Active Directory. For these queues, it is not necessary to know the system where they are located. You can find private queues only if you know the name of the system where the queue is located.

You can find public queues in the Active Directory domain by searching for the queue's label, category, or format name. You can also get all queues on a machine. The class `MessageQueue` has static methods to search for queues: `GetPublicQueuesByLabel`, `GetPublicQueuesByCategory`, and `GetPublicQueuesByMachine`. The method `GetPublicQueues` returns an array of all public queues in the domain (code file `WorkingWithQueues/FindQueues/Program.cs`):

```
using System;
using System.Messaging;

namespace Wrox.ProCSharp.Messaging
{
  class Program
  {
    static void Main()
    {
      foreach (var queue in MessageQueue.GetPublicQueues())
```

```
        {
          Console.WriteLine(queue.Path);
        }
      }
    }
  }
```

The method `GetPublicQueues` is overloaded. One version enables passing an instance of the `MessageQueueCriteria` class. With this class, you can search for queues created or modified before or after a certain time, and you can also look for a category, label, or machine name.

You can search for private queues with the static method `GetPrivateQueuesByMachine`. This method returns all private queues from a specific system.

Opening Known Queues

If the name of the queue is known, it is not necessary to search for it. Queues can be opened by using the path or format name. They both can be set in the constructor of the `MessageQueue` class.

Pathname

The path specifies the machine name and the queue name to open the queue. This code example opens the queue `MyPublicQueue` on the local host. To be sure that the queue exists, you use the static method `MessageQueue.Exists` (code file `WorkingWithQueues/OpenQueue/Program.cs`):

```
using System;
using System.Messaging;

namespace Wrox.ProCSharp.Messaging
{
  class Program
  {
    static void Main()
    {
      if (MessageQueue.Exists(@".\MyPublicQueue"))
      {
        var queue = new MessageQueue(@".\MyPublicQueue");
        //...

      }
      else
      {
        Console.WriteLine("Queue .\MyPublicQueue not existing");
      }
    }
  }
}
```

Depending on the queue type, different identifiers are required when queues are opened. The following table shows the syntax of the queue name for specific types.

QUEUE TYPE	SYNTAX
Public queue	MachineName\QueueName
Private queue	MachineName\Private$\QueueName
Journal queue	MachineName\QueueName\Journal$
Machine journal queue	MachineName\Journal$
Machine dead-letter queue	MachineName\DeadLetter$
Machine transactional dead-letter queue	MachineName\XactDeadLetter$

When you use the pathname to open public queues, it is necessary to pass the machine name. If the machine name is not known, the format name can be used instead. The pathname for private queues can be used only on the local system. The format name must be used to access private queues remotely.

Format Name

Instead of the pathname, you can use the format name to open a queue. The format name is used for searching the queue in the Active Directory to get the host where the queue is located. In a disconnected environment where the queue cannot be reached at the time the message is sent, you must use the format name:

```
var queue = new MessageQueue(
    @"FormatName:PUBLIC=09816AFF-3608-4c5d-B892-69754BA151FF");
```

The format name has some different uses. You can use it to open private queues and to specify a protocol that should be used:

➤ To access a private queue, the string that must be passed to the constructor is `FormatName:PRIVATE=MachineGUID\QueueNumber`. The queue number for private queues is generated when the queue is created. You can see the queue numbers in the `<windows>\System32\msmq\storage\lqs` directory.

➤ With `FormatName:DIRECT=Protocol:MachineAddress\QueueName`, you can specify the protocol that should be used to send the message. The HTTP protocol is supported since Message Queuing 3.0.

➤ `FormatName:DIRECT=OS:MachineName\QueueName` is another way to specify a queue using the format name. This way you don't need to specify the protocol but still can use the machine name with the format name.

Sending a Message

You can use the `Send` method of the `MessageQueue` class to send a message to the queue. The object passed as an argument of the `Send` method is serialized to the associated queue. The `Send` method is overloaded so that a label and a `MessageQueueTransaction` object can be passed. Transactional behavior of Message Queuing is discussed in the section "Transactional Queues."

The code example first checks if the queue exists. If it doesn't exist, a queue is created. Then the queue is opened and the message `Sample Message` is sent to the queue using the `Send` method.

The pathname specifies a dot (just like a period) for the server name, which is the local system. Pathnames to private queues work only locally (code file `WorkingWithQueues/SendMessage/Program.cs`):

```
using System;
using System.Messaging;

namespace Wrox.ProCSharp.Messaging
{
  class Program
  {
    static void Main()
    {
      try
      {
        if (!MessageQueue.Exists(@".\Private$\MyPrivateQueue"))
        {
          MessageQueue.Create(@".\Private$\MyPrivateQueue");
        }
        var queue = new MessageQueue(@".\Private$\MyPrivateQueue");

        queue.Send("Sample Message", "Label");
      }
```

```
        catch (MessageQueueException ex)
        {
          Console.WriteLine(ex.Message);
        }
      }
    }
  }
```

Figure 47-7 shows the Computer Management admin tool where you can see the message that arrived in the queue.

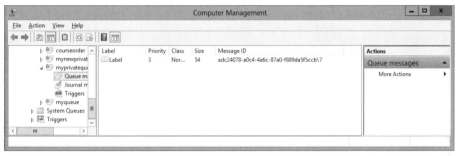

FIGURE 47-7

By opening the message and selecting the Body tab (see Figure 47-8) of the dialog box, you can see that the message was formatted using XML. Determining how the message is formatted is the function of the formatter that's associated with the message queue.

Message Formatter

The format in which messages are transferred to the queue depends on the formatter. The MessageQueue class has a Formatter property through which a formatter can be assigned. The default formatter, XmlMessageFormatter, formats the message in XML syntax as shown in the previous example.

A message formatter implements the interface IMessageFormatter. Three message formatters are available with the namespace System.Messaging:

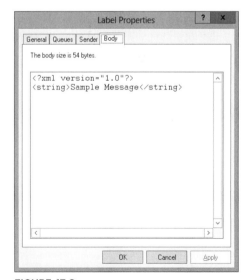

FIGURE 47-8

➤ The XmlMessageFormatter is the default formatter. It serializes objects using XML. See Chapter 34, "Manipulating XML," for more on XML formatting.

➤ With the BinaryMessageFormatter, messages are serialized in a binary format. These messages are shorter than the messages formatted using XML.

➤ The ActiveXMessageFormatter is a binary formatter so that messages can be read or written with COM objects. Using this formatter, you can write a message to the queue with a .NET class and to read the message from the queue with a COM object or vice versa.

The sample message shown in Figure 47-8 with XML is formatted with the BinaryMessageFormatter in Figure 47-9.

Sending Complex Messages

Instead of passing strings, you can pass objects to the Send method of the MessageQueue class. The type of the class must fulfill some specific requirements, but they depend on the formatter.

For the binary formatter, the class must be serializable with the [Serializable] attribute. With the .NET runtime serialization, all fields are serialized. (This includes private fields.) Custom serialization can be defined by implementing the interface ISerializable. You can read more about the .NET runtime serialization in Chapter 24, "Manipulating Files and the Registry."

XML serialization takes place with the XML formatter. With XML serialization, all public fields and properties are serialized. The XML serialization can be influenced by using attributes from the System.Xml.Serialization namespace. You can read more about XML serialization in Chapter 34.

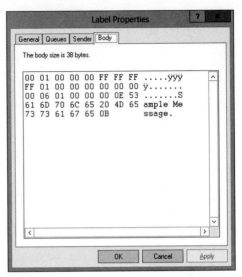

FIGURE 47-9

Receiving Messages

To read messages, again, you can use the MessageQueue class. With the Receive method, a single message is read and removed from the queue. If messages are sent with different priorities, the message with the highest priority is read. Reading messages with the same priority may mean that the first message sent is not the first message read because the order of messages across the network is not guaranteed. For a guaranteed order, you should use transactional message queues.

In the following example, a message is read from the private queue MyPrivateQueue. Previously, a simple string was passed to the message. When you read a message using the XmlMessageFormatter, you must pass the types of the objects that are read to the constructor of the formatter. In the example, the type System.String is passed to the argument array of the XmlMessageFormatter constructor. This constructor enables either a String array that contains the types as strings to be passed or a Type array.

The message is read with the Receive method, and then the message body is written to the console (code file WorkingWithQueues/SendMessage/Program.cs):

```
using System;
using System.Messaging;

namespace Wrox.ProCSharp.Messaging
{
  class Program
  {
    static void Main()
    {
      var queue = new MessageQueue(@".\Private$\MyPrivateQueue");
      queue.Formatter = new XmlMessageFormatter(
          new string[] {"System.String"});

      Message message = queue.Receive();
      Console.WriteLine(message.Body);
    }
  }
}
```

The `Receive` message behaves synchronously and waits until a message is in the queue if there is none.

Enumerating Messages

Instead of reading message by message with the `Receive` method, you can use an enumerator to walk through all messages. The `MessageQueue` class implements the interface `IEnumerable` and thus can be used with a `foreach` statement. Here, the messages are not removed from the queue, but you get just a peek at the messages to get their content:

```
var queue = new MessageQueue(@".\Private$\MyPrivateQueue");
queue.Formatter = new XmlMessageFormatter(
    new string[] {"System.String"});

foreach (Message message in queue)
{
    Console.WriteLine(message.Body);
}
```

Instead of using the `IEnumerable` interface, you can use the class `MessageEnumerator`. `MessageEnumerator` implements the interface `IEnumerator` but has some more features. With the `IEnumerable` interface, the messages are not removed from the queue. The method `RemoveCurrent` of the `MessageEnumerator` removes the message from the current cursor position of the enumerator.

In the example, the `MessageQueue` method `GetMessageEnumerator`accesses the `MessageEnumerator`. The `MoveNext` method takes a peek message by message with the `MessageEnumerator`. The `MoveNext` method is overloaded to allow a time span as an argument. This is one of the big advantages when using this enumerator. Here, the thread can wait until a message arrives in the queue, but only for the specified time span. The `Current` property, which is defined by the `IEnumerator` interface, returns a reference to a message:

```
var queue = new MessageQueue(@".\Private$\MyPrivateQueue");
queue.Formatter = new XmlMessageFormatter(
    new string[] {"System.String"});

using (MessageEnumerator messages = queue.GetMessageEnumerator())
{
    while (messages.MoveNext(TimeSpan.FromMinutes(30)))
    {
        Message message = messages.Current;
        Console.WriteLine(message.Body);
    }
}
```

Asynchronous Read

The `Receive` method of the `MessageQueue` class waits until a message from the queue can be read. To avoid blocking the thread, you can specify a timeout in an overloaded version of the `Receive` method. To read the message from the queue after the timeout, you must invoke `Receive`again. Instead of polling for messages, the asynchronous method `BeginReceive` can be called. Before starting the asynchronous read with `BeginReceive`, you should set the event `ReceiveCompleted`. The `ReceiveCompleted` event requires a `ReceiveCompletedEventHandler` delegate that references the method invoked when a message arrives in the queue and can be read. In the example, the method `MessageArrived` passes to the `ReceivedCompletedEventHandler` delegate (code file `WorkingWithQueues/ReceiveMessageAsync/Program.cs`):

```
var queue = new MessageQueue(@".\Private$\MyPrivateQueue");
queue.Formatter = new XmlMessageFormatter(
    new string[] {"System.String"});
```

```
queue.ReceiveCompleted += MessageArrived;
queue.BeginReceive();
// thread does not wait
```

The handler method `MessageArrived` requires two parameters. The first parameter is the origin of the event, the `MessageQueue`. The second parameter is of type `ReceiveCompletedEventArgs` that contains the message and the asynchronous result. In the example, the method `EndReceive` from the queue is invoked to get the result of the asynchronous method, the message:

```
public static void MessageArrived(object source, ReceiveCompletedEventArgs e)
{
    MessageQueue queue = (MessageQueue)source;
    Message message = queue.EndReceive(e.AsyncResult);
    Console.WriteLine(message.Body);
}
```

If the message should not be removed from the queue, the `BeginPeek` and `EndPeek` methods can be used with asynchronous I/O.

COURSE ORDER APPLICATION

To demonstrate the use of Message Queuing, in this section you create a sample solution to order courses. The sample solution is made up of three assemblies:

➤ A component library (`CourseOrder`) that includes entity classes for the messages sent and received in the queue

➤ A WPF application (`CourseOrderSender`) that sends messages to the message queue

➤ A WPF application (`CourseOrderReceiver`) that receives messages from the message queue

Course Order Class Library

Both the sending and the receiving application need the order information. For this reason, the entity classes are put into a separate assembly. The `CourseOrder` assembly includes three entity classes: `CourseOrder`, `Course`, and `Customer` and a base class `BindableBase`. With the sample application, not all properties are implemented as they would be in a real application, but just enough properties to show the concept.

In the file `BindableBase.cs`, the class `BindableBase` is defined. This class implements the interface `INotifyPropertyChanged` and offers the method `SetProperty` that can be called from derived classes within a property setter (code file `CourseOrderApplication/CourseOrder/BindableBase.cs`).

```
using System.Collections.Generic;
using System.ComponentModel;
using System.Runtime.CompilerServices;

namespace Wrox.ProCSharp.Messaging
{
    public abstract class BindableBase : INotifyPropertyChanged
    {
        protected void SetProperty<T>(ref T prop, T value,
            [CallerMemberName] string callerName = "")
        {
            if (!EqualityComparer<T>.Default.Equals(prop, value))
            {
                prop = value;
                OnPropertyChanged(callerName);
            }
        }
```

```
      protected virtual void OnPropertyChanged(string propertyName)
      {
        PropertyChangedEventHandler propertyChanged = PropertyChanged;
        if (propertyChanged != null)
        {
          propertyChanged(this, new PropertyChangedEventArgs(propertyName));
        }
      }

      public event PropertyChangedEventHandler PropertyChanged;
    }
  }
```

In the file `Course.cs`, the class `Course` is defined. This class has just one property for the title of the course (code file `CourseOrderApplication/CourseOrder/Course.cs`):

```
  public class Course : BindableBase
  {
    private string title;
    public string Title
    {
      get { return title; }
      set
      {
        SetProperty(ref title, value);
      }
    }
  }
```

The file `Customer.cs` includes the class `Customer`, which includes properties for the company and contact names (code file `CourseOrderApplication/CourseOrder/Customer.cs`):

```
  public class Customer : BindableBase
  {
    private string company;
    public string Company
    {
      get { return company; }
      set
      {
        SetProperty(ref company, value);
      }
    }

    private string contact;
    public string Contact
    {
      get { return contact; }
      set
      {
        SetProperty(contact, value);
      }
    }
  }
```

The class `CourseOrder` in the file `CourseOrder.cs` maps a customer and a course inside an order and defines whether the order is high priority. This class also defines the name of the queue that is set to a format name of a public queue. The format name is used to send the message, even if the queue cannot be reached currently. You can get the format name by using the Computer Management snap-in to read the ID of the message queue. If you don't have access to an Active Directory to create a public queue, you can easily

change the code to use a private queue (code file `CourseOrderApplication/CourseOrder/`
`CourseOrder.cs`):

```
public class CourseOrder : BindableBase
{
  public const string CourseOrderQueueName =
      "FormatName:Public=D99CE5F3-4282-4a97-93EE-E9558B15EB13";

  private Customer customer;
  public Customer Customer
  {
    get { return customer; }
    set
    {
      SetProperty(ref customer, value);
    }
  }

  private Course course;
  public Course Course
  {
    get { return course; }
    set
    {
      SetProperty(ref course, value);
    }
  }
}
```

Course Order Message Sender

The second part of the solution is a Windows application called
`CourseOrderSender`. With this application, course orders are sent
to the message queue. The assemblies `System.Messaging` and
`CourseOrder` must be referenced.

The user interface of this application is shown in Figure 47-10. A
combo box enables selecting an available course, and some text
box controls enable entering some text by the user before submitting
the order.

The XAML code makes use of WPF data binding as shown
in the code snippet. The `ComboBox` is bound to the property `Courses` that returns a list of available courses (code
file `CourseOrderApplication/CourseOrderSender/`
`CourseOrderWindow.xaml`).

FIGURE 47-10

```
<CheckBox Grid.Row="3" Grid.Column="0"
    IsChecked="{Binding MessageConfiguration.HighPriority,
        Mode=OneWayToSource}">
  High Priority</CheckBox>
<ComboBox ItemsSource="{Binding Courses}" Grid.Row="0" Grid.Column="1"
    SelectedItem="{Binding CourseOrder.Course.Title, Mode=OneWayToSource}" />
<TextBox Text="{Binding CourseOrder.Customer.Company}" Grid.Row="1"
    Grid.Column="1" />
<TextBox Text="{Binding CourseOrder.Customer.Contact}" Grid.Row="2"
    Grid.Column="1" />
<Button Click="buttonSubmit_Click" Grid.Row="3" Grid.Column="1">
  Submit the Order</Button>
```

The properties bound from the code-behind file are shown in the following code snippet. The `Courses` property just returns a string collection that contains available courses. The `CourseOrder` property of type `CourseOrder` receives the input data from the user. The `CourseOrder` class was shown earlier creating the course order class library (code file `CourseOrderApplication/CourseOrderSender/CourseOrderWindow.xaml.xs`):

```
public partial class CourseOrderWindow : Window
{
    private readonly ObservableCollection<string> courseList =
        new ObservableCollection<string>();
    private readonly CourseOrder courseOrder = new CourseOrder();
    private readonly MessageConfiguration messageConfiguration =
        new MessageConfiguration();

    public CourseOrderWindow()
    {
        InitializeComponent();
        FillCourses();
        this.DataContext = this;
    }

    public IEnumerable<string> Courses
    {
        get
        {
            return courseList;
        }
    }

    private void FillCourses()
    {
        courseList.Add("Parallel .NET Programming");
        courseList.Add("Data Access with the ADO.NET Entity Framework");
        courseList.Add("Distributed Solutions with WCF");
        courseList.Add("Windows 8 Metro Apps with XAML and C#");
    }

    public CourseOrder CourseOrder
    {
        get
        {
            return courseOrder;
        }
    }
    public MessageConfiguration MessageConfiguration
    {
        get
        {
            return messageConfiguration;
        }
    }
}
```

When the Submit the Order button is clicked, the handler method `buttonSubmit_Click` is invoked. With this method, a `MessageQueue` instance is created to open a message queue with a format name. With the `Send` method, the `courseOrder` object is passed to write the message to the queue (code file `CourseOrderApplication/CourseOrderSender/CourseOrderWindow.xaml.cs`):

```
private void buttonSubmit_Click(object sender, RoutedEventArgs e)
{
    try
```

```
    {
      using (var queue = new MessageQueue(CourseOrder.CourseOrderQueueName))
      {
        queue.Send(courseOrder, String.Format("Course Order {{{0}}}",
            courseOrder.Customer.Company));
      }

      MessageBox.Show("Course Order submitted", "Course Order",
          MessageBoxButton.OK, MessageBoxImage.Information);
    }
    catch (MessageQueueException ex)
    {
      MessageBox.Show(ex.Message, "Course Order Error",
          MessageBoxButton.OK, MessageBoxImage.Error);
    }
  }
}
```

Sending Priority and Recoverable Messages

Messages can be prioritized by setting the `Priority` property of the `Message` class. If messages are specially configured, a `Message` object must be created where the body of the message is passed in the constructor.

In the example, the priority is set to `MessagePriority.High` or `MessagePriority.Normal` depending on the selection of the user that manifests with the `MessageConfiguration.HighPriority` property that is bound to a check box setting. `MessagePriority` is an enumeration that enables you to set values from `Lowest` (0) to `Highest` (7). The default value, `Normal`, has a priority value of 3.

To make the message recoverable, the property `Recoverable` is set to `true`:

```
    private void buttonSubmit_Click(object sender, RoutedEventArgs e)
    {
      try
      {
        using (var queue = new MessageQueue(CourseOrder.CourseOrderQueueName))
        using (var message = new Message(courseOrder)
          {
            Recoverable = true,
            Priority = MessageConfiguration.HighPriority == true ?
                MessagePriority.High : MessagePriority.Normal
          })
        {
          queue.Send(message, String.Format("Course Order {{{0}}}",
              courseOrder.Customer.Company));
        }

        MessageBox.Show("Course Order submitted", "Course Order",
            MessageBoxButton.OK, MessageBoxImage.Information);
      }
      catch (MessageQueueException ex)
      {
        MessageBox.Show(ex.Message, "Course Order Error",
            MessageBoxButton.OK, MessageBoxImage.Error);
      }
    }
```

By running the application, you can add course orders to the message queue (see Figure 47-11).

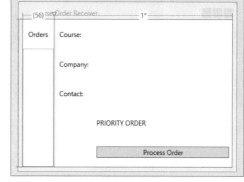

FIGURE 47-11

FIGURE 47-12

Course Order Message Receiver

The design view of the Course Order receiving application that reads messages from the queue is shown in Figure 47-12. This application displays labels of every order in the `listOrders` list box. When an order is selected, the content of the order displays with the controls on the right side of the application.

As with the previous WPF application, the receiving application makes use of data binding as well. Here, the `ListBox` is bound to the `OrdersList` property that returns a list of all orders. A `Grid` that contains the controls for the selected order from the list box is bound to the property `SelectedCourseInfo`. The property `SelectedCourseInfo` is of type `CourseOrderInfo`. This class is created for defining the information needed by the child controls of this grid. `CourseOrderInfo` implements the properties `Course`, `Company`, `Contact`... (code file `CourseOrderApplication/CourseOrderReceiver/CourseOrderReceiverWindow.xaml`):

```
<Grid Grid.Column="0">
  <Grid.RowDefinitions>
    <RowDefinition Height="*" />
    <RowDefinition Height="4*" />
  </Grid.RowDefinitions>
  <Label Grid.Row="0" Content="Orders"/>
  <ListBox x:Name="listOrders" Grid.Row="1" ItemsSource="{Binding OrdersList}"
      SelectionChanged="listOrders_SelectionChanged" />
</Grid>
<GridSplitter Grid.Column="1" HorizontalAlignment="Left" Width="3" />
<Grid Grid.Column="1" IsEnabled="True"
    DataContext="{Binding SelectedCourseInfo}" >
  <Grid.RowDefinitions>
    <RowDefinition />
    <RowDefinition />
    <RowDefinition />
    <RowDefinition />
    <RowDefinition />
  </Grid.RowDefinitions>
  <Grid.ColumnDefinitions>
    <ColumnDefinition Width="Auto" />
    <ColumnDefinition Width="*" />
  </Grid.ColumnDefinitions>
  <Label Grid.Row="0" Grid.Column="0" Content="Course:"/>
  <Label Grid.Row="1" Grid.Column="0" Content="Company:"/>
  <Label Grid.Row="2" Grid.Column="0" Content="Contact:"/>
  <TextBlock Text="{Binding Course}" Grid.Row="0" Grid.Column="1" />
  <TextBlock Text="{Binding Company}" Grid.Row="1" Grid.Column="1" />
  <TextBlock Text="{Binding Contact}" Grid.Row="2" Grid.Column="1" />
```

```
<TextBlock Grid.Row="3" Grid.Column="1" Text="PRIORITY ORDER"
    Visibility="{Binding HighPriority}"/>
<Button Grid.Row="4" Grid.Column="1" Content="Process Order"
    IsEnabled="{Binding EnableProcessing}"
    Click="buttonProcessOrder_Click"/>
```

The code for the class `CourseOrderInfo` is shown in the next code snippet. This class derives from the base class `BindableBase` shown earlier for an implementation of the interface `INotifyPropertyChanged` and defines all the properties needed for data binding from XAML (code file `CourseOrderApplication/CourseOrderReceiver/CourseOrderInfo.cs`):

```csharp
using System.Windows;

namespace Wrox.ProCSharp.Messaging
{
  public class CourseOrderInfo : BindableBase
  {
    public CourseOrderInfo()
    {
      Clear();
    }

    private MessageInfo messageInfo;
    public MessageInfo MessageInfo
    {
      get { return messageInfo; }
      set
      {
        SetProperty(ref messageInfo, value);
      }
    }

    private string course;
    public string Course
    {
      get { return course; }
      set
      {
        SetProperty(ref course, value);
      }
    }

    private string company;
    public string Company
    {
      get { return company; }
      set
      {
        SetProperty(ref company, value);
      }
    }

    private string contact;
    public string Contact
    {
      get { return contact; }
      set
      {
        SetProperty(ref contact, value);
      }
    }
```

```
        private bool enableProcessing;
        public bool EnableProcessing
        {
          get
          {
            return enableProcessing;
          }
          set
          {
            SetProperty(ref enableProcessing, value);
          }
        }

        private Visibility highPriority;
        public Visibility HighPriority
        {
          get
          {
            return highPriority;
          }
          set
          {
            SetProperty(ref highPriority, value);
          }
        }

        public void Clear()
        {
          Course = string.Empty;
          Company = string.Empty;
          Contact = string.Empty;
          EnableProcessing = false;
          HighPriority = Visibility.Hidden;
        }
      }
    }
```

In the constructor of the `Window` class `CourseOrderReceiverWindow`, the `MessageQueue` object is created that references the same queue that was used with the sending application. For reading messages, the `XmlMessageFormatter` with the types that are read is associated with the queue using the `Formatter` property.

To display the available messages in the list, a new task is created that peeks at messages in the background. The task's main method is `PeekMessages` (code file `CourseOrderApplication/CourseOrderReceiver/CourseOrderReceiverWindow.xaml.cs`):

```
using System;
using System.Collections.ObjectModel;
using System.Messaging;
using System.Threading.Tasks;
using System.Windows;
using System.Windows.Controls;
using System.Windows.Data;
using System.Windows.Threading;

namespace Wrox.ProCSharp.Messaging
{
  public partial class CourseOrderReceiverWindow : Window
  {
    private MessageQueue ordersQueue;
    private ObservableCollection<MessageInfo> ordersList =
```

```
          new ObservableCollection<MessageInfo>();
  private object syncOrdersList = new object();

  public ObservableCollection<MessageInfo> OrdersList
  {
    get
    {
      return ordersList;
    }
  }

  protected override void OnClosed(EventArgs e)
  {
    base.OnClosed(e);
    if (ordersQueue != null)
      ordersQueue.Dispose();
  }

  public CourseOrderReceiverWindow()
  {
    InitializeComponent();
    this.DataContext = this;
    BindingOperations.EnableCollectionSynchronization(ordersList,
        syncOrdersList);

    ordersQueue = new MessageQueue(CourseOrder.CourseOrderQueueName);

    ordersQueue.Formatter = new XmlMessageFormatter(
      new Type[]
        {
          typeof(CourseOrder),
          typeof(Customer),
          typeof(Course)
        });

    // start the task that fills the ListBox with orders
    Task.Factory.StartNew(PeekMessages);
  }
```

> **NOTE** *You can read more about tasks in Chapter 21, "Tasks, Threads, and Synchronization".*

The task's main method, PeekMessages, uses the enumerator of the message queue to display all messages. Within the while loop, the messagesEnumerator checks to see if there is a new message in the queue. If there is no message in the queue, the task waits 3 hours for the next message to arrive before it exits.

```
  private void PeekMessages()
  {
    try
    {
      using (MessageEnumerator messagesEnumerator =
          ordersQueue.GetMessageEnumerator2())
      {
        while (messagesEnumerator.MoveNext(TimeSpan.FromHours(3)))
        {
          var messageInfo = new MessageInfo
          {
            Id = messagesEnumerator.Current.Id,
```

```
                Label = messagesEnumerator.Current.Label
            };

            ordersList.Add(messageInfo);
        }
    }
    MessageBox.Show("No orders in the last 3 hours. Exiting thread",
        "Course Order Receiver", MessageBoxButton.OK,
        MessageBoxImage.Information);
}
catch (MessageQueueException ex)
{
    MessageBox.Show(ex.Message, "Error", MessageBoxButton.OK,
        MessageBoxImage.Error);
}
}
```

The `ListBox` control contains elements of the `MessageInfo` class. This class is used to display the labels of the messages in the list box but to keep the ID of the message hidden. The ID of the message can be used to read the message at a later time (code file `CourseOrderApplication/CourseOrderReceiver/MessageInfo.cs`):

```
private class MessageInfo
{
    public string Label { get; set; }
    public string Id { get; set; }

    public override string ToString()
    {
        return Label;
    }
}
```

The `ListBox` control has the `SelectedIndexChanged` event associated with the method `listOrders_SelectionChanged`. This method gets the `LabelIdMapping` object from the current selection and uses the ID to peek at the message once more with the `PeekById` method. Then the content of the message displays in the `TextBox` control. Because by default the priority of the message is not read, the property `MessageReadPropertyFilter` must be set to receive the `Priority` (code file `CourseOrderApplication/CourseOrderReceiver/CourseOrderReceiverWindow.xaml.cs`):

```
private void listOrders_SelectionChanged(object sender,
    SelectionChangedEventArgs e)
{
    var messageInfo = (sender as ListBox).SelectedItem as MessageInfo;
    if (messageInfo == null)
        return;

    ordersQueue.MessageReadPropertyFilter.Priority = true;
    Message message = ordersQueue.PeekById(messageInfo.Id);

    var order = message.Body as CourseOrder;
    if (order != null)
    {
        selectedCourseInfo.MessageInfo = messageInfo;
        selectedCourseInfo.Course = order.Course.Title;
        selectedCourseInfo.Company = order.Customer.Company;
        selectedCourseInfo.Contact = order.Customer.Contact;
        selectedCourseInfo.EnableProcessing = true;

        if (message.Priority > MessagePriority.Normal)
```

```
    {
      selectedCourseInfo.HighPriority = Visibility.Visible;
    }
    else
    {
      selectedCourseInfo.HighPriority = Visibility.Hidden;
    }
  }
  else
  {
    MessageBox.Show("The selected item is not a course order",
          "Course Order Receiver", MessageBoxButton.OK,
          MessageBoxImage.Warning);
  }
}
```

When the Process Order button is clicked, the handler method `OnProcessOrder` is invoked. Here again, the currently selected message from the list box is referenced, and the message is removed from the queue by calling the method `ReceiveById`:

```
private void buttonProcessOrder_Click(object sender, RoutedEventArgs e)
{
  Message message = ordersQueue.ReceiveById(
      SelectedCourseInfo.MessageInfo.Id);

  ordersList.Remove(SelectedCourseInfo.MessageInfo);

  listOrders.SelectedIndex = -1;
  selectedCourseInfo.Clear();

  MessageBox.Show("Course order processed", "Course Order Receiver",
      MessageBoxButton.OK, MessageBoxImage.Information);
}
```

Figure 47-13 shows the running receiving application that lists four orders in the queue, and one order is currently selected.

RECEIVING RESULTS

With the current version of the sample application, the sending application never knows if the message is ever dealt with. To get results from the receiver, you can use acknowledgment queues or response queues.

Acknowledgment Queues

With an acknowledgment queue, the sending application can get information about the status of the message. With acknowledgments, you can define if you would like to receive an answer, if everything went

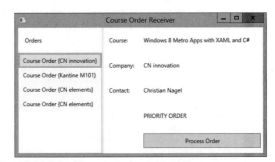

FIGURE 47-13

okay, or if something went wrong. For example, acknowledgments can be sent when the message reaches the destination queue or when the message is read, or if it didn't reach the destination queue or was not read before a timeout elapsed.

In the example, the `AdministrationQueue` of the `Message` class is set to the `CourseOrderAck` queue, which must be created similar to a normal queue. This queue is just used the other way around: The original sender receives acknowledgments. The `AcknowledgeType` property is set to `AcknowledgeTypes.FullReceive` to get an acknowledgment when the message is read:

```
var message = new Message(order);

message.AdministrationQueue = new MessageQueue(@".\CourseOrderAck");
message.AcknowledgeType = AcknowledgeTypes.FullReceive;

queue.Send(message, String.Format("Course Order {{0}}",
        order.Customer.Company);

string id = message.Id;
```

The *correlation ID* determines what acknowledgment message belongs to which message sent. Every message sent has an ID, and the acknowledgment message sent in response to that message holds the ID of the originating message as its correlation ID. The messages from the acknowledgment queue can be read using `MessageQueue.ReceiveByCorrelationId` to receive the associated acknowledgment.

Instead of using acknowledgments, the dead-letter queue can be used for messages that didn't arrive at their destination. With the `UseDeadLetterQueue` property of the `Message` class set to `true`, the message is copied to the dead-letter queue if it didn't arrive at the target queue before the timeout was reached.

Timeouts can be set with the `Message` properties `TimeToReachQueue` and `TimeToBeReceived`.

Response Queues

If more information than an acknowledgment is needed from the receiving application, a response queue can be used. A response queue is like a normal queue, but the original sender uses the queue as a receiver, and the original receiver uses the response queue as a sender.

The sender must assign the response queue with the `ResponseQueue` property of the `Message` class. The sample code here shows how the receiver uses the response queue to return a response message. With the response message `responseMessage`, the property `CorrelationId` is set to the ID of the original message. This way the client application knows to which message the answer belongs. This is similar to acknowledgment queues. The response message is sent with the `Send` method of the `MessageQueue` object that is returned from the `ResponseQueue` property:

```
public void ReceiveMessage(Message message)
{
    var responseMessage = new Message("response")
    {
        CorrelationId = message.Id
    }

    message.ResponseQueue.Send(responseMessage);
}
```

TRANSACTIONAL QUEUES

With recoverable messages, it is not guaranteed that the messages arrives in order and just once. Failures on the network can cause messages to arrive multiple times; this happens also if both the sender and receiver have multiple network protocols installed that are used by Message Queuing.

Transactional queues can be used when these guarantees are required:

➤   Messages arrive in the same order they have been sent.

➤   Messages arrive only once.

With transactional queues, a single transaction doesn't span the sending and receiving of messages. The nature of Message Queuing is that the time between send and receive can be quite long. In contrast, transactions should be short. With Message Queuing, the first transaction is used to send the message into the queue, the second transaction forwards the message on the network, and the third transaction is used to receive the messages.

The next example shows how to create a transactional message queue and how to send messages using a transaction.

A transactional message queue is created by passing true with the second parameter of the MessageQueue. Create method.

If you want to write multiple messages to a queue within a single transaction, you must instantiate a MessageQueueTransaction object and invoke the Begin method. When you finish sending all messages that belong to the transaction, the Commit method of the MessageQueueTransaction object must be called. To cancel a transaction (and have no messages written to the queue), the Abort method must be called, as you can see within the catch block:

```csharp
using System;
using System.Messaging;

namespace Wrox.ProCSharp.Messaging
{
  class Program
  {
    static void Main()
    {
      if (!MessageQueue.Exists(@".\MyTransactionalQueue"))
      {
        MessageQueue.Create(@".\MyTransactionalQueue", true);
      }

      var queue = new MessageQueue(@".\MyTransactionalQueue");
      var transaction = new MessageQueueTransaction();

      try
      {
        transaction.Begin();
        queue.Send("a", transaction);
        queue.Send("b", transaction);
        queue.Send("c", transaction);
        transaction.Commit();
      }
      catch
      {
        transaction.Abort();
      }
    }
  }
}
```

MESSAGE QUEUING WITH WCF

Chapter 43, "Windows Communication Foundation," covers the architecture and core features of WCF. With WCF, you can configure a Message Queuing binding that makes use of the Windows Message Queuing architecture. With this, WCF offers an abstraction layer to Message Queuing. Figure 47-14 explains the architecture using a simple picture. The client application invokes a method of a WCF proxy to send a message to the queue. The message is created by the proxy. For the client developer, there's no need to know that a message is sent to the queue. The client developer just invokes a method of the proxy. The proxy abstracts deals with the classes from the System.Messaging namespace and sends a message to the queue. The MSMQ listener channel on the service side reads messages from the queue, converts them to method calls, and invokes the method calls with the service.

Next, the Course Ordering application converts to make use of Message Queuing from a WCF viewpoint. With this solution, the three earlier projects are modified, and one more assembly is added that includes the contract of the WCF service:

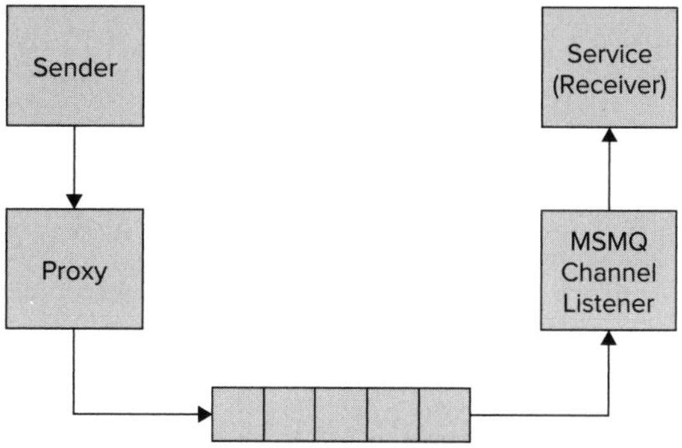

➤ The component library (CourseOrder) includes entity classes for the messages that are sent across the wire. These entity classes are modified to fulfill the data contract for serialization with WCF.

➤ A new library is added (CourseOrderService) that defines the contract offered by the service.

FIGURE 47-14

➤ The WPF sender application (CourseOrderSender) is modified to not send messages but instead invoke methods of a WCF proxy.

➤ The WPF receiving application (CourseOrderReceiver) is modified to make use of the WCF service that implements the contract.

Entity Classes with a Data Contract

In the library CourseOrder, the classes Course, Customer, and CourseOrder are modified to apply the data contract with the attributes [DataContract] and [DataMember]. For using these attributes, you must reference the assembly System.Runtime.Serialization and import the namespace System.Runtime .Serialization (code file CourseOrderApplicationWCF/CourseOrder/Course.cs):

```csharp
using System.Runtime.Serialization;

namespace Wrox.ProCSharp.Messaging
{
  [DataContract]
  public class Course
  {
    [DataMember]
    public string Title { get; set; }
  }
}
```

The Customer class requires the data contract attributes as well (code file CourseOrderApplicationWCF/ CourseOrder/Customer.cs):

```csharp
[DataContract]
public class Customer
{
  [DataMember]
  public string Company { get; set; }

  [DataMember]
  public string Contact { get; set; }
}
```

With the class CourseOrder, not only the data contract attributes are added, but an override of the ToString method as well to have a default string representation of these objects (code file CourseOrderApplicationWCF/CourseOrder/CourseOrder.cs):

```csharp
[DataContract]
public class CourseOrder
```

```
    {
      [DataMember]
      public Customer Customer { get; set; }

      [DataMember]
      public Course Course { get; set; }

      public override string ToString()
      {
        return String.Format("Course Order {{{0}}}", Customer.Company);
      }
    }
```

WCF Service Contract

To offer the service with a WCF service contract, add a WCF service library with the name CourseOrderServiceContract. The contract is defined by the interface ICourseOrderService. This contract needs the attribute [ServiceContract]. If you want to restrict using this interface only with message queues, you can apply the [DeliveryRequirements] attribute and assign the property QueuedDeliveryRequirements. Possible values of the enumeration QueuedDeliveryRequirementsMode are Required, Allowed, and NotAllowed. The method AddCourseOrder is offered by the service. Methods used by Message Queuing can have only input parameters. Because the sender and receiver can run independent of each other, the sender cannot expect an immediate result. With the attribute [OperationContract], the IsOneWay property is set. The caller of this operation does not wait for an answer from the service (code file CourseOrderApplicationWCF/CourseOrderServiceContract/ICourseOrderService.cs):

```
using System.ServiceModel;

namespace Wrox.ProCSharp.Messaging
{
  [ServiceContract]
  [DeliveryRequirements(
      QueuedDeliveryRequirements=QueuedDeliveryRequirementsMode.Required)]
  public interface ICourseOrderService
  {
    [OperationContract(IsOneWay = true)]
    void AddCourseOrder(CourseOrder courseOrder);
  }
}
```

> **NOTE** *You can use acknowledgment and response queues to get answers to the client.*

WCF Message Receiver Application

The WPF application CourseOrderReceiver is now modified to implement the WCF service and receive the messages. References to the assembly System.ServiceModel and the WCF contract assembly CourseOrderServiceContract are required.

The class CourseOrderService implements the interface ICourseOrderService. With the implementation, the event CourseOrderAdded is fired. The WPF application registers to this event to receive CourseOrder objects.

Because WPF controls are bound to a single thread, the property UseSynchronizationContext is set with the [ServiceBehavior] attribute. This is a feature of the WCF runtime to pass the method call invocation to the thread defined by the synchronization context of the WPF application (code file `CourseOrderApplicationWCF/CourseOrderReceiver/CourseOrderService.cs`):

```
using System.ServiceModel;

namespace Wrox.ProCSharp.Messaging
{
  [ServiceBehavior(UseSynchronizationContext=true)]

  public class CourseOrderService: ICourseOrderService
  {
    public static event EventHandler<CourseOrderEventArgs>
        CourseOrderAdded;

    public void AddCourseOrder(CourseOrder courseOrder)
    {
      var courseOrderAdded = CourseOrderAdded;
      if (courseOrderAdded != null)
      {
        courseOrderAdded(this, new CourseOrderEventArgs(courseOrder));
      }
    }
  }

  public class CourseOrderEventArgs : EventArgs
  {
    public CourseOrderEventArgs(CourseOrder courseOrder)
    {
      this.CourseOrder = courseOrder;
    }
    public CourseOrder CourseOrder { get; private set; }
  }
}
```

> **NOTE** *Chapter 21, "Tasks, Threads, and Synchronization", explains the synchronization context.*

With the constructor of the class `CourseReceiverWindow`, a `ServiceHost` object is instantiated and opened to start the listener. The binding of the listener is done in the application configuration file.

In the constructor, the event `CourseOrderAdded` of the `CourseOrderService` is subscribed. Because the only thing that happens here is adding the received `CourseOrder` object to a collection, a simple Lambda expression is used.

> **NOTE** *Lambda expressions are explained in Chapter 8, "Delegates, Lambdas, and Events."*

The collection class used here is `ObservableCollection<T>` from the namespace `System.Collections.ObjectModel`. This collection class implements the interface `INotifyCollectionChanged`, and thus the WPF controls bound to the collection are informed about dynamic changes to the list (code file `CourseOrderApplicationWCF/CourseOrderReceiver/CourseOrderReceiverWindow.xaml.cs`):

```
using System;
using System.Collections.ObjectModel;
using System.ServiceModel;
using System.Windows;
```

```
namespace Wrox.ProCSharp.Messaging
{
  public partial class CourseOrderReceiverWindow : Window
  {
    private ObservableCollection<CourseOrder> courseOrders =
        new ObservableCollection<CourseOrder>();

    public CourseOrderReceiverWindow()
    {
      InitializeComponent();
      this.DataContext = courseOrders;
      CourseOrderService.CourseOrderAdded += (sender, e) =>
        {
          courseOrders.Add(e.CourseOrder);
          buttonProcessOrder.IsEnabled = true;
        };

      var host = new ServiceHost(typeof(CourseOrderService));
      try
      {
        host.Open();
      }
      catch (Exception ex)
      {
        Console.WriteLine(ex.Message);
      }
    }
  }
}
```

The data binding of the WPF elements in the XAML code is now changed to use the new collection. The ListBox is bound to the data context, and the single-item controls are bound to properties of the current item of the data context (code file CourseOrderApplicationWCF/CourseOrderReceiver/CourseOrderReceiverWindow.xaml):

```
<ListBox x:Name="listOrders" Grid.Row="1" ItemsSource="{Binding}"
    IsSynchronizedWithCurrentItem="True" />
<!-- ... -->

<TextBlock Text="{Binding Course.Title}" Grid.Row="0" Grid.Column="1" />
<TextBlock Text="{Binding Customer.Company}" Grid.Row="1" Grid.Column="1" />
<TextBlock Text="{Binding Customer.Contact}" Grid.Row="2" Grid.Column="1" />
```

The application configuration file defines the netMsmqBinding. For reliable messaging, transactional queues are required. To receive and send messages to nontransactional queues, the exactlyOnce property must be set to false (config file CourseOrderApplicationWCF/CourseOrderReceiver/app.config):

```
<?xml version="1.0"?>
<configuration>
  <startup>
    <supportedRuntime version="v4.0" sku=".NETFramework,Version=v4.5"/>
  </startup>
  <system.serviceModel>
    <bindings>
      <netMsmqBinding>
        <binding name="NonTransactionalQueueBinding" exactlyOnce="false">
          <security mode="None" />
        </binding>
      </netMsmqBinding>
    </bindings>
    <services>
      <service name="Wrox.ProCSharp.Messaging.CourseOrderService">
```

```
        <endpoint address="net.msmq://localhost/private/courseorder"
          binding="netMsmqBinding"
          bindingConfiguration="NonTransactionalQueueBinding"
          name="OrderQueueEP"
          contract="Wrox.ProCSharp.Messaging.ICourseOrderService" />
      </service>
    </services>
  </system.serviceModel>
</configuration>
```

The `Click` event handler of the `buttonProcessOrder` button removes the selected course order from the collection class (code file `CourseOrderApplicationWCF/CourseOrderReceiver/CourseOrderReceiverWindow.xaml.cs`):

```
private void buttonProcessOrder_Click(object sender, RoutedEventArgs e)
{
  var courseOrder = listOrders.SelectedItem as CourseOrder;
  courseOrders.Remove(courseOrder);
  listOrders.SelectedIndex = -1;
  buttonProcessOrder.IsEnabled = false;

  MessageBox.Show("Course order processed", "Course Order Receiver",
        MessageBoxButton.OK, MessageBoxImage.Information);

}
```

WCF Message Sender Application

The sending application is modified to make use of a WCF proxy class. For the contract of the service, the assembly `CourseOrderServiceContract` is referenced, and the assembly `System.ServiceModel` is required for use of the WCF classes.

In the `Click` event handler of the `buttonSubmit` control, the `ChannelFactory` class returns a proxy. The proxy sends a message to the queue by invoking the method `AddCourseOrder` (code file `CourseOrderApplicationWCF/CourseOrderSender/CourseOrderWindow.xaml.cs`):

```
private void buttonSubmit_Click(object sender, RoutedEventArgs e)
{
  try
  {
    var factory = new ChannelFactory<ICourseOrderService>("queueEndpoint");
    ICourseOrderService proxy = factory.CreateChannel();
    proxy.AddCourseOrder(CourseOrder);
    factory.Close();

    MessageBox.Show("Course Order submitted", "Course Order",
        MessageBoxButton.OK, MessageBoxImage.Information);
  }
  catch (MessageQueueException ex)
  {
    MessageBox.Show(ex.Message, "Course Order Error",
        MessageBoxButton.OK, MessageBoxImage.Error);
  }
}
```

The application configuration file defines the client part of the WCF connection. Again, the `netMsmqBinding` is used (config file `CourseOrderApplicationWCF/CourseOrderSender/app.config`):

```
<?xml version="1.0"?>
<configuration>
  <startup>
```

```
      <supportedRuntime version="v4.0" sku=".NETFramework,Version=v4.5"/>
    </startup>
    <system.serviceModel>
      <bindings>
        <netMsmqBinding>
          <binding name="nonTransactionalQueueBinding" exactlyOnce="false">
            <security mode="None" />
          </binding>
        </netMsmqBinding>
      </bindings>
      <client>
        <endpoint address="net.msmq://localhost/private/courseorder"
          binding="netMsmqBinding"
          bindingConfiguration="nonTransactionalQueueBinding"
          contract="Wrox.ProCSharp.Messaging.ICourseOrderService"
          name="queueEndpoint"
          kind="" endpointConfiguration="" />
      </client>
    </system.serviceModel>
  </configuration>
```

When you start the application now, it works in a similar way as before. There is no longer a need to use classes of the System.Messaging namespace to send and receive messages. Instead, you write the application in a similar way as using TCP or HTTP channels with WCF.

However, to create message queues and to purge messages, you still need the MessageQueue class. WCF is only an abstraction to send and receive messages.

> **NOTE** *If you need to have a* System.Messaging *application to communicate with a WCF application, you can do so by using the* msmqIntegrationBinding *instead of the netMsmqBinding. This binding uses the message format used with COM and* System .Messaging.

MESSAGE QUEUE INSTALLATION

Message queues can be created with the MessageQueue.Create method. However, the user running an application usually doesn't have the administrative privileges required to create message queues.

Usually, message queues are created with an installation program, using the class MessageQueueInstaller. If an installer class is part of an application, the command-line utility installutil.exe (or a Windows Installation Package) invokes the Install method of the installer.

Visual Studio has special support for using the MessageQueueInstaller with Windows Forms applications. If a MessageQueue component is dropped from the toolbox onto the form, the smart tag of the component enables you to add an installer with the menu entry Add Installer. The MessageQueueInstaller object can be configured with the properties editor to define transactional queues, journal queues, the type of the formatter, the base priority, and so on.

> **NOTE** *Installers are discussed in Chapter 18, "Deployment."*

SUMMARY

In this chapter, you've seen how to use Message Queuing. Message Queuing is an important technology that offers not only asynchronous but also disconnected communication. The sender and receiver can run at different times, which makes Message Queuing an option for smart clients and also useful to distribute the load on the server over time.

The most important classes with Message Queuing are `Message` and `MessageQueue`. The `MessageQueue` class enables sending, receiving, and peeking at messages, and the `Message` class defines the content that is sent.

WCF offers an abstraction to Message Queuing. You can use the concepts offered by WCF to send messages by calling methods of a proxy and to receive messages by implementing a service.

INDEX

U

Y

Z

Try Safari Books Online FREE
for 15 days and take 15% off for up to 6 Months*

Gain unlimited subscription access to thousands of books and videos.

With Safari Books Online, learn without limits from thousands of technology, digital media and professional development books and videos from hundreds of leading publishers. With a monthly or annual unlimited access subscription, you get:

- Anytime, anywhere mobile access with Safari To Go apps for iPad, iPhone and Android

- Hundreds of expert-led instructional videos on today's hottest topics

- Sample code to help accelerate a wide variety of software projects

- Robust organizing features including favorites, highlights, tags, notes, mash-ups and more

- Rough Cuts pre-published manuscripts

START YOUR FREE TRIAL TODAY!
Visit: www.safaribooksonline.com/wrox

*Discount applies to new Safari Library subscribers only and is valid for the first 6 consecutive monthly billing cycles. Safari Library is not available in all countries.

An Imprint of WILEY
Now you know.